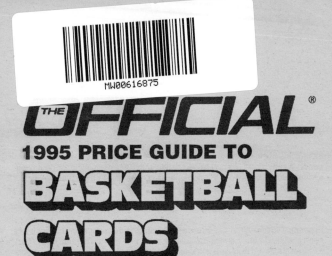

THE OFFICIAL®
1995 PRICE GUIDE TO
BASKETBALL CARDS

BY
DR. JAMES BECKETT

FOURTH EDITION

HOUSE OF COLLECTIBLES • NEW YORK

© 1994 by James Beckett III

All rights reserved under International
and Pan-American Copyright Conventions.

This is a registered trademark of Random House, Inc.

Published by:
House of Collectibles
201 East 50th Street
New York, New York 10022

Distributed by Ballantine Books, a division of Random House, Inc.,
New York, and simultaneously in Canada by
Random House of Canada Limited, Toronto.

Manufactured in the United States of America

ISSN: 1062-6980

ISBN: 0-876-37943-9

Fourth Edition: December 1994

10 9 8 7 6 5 4 3 2 1

Table of Contents

About the Author

Jim Beckett, the leading authority on sport card values in the United States, maintains a wide range of activities in the world of sports. He possesses one of the finest collections of sports cards and autographs in the world, has made numerous appearances on radio and television, and has been frequently cited in many national publications. He was awarded the first "Special Achievement Award" for Contributions to the Hobby by the National Sports Collectors Convention in 1980, the "Jock-Jaspersen Award" for Hobby Dedication in 1983, and the "Buck Barker, Spirit of the Hobby" Award in 1991.

Dr. Beckett is the author of *The Sport Americana Baseball Card Price Guide, The Official Price Guide to Baseball Cards, The Sport Americana Price Guide to Baseball Collectibles, The Sport Americana Baseball Memorabilia and Autograph Price Guide, The Sport Americana Football Card Price Guide, The Official Price Guide to Football Cards, The Sport Americana Hockey Card Price Guide, The Official Price Guide to Hockey Cards, The Sport Americana Basketball Card Price Guide and Alphabetical Checklist, The Official Price Guide to Basketball Cards,* and *The Sport Americana Baseball Card Alphabetical Checklist.* In addition, he is the founder, publisher, and editor of *Beckett Baseball Card Monthly, Beckett Basketball Monthly, Beckett Football Card Monthly, Beckett Hockey Monthly, Beckett Focus on Future Stars, Beckett Tribute,* and *Beckett Racing Monthly* magazines.

Jim Beckett received his Ph.D. in Statistics from Southern Methodist University in 1975. Prior to starting Beckett Publications in 1984, Dr. Beckett served as an Associate Professor of Statistics at Bowling Green State University and as a Vice President of a consulting firm in Dallas, Texas. He currently resides in Dallas with his wife, Patti, and their daughters, Christina, Rebecca, and Melissa.

How To Use This Book

Isn't it great? Every year this book gets bigger and bigger with all the new sets coming out. But even more exciting is that every year there are more attractive choices and, subsequently, more interest in the cards we love so much. This edition has been enhanced and expanded from the previous edition. The cards you collect — who appears on them, what they look like, where they are from, and (most important to most of you) what their current values are — are enumerated within. Many of the features contained in the other *Beckett Price Guides* have been incorporated into this volume since condition grading, terminology, and many other aspects of collecting are common to the card hobby in general. We hope you find the book both interesting and useful in your collecting pursuits.

The *Beckett Guide* has been successful where other attempts have failed because it is complete, current, and valid. This Price Guide contains not just one, but three prices by condition for all the basketball cards listed. These account for most of the basketball cards in existence. The prices were added to the card lists just prior to printing and reflect not the author's opinions or desires but the going retail prices for each card, based on the marketplace (sports memorabilia conventions and shows, sports card shops, hobby papers, current mail-order catalogs, local club meetings, auction results, and other first-hand reportings of actually realized prices).

What is the best price guide available on the market today? Of course card sellers will prefer the price guide with the highest prices, while card buyers will naturally prefer the one with the lowest prices. Accuracy, however, is the true

test. Use the price guide used by more collectors and dealers than all the others combined. Look for the Beckett name. I won't put my name on anything I won't stake my reputation on. Not the lowest and not the highest — but the most accurate, with integrity.

To facilitate your use of this book, read the complete introductory section on the following pages before going to the pricing pages. Every collectible field has its own terminology; we've tried to capture most of these terms and definitions in our glossary. Please read carefully the section on grading and the condition of your cards, as you will not be able to determine which price column is appropriate for a given card without first knowing its condition.

Advertising

Within this Price Guide you will find advertisements for sports memorabilia material, mail order, and retail sports collectibles establishments. All advertisements were accepted in good faith based on the reputation of the advertiser; however, neither the author, the publisher, the distributors, nor the other advertisers in this Price Guide accept any responsibility for any particular advertiser not complying with the terms of his or her ad.

Readers also should be aware that prices in advertisements are subject to change over the annual period before a new edition of this volume is issued each spring. When replying to an advertisement late in the basketball year, the reader should take this into account, and contact the dealer by phone or in writing for up-to-date price information. Should you come into contact with any of the advertisers in this guide as a result of their advertisement herein, please mention this source as your contact.

Prices in this Guide

Prices found in this guide reflect current retail rates just prior to the printing of this book. They do not reflect the FOR SALE prices of the author, the publisher, the distributors, the advertisers, or any card dealers associated with this guide. No one is obligated in any way to buy, sell or trade his or her cards based on these prices. The price listings were compiled by the author from actual buy/sell transactions at sports conventions, sports card shops, buy/sell advertisements in the hobby papers, for sale prices from dealer catalogs and price lists, and discussions with leading hobbyists in the U.S. and Canada. All prices are in U.S. dollars.

Acknowledgments

A great deal of diligence, hard work, and dedicated effort went into this year's volume. The high standards to which we hold ourselves, however, could not have been met without the expert input and generous amount of time contributed by many people. Our sincere thanks are extended to each and every one of you.

A complete list of these invaluable contributors appears after the Price Guide section.

The Official

Price Guide

to

Basketball Cards

1993 Basketball Cards Year in Review

by Bob Brill

Our hobby had a tough act to follow entering the 1993-94 collecting season. The debut of Shaquille O'Neal, coupled with a sensational rookie crop and the hoopla over the Dream Team, had pushed the basketball market into the stratosphere. Yet believe it or not, officials with the NBA say the post-Shaq Attaq season was even bigger.

"This year was better for the NBA and its partners because of the move toward premium products as well as an excellent group of rookies," said Donna Goldsmith, who heads up Group Marketing at NBA Properties. "Ours was the only sport to show an increase in dollar sales as well as cards sold."

The beat rolled on because of several reasons: another exciting rookie class, the natural collector/dealer anticipation coming off a banner year, the bonus of three USA Basketball/Dream Team II sets and the influx of new premium brands.

The Next Wave

Talented rookies such as Chris Webber, Anfernee Hardaway and Jamal Mashburn all built on the momentum unleashed by the O'Neal gang. Neither dominated like the slam-dunking Shaq, yet collectively they did follow in the footsteps of Alonzo Mourning and the other members of the strongest rookie class ever. Probably more than in any other sport, rookies, because of their immediate impact on a 12-man roster, drive basketball cards.

A year before, Charles Barkley emerged as a challenger to Michael Jordan. Last season, Hakeem Olajuwon took the quantum leap from star to superstar. Only Hakeem did Barkley one better by leading his team to a title.

Despite the Dream's MVP season, Jordan stole the show without ever lacing up a pair of sneakers. He left for baseball and 10-hour bus rides in stunning fashion, causing hobbyists to fill out their Jordan basketball collections and begin chasing his various baseball issues. Since his batting average just escaped the Mendoza line, he could return to the court and give a boost to his already prolific basketball cards. Michael remains a magical name and will always sell, especially if he returns to the NBA.

Star Search

No one player could fill the void left by Jordan. Veterans such as Olajuwon and Patrick Ewing picked up some of the slack, and collectors looked to their cards from the Star Company and Fleer sets from the 1980s. Unfortunately, consistent rumors of counterfeited and reprinted Star material scared off many buyers, causing a softening of the market. Star cards became more affordable, but some dealers were left reeling from the aftershocks.

The one area that showed very little movement was vintage (pre-1981) basketball. Exceptions to this longstanding trend were pre-1970s material. The 1948 Bowman set continued as one of the most popular high-dollar vintage issues of any sport. Also, high-grade 1957-58 Topps and the relatively more affordable 1961-62 Fleer singles remained strong sellers.

Some of the individual 1970s cards of Julius Erving, Pete Maravich and Bill Walton spurred some activity. But taken as a whole, material from the 1970s remained generally soft. Many collectors just don't seem to identify with "the old guys."

Stadium Club, for one, tapped into that youthful trend on its 1993-94 card backs. While few people read card backs, Topps did something noticeable. They turned to an "MTV style" with short, catchy one-liners. "Basketball is hip-hop, it's entertainment," said Bob Aniello, Stadium Club brand manager. "We wanted something that tied itself to the sport of today."

The NBA declined to expand the market to new manufacturers, but as with the other leagues, each licensed company was allowed to deliver more brands. Superpremium cards like Topps Finest raised the stakes. In 1992-93 only SkyBox was allowed to market Olympic cards. In 1993-94, Upper Deck and Fleer, offering Flair as its USAB line, joined the mix.

Chasing a Dream

In the ever-expanding universe of inserts, the parallel set came into its own. Hoops, celebrating its Fifth Anniversary, offered a gold card per pack. Upper Deck introduced SE Basketball and added two parallel sets: Electric Court cards came at a rate of one per pack, and Electric Gold cards popped up one per box.

Topps, which started the parallel Gold card tradition in 1992-93, continued to insert them one per pack, while its high-dollar Finest Refractors and Stadium Club First Day Issues posed a challenge for even well-heeled collectors. Fleer took another direction and guaranteed various inserts one per pack, upping the insert phenomena to a new level.

Some of the more popular inserts were Fleer Towers of Power, Stadium Club Frequent Flyers and Super Teams, Ultra All-Defensive and Scoring Kings, and Upper Deck Mr. June and Upper Deck SE Die-Cut All-Stars.

The clamor for inserts wasn't restricted only to 1993-94 product. Some 1992-93 chase cards, most notably Fleer Team Leaders and Fleer Total D, soared in value. As Jordan and Olajuwon fans began to fill out their collections, they discovered that some of the inserts of the previous year were tougher to locate than originally believed. The results were huge price jumps in some of the scarcer non-hobby distributed Fleer products and an increased interest across the board in other sleeper insert sets.

Draft redemption cards slipped by virtually no one. One year before, Classic scored the equivalent of a quadruple double by wrapping up O'Neal through the calendar year 1992. That promotional coup touched off a redemption card bonanza in 1993-94. Nearly every cardmaker issued first-series draft redemption cards exchangeable for special cards through the mail.

Waiting Game

When it came to escalating card values, collectors got smarter. They learned that values often drop soon after the cards are released, and collectors began waiting before buying them. The exception was Finest. Because of the surge of 1993 Finest baseball, boxes of Finest basketball pre-sold like hotcakes. But sure enough, about three weeks after the product was live, sets and singles were selling for considerably less, but still far above issue cost.

The increased popularity of all basketball cards led to greater numbers of them flying off of racks at such retail outlets as Wal-Mart, which expanded with the acquisition of Pace stores. This marketing trend was not applauded by many dealers, but it can be argued potential first-time collectors were exposed to a wealth of new cards for the first time.

To cover all bases, so to speak, card manufacturers began to use the segmentation strategy employed in the baseball card market. Now, almost every cardmaker uses a three-brand strategy: a low-end (let's get them started in the hobby) brand, a medium priced brand for every-day collectors and a high-end brand for upwardly mobile hobbyists. Upper Deck epitomized this strategy, and in the 1994-95 season will have it fully in place with its base line, Collector's Choice.

Collector's Choice, with a suggested retail of $1 a pack, is designed to excite youngsters about collecting cards. Upper Deck basketball covers the mainstream (the company's SE line will disappear), and SP fills the super-premium slot.

Fleer will continue its base series, followed by Ultra for mid-level collectors. Superpremium Flair joins the game in 1994-95, and Jam Session, which in 1993-94 reintroduced oversize or tall boy cards, is aimed at younger collectors. Jam Session fared moderately well, much better than Classic's Draft Pick version of the tall boy (Futures). Collectors have not flocked to this larger format, which includes the Topps cards of the early 1970s, despite its natural fit for tall basketball players.

Topps again defined the cutting edge with the release of its superpremium Finest. A chromium card, Finest built on the sharp-dressed success carved out by Stadium Club during the cardmaker's comeback season of 1992-93.

Again this past season, SkyBox International enjoyed success with its base brand, Hoops. Hoops traditionally sells well and is a mainstay for many dealers. The firm's premium line, SkyBox, took a bit of a dive despite an attractive design. USA Basketball continues to rack up points, and a lot of promotions to help store owners and other contests kept the name of SkyBox in the lead on several fronts. Look for a new brand from the North Carolina company for the 1994-95 season.

The future of our hobby promises more defined product segmentation, meaning more products but lower production numbers. The strong growth of the last couple of years should slow somewhat, but everything is in place for slight expansion, at the very least. Another powerful rookie class is in place, and collectors can expect Glenn Robinson, Jason Kidd and Grant Hill to follow in the footsteps of Webber, Hardaway and Mashburn.

Unfortunately, a Shaq comes along once in a decade. If there is another out there, the market could soar to greater levels. For now, collectors and dealers will have to be content with a stable but still strong market.

Drawing Cards

Card movement hinges primarily on what happens on the court. Here are some of the players who turned in noteworthy performances last season.

Chris Webber bucked the odds stacked against his grabbing hobby stardom: toiling out of a major media spotlight for the banged-up Warriors and playing out of position at center instead of power forward. His Rookie of the Year season only served to boost his tough-to-pull 1993-94 parallel cards, including Topps Finest Refractors (#212), Stadium Club First Day Issue (#224) and Upper Deck SE Electric Gold (#4).

Anfernee Hardaway did the near-impossible by emerging from Shaq's immense shadow in Orlando. In all fairness, Penny isn't the second coming of Magic Johnson, but if he comes close, his already tough 1993-94 SkyBox Draft Picks (#3) and Upper Deck SE Die Cut All-Star (#E12) could become even more of a catch.

Shaquille O'Neal may have been a victim of his phenomenal success. Collectors backed off of Shaq-mania just a bit, but 10 years from now, new fans will discover his Rookie Cards. Nevertheless, ardent collectors added his 1993-94 Ultra Award Winners (#4) and Upper Deck SE Die Cut All-Star (#E13) to the upper reaches of their want lists.

Hakeem Olajuwon blew past Patrick Ewing and Robinson to become the game's, and the hobby's, preeminent center. Nothing like an MVP award and a world championship to jazz up a card back. His 1986-87 Fleer RC (#82) doubled in value over the course of the calendar year.

Bob Brill is the publisher of the hobby newsletter "The Brill Report."

Introduction

Welcome to the exciting world of sports card collecting, one of America's most popular avocations. You have made a good choice in buying this book, since it will open up to you the entire panorama of this field in the simplest, most concise way. It is estimated that more than a third of a million different sports cards have been issued during the past century. And the number of total cards put out by all manufacturers last year has been estimated at several billion, with an initial wholesale price of more than $1 billion. Sales of older cards by dealers may account for a like amount. With all that cardboard available in the marketplace, it should be no surprise that several million sports fans like you collect sports cards today.

The growth of *Beckett Baseball Card Monthly*, *Beckett Basketball Monthly*, *Beckett Football Card Monthly*, *Beckett Hockey Monthly*, and *Beckett Focus on Future Stars* is another indication of the unprecedented popularity of sports cards. Founded in 1984 by Dr. James Beckett, the author of this Price Guide, *Beckett Baseball Card Monthly* has reached the pinnacle of the sports card hobby, with more than half a million readers anxiously awaiting each enjoyable and informative issue. The other four magazines have met similar success, with hundreds of thousands of readers devoted to each publication.

So collecting sports cards — while still pursued as a hobby with youthful exuberance by kids in the neighborhood — has also taken on the trappings of an industry, with thousands of full- and part-time card dealers, as well as vendors of supplies, clubs and conventions. In fact, each year since 1980 thousands of hobbyists have assembled for a National Sports Collectors Convention, at which hundreds of dealers have displayed their wares, seminars have been conducted, autographs penned by sports notables, and millions of cards changed hands. These colossal affairs have been staged in Los Angeles, Detroit, St. Louis, Chicago, New York, Anaheim, Arlington (Texas), San Francisco, Atlantic City, Houston and Atlanta. So sports card collecting really is national in scope!

This increasing interest has been reflected in card values. As more collectors compete for available supplies, card prices (especially for premium-grade cards) rise. There has been a strong advance in sports card prices during the past decade, and a quick perusal of prices in this book compared to the figures in earlier editions of this Price Guide will demonstrate this. Which brings us back around again to the book you have in your hands. It is the best annual guide available to this exciting world of basketball cards. Read it and use it. May your enjoyment and your card collection increase in the coming months and years.

How to Collect

Each collection is personal and reflects the individuality of its owner. There are no set rules on how to collect cards. Since card collecting is a hobby or leisure pastime, what you collect, how much you collect, and how much time and money you spend collecting are entirely up to you. The funds you have available for collecting and your own personal taste should determine how you collect. The information and ideas presented here are intended to help you get the most enjoyment from this hobby.

It is impossible to collect every card ever produced. Therefore, beginners as well as intermediate and advanced collectors usually specialize in some way. One of the reasons this hobby is popular is that individual collectors can define and tailor their collecting methods to match their own tastes. To give you some ideas of the various approaches to collecting, we will list some of the more popular areas of specialization.

Many collectors select complete sets from particular years. For example, they may concentrate on assembling complete sets from all the years since their birth or since they became avid sports fans. They may try to collect a card for every player during that specified period of time. Many others wish to acquire only certain players. Usually such players are the superstars of the sport, but occasionally collectors will specialize in all the cards of players who attended a particular college or came from a certain town. Some collectors are only interested in the first cards or Rookie Cards of certain players.

Another fun way to collect cards is by team. Most fans have a favorite team, and it is natural for that loyalty to be translated into a desire for cards of the players on that favorite team. For most of the recent years, team sets (all the cards from a given team for that year) are readily available at a reasonable price. *The Sport Americana Team Football and Basketball Card Checklist* will open up this field to the collector.

Obtaining Cards

Several avenues are open to card collectors. Cards still can be purchased in the traditional way: by the pack at the local discount, grocery or convenience stores. But there are also thousands of card shops across the country that specialize in selling cards individually or by the pack, box, or set. Another alternative is the thousands of card shows held each month around the country, which feature anywhere from five to 800 tables of sports cards and memorabilia for sale.

For many years, it has been possible to purchase complete sets of cards through mail-order advertisers found in traditional sports media publications, such as *The Sporting News, Football Digest, Street & Smith* yearbooks, and others. These sets also are advertised in the card collecting periodicals. Many collectors will begin by subscribing to at least one of the hobby periodicals, all with good up-to-date information. In fact, subscription offers can be found in the advertising section of this book.

Most serious card collectors obtain old (and new) cards from one or more of several main sources: (1) trading or buying from other collectors or dealers; (2) responding to sale or auction ads in the hobby publications; (3) buying at a local hobby store; and/or (4) attending sports collectibles shows or conventions.

We advise that you try all four methods since each has its own distinct advantages: (1) trading is a great way to make new friends; (2) hobby periodicals help you keep up with what's going on in the hobby (including when and where the conventions are happening); (3) stores provide the opportunity to enjoy personalized service and consider a great diversity of material in a relaxed sports-oriented atmosphere; and (4) shows allow you to choose from multiple dealers and thousands of cards under one roof in a competitive situation.

Preserving Your Cards

Cards are fragile. They must be handled properly in order to retain their value. Careless handling can easily result in creased or bent cards. It is, however, not recommended that tweezers or tongs be used to pick up your cards since such utensils might mar or indent card surfaces and thus reduce those cards' conditions and values. In general, your cards should be handled directly as little as possible. This is sometimes easier to say than to do.

Although there are still many who use custom boxes, storage trays, or even shoe boxes, plastic sheets are the preferred method of many collectors for storing cards. A collection stored in plastic pages in a three-ring album allows you to view your collection at any time without the need to touch the card itself.

Cards can also be kept in single holders (of various types and thickness) designed for the enjoyment of each card individually. For a large collection, some collectors may use a combination of the above methods. When purchasing plastic sheets for your cards, be sure that you find the pocket size that fits the cards snugly. Don't put your 1969-70 Topps in a sheet designed to fit 1992-93 Topps.

Most hobby and collectibles shops and virtually all collectors' conventions will have these plastic pages available in quantity for the various sizes offered, or you can purchase them directly from the advertisers in this book. Also, remember that pocket size isn't the only factor to consider when looking for plastic sheets. Other factors such as safety, economy, appearance, availability, or personal preference also may indicate which types of sheets a collector may want to buy.

Damp, sunny and/or hot conditions — no, this is not a weather forecast — are three elements to avoid in extremes if you are interested in preserving your collection. Too much (or too little) humidity can cause gradual deterioration of a card. Direct, bright sun (or fluorescent light) over time will bleach out the color of a card. Extreme heat accelerates the decomposition of the card. On the other hand, many cards have lasted more than 50 years without much scientific intervention. So be cautious, even if the above factors typically present a problem only when present in the extreme. It never hurts to be prudent.

Collecting vs. Investing

Collecting individual players and collecting complete sets are both popular vehicles for investment and speculation. Most investors and speculators stock up on complete sets or on quantities of players they think have good investment potential.

There is obviously no guarantee in this book, or anywhere else for that matter, that cards will outperform the stock market or other investment alternatives in the future. After all, basketball cards do not pay quarterly dividends and cards cannot be sold at their "current values" as easily as stocks or bonds.

Nevertheless, investors have noticed a favorable long-term trend in the past performance of sports collectibles, and certain cards and sets have outperformed just about any other investment in some years. Many hobbyists maintain that the best investment is and always will be the building of a collection, which traditionally has held up better than outright speculation.

Some of the obvious questions are: Which cards? When to buy? When to sell? The best investment you can make is in your own education. The more you know about your collection and the hobby, the more informed the decisions you will be able to make. We're not selling investment tips. We're selling information about the current value of basketball cards. It's up to you to use that information to your best advantage.

Glossary/Legend

Our glossary defines terms frequently used in the card collecting hobby. Many of these terms are also common to other types of sports memorabilia collecting. Some terms may have several meanings depending on use and context.

ABA - American Basketball Association.
ACC - Accomplishment.
ACO - Assistant Coach Card.
AF - Atlantic Finest.
AL - Active Leader.
ART - All-Rookie Team.

AS - All-Star.

ASA - All-Star Advice.

ASW - All-Star Weekend.

AUTO - Autograph.

AW - Award Winner.

BC - Bonus Card.

BRICK - A group or "lot" or cards, usually 50 or more having common characteristics, that is intended to be bought, sold, or traded as a unit.

BT - Beam Team or Breakaway Threats.

CBA - Continental Basketball Association.

CC - Classic Confrontation.

CF - Changing Faces or Central Finest.

CL - Checklist card. A card that lists in order the cards and players in the set or series. Older checklist cards in Mint condition that have not been checked off are very desirable and command large premiums.

CO - Coach card.

COIN - A small disc of metal or plastic portraying a player in its center.

COLLECTOR - A person who engages in the hobby of collecting cards primarily for his own enjoyment, with any profit motive being secondary.

COMBINATION CARD - A single card depicting two or more players (not including team cards).

COMMON CARD - The typical card of any set; it has no premium value accruing from subject matter, numerical scarcity, popular demand, or anomaly.

CONVENTION ISSUE - A set produced in conjunction with a sports collectibles convention to commemorate or promote the show. Most recent convention issues could also be classified as promo sets.

COR - Corrected card. A version of an error card that was fixed by the manufacturer.

COUPON - See Tab.

DEALER - A person who engages in buying, selling, and trading sports collectibles or supplies. A dealer may also be a collector, but as a dealer, he anticipates a profit.

DIE-CUT - A card with part of its stock partially cut for ornamental reasons.

DISC - A circular-shaped card.

DISPLAY SHEET - A clear, plastic page that is punched for insertion into a binder (with standard three-ring spacing) containing pockets for displaying cards. Many different styles of sheets exist with pockets of varying sizes to hold the many differing card formats. The vast majority of current cards measure 2 1/2 by 3 1/2 inches and fit in nine-pocket sheets.

DP - Double Print. A card that was printed in approximately double the quantity compared to other cards in the same series, or draft pick card.

EB - Executive Board.

ERR - Error card. A card with erroneous information, spelling, or depiction on either side of the card. Most errors are never corrected by the producing card company.

FACE - In Your Face card.

FAN - Fanimation card.

FF - Frequent Flyer.

FIN - Finals.

FLB - Flashback.

FPM - Future Playoff MVP's.

FSL - Future Scoring Leaders.

FULL SHEET - A complete sheet of cards that has not been cut into individual cards by the manufacturer. Also called an uncut sheet.

GF - Ground Force.

GI - Game Images.

GQ - Gentleman's Quarterly.

HL - Highlight card.

HOF - Hall of Fame, or Hall of Famer (also abbreviated HOFer).

HOR - Horizontal pose on a card as opposed to the standard vertical orientation found on most cards.

IA - In Action card. A special type of card depicting a player in an action photo, such as the 1982 Topps cards.

INSERT - A card of a different type, e.g., a poster, or any other sports collectible contained and sold in the same package along with a card or cards of a major set.

IS - Inside Stuff.

ISSUE - Synonymous with set, but usually used in conjunction with a manufacturer, e.g., a Topps issue.

JWA - John Wooden Award.

JS - Jam Session card.

KID - Kid Picture card.

LEGITIMATE ISSUE - A set produced to promote or boost sales of a product or service, e.g., bubble gum, cereal, cigarettes, etc. Most collector issues are not legitimate issues in this sense.

LID - A circular-shaped card (possibly with tab) that forms the top of the container for the product being promoted.

MAG - Magic of SkyBox cards.

MAJOR SET - A set produced by a national manufacturer of cards, containing a large number of cards. Usually 100 or more different cards comprise a major set.

MC - Members Choice.

MEM - Memorial.

MF - Midwest Finest.

MO - McDonald's Open.

MINI - A small card or stamp (the 1991-92 SkyBox Canadian set, for example).

MS - Milestone.

MVP - Most Valuable Player.

NNO - No number on back.

NW - New Wave.

NY - New York.

OBVERSE - The front, face, or pictured side of the card.

OLY - Olympic card.

PANEL - An extended card that is composed of multiple individual cards.

PC - Poster card.

PERIPHERAL SET - A loosely defined term that applies to any non-regular issue set. This term most often is used to describe food issue, giveaway, regional or sendaway sets that contain a fairly small number of cards and are not accepted by the hobby as major sets.

PF - Pacific Finest

POY - Player of the Year.

PREMIUM - A card, sometimes on photographic stock, that is purchased or obtained in conjunction with (or redeemed for) another card or product. This term applies mainly to older products, as newer cards distributed in this manner are generally lumped together as peripheral sets.

PREMIUM CARDS - A class of products introduced recently, intended to have higher quality card stock and photography than regular cards, but more limited production and higher cost. Defining what is and isn't a premium card is somewhat subjective.

PROMOTIONAL SET - A set, usually containing a small number of cards, issued by a national card producer and distributed in limited quantities or to a select group of people, such as major show attendees or dealers with whole-sale accounts. Presumably, the purpose of a promo set is to stir up demand for an upcoming set. Also called a preview, prototype or test set.

PV - Pro Visions.

QP - Quadruple Point.

RARE - A card or series of cards of very limited availability. Unfortunately, "rare" is a subjective term sometimes used indiscriminately. Using the strict definitions, rare cards are harder to obtain than scarce cards.

RB - Record Breaker card.

RC - Rookie Card. A player's first appearance on a regular issue card from one of the major card companies. Each company has only one regular issue set per season, and that is the widely available traditional set. With a few exceptions, each player has only one RC in any given set. A Rookie Card cannot be an All-Star, Highlight, In Action, League Leader, Super Action or Team Leader card. It can, however, be a coach card or draft pick card.

REGIONAL - A card issued and distributed only in a limited geographical area of the country. The producer may or may not be a major, national producer of trading cards. The key is whether the set was distributed nationally in any form or not.

REVERSE - The back or narrative side of the card.

REV NEG - Reversed or flopped photo side of the card. This is a major type of error card, but only some are corrected.

RIS - Rising Star.

ROY - Rookie of the Year.

SA - Super Action card. Similar to an In Action card.

SAL - SkyBox Salutes

SASE - Self-addressed, stamped envelope.

SC - Supreme Court.

SCARCE - A card or series of cards of limited availability. This subjective term is sometimes used indiscriminately to promote or hype value. Using strict definitions, scarce cards are easier to obtain than rare cards.

SD - Slam Dunk.

SERIES - The entire set of cards issued by a particular producer in a particular year, e.g., the 1978-79 Topps series. Also, within a particular set, series can refer to a group of (consecutively numbered) cards printed at the same time, e.g., the first series of the 1972-73 Topps set (#1 through #132).

SET - One each of an entire run of cards of the same type, produced by a particular manufacturer during a single season. In other words, if you have a complete set of 1989-90 Fleer cards, then you have every card from #1 up to and including #132; i.e., all the different cards that were produced.

SHOOT - Shooting Star.

SHOW - A large gathering of dealers and collectors at a single location for the purpose of buying, selling, and trading sorts cards and memorabilia. Conventions are open to the public and sometimes also feature autograph guests, door prizes, films, contests, etc.

SKED - Schedules.

SKL - Skylights.

SKY - Sky Masters.

SM - Signature Moves.

SP - Single or Short Print. A card which was printed in lesser quantity compared to the other cards in the same series (also see DP). This term only can be used in a relative sense and in reference to one particular set. For instance, the 1989-90 Hoops Pistons Championship card (#353A) is less common than the other cards in that set, but it isn't necessarily scarcer than regular cards of any other set.

SPECIAL CARD - A card that portrays something other than a single player or team.

SS - Star Stats.

ST - Scoring Threats card.

STAR CARD - A card that portrays a player of some repute, usually determined by his ability, but sometimes referring to sheer popularity.

STAY - Stay in School.

STICKER - A card-like item with a removable layer that can be affixed to another surface. Example: 1986-87 through 1989-90 Fleer bonus cards.

STOCK - The cardboard or paper on which the card is printed.

SUPERSTAR CARD - A card that portrays a superstar, e.g., a Hall of Fame member or a player whose current performance may eventually warrant serious Hall of Fame consideration.

SY - Schoolyard Stars.

TC - Team card or team checklist card.

TD - Triple Double. A term used for having double digit totals in three categories.

TEAM CARD - A card that depicts an entire team, notably the 1989-90 and 1990-91 NBA Hoops Detroit Pistons championship cards and the 1991-92 NBA Hoops subset.

TEST SET - A set, usually containing a small number of cards, issued by a national producer and distributed in a limited section of the country or to a select group of people. Presumably, the purpose of a test set is to measure market appeal for a particular type of card. Also called a promo or prototype set.

TFC - Team Fact card.

TH - Team Headlines.

THEN - Then and Now.

TL - Team Leader.

TO - Tip-off.

TP - Top Prospects.

TR - Traded card.

TRIB - Tribune.

TRV - Trivia.

TT - Team Tickets card.

TW - Teamwork.

UER - Uncorrected Error card.

USA - Team USA.

VAR - Variation card. One of two or more cards from the same series, with the same card number (or player with identical pose, if the series is unnumbered) differing from one another in some aspect, from the printing, stock or other feature of the card. This is often caused when the manufacturer of the cards notices an error in a particular card, corrects the error and then resumes the print run. In this case there will be two versions or variations of the same card. Sometimes one of the variations is relatively scarce. Variations also can result from accidental or deliberate design changes, information updates, photo substitutions, etc.

VERT - Vertical pose on a card.

XRC - Extended Rookie Card. A player's first appearance on a card, but issued in a set that was not distributed nationally nor in packs. In basketball sets, this term only refers to the 1983, '84 and '85 Star Company sets.

YB - Yearbook.

20A - Twenty assist club.

50P - Fifty point club.

6M - Sixth Man.

! - Conditional sensitive card or set (see **Grading Your Cards**).

Understanding Card Values

Determining Value

Why are some cards more valuable than others? Obviously, the economic laws of supply and demand are applicable to card collecting just as they are to any other field where a commodity is bought, sold or traded in a free, unregulated market.

Supply (the number of cards available on the market) is less than the total number of cards originally produced since attrition diminishes that original quantity. Each year a percentage of cards is typically thrown away, destroyed or otherwise lost to collectors. This percentage is much, much smaller today than it was in the past because more and more people have become increasingly aware of the value of their cards.

For those who collect only Mint condition cards, the supply of older cards can be quite small indeed. Until recently, collectors were not so conscious of the need to preserve the condition of their cards. For this reason, it is difficult to know exactly how many 1957-58 Topps are currently available, Mint or otherwise. It is generally accepted that there are fewer 1957-58 Topps available than 1969-70, 1979-80 or 1992-93 Topps cards. If demand were equal for each of these sets, the law of supply and demand would increase the price for the least available sets.

Demand, however, is never equal for all sets, so price correlations can be complicated. The demand for a card is influenced by many factors. These include: (1) the age of the card; (2) the number of cards printed; (3) the player(s) portrayed on the card; (4) the attractiveness and popularity of the set; and (5) the physical condition of the card.

In general, (1) the older the card, (2) the fewer the number of the cards printed, (3) the more famous, popular and talented the player, (4) the more attractive and popular the set, and (5) the better the condition of the card, the higher the value of the card will be. There are exceptions to all but one of these factors: the condition of the card. Given two cards similar in all respects except condition, the one in the best condition will always be valued higher.

While those guidelines help to establish the value of a card, the countless exceptions and peculiarities make any simple, direct mathematical formula to determine card values impossible.

Regional Variation

Since the market varies from region to region, card prices of local players may be higher. This is known as a regional premium. How significant the premium is — and if there is any premium at all — depends on the local popularity of the team and the player.

The largest regional premiums usually do not apply to superstars, who often are so well known nationwide that the prices of their key cards are too high for local dealers to realize a premium.

Lesser stars often command the strongest premiums. Their popularity is concentrated in their home region, creating local demand that greatly exceeds overall demand.

Regional premiums can apply to popular retired players and sometimes can be found in the areas where the players grew up or starred in college.

A regional discount is the converse of a regional premium. Regional discounts occur when a player has been so popular in his region for so long that local collectors and dealers have accumulated quantities of his cards. The abundant supply may make the cards available in that area at the lowest prices anywhere.

Set Prices

A somewhat paradoxical situation exists in the price of a complete set vs. the combined cost of the individual cards in the set. In nearly every case, the sum of the prices for the individual cards is higher than the cost for the complete set. This is prevalent especially in the cards of the past few years. The reasons for this apparent anomaly stem from the habits of collectors and from the carrying costs to dealers. Today, each card in a set normally is produced in the same quantity as all others in its set.

Many collectors pick up only stars, superstars and particular teams. As a result, the dealer is left with a shortage of certain player cards and an abundance of others. He therefore incurs an expense in simply "carrying" these less desirable cards in stock. On the other hand, if he sells a complete set, he gets rid of large numbers of cards at one time. For this reason, he generally is willing to receive less money for a complete set. By doing this, he recovers all of his costs and also makes a profit.

Set prices do not include rare card varieties, unless specifically stated. Of course, the prices for sets do include one example of each type for the given set, but this is the least expensive variety.

Scarce Series

Only a select few basketball sets contain scarce series: 1948 Bowman, 1970-71 and 1972-73 Topps, 1983-84, 1984-85 and 1985-86 Star. The 1948 Bowman set was printed on two 36-card sheets, the second of which was issued in significantly lower quantities. The two Topps scarce series are only marginally tougher than the set as a whole. The Star Company scarcities relate to particular team sets that, to different extents, were less widely distributed.

We are always looking for information or photographs of printing sheets of cards for research. Each year, we try to update the hobby's knowledge of distribution anomalies. Please let us know at the address in this book if you have first-hand knowledge that would be helpful in this pursuit.

Grading Your Cards

Each hobby has its own grading terminology — stamps, coins, comic books, record collecting, etc. Collectors of sports cards are no exception. The one invariable criterion for determining the value of a card is its condition: the better the condition of the card, the more valuable it is. Condition grading, however, is subjective. Individual card dealers and collectors differ in the strictness of their grading, but the stated condition of a card should be determined without regard to whether it is being bought or sold.

No allowance is made for age. A 1961-62 Fleer card is judged by the same standards as a 1991-92 Fleer card. But there are specific sets and cards that are condition sensitive because of their border color, consistently poor centering, etc. Such cards and sets sometimes command premiums above the listed percentages in Mint condition.

Centering

Current centering terminology uses numbers representing the percentage of border on either side of the main design. Obviously, centering is diminished in importance for borderless cards such as Stadium Club.

Slightly Off-Center (60/40): A slightly off-center card is one that upon close inspection is found to have one border bigger than the opposite border. This degree once was offensive to only purists, but now some hobbyists try to avoid cards that are anything other than perfectly centered.

Off-Center (70/30): An off-center card has one border that is noticeably more than twice as wide as the opposite border.

Badly Off-Center (80/20 or worse): A badly off-center card has virtually no border on one side of the card.

Miscut: A miscut card actually shows part of the adjacent card in its larger border and consequently a corresponding amount of its card is cut off.

Corner Wear

Corner wear is the most scrutinized grading criteria in the hobby. These are the major categories of corner wear:

Corner with a slight touch of wear: The corner still is sharp, but there is a slight touch of wear showing. On a dark-bordered card, this shows as a dot of white.

Fuzzy corner: The corner still comes to a point, but the point has just begun to fray. A slightly "dinged" corner is considered the same as a fuzzy corner.

Slightly rounded corner: The fraying of the corner has increased to where there is only a hint of a point. Mild layering may be evident. A "dinged" corner is considered the same as a slightly rounded corner.

Rounded corner: The point is completely gone. Some layering is noticeable.

Badly rounded corner: The corner is completely round and rough. Severe layering is evident.

Creases

A third common defect is the crease. The degree of creasing in a card is difficult to show in a drawing or picture. On giving the specific condition of an expensive card for sale, the seller should note any creases additionally. Creases can be categorized as to severity according to the following scale.

Light Crease: A light crease is a crease that is barely noticeable upon close inspection. In fact, when cards are in plastic sheets or holders, a light crease may not be seen (until the card is taken out of the holder). A light crease on the front is much more serious than a light crease on the card back only.

Medium Crease: A medium crease is noticeable when held and studied at arm's length by the naked eye, but does not overly detract from the appearance of the card. It is an obvious crease, but not one that breaks the picture surface of the card.

Heavy Crease: A heavy crease is one that has torn or broken through the card's picture surface, e.g., puts a tear in the photo surface.

Alterations

Deceptive Trimming: This occurs when someone alters the card in order (1) to shave off edge wear, (2) to improve the sharpness of the corners, or (3) to improve centering — obviously their objective is to falsely increase the perceived value of the card to an unsuspecting buyer. The shrinkage usually is evident only if the trimmed card is compared to an adjacent full-sized card or if the trimmed card is itself measured.

Obvious Trimming: Obvious trimming is noticeable and unfortunate. It is usually performed by non-collectors who give no thought to the present or future value of their cards.

Deceptively Retouched Borders: This occurs when the borders (especially on those cards with dark borders) are touched up on the edges and cor-

Centering

Well-centered

Slightly Off-centered

Off-centered

Badly Off-centered

Miscut

ners with magic marker or crayons of appropriate color in order to make the card appear to be Mint.

Categorization of Defects

Miscellaneous Flaws

The following are common minor flaws that, depending on severity, lower a card's condition by one to four grades and often render it no better than Excellent-Mint: bubbles (lumps in surface), gum and wax stains, diamond cutting (slanted borders), notching, off-centered backs, paper wrinkles, scratched-off cartoons or puzzles on back, rubber band marks, scratches, surface impressions and warping.

The following are common serious flaws that, depending on severity, lower a card's condition at least four grades and often render it no better than Good: chemical or sun fading, erasure marks, mildew, miscutting (severe off-centering), holes, bleached or retouched borders, tape marks, tears, trimming, water or coffee stains and writing.

Condition Guide

Grades

Mint (Mt) - A card with no flaws or wear. The card has four perfect corners, 60/40 or better centering from top to bottom and from left to right, original gloss, smooth edges and original color borders. A Mint card does not have print spots, color or focus imperfections.

Near Mint-Mint (NrMt-Mt) - A card with one minor flaw. Any one of the following would lower a Mint card to Near Mint-Mint: one corner with a slight touch of wear, barely noticeable print spots, color or focus imperfections. The card must have 60/40 or better centering in both directions, original gloss, smooth edges and original color borders.

Near Mint (NrMt) - A card with one minor flaw. Any one of the following would lower a Mint card to Near Mint: one fuzzy corner or two to four corners with slight touches of wear, 70/30 to 60/40 centering, slightly rough edges, minor print spots, color or focus imperfections. The card must have original gloss and original color borders.

Excellent-Mint (ExMt) - A card with two or three fuzzy, but not rounded, corners and centering no worse than 80/20. The card may have no more than two of the following: slightly rough edges, very slightly discolored borders, minor print spots, color or focus imperfections. The card must have original gloss.

Excellent (Ex) - A card with four fuzzy but definitely not rounded corners and centering no worse than 80/20. The card may have a small amount of original gloss lost, rough edges, slightly discolored borders and minor print spots, color or focus imperfections.

Very Good (Vg) - A card that has been handled but not abused: slightly rounded corners with slight layering, slight notching on edges, a significant amount of gloss lost from the surface but no scuffing and moderate discoloration of borders. The card may have a few light creases.

Good (G), Fair (F), Poor (P) - A well-worn, mishandled or abused card: badly rounded and layered corners, scuffing, most or all original gloss missing, seriously discolored borders, moderate or heavy creases, and one or more serious flaws. The grade of Good, Fair or Poor depends on the severity of wear and flaws. Good, Fair and Poor cards generally are used only as fillers.

The most widely used grades are defined above. Obviously, many cards will not perfectly fit one of the definitions.

Corner Wear

The partial cards here have been photographed at 300%. This was done in order to magnify each card's corner wear to such a degree that differences could be shown on a printed page.

This 1986-87 Fleer Mark Aguirre card has a touch of wear. Notice the extremely slight fraying on the corner.

This 1986-87 Fleer Isiah Thomas card has a fuzzy corner. Notice that there is no longer a sharp corner.

This 1986-87 Fleer Wayman Tisdale card has a slightly rounded corner evident by the lack of a sharp point and heavy wear on both edges.

This 1986-87 Fleer Herb Williams card displays a badly rounded corner. Notice a large portion of missing cardboard accompanied by heavy wear and excessive fraying.

This 1986-87 Fleer Maurice Cheeks card displays several creases of varying degrees. Light creases (left side of the card) may not break the card's surface, while heavy creases (right side) will.

Therefore, categories between the major grades known as in-between grades are used, such as Good to Very Good (G-Vg), Very Good to Excellent (VgEx), and Excellent-Mint to Near Mint (ExMt-NrMt). Such grades indicate a card with all qualities of the lower category but with at least a few qualities of the higher category.

This *Price Guide* book lists each card and set in three grades, with the middle grade valued at about 40-45% of the top grade, and the bottom grade valued at about 10-15% of the top grade.

The value of cards that fall between the listed columns can also be calculated using a percentage of the top grade. For example, a card that falls between the top and middle grades (Ex, ExMt or NrMt in most cases) will generally be valued at anywhere from 50% to 90% of the top grade.

Similarly, a card that falls between the middle and bottom grades (G-Vg, Vg or VgEx in most cases) will generally be valued at anywhere from 20% to 40% of the top grade.

There are also cases where cards are in better condition than the top grade or worse than the bottom grade. Cards that grade worse than the lowest grade are generally valued at 5-10% of the top grade.

When a card exceeds the top grade by one — such as NrMt-Mt when the top grade is NrMt, or Mint when the top grade is NrMt-Mt — a premium of up to 50% is possible, with 10-20% the usual norm.

When a card exceeds the top grade by two — such as Mint when the top grade is NrMt, or NrMt-Mt when the top grade is ExMt — a premium of 25-50% is the usual norm. But certain condition sensitive cards or sets, particularly those from the pre-war era, can bring premiums of up to 100% or even more.

Unopened packs, boxes and factory-collated sets are considered Mint in their unknown (and presumed perfect) state. Once opened, however, each card can be graded (and valued) in its own right by taking into account any defects that may be present in spite of the fact that the card has never been handled.

Selling Your Cards

Just about every collector sells cards or will sell cards eventually. Someday you may be interested in selling your duplicates or maybe even your whole collection. You may sell to other collectors, friends or dealers. You may even sell cards you purchased from a certain dealer back to that same dealer. In any event, it helps to know some of the mechanics of the typical transaction between buyer and seller.

Dealers will buy cards in order to resell them to other collectors who are interested in the cards. Dealers will always pay a higher percentage for items that (in their opinion) can be resold quickly, and a much lower percentage for those items that are perceived as having low demand and hence are slow moving. In either case, dealers must buy at a price that allows for the expense of doing business and a margin for profit.

If you have cards for sale, the best advice we can give is that you get several offers for your cards — either from card shops or at a card show — and take the best offer, all things considered. Note, the "best" offer may not be the one for the highest amount. And remember, if a dealer really wants your cards, he won't let you get away without making his best competitive offer. Another alternative is to place your cards in an auction as one or several lots.

Many people think nothing of going into a department store and paying $15 for an item of clothing for which the store paid $5. But if you were selling your $15 card to a dealer and he offered you $5 for it, you might think his mark-up unreasonable. To complete the analogy: most department stores (and card dealers) that consistently pay $10 for $15 items eventually go out of business.

An exception is when the dealer has lined up a willing buyer for the item(s) you are attempting to sell, or if the cards are so Hot that it's likely he'll have to hold the cards for only a short period of time.

In those cases, an offer of up to 75 percent of book value still will allow the dealer to make a reasonable profit considering the short time he will need to hold the merchandise. In general, however, most cards and collections will bring offers in the range of 25 to 50 percent of retail price. Also consider that most material from the past five to 10 years is plentiful. If that's what you're selling, don't be surprised if your best offer is well below that range.

Interesting Notes

The first card numerically of an issue is the single card most likely to obtain excessive wear. Consequently, you typically will find the price on the #1 card (in NrMt or Mint condition) somewhat higher than might otherwise be the case. Similarly, but to a lesser extent (because normally the less important, reverse side of the card is the one exposed), the last card numerically in an issue also is prone to abnormal wear. This extra wear and tear occurs because the first and last cards are exposed to the elements (human element included) more than any other cards. They are generally end cards in any brick formations, rubber bandings, stackings on wet surfaces, and like activities.

Sports cards have no intrinsic value. The value of a card, like the value of other collectibles, can be determined only by you and your enjoyment in viewing and possessing these cardboard treasures.

Remember, the buyer ultimately determines the price of each card. You are the determining price factor because you have the ability to say "No" to the price of any card by not exchanging your hard-earned money for a given card. When the cost of a trading card exceeds the enjoyment you will receive from it, your answer should be "No." We assess and report the prices. You set them!

We are always interested in receiving the price input of collectors and dealers from around the country. We happily credit all contributors. We welcome your opinions, since your contributions assist us in ensuring a better guide each year. If you would like to join our survey list for the next editions of this book and others authored by Dr. Beckett, please send your name and address to Dr. James Beckett, 15850 Dallas Parkway, Dallas, Texas 75248.

History of Basketball Cards

The earliest basketball collectibles known are team postcards issued at the turn of the 20th century. Many of these postcards feature collegiate or high school teams of that day. Postcards were intermittently issued throughout the first half of the 20th century, with the bulk of them coming out in the 1920s and '30s. Unfortunately, the cataloging of these collectibles is sporadic at best. In addition, many collectors consider these postcards as memorabilia more so than trading cards, thus their exclusion from this book.

In 1910, College Athlete Felts (catalog number B-33) made their debut. Of a total of 270 felts, 20 featured basketball plays.

The first true basketball trading cards were issued by Murad cigarettes in 1911. The T-51 Murad cards depict a number of various sports and colleges, including four basketball cards (Luther, Northwestern, Williams and Xavier). In addition to these small (2-by-3 inch) cards, Murad issued a large (8-by-5 inch) basketball card featuring Williams college (catalog number T-6) as part of another multisport set.

The first basketball cards ever to be issued in gum packs were distributed in 1933 by Goudey in their multisport Sport Kings set. Four cards from the complete 48-card set feature Boston Celtics basketball players Nat Holman, Ed Wachter, Joe Lapchick and Eddie Burke.

The period of growth that the NBA experienced from 1948 to 1951 marked the first initial boom, both for that sport and the cards that chronicle it. In 1948, Bowman created the first trading card set exclusively devoted to basketball cards, ushering in the modern era of hoops collectibles. The 72-card Bowman set contains the Rookie Card of HOFer George Mikan, one of the most valuable, and important, basketball cards in the hobby. Mikan, pro basketball's first dominant big man, set the stage for Bill Russell, Wilt Chamberlain and all of the other legendary centers who have played the game since.

In addition to the Bowman release, Topps included 11 basketball cards in its 252-card multisport 1948 Magic Photo set. Five of the cards feature individual players (including collegiate great "Easy" Ed Macauley), another five feature colleges, and one additional card highlights a Manhattan-Dartmouth game. These 11 cards represent Topps first effort to produce basketball trading cards. Kellogg's also created an 18-card multisport set of trading cards in 1948 that were inserted into boxes of Pep cereal. The only basketball card in the set features Mikan. Throughout 1948 and 1949, the Exhibit Supply Company of Chicago issued oversized thick-stock multisport trading cards in conjunction with the 1948 Olympic games. Six basketball players were featured, including HOFers Mikan and Joe Fulks, among others. The cards were distributed through penny arcade machines.

In 1950-51, Scott's Chips issued a 13-card set featuring the Minneapolis Lakers. The cards were issued in Scott's Potato and Cheese Potato Chip boxes. The cards are extremely scarce today due to the fact that many were redeemed back in 1950-51 in exchange for game tickets and signed team pictures. This set contains possibly the scarcest Mikan issue in existence. In 1951, a Philadelphia-based meat company called Berk Ross issued a four-series, 72-card multisport set. The set contains five different basketball players, including the first cards of HOFers Bob Cousy and Bill Sharman.

Wheaties issued an oversized six-card multisport set on the backs of its cereal boxes in 1951. The only basketball player featured in the set is Mikan.

In 1952, Wheaties expanded the cereal box set to 30 cards, including six issues featuring basketball players of that day. Of these six cards, two feature Mikan (a portrait and an action shot). The 1952 cards are significantly smaller than the previous year's issue. That same year, the 32-card Bread for Health set was issued. The set was one of the few trading card issues of that decade exclusively devoted to the sport of basketball. The cards are actually bread end labels and were probably meant to be housed in an album. To date, the only companies known to have issued this set are Fisher's Bread in the New Jersey, New York and Pennsylvania areas and NBC Bread in the Michigan area.

One must skip ahead to 1957-58 to find the next major basketball issue, again produced by Topps. Its 80-card basketball set from that year is recognized within the hobby as the second major modern basketball issue, including Rookie Cards of all-time greats such as Bill Russell, Bob Cousy and Bob Pettit.

In 1960, Post cereal created a nine-card multisport set by devoting most of the back of the actual cereal boxes to full color picture frames of the athletes. Celtics HOFers Bob Cousy and Bill Sharman are the two featured basketball players.

In 1961-62, Fleer issued the third major modern basketball set. The 66-card set contains the Rookie Cards of all-time greats such as Wilt Chamberlain, Oscar Robertson and Jerry West. That same year, Bell Brand Potato Chips inserted trading cards (one per bag) featuring the L.A. Lakers team of that year and including scarce, early issues of HOFers Jerry West and Elgin Baylor.

From 1963 to 1968 no major companies manufactured basketball cards. Kahn's (an Ohio-based meat company) issued small regional basketball sets from 1957-58 through 1965-66 (including the first cards of Jerry West and Oscar Robertson in its 1960-61 set). All of the Kahn's sets feature members of the Cincinnati Royals, except for the few issues featuring Laker Jerry West.

In 1968, Topps printed a very limited quantity of standard-size black-and-white test issue cards, preluding its 1969-70 nationwide return to the basketball card market.

The 1969-70 Topps set began a 13-year run of producing nationally distributed basketball card sets which ended in 1981-82. This was about the time the league's popularity bottomed out and was about to begin its ascent to the lofty level it's at today.

Topps' run included several sets that are troublesome for today's collectors. The 1969-70, 1970-71 and 1976-77 sets are larger than standard size, thus making them hard to store and preserve. The 1980-81 set consists of standard-size panels containing three cards each. Completing and cataloging the 1980-81 set (which features the classic Larry Bird RC/Magic Johnson RC/Julius Erving panel) is challenging, to say the least.

In 1983, this basketball card void was filled by the Star Company, a small company which issued three attractive sets of basketball cards, along with a plethora of peripheral sets. Star's 1983-84 premiere offering was issued in four groups, with the first series (cards 1-100) very difficult to obtain, as many of the early team subsets were miscut and destroyed before release. The 1984-85 and 1985-86 sets were more widely and evenly distributed. Even so, players' initial appearances on any of the three Star Company sets are considered Extended Rookie Cards, not regular Rookie Cards, because of the relatively limited distribution. Chief among these is Michael Jordan's 1984-85 Star XRC, the most valuable sports card issued in a 1980s major set.

Then, in 1986, Fleer took over the rights to produce cards for the NBA. Their 1986-87, 1987-88 and 1988-89 sets each contain 132 attractive, colorful cards depicting mostly stars and superstars. They were sold in the familiar wax pack format (12 cards and one sticker per pack). Fleer increased its set size to 168 in 1989-90, and was joined by NBA Hoops, which produced a 300-card first series (containing David Robinson's only Rookie Card) and a 52-card second series. The demand for all three Star Company sets, along with the first four Fleer sets and the premiere NBA Hoops set, skyrocketed during the early part of 1990.

The basketball card market stabilized somewhat in 1990-91, with both Fleer and Hoops stepping up production tremendously. A new major set, SkyBox, also made a splash in the market with its unique "high-tech" cards featuring computer-generated backgrounds. Because of overproduction, none of the three major 1990-91 sets have experienced significant price growth, although the increased competition apparently has led to higher quality and more innovative products.

Another milestone in 1990-91 was the first-time inclusion of current rookies in update sets (NBA Hoops and SkyBox Series II, Fleer Update). The NBA Hoops and SkyBox issues contain just the 11 lottery picks, while Fleer's 100-card boxed set includes all rookies of any significance. A small company called "Star Pics" (not to be confused with Star Company) tried to fill this niche by printing a 70-card set in late 1990, but because the set was not licensed by the NBA, it is not considered a major set by the majority of collectors. It does, however, contain the first nationally distributed cards of 1990-91 rookies such as Derrick Coleman and Kendall Gill, among others.

In 1991-92, the draft pick set market that Star Pics opened in 1990-91 expanded to include several competitors. More significantly, that season brought with it the three established NBA card brands plus Upper Deck, known throughout the hobby for its high quality card stock and photography in other sports. Upper Deck's first basketball set probably captured NBA action better than any previous set. But its value — like all other major 1990-91 and 1991-92 NBA sets — declined because of overproduction.

On the bright side, the historic entrance of NBA players to Olympic competition kept interest in basketball cards going long after the Chicago Bulls won their second straight NBA championship. So for at least one year, the basketball card market — probably the most seasonal of the four major team sports — remained in the spotlight for an extended period of time.

The 1992-93 season will be remembered as the year of Shaq — the debut campaign of the most heralded rookie in many years. Shaquille O'Neal headlined the most promising rookie class in NBA history, sparking unprecedented interest in basketball cards. Among O'Neal's many talented rookie companions were Alonzo Mourning, Christian Laettner, Harold Miner, Tom Gugliotta and Latrell Sprewell.

Classic Games, known primarily for producing draft picks and minor league baseball cards, signed O'Neal to an exclusive contract through 1992, thus postponing the appearances of O'Neal's NBA-licensed cards.

Shaquille's Classic and NBA cards, particularly the inserts, became some of the most sought-after collectibles in years. As a direct result of O'Neal and his fellow rookie standouts, the basketball card market achieved a new level of popularity in 1993.

The hobby rode that crest of popularity throughout the 1993-94 season. Michael Jordan may have retired, but his absence only spurred interest in some of his tougher inserts. Another strong rookie class followed Shaq, and Reggie Miller elevated his collectibility to a superstar level. Hakeem Olajuwon, by leading the Rockets to an NBA title, boosted his early cards to levels surpassed only by Jordan.

No new cardmakers came on board, but superpremium Topps Finest raised the stakes, and the parallel set came into its own.

Additional Reading

With the increase in popularity of the hobby in recent years, there has been a corresponding increase in available literature. Below is a list of the books and periodicals that receive our highest recommendation and that we hope will further advance your knowledge and enjoyment of our great hobby.

The Sport Americana Baseball Card Price Guide by Dr. James Beckett (Sixteenth Edition, $16.95, released 1994, published by Edgewater Book Company) — the most comprehensive Price Guide and checklist ever issued on baseball cards.

The Official Price Guide to Baseball Cards by Dr. James Beckett (Fourteenth Edition, $6.99, released 1994, published by The House of Collectibles) — an abridgment of *The Sport Americana Price Guide* in a convenient and economical pocket-size format providing Dr. Beckett's pricing of the major baseball sets since 1948.

The Sport Americana Football Price Guide by Dr. James Beckett (Eleventh Edition, $16.95, released 1994, published by Edgewater Book Company) — The most comprehensive Price Guide and checklist ever issued on football cards.

The Official Price Guide to Football Cards by Dr. James Beckett (Fourteenth Edition, $6.99, released 1993, published by The House of Collectibles) — an abridgment of *The Sport Americana Price Guide* listed above in a convenient and economical pocket-size format providing Dr. Beckett's pricing of the major football sets since 1948.

The Sport Americana Hockey Card Price Guide by Dr. James Beckett (Third Edition, $14.95, released 1994, published by Edgewater Book Company) — the most comprehensive Price Guide and checklist ever issued on hockey cards.

The Official Price Guide to Hockey Cards by Dr. James Beckett (Third Edition, $6.99, released 1993, published by The House of Collectibles) — an abridgment of *The Sport Americana Price Guide* listed above in a convenient and economical pocket-size format providing Dr. Beckett's pricing of the major hockey sets since 1951.

The Sport Americana Basketball Card Price Guide and Alphabetical Checklist by Dr. James Beckett (Third Edition, $14.95, released 1993, published by Edgewater Book Company) — the most comprehensive combination Price Guide and alphabetical checklist ever issued on basketball cards.

The Sport Americana Baseball Card Alphabetical Checklist by Dr. James Beckett (Sixth Edition, $15.95, released 1994, published by Edgewater Book Company) — an alphabetical listing, by the last name of the player portrayed on the card, of virtually all baseball cards (major league and minor league) produced up through the 1994 major sets.

The Sport Americana Price Guide to the Non-Sports Cards 1930-1960 by Christopher Benjamin (Second Edition, $14.95, released 1993, published by Edgewater Book Company) — the definitive guide to virtually all popular non-sports American tobacco and bubblegum cards issued between 1930 and 1960. In addition to cards, illustrations and prices for wrappers also are included.

The Sport Americana Price Guide to the Non-Sports Cards by Christopher Benjamin (Fourth Edition, $14.95, released 1992, published by Edgewater Book Company) — the definitive guide to all popular non-sports American cards. In addition to cards, illustrations and prices for wrappers also are included. This volume covers non-sports cards from 1961 to 1992.

The Sport Americana Baseball Address List by Jack Smalling (Eighth Edition, $13.95, released 1994, published by Edgewater Book Company) — the definitive guide for autograph hunters, giving addresses and deceased information for virtually all Major League Baseball players past and present.

The Sport Americana Team Baseball Card Checklist by Jeff Fritsch (Sixth Edition, $12.95, released 1992, published by Edgewater Book Company) — includes all Topps, Bowman, Donruss, Fleer, Score, Play Ball, Goudey, and Upper Deck cards, with the players portrayed on the cards listed with the teams for whom they played. The book is invaluable to the collector who specializes in an individual team because it is the most complete baseball card team checklist available.

The Sport Americana Team Football and Basketball Card Checklist by Jeff Fritsch and Jane Fritsch-Gavin (Second Edition, $12.95, released 1993, published by Edgewater Book Company) — the book is invaluable to the collector who specializes in an individual team because it is the most complete football and basketball card team checklist available.

The Encyclopedia of Baseball Cards, Volume I: 19th Century Cards by Lew Lipset ($11.95, released 1983, published by the author) — everything you ever wanted to know about 19th century cards.

The Encyclopedia of Baseball Cards, Volume II: Early Gum and Candy Cards by Lew Lipset ($10.95, released 1984, published by the author) — everything you ever wanted to know about early candy and gum cards.

The Encyclopedia of Baseball Cards, Volume III: 20th Century Tobacco Cards, 1909-1932 by Lew Lipset ($12.95, released 1986, published by the author) — everything you ever wanted to know about old tobacco cards.

Beckett Baseball Card Monthly, published and edited by Dr. James Beckett, contains the most extensive and accepted monthly Price Guide, collectible glossy superstar covers, colorful feature articles, "who's Hot and who's Cold" section, Convention Calendar, tips for beginners, "Readers Write" letters to and responses from the editor, information on errors and varieties, autograph collecting tips and profiles of the sport's Hottest stars. Published every month, *BBCM* is the hobby's largest paid circulation periodical. *Beckett Football Card Monthly, Beckett Basketball Monthly, Beckett Hockey Monthly, Beckett Focus on Future Stars®, Beckett Tribute,* and *Beckett Racing Monthly* were built on the success of *BBCM*.

1948 Bowman

The 1948 Bowman basketball card set of 72 cards was the company's only basketball issue. It was also the only major basketball issue until 1957-58. Cards in the set measure 2 1/16" by 2 1/2". The set is in color and features both player cards and diagram cards. The player cards in the second series are sometimes found without the red or blue printing on the card front, leaving only a gray background. These gray-front cards are more difficult to find, as they are printing errors where the printer apparently ran out of red or blue ink that was supposed to print on the player's uniform. The key Rookie Cards in this set are Carl Braun, Joe Fulks, William "Red" Holzman, George Mikan, Jim Pollard, and Max Zaslofsky.

	NRMT	VG-E	GOOD
COMPLETE SET (72)	8000.00	4000.00	800.00
COMMON PLAYER (1-36)	50.00	25.00	5.00
COMMON PLAYER (37-72)	100.00	50.00	10.00
☐ 1 Ernie Calverley	160.00	80.00	16.00
Providence Steamrollers			
☐ 2 Ralph Hamilton	50.00	25.00	5.00
Ft. Wayne Pistons			
☐ 3 Gale Bishop	50.00	25.00	5.00
Philadelphia Warriors			
☐ 4 Fred Lewis CO	60.00	30.00	6.00
Indianapolis Jets			
☐ 5 Basketball Play	35.00	17.50	3.50
Single cut off post			
☐ 6 Bob Ferrick	60.00	30.00	6.00
Washington Capitols			
☐ 7 John Logan	50.00	25.00	5.00
St. Louis Bombers			
☐ 8 Mel Riebe	50.00	25.00	5.00
Boston Celtics			
☐ 9 Andy Phillip	135.00	70.00	13.50
Chicago Stags			
☐ 10 Bob Davies	135.00	70.00	13.50
Rochester Royals			
☐ 11 Basketball Play	35.00	17.50	3.50
Single cut with			
return pass to post			
☐ 12 Kenny Sailors	60.00	30.00	6.00
Providence Steamrollers			
☐ 13 Paul Armstrong	50.00	25.00	5.00
Ft. Wayne Pistons			
☐ 14 Howard Dallmar	60.00	30.00	6.00
Philadelphia Warriors			
☐ 15 Bruce Hale	60.00	30.00	6.00
Indianapolis Jets			
☐ 16 Sid Hertzberg	50.00	25.00	5.00
Washington Capitols			
☐ 17 Basketball Play	35.00	17.50	3.50
Single cut			

☐ 18 Red Rocha	50.00	25.00	5.00
St. Louis Bombers			
☐ 19 Eddie Ehlers	50.00	25.00	5.00
Boston Celtics			
☐ 20 Ellis(Gene) Vance	50.00	25.00	5.00
Chicago Stags			
☐ 21 Andrew(Fuzzy) Levane	60.00	30.00	6.00
Rochester Royals			
☐ 22 Earl Shannon	50.00	25.00	5.00
Providence Steamrollers			
☐ 23 Basketball Play	35.00	17.50	3.50
Double cut off post			
☐ 24 Leo(Crystal) Klier	50.00	25.00	5.00
Ft. Wayne Pistons			
☐ 25 George Senesky	50.00	25.00	5.00
Philadelphia Warriors			
☐ 26 Price Brookfield	50.00	25.00	5.00
Indianapolis Jets			
☐ 27 John Norlander	50.00	25.00	5.00
Washington Capitols			
☐ 28 Don Putman	50.00	25.00	5.00
St. Louis Bombers			
☐ 29 Basketball Play	35.00	17.50	3.50
Double post			
☐ 30 Jack Garfinkel	50.00	25.00	5.00
Boston Celtics			
☐ 31 Chuck Gilmur	50.00	25.00	5.00
Chicago Stags			
☐ 32 William Holzman	425.00	210.00	42.50
Rochester Royals			
☐ 33 Jack Smiley	50.00	25.00	5.00
Ft. Wayne Pistons			
☐ 34 Joe Fulks	425.00	210.00	42.50
Philadelphia Warriors			
☐ 35 Basketball Play	35.00	17.50	3.50
Screen play			
☐ 36 Hal Tidrick	50.00	25.00	5.00
Indianapolis Jets			
☐ 37 Don(Swede) Carlson	100.00	50.00	10.00
Minneapolis Lakers			
☐ 38 Buddy Jeanette CO	135.00	70.00	13.50
Baltimore Bullets			
☐ 39 Ray Kuka	100.00	50.00	10.00
New York Knicks			
☐ 40 Stan Miasek	100.00	50.00	10.00
Chicago Stags			
☐ 41 Basketball Play	70.00	35.00	7.00
Double screen			
☐ 42 George Nostrand	100.00	50.00	10.00
Providence Steamrollers			
☐ 43 Chuck Halbert	110.00	55.00	11.00
Boston Celtics			
☐ 44 Arnie Johnson	100.00	50.00	10.00
Rochester Royals			
☐ 45 Bob Doll	100.00	50.00	10.00
St. Louis Bombers			
☐ 46 Horace McKinney	135.00	70.00	13.50
Washington Capitols			
☐ 47 Basketball Play	70.00	35.00	7.00
Out of bounds			
☐ 48 Ed Sadowski	100.00	50.00	10.00
Philadelphia Warriors			
☐ 49 Bob Kinney	100.00	50.00	10.00
Ft. Wayne Pistons			
☐ 50 Charles(Hawk) Black	100.00	50.00	10.00
Indianapolis Jets			
☐ 51 Jack Dwan	100.00	50.00	10.00
Minneapolis Lakers			
☐ 52 Cornelius Simmons	110.00	55.00	11.00
Baltimore Bullets			
☐ 53 Basketball Play	70.00	35.00	7.00
Out of bounds			
☐ 54 Bud Palmer	135.00	70.00	13.50

	New York Knicks			
☐ 55	Max Zaslofsky	300.00	150.00	30.00
	Chicago Stags			
☐ 56	Lee Roy Robbins	100.00	50.00	10.00
	Providence Steamrollers			
☐ 57	Arthur Spector	100.00	50.00	10.00
	Boston Celtics			
☐ 58	Arnie Risen	135.00	70.00	13.50
	Rochester Royals			
☐ 59	Basketball Play	70.00	35.00	7.00
	Out of bounds play			
☐ 60	Ariel Maughan	100.00	50.00	10.00
	St. Louis Bombers			
☐ 61	Dick O'Keefe	100.00	50.00	10.00
	Washington Capitols			
☐ 62	Herman Schaefer	100.00	50.00	10.00
	Minneapolis Lakers			
☐ 63	John Mahnken	100.00	50.00	10.00
	Baltimore Bullets			
☐ 64	Tommy Byrnes	100.00	50.00	10.00
	New York Knicks			
☐ 65	Basketball Play	70.00	35.00	7.00
	Held ball			
☐ 66	Jim Pollard	375.00	190.00	38.00
	Minneapolis Lakers			
☐ 67	Lee Mogus	100.00	50.00	10.00
	Baltimore Bullets			
☐ 68	Lee Knorek	100.00	50.00	10.00
	New York Knicks			
☐ 69	George Mikan	4500.00	1900.00	700.00
	Minneapolis Lakers			
☐ 70	Walter Budko	100.00	50.00	10.00
	Baltimore Bullets			
☐ 71	Basketball Play	70.00	35.00	7.00
	Guards Play			
☐ 72	Carl Braun	250.00	80.00	20.00
	New York Knicks			

1991 Classic Draft Picks

This 50-card set of basketball draft picks was produced by Classic Games, Inc. and features 48 players picked in the first two rounds of the 1991 NBA draft. A total of 450,000 sets were issued, and each set is accompanied by a letter of limited edition. The cards were only available for sale in these factory-sealed complete sets with no wax product being produced. The cards measure the standard size (2 1/2" by 3 1/2"). The fronts feature a glossy color action photo of each player. The backs have statistics and biographical information. Special cards included in the set are a commemorative number one draft choice card of Larry Johnson and a "One-on-One" card of Billy Owens slam-dunking over Johnson.

	MINT	EXC	G-VG
COMPLETE SET (50)	5.00	2.00	.50
COMMON PLAYER (1-50)	.04	.02	.00
☐ 1 Larry Johnson UNLV	1.50	.60	.15
☐ 2 Billy Owens Syracuse	.50	.20	.05
☐ 3 Dikembe Mutombo Georgetown	.75	.30	.07
☐ 4 Mark Macon Temple	.10	.04	.01
☐ 5 Brian Williams Arizona	.20	.08	.02
☐ 6 Terrell Brandon Oregon	.20	.08	.02
☐ 7 Greg Anthony UNLV	.15	.06	.01
☐ 8 Dale Davis Clemson	.40	.16	.04
☐ 9 Anthony Avent Seton Hall	.15	.06	.01
☐ 10 Chris Gatling Old Dominion	.15	.06	.01
☐ 11 Victor Alexander Iowa State	.15	.06	.01
☐ 12 Kevin Brooks Southwest Louisiana	.07	.03	.01
☐ 13 Eric Murdock Providence	.35	.14	.03
☐ 14 LeRon Ellis Syracuse	.10	.04	.01
☐ 15 Stanley Roberts LSU	.12	.05	.01
☐ 16 Rick Fox North Carolina	.30	.12	.03
☐ 17 Pete Chilcutt North Carolina	.15	.06	.01
☐ 18 Kevin Lynch Minnesota	.07	.03	.01
☐ 19 George Ackles UNLV	.04	.02	.00
☐ 20 Rodney Monroe North Carolina State	.07	.03	.01
☐ 21 Randy Brown New Mexico State	.10	.04	.01
☐ 22 Chad Gallagher Creighton	.04	.02	.00
☐ 23 Donald Hodge Temple	.07	.03	.01
☐ 24 Myron Brown Slippery Rock	.07	.03	.01
☐ 25 Mike Iuzzolino St. Francis	.07	.03	.01
☐ 26 Chris Corchiani North Carolina State	.10	.04	.01
☐ 27 Elliott Perry UER Memphis State	.07	.03	.01
☐ 28 Joe Wylie Miami (FL)	.04	.02	.00
☐ 29 Jimmy Oliver Purdue	.04	.02	.00
☐ 30 Doug Overton LaSalle	.10	.04	.01
☐ 31 Sean Green Iona	.07	.03	.01
☐ 32 Steve Hood James Madison	.04	.02	.00
☐ 33 Lamont Strothers Chris. Newport	.07	.03	.01
☐ 34 Alvaro Teheran Houston	.04	.02	.00
☐ 35 Bobby Phills Southern	.15	.06	.01

☐ 36	Richard Dumas DNP (Spain/Okla.St.)	.10	.04	.01
☐ 37	Keith Hughes Rutgers	.04	.02	.00
☐ 38	Isaac Austin Arizona State	.04	.02	.00
☐ 39	Greg Sutton Oral Roberts	.04	.02	.00
☐ 40	Joey Wright Texas	.04	.02	.00
☐ 41	Anthony Jones Oral Roberts	.04	.02	.00
☐ 42	Von McDade Milwaukee/Wisconsin	.04	.02	.00
☐ 43	Marcus Kennedy E. Michigan	.04	.02	.00
☐ 44	Larry Johnson UNLV Top Pick	.50	.20	.05
☐ 45	Larry Johnson and Billy Owens UNLV and Syracuse	.30	.12	.03
☐ 46	Anderson Hunt UNLV	.07	.03	.01
☐ 47	Darrin Chancellor S. Mississippi	.04	.02	.00
☐ 48	Damon Lopez Fordham	.04	.02	.00
☐ 49	Thomas Jordan DNP (Spain/Okla.St.)	.04	.02	.00
☐ 50	Tony Farmer Nebraska	.04	.02	.00

1991 Classic Four-Sport

This 230-card multi-sport set includes all 200 draft picks players from the four Classic Draft Picks sets (football, baseball, basketball, and hockey), plus an additional 30 draft picks not previously found in these other sets. The standard-size (2 1/2" by 3 1/2") cards display new color player photos, with blue-gray marbled borders. The "1991 Classic Draft Picks" emblem appears as a wine-colored wax seal. The full color backs present biographical information and statistics. Appended to the 230-card set is a special ten-card bonus subset, with nine silver bordered cards and a tenth "Gold Card" featuring Raghib "Rocket" Ismail. A five-card Ismail subset is also to be found within the nine silver bordered cards. A final special subset within the 230 cards consists of five cards highlighting the publicized one-on-one game between Billy Owens and Larry Johnson. As an additional incentive to collectors, Classic randomly inserted over 60,000 autographed cards into the 15-card foil packs; it is claimed that each case should contain two or more autographed cards. The autographed cards fea-

ture 61 different players, approximately two-thirds of whom were hockey players. The production run for the English version was 25,000 cases, and a bilingual version of the set was also produced at 20 percent of the English production. The French versions are valued the same as the English cards. The major subdivisions of set are according to sport: hockey (2-50), baseball (51-101), football (102-148), and basketball (149-202). The cards are numbered on the back and checklisted below accordingly.

		MINT	EXC	G-VG
COMPLETE SET (230)		15.00	6.00	1.50
COMMON PLAYER (1-230)		.05	.02	.00
☐ 1	Future Stars	1.00	.40	.10
	Larry Johnson			
	Brien Taylor			
	Russell Maryland			
	Eric Lindros			
☐ 2	Pat Falloon	.60	.24	.06
☐ 3	Scott Niedermayer	.60	.24	.06
☐ 4	Scott Lachance	.20	.08	.02
☐ 5	Peter Forsberg	1.00	.40	.10
☐ 6	Alex Stojanov	.05	.02	.00
☐ 7	Richard Matvichuk	.12	.05	.01
☐ 8	Patrick Poulin	.20	.08	.02
☐ 9	Martin Lapointe	.20	.08	.02
☐ 10	Tyler Wright	.12	.05	.01
☐ 11	Philippe Boucher	.10	.04	.01
☐ 12	Pat Peake	.40	.16	.04
☐ 13	Markus Naslund	.15	.06	.01
☐ 14	Brent Bilodeau	.12	.05	.01
☐ 15	Glen Murray	.20	.08	.02
☐ 16	Niklas Sundblad	.08	.03	.01
☐ 17	Martin Rucinsky	.15	.06	.01
☐ 18	Trevor Halverson	.08	.03	.01
☐ 19	Dean McAmmond	.12	.05	.01
☐ 20	Ray Whitney	.20	.08	.02
☐ 21	Rene Corbet	.12	.05	.01
☐ 22	Eric Lavigne	.08	.03	.01
☐ 23	Zigmund Palffy	.20	.08	.02
☐ 24	Steve Staios	.12	.05	.01
☐ 25	Jim Campbell	.12	.05	.01
☐ 26	Jassen Cullimore	.08	.03	.01
☐ 27	Martin Hamrlik	.10	.04	.01
☐ 28	Jamie Pushor	.08	.03	.01
☐ 29	Donevan Hextall	.08	.03	.01
☐ 30	Andrew Verner	.12	.05	.01
☐ 31	Jason Dawe	.15	.06	.01
☐ 32	Jeff Nelson	.12	.05	.01
☐ 33	Darcy Werenka	.10	.04	.01
☐ 34	Jozef Stumpel	.20	.08	.02
☐ 35	Francois Groleau	.08	.03	.01
☐ 36	Guy Leveque	.12	.05	.01
☐ 37	Jamie Matthews	.08	.03	.01
☐ 38	Dody Wood	.08	.03	.01
☐ 39	Yanic Perreault	.12	.05	.01
☐ 40	Jamie McLennan	.20	.08	.02
☐ 41	Yanick Dupre UER	.10	.04	.01
	(Yanic misspelled on both sides)			
☐ 42	Sandy McCarthy	.12	.05	.01
☐ 43	Chris Osgood	.25	.10	.02
☐ 44	Fredrik Lindquist	.08	.03	.01
☐ 45	Jason Young	.08	.03	.01
☐ 46	Steve Konowalchuk	.12	.05	.01
☐ 47	Michael Nylander UER	.20	.08	.02
☐ 48	Shane Peacock	.08	.03	.01
☐ 49	Yves Sarault	.05	.02	.00
☐ 50	Marcel Cousineau	.08	.03	.01
☐ 51	Brien Taylor	.20	.08	.02
☐ 52	Mike Kelly	.35	.14	.03
☐ 53	David McCarty	.30	.12	.03
☐ 54	Dmitri Young	.30	.12	.03
☐ 55	Joe Vitiello	.30	.12	.03

☐	56	Mark Smith	.15	.06	.01
☐	57	Tyler Green	.15	.06	.01
☐	58	Shawn Estes UER	.10	.04	.01
		(Reversed negative)			
☐	59	Doug Glanville	.15	.06	.01
☐	60	Manny Ramirez	1.25	.50	.12
☐	61	Cliff Floyd	1.25	.50	.12
☐	62	Tyrone Hill	.15	.06	.01
☐	63	Eduardo Perez	.25	.10	.02
☐	64	Al Shirley	.10	.04	.01
☐	65	Benji Gil	.20	.08	.02
☐	66	Calvin Reese	.10	.04	.01
☐	67	Allen Watson	.30	.12	.03
☐	68	Brian Barber	.15	.06	.01
☐	69	Aaron Sele	.90	.36	.09
☐	70	Jon Farrell UER	.10	.04	.01
☐	71	Scott Ruffcorn	.40	.16	.04
☐	72	Brent Gates	.35	.14	.03
☐	73	Scott Stahoviak	.10	.04	.01
☐	74	Tom McKinnon	.10	.04	.01
☐	75	Shawn Livsey	.10	.04	.01
☐	76	Jason Pruitt	.10	.04	.01
☐	77	Greg Anthony	.08	.03	.01
		(Baseball)			
☐	78	Justin Thompson	.20	.08	.02
☐	79	Steve Whitaker	.10	.04	.01
☐	80	Jorge Fabregas	.20	.08	.02
☐	81	Jeff Ware	.08	.03	.01
☐	82	Bobby Jones	.50	.20	.05
☐	83	J.J. Johnson	.20	.08	.02
☐	84	Mike Rossiter	.10	.04	.01
☐	85	Dan Cholowsky	.12	.05	.01
☐	86	Jimmy Gonzalez	.10	.04	.01
☐	87	Trever Miller UER	.10	.04	.01
☐	88	Scott Hatteberg	.12	.05	.01
☐	89	Mike Groppuso	.10	.04	.01
☐	90	Ryan Long	.10	.04	.01
☐	91	Eddie Williams	.10	.04	.01
☐	92	Mike Durant	.10	.04	.01
☐	93	Buck McNabb	.10	.04	.01
☐	94	Jimmy Lewis	.10	.04	.01
☐	95	Eddie Ramos	.10	.04	.01
☐	96	Terry Horn	.10	.04	.01
☐	97	Jon Barnes	.10	.04	.01
☐	98	Shawn Curran	.10	.04	.01
☐	99	Tommy Adams	.10	.04	.01
☐	100	Trevor Mallory	.10	.04	.01
☐	101	Frankie Rodriguez	.40	.16	.04
☐	102	Raghib(Rocket) Ismail	1.25	.50	.12
☐	103	Russell Maryland	.30	.12	.03
☐	104	Eric Turner	.15	.06	.01
☐	105	Bruce Pickens	.10	.04	.01
☐	106	Mike Croel	.20	.08	.02
☐	107	Todd Lyght	.20	.08	.02
☐	108	Eric Swann	.25	.10	.02
☐	109	Antone Davis	.10	.04	.01
☐	110	Stanley Richard	.20	.08	.02
		("Sheriff")			
☐	111	Pat Harlow	.10	.04	.01
☐	112	Alvin Harper	.75	.30	.07
☐	113	Mike Pritchard	.60	.24	.06
☐	114	Leonard Russell	.50	.20	.05
☐	115	Dan McGwire	.12	.05	.01
☐	116	Bobby Wilson	.10	.04	.01
☐	117	Vinnie Clark	.10	.04	.01
☐	118	Kelvin Pritchett	.12	.05	.01
☐	119	Harvey Williams	.20	.08	.02
☐	120	Stan Thomas	.10	.04	.01
☐	121	Randal Hill	.40	.16	.04
☐	122	Todd Marinovich	.10	.04	.01
☐	123	Henry Jones	.25	.10	.02
☐	124	Mike Dumas	.10	.04	.01
☐	125	Ed King	.10	.04	.01

☐	126	Reggie Johnson	.10	.04	.01
☐	127	Roman Phifer	.12	.05	.01
☐	128	Mike Jones	.10	.04	.01
☐	129	Brett Favre	1.25	.50	.12
☐	130	Browning Nagle	.10	.04	.01
☐	131	Esera Tuaolo	.10	.04	.01
☐	132	George Thornton	.08	.03	.01
☐	133	Dixon-Edwards	.12	.05	.01
☐	134	Darryl Lewis UER	.10	.04	.01
☐	135	Eric Bieniemy	.15	.06	.01
☐	136	Shane Curry	.05	.02	.00
☐	137	Jerome Henderson	.10	.04	.01
☐	138	Wesley Carroll	.10	.04	.01
☐	139	Nick Bell	.20	.08	.02
☐	140	John Flannery	.08	.03	.01
☐	141	Ricky Watters	1.00	.40	.10
☐	142	Jeff Graham	.25	.10	.02
☐	143	Eric Moten	.10	.04	.01
☐	144	Jesse Campbell	.10	.04	.01
☐	145	Chris Zorich	.30	.12	.03
☐	146	Doug Thomas	.12	.05	.01
☐	147	Phil Hansen	.15	.06	.01
☐	148	Reggie Barrett	.10	.04	.01
☐	149	Larry Johnson	1.25	.50	.12
☐	150	Billy Owens	.40	.16	.04
☐	151	Dikembe Mutombo	.60	.24	.06
☐	152	Mark Macon	.10	.04	.01
☐	153	Brian Williams	.15	.06	.01
☐	154	Terrell Brandon	.15	.06	.01
☐	155	Greg Anthony	.12	.05	.01
		(Basketball)			
☐	156	Dale Davis	.30	.12	.03
☐	157	Anthony Avent	.12	.05	.01
☐	158	Chris Gatling	.12	.05	.01
☐	159	Victor Alexander	.12	.05	.01
☐	160	Kevin Brooks	.08	.03	.01
☐	161	Eric Murdock	.25	.10	.02
☐	162	LeRon Ellis	.10	.04	.01
☐	163	Stanley Roberts	.10	.04	.01
☐	164	Rick Fox	.20	.08	.02
☐	165	Pete Chilcutt	.12	.05	.01
☐	166	Kevin Lynch	.08	.03	.01
☐	167	George Ackles	.08	.03	.01
☐	168	Rodney Monroe	.08	.03	.01
☐	169	Randy Brown	.10	.04	.01
☐	170	Chad Gallagher	.05	.02	.00
☐	171	Donald Hodge	.08	.03	.01
☐	172	Myron Brown	.08	.03	.01
☐	173	Mike Iuzzolino	.08	.03	.01
☐	174	Chris Corchiani	.10	.04	.01
☐	175	Elliot Perry UER	.08	.03	.01
☐	176	Joe Wylie	.05	.02	.00
☐	177	Jimmy Oliver	.08	.03	.01
☐	178	Doug Overton	.10	.04	.01
☐	179	Sean Green	.08	.03	.01
☐	180	Steve Hood	.05	.02	.00
☐	181	Lamont Strothers	.08	.03	.01
☐	182	Alvaro Teheran	.05	.02	.00
☐	183	Bobby Phills	.12	.05	.01
☐	184	Richard Dumas	.10	.04	.01
☐	185	Keith Hughes	.05	.02	.00
☐	186	Isaac Austin	.05	.02	.00
☐	187	Greg Sutton	.05	.02	.00
☐	188	Joey Wright	.05	.02	.00
☐	189	Anthony Jones	.05	.02	.00
☐	190	Von McDade	.05	.02	.00
☐	191	Marcus Kennedy	.05	.02	.00
☐	192	Larry Johnson	.40	.16	.04
		(Number One Pick)			
☐	193	Classic One on One II	.15	.06	.01
☐	194	Anderson Hunt	.08	.03	.01
☐	195	Darrin Chancellor	.05	.02	.00
☐	196	Damon Lopez	.05	.02	.00

			MINT	EXC	G-VG
☐	197	Thomas Jordan	.05	.02	.00
☐	198	Tony Farmer	.05	.02	.00
☐	199	Billy Owens (Number Three Pick)	.15	.06	.01
☐	200	Owens Takes 4-3 Lead (Billy Owens)	.15	.06	.01
☐	201	Johnson Slams for 6-6 Tie (Larry Johnson)	.15	.06	.01
☐	202	Score Tied with :49 Left	.15	.06	.01
☐	203	Gary Brown	1.50	.60	.15
☐	204	Rob Carpenter	.12	.05	.01
☐	205	Ricky Ervins	.15	.06	.01
☐	206	Donald Hollas	.10	.04	.01
☐	207	Greg Lewis	.10	.04	.01
☐	208	Darren Lewis	.10	.04	.01
☐	209	Anthony Morgan	.08	.03	.01
☐	210	Chris Smith	.05	.02	.00
☐	211	Perry Carter	.05	.02	.00
☐	212	Melvin Cheatum	.05	.02	.00
☐	213	Jerome Harmon	.08	.03	.01
☐	214	Keith(Mr.) Jennings	.15	.06	.01
☐	215	Brian Shorter	.05	.02	.00
☐	216	Dexter Davis	.10	.04	.01
☐	217	Ed McCaffrey	.30	.12	.03
☐	218	Joey Hamilton	.60	.24	.06
☐	219	Marc Kroon	.15	.06	.01
☐	220	Moe Gardner	.12	.05	.01
☐	221	Jon Vaughn	.20	.08	.02
☐	222	Lawrence Dawsey	.20	.08	.02
☐	223	Michael Stonebreaker	.08	.03	.01
☐	224	Shawn Moore	.20	.08	.02
☐	225	Shawn Green	.50	.20	.05
☐	226	Scott Pisciotta	.15	.06	.01
☐	227	Checklist 1	.05	.02	.00
☐	228	Checklist 2	.05	.02	.00
☐	229	Checklist 3	.05	.02	.00
☐	230	Checklist 4	.08	.03	.01

1991 Classic Four-Sport Autographs

Yves Sarault   LW

Congratulations! You have just received this extremely Limited Classic Draft Pick Collection Autograph Card.

The 1991 Classic Draft Collection Autograph set consists of 61 standard-size (2 1/2" by 3 1/2") cards. They were randomly inserted throughout the foil packs. Listed after the player's name is how many cards were autographed by that player. An "A" suffix after the regular card number is used here for convenience.

	MINT	EXC	G-VG
COMPLETE SET (61)	1000.00	400.00	100.00
COMMON CARD	10.00	4.00	1.00

☐	2A Pat Falloon/1100	50.00	20.00	5.00
☐	3A S.Niedermayer/1250	50.00	20.00	5.00
☐	4A Scott Lachance/1100	15.00	6.00	1.50
☐	6A Alex Stojanov/950	10.00	4.00	1.00
☐	8A Patrick Poulin/1100	15.00	6.00	1.50
☐	10A Tyler Wright/950	10.00	4.00	1.00
☐	11A Philippe Boucher/1150	10.00	4.00	1.00
☐	12A Pat Peake/1100	35.00	14.00	3.50
☐	14A Brent Bilodeau/1000	10.00	4.00	1.00
☐	15A Glen Murray/1100	15.00	6.00	1.50
☐	16A Niklas Sundblad/900	10.00	4.00	1.00
☐	17A Martin Rucinsky/1100	10.00	4.00	1.00
☐	18A Trevor Halverson/1100	10.00	4.00	1.00
☐	19A Dean McAmmond/1100	10.00	4.00	1.00
☐	20A Ray Whitney/2600	10.00	4.00	1.00
☐	21A Rene Corbet/950	10.00	4.00	1.00
☐	22A Eric Lavigne/1100	10.00	4.00	1.00
☐	24A Steve Staios/1100	10.00	4.00	1.00
☐	25A Jim Campbell/1100	10.00	4.00	1.00
☐	26A Jassen Cullimore/1000	10.00	4.00	1.00
☐	28A Jamie Pushor/1050	10.00	4.00	1.00
☐	29A Donevan Hextall/1100	10.00	4.00	1.00
☐	30A Andrew Verner/1200	10.00	4.00	1.00
☐	31A Jason Dawe/950	15.00	6.00	1.50
☐	32A Jeff Nelson/1100	10.00	4.00	1.00
☐	33A Darcy Werenka/1150	10.00	4.00	1.00
☐	35A Francois Groleau/1150	10.00	4.00	1.00
☐	36A Guy Leveque/1150	10.00	4.00	1.00
☐	37A Jamie Matthews/1100	10.00	4.00	1.00
☐	38A Dody Wood/1050	10.00	4.00	1.00
☐	39A Yanic Perreault/1100	10.00	4.00	1.00
☐	40A Jamie McLennan/1100	15.00	6.00	1.50
☐	41A Yanick Dupre/1050	10.00	4.00	1.00
☐	42A Sandy McCarthy/1150	10.00	4.00	1.00
☐	43A Chris Osgood/1100	25.00	10.00	2.50
☐	44A Fredr.Lindquist/1100	10.00	4.00	1.00
☐	45A Jason Young/1200	10.00	4.00	1.00
☐	46A S.Konowalchuk/1350	10.00	4.00	1.00
☐	47A Michael Nylander/1100	15.00	6.00	1.50
☐	48A Shane Peacock/1150	10.00	4.00	1.00
☐	49A Yves Sarault/1150	10.00	4.00	1.00
☐	50A Marcel Cousineau/1100	10.00	4.00	1.00
☐	51A Brien Taylor/2600	20.00	8.00	2.00
☐	52A Mike Kelly/2600	30.00	12.00	3.00
☐	53A David McCarty/2450	25.00	10.00	2.50
☐	54A Dmitri Young/2600	30.00	12.00	3.00
☐	55A Joe Vitiello/1900	15.00	6.00	1.50
☐	56A Mark Smith/1700	15.00	6.00	1.50
☐	58A Shawn Estes/2000	10.00	4.00	1.00
☐	59A Doug Glanville/2000	10.00	4.00	1.00
☐	61A Cliff Floyd/2000	90.00	36.00	9.00
☐	62A Tyrone Hill/1000	10.00	4.00	1.00
☐	63A Eduardo Perez/950	30.00	12.00	3.00
☐	101A F.Rodriguez/1450	40.00	16.00	4.00
☐	102A Rocket Ismail/2000	75.00	30.00	7.50
☐	103A Russell Maryland/1000	25.00	10.00	2.50
☐	150A Billy Owens/2500	30.00	12.00	3.00
☐	151A Dikembe Mutombo/1000	60.00	24.00	6.00
☐	153A Brian Williams/1500	10.00	4.00	1.00
☐	163A Stanley Roberts/2000	10.00	4.00	1.00
☐	218A Joey Hamilton/2000	30.00	12.00	3.00

1991 Classic Four-Sport LPs

Cards from this ten-card bonus subset were randomly inserted in 1991 Classic Draft Picks Collection foil packs. The cards are distinguished from the regular issue in that nine of them have a silver inner border while one has a gold inner border. A five-card Ismail subset is also to be found within the nine silver-bordered cards. The "1991 Classic Draft Picks" emblem appears as a wine-colored wax seal at the upper left corner. The horizontally oriented backs carry brief comments superimposed over a dusted version of Classic's wax seal emblem. The cards are numbered on the back.

"The Final Shot"

	MINT	EXC	G-VG
COMPLETE SET (10)	25.00	10.00	2.50
COMMON CARD (LP1-LP10)	1.50	.60	.15
☐ LP1 Rocket Lands In Canada	2.00	.80	.20
☐ LP2 Rocket Surveys The Future	2.00	.80	.20
☐ LP3 Rocket Launch	2.00	.80	.20
☐ LP4 Track Star (Rocket Ismail)	2.00	.80	.20
☐ LP5 Rocket Knows Classic	2.00	.80	.20
☐ LP6 Johnson's Guns (Larry Johnson)	6.00	2.40	.60
☐ LP7 Brien Taylor	1.50	.60	.15
☐ LP8 Classic Gold Card SP	10.00	4.00	1.00
☐ LP9 The Final Shot (Larry Johnson and Billy Owens)	4.00	1.60	.40
☐ LP10 Russell Maryland (Number One Pick)	1.75	.70	.17

1992 Classic BK Previews

These Classic Basketball Draft Picks preview cards were randomly inserted in the 1992 Classic Football Draft Picks 15-card foil packs. Only 10,000 of each card were produced. The standard-size cards (2 1/2" by 3 1/2") cards feature on the front glossy color action player photos enclosed by white borders. The Classic logo, player's name, and position

appear in a silver stripe beneath the picture. The backs read repeatedly "For Promotional Purposes Only" as well as bearing an advertisement and the Classic logo. The cards are numbered on the back.

	MINT	EXC	G-VG
COMPLETE SET (5)	150.00	60.00	15.00
COMMON PLAYER (1-5)	6.00	2.40	.60
☐ 1 Shaquille O'Neal LSU	100.00	40.00	10.00
☐ 2 Alonzo Mourning Georgetown	50.00	20.00	5.00
☐ 3 Don MacLean UCLA	15.00	6.00	1.50
☐ 4 Walt Williams Maryland	6.00	2.40	.60
☐ 5 Christian Laettner Duke	12.00	5.00	1.20

1992 Classic Draft

The 1992 Classic Basketball Draft Picks set contains 100 standard-size (2 1/2" by 3 1/2") cards, including all 54 drafted players. The set features the first nationally distributed 1992 trading card of NBA first overall pick Shaquille O'Neal as well as the only draft cards of second pick Alonzo Mourning and fourth pick Jimmy Jackson. The set also includes a Flashback (95-98) subset. The fronts feature glossy color action photos bordered in white. The player's name appears in a silver stripe beneath the picture, which intersects the Classic logo at the lower left corner. The backs have a second color player photo and present biographical information, complete college statistics, and a scouting report. The cards are numbered on the back. Cards 61-100 were only available in 15-card foil packs as the blister sets contained only cards 1-60. The production run was reportedly 28,000 ten-box cases and 125,000 60-card factory blister sets .

	MINT	EXC	G-VG
COMPLETE FOIL SET (100)	15.00	6.00	1.50
COMPLETE BLISTER SET (61)	15.00	6.00	1.50
COMMON PLAYER (1-60)	.05	.02	.00
COMMON PLAYER (61-100)	.05	.02	.00
☐ 1 Shaquille O'Neal LSU	5.00	2.00	.50
☐ 2 Walt Williams Maryland	.30	.12	.03
☐ 3 Lee Mayberry Arkansas	.20	.08	.02
☐ 4 Tony Bennett Wisconsin (Green Bay)	.15	.06	.01
☐ 5 Litteral Green Georgia	.10	.04	.01

☐ 6 Chris Smith	.25	.10	.02
Connecticut			
☐ 7 Henry Williams	.05	.02	.00
NC (Charlotte)			
☐ 8 Terrell Lowery	.25	.10	.02
Loyola			
☐ 9 Radenko Dobras	.05	.02	.00
South Florida			
☐ 10 Curtis Blair	.05	.02	.00
Richmond			
☐ 11 Randy Woods	.10	.04	.01
La Salle			
☐ 12 Todd Day	.30	.12	.03
Arkansas			
☐ 13 Anthony Peeler	.35	.14	.03
Missouri			
☐ 14 Darin Archbold	.05	.02	.00
Butler			
☐ 15 Benford Williams	.05	.02	.00
Texas			
☐ 16 Terrence Lewis	.05	.02	.00
Washington State			
☐ 17 James McCoy	.05	.02	.00
Massachusetts			
☐ 18 Damon Patterson	.05	.02	.00
Oklahoma			
☐ 19 Bryant Stith	.50	.20	.05
Virginia			
☐ 20 Doug Christie	.40	.16	.04
Pepperdine			
☐ 21 Latrell Sprewell	1.75	.70	.17
Alabama			
☐ 22 Hubert Davis	.30	.12	.03
North Carolina			
☐ 23 David Booth	.05	.02	.00
DePaul			
☐ 24 David Johnson	.08	.03	.01
Syracuse			
☐ 25 Jon Barry	.20	.08	.02
Georgia Tech			
☐ 26 Everick Sullivan	.05	.02	.00
Louisville			
☐ 27 Brian Davis	.10	.04	.01
Duke			
☐ 28 Clarence Weatherspoon	.90	.36	.09
Southern Mississippi			
☐ 29 Malik Sealy	.15	.06	.01
St. John's			
☐ 30 Matt Geiger	.25	.10	.02
Georgia Tech			
☐ 31 Jimmy Jackson	1.50	.60	.15
Ohio State			
☐ 32 Matt Steigenga	.08	.03	.01
Michigan State			
☐ 33 Robert Horry	.90	.36	.09
Alabama			
☐ 34 Marlon Maxey	.12	.05	.01
UTEP			
☐ 35 Reggie Slater	.05	.02	.00
Wyoming			
☐ 36 Lucius Davis	.08	.03	.01
UC Santa Barbara			
☐ 37 Chris King	.10	.04	.01
Wake Forest			
☐ 38 Dexter Cambridge	.05	.02	.00
Texas			
☐ 39 Alonzo Jamison	.08	.03	.01
Kansas			
☐ 40 Anthony Tucker	.05	.02	.00
Wake Forest			
☐ 41 Tracy Murray	.20	.08	.02
UCLA			
☐ 42 Vernel Singleton	.05	.02	.00

☐ 43	Christian Laettner Duke LSU	.60	.24	.06
☐ 44	Don MacLean UCLA	.75	.30	.07
☐ 45	Adam Keefe Stanford	.12	.05	.01
☐ 46	Tom Gugliotta North Carolina State	.75	.30	.07
☐ 47	LaPhonso Ellis Notre Dame	.90	.36	.09
☐ 48	Byron Houston Oklahoma	.15	.06	.01
☐ 49	Oliver Miller Arkansas	.35	.14	.03
☐ 50	Ron "Popeye" Jones Murray State	.08	.03	.01
☐ 51	P.J. Brown Louisiana Tech	.05	.02	.00
☐ 52	Eric Anderson Indiana	.10	.04	.01
☐ 53	Darren Morningstar Pittsburgh	.05	.02	.00
☐ 54	Isaiah Morris Arkansas	.08	.03	.01
☐ 55	Stephen Howard DePaul	.05	.02	.00
☐ 56	Reggie Smith TCU	.10	.04	.01
☐ 57	Elmore Spencer UNLV	.25	.10	.02
☐ 58	Sean Rooks Arizona	.20	.08	.02
☐ 59	Robert Werdann St. John's	.08	.03	.01
☐ 60	Alonzo Mourning Georgetown	2.50	1.00	.25
☐ 61	Steve Rogers Alabama State	.05	.02	.00
☐ 62	Tim Burroughs Jacksonville	.05	.02	.00
☐ 63	Ed Book Canisius	.05	.02	.00
☐ 64	Herb Jones Cincinnati	.08	.03	.01
☐ 65	Mik Kilgore Temple	.05	.02	.00
☐ 66	Ken Leeks Central Florida	.05	.02	.00
☐ 67	Sam Mack Houston	.05	.02	.00
☐ 68	Sean Miller Pittsburgh	.05	.02	.00
☐ 69	Craig Upchurch Houston	.05	.02	.00
☐ 70	Van Usher Tennessee Tech	.05	.02	.00
☐ 71	Corey Williams Oklahoma State	.05	.02	.00
☐ 72	Duane Cooper USC	.08	.03	.01
☐ 73	Brett Roberts Morehead State	.10	.04	.01
☐ 74	Elmer Bennett Notre Dame	.08	.03	.01
☐ 75	Brent Price Oklahoma	.12	.05	.01
☐ 76	Daimon Sweet Notre Dame	.08	.03	.01
☐ 77	Darrick Martin UCLA	.05	.02	.00
☐ 78	Gerald Madkins UCLA	.10	.04	.01

☐ 79 Jo Jo English	.10	.04	.01
South Carolina			
☐ 80 Alex Blackwell	.08	.03	.01
Monmouth			
☐ 81 Anthony Dade	.05	.02	.00
Louisiana Tech			
☐ 82 Matt Fish	.05	.02	.00
NC (Wilmington)			
☐ 83 Byron Tucker	.05	.02	.00
George Mason			
☐ 84 Harold Miner	.40	.16	.04
USC			
☐ 85 Greg Dennis	.05	.02	.00
East Tennessee State			
☐ 86 Jeff Roulston	.05	.02	.00
South Carolina			
☐ 87 Keir Rogers	.05	.02	.00
Loyola (Illinois)			
☐ 88 Billy Law	.05	.02	.00
Colorado			
☐ 89 Geoff Lear	.05	.02	.00
Pepperdine			
☐ 90 Lambert Shell	.05	.02	.00
Bridgeport			
☐ 91 Elbert Rogers	.05	.02	.00
Alabama (Birmingham)			
☐ 92 Ron Ellis	.05	.02	.00
Louisiana Tech			
☐ 93 Predrag Danilovic	.05	.02	.00
☐ 94 Calvin Talford	.05	.02	.00
East Tennessee State			
☐ 95 Stacey Augmon	.12	.05	.01
UNLV			
Flashback 1			
☐ 96 Steve Smith	.12	.05	.01
Michigan State			
Flashback 2			
☐ 97 Billy Owens	.12	.05	.01
Syracuse			
Flashback 3			
☐ 98 Dikembe Mutombo	.20	.08	.02
Georgetown			
Flashback 4			
☐ 99 Checklist 1-50	.05	.02	.00
☐ 100 Checklist 51-100	.08	.03	.01
☐ NNO Christian Laettner BC	1.25	.50	.12
(Bonus Card found			
only in blister sets)			

1992 Classic Draft Gold

This 101-card set features all 54 drafted players and measures the standard size (2 1/2" by 3 1/2"). Only 8,500 sequentially numbered sets were produced, and each set was packaged in a walnut display case. Each set included an individually numbered Shaquille O'Neal autograph card. The fronts feature action color player photos with white borders. The player's name and position are gold foil stamped in a black border stripe at the bottom. The Classic Draft Picks Gold logo overlaps the stripe and the photo at the lower left corner. The white background on the backs displays a vertical action color picture and a scouting report, while the player's name (in a gold stripe), biography, and statistics appear horizontally. The cards are numbered on the back. Gold star cards are valued at three to six times the corresponding value of the regular card.

	MINT	EXC	G-VG
COMPLETE FACT.SET (101)	275.00	110.00	27.00
COMMON PLAYER (1-100)	.30	.12	.03

	MINT	EXC	G-VG
☐ AU Shaquille O'Neal AU	180.00	75.00	18.00
LSU			
(Certified autograph, one of 8500)			

1992 Classic Draft LPs

This ten-card set, subtitled "Top Ten Pick", features the top ten picks of the 1992 NBA Draft. These standard size (2 1/2" by 3 1/2") cards were randomly inserted in 1992 Classic Draft Picks 15-card foil packs. The fronts feature glossy color action photos enclosed by white borders. The player's name appears in a silver foil stripe beneath the picture, which intersects the Classic logo at the lower left corner. The production figures "1 of 56,000" and the "Top Ten Pick" emblem at the card top are also silver foil. The horizontally oriented backs have a silver background and feature a second color player photo and player profile. The cards are numbered on the back with an "LP" (limited print) prefix.

	MINT	EXC	G-VG
COMPLETE SET (10)	100.00	40.00	10.00
COMMON PLAYER (LP1-LP10)	1.00	.40	.10
☐ LP1 Shaquille O'Neal	50.00	20.00	5.00
LSU			
☐ LP2 Alonzo Mourning	25.00	10.00	2.50
Georgetown			
☐ LP3 Christian Laettner	6.00	2.40	.60
Duke			
☐ LP4 Jimmy Jackson	15.00	6.00	1.50
Ohio State			
☐ LP5 LaPhonso Ellis	9.00	3.75	.90

		MINT	EXC	G-VG
	Notre Dame			
☐ LP6 Tom Gugliotta		7.50	3.00	.75
	North Carolina State			
☐ LP7 Walt Williams		3.00	1.20	.30
	Maryland			
☐ LP8 Todd Day		3.00	1.20	.30
	Arkansas			
☐ LP9 Clarence Weatherspoon		9.00	3.75	.90
	Southern Mississippi			
☐ LP10 Adam Keefe		1.00	.40	.10
	Stanford			

1992 Classic Magicians

Inserted one per jumbo pack, this 20-card standard-size (2 1/2" by 3 1/2") set features white-bordered color action shots on the fronts. Each card displays the player's name in blue lettering inside a silver foil stripe at the bottom of the photo, with the player's position appearing just beneath inside a black bar, and the Classic logo atop the foil to the left. The silver foil Magician logo in the top right rounds out the front. The backs have narrow-cropped color action photos on their right sides and silver stripes down the left with the player's name. Scouting reports and horizontally oriented biography and stats appear between. Cards 2, 4 and 5 have "'91 Flashback" printed in white across the tops of the fronts. The cards are numbered on the back with a "BC" prefix.

		MINT	EXC	G-VG
COMPLETE SET (20)		14.00	5.75	1.40
COMMON PLAYER (BC1-BC20)		.25	.10	.02
☐ BC1 Doug Christie		.75	.30	.07
	Pepperdine			
☐ BC2 Billy Owens FLB		.60	.24	.06
	Syracuse			
☐ BC3 Latrell Sprewell		3.50	1.40	.35
	Alabama			
☐ BC4 Stacey Augmon FLB		.60	.24	.06
	UNLV			
☐ BC5 Steve Smith FLB		.60	.24	.06
	Michigan State			
☐ BC6 Jon Barry		.40	.16	.04
	Georgia Tech			
☐ BC7 Christian Laettner		1.25	.50	.12
	Duke			
☐ BC8 Jimmy Jackson		3.00	1.20	.30
	Ohio State			
☐ BC9 Tracy Murray		.40	.16	.04
	UCLA			
☐ BC10 Walt Williams		.60	.24	.06
	Maryland			
☐ BC11 Todd Day		.60	.24	.06
	Arkansas			
☐ BC12 Dave Johnson		.25	.10	.02

	MINT	EXC	G-VG
□ BC13 Byron Houston Syracuse	.30	.12	.03
□ BC14 Robert Horry Oklahoma State	1.75	.70	.17
□ BC15 Harold Miner Alabama	.75	.30	.07
□ BC16 Bryant Stith USC	1.00	.40	.10
□ BC17 Malik Sealy Virginia	.30	.12	.03
□ BC18 Randy Woods St. John's	.25	.10	.02
□ BC19 Anthony Peeler La Salle	.75	.30	.07
□ BC20 Lee Mayberry Missouri	.40	.16	.04
Arkansas			

1992 Classic Four-Sport Previews

These five preview cards were randomly inserted in baseball and hockey draft picks foil packs. According to the backs, just 10,000 of each card were produced. The cards measure the standard size (2 1/2" by 3 1/2"). The fronts display the full-bleed glossy color player photos. At the upper right corner, the word "Preview" surmounts the Classic logo. This logo overlays a black stripe that runs down the left side and features the player's name and position. The gray backs have the word "Preview" in red lettering at the top and are accented by short purple diagonal stripes on each side. Between the stripes are a congratulations and an advertisement. The cards are numbered on the back with a "CC" prefix for convenience.

	MINT	EXC	G-VG
COMPLETE SET (5)	75.00	30.00	7.50
COMMON PLAYER (CC1-CC5)	3.00	1.20	.30
□ CC1 Shaquille O'Neal	50.00	20.00	5.00
□ CC2 Desmond Howard	3.50	1.40	.35
□ CC3 Roman Hamrlik	4.00	1.60	.40
□ CC4 Phil Nevin	3.00	1.20	.30
□ CC5 Alonzo Mourning	25.00	10.00	2.50

1992 Classic Four-Sport

The 1992 Classic Draft Picks Collection consists of 325 standard-size (2 1/2" by 3 1/2") cards, featuring the top picks from football, basketball, baseball, and hockey drafts. Only 40,000 12-box foil cases were produced. Randomly inserted in the 12-card packs were over 100,000 autograph cards from over 50 of the top draft picks from basketball, football, base-

ball, and hockey, including cards autographed by Shaquille O'Neal, Desmond Howard, Roman Hamrlik, and Phil Nevin. Also inserted in the packs were "Instant Win Giveway Cards" that entitled the collector to the 500,000.00 sports memorabilia giveway that Classic offered in this contest. Finally a 25-card limited print, foil-stamped insert set, which included the special "Future Superstars" card and the "King and His Heir" card, was randomly collated into the packs; only 46,080 of each LP card was produced.

		MINT	EXC	G-VG
	COMPLETE SET (325)	20.00	8.00	2.00
	COMMON PLAYER (1-325)	.05	.02	.00
☐ 1	Shaquille O'Neal	4.00	1.60	.40
☐ 2	Walt Williams	.25	.10	.02
☐ 3	Lee Mayberry	.15	.06	.01
☐ 4	Tony Bennett	.12	.05	.01
☐ 5	Litteral Green	.10	.04	.01
☐ 6	Chris Smith	.20	.08	.02
☐ 7	Henry Williams	.05	.02	.00
☐ 8	Terrell Lowery	.20	.08	.02
☐ 9	Curtis Blair	.05	.02	.00
☐ 10	Randy Woods	.10	.04	.01
☐ 11	Todd Day	.25	.10	.02
☐ 12	Anthony Peeler	.25	.10	.02
☐ 13	Darin Archbold	.05	.02	.00
☐ 14	Benford Williams	.05	.02	.00
☐ 15	Damon Patterson	.05	.02	.00
☐ 16	Bryant Stith	.40	.16	.04
☐ 17	Doug Christie	.30	.12	.03
☐ 18	Latrell Sprewell	1.25	.50	.12
☐ 19	Hubert Davis	.25	.10	.02
☐ 20	David Booth	.05	.02	.00
☐ 21	Dave Johnson	.08	.03	.01
☐ 22	Jon Barry	.15	.06	.01
☐ 23	Everick Sullivan	.05	.02	.00
☐ 24	Brian Davis	.10	.04	.01
☐ 25	Clarence Weatherspoon	.75	.30	.07
☐ 26	Malik Sealy	.12	.05	.01
☐ 27	Matt Geiger	.20	.08	.02
☐ 28	Jimmy Jackson	1.25	.50	.12
☐ 29	Matt Steigenga	.08	.03	.01
☐ 30	Robert Horry	.75	.30	.07
☐ 31	Marlon Maxey	.10	.04	.01
☐ 32	Chris King	.05	.02	.00
☐ 33	Dexter Cambridge	.05	.02	.00
☐ 34	Alonzo Jamison	.08	.03	.01
☐ 35	Anthony Tucker	.05	.02	.00
☐ 36	Tracy Murray	.15	.06	.01
☐ 37	Vernel Singleton	.05	.02	.00
☐ 38	Christian Laettner	.50	.20	.05
☐ 39	Don MacLean	.60	.24	.06
☐ 40	Adam Keefe	.10	.04	.01
☐ 41	Tom Gugliotta	.60	.24	.06
☐ 42	LaPhonso Ellis	.75	.30	.07

□	#	Name			
□	43	Byron Houston	.12	.05	.01
□	44	Oliver Miller	.25	.10	.02
□	45	Ron (Popeye) Jones	.08	.03	.01
□	46	P.J. Brown	.05	.02	.00
□	47	Eric Anderson	.10	.04	.01
□	48	Darren Morningstar	.05	.02	.00
□	49	Isaiah Morris	.08	.03	.01
□	50	Stephen Howard	.05	.02	.00
□	51	Elmore Spencer	.20	.08	.02
□	52	Sean Rooks	.15	.06	.01
□	53	Robert Werdann	.08	.03	.01
□	54	Alonzo Mourning	2.00	.80	.20
□	55	Steve Rogers	.05	.02	.00
□	56	Tim Burroughs	.05	.02	.00
□	57	Herb Jones	.08	.03	.01
□	58	Sean Miller	.05	.02	.00
□	59	Corey Williams	.08	.03	.01
□	60	Duane Cooper	.08	.03	.01
□	61	Brett Roberts	.10	.04	.01
□	62	Elmer Bennett	.08	.03	.01
□	63	Brent Price	.10	.04	.01
□	64	Daimon Sweet	.08	.03	.01
□	65	Darrick Martin	.08	.03	.01
□	66	Gerald Madkins	.08	.03	.01
□	67	Jo Jo English	.10	.04	.01
□	68	Matt Fish	.05	.02	.00
□	69	Harold Minor	.30	.12	.03
□	70	Greg Dennis	.05	.02	.00
□	71	Jeff Roulston	.05	.02	.00
□	72	Keir Rogers	.05	.02	.00
□	73	Geoff Lear	.05	.02	.00
□	74	Ron Ellis	.08	.03	.01
□	75	Predrag Danilovic	.05	.02	.01
□	76	Desmond Howard	.60	.24	.06
□	77	David Klingler	.60	.24	.06
□	78	Quentin Coryatt	.75	.30	.07
□	79	Bill Johnson	.10	.04	.01
□	80	Eugene Chung	.10	.04	.01
□	81	Derek Brown	.40	.16	.04
□	82	Carl Pickens	.75	.30	.07
□	83	Chris Mims	.25	.10	.02
□	84	Charles Davenport	.12	.05	.01
□	85	Ray Roberts	.10	.04	.01
□	86	Chuck Smith	.10	.04	.01
□	87	Tony Smith RB	.20	.08	.02
□	88	Ken Swilling	.08	.03	.01
□	89	Greg Skrepenak	.10	.04	.01
□	90	Phillippi Sparks	.10	.04	.01
□	91	Alonzo Spellman	.15	.06	.01
□	92	Bernard Dafney	.10	.04	.01
□	93	Edgar Bennett	.90	.36	.09
□	94	Shane Dronett	.15	.06	.01
□	95	Jeremy Lincoln	.12	.05	.01
□	96	Dion Lambert	.10	.04	.01
□	97	Siran Stacy	.10	.04	.01
□	98	Tony Sacca	.10	.04	.01
□	99	Sean Lumpkin	.12	.05	.01
□	100	Tommy Vardell	.50	.20	.05
□	101	Keith Hamilton	.25	.10	.02
□	102	Sean Gilbert	.75	.30	.07
□	103	Casey Weldon	.20	.08	.02
□	104	Marc Boutte	.12	.05	.01
□	105	Arthur Marshall	.20	.08	.02
□	106	Santana Dotson	.25	.10	.02
□	107	Ronnie West	.08	.03	.01
□	108	Mike Pawlawski	.08	.03	.01
□	109	Dale Carter	.20	.08	.02
□	110	Carlos Snow	.08	.03	.01
□	111	Mark D'Onofrio	.10	.04	.01
□	112	Matt Blundin	.25	.10	.02
□	113	Patrick Rowe	.10	.04	.01
□	114	Joel Steed	.10	.04	.01
□	115	Erick Anderson	.10	.04	.01

☐ 116	Rodney Culver	.20	.08	.02
☐ 117	Chris Hakel	.10	.04	.01
☐ 118	Kevin Smith	.25	.10	.02
☐ 119	Robert Brooks	.12	.05	.01
☐ 120	Bucky Richardson	.20	.08	.02
☐ 121	Steve Israel	.10	.04	.01
☐ 122	Marco Coleman	.75	.30	.07
☐ 123	Johnny Mitchell	.75	.30	.07
☐ 124	Scottie Graham	.50	.20	.05
☐ 125	Keith Goganious	.10	.04	.01
☐ 126	Tommy Maddox	.50	.20	.05
☐ 127	Terrell Buckley	.50	.20	.05
☐ 128	Dana Hall	.12	.05	.01
☐ 129	Ty Detmer	.40	.16	.04
☐ 130	Darryl Williams	.15	.06	.01
☐ 131	Jason Hanson	.25	.10	.02
☐ 132	Leon Searcy	.10	.04	.01
☐ 133	Will Furrer	.25	.10	.02
☐ 134	Darren Woodson	.20	.08	.02
☐ 135	Corey Widmer	.10	.04	.01
☐ 136	Larry Tharpe	.10	.04	.01
☐ 137	Lance Olberding	.08	.03	.01
☐ 138	Stacey Dillard	.10	.04	.01
☐ 139	Anthony Hamlet	.05	.02	.00
☐ 140	Mike Evans	.08	.03	.01
☐ 141	Chester McGlockton	.12	.05	.01
☐ 142	Marquez Pope	.12	.05	.01
☐ 143	Tyrone Legette	.10	.04	.01
☐ 144	Derrick Moore	.20	.08	.02
☐ 145	Calvin Holmes	.08	.03	.01
☐ 146	Eddie Robinson Jr.	.15	.06	.01
☐ 147	Robert Jones	.15	.06	.01
☐ 148	Ricardo McDonald	.10	.04	.01
☐ 149	Howard Dinkins	.10	.04	.01
☐ 150	Todd Collins	.12	.05	.01
☐ 151	Roman Hamrlik	.20	.08	.02
☐ 152	Alexei Yashin	.75	.30	.07
☐ 153	Mike Rathje	.15	.06	.01
☐ 154	Darius Kasparaitis	.15	.06	.01
☐ 155	Cory Stillman	.12	.05	.01
☐ 156	Robert Petrovicky	.15	.06	.01
☐ 157	Andrei Nazarov	.12	.05	.01
☐ 158	Jason Bowen	.12	.05	.01
☐ 159	Jason Smith	.10	.04	.01
☐ 160	David Wilkie	.10	.04	.01
☐ 161	Curtis Bowen	.12	.05	.01
☐ 162	Grant Marshall	.12	.05	.01
☐ 163	Valeri Bure	.50	.20	.05
☐ 164	Jeff Shantz	.12	.05	.01
☐ 165	Justin Hocking	.10	.04	.01
☐ 166	Mike Pecca	.15	.06	.01
☐ 167	Marc Hussey	.10	.04	.01
☐ 168	Sandy Allan	.10	.04	.01
☐ 169	Kirk Maltby	.12	.05	.01
☐ 170	Cale Hulse	.10	.04	.01
☐ 171	Sylvain Cloutier	.10	.04	.01
☐ 172	Martin Gendron	.15	.06	.01
☐ 173	Kevin Smyth	.10	.04	.01
☐ 174	Jason McBain	.10	.04	.01
☐ 175	Lee J. Leslie	.10	.04	.01
☐ 176	Ralph Intranuovo	.12	.05	.01
☐ 177	Martin Reichel	.10	.04	.01
☐ 178	Stefan Ustorf	.10	.04	.01
☐ 179	Jarkko Varvio	.15	.06	.01
☐ 180	Martin Straka	.60	.24	.06
☐ 181	Libor Polasek	.12	.05	.01
☐ 182	Jozef Cierny	.10	.04	.01
☐ 183	Sergei Krivokrasov	.15	.06	.01
☐ 184	Sergei Gonchar	.12	.05	.01
☐ 185	Boris Mironov	.15	.06	.01
☐ 186	Denis Metyluk	.10	.04	.01
☐ 187	Sergei Klimovich	.12	.05	.01
☐ 188	Sergei Brylin	.12	.05	.01

☐	189	Andrei Nikolishin	.10	.04	.01
☐	190	Alexander Cherbayev	.15	.06	.01
☐	191	Vitali Tomilin	.10	.04	.01
☐	192	Sandy Moger	.10	.04	.01
☐	193	Darrin Madeley	.12	.05	.01
☐	194	Denny Felsner	.12	.05	.01
☐	195	Dwayne Norris	.10	.05	.01
☐	196	Joby Messier	.10	.04	.01
☐	197	Michael Stewart	.10	.04	.01
☐	198	Scott Thomas	.10	.04	.01
☐	199	Daniel Laperriere	.10	.04	.01
☐	200	Martin Lacroix	.10	.04	.01
☐	201	Scott LaGrand	.12	.05	.01
☐	202	Scott Pellerin	.10	.04	.01
☐	203	Jean-Yves Roy	.12	.05	.01
☐	204	Rob Gaudreau	.15	.06	.01
☐	205	Jeff McLean	.10	.04	.01
☐	206	Dallas Drake	.15	.06	.01
☐	207	Doug Zmolek	.12	.05	.01
☐	208	Duane Derksen	.10	.04	.01
☐	209	Jim Cummins	.10	.04	.01
☐	210	Lonnie Loach	.10	.04	.01
☐	211	Rob Zamuner	.12	.05	.01
☐	212	Brad Werenka	.15	.06	.01
☐	213	Brent Grieve	.12	.05	.01
☐	214	Sean Hill	.15	.06	.01
☐	215	Peter Ciavaglia	.10	.04	.01
☐	216	Jason Ruff	.10	.04	.01
☐	217	Shawn McCosh	.10	.04	.01
☐	218	Dave Tretowicz	.10	.04	.01
☐	219	Mike Vukonich	.10	.04	.01
☐	220	Kevin Wortman	.10	.04	.01
☐	221	Jason Muzzatti	.12	.05	.01
☐	222	Dmitri Kvartalnov	.15	.06	.01
☐	223	Ray Whitney	.15	.06	.01
☐	224	Manon Rheaume	5.00	2.00	.50
☐	225	Viktor Kozlov	.40	.16	.04
☐	226	Phil Nevin	.50	.20	.05
☐	227	Paul Shuey	.30	.12	.03
☐	228	B.J. Wallace	.20	.08	.02
☐	229	Jeffrey Hammonds	1.50	.60	.15
☐	230	Chad Mottola	.30	.12	.03
☐	231	Derek Jeter	.60	.24	.06
☐	232	Michael Tucker	.50	.20	.05
☐	233	Derek Wallace	.12	.05	.01
☐	234	Kenny Felder	.12	.05	.01
☐	235	Chad McConnell	.20	.08	.02
☐	236	Sean Lowe	.10	.04	.01
☐	237	Ricky Greene	.12	.05	.01
☐	238	Chris Roberts	.20	.08	.02
☐	239	Shannon Stewart	.25	.10	.02
☐	240	Benji Grigsby	.12	.05	.01
☐	241	Jamie Arnold	.15	.06	.01
☐	242	Rick Helling	.25	.10	.02
☐	243	Jason Kendall	.20	.08	.02
☐	244	Todd Steverson	.20	.08	.02
☐	245	Dan Serafini	.15	.06	.01
☐	246	Jeff Schmidt	.10	.04	.01
☐	247	Sherard Clinkscales	.10	.04	.01
☐	248	Ryan Luzinski	.15	.06	.01
☐	249	Shon Walker	.15	.06	.01
☐	250	Brandon Cromer	.10	.04	.01
☐	251	Dave Landaker	.12	.05	.01
☐	252	Michael Mathews	.10	.04	.01
☐	253	Brian Sackinsky	.12	.05	.01
☐	254	Jon Lieber	.40	.16	.04
☐	255	Jim Rosenbohm	.10	.04	.01
☐	256	DeShawn Warren	.10	.04	.01
☐	257	Mike Buddie	.10	.04	.01
☐	258	Chris Smith	.15	.06	.01
☐	259	Dwain Bostic	.12	.05	.01
☐	260	Bobby Hughes	.20	.08	.02
☐	261	Rick Magdellano	.10	.04	.01

☐	262	Bob Wolcott	.12	.05	.01
☐	263	Mike Gulan	.12	.05	.01
☐	264	Yuri Sanchez	.12	.05	.01
☐	265	Tony Sheffield	.10	.04	.01
☐	266	Dan Melendez	.10	.04	.01
☐	267	Jason Giambi	.20	.08	.02
☐	268	Ritchie Moody	.10	.04	.01
☐	269	Trey Beamon	.30	.12	.03
☐	270	Tim Crabtree	.10	.04	.01
☐	271	Chad Roper	.12	.05	.01
☐	272	Mark Thompson	.15	.06	.01
☐	273	Marquis Riley	.10	.04	.01
☐	274	Tom Knauss	.10	.04	.01
☐	275	Chris Holt	.15	.06	.01
☐	276	Jonathan Nunnally	.15	.06	.01
☐	277	Everett Stull	.10	.04	.01
☐	278	Billy Owens	.30	.12	.03
☐	279	Todd Etler	.12	.05	.01
☐	280	Benji Simonton	.30	.12	.03
☐	281	Dwight Maness	.10	.04	.01
☐	282	Chris Eddy	.10	.04	.01
☐	283	Brant Brown	.15	.06	.01
☐	284	Kurt Ehmann	.10	.04	.01
☐	285	Chris Widger	.10	.04	.01
☐	286	Steve Montgomery	.10	.04	.01
☐	287	Chris Gomez	.60	.24	.06
☐	288	Jared Baker	.10	.04	.01
☐	289	Doug Hecker	.10	.04	.01
☐	290	David Spykstra	.10	.04	.01
☐	291	Scott Miller	.10	.04	.01
☐	292	Carey Paige	.12	.05	.01
☐	293	Dave Manning	.10	.04	.01
☐	294	James Keefe	.10	.04	.01
☐	295	Levon Largusa	.12	.05	.01
☐	296	Roger Bailey	.10	.04	.01
☐	297	Rich Ireland	.10	.04	.01
☐	298	Matt Williams	.10	.04	.01
☐	299	Scott Gentile	.10	.04	.01
☐	300	Hut Smith	.10	.04	.01
☐	301	Dave Brown	.25	.10	.02
☐	302	Bobby Bonds Jr.	.12	.05	.01
☐	303	Reggie Smith	.10	.04	.01
☐	304	Preston Wilson	.25	.10	.02
☐	305	John Burke	.25	.10	.02
☐	306	Rodney Henderson	.20	.08	.02
☐	307	Pete Janicki	.15	.06	.01
☐	308	Brien Taylor FLB	.12	.05	.01
☐	309	Mike Kelly FLB	.20	.08	.02
☐	310	Rocket Ismail FLB	.40	.16	.04
☐	311	Billy Owens FLB	.10	.04	.01
☐	312	Dikembe Mutombo FLB	.15	.06	.01
☐	313	Ty Detmer and Desmond Howard	.30	.12	.03
☐	314	Jim Pittsley	.20	.08	.02
☐	315	Christian Laettner JWA	.20	.08	.02
☐	316	Harold Miner JWA	.12	.05	.01
☐	317	Jimmy Jackson JWA	.50	.20	.05
☐	318	Shaquille O'Neal JWA	2.00	.80	.20
☐	319	Alonzo Mourning JWA	1.00	.40	.10
☐	320	Checklist 1	.05	.02	.00
☐	321	Checklist 2	.05	.02	.00
☐	322	Checklist 3	.05	.02	.00
☐	323	Checklist 4	.05	.02	.00
☐	324	Checklist 5	.05	.02	.00
☐	325	Checklist 6	.08	.03	.01

1992 Classic Four-Sport Gold

This 326-card set features all 325 cards of the regular set plus an additional "Future Superstars" autographed card. The cards measure the standard size (2 1/2" by 3 1/2"). Only

9,500 sequentially numbered sets were produced, and each set was packaged in a walnut display case. The cards are numbered on the back. Gold star cards are valued at three to six times the corresponding value of the regular card.

	MINT	EXC	G-VG
COMPLETE FACT.SET (326)	200.00	80.00	20.00
COMMON PLAYER (1-325)	.40	.16	.04
☐ AU Future Superstars AU	100.00	40.00	10.00

Phil Nevin
Shaquille O'Neal
Desmond Howard
Roman Hamrlik
(Certified autograph,
one of 9500)

1992 Classic Four-Sport Autographs

The 1992 Classic Draft Collection Autograph set consists of 54 standard-size (2 1/2" by 3 1/2") cards. They were randomly inserted throughout the foil packs. Listed after the player's name is how many cards were autographed by that player. An "A" suffix after the regular card number is used here for convenience. Jan Caloun and Jan Vopat were not included in the regular set.

	MINT	EXC	G-VG
COMPLETE SET (54)	2800.00	1200.00	250.00
COMMON CARD	10.00	4.00	1.00

☐ 1A Shaquille O'Neal/150	1800.00	750.00	175.00
☐ 2A Walt Williams/2550	15.00	6.00	1.50
☐ 3A Lee Mayberry/2575	10.00	4.00	1.00
☐ 11A Todd Day/1575	20.00	8.00	2.00
☐ 25A C.Weatherspoon/1575	40.00	16.00	4.00
☐ 26A Malik Sealy/1575	10.00	4.00	1.00
☐ 28A Jimmy Jackson/1575	65.00	26.00	6.50
☐ 36A Tracy Murray/1450	10.00	4.00	1.00
☐ 38A C.Laettner/725	45.00	18.00	4.50
☐ 39A Don MacLean/2575	30.00	12.00	3.00
☐ 40A Adam Keefe/1575	10.00	4.00	1.00
☐ 54A Alonzo Mourning/975	200.00	80.00	20.00
☐ 69A Harold Miner/1475	20.00	8.00	2.00
☐ 76A Desmond Howard/975	40.00	16.00	4.00
☐ 77A David Klingler/1125	35.00	14.00	3.50
☐ 78A Quentin Coryatt/3500	25.00	10.00	2.50
☐ 82A Carl Pickens/1475	35.00	14.00	3.50
☐ 87A Tony Smith/3450	10.00	4.00	1.00
☐ 97A Siran Stacy/4325	10.00	4.00	1.00
☐ 98A Tony Sacca/1575	10.00	4.00	1.00
☐ 103A Casey Weldon/4350	15.00	6.00	1.50
☐ 112A Matt Blundin/1575	30.00	12.00	3.00
☐ 127A Terrell Buckley/1475	25.00	10.00	2.50
☐ 129A Ty Detmer/1475	15.00	6.00	1.50
☐ 144A Derrick Moore/1575	15.00	6.00	1.50
☐ 151A Roman Hamrlik/1550	15.00	6.00	1.50
☐ 153A Mike Rathje/2075	10.00	4.00	1.00
☐ 155A Cory Stillman/2125	10.00	4.00	1.00
☐ 158A Jason Bowen/2075	10.00	4.00	1.00
☐ 159A Jason Smith/2075	10.00	4.00	1.00
☐ 165A Justin Hocking/2075	10.00	4.00	1.00
☐ 170A Cale Hulse/1850	10.00	4.00	1.00
☐ 181A Libor Polasek/1950	10.00	4.00	1.00
☐ 185A Boris Mironov/2075	10.00	4.00	1.00
☐ 192A Sandy Moger/1075	10.00	4.00	1.00
☐ 195A Dwayne Norris/1075	10.00	4.00	1.00
☐ 196A Joby Messier/1075	10.00	4.00	1.00
☐ 207A Doug Zmolek/1075	30.00	12.00	3.00
☐ 226A Phil Nevin/1075	15.00	6.00	1.50
☐ 227A Paul Shuey/4050	60.00	24.00	6.00
☐ 229A Jeffrey Hammonds/2950	35.00	14.00	3.50
☐ 231A Derek Jeter/1125	10.00	4.00	1.00
☐ 233A Derek Wallace/1475	10.00	4.00	1.00
☐ 241A Jamie Arnold/1575	15.00	6.00	1.50
☐ 242A Rick Helling/2875	10.00	4.00	1.00
☐ 245A Dan Serafini/1475	10.00	4.00	1.00
☐ 248A Ryan Luzinski/1575	10.00	4.00	1.00
☐ 253A Brian Sackinsky/1575	10.00	4.00	1.00
☐ 259A Dwain Bostic/2075	10.00	4.00	1.00
☐ 290A David Spykstra/1575	15.00	6.00	1.50
☐ 301A Dave Brown/1575	10.00	4.00	1.00
☐ 307A Pete Janicki/1875	15.00	6.00	1.50
☐ NNO Jan Caloun/1975	10.00	4.00	1.00
☐ NNO Jan Vopat/1775			

1992 Classic Four-Sport BCs

Randomly inserted in Classic Draft Picks Collection jumbo packs, these 20 bonus cards measure the standard size (2 1/2" by 3 1/2"). The fronts feature full-bleed glossy color action player photos. A silver foil strip runs down the card face near the left edge and carries the player's name and position. On a silver panel edged by a dark gray stripe, the backs carry statistics, biography, and career summary; a color player photo running down the right edge rounds out the back. The cards are numbered on the dark gray stripe and arranged according to sport as follows: basketball (1-6), hockey (7-12), football (13-17), and baseball (18-20). A randomly inserted Future Superstars card has a picture of all four players on its front, shot against a horizon with dark clouds and lightning; the back indicates that just 10,000 of these cards were produced.

	MINT	EXC	G-VG
COMPLETE SET (21)	25.00	10.00	2.50
COMMON PLAYER (BC1-BC20)	.40	.16	.04
☐ BC1 Alonzo Mourning	4.00	1.60	.40
Georgetown			
☐ BC2 Christian Laettner	1.00	.40	.10
Duke			
☐ BC3 Jim Jackson	2.50	1.00	.25
Ohio State			
☐ BC4 Tom Gugliotta	1.25	.50	.12
North Carolina State			
☐ BC5 Walt Williams	.50	.20	.05
Maryland			
☐ BC6 Harold Miner	.60	.24	.06
USC			
☐ BC7 Roman Hamrlik	.40	.16	.04
☐ BC8 Valeri Bure	1.00	.40	.10
☐ BC9 Dallas Drake	.40	.16	.04
☐ BC10 Dmitri Kvartalnov	.50	.20	.05
☐ BC11 Manon Rheaume	10.00	4.00	1.00
☐ BC12 Viktor Kozlov	.50	.20	.05
☐ BC13 Desmond Howard	1.25	.50	.12
Michigan			
☐ BC14 David Klingler	1.25	.50	.12
Houston			
☐ BC15 Terrell Buckley	1.00	.40	.10
Florida State			
☐ BC16 Quentin Coryatt	1.50	.60	.15
Texas A and M			
☐ BC17 Carl Pickens	1.50	.60	.15
Tennessee			
☐ BC18 Phil Nevin	1.00	.40	.10
Cal State Fullerton			
☐ BC19 Jeffrey Hammonds	3.00	1.20	.30
Stanford			
☐ BC20 Michael Tucker	1.00	.40	.10
Longwood			
☐ FS1 Future Superstars	40.00	16.00	4.00
Phil Nevin			
Shaquille O'Neal			
Desmond Howard			
Roman Hamrlik			

1992 Classic Four-Sport LPs

Randomly inserted in foil packs, this 25-card standard-size (2 1/2" by 3 1/2") limited print set features full-bleed glossy color action player photos on the fronts. A vertical gold foil stripe

runs down each card face near the left edge and carries the player's name and position. Parallel to the stripe, "One of 46,080" appears in gold foil characters. The backs carry a brief biography in a silver panel edged on the left by a dark green stripe that contains the player's name and position. A color player photo along the right edge completes the back. The sports represented are football (1-7, 16), basketball (8-14), baseball (17-21), and hockey (22-25). The cards are numbered on the back with an "LP" prefix.

	MINT	EXC	G-VG
COMPLETE SET (25)	135.00	54.00	13.50
COMMON CARD (LP1-LP25)	1.25	.50	.12
☐ LP1 Desmond Howard	3.50	1.40	.35
☐ LP2 David Klingler	3.50	1.40	.35
☐ LP3 Tommy Maddox	3.50	1.40	.35
☐ LP4 Casey Weldon	1.50	.60	.15
☐ LP5 Tony Smith RB	1.25	.50	.12
☐ LP6 Terrell Buckley	2.50	1.00	.25
☐ LP7 Carl Pickens	4.00	1.60	.40
☐ LP8 Shaquille O'Neal	50.00	20.00	5.00
☐ LP9 Jimmy Jackson	15.00	6.00	1.50
☐ LP10 Alonzo Mourning	25.00	10.00	2.50
☐ LP11 Christian Laettner	6.00	2.40	.60
☐ LP12 Harold Miner	4.00	1.60	.40
☐ LP13 Todd Day	3.00	1.20	.30
☐ LP14 The King and	20.00	8.00	2.00
His Heir			
Kareem Abdul-Jabbar			
Shaquille O'Neal			
☐ LP15 Future Superstars	20.00	8.00	2.00
Phil Nevin			
Shaquille O'Neal			
Roman Hamrlik			
Desmond Howard			
☐ LP16 Classic Quarterbacks	3.00	1.20	.30
Matt Blundin			
David Klingler			
Tommy Maddox			
Mike Pawlawski			
Tony Sacca			
Casey Weldon			
☐ LP17 Phil Nevin	2.50	1.00	.25
☐ LP18 Jeffrey Hammonds	8.00	3.25	.80
☐ LP19 Paul Shuey	1.75	.70	.17
☐ LP20 Ryan Luzinski UER	1.25	.50	.12
☐ LP21 Brien Taylor	2.00	.80	.20
☐ LP22 Roman Hamrlik	3.50	1.40	.35
☐ LP23 Mike Rathje	1.50	.60	.15
☐ LP24 Valeri Bure	7.00	2.80	.70
☐ LP25 Alexei Yashin	8.00	3.25	.80

1993 Classic Draft Previews

These basketball cards were randomly inserted in 1993 Classic Football Draft Picks foil packs as well as 1993 Classic NFL Pro Line Collection packs. Reportedly 17,500 of each card were produced and randomly inserted an average of two cards per case, evenly distributed through both products. The cards measure the standard size (2 1/2" by 3 1/2"). The fronts feature color player action shots with simulated pinewood borders. The player's name and position appear in a colored stripe at the bottom of the photo. The red-bordered back carries a basketball icon and the number of cards produced. The cards are unnumbered and are checklisted below in alphabetical order.

	MINT	EXC	G-VG
COMPLETE SET (4)	100.00	40.00	10.00
COMMON PLAYER (BK1-BK4)	7.00	2.80	.70
☐ BK1 Anfernee Hardaway Memphis State	30.00	12.00	3.00
☐ BK2 Allan Houston UER (Misspelled Alan) Tennessee	7.00	2.80	.70
☐ BK3 Jamal Mashburn Kentucky	25.00	10.00	2.50
☐ BK4 Chris Webber Michigan	40.00	16.00	4.00

1993 Classic Draft Picks

The 1993 Classic Draft Picks set consists of 110 standard-size (2 1/2" by 3 1/2") cards. Randomly inserted throughout the foil packs were the following subsets: ten limited-print, foil-stamped cards, five Hockey Draft Picks preview cards, three superhero cards, and a five-card visually interlocking set of clear acetate cards. The production run was limited to 32,500 ten-box cases. The fronts feature color action player photos with simulated pinewood borders. The player's name and position, along with the 1993 Classic Draft Picks logo, appears in a white bar across the base of each picture. The simulated pinewood design continues on the horizontal back. The player's name appears at the top in an ellipse that is of a lighter-colored simulated pinewood. Stats are displayed in a lighter-colored rectangle at the bottom. A narrow-cropped pinewood-bordered player color action shot along the left side rounds out the card. The cards are numbered on the back.

	MINT	EXC	G-VG
COMPLETE SET (110)	8.00	3.25	.80
COMMON PLAYER (1-110)	.05	.02	.00
☐ 1 Chris Webber Michigan	2.50	1.00	.25
☐ 2 Anfernee Hardaway Memphis State	2.00	.80	.20
☐ 3 Jamal Mashburn Kentucky	1.00	.40	.10

JAMAL MASHBURN   SF

☐ 4 J.R. Rider	1.00	.40	.10
UNLV			
☐ 5 Vin Baker	.75	.30	.07
Hartford			
☐ 6 Rodney Rogers	.40	.16	.04
Wake Forest			
☐ 7 Lindsey Hunter	.40	.16	.04
Jackson State			
☐ 8 Allan Houston	.25	.10	.02
Tennessee			
☐ 9 George Lynch	.40	.16	.04
North Carolina			
☐ 10 Toni Kukoc	.60	.24	.06
(Croatia)			
☐ 11 Ashraf Amaya	.05	.02	.00
Southern Illinois			
☐ 12 Mark Bell	.08	.03	.01
Western Kentucky			
☐ 13 John Best	.08	.03	.01
Tennessee Tech			
☐ 14 Corie Blount	.12	.05	.01
Cincinnati			
☐ 15 Dexter Boney	.05	.02	.00
UNLV			
☐ 16 Tim Brooks	.05	.02	.00
Tennessee (Chattanooga)			
☐ 17 James Bryson	.05	.02	.00
Villanova			
☐ 18 Evers Burns	.10	.04	.01
Maryland			
☐ 19 Scott Burrell	.15	.06	.01
Connecticut			
☐ 20 Sam Cassell	.60	.24	.06
Florida State			
☐ 21 Derrick Chandler	.05	.02	.00
Nebraska			
☐ 22 Sam Crawford	.08	.03	.01
New Mexico State			
☐ 23 Ron Curry	.05	.02	.00
Marquette			
☐ 24 William Davis	.05	.02	.00
James Madison			
☐ 25 Rodney Dobard	.05	.02	.00
Florida State			
☐ 26 Tony Dunkin	.05	.02	.00
Coastal Carolina			
☐ 27 Spencer Dunkley	.08	.03	.01
Delaware			
☐ 28 Bill Edwards	.05	.02	.00
Wright State			
☐ 29 Bryan Edwards	.05	.02	.00
James Madison			

☐ 30 Doug Edwards Florida State	.10	.04	.01
☐ 31 Chuck Evans Mississippi State	.05	.02	.00
☐ 32 Terry Evans Oklahoma	.05	.02	.00
☐ 33 Will Flemons Texas Tech	.05	.02	.00
☐ 34 Alphonso Ford Miss. Valley State	.05	.02	.00
☐ 35 Brian Gilgeous American	.05	.02	.00
☐ 36 Josh Grant Utah	.10	.04	.01
☐ 37 Evric Gray UNLV	.05	.02	.00
☐ 38 Geert Hammink LSU	.08	.03	.01
☐ 39 Lucious Harris Long Beach State	.12	.05	.01
☐ 40 Joe Harvell Mississippi	.05	.02	.00
☐ 41 Antonio Harvey Pfeiffer College	.10	.04	.01
☐ 42 Scott Haskin Oregon State	.10	.04	.01
☐ 43 Brian Hendrick California	.05	.02	.00
☐ 44 Sascha Hupmann Evansville	.05	.02	.00
☐ 45 Stanley Jackson Alabama (Birmingham)	.10	.04	.01
☐ 46 Ervin Johnson New Orleans	.10	.04	.01
☐ 47 Adonis Jordan Kansas	.10	.04	.01
☐ 48 Warren Kidd Middle Tennessee State	.10	.04	.01
☐ 49 Malcolm Mackey Georgia Tech	.10	.04	.01
☐ 50 Rich Manning Washington	.05	.02	.00
☐ 51 Chris McNeal Pittsburgh	.05	.02	.00
☐ 52 Conrad McRae Syracuse	.05	.02	.00
☐ 53 Lance Miller Villanova	.05	.02	.00
☐ 54 Chris Mills Arizona	.40	.16	.04
☐ 55 Matt Nover Indiana	.08	.03	.01
☐ 56 Charles(Bo) Outlaw Houston	.05	.02	.00
☐ 57 Eric Pauley Kansas	.05	.02	.00
☐ 58 Mike Peplowski Michigan State	.08	.03	.01
☐ 59 Stacey Poole Florida	.05	.02	.00
☐ 60 Anthony Reed Tulane	.05	.02	.00
☐ 61 Eric Riley Michigan	.10	.04	.01
☐ 62 Darrin Robinson Sacred Heart	.05	.02	.00
☐ 63 Jackie Robinson So. Carolina State	.05	.02	.00
☐ 64 James Robinson Alabama	.12	.05	.01
☐ 65 Bryon Russell Long Beach State	.15	.06	.01
☐ 66 Brent Scott	.05	.02	.00

		Rice			
☐	67	Bennie Seltzer	.05	.02	.00
		Washington State			
☐	68	Ed Stokes	.08	.03	.01
		Arizona			
☐	69	Antoine Stoudamire	.05	.02	.00
		Oregon			
☐	70	Dirk Surles	.05	.02	.00
		George Washington			
☐	71	Justus Thigpen	.05	.02	.00
		Iowa State			
☐	72	Kevin Thompson	.10	.04	.01
		North Carolina State			
☐	73	Ray Thompson	.05	.02	.00
		Oral Roberts			
☐	74	Gary Trost	.05	.02	.00
		Brigham Young			
☐	75	Nick Van Exel	.50	.20	.05
		Cincinnati			
☐	76	Jerry Walker	.05	.02	.00
		Seton Hall			
☐	77	Rex Walters	.10	.04	.01
		Kansas			
☐	78	Leonard White	.05	.02	.00
		Southern			
☐	79	Chris Whitney	.10	.04	.01
		Clemson			
☐	80	Steve Worthy	.05	.02	.00
		Rutgers			
☐	81	Alex Wright	.05	.02	.00
		Central State			
☐	82	Luther Wright	.10	.04	.01
		Seton Hall			
☐	83	Mark Buford	.05	.02	.00
		Miss. Valley State			
☐	84	Keith Bullock	.05	.02	.00
		Manhattan			
☐	85	Mitchell Butler	.20	.08	.02
		UCLA			
☐	86	Brian Clifford	.05	.02	.00
		Niagara			
☐	87	Terry Dehere	.12	.05	.01
		Seton Hall			
☐	88	Acie Earl	.12	.05	.01
		Iowa			
☐	89	Greg Graham	.10	.04	.01
		Indiana			
☐	90	Angelo Hamilton	.05	.02	.00
		Oklahoma			
☐	91	Thomas Hill	.08	.03	.01
		Duke			
☐	92	Alex Holcombe	.05	.02	.00
		Baylor			
☐	93	Khari Jaxon	.05	.02	.00
		New Mexico			
☐	94	Darnell Mee	.12	.05	.01
		Western Kentucky			
☐	95	Sherron Mills	.05	.02	.00
		Virginia Commonwealth			
☐	96	Gheorge Muresan	.25	.10	.02
		(Romania)			
☐	97	Marcelo Nicola	.05	.02	.00
		UTEP			
☐	98	Julius Nwosu	.05	.02	.00
		Liberty			
☐	99	Richard Petruska	.10	.04	.01
		UCLA			
☐	100	Bryan Sallier	.05	.02	.00
		Oklahoma			
☐	101	Harper Williams	.05	.02	.00
		Massachusetts			
☐	102	Ike Williams	.05	.02	.00
		New Mexico			

		MINT	EXC	G-VG
☐ 103	Byron Wilson.................... Utah	.05	.02	.00
☐ 104	Shaquille O'Neal FLB.......... LSU	.60	.24	.06
☐ 105	Alonzo Mourning FLB.......... Georgetown	.30	.12	.03
☐ 106	Christian Laettner FLB......... Duke	.10	.04	.01
☐ 107	Jimmy Jackson FLB............ Ohio State	.20	.08	.02
☐ 108	Harold Miner FLB.............. USC	.08	.03	.01
☐ 109	Checklist 1....................	.05	.02	.00
☐ 110	Checklist 2....................	.05	.02	.00

1993 Classic Draft Gold

This parallel set to the regular '93 Classic also features one Mashburn and one Webber autograph card included per '93 Classic Gold set. Both players each signed 9500 cards. Except for the gold-foil highlights, the standard-size (2 1/2" by 3 1/2") cards are identical to their regular '93 Classic counterparts. The cards are numbered on the back. Gold stars are valued at three to six times the corresponding value of the regular card.

		MINT	EXC	G-VG
COMPLETE FACT.SET (112).......................		200.00	80.00	20.00
COMMON PLAYER (1-110)........................		.30	.12	.03
☐ AU	Jamal Mashburn AU....................... Kentucky (Certified autograph, one of 9500)	50.00	20.00	5.00
☐ AU	Chris Webber AU.......................... Michigan (Certified autograph, one of 9500)	100.00	40.00	10.00

1993 Classic Draft Acetate Stars

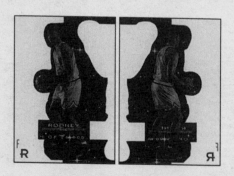

These five acetate cards were randomly inserted in foil packs. By visually interlocking these cards, the collector created a "Draft Stars" panoramic image featuring Webber, Hardaway, Mashburn, Rider, and Rogers. These visually interlocking clear plastic acetate cards were inserted on an average of three per ten-box case of 1993 Classic Basketball Draft Picks. The cards are unnumbered and checklisted below in alphabetical order.

	MINT	EXC	G-VG
COMPLETE SET (5)	40.00	16.00	4.00
COMMON PLAYER (AD1-AD5)	3.50	1.40	.35
☐ AD1 Anfernee Hardaway	14.00	5.75	1.40
Memphis St.			
☐ AD2 Jamal Mashburn	7.00	2.80	.70
Kentucky			
☐ AD3 J.R. Rider	7.00	2.80	.70
UNLV			
☐ AD4 Rodney Rogers	3.50	1.40	.35
Wake Forest			
☐ AD5 Chris Webber	16.00	6.50	1.60
Michigan			

1993 Classic Draft Chromium Stars

Inserted one per jumbo pack, these 20 standard-size (2 1/2" by 3 1/2") cards feature on their metallic fronts borderless color player action shots. The player's name and position appear within the silver bar near the bottom. The horizontal simulated pinewood back carries a narrow-cropped color player action shot on the left. The player's name and biography appear at the top, followed below by a congratulatory message and statistics. The cards are numbered on the back with a "DS" prefix.

	MINT	EXC	G-VG
COMPLETE SET (20)	20.00	8.00	2.00
COMMON PLAYER (DS21-DS40)	.40	.16	.04
☐ DS21 Vin Baker	1.75	.70	.17
Hartford			
☐ DS22 Terry Dehere	.40	.16	.04
Seton Hall			
☐ DS23 Sam Cassell	1.50	.60	.15
Florida State			
☐ DS24 Doug Edwards	.40	.16	.04
Florida State			
☐ DS25 Greg Graham	.40	.16	.04
Indiana			

	MINT	EXC	G-VG
☐ DS26 Scott Haskin	.40	.16	.04
Oregon State			
☐ DS27 Allan Houston	.75	.30	.07
Tennessee			
☐ DS28 Toni Kukoc	1.50	.60	.15
Benetton			
☐ DS29 George Lynch	1.00	.40	.10
North Carolina			
☐ DS30 Jamal Mashburn	2.00	.80	.20
Kentucky			
☐ DS31 Harold Miner	.40	.16	.04
Miami Heat			
☐ DS32 Rex Walters	.40	.16	.04
Kansas			
☐ DS33 James Robinson	.40	.16	.04
Alabama			
☐ DS34 Rodney Rogers	1.00	.40	.10
Wake Forrest			
☐ DS35 Luther Wright	.40	.16	.04
Seton Hall			
☐ DS36 Alonzo Mourning	1.50	.60	.15
Charlotte Hornets			
☐ DS37 Anfernee Hardaway	4.00	1.60	.40
Memphis State			
☐ DS38 Isaiah Rider	2.00	.80	.20
UNLV			
☐ DS39 Lindsey Hunter	1.00	.40	.10
Jackson State			
☐ DS40 Chris Webber	5.00	2.00	.50
Michigan			

1993 Classic Draft Illustrated

Drawn by artist Craig Hamilton, these three cards display images of basketball superstars and they were reportedly inserted on an average of three per ten-box case. Measuring the standard-size (2 1/2" by 3 1/2"), the fronts feature full-bleed artistic portraits of exaggerated action scenes. The player's name and position appear in a white bar across the bottom, and 1993 Classic Draft Picks logo overlays the bar. On a background consisting of a ghosted blow-up of the front portrait, the backs have a narrowly-cropped color player picture and a player profile. The production figures ("1 of 39,000") round out the back. The cards are numbered on the back with an "SS" prefix.

	MINT	EXC	G-VG
COMPLETE SET (3)	30.00	12.00	3.00
COMMON PLAYER (SS1-SS3)	7.00	2.80	.70

		MINT	EXC	G-VG
☐ SS1	Chris Webber	16.00	6.50	1.60
	Michigan			
☐ SS2	Jamal Mashburn	7.00	2.80	.70
	Kentucky			
☐ SS3	Anfernee Hardaway	14.00	5.75	1.40
	Memphis St.			

1993 Classic Draft LPs

These ten standard-size (2 1/2" by 3 1/2") cards were randomly inserted on an average of two per box of 1993 Classic Basketball Draft Picks. The fronts feature full-bleed color action player photos. The player's name and position appear in a holographic bar at the bottom, with the production run figures ("1 of 74,500") in holographic lettering immediately above. Also the 1993 Classic Draft Picks logo overlays the holographic bar. On a woodgrain-textured silver background, the horizontal backs carry a narrowly-cropped color player picture on the left and a player profile on the right. The player's name appears in a silver foil oval at the top. The cards are numbered on the back with an "LP" prefix.

		MINT	EXC	G-VG
COMPLETE SET (10)		40.00	16.00	4.00
COMMON PLAYER (LP1-LP10)		2.00	.80	.20
☐ LP1	Chris Webber	12.00	5.00	1.20
	Michigan			
☐ LP2	Anfernee Hardaway	10.00	4.00	1.00
	Memphis St.			
☐ LP3	Jamal Mashburn	5.00	2.00	.50
	Kentucky			
☐ LP4	J.R. Rider	5.00	2.00	.50
	UNLV			
☐ LP5	Vin Baker	3.50	1.40	.35
	Hartford			
☐ LP6	Rodney Rogers	2.50	1.00	.25
	Wake Forest			
☐ LP7	Lindsey Hunter	2.00	.80	.20
	Jackson St.			
☐ LP8	Toni Kukoc	3.00	1.20	.30
	Italy			
☐ LP9	Shaquille O'Neal FLB	6.00	2.40	.60
	LSU			
☐ LP10	Alonzo Mourning FLB	3.00	1.20	.30
	Georgetown			

1993 Classic Draft Special Bonus

Issued one per jumbo sheet, these 20 standard-size (2 1/2" by 3 1/2") cards feature on their fronts borderless color player action shots. The player's name and position appear within the gold-foil bar near the bottom. The horizontal simulated pinewood back carries a narrow-cropped color player action shot on the left. The player's name and biography appear at the top, followed below by a scouting report and statistics. The cards are numbered on the back with an "SB" prefix.

	MINT	EXC	G-VG
COMPLETE SET (20)	20.00	8.00	2.00
COMMON PLAYER (SB1-SB20)	.40	.16	.04
☐ NNO Chris Webber Special Michigan	12.00	5.00	1.20
☐ SB1 Chris Webber Michigan	5.00	2.00	.50
☐ SB2 Anfernee Hardaway Memphis State	4.00	1.60	.40
☐ SB3 Jamal Mashburn Kentucky	2.00	.80	.20
☐ SB4 Isaiah Rider UNLV	2.00	.80	.20
☐ SB5 Rodney Rogers Wake Forrest	1.00	.40	.10
☐ SB6 Vin Baker Hartford	1.75	.70	.17
☐ SB7 Lindsey Hunter Jackson State	1.00	.40	.10
☐ SB8 Allan Houston Tennessee	.75	.30	.07
☐ SB9 Toni Kukoc Benetton	1.50	.60	.15
☐ SB10 Acie Earl Iowa	.40	.16	.04
☐ SB11 George Lynch North Carolina	1.00	.40	.10
☐ SB12 Terry Dehere Seton Hall	.40	.16	.04
☐ SB13 Rex Walters Kansas	.40	.16	.04
☐ SB14 Harold Miner Miami Heat	.40	.16	.04
☐ SB15 Scott Haskin Oregon State	.40	.16	.04
☐ SB16 Doug Edwards Florida State	.40	.16	.04
☐ SB17 Greg Graham Indiana	.40	.16	.04

		MINT	EXC	G-VG
☐ SB18 Christian Laettner		.50	.20	.05
Minnesota Timberwolves				
☐ SB19 Alonzo Mourning		1.50	.60	.15
Charlotte Hornets				
☐ SB20 Shaquille O'Neal		3.00	1.20	.30
Orlando Magic				

1993 Classic Four-Sport Previews

Issued as unnumbered inserts in '93 Classic hockey packs, these five cards measure the standard size (2 1/2" by 3 1/2"). The fronts are similar in design to regular 1993 Classic Four-Sport cards. The backs carry a congratulatory message. The cards are unnumbered and checklisted below in alphabetical order.

	MINT	EXC	G-VG
COMPLETE SET (5)	75.00	30.00	7.50
COMMON PLAYER (CC1-CC5)	6.00	2.40	.60
☐ CC1 Alexandre Daigle	12.00	5.00	1.20
☐ CC2 Jeff Granger	6.00	2.40	.60
☐ CC3 Rick Mirer	20.00	8.00	2.00
☐ CC4 Chris Webber	35.00	14.00	3.50
☐ CC5 Toni Kukoc	10.00	4.00	1.00

1993 Classic Four-Sport

The 1993 Classic Four-Sport Draft Pick Collection set consists of 325 standard-size (2 1/2" by 3 1/2") cards of the top 1993 draft picks from football, basketball, baseball, and hockey. Just 49,500 sequentially numbered 12-box cases were produced. Randomly inserted throughout the foil packs were a 15-card Tri-Card subset, a 25-card LP subset, a 12-card Acetate subset, and over 30,000 autograph cards. The borderless fronts feature color player action shots, with the player's name appearing vertically in green and gold-foil lettering within a ghosted strip near the right edge. The gold-foil Classic Four-Sport logo rests at the lower right. The back carries a narrow-cropped color player action shot on the right, and player statistics, biography, and career highlights on the left within a gray lithic background. The set includes two topical subsets: John R. Wooden Award (310-314) and All-Rookie Basketball Team (315-319). The cards are numbered on the back.

	MINT	EXC	G-VG
COMPLETE SET (325)	16.00	6.50	1.60
COMMON PLAYER (1-325)	.05	.02	.00

	MINT	EXC	G-VG
☐ 1 Chris Webber	2.00	.80	.20
☐ 2 Anfernee Hardaway	1.50	.60	.15
☐ 3 Jamal Mashburn	.90	.36	.09
☐ 4 Isaiah Rider	.90	.36	.09
☐ 5 Vin Baker	.60	.24	.06
☐ 6 Rodney Rogers	.30	.12	.03
☐ 7 Lindsey Hunter	.30	.12	.03
☐ 8 Allan Houston	.20	.08	.02
☐ 9 George Lynch	.30	.12	.03
☐ 10 Toni Kukoc	.50	.20	.05
☐ 11 Ashraf Amaya	.05	.02	.00
☐ 12 Mark Bell	.08	.03	.01
☐ 13 Corie Blount	.10	.04	.01
☐ 14 Dexter Boney	.08	.03	.01
☐ 15 Tim Brooks	.05	.02	.00
☐ 16 James Bryson	.05	.02	.00
☐ 17 Evers Burns	.10	.04	.01
☐ 18 Scott Burrell	.12	.05	.01
☐ 19 Sam Cassell	.50	.20	.05
☐ 20 Sam Crawford	.08	.03	.01
☐ 21 Ron Curry	.05	.02	.00
☐ 22 William Davis	.05	.02	.00
☐ 23 Rodney Dobard	.05	.02	.00
☐ 24 Tony Dunkin	.08	.03	.01
☐ 25 Spencer Dunkley	.08	.03	.01
☐ 26 Bryan Edwards	.05	.02	.00
☐ 27 Doug Edwards	.10	.04	.01
☐ 28 Chuck Evans	.05	.02	.00
☐ 29 Terry Evans	.05	.02	.00
☐ 30 Will Flemons	.05	.02	.00
☐ 31 Alphonso Ford	.05	.02	.00
☐ 32 Josh Grant	.10	.04	.01
☐ 33 Eric Gray	.05	.02	.00
☐ 34 Geert Hammink	.08	.03	.01
☐ 35 Joe Harvell	.05	.02	.00
☐ 36 Scott Haskin	.10	.04	.01
☐ 37 Brian Hendrick	.05	.02	.00
☐ 38 Sascha Hupmann	.05	.02	.00
☐ 39 Stanley Jackson	.10	.04	.01
☐ 40 Ervin Johnson	.10	.04	.01
☐ 41 Adonis Jordan	.08	.03	.01
☐ 42 Malcolm Mackey	.10	.04	.01
☐ 43 Rich Manning	.08	.03	.01
☐ 44 Chris McNeal	.05	.02	.00
☐ 45 Conrad McRae	.08	.03	.01
☐ 46 Lance Miller	.05	.02	.00
☐ 47 Chris Mills	.30	.12	.03
☐ 48 Matt Nover	.08	.03	.01
☐ 49 Charles(Bo) Outlaw	.05	.02	.00
☐ 50 Eric Pauley	.05	.02	.00
☐ 51 Mike Peplowski	.10	.04	.01
☐ 52 Stacey Poole	.05	.02	.00
☐ 53 Anthony Reed	.05	.02	.00
☐ 54 Eric Riley	.10	.04	.01
☐ 55 Darrin Robinson	.05	.02	.00
☐ 56 James Robinson	.10	.04	.01
☐ 57 Bryon Russell	.12	.05	.01
☐ 58 Brent Scott	.08	.03	.01
☐ 59 Bennie Seltzer	.05	.02	.00
☐ 60 Ed Stokes	.08	.03	.01
☐ 61 Antoine Stoudamire	.05	.02	.00
☐ 62 Dirkk Surles	.05	.02	.00
☐ 63 Justus Thigpen	.08	.03	.01
☐ 64 Kevin Thompson	.10	.04	.01
☐ 65 Ray Thompson	.05	.02	.00
☐ 66 Gary Trost	.05	.02	.00
☐ 67 Nick Van Exel	.40	.16	.04
☐ 68 Jerry Walker	.05	.02	.00
☐ 69 Rex Walters	.10	.04	.01

☐ 70 Chris Whitney	.10	.04	.01
☐ 71 Steve Worthy	.05	.02	.00
☐ 72 Luther Wright	.10	.04	.01
☐ 73 Mark Buford	.05	.02	.00
☐ 74 Mitchell Butler	.15	.06	.01
☐ 75 Brian Clifford	.05	.02	.00
☐ 76 Terry Dehere	.10	.04	.01
☐ 77 Acie Earl	.10	.04	.01
☐ 78 Greg Graham	.10	.04	.01
☐ 79 Angelo Hamilton	.05	.02	.00
☐ 80 Thomas Hill	.08	.03	.01
☐ 81 Khari Jaxon	.05	.02	.00
☐ 82 Darnell Mee	.10	.04	.01
☐ 83 Sherron Mills	.05	.02	.00
☐ 84 Gheorghe Muresan	.20	.08	.02
☐ 85 Eddie Rivera	.05	.02	.00
☐ 86 Richard Petruska	.10	.04	.01
☐ 87 Bryan Sallier	.08	.03	.01
☐ 88 Harper Williams	.05	.02	.00
☐ 89 Ike Williams	.05	.02	.00
☐ 90 Byron Wilson	.05	.02	.00
☐ 91 Drew Bledsoe	1.25	.50	.12
☐ 92 Rick Mirer	1.25	.50	.12
☐ 93 Garrison Hearst	.30	.12	.03
☐ 94 Marvin Jones	.20	.08	.02
☐ 95 John Copeland	.20	.08	.02
☐ 96 Eric Curry	.25	.10	.02
☐ 97 Curtis Conway	.30	.12	.03
☐ 98 Willie Roaf	.25	.10	.02
☐ 99 Lincoln Kennedy	.12	.05	.01
☐ 100 Jerome Bettis	1.50	.60	.15
☐ 101 Mike Compton	.10	.04	.01
☐ 102 John Gerak	.10	.04	.01
☐ 103 Will Shields	.10	.04	.01
☐ 104 Ben Coleman	.10	.04	.01
☐ 105 Ernest Dye	.10	.04	.01
☐ 106 Lester Holmes	.10	.04	.01
☐ 107 Brad Hopkins	.10	.04	.01
☐ 108 Everett Lindsay	.10	.04	.01
☐ 109 Todd Rucci	.10	.04	.01
☐ 110 Lance Gunn	.10	.04	.01
☐ 111 Elvis Grbac	.20	.08	.02
☐ 112 Shane Matthews	.15	.06	.01
☐ 113 Rudy Harris	.10	.04	.01
☐ 114 Richie Anderson	.12	.05	.01
☐ 115 Derek Brown	.35	.14	.03
☐ 116 Roger Harper	.12	.05	.01
☐ 117 Terry Kirby	.75	.30	.07
☐ 118 Natrone Means	.75	.30	.07
☐ 119 Glyn Milburn	.50	.20	.05
☐ 120 Adrian Murrell	.15	.06	.01
☐ 121 Lorenzo Neal	.20	.08	.02
☐ 122 Roosevelt Potts	.50	.20	.05
☐ 123 Kevin Williams WR	.50	.20	.05
☐ 124 Fred Baxter	.10	.04	.01
☐ 125 Troy Drayton	.15	.06	.01
☐ 126 Chris Gedney	.10	.04	.01
☐ 127 Irv Smith	.12	.05	.01
☐ 128 Olanda Truitt	.12	.05	.01
☐ 129 Victor Bailey	.30	.12	.03
☐ 130 Horace Copeland	.30	.12	.03
☐ 131 Ron Dickerson Jr.	.10	.04	.01
☐ 132 Willie Harris	.05	.02	.00
☐ 133 Tyrone Hughes	.25	.10	.02
☐ 134 Qadry Ismail	.50	.20	.05
☐ 135 Reggie Brooks	.75	.30	.07
☐ 136 Sean LaChapelle	.12	.05	.01
☐ 137 O.J. McDuffie	.60	.24	.06
☐ 138 Henny Shedd	.05	.02	.00
☐ 139 Brian Stablein	.05	.02	.00
☐ 140 Lamar Thomas	.25	.10	.02
☐ 141 Kevin Williams RB	.12	.05	.01
☐ 142 Othello Henderson	.10	.04	.01

☐	143	Kevin Henry	.10	.04	.01
☐	144	Todd Kelly	.10	.04	.01
☐	145	Devon McDonald	.10	.04	.01
☐	146	Michael Strahan	.10	.04	.01
☐	147	Dan Williams	.10	.04	.01
☐	148	Gilbert Brown	.10	.04	.01
☐	149	Mark Caesar	.05	.02	.00
☐	150	John Parrella	.10	.04	.01
☐	151	Leonard Renfro	.10	.04	.01
☐	152	Coleman Rudolph	.10	.04	.01
☐	153	Ronnie Bradford	.10	.04	.01
☐	154	Tom Carter	.20	.08	.02
☐	155	Deon Figures	.20	.08	.02
☐	156	Derrick Frazier	.10	.04	.01
☐	157	Darrien Gordon	.20	.08	.02
☐	158	Carlton Gray	.10	.04	.01
☐	159	Adrian Hardy	.10	.04	.01
☐	160	Mike Reid	.10	.04	.01
☐	161	Thomas Smith	.10	.04	.01
☐	162	Robert O'Neal	.10	.04	.01
☐	163	Chad Brown	.10	.04	.01
☐	164	Demetrius DuBose	.12	.05	.01
☐	165	Reggie Givens	.05	.02	.00
☐	166	Travis Hill	.05	.02	.00
☐	167	Rich McKenzie	.10	.04	.01
☐	168	Darrin Smith	.20	.08	.02
☐	169	Steve Tovar	.12	.05	.01
☐	170	Patrick Bates	.15	.06	.01
☐	171	Dan Footman	.10	.04	.01
☐	172	Ryan McNeil	.12	.05	.01
☐	173	Danan Hughes	.12	.05	.01
☐	174	Mark Brunell	.20	.08	.02
☐	175	Ron Moore	.60	.24	.06
☐	176	Antonio London	.10	.04	.01
☐	177	Steve Everitt	.12	.05	.01
☐	178	Wayne Simmons	.10	.04	.01
☐	179	Robert Smith	.30	.12	.03
☐	180	Dana Stubblefield	.25	.10	.02
☐	181	George Teague	.20	.08	.02
☐	182	Carl Simpson	.10	.04	.01
☐	183	Billy Joe Hobert	.25	.10	.02
☐	184	Gino Torretta	.30	.12	.03
☐	185	Alexandre Daigle	.50	.20	.05
☐	186	Chris Pronger	.30	.12	.03
☐	187	Chris Gratton	.30	.12	.03
☐	188	Paul Kariya	.60	.24	.06
☐	189	Rob Niedermayer	.30	.12	.03
☐	190	Viktor Kozlov	.25	.10	.02
☐	191	Jason Arnott	.75	.30	.07
☐	192	Niklas Sundstrom	.15	.06	.01
☐	193	Todd Harvey	.20	.08	.02
☐	194	Jocelyn Thibault	.15	.06	.01
☐	195	Kenny Jonsson	.15	.06	.01
☐	196	Denis Pederson	.10	.04	.01
☐	197	Adam Deadmarsh	.10	.04	.01
☐	198	Mats Lindgren	.12	.05	.01
☐	199	Nick Stadjuhar	.10	.04	.01
☐	200	Jason Allison	.20	.08	.02
☐	201	Jesper Mattsson	.12	.05	.01
☐	202	Saku Koivu	.25	.10	.02
☐	203	Anders Eriksson	.10	.04	.01
☐	204	Todd Bertuzzi	.12	.05	.01
☐	205	Eric Lecompte	.10	.04	.01
☐	206	Nikolai Tsulugin	.12	.05	.01
☐	207	Janne Niinimaa	.10	.04	.01
☐	208	Maxim Bets	.15	.06	.01
☐	209	Rory Fitzpatrick	.10	.04	.01
☐	210	Eric Manlow	.15	.06	.01
☐	211	David Roche	.15	.06	.01
☐	212	Vladimir Chebaturkin	.10	.04	.01
☐	213	Bill McCauley	.10	.04	.01
☐	214	Chad Lang	.15	.06	.01
☐	215	Cosmo DuPaul	.15	.06	.01

☐	216	Bob Wren	.15	.06	.01
☐	217	Chris Simon	.15	.06	.01
☐	218	Ryan Brown	.10	.04	.01
☐	219	Mikhail Shtalenkov	.15	.06	.01
☐	220	Vladimir Krechin	.10	.04	.01
☐	221	Jason Saal	.10	.04	.01
☐	222	Dion Darling	.10	.04	.01
☐	223	Chris Helleher	.10	.04	.01
☐	224	Antti Aalto	.10	.04	.01
☐	225	Alain Nasreddine	.10	.04	.01
☐	226	Paul Vincent	.10	.04	.01
☐	227	Manny Legace	.15	.06	.01
☐	228	Igor Chibirev	.10	.04	.01
☐	229	Tom Noble	.10	.04	.01
☑	230	Mike Bales	.10	.04	.01
☑	231	Jozef Cierny	.10	.04	.01
☑	232	Ivan Droppa	.10	.04	.01
☑	233	Anatoli Fedotov	.10	.04	.01
☑	234	Martin Gendron	.12	.05	.01
☐	235	Daniel Guerard	.10	.04	.01
☐	236	Corey Hirsch	.15	.06	.01
☐	237	Steven King	.10	.04	.01
☐	238	Sergei Krivokrassov	.12	.05	.01
☐	239	Darrin Madeley	.15	.06	.01
☐	240	Grant Marshall	.10	.04	.01
☐	241	Sandy McCarthy	.10	.04	.01
☐	242	Bill McDougall	.15	.06	.01
☐	243	Dean Melanson	.10	.04	.01
☐	244	Roman Oksiuta	.10	.04	.01
☐	245	Robert Petrovicky	.10	.04	.01
☐	246	Mike Rathje	.10	.04	.01
☐	247	Eldon Reddick	.15	.06	.01
☐	248	Andrei Trefilov	.12	.05	.01
☐	249	Jiri Slegr	.10	.04	.01
☐	250	Leonid Toropchenko	.10	.04	.01
☐	251	Dody Wood	.08	.03	.01
☐	252	Kevin Paden	.10	.04	.01
☐	253	Manon Rheaume	2.00	.80	.20
☐	254	Cammi Granato	.75	.30	.07
☐	255	Patrick Charboneau	.15	.06	.01
☐	256	Curtis Bowen	.10	.04	.01
☐	257	Kevin Brown	.12	.05	.01
☐	258	Valeri Bure	.25	.10	.02
☐	259	Janne Laukkanen	.10	.04	.01
☐	260	Alex Rodriguez	1.50	.60	.15
☐	261	Darren Dreifort	.30	.12	.03
☐	262	Matt Brunson	.15	.06	.01
☐	263	Matt Drews	.15	.06	.01
☐	264	Wayne Gomes	.15	.06	.01
☐	265	Jeff Granger	.20	.08	.02
☐	266	Steve Soderstrom	.15	.06	.01
☐	267	Brooks Kieschnick	.75	.30	.07
☐	268	Daron Kirkreit	.20	.08	.02
☐	269	Billy Wagner	.30	.12	.03
☐	270	Alan Benes	.35	.14	.03
☐	271	Scott Christman	.12	.05	.01
☐	272	Willie Adams	.20	.08	.02
☐	273	Jermaine Allensworth	.25	.10	.02
☐	274	Jason Baker	.15	.06	.01
☐	275	Brian Banks	.10	.04	.01
☐	276	Marc Barcelo	.20	.08	.02
☐	277	Jeff D'Amico IF	.10	.04	.01
		(Redmond High;			
		see also card 306)			
☐	278	Todd Dunn	.25	.10	.02
☐	279	Dan Ehler	.10	.04	.01
☐	280	Tony Fuduric	.10	.04	.01
☐	281	Ryan Hancock	.15	.06	.01
☐	282	Vee Hightower	.10	.04	.01
☐	283	Andre King	.15	.06	.01
		(See also card 288)			
☐	284	Brett King	.10	.04	.01
☐	285	Derek Lee	.30	.12	.03

☐ 286	Andrew Lorraine	.25	.10	.02
☐ 287	Eric Ludwick	.15	.06	.01
☐ 288	Ryan McGuire UER	.30	.12	.03
	(Card misnumbered 283; should be 288)			
☐ 289	Anthony Medrano	.10	.04	.01
☐ 290	Joel Moore	.15	.06	.01
☐ 291	Dan Perkins	.10	.04	.01
☐ 292	Kevin Pickford	.10	.04	.01
☐ 293	Jon Ratliff	.20	.08	.02
☐ 294	Bryan Rekar	.15	.06	.01
☐ 295	Andy Rice	.10	.04	.01
☐ 296	Carl Schulz	.15	.06	.01
☐ 297	Chris Singleton	.15	.06	.01
☐ 298	Cameron Smith	.10	.04	.01
☐ 299	Marc Valdes	.15	.06	.01
☐ 300	Joe Wagner	.15	.06	.01
☐ 301	John Wasdin	.25	.10	.02
☐ 302	Pat Watkins	.40	.16	.04
☐ 303	Dax Winslett	.10	.04	.01
☐ 304	Jamey Wright	.25	.10	.02
☐ 305	Kelly Wunsch	.15	.06	.01
☐ 306	Jeff D'Amico P UER	.20	.08	.02
	(Northeast High; card misnumbered 277, should be 306)			
☐ 307	Brian Anderson	.30	.12	.03
☐ 308	Trot Nixon	1.00	.40	.10
☐ 309	Kirk Presley	.75	.30	.07
☐ 310	John R. Wooden	.15	.06	.01
☐ 311	Chris Webber JWA	1.00	.40	.10
☐ 312	Jamal Mashburn JWA	.35	.14	.03
☐ 313	Anfernee Hardaway JWA	.60	.24	.06
☐ 314	Terry Dehere JWA	.10	.04	.01
☐ 315	Shaquille O'Neal ART	.60	.24	.06
☐ 316	Alonzo Mourning ART	.50	.20	.05
☐ 317	Christian Laettner ART	.10	.04	.01
☐ 318	Jimmy Jackson ART	.20	.08	.02
☐ 319	Harold Miner ART	.08	.03	.01
☐ 320	Checklist 1	.05	.02	.00
☐ 321	Checklist 2	.05	.02	.00
☐ 322	Checklist 3	.05	.02	.00
☐ 323	Checklist 4	.05	.02	.00
☐ 324	Checklist 5	.05	.02	.00
☐ 325	Checklist 6	.05	.02	.00
☐ NNO	Jamal Mashburn	2.50	1.00	.25
	Draft Star Mail-In			

1993 Classic Four-Sport Gold

This parallel issue to the '93 Classic Four-Sport set consists of the 325 Gold versions of the regular set, plus four player autograph cards that were inserted into each factory gold set. Each of the four players autographed 3900 cards. Aside from the special gold-foil highlights (such as the ghosted stripe carrying the player's name being offset by gold-foil lines) the cards are identical to the regular '93 Classic Four-Sport cards. The cards are numbered on the back. Gold stars are valued at three to six times the corresponding value of the regular card.

	MINT	EXC	G-VG
COMPLETE SET (329)	250.00	100.00	25.00
COMMON PLAYER (1-325)	.40	.16	.04
☐ AU Jerome Bettis AU	45.00	18.00	4.50
☐ AU Chris Gratton AU	20.00	8.00	2.00
☐ AU Alonzo Mourning AU	45.00	18.00	4.50
☐ AU Alex Rodriguez AU	45.00	18.00	4.50

1993 Classic Four-Sport Acetates

Randomly inserted throughout the 1993 Classic Four-Sport foil packs, this 12-card standard-size (2 1/2" by 3 1/2") acetate set features on its fronts clear-bordered color player action cutouts set on basketball, football, baseball, or hockey stick backgrounds. The back carries the player's name at the lower left, with career highlights appearing above. The cards are unnumbered but carry letter designations. They are checklisted below in the order that spells '93 Rookie Class.

	MINT	EXC	G-VG
COMPLETE SET (12)	70.00	28.00	7.00
COMMON PLAYER (1-12)	2.50	1.00	.25
☐ 1 Chris Webber	15.00	6.00	1.50
☐ 2 Anfernee Hardaway	12.00	5.00	1.20
☐ 3 Jamal Mashburn	8.00	3.25	.80
☐ 4 Isaiah Rider	8.00	3.25	.80
☐ 5 Toni Kukoc	4.00	1.60	.40
☐ 6 Drew Bledsoe	9.00	3.75	.90
☐ 7 Rick Mirer	9.00	3.75	.90
☐ 8 Garrison Hearst	3.00	1.20	.30
☐ 9 Alex Rodriguez	12.00	5.00	1.20
☐ 10 Jeff Granger	2.50	1.00	.25
☐ 11 Alexandre Daigle	5.00	2.00	.50
☐ 12 Chris Pronger	4.00	1.60	.40

1993 Classic Four-Sport Autographs

Randomly inserted in '93 Classic Four-Sport packs, these 26 standard-size (2 1/2" by 3 1/2") cards feature on their fronts borderless color player action shots. Within a ghosted stripe near the right edge, the player's first name appears in vertical gold-foil lettering and his last name in vertical green-colored lettering. The player's autograph appears in blue ink across the card face. A fraction representing the card's production number over the number of cards produced appears in blue ink at the lower left. The back carries a congratulatory message. The cards are listed below by their corresponding regular card numbers, except for Jennings and Klippenstein, which are shown as unnumbered cards (NNO) at the end of the checklist, since they are not in the regular set. The number of cards each player signed is shown beneath the card listing. The Rider card may have been autopenned.

	MINT	EXC	G-VG
COMPLETE SET (26)	2700.00	1100.00	250.00
COMMON PLAYER (1-26)	10.00	4.00	1.00
☐ 1A Chris Webber	450.00	180.00	45.00
AU/550			
☐ 3A Jamal Mashburn	135.00	54.00	13.50
AU/800			
☐ 4A Isaiah Rider	40.00	16.00	4.00
AU/4100			
☐ 6A Rodney Rogers	20.00	8.00	2.00
AU/4000			
☐ 7A Acie Earl	20.00	8.00	2.00
AU/550			
☐ 91A Drew Bledsoe	225.00	90.00	22.00
AU/275			
☐ 92A Rick Mirer	200.00	80.00	20.00
AU/375			
☐ 93A Garrison Hearst	35.00	14.00	3.50
AU/650			
☐ 94A Marvin Jones	15.00	6.00	1.50
AU/3650			
☐ 184A Gino Torretta	30.00	12.00	3.00
AU/3200			
☐ 189A Rob Niedermayer	20.00	8.00	2.00
AU/4500			
☐ 196A Denis Pederson	10.00	4.00	1.00
AU/2050			
☐ 197A Adam Deadmarsh	10.00	4.00	1.00
AU/4250			
☐ 218A Ryan Brown	10.00	4.00	1.00
AU/900			
☐ 222A Dion Darling	10.00	4.00	1.00
AU/1500			
☐ 253A Manon Rheaume	150.00	60.00	15.00
AU/1250			
☐ 260A Alex Rodriguez	50.00	20.00	5.00
AU/4300			
☐ 261A Darren Dreifort	20.00	8.00	2.00
AU/3875			

	MINT	EXC	G-VG
☐ 265A Jeff Granger	80.00	32.00	8.00
AU/150			
☐ 267A Brooks Kieschnick	100.00	40.00	10.00
AU/450			
☐ 268A Daron Kirkreit	40.00	16.00	4.00
AU/275			
☐ 310A John Wooden	375.00	150.00	37.00
AU/150			
☐ 315A Shaquille O'Neal	450.00	180.00	45.00
AU/500			
☐ 316A Alonzo Mourning	300.00	120.00	30.00
AU/400			
☐ NNO Jason Jennings	15.00	6.00	1.50
AU/1475			
☐ NNO Wade Klippenstein	15.00	6.00	1.50
AU/800			

1993 Classic Four-Sport Chromium Draft Stars

Inserted one per jumbo pack, these 20 standard-size (2 1/2" by 3 1/2") cards feature color player action cutouts on their borderless metallic fronts. The player's name, along with the production number (1 of 80,000), appear vertically in gold foil at the lower left. The back carries a narrow-cropped color player action shot on the right. The player's biography and career highlights appear on the left, within a gray lithic background. The cards are numbered on the back with a "DS" prefix.

	MINT	EXC	G-VG
COMPLETE SET (20)	25.00	10.00	2.50
COMMON PLAYER (DS41-DS60)	.50	.20	.05
☐ DS41 Chris Webber	4.00	1.60	.40
☐ DS42 Anfernee Hardaway	3.00	1.20	.30
☐ DS43 Jamal Mashburn	1.75	.70	.17
☐ DS44 Isaiah Rider	1.75	.70	.17
☐ DS45 Toni Kukoc	1.25	.50	.12
☐ DS46 Rodney Rogers	.60	.24	.06
☐ DS47 Chris Mills	.60	.24	.06
☐ DS48 Drew Bledsoe	2.50	1.00	.25
☐ DS49 Rick Mirer	2.50	1.00	.25
☐ DS50 Garrison Hearst	.60	.24	.06
☐ DS51 Jerome Bettis	3.00	1.20	.30
☐ DS52 Terry Kirby	1.50	.60	.15
☐ DS53 Glyn Milburn	1.00	.40	.10
☐ DS54 Reggie Brooks	1.50	.60	.15
☐ DS55 Alex Rodriguez	3.00	1.20	.30
☐ DS56 Brooks Kieschnick	1.50	.60	.15

		MINT	EXC	G-VG
☐ DS57	Jeff Granger	.50	.20	.05
☐ DS58	Alexandre Daigle	1.25	.50	.12
☐ DS59	Chris Pronger	.75	.30	.07
☐ DS60	Chris Gratton	.75	.30	.07

1993 Classic Four-Sport LPs

Randomly inserted throughout the 1993 Classic Four-Sport foil packs, this 25-card standard-size (2 1/2" by 3 1/2") set features the hottest draft pick players in 1993. The borderless fronts feature color player action shots. The player's name appears vertically at the lower left. The production number (1 of 63,400) appears in gold foil at the lower right. The back carries a narrow-cropped color player action shot on the right. The player's career highlights appear on the left, within a gray lithic background. The cards are numbered on the back with an "LP" prefix.

		MINT	EXC	G-VG
COMPLETE SET (25)		75.00	30.00	7.50
COMMON PLAYER (1-25)		2.00	.80	.20
☐ LP1	Four-in-One Card	5.00	2.00	.50
	Chris Webber			
	Drew Bledsoe			
	Alex Rodriguez			
	Alexandre Daigle			
☐ LP2	Chris Webber	12.00	5.00	1.20
☐ LP3	Anfernee Hardaway	9.00	3.75	.90
☐ LP4	Jamal Mashburn	6.00	2.40	.60
☐ LP5	Isaiah Rider	6.00	2.40	.60
☐ LP6	Shaquille O'Neal	6.00	2.40	.60
☐ LP7	Toni Kukoc	3.00	1.20	.30
☐ LP8	Rodney Rogers	2.50	1.00	.25
☐ LP9	Lindsey Hunter	2.00	.80	.20
☐ LP10	Drew Bledsoe	7.00	2.80	.70
☐ LP11	Rick Mirer	7.00	2.80	.70
☐ LP12	Garrison Hearst	2.00	.80	.20
☐ LP13	Jerome Bettis	7.50	3.00	.75
☐ LP14	Marvin Jones	2.00	.80	.20
☐ LP15	Terry Kirby	4.00	1.60	.40
☐ LP16	Glyn Milburn	3.00	1.20	.30
☐ LP17	Reggie Brooks	4.00	1.60	.40
☐ LP18	Alex Rodriguez	9.00	3.75	.90
☐ LP19	Darren Dreifort	2.50	1.00	.25
☐ LP20	Jeff Granger	2.00	.80	.20
☐ LP21	Brooks Kieschnick	4.00	1.60	.40
☐ LP22	Alexandre Daigle	3.50	1.40	.35
☐ LP23	Chris Pronger	2.50	1.00	.25
☐ LP24	Chris Gratton	2.50	1.00	.25
☐ LP25	Paul Kariya	3.50	1.40	.35

1993 Classic Four-Sport LP Jumbos

*Random inserts in hobby boxes, these five oversized cards measure approximately 3 1/2"
by 5" and feature on their fronts borderless color player action shots. Within a ghosted stripe
near the right edge, the player's first name appears in vertical gold-foil lettering and his last
name in vertical green-colored lettering. The back carries a narrow-cropped color player
action shot on the right. The player's name, statistics, biography, and career highlights,
along with the card's production number out of 8,000 produced, appear on a gray lithic
background to the left. The cards are numbered on the back as "X of 5."*

	MINT	EXC	G-VG
COMPLETE SET (5)	40.00	16.00	4.00
COMMON PLAYER (1-5)	6.00	2.40	.60
☐ 1 Drew Bledsoe	9.00	3.75	.90
☐ 2 Alexandre Daigle	6.00	2.40	.60
☐ 3 Alex Rodriguez	12.00	5.00	1.20
☐ 4 Chris Webber	15.00	6.00	1.50
☐ 5 Four in One	7.00	2.80	.70

1993 Classic Four-Sport Power Pick Bonus

*Issued one per jumbo sheet, these 20 standard-size (2 1/2" by 3 1/2") cards feature on their
borderless fronts color player action shots, the backgrounds for which are faded to black-
and-white. The player's name and the sets production number (1 of 80,000) appear in
green-foil cursive lettering near the bottom. On a gray lithic background, the back carries a
color player action cutout on the right, with the player's biography and career highlights
appearing alongside on the left. The cards are numbered on the back with a "PP" prefix.*

	MINT	EXC	G-VG
COMPLETE SET (20)	25.00	10.00	2.50
COMMON PLAYER (PP1-PP20)	.50	.20	.05
☐ NNO Four in One Special	10.00	4.00	1.00
☐ PP1 Chris Webber	4.00	1.60	.40
☐ PP2 Anfernee Hardaway	3.00	1.20	.30
☐ PP3 Jamal Mashburn	1.75	.70	.17
☐ PP4 Isaiah Rider	1.75	.70	.17
☐ PP5 Toni Kukoc	1.25	.50	.12
☐ PP6 Rodney Rogers	.60	.24	.06
☐ PP7 Chris Mills	.60	.24	.06
☐ PP8 Drew Bledsoe	2.50	1.00	.25
☐ PP9 Rick Mirer	2.50	1.00	.25
☐ PP10 Garrison Hearst	.60	.24	.06
☐ PP11 Jerome Bettis	3.00	1.20	.30
☐ PP12 Terry Kirby	1.50	.60	.15
☐ PP13 Glyn Milburn	1.00	.40	.10
☐ PP14 Reggie Brooks	1.50	.60	.15
☐ PP15 Alex Rodriguez	3.00	1.20	.30
☐ PP16 Brooks Kieschnick	1.50	.60	.15
☐ PP17 Jeff Granger	.50	.20	.05
☐ PP18 Alexandre Daigle	1.25	.50	.12
☐ PP19 Chris Pronger	.75	.30	.07
☐ PP20 Chris Gratton	.75	.30	.07

1993 Classic Four-Sport Tri-Cards

Randomly inserted throughout the 1993 Classic Four-Sport foil packs, this set features five standard-size (2 1/2" by 3 1/2") cards with three players on each card separated by perforations. The horizontal fronts feature three separate color player action shots, with each player's name appearing in green and gold-foil lettering at the bottom of his strip. The back carries three color player head shots on the left, stacked one upon the other. To the right of each head shot is the player's name and biography within a gray lithic background. The cards are numbered on the back with a "TC" prefix.

	MINT	EXC	G-VG
COMPLETE SET (5)	60.00	24.00	6.00
COMMON PLAYER (TC1-TC5)	7.00	2.80	.70
☐ TC1 Anfernee Hardaway	20.00	8.00	2.00
TC6 Shaquile O'Neal			
TC11 Chris Webber			
☐ TC2 Drew Bledsoe	12.00	5.00	1.20
TC7 Rick Mirer			
TC12 Garrison Hearst			
☐ TC3 Jeff Granger	9.00	3.75	.90
TC8 Brooks Kieschnick			
TC13 Alex Rodriguez			

1993 Classic McDonald's Four-Sport

Classic has produced this 35-card four-sport set for a promotion at McDonald's restaurants in central and southeastern Pennsylvania, southern New Jersey, Delaware, and central Florida. Measuring the standard size (2 1/2" by 3 1/2"), the cards were distributed in five-card packs. A five-card "limited production" subset was randomly inserted throughout these packs. The promotion also featured instant win cards awarding 2,000 pieces of autographed Score Board memorabilia. An autographed Chris Webber card was also randomly inserted in the packs on a limited basis. The fronts feature full-bleed action photos except on the right side, where a dark gray stripe carries the player's name and position in gold foil lettering. Between a dark gray stripe and a narrowly-cropped player photo, the backs have gray panel displaying biography and career summary. The set is arranged according to sports as follows: football (1-10), baseball (11, 26, 31-35), hockey (12-20), and basketball (21-25, 27-30). The cards are numbered on the back in the upper left, and the McDonald's trademark is gold foil stamped toward the bottom.

	MINT	EXC	G-VG
COMPLETE SET (35)	10.00	4.00	1.00
COMMON PLAYER (1-35)	.05	.02	.00
☐ 1 Troy Aikman	1.00	.40	.10
☐ 2 Drew Bledsoe	1.25	.50	.12
☐ 3 Eric Curry	.25	.10	.02
☐ 4 Garrison Hearst	.30	.12	.03
☐ 5 Lester Holmes	.10	.04	.01
☐ 6 Marvin Jones	.20	.08	.02
☐ 7 O.J. McDuffie	.60	.24	.06
☐ 8 Rick Mirer	1.25	.50	.12
☐ 9 Leonard Renfro	.10	.04	.01
☐ 10 Jerry Rice	.30	.12	.03
☐ 11 Darren Daulton	.15	.06	.01
☐ 12 Vyacheslav Butsayev	.10	.04	.01
☐ 13 Kevin Dineen	.15	.06	.01
☐ 14 Andre Faust	.10	.04	.01
☐ 15 Roman Hamrlik	.15	.06	.01
☐ 16 Mark Recchi		.80	.20
☐ 17 Manon Rheaume	2.00		
☐ 18 Dominic Roussel	.30	.12	.03
☐ 19 Teemu Selanne	.50	.20	.05
☐ 20 Tommy Soderstrom	.15	.06	.01
☐ 21 Anfernee Hardaway	1.50	.60	.15

☐ 22	Jimmy Jackson	.50	.20	.05
☐ 23	Christian Laettner	.25	.10	.02
☐ 24	Jamal Mashburn	.90	.36	.09
☐ 25	Harold Miner	.08	.03	.01
☐ 26	Bull and Baby Bull	.08	.03	.01
	Greg Luzinski			
	Ryan Luzinski			
☐ 27	Alonzo Mourning	1.00	.40	.10
☐ 28	Shaquille O'Neal	1.50	.60	.15
☐ 29	Clarence Weatherspoon	.30	.12	.03
☐ 30	Chris Webber	2.00	.80	.20
☐ 31	Chad McConnell	.15	.06	.01
☐ 32	Phil Nevin	.30	.12	.03
☐ 33	Paul Shuey	.15	.06	.01
☐ 34	Derek Wallace	.08	.03	.01
☐ 35	Trench Warfare	.05	.02	.00
	Leonard Renfro			
	Lester Holmes			

1993 Classic McDonald's Four-Sport LPs

Measuring the standard size (2 1/2" by 3 1/2"), these five limited production cards were randomly inserted in 1993 Classic McDonald's five-card packs. Chris Webber, the number one pick in the NBA draft, autographed 1,250 of his cards. The front features a glossy color player action photo that is borderless except for the gold foil band on the right edge, which contains the player's name and position. Printed vertically, and parallel and next to the gold foil band, "1 of 16,750" appears in gold foil. The Classic Four Sport logo appears in the upper right. The back has a narrow-cropped color player action photo along the right edge, a dark green band along the left edge that contains the player's name in gold foil, and brief highlights of the player's career printed in the middle silver panel. The McDonald's logo is gold-foil stamped at the bottom. The cards are numbered on the back in gold foil with an "LP" prefix.

		MINT	EXC	G-VG
	COMPLETE SET (5)	30.00	12.00	3.00
	COMMON CARD (LP1-LP5)	1.00	.40	.10
☐ LP1	Darren Daulton	2.00	.80	.20
☐ LP2	Trench Warfare	1.00	.40	.10
	Leonard Renfro			
	Lester Holmes			
☐ LP3	Alonzo Mourning	8.00	3.25	.80
☐ LP4	Manon Rheaume	20.00	8.00	2.00
☐ LP5	Steve Young	3.00	1.20	.30
☐ NNO	Chris Webber AU/1250	175.00	70.00	18.00
	(Certified autograph)			

1993 Classic Futures

These 100 cards measure approximately 2 1/2" by 4 3/4" and feature on their fronts color player action shots with backgrounds that have been thrown out of focus. The card has white borders at the top and bottom. The player's name and position appear in gold-foil lettering within the bottom white margin. The same border design is duplicated on the back, which carries a narrow-cropped color player action shot on the left, and biography, career highlights and statistics on the right. The cards are numbered on the back.

	MINT	EXC	G-VG
COMPLETE SET (100)	12.00	5.00	1.20
COMMON PLAYER (1-100)	.10	.04	.01
☐ 1 Chris Webber	4.00	1.60	.40
Michigan			
☐ 2 Bill Edwards	.10	.04	.01
Wright State			
☐ 3 Anfernee Hardaway	3.00	1.20	.30
Memphis State			
☐ 4 Bryan Edwards	.10	.04	.01
James Madison			
☐ 5 Jamal Mashburn	1.50	.60	.15
Kentucky			
☐ 6 Doug Edwards	.15	.06	.01
Florida State			
☐ 7 Isaiah Rider	1.50	.60	.15
UNLV			
☐ 8 Chuck Evans	.10	.04	.01
Mississippi State			
☐ 9 Vin Baker	1.25	.50	.12
Hartford			
☐ 10 Terry Evans	.10	.04	.01
Oklahoma			
☐ 11 Rodney Rogers	.60	.24	.06
Wake Forest			
☐ 12 Will Flemons	.10	.04	.01
Texas Tech			
☐ 13 Lindsey Hunter	.60	.24	.06
Jackson State			
☐ 14 Alphonso Ford	.10	.04	.01
Mississippi Valley			
☐ 15 Allan Houston	.40	.16	.04
Tennessee			

☐ 16 Josh Grant	.15	.06	.01
Utah			
☐ 17 George Lynch	.60	.24	.06
North Carolina			
☐ 18 Evric Gray	.10	.04	.01
UNLV			
☐ 19 Toni Kukoc	.90	.36	.09
Benetton			
☐ 20 Geert Hammink	.10	.04	.01
LSU			
☐ 21 Ashraf Amaya	.10	.04	.01
Southern Illinois			
☐ 22 Lucious Harris	.20	.08	.02
Long Beach State			
☐ 23 Mark Bell	.10	.04	.01
Western Kentucky			
☐ 24 Joe Harvell	.10	.04	.01
Mississippi			
☐ 25 Corie Blount	.20	.08	.02
Cincinnati			
☐ 26 Antonio Harvey	.15	.06	.01
Pfeiffer			
☐ 27 Dexter Boney	.10	.04	.01
UNLV			
☐ 28 Scott Haskin	.15	.06	.01
Oregon State			
☐ 29 Tim Brooks	.10	.04	.01
Tennessee Chattanooga			
☐ 30 Brian Hendrick	.10	.04	.01
California			
☐ 31 James Bryson	.10	.04	.01
Villanova			
☐ 32 Sascha Hupmann	.10	.04	.01
Evansville			
☐ 33 Evers Burns	.15	.06	.01
Maryland			
☐ 34 Stanley Jackson	.15	.06	.01
UAB			
☐ 35 Scott Burrell	.25	.10	.02
Connecticut			
☐ 36 Ervin Johnson	.15	.06	.01
New Orleans			
☐ 37 Sam Cassell	.90	.36	.09
Florida State			
☐ 38 Adonis Jordan	.15	.06	.01
Kansas			
☐ 39 Sam Crawford	.10	.04	.01
New Mexico State			
☐ 40 Warren Kidd	.15	.06	.01
Mid Tennessee State			
☐ 41 Ron Curry	.10	.04	.01
Marquette			
☐ 42 Malcolm Mackey	.15	.06	.01
Georgia Tech			
☐ 43 William Davis	.10	.04	.01
James Madison			
☐ 44 Rich Manning	.15	.06	.01
Washington			
☐ 45 Rodney Dobard	.10	.04	.01
Florida State			
☐ 46 Chris McNeal	.10	.04	.01
Pittsburgh			
☐ 47 Tony Dunkin	.10	.04	.01
Coastal Carolina			
☐ 48 Conrad McRae	.10	.04	.01
Syracuse			
☐ 49 Spencer Dunkley	.10	.04	.01
Delaware			
☐ 50 Lance Miller	.10	.04	.01
Villanova			
☐ 51 Chris Mills	.60	.24	.06
Arizona			
☐ 52 Chris Whitney	.15	.06	.01

	Clemson		
☐ 53 Matt Nover	.15	.06	.01
	Indiana		
☐ 54 Steve Worthy	.10	.04	.01
	Rutgers		
☐ 55 Charles Outlaw	.10	.04	.01
	Houston		
☐ 56 Luther Wright	.15	.06	.01
	Seton Hall		
☐ 57 Eric Pauley	.10	.04	.01
	Kansas		
☐ 58 Mark Buford	.10	.04	.01
	Mississippi Valley		
☐ 59 Mike Peplowski	.15	.06	.01
	Michigan State		
☐ 60 Mitchell Butler	.30	.12	.03
	UCLA		
☐ 61 Stacey Poole	.10	.04	.01
	Florida		
☐ 62 Brian Clifford	.10	.04	.01
	Niagara		
☐ 63 Anthony Reed	.10	.04	.01
	Tulane		
☐ 64 Terry Dehere	.20	.08	.02
	Seton Hall		
☐ 65 Eric Riley	.15	.06	.01
	Michigan		
☐ 66 Acie Earl	.20	.08	.02
	Iowa		
☐ 67 Darrin Robinson	.10	.04	.01
	Sacred Heart		
☐ 68 Greg Graham	.15	.06	.01
	Indiana		
☐ 69 James Robinson	.20	.08	.02
	Alabama		
☐ 70 Angelo Hamilton	.10	.04	.01
	Oklahoma		
☐ 71 Bryon Russell	.25	.10	.02
	Long Beach State		
☐ 72 Thomas Hill	.15	.06	.01
	Duke		
☐ 73 Brent Scott	.10	.04	.01
	Rice		
☐ 74 Khari Jaxon	.10	.04	.01
	New Mexico		
☐ 75 Bennie Seltzer	.10	.04	.01
	Washington State		
☐ 76 Darnell Mee	.20	.08	.02
	Western Kentucky		
☐ 77 Ed Stokes	.15	.06	.01
	Arizona		
☐ 78 Sherron Mills	.10	.04	.01
	VCU		
☐ 79 Antoine Stoudamire	.10	.04	.01
	Oregon		
☐ 80 Gheorghe Muresan	.40	.16	.04
	Pau Orthez		
☐ 81 Dirkk Surles	.10	.04	.01
	George Washington		
☐ 82 Eddie Vivera	.10	.04	.01
	UTEP		
☐ 83 Justus Thigpen	.10	.04	.01
	Iowa State		
☐ 84 Julius Nwosu	.10	.04	.01
	Liberty		
☐ 85 Kevin Thompson	.15	.06	.01
	North Carolina State		
☐ 86 Richard Petruska	.15	.06	.01
	UCLA		
☐ 87 Ray Thompson	.10	.04	.01
	Oral Roberts		
☐ 88 Bryan Sallier	.10	.04	.01
	Oklahoma		

☐ 89	Gary Trost	.10	.04	.01
	BYU			
☐ 90	Harper Williams	.10	.04	.01
	Massachusetts			
☐ 91	Nick Van Exel	.75	.30	.07
	Cincinnati			
☐ 92	Ike Williams	.10	.04	.01
	New Mexico			
☐ 93	Jerry Walker	.10	.04	.01
	Seton Hall			
☐ 94	Bryon Wilson	.10	.04	.01
	Utah			
☐ 95	Rex Walters	.15	.06	.01
	Kansas			
☐ 96	Alex Holcombe	.10	.04	.01
	Baylor			
☐ 97	Leonard White	.10	.04	.01
	Southern			
☐ 98	Alex Wright	.10	.04	.01
	Central Oklahoma			
☐ 99	Checklist 1-50	.10	.04	.01
☐ 100	Checklist 51-100	.10	.04	.01
☐ NNO	Shaquille O'Neal	100.00	40.00	10.00
	Acetate			

1993 Classic Futures LPs

This 1993-94 Classic Futures Limited Edition five-card set had a production of 29,500. The cards measure approximately 2 1/2" by 4 3/4". The fronts contain full-bleed color action player photos. The player's name is printed in bold lettering within a wide white bar across the lower edge. The white backs have the number of cards produced prominently displayed across the top of the card. Below is biography, career summary and statistics. The player's name is printed at the bottom. The cards are unnumbered and checklisted below in draft order.

	MINT	EXC	G-VG
COMPLETE SET (5)	45.00	18.00	4.50
COMMON PLAYER (LP1-LP5)	5.00	2.00	.50

			MINT	EXC	G-VG
☐	LP1	Chris Webber	18.00	7.25	1.80
		Michigan			
☐	LP2	Anfernee Hardaway	15.00	6.00	1.50
		Memphis State			
☐	LP3	Jamal Mashburn	8.00	3.25	.80
		Kentucky			
☐	LP4	Isaiah Rider	8.00	3.25	.80
		UNLV			
☐	LP5	Toni Kukoc	5.00	2.00	.50
		Benneton			

1993 Classic Futures Team

Randomly inserted in packs, these five cards measure approximately 2 1/2" by 4 3/4" and feature on their fronts elliptical color player action shots set on white backgrounds. The player's name and position appear in gold-foil lettering at the bottom. The back carries a color player action shot at the top and career highlights at the bottom. The cards are numbered on the back with a "CFT" prefix.

	MINT	EXC	G-VG
COMPLETE SET (5)	30.00	12.00	3.00
COMMON PLAYER (CFT1-CFT5)	3.00	1.20	.30
☐ CFT1 Chris Webber	12.00	5.00	1.20
Michigan			
☐ CFT2 Anfernee Hardaway	10.00	4.00	1.00
Memphis State			
☐ CFT3 Jamal Mashburn	5.00	2.00	.50
Kentucky			
☐ CFT4 Isaiah Rider	5.00	2.00	.50
UNLV			
☐ CFT5 Toni Kukoc	3.00	1.20	.30
Benneton			

1994 Classic Previews

Randomly inserted in '94 Classic football and ProLine football packs, these five standard-size (2 1/2" by 3 1/2") cards feature color player action shots on their borderless fronts. The player's name and position appear in a black bar near the bottom. The back carries a congratulatory message. The cards are unnumbered and checklisted below. The complete set was also available using a redemption card. This offer expired Oct. 1, 1994.

	MINT	EXC	G-VG
COMPLETE SET (5)	90.00	36.00	9.00
COMMON PLAYER (BP1-BP5)	10.00	4.00	1.00
☐ BP1 Eric Montross North Carolina	15.00	6.00	1.50
☐ BP2 Jason Kidd California	25.00	10.00	2.50
☐ BP3 Yinka Dare George Washington	10.00	4.00	1.00
☐ BP4 Glenn Robinson Purdue	40.00	16.00	4.00
☐ BP5 Clifford Rozier Louisville	10.00	4.00	1.00

1994 Classic Draft

These 105 standard-size (2 1/2" by 3 1/2") cards feature borderless color player action shots on their fronts. The player's name and position appear within a black bar near the bottom. The back carries another borderless color player action shot, which is gradually ghosted toward the bottom. The player's name and position appear at the top; statistics and career highlights appear near the bottom. Dick Vitale's facsimile autograph at the lower right rounds out the card. The cards are numbered on the back.

	MINT	EXC	G-VG
COMPLETE SET (105)	10.00	4.00	1.00
COMMON PLAYER (1-105)	.05	.02	.00
☐ 1 Glenn Robinson	2.00	.80	.20
Purdue			
☐ 2 Jason Kidd	1.25	.50	.12
California			
☐ 3 Charlie Ward	.40	.16	.04
Florida State			
☐ 4 Grant Hill	1.25	.50	.12
Duke			
☐ 5 Juwan Howard	.60	.24	.06
Michigan			
☐ 6 Eric Montross	.40	.16	.04
North Carolina			
☐ 7 Carlos Rogers	.25	.10	.02
Tennessee State			
☐ 8 Wesley Person	.20	.08	.02
Auburn			
☐ 9 Anthony Miller	.12	.05	.01
Michigan State			
☐ 10 Dwayne Morton	.12	.05	.01
Louisville			
☐ 11 Chris Mills ART	.05	.02	.00
Cleveland Cavaliers			
☐ 12 Jamal Mashburn ART	.12	.05	.01
Dallas Mavericks			
☐ 13 Chris Webber ART	.30	.12	.03
Golden State Warriors			
☐ 14 Anfernee Hardaway ART	.25	.10	.02
Golden State Warriors			
☐ 15 Isaiah Rider ART	.12	.05	.01
Minnesota Timberwolves			
☐ 16 Billy McCaffrey	.10	.04	.01
Vanderbilt			
☐ 17 Steve Woodberry	.05	.02	.00
Kansas			
☐ 18 Damon Bailey	.30	.12	.03
Indiana			
☐ 19 Deon Thomas	.15	.06	.01
Illinois			
☐ 20 Dontonio Wingfield	.15	.06	.01
Cincinnati			
☐ 21 Albert Burditt	.12	.05	.01
Texas			
☐ 22 Aaron McKie	.25	.10	.02
Temple			
☐ 23 Steve Smith	.05	.02	.00
Arizona State			
☐ 24 Tony Dumas	.15	.06	.01
Missouri-K.C.			
☐ 25 Adrian Autry	.08	.03	.01
Syracuse			
☐ 26 Monty Williams	.25	.10	.02
Notre Dame			
☐ 27 Askia Jones	.05	.02	.00
Kansas State			
☐ 28 Howard Eisley	.15	.06	.01
Boston College			
☐ 29 Brian Grant	.25	.10	.02
Xavier			
☐ 30 Eddie Jones	.30	.12	.03
Temple			
☐ 31 Dickey Simpkins	.20	.08	.02
Providence			

☐ 32 Michael Smith .... .12 Providence		.05	.01
☐ 33 Clifford Rozier .... .30 Louisville		.12	.03
☐ 34 Travis Ford .... .15 Kentucky		.06	.01
☐ 35 Jervaughn Scales .... .05 Southern		.02	.00
☐ 36 Tracy Webster .... .05 Wisconsin		.02	.00
☐ 37 Brooks Thompson .... .15 Oklahoma State		.06	.01
☐ 38 Jim McIlvaine .... .15 Marquette		.06	.01
☐ 39 Eric Piatkowski .... .20 Nebraska		.08	.02
☐ 40 Arturas Karnishovas .... .08 Seton Hall		.03	.01
☐ 41 Rodney Dent .... .20 Kentucky		.08	.02
☐ 42 Robert Shannon .... .05 UAB		.02	.00
☐ 43 Derrick Phelps .... .10 North Carolina		.04	.01
☐ 44 Brian Reese .... .10 North Carolina		.04	.01
☐ 45 Kevin Salvadori .... .05 North Carolina		.02	.00
☐ 46 Shon Tarver .... .05 UCLA		.02	.00
☐ 47 Anthony Goldwire .... .12 Houston		.05	.01
☐ 48 Jamie Watson .... .12 South Carolina		.05	.01
☐ 49 Damon Key .... .05 Marquette		.02	.00
☐ 50 Kevin Rankin .... .05 Northwestern		.02	.00
☐ 51 Khalid Reeves .... .30 Arizona		.12	.03
☐ 52 Doremus Benneman .... .05 Siena		.02	.00
☐ 53 Sharone Wright .... .35 Clemson		.14	.03
☐ 54 Melvin Simon .... .05 New Orleans		.02	.00
☐ 55 Andrei Fetisov .... .12 Forum Valladolid		.05	.01
☐ 56 Barry Brown .... .05 Jacksonville		.02	.00
☐ 57 B.J. Tyler .... .15 Texas		.06	.01
☐ 58 Lawrence Funderburke .... .15 Ohio State		.06	.01
☐ 59 Darrin Hancock .... .15 Kansas		.06	.01
☐ 60 Gaylon Nickerson .... .12 NW Oklahoma		.05	.01
☐ 61 Jeff Webster .... .12 Oklahoma		.05	.01
☐ 62 Derrick Alston .... .12 Duquesne		.05	.01
☐ 63 Kendrick Warren .... .05 VCU		.02	.00
☐ 64 Yinka Dare .... .30 G. Washington		.12	.03
☐ 65 Shawnelle Scott .... .12 St. John's		.05	.01
☐ 66 Patrick Ewing CEN .... .10 New York Knicks		.04	.01
☐ 67 Dikembe Mutombo CEN .... .05 Denver Nuggets		.02	.00
☐ 68 Alonzo Mourning CEN .... .15		.06	.01

	Charlotte Hornets			
☐ 69	Shaquille O'Neal CEN	.30	.12	.03
	Orlando Magic			
☐ 70	Hakeem Olajuwon CEN	.12	.05	.01
	Houston Rockets			
☐ 71	Thomas Hamilton	.05	.02	.00
	MLK High School			
☐ 72	Joey Brown	.05	.02	.00
	Georgetown			
☐ 73	Voshon Lenard	.15	.06	.01
	Minnesota			
☐ 74	Donyell Marshall	.75	.30	.07
	Connecticut			
☐ 75	Abdul Fox	.05	.02	.00
	Rhode Island			
☐ 76	Checklist	.05	.02	.00
☐ 77	Checklist	.05	.02	.00
☐ 78	Jalen Rose	.35	.14	.03
	Michigan			
☐ 79	Trevor Ruffin	.05	.02	.00
	Hawaii			
☐ 80	Sam Mitchell	.05	.02	.00
	Cleveland State			
☐ 81	Dick Vitale ANN	.30	.12	.03
☐ 82	Charlie Ward 2-Sport	.40	.16	.04
	Florida State			
☐ 83	Cornell Parker	.05	.02	.00
	Virginia			
☐ 84	Clayton Ritter	.05	.02	.00
	James Madison			
☐ 85	Carl Ray Harris	.05	.02	.00
	Fresno State			
☐ 86	Randy Blocker	.05	.02	.00
	Northern Iowa			
☐ 87	Chuck Graham	.05	.02	.00
	Florida State			
☐ 88	Greg Minor	.15	.06	.01
	Louisville			
☐ 89	Bill Curley	.15	.06	.01
	Boston College			
☐ 90	Harry Moore	.05	.02	.00
	St. Bonaventure			
☐ 91	Melvin Booker	.08	.03	.01
	Missouri			
☐ 92	Gary Collier	.12	.05	.01
	Tulsa			
☐ 93	Myron Walker	.05	.02	.00
	Robert Morris			
☐ 94	Jamie Brandon	.05	.02	.00
	LSU			
☐ 95	Eric Mobley	.15	.06	.01
	Pittsburgh			
☐ 96	Byron Starks	.05	.02	.00
	SW Louisiana			
☐ 97	Antonio Lang	.20	.08	.02
	Duke			
☐ 98	Jevon Crudup	.12	.05	.01
	Missouri			
☐ 99	Robert Churchwell	.05	.02	.00
	Georgetown			
☐ 100	Aaron Swinson	.05	.02	.00
	Auburn			
☐ 101	Glenn Robinson COMIC	1.25	.50	.12
	Purdue			
☐ 102	Jason Kidd COMIC	.75	.30	.07
	California			
☐ 103	Juwan Howard COMIC	.35	.14	.03
	Michigan			
☐ 104	Charlie Ward COMIC	.25	.10	.02
	Florida State			
☐ 105	Eric Montross COMIC	.25	.10	.02
	North Carolina			

1994 Classic Draft Gold

Inserted one per '94 Classic pack, the 105 standard-size (2 1/2" by 3 1/2") cards of this parallel set feature borderless color player action shots on their fronts. The player's name and position are stamped within a gold-foil bar near the bottom. The back carries another borderless color player action shot, which is gradually ghosted toward the bottom. The player's name and position appear at the top; statistics and career highlights appear near the bottom. Dick Vitale's facsimile autograph at the lower right rounds out the card. The cards are numbered on the back. Gold stars are valued at two to four times the price of the regular issue corresponding card.

	MINT	EXC	G-VG
COMPLETE SET (105)	40.00	16.00	4.00
COMMON PLAYER (1-105)	.15	.06	.01

1994 Classic Vitale's PTPers

Randomly inserted in packs, these 15 standard-size (2 1/2" by 3 1/2") cards feature on their borderless metallic fronts color player action cutouts set on multicolored backgrounds. The player's name appears within a colored stripe across the bottom. The back carries a color player action shot on the right and career highlights on a yellow panel on the left. A color cutout of Dick Vitale and his facsimile autograph at the bottom round out the card. The cards are numbered on the back with a "PTP" prefix.

	MINT	EXC	G-VG
COMPLETE SET (15)	65.00	26.00	6.50
COMMON CARD (PTP1-PTP15)	2.00	.80	.20

☐ PTP1 Glenn Robinson	15.00	6.00	1.50
Purdue			
☐ PTP2 Jason Kidd	10.00	4.00	1.00
California			
☐ PTP3 Grant Hill	10.00	4.00	1.00
Duke			
☐ PTP4 Sharone Wright	4.00	1.60	.40
Clemson			
☐ PTP5 Juwan Howard	6.00	2.40	.60
Michigan			
☐ PTP6 Billy McCaffrey	2.00	.80	.20
Vanderbilt			
☐ PTP7 Khalid Reeves	3.50	1.40	.35
Arizona			
☐ PTP8 Eddie Jones	3.50	1.40	.35
Temple			
☐ PTP9 Clifford Rozier	3.50	1.40	.35
Louisville			
☐ PTP10 Charlie Ward	5.00	2.00	.50
Florida State			
☐ PTP11 Eric Montross	5.00	2.00	.50
North Carolina			
☐ PTP12 Wesley Person	2.50	1.00	.25
Auburn			
☐ PTP13 Yinka Dare	3.50	1.40	.35
G. Washington			
☐ PTP14 Dontonio Wingfield	2.00	.80	.20
Cincinnati			
☐ PTP15 Carlos Rogers	3.00	1.20	.30
Tennessee State			

1994 Classic Images *

These 150 standard-size (2 1/2" by 3 1/2") cards feature on their borderless fronts color player action shots with backgrounds that have been thrown out of focus. The player's name and position appear in gold-foil lettering within a black strip near the bottom. The gold-foil Classic Images logo appears in an upper corner. The back carries a narrow-cropped color player action shot on the right. On the white background to the left, career highlights, biography and statistics are displayed. The cards are numbered on the back. The set closes with Classic Headlines (128-147) and checklists (148-150). A redemption card inserted one per case entitled the collector to one set of basketball draft preview cards.

	MINT	EXC	G-VG
COMPLETE SET (150)	18.00	7.25	1.80
COMMON PLAYER (1-150)	.05	.02	.00
☐ 1 Drew Bledsoe	1.25	.50	.12
☐ 2 Chris Webber	2.00	.80	.20
☐ 3 Alex Rodriguez	1.50	.60	.15

	#	Player			
☐	4	Alexandre Daigle	.50	.20	.05
☐	5	Rick Mirer	1.25	.50	.12
☐	6	Anfernee Hardaway	1.50	.60	.15
☐	7	Jeff D'Amico P	.20	.08	.02
☐	8	Chris Pronger	.30	.12	.03
☐	9	Robert Smith	.30	.12	.03
☐	10	Sherron Mills	.05	.02	.00
☐	11	Alan Benes	.35	.14	.03
☐	12	Warren Kidd	.12	.05	.01
☐	13	Bryon Russell	.12	.05	.01
☐	14	Mike Peplowski	.10	.04	.01
☐	15	Jeff Granger	.15	.06	.01
☐	16	Jim Montgomery	.12	.05	.01
☐	17	Todd Marchant	.15	.06	.01
☐	18	Doug Edwards	.10	.04	.01
☐	19	Daron Kirkreit	.20	.08	.02
☐	20	Mike Dunham	.12	.05	.01
☐	21	Garth Snow	.20	.08	.02
☐	22	Darnell Mee	.10	.04	.01
☐	23	Billy Wagner	.30	.12	.03
☐	24	Barry Richter	.12	.05	.01
☐	25	Lincoln Kennedy	.12	.05	.01
☐	26	Jerome Bettis	1.50	.60	.15
☐	27	Corie Blount	.10	.04	.01
☐	28	Matt Martin	.15	.06	.01
☐	29	Deon Figures	.20	.08	.02
☐	30	Rob Niedermayer	.30	.12	.03
☐	31	Brian Anderson	.30	.12	.03
☐	32	Jesse Belanger	.20	.08	.02
☐	33	George Teague	.20	.08	.02
☐	34	Chris Schwab	.25	.10	.02
☐	35	Peter Ferraro	.25	.10	.02
☐	36	Shaquille O'Neal Rap	1.00	.40	.10
☐	37	Matt Brunson	.15	.06	.01
☐	38	Ted Drury	.15	.06	.01
☐	39	Glyn Milburn	.50	.20	.05
☐	40	George Lynch	.30	.12	.03
☐	41	Gheorghe Muresan	.20	.08	.02
☐	42	Kirk Presley	.75	.30	.07
☐	43	Derek Plante	.40	.16	.04
☐	44	Gino Torretta	.30	.12	.03
☐	45	Roger Harper	.12	.05	.01
☐	46	Jim Campbell	.10	.04	.01
☐	47	Chris Carpenter	.20	.08	.02
☐	48	Victor Bailey	.30	.12	.03
☐	49	Kelly Wunsch	.15	.06	.01
☐	50	Isaiah Rider	.90	.36	.09
☐	51	Jon Ratliff	.20	.08	.02
☐	52	Wayne Gomes	.15	.06	.01
☐	53	Thomas Smith	.10	.04	.01
☐	54	Trot Nixon	1.00	.40	.10
☐	55	Andre King	.15	.06	.01
☐	56	Chris Osgood	.25	.10	.02
☐	57	Reggie Brooks	.75	.30	.07
☐	58	Ron Moore	.60	.24	.06
☐	59	Vin Baker	.60	.24	.06
☐	60	Rodney Rogers	.30	.12	.03
☐	61	Dan Footman	.10	.04	.01
☐	62	Jason Arnott	.75	.30	.07
☐	63	Darren Dreifort	.30	.12	.03
☐	64	Tom Carter	.20	.08	.02
☐	65	Qadry Ismail	.50	.20	.05
☐	66	Josh Grant	.10	.04	.01
☐	67	Luther Wright	.10	.04	.01
☐	68	Allan Houston	.20	.08	.02
☐	69	Brooks Kieschnick	.75	.30	.07
☐	70	Marvin Jones	.20	.08	.02
☐	71	Garrison Hearst	.30	.12	.03
☐	72	John Copeland	.20	.08	.02
☐	73	Darrien Gordon	.20	.08	.02
☐	74	Jocelyn Thibault	.15	.06	.01
☐	75	Lindsey Hunter	.30	.12	.03
☐	76	Scott Burrell	.12	.05	.01

☐ 77	Torii Hunter	.15	.06	.01
☐ 78	Chad Brown	.10	.04	.01
☐ 79	Sam Cassell	.50	.20	.05
☐ 80	Steve Soderstrom	.15	.06	.01
☐ 81	Jimmy Jackson	.30	.12	.03
☐ 82	Irv Smith	.12	.05	.01
☐ 83	Troy Drayton	.15	.06	.01
☐ 84	Chris Mills	.30	.12	.03
☐ 85	Derrek Lee	.30	.12	.03
☐ 86	Chris Gratton	.30	.12	.03
☐ 87	Carlton Gray	.10	.04	.01
☐ 88	Billy Joe Hobert	.25	.10	.02
☐ 89	Acie Earl	.10	.04	.01
☐ 90	Terry Dehere	.10	.04	.01
☐ 91	Carl Simpson	.10	.04	.01
☐ 92	Mike Rathje	.10	.04	.01
☐ 93	Jay Powell	.20	.08	.02
☐ 94	James Robinson	.10	.04	.01
☐ 95	Roosevelt Potts	.50	.20	.05
☐ 96	Jamal Mashburn	.90	.36	.09
☐ 97	Derek Brown RB	.08	.03	.01
☐ 98	Ed Stokes	.10	.04	.01
☐ 99	Ervin Johnson	.10	.04	.01
☐ 100	Nick Van Exel	.40	.16	.04
☐ 101	Martin Brodeur	.40	.16	.04
☐ 102	Curtis Conway	.30	.12	.03
☐ 103	Lamar Thomas	.25	.10	.02
☐ 104	Willie Roaf	.25	.10	.02
☐ 105	Matt Drews	.15	.06	.01
☐ 106	Paul Kariya	.60	.24	.06
☐ 107	Eric Curry	.25	.10	.02
☐ 108	Todd Kelly	.10	.04	.01
☐ 109	Rex Walters	.10	.04	.01
☐ 110	Chris Whitney	.10	.04	.01
☐ 111	Manon Rheaume	2.00	.80	.20
☐ 112	Alonzo Mourning	.50	.20	.05
☐ 113	Lucious Harris	.12	.05	.01
☐ 114	Horace Copeland	.30	.12	.03
☐ 115	Scott Christman	.12	.05	.01
☐ 116	Terry Kirby	.75	.30	.07
☐ 117	Demetrius DuBose	.12	.05	.01
☐ 118	Will Shields	.10	.04	.01
☐ 119	Natrone Means	.75	.30	.07
☐ 120	O.J. McDuffie	.60	.24	.06
☐ 121	Felix Potvin	.60	.24	.06
☐ 122	Dino Radja	.40	.16	.04
☐ 123	Harold Miner	.10	.04	.01
☐ 124	Greg Graham	.10	.04	.01
☐ 125	Alexei Yashin	.50	.20	.05
☐ 126	Kevin Williams WR	.50	.20	.05
☐ 127	Lorenzo Neal	.20	.08	.02
☐ 128	Shaquille O'Neal BW	.30	.12	.03
☐ 129	Drew Bledsoe BW	.40	.16	.04
☐ 130	Alexei Yashin BW	.20	.08	.02
☐ 131	Kirk Presley BW	.30	.12	.03
☐ 132	Chris Webber BW	1.00	.40	.10
☐ 133	Rick Mirer BW	.50	.20	.05
☐ 134	Anfernee Hardaway BW	.60	.24	.06
☐ 135	Chris Pronger BW	.10	.04	.01
☐ 136	Alonzo Mourning BW	.20	.08	.02
☐ 137	Jerome Bettis BW	.60	.24	.06
☐ 138	Chris Gratton BW	.10	.04	.01
☐ 139	Trot Nixon BW	.40	.16	.04
☐ 140	Terry Kirby BW	.30	.12	.03
☐ 141	Jamal Mashburn BW	.35	.14	.03
☐ 142	Jason Arnott BW	.30	.12	.03
☐ 143	Alex Rodriguez BW	.60	.24	.06
☐ 144	Derek Brown RB BW	.12	.05	.01
☐ 145	Isaiah Rider BW	.35	.14	.03
☐ 146	Harold Miner BW	.08	.03	.01
☐ 147	Manon Rheaume BW	2.50	1.00	.25
☐ 148	Checklist 1	.05	.02	.00
☐ 149	Checklist 2	.05	.02	.00

☐ 150 Checklist 3	.05	.02	.00
☐ NNO BK Preview	75.00	30.00	7.50
Redemption Card			

1994 Classic Images Acetates *

Randomly inserted in 1994 Classic Images packs (four per case; 6,500 of each), these four standard-size (2 1/2" by 3 1/2") clear acetate cards feature color player action cutouts on their fronts. The player's name appears in vertical lettering within a black bar at the upper right. The back carries a ghosted action cutout, which also utilizes the reverse image of the front's cutout. The player's name appears in vertical lettering within a black bar at the upper left. Career highlights appear over the ghosted panel at the bottom. The cards are numbered on the back.

	MINT	EXC	G-VG
COMPLETE SET (4)	60.00	24.00	6.00
COMMON PLAYER (1-4)	9.00	3.75	.90
☐ 1 Chris Webber	25.00	10.00	2.50
☐ 2 Jerome Bettis	20.00	8.00	2.00
☐ 3 Steve Young	9.00	3.75	.90
☐ 4 Hakeem Olajuwon	18.00	7.25	1.80

1994 Classic Images Chrome *

Randomly inserted in 1994 Classic Images packs, these 20 limited print (9,750 of each) cards measure the standard size (2 1/2" by 3 1/2") and feature color player action shots on their borderless metallic fronts. The player's name appears in gold-colored lettering at the top. The set logo rests at the bottom of the card, and is also displayed behind the player. The back carries the player's name in the white margin at the top, followed below by an action close-up and career highlights on a white background. The cards are numbered on the back with a "CC" prefix.

	MINT	EXC	G-VG
COMPLETE SET (20)	120.00	50.00	12.00
COMMON PLAYER (CC1-CC20)	3.00	1.20	.30
☐ CC1 Chris Webber	18.00	7.25	1.80
☐ CC2 Anfernee Hardaway	15.00	6.00	1.50
☐ CC3 Jimmy Jackson	4.00	1.60	.40
☐ CC4 Nick Van Exel	4.00	1.60	.40
☐ CC5 Jamal Mashburn	8.00	3.25	.80
☐ CC6 Isaiah Rider	8.00	3.25	.80
☐ CC7 Drew Bledsoe	9.00	3.75	.90
☐ CC8 Jerome Bettis	10.00	4.00	1.00
☐ CC9 Terry Kirby	7.00	2.80	.70
☐ CC10 Dana Stubblefield	3.00	1.20	.30
☐ CC11 Rick Mirer	10.00	4.00	1.00
☐ CC12 Cammi Granato	7.00	2.80	.70
☐ CC13 Alexei Yashin	4.00	1.60	.40
☐ CC14 Alexandre Daigle	4.00	1.60	.40
☐ CC15 Manon Rheaume	18.00	7.25	1.80
☐ CC16 Radek Bonk	10.00	4.00	1.00
☐ CC17 Alex Rodriguez	15.00	6.00	1.50
☐ CC18 Kirk Presley	7.00	2.80	.70
☐ CC19 Trot Nixon	9.00	3.75	.90
☐ CC20 Brooks Kieschnick	7.00	2.80	.70

1994 Classic Images Marshall Faulk

Randomly inserted in 1994 Classic Images packs (three per case; 3,250 each), these six standard-size (2 1/2" by 3 1/2") cards feature color player action shots on their fronts. The photos are borderless, except at a lower corner, where a blue triangular area carries the player's position. The player's name an team helmet appears in the other corner. The back carries a borderless color player action shot that is ghosted, except for the area around the player's head. Career highlights appear below. The cards are numbered on the back with an "M" prefix. Card M5 is redeemable for a Classic Images Chrome sheet.

	MINT	EXC	G-VG
COMPLETE SET (6)	120.00	50.00	12.00
COMMON CARD (M1-M6)	10.00	4.00	1.00
☐ M1 Tampa Bay Buccaneers	10.00	4.00	1.00

☐ M2 Cincinnati Bengals	10.00	4.00	1.00
☐ M3 Chicago Bears	10.00	4.00	1.00
☐ M4 New England Patriots	10.00	4.00	1.00
☐ M5 Indianapolis Colts	75.00	30.00	7.50
☐ M6 Field Card	10.00	4.00	1.00

1994 Classic Images Sudden Impact *

Inserted one per '94 Classic Images pack, these 20 gold foil-board cards measure the standard-size (2 1/2" by 3 1/2"). The gold metallic fronts feature borderless color player action shots on backgrounds that have been thrown out of focus. The player's name and position appear in vertical lettering within a black strip across the card near the right edge. The back carries a color player action shot at the top, followed below by career highlights on a white panel. The player's name appears in vertical black lettering within a ghosted action strip at the left edge. The cards are numbered on the back with an "SI" prefix.

	MINT	EXC	G-VG
COMPLETE SET (20)	12.00	5.00	1.20
COMMON PLAYER (SI1-SI20)	.10	.04	.01
☐ SI1 Carlos Delgado	.75	.30	.07
☐ SI2 Vin Baker	.60	.24	.06
☐ SI3 Derek Jeter	.50	.20	.05
☐ SI4 Alex Rodriguez	1.50	.60	.15
☐ SI5 Alexandre Daigle	.50	.20	.05
☐ SI6 Rob Niedermayer	.30	.12	.03
☐ SI7 Jocelyn Thibault	.10	.04	.01
☐ SI8 Derek Plante	.40	.16	.04
☐ SI9 Shaquille O'Neal	1.00	.40	.10
☐ SI10 Alonzo Mourning	.50	.20	.05
☐ SI11 Harold Miner	.10	.04	.01
☐ SI12 Chris Webber	2.00	.80	.20
☐ SI13 Anfernee Hardaway	1.50	.60	.15
☐ SI14 Jamal Mashburn	.90	.36	.09
☐ SI15 Drew Bledsoe	1.25	.50	.12
☐ SI16 Rick Mirer	1.25	.50	.12
☐ SI17 Derek Brown RB	.35	.14	.03
☐ SI18 Ron Moore	.60	.24	.06
☐ SI19 Jerome Bettis	1.50	.60	.15
☐ SI20 Dino Radja	.40	.16	.04

1994-95 Collector's Choice

These 210 standard-size (2 1/2" by 3 1/2") cards comprising Upper Deck's '94-95 Collector's Choice set have white-bordered fronts that feature color player action shots. The player's

name, team, and position appear in a lower corner. The back carries another color player action shot at the top, with statistics and career highlights displayed below. The cards are numbered on the back. The following subsets are included in this set: Tip-Off (166-192), All-Star Advice (193-198), and NBA Profiles (199-206). A card from the parallel Silver Signature insert set was included in every pack.

	MINT	EXC	G-VG
COMPLETE SERIES 1 (210)	15.00	6.75	1.90
COMMON PLAYER (1-210)	.05	.02	.01
☐ 1 Anfernee Hardaway Orlando Magic	.75	.35	.09
☐ 2 Moses Malone Philadelphia 76ers	.10	.05	.01
☐ 3 Steve Smith Miami Heat	.10	.05	.01
☐ 4 Chris Webber Golden State Warriors	1.00	.45	.13
☐ 5 Donald Royal Orlando Magic	.05	.02	.01
☐ 6 Avery Johnson Golden State Warriors	.05	.02	.01
☐ 7 Kevin Johnson Phoenix Suns	.10	.05	.01
☐ 8 Doug Christie Los Angeles Lakers	.08	.04	.01
☐ 9 Derrick McKey Indiana Pacers	.05	.02	.01
☐ 10 Dennis Rodman San Antonio Spurs	.08	.04	.01
☐ 11 Scott Skiles Orlando Magic	.05	.02	.01
☐ 12 Johnny Dawkins Philadelphia 76ers	.15	.07	.02
☐ 13 Kendall Gill Seattle Supersonics	.08	.04	.01
☐ 14 Jeff Hornacek Utah Jazz	.08	.04	.01
☐ 15 Latrell Sprewell Golden State Warriors	.30	.14	.04
☐ 16 Lucious Harris Dallas Mavericks	.05	.02	.01
☐ 17 Chris Mullin Golden State Warriors	.15	.07	.02
☐ 18 John Williams Cleveland Cavaliers	.08	.04	.01
☐ 19 Tony Campbell Dallas Mavericks	.05	.02	.01
☐ 20 LaPhonso Ellis Denver Nuggets	.10	.05	.01
☐ 21 Gerald Wilkins Cleveland Cavaliers	.05	.02	.01
☐ 22 Clyde Drexler	.20	.09	.03

	Portland Trail Blazers			
☐ 23	Michael Jordan	2.00	.90	.25
	Chicago Bulls			
☐ 24	George Lynch	.08	.04	.01
	Los Angeles Lakers			
☐ 25	Mark Price	.10	.05	.01
	Cleveland Cavaliers			
☐ 26	James Robinson	.05	.02	.01
	Portland Trail Blazers			
☐ 27	Elmore Spencer	.05	.02	.01
	Los Angeles Clippers			
☐ 28	Stacey King	.05	.02	.01
	Minnesota Timberwolves			
☐ 29	Corie Blount	.05	.02	.01
	Chicago Bulls			
☐ 30	Dell Curry	.08	.04	.01
	Charlotte Hornets			
☐ 31	Reggie Miller	.20	.09	.03
	Indiana Pacers			
☐ 32	Karl Malone	.25	.11	.03
	Utah Jazz			
☐ 33	Scottie Pippen	.30	.14	.04
	Chicago Bulls			
☐ 34	Hakeem Olajuwon	.75	.35	.09
	Houston Rockets			
☐ 35	Clarence Weatherspoon	.10	.05	.01
	Philadelphia 76ers			
☐ 36	Kevin Edwards	.05	.02	.01
	New Jersey Nets			
☐ 37	Pete Myers	.05	.02	.01
	Chicago Bulls			
☐ 38	Jeff Turner	.05	.02	.01
	Orlando Magic			
☐ 39	Ennis Whatley	.05	.02	.01
	Atlanta Hawks			
☐ 40	Calbert Cheaney	.15	.07	.02
	Washington Bullets			
☐ 41	Glen Rice	.10	.05	.01
	Miami Heat			
☐ 42	Vin Baker	.25	.11	.03
	Milwaukee Bucks			
☐ 43	Grant Long	.05	.02	.01
	Miami Heat			
☐ 44	Derrick Coleman	.20	.09	.03
	New Jersey Nets			
☐ 45	Rik Smits	.08	.04	.01
	Indiana Pacers			
☐ 46	Chris Smith	.05	.02	.01
	Minnesota Timberwolves			
☐ 47	Carl Herrera	.05	.02	.01
	Houston Rockets			
☐ 48	Bob Martin	.05	.02	.01
	Los Angeles Clippers			
☐ 49	Terrell Brandon	.05	.02	.01
	Cleveland Cavaliers			
☐ 50	David Robinson	.50	.23	.06
	San Antonio Spurs			
☐ 51	Danny Ferry	.05	.02	.01
	Cleveland Cavaliers			
☐ 52	Buck Williams	.10	.05	.01
	Portland Trail Blazers			
☐ 53	Josh Grant	.05	.02	.01
	Golden State Warriors			
☐ 54	Ed Pinckney	.05	.02	.01
	Boston Celtics			
☐ 55	Dikembe Mutombo	.15	.07	.02
	Denver Nuggets			
☐ 56	Clifford Robinson	.10	.05	.01
	Portland Trail Blazers			
☐ 57	Luther Wright	.05	.02	.01
	Utah Jazz			
☐ 58	Scott Burrell	.05	.02	.01
	Charlotte Hornets			

☐ 59 Stacey Augmon Atlanta Hawks	.10	.05	.01
☐ 60 Jeff Malone Philadelphia 76ers	.08	.04	.01
☐ 61 Byron Houston Golden State Warriors	.05	.02	.01
☐ 62 Anthony Peeler Los Angeles Lakers	.08	.04	.01
☐ 63 Michael Adams Washington Bullets	.08	.04	.01
☐ 64 Negele Knight San Antonio Spurs	.05	.02	.01
☐ 65 Terry Cummings San Antonio Spurs	.08	.04	.01
☐ 66 Christian Laettner Minnesota Timberwolves	.10	.05	.01
☐ 67 Tracy Murray Portland Trail Blazers	.05	.02	.01
☐ 68 Sedale Threatt Los Angeles Lakers	.05	.02	.01
☐ 69 Dan Majerle Phoenix Suns	.10	.05	.01
☐ 70 Frank Brickowski Charlotte Hornets	.08	.04	.01
☐ 71 Ken Norman Milwaukee Bucks	.08	.04	.01
☐ 72 Charles Smith New York Knicks	.05	.02	.01
☐ 73 Adam Keefe Atlanta Hawks	.05	.02	.01
☐ 74 P.J. Brown New Jersey Nets	.05	.02	.01
☐ 75 Kevin Duckworth Washington Bullets	.05	.02	.01
☐ 76 Shawn Bradley Philadelphia 76ers	.15	.07	.02
☐ 77 Darnell Mee Denver Nuggets	.05	.02	.01
☐ 78 Nick Anderson Orlando Magic	.08	.04	.01
☐ 79 Mark West Phoenix Suns	.05	.02	.01
☐ 80 B.J. Armstrong Chicago Bulls	.10	.05	.01
☐ 81 Dennis Scott Orlando Magic	.08	.04	.01
☐ 82 Lindsey Hunter Detroit Pistons	.15	.07	.02
☐ 83 Derek Strong Milwaukee Bucks	.05	.02	.01
☐ 84 Mike Brown Minnesota Timberwolves	.05	.02	.01
☐ 85 Antonio Harvey Los Angeles Lakers	.05	.02	.01
☐ 86 Anthony Bonner New York Knicks	.05	.02	.01
☐ 87 Sam Cassell Houston Rockets	.15	.07	.02
☐ 88 Harold Miner Miami Heat	.08	.04	.01
☐ 89 Spud Webb Sacramento Kings	.10	.05	.01
☐ 90 Mookie Blaylock Atlanta Hawks	.08	.04	.01
☐ 91 Greg Anthony New York Knicks	.05	.02	.01
☐ 92 Richard Petruska Houston Rockets	.05	.02	.01
☐ 93 Sean Rooks Dallas Mavericks	.05	.02	.01
☐ 94 Ervin Johnson Seattle Supersonics	.05	.02	.01
☐ 95 Randy Brown	.05	.02	.01

☐ 96	Orlando Woolridge	.08	.04	.01
	Sacramento Kings			
☐ 97	Charles Oakley	.10	.05	.01
	Philadelphia 76ers			
☐ 98	Craig Ehlo	.05	.02	.01
	New York Knicks			
☐ 99	Derek Harper	.08	.04	.01
	Atlanta Hawks			
☐ 100	Doug Edwards	.05	.02	.01
	New York Knicks			
☐ 101	Muggsy Bogues	.10	.05	.01
	Atlanta Hawks			
☐ 102	Mitch Richmond	.10	.05	.01
	Charlotte Hornets			
☐ 103	Mahmoud Abdul-Rauf	.08	.04	.01
	Sacramento Kings			
☐ 104	Joe Dumars	.15	.07	.02
	Denver Nuggets			
☐ 105	Eric Riley	.05	.02	.01
	Detroit Pistons			
☐ 106	Terry Mills	.08	.04	.01
	Houston Rockets			
☐ 107	Toni Kukoc	.15	.07	.02
	Detroit Pistons			
☐ 108	Jon Koncak	.05	.02	.01
	Chicago Bulls			
☐ 109	Haywoode Workman	.05	.02	.01
	Atlanta Hawks			
☐ 110	Todd Day	.08	.04	.01
	Indiana Pacers			
☐ 111	Detlef Schrempf	.10	.05	.01
	Milwaukee Bucks			
☐ 112	David Wesley	.05	.02	.01
	Seattle Supersonics			
☐ 113	Mark Jackson	.08	.04	.01
	New Jersey Nets			
☐ 114	Doug Overton	.05	.02	.01
	Los Angeles Clippers			
☐ 115	Vinny Del Negro	.05	.02	.01
	Washington Bullets			
☐ 116	Loy Vaught	.08	.04	.01
	San Antonio Spurs			
☐ 117	Mike Peplowski	.05	.02	.01
	Los Angeles Clippers			
☐ 118	Bimbo Coles	.05	.02	.01
	Sacramento Kings			
☐ 119	Rex Walters	.05	.02	.01
	Miami Heat			
☐ 120	Sherman Douglas	.05	.02	.01
	New Jersey Nets			
☐ 121	David Benoit	.05	.02	.01
	Boston Celtics			
☐ 122	John Salley	.05	.02	.01
	Utah Jazz			
☐ 123	Cedric Ceballos	.10	.05	.01
	Miami Heat			
☐ 124	Chris Mills	.08	.04	.01
	Phoenix Suns			
☐ 125	Robert Horry	.10	.05	.01
	Cleveland Cavaliers			
☐ 126	Johnny Newman	.05	.02	.01
	Houston Rockets			
☐ 127	Malcolm Mackey	.05	.02	.01
	New Jersey Nets			
☐ 128	Terry Dehere	.05	.02	.01
	Phoenix Suns			
☐ 129	Dino Radja	.15	.07	.02
	Los Angeles Clippers			
☐ 130	Tree Rollins	.05	.02	.01
	Boston Celtics			
☐ 131	Xavier McDaniel	.08	.04	.01
	Charlotte Hornets			
	Boston Celtics			

☐ 132	Bobby Hurley	.15	.07	.02
	Sacramento Kings			
☐ 133	Alonzo Mourning	.50	.23	.06
	Charlotte Hornets			
☐ 134	Isaiah Rider	.40	.18	.05
	Minnesota Timberwolves			
☐ 135	Antoine Carr	.05	.02	.01
	San Antonio Spurs			
☐ 136	Robert Pack	.05	.02	.01
	Denver Nuggets			
☐ 137	Walt Williams	.08	.04	.01
	Sacramento Kings			
☐ 138	Tyrone Corbin	.05	.02	.01
	Utah Jazz			
☐ 139	Popeye Jones	.05	.02	.01
	Dallas Mavericks			
☐ 140	Shawn Kemp	.30	.14	.04
	Seattle Supersonics			
☐ 141	Thurl Bailey	.05	.02	.01
	Minnesota Timberwolves			
☐ 142	James Worthy	.10	.05	.01
	Los Angeles Lakers			
☐ 143	Scott Haskin	.05	.02	.01
	Indiana Pacers			
☐ 144	Hubert Davis	.05	.02	.01
	New York Knicks			
☐ 145	A.C. Green	.08	.04	.01
	Phoenix Suns			
☐ 146	Dale Davis	.08	.04	.01
	Indiana Pacers			
☐ 147	Nate McMillan	.05	.02	.01
	Seattle Supersonics			
☐ 148	Chris Morris	.05	.02	.01
	New Jersey Nets			
☐ 149	Will Perdue	.05	.02	.01
	Chicago Bulls			
☐ 150	Felton Spencer	.05	.02	.01
	Utah Jazz			
☐ 151	Rod Strickland	.08	.04	.01
	Portland Trail Blazers			
☐ 152	Blue Edwards	.05	.02	.01
	Milwaukee Bucks			
☐ 153	John Williams	.05	.02	.01
	Los Angeles Clippers			
☐ 154	Rodney Rogers	.08	.04	.01
	Denver Nuggets			
☐ 155	Acie Earl	.05	.02	.01
	Boston Celtics			
☐ 156	Hersey Hawkins	.08	.04	.01
	Charlotte Hornets			
☐ 157	Jamal Mashburn	.40	.18	.05
	Dallas Mavericks			
☐ 158	Don MacLean	.08	.04	.01
	Washington Bullets			
☐ 159	Micheal Williams	.08	.04	.01
	Minnesota Timberwolves			
☐ 160	Kenny Gattison	.05	.02	.01
	Charlotte Hornets			
☐ 161	Rich King	.05	.02	.01
	Seattle Supersonics			
☐ 162	Allan Houston	.05	.02	.01
	Detroit Pistons			
☐ 163	Hoop-it up	.05	.02	.01
	Men's Champions			
☐ 164	Hoop-it up	.05	.02	.01
	Women's Champions			
☐ 165	Hoop-it up	.05	.02	.01
	Slam-Dunk Champions			
☐ 166	Danny Manning TO	.10	.05	.01
	Atlanta Hawks			
☐ 167	Robert Parish TO	.08	.04	.01
	Boston Celtics			
☐ 168	Alonzo Mourning TO	.25	.11	.03

☐ 169	Charlotte Hornets Scottie Pippen TO	.15	.07	.02
☐ 170	Chicago Bulls Mark Price TO	.08	.04	.01
☐ 171	Cleveland Cavaliers Jamal Mashburn TO	.40	.18	.05
☐ 172	Dallas Mavericks Dikembe Mutombo TO	.10	.05	.01
☐ 173	Denver Nuggets Joe Dumars TO	.10	.05	.01
☐ 174	Detroit Pistons Chris Webber TO	.50	.23	.06
☐ 175	Golden State Warriors Hakeem Olajuwon TO	.40	.18	.05
☐ 176	Houston Rockets Reggie Miller TO	.10	.05	.01
☐ 177	Indiana Pacers Ron Harper TO	.08	.04	.01
☐ 178	Los Angeles Clippers Nick Van Exel TO	.10	.05	.01
☐ 179	Los Angeles Lakers Steve Smith TO	.08	.04	.01
☐ 180	Miami Heat Vin Baker TO	.05	.02	.01
☐ 181	Milwaukee Bucks Isaiah Rider TO	.20	.09	.03
☐ 182	Minnesota Timberwolves Derrick Coleman TO	.10	.05	.01
☐ 183	New Jersey Nets Patrick Ewing TO	.15	.07	.02
☐ 184	New York Knicks Shaquille O'Neal TO	.75	.35	.09
☐ 185	Orlando Magic Clarence Weatherspoon TO	.10	.05	.01
☐ 186	Philadelphia 76ers Charles Barkley TO	.25	.11	.03
☐ 187	Phoenix Suns Clyde Drexler TO	.10	.05	.01
☐ 188	Portland Trail Blazers Mitch Richmond TO	.08	.04	.01
☐ 189	Sacramento Kings David Robinson TO	.25	.11	.03
☐ 190	San Antonio Spurs Shawn Kemp TO	.15	.07	.02
☐ 191	Seattle Supersonics Karl Malone TO	.12	.05	.02
☐ 192	Utah Jazz Tom Gugliotta TO	.10	.05	.01
☐ 193	Washington Bullets Kenny Anderson ASA	.10	.05	.01
☐ 194	New Jersey Nets Alonzo Mourning ASA	.25	.11	.03
☐ 195	Charlotte Hornets Mark Price ASA	.08	.04	.01
☐ 196	Cleveland Cavaliers John Stockton ASA	.10	.05	.01
☐ 197	Utah Jazz Shaquille O'Neal ASA	.75	.35	.09
☐ 198	Orlando Magic Latrell Sprewell ASA	.15	.07	.02
☐ 199	Golden State Warriors Charles Barkley PRO	.25	.11	.03
☐ 200	Phoenix Suns Chris Webber PRO	.50	.23	.06
☐ 201	Golden State Warriors Patrick Ewing PRO	.12	.05	.02
☐ 202	New York Knicks Dennis Rodman PRO	.05	.02	.01
☐ 203	San Antonio Spurs Shawn Kemp PRO	.15	.07	.02
☐ 204	Seattle Supersoncis Michael Jordan PRO	1.00	.45	.13
	Chicago Bulls			

				MINT	EXC	G-VG
☐	205	Shaquille O'Neal PRO		.75	.35	.09
		Orlando Magic				
☐	206	Larry Johnson PRO		.15	.07	.02
		Charlotte Hornets				
☐	207	Tim Hardaway CL		.10	.05	.01
		Golden State Warriors				
☐	208	John Stockton CL		.10	.05	.01
		Utah Jazz				
☐	209	Harold Miner CL		.08	.04	.01
		Miami Heat				
☐	210	B.J. Armstrong CL		.10	.05	.01
		Chicago Bulls				
☐	NNO	Draft Trade Winner Card		5.00	2.30	.60

1994-95 Collector's Choice
Silver Signature

Issued one per Collector's Choice pack, these 210 standard-size (2 1/2" by 3 1/2")cards comprise a parallel set to the regular Collector's Choice issue. The silver-bordered fronts feature color player action shots. The player's name, team, and position appear in a lower corner. The player's facsimile autograph appears in silver-foil near the bottom. The back carries another color player action shot at the top, with statistics and career highlights displayed below. The cards are numbered on the back. The following subsets are included in this set: Tip-Off (166-192), All-Star Advice (193-198), and NBA Profiles (199-206).

	MINT	EXC	G-VG
COMPLETE SERIES 1 (210)	75.00	34.00	9.50
COMMON SILVER (1-210)	.15	.07	.02
*UNLISTED STARS: 2.5X to 5X VALUE			

1994-95 Collector's Choice Crash the
Game

Randomly inserted in first-series hobby packs only, these 15 standard-size (2 1/2" by 3 1/2") cards feature on their fronts action player color shots set on grainy backgrounds faded to black-and-white. The player's name and team name appear in white lettering within the black margin at the top. The back carries the rules on how to play the 2,000-point game. The cards are numbered on the back with an "S" prefix.

	MINT	EXC	G-VG
COMPLETE 2000 PT SET (15)	90.00	40.00	11.50
COMMON PLAYER (S1-S15)	2.00	.90	.25

☐ S1	Charles Barkley	8.00	3.60	1.00
	Phoenix Suns			
☐ S2	Derrick Coleman	3.00	1.35	.40
	New Jersey Nets			
☐ S3	Joe Dumars	2.00	.90	.25
	Detroit Pistons			
☐ S4	Patrick Ewing	6.00	2.70	.75
	New York Knicks			
☐ S5	Karl Malone	4.00	1.80	.50
	Utah Jazz			
☐ S6	Reggie Miller	3.00	1.35	.40
	Indiana Pacers			
☐ S7	Shaquille O'Neal	20.00	9.00	2.50
	Orlando Magic			
☐ S8	Hakeem Olajuwon	10.00	4.50	1.25
	Houston Rockets			
☐ S9	Scottie Pippen	6.00	2.70	.75
	Chicago Bulls			
☐ S10	Glen Rice	2.00	.90	.25
	Miami Heat			
☐ S11	Mitch Richmond	2.00	.90	.25
	Sacramento Kings			
☐ S12	David Robinson	8.00	3.60	1.00
	San Antonio Spurs			
☐ S13	Latrell Sprewell	5.00	2.30	.60
	Golden State Warriors			
☐ S14	Chris Webber	15.00	6.75	1.90
	Golden State Warriors			
☐ S15	Dominique Wilkins	5.00	2.30	.60
	Los Angeles Clippers			

1991 Courtside Draft Pix

The 1991 Courtside Draft Pix basketball set consists of 45 cards measuring the standard size (2 1/2" by 3 1/2"). All 198,000 sets produced are numbered and distributed as complete sets in their own custom boxes each accompanied by a certificate with a unique serial number. It has also been reported that 30,000 autographed cards were randomly inserted in the 9,900 cases. The card front features a color action player photo. The design of the card fronts features a color rectangle (either pearlized red, blue, or green) on a pearlized white background, with two border stripes in the same color intersecting at the upper right corner. The player's name appears at the upper right corner of the card face, with the words "Courtside 1991" at the bottom. The backs reflect the color on the fronts and present stats (biographical), college record (year by year statistics), and player profile. The cards are numbered on the back. The unnumbered Larry Johnson sendaway card is not included in the complete set price below. The autographed cards are valued at 25 to 50 times the prices listed below.

	MINT	EXC	G-VG
COMPLETE SET (45)	5.00	2.00	.50
COMMON PLAYER (1-45)	.04	.02	.00
☐ 1 Larry Johnson First Draft Pick UNLV	.40	.16	.04
☐ 2 George Ackles UNLV	.04	.02	.00
☐ 3 Kenny Anderson Georgia Tech	.75	.30	.07
☐ 4 Greg Anthony UNLV	.15	.06	.01
☐ 5 Anthony Avent Seton Hall	.15	.06	.01
☐ 6 Terrell Brandon Oregon	.20	.08	.02
☐ 7 Kevin Brooks Southwestern Louisiana	.07	.03	.01
☐ 8 Marc Brown Siena	.04	.02	.00
☐ 9 Myron Brown Slippery Rock	.07	.03	.01
☐ 10 Randy Brown New Mexico State	.10	.04	.01
☐ 11 Darrin Chancellor Southern Mississippi	.04	.02	.00
☐ 12 Pete Chilcutt North Carolina	.15	.06	.01
☐ 13 Chris Corchiani North Carolina State	.10	.04	.01
☐ 14 John Crotty Virginia	.10	.04	.01
☐ 15 Dale Davis Clemson	.40	.16	.04
☐ 16 Marty Dow San Diego State	.04	.02	.00
☐ 17 Richard Dumas Oklahoma State	.10	.04	.01
☐ 18 LeRon Ellis Syracuse	.10	.04	.01
☐ 19 Tony Farmer Nebraska	.04	.02	.00
☐ 20 Roy Fisher California	.04	.02	.00
☐ 21 Rick Fox North Carolina	.30	.12	.03
☐ 22 Chad Gallagher Creighton	.04	.02	.00
☐ 23 Chris Gatling Old Dominion	.15	.06	.01
☐ 24 Sean Green	.07	.03	.01

☐ 25	Reggie Hanson Kentucky	.07	.03	.01
☐ 26	Donald Hodge Temple	.07	.03	.01
☐ 27	Steve Hood James Madison	.04	.02	.00
☐ 28	Keith Hughes Rutgers	.04	.02	.00
☐ 29	Mike Iuzzolino St.Francis	.07	.03	.01
☐ 30	Keith Jennings East Tenn. State	.15	.06	.01
☐ 31	Larry Johnson UNLV	1.50	.60	.15
☐ 32	Treg Lee Ohio State	.07	.03	.01
☐ 33	Cedric Lewis Maryland	.04	.02	.00
☐ 34	Kevin Lynch Minnesota	.07	.03	.01
☐ 35	Mark Macon Temple	.10	.04	.01
☐ 36	Jason Matthews Pittsburgh	.04	.02	.00
☐ 37	Eric Murdock Providence	.35	.14	.03
☐ 38	Jimmy Oliver Purdue	.04	.02	.00
☐ 39	Doug Overton LaSalle	.10	.04	.01
☐ 40	Elliot Perry Memphis State	.07	.03	.01
☐ 41	Brian Shorter Pittsburgh	.04	.02	.00
☐ 42	Alvaro Teheran Houston	.04	.02	.00
☐ 43	Joey Wright Texas	.04	.02	.00
☐ 44	Joe Wylie Miami (FL)	.04	.02	.00
☐ 45	Larry Johnson Collegiate Player of the Year	.40	.16	.04
☐ NNO	Larry Johnson SP (Sendaway)	4.00	1.60	.40

1993-94 Finest

The premier edition of the 1993-94 Topps Finest basketball set contains 220 cards, subdivided into 180 player cards, plus a 40-card subset of ten of the best players in each of the four divisions as follows: Atlantic (90-99), Central (100-109), Midwest (110-119), and Pacific (120-129). The seven-card packs included six player cards plus one subset card and retailed for about 4.00. Also, Refractors were offered for each of the 220 cards. One of these were inserted in every nine packs. Topps also issued a 14-card jumbo pack for 8.00, which included 11 regulars, two subsets, and a jumbo-only Main Attraction chase card. The 27-card chase set included one card for each NBA team. The rainbow colored metallic front features a color action cutout on a metalic marble background. The players name appears in the blue horizonal bar in the upper left. The white bordered back features a color player cutout on the left inset in a marble textured background. The players name and position appears in the gold bar in the upper right with the player's bigraphy, statistics and profile below. The cards are numbered on the back.

		MINT	EXC	G-VG
	COMPLETE SET (220)	150.00	70.00	19.00
	COMMON PLAYER (1-220)	.40	.18	.05
☐ 1	Michael Jordan	25.00	11.50	3.10
☐ 2	Larry Bird	10.00	4.50	1.25
☐ 3	Shaquille O'Neal Orlando Magic	20.00	9.00	2.50

☐ 4	Benoit Benjamin	.40	.18	.05
	New Jersey Nets			
☐ 5	Ricky Pierce	.60	.25	.08
	Seattle Supersonics			
☐ 6	Ken Norman	.40	.18	.05
	Milwaukee Bucks			
☐ 7	Victor Alexander	.40	.18	.05
	Golden State Warriors			
☐ 8	Mark Jackson	.60	.25	.08
	Los Angeles Clippers			
☐ 9	Mark West	.40	.18	.05
	Phoenix Suns			
☐ 10	Don MacLean	.60	.25	.08
	Washington Bullets			
☐ 11	Reggie Miller	3.00	1.35	.40
	Indiana Pacers			
☐ 12	Sarunas Marciulionis	.40	.18	.05
	Golden State Warriors			
☐ 13	Craig Ehlo	.40	.18	.05
	Atlanta Hawks			
☐ 14	Toni Kukoc	3.50	1.55	.45
	Chicago Bulls			
☐ 15	Glen Rice	.75	.35	.09
	Miami Heat			
☐ 16	Otis Thorpe	.60	.25	.08
	Houston Rockets			
☐ 17	Reggie Williams	.40	.18	.05
	Denver Nuggets			
☐ 18	Charles Smith	.40	.18	.05
	New York Knicks			
☐ 19	Micheal Williams	.60	.25	.08
	Minnesota Timberwolves			
☐ 20	Tom Chambers	.60	.25	.08
	Utah Jazz			
☐ 21	David Robinson	8.00	3.60	1.00
	San Antonio Spurs			
☐ 22	Jamal Mashburn	8.00	3.60	1.00
	Dallas Mavericks			
☐ 23	Clifford Robinson	.75	.35	.09
	Portland Trail Blazers			
☐ 24	Acie Earl	1.00	.45	.13
	Boston Celtics			
☐ 25	Danny Ferry	.40	.18	.05
	Cleveland Cavaliers			
☐ 26	Bobby Hurley	3.50	1.55	.45
	Sacramento Kings			
☐ 27	Eddie Johnson	.40	.18	.05
	Charlotte Hornets			
☐ 28	Detlef Schrempf	.75	.35	.09
	Seattle Supersonics			
☐ 29	Mike Brown	.40	.18	.05
	Minnesota Timberwolves			

☐ 30 Latrell Sprewell 6.00	2.70	.75
Golden State Warriors		
☐ 31 Derek Harper .... .60	.25	.08
New York Knicks		
☐ 32 Stacey Augmon .... .75	.35	.09
Atlanta Hawks		
☐ 33 Pooh Richardson .... .40	.18	.05
Indiana Pacers		
☐ 34 Larry Krystkowiak .... .40	.18	.05
Orlando Magic		
☐ 35 Pervis Ellison .... .40	.18	.05
Washington Bullets		
☐ 36 Jeff Malone .... .60	.25	.08
Philadelphia 76ers		
☐ 37 Sean Elliott .... .60	.25	.08
Detroit Pistons		
☐ 38 John Paxson .... .40	.18	.05
Chicago Bulls		
☐ 39 Robert Parish .... .75	.35	.09
Boston Celtics		
☐ 40 Mark Aguirre .... .75	.35	.09
Los Angeles Clippers		
☐ 41 Danny Ainge .... .75	.35	.09
Phoenix Suns		
☐ 42 Brian Shaw .... .40	.18	.05
Miami Heat		
☐ 43 Laphonso Ellis 2.00	.90	.25
Denver Nuggets		
☐ 44 Carl Herrera .... .40	.18	.05
Houston Rockets		
☐ 45 Terry Cummings .... .60	.25	.08
San Antonio Spurs		
☐ 46 Chris Dudley .... .40	.18	.05
Portland Trail Blazers		
☐ 47 Anthony Mason .... .40	.18	.05
New York Knicks		
☐ 48 Chris Morris .... .40	.18	.05
New Jersey Nets		
☐ 49 Todd Day .... .60	.25	.08
Milwaukee Bucks		
☐ 50 Nick Van Exel 3.50	1.55	.45
Los Angeles Lakers		
☐ 51 Larry Nance .... .60	.25	.08
Cleveland Cavaliers		
☐ 52 Derrick McKey .... .40	.18	.05
Indiana Pacers		
☐ 53 Muggsy Bogues .... .75	.35	.09
Charlotte Hornets		
☐ 54 Andrew Lang .... .40	.18	.05
Atlanta Hawks		
☐ 55 Chuck Person .... .60	.25	.08
Minnesota Timberwolves		
☐ 56 Michael Adams .... .60	.25	.08
Washington Bullets		
☐ 57 Spud Webb .... .75	.35	.09
Sacramento Kings		
☐ 58 Scott Skiles .... .40	.18	.05
Orlando Magic		
☐ 59 A.C. Green .... .60	.25	.08
Phoenix Suns		
☐ 60 Terry Mills .... .60	.25	.08
Detroit Pistons		
☐ 61 Xavier McDaniel .... .60	.25	.08
Boston Celtics		
☐ 62 B.J. Armstrong .... .75	.35	.09
Chicago Bulls		
☐ 63 Donald Hodge .... .40	.18	.05
Dallas Mavericks		
☐ 64 Gary Grant .... .40	.18	.05
Los Angeles Clippers		
☐ 65 Billy Owens .... .60	.25	.08
Golden State Warriors		
☐ 66 Greg Anthony .... .40	.18	.05

	New York Knicks			
☐ 67	Jay Humphries	.40	.18	.05
	Utah Jazz			
☐ 68	Lionel Simmons	.60	.25	.08
	Sacramento Kings			
☐ 69	Dana Barros	.40	.18	.05
	Philadelphia 76ers			
☐ 70	Steve Smith	.60	.25	.08
	Miami Heat			
☐ 71	Ervin Johnson	1.00	.45	.13
	Seattle Supersonics			
☐ 72	Sleepy Floyd	.40	.18	.05
	San Antonio Spurs			
☐ 73	Blue Edwards	.40	.18	.05
	Milwaukee Bucks			
☐ 74	Clyde Drexler	3.00	1.35	.40
	Portland Trail Blazers			
☐ 75	Elden Campbell	.40	.18	.05
	Los Angeles Lakers			
☐ 76	Hakeem Olajuwon	10.00	4.50	1.25
	Houston Rockets			
☐ 77	Clarence Weatherspoon	.75	.35	.09
	Philadelphia 76ers			
☐ 78	Kevin Willis	.60	.25	.08
	Atlanta Hawks			
☐ 79	Isaiah Rider	8.00	3.60	1.00
	Minnesota Timberwolves			
☐ 80	Derrick Coleman	3.00	1.35	.40
	New Jersey Nets			
☐ 81	Nick Anderson	.60	.25	.08
	Orlando Magic			
☐ 82	Bryant Stith	.60	.25	.08
	Denver Nuggets			
☐ 83	Johnny Newman	.40	.18	.05
	New Jersey Nets			
☐ 84	Clabert Cheaney	3.50	1.55	.45
	Washington Bullets			
☐ 85	Oliver Miller	.75	.35	.09
	Phoenix Suns			
☐ 86	Loy Vaught	.60	.25	.08
	Los Angeles Clippers			
☐ 87	Isiah Thomas	2.50	1.15	.30
	Detroit Pistons			
☐ 88	Dee Brown	.40	.18	.05
	Boston Celtics			
☐ 89	Horace Grant	.75	.35	.09
	Chicago Bulls			
☐ 90	Patrick Ewing AF	3.50	1.55	.45
	New York Knicks			
☐ 91	Clarence Weatherspoon AF	1.00	.45	.13
	Philadelphia 76ers			
☐ 92	Rony Seikaly AF	1.00	.45	.13
	Miami Heat			
☐ 93	Dino Radja AF	1.50	.65	.19
	Boston Celtics			
☐ 94	Kenny Anderson AF	1.50	.65	.19
	New Jersey Nets			
☐ 95	John Starks AF	.75	.35	.09
	New York Knicks			
☐ 96	Tom Gugliotta AF	.75	.35	.09
	Washington Bullets			
☐ 97	Steve Smith AF	.75	.35	.09
	Miami Heat			
☐ 98	Derrick Coleman AF	1.50	.65	.19
	New Jersey Nets			
☐ 99	Shaquille O'Neal AF	12.00	5.50	1.50
	Orlando Magic			
☐ 100	Brad Daugherty CF	1.00	.45	.13
	Cleveland Cavaliers			
☐ 101	Horace Grant CF	1.00	.45	.13
	Chicago Bulls			
☐ 102	Dominique Wilkins CF	3.00	1.35	.40
	Atlanta Hawks			

☐ 103	Joe Dumars CF Detroit Pistons	.50	.23	.06
☐ 104	Alonzo Mourning CF Charlotte Hornets	5.00	2.30	.60
☐ 105	Scottie Pippen CF Chicago Bulls	3.50	1.55	.45
☐ 106	Reggie Miller CF Indiana Pacers	.50	.23	.06
☐ 107	Mark Price CF Cleveland Cavaliers	1.00	.45	.13
☐ 108	Ken Norman CF Milwaukee Bucks	.50	.23	.06
☐ 109	Larry Johnson CF Charlotte Hornets	3.50	1.55	.45
☐ 110	Jamal Mashburn MF Dallas Mavericks	3.00	1.35	.40
☐ 111	Christian Laettner MF Minnesota Timberwolves	.75	.35	.09
☐ 112	Karl Malone MF Utah Jazz	2.50	1.15	.30
☐ 113	Dennis Rodman MF San Antonio Spurs	.75	.35	.09
☐ 114	Mahmoud Abdul-Rauf MF Denver Nuggets	.50	.23	.06
☐ 115	Hakeem Olajuwon MF Houston Rockets	6.00	2.70	.75
☐ 116	Jim Jackson MF Dallas Mavericks	3.00	1.35	.40
☐ 117	John Stockton MF Utah Jazz	2.00	.90	.25
☐ 118	David Robinson MF San Antonio Spurs	5.00	2.30	.60
☐ 119	Dikembe Mutombo MF Denver Nuggets	1.00	.45	.13
☐ 120	Vlade Divac PF Los Angeles Lakers	.50	.23	.06
☐ 121	Dan Majerle PF Phoenix Suns	1.00	.45	.13
☐ 122	Chris Mullin PF Golden State Warriors	1.50	.65	.19
☐ 123	Shawn Kemp PF Seattle Supersonics	3.50	1.55	.45
☐ 124	Danny Manning PF Los Angeles Clippers	1.00	.45	.13
☐ 125	Charles Barkley PF Phoenix Suns	5.00	2.30	.60
☐ 126	Mitch Richmond PF Sacramento Kings	1.00	.45	.13
☐ 127	Tim Hardaway PF Golden State Warriors	1.00	.45	.13
☐ 128	Detlef Schrempf PF Seattle Supersonics	1.00	.45	.13
☐ 129	Clyde Drexler PF Portland Trail Blazers	2.00	.90	.25
☐ 130	Christian Laettner Minnesota Timberwolves	.60	.25	.08
☐ 131	Rodney Rogers Denver Nuggets	2.00	.90	.25
☐ 132	Rik Smits Indiana Pacers	.60	.25	.08
☐ 133	Chris Mills Cleveland Cavaliers	2.00	.90	.25
☐ 134	Corie Blount Chicago Bulls	1.25	.55	.16
☐ 135	Mookie Blaylock Atlanta Hawks	.60	.25	.08
☐ 136	Jim Jackson Dallas Mavericks	4.00	1.80	.50
☐ 137	Tom Gugliotta Washington Bullets	.60	.25	.08
☐ 138	Dennis Scott Orlando Magic	.60	.25	.08
☐ 139	Vin Baker	6.00	2.70	.75

	Milwaukee Bucks			
☐ 140	Gary Payton	.40	.18	.05
	Seattle Supersonics			
☐ 141	Sedale Threatt	.40	.18	.05
	Los Angeles Lakers			
☐ 142	Orlando Woolridge	.60	.25	.08
	Philadelphia 76ers			
☐ 143	Avery Johnson	.40	.18	.05
	Golden State Warriors			
☐ 144	Charles Oakley	.75	.35	.09
	New York Knicks			
☐ 145	Harvey Grant	.40	.18	.05
	Portland Trail Blazers			
☐ 146	Bimbo Coles	.40	.18	.05
	Miami Heat			
☐ 147	Vernon Maxwell	.60	.25	.08
	Houston Rockets			
☐ 148	Danny Manning	2.50	1.15	.30
	Los Angeles Clippers			
☐ 149	Hersey Hawkins	.60	.25	.08
	Charlotte Hornets			
☐ 150	Kevin Gamble	.40	.18	.05
	Boston Celtics			
☐ 151	Johnny Dawkins	.40	.18	.05
	Philadelphia 76ers			
☐ 152	Olden Polynice	.40	.18	.05
	Sacramento Kings			
☐ 153	Kevin Edwards	.40	.18	.05
	New Jersey Nets			
☐ 154	Willie Anderson	.40	.18	.05
	San Antonio Spurs			
☐ 155	Wayman Tisdale	.60	.25	.08
	Sacramento Kings			
☐ 156	Popeye Jones	1.50	.65	.19
	Dallas Mavericks			
☐ 157	Dan Majerle	.75	.35	.09
	Phoenix Suns			
☐ 158	Rex Chapman	.40	.18	.05
	Washington Bullets			
☐ 159	Shawn Kemp	6.00	2.70	.75
	Seattle Supersonics			
☐ 160	Eric Murdock	.60	.25	.08
	Milwaukee Bucks			
☐ 161	Randy White	.40	.18	.05
	Dallas Mavericks			
☐ 162	Larry Johnson	5.00	2.30	.60
	Charlotte Hornets			
☐ 163	Dominique Wilkins	5.00	2.30	.60
	Atlanta Hawks			
☐ 164	Dikembe Mutombo	2.50	1.15	.30
	Denver Nuggets			
☐ 165	Patrick Ewing	6.00	2.70	.75
	New York Knicks			
☐ 166	Jerome Kersey	.40	.18	.05
	Portland Trail Blazers			
☐ 167	Dale Davis	.60	.25	.08
	Indiana Pacers			
☐ 168	Ron Harper	.60	.25	.08
	Los Angeles Clippers			
☐ 169	Sam Cassell	4.00	1.80	.50
	Houston Rockets			
☐ 170	Bill Cartwright	.40	.18	.05
	Chicago Bulls			
☐ 171	John Williams	.60	.25	.08
	Cleveland Cavaliers			
☐ 172	Dino Radja	3.00	1.35	.40
	Boston Celtics			
☐ 173	Dennis Rodman	.60	.25	.08
	San Antonio Spurs			
☐ 174	Kenny Anderson	2.50	1.15	.30
	New Jersey Nets			
☐ 175	Robert Horry	.75	.35	.09
	Houston Rockets			

☐ 176	Chris Mullin Golden State Warriors	2.50	1.15	.30
☐ 177	John Salley Miami Heat	.40	.18	.05
☐ 178	Scott Burrell Charlotte Hornets	1.50	.65	.19
☐ 179	Mitch Richmond Sacramento Kings	.75	.35	.09
☐ 180	Lee Mayberry Milwaukee Bucks	.40	.18	.05
☐ 181	James Worthy Los Angeles Lakers	.75	.35	.09
☐ 182	Rick Fox Boston Celtics	.40	.18	.05
☐ 183	Kevin Johnson Phoenix Suns	.75	.35	.09
☐ 184	Lindsey Hunter Detroit Pistons	3.00	1.35	.40
☐ 185	Marlon Maxey Phoenix Suns	.40	.18	.05
☐ 186	Sam Perkins Seattle Supersonics	.60	.25	.08
☐ 187	Kevin Duckworth Washington Bullets	.40	.18	.05
☐ 188	Jeff Hornacek Utah Jazz	.60	.25	.08
☐ 189	Anfernee Hardaway Orlando Magic	15.00	6.75	1.90
☐ 190	Rex Walters New Jersey Nets	1.00	.45	.13
☐ 191	Mahmoud Abdul-Rauf Denver Nuggets	.40	.18	.05
☐ 192	Terry Dehere Los Angeles Clippers	1.25	.55	.16
☐ 193	Brad Daugherty Cleveland Cavaliers	.75	.35	.09
☐ 194	John Starks New York Knicks	.75	.35	.09
☐ 195	Rod Strickland Portland Trail Blazers	.60	.25	.08
☐ 196	Luther Wright Utah Jazz	1.00	.45	.13
☐ 197	Vlade Divac Los Angeles Lakers	.40	.18	.05
☐ 198	Tim Hardaway Golden State Warriors	.75	.35	.09
☐ 199	Joe Dumars Detroit Pistons	2.50	1.15	.30
☐ 200	Charles Barkley Phoenix Suns	8.00	3.60	1.00
☐ 201	Alonzo Mourning Orlando Magic	8.00	3.60	1.00
☐ 202	Doug West Minnesota Timberwolves	.40	.18	.05
☐ 203	Anthony Avent Orlando Magic	.40	.18	.05
☐ 204	Lloyd Daniels San Antonio Spurs	.40	.18	.05
☐ 205	Mark Price Cleveland Cavaliers	.75	.35	.09
☐ 206	Rumeal Robinson Charlotte Hornets	.40	.18	.05
☐ 207	Kendall Gill Seattle Supersonics	.60	.25	.08
☐ 208	Scottie Pippen Chicago Bulls	6.00	2.70	.75
☐ 209	Kenny Smith Houston Rockets	.40	.18	.05
☐ 210	Walt Williams Sacramento Kings	.60	.25	.08
☐ 211	Hubert Davis New York Knicks	.40	.18	.05
☐ 212	Chris Webber	20.00	9.00	2.50

			MINT	EXC	G-VG
	Golden State Warriors				
☐ 213	Rony Seikaly	.75	.35	.09	
	Miami Heat				
☐ 214	Sam Bowie	.40	.18	.05	
	Los Angeles Lakers				
☐ 215	Karl Malone	4.00	1.80	.50	
	Utah Jazz				
☐ 216	Malik Sealy	.40	.18	.05	
	Indiana Pacers				
☐ 217	Dale Ellis	.60	.25	.08	
	Indiana Pacers				
☐ 218	Harold Miner	.60	.25	.08	
	Miami Heat				
☐ 219	John Stockton	3.00	1.35	.40	
	Utah Jazz				
☐ 220	Shawn Bradley	3.50	1.55	.45	
	Philadelphia 76ers				

1993-94 Finest Refractors

These special Refractor cards were produced for all 220 Finest cards; they were randomly inserted at a rate of one in every nine Finest packs. The rainbow-colored front features a color action cutout on a metallic background. The player's name appears in the blue horizonal bar at the upper left. The white-bordered back features a color player cutout on the left. The player's name and position appear in the gold bar at the upper right with the player's biography, statistics and profile below. The cards are numbered on the back. The cards listed below are those that do not conform to the multiplier.

		MINT	EXC	G-VG
COMPLETE SET (220)		3000.00	1350.00	375.00
COMMON PLAYER (1-220)		4.00	1.80	.50
*UNLISTED STARS: 3X to 8X VALUE				
*UNLISTED ROOKIES: 3X to 8X VALUE				
☐ 1	Michael Jordan TRIB	300.00	135.00	38.00
☐ 2	Larry Bird TRIB	100.00	45.00	12.50
☐ 3	Shaquille O'Neal	200.00	90.00	25.00
	Orlando Magic			
☐ 21	David Robinson	70.00	32.00	8.75
	San Antonio Spurs			
☐ 22	Jamal Mashburn	60.00	27.00	7.50
	Dallas Mavericks			
☐ 30	Latrell Sprewell	60.00	27.00	7.50
	Golden State Warriors			
☐ 76	Hakeem Olajuwon	100.00	45.00	12.50
	Houston Rockets			
☐ 79	Isaiah Rider	60.00	27.00	7.50
	Minnesota Timberwolves			
☐ 99	Shaquille O'Neal AF	100.00	45.00	12.50

		Orlando Magic			
☐	104	Alonzo Mourning CF	45.00	20.00	5.75
		Charlotte Hornets			
☐	110	Jamal Mashburn MF	4.00	1.80	.50
		Dallas Mavericks			
☐	115	Hakeem Olajuwon MF	50.00	23.00	6.25
		Houston Rockets			
☐	118	David Robinson MF	35.00	16.00	4.40
		San Antonio Spurs			
☐	125	Charles Barkley PF	35.00	16.00	4.40
		Phoenix Suns			
☐	136	Jim Jackson	40.00	18.00	5.00
		Dallas Mavericks			
☐	139	Vin Baker	40.00	18.00	5.00
		Milwaukee Bucks			
☐	159	Shawn Kemp UER	50.00	23.00	6.25
		Seattle Supersonics			
		(Misnumbered 136)			
☐	162	Larry Johnson	40.00	18.00	5.00
		Charlotte Hornets			
☐	163	Dominique Wilkins	40.00	18.00	5.00
		Atlanta Hawks			
☐	165	Patrick Ewing	50.00	23.00	6.25
		New York Knicks			
☐	189	Anfernee Hardaway	150.00	70.00	19.00
		Orlando Magic			
☐	200	Charles Barkley	70.00	32.00	8.75
		Phoenix Suns			
☐	201	Alonzo Mourning	90.00	40.00	11.50
		Orlando Magic			
☐	208	Scottie Pippen	50.00	23.00	6.25
		Chicago Bulls			
☐	212	Chris Webber	200.00	90.00	25.00
		Golden State Warriors			
☐	215	Karl Malone	35.00	16.00	4.40
		Utah Jazz			

1993-94 Finest Main Attraction

One of these chase cards was randomly inserted in 14-card jumbos packs only. Each NBA team is represented by one card in this standard size (2 1/2" by 3 1/2") set. The rainbow colored metallic front features a semi-embossed color action cutout on textured metallic background. The players name appears in metallic gold on the orange colored horizonal bar in the lower left. The brick textured bordered back features a color action shot with a gold border. The players name and position appears vertically in black on the left side of the photo. Player's statistics and profile appear below the photo. The cards are numbered on the back "X" of 27..

	MINT	EXC	G-VG
COMPLETE SET (27)	175.00	80.00	22.00
COMMON PLAYER (1-27)	3.00	1.35	.40
☐ 1 Dominique Wilkins	10.00	4.50	1.25
Atlanta Hawks			
☐ 2 Dino Radja	6.00	2.70	.75
Boston Celtics			
☐ 3 Larry Johnson	10.00	4.50	1.25
Charlotte Hornets			
☐ 4 Scottie Pippen	12.00	5.50	1.50
Chicago Bulls			
☐ 5 Mark Price	3.50	1.55	.45
Cleveland Cavaliers			
☐ 6 Jamal Mashburn	14.00	6.25	1.75
Dallas Mavericks			
☐ 7 Mahmoud Abdul-Rauf	3.00	1.35	.40
Denver Nuggets			
☐ 8 Joe Dumars	4.00	1.80	.50
Detroit Piston			
☐ 9 Chris Webber	40.00	18.00	5.00
Golden State Warriors			
☐ 10 Hakeem Olajuwon	20.00	9.00	2.50
Houston Rockets			
☐ 11 Reggie Miller	5.00	2.30	.60
Indiana Pacers			
☐ 12 Danny Manning	4.00	1.80	.50
Los Angeles Clippers			
☐ 13 Doug Christie	3.00	1.35	.40
Los Angeles Lakers			
☐ 14 Steve Smith	3.50	1.55	.45
Miami Heat			
☐ 15 Eric Murdock	3.00	1.35	.40
Milwaukee Bucks			
☐ 16 Isaiah Rider	14.00	6.25	1.75
Minnesota Timberwolves			
☐ 17 Derrick Coleman	5.00	2.30	.60
New Jersey Nets			
☐ 18 Patrick Ewing	12.00	5.50	1.50
New York Knicks			
☐ 19 Shaquille O'Neal	40.00	18.00	5.00
Orlando Magic			
☐ 20 Shawn Bradley	6.00	2.70	.75
Philadelphia 76ers			
☐ 21 Charles Barkley	15.00	6.75	1.90
Phoenix Suns			
☐ 22 Clyde Drexler	5.00	2.30	.60
Portland Trail Blazers			
☐ 23 Mitch Richmond	3.50	1.55	.45
Sacramento Kings			
☐ 24 David Robinson	15.00	6.75	1.90
San Antonio Spurs			
☐ 25 Shawn Kemp	12.00	5.50	1.50
Seattle Supersonics			
☐ 26 Karl Malone	8.00	3.60	1.00
Utah Jazz			
☐ 27 Tom Gugliotta	4.00	1.80	.50
Washington Bullets			

1994 Flair USA

The 120 standard-size (2 1/2" by 3 1/2") cards comprising this set pay tribute to the players of 1994 Team USA. Each player has several cards highlighting various stages in his career. The cards are thicker than traditional basketball cards. The borderless fronts feature two blended color player photos. The player's name appears in gold-foil lettering near the bottom. The borderless back carries a posed color player photo with player information appearing in silver-foil lettering toward the bottom. The cards are numbered on the back. The set concludes with a USA Basketball Women's Team Legends (113-118) subset and checklists (119-120).

	MINT	EXC	G-VG
COMPLETE SET (120)	50.00	23.00	6.25
COMMON PLAYER (1-120)	.25	.11	.03
☐ 1 Don Chaney CO	.25	.11	.03
Career Highlights			
☐ 2 Don Chaney CO	.25	.11	.03
Personal Note			
☐ 3 Pete Gillen CO	.25	.11	.03
Career Highlights			
☐ 4 Pete Gillen CO	.25	.11	.03
Personal Note			
☐ 5 Rick Majerus CO	.25	.11	.03
Career Highlights			
☐ 6 Rick Majerus CO	.25	.11	.03
Personal Note			
☐ 7 Don Nelson CO	.25	.11	.03
Career Highlights			
☐ 8 Don Nelson CO	.25	.11	.03
Personal Note			
☐ 9 Derrick Coleman	.60	.25	.08
Strong Suit			
☐ 10 Derrick Coleman	.60	.25	.08
Career Highlights			
☐ 11 Derrick Coleman	.60	.25	.08
Golden Moment			
☐ 12 Derrick Coleman	.60	.25	.08
Biography			
☐ 13 Derrick Coleman	.60	.25	.08
Rookie Year			
☐ 14 Derrick Coleman	.60	.25	.08
Weights and Measures			
☐ 15 Derrick Coleman	.60	.25	.08
Personal Note			
☐ 16 Joe Dumars	.50	.23	.06
Dreamscapes			
☐ 17 Joe Dumars	.50	.23	.06
Strong Suit			
☐ 18 Joe Dumars	.50	.23	.06
Career Highlights			
☐ 19 Joe Dumars	.50	.23	.06
Golden Moment			
☐ 20 Joe Dumars	.50	.23	.06
Biography			
☐ 21 Joe Dumars	.50	.23	.06
Rookie Year			
☐ 22 Joe Dumars	.50	.23	.06
Weights and Measures			
☐ 23 Joe Dumars	.50	.23	.06
Personal Note			
☐ 24 Joe Dumars	.50	.23	.06
Dreamscapes			
☐ 25 Tim Hardaway	.40	.18	.05

	Strong Suit			
☐ 26	Tim Hardaway	.40	.18	.05
	Career Highlights			
☐ 27	Tim Hardaway	.40	.18	.05
	Golden Moment			
☐ 28	Tim Hardaway	.40	.18	.05
	Biography			
☐ 29	Tim Hardaway	.40	.18	.05
	Rookie Year			
☐ 30	Tim Hardaway	.40	.18	.05
	Weights and Measures			
☐ 31	Tim Hardaway	.40	.18	.05
	Personal Note			
☐ 32	Tim Hardaway	.40	.18	.05
	Dreamscapes			
☐ 33	Larry Johnson	1.00	.45	.13
	Strong Suit			
☐ 34	Larry Johnson	1.00	.45	.13
	Career Highlights			
☐ 35	Larry Johnson	1.00	.45	.13
	Golden Moments			
☐ 36	Larry Johnson	1.00	.45	.13
	Biography			
☐ 37	Larry Johnson	1.00	.45	.13
	Rookie Year			
☐ 38	Larry Johnson	1.00	.45	.13
	Weights and Measures			
☐ 39	Larry Johnson	1.00	.45	.13
	Personal Note			
☐ 40	Larry Johnson	1.00	.45	.13
	Dreamscapes			
☐ 41	Shawn Kemp	1.25	.55	.16
	Strong Suit			
☐ 42	Shawn Kemp	1.25	.55	.16
	Career Highlights			
☐ 43	Shawn Kemp	1.25	.55	.16
	Golden Moment			
☐ 44	Shawn Kemp	1.25	.55	.16
	Biography			
☐ 45	Shawn Kemp	1.25	.55	.16
	Rookie Year			
☐ 46	Shawn Kemp	1.25	.55	.16
	Weights and Measures			
☐ 47	Shawn Kemp	1.25	.55	.16
	Personal Note			
☐ 48	Shawn Kemp	1.25	.55	.16
	Dreamscapes			
☐ 49	Dan Majerle	.40	.18	.05
	Strong Suit			
☐ 50	Dan Majerle	.40	.18	.05
	Career Highlights			
☐ 51	Dan Majerle	.40	.18	.05
	Golden Moment			
☐ 52	Dan Majerle	.40	.18	.05
	Biography			
☐ 53	Dan Majerle	.40	.18	.05
	Rookie Year			
☐ 54	Dan Majerle	.40	.18	.05
	Weights and Measures			
☐ 55	Dan Majerle	.40	.18	.05
	Personal Note			
☐ 56	Dan Majerle	.40	.18	.05
	Dreamscapes			
☐ 57	Reggie Miller	.60	.25	.08
	Strong Suit			
☐ 58	Reggie Miller	.60	.25	.08
	Career Highlights			
☐ 59	Reggie Miller	.60	.25	.08
	Golden Moments			
☐ 60	Reggie Miller	.60	.25	.08
	Biography			
☐ 61	Reggie Miller	.60	.25	.08
	Rookie Year			

☐ 62	Reggie Miller	.60	.25	.08
	Weights and Measures			
☐ 63	Reggie Miller	.60	.25	.08
	Personal Note			
☐ 64	Reggie Miller	.60	.25	.08
	Dreamscapes			
☐ 65	Alonzo Mourning	2.00	.90	.25
	Strong Suit			
☐ 66	Alonzo Mourning	2.00	.90	.25
	Career Highlights			
☐ 67	Alonzo Mourning	2.00	.90	.25
	Golden Moment			
☐ 68	Alonzo Mourning	2.00	.90	.25
	Biography			
☐ 69	Alonzo Mourning	2.00	.90	.25
	Rookie Year			
☐ 70	Alonzo Mourning	2.00	.90	.25
	Weights and Measures			
☐ 71	Alonzo Mourning	2.00	.90	.25
	Personal Note			
☐ 72	Alonzo Mourning	2.00	.90	.25
	Dreamscapes			
☐ 73	Shaquille O'Neal	5.00	2.30	.60
	Strong Suit			
☐ 74	Shaquille O'Neal	5.00	2.30	.60
	Career Highlights			
☐ 75	Shaquille O'Neal	5.00	2.30	.60
	Golden Moment			
☐ 76	Shaquille O'Neal	5.00	2.30	.60
	Biography			
☐ 77	Shaquille O'Neal	5.00	2.30	.60
	Rookie Year			
☐ 78	Shaquille O'Neal	5.00	2.30	.60
	Weights and Measures			
☐ 79	Shaquille O'Neal	5.00	2.30	.60
	Personal Note			
☐ 80	Shaquille O'Neal	5.00	2.30	.60
	Dreamscapes			
☐ 81	Mark Price	.40	.18	.05
	Strong Suit			
☐ 82	Mark Price	.40	.18	.05
	Career Highlights			
☐ 83	Mark Price	.40	.18	.05
	Golden Moment			
☐ 84	Mark Price	.40	.18	.05
	Biography			
☐ 85	Mark Price	.40	.18	.05
	Rookie Year			
☐ 86	Mark Price	.40	.18	.05
	Weights and Measures			
☐ 87	Mark Price	.40	.18	.05
	Personal Note			
☐ 88	Mark Price	.40	.18	.05
	Dreamscapes			
☐ 89	Steve Smith	.40	.18	.05
	Strong Suit			
☐ 90	Steve Smith	.40	.18	.05
	Career Highlights			
☐ 91	Steve Smith	.40	.18	.05
	Golden Moment			
☐ 92	Steve Smith	.40	.18	.05
	Biography			
☐ 93	Steve Smith	.40	.18	.05
	Rookie Year			
☐ 94	Steve Smith	.40	.18	.05
	Weights and Measures			
☐ 95	Steve Smith	.40	.18	.05
	Personal Note			
☐ 96	Steve Smith	.40	.18	.05
	Dreamscapes			
☐ 97	Isiah Thomas	.50	.23	.06
	Strong Suit			
☐ 98	Isiah Thomas	.50	.23	.06

	Career Highlights			
☐ 99	Isiah Thomas	.50	.23	.06
	Golden Moment			
☐ 100	Isiah Thomas	.50	.23	.06
	Biography			
☐ 101	Isiah Thomas	.50	.23	.06
	Rookie Year			
☐ 102	Isiah Thomas	.50	.23	.06
	Weights and Measures			
☐ 103	Isiah Thomas	.50	.23	.06
	Personal Note			
☐ 104	Isiah Thomas	.50	.23	.06
	Dreamscapes			
☐ 105	Dominique Wilkins	1.00	.45	.13
	Strong Suit			
☐ 106	Dominique Wilkins	1.00	.45	.13
	Career Highlights			
☐ 107	Dominique Wilkins	1.00	.45	.13
	Golden Moment			
☐ 108	Dominique Wilkins	1.00	.45	.13
	Biography			
☐ 109	Dominique Wilkins	1.00	.45	.13
	Rookie Year			
☐ 110	Dominique Wilkins	1.00	.45	.13
	Weights and Measures			
☐ 111	Dominique Wilkins	1.00	.45	.13
	Personal Note			
☐ 112	Dominique Wilkins	1.00	.45	.13
	Dreamscapes			
☐ 113	Carol Blazejowski	.25	.11	.03
☐ 114	Teresa Edwards	.25	.11	.03
☐ 115	Nancy Lieberman-Cline	.25	.11	.03
☐ 116	Ann Meyers	.25	.11	.03
☐ 117	Pat Summitt CO	.25	.11	.03
☐ 118	Lynette Woodard	.25	.11	.03
☐ 119	Checklist	1.00	.45	.13
☐ 120	Checklist	1.00	.45	.13

1961-62 Fleer

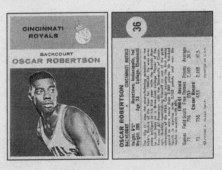

The 1961-62 Fleer set was the company's only major basketball issue until the 1986-87 season. The cards were issued in five-cent wax packs. The cards in the set measure the standard, 2 1/2" by 3 1/2". Cards numbered 45 to 66 are action shots (designated IA) of players elsewhere in the set. Both the regular cards and the IA cards are numbered alphabetically within that particular subgroup. No known scarcities exist, although the set is quite popular since it contains the first mainstream basketball cards of many of the game's all-time greats including Elgin Baylor, Wilt Chamberlain, Oscar Robertson, and Jerry West. Many of the cards are frequently found with centering problems.

	NRMT	VG-E	GOOD
COMPLETE SET (66)	4200.00	1900.00	525.00
COMMON PLAYER (1-44)	15.00	6.75	1.90
COMMON PLAYER (45-66)	12.50	5.75	1.55
☐ 1 Al Attles Philadelphia Warriors	100.00	22.00	5.00
☐ 2 Paul Arizin Philadelphia Warriors	35.00	16.00	4.40
☐ 3 Elgin Baylor Los Angeles Lakers	375.00	170.00	47.50
☐ 4 Walt Bellamy Chicago Packers	50.00	23.00	6.25
☐ 5 Arlen Bockhorn Cincinnati Royals	15.00	6.75	1.90
☐ 6 Bob Boozer Cincinnati Royals	20.00	9.00	2.50
☐ 7 Carl Braun Boston Celtics	20.00	9.00	2.50
☐ 8 Wilt Chamberlain Philadelphia Warriors	1350.00	600.00	170.00
☐ 9 Larry Costello Syracuse Nationals	20.00	9.00	2.50
☐ 10 Bob Cousy Boston Celtics	225.00	100.00	28.00
☐ 11 Walter Dukes Detroit Pistons	15.00	6.75	1.90
☐ 12 Wayne Embry Cincinnati Royals	35.00	16.00	4.40
☐ 13 Dave Gambee Syracuse Nationals	15.00	6.75	1.90
☐ 14 Tom Gola Philadelphia Warriors	40.00	18.00	5.00
☐ 15 Sihugo Green St. Louis Hawks	20.00	9.00	2.50
☐ 16 Hal Greer Syracuse Nationals	75.00	34.00	9.50
☐ 17 Richie Guerin New York Knicks	40.00	18.00	5.00
☐ 18 Cliff Hagan St. Louis Hawks	35.00	16.00	4.40
☐ 19 Tom Heinsohn Boston Celtics	75.00	34.00	9.50
☐ 20 Bailey Howell Detroit Pistons	40.00	18.00	5.00
☐ 21 Rod Hundley Los Angeles Lakers	40.00	18.00	5.00
☐ 22 K.C. Jones Boston Celtics	85.00	38.00	10.50
☐ 23 Sam Jones Boston Celtics	85.00	38.00	10.50
☐ 24 Phil Jordan New York Knicks	15.00	6.75	1.90
☐ 25 John Kerr Syracuse Nationals	30.00	13.50	3.80
☐ 26 Rudy LaRusso Los Angeles Lakers	30.00	13.50	3.80
☐ 27 George Lee Detroit Pistons	15.00	6.75	1.90
☐ 28 Bob Leonard Chicago Packers	18.00	8.00	2.30
☐ 29 Clyde Lovellette St. Louis Hawks	30.00	13.50	3.80
☐ 30 John McCarthy St. Louis Hawks	15.00	6.75	1.90
☐ 31 Tom Meschery Philadelphia Warriors	22.00	10.00	2.80
☐ 32 Willie Naulls New York Knicks	20.00	9.00	2.50
☐ 33 Don Ohl Detroit Pistons	22.00	10.00	2.80
☐ 34 Bob Pettit St. Louis Hawks	75.00	34.00	9.50

☐ 35	Frank Ramsey	30.00	13.50	3.80
	Boston Celtics			
☐ 36	Oscar Robertson	500.00	230.00	65.00
	Cincinnati Royals			
☐ 37	Guy Rodgers	25.00	11.50	3.10
	Philadelphia Warriors			
☐ 38	Bill Russell	500.00	230.00	65.00
	Boston Celtics			
☐ 39	Dolph Schayes	40.00	18.00	5.00
	Syracuse Nationals			
☐ 40	Frank Selvy	20.00	9.00	2.50
	Los Angeles Lakers			
☐ 41	Gene Shue	25.00	11.50	3.10
	Detroit Pistons			
☐ 42	Jack Twyman	35.00	16.00	4.40
	Cincinnati Royals			
☐ 43	Jerry West	700.00	325.00	90.00
	Los Angeles Lakers			
☐ 44	Len Wilkens UER	120.00	55.00	15.00
	St. Louis Hawks			
	(Misspelled Wilkins			
	on card front)			
☐ 45	Paul Arizin IA	20.00	9.00	2.50
	Philadelphia Warriors			
☐ 46	Elgin Baylor IA	100.00	45.00	12.50
	Los Angeles Lakers			
☐ 47	Wilt Chamberlain IA	375.00	170.00	47.50
	Philadelphia Warriors			
☐ 48	Larry Costello IA	12.50	5.75	1.55
	Syracuse Nationals			
☐ 49	Bob Cousy IA	75.00	34.00	9.50
	Boston Celtics			
☐ 50	Walter Dukes IA	12.50	5.75	1.55
	Detroit Pistons			
☐ 51	Tom Gola IA	20.00	9.00	2.50
	Philadelphia Warriors			
☐ 52	Richie Guerin IA	20.00	9.00	2.50
	New York Knicks			
☐ 53	Cliff Hagan IA	25.00	11.50	3.10
	St. Louis Hawks			
☐ 54	Tom Heinsohn IA	35.00	16.00	4.40
	Boston Celtics			
☐ 55	Bailey Howell IA	20.00	9.00	2.50
	Detroit Pistons			
☐ 56	John Kerr IA	25.00	11.50	3.10
	Syracuse Nationals			
☐ 57	Rudy LaRusso IA	20.00	9.00	2.50
	Los Angeles Lakers			
☐ 58	Clyde Lovellette IA	25.00	11.50	3.10
	St. Louis Hawks			
☐ 59	Bob Pettit IA	45.00	20.00	5.75
	St. Louis Hawks			
☐ 60	Frank Ramsey IA	20.00	9.00	2.50
	Boston Celtics			
☐ 61	Oscar Robertson IA	150.00	70.00	19.00
	Cincinnati Royals			
☐ 62	Bill Russell IA	225.00	100.00	28.00
	Boston Celtics			
☐ 63	Dolph Schayes IA	25.00	11.50	3.10
	Syracuse Nationals			
☐ 64	Gene Shue IA	15.00	6.75	1.90
	Detroit Pistons			
☐ 65	Jack Twyman IA	20.00	9.00	2.50
	Cincinnati Royals			
☐ 66	Jerry West IA	275.00	95.00	22.00
	Los Angeles Lakers			

1986-87 Fleer

This 132-card set features 131 prominent NBA players plus a checklist card. Cards measure the standard 2 1/2" by 3 1/2". The photo on the front is inside a red, white, and blue frame. A

Fleer "Premier" logo appears in the upper corner of the card front. The card backs are print-ed in red and blue on white card stock. The card numbers correspond to the alphabetical order of the player's names. Wax boxes contained 36 wax packs each containing 12 player cards, a piece of gum, and an insert sticker card. Several cards have special "Traded" nota-tions on them if the player was traded after his picture was selected. Since only the Star Company had been issuing basketball cards nationally since 1983, most of the players in this Fleer set already had cards which are considered XRC's, Extended Rookie Cards. However, since this Fleer set was the first nationally available set in packs since the 1981-82 Topps issue, most of the players in the set are considered Rookie Cards. Therefore, the key Rookie Cards in this set, who had cards in previous Star sets are Charles Barkley, Clyde Drexler, Patrick Ewing, Michael Jordan, Hakeem Olajuwon, Isiah Thomas, and Dominique Wilkins. The key Rookie Cards in this set, who had not previously appeared on cards, are Joe Dumars, Karl Malone, and Chris Mullin. It's important to note that some of the more expensive cards in this set (especially Michael Jordan) have been counterfeited in the past few years. Checking key detailed printing areas such as the "Fleer Premier" logo on the front and the players' association logo on the back under eight or ten power magnifica-tion usually detects the legitimate from the counterfeits. The cards are condition sensitive due to dark borders and centering problems.

	MINT	EXC	G-VG
COMPLETE w/Stickers(143)	1600.00	700.00	200.00
COMPLETE SET (132)	1500.00	700.00	190.00
COMMON PLAYER (1-132)	2.00	.90	.25
☐ 1 Kareem Abdul-Jabbar	12.00	5.50	1.50
Los Angeles Lakers			
☐ 2 Alvan Adams	2.25	1.00	.30
Phoenix Suns			
☐ 3 Mark Aguirre	5.00	2.30	.60
Dallas Mavericks			
☐ 4 Danny Ainge	18.00	8.00	2.30
Boston Celtics			
☐ 5 John Bagley	2.50	1.15	.30
Cleveland Cavaliers			
☐ 6 Thurl Bailey	3.00	1.35	.40
Utah Jazz			
☐ 7 Charles Barkley	150.00	70.00	19.00
Philadelphia 76ers			
☐ 8 Benoit Benjamin	2.50	1.15	.30
Los Angeles Clippers			
☐ 9 Larry Bird	50.00	23.00	6.25
Boston Celtics			
☐ 10 Otis Birdsong	2.25	1.00	.30
New Jersey Nets			
☐ 11 Rolando Blackman	5.00	2.30	.60
Dallas Mavericks			
☐ 12 Manute Bol	2.50	1.15	.30
Washington Bullets			
☐ 13 Sam Bowie	3.00	1.35	.40
Portland Trail Blazers			
☐ 14 Joe Barry Carroll	2.25	1.00	.30
Golden State Warriors			
☐ 15 Tom Chambers	8.00	3.60	1.00

	Seattle Supersonics			
☐ 16	Maurice Cheeks	3.50	1.55	.45
	Philadelphia 76ers			
☐ 17	Michael Cooper	3.50	1.55	.45
	Los Angeles Lakers			
☐ 18	Wayne Cooper	2.00	.90	.25
	Denver Nuggets			
☐ 19	Pat Cummings	2.00	.90	.25
	New York Knicks			
☐ 20	Terry Cummings	5.00	2.30	.60
	Milwaukee Bucks			
☐ 21	Adrian Dantley	3.50	1.55	.45
	Utah Jazz			
☐ 22	Brad Davis	2.50	1.15	.30
	Dallas Mavericks			
☐ 23	Walter Davis	3.50	1.55	.45
	Phoenix Suns			
☐ 24	Darryl Dawkins	3.00	1.35	.40
	New Jersey Nets			
☐ 25	Larry Drew	2.00	.90	.25
	Sacramento Kings			
☐ 26	Clyde Drexler	35.00	16.00	4.40
	Portland Trail Blazers			
☐ 27	Joe Dumars	30.00	13.50	3.80
	Detroit Pistons			
☐ 28	Mark Eaton	3.00	1.35	.40
	Utah Jazz			
☐ 29	James Edwards	2.25	1.00	.30
	Phoenix Suns			
☐ 30	Alex English	3.50	1.55	.45
	Denver Nuggets			
☐ 31	Julius Erving	18.00	8.00	2.30
	Philadelphia 76ers			
☐ 32	Patrick Ewing	90.00	40.00	11.50
	New York Knicks			
☐ 33	Vern Fleming	4.00	1.80	.50
	Indiana Pacers			
☐ 34	Sleepy Floyd	3.00	1.35	.40
	Golden State Warriors			
☐ 35	World B. Free	2.50	1.15	.30
	Cleveland Cavaliers			
☐ 36	George Gervin	5.00	2.30	.60
	Chicago Bulls			
☐ 37	Artis Gilmore	3.50	1.55	.45
	San Antonio Spurs			
☐ 38	Mike Gminski	2.25	1.00	.30
	New Jersey Nets			
☐ 39	Rickey Green	2.25	1.00	.30
	Utah Jazz			
☐ 40	Sidney Green	2.00	.90	.25
	Chicago Bulls			
☐ 41	David Greenwood	2.00	.90	.25
	San Antonio Spurs			
☐ 42	Darrell Griffith	2.25	1.00	.30
	Utah Jazz			
☐ 43	Bill Hanzlik	2.00	.90	.25
	Denver Nuggets			
☐ 44	Derek Harper	8.00	3.60	1.00
	Dallas Mavericks			
☐ 45	Gerald Henderson	2.00	.90	.25
	Seattle Supersonics			
☐ 46	Roy Hinson	2.00	.90	.25
	Philadelphia 76ers			
☐ 47	Craig Hodges	3.00	1.35	.40
	Milwaukee Bucks			
☐ 48	Phil Hubbard	2.00	.90	.25
	Cleveland Cavaliers			
☐ 49	Jay Humphries	3.00	1.35	.40
	Phoenix Suns			
☐ 50	Dennis Johnson	3.50	1.55	.45
	Boston Celtics			
☐ 51	Eddie Johnson	5.00	2.30	.60
	Sacramento Kings			

☐ 52	Frank Johnson	2.50	1.15	.30
	Washington Bullets		
☐ 53	Magic Johnson	35.00	16.00	4.40
	Los Angeles Lakers		
☐ 54	Marques Johnson	2.25	1.00	.30
	Los Angeles Clippers		
	(Decimal point missing,		
	rookie year scoring avg.)		
☐ 55	Steve Johnson UER	2.00	.90	.25
	San Antonio Spurs		
	(photo actually		
	David Greenwood)		
☐ 56	Vinnie Johnson	2.25	1.00	.30
	Detroit Pistons		
☐ 57	Michael Jordan	750.00	350.00	95.00
	Chicago Bulls		
☐ 58	Clark Kellogg	2.50	1.15	.30
	Indiana Pacers		
☐ 59	Albert King	2.00	.90	.25
	New Jersey Nets		
☐ 60	Bernard King	3.50	1.55	.45
	New York Knicks		
☐ 61	Bill Laimbeer	3.00	1.35	.40
	Detroit Pistons		
☐ 62	Allen Leavell	2.00	.90	.25
	Houston Rockets		
☐ 63	Lafayette Lever	2.50	1.15	.30
	Denver Nuggets		
☐ 64	Alton Lister	2.25	1.00	.30
	Seattle Supersonics		
☐ 65	Lewis Lloyd	2.00	.90	.25
	Houston Rockets		
☐ 66	Maurice Lucas	2.50	1.15	.30
	Los Angeles Lakers		
☐ 67	Jeff Malone	6.00	2.70	.75
	Washington Bullets		
☐ 68	Karl Malone	60.00	27.00	7.50
	Utah Jazz		
☐ 69	Moses Malone	5.00	2.30	.60
	Washington Bullets		
☐ 70	Cedric Maxwell	2.00	.90	.25
	Los Angeles Clippers		
☐ 71	Rodney McCray	2.50	1.15	.30
	Houston Rockets		
☐ 72	Xavier McDaniel	8.00	3.60	1.00
	Seattle Supersonics		
☐ 73	Kevin McHale	5.00	2.30	.60
	Boston Celtics		
☐ 74	Mike Mitchell	2.00	.90	.25
	San Antonio Spurs		
☐ 75	Sidney Moncrief	3.50	1.55	.45
	Milwaukee Bucks		
☐ 76	Johnny Moore	2.00	.90	.25
	San Antonio Spurs		
☐ 77	Chris Mullin	30.00	13.50	3.80
	Golden State Warriors		
☐ 78	Larry Nance	10.00	4.50	1.25
	Phoenix Suns		
☐ 79	Calvin Natt	2.00	.90	.25
	Denver Nuggets		
☐ 80	Norm Nixon	2.25	1.00	.30
	Los Angeles Clippers		
☐ 81	Charles Oakley	15.00	6.75	1.90
	Chicago Bulls		
☐ 82	Hakeem Olajuwon	165.00	75.00	21.00
	Houston Rockets		
☐ 83	Louis Orr	2.00	.90	.25
	New York Knicks		
☐ 84	Robert Parish UER	5.00	2.30	.60
	Boston Celtics		
	(Misspelled Parrish		
	on both sides)		
☐ 85	Jim Paxson	2.00	.90	.25

	Portland Trail Blazers		
☐ 86	Sam Perkins	8.00	3.60	1.00
	Dallas Mavericks		
☐ 87	Ricky Pierce	8.00	3.60	1.00
	Milwaukee Bucks		
☐ 88	Paul Pressey	2.50	1.15	.30
	Milwaukee Bucks		
☐ 89	Kurt Rambis	3.00	1.35	.40
	Los Angeles Lakers		
☐ 90	Robert Reid	2.00	.90	.25
	Houston Rockets		
☐ 91	Doc Rivers	6.00	2.70	.75
	Atlanta Hawks		
☐ 92	Alvin Robertson	5.00	2.30	.60
	San Antonio Spurs		
☐ 93	Cliff Robinson	2.00	.90	.25
	Philadelphia 76ers		
☐ 94	Tree Rollins	2.25	1.00	.30
	Atlanta Hawks		
☐ 95	Dan Roundfield	2.50	1.15	.30
	Washington Bullets		
☐ 96	Jeff Ruland	2.00	.90	.25
	Philadelphia 76ers		
☐ 97	Ralph Sampson	3.00	1.35	.40
	Houston Rockets		
☐ 98	Danny Schayes	2.50	1.15	.30
	Denver Nuggets		
☐ 99	Byron Scott	6.00	2.70	.75
	Los Angeles Lakers		
☐ 100	Purvis Short	2.00	.90	.25
	Golden State Warriors		
☐ 101	Jerry Sichting	2.00	.90	.25
	Boston Celtics		
☐ 102	Jack Sikma	3.00	1.35	.40
	Milwaukee Bucks		
☐ 103	Derek Smith	2.00	.90	.25
	Los Angeles Clippers		
☐ 104	Larry Smith	2.25	1.00	.30
	Golden State Warriors		
☐ 105	Rory Sparrow	2.00	.90	.25
	New York Knicks		
☐ 106	Steve Stipanovich	2.00	.90	.25
	Indiana Pacers		
☐ 107	Terry Teagle	2.00	.90	.25
	Golden State Warriors		
☐ 108	Reggie Theus	3.00	1.35	.40
	Sacramento Kings		
☐ 109	Isiah Thomas	30.00	13.50	3.80
	Detroit Pistons		
☐ 110	LaSalle Thompson	2.50	1.15	.30
	Sacramento Kings		
☐ 111	Mychal Thompson	2.25	1.00	.30
	Portland Trail Blazers		
☐ 112	Sedale Threatt	5.00	2.30	.60
	Philadelphia 76ers		
☐ 113	Wayman Tisdale	6.00	2.70	.75
	Indiana Pacers		
☐ 114	Andrew Toney	2.00	.90	.25
	Philadelphia 76ers		
☐ 115	Kelly Tripucka	2.25	1.00	.30
	Detroit Pistons		
☐ 116	Mel Turpin	2.25	1.00	.30
	Cleveland Cavaliers		
☐ 117	Kiki Vandeweghe	3.00	1.35	.40
	Portland Trail Blazers		
☐ 118	Jay Vincent	2.00	.90	.25
	Dallas Mavericks		
☐ 119	Bill Walton	8.00	3.60	1.00
	Boston Celtics (Missing decimal points on four lines of FG Percentage)		
☐ 120	Spud Webb	8.00	3.60	1.00
	Atlanta Hawks		

☐ 121	Dominique Wilkins	75.00	34.00	9.50
	Atlanta Hawks			
☐ 122	Gerald Wilkins	6.00	2.70	.75
	New York Knicks			
☐ 123	Buck Williams	8.00	3.60	1.00
	New Jersey Nets			
☐ 124	Gus Williams	2.25	1.00	.30
	Washington Bullets			
☐ 125	Herb Williams	2.50	1.15	.30
	Indiana Pacers			
☐ 126	Kevin Willis	15.00	6.75	1.90
	Atlanta Hawks			
☐ 127	Randy Wittman	2.00	.90	.25
	Atlanta Hawks			
☐ 128	Al Wood	2.00	.90	.25
	Seattle Supersonics			
☐ 129	Mike Woodson	2.00	.90	.25
	Sacramento Kings			
☐ 130	Orlando Woolridge	3.00	1.35	.40
	Chicago Bulls			
☐ 131	James Worthy	18.00	8.00	2.30
	Los Angeles Lakers			
☐ 132	Checklist 1-132	10.00	.90	.25

1986-87 Fleer Stickers

This set of 11 stickers was distributed in the wax packs (one per pack) with the Fleer regular 132-card issue. The stickers are 2 1/2" by 3 1/2". The backs of the sticker cards are printed in blue and red on white card stock. The set numbering of the stickers is alphabetical by player's name. Based on the one-to-twelve proportion of stickers to regular cards in the wax packs, there are theoretically an equal number of sticker sets and regular sets. The cards are frequently found off-centered.

		MINT	EXC	G-VG
	COMPLETE SET (11)	150.00	70.00	19.00
	COMMON STICKER (1-11)	2.00	.90	.25
☐ 1	Kareem Abdul-Jabbar	6.00	2.70	.75
	Los Angeles Lakers			
☐ 2	Larry Bird	18.00	8.00	2.30
	Boston Celtics			
☐ 3	Adrian Dantley	2.00	.90	.25
	Utah Jazz			
☐ 4	Alex English	2.00	.90	.25
	Denver Nuggets			
☐ 5	Julius Erving	7.00	3.10	.85

		MINT	EXC	G-VG
	Philadelphia 76ers			
☐ 6	Patrick Ewing	15.00	6.75	1.90
	New York Knicks			
☐ 7	Magic Johnson	15.00	6.75	1.90
	Los Angeles Lakers			
☐ 8	Michael Jordan	90.00	40.00	11.50
	Chicago Bulls			
☐ 9	Hakeem Olajuwon	30.00	13.50	3.80
	Houston Rockets			
☐ 10	Isiah Thomas	7.00	3.10	.85
	Detroit Pistons			
☐ 11	Dominique Wilkins	12.00	5.50	1.50
	Atlanta Hawks			

1987-88 Fleer

The 1987-88 Fleer basketball set contains 132 standard size (2 1/2" by 3 1/2") cards featuring 131 of the NBA's better-known players, plus a checklist. Wax boxes contained 36 wax packs each containing 12 player cards, a piece of gum, and an insert sticker card. The fronts are white with gray horizontal stripes. The backs are red, white, and blue and show each player's complete NBA statistics. The cards are numbered essentially in alphabetical order. The key "pure" Rookie Cards in this set are Brad Daugherty, A.C. Green, Ron Harper, Chuck Person, Terry Porter, Detlef Schrempf, and Hot Rod Williams. Other key Rookie Cards in this set, who had already had cards in previous Star sets, are Dale Ellis, Jerome Kersey, John Paxson, and Otis Thorpe. The cards are frequently found off-centered.

		MINT	EXC	G-VG
	COMPLETE w/Stickers (143)	350.00	160.00	45.00
	COMPLETE SET (132)	300.00	135.00	38.00
	COMMON PLAYER (1-132)	1.00	.45	.13
☐ 1	Kareem Abdul-Jabbar	8.00	2.00	.50
	Los Angeles Lakers			
☐ 2	Alvan Adams	1.25	.55	.16
	Phoenix Suns			
☐ 3	Mark Aguirre	1.50	.65	.19
	Dallas Mavericks			
☐ 4	Danny Ainge	4.00	1.80	.50
	Boston Celtics			
☐ 5	John Bagley	1.00	.45	.13
	Cleveland Cavaliers			
☐ 6	Thurl Bailey UER	1.25	.55	.16
	Utah Jazz			
	(reverse negative)			
☐ 7	Greg Ballard	1.00	.45	.13
	Golden State Warriors			
☐ 8	Gene Banks	1.00	.45	.13

☐ 9	Charles Barkley Chicago Bulls Philadelphia 76ers	35.00	16.00	4.40
☐ 10	Benoit Benjamin Los Angeles Clippers	1.00	.45	.13
☐ 11	Larry Bird Boston Celtics	30.00	13.50	3.80
☐ 12	Rolando Blackman Dallas Mavericks	1.50	.65	.19
☐ 13	Manute Bol Washington Bullets	1.00	.45	.13
☐ 14	Tony Brown New Jersey Nets	1.00	.45	.13
☐ 15	Michael Cage Los Angeles Clippers	2.00	.90	.25
☐ 16	Joe Barry Carroll Golden State Warriors	1.25	.55	.16
☐ 17	Bill Cartwright New York Knicks	1.50	.65	.19
☐ 18	Terry Catledge Washington Bullets	1.00	.45	.13
☐ 19	Tom Chambers Seattle Supersonics	2.00	.90	.25
☐ 20	Maurice Cheeks Philadelphia 76ers	1.75	.80	.22
☐ 21	Michael Cooper Los Angeles Lakers	1.50	.65	.19
☐ 22	Dave Corzine Chicago Bulls	1.00	.45	.13
☐ 23	Terry Cummings Milwaukee Bucks	1.50	.65	.19
☐ 24	Adrian Dantley Detroit Pistons	1.75	.80	.22
☐ 25	Brad Daugherty Cleveland Cavaliers	10.00	4.50	1.25
☐ 26	Walter Davis Phoenix Suns	1.75	.80	.22
☐ 27	Johnny Dawkins San Antonio Spurs	2.00	.90	.25
☐ 28	James Donaldson Dallas Mavericks	1.00	.45	.13
☐ 29	Larry Drew Los Angeles Clippers	1.00	.45	.13
☐ 30	Clyde Drexler Portland Trail Blazers	9.00	4.00	1.15
☐ 31	Joe Dumars Detroit Pistons	8.00	3.60	1.00
☐ 32	Mark Eaton Utah Jazz	1.25	.55	.16
☐ 33	Dale Ellis Seattle Supersonics	5.00	2.30	.60
☐ 34	Alex English Denver Nuggets	1.75	.80	.22
☐ 35	Julius Erving Philadelphia 76ers	12.00	5.50	1.50
☐ 36	Mike Evans Denver Nuggets	1.00	.45	.13
☐ 37	Patrick Ewing New York Knicks	20.00	9.00	2.50
☐ 38	Vern Fleming Indiana Pacers	1.25	.55	.16
☐ 39	Sleepy Floyd Golden State Warriors	1.25	.55	.16
☐ 40	Artis Gilmore San Antonio Spurs	1.75	.80	.22
☐ 41	Mike Gminski UER New Jersey Nets (reversed negative)	1.25	.55	.16
☐ 42	A.C. Green Los Angeles Lakers	12.00	5.50	1.50
☐ 43	Rickey Green Utah Jazz	1.25	.55	.16
☐ 44	Sidney Green Detroit Pistons	1.00	.45	.13

☐ 45	David Greenwood	1.00	.45	.13
	San Antonio Spurs			
☐ 46	Darrell Griffith	1.25	.55	.16
	Utah Jazz			
☐ 47	Bill Hanzlik	1.00	.45	.13
	Denver Nuggets			
☐ 48	Derek Harper	2.00	.90	.25
	Dallas Mavericks			
☐ 49	Ron Harper	9.00	4.00	1.15
	Cleveland Cavaliers			
☐ 50	Gerald Henderson	1.00	.45	.13
	New York Knicks			
☐ 51	Roy Hinson	1.00	.45	.13
	Philadelphia 76ers			
☐ 52	Craig Hodges	1.25	.55	.16
	Milwaukee Bucks			
☐ 53	Phil Hubbard	1.00	.45	.13
	Cleveland Cavaliers			
☐ 54	Dennis Johnson	1.75	.80	.22
	Boston Celtics			
☐ 55	Eddie Johnson	1.50	.65	.19
	Sacramento Kings			
☐ 56	Magic Johnson	20.00	9.00	2.50
	Los Angeles Lakers			
☐ 57	Steve Johnson	1.00	.45	.13
	Portland Trail Blazers			
☐ 58	Vinnie Johnson	1.25	.55	.16
	Detroit Pistons			
☐ 59	Michael Jordan	175.00	80.00	22.00
	Chicago Bulls			
☐ 60	Jerome Kersey	2.00	.90	.25
	Portland Trail Blazers			
☐ 61	Bill Laimbeer	1.50	.65	.19
	Detroit Pistons			
☐ 62	Lafayette Lever UER	1.25	.55	.16
	Denver Nuggets (Photo actually Otis Smith)			
☐ 63	Cliff Levingston	1.00	.45	.13
	Atlanta Hawks			
☐ 64	Alton Lister	1.00	.45	.13
	Seattle Supersonics			
☐ 65	John Long	1.00	.45	.13
	Indiana Pacers			
☐ 66	John Lucas	1.50	.65	.19
	Milwaukee Bucks			
☐ 67	Jeff Malone	1.50	.65	.19
	Washington Bullets			
☐ 68	Karl Malone	15.00	6.75	1.90
	Utah Jazz			
☐ 69	Moses Malone	3.00	1.35	.40
	Washington Bullets			
☐ 70	Cedric Maxwell	1.00	.45	.13
	Houston Rockets			
☐ 71	Tim McCormick	1.00	.45	.13
	Philadelphia 76ers			
☐ 72	Rodney McCray	1.00	.45	.13
	Houston Rockets			
☐ 73	Xavier McDaniel	2.00	.90	.25
	Seattle Supersonics			
☐ 74	Kevin McHale	3.00	1.35	.40
	Boston Celtics			
☐ 75	Nate McMillan	5.00	2.30	.60
	Seattle Supersonics			
☐ 76	Sidney Moncrief	1.75	.80	.22
	Milwaukee Bucks			
☐ 77	Chris Mullin	8.00	3.60	1.00
	Golden State Warriors			
☐ 78	Larry Nance	2.50	1.15	.30
	Phoenix Suns			
☐ 79	Charles Oakley	3.50	1.55	.45
	Chicago Bulls			
☐ 80	Hakeem Olajuwon	40.00	18.00	5.00

☐ 81	Robert Parish UER	Houston Rockets	3.00	1.35	.40
	Boston Celtics (Misspelled Parrish on both sides)				
☐ 82	Jim Paxson	Portland Trail Blazers	1.00	.45	.13
☐ 83	John Paxson	Chicago Bulls	5.00	2.30	.60
☐ 84	Sam Perkins	Dallas Mavericks	2.00	.90	.25
☐ 85	Chuck Person	Indiana Pacers	4.00	1.80	.50
☐ 86	Jim Peterson	Houston Rockets	1.00	.45	.13
☐ 87	Ricky Pierce	Milwaukee Bucks	1.75	.80	.22
☐ 88	Ed Pinckney	Phoenix Suns	1.50	.65	.19
☐ 89	Terry Porter	Portland Trail Blazers (College Wisconsin, should be Wisconsin - Stevens Point)	8.00	3.60	1.00
☐ 90	Paul Pressey	Milwaukee Bucks	1.00	.45	.13
☐ 91	Robert Reid	Houston Rockets	1.00	.45	.13
☐ 92	Doc Rivers	Atlanta Hawks	1.50	.65	.19
☐ 93	Alvin Robertson	San Antonio Spurs	1.50	.65	.19
☐ 94	Tree Rollins	Atlanta Hawks	1.25	.55	.16
☐ 95	Ralph Sampson	Houston Rockets	1.25	.55	.16
☐ 96	Mike Sanders	Phoenix Suns	1.00	.45	.13
☐ 97	Detlef Schrempf	Dallas Mavericks	15.00	6.75	1.90
☐ 98	Byron Scott	Los Angeles Lakers	1.50	.65	.19
☐ 99	Jerry Sichting	Boston Celtics	1.00	.45	.13
☐ 100	Jack Sikma	Milwaukee Bucks	1.50	.65	.19
☐ 101	Larry Smith	Golden State Warriors	1.25	.55	.16
☐ 102	Rory Sparrow	New York Knicks	1.00	.45	.13
☐ 103	Steve Stipanovich	Indiana Pacers	1.00	.45	.13
☐ 104	Jon Sundvold	San Antonio Spurs	1.00	.45	.13
☐ 105	Reggie Theus	Sacramento Kings	1.50	.65	.19
☐ 106	Isiah Thomas	Detroit Pistons	8.00	3.60	1.00
☐ 107	LaSalle Thompson	Sacramento Kings	1.25	.55	.16
☐ 108	Mychal Thompson	Los Angeles Lakers	1.25	.55	.16
☐ 109	Otis Thorpe	Sacramento Kings	10.00	4.50	1.25
☐ 110	Sedale Threatt	Chicago Bulls	1.50	.65	.19
☐ 111	Waymon Tisdale	Indiana Pacers	1.50	.65	.19
☐ 112	Kelly Tripucka	Utah Jazz	1.25	.55	.16
☐ 113	Trent Tucker	New York Knicks	1.50	.65	.19
☐ 114	Terry Tyler	Sacramento Kings	1.00	.45	.13

		MINT	EXC	G-VG
☐ 115	Darnell Valentine	1.00	.45	.13
	Los Angeles Clippers			
☐ 116	Kiki Vandeweghe	1.25	.55	.16
	Portland Trail Blazers			
☐ 117	Darrell Walker	1.50	.65	.19
	Denver Nuggets			
☐ 118	Dominique Wilkins	18.00	8.00	2.30
	Atlanta Hawks			
☐ 119	Gerald Wilkins	1.50	.65	.19
	New York Knicks			
☐ 120	Buck Williams	2.00	.90	.25
	New Jersey Nets			
☐ 121	Herb Williams	1.00	.45	.13
	Indiana Pacers			
☐ 122	John Williams	1.25	.55	.16
	Washington Bullets			
☐ 123	John Williams	5.00	2.30	.60
	Cleveland Cavaliers			
☐ 124	Kevin Willis	3.00	1.35	.40
	Atlanta Hawks			
☐ 125	David Wingate	1.50	.65	.19
	Philadelphia 76ers			
☐ 126	Randy Wittman	1.00	.45	.13
	Atlanta Hawks			
☐ 127	Leon Wood	1.00	.45	.13
	New Jersey Nets			
☐ 128	Mike Woodson	1.00	.45	.13
	Los Angeles Clippers			
☐ 129	Orlando Woolridge	1.25	.55	.16
	New Jersey Nets			
☐ 130	James Worthy	4.00	1.80	.50
	Los Angeles Lakers			
☐ 131	Danny Young	1.00	.45	.13
	Seattle Supersonics			
☐ 132	Checklist 1-132	3.00	.45	.13

1987-88 Fleer Stickers

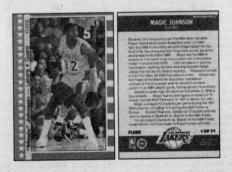

The 1987-88 Fleer Stickers is an 11-card standard size (2 1/2" by 3 1/2") set issued as an insert in wax packs with the regular 132-card set. The fronts are red, white, blue, and yellow. The backs are white and blue, and contain career highlights. One sticker was included in each wax pack. Based on the one-to-twelve proportion of stickers to regular cards in the wax packs, there are theoretically an equal number of sticker sets and regular sets. Virtually all cards from this set have wax-stained backs as a result of the packaging.

	MINT	EXC	G-VG
COMPLETE SET (11)	60.00	27.00	7.50
COMMON STICKER (1-11)	1.25	.55	.16

☐ 1	Magic Johnson	10.00	4.50	1.25
	Los Angeles Lakers			
☐ 2	Michael Jordan	40.00	18.00	5.00
	Chicago Bulls			
	(In text, votes mis-			
	spelled as voites)			
☐ 3	Hakeem Olajuwon UER	15.00	6.75	1.90
	Houston Rockets			
	(Misspelled Olajuwan			
	on card back)			
☐ 4	Larry Bird	15.00	6.75	1.90
	Boston Celtics			
☐ 5	Kevin McHale	1.50	.65	.19
	Boston Celtics			
☐ 6	Charles Barkley	12.00	5.50	1.50
	Philadelphia 76ers			
☐ 7	Dominique Wilkins	7.00	3.10	.85
	Atlanta Hawks			
☐ 8	Kareem Abdul-Jabbar	4.00	1.80	.50
	Los Angeles Lakers			
☐ 9	Mark Aguirre	1.25	.55	.16
	Dallas Mavericks			
☐ 10	Chuck Person	1.50	.65	.19
	Indiana Pacers			
☐ 11	Alex English	1.25	.55	.16
	Denver Nuggets			

1988-89 Fleer

The 1988-89 Fleer basketball set contains 132 standard size (2 1/2" by 3 1/2") cards. There are 119 regular cards, plus 12 All-Star cards and a checklist. This set was issued in wax packs of 12 cards, gum, and a sticker. Wax boxes contained 36 wax packs. The outer borders are white and gray, while the inner borders correspond to the team colors. The backs are greenish, and show full NBA statistics with limited biographical information. The set is ordered alphabetically in team subsets (with a few exceptions due to late trades). The teams themselves are also presented in alphabetical order, Atlanta Hawks (1-6, 98, and 118), Boston Celtics (8-12), Charlotte Hornets (13-14), Chicago Bulls (15-17 and 19-21), Cleveland Cavaliers (22-26), Dallas Mavericks (27-32), Denver Nuggets (33-38), Detroit Pistons (39-45), Golden State Warriors (46-49), Houston Rockets (50-54 and 63), Indiana Pacers (55-60), Los Angeles Clippers (61), Los Angeles Lakers (64-70), Miami Heat (71-72), Milwaukee Bucks (73-76), New Jersey Nets (77-79 and 102), New York Knicks (18 and 80-84), Philadelphia 76ers (85-88), Phoenix Suns (89-91 and 106), Portland Trail Blazers (92-96), Sacramento Kings (7, 97, and 99-100), San Antonio Spurs (101 and 103-105), Seattle Supersonics (62 and 107-110), Utah Jazz (111-115), Washington Bullets (116-117 and 119), and All-Stars (120-131). The key Rookie Cards in this set are Michael Adams, Muggsy Bogues, Dell Curry, Kevin Duckworth, Horace Grant, Mark Jackson, Reggie Miller, Derrick McKey, Scottie Pippen, Dennis Rodman, Mark Price, and Kenny Smith. There is also a Rookie Card of John Stockton who had previously only appeared in Star Company sets.

	MINT	EXC	G-VG
COMPLETE w/Stickers (143)	150.00	70.00	19.00
COMPLETE SET (132)	130.00	57.50	16.50
COMMON PLAYER (1-132)	.25	.11	.03
☐ 1 Antoine Carr	1.00	.45	.13
☐ 2 Cliff Levingston	.25	.11	.03
☐ 3 Doc Rivers	.60	.25	.08
☐ 4 Spud Webb	.60	.25	.08
☐ 5 Dominique Wilkins	5.00	2.30	.60
☐ 6 Kevin Willis	1.00	.45	.13
☐ 7 Randy Wittman	.25	.11	.03
☐ 8 Danny Ainge	1.00	.45	.13
☐ 9 Larry Bird	10.00	4.50	1.25
☐ 10 Dennis Johnson	.60	.25	.08
☐ 11 Kevin McHale	1.25	.55	.16
☐ 12 Robert Parish	1.25	.55	.16
☐ 13 Tyrone Bogues	4.00	1.80	.50
☐ 14 Dell Curry	3.00	1.35	.40
☐ 15 Dave Corzine	.25	.11	.03
☐ 16 Horace Grant	10.00	4.50	1.25
☐ 17 Michael Jordan	50.00	23.00	6.25
☐ 18 Charles Oakley	.35	.16	.04
☐ 19 John Paxson	.75	.35	.09
☐ 20 Scottie Pippen UER	50.00	23.00	6.25
(Misspelled Pippin			
on card back)			
☐ 21 Brad Sellers	.25	.11	.03
☐ 22 Brad Daugherty	2.00	.90	.25
☐ 23 Ron Harper	1.50	.65	.19
☐ 24 Larry Nance	.75	.35	.09
☐ 25 Mark Price	12.00	5.50	1.50
☐ 26 Hot Rod Williams	1.00	.45	.13
☐ 27 Mark Aguirre	.35	.16	.04
☐ 28 Rolando Blackman	.50	.23	.06
☐ 29 James Donaldson	.25	.11	.03
☐ 30 Derek Harper	.60	.25	.08
☐ 31 Sam Perkins	.60	.25	.08
☐ 32 Roy Tarpley	.75	.35	.09
☐ 33 Michael Adams	3.00	1.35	.40
☐ 34 Alex English	.60	.25	.08
☐ 35 Lafayette Lever	.25	.11	.03
☐ 36 Blair Rasmussen	.25	.11	.03
☐ 37 Danny Schayes	.25	.11	.03
☐ 38 Jay Vincent	.25	.11	.03
☐ 39 Adrian Dantley	.50	.23	.06
☐ 40 Joe Dumars	2.00	.90	.25
☐ 41 Vinnie Johnson	.30	.14	.04
☐ 42 Bill Laimbeer	.35	.16	.04
☐ 43 Dennis Rodman	12.00	5.50	1.50
☐ 44 John Salley	1.00	.45	.13
☐ 45 Isiah Thomas	2.00	.90	.25
☐ 46 Winston Garland	.50	.23	.06
☐ 47 Rod Higgins	.25	.11	.03
☐ 48 Chris Mullin	2.00	.90	.25
☐ 49 Ralph Sampson	.30	.14	.04
☐ 50 Joe Barry Carroll	.30	.14	.04
☐ 51 Sleepy Floyd	.30	.14	.04
☐ 52 Rodney McCray	.25	.11	.03
☐ 53 Hakeem Olajuwon	10.00	4.50	1.25
☐ 54 Purvis Short	.25	.11	.03
☐ 55 Vern Fleming	.30	.14	.04
☐ 56 John Long	.25	.11	.03
☐ 57 Reggie Miller	18.00	8.00	2.30
☐ 58 Chuck Person	.60	.25	.08
☐ 59 Steve Stipanovich	.25	.11	.03
☐ 60 Waymon Tisdale	.60	.25	.08
☐ 61 Benoit Benjamin	.25	.11	.03
☐ 62 Michael Cage	.25	.11	.03
☐ 63 Mike Woodson	.25	.11	.03
☐ 64 Kareem Abdul-Jabbar	4.00	1.80	.50
☐ 65 Michael Cooper	.50	.23	.06
☐ 66 A.C. Green	2.50	1.15	.30

☐ 67	Magic Johnson	8.00	3.60	1.00
☐ 68	Byron Scott	.60	.25	.08
☐ 69	Mychal Thompson	.30	.14	.04
☐ 70	James Worthy	1.00	.45	.13
☐ 71	Duane Washington	.25	.11	.03
☐ 72	Kevin Williams	.25	.11	.03
☐ 73	Randy Breuer	.25	.11	.03
☐ 74	Terry Cummings	.50	.23	.06
☐ 75	Paul Pressey	.25	.11	.03
☐ 76	Jack Sikma	.50	.23	.06
☐ 77	John Bagley	.25	.11	.03
☐ 78	Roy Hinson	.25	.11	.03
☐ 79	Buck Williams	.60	.25	.08
☐ 80	Patrick Ewing	6.00	2.70	.75
☐ 81	Sidney Green	.25	.11	.03
☐ 82	Mark Jackson	3.00	1.35	.40
☐ 83	Kenny Walker	.25	.11	.03
☐ 84	Gerald Wilkins	.50	.23	.06
☐ 85	Charles Barkley	8.00	3.60	1.00
☐ 86	Maurice Cheeks	.60	.25	.08
☐ 87	Mike Gminski	.30	.14	.04
☐ 88	Cliff Robinson	.25	.11	.03
☐ 89	Armon Gilliam	1.00	.45	.13
☐ 90	Eddie Johnson	.50	.23	.06
☐ 91	Mark West	.50	.23	.06
☐ 92	Clyde Drexler	2.50	1.15	.30
☐ 93	Kevin Duckworth	.75	.35	.09
☐ 94	Steve Johnson	.25	.11	.03
☐ 95	Jerome Kersey	.30	.14	.04
☐ 96	Terry Porter (College Wisconsin, should be Wisconsin Stevens Point)	1.50	.65	.19
☐ 97	Joe Kleine	.50	.23	.06
☐ 98	Reggie Theus	.35	.16	.04
☐ 99	Otis Thorpe	2.00	.90	.25
☐ 100	Kenny Smith (College NC State, should be North Carolina)	3.00	1.35	.40
☐ 101	Greg Anderson	.50	.23	.06
☐ 102	Walter Berry	.25	.11	.03
☐ 103	Frank Brickowski	1.25	.55	.16
☐ 104	Johnny Dawkins	.30	.14	.04
☐ 105	Alvin Robertson	.50	.23	.06
☐ 106	Tom Chambers (Born 6/2/59, should be 6/21/59)	.60	.25	.08
☐ 107	Dale Ellis	.75	.35	.09
☐ 108	Xavier McDaniel	.60	.25	.08
☐ 109	Derrick McKey	3.00	1.35	.40
☐ 110	Nate McMillan UER (Photo actually Kevin Williams)	.30	.14	.04
☐ 111	Thurl Bailey	.30	.14	.04
☐ 112	Mark Eaton	.30	.14	.04
☐ 113	Bobby Hansen	.25	.11	.03
☐ 114	Karl Malone	4.00	1.80	.50
☐ 115	John Stockton	20.00	9.00	2.50
☐ 116	Bernard King	.60	.25	.08
☐ 117	Jeff Malone	.50	.23	.06
☐ 118	Moses Malone	1.00	.45	.13
☐ 119	John Williams	.25	.11	.03
☐ 120	Michael Jordan AS Chicago Bulls	15.00	6.75	1.90
☐ 121	Mark Jackson AS New York Knicks	.75	.35	.09
☐ 122	Byron Scott AS Los Angeles Lakers	.25	.11	.03
☐ 123	Magic Johnson AS Los Angeles Lakers	4.00	1.80	.50
☐ 124	Larry Bird AS Boston Celtics	5.00	2.30	.60

☐ 125 Dominique Wilkins AS	2.50	1.15	.30
Atlanta Hawks			
☐ 126 Hakeem Olajuwon AS	5.00	2.30	.60
Houston Rockets			
☐ 127 John Stockton AS	3.00	1.35	.40
Utah Jazz			
☐ 128 Alvin Robertson AS	.25	.11	.03
San Antonio Spurs			
☐ 129 Charles Barkley AS	4.00	1.80	.50
Philadelphia 76ers			
(Back says Buck Williams			
is member of Jets,			
should be Nets)			
☐ 130 Patrick Ewing AS	3.00	1.35	.40
New York Knicks			
☐ 131 Mark Eaton AS	.25	.11	.03
Utah Jazz			
☐ 132 Checklist 1-132	.40	.11	.03

1988-89 Fleer Stickers

The 1988-89 Fleer Basketball Super Star Stickers is an 11-card standard size (2 1/2" by 3 1/2") set issued as a one per pack insert along with 12 cards from the the regular 132-card set. The fronts are baby blue, red, and white. The backs are blue and pink and contain career highlights. The set is ordered alphabetically. Based on the one-to-twelve proportion of stickers to regular cards in the wax packs, there are theoretically an equal number of sticker sets and regular sets. Virtually all cards from this set have wax-stained backs as a result of the packaging.

	MINT	EXC	G-VG
COMPLETE SET (11)	25.00	11.50	3.10
COMMON STICKER (1-11)	.40	.18	.05
☐ 1 Mark Aguirre	.40	.18	.05
Dallas Mavericks			
☐ 2 Larry Bird	5.00	2.30	.60
Boston Celtics			
☐ 3 Clyde Drexler	1.25	.55	.16
Portland Trail Blazers			
☐ 4 Alex English	.40	.18	.05
Denver Nuggets			
☐ 5 Patrick Ewing	3.00	1.35	.40
New York Knicks			
☐ 6 Magic Johnson	4.00	1.80	.50
Los Angeles Lakers			
☐ 7 Michael Jordan	15.00	6.75	1.90
Chicago Bulls			
☐ 8 Karl Malone	2.00	.90	.25
Utah Jazz			
☐ 9 Kevin McHale	.75	.35	.09
Boston Celtics			

☐ 10	Isiah Thomas	1.00	.45	.13
	Detroit Pistons			
☐ 11	Dominique Wilkins	2.50	1.15	.30
	Atlanta Hawks			

1989-90 Fleer

The 1989-90 Fleer basketball set consists of 168 cards measuring the standard size (2 1/2"
by 3 1/2"). The cards were distributed in 12-card wax packs and in 36-card rack packs. The
fronts feature color action player photos, with various color borders between white inner and
outer borders. The player's name and position appear in the upper left corner, with the team
logo superimposed over the upper right corner of the picture. The horizontally oriented
backs have black lettering on red, pink, and white background and present career statistics,
biographical information, and a performance index. The set is ordered alphabetically in team
subsets (with a few exceptions due to late trades). The teams themselves are also presented in alphabetical order, Atlanta Hawks (1-7), Boston Celtics (8-14), Charlotte Hornets (15-
18), Chicago Bulls (19-23), Cleveland Cavaliers (25-31), Dallas Mavericks (32-37), Denver
Nuggets (38-43), Detroit Pistons (44-51), Golden State Warriors (52-57), Houston Rockets
(58-63), Indiana Pacers (64-68), Los Angeles Clippers (69-74), Los Angeles Lakers (75-80),
Miami Heat (81-84), Milwaukee Bucks (85-91), Minnesota Timberwolves (92-94), New
Jersey Nets (95-99), New York Knicks (100-111), Orlando Magic (108-111), Philadelphia
76ers (112-118), Phoenix Suns (119-125), Portland Trail Blazers (126-132), Sacramento
Kings (133-139), San Antonio Spurs (140-144), Seattle Supersonics (24 and 145-150), Utah
Jazz (151-156), Washington Bullets (157-162), and All-Star Game Combos (163-167).
Rookie Cards included in this set are Willie Anderson, Rex Chapman, Hersey Hawkins, Jeff
Hornacek, Kevin Johnson, Reggie Lewis, Grant Long, Dan Majerle, Danny Manning, Vernon
Maxwell, Chris Morris, Johnny Newman, Ken Norman, Mitch Richmond, Rony Seikaly, Brian
Shaw, Scott Skiles, Charles Smith, Rik Smits, Rod Strickland, and Reggie Williams.

	MINT	EXC	G-VG
COMPLETE w/Stickers (179)	40.00	18.00	5.00
COMPLETE SET (168)	35.00	16.00	4.40
COMMON PLAYER (1-162)	.15	.07	.02
☐ 1 John Battle	.40	.18	.05
☐ 2 Jon Koncak	.40	.18	.05
☐ 3 Cliff Levingston	.15	.07	.02
☐ 4 Moses Malone	.40	.18	.05
☐ 5 Glenn Rivers	.20	.09	.03
☐ 6 Spud Webb UER	.25	.11	.03
(Points per 48 minutes			
incorrect at 2.6)			
☐ 7 Dominique Wilkins	1.75	.80	.22
☐ 8 Larry Bird	4.00	1.80	.50
☐ 9 Dennis Johnson	.25	.11	.03
☐ 10 Reggie Lewis	4.00	1.80	.50
☐ 11 Kevin McHale	.40	.18	.05
☐ 12 Robert Parish	.40	.18	.05
☐ 13 Ed Pinckney	.15	.07	.02

☐ 14 Brian Shaw	1.00	.45	.13
☐ 15 Rex Chapman	1.00	.45	.13
☐ 16 Kurt Rambis	.20	.09	.03
☐ 17 Robert Reid	.15	.07	.02
☐ 18 Kelly Tripucka	.20	.09	.03
☐ 19 Bill Cartwright UER	.20	.09	.03
(First season 1978-80, should be 1979-80)			
☐ 20 Horace Grant	1.00	.45	.13
☐ 21 Michael Jordan	15.00	6.75	1.90
☐ 22 John Paxson	.20	.09	.03
☐ 23 Scottie Pippen	5.00	2.30	.60
☐ 24 Brad Sellers	.15	.07	.02
☐ 25 Brad Daugherty	.50	.23	.06
☐ 26 Craig Ehlo	1.00	.45	.13
☐ 27 Ron Harper	.40	.18	.05
☐ 28 Larry Nance	.25	.11	.03
☐ 29 Mark Price	1.00	.45	.13
☐ 30 Mike Sanders	.15	.07	.02
☐ 31A John Williams ERR	.75	.35	.09
Washington Bullets			
☐ 31B John Williams COR	.20	.09	.03
Cleveland Cavaliers			
☐ 32 Rolando Blackman UER	.20	.09	.03
(Career blocks and points listed as 1961 and 2127, should be 196 and 12,127)			
☐ 33 Adrian Dantley	.25	.11	.03
☐ 34 James Donaldson	.15	.07	.02
☐ 35 Derek Harper	.20	.09	.03
☐ 36 Sam Perkins	.25	.11	.03
☐ 37 Herb Williams	.15	.07	.02
☐ 38 Michael Adams	.20	.09	.03
☐ 39 Walter Davis	.25	.11	.03
☐ 40 Alex English	.25	.11	.03
☐ 41 Lafayette Lever	.15	.07	.02
☐ 42 Blair Rasmussen	.15	.07	.02
☐ 43 Dan Schayes	.15	.07	.02
☐ 44 Mark Aguirre	.25	.11	.03
☐ 45 Joe Dumars	.75	.35	.09
☐ 46 James Edwards	.20	.09	.03
☐ 47 Vinnie Johnson	.20	.09	.03
☐ 48 Bill Laimbeer	.25	.11	.03
☐ 49 Dennis Rodman	1.00	.45	.13
☐ 50 Isiah Thomas	.75	.35	.09
☐ 51 John Salley	.20	.09	.03
☐ 52 Manute Bol	.15	.07	.02
☐ 53 Winston Garland	.15	.07	.02
☐ 54 Rod Higgins	.15	.07	.02
☐ 55 Chris Mullin	.75	.35	.09
☐ 56 Mitch Richmond	5.00	2.30	.60
☐ 57 Terry Teagle	.15	.07	.02
☐ 58 Derrick Chievous UER	.15	.07	.02
(Stats correctly say 81 games in '88-89, text says 82)			
☐ 59 Sleepy Floyd	.20	.09	.03
☐ 60 Tim McCormick	.15	.07	.02
☐ 61 Hakeem Olajuwon	4.00	1.80	.50
☐ 62 Otis Thorpe	.60	.25	.08
☐ 63 Mike Woodson	.15	.07	.02
☐ 64 Vern Fleming	.20	.09	.03
☐ 65 Reggie Miller	1.75	.80	.22
☐ 66 Chuck Person	.20	.09	.03
☐ 67 Detlef Schrempf	1.50	.65	.19
☐ 68 Rik Smits	2.00	.90	.25
☐ 69 Benoit Benjamin	.15	.07	.02
☐ 70 Gary Grant	.50	.23	.06
☐ 71 Danny Manning	6.00	2.70	.75
☐ 72 Ken Norman	1.00	.45	.13
☐ 73 Charles Smith	1.00	.45	.13
☐ 74 Reggie Williams	1.00	.45	.13
☐ 75 Michael Cooper	.25	.11	.03

☐	76	A.C. Green	.75	.35	.09
☐	77	Magic Johnson	3.00	1.35	.40
☐	78	Byron Scott	.20	.09	.03
☐	79	Mychal Thompson	.20	.09	.03
☐	80	James Worthy	.40	.18	.05
☐	81	Kevin Edwards	1.00	.45	.13
☐	82	Grant Long	1.00	.45	.13
☐	83	Rony Seikaly	2.50	1.15	.30
☐	84	Rory Sparrow	.15	.07	.02
☐	85	Greg Anderson UER	.15	.07	.02
		(Stats show 1988-89 as 19888-89)			
☐	86	Jay Humphries	.15	.07	.02
☐	87	Larry Krystkowiak	.40	.18	.05
☐	88	Ricky Pierce	.25	.11	.03
☐	89	Paul Pressey	.15	.07	.02
☐	90	Alvin Robertson	.20	.09	.03
☐	91	Jack Sikma	.25	.11	.03
☐	92	Steve Johnson	.15	.07	.02
☐	93	Rick Mahorn	.20	.09	.03
☐	94	David Rivers	.20	.09	.03
☐	95	Joe Barry Carroll	.15	.07	.02
☐	96	Lester Conner UER	.15	.07	.02
		(Garden State in stats, should be Golden State)			
☐	97	Roy Hinson	.15	.07	.02
☐	98	Mike McGee	.15	.07	.02
☐	99	Chris Morris	1.00	.45	.13
☐	100	Patrick Ewing	2.00	.90	.25
☐	101	Mark Jackson	.15	.07	.02
☐	102	Johnny Newman	1.00	.45	.13
☐	103	Charles Oakley	.25	.11	.03
☐	104	Rod Strickland	2.50	1.15	.30
☐	105	Trent Tucker	.20	.09	.03
☐	106	Kiki Vandeweghe	.20	.09	.03
☐	107A	Gerald Wilkins	.20	.09	.03
		(U. of Tennessee)			
☐	107B	Gerald Wilkins	.20	.09	.03
		(U. of Tenn.)			
☐	108	Terry Catledge	.15	.07	.02
☐	109	Dave Corzine	.15	.07	.02
☐	110	Scott Skiles	1.00	.45	.13
☐	111	Reggie Theus	.25	.11	.03
☐	112	Ron Anderson	.15	.07	.02
☐	113	Charles Barkley	3.00	1.35	.40
☐	114	Scott Brooks	.50	.23	.06
☐	115	Maurice Cheeks	.25	.11	.03
☐	116	Mike Gminski	.15	.07	.02
☐	117	Hersey Hawkins UER	2.00	.90	.25
		(Born 9/29/65, should be 9/9/65)			
☐	118	Christian Welp	.15	.07	.02
☐	119	Tom Chambers	.25	.11	.03
☐	120	Armon Gilliam	.20	.09	.03
☐	121	Jeff Hornacek	2.00	.90	.25
☐	122	Eddie Johnson	.20	.09	.03
☐	123	Kevin Johnson	6.00	2.70	.75
☐	124	Dan Majerle	5.00	2.30	.60
☐	125	Mark West	.15	.07	.02
☐	126	Richard Anderson	.15	.07	.02
☐	127	Mark Bryant	.15	.07	.02
☐	128	Clyde Drexler	1.00	.45	.13
☐	129	Kevin Duckworth	.20	.09	.03
☐	130	Jerome Kersey	.20	.09	.03
☐	131	Terry Porter	.25	.11	.03
☐	132	Buck Williams	.25	.11	.03
☐	133	Danny Ainge	.40	.18	.05
☐	134	Ricky Berry	.15	.07	.02
☐	135	Rodney McCray	.15	.07	.02
☐	136	Jim Petersen	.15	.07	.02
☐	137	Harold Pressley	.15	.07	.02
☐	138	Kenny Smith	.20	.09	.03
☐	139	Wayman Tisdale	.20	.09	.03

☐ 140	Willie Anderson	1.00	.45	.13
☐ 141	Frank Brickowski	.20	.09	.03
☐ 142	Terry Cummings	.20	.09	.03
☐ 143	Johnny Dawkins	.20	.09	.03
☐ 144	Vern Maxwell	2.50	1.15	.30
☐ 145	Michael Cage	.15	.07	.02
☐ 146	Dale Ellis	.20	.09	.03
☐ 147	Alton Lister	.15	.07	.02
☐ 148	Xavier McDaniel UER	.25	.11	.03
	(All-Rookie team in 1985, not 1988)			
☐ 149	Derrick McKey	.20	.09	.03
☐ 150	Nate McMillan	.20	.09	.03
☐ 151	Thurl Bailey	.15	.07	.02
☐ 152	Mark Eaton	.20	.09	.03
☐ 153	Darrell Griffith	.15	.07	.02
☐ 154	Eric Leckner	.15	.07	.19
☐ 155	Karl Malone	1.50	.65	.19
☐ 156	John Stockton	2.00	.90	.25
☐ 157	Mark Alarie	.15	.07	.02
☐ 158	Ledell Eackles	.15	.07	.02
☐ 159	Bernard King	.25	.11	.03
☐ 160	Jeff Malone	.15	.07	.02
☐ 161	Darrell Walker	.15	.07	.02
☐ 162A	John Williams ERR	.75	.35	.09
	Cleveland Cavaliers			
☐ 162B	John Williams COR	.20	.09	.03
	Washington Bullets			
☐ 163	All Star Game	.50	.23	.06
	Karl Malone			
	John Stockton			
☐ 164	All Star Game	1.00	.45	.13
	Hakeem Olajuwon			
	Clyde Drexler			
☐ 165	All Star Game	.50	.23	.06
	Dominique Wilkins			
	Moses Malone			
☐ 166	All Star Game UER	.30	.14	.04
	Brad Daugherty			
	Mark Price			
	(Bio says Nance had 204 blocks, should be 206)			
☐ 167	All Star Game	.50	.23	.06
	Patrick Ewing			
	Mark Jackson			
☐ 168	Checklist 1-168	.20	.07	.02

1989-90 Fleer Stickers

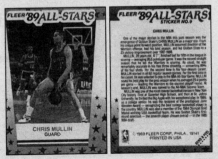

This set of 11 insert stickers features NBA All-Stars and measures the standard size (2 1/2" by 3 1/2"). One All-Star sticker was inserted in each 12-card wax pack. The front has a color

action player photo. An aqua stripe with dark blue stars traverses the card top, and the same pattern reappears about halfway down the card face. The words "Fleer '89 All-Stars" appear at the top of the picture, with the player's name and position immediately below the picture. The back has a star pattern similar to the front. A career summary is printed in blue on a white background. The stickers are numbered on the back and checklisted below accordingly.

	MINT	EXC	G-VG
COMPLETE SET (11)	8.00	3.60	1.00
COMMON STICKER (1-11)	.15	.07	.02
☐ 1 Karl Malone Utah Jazz	.75	.35	.09
☐ 2 Hakeem Olajuwon Houston Rockets	2.00	.90	.25
☐ 3 Michael Jordan Chicago Bulls	6.00	2.70	.75
☐ 4 Charles Barkley Philadelphia 76ers	1.50	.65	.19
☐ 5 Magic Johnson Los Angeles Lakers	1.50	.65	.19
☐ 6 Isiah Thomas Detroit Pistons	.40	.18	.05
☐ 7 Patrick Ewing New York Knicks	1.00	.45	.13
☐ 8 Dale Ellis Seattle Supersonics	.15	.07	.02
☐ 9 Chris Mullin Golden State Warriors	.40	.18	.05
☐ 10 Larry Bird Boston Celtics	2.00	.90	.25
☐ 11 Tom Chambers Phoenix Suns	.15	.07	.02

1990-91 Fleer

The 1990-91 Fleer set contains 198 cards measuring the standard size (2 1/2" by 3 1/2"). The cards were available in 12-card wax packs, 23-card cello packs, and 36-card rack packs. The fronts feature a color action player photo, with a white inner border and a two-color (red on top and bottom, blue on sides) outer border on a white card face. The team logo is superimposed at the upper left corner of the picture, with the player's name and position appearing below the picture. The backs are printed in black, gray, and yellow, and present biographical and statistical information. The cards are numbered on the back. The set is ordered alphabetically in team subsets (with a few exceptions due to late trades). The teams themselves are also presented in alphabetical order, Atlanta Hawks (1-7), Boston Celtics (8-15), Charlotte Hornets (16-21), Chicago Bulls (22-30 and 120), Cleveland Cavaliers (31-37), Dallas Mavericks (38-45 and 50), Denver Nuggets (46-53), Detroit Pistons (54-61), Golden State Warriors (62-68), Houston Rockets (69-75), Indiana Pacers (76-83), Los Angeles Clippers (84-89), Los Angeles Lakers (90-97), Miami Heat (98-103),

Milwaukee Bucks (104-110), Minnesota Timberwolves (111-116 and 140), New Jersey Nets (117-123 and 136), New York Knicks (124-131), Orlando Magic (132-135 and 137), Philadelphia 76ers (138-139 and 141-145), Phoenix Suns (146-153), Portland Trail Blazers (154-161), Sacramento Kings (162-167 and 186-187), San Antonio Spurs (168-174), Seattle Supersonics (175-181), Utah Jazz (182-189 and 195), and Washington Bullets (164, 190-194, and 196). The description, All-American, is properly capitalized on the back of cards 134 and 144, but is not capitalized on cards 20, 29, 51, 53, 59, 70, 119, 130, 178, and 192. Notable Rookie Cards in the set are Nick Anderson, B.J. Armstrong, Mookie Blaylock, Vlade Divac, Sherman Douglas, Sean Elliott, Pervis Ellison, Danny Ferry, Tim Hardaway, Shawn Kemp, Sarunas Marciulionis, Glen Rice, Pooh Richardson, and Cliff Robinson.

	MINT	EXC	G-VG
COMPLETE SET (198)	6.00	2.70	.75
COMMON PLAYER (1-198)	.05	.02	.01
☐ 1 John Battle UER	.05	.02	.01
(Drafted in '84, should be '85)			
☐ 2 Cliff Levingston	.05	.02	.01
☐ 3 Moses Malone	.10	.05	.01
☐ 4 Kenny Smith	.05	.02	.01
☐ 5 Spud Webb	.10	.05	.01
☐ 6 Dominique Wilkins	.25	.11	.03
☐ 7 Kevin Willis	.08	.04	.01
☐ 8 Larry Bird	.75	.35	.09
☐ 9 Dennis Johnson	.10	.05	.01
☐ 10 Joe Kleine	.05	.02	.01
☐ 11 Reggie Lewis	.15	.07	.02
☐ 12 Kevin McHale	.10	.05	.01
☐ 13 Robert Parish	.10	.05	.01
☐ 14 Jim Paxson	.05	.02	.01
☐ 15 Ed Pinckney	.10	.05	.01
☐ 16 Tyrone Bogues	.08	.04	.01
☐ 17 Rex Chapman	.08	.04	.01
☐ 18 Dell Curry	.08	.04	.01
☐ 19 Armon Gilliam	.05	.02	.01
☐ 20 J.R. Reid	.15	.07	.02
☐ 21 Kelly Tripucka	.08	.04	.01
☐ 22 B.J. Armstrong	.75	.35	.09
☐ 23A Bill Cartwright ERR	.50	.23	.06
(No decimal points in FGP and FTP)			
☐ 23B Bill Cartwright COR	.08	.04	.01
☐ 24 Horace Grant	.10	.05	.01
☐ 25 Craig Hodges	.05	.02	.01
☐ 26 Michael Jordan UER	2.50	1.15	.30
(Led NBA in scoring 4 years, not 3)			
☐ 27 Stacey King UER	.10	.05	.01
(Comma missing between progressed and Stacy)			
☐ 28 John Paxson	.08	.04	.01
☐ 29 Will Perdue	.05	.02	.01
☐ 30 Scottie Pippen UER	.40	.18	.05
(Born AR, not AK)			
☐ 31 Brad Daugherty	.10	.05	.01
☐ 32 Craig Ehlo	.08	.04	.01
☐ 33 Danny Ferry	.10	.05	.01
☐ 34 Steve Kerr	.05	.02	.01
☐ 35 Larry Nance	.08	.04	.01
☐ 36 Mark Price UER	.10	.05	.01
(Drafted by Cleveland, should be Dallas)			
☐ 37 Hot Rod Williams	.08	.04	.01
☐ 38 Rolando Blackman	.08	.04	.01
☐ 39A Adrian Dantley ERR	.50	.23	.06
(No decimal points in FGP and FTP)			
☐ 39B Adrian Dantley COR	.10	.05	.01
☐ 40 Brad Davis	.05	.02	.01
☐ 41 James Donaldson UER	.05	.02	.01
(Text says in committed, should be is committed)			

☐ 42	Derek Harper	.08	.04	.01
☐ 43	Sam Perkins UER	.10	.05	.01
	(First line of text should be intact)			
☐ 44	Bill Wennington	.05	.02	.01
☐ 45	Herb Williams	.05	.02	.01
☐ 46	Michael Adams	.08	.04	.01
☐ 47	Walter Davis	.10	.05	.01
☐ 48	Alex English UER	.10	.05	.01
	(Stats missing from '76-77 through '79-80)			
☐ 49	Bill Hanzlik	.05	.02	.01
☐ 50	Lafayette Lever UER	.05	.02	.01
	(Born AR, not AK)			
☐ 51	Todd Lichti	.05	.02	.01
☐ 52	Blair Rasmussen	.05	.02	.01
☐ 53	Dan Schayes	.05	.02	.01
☐ 54	Mark Aguirre	.10	.05	.01
☐ 55	Joe Dumars	.15	.07	.02
☐ 56	James Edwards	.05	.02	.01
☐ 57	Vinnie Johnson	.08	.04	.01
☐ 58	Bill Laimbeer	.10	.05	.01
☐ 59	Dennis Rodman UER	.08	.04	.01
	(College misspelled as coilege on back)			
☐ 60	John Salley	.08	.04	.01
☐ 61	Isiah Thomas	.15	.07	.02
☐ 62	Manute Bol	.05	.02	.01
☐ 63	Tim Hardaway	.75	.35	.09
☐ 64	Rod Higgins	.05	.02	.01
☐ 65	Sarunas Marciulionis	.10	.05	.01
☐ 66	Chris Mullin	.15	.07	.02
☐ 67	Mitch Richmond	.20	.09	.03
☐ 68	Terry Teagle	.05	.02	.01
☐ 69	Anthony Bowie UER	.10	.05	.01
	(Seasons, not seeasons)			
☐ 70	Sleepy Floyd	.05	.02	.01
☐ 71	Buck Johnson	.05	.02	.01
☐ 72	Vernon Maxwell	.08	.04	.01
☐ 73	Hakeem Olajuwon	.75	.35	.09
☐ 74	Otis Thorpe	.08	.04	.01
☐ 75	Mitchell Wiggins	.05	.02	.01
☐ 76	Vern Fleming	.05	.02	.01
☐ 77	George McCloud	.05	.02	.01
☐ 78	Reggie Miller	.15	.07	.02
☐ 79	Chuck Person	.08	.04	.01
☐ 80	Mike Sanders	.05	.02	.01
☐ 81	Detlef Schrempf	.10	.05	.01
☐ 82	Rik Smits	.10	.05	.01
☐ 83	LaSalle Thompson	.08	.04	.01
☐ 84	Benoit Benjamin	.05	.02	.01
☐ 85	Winston Garland	.05	.02	.01
☐ 86	Ron Harper	.08	.04	.01
☐ 87	Danny Manning	.25	.11	.03
☐ 88	Ken Norman	.08	.04	.01
☐ 89	Charles Smith	.08	.04	.01
☐ 90	Michael Cooper	.10	.05	.01
☐ 91	Vlade Divac	.25	.11	.03
☐ 92	A.C. Green	.08	.04	.01
☐ 93	Magic Johnson	.50	.23	.06
☐ 94	Byron Scott	.08	.04	.01
☐ 95	Mychal Thompson UER	.08	.04	.01
	(Missing '78-79 stats from Portland)			
☐ 96	Orlando Woolridge	.08	.04	.01
☐ 97	James Worthy	.10	.05	.01
☐ 98	Sherman Douglas	.25	.11	.03
☐ 99	Kevin Edwards	.08	.04	.01
☐ 100	Grant Long	.08	.04	.01
☐ 101	Glen Rice	.75	.35	.09
☐ 102	Rony Seikaly UER	.10	.05	.01
	(Ron on front)			
☐ 103	Billy Thompson	.05	.02	.01

☐ 104	Jeff Grayer	.05	.02	.01
☐ 105	Jay Humphries	.05	.02	.01
☐ 106	Ricky Pierce	.08	.04	.01
☐ 107	Paul Pressey	.05	.02	.01
☐ 108	Fred Roberts	.05	.02	.01
☐ 109	Alvin Robertson	.08	.04	.01
☐ 110	Jack Sikma	.10	.05	.01
☐ 111	Randy Breuer	.05	.02	.01
☐ 112	Tony Campbell	.05	.02	.01
☐ 113	Tyrone Corbin	.08	.04	.01
☐ 114	Sam Mitchell UER	.05	.02	.01
	(Mercer University, not Mercer College)			
☐ 115	Tod Murphy UER	.05	.02	.01
	(Born Long Beach, not Lakewood)			
☐ 116	Pooh Richardson	.15	.07	.02
☐ 117	Mookie Blaylock	.50	.23	.06
☐ 118	Sam Bowie	.08	.04	.01
☐ 119	Lester Conner	.05	.02	.01
☐ 120	Dennis Hopson	.05	.02	.01
☐ 121	Chris Morris	.05	.02	.01
☐ 122	Charles Shackleford	.05	.02	.01
☐ 123	Purvis Short	.05	.02	.01
☐ 124	Maurice Cheeks	.10	.05	.01
☐ 125	Patrick Ewing	.30	.14	.04
☐ 126	Mark Jackson	.08	.04	.01
☐ 127A	Johnny Newman ERR	.50	.23	.06
	(Jr. misprinted as J. on card back)			
☐ 127B	Johnny Newman COR	.05	.02	.01
☐ 128	Charles Oakley	.10	.05	.01
☐ 129	Trent Tucker	.05	.02	.01
☐ 130	Kenny Walker	.05	.02	.01
☐ 131	Gerald Wilkins	.08	.04	.01
☐ 132	Nick Anderson	.40	.18	.05
☐ 133	Terry Catledge	.05	.02	.01
☐ 134	Sidney Green	.05	.02	.01
☐ 135	Otis Smith	.05	.02	.01
☐ 136	Reggie Theus	.08	.04	.01
☐ 137	Sam Vincent	.05	.02	.01
☐ 138	Ron Anderson	.05	.02	.01
☐ 139	Charles Barkley UER	.50	.23	.06
	(FG Percentage .545.)			
☐ 140	Scott Brooks UER	.05	.02	.01
	('89-89 Philadelphia in wrong typeface)			
☐ 141	Johnny Dawkins	.05	.02	.01
☐ 142	Mike Gminski	.05	.02	.01
☐ 143	Hersey Hawkins	.10	.05	.01
☐ 144	Rick Mahorn	.08	.04	.01
☐ 145	Derek Smith	.05	.02	.01
☐ 146	Tom Chambers	.10	.05	.01
☐ 147	Jeff Hornacek	.10	.05	.01
☐ 148	Eddie Johnson	.08	.04	.01
☐ 149	Kevin Johnson	.25	.11	.03
☐ 150A	Dan Majerle ERR	1.00	.45	.13
	(Award in 1988; three-time selection)			
☐ 150B	Dan Majerle COR	.20	.09	.03
	(Award in 1989; three-time selection)			
☐ 151	Tim Perry	.05	.02	.01
☐ 152	Kurt Rambis	.08	.04	.01
☐ 153	Mark West	.05	.02	.01
☐ 154	Clyde Drexler	.20	.09	.03
☐ 155	Kevin Duckworth	.05	.02	.01
☐ 156	Byron Irvin	.05	.02	.01
☐ 157	Jerome Kersey	.05	.02	.01
☐ 158	Terry Porter	.10	.05	.01
☐ 159	Cliff Robinson	.75	.35	.09
☐ 160	Buck Williams	.10	.05	.01
☐ 161	Danny Young	.05	.02	.01

☐ 162	Danny Ainge	.10	.05	.01
☐ 163	Antoine Carr	.05	.02	.01
☐ 164	Pervis Ellison	.15	.07	.02
☐ 165	Rodney McCray	.05	.02	.01
☐ 166	Harold Pressley	.05	.02	.01
☐ 167	Wayman Tisdale	.08	.04	.01
☐ 168	Willie Anderson	.05	.02	.01
☐ 169	Frank Brickowski	.08	.04	.01
☐ 170	Terry Cummings	.08	.04	.01
☐ 171	Sean Elliott	.25	.11	.03
☐ 172	David Robinson	1.00	.45	.13
☐ 173	Rod Strickland	.08	.04	.01
☐ 174	David Wingate	.05	.02	.01
☐ 175	Dana Barros	.15	.07	.02
☐ 176	Michael Cage UER	.05	.02	.01
	(Born AR, not AK)			
☐ 177	Dale Ellis	.08	.04	.01
☐ 178	Shawn Kemp	2.50	1.15	.30
☐ 179	Xavier McDaniel	.10	.05	.01
☐ 180	Derrick McKey	.05	.02	.01
☐ 181	Nate McMillan	.08	.04	.01
☐ 182	Thurl Bailey	.05	.02	.01
☐ 183	Mike Brown	.05	.02	.01
☐ 184	Mark Eaton	.08	.04	.01
☐ 185	Blue Edwards	.15	.07	.02
☐ 186	Bob Hansen	.05	.02	.01
☐ 187	Eric Leckner	.05	.02	.01
☐ 188	Karl Malone	.25	.11	.03
☐ 189	John Stockton	.20	.09	.03
☐ 190	Mark Alarie	.05	.02	.01
☐ 191	Ledell Eackles	.05	.02	.01
☐ 192A	Harvey Grant	1.00	.45	.13
	(First name on card front in black)			
☐ 192B	Harvey Grant	.10	.05	.01
	(First name on card front in white)			
☐ 193	Tom Hammonds	.10	.05	.01
☐ 194	Bernard King	.10	.05	.01
☐ 195	Jeff Malone	.08	.04	.01
☐ 196	Darrell Walker	.05	.02	.01
☐ 197	Checklist 1-99	.05	.02	.01
☐ 198	Checklist 100-198	.05	.02	.01

1990-91 Fleer All-Stars

These 1990-91 Fleer All-Star inserts measure the standard size (2 1/2" by 3 1/2"). These inserts were randomly inserted at a rate of approximately one per five 12-card wax packs *and hence are more difficult to find than the Fleer All-Star sticker inserts of the previous years. The fronts feature a color action photo, framed by a basketball hoop and net on an aqua background. An orange stripe at the top represents the bottom of the backboard and has the words "Fleer '90 All-Stars." The player's name and position are given at the bottom between stars. The backs are printed in blue and pink with white borders and have career summaries. The cards are numbered on the back.*

	MINT	EXC	G-VG
COMPLETE SET (12)	8.00	3.60	1.00
COMMON PLAYER (1-12)	.20	.09	.03
☐ 1 Charles Barkley Philadelphia 76ers	1.25	.55	.16
☐ 2 Larry Bird Boston Celtics	1.50	.65	.19
☐ 3 Hakeem Olajuwon Houston Rockets	1.50	.65	.19
☐ 4 Magic Johnson Los Angeles Lakers	1.25	.55	.16
☐ 5 Michael Jordan Chicago Bulls	5.00	2.30	.60
☐ 6 Isiah Thomas Detroit Pistons	.30	.14	.04
☐ 7 Karl Malone Utah Jazz	.50	.23	.06
☐ 8 Tom Chambers Phoenix Suns	.20	.09	.03
☐ 9 John Stockton Utah Jazz	.40	.18	.05
☐ 10 David Robinson San Antonio Spurs	2.50	1.15	.30
☐ 11 Clyde Drexler Portland Trail Blazers	.40	.18	.05
☐ 12 Patrick Ewing New York Knicks	.75	.35	.09

1990-91 Fleer Rookie Sensations

These Rookie Sensation cards measure the standard size (2 1/2" by 3 1/2"). These inserts were distributed randomly at a rate of approximately one per six 23-card cello packs and thus are considered a tough insert set to complete. The fronts feature color action player photos, with white and red borders on an aqua background. A basketball overlays the lower left corner of the picture, with the words "Rookie Sensation" in yellow lettering, and the player's name appearing in white lettering in the bottom red border. The backs are printed in black and red on gray background (with white borders), and present summaries of their college careers and rookie seasons. The cards are numbered on the back.

	MINT	EXC	G-VG
COMPLETE SET (10)	50.00	23.00	6.25
COMMON PLAYER (1-10)	1.00	.45	.13

☐ 1 David Robinson UER ... 30.00 — 13.50 — 3.80
  San Antonio Spurs
  (Text has 1988-90 season,
  should be 1989-90)
☐ 2 Sean Elliott UER ... 3.00 — 1.35 — .40
  San Antonio Spurs
  (Misspelled Elliot
  on card front)
☐ 3 Glen Rice ... 10.00 — 4.50 — 1.25
  Miami Heat
☐ 4 J.R. Reid ... 1.50 — .65 — .19
  Charlotte Hornets
☐ 5 Stacey King ... 1.00 — .45 — .13
  Chicago Bulls
☐ 6 Pooh Richardson ... 1.50 — .65 — .19
  Minnesota Timberwolves
☐ 7 Nick Anderson ... 5.00 — 2.30 — .60
  Orlando Magic
☐ 8 Tim Hardaway ... 10.00 — 4.50 — 1.25
  Golden State Warriors
☐ 9 Vlade Divac ... 3.00 — 1.35 — .40
  Los Angeles Lakers
☐ 10 Sherman Douglas ... 3.00 — 1.35 — .40
  Miami Heat

1990-91 Fleer Update

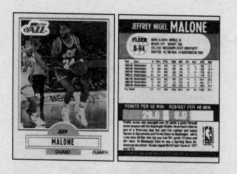

These cards are the same size (2 1/2" by 3 1/2") and design as the regular issue. Cards were distributed exclusively through hobby dealers in complete set factory-sealed boxes. The set numbering is arranged alphabetically by team as follows: Atlanta Hawks (1-5), Boston Celtics (6-10), Charlotte Hornets (11-13), Chicago Bulls (14-15), Cleveland Cavaliers (16-18), Dallas Mavericks (19-23), Cleveland Cavaliers (24-27), Detroit Pistons (28-30), Golden State Warriors (31-34), Houston Rockets (35-36), Indiana Pacers (37-39), Los Angeles Clippers (40-42), Los Angeles Lakers (43-46), Miami Heat (47-50), Milwaukee Bucks (51-55), Minnesota Timberwolves (56-58), New Jersey Nets (59-62), New York Knicks (63-66), Orlando Magic (67), Philadelphia 76ers (68-73), Phoenix Suns (74-77), Portland Trail Blazers (78-81), Sacramento Kings (82-87), San Antonio Spurs (88-91), Seattle Supersonics (92-93), Utah Jazz (94-96), and Washington Bullets (97-99). The card numbers have a "U" prefix. Rookie Cards include Dee Brown, Elden Campbell, Cedric Ceballos, Derrick Coleman, Kendall Gill, Tyrone Hill, Chris Jackson, Gary Payton, Drazen Petrovic, Dennis Scott, Lionel Simmons, Loy Vaught and Doug West.

	MINT	EXC	G-VG
COMPLETE SET (100)...........................	8.00	3.60	1.00
COMMON PLAYER (U1-U100).................	.05	.02	.01
☐ U1 Jon Koncak..................................	.05	.02	.01
☐ U2 Tim McCormick..........................	.05	.02	.01
☐ U3 Glenn Rivers.............................	.08	.04	.01
☐ U4 Rumeal Robinson......................	.10	.05	.01
☐ U5 Trevor Wilson...........................	.05	.02	.01
☐ U6 Dee Brown...............................	.75	.35	.09
☐ U7 Dave Popson............................	.05	.02	.01
☐ U8 Kevin Gamble...........................	.05	.02	.01
☐ U9 Brian Shaw..............................	.05	.02	.01
☐ U10 Michael Smith.........................	.05	.02	.01
☐ U11 Kendall Gill............................	1.00	.45	.13
☐ U12 Johnny Newman......................	.05	.02	.01
☐ U13 Steve Scheffler.......................	.05	.02	.01
☐ U14 Dennis Hopson........................	.05	.02	.01
☐ U15 Cliff Levingston.......................	.05	.02	.01
☐ U16 Chucky Brown..........................	.05	.02	.01
☐ U17 John Morton............................	.05	.02	.01
☐ U18 Gerald Paddio..........................	.05	.02	.01
☐ U19 Alex English...........................	.10	.05	.01
☐ U20 Fat Lever...............................	.05	.02	.01
☐ U21 Rodney McCray........................	.05	.02	.01
☐ U22 Roy Tarpley............................	.05	.02	.01
☐ U23 Randy White............................	.10	.05	.01
☐ U24 Anthony Cook...........................	.05	.02	.01
☐ U25 Chris Jackson.........................	1.25	.55	.16
☐ U26 Marcus Liberty........................	.05	.02	.01
☐ U27 Orlando Woolridge....................	.08	.04	.01
☐ U28 William Bedford........................	.05	.02	.01
☐ U29 Lance Blanks..........................	.05	.02	.01
☐ U30 Scott Hastings........................	.05	.02	.01
☐ U31 Tyrone Hill.............................	.50	.23	.06
☐ U32 Les Jepsen............................	.05	.02	.01
☐ U33 Steve Johnson........................	.05	.02	.01
☐ U34 Kevin Pritchard.......................	.05	.02	.01
☐ U35 Dave Jamerson........................	.05	.02	.01
☐ U36 Kenny Smith...........................	.05	.02	.01
☐ U37 Greg Dreiling..........................	.05	.02	.01
☐ U38 Kenny Williams........................	.20	.09	.03
☐ U39 Micheal Williams UER...............	.08	.04	.01
☐ U40 Gary Grant.............................	.05	.02	.01
☐ U41 Bo Kimble..............................	.05	.02	.01
☐ U42 Loy Vaught............................	.40	.18	.05
☐ U43 Elden Campbell.......................	.40	.18	.05
☐ U44 Sam Perkins..........................	.10	.05	.01
☐ U45 Tony Smith............................	.15	.07	.02
☐ U46 Terry Teagle...........................	.05	.02	.01
☐ U47 Willie Burton...........................	.15	.07	.02
☐ U48 Bimbo Coles...........................	.15	.07	.02
☐ U49 Terry Davis............................	.10	.05	.01
☐ U50 Alec Kessler...........................	.05	.02	.01
☐ U51 Greg Anderson........................	.05	.02	.01
☐ U52 Frank Brickowski......................	.08	.04	.01
☐ U53 Steve Henson..........................	.05	.02	.01
☐ U54 Brad Lohaus...........................	.05	.02	.01
☐ U55 Dan Schayes...........................	.05	.02	.01
☐ U56 Gerald Glass..........................	.05	.02	.01
☐ U57 Felton Spencer........................	.25	.11	.03
☐ U58 Doug West.............................	.60	.25	.08
☐ U59 Jud Buechler..........................	.05	.02	.01
☐ U60 Derrick Coleman......................	3.00	1.35	.40
☐ U61 Tate George...........................	.05	.02	.01
☐ U62 Reggie Theus..........................	.08	.04	.01
☐ U63 Greg Grant.............................	.05	.02	.01
☐ U64 Jerrod Mustaf.........................	.05	.02	.01
☐ U65 Eddie Lee Wilkins.....................	.05	.02	.01
☐ U66 Michael Ansley........................	.05	.02	.01
☐ U67 Jerry Reynolds........................	.05	.02	.01
☐ U68 Dennis Scott...........................	.60	.25	.08
☐ U69 Manute Bol.............................	.05	.02	.01

☐	U70	Armon Gilliam	.05	.02	.01
☐	U71	Brian Oliver	.05	.02	.01
☐	U72	Kenny Payne	.05	.02	.01
☐	U73	Jayson Williams	.05	.02	.01
☐	U74	Kenny Battle	.05	.02	.01
☐	U75	Cedric Ceballos	1.50	.65	.19
☐	U76	Negele Knight	.15	.07	.02
☐	U77	Xavier McDaniel	.10	.05	.01
☐	U78	Alaa Abdelnaby	.15	.07	.02
☐	U79	Danny Ainge	.10	.05	.01
☐	U80	Mark Bryant	.05	.02	.01
☐	U81	Drazen Petrovic	.75	.35	.09
☐	U82	Anthony Bonner	.15	.07	.02
☐	U83	Duane Causwell	.15	.07	.02
☐	U84	Bobby Hansen	.05	.02	.01
☐	U85	Eric Leckner	.05	.02	.01
☐	U86	Travis Mays	.05	.02	.01
☐	U87	Lionel Simmons	.75	.35	.09
☐	U88	Sidney Green	.05	.02	.01
☐	U89	Tony Massenburg	.05	.02	.01
☐	U90	Paul Pressey	.05	.02	.01
☐	U91	Dwayne Schintzius	.10	.05	.01
☐	U92	Gary Payton	1.50	.65	.19
☐	U93	Olden Polynice	.05	.02	.01
☐	U94	Jeff Malone	.08	.04	.01
☐	U95	Walter Palmer	.05	.02	.01
☐	U96	Delaney Rudd	.05	.02	.01
☐	U97	Pervis Ellison	.25	.11	.03
☐	U98	A.J. English	.05	.02	.01
☐	U99	Greg Foster	.05	.02	.01
☐	U100	Checklist 1-100	.05	.02	.01

1991-92 Fleer

The complete 1991-92 Fleer basketball card set contains 400 cards measuring the standard size (2 1/2" by 3 1/2"). The set was distributed in two series of 240 and 160 cards, respectively. The cards were distributed in 12-card wax packs, 23-card cello packs, and 36-card rack packs. The fronts feature color action player photos, bordered by a red stripe on the bottom, and gray and red stripes on the top. A 3/4" blue stripe checkered with black NBA logos runs the length of the card and serves as the left border of the picture. The team logo, player's name, and position are printed in white lettering in this stripe. The picture is bordered on the right side by a thin gray stripe and a thicker blue one. The backs present career summaries and are printed with black lettering on various pastel colors, superimposed over a wooden basketball floor background. The cards are numbered and checklisted below alphabetically within and according to teams as follows: Atlanta Hawks (1-7), Boston Celtics (8-16), Charlotte Hornets (17-24), Chicago Bulls (25-33), Cleveland Cavaliers (34-41), Dallas Mavericks (42-48), Denver Nuggets (49-56), Detroit Pistons (57-64), Golden State Warriors (65-72), Houston Rockets (73-80), Indiana Pacers (81-88), L.A. Clippers (86-

96), L.A. Lakers (97-104), Miami Heat (105-112), Milwaukee Bucks (113-120), Minnesota Timberwolves (121-127), New Jersey Nets (128-134), New York Knicks (135-142), Orlando Magic (143-149), Philadelphia 76ers (150-157), Phoenix Suns (158-165), Portland Trail Blazers (166-173), Sacramento Kings (174-181), San Antonio Spurs (182-188), Seattle Supersonics (189-196), Utah Jazz (197-203), and Washington Bullets (204-209). Other subsets within the set are All-Stars (210-219), League Leaders (220-226), Slam Dunk (227-232), All Star Game Highlights (233-238), Atlanta Hawks (241-246), Boston Celtics (247-251), Charlotte Hornets (252-255), Chicago Bulls (256-259), Cleveland Cavaliers (260-265), Dallas Mavericks (266-271), Denver Nuggets (272-277), Detroit Pistons (278-283), Golden State Warriors (284-288), Houston Rockets (289-292), Indiana Pacers (293-295), Los Angeles Clippers (296-299), Los Angeles Lakers (300-304), Miami Heat (305-309), Milwaukee Bucks (310-315), Minnesota Timberwolves (316-321), New Jersey Nets (322-325), New York Knicks (326-330), Orlando Magic (331-334), Philadelphia 76ers (335-338), Phoenix Suns (339-343), Portland Trail Blazers (344-346), Sacramento Kings (347-352), San Antonio Spurs (353-356), Seattle Supersonics (357-361), Utah Jazz (362-366), and Washington Bullets (367-371), Team Leaders (372-398), and checklist cards (399-400). The second series was intended to include primarily rookies and traded veterans. Special Dikembe Mutombo and Dominique Wilkins cards were randomly inserted into second series packs, and each player signed over 2,000 of his cards. There are no key Rookie Cards in the first series; the key Rookie Cards in the second series are Kenny Anderson, Stacey Augmon, Larry Johnson, Dikembe Mutombo, Billy Owens, Steve Smith, and John Starks.

	MINT	EXC	G-VG
COMPLETE SET (400)	10.00	4.50	1.25
COMPLETE SERIES 1 (240)	4.00	1.80	.50
COMPLETE SERIES 2 (160)	6.00	2.70	.75
COMMON PLAYER (1-240)	.05	.02	.01
COMMON PLAYER (241-400)	.05	.02	.01
☐ 1 John Battle	.05	.02	.01
☐ 2 Jon Koncak	.05	.02	.01
☐ 3 Rumeal Robinson	.05	.02	.01
☐ 4 Spud Webb	.10	.05	.01
☐ 5 Bob Weiss CO	.05	.02	.01
☐ 6 Dominique Wilkins	.20	.09	.03
☐ 7 Kevin Willis	.08	.04	.01
☐ 8 Larry Bird	.60	.25	.08
☐ 9 Dee Brown	.05	.02	.01
☐ 10 Chris Ford CO	.05	.02	.01
☐ 11 Kevin Gamble	.05	.02	.01
☐ 12 Reggie Lewis	.10	.05	.01
☐ 13 Kevin McHale	.10	.05	.01
☐ 14 Robert Parish	.10	.05	.01
☐ 15 Ed Pinckney	.05	.02	.01
☐ 16 Brian Shaw	.05	.02	.01
☐ 17 Tyrone Bogues	.10	.05	.01
☐ 18 Rex Chapman	.05	.02	.01
☐ 19 Dell Curry	.08	.04	.01
☐ 20 Kendall Gill	.08	.04	.01
☐ 21 Eric Leckner	.05	.02	.01
☐ 22 Gene Littles CO	.05	.02	.01
☐ 23 Johnny Newman	.05	.02	.01
☐ 24 J.R. Reid	.05	.02	.01
☐ 25 B.J. Armstrong	.15	.07	.02
☐ 26 Bill Cartwright	.08	.04	.01
☐ 27 Horace Grant	.10	.05	.01
☐ 28 Phil Jackson CO	.08	.04	.01
☐ 29 Michael Jordan	2.00	.90	.25
☐ 30 Cliff Levingston	.05	.02	.01
☐ 31 John Paxson	.08	.04	.01
☐ 32 Will Perdue	.05	.02	.01
☐ 33 Scottie Pippen	.25	.11	.03
☐ 34 Brad Daugherty	.10	.05	.01
☐ 35 Craig Ehlo	.05	.02	.01
☐ 36 Danny Ferry	.05	.02	.01
☐ 37 Larry Nance	.08	.04	.01
☐ 38 Mark Price	.10	.05	.01
☐ 39 Darnell Valentine	.05	.02	.01
☐ 40 Hot Rod Williams	.08	.04	.01
☐ 41 Lenny Wilkens CO	.08	.04	.01
☐ 42 Richie Adubato CO	.05	.02	.01
☐ 43 Rolando Blackman	.08	.04	.01
☐ 44 James Donaldson	.05	.02	.01

☐	45	Derek Harper	.08	.04	.01
☐	46	Rodney McCray	.05	.02	.01
☐	47	Randy White	.05	.02	.01
☐	48	Herb Williams	.05	.02	.01
☐	49	Chris Jackson	.05	.02	.01
☐	50	Marcus Liberty	.05	.02	.01
☐	51	Todd Lichti	.05	.02	.01
☐	52	Blair Rasmussen	.05	.02	.01
☐	53	Paul Westhead CO	.05	.02	.01
☐	54	Reggie Williams	.08	.04	.01
☐	55	Joe Wolf	.05	.02	.01
☐	56	Orlando Woolridge	.08	.04	.01
☐	57	Mark Aguirre	.10	.05	.01
☐	58	Chuck Daly CO	.08	.04	.01
☐	59	Joe Dumars	.15	.07	.02
☐	60	James Edwards	.05	.02	.01
☐	61	Vinnie Johnson	.08	.04	.01
☐	62	Bill Laimbeer	.10	.05	.01
☐	63	Dennis Rodman	.08	.04	.01
☐	64	Isiah Thomas	.15	.07	.02
☐	65	Tim Hardaway	.15	.07	.02
☐	66	Rod Higgins	.05	.02	.01
☐	67	Tyrone Hill	.05	.02	.01
☐	68	Sarunas Marciulionis	.08	.04	.01
☐	69	Chris Mullin	.15	.07	.02
☐	70	Don Nelson CO	.08	.04	.01
☐	71	Mitch Richmond	.10	.05	.01
☐	72	Tom Tolbert	.05	.02	.01
☐	73	Don Chaney CO	.08	.04	.01
☐	74	Eric(Sleepy) Floyd	.05	.02	.01
☐	75	Buck Johnson	.05	.02	.01
☐	76	Vernon Maxwell	.08	.04	.01
☐	77	Hakeem Olajuwon	.60	.25	.08
☐	78	Kenny Smith	.05	.02	.01
☐	79	Larry Smith	.08	.04	.01
☐	80	Otis Thorpe	.08	.04	.01
☐	81	Vern Fleming	.05	.02	.01
☐	82	Bob Hill CO	.05	.02	.01
☐	83	Reggie Miller	.15	.07	.02
☐	84	Chuck Person	.08	.04	.01
☐	85	Detlef Schrempf	.10	.05	.01
☐	86	Rik Smits	.08	.04	.01
☐	87	LaSalle Thompson	.08	.04	.01
☐	88	Micheal Williams	.08	.04	.01
☐	89	Gary Grant	.05	.02	.01
☐	90	Ron Harper	.08	.04	.01
☐	91	Bo Kimble	.05	.02	.01
☐	92	Danny Manning	.15	.07	.02
☐	93	Ken Norman	.08	.04	.01
☐	94	Olden Polynice	.05	.02	.01
☐	95	Mike Schuler CO	.05	.02	.01
☐	96	Charles Smith	.08	.04	.01
☐	97	Vlade Divac	.08	.04	.01
☐	98	Mike Dunleavy CO	.05	.02	.01
☐	99	A.C. Green	.08	.04	.01
☐	100	Magic Johnson	.40	.18	.05
☐	101	Sam Perkins	.08	.04	.01
☐	102	Byron Scott	.08	.04	.01
☐	103	Terry Teagle	.05	.02	.01
☐	104	James Worthy	.10	.05	.01
☐	105	Willie Burton	.05	.02	.01
☐	106	Bimbo Coles	.05	.02	.01
☐	107	Sherman Douglas	.05	.02	.01
☐	108	Kevin Edwards	.05	.02	.01
☐	109	Grant Long	.05	.02	.01
☐	110	Kevin Loughery CO	.05	.02	.01
☐	111	Glen Rice	.15	.07	.02
☐	112	Rony Seikaly	.10	.05	.01
☐	113	Frank Brickowski	.08	.04	.01
☐	114	Dale Ellis	.08	.04	.01
☐	115	Del Harris CO	.05	.02	.01
☐	116	Jay Humphries	.05	.02	.01
☐	117	Fred Roberts	.05	.02	.01

☐	118	Alvin Robertson	.08	.04	.01
☐	119	Dan Schayes	.05	.02	.01
☐	120	Jack Sikma	.10	.05	.01
☐	121	Tony Campbell	.05	.02	.01
☐	122	Tyrone Corbin	.05	.02	.01
☐	123	Sam Mitchell	.05	.02	.01
☐	124	Tod Murphy	.05	.02	.01
☐	125	Pooh Richardson	.05	.02	.01
☐	126	Jim Rodgers CO	.05	.02	.01
☐	127	Felton Spencer	.05	.02	.01
☐	128	Mookie Blaylock	.08	.04	.01
☐	129	Sam Bowie	.08	.04	.01
☐	130	Derrick Coleman	.30	.14	.04
☐	131	Chris Dudley	.05	.02	.01
☐	132	Bill Fitch CO	.05	.02	.01
☐	133	Chris Morris	.05	.02	.01
☐	134	Drazen Petrovic	.08	.04	.01
☐	135	Maurice Cheeks	.10	.05	.01
☐	136	Patrick Ewing	.25	.11	.03
☐	137	Mark Jackson	.08	.04	.01
☐	138	Charles Oakley	.10	.05	.01
☐	139	Pat Riley CO	.08	.04	.01
☐	140	Trent Tucker	.05	.02	.01
☐	141	Kiki Vandeweghe	.08	.04	.01
☐	142	Gerald Wilkins	.08	.04	.01
☐	143	Nick Anderson	.10	.05	.01
☐	144	Terry Catledge	.05	.02	.01
☐	145	Matt Guokas CO	.05	.02	.01
☐	146	Jerry Reynolds	.05	.02	.01
☐	147	Dennis Scott	.08	.04	.01
☐	148	Scott Skiles	.08	.04	.01
☐	149	Otis Smith	.05	.02	.01
☐	150	Ron Anderson	.05	.02	.01
☐	151	Charles Barkley	.40	.18	.05
☐	152	Johnny Dawkins	.05	.02	.01
☐	153	Armon Gilliam	.08	.04	.01
☐	154	Hersey Hawkins	.08	.04	.01
☐	155	Jim Lynam CO	.05	.02	.01
☐	156	Rick Mahorn	.08	.04	.01
☐	157	Brian Oliver	.05	.02	.01
☐	158	Tom Chambers	.10	.05	.01
☐	159	Cotton Fitzsimmons CO	.05	.02	.01
☐	160	Jeff Hornacek	.10	.05	.01
☐	161	Kevin Johnson	.15	.07	.02
☐	162	Negele Knight	.05	.02	.01
☐	163	Dan Majerle	.10	.05	.01
☐	164	Xavier McDaniel	.10	.05	.01
☐	165	Mark West	.05	.02	.01
☐	166	Rick Adelman CO	.08	.04	.01
☐	167	Danny Ainge	.10	.05	.01
☐	168	Clyde Drexler	.15	.07	.02
☐	169	Kevin Duckworth	.05	.02	.01
☐	170	Jerome Kersey	.05	.02	.01
☐	171	Terry Porter	.08	.04	.01
☐	172	Cliff Robinson	.15	.07	.02
☐	173	Buck Williams	.10	.05	.01
☐	174	Antoine Carr	.05	.02	.01
☐	175	Duane Causwell	.05	.02	.01
☐	176	Jim Les	.05	.02	.01
☐	177	Travis Mays	.05	.02	.01
☐	178	Dick Motta CO	.05	.02	.01
☐	179	Lionel Simmons	.08	.04	.01
☐	180	Rory Sparrow	.05	.02	.01
☐	181	Wayman Tisdale	.08	.04	.01
☐	182	Willie Anderson	.05	.02	.01
☐	183	Larry Brown CO	.08	.04	.01
☐	184	Terry Cummings	.08	.04	.01
☐	185	Sean Elliott	.08	.04	.01
☐	186	Paul Pressey	.05	.02	.01
☐	187	David Robinson	.50	.23	.06
☐	188	Rod Strickland	.08	.04	.01
☐	189	Benoit Benjamin	.05	.02	.01
☐	190	Eddie Johnson	.08	.04	.01

☐ 191	K.C. Jones CO	.08	.04	.01
☐ 192	Shawn Kemp	.75	.35	.09
☐ 193	Derrick McKey	.05	.02	.01
☐ 194	Gary Payton	.15	.07	.02
☐ 195	Ricky Pierce	.08	.04	.01
☐ 196	Sedale Threatt	.05	.02	.01
☐ 197	Thurl Bailey	.05	.02	.01
☐ 198	Mark Eaton	.05	.02	.01
☐ 199	Blue Edwards	.05	.02	.01
☐ 200	Jeff Malone	.08	.04	.01
☐ 201	Karl Malone	.20	.09	.03
☐ 202	Jerry Sloan CO	.05	.02	.01
☐ 203	John Stockton	.15	.07	.02
☐ 204	Ledell Eackles	.05	.02	.01
☐ 205	Pervis Ellison	.08	.04	.01
☐ 206	A.J. English	.05	.02	.01
☐ 207	Harvey Grant	.05	.02	.01
☐ 208	Bernard King	.05	.02	.01
☐ 209	Wes Unseld CO	.10	.05	.01
☐ 210	Kevin Johnson AS	.10	.05	.01
☐ 211	Michael Jordan AS	1.00	.45	.13
☐ 212	Dominique Wilkins AS	.10	.05	.01
☐ 213	Charles Barkley AS	.20	.09	.03
☐ 214	Hakeem Olajuwon AS	.30	.14	.04
☐ 215	Patrick Ewing AS	.15	.07	.02
☐ 216	Tim Hardaway AS	.10	.05	.01
☐ 217	John Stockton AS	.10	.05	.01
☐ 218	Chris Mullin AS	.10	.05	.01
☐ 219	Karl Malone AS	.10	.05	.01
☐ 220	Michael Jordan LL	1.00	.45	.13
☐ 221	John Stockton LL	.10	.05	.01
☐ 222	Alvin Robertson LL	.05	.02	.01
☐ 223	Hakeem Olajuwon LL	.30	.14	.04
☐ 224	Buck Williams LL	.05	.02	.01
☐ 225	David Robinson LL	.25	.11	.03
☐ 226	Reggie Miller LL	.10	.05	.01
☐ 227	Blue Edwards SD	.05	.02	.01
☐ 228	Dee Brown SD	.05	.02	.01
☐ 229	Rex Chapman SD	.05	.02	.01
☐ 230	Kenny Smith SD	.05	.02	.01
☐ 231	Shawn Kemp SD	.40	.18	.05
☐ 232	Kendall Gill SD	.08	.04	.01
☐ 233	'91 All Star Game	.05	.02	.01
	Enemies - A Love Story			
	(East Bench Scene)			
☐ 234	'91 All Star Game	.08	.04	.01
	A Game of Contrasts			
	(Drexler over McHale)			
☐ 235	'91 All Star Game	.05	.02	.01
	Showtime			
	(Alvin Robertson)			
☐ 236	'91 All Star Game	.10	.05	.01
	Unstoppable Force			
	vs. Unbeatable Man			
	(Ewing rejects K.Malone)			
☐ 237	'91 All Star Game	.05	.02	.01
	Just Me and the Boys			
	(Rebounding Scene)			
☐ 238	'91 All Star Game	.10	.05	.01
	Unforgettable			
	(Jordan reverse lay-in)			
☐ 239	Checklist 1-120	.05	.02	.01
☐ 240	Checklist 121-240	.05	.02	.01
☐ 241	Stacey Augmon	.40	.18	.05
☐ 242	Maurice Cheeks	.10	.05	.01
☐ 243	Paul Graham	.10	.05	.01
☐ 244	Rodney Monroe	.05	.02	.01
☐ 245	Blair Rasmussen	.05	.02	.01
☐ 246	Alexander Volkov	.05	.02	.01
☐ 247	John Bagley	.05	.02	.01
☐ 248	Rick Fox	.25	.11	.03
☐ 249	Rickey Green	.05	.02	.01
☐ 250	Joe Kleine	.05	.02	.01

☐	251 Stojko Vrankovic	.05	.02	.01
☐	252 Allan Bristow CO	.05	.02	.01
☐	253 Kenny Gattison	.05	.02	.01
☐	254 Mike Gminski	.05	.02	.01
☐	255 Larry Johnson	2.00	.90	.25
☐	256 Bobby Hansen	.05	.02	.01
☐	257 Craig Hodges	.05	.02	.01
☐	258 Stacey King	.15	.07	.02
☐	259 Scott Williams	.05	.02	.01
☐	260 John Battle	.05	.02	.01
☐	261 Winston Bennett	.15	.07	.02
☐	262 Terrell Brandon	.15	.07	.02
☐	263 Henry James	.05	.02	.01
☐	264 Steve Kerr	.05	.02	.01
☐	265 Jimmy Oliver	.05	.02	.01
☐	266 Brad Davis	.05	.02	.01
☐	267 Terry Davis	.05	.02	.01
☐	268 Donald Hodge	.05	.02	.01
☐	269 Mike Iuzzolino	.05	.02	.01
☐	270 Fat Lever	.05	.02	.01
☐	271 Doug Smith	.15	.07	.02
☐	272 Greg Anderson	.05	.02	.01
☐	273 Kevin Brooks	.05	.02	.01
☐	274 Walter Davis	.10	.05	.01
☐	275 Winston Garland	.05	.02	.01
☐	276 Mark Macon	.05	.02	.01
☐	277A Dikembe Mutombo (Fleer '91 on front)	.75	.35	.09
☐	277B Dikembe Mutombo (Fleer '91-92 on front)	.75	.35	.09
☐	278 William Bedford	.05	.02	.01
☐	279 Lance Blanks	.05	.02	.01
☐	280 John Salley	.05	.02	.01
☐	281 Charles Thomas	.05	.02	.01
☐	282 Darrell Walker	.05	.02	.01
☐	283 Orlando Woolridge	.08	.04	.01
☐	284 Victor Alexander	.15	.07	.02
☐	285 Vincent Askew	.05	.02	.01
☐	286 Mario Elie	.20	.09	.03
☐	287 Alton Lister	.05	.02	.01
☐	288 Billy Owens	.40	.18	.05
☐	289 Matt Bullard	.05	.02	.01
☐	290 Carl Herrera	.20	.09	.03
☐	291 Tree Rollins	.05	.02	.01
☐	292 John Turner	.05	.02	.01
☐	293 Dale Davis UER (Photo on back actually Sean Green)	.30	.14	.04
☐	294 Sean Green	.05	.02	.01
☐	295 Kenny Williams	.05	.02	.01
☐	296 James Edwards	.05	.02	.01
☐	297 LeRon Ellis	.10	.05	.01
☐	298 Doc Rivers	.08	.04	.01
☐	299 Loy Vaught	.08	.04	.01
☐	300 Elden Campbell	.05	.02	.01
☐	301 Jack Haley	.05	.02	.01
☐	302 Keith Owens	.05	.02	.01
☐	303 Tony Smith	.05	.02	.01
☐	304 Sedale Threatt	.05	.02	.01
☐	305 Keith Askins	.05	.02	.01
☐	306 Alec Kessler	.05	.02	.01
☐	307 John Morton	.05	.02	.01
☐	308 Alan Ogg	.05	.02	.01
☐	309 Steve Smith	.50	.23	.06
☐	310 Lester Conner	.05	.02	.01
☐	311 Jeff Grayer	.05	.02	.01
☐	312 Frank Hamblen CO	.05	.02	.01
☐	313 Steve Henson	.05	.02	.01
☐	314 Larry Krystkowiak	.05	.02	.01
☐	315 Moses Malone	.10	.05	.01
☐	316 Thurl Bailey	.05	.02	.01
☐	317 Randy Breuer	.05	.02	.01
☐	318 Scott Brooks	.05	.02	.01

☐ 319	Gerald Glass	.05	.02	.01
☐ 320	Luc Longley	.15	.07	.02
☐ 321	Doug West	.08	.04	.01
☐ 322	Kenny Anderson	.75	.35	.09
☐ 323	Tate George	.05	.02	.01
☐ 324	Terry Mills	.40	.18	.05
☐ 325	Greg Anthony	.15	.07	.02
☐ 326	Anthony Mason	.30	.14	.04
☐ 327	Tim McCormick	.05	.02	.01
☐ 328	Xavier McDaniel	.10	.05	.01
☐ 329	Brian Quinnett	.05	.02	.01
☐ 330	John Starks	.50	.23	.06
☐ 331	Stanley Roberts	.10	.05	.01
☐ 332	Jeff Turner	.05	.02	.01
☐ 333	Sam Vincent	.05	.02	.01
☐ 334	Brian Williams	.20	.09	.03
☐ 335	Manute Bol	.05	.02	.01
☐ 336	Kenny Payne	.05	.02	.01
☐ 337	Charles Shackleford	.05	.02	.01
☐ 338	Jayson Williams	.05	.02	.01
☐ 339	Cedric Ceballos	.10	.05	.01
☐ 340	Andrew Lang	.05	.02	.01
☐ 341	Jerrod Mustaf	.05	.02	.01
☐ 342	Tim Perry	.05	.02	.01
☐ 343	Kurt Rambis	.05	.02	.01
☐ 344	Alaa Abdelnaby	.08	.04	.01
☐ 345	Robert Pack	.05	.02	.01
☐ 346	Danny Young	.20	.09	.03
☐ 347	Anthony Bonner	.05	.02	.01
☐ 348	Pete Chilcutt	.05	.02	.01
☐ 349	Rex Hughes CO	.05	.02	.01
☐ 350	Mitch Richmond	.10	.05	.01
☐ 351	Dwayne Schintzius	.05	.02	.01
☐ 352	Spud Webb	.10	.05	.01
☐ 353	Antoine Carr	.05	.02	.01
☐ 354	Sidney Green	.05	.02	.01
☐ 355	Vinnie Johnson	.08	.04	.01
☐ 356	Greg Sutton	.05	.02	.01
☐ 357	Dana Barros	.05	.02	.01
☐ 358	Michael Cage	.05	.02	.01
☐ 359	Marty Conlon	.05	.02	.01
☐ 360	Rich King	.05	.02	.01
☐ 361	Nate McMillan	.08	.04	.01
☐ 362	David Benoit	.10	.05	.01
☐ 363	Mike Brown	.05	.02	.01
☐ 364	Tyrone Corbin	.05	.02	.01
☐ 365	Eric Murdock	.30	.14	.04
☐ 366	Delaney Rudd	.05	.02	.01
☐ 367	Michael Adams	.08	.04	.01
☐ 368	Tom Hammonds	.05	.02	.01
☐ 369	Larry Stewart	.10	.05	.01
☐ 370	Andre Turner	.05	.02	.01
☐ 371	David Wingate	.05	.02	.01
☐ 372	Dominique Wilkins TL Atlanta Hawks	.10	.05	.01
☐ 373	Larry Bird TL Boston Celtics	.30	.14	.04
☐ 374	Rex Chapman TL Charlotte Hornets	.05	.02	.01
☐ 375	Michael Jordan TL Chicago Bulls	1.00	.45	.13
☐ 376	Brad Daugherty TL Cleveland Cavaliers	.08	.04	.01
☐ 377	Derek Harper TL Dallas Mavericks	.08	.04	.01
☐ 378	Dikembe Mutombo TL Denver Nuggets	.25	.11	.03
☐ 379	Joe Dumars TL Detroit Pistons	.08	.04	.01
☐ 380	Chris Mullin TL Golden State Warriors	.10	.05	.01
☐ 381	Hakeem Olajuwon TL Houston Rockets	.30	.14	.04

		MINT	EXC	G-VG
☐ 382	Chuck Person TL	.05	.02	.01
	Indiana Pacers			
☐ 383	Charles Smith TL	.08	.04	.01
	Los Angeles Clippers			
☐ 384	James Worthy TL	.08	.04	.01
	Los Angeles Lakers			
☐ 385	Glen Rice TL	.10	.05	.01
	Miami Heat			
☐ 386	Alvin Robertson TL	.08	.04	.01
	Milwaukee Bucks			
☐ 387	Tony Campbell TL	.05	.02	.01
	Minnesota Timberwolves			
☐ 388	Derrick Coleman TL	.15	.07	.02
	New Jersey Nets			
☐ 389	Patrick Ewing TL	.15	.07	.02
	New York Knicks			
☐ 390	Scott Skiles TL	.05	.02	.01
	Orlando Magic			
☐ 391	Charles Barkley TL	.20	.09	.03
	Philadelphia 76ers			
☐ 392	Kevin Johnson TL	.10	.05	.01
	Phoenix Suns			
☐ 393	Clyde Drexler TL	.10	.05	.01
	Portland Trail Blazers			
☐ 394	Lionel Simmons TL	.05	.02	.01
	Sacramento Kings			
☐ 395	David Robinson TL	.25	.11	.03
	San Antonio Spurs			
☐ 396	Ricky Pierce TL	.05	.02	.01
	Seattle Supersonics			
☐ 397	John Stockton TL	.10	.05	.01
	Utah Jazz			
☐ 398	Michael Adams TL	.05	.02	.01
	Washington Bullets			
☐ 399	Checklist	.05	.02	.01
☐ 400	Checklist	.05	.02	.01

1991-92 Fleer Pro Visions

This six-card set measures the standard size (2 1/2" by 3 1/2") and showcases outstanding NBA players. The set was distributed as a random insert in 1991-92 Fleer first series 12-card plastic-wrap packs at a rate of approximately one per six packs. The fronts feature a color player portrait by sports artist Terry Smith. The portrait is bordered on all sides by white, with the player's name in red lettering below the picture. The backs present biographical information and career summary in black lettering on a color background (with white borders). The cards are numbered on the back.

	MINT	EXC	G-VG
COMPLETE SET (6)	4.00	1.80	.50
COMMON PLAYER (1-6)	.50	.23	.06

		MINT	EXC	G-VG
☐ 1	David Robinson San Antonio Spurs	1.00	.45	.13
☐ 2	Michael Jordan Chicago Bulls	3.00	1.35	.40
☐ 3	Charles Barkley Philadelphia 76ers	.75	.35	.09
☐ 4	Patrick Ewing New York Knicks	.50	.23	.06
☐ 5	Karl Malone Utah Jazz	.40	.18	.05
☐ 6	Magic Johnson Los Angeles Lakers	.75	.35	.09

1991-92 Fleer Rookie Sensations

This ten-card set showcases outstanding rookies from the 1990-91 season and measures the standard size (2 1/2" by 3 1/2"). The set was distributed as a random insert in 1991-92 Fleer 23-card cello packs at a rate of approximately one per one to two packs. The card fronts feature a color player photo inside a basketball rim and net. The picture is bordered in magenta on all sides. The words "Rookie Sensations" appear above the picture, and player information is given below the picture. An orange basketball with the words "Fleer '91" appears in the upper left corner on both sides of the card. The back has a magenta border and includes highlights of the player's rookie season. The cards are numbered on the back.

		MINT	EXC	G-VG
COMPLETE SET (10)		15.00	6.75	1.90
COMMON PLAYER (1-10)		.50	.23	.06
☐ 1	Lionel Simmons	1.50	.65	.19
☐ 2	Dennis Scott	.75	.35	.09
☐ 3	Derrick Coleman	6.00	2.70	.75
☐ 4	Kendall Gill	2.00	.90	.25
☐ 5	Travis Mays	.50	.23	.06
☐ 6	Felton Spencer	.50	.23	.06
☐ 7	Willie Burton	.50	.23	.06
☐ 8	Chris Jackson	2.50	1.15	.30
☐ 9	Gary Payton	3.00	1.35	.40
☐ 10	Dee Brown	1.50	.65	.19

1991-92 Fleer Schoolyard

This six-card set of "Schoolyard Stars" measures the standard size (2 1/2" by 3 1/2"). The set was distributed only in 1991-92 Fleer 36-card rack packs at a rate of one per pack. The card front features color action player photos. The photos are bordered on the left and bot-

tom by a black stripe and a broken pink stripe. Yellow stripes traverse the card top and bottom, and the background is a gray cement-colored design. The back has a similar layout
and presents a basketball tip in black lettering on white. The cards are numbered on the
back.

	MINT	EXC	G-VG
COMPLETE SET (6)...	8.00	3.60	1.00
COMMON PLAYER (1-6)..	.75	.35	.09
☐ 1 Chris Mullin..	1.50	.65	.19
Golden State Warriors			
☐ 2 Isiah Thomas..	1.50	.65	.19
Detroit Pistons			
☐ 3 Kevin McHale..	1.00	.45	.13
Boston Celtics			
☐ 4 Kevin Johnson...	1.50	.65	.19
Phoenix Suns			
☐ 5 Karl Malone..	3.00	1.35	.40
Utah Jazz			
☐ 6 Alvin Robertson...	.75	.35	.09
Milwaukee Bucks			

1991-92 Fleer Dikembe Mutombo

This 12-card subset was randomly inserted in 1991-92 Fleer second series 12-card wax
packs at a rate of approximately one per six packs. The cards measure the standard size (2
1/2" by 3 1/2"). The front borders are dark red and checkered with miniature black NBA
logos. The background of the color action photo is ghosted so that the featured player
stands out, and the color of the lettering on the front is mustard. On a pink background, the

back has a color close-up photo and a summary of the player's performance. The cards are numbered on the back. Mutombo autographed over 2,000 of these cards.

	MINT	EXC	G-VG
COMPLETE SET (12)	5.00	2.30	.60
COMMON MUTOMBO (1-12)	.50	.23	.06
☐ 1 Dikembe Mutombo	.50	.23	.06
Childhood in Zaire			
☐ 2 Dikembe Mutombo	.50	.23	.06
Georgetown Start			
☐ 3 Dikembe Mutombo	.50	.23	.06
Arrival on			
college scene			
☐ 4 Dikembe Mutombo	.50	.23	.06
Capping college career			
☐ 5 Dikembe Mutombo	.50	.23	.06
NBA Draft			
☐ 6 Dikembe Mutombo	.50	.23	.06
First NBA games			
☐ 7 Dikembe Mutombo	.50	.23	.06
Offensive skills			
☐ 8 Dikembe Mutombo	.50	.23	.06
What he has meant			
to the Nuggets			
☐ 9 Dikembe Mutombo	.50	.23	.06
Work Habits			
☐ 10 Dikembe Mutombo	.50	.23	.06
Charmed Denver			
☐ 11 Dikembe Mutombo	.50	.23	.06
The Future			
☐ 12 Dikembe Mutombo	.50	.23	.06
The Mutombo Legend			
☐ AU Dikembe Mutombo	80.00	36.00	10.00
(Certified autograph)			

1991-92 Fleer Dominique Wilkins

Cards from this 12-card subset were randomly inserted in 1991-92 Fleer second series 12-card wax packs at a rate of approximately one per six wax packs. The cards measure the standard size (2 1/2" by 3 1/2"). The front borders are dark red and checkered with miniature black NBA logos. The background of the color action photo is ghosted so that the featured player stands out, and the color of the lettering on the front is mustard. On a pink background, the back has a color close-up photo and a summary of the player's performance. The cards are numbered on the back. Wilkins personally autographed over 2,000 of these cards.

	MINT	EXC	G-VG
COMPLETE SET (12)..	5.00	2.30	.60
COMMON D.WILKINS (1-12)................................	.50	.23	.06
☐ 1 Dominique Wilkins .... Overview	.50	.23	.06
☐ 2 Dominique Wilkins .... College	.50	.23	.06
☐ 3 Dominique Wilkins .... Early years	.50	.23	.06
☐ 4 Dominique Wilkins .... Early Career	.50	.23	.06
☐ 5 Dominique Wilkins .... Dominique Emerges	.50	.23	.06
☐ 6 Dominique Wilkins .... Another milestone	.50	.23	.06
☐ 7 Dominique Wilkins .... Wilkins continues to shine	.50	.23	.06
☐ 8 Dominique Wilkins .... Best all-round season	.50	.23	.06
☐ 9 Dominique Wilkins .... Charitable Causes	.50	.23	.06
☐ 10 Dominique Wilkins .... Durability	.50	.23	.06
☐ 11 Dominique Wilkins .... Career Numbers	.50	.23	.06
☐ 12 Dominique Wilkins .... Future	.50	.23	.06
☐ AU Dominique Wilkins .... (Certified autograph)	100.00	45.00	12.50

1992-93 Fleer

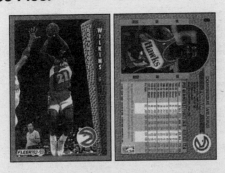

The complete 1992-93 Fleer basketball set contains 444 standard-size (2 1/2" by 3 1/2") cards. The set was distributed in two series of 264 and 180 cards, respectively. First series cards were distributed in 17-card plastic-wrap packs, 32-card cello packs, and 42-card rack packs. Second series cards were distributed in 15-card plastic-wrap packs and 32-card cello packs. The fronts display color action player photos, enclosed by metallic bronze borders and accented on the right by two pebble-grain colored stripes. On a tan pebble-grain background, the horizontally oriented backs have a color close-up photo in the shape of the lane under the basket. Biography, career statistics, and player profile are included on the back. The cards are numbered on the back and checklisted below alphabetically according to teams as follows: Atlanta Hawks (1-9), Boston Celtics (10-19), Charlotte Hornets (20-27), Chicago Bulls (28-37), Cleveland Cavaliers (38-46), Dallas Mavericks (47-53), Denver Nuggets (54-61), Detroit Pistons (62-71), Golden State Warriors (72-79), Houston Rockets (80-87), Indiana Pacers (88-96), Los Angeles Clippers (97-105), Los Angeles Lakers (106-114), Miami Heat (115-123), Milwaukee Bucks (124-130), Minnesota Timberwolves (131-139), New Jersey Nets (140-147), New York Knicks (148-157), Orlando Magic (158-165),

Philadelphia 76ers (166-176), Phoenix Suns (177-184), Portland Trail Blazers (185-193), Sacramento Kings (194-200), San Antonio Spurs (201-208), Seattle Supersonics (209-217), Utah Jazz (218-227), and Washington Bullets (228-237), League Leaders (238-245), Award Winners (246-249), Pro-Visions (250-255), Schoolyard Stars (256-264), Slam Dunk (265-300), Atlanta Hawks (301-304), Boston Celtics (305-307), Charlotte Hornets (308-312), Chicago Bulls (313-316), Cleveland Cavaliers (317-320), Dallas Mavericks (321-326), Denver Nuggets (327-332), Detroit Pistons (333-337), Golden State Warriors (338-343), Houston Rockets (344-348), Indiana Pacers (349-354), Los Angeles Clippers (355-361), Los Angeles Lakers (362-365), Miami Heat (366-370), Milwaukee Bucks (371-377), Minnesota Timberwolves (378-384), New Jersey Nets (385-391), New York Knicks (392-398), Orlando Magic (399-403), Philadelphia 76ers (404-409), Phoenix Suns (410-414), Portland Trail Blazers (415-420), Sacramento Kings (421-424), San Antonio Spurs (425-429), Seattle Supersonics (430-431), Utah Jazz (432-436), and Washington Bullets (437-442). The Slam Dunk subset is divided into five categories: Power, Grace, Champions, Little Big Men, and Great Defenders. Randomly inserted throughout the packs were more than 3,000 (Slam Dunk) cards signed by former NBA players Darryl Dawkins and Kenny Walker as well as by current NBA star Shawn Kemp. According to Fleer's advertising material, odds of finding a signed slam dunk card are one in 5,000 packs. Rookie Cards include Laphonso Ellis, Tom Gugliotta, Robert Horry, Christian Laettner, Don McLean, Harold Miner, Alonzo Mourning, Shaquille O'Neal, Latrell Sprewell, Clarence Weatherspoon and Walt Williams. Larry Johnson is spotlighted on a 12-card signature series, and he autographed more than 2,000 of these cards, which were randomly inserted in all first series packs. Collectors were also able to receive three additional Johnson cards and the premiere edition of NBA Inside Stuff magazine by sending in ten wrappers and 1.00 in a mail-in offer. A second series mail-in offer featuring an "All-Star Slam Dunk Team" card and an issue of Inside Stuff was available (expiring 6/30/93) in return for ten second series wrappers plus a dollar.

	MINT	EXC	G-VG
COMPLETE SET (444)	30.00	13.50	3.80
COMPLETE SERIES 1 (264)	10.00	4.50	1.25
COMPLETE SERIES 2 (180)	20.00	9.00	2.50
COMMON PLAYER (1-264)	.05	.02	.01
COMMON PLAYER (265-444)	.05	.02	.01
☐ 1 Stacey Augmon	.10	.05	.01
☐ 2 Duane Ferrell	.05	.02	.01
☐ 3 Paul Graham	.05	.02	.01
☐ 4A Jon Koncak	.08	.04	.01
(Shooting pose on back)			
☐ 4B Jon Koncak	.08	.04	.01
(No ball visible in photo on back)			
☐ 5 Blair Rasmussen	.05	.02	.01
☐ 6 Rumeal Robinson	.05	.02	.01
☐ 7 Bob Weiss CO	.05	.02	.01
☐ 8 Dominique Wilkins	.30	.14	.04
☐ 9 Kevin Willis	.08	.04	.01
☐ 10 John Bagley	.05	.02	.01
☐ 11 Larry Bird	.75	.35	.09
☐ 12 Dee Brown	.05	.02	.01
☐ 13 Chris Ford CO	.05	.02	.01
☐ 14 Rick Fox	.08	.04	.01
☐ 15 Kevin Gamble	.05	.02	.01
☐ 16 Reggie Lewis	.10	.05	.01
☐ 17 Kevin McHale	.10	.05	.01
☐ 18 Robert Parish	.10	.05	.01
☐ 19 Ed Pinckney	.05	.02	.01
☐ 20 Muggsy Bogues	.10	.05	.01
☐ 21 Allan Bristow CO	.05	.02	.01
☐ 22 Dell Curry	.08	.04	.01
☐ 23 Kenny Gattison	.05	.02	.01
☐ 24 Kendall Gill	.08	.04	.01
☐ 25 Larry Johnson	.50	.23	.06
☐ 26 Johnny Newman	.05	.02	.01
☐ 27 J.R. Reid	.10	.05	.01
☐ 28 B.J. Armstrong	.05	.02	.01
☐ 29 Bill Cartwright	.08	.04	.01
☐ 30 Horace Grant	.10	.05	.01
☐ 31 Phil Jackson CO	.08	.04	.01
☐ 32 Michael Jordan	2.00	.90	.25
☐ 33 Stacey King	.05	.02	.01
☐ 34 Cliff Levingston	.05	.02	.01
☐ 35 John Paxson	.08	.04	.01

☐ 36	Scottie Pippen	.40	.18	.05
☐ 37	Scott Williams	.05	.02	.01
☐ 38	John Battle	.05	.02	.01
☐ 39	Terrell Brandon	.05	.02	.01
☐ 40	Brad Daugherty	.10	.05	.01
☐ 41	Craig Ehlo	.05	.02	.01
☐ 42	Larry Nance	.08	.04	.01
☐ 43	Mark Price	.10	.05	.01
☐ 44	Mike Sanders	.05	.02	.01
☐ 45	Lenny Wilkens CO	.08	.04	.01
☐ 46	Hot Rod Williams	.08	.04	.01
☐ 47	Richie Adubato CO	.05	.02	.01
☐ 48	Terry Davis	.05	.02	.01
☐ 49	Derek Harper	.08	.04	.01
☐ 50	Donald Hodge	.05	.02	.01
☐ 51	Mike Iuzzolino	.05	.02	.01
☐ 52	Rodney McCray	.05	.02	.01
☐ 53	Doug Smith	.05	.02	.01
☐ 54	Greg Anderson	.05	.02	.01
☐ 55	Winston Garland	.05	.02	.01
☐ 56	Dan Issel CO	.08	.04	.01
☐ 57	Chris Jackson	.08	.04	.01
☐ 58	Marcus Liberty	.08	.04	.01
☐ 59	Mark Macon	.05	.02	.01
☐ 60	Dikembe Mutombo	.20	.09	.03
☐ 61	Reggie Williams	.08	.04	.01
☐ 62	Mark Aguirre	.10	.05	.01
☐ 63	Joe Dumars	.15	.07	.02
☐ 64	Bill Laimbeer	.10	.05	.01
☐ 65	Olden Polynice	.05	.02	.01
☐ 66	Dennis Rodman	.08	.04	.01
☐ 67	Ron Rothstein CO	.05	.02	.01
☐ 68	John Salley	.05	.02	.01
☐ 69	Isiah Thomas	.15	.07	.02
☐ 70	Darrell Walker	.05	.02	.01
☐ 71	Orlando Woolridge	.08	.04	.01
☐ 72	Victor Alexander	.05	.02	.01
☐ 73	Mario Elie	.05	.02	.01
☐ 74	Tim Hardaway	.10	.05	.01
☐ 75	Tyrone Hill	.05	.02	.01
☐ 76	Sarunas Marciulionis	.08	.04	.01
☐ 77	Chris Mullin	.15	.07	.02
☐ 78	Don Nelson CO	.08	.04	.01
☐ 79	Billy Owens	.10	.05	.01
☐ 80	Sleepy Floyd UER	.05	.02	.01
	(Went past 4000 assist mark, not 2000)			
☐ 81	Avery Johnson	.05	.02	.01
☐ 82	Buck Johnson	.05	.02	.01
☐ 83	Vernon Maxwell	.08	.04	.01
☐ 84	Hakeem Olajuwon	.75	.35	.09
☐ 85	Kenny Smith	.05	.02	.01
☐ 86	Otis Thorpe	.08	.04	.01
☐ 87	Rudy Tomjanovich CO	.05	.02	.01
☐ 88	Dale Davis	.08	.04	.01
☐ 89	Vern Fleming	.05	.02	.01
☐ 90	Bob Hill CO	.05	.02	.01
☐ 91	Reggie Miller	.20	.09	.03
☐ 92	Chuck Person	.08	.04	.01
☐ 93	Detlef Schrempf	.10	.05	.01
☐ 94	Rik Smits	.08	.04	.01
☐ 95	LaSalle Thompson	.08	.04	.01
☐ 96	Micheal Williams	.08	.04	.01
☐ 97	Larry Brown CO	.08	.04	.01
☐ 98	James Edwards	.05	.02	.01
☐ 99	Gary Grant	.05	.02	.01
☐ 100	Ron Harper	.08	.04	.01
☐ 101	Danny Manning	.15	.07	.02
☐ 102	Ken Norman	.05	.02	.01
☐ 103	Doc Rivers	.08	.04	.01
☐ 104	Charles Smith	.05	.02	.01
☐ 105	Loy Vaught	.08	.04	.01
☐ 106	Elden Campbell	.05	.02	.01

☐ 107	Vlade Divac	.08	.04	.01
☐ 108	A.C. Green	.08	.04	.01
☐ 109	Sam Perkins	.08	.04	.01
☐ 110	Randy Pfund CO	.05	.02	.01
☐ 111	Byron Scott	.08	.04	.01
☐ 112	Terry Teagle	.05	.02	.01
☐ 113	Sedale Threatt	.05	.02	.01
☐ 114	James Worthy	.10	.05	.01
☐ 115	Willie Burton	.05	.02	.01
☐ 116	Bimbo Coles	.08	.04	.01
☐ 117	Kevin Edwards	.05	.02	.01
☐ 118	Grant Long	.05	.02	.01
☐ 119	Kevin Loughery CO	.05	.02	.01
☐ 120	Glen Rice	.10	.05	.01
☐ 121	Rony Seikaly	.10	.05	.01
☐ 122	Brian Shaw	.05	.02	.01
☐ 123	Steve Smith	.15	.07	.02
☐ 124	Frank Brickowski	.08	.04	.01
☐ 125	Mike Dunleavy CO	.05	.02	.01
☐ 126	Blue Edwards	.08	.04	.01
☐ 127	Moses Malone	.10	.05	.01
☐ 128	Eric Murdock	.08	.04	.01
☐ 129	Fred Roberts	.05	.02	.01
☐ 130	Alvin Robertson	.08	.04	.01
☐ 131	Thurl Bailey	.05	.02	.01
☐ 132	Tony Campbell	.05	.02	.01
☐ 133	Gerald Glass	.05	.02	.01
☐ 134	Luc Longley	.05	.02	.01
☐ 135	Sam Mitchell	.05	.02	.01
☐ 136	Pooh Richardson	.05	.02	.01
☐ 137	Jimmy Rodgers CO	.05	.02	.01
☐ 138	Felton Spencer	.05	.02	.01
☐ 139	Doug West	.05	.02	.01
☐ 140	Kenny Anderson	.20	.09	.03
☐ 141	Mookie Blaylock	.08	.04	.01
☐ 142	Sam Bowie	.05	.02	.01
☐ 143	Derrick Coleman	.20	.09	.03
☐ 144	Chuck Daly CO	.08	.04	.01
☐ 145	Terry Mills	.10	.05	.01
☐ 146	Chris Morris	.05	.02	.01
☐ 147	Drazen Petrovic	.08	.04	.01
☐ 148	Greg Anthony	.05	.02	.01
☐ 149	Rolando Blackman	.08	.04	.01
☐ 150	Patrick Ewing	.40	.18	.05
☐ 151	Mark Jackson	.08	.04	.01
☐ 152	Anthony Mason	.08	.04	.01
☐ 153	Xavier McDaniel	.08	.04	.01
☐ 154	Charles Oakley	.10	.05	.01
☐ 155	Pat Riley CO	.08	.04	.01
☐ 156	John Starks	.10	.05	.01
☐ 157	Gerald Wilkins	.05	.02	.01
☐ 158	Nick Anderson	.08	.04	.01
☐ 159	Anthony Bowie	.05	.02	.01
☐ 160	Terry Catledge	.05	.02	.01
☐ 161	Matt Guokas CO	.05	.02	.01
☐ 162	Stanley Roberts	.05	.02	.01
☐ 163	Dennis Scott	.08	.04	.01
☐ 164	Scott Skiles	.08	.04	.01
☐ 165	Brian Williams	.05	.02	.01
☐ 166	Ron Anderson	.05	.02	.01
☐ 167	Manute Bol	.05	.02	.01
☐ 168	Johnny Dawkins	.05	.02	.01
☐ 169	Armon Gilliam	.05	.02	.01
☐ 170	Hersey Hawkins	.08	.04	.01
☐ 171	Jeff Hornacek	.08	.04	.01
☐ 172	Andrew Lang	.05	.02	.01
☐ 173	Doug Moe CO	.05	.02	.01
☐ 174	Tim Perry	.05	.02	.01
☐ 175	Jeff Ruland	.08	.04	.01
☐ 176	Charles Shackleford	.05	.02	.01
☐ 177	Danny Ainge	.10	.05	.01
☐ 178	Charles Barkley	.50	.23	.06
☐ 179	Cedric Ceballos	.10	.05	.01

☐ 180	Tom Chambers	.08	.04	.01
☐ 181	Kevin Johnson	.10	.05	.01
☐ 182	Dan Majerle	.10	.05	.01
☐ 183	Mark West UER	.05	.02	.01
	(Needs 33 blocks to			
	reach 1000, not 31)			
☐ 184	Paul Westphal CO	.05	.02	.01
☐ 185	Rick Adelman CO	.08	.04	.01
☐ 186	Clyde Drexler	.20	.09	.03
☐ 187	Kevin Duckworth	.05	.02	.01
☐ 188	Jerome Kersey	.05	.02	.01
☐ 189	Robert Pack	.08	.04	.01
☐ 190	Terry Porter	.10	.05	.01
☐ 191	Cliff Robinson	.08	.04	.01
☐ 192	Rod Strickland	.10	.05	.01
☐ 193	Buck Williams	.05	.02	.01
☐ 194	Anthony Bonner	.05	.02	.01
☐ 195	Duane Causwell	.05	.02	.01
☐ 196	Mitch Richmond	.10	.05	.01
☐ 197	Garry St. Jean CO	.05	.02	.01
☐ 198	Lionel Simmons	.08	.04	.01
☐ 199	Wayman Tisdale	.08	.04	.01
☐ 200	Spud Webb	.10	.05	.01
☐ 201	Willie Anderson	.05	.02	.01
☐ 202	Antoine Carr	.05	.02	.01
☐ 203	Terry Cummings	.08	.04	.01
☐ 204	Sean Elliott	.08	.04	.01
☐ 205	Dale Ellis	.08	.04	.01
☐ 206	Vinnie Johnson	.08	.04	.01
☐ 207	David Robinson	.50	.23	.06
☐ 208	Jerry Tarkanian CO	.20	.09	.03
☐ 209	Benoit Benjamin	.05	.02	.01
☐ 210	Michael Cage	.05	.02	.01
☐ 211	Eddie Johnson	.05	.02	.01
☐ 212	George Karl CO	.75	.35	.09
☐ 213	Shawn Kemp	.75	.35	.09
☐ 214	Derrick McKey	.05	.02	.01
☐ 215	Nate McMillan	.05	.02	.01
☐ 216	Gary Payton	.10	.05	.01
☐ 217	Ricky Pierce	.08	.04	.01
☐ 218	David Benoit	.05	.02	.01
☐ 219	Mike Brown	.05	.02	.01
☐ 220	Tyrone Corbin	.05	.02	.01
☐ 221	Mark Eaton	.05	.02	.01
☐ 222	Jay Humphries	.05	.02	.01
☐ 223	Larry Krystkowiak	.05	.02	.01
☐ 224	Jeff Malone	.08	.04	.01
☐ 225	Karl Malone	.25	.11	.03
☐ 226	Jerry Sloan CO	.05	.02	.01
☐ 227	John Stockton	.20	.09	.03
☐ 228	Michael Adams	.08	.04	.01
☐ 229	Rex Chapman	.05	.02	.01
☐ 230	Ledell Eackles	.05	.02	.01
☐ 231	Pervis Ellison	.05	.02	.01
☐ 232	A.J. English	.05	.02	.01
☐ 233	Harvey Grant	.05	.02	.01
☐ 234	LaBradford Smith	.05	.02	.01
☐ 235	Larry Stewart	.05	.02	.01
☐ 236	Wes Unseld CO	.08	.04	.01
☐ 237	David Wingate	.05	.02	.01
☐ 238	Michael Jordan LL	1.00	.45	.13
	Scoring			
☐ 239	Dennis Rodman LL	.05	.02	.01
	Rebounding			
☐ 240	John Stockton LL	.10	.05	.01
	Assists/Steals			
☐ 241	Buck Williams LL	.05	.02	.01
	Field Goal Percentage			
☐ 242	Mark Price LL	.08	.04	.01
	Free Throw Percentage			
☐ 243	Dana Barros LL	.05	.02	.01
	Three Point Percentage			
☐ 244	David Robinson LL	.25	.11	.03

☐ 289	Dennis Rodman SD	.05	.02	.01
	Detroit Pistons			
☐ 290	Blue Edwards SD	.05	.02	.01
☐ 291	Patrick Ewing SD	.20	.09	.03
	New York Knicks			
☐ 292	Larry Johnson SD	.25	.11	.03
	Charlotte Hornets			
☐ 293	Jerome Kersey SD	.05	.02	.01
	Portland Trail Blazers			
☐ 294	Hakeem Olajuwon SD	.40	.18	.05
	Houston Rockets			
☐ 295	Stacey Augmon SD	.08	.04	.01
	Atlanta Hawks			
☐ 296	Derrick Coleman SD	.10	.05	.01
	New Jersey Nets			
☐ 297	Kendall Gill SD	.05	.02	.01
	Charlotte Hornets			
☐ 298	Shaquille O'Neal SD	2.00	.90	.25
	Orlando Magic			
☐ 299	Scottie Pippen SD	.20	.09	.03
	Chicago Bulls			
☐ 300	Darryl Dawkins SD	.08	.04	.01
	Philadelphia 76ers			
☐ 301	Mookie Blaylock	.08	.04	.01
☐ 302	Adam Keefe	.10	.05	.01
☐ 303	Travis Mays	.05	.02	.01
☐ 304	Morlon Wiley	.05	.02	.01
☐ 305	Sherman Douglas	.05	.02	.01
☐ 306	Joe Kleine	.05	.02	.01
☐ 307	Xavier McDaniel	.08	.04	.01
☐ 308	Tony Bennett	.10	.02	.01
☐ 309	Tom Hammonds	.05	.02	.01
☐ 310	Kevin Lynch	.05	.02	.01
☐ 311	Alonzo Mourning	3.00	1.35	.40
☐ 312	David Wingate	.05	.02	.01
☐ 313	Rodney McCray	.05	.02	.01
☐ 314	Will Perdue	.05	.02	.01
☐ 315	Trent Tucker	.05	.02	.01
☐ 316	Corey Williams	.05	.02	.01
☐ 317	Danny Ferry	.05	.02	.01
☐ 318	Jay Guidinger	.05	.02	.01
☐ 319	Jerome Lane	.05	.02	.01
☐ 320	Gerald Wilkins	.05	.02	.01
☐ 321	Stephen Bardo	.05	.02	.01
☐ 322	Walter Bond	.05	.02	.01
☐ 323	Brian Howard	.05	.02	.01
☐ 324	Tracy Moore	.05	.02	.01
☐ 325	Sean Rooks	.15	.07	.02
☐ 326	Randy White	.05	.02	.01
☐ 327	Kevin Brooks	.05	.02	.01
☐ 328	LaPhonso Ellis	.75	.35	.09
☐ 329	Scott Hastings	.05	.02	.01
☐ 330	Todd Lichti	.05	.02	.01
☐ 331	Robert Pack	.05	.02	.01
☐ 332	Bryant Stith	.40	.18	.05
☐ 333	Gerald Glass	.05	.02	.01
☐ 334	Terry Mills	.10	.05	.01
☐ 335	Isaiah Morris	.05	.02	.01
☐ 336	Mark Randall	.05	.02	.01
☐ 337	Danny Young	.05	.02	.01
☐ 338	Chris Gatling	.05	.02	.01
☐ 339	Jeff Grayer	.05	.02	.01
☐ 340	Byron Houston	.10	.05	.01
☐ 341	Keith Jennings	.10	.05	.01
☐ 342	Alton Lister	.05	.02	.01
☐ 343	Latrell Sprewell	2.00	.90	.25
☐ 344	Scott Brooks	.05	.02	.01
☐ 345	Matt Bullard	.05	.02	.01
☐ 346	Carl Herrera	.05	.02	.01
☐ 347	Robert Horry	.75	.35	.09
☐ 348	Tree Rollins	.05	.02	.01
☐ 349	Greg Dreiling	.05	.02	.01
☐ 350	George McCloud	.05	.02	.01

☐	351	Sam Mitchell	.05	.02	.01
☐	352	Pooh Richardson	.05	.02	.01
☐	353	Malik Sealy	.10	.05	.01
☐	354	Kenny Williams	.05	.02	.01
☐	355	Jaren Jackson	.05	.02	.01
☐	356	Mark Jackson	.08	.04	.01
☐	357	Stanley Roberts	.05	.02	.01
☐	358	Elmore Spencer	.15	.07	.02
☐	359	Kiki Vandeweghe	.08	.04	.01
☐	360	John S. Williams	.05	.02	.01
☐	361	Randy Woods	.05	.02	.01
☐	362	Duane Cooper	.05	.02	.01
☐	363	James Edwards	.05	.02	.01
☐	364	Anthony Peeler	.30	.14	.04
☐	365	Tony Smith	.05	.02	.01
☐	366	Keith Askins	.05	.02	.01
☐	367	Matt Geiger	.15	.07	.02
☐	368	Alec Kessler	.05	.02	.01
☐	369	Harold Miner	.40	.18	.05
☐	370	John Salley	.05	.02	.01
☐	371	Anthony Avent	.10	.05	.01
☐	372	Todd Day	.40	.18	.05
☐	373	Blue Edwards	.08	.04	.01
☐	374	Brad Lohaus	.05	.02	.01
☐	375	Lee Mayberry	.10	.05	.01
☐	376	Eric Murdock	.08	.04	.01
☐	377	Dan Schayes	.05	.02	.01
☐	378	Lance Blanks	.05	.02	.01
☐	379	Christian Laettner	.75	.35	.09
☐	380	Bob McCann	.05	.02	.01
☐	381	Chuck Person	.08	.04	.01
☐	382	Brad Sellers	.05	.02	.01
☐	383	Chris Smith	.10	.05	.01
☐	384	Micheal Williams	.08	.04	.01
☐	385	Rafael Addison	.05	.02	.01
☐	386	Chucky Brown	.05	.02	.01
☐	387	Chris Dudley	.05	.02	.01
☐	388	Tate George	.05	.02	.01
☐	389	Rick Mahorn	.08	.04	.01
☐	390	Rumeal Robinson	.05	.02	.01
☐	391	Jayson Williams	.05	.02	.01
☐	392	Eric Anderson	.05	.02	.01
☐	393	Rolando Blackman	.08	.04	.01
☐	394	Tony Campbell	.05	.02	.01
☐	395	Hubert Davis	.40	.18	.05
☐	396	Doc Rivers	.08	.04	.01
☐	397	Charles Smith	.05	.02	.01
☐	398	Herb Williams	.05	.02	.01
☐	399	Litterial Green	.10	.05	.01
☐	400	Greg Kite	.05	.02	.01
☐	401	Shaquille O'Neal	6.00	2.70	.75
☐	402	Jerry Reynolds	.05	.02	.01
☐	403	Jeff Turner	.05	.02	.01
☐	404	Greg Grant	.05	.02	.01
☐	405	Jeff Hornacek	.08	.04	.01
☐	406	Andrew Lang	.05	.02	.01
☐	407	Kenny Payne	.05	.02	.01
☐	408	Tim Perry	.05	.02	.01
☐	409	Clarence Weatherspoon	.75	.35	.09
☐	410	Danny Ainge	.10	.05	.01
☐	411	Charles Barkley	.50	.23	.06
☐	412	Negele Knight	.05	.02	.01
☐	413	Oliver Miller	.40	.18	.05
☐	414	Jerrod Mustaf	.05	.02	.01
☐	415	Mark Bryant	.05	.02	.01
☐	416	Mario Elie	.05	.02	.01
☐	417	Dave Johnson	.05	.02	.01
☐	418	Tracy Murray	.10	.05	.01
☐	419	Reggie Smith	.05	.02	.01
☐	420	Rod Strickland	.08	.04	.01
☐	421	Randy Brown	.05	.02	.01
☐	422	Pete Chilcutt	.05	.02	.01
☐	423	Jim Les	.05	.02	.01

			MINT	EXC	G-VG
☐	424	Walt Williams	.40	.18	.05
☐	425	Lloyd Daniels	.10	.05	.01
☐	426	Vinny Del Negro	.05	.02	.01
☐	427	Dale Ellis	.08	.04	.01
☐	428	Sidney Green	.05	.02	.01
☐	429	Avery Johnson	.05	.02	.01
☐	430	Dana Barros	.05	.02	.01
☐	431	Rich King	.05	.02	.01
☐	432	Isaac Austin	.05	.02	.01
☐	433	John Crotty	.05	.02	.01
☐	434	Stephen Howard	.05	.02	.01
☐	435	Jay Humphries	.05	.02	.01
☐	436	Larry Krystkowiak	.05	.02	.09
☐	437	Tom Gugliotta	.75	.35	.09
☐	438	Buck Johnson	.05	.02	.01
☐	439	Charles Jones	.05	.02	.01
☐	440	Don MacLean	.50	.23	.06
☐	441	Doug Overton	.05	.02	.01
☐	442	Brent Price	.10	.05	.01
☐	443	Checklist 1	.05	.02	.01
☐	444	Checklist 2	.05	.02	.01
☐	SD266	Shawn Kemp AU	200.00	90.00	25.00
		(Certified Autograph)			
☐	SD277	Darrell Walker AU	15.00	6.75	1.90
		(Certified Autograph)			
☐	SD300	Darryl Dawkins AU	40.00	18.00	5.00
		(Certified Autograph)			

1992-93 Fleer All-Stars

These 24 1992-93 Fleer All-Star cards were randomly inserted exclusively into first series plastic-wrap 17-card packs and feature outstanding players from the Eastern (1-12) and Western (13-24) Conference. According to Fleer's advertising materials, the odds of pulling an All-Star insert are approximately one per nine packs. The cards measure the standard size (2 1/2" by 3 1/2"). The horizontal fronts display two color images of the featured player against a gradated silver-blue background. The cards are bordered by a darker silver-blue, and the player's name is gold-foil stamped at the lower right corner. The Orlando All-Star Weekend logo is in the upper right and the team logo in the lower left corner. The backs are white with silver-blue borders and present career highlights, the player's name, and the Orlando All-Star Weekend logo. The cards are numbered on the back.

	MINT	EXC	G-VG
COMPLETE SET (24)	40.00	18.00	5.00
COMMON PLAYER (1-24)	.75	.35	.09
☐ 1 Michael Adams	.75	.35	.09
Washington Bullets			
☐ 2 Charles Barkley	6.00	2.70	.75
Phoenix Suns			
☐ 3 Brad Daugherty	.90	.40	.11
Cleveland Cavaliers			

☐ 4	Joe Dumars	1.25	.55	.16
	Detroit Pistons			
☐ 5	Patrick Ewing	4.00	1.80	.50
	New York Knicks			
☐ 6	Michael Jordan	20.00	9.00	2.50
	Chicago Bulls			
☐ 7	Reggie Lewis	1.00	.45	.13
	Boston Celtics			
☐ 8	Scottie Pippen	4.00	1.80	.50
	Chicago Bulls			
☐ 9	Mark Price	1.00	.45	.13
	Cleveland Cavaliers			
☐ 10	Dennis Rodman	.75	.35	.09
	Detroit Pistons			
☐ 11	Isiah Thomas	1.25	.55	.16
	Detroit Pistons			
☐ 12	Kevin Willis	.90	.40	.11
	Atlanta Hawks			
☐ 13	Clyde Drexler	1.50	.65	.19
	Portland Trail Blazers			
☐ 14	Tim Hardaway	1.00	.45	.13
	Golden State Warriors			
☐ 15	Jeff Hornacek	.75	.35	.09
	Philadelphia 76ers			
☐ 16	Dan Majerle	1.00	.45	.13
	Phoenix Suns			
☐ 17	Karl Malone	2.50	1.15	.30
	Utah Jazz			
☐ 18	Chris Mullin	1.25	.55	.16
	Golden State Warriors			
☐ 19	Dikembe Mutombo	2.00	.90	.25
	Denver Nuggets			
☐ 20	Hakeem Olajuwon	7.00	3.10	.85
	Houston Rockets			
☐ 21	David Robinson	6.00	2.70	.75
	San Antonio Spurs			
☐ 22	John Stockton	1.50	.65	.19
	Utah Jazz			
☐ 23	Otis Thorpe	.90	.40	.11
	Houston Rockets			
☐ 24	James Worthy	.90	.40	.11
	Los Angeles Lakers			

1992-93 Fleer Larry Johnson

Larry Johnson, the 1991-92 NBA Rookie of the Year, is featured in this 15-card signature series. The first 12 cards were available as random inserts in all forms of Fleer's first series packaging. According to information printed on the wrappers the odds of pulling a Larry Johnson insert from a 17-card pack were one in 18, from a 32-card cello pack were one in 13, and from a 42-card rack pack were one in six. In addition, Larry personally autographed more than 2,000 of these cards, which were randomly inserted in the wax packs. According to Fleer's advertising materials, the odds of finding a signed Larry Johnson were approxi-

mately one in 15,000 packs. Collectors were also able to receive three additional Johnson cards and the premiere edition of *NBA Inside Stuff* magazine by sending in ten wrappers and 1.00 in a mail-in offer expiring 6/30/93. These standard-size (2 1/2" by 3 1/2") cards feature color player photos framed by thin orange and blue borders on a silver-blue card face. The player's name and the words "NBA Rookie of the Year" are gold foil-stamped at the top. The backs feature an orange panel that summarizes Johnson's game and demeanor. His name and "NBA Rookie of the Year" appear at the top in a lighter orange. The cards are numbered on the back.

	MINT	EXC	G-VG
COMPLETE SET (12)	10.00	4.50	1.25
COMMON L.JOHNSON (1-12)	1.00	.45	.13
COMMON SEND-OFF (13-15)	5.00	2.30	.60
☐ 1 Larry Johnson (Holding up Hornets' home jersey)	1.00	.45	.13
☐ 2 Larry Johnson (Driving through traffic against Knicks)	1.00	.45	.13
☐ 3 Larry Johnson (Turned to the side, holding ball over head)	1.00	.45	.13
☐ 4 Larry Johnson (Shooting jumpshot)	1.00	.45	.13
☐ 5 Larry Johnson (Smiling, holding ball at chest level)	1.00	.45	.13
☐ 6 Larry Johnson (Dribbling into a no-look pass)	1.00	.45	.13
☐ 7 Larry Johnson (Posting up down low)	1.00	.45	.13
☐ 8 Larry Johnson (Shooting ball in lane)	1.00	.45	.13
☐ 9 Larry Johnson (Going for tip-in in home jersey)	1.00	.45	.13
☐ 10 Larry Johnson (In warm-up suit)	1.00	.45	.13
☐ 11 Larry Johnson (High-fiving during pre-game introductions)	1.00	.45	.13
☐ 12 Larry Johnson (Dribbling with his left hand)	1.00	.45	.13
☐ 13 Larry Johnson	5.00	2.30	.60
☐ 14 Larry Johnson	5.00	2.30	.60
☐ 15 Larry Johnson	5.00	2.30	.60
☐ AU Larry Johnson AU (Certified autograph)	150.00	70.00	19.00

1992-93 Fleer Rookie Sensations

Randomly inserted in first series 32-card cello packs, this 12-card set measures the standard size (2 1/2" by 3 1/2") and features the player in action against a computer-generated team emblem on a gradated purple background. The odds of pulling a Rookie Sensation is reportedly approximately one per five packs. The words "Rookie Sensations" and the player's name are gold foil-stamped at the bottom. The backs display career highlights on a mint-green face with a purple border. The cards are numbered on the back.

	MINT	EXC	G-VG
COMPLETE SET (12)	50.00	23.00	6.25
COMMON PLAYER (1-12)	2.00	.90	.25
☐ 1 Greg Anthony New York Knicks	2.00	.90	.25
☐ 2 Stacey Augmon Atlanta Hawks	6.00	2.70	.75
☐ 3 Terrell Brandon Cleveland Cavaliers	2.00	.90	.25
☐ 4 Rick Fox	3.00	1.35	.40

Rookie Sensations
STACEY AUGMON

	Boston Celtics			
☐ 5	Larry Johnson	30.00	13.50	3.80
	Charlotte Hornets			
☐ 6	Mark Macon	2.00	.90	.25
	Denver Nuggets			
☐ 7	Dikembe Mutombo	12.00	5.50	1.50
	Denver Nuggets			
☐ 8	Billy Owens	6.00	2.70	.75
	Golden State Warriors			
☐ 9	Stanley Roberts	3.00	1.35	.40
	Orlando Magic			
☐ 10	Doug Smith	3.00	1.35	.40
	Dallas Mavericks			
☐ 11	Steve Smith	8.00	3.60	1.00
	Miami Heat			
☐ 12	Larry Stewart	3.00	1.35	.40
	Washington Bullets			

1992-93 Fleer Sharpshooters

Randomly inserted in second series 15-card plastic-wrap packs, these 18 standard-size (2 1/2" by 3 1/2") cards feature some of the NBA's best shooters. According to Fleer's advertising materials, the odds of finding a Sharpshooter card are approximately one per three to five packs. The color action photos on the fronts are odd-shaped, overlaying a purple geometric shape and resting on a silver card face. The "Sharp Shooter" logo is gold-foil stamped at the upper left corner, while the player's name is gold-foil stamped below the picture. On a wheat-colored panel inside blue borders, the backs present a player profile. The cards are numbered on the back.

	MINT	EXC	G-VG
COMPLETE SET (18)	8.00	3.60	1.00
COMMON PLAYER (1-18)	.40	.18	.05

☐ 1 Reggie Miller	1.00	.45	.13
Indiana Pacers			
☐ 2 Dana Barros	.40	.18	.05
Seattle Supersonics			
☐ 3 Jeff Hornacek	.50	.23	.06
Philadelphia 76ers			
☐ 4 Drazen Petrovic	.50	.23	.06
New Jersey Nets			
☐ 5 Glen Rice	.60	.25	.08
Miami Heat			
☐ 6 Terry Porter	.50	.23	.06
Portland Trail Blazers			
☐ 7 Mark Price	.60	.25	.08
Cleveland Cavaliers			
☐ 8 Michael Adams	.50	.23	.06
Washington Bullets			
☐ 9 Hersey Hawkins	.50	.23	.06
Philadelphia 76ers			
☐ 10 Chuck Person	.50	.23	.06
Minnesota Timberwolves			
☐ 11 John Stockton	1.00	.45	.13
Utah Jazz			
☐ 12 Dale Ellis	.50	.23	.06
San Antonio Spurs			
☐ 13 Clyde Drexler	1.00	.45	.13
Portland Trail Blazers			
☐ 14 Mitch Richmond	.60	.25	.08
Golden State Warriors			
☐ 15 Craig Ehlo	.40	.18	.05
Cleveland Cavaliers			
☐ 16 Dell Curry	.40	.18	.05
Charlotte Hornets			
☐ 17 Chris Mullin	.75	.35	.09
Golden State Warriors			
☐ 18 Rolando Blackman	.50	.23	.06
New York Knicks			

1992-93 Fleer Team Leaders

The 1992-93 Fleer Team Leaders were inserted into five of every six first series 42-card rack packs. A Larry Johnson insert card was available one per six rack packs. These 27 standard size (2 1/2" by 3 1/2") cards feature a key member of each NBA team. The color action photos on the front are surrounded by thick dark blue borders, covered by a slick UV coating and stamped with gold foil printing. The full-color card backs include a player head shot accompanied by written text summarizing the player's career. The cards are numbered on the back in alphabetical order by team.

	MINT	EXC	G-VG
COMPLETE SET (27)	600.00	275.00	75.00
COMMON PLAYER (1-27)	8.00	3.60	1.00
☐ 1 Dominique Wilkins	35.00	16.00	4.40
Atlanta Hawks			
☐ 2 Reggie Lewis	10.00	4.50	1.25
Boston Celtics			
☐ 3 Larry Johnson	60.00	27.00	7.50
Charlotte Hornets			
☐ 4 Michael Jordan	250.00	115.00	31.00
Chicago Bulls			
☐ 5 Mark Price	10.00	4.50	1.25
Cleveland Cavaliers			
☐ 6 Terry Davis	8.00	3.60	1.00
Dallas Mavericks			
☐ 7 Dikembe Mutombo	25.00	11.50	3.10
Denver Nuggets			
☐ 8 Isiah Thomas	15.00	6.75	1.90
Detroit Pistons			
☐ 9 Chris Mullin	15.00	6.75	1.90
Golden State Warriors			
☐ 10 Hakeem Olajuwon	85.00	38.00	10.50
Houston Rockets			

		MINT	EXC	G-VG
☐ 11	Reggie Miller Indiana Pacers	20.00	9.00	2.50
☐ 12	Danny Manning Los Angeles Clippers	15.00	6.75	1.90
☐ 13	James Worthy Los Angeles Lakers	10.00	4.50	1.25
☐ 14	Glen Rice Miami Heat	10.00	4.50	1.25
☐ 15	Alvin Robertson Milwaukee Bucks	8.00	3.60	1.00
☐ 16	Tony Campbell Minnesota Timberwolves	8.00	3.60	1.00
☐ 17	Derrick Coleman New Jersey Nets	20.00	9.00	2.50
☐ 18	Patrick Ewing New York Knicks	50.00	23.00	6.25
☐ 19	Scott Skiles Orlando Magic	8.00	3.60	1.00
☐ 20	Hersey Hawkins Philadelphia 76ers	9.00	4.00	1.15
☐ 21	Kevin Johnson Phoenix Suns	15.00	6.75	1.90
☐ 22	Clyde Drexler Portland Trail Blazers	20.00	9.00	2.50
☐ 23	Mitch Richmond Sacramento Kings	10.00	4.50	1.25
☐ 24	David Robinson San Antonio Spurs	60.00	27.00	7.50
☐ 25	Ricky Pierce Seattle Supersonics	8.00	3.60	1.00
☐ 26	Karl Malone Utah Jazz	30.00	13.50	3.80
☐ 27	Pervis Ellison Washington Bullets	8.00	3.60	1.00

1992-93 Fleer Total D

The 1992-93 Fleer Total D cards were randomly inserted into second series 32-card cello packs. According to Fleer's advertising materials, the odds of pulling a Total D card were approximately one per five packs. These 15 standard size (2 1/2" by 3 1/2") cards feature some of the NBA's top defensive players. Card fronts feature colorized players against a black border, covered with a slick UV coating and gold stamped lettering. The full-color card backs feature small player head shots accompanied by text describing the player's defensive abilities. The cards are numbered on the back.

		MINT	EXC	G-VG
COMPLETE SET (15)		225.00	100.00	28.00
COMMON PLAYER (1-15)		5.00	2.30	.60
☐ 1	David Robinson San Antonio Spurs	30.00	13.50	3.80

☐ 2 Dennis Rodman	6.00	2.70	.75
Detroit Pistons			
☐ 3 Scottie Pippen	25.00	11.50	3.10
Chicago Bulls			
☐ 4 Joe Dumars	8.00	3.60	1.00
Detroit Pistons			
☐ 5 Michael Jordan	125.00	57.50	15.50
Chicago Bulls			
☐ 6 John Stockton	10.00	4.50	1.25
Utah Jazz			
☐ 7 Patrick Ewing	25.00	11.50	3.10
New York Knicks			
☐ 8 Micheal Williams	5.00	2.30	.60
Minnesota Timberwolves			
☐ 9 Larry Nance	6.00	2.70	.75
Cleveland Cavaliers			
☐ 10 Buck Williams	6.00	2.70	.75
Portland Trail Blazers			
☐ 11 Alvin Robertson	5.00	2.30	.60
Milwaukee Bucks			
☐ 12 Dikembe Mutombo	12.00	5.50	1.50
Denver Nuggets			
☐ 13 Mookie Blaylock	5.00	2.30	.60
Atlanta Hawks			
☐ 14 Hakeem Olajuwon	45.00	20.00	5.75
Houston Rockets			
☐ 15 Rony Seikaly	6.00	2.70	.75
Miami Heat			

1993-94 Fleer

The 1993-94 Fleer basketball card set contains 400 cards measuring the standard size (2 1/2" by 3 1/2"). The fronts are UV-coated and feature color action player photos and are enclosed by white borders. The player's name appears in the lower left and is superimposed over a colorful florescent background. The backs feature full-color printing and bold graphics combining the player's picture, name, and complete statistics. With the exception of card numbers 131, 174, and 216, the cards are numbered and checklisted below alphabetically within and according to teams as follows: Atlanta Hawks (1-8), Boston Celtics (9-16), Charlotte Hornets (17-24), Chicago Bulls (25-33), Cleveland Cavaliers (34-42), Dallas Mavericks (43-49), Denver Nuggets (50-57), Detroit Pistons (58-65), Golden State Warriors (66-73), Houston Rockets (74-81), Indiana Pacers (82-89), Los Angeles Clippers (90-97), Los Angeles Lakers (98-105), Miami Heat (106-113), Milwaukee Bucks (114-121), Minnesota Timberwolves (122-128), New Jersey Nets (129-136), New York Knicks (137-146), Orlando Magic (147-154), Philadelphia 76ers (155-161), Phoenix Suns (162-171), Portland Trail Blazers (172-180), Sacramento Kings (181-187), San Antonio Spurs (188-196), Seattle Supersonics (197-204), Utah Jazz (205-212), Washington Bullets (213-220), NBA League Leaders (221-228), NBA Award Winners (229-232), Pro-Visions (223-237), and checklists (238-240). Players traded since the first series are pictured with their new team in a 160-card second series (241-400) offering. Rookie Cards include Vin Baker, Shawn Bradley, Sam Cassell, Calbert Cheaney, Anfernee Hardaway, Lindsey Hunter, Bobby Hurley, Toni Kukoc, Jamal Mashburn, Dino Rajda, Isaiah Rider, Nick Van Exel and Chris Webber.

	MINT	EXC	G-VG
COMPLETE SET (400)	20.00	9.00	2.50
COMPLETE SERIES 1 (240)	10.00	4.50	1.25
COMPLETE SERIES 2 (160)	10.00	4.50	1.25
COMMON PLAYER (1-240)	.05	.02	.01
COMMON PLAYER (241-400)	.05	.02	.01
☐ 1 Stacey Augmon	.10	.05	.01
☐ 2 Mookie Blaylock	.08	.04	.01
☐ 3 Duane Ferrell	.05	.02	.01
☐ 4 Paul Graham	.05	.02	.01
☐ 5 Adam Keefe	.05	.02	.01
☐ 6 Jon Koncak	.05	.02	.01
☐ 7 Dominique Wilkins	.25	.11	.03
☐ 8 Kevin Willis	.08	.04	.01
☐ 9 Alaa Abdelnaby	.05	.02	.01
☐ 10 Dee Brown	.05	.02	.01
☐ 11 Sherman Douglas	.05	.02	.01
☐ 12 Rick Fox	.05	.02	.01
☐ 13 Kevin Gamble	.05	.02	.01
☐ 14 Reggie Lewis	.10	.05	.01
☐ 15 Xavier McDaniel	.08	.04	.01
☐ 16 Robert Parish	.10	.05	.01
☐ 17 Muggsy Bogues	.10	.05	.01
☐ 18 Dell Curry	.08	.04	.01
☐ 19 Kenny Gattison	.05	.02	.01
☐ 20 Kendall Gill	.08	.04	.01
☐ 21 Larry Johnson	.25	.11	.03
☐ 22 Alonzo Mourning	.50	.23	.06
☐ 23 Johnny Newman	.05	.02	.01
☐ 24 David Wingate	.05	.02	.01
☐ 25 B.J. Armstrong	.10	.05	.01
☐ 26 Bill Cartwright	.08	.04	.01
☐ 27 Horace Grant	.10	.05	.01
☐ 28 Michael Jordan	2.00	.90	.25
☐ 29 Stacey King	.05	.02	.01
☐ 30 John Paxson	.08	.04	.01
☐ 31 Will Perdue	.05	.02	.01
☐ 32 Scottie Pippen	.30	.14	.04
☐ 33 Scott Williams	.05	.02	.01
☐ 34 Terrell Brandon	.05	.02	.01
☐ 35 Brad Daugherty	.10	.05	.01
☐ 36 Craig Ehlo	.05	.02	.01
☐ 37 Danny Ferry	.05	.02	.01
☐ 38 Larry Nance	.08	.04	.01
☐ 39 Mark Price	.10	.05	.01
☐ 40 Mike Sanders	.05	.02	.01
☐ 41 Gerald Wilkins	.05	.02	.01
☐ 42 John(Hot Rod) Williams	.08	.04	.01
☐ 43 Terry Davis	.05	.02	.01
☐ 44 Derek Harper	.08	.04	.01
☐ 45 Mike Iuzzolino	.05	.02	.01

☐	46	Jim Jackson	.25	.11	.03
☐	47	Sean Rooks	.05	.02	.01
☐	48	Doug Smith	.05	.02	.01
☐	49	Randy White	.05	.02	.01
☐	50	Mahmoud Abdul-Rauf	.05	.02	.01
☐	51	LaPhonso Ellis	.10	.05	.01
☐	52	Marcus Liberty	.05	.02	.01
☐	53	Mark Macon	.05	.02	.01
☐	54	Dikembe Mutombo	.10	.05	.01
☐	55	Robert Pack	.05	.02	.01
☐	56	Bryant Stith	.08	.04	.01
☐	57	Reggie Williams	.05	.02	.01
☐	58	Mark Aguirre	.10	.05	.01
☐	59	Joe Dumars	.15	.07	.02
☐	60	Bill Laimbeer	.10	.05	.01
☐	61	Terry Mills	.05	.02	.01
☐	62	Olden Polynice	.08	.04	.01
☐	63	Alvin Robertson	.08	.04	.01
☐	64	Dennis Rodman	.15	.07	.02
☐	65	Isiah Thomas	.15	.07	.02
☐	66	Victor Alexander	.05	.02	.01
☐	67	Tim Hardaway	.10	.05	.01
☐	68	Tyrone Hill	.05	.02	.01
☐	69	Byron Houston	.05	.02	.01
☐	70	Sarunas Marciulionis	.08	.04	.01
☐	71	Chris Mullin	.15	.07	.02
☐	72	Billy Owens	.08	.04	.01
☐	73	Latrell Sprewell	.40	.18	.05
☐	74	Scott Brooks	.05	.02	.01
☐	75	Matt Bullard	.05	.02	.01
☐	76	Carl Herrera	.05	.02	.01
☐	77	Robert Horry	.10	.05	.01
☐	78	Vernon Maxwell	.08	.04	.01
☐	79	Hakeem Olajuwon	.75	.35	.09
☐	80	Kenny Smith	.05	.02	.01
☐	81	Otis Thorpe	.08	.04	.01
☐	82	Dale Davis	.08	.04	.01
☐	83	Vern Fleming	.05	.02	.01
☐	84	George McCloud	.05	.02	.01
☐	85	Reggie Miller	.15	.07	.02
☐	86	Sam Mitchell	.05	.02	.01
☐	87	Pooh Richardson	.05	.02	.01
☐	88	Detlef Schrempf	.10	.05	.01
☐	89	Rik Smits	.08	.04	.01
☐	90	Gary Grant	.05	.02	.01
☐	91	Ron Harper	.08	.04	.01
☐	92	Mark Jackson	.08	.04	.01
☐	93	Danny Manning	.10	.05	.01
☐	94	Ken Norman	.05	.02	.01
☐	95	Stanley Roberts	.05	.02	.01
☐	96	Loy Vaught	.08	.04	.01
☐	97	John Williams	.05	.02	.01
☐	98	Elden Campbell	.05	.02	.01
☐	99	Doug Christie	.08	.04	.01
☐	100	Duane Cooper	.05	.02	.01
☐	101	Vlade Divac	.08	.04	.01
☐	102	A.C. Green	.08	.04	.01
☐	103	Anthony Peeler	.08	.04	.01
☐	104	Sedale Threatt	.05	.02	.01
☐	105	James Worthy	.10	.05	.01
☐	106	Bimbo Coles	.05	.02	.01
☐	107	Grant Long	.05	.02	.01
☐	108	Harold Miner	.08	.04	.01
☐	109	Glen Rice	.10	.05	.01
☐	110	John Salley	.05	.02	.01
☐	111	Rony Seikaly	.10	.05	.01
☐	112	Brian Shaw	.05	.02	.01
☐	113	Steve Smith	.08	.04	.01
☐	114	Anthony Avent	.05	.02	.01
☐	115	Jon Barry	.08	.04	.01
☐	116	Frank Brickowski	.08	.04	.01
☐	117	Todd Day	.08	.04	.01
☐	118	Blue Edwards	.05	.02	.01

☐ 119 Brad Lohaus	.05	.02	.01
☐ 120 Lee Mayberry	.05	.02	.01
☐ 121 Eric Murdock	.08	.04	.01
☐ 122 Thurl Bailey	.05	.02	.01
☐ 123 Christian Laettner	.08	.04	.01
☐ 124 Luc Longley	.05	.02	.01
☐ 125 Chuck Person	.08	.04	.01
☐ 126 Felton Spencer	.05	.02	.01
☐ 127 Doug West	.05	.02	.01
☐ 128 Micheal Williams	.08	.04	.01
☐ 129 Rafael Addison	.05	.02	.01
☐ 130 Kenny Anderson	.15	.07	.02
☐ 131 Sam Bowie	.05	.02	.01
☐ 132 Chucky Brown	.05	.02	.01
☐ 133 Derrick Coleman	.20	.09	.03
☐ 134 Chris Dudley	.05	.02	.01
☐ 135 Chris Morris	.05	.02	.01
☐ 136 Rumeal Robinson	.05	.02	.01
☐ 137 Greg Anthony	.05	.02	.01
☐ 138 Rolando Blackman	.08	.04	.01
☐ 139 Tony Campbell	.05	.02	.01
☐ 140 Hubert Davis	.05	.02	.01
☐ 141 Patrick Ewing	.30	.14	.04
☐ 142 Anthony Mason	.05	.02	.01
☐ 143 Charles Oakley	.10	.05	.01
☐ 144 Doc Rivers	.08	.04	.01
☐ 145 Charles Smith	.05	.02	.01
☐ 146 John Starks	.10	.05	.01
☐ 147 Nick Anderson	.08	.04	.01
☐ 148 Anthony Bowie	.05	.02	.01
☐ 149 Shaquille O'Neal	1.50	.65	.19
☐ 150 Donald Royal	.05	.02	.01
☐ 151 Dennis Scott	.08	.04	.01
☐ 152 Scott Skiles	.05	.02	.01
☐ 153 Tom Tolbert	.05	.02	.01
☐ 154 Jeff Turner	.05	.02	.01
☐ 155 Ron Anderson	.05	.02	.01
☐ 156 Johnny Dawkins	.05	.02	.01
☐ 157 Hersey Hawkins	.08	.04	.01
☐ 158 Jeff Hornacek	.08	.04	.01
☐ 159 Andrew Lang	.05	.02	.01
☐ 160 Tim Perry	.05	.02	.01
☐ 161 Clarence Weatherspoon	.10	.05	.01
☐ 162 Danny Ainge	.10	.05	.01
☐ 163 Charles Barkley	.40	.18	.05
☐ 164 Cedric Ceballos	.10	.05	.01
☐ 165 Tom Chambers	.08	.04	.01
☐ 166 Richard Dumas	.08	.04	.01
☐ 167 Kevin Johnson	.10	.05	.01
☐ 168 Negele Knight	.05	.02	.01
☐ 169 Dan Majerle	.10	.05	.01
☐ 170 Oliver Miller	.10	.05	.01
☐ 171 Mark West	.05	.02	.01
☐ 172 Mark Bryant	.05	.02	.01
☐ 173 Clyde Drexler	.20	.09	.03
☐ 174 Kevin Duckworth	.05	.02	.01
☐ 175 Mario Elie	.05	.02	.01
☐ 176 Jerome Kersey	.05	.02	.01
☐ 177 Terry Porter	.08	.04	.01
☐ 178 Cliff Robinson	.10	.05	.01
☐ 179 Rod Strickland	.08	.04	.01
☐ 180 Buck Williams	.10	.05	.01
☐ 181 Anthony Bonner	.05	.02	.01
☐ 182 Duane Causwell	.05	.02	.01
☐ 183 Mitch Richmond	.10	.05	.01
☐ 184 Lionel Simmons	.08	.04	.01
☐ 185 Wayman Tisdale	.08	.04	.01
☐ 186 Spud Webb	.10	.05	.01
☐ 187 Walt Williams	.08	.04	.01
☐ 188 Antoine Carr	.05	.02	.01
☐ 189 Terry Cummings	.08	.04	.01
☐ 190 Lloyd Daniels	.05	.02	.01
☐ 191 Vinny Del Negro	.05	.02	.01

☐ 192	Sean Elliott	.08	.04	.01
☐ 193	Dale Ellis	.08	.04	.01
☐ 194	Avery Johnson	.05	.02	.01
☐ 195	J.R. Reid	.05	.02	.01
☐ 196	David Robinson	.40	.18	.05
☐ 197	Michael Cage	.05	.02	.01
☐ 198	Eddie Johnson	.05	.02	.01
☐ 199	Shawn Kemp	.30	.14	.04
☐ 200	Derrick McKey	.05	.02	.01
☐ 201	Nate McMillan	.05	.02	.01
☐ 202	Gary Payton	.10	.05	.01
☐ 203	Sam Perkins	.08	.04	.01
☐ 204	Ricky Pierce	.08	.04	.01
☐ 205	David Benoit	.05	.02	.01
☐ 206	Tyrone Corbin	.05	.02	.01
☐ 207	Mark Eaton	.05	.02	.01
☐ 208	Jay Humphries	.05	.02	.01
☐ 209	Larry Krystkowiak	.05	.02	.01
☐ 210	Jeff Malone	.08	.04	.01
☐ 211	Karl Malone	.25	.11	.03
☐ 212	John Stockton	.15	.07	.02
☐ 213	Michael Adams	.08	.04	.01
☐ 214	Rex Chapman	.05	.02	.01
☐ 215	Pervis Ellison	.05	.02	.01
☐ 216	Harvey Grant	.05	.02	.01
☐ 217	Tom Gugliotta	.08	.04	.01
☐ 218	Buck Johnson	.05	.02	.01
☐ 219	LaBradford Smith	.05	.02	.01
☐ 220	Larry Stewart	.05	.02	.01
☐ 221	B.J. Armstrong LL Chicago Bulls 3-Pt Field Goal Percentage Leader	.10	.05	.01
☐ 222	Cedric Ceballos LL Phoenix Suns FG Percentage Leader	.08	.04	.01
☐ 223	Larry Johnson LL Charlotte Hornets Minutes Played Leader	.12	.05	.02
☐ 224	Michael Jordan LL Chicago Bulls Scoring/Steals Leader	1.00	.45	.13
☐ 225	Hakeem Olajuwon LL Houston Rockets Shot Block Leader	.40	.18	.05
☐ 226	Mark Price LL Cleveland Cavaliers FT Percentage Leader	.08	.04	.01
☐ 227	Dennis Rodman LL Detroit Pistons Rebounding Leader	.05	.02	.01
☐ 228	John Stockton LL Utah Jazz Assists Leader	.10	.05	.01
☐ 229	Charles Barkley AW Phoenix Suns Most Valuable Player	.20	.09	.03
☐ 230	Hakeem Olajuwon AW Houston Rockets Defensive POY	.40	.18	.05
☐ 231	Shaquille O'Neal AW Orlando Magic Rookie of the Year	.75	.35	.09
☐ 232	Cliff Robinson AW Portland Trail Blazers Sixth Man Award	.08	.04	.01
☐ 233	Shawn Kemp PV Seattle Supersonics	.15	.07	.02
☐ 234	Alonzo Mourning PV Charlotte Hornets	.25	.11	.03
☐ 235	Hakeem Olajuwon PV Houston Rockets	.40	.18	.05
☐ 236	John Stockton PV	.10	.05	.01

	Utah Jazz			
☐ 237	Dominique Wilkins PV	.12	.05	.02
	Atlanta Hawks			
☐ 238	Checklist 1-85	.05	.02	.01
☐ 239	Checklist 86-165	.05	.02	.01
☐ 240	Checklist 166-240 UER	.05	.02	.01
	(237 listed as Cliff Robinson;			
	should be Dominique Wilkins)			
☐ 241	Doug Edwards	.10	.05	.01
☐ 242	Craig Ehlo	.05	.02	.01
☐ 243	Andrew Lang	.05	.02	.01
☐ 244	Ennis Whatley	.05	.02	.01
☐ 245	Chris Corchiani	.05	.02	.01
☐ 246	Acie Earl	.10	.05	.01
☐ 247	Jimmy Oliver	.05	.02	.01
☐ 248	Ed Pinckney	.05	.02	.01
☐ 249	Dino Radja	.40	.18	.05
☐ 250	Matt Wenstrom	.10	.05	.01
☐ 251	Tony Bennett	.05	.02	.01
☐ 252	Scott Burrell	.15	.07	.02
☐ 253	LeRon Ellis	.05	.02	.01
☐ 254	Hersey Hawkins	.08	.04	.01
☐ 255	Eddie Johnson	.05	.02	.01
☐ 256	Corie Blount	.10	.05	.01
☐ 257	Jo Jo English	.10	.05	.01
☐ 258	Dave Johnson	.10	.05	.01
☐ 259	Steve Kerr	.05	.02	.01
☐ 260	Toni Kukoc	.40	.18	.05
☐ 261	Pete Myers	.05	.02	.01
☐ 262	Bill Wennington	.05	.02	.01
☐ 263	John Battle	.05	.02	.01
☐ 264	Tyrone Hill	.05	.02	.01
☐ 265	Gerald Madkins	.05	.02	.01
☐ 266	Chris Mills	.10	.05	.01
☐ 267	Bobby Phills	.25	.11	.03
☐ 268	Greg Dreiling	.05	.02	.01
☐ 269	Lucious Harris	.10	.05	.01
☐ 270	Donald Hodge	.05	.02	.01
☐ 271	Popeye Jones	.15	.07	.02
☐ 272	Tim Legler	.10	.05	.01
☐ 273	Fat Lever	.05	.02	.01
☐ 274	Jamal Mashburn	1.00	.45	.13
☐ 275	Darren Morningstar	.10	.05	.01
☐ 276	Tom Hammonds	.05	.02	.01
☐ 277	Darnell Mee	.10	.05	.01
☐ 278	Rodney Rogers	.25	.11	.03
☐ 279	Brian Williams	.05	.02	.01
☐ 280	Greg Anderson	.05	.02	.01
☐ 281	Sean Elliott	.05	.02	.01
☐ 282	Allan Houston	.08	.04	.01
☐ 283	Lindsey Hunter	.15	.07	.02
☐ 284	Marcus Liberty	.40	.18	.05
☐ 285	Mark Macon	.05	.02	.01
☐ 286	David Wood	.05	.02	.01
☐ 287	Jud Buechler	.05	.02	.01
☐ 288	Chris Gatling	.05	.02	.01
☐ 289	Josh Grant	.10	.05	.01
☐ 290	Jeff Grayer	.05	.02	.01
☐ 291	Avery Johnson	.05	.02	.01
☐ 292	Chris Webber	2.50	1.15	.30
☐ 293	Sam Cassell	.50	.23	.06
☐ 294	Mario Elie	.05	.02	.01
☐ 295	Richard Petruska	.10	.05	.01
☐ 296	Eric Riley	.10	.05	.01
☐ 297	Antonio Davis	.25	.11	.03
☐ 298	Scott Haskin	.10	.05	.01
☐ 299	Derrick McKey	.05	.02	.01
☐ 300	Byron Scott	.08	.04	.01
☐ 301	Malik Sealy	.05	.02	.01
☐ 302	LaSalle Thompson	.08	.04	.01
☐ 303	Kenny Williams	.05	.02	.01
☐ 304	Haywoode Workman	.05	.02	.01
☐ 305	Mark Aguirre	.10	.05	.01

☐ 306 Terry Dehere	.10	.05	.01
☐ 307 Bob Martin	.10	.05	.01
☐ 308 Elmore Spencer	.05	.02	.01
☐ 309 Tom Tolbert	.05	.02	.01
☐ 310 Randy Woods	.05	.02	.01
☐ 311 Sam Bowie	.05	.02	.01
☐ 312 James Edwards	.10	.05	.01
☐ 313 Antonio Harvey	.25	.11	.03
☐ 314 George Lynch	.05	.02	.01
☐ 315 Tony Smith	.40	.18	.05
☐ 316 Nick Van Exel	.05	.02	.01
☐ 317 Manute Bol	.05	.02	.01
☐ 318 Willie Burton	.05	.02	.01
☐ 319 Matt Geiger	.05	.02	.01
☐ 320 Alec Kessler	.60	.25	.08
☐ 321 Vin Baker	.05	.02	.01
☐ 322 Ken Norman	.05	.02	.01
☐ 323 Dan Schayes	.10	.05	.01
☐ 324 Derek Strong	.05	.02	.01
☐ 325 Mike Brown	.10	.05	.01
☐ 326 Brian Davis	.05	.02	.01
☐ 327 Tellis Frank	.05	.02	.01
☐ 328 Marlon Maxey	1.00	.45	.13
☐ 329 Isaiah Rider	.05	.02	.01
☐ 330 Chris Smith	.05	.02	.01
☐ 331 Benoit Benjamin	.15	.07	.02
☐ 332 P.J. Brown	.05	.02	.01
☐ 333 Kevin Edwards	.05	.02	.01
☐ 334 Armon Gilliam	.05	.02	.01
☐ 335 Rick Mahorn	.05	.02	.01
☐ 336 Dwayne Schintzius	.10	.05	.01
☐ 337 Rex Walters	.10	.05	.01
☐ 338 David Wesley	.05	.02	.01
☐ 339 Jayson Williams	.05	.02	.01
☐ 340 Anthony Bonner	.05	.02	.01
☐ 341 Herb Williams	.05	.02	.01
☐ 342 Litterial Green	2.00	.90	.25
☐ 343 Anfernee Hardaway	.05	.02	.01
☐ 344 Greg Kite	.05	.02	.01
☐ 345 Larry Krystkowiak	.05	.02	.01
☐ 346 Todd Lichti	.10	.05	.01
☐ 347 Keith Tower	.05	.02	.01
☐ 348 Dana Barros	.40	.18	.05
☐ 349 Shawn Bradley	.10	.05	.01
☐ 350 Michael Curry	.10	.05	.01
☐ 351 Greg Graham	.10	.05	.01
☐ 352 Warren Kidd	.10	.05	.01
☐ 353 Moses Malone	.08	.04	.01
☐ 354 Orlando Woolridge	.05	.02	.01
☐ 355 Duane Cooper	.10	.05	.01
☐ 356 Joe Courtney	.08	.04	.01
☐ 357 A.C. Green	.05	.02	.01
☐ 358 Frank Johnson	.05	.02	.01
☐ 359 Joe Kleine	.10	.05	.01
☐ 360 Malcolm Mackey	.05	.02	.01
☐ 361 Jerrod Mustaf	.05	.02	.01
☐ 362 Chris Dudley	.05	.02	.01
☐ 363 Harvey Grant	.05	.02	.01
☐ 364 Tracy Murray	.15	.07	.02
☐ 365 James Robinson	.05	.02	.01
☐ 366 Reggie Smith	.10	.05	.01
☐ 367 Kevin Thompson	.05	.02	.01
☐ 368 Randy Breuer	.10	.05	.01
☐ 369 Randy Brown	.05	.02	.01
☐ 370 Evers Burns	.40	.18	.05
☐ 371 Pete Chilcutt	.05	.02	.01
☐ 372 Bobby Hurley	.10	.05	.01
☐ 373 Jim Les	.05	.02	.01
☐ 374 Mike Peplowski	.05	.02	.01
☐ 375 Willie Anderson	.05	.02	.01
☐ 376 Sleepy Floyd	.05	.02	.01
☐ 377 Negele Knight	.08	.04	.01
☐ 378 Dennis Rodman			

☐	379	Chris Whitney	.10	.05	.01
☐	380	Vincent Askew	.05	.02	.01
☐	381	Kendall Gill	.08	.04	.01
☐	382	Ervin Johnson	.10	.05	.01
☐	383	Chris King	.10	.05	.01
☐	384	Rich King	.05	.02	.01
☐	385	Steve Scheffler	.05	.02	.01
☐	386	Detlef Schrempf	.10	.05	.01
☐	387	Tom Chambers	.08	.04	.01
☐	388	John Crotty	.05	.02	.01
☐	389	Bryon Russell	.15	.07	.02
☐	390	Felton Spencer	.05	.02	.01
☐	391	Luther Wright	.10	.05	.01
☐	392	Mitchell Butler	.10	.05	.01
☐	393	Calbert Cheaney	.40	.18	.05
☐	394	Kevin Duckworth	.05	.02	.01
☐	395	Don MacLean	.08	.04	.01
☐	396	Gheorghe Muresan	.15	.07	.02
☐	397	Doug Overton	.05	.02	.01
☐	398	Brent Price	.05	.02	.01
☐	399	Checklist	.05	.02	.01
☐	400	Checklist	.05	.02	.01

1993-94 Fleer All-Stars

Randomly inserted in 1993-94 Fleer first series foil packs, this 24-card set features the top twelve players from the Eastern Conference (1-12) and the Western Conference (13-24). According to information on the wrappers, All-Stars are randomly inserted into one of every 10 packs. The inserts measure the standard size (2 1/2" by 3 1/2"). The fronts are UV-coated and feature color action player photos enclosed by purple borders. The NBA All-Star logo appears in the lower left or right corner. The player's name is stamped in gold foil and appears at the bottom. The backs are also UV-coated and feature a full-color shot of the player along with a statistical performance sketch from the previous year.

	MINT	EXC	G-VG
COMPLETE SET (24)	30.00	13.50	3.80
COMMON PLAYER (1-24)	.50	.23	.06
☐ 1 Brad Daugherty	.50	.23	.06
Cleveland Cavaliers			
☐ 2 Joe Dumars	.75	.35	.09
Detroit Pistons			
☐ 3 Patrick Ewing	2.50	1.15	.30
New York Knicks			
☐ 4 Larry Johnson	2.00	.90	.25
Charlotte Hornets			
☐ 5 Michael Jordan	12.00	5.50	1.50
Chicago Bulls			
☐ 6 Larry Nance	.50	.23	.06
Cleveland Cavaliers			

☐ 7 Shaquille O'Neal	8.00	3.60	1.00
Orlando Magic			
☐ 8 Scottie Pippen UER	2.50	1.15	.30
Chicago Bulls			
(Name spelled Pipen on front)			
☐ 9 Mark Price	.50	.23	.06
Cleveland Cavaliers			
☐ 10 Detlef Schrempf	.60	.25	.08
Indiana Pacers			
☐ 11 Isiah Thomas	.75	.35	.09
Detroit Pistons			
☐ 12 Dominique Wilkins	2.00	.90	.25
Atlanta Hawks			
☐ 13 Charles Barkley	3.00	1.35	.40
Phoenix Suns			
☐ 14 Clyde Drexler	1.00	.45	.13
Portland Trail Blazers			
☐ 15 Sean Elliott	.50	.23	.06
San Antonio Spurs			
☐ 16 Tim Hardaway	.50	.23	.06
Golden State Warriors			
☐ 17 Shawn Kemp	2.50	1.15	.30
Seattle Supersonics			
☐ 18 Dan Majerle	.60	.25	.08
Phoenix Suns			
☐ 19 Karl Malone	1.75	.80	.22
Utah Jazz			
☐ 20 Danny Manning	.75	.35	.09
Los Angeles Clippers			
☐ 21 Hakeem Olajuwon	4.00	1.80	.50
Houston Rockets			
☐ 22 Terry Porter	.50	.23	.06
Portland Trail Blazers			
☐ 23 David Robinson	3.00	1.35	.40
San Antonio Spurs			
☐ 24 John Stockton	1.00	.45	.13
Utah Jazz			

1993-94 Fleer Clyde Drexler

Subtitled "Career Highlights" and randomly inserted in all 1993-94 Fleer first series packs, this 12-card standard-size (2 1/2" by 3 1/2") set captures the greatest moments in Drexler's career. Drexler autographed more than 2,000 of his cards. Moreover, the collector could acquire four additional cards and an issue of NBA Inside Stuff magazine through a mail-in for ten wrappers plus 1.50. The front features a unique two photo design, one color, and the other red-screened, serving as the background. The player's name as well as the Fleer logo appear at the top of the card in gold foil. The bottom of the card carries the words "Career Highlights," also stamped in gold foil. The back of the cards carry information about Drexler, with another red-screened photo again as the background. The cards are numbered on the back.

	MINT	EXC	G-VG
COMPLETE SET (12)	5.00	2.30	.60
COMMON DREXLER (1-12)	.50	.23	.06
COMMON SEND-OFF (13-16)	1.00	.45	.13
☐ 1 Clyde Drexler (Ball in right hand, pointing with left)	.50	.23	.06
☐ 2 Clyde Drexler (Holding ball aloft with right hand)	.50	.23	.06
☐ 3 Clyde Drexler (Wearing red shoes, left-hand dribble)	.50	.23	.06
☐ 4 Clyde Drexler (Wearing red shoes, right-hand dribble)	.50	.23	.06
☐ 5 Clyde Drexler (Making ready to slam dunk with both hands)	.50	.23	.06
☐ 6 Clyde Drexler (Wearing white shoes, right-hand dribble)	.50	.23	.06
☐ 7 Clyde Drexler (Right-hand dribble; half of ball visible)	.50	.23	.06
☐ 8 Clyde Drexler (Right hand under ball, left hand alongside)	.50	.23	.06
☐ 9 Clyde Drexler (Receiving or passing ball)	.50	.23	.06
☐ 10 Clyde Drexler (Both hands above head; right hand near ball)	.50	.23	.06
☐ 11 Clyde Drexler (Left foot off floor; right-hand dribble)	.50	.23	.06
☐ 12 Clyde Drexler (In NBA All-Star uniform)	.50	.23	.06
☐ 13 Clyde Drexler (Right-hand dribble, looking over defense)	1.00	.45	.13
☐ 14 Clyde Drexler (Dribbling down court with right hand)	1.00	.45	.13
☐ 15 Clyde Drexler (Shooting, with Pippen defending)	1.00	.45	.13
☐ 16 Clyde Drexler (Bringing ball upcourt, black uniform)	1.00	.45	.13
☐ AU Clyde Drexler AU (Certified autograph)	90.00	40.00	11.50

1993-94 Fleer First Year Phenoms

These ten standard-size (2 1/2" by 3 1/2") cards were randomly inserted in all types of 1993-94 Fleer second-series packs. The yellow-bordered fronts feature color player action cutouts superposed upon purple, yellow, and black florescent basketball court designs. The player's name appears vertically in gold foil near one corner, and the gold-foil set logo appears at the bottom left. The horizontal back sports a similar florescent design. A color player close-up cutout appears on one side; his name, team, and career highlights appear on the other. The cards are numbered on the back as "X of 10."

	MINT	EXC	G-VG
COMPLETE SET (10)	15.00	6.75	1.90
COMMON PLAYER (1-10)	.75	.35	.09

☐ 1	Shawn Bradley	.75	.35	.09
	Philadelphia 76ers			
☐ 2	Anfernee Hardaway	4.00	1.80	.50
	Orlando Magic			
☐ 3	Lindsey Hunter	.75	.35	.09
	Detroit Pistons			
☐ 4	Bobby Hurley	.75	.35	.09
	Sacramento Kings			
☐ 5	Toni Kukoc	.75	.35	.09
	Chicago Bulls			
☐ 6	Jamal Mashburn	2.00	.90	.25
	Dallas Mavericks			
☐ 7	Dino Radja	.75	.35	.09
	Boston Celtics			
☐ 8	Isaiah Rider	2.00	.90	.25
	Minnesota Timberwolves			
☐ 9	Nick Van Exel	.75	.35	.09
	Los Angeles Lakers			
☐ 10	Chris Webber	5.00	2.30	.60
	Golden State Warriors			

1993-94 Fleer Internationals

This 12-card insert set features NBA players born outside the United States and measures the standard size (2 1/2" by 3 1/2"). The fronts are UV-coated and feature a color player photo superimposed over a map of his country of origin. The player's name appears at the top of the card and is gold foil stamped. The backs are also UV-coated and feature a color shot of the player along with a brief biographical sketch. These inserts came randomly packed approximately one in every ten first series wax packs. The cards are numbered on the back.

	MINT	EXC	G-VG
COMPLETE SET (12)	5.00	2.30	.60
COMMON PLAYER (1-12)	.50	.23	.06
☐ 1 Alaa Abdelnaby	.50	.23	.06
Boston Celtics			
☐ 2 Vlade Divac	.50	.23	.06
Los Angeles Lakers			
☐ 3 Patrick Ewing	2.50	1.15	.30
New York Knicks			
☐ 4 Carl Herrera	.50	.23	.06
Houston Rockets			
☐ 5 Luc Longley	.50	.23	.06
Minnesota Timberwolves			
☐ 6 Sarunas Marciulionis	.75	.35	.09
Golden State Warriors			
☐ 7 Dikembe Mutombo	.75	.35	.09
Denver Nuggets			
☐ 8 Rumeal Robinson	.50	.23	.06
New Jersey Nets			
☐ 9 Detlef Schrempf	.75	.35	.09
Indiana Pacers			
☐ 10 Rony Seikaly	.75	.35	.09
Miami Heat			
☐ 11 Rik Smits	.50	.23	.06
Indiana Pacers			
☐ 12 Dominique Wilkins	2.00	.90	.25
Atlanta Hawks			

1993-94 Fleer Living Legends

These six standard-size (2 1/2" by 3 1/2") cards were randomly inserted in all types of 1993-94 Fleer second-series packs. The horizontal fronts feature color player action cutouts superposed upon a borderless metallic motion-streaked background. The player's name and the set's logo appear at the bottom in gold foil. The horizontal back carries a color player close-up cutout on one side; his name, team, and career highlights appear on the other. The cards are numbered on the back as "X of 6."

	MINT	EXC	G-VG
COMPLETE SET (6)	60.00	27.00	7.50
COMMON PLAYER (1-6)	6.00	2.70	.75
☐ 1 Charles Barkley	10.00	4.50	1.25
Phoenix Suns			
☐ 2 Larry Bird	12.00	5.50	1.50

Boston Celtics			
☐ 3 Patrick Ewing	8.00	3.60	1.00
New York Knicks			
☐ 4 Michael Jordan	35.00	16.00	4.40
Chicago Bulls			
☐ 5 Hakeem Olajuwon	12.00	5.50	1.50
Houston Rockets			
☐ 6 Dominique Wilkins	6.00	2.70	.75
Atlanta Hawks			

1993-94 Fleer Lottery Exchange

This 11-card standard-size (2 1/2" by 3 1/2") set features college stars chosen in the '93 NBA Draft Lottery who signed up with their teams by November 1, 1993. It could be obtained in exchange for the randomly inserted Draft Exchange Card. The cards are numbered on the back.

	MINT	EXC	G-VG
COMPLETE SET (11)	25.00	11.50	3.10
COMMON PLAYER (1-11)	.50	.23	.06
☐ 1 Chris Webber	10.00	4.50	1.25
Golden State Warriors			
☐ 2 Shawn Bradley	1.50	.65	.19
Philadelphia 76ers			
☐ 3 Anfernee Hardaway	8.00	3.60	1.00
Orlando Magic			
☐ 4 Jamal Mashburn	4.00	1.80	.50
Dallas Mavericks			
☐ 5 Isaiah Rider	4.00	1.80	.50
Minnesota Timberwolves			
☐ 6 Calbert Cheaney	1.50	.65	.19
Washington Bullets			
☐ 7 Bobby Hurley	1.50	.65	.19
Sacramento Kings			
☐ 8 Vin Baker	3.00	1.35	.40
Milwaukee Bucks			
☐ 9 Rodney Rogers	1.00	.45	.13
Denver Nuggets			
☐ 10 Lindsey Hunter	1.50	.65	.19
Detroit Pistons			
☐ 11 Allan Houston	.50	.23	.06
Detroit Pistons			
☐ NNO Expired Exchange Card	3.00	1.35	.40

1993-94 Fleer NBA Superstars

These 20 standard-size (2 1/2" by 3 1/2") cards were randomly inserted in 1993-94 Fleer second-series 15-card packs. The fronts feature color player action cutouts superposed upon multiple color action shots on the right side, and the player's name in team color-coded vertical block lettering on the left. The set's title appears vertically along the left edge in gold foil. The horizontal back carries a color player close-up cutout on one side; his name, team, and career highlights appear on the other. The cards are numbered on the back as "X of 20."

	MINT	EXC	G-VG
COMPLETE SET (20)	15.00	6.75	1.90
COMMON PLAYER (1-20)	.25	.11	.03
☐ 1 Mahmoud Abdul-Rauf Denver Nuggets	.25	.11	.03
☐ 2 Charles Barkley Phoenix Suns	1.50	.65	.19
☐ 3 Derrick Coleman New Jersey Nets	.50	.23	.06
☐ 4 Clyde Drexler Portland Trail Blazers	.50	.23	.06
☐ 5 Joe Dumars Detroit Pistons	.40	.18	.05
☐ 6 Patrick Ewing New York Knicks	1.25	.55	.16
☐ 7 Michael Jordan Chicago Bulls	6.00	2.70	.75
☐ 8 Shawn Kemp Seattle Supersonics	1.25	.55	.16
☐ 9 Christian Laettner Minnesota Timberwolves	.40	.18	.05
☐ 10 Karl Malone Utah Jazz	1.00	.45	.13
☐ 11 Danny Manning Los Angeles Clippers	.40	.18	.05
☐ 12 Reggie Miller Indiana Pacers	.50	.23	.06
☐ 13 Alonzo Mourning Charlotte Hornets	1.50	.65	.19
☐ 14 Chris Mullin Golden State Warriors	.40	.18	.05
☐ 15 Hakeem Olajuwon Houston Rockets	2.00	.90	.25
☐ 16 Shaquille O'Neal Orlando Magic	4.00	1.80	.50
☐ 17 Mark Price Cleveland Cavaliers	.25	.11	.03
☐ 18 Mitch Richmond	.25	.11	.03

Sacramento Kings
□ 19 David Robinson.................................. 1.50 .65 .19
San Antonio Spurs
□ 20 Dominique Wilkins........................... 1.00 .45 .13
Atlanta Hawks

1993-94 Fleer Rookie Sensations

Randomly inserted in 29-card series one cello packs, these 24 standard-size (2 1/2" by 3 1/2") UV-coated cards feature color player action photos on the fronts within silver-colored borders. Each player photo is superposed upon a card design that has a basketball "earth" at the card bottom radiating "spotlight" beams that shade from yellow to magenta on a sky blue background. The player's name and the Rookie Sensations logo, both stamped in gold foil, appear in the lower left. Bordered in silver, the backs feature color closeups of the players in the lower right or left. Blue "sky" and two intersecting yellow-to-magenta "spotlight" beams form the background. The player's name appears in silver-colored lettering at the top of the card above the player's NBA rookie-year highlights. The cards are numbered on the back. Odds of finding a Rookie Sensations card are approximately one in every five packs.

	MINT	EXC	G-VG
COMPLETE SET (24)...	70.00	32.00	8.75
COMMON PLAYER (1-24)......................................	1.00	.45	.13
□ 1 Anthony Avent................................	1.00	.45	.13
Milwaukee Bucks			
□ 2 Doug Christie.................................	1.50	.65	.19
Los Angeles Lakers			
□ 3 Lloyd Daniels................................	1.00	.45	.13
San Antonio Spurs			
□ 4 Hubert Davis................................	1.50	.65	.19
New York Knicks			
□ 5 Todd Day.....................................	1.50	.65	.19
Milwaukee Bucks			
□ 6 Richard Dumas.............................	1.00	.45	.13
Phoenix Suns			
□ 7 LaPhonso Ellis.............................	3.00	1.35	.40
Denver Nuggets			
□ 8 Tom Gugliotta...............................	3.00	1.35	.40
Washington Bullets			
□ 9 Robert Horry.................................	3.00	1.35	.40
Houston Rockets			
□ 10 Byron Houston.............................	1.00	.45	.13
Golden State Warriors			
□ 11 Jim Jackson UER........................	6.00	2.70	.75
Dallas Mavericks			
(Text on back states he played			
in Big East; he played in Big Ten)			
□ 12 Adam Keefe................................	1.00	.45	.13
Atlanta Hawks			

☐ 13	Christian Laettner Minnesota Timberwolves	3.00	1.35	.40
☐ 14	Lee Mayberry Milwaukee Bucks	1.00	.45	.13
☐ 15	Oliver Miller Phoenix Suns	1.50	.65	.19
☐ 16	Harold Miner Miami Heat	1.50	.65	.19
☐ 17	Alonzo Mourning Charlotte Hornets	10.00	4.50	1.25
☐ 18	Shaquille O'Neal Orlando Magic	25.00	11.50	3.10
☐ 19	Anthony Peeler Los Angeles Lakers	1.00	.45	.13
☐ 20	Sean Rooks Dallas Mavericks	1.00	.45	.13
☐ 21	Latrell Sprewell Golden State Warriors	8.00	3.60	1.00
☐ 22	Bryant Stith Denver Nuggets	1.50	.65	.19
☐ 23	Clarence Weatherspoon Philadelphia 76ers	3.00	1.35	.40
☐ 24	Walt Williams Sacramento Kings	1.50	.65	.19

1993-94 Fleer Sharpshooters

These ten standard-size (2 1/2" by 3 1/2") cards were randomly inserted in 1993-94 Fleer second-series 15-card packs. The fronts feature color player action cutouts superposed upon color-screened action shots. The player's name appears at the upper right in gold foil. The set's logo appears at the bottom left. The black horizontal back carries a color player close-up cutout on one side; his name, card title, and career highlights appear on the other. The cards are numbered on the back as "X of 10."

		MINT	EXC	G-VG
COMPLETE SET (10)		25.00	11.50	3.10
COMMON PLAYER (1-10)		.75	.35	.09
☐ 1	Tom Gugliotta Washington Bullets	1.00	.45	.13
☐ 2	Jim Jackson Dallas Mavericks	2.50	1.15	.30
☐ 3	Michael Jordan Chicago Bulls	15.00	6.75	1.90
☐ 4	Dan Majerle Phoenix Suns	1.00	.45	.13

☐ 5 Mark Price	.75	.35	.09
Cleveland Cavaliers			
☐ 6 Glen Rice	.75	.35	.09
Miami Heat			
☐ 7 Mitch Richmond	.75	.35	.09
Sacramento Kings			
☐ 8 Latrell Sprewell	4.00	1.80	.50
Golden State Warriors			
☐ 9 John Starks	1.00	.45	.13
New York Knicks			
☐ 10 Dominique Wilkins	2.50	1.15	.30
Atlanta Hawks			

1993-94 Fleer Towers Of Power

These 30 standard-size (2 1/2" by 3 1/2") cards were randomly inserted in 1993-94 Fleer second-series 21-card cello packs. The fronts feature color player action cutouts super-posed upon borderless backgrounds of city skylines. The player's name appears in gold foil in a lower corner. The gold-foil set logo appears in an upper corner. The back has the same borderless skyline background photo as the front and carries a color player cutout on one side, and his career highlights on the other. The cards are numbered on the back as "X of 30."

	MINT	EXC	G-VG
COMPLETE SET (30)	130.00	57.50	16.50
COMMON PLAYER (1-30)	2.00	.90	.25
☐ 1 Charles Barkley	10.00	4.50	1.25
Phoenix Suns			
☐ 2 Shawn Bradley	4.00	1.80	.50
Philadelphia 76ers			
☐ 3 Derrick Coleman	3.00	1.35	.40
New Jersey Nets			
☐ 4 Brad Daugherty	2.25	1.00	.30
Cleveland Cavaliers			
☐ 5 Dale Davis	2.25	1.00	.30
Indiana Pacers			
☐ 6 Vlade Divac	2.00	.90	.25
Los Angeles Lakers			
☐ 7 Patrick Ewing	8.00	3.60	1.00
New York Knicks			
☐ 8 Horace Grant	2.00	.90	.25
Chicago Bulls			
☐ 9 Tom Gugliotta	2.50	1.15	.30
Washington Bullets			
☐ 10 Larry Johnson	6.00	2.70	.75
Charlotte Hornets			
☐ 11 Shawn Kemp	8.00	3.60	1.00

☐ 12	Christian Laettner	2.50	1.15	.30
	Minnesota Timberwolves			
☐ 13	Karl Malone	5.00	2.30	.60
	Utah Jazz			
☐ 14	Danny Manning	2.50	1.15	.30
	Los Angeles Clippers			
☐ 15	Jamal Mashburn	10.00	4.50	1.25
	Dallas Mavericks			
☐ 16	Oliver Miller	2.00	.90	.25
	Phoenix Suns			
☐ 17	Alonzo Mourning	10.00	4.50	1.25
	Charlotte Hornets			
☐ 18	Dikembe Mutombo	2.50	1.15	.30
	Denver Nuggets			
☐ 19	Ken Norman	2.00	.90	.25
	Milwaukee Bucks			
☐ 20	Hakeem Olajuwon	12.00	5.50	1.50
	Houston Rockets			
☐ 21	Shaquille O'Neal	25.00	11.50	3.10
	Orlando Magic			
☐ 22	Robert Parish	2.25	1.00	.30
	Boston Celtics			
☐ 23	Olden Polynice	2.00	.90	.25
	Detroit Pistons			
☐ 24	Clifford Robinson	2.25	1.00	.30
	Portland Trail Blazers			
☐ 25	David Robinson	10.00	4.50	1.25
	San Antonio Spurs			
☐ 26	Dennis Rodman	2.00	.90	.25
	San Antonio Spurs			
☐ 27	Rony Seikaly	2.25	1.00	.30
	Miami Heat			
☐ 28	Wayman Tisdale	2.00	.90	.25
	Sacramento Kings			
☐ 29	Chris Webber	25.00	11.50	3.10
	Golden State Warriors			
☐ 30	Dominique Wilkins	6.00	2.70	.75
	Atlanta Hawks			

1994-95 Fleer

The 240 cards comprising Fleer's '94-95 first-series measure the standard size (2 1/2" by 3 1/2") and feature color player action shots on their white-bordered fronts. The player's name, team, and position appear in team-colored lettering set on an irregular team-colored foil patch at the lower left. The black-bordered back carries a color player action shot on the left side, with the player's name, biography, team logo, and statistics displayed on a team-colored background on the right. The cards are numbered on the back, grouped alphabetically within teams, and checklisted below alphabetically according to teams as follows: Atlanta Hawks (1-9), Boston Celtics (10-18), Charlotte Hornets (19-28), Chicago Bulls (29-37),

Cleveland Cavaliers (38-46), Dallas Mavericks (47-55), Denver Nuggets (56-63), Detroit Pistons (64-69), Golden State Warriors (70-78), Houston Rockets (79-87), Indiana Pacers (88-96), Los Angeles Clippers (97-105), Los Angeles Lakers (106-114), Miami Heat (115-122), Milwaukee Bucks (123-130), Minnesota Timberwolves (131-138), New Jersey Nets (139-146), New York Knicks (147-156), Orlando Magic (157-164), Philadelphia 76ers (165-173), Phoenix Suns (174-182), Portland Trail Blazers (183-191), Sacramento Kings (192-200), San Antonio Spurs (201-209), Seattle Supersonics (210-218), Utah Jazz (219-227), and Washington Bullets (228-236).

	MINT	EXC	G-VG
COMPLETE SERIES 1 (240)	15.00	6.75	1.90
COMMON PLAYER (1-240)	.05	.02	.01
☐ 1 Stacey Augmon	.10	.05	.01
☐ 2 Mookie Blaylock	.08	.04	.01
☐ 3 Craig Ehlo	.05	.02	.01
☐ 4 Duane Ferrell	.05	.02	.01
☐ 5 Adam Keefe	.05	.02	.01
☐ 6 Jon Koncak	.05	.02	.01
☐ 7 Andrew Lang	.05	.02	.01
☐ 8 Danny Manning	.10	.05	.01
☐ 9 Kevin Willis	.08	.04	.01
☐ 10 Dee Brown	.08	.04	.01
☐ 11 Sherman Douglas	.05	.02	.01
☐ 12 Acie Earl	.05	.02	.01
☐ 13 Rick Fox	.05	.02	.01
☐ 14 Kevin Gamble	.05	.02	.01
☐ 15 Xavier McDaniel	.08	.04	.01
☐ 16 Robert Parish	.10	.05	.01
☐ 17 Ed Pinckney	.05	.02	.01
☐ 18 Dino Radja	.15	.07	.02
☐ 19 Muggsy Bogues	.10	.05	.01
☐ 20 Frank Brickowski	.05	.02	.01
☐ 21 Scott Burrell	.05	.02	.01
☐ 22 Dell Curry	.08	.04	.01
☐ 23 Kenny Gattison	.05	.02	.01
☐ 24 Hersey Hawkins	.08	.04	.01
☐ 25 Eddie Johnson	.05	.02	.01
☐ 26 Larry Johnson	.25	.11	.03
☐ 27 Alonzo Mourning	.50	.23	.06
☐ 28 David Wingate	.05	.02	.01
☐ 29 B.J. Armstrong	.10	.05	.01
☐ 30 Horace Grant	.10	.05	.01
☐ 31 Steve Kerr	.05	.02	.01
☐ 32 Toni Kukoc	.15	.07	.02
☐ 33 Luc Longley	.05	.02	.01
☐ 34 Pete Myers	.05	.02	.01
☐ 35 Scottie Pippen	.30	.14	.04
☐ 36 Bill Wennington	.05	.02	.01
☐ 37 Scott Williams	.05	.02	.01
☐ 38 Terrell Brandon	.05	.02	.01
☐ 39 Brad Daugherty	.10	.05	.01
☐ 40 Tyrone Hill	.05	.02	.01
☐ 41 Chris Mills	.08	.04	.01
☐ 42 Larry Nance	.05	.02	.01
☐ 43 Bobby Phills	.05	.02	.01
☐ 44 Mark Price	.10	.05	.01
☐ 45 Gerald Wilkins	.05	.02	.01
☐ 46 John Williams	.08	.04	.01
☐ 47 Lucious Harris	.05	.02	.01
☐ 48 Donald Hodge	.05	.02	.01
☐ 49 Jim Jackson	.20	.09	.03
☐ 50 Popeye Jones	.05	.02	.01
☐ 51 Tim Legler	.05	.02	.01
☐ 52 Fat Lever	.05	.02	.01
☐ 53 Jamal Mashburn	.40	.18	.05
☐ 54 Sean Rooks	.05	.02	.01
☐ 55 Doug Smith	.05	.02	.01
☐ 56 Mahmoud Abdul-Rauf	.05	.02	.01
☐ 57 LaPhonso Ellis	.10	.05	.01
☐ 58 Dikembe Mutombo	.15	.07	.02
☐ 59 Robert Pack	.05	.02	.01
☐ 60 Rodney Rogers	.08	.04	.01

☐	61	Bryant Stith	.08	.04	.01
☐	62	Brian Williams	.05	.02	.01
☐	63	Reggie Williams	.05	.02	.01
☐	64	Greg Anderson	.05	.02	.01
☐	65	Joe Dumars	.15	.07	.02
☐	66	Sean Elliott	.05	.02	.01
☐	67	Allan Houston	.05	.02	.01
☐	68	Lindsey Hunter	.15	.07	.02
☐	69	Terry Mills	.08	.04	.01
☐	70	Victor Alexander	.05	.02	.01
☐	71	Chris Gatling	.05	.02	.01
☐	72	Tim Hardaway	.10	.05	.01
☐	73	Keith Jennings	.05	.02	.01
☐	74	Avery Johnson	.05	.02	.01
☐	75	Chris Mullin	.15	.07	.02
☐	76	Billy Owens	.05	.02	.01
☐	77	Latrell Sprewell	.30	.14	.04
☐	78	Chris Webber	1.00	.45	.13
☐	79	Scott Brooks	.05	.02	.01
☐	80	Sam Cassell	.15	.07	.02
☐	81	Mario Elie	.05	.02	.01
☐	82	Carl Herrera	.05	.02	.01
☐	83	Robert Horry	.10	.05	.01
☐	84	Vernon Maxwell	.08	.04	.01
☐	85	Hakeem Olajuwon	.75	.35	.09
☐	86	Kenny Smith	.05	.02	.01
☐	87	Otis Thorpe	.08	.04	.01
☐	88	Antonio Davis	.08	.04	.01
☐	89	Dale Davis	.08	.04	.01
☐	90	Vern Fleming	.05	.02	.01
☐	91	Derrick McKey	.05	.02	.01
☐	92	Reggie Miller	.20	.09	.03
☐	93	Pooh Richardson	.05	.02	.01
☐	94	Byron Scott	.08	.04	.01
☐	95	Rik Smits	.08	.04	.01
☐	96	Haywoode Workman	.05	.02	.01
☐	97	Terry Dehere	.05	.02	.01
☐	98	Harold Ellis	.05	.02	.01
☐	99	Gary Grant	.05	.02	.01
☐	100	Ron Harper	.08	.04	.01
☐	101	Mark Jackson	.08	.04	.01
☐	102	Stanley Roberts	.05	.02	.01
☐	103	Elmore Spencer	.05	.02	.01
☐	104	Loy Vaught	.08	.04	.01
☐	105	Dominique Wilkins	.25	.11	.03
☐	106	Elden Campbell	.05	.02	.01
☐	107	Doug Christie	.08	.04	.01
☐	108	Vlade Divac	.05	.02	.01
☐	109	George Lynch	.08	.04	.01
☐	110	Anthony Peeler	.08	.04	.01
☐	111	Tony Smith	.05	.02	.01
☐	112	Sedale Threatt	.05	.02	.01
☐	113	Nick Van Exel	.15	.07	.02
☐	114	James Worthy	.05	.02	.01
☐	115	Bimbo Coles	.05	.02	.01
☐	116	Grant Long	.05	.02	.01
☐	117	Harold Miner	.08	.04	.01
☐	118	Glen Rice	.10	.05	.01
☐	119	John Salley	.05	.02	.01
☐	120	Rony Seikaly	.10	.05	.01
☐	121	Brian Shaw	.05	.02	.01
☐	122	Steve Smith	.10	.05	.01
☐	123	Vin Baker	.25	.11	.03
☐	124	Jon Barry	.05	.02	.01
☐	125	Todd Day	.05	.02	.01
☐	126	Blue Edwards	.05	.02	.01
☐	127	Lee Mayberry	.05	.02	.01
☐	128	Eric Murdock	.08	.04	.01
☐	129	Ken Norman	.05	.02	.01
☐	130	Derek Strong	.05	.02	.01
☐	131	Thurl Bailey	.05	.02	.01
☐	132	Stacey King	.05	.02	.01
☐	133	Christian Laettner	.08	.04	.01

☐ 134	Chuck Person	.08	.04	.01
☐ 135	Isaiah Rider	.40	.18	.05
☐ 136	Chris Smith	.05	.02	.01
☐ 137	Doug West	.05	.02	.01
☐ 138	Micheal Williams	.08	.04	.01
☐ 139	Kenny Anderson	.15	.07	.02
☐ 140	Benoit Benjamin	.05	.02	.01
☐ 141	P.J. Brown	.05	.02	.01
☐ 142	Derrick Coleman	.20	.09	.03
☐ 143	Kevin Edwards	.05	.02	.01
☐ 144	Armon Gilliam	.05	.02	.01
☐ 145	Chris Morris	.05	.02	.01
☐ 146	Johnny Newman	.05	.02	.01
☐ 147	Greg Anthony	.05	.02	.01
☐ 148	Anthony Bonner	.05	.02	.01
☐ 149	Hubert Davis	.05	.02	.01
☐ 150	Patrick Ewing	.30	.14	.04
☐ 151	Derek Harper	.08	.04	.01
☐ 152	Anthony Mason	.05	.02	.01
☐ 153	Charles Oakley	.10	.05	.01
☐ 154	Doc Rivers	.08	.04	.01
☐ 155	Charles Smith	.05	.02	.01
☐ 156	John Starks	.05	.02	.01
☐ 157	Nick Anderson	.05	.02	.01
☐ 158	Anthony Avent	.05	.02	.01
☐ 159	Anfernee Hardaway	.75	.35	.09
☐ 160	Shaquille O'Neal	1.50	.65	.19
☐ 161	Donald Royal	.05	.02	.01
☐ 162	Dennis Scott	.08	.04	.01
☐ 163	Scott Skiles	.05	.02	.01
☐ 164	Jeff Turner	.05	.02	.01
☐ 165	Dana Barros	.05	.02	.01
☐ 166	Shawn Bradley	.15	.07	.02
☐ 167	Greg Graham	.05	.02	.01
☐ 168	Eric Leckner	.05	.02	.01
☐ 169	Jeff Malone	.08	.04	.01
☐ 170	Moses Malone	.10	.05	.01
☐ 171	Tim Perry	.05	.02	.01
☐ 172	Clarence Weatherspoon	.10	.05	.01
☐ 173	Orlando Woolridge	.08	.04	.01
☐ 174	Danny Ainge	.10	.05	.01
☐ 175	Charles Barkley	.50	.23	.06
☐ 176	Cedric Ceballos	.10	.05	.01
☐ 177	A.C. Green	.08	.04	.01
☐ 178	Kevin Johnson	.10	.05	.01
☐ 179	Joe Kleine	.05	.02	.01
☐ 180	Dan Majerle	.10	.05	.01
☐ 181	Oliver Miller	.08	.04	.01
☐ 182	Mark West	.05	.02	.01
☐ 183	Clyde Drexler	.20	.09	.03
☐ 184	Harvey Grant	.05	.02	.01
☐ 185	Jerome Kersey	.05	.02	.01
☐ 186	Tracy Murray	.05	.02	.01
☐ 187	Terry Porter	.08	.04	.01
☐ 188	Clifford Robinson	.08	.04	.01
☐ 189	James Robinson	.05	.02	.01
☐ 190	Rod Strickland	.08	.04	.01
☐ 191	Buck Williams	.05	.02	.01
☐ 192	Duane Causwell	.05	.02	.01
☐ 193	Bobby Hurley	.15	.07	.02
☐ 194	Olden Polynice	.05	.02	.01
☐ 195	Mitch Richmond	.10	.05	.01
☐ 196	Lionel Simmons	.08	.04	.01
☐ 197	Wayman Tisdale	.08	.04	.01
☐ 198	Spud Webb	.10	.05	.01
☐ 199	Walt Williams	.08	.04	.01
☐ 200	Trevor Wilson	.05	.02	.01
☐ 201	Willie Anderson	.05	.02	.01
☐ 202	Antoine Carr	.05	.02	.01
☐ 203	Terry Cummings	.08	.04	.01
☐ 204	Vinny Del Negro	.05	.02	.01
☐ 205	Dale Ellis	.08	.04	.01
☐ 206	Negele Knight	.05	.02	.01

☐ 207	J.R. Reid	.05	.02	.01
☐ 208	David Robinson	.50	.23	.06
☐ 209	Dennis Rodman	.08	.04	.01
☐ 210	Vincent Askew	.05	.02	.01
☐ 211	Michael Cage	.05	.02	.01
☐ 212	Kendall Gill	.08	.04	.01
☐ 213	Shawn Kemp	.30	.14	.04
☐ 214	Nate McMillan	.05	.02	.01
☐ 215	Gary Payton	.10	.05	.01
☐ 216	Sam Perkins	.05	.02	.01
☐ 217	Ricky Pierce	.05	.02	.01
☐ 218	Detlef Schrempf	.10	.05	.01
☐ 219	David Benoit	.05	.02	.01
☐ 220	Tom Chambers	.08	.04	.01
☐ 221	Tyrone Corbin	.05	.02	.01
☐ 222	Jeff Hornacek	.08	.04	.01
☐ 223	Jay Humphries	.05	.02	.01
☐ 224	Karl Malone	.25	.11	.03
☐ 225	Bryon Russell	.05	.02	.01
☐ 226	Felton Spencer	.05	.02	.01
☐ 227	John Stockton	.20	.09	.03
☐ 228	Michael Adams	.08	.04	.01
☐ 229	Rex Chapman	.05	.02	.01
☐ 230	Calbert Cheaney	.15	.07	.02
☐ 231	Kevin Duckworth	.05	.02	.01
☐ 232	Pervis Ellison	.05	.02	.01
☐ 233	Tom Gugliotta	.08	.04	.01
☐ 234	Don MacLean	.08	.04	.01
☐ 235	Gheorghe Muresan	.05	.02	.01
☐ 236	Brent Price	.05	.02	.01
☐ 237	Toronto Raptors Logo Card	.15	.07	.02
☐ 238	Checklist	.05	.02	.01
☐ 239	Checklist	.05	.02	.01
☐ 240	Checklist	.05	.02	.01
☐ NNO	Lottery Exchange Card	30.00	13.50	3.80

1994-95 Fleer All-Defensive

Randomly inserted in all first-series packs, these 10 standard-size (2 1/2" by 3 1/2") cards feature on their borderless fronts color player action shots, the backgrounds of which have been faded to black-and-white. The player's name and first or second team designation appear in silver-foil lettering near the bottom. On a color-screened background, the back carries a color player cutout on one side and career highlights on the other. The cards are numbered on the back as "X of 10."

	MINT	EXC	G-VG
COMPLETE SET (10)	10.00	4.50	1.25
COMMON PLAYER (1-10)	.50	.23	.06
☐ 1 Mookie Blaylock	.50	.23	.06
Atlanta Hawks			
☐ 2 Charles Oakley	.50	.23	.06

New York Knicks			
☐ 3 Hakeem Olajuwon	4.00	1.80	.50
Orlando Magic			
☐ 4 Gary Payton	.50	.23	.06
Seattle Seahawks			
☐ 5 Scottie Pippen	2.50	1.15	.30
Chicago Bulls			
☐ 6 Horace Grant	.50	.23	.06
Chicago Bulls			
☐ 7 Nate McMillan	.50	.23	.06
Seattle Seahawks			
☐ 8 David Robinson	3.00	1.35	.40
San Antonio Spurs			
☐ 9 Dennis Rodman	.50	.23	.06
San Antonio Spurs			
☐ 10 Latrell Sprewell	2.00	.90	.25
Golden State Warriors			

1994-95 Fleer All-Stars

Randomly inserted in all first-series packs, these 10 standard-size (2 1/2" by 3 1/2") cards feature on their borderless fronts color player action shots, the backgrounds of which have been faded to black-and-white. The player's name and first or second team designation appear in silver-foil lettering near the bottom. On a color-screened background, the back carries a color player cutout on one side and career highlights on the other. The cards are numbered on the back as "X of 10."

	MINT	EXC	G-VG
COMPLETE SET (26)	20.00	9.00	2.50
COMMON PLAYER (1-26)	.25	.11	.03
☐ 1 Kenny Anderson	.50	.23	.06
New Jersey Nets			
☐ 2 B.J. Armstrong	.25	.11	.03
Chicago Bulls			
☐ 3 Mookie Blaylock	.25	.11	.03
Atlanta Hawks			
☐ 4 Derrick Coleman	.60	.25	.08
New Jersey Nets			
☐ 5 Patrick Ewing	1.25	.55	.16
New York Knicks			
☐ 6 Horace Grant	.25	.11	.03
Chicago Bulls			
☐ 7 Alonzo Mourning	1.50	.65	.19
Charlotte Hornets			
☐ 8 Charles Oakley	.25	.11	.03
New York Knicks			
☐ 9 Shaquille O'Neal	4.00	1.80	.50
Orlando Magic			
☐ 10 Scottie Pippen	1.25	.55	.16
Chicago Bulls			
☐ 11 Mark Price	.25	.11	.03

		MINT	EXC	G-VG
☐ 12	John Starks Cleveland Cavaliers	.25	.11	.03
☐ 13	Dominique Wilkins New York Knicks	1.00	.45	.13
☐ 14	Charles Barkley Atlanta Hawks	1.50	.65	.19
☐ 15	Clyde Drexler Phoenix Suns	.60	.25	.08
☐ 16	Kevin Johnson Portland Trail Blazers	.25	.11	.03
☐ 17	Shawn Kemp Phoenix Suns	1.25	.55	.16
☐ 18	Karl Malone Seattle Supersonics	1.00	.45	.13
☐ 19	Danny Manning Utah Jazz	.25	.11	.03
☐ 20	Hakeem Olajuwon Los Angeles Clippers	2.00	.90	.25
☐ 21	Gary Payton Houston Rockets	.25	.11	.03
☐ 22	Mitch Richmond Seattle Supersonics	.25	.11	.03
☐ 23	Clifford Robinson Sacramento Kings	.25	.11	.03
☐ 24	David Robinson Portland Trail Blazers	1.50	.65	.19
☐ 25	Latrell Sprewell San Antonio Spurs	1.00	.45	.13
☐ 26	John Stockton Golden State Warriors	.60	.25	.08
	Utah Jazz			

1994-95 Fleer Award Winners

These four standard-size (2 1/2" by 3 1/2") cards were random inserts in first-series Fleer packs . The horizontal fronts feature multiple player images. The player's name and his award appear at the bottom in gold-foil lettering. The horizontal back carries a color player close-up on one side and career highlights on the other. The cards are numbered on the back as "X of 4.".

		MINT	EXC	G-VG
	COMPLETE SET (4)	10.00	4.50	1.25
	COMMON PLAYER (1-4)	.50	.23	.06
☐ 1	Dell Curry Charlotte Hornets	.50	.23	.06
☐ 2	Don MacLean Washington Bullets	.75	.35	.09
☐ 3	Hakeem Olajuwon Houston Rockets	4.00	1.80	.50
☐ 4	Chris Webber Golden State Warriors	6.00	2.70	.75

1994-95 Fleer Career Achievement

Randomly inserted in first-series Fleer packs, these six standard-size (2 1/2" by 3 1/2") cards feature color player action cutouts on their borderless metallic fronts. The player's name appears in gold-foil lettering in a lower corner. The back carries a color player close-up in a lower corner, with career highlights appearing above and alongside. The cards are numbered on the back as "X of 6."

	MINT	EXC	G-VG
COMPLETE SET (6)	50.00	23.00	6.25
COMMON PLAYER (1-6)	5.00	2.30	.60
☐ 1 Patrick Ewing	12.00	5.50	1.50
New York Knicks			
☐ 2 Karl Malone	8.00	3.60	1.00
Utah Jazz			
☐ 3 Hakeem Olajuwon	15.00	6.75	1.90
Houston Rockets			
☐ 4 Robert Parish	5.00	2.30	.60
Boston Celtics			
☐ 5 Scottie Pippen	12.00	5.50	1.50
Chicago Bulls			
☐ 6 Dominique Wilkins	10.00	4.50	1.25
Los Angeles Clippers			

1994-95 Fleer League Leaders

Randomly inserted in first-series Fleer packs, these eight standard-size (2 1/2" by 3 1/2") cards feature on their horizontal fronts color player action cutouts set on hardwood backgrounds. The player's name and the category in which he led the NBA appear in gold-foil lettering at the bottom. On a hardwood background, the horizontal back carries a color player close-up on one side and career highlights on the other. The cards are numbered on the back as "X of 8."

	MINT	EXC	G-VG
COMPLETE SET (8)	10.00	4.50	1.25
COMMON PLAYER (1-8)	.50	.23	.06
☐ 1 Mahmoud Abdul-Rauf Denver Nuggets	.50	.23	.06
☐ 2 Nate McMillan Seattle Seahawks	.50	.23	.06
☐ 3 Tracy Murray Portland Trail Blazers	.50	.23	.06
☐ 4 Dikembe Mutombo Denver Nuggets	1.00	.45	.13
☐ 5 Shaquille O'Neal Orlando Magic	8.00	3.60	1.00
☐ 6 David Robinson San Antonio Spurs	3.00	1.35	.40
☐ 7 Dennis Rodman San Antonio Spurs	.50	.23	.06
☐ 8 John Stockton Utah Jazz	1.25	.55	.16

1994-95 Fleer Pro-Visions

Randomly inserted in all first-series packs, these nine standard-size (2 1/2" by 3 1/2") cards feature on their borderless fronts color paintings of the players on fanciful backgrounds. The player's name appears in gold-foil lettering in a lower corner. The back carries career highlights on a colorful ghosted abstract background. The cards are numbered on the back as "X of 10."

	MINT	EXC	G-VG
COMPLETE SET (9)	6.00	2.70	.75
COMMON PLAYER (1-9)	.25	.11	.03
☐ 1 Jamal Mashburn Dallas Mavericks	1.00	.45	.13
☐ 2 John Starks New York Knicks	.25	.11	.03
☐ 3 Toni Kukoc Chicago Bulls	.50	.23	.06
☐ 4 Derrick Coleman New Jersey Nets	.60	.25	.08
☐ 5 Chris Webber Golden State Warriors	3.00	1.35	.40
☐ 6 Dennis Rodman San Antonio Spurs	.25	.11	.03
☐ 7 Gary Payton Seattle Supersonics	.25	.11	.03
☐ 8 Anfernee Hardaway Orlando Magic	2.00	.90	.25
☐ 9 Dan Majerle Phoenix Suns	.25	.11	.03

1994-95 Fleer Triple Threats

Randomly inserted in all first-series packs, these 10 standard-size (2 1/2" by 3 1/2") cards feature on their borderless fronts multiple color player action cutouts on black backgrounds highlighted by colorful basketball court designs. The player's name appears in gold-foil lettering in a lower corner. This background design continues on the back, which carries a color player cutout on one side and career highlights in a ghosted strip on the other. The cards are numbered on the back as "X of 10."

	MINT	EXC	G-VG
COMPLETE SET (10)	10.00	4.50	1.25
COMMON PLAYER (1-10)	.50	.23	.06
☐ 1 Mookie Blaylock	.50	.23	.06
Atlanta Hawks			
☐ 2 Patrick Ewing	1.25	.55	.16
New York Knicks			
☐ 3 Shawn Kemp	1.25	.55	.16
Seattle Supersonics			
☐ 4 Karl Malone	1.00	.45	.13
Utah Jazz			
☐ 5 Reggie Miller	.75	.35	.09
Indiana Pacers			
☐ 6 Hakeem Olajuwon	2.00	.90	.25
Houston Rockets			
☐ 7 Shaquille O'Neal	4.00	1.80	.50
Orlando Magic			
☐ 8 Scottie Pippen	1.25	.55	.16
Chicago Bulls			
☐ 9 David Robinson	1.50	.65	.19
San Antonio Spurs			
☐ 10 Latrell Sprewell	1.00	.45	.13
Golden State Warriors			

1991 Front Row 50

The 1991 Front Row Basketball Draft Pick set contains 50 cards measuring the standard-size (2 1/2" by 3 1/2"). For the American version, Front Row produced approximately 150,000 factory sets and 600 wax cases, for a total press run of about 187,000 sets. The factory sets come with an official certificate of authenticity that bears a unique serial number. Two bilingual versions were also printed. The Japanese/English version features the same players as in the American version, but with different production quantities (62,000 factory sets and 600 wax cases). The Italian/English version features many different players and has 100 cards, with production quantities of 30,000 factory sets and 3,000 wax cases. Finally the bonus card in the American version could be redeemed for two Italian Promotional cards and an additional card number 50 to replace the returned bonus card.

The front design features glossy color action player photos with white borders. The player's name appears in a green stripe beneath the picture. The backs have different smaller color photos (upper right corner) as well as biography, college statistics, and achievements superimposed on a gray background with an orange basketball. The set also includes a second (career highlights) card of some players (39-43), and a subset devoted to Larry Johnson (44-49). The cards are numbered on the back. The Japanese sets are valued the same as the American version. Gold versions of the cards are valued at four times the values below; silver versions of the cards are valued at two times the values below.

	MINT	EXC	G-VG
COMPLETE SET (50)	4.00	1.60	.40
COMMON PLAYER (1-50)	.04	.02	.00
☐ 1 Larry Johnson UNLV	1.50	.60	.15
☐ 2 Kenny Anderson Georgia Tech	.75	.30	.07
☐ 3 Rick Fox North Carolina	.30	.12	.03
☐ 4 Pete Chilcutt North Carolina	.15	.06	.01
☐ 5 George Ackles UNLV	.07	.03	.01
☐ 6 Mark Macon Temple	.10	.04	.01
☐ 7 Greg Anthony UNLV	.15	.06	.01
☐ 8 Mike Iuzzolino St. Francis	.07	.03	.01
☐ 9 Anthony Avent Seton Hall	.15	.06	.01
☐ 10 Terrell Brandon Oregon	.20	.08	.02
☐ 11 Kevin Brooks SW Louisiana	.07	.03	.01
☐ 12 Myron Brown Slippery Rock	.07	.03	.01
☐ 13 Chris Corchiani North Carolina State	.10	.04	.01
☐ 14 Chris Gatling Old Dominion	.15	.06	.01
☐ 15 Marcus Kennedy Eastern Michigan	.04	.02	.00
☐ 16 Eric Murdock Providence	.35	.14	.03
☐ 17 Tony Farmer Nebraska	.04	.02	.00
☐ 18 Keith Hughes Rutgers	.04	.02	.00
☐ 19 Kevin Lynch Minnesota	.07	.03	.01
☐ 20 Chad Gallagher Creighton	.04	.02	.00

☐ 21	Darrin Chancellor	.04	.02	.00
	Southern Mississippi			
☐ 22	Jimmy Oliver	.04	.02	.00
	Purdue			
☐ 23	Von McDade	.04	.02	.00
	Wisconsin-Milwaukee			
☐ 24	Donald Hodge	.07	.03	.01
	Temple			
☐ 25	Randy Brown	.10	.04	.01
	New Mexico State			
☐ 26	Doug Overton	.10	.04	.01
	LaSalle			
☐ 27	LeRon Ellis	.10	.04	.01
	Syracuse			
☐ 28	Sean Green	.07	.03	.01
	Iona			
☐ 29	Elliot Perry	.07	.03	.01
	Memphis State			
☐ 30	Richard Dumas	.10	.04	.01
	Oklahoma State			
☐ 31	Dale Davis	.40	.16	.04
	Clemson			
☐ 32	Lamont Strothers	.07	.03	.01
	Christopher Newport			
☐ 33	Steve Hood	.04	.02	.00
	James Madison			
☐ 34	Joey Wright	.04	.02	.00
	Texas			
☐ 35	Patrick Eddie	.04	.02	.00
	Mississippi			
☐ 36	Joe Wylie	.04	.02	.00
	Miami			
☐ 37	Bobby Phills	.15	.06	.01
	Southern			
☐ 38	Alvaro Teheran	.04	.02	.00
	Houston			
☐ 39	Dale Davis	.20	.08	.02
	Career Highlights			
☐ 40	Rick Fox	.15	.06	.01
	Career Highlights			
☐ 41	Terrell Brandon	.10	.04	.01
	Career Highlights			
☐ 42	Greg Anthony	.07	.03	.01
	Career Highlights			
☐ 43	Mark Macon	.07	.03	.01
	Career Highlights			
☐ 44	Larry Johnson	.50	.20	.05
	Career Highlights			
☐ 45	Larry Johnson	.50	.20	.05
	First in the Nation			
☐ 46	Larry Johnson	.50	.20	.05
	Power			
☐ 47	Larry Johnson	.50	.20	.05
	A Class Act			
☐ 48	Larry Johnson	.50	.20	.05
	Flashback			
☐ 49	Larry Johnson	.50	.20	.05
	Up Close and Personal			
☐ 50A	Bonus Card	.50	.20	.05
☐ 50B	Marty Conlon	.10	.04	.01
	Providence			

1991 Front Row Update

The 1991 Front Row Update basketball set completes the 1991 Front Row Draft Picks set. Each card was accompanied by a certificate of authenticity that bears a unique serial number, with the production run reported to be 50,000 sets. The cards measure the standard size (2 1/2" by 3 1/2"). The fronts feature glossy color action player photos enclosed by white borders. A basketball backboard and rim with the words "Update 92" appears in the lower left corner, with the player's name and position in a dark green stripe beneath the picture. On a

gray background with an orange basketball, the backs carry biography, color close-up photo, statistics, and achievements. The cards are numbered on the back. Gold versions of the cards are valued at three times the values below; silver versions of the cards are valued at two times the values below.

	MINT	EXC	G-VG
COMPLETE SET (50)	3.00	1.20	.30
COMMON PLAYER (51-100)	.04	.02	.00
☐ 51 Billy Owens Syracuse	.50	.20	.05
☐ 52 Dikembe Mutombo Georgetown	.75	.30	.07
☐ 53 Steve Smith Michigan State	.50	.20	.05
☐ 54 Luc Longley New Mexico	.20	.08	.02
☐ 55 Doug Smith Missouri	.15	.06	.01
☐ 56 Stacey Augmon UNLV	.50	.20	.05
☐ 57 Brian Williams Arizona	.20	.08	.02
☐ 58 Stanley Roberts LSU	.12	.05	.01
☐ 59 Rodney Monroe North Carolina State	.07	.03	.01
☐ 60 Isaac Austin Arizona State	.04	.02	.00
☐ 61 Rich King Nebraska	.10	.04	.01
☐ 62 Victor Alexander Iowa State	.15	.06	.01
☐ 63 LaBradford Smith Louisville	.07	.03	.01
☐ 64 Greg Sutton Oklahoma City	.04	.02	.00
☐ 65 John Turner Phillips	.04	.02	.00
☐ 66 Joao Viana Nassuna	.04	.02	.00
☐ 67 Charles Thomas Eastern Michigan	.04	.02	.00
☐ 68 Carl Thomas Eastern Michigan	.04	.02	.00
☐ 69 Tharon Mayes Florida State	.04	.02	.00
☐ 70 David Benoit Alabama	.20	.08	.02
☐ 71 Corey Crowder Kentucky Wesleyan	.04	.02	.00
☐ 72 Larry Stewart Coppin State	.10	.04	.01

☐ 73 Steve Bardo	.04	.02	.00
Illinois			
☐ 74 Paris McCurdy	.04	.02	.00
Ball State			
☐ 75 Robert Pack	.25	.10	.02
USC			
☐ 76 Doug Lee	.04	.02	.00
Purdue			
☐ 77 Tom Copa	.04	.02	.00
Marquette			
☐ 78 Keith Owens	.04	.02	.00
UCLA			
☐ 79 Mike Goodson	.04	.02	.00
Pittsburgh			
☐ 80 John Crotty	.10	.04	.01
Virginia			
☐ 81 Sean Muto	.04	.02	.00
St. John's			
☐ 82 Chancellor Nichols	.04	.02	.00
James Madison			
☐ 83 Stevie Thompson	.04	.02	.00
Syracuse			
☐ 84 Demetrius Calip	.04	.02	.00
Michigan			
☐ 85 Clifford Martin	.04	.02	.00
Idaho			
☐ 86 Andy Kennedy	.04	.02	.00
Alabama (Birmingham)			
☐ 87 Oliver Taylor	.04	.02	.00
Seton Hall			
☐ 88 Gary Waites	.04	.02	.00
Alabama			
☐ 89 Matt Roe	.04	.02	.00
Maryland			
☐ 90 Cedric Lewis	.04	.02	.00
Maryland			
☐ 91 Emanuel Davis	.04	.02	.00
Deleware State			
☐ 92 Jackie Jones	.04	.02	.00
Oklahoma			
☐ 93 Clifford Scales	.04	.02	.00
Nebraska			
☐ 94 Cameron Burns	.04	.02	.00
Mississippi State			
☐ 95 Clinton Venable	.04	.02	.00
Bowling Green			
☐ 96 Ken Redfield	.04	.02	.00
Michigan State			
☐ 97 Melvin Newbern	.04	.02	.00
Minnesota			
☐ 98 Chris Harris	.04	.02	.00
Illinois (Chicago)			
☐ 99 Bonus Card	.50	.20	.05
☐ 100 Checklist	.07	.03	.01

1991 Front Row Italian/English 100

The 1991 Front Row Italian/English Basketball Draft Pick set contains 100 cards measuring standard size (2 1/2" by 3 1/2"). Each factory set comes with an official certificate of authenticity that bears a unique serial number. This set is distinguished from the American version by length (100 instead of 50 cards), different production quantities (30,000 factory sets and 3,000 wax cases), and a red stripe on the card front. The front design features glossy color action player photos with white borders. The player's name appears in a red stripe beneath the picture. The backs have different smaller color photos (upper right corner) as well as biography, college statistics, and achievements superimposed on a gray background with an orange basketball. The set also includes a second (career highlights) card of some players (39-43), a subset devoted to Larry Johnson (44-49), and two "Retrospect" cards (96-97). The cards are numbered on the back.

	MINT	EXC	G-VG
COMPLETE SET (100)	5.00	2.00	.50
COMMON PLAYER (1-50)	.04	.02	.00
COMMON PLAYER (51-100)	.04	.02	.00
☐ 1 Larry Johnson UNLV	1.50	.60	.15
☐ 2 Kenny Anderson Georgia Tech	.75	.30	.07
☐ 3 Rick Fox North Carolina	.30	.12	.03
☐ 4 Pete Chilcutt North Carolina	.15	.06	.01
☐ 5 George Ackles UNLV	.07	.03	.01
☐ 6 Mark Macon Temple	.10	.04	.01
☐ 7 Greg Anthony UNLV	.15	.06	.01
☐ 8 Mike Iuzzolino St. Francis	.07	.03	.01
☐ 9 Anthony Avent Seton Hall	.15	.06	.01
☐ 10 Terrell Brandon Oregon	.20	.08	.02
☐ 11 Kevin Brooks SW Louisiana	.07	.03	.01
☐ 12 Myron Brown Slippery Rock	.07	.03	.01
☐ 13 Chris Corchiani North Carolina State	.10	.04	.01
☐ 14 Chris Gatling Old Dominion	.15	.06	.01
☐ 15 Marcus Kennedy Eastern Michigan	.04	.02	.00
☐ 16 Eric Murdock Providence	.35	.14	.03
☐ 17 Tony Farmer Nebraska	.04	.02	.00
☐ 18 Keith Hughes Rutgers	.04	.02	.00
☐ 19 Kevin Lynch Minnesota	.07	.03	.01
☐ 20 Chad Gallagher Creighton	.04	.02	.00
☐ 21 Darrin Chancellor Southern Mississippi	.04	.02	.00
☐ 22 Jimmy Oliver Purdue	.04	.02	.00
☐ 23 Von McDade Wisconsin-Milwaukee	.04	.02	.00
☐ 24 Donald Hodge	.07	.03	.01

	Temple			
☐ 25	Randy Brown	.10	.04	.01
	New Mexico State			
☐ 26	Doug Overton	.10	.04	.01
	LaSalle			
☐ 27	LeRon Ellis	.10	.04	.01
	Syracuse			
☐ 28	Sean Green	.07	.03	.01
	Iona			
☐ 29	Elliot Perry	.07	.03	.01
	Memphis State			
☐ 30	Richard Dumas	.10	.04	.01
	Oklahoma State			
☐ 31	Dale Davis	.40	.16	.04
	Clemson			
☐ 32	Lamont Strothers	.07	.03	.01
	Christopher Newport			
☐ 33	Steve Hood	.04	.02	.00
	James Madison			
☐ 34	Joey Wright	.04	.02	.00
	Texas			
☐ 35	Patrick Eddie	.04	.02	.00
	Mississippi			
☐ 36	Joe Wylie	.04	.02	.00
	Miami			
☐ 37	Bobby Phills	.15	.06	.01
	Southern			
☐ 38	Alvaro Teheran	.04	.02	.00
	Houston			
☐ 39	Dale Davis	.20	.08	.02
	Career Highlights			
☐ 40	Rick Fox	.15	.06	.01
	Career Highlights			
☐ 41	Terrell Brandon	.10	.04	.01
	Career Highlights			
☐ 42	Greg Anthony	.07	.03	.01
	Career Highlights			
☐ 43	Mark Macon	.07	.03	.01
	Career Highlights			
☐ 44	Larry Johnson	.50	.20	.05
	Career Highlights			
☐ 45	Larry Johnson	.50	.20	.05
	First in the Nation			
☐ 46	Larry Johnson	.50	.20	.05
	Power			
☐ 47	Larry Johnson	.50	.20	.05
	A Class Act			
☐ 48	Larry Johnson	.50	.20	.05
	Flashback			
☐ 49	Larry Johnson	.50	.20	.05
	Up Close and Personal			
☐ 50A	Bonus Card	.50	.20	.05
☐ 50B	Marty Conlon	.10	.04	.01
	Providence			
☐ 51	Mike Goodson	.04	.02	.00
	Pittsburgh			
☐ 52	Drexel Deveaux	.04	.02	.00
	Tampa			
☐ 53	Sean Muto	.04	.02	.00
	St. John's			
☐ 54	Keith Owens	.04	.02	.00
	UCLA			
☐ 55	Joao Viana	.04	.02	.00
	Nassuna			
☐ 56	Chancellor Nichols	.04	.02	.00
	James Madison			
☐ 57	Charles Thomas	.04	.02	.00
	Eastern Michigan			
☐ 58	Carl Thomas	.04	.02	.00
	Eastern Michigan			
☐ 59	Anthony Blakley	.04	.02	.00
	Panhandle State			
☐ 60	Demetrius Calip	.04	.02	.00
	Michigan			

☐ 61	Dale Turnquist .04 Bethel College	.02	.00
☐ 62	Carlos Funchess .04 Northeast Louisiana	.02	.00
☐ 63	Tharon Mayes .04 Florida State	.02	.00
☐ 64	Andy Kennedy .04 Alabama - Birmingham	.02	.00
☐ 65	Oliver Taylor .04 Seton Hall	.02	.00
☐ 66	David Benoit .20 Alabama	.08	.02
☐ 67	Gary Waites .04 Alabama	.02	.00
☐ 68	Corey Crowder .04 Kentucky Wesleyan	.02	.00
☐ 69	Sydney Grider .04 Southwestern Louisiana -	.02	.00
☐ 70	Derek Strong .07 Xavier	.03	.01
☐ 71	Larry Stewart .10 Coppin State	.04	.01
☐ 72	Matt Roe .04 Maryland	.02	.00
☐ 73	Cedric Lewis .04 Maryland	.02	.00
☐ 74	Anthony Houston .04 St. Mary's	.02	.00
☐ 75	Steve Bardo .04 Illinois	.02	.00
☐ 76	Marc Brown .04 Siena	.02	.00
☐ 77	Michael Cutright .04 McNeese State	.02	.00
☐ 78	Emanuel Davis .04 Deleware State	.02	.00
☐ 79	Paris McCurdy .04 Ball State	.02	.00
☐ 80	Jackie Jones .04 Oklahoma State	.02	.00
☐ 81	Mark Peterson .04 Rutgers	.02	.00
☐ 82	Clifford Scales .04 Nebraska	.02	.00
☐ 83	Robert Pack .25 USC	.10	.02
☐ 84	Doug Lee .04 Purdue	.02	.00
☐ 85	Cameron Burns .04 Mississippi State	.02	.00
☐ 86	Tom Copa .04 Marquette	.02	.00
☐ 87	Clinton Venable .04 Bowling Green State	.02	.00
☐ 88	Ken Redfield .04 Michigan State	.02	.00
☐ 89	Melvin Newbern .04 Minnesota	.02	.00
☐ 90	Darren Henrie .04 David Lipscomb	.02	.00
☐ 91	Chris Harris .04 Illinois (Chicago)	.02	.00
☐ 92	John Crotty .10 Virginia	.04	.01
☐ 93	Paul Graham .10 Ohio	.04	.01
☐ 94	Stevie Thompson .04 Syracuse	.02	.00
☐ 95	Clifford Martin .04 Idaho	.02	.00
☐ 96	Brian Shaw .07 UC Santa Barbara	.03	.01
☐ 97	Danny Ferry .07	.03	.01

		MINT	EXC	G-VG
	Duke			
☐ 98	Doug Loescher	.04	.02	.00
☐ 99	Checklist	.04	.02	.00
☐ 100	Bonus Card	.50	.20	.05

1991-92 Front Row Premier

The 1991-92 Front Row Premier set contains 120 standard-size (2 1/2" by 3 1/2") cards. No factory sets were made, and the production run was limited to 2,500 waxbox cases, with 360 cards per box. The set included five bonus cards (86, 88, 90, 91, 93) that were redeemable through a mail-in offer for unnamed player cards. Moreover, limited edition cards as well as gold, silver, and autographed cards were randomly inserted in the wax packs. The glossy color player photos on the fronts are enclosed by borders with different shades of white and blue. The player's name appears in a silver stripe beneath the picture. The backs have biography, statistics, and achievements superimposed on an orange basketball icon. The cards are numbered on the back.

		MINT	EXC	G-VG
COMPLETE SET (120)		8.00	3.25	.80
COMMON PLAYER (1-120)		.04	.02	.00
☐ 1	Rich King	.10	.04	.01
	Nebraska			
☐ 2	Kenny Anderson	.75	.30	.07
	Georgia Tech			
☐ 3	Billy Owens ACC	.15	.06	.01
	Syracuse			
☐ 4	Ken Redfield	.04	.02	.00
	Michigan State			
☐ 5	Robert Pack	.25	.10	.02
	USC			
☐ 6	Clinton Venable	.04	.02	.00
	Bowling Green			
☐ 7	Tom Copa	.04	.02	.00
	Marquette			
☐ 8	Rick Fox HL	.10	.04	.01
	North Carolina			
☐ 9	Cameron Burns	.04	.02	.00
	Mississippi State			
☐ 10	Doug Lee	.04	.02	.00
	Purdue			
☐ 11	LaBradford Smith	.07	.03	.01
	Louisville			
☐ 12	Clifford Scales	.04	.02	.00
	Nebraska			
☐ 13	Mark Peterson	.04	.02	.00
	Rutgers			
☐ 14	Jackie Jones	.04	.02	.00
	Oklahoma			
☐ 15	Paris McCurdy	.04	.02	.00
	Ball State			
☐ 16	Dikembe Mutombo ACC	.25	.10	.02
	Georgetown			
☐ 17	Emanuel Davis	.04	.02	.00
	Delaware State			
☐ 18	Michael Cutright	.04	.02	.00
	McNeese State			
☐ 19	Marc Brown	.04	.02	.00
	Siena			
☐ 20	Steve Bardo	.04	.02	.00
	Illinois			
☐ 21	John Turner	.04	.02	.00
	Phillips			
☐ 22	Anthony Houston	.04	.02	.00
	St. Mary's			
☐ 23	Cedric Lewis	.04	.02	.00
	Maryland			

☐ 24	Matt Roe Maryland	.04	.02	.00
☐ 25	Larry Stewart Coppin State	.10	.04	.01
☐ 26	Derek Strong Xavier	.07	.03	.01
☐ 27	Sydney Grider Southwestern Louisiana	.04	.02	.00
☐ 28	Corey Crowder Kentucky Wesleyan	.04	.02	.00
☐ 29	Gary Waites Alabama	.04	.02	.00
☐ 30	David Benoit Alabama	.20	.08	.02
☐ 31	Larry Johnson ACC UNLV	.40	.16	.04
☐ 32	Oliver Taylor UER Seton Hall (Chris Corchiani's name on back)	.04	.02	.00
☐ 33	Andy Kennedy Alabama-Birmingham	.04	.02	.00
☐ 34	Tharon Mayes Florida State	.04	.02	.00
☐ 35	Carlos Funchess Northeast Louisiana	.04	.02	.00
☐ 36	Dale Turnquist Bethel	.04	.02	.00
☐ 37	Luc Longley New Mexico	.20	.08	.02
☐ 38	Demetrius Calip Michigan	.04	.02	.00
☐ 39	Anthony Blakley Panhandle State	.04	.02	.00
☐ 40	Carl Thomas Eastern Michigan	.04	.02	.00
☐ 41	Charles Thomas Eastern Michigan	.04	.02	.00
☐ 42	Chancellor Nichols James Madison	.04	.02	.00
☐ 43	Joao Viana Nassuna	.04	.02	.00
☐ 44	Keith Owens UCLA	.04	.02	.00
☐ 45	Sean Muto St. Johns	.04	.02	.00
☐ 46	Drexel Deveaux Tampa	.04	.02	.00
☐ 47	Stacey Augmon ACC UNLV	.15	.06	.01
☐ 48	Mike Goodson Pittsburgh	.04	.02	.00
☐ 49	Marty Conlon Providence	.07	.03	.01
☐ 50	Mark Macon Temple	.10	.04	.01
☐ 51	Greg Anthony UNLV	.15	.06	.01
☐ 52	Dale Davis Clemson	.40	.16	.04
☐ 53	Isaac Austin Arizona State	.04	.02	.00
☐ 54	Alvaro Teheran Houston	.04	.02	.00
☐ 55	Bobby Phills Southern	.15	.06	.01
☐ 56	Joe Wylie Miami	.04	.02	.00
☐ 57	Patrick Eddie Mississippi	.04	.02	.00
☐ 58	Joey Wright Texas	.04	.02	.00
☐ 59	Steve Hood	.04	.02	.00

James Maidson			
☐ 60. Lamont Strothers	.07	.03	.01
Christopher Newport			
☐ 61 Victor Alexander	.15	.06	.01
Iowa State			
☐ 62 Richard Dumas	.10	.04	.01
Oklahoma State			
☐ 63 Elliot Perry	.07	.03	.01
Memphis State			
☐ 64 Sean Green	.07	.03	.01
Iona			
☐ 65 Rick Fox	.30	.12	.03
North Carolina			
☐ 66 LeRon Ellis	.10	.04	.01
Syracuse			
☐ 67 Doug Overton	.10	.04	.01
LaSalle			
☐ 68 Randy Brown	.10	.04	.01
New Mexico State			
☐ 69 Donald Hodge	.07	.03	.01
Temple			
☐ 70 Von McDade	.04	.02	.00
Wisconsin-Milwaukee			
☐ 71 Greg Sutton	.04	.02	.00
Oral Roberts			
☐ 72 Jimmy Oliver	.04	.02	.00
Purdue			
☐ 73 Terrell Brandon HL	.10	.04	.01
Oregon			
☐ 74 Darrin Chancellor	.04	.02	.00
Southern Mississippi			
☐ 75 Chad Gallagher	.04	.02	.00
Creighton			
☐ 76 Kevin Lynch	.07	.03	.01
Minnesota			
☐ 77 Keith Hughes	.04	.02	.00
Rutgers			
☐ 78 Tony Farmer	.04	.02	.00
Nebraska			
☐ 79 Eric Murdock	.35	.14	.03
Providence			
☐ 80 Marcus Kennedy	.04	.02	.00
Eastern Michigan			
☐ 81 Larry Johnson	1.50	.60	.15
UNLV			
☐ 82 Stacey Augmon	.50	.20	.05
UNLV			
☐ 83 Dikembe Mutombo	.75	.30	.07
Georgetown			
☐ 84 Steve Smith	.50	.20	.05
Michigan State			
☐ 85 Billy Owens UER	.50	.20	.05
Syracuse			
☐ 86 Bonus Card 1	.15	.06	.01
Stanley Roberts			
LSU			
☐ 87 Brian Shaw	.07	.03	.01
UC Santa Barbara			
☐ 88 Bonus Card 2	.15	.06	.01
Rodney Monroe			
North Carolina State			
☐ 89 LaBradford Smith HL	.07	.03	.01
Louisville			
☐ 90 Bonus Card 3	.15	.06	.01
Mark Randall			
Kansas			
☐ 91 Bonus Card 4	.15	.06	.01
Brian Williams			
Arizona			
☐ 92 Danny Ferry FLB	.07	.03	.01
Duke			
☐ 93 Bonus Card 5	.15	.06	.01
Shawn Vandiver			
Colorado			

☐ 94	Doug Smith HL Missouri	.07	.03	.01
☐ 95	Luc Longley HL New Mexico	.10	.04	.01
☐ 96	Billy Owens HL Syracuse	.15	.06	.01
☐ 97	Steve Smith HL Michigan State	.15	.06	.01
☐ 98	Dikembe Mutombo HL Georgetown	.25	.10	.02
☐ 99	Stacey Augmon HL UNLV	.15	.06	.01
☐ 100	Larry Johnson HL UNLV	.40	.16	.04
☐ 101	Chris Gatling Old Dominion	.15	.06	.01
☐ 102	Chris Corchiani North Carolina State	.10	.04	.01
☐ 103	Myron Brown Slippery Rock	.07	.03	.01
☐ 104	Kevin Brooks Southwestern Louisiana	.07	.03	.01
☐ 105	Anthony Avent Seton Hall	.15	.06	.01
☐ 106	Steve Smith ACC Michigan State	.15	.06	.01
☐ 107	Mike Iuzzolino Saint Francis	.07	.03	.01
☐ 108	George Ackles UNLV	.07	.03	.01
☐ 109	Melvin Newbern Minnesota	.04	.02	.00
☐ 110	Robert Pack HL USC	.10	.04	.01
☐ 111	Darren Henrie David Lipscomb	.04	.02	.00
☐ 112	Chris Harris Illinois-Chicago	.04	.02	.00
☐ 113	John Crotty Virginia	.10	.04	.01
☐ 114	Terrell Brandon Oregon	.20	.08	.02
☐ 115	Paul Graham Ohio	.10	.04	.01
☐ 116	Stevie Thompson Syracuse	.04	.02	.00
☐ 117	Clifford Martin Idaho	.04	.02	.00
☐ 118	Doug Smith Missouri	.15	.06	.01
☐ 119	Pete Chilcutt North Carolina	.15	.06	.01
☐ 120	Checklist Card	.07	.03	.01

1992 Front Row Draft Picks

The 1992 Front Row Draft Picks basketball set consists of 100 standard-size (2 1/2" by 3 1/2") cards. The set was sold in a cardboard box, and the back panel carries the set serial number and total production run (150,000). The fronts features color action player photos. Teal borders shading from dark to light surround the pictures. A gradated orange vertical bar containing the player's name is superimposed over one side of the photo. The Front Row Draft Picks logo appears below it. The miniature representation of the team mascot appears in the lower left corner. The horizontal backs display biography, collegiate statistics, and career highlights on a teal background with white borders. An orange bar similar to the one on the front runs down the right edge and contains the words "Draft Picks '92". Four cards (90, 92, 96, and 99) have player photos instead of text on their backs. The cards are numbered on the back. Gold versions of the cards are valued at four times the values below; silver versions of the cards are valued at two times the values below.

	MINT	EXC	G-VG
COMPLETE SET (100)	8.00	3.25	.80
COMMON PLAYER (1-100)	.04	.02	.00
☐ 1 Eric Anderson	.10	.04	.01
Indiana			
☐ 2 Darin Archbold	.04	.02	.00
Butler			
☐ 3 Woody Austin	.04	.02	.00
Purdue			
☐ 4 Mark Baker	.04	.02	.00
Ohio State			
☐ 5 Jon Barry	.20	.08	.02
Georgia Tech			
☐ 6 Elmer Bennett	.07	.03	.01
Notre Dame			
☐ 7 Tony Bennett	.15	.06	.01
Wisconsin-Green Bay			
☐ 8 Alex Blackwell	.07	.03	.01
Monmouth			
☐ 9 Curtis Blair	.04	.02	.00
Richmond			
☐ 10 Ed Book	.04	.02	.00
Canisius			
☐ 11 Marques Bragg	.04	.02	.00
Providence			
☐ 12 P.J. Brown	.04	.02	.00
Louisiana Tech			
☐ 13 Anthony Buford	.04	.02	.00
Cincinnati			
☐ 14 Dexter Cambridge	.04	.02	.00
Texas			
☐ 15 Brian Davis	.10	.04	.01
Duke			
☐ 16 Lucius Davis	.07	.03	.01
UC Santa Barbara			
☐ 17 Todd Day	.30	.12	.03
Arkansas			
☐ 18 Greg Dennis	.04	.02	.00
East Tennessee State			
☐ 19 Radenko Dobras	.04	.02	.00
South Florida			
☐ 20 Harold Ellis	.25	.10	.02
Morehouse			
☐ 21 Chris King	.10	.04	.01
Wake Forest			
☐ 22 Jo Jo English	.10	.04	.01
South Carolina			
☐ 23 Deron Feldhaus	.07	.03	.01
Kentucky			
☐ 24 Matt Geiger	.25	.10	.02
Georgia Tech			

☐ 25	Lewis Geter	.04	.02	.00
	Ohio University			
☐ 26	George Gilmore	.04	.02	.00
	Chaminade			
☐ 27	Litterial Green	.10	.04	.01
	Georgia			
☐ 28	Tom Gugliotta	.75	.30	.07
	North Carolina State			
☐ 29	Jim Havrilla	.04	.02	.00
	Western Michigan			
☐ 30	Robert Horry	.90	.36	.09
	Alabama			
☐ 31	Stephen Howard	.07	.03	.01
	DePaul			
☐ 32	Alonzo Jamison	.07	.03	.01
	Kansas			
☐ 33	David Johnson	.07	.03	.01
	Syracuse			
☐ 34	Herb Jones	.07	.03	.01
	Cincinnati			
☐ 35	Popeye Jones	.07	.03	.01
	Murray State			
☐ 36	Adam Keefe	.12	.05	.01
	Stanford			
☐ 37	Dan Cyrulik	.04	.02	.00
	Connecticut			
☐ 38	Ken Leeks	.04	.02	.00
	Central Florida			
☐ 39	Ricardo Leonard	.04	.02	.00
	Old Dominion			
☐ 40	Gerald Madkins	.04	.02	.00
	UCLA			
☐ 41	Eric Manuel	.04	.02	.00
	Oklahoma City			
☐ 42	Marlon Maxey	.12	.05	.01
	UTEP			
☐ 43	Jim McCoy	.04	.02	.00
	Massachusetts			
☐ 44	Oliver Miller	.35	.14	.03
	Arkansas			
☐ 45	Sean Miller	.04	.02	.00
	Pittsburgh			
☐ 46	Darren Morningstar	.04	.02	.00
	Pittsburgh			
☐ 47	Isaiah Morris	.07	.03	.01
	Arkansas			
☐ 48	James Moses	.04	.02	.00
	Iowa			
☐ 49	Doug Christie	.40	.16	.04
	Pepperdine			
☐ 50	Damon Patterson	.04	.02	.00
	Oklahoma			
☐ 51	John Pelphrey	.07	.03	.01
	Kentucky			
☐ 52	Brent Price	.12	.05	.01
	Oklahoma			
☐ 53	Brett Roberts	.10	.04	.01
	Morehead State			
☐ 54	Steve Rogers	.04	.02	.00
	Alabama State			
☐ 55	Sean Rooks	.20	.08	.02
	Arizona			
☐ 56	Malik Sealy	.15	.06	.01
	St. John's			
☐ 57	Tom Schurfranz	.04	.02	.00
	Bellarmine Kentucky			
☐ 58	David Scott	.04	.02	.00
	Miami (Ohio)			
☐ 59	Rod Sellers	.07	.03	.01
	Connecticut			
☐ 60	Vernel Singleton	.04	.02	.00
	LSU			
☐ 61	Reggie Slater	.04	.02	.00

☐ 62	Wyoming Elmore Spencer	.25	.10	.02
☐ 63	UNLV Chris Smith	.25	.10	.02
☐ 64	Connecticut Latrell Sprewell	1.75	.70	.17
☐ 65	Alabama Matt Steigenga	.07	.03	.01
☐ 66	Michigan State Bryant Stith	.50	.20	.05
☐ 67	Virginia Daimon Sweet	.07	.03	.01
☐ 68	Notre Dame Craig Upchurch	.04	.02	.00
☐ 69	Houston Van Usher	.04	.02	.00
☐ 70	Tennessee Tech Tony Watts	.04	.02	.00
☐ 71	Mississippi State Clarence Weatherspoon	.90	.36	.09
☐ 72	Southern Mississippi Robert Werdann	.07	.03	.01
☐ 73	St. John's Benford Williams	.04	.02	.00
☐ 74	Texas Corey Williams	.04	.02	.00
☐ 75	Oklahoma State Henry Williams	.04	.02	.00
☐ 76	UNC-Charlotte Tim Burroughs	.04	.02	.00
☐ 77	Jacksonville Florida Erik Wilson	.04	.02	.00
☐ 78	Virginia Tech Randy Woods	.10	.04	.01
☐ 79	LaSalle Kendall Youngblood	.04	.02	.00
☐ 80	Utah State Terry Boyd	.04	.02	.00
☐ 81	Western Carolina Tracy Murray	.20	.08	.02
☐ 82	UCLA Reggie Smith	.10	.04	.01
☐ 83	Texas Christian Lee Mayberry	.20	.08	.02
☐ 84	Arkansas Matt Fish	.04	.02	.00
☐ 85	UNC Wilmington Hubert Davis	.30	.12	.03
☐ 86	North Carolina Duane Cooper	.07	.03	.01
☐ 87	USC Anthony Peeler	.35	.14	.03
☐ 88	Missouri Harold Miner	.40	.16	.04
☐ 89	USC Harold Miner "Miner on Dunking"	.12	.05	.01
☐ 90	USC Harold Miner (Action on both sides)	.12	.05	.01
☐ 91	USC Christian Laettner	.60	.24	.06
☐ 92	Duke Christian Laettner (Action shot on front, portrait on back)	.20	.08	.02
☐ 93	Duke Christian Laettner and Brian Davis	.20	.08	.02
☐ 94	Duke "A Devilish Duo" Walt Williams	.30	.12	.03
	Maryland			

☐ 95 Walt Williams	.10	.04	.01
"ACC Terror"			
Maryland			
☐ 96 Walt Williams	.10	.04	.01
(Action shot on			
front, portrait on back)			
Maryland			
☐ 97 LaPhonso Ellis	.90	.36	.09
Notre Dame			
☐ 98 LaPhonso Ellis	.30	.12	.03
"The Ellis File"			
Notre Dame			
☐ 99 Laphonso Ellis	.30	.12	.03
(Action shot on			
front, portrait on back)			
Notre Dame			
☐ 100 Checklist 1-100	.04	.02	.00

1992 Front Row Dream Picks

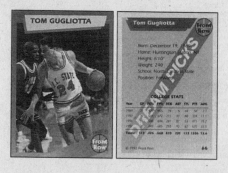

The 1992 Front Row Dream Picks basketball set contains 100 cards measuring the standard size (2 1/2" by 3 1/2"). The set features five cards each of the top ten players who signed with Front Row from the 1991 NBA Draft and five cards of the top ten from the 1992 draft. The fronts display color action player photos bordered in purple. The player's name appears above the picture in a yellow bar accented by a red shadow border. The Front Row logo appears at the lower right corner in an orange diagonal stripe. The backs are predominantly yellow and present career summary and highlights. The words "Dream Picks" appear in an orange diagonal stripe on the back. The fifth card of each five-card set has a second color player photo on its back. The cards are numbered on the back. Gold versions of the cards are valued at three times the values below; silver versions of the cards are valued at two times the values below.

	MINT	EXC	G-VG
COMPLETE SET (100)	8.00	3.25	.80
COMMON PLAYER (1-100)	.04	.02	.00
☐ 1 Larry Johnson	.50	.20	.05
UNLV			
College Stats			
☐ 2 Larry Johnson	.40	.16	.04
Career Highlights			
☐ 3 Larry Johnson	.40	.16	.04
NBA All-Rookie Team			
☐ 4 Larry Johnson	.40	.16	.04
NBA Rookie of the Year			

☐ 5	Larry Johnson	.40	.16	.04
☐ 6	Dikembe Mutombo	.20	.08	.02
	Georgetown			
	College Stats			
☐ 7	Dikembe Mutombo	.20	.08	.02
	Career Highlights			
☐ 8	Dikembe Mutombo	.20	.08	.02
	NBA All-Rookie Team			
☐ 9	Dikembe Mutombo	.20	.08	.02
	NBA All-Star			
☐ 10	Dikembe Mutombo	.20	.08	.02
☐ 11	Stacey Augmon	.12	.05	.01
	UNLV			
	College Stats			
☐ 12	Stacey Augmon	.12	.05	.01
	Career Highlights			
☐ 13	Stacey Augmon	.12	.05	.01
	NBA All-Rookie Team			
☐ 14	Stacey Augmon	.12	.05	.01
	Defensive Specialist			
☐ 15	Stacey Augmon	.12	.05	.01
☐ 16	Billy Owens	.12	.05	.01
	Syracuse			
	College Stats			
☐ 17	Billy Owens	.12	.05	.01
	Career Highlights			
☐ 18	Billy Owens	.12	.05	.01
	NBA All-Rookie Team			
☐ 19	Billy Owens	.12	.05	.01
	A Proven Winner			
☐ 20	Billy Owens	.12	.05	.01
☐ 21	Clarence Weatherspoon	.30	.12	.03
	Southern Miss.			
	College Stats			
☐ 22	Clarence Weatherspoon	.30	.12	.03
	Career Highlights			
☐ 23	Clarence Weatherspoon	.30	.12	.03
	NBA Scouting Report			
☐ 24	Clarence Weatherspoon	.30	.12	.03
	Flexible Golden Eagle			
☐ 25	Clarence Weatherspoon	.30	.12	.03
☐ 26	Steve Smith	.12	.05	.01
	Michigan State			
	College Stats			
☐ 27	Steve Smith	.12	.05	.01
	Career Highlights			
☐ 28	Steve Smith	.12	.05	.01
	NBA All-Rookie Team			
☐ 29	Steve Smith	.12	.05	.01
	Withstanding the Heat			
☐ 30	Steve Smith	.12	.05	.01
☐ 31	Larry Stewart	.04	.02	.00
	Coppin State			
	College Stats			
☐ 32	Larry Stewart	.04	.02	.00
	Career Highlights			
☐ 33	Larry Stewart	.04	.02	.00
	NBA All-Rookie Team			
☐ 34	Larry Stewart	.04	.02	.00
	Against the Odds			
☐ 35	Larry Stewart	.04	.02	.00
☐ 36	Rick Fox	.07	.03	.01
	North Carolina			
	College Stats			
☐ 37	Rick Fox	.07	.03	.01
	Career Highlights			
☐ 38	Rick Fox	.07	.03	.01
	NBA All-Rookie Team			
☐ 39	Rick Fox	.07	.03	.01
	Divine Intervention			
☐ 40	Rick Fox	.07	.03	.01
☐ 41	Christian Laettner	.20	.08	.02
	Duke			

	College Stats			
☐ 42	Christian Laettner	.20	.08	.02
	Career Highlights			
☐ 43	Christian Laettner	.20	.08	.02
	NBA Scouting Report			
☐ 44	Christian Laettner	.20	.08	.02
	Championship Season			
☐ 45	Christian Laettner	.20	.08	.02
☐ 46	Bryant Stith	.07	.03	.01
	Virginia			
	College Stats			
☐ 47	Bryant Stith	.07	.03	.01
	Career Highlights			
☐ 48	Bryant Stith	.07	.03	.01
	NBA Scouting Report			
☐ 49	Bryant Stith	.07	.03	.01
	A Change in Perspective			
☐ 50	Bryant Stith	.07	.03	.01
☐ 51	Harold Miner	.12	.05	.01
	USC			
	College Stats			
☐ 52	Harold Miner	.12	.05	.01
	Career Highlights			
☐ 53	Harold Miner	.12	.05	.01
	NBA Scouting Report			
☐ 54	Harold Miner	.12	.05	.01
	An Encounter With Michael			
☐ 55	Harold Miner	.12	.05	.01
☐ 56	Mark Macon	.04	.02	.00
	Temple			
	College Stats			
☐ 57	Mark Macon	.04	.02	.00
	Career Highlights			
☐ 58	Mark Macon	.04	.02	.00
	NBA All-Rookie Team			
☐ 59	Mark Macon	.04	.02	.00
	Stealing the Show			
☐ 60	Mark Macon	.04	.02	.00
☐ 61	Adam Keefe	.04	.02	.00
	Stanford			
	College Stats			
☐ 62	Adam Keefe	.04	.02	.00
	Career Highlights			
☐ 63	Adam Keefe	.04	.02	.00
	NBA Scouting Report			
☐ 64	Adam Keefe	.04	.02	.00
	Premier Big Man			
☐ 65	Adam Keefe	.04	.02	.00
☐ 66	Tom Gugliotta	.25	.10	.02
	North Carolina State			
	College Stats			
☐ 67	Tom Gugliotta	.25	.10	.02
	Career Highlights			
☐ 68	Tom Gugliotta	.25	.10	.02
	NBA Scouting Report			
☐ 69	Tom Gugliotta	.25	.10	.02
	Most Improved			
☐ 70	Tom Gugliotta	.25	.10	.02
☐ 71	Todd Day	.10	.04	.01
	Arkansas			
	College Stats			
☐ 72	Todd Day	.10	.04	.01
	Career Highlights			
☐ 73	Todd Day	.10	.04	.01
	NBA Scouting Report			
☐ 74	Todd Day	.10	.04	.01
	One Bright Day			
☐ 75	Todd Day	.10	.04	.01
☐ 76	Walt Williams	.10	.04	.01
	Maryland			
	College Stats			
☐ 77	Walt Williams	.10	.04	.01
	Career Highlights			

☐ 78 Walt Williams	.10	.04	.01
NBA Scouting Report			
☐ 79 Walt Williams	.10	.04	.01
Nation's Longest Streaks			
☐ 80 Walt Williams	.10	.04	.01
☐ 81 Malik Sealy	.07	.03	.01
St. Johns			
College Stats			
☐ 82 Malik Sealy	.07	.03	.01
Career Highlights			
☐ 83 Malik Sealy	.07	.03	.01
NBA Scouting Report			
☐ 84 Malik Sealy	.07	.03	.01
Malik Wear			
☐ 85 Malik Sealy	.07	.03	.01
☐ 86 Stanley Roberts	.07	.03	.01
LSU			
College Stats			
☐ 87 Stanley Roberts	.07	.03	.01
Career Highlights			
☐ 88 Stanley Roberts	.07	.03	.01
NBA All-Rookie Team			
☐ 89 Stanley Roberts	.07	.03	.01
The Spanish League			
☐ 90 Stanley Roberts	.07	.03	.01
☐ 91 LaPhonso Ellis	.30	.12	.03
Notre Dame			
College Stats			
☐ 92 LaPhonso Ellis	.30	.12	.03
Career Highlights			
☐ 93 LaPhonso Ellis	.30	.12	.03
NBA Scouting Report			
☐ 94 LaPhonso Ellis	.30	.12	.03
Dream Come True			
☐ 95 LaPhonso Ellis	.07	.03	.01
☐ 96 Terrell Brandon	.07	.03	.01
Oregon			
College Stats			
☐ 97 Terrell Brandon	.07	.03	.01
Career Highlights			
☐ 98 Terrell Brandon	.07	.03	.01
NBA All-Rookie Team			
☐ 99 Terrell Brandon	.07	.03	.01
Quickest in the League			
☐ 100 Terrell Brandon	.07	.03	.01

1989-90 Hoops

*The complete 1989-90 Hoops set contains 352 cards measuring the standard size (2 1/2"
by 3 1/2"). The cards were issued in two series of 300 and 52 cards. The fronts feature color
action player photos, bordered by a basketball lane in one of the team's colors. On a white
card face the player's name appears in black lettering above the picture. The backs have
head shots of the players, biographical information, and statistics, all printed on a pale yellow background with white borders. The cards are numbered on the backs. The key Rookie
Card in this set is David Robinson's card number 138, which only appeared in this first
series of Hoops. Beware of David Robinson counterfeit cards which are distinguishable primarily by comparison to a real card or under magnification. Other notable Rookie Cards in
the set are Hersey Hawkins, Jeff Hornacek, Kevin Johnson, Reggie Lewis, Dan Majerle,
Danny Manning, Vernon Maxwell, Mitch Richmond, Rony Seikaly and Rod Strickland. The
second series features the expansion teams (Minnesota and Orlando), traded players, a
special NBA Championship card of the Detroit Pistons, and a David Robinson In Action
(310) card. Cards numbered 301, 305, 307, 308, 318, 322, 328, 339, and 343 all have basketball misspelled as baasketball on the bottom of the card back. Since the original card
number 86 Detroit Pistons World Champs was so difficult for collectors to find in packs,
Hoops produced another edition of the card that was available direct from the company for
free with additional copies available for only 35 cents per card. The short prints (SP below)
in the first series are those cards which were dropped to make room for the new second
series cards on the printing sheet.*

	MINT	**EXC**	**G-VG**
COMPLETE SET (352)	40.00	18.00	5.00
COMPLETE SERIES 1 (300)	35.00	16.00	4.40
COMPLETE SERIES 2 (52)	5.00	2.30	.60
COMMON PLAYER (1-300)	.05	.02	.01
COMMON PLAYER (301-352)	.05	.02	.01

	MINT	EXC	G-VG
☐ 1 Joe Dumars Detroit Pistons	.20	.09	.03
☐ 2 Tree Rollins Cleveland Cavaliers	.08	.04	.01
☐ 3 Kenny Walker New York Knicks	.05	.02	.01
☐ 4 Mychal Thompson Los Angeles Lakers	.08	.04	.01
☐ 5 Alvin Robertson SP San Antonio Spurs	.20	.09	.03
☐ 6 Vinny Del Negro Sacramento Kings	.15	.07	.02
☐ 7 Greg Anderson SP San Antonio Spurs	.15	.07	.02
☐ 8 Rod Strickland New York Knicks	.60	.25	.08
☐ 9 Ed Pinckney Boston Celtics	.05	.02	.01
☐ 10 Dale Ellis Seattle Supersonics	.08	.04	.01
☐ 11 Chuck Daly CO Detroit Pistons	.40	.18	.05
☐ 12 Eric Leckner Utah Jazz	.05	.02	.01
☐ 13 Charles Davis Chicago Bulls	.05	.02	.01
☐ 14 Cotton Fitzsimmons CO Phoenix Suns (No NBA logo on back in bottom right)	.05	.02	.01
☐ 15 Byron Scott Los Angeles Lakers	.08	.04	.01
☐ 16 Derrick Chievous Houston Rockets	.05	.02	.01
☐ 17 Reggie Lewis Boston Celtics	1.00	.45	.13
☐ 18 Jim Paxson Boston Celtics	.05	.02	.01
☐ 19 Tony Campbell Los Angeles Lakers	.20	.09	.03
☐ 20 Rolando Blackman Dallas Mavericks	.08	.04	.01
☐ 21 Michael Jordan AS Chicago Bulls	1.50	.65	.19
☐ 22 Cliff Levingston	.05	.02	.01

	Atlanta Hawks			
☐ 23	Roy Tarpley	.05	.02	.01
	Dallas Mavericks			
☐ 24	Harold Pressley UER	.05	.02	.01
	Sacramento Kings			
	(Cinderella misspelled			
	as cindarella)			
☐ 25	Larry Nance	.10	.05	.01
	Cleveland Cavaliers			
☐ 26	Chris Morris	.25	.11	.03
	New Jersey Nets			
☐ 27	Bob Hansen UER	.05	.02	.01
	Utah Jazz			
	(Drafted in '84,			
	should say '83)			
☐ 28	Mark Price AS	.08	.04	.01
	Cleveland Cavaliers			
☐ 29	Reggie Miller	.40	.18	.05
	Indiana Pacers			
☐ 30	Karl Malone	.35	.16	.04
	Utah Jazz			
☐ 31	Sidney Lowe SP	.15	.07	.02
	Charlotte Hornets			
☐ 32	Ron Anderson	.05	.02	.01
	Philadelphia 76ers			
☐ 33	Mike Gminski	.05	.02	.01
	Philadelphia 76ers			
☐ 34	Scott Brooks	.15	.07	.02
	Philadelphia 76ers			
☐ 35	Kevin Johnson	1.50	.65	.19
	Phoenix Suns			
☐ 36	Mark Bryant	.05	.02	.01
	Portland Trail Blazers			
☐ 37	Rik Smits	.60	.25	.08
	Indiana Pacers			
☐ 38	Tim Perry	.15	.07	.02
	Phoenix Suns			
☐ 39	Ralph Sampson	.08	.04	.01
	Golden State Warriors			
☐ 40	Danny Manning UER	1.50	.65	.19
	Los Angeles Clippers			
	(Missing 1988			
	in draft info)			
☐ 41	Kevin Edwards	.25	.11	.03
	Miami Heat			
☐ 42	Paul Mokeski	.05	.02	.01
	Milwaukee Bucks			
☐ 43	Dale Ellis AS	.05	.02	.01
	Seattle Supersonics			
☐ 44	Walter Berry	.05	.02	.01
	Houston Rockets			
☐ 45	Chuck Person	.08	.04	.01
	Indiana Pacers			
☐ 46	Rick Mahorn SP	.20	.09	.03
	Detroit Pistons			
☐ 47	Joe Kleine	.05	.02	.01
	Boston Celtics			
☐ 48	Brad Daugherty AS	.10	.05	.01
	Cleveland Cavaliers			
☐ 49	Mike Woodson	.05	.02	.01
	Houston Rockets			
☐ 50	Brad Daugherty	.15	.07	.02
	Cleveland Cavaliers			
☐ 51	Shelton Jones SP	.15	.07	.02
	Philadelphia 76ers			
☐ 52	Michael Adams	.08	.04	.01
	Denver Nuggets			
☐ 53	Wes Unseld CO	.08	.04	.01
	Washington Bullets			
☐ 54	Rex Chapman	.25	.11	.03
	Charlotte Hornets			
☐ 55	Kelly Tripucka	.08	.04	.01
	Charlotte Hornets			

☐ 56 Rickey Green	.05	.02	.01
Milwaukee Bucks			
☐ 57 Frank Johnson SP	.20	.09	.03
Houston Rockets			
☐ 58 Johnny Newman	.25	.11	.03
New York Knicks			
☐ 59 Billy Thompson	.05	.02	.01
Miami Heat			
☐ 60 Stu Jackson CO	.05	.02	.01
New York Knicks			
☐ 61 Walter Davis	.10	.05	.01
Denver Nuggets			
☐ 62 Brian Shaw SP UER	.75	.35	.09
Boston Celtics			
(Gary Grant led rookies			
in assists, not Shaw)			
☐ 63 Gerald Wilkins	.08	.04	.01
New York Knicks			
☐ 64 Armon Gilliam	.08	.04	.01
Phoenix Suns			
☐ 65 Maurice Cheeks SP	.25	.11	.03
Philadelphia 76ers			
☐ 66 Jack Sikma	.10	.05	.01
Milwaukee Bucks			
☐ 67 Harvey Grant	.25	.11	.03
Washington Bullets			
☐ 68 Jim Lynam CO	.05	.02	.01
Philadelphia 76ers			
☐ 69 Clyde Drexler AS	.15	.07	.02
Portland Trail Blazers			
☐ 70 Xavier McDaniel	.10	.05	.01
Seattle Supersonics			
☐ 71 Danny Young	.05	.02	.01
Portland Trail Blazers			
☐ 72 Fennis Dembo	.05	.02	.01
Detroit Pistons			
☐ 73 Mark Acres SP	.15	.07	.02
Boston Celtics			
☐ 74 Brad Lohaus SP	.25	.11	.03
Sacramento Kings			
☐ 75 Manute Bol	.05	.02	.01
Golden State Warriors			
☐ 76 Purvis Short	.05	.02	.01
Houston Rockets			
☐ 77 Allen Leavell	.05	.02	.01
Houston Rockets			
☐ 78 Johnny Dawkins SP	.20	.09	.03
San Antonio Spurs			
☐ 79 Paul Pressey	.05	.02	.01
Milwaukee Bucks			
☐ 80 Patrick Ewing	.50	.23	.06
New York Knicks			
☐ 81 Bill Wennington	.15	.07	.02
Dallas Mavericks			
☐ 82 Danny Schayes	.05	.02	.01
Denver Nuggets			
☐ 83 Derek Smith	.05	.02	.01
Philadelphia 76ers			
☐ 84 Moses Malone AS	.10	.05	.01
Atlanta Hawks			
☐ 85 Jeff Malone	.08	.04	.01
Washington Bullets			
☐ 86 Otis Smith SP	.15	.07	.02
Golden State Warriors			
☐ 87 Trent Tucker	.05	.02	.01
New York Knicks			
☐ 88 Robert Reid	.05	.02	.01
Charlotte Hornets			
☐ 89 John Paxson	.08	.04	.01
Chicago Bulls			
☐ 90 Chris Mullin	.20	.09	.03
Golden State Warriors			
☐ 91 Tom Garrick	.05	.02	.01

	Los Angeles Clippers			
☐ 92	Willis Reed CO SP UER	.25	.11	.03
	New Jersey Nets			
	(Gambling, should			
	be Grambling)			
☐ 93	Dave Corzine SP	.15	.07	.02
	Chicago Bulls			
☐ 94	Mark Alarie	.05	.02	.01
	Washington Bullets			
☐ 95	Mark Aguirre	.10	.05	.01
	Detroit Pistons			
☐ 96	Charles Barkley AS	.40	.18	.05
	Philadelphia 76ers			
☐ 97	Sidney Green SP	.15	.07	.02
	New York Knicks			
☐ 98	Kevin Willis	.15	.07	.02
	Atlanta Hawks			
☐ 99	Dave Hoppen	.05	.02	.01
	Charlotte Hornets			
☐ 100	Terry Cummings SP	.20	.09	.03
	Milwaukee Bucks			
☐ 101	Dwayne Washington SP	.15	.07	.02
	Miami Heat			
☐ 102	Larry Brown CO	.08	.04	.01
	San Antonio Spurs			
☐ 103	Kevin Duckworth	.05	.02	.01
	Portland Trail Blazers			
☐ 104	Uwe Blab SP	.15	.07	.02
	Dallas Mavericks			
☐ 105	Terry Porter	.10	.05	.01
	Portland Trail Blazers			
☐ 106	Craig Ehlo	.30	.14	.04
	Cleveland Cavaliers			
☐ 107	Don Casey CO	.05	.02	.01
	Los Angeles Clippers			
☐ 108	Pat Riley CO	.08	.04	.01
	Los Angeles Lakers			
☐ 109	John Salley	.08	.04	.01
	Detroit Pistons			
☐ 110	Charles Barkley	.75	.35	.09
	Philadelphia 76ers			
☐ 111	Sam Bowie SP	.20	.09	.03
	Portland Trail Blazers			
☐ 112	Earl Cureton	.05	.02	.01
	Charlotte Hornets			
☐ 113	Craig Hodges UER	.05	.02	.01
	Chicago Bulls			
	(3-pointing shooting)			
☐ 114	Benoit Benjamin	.05	.02	.01
	Los Angeles Clippers			
☐ 115A	Spud Webb ERR SP	.30	.14	.04
	Atlanta Hawks			
	(Signed 9/27/89)			
☐ 115B	Spud Webb COR	.10	.05	.01
	Atlanta Hawks			
	(Second series;			
	signed 9/26/85)			
☐ 116	Karl Malone AS	.20	.09	.03
	Utah Jazz			
☐ 117	Sleepy Floyd	.08	.04	.01
	Houston Rockets			
☐ 118	John Williams	.08	.04	.01
	Cleveland Cavaliers			
☐ 119	Michael Holton	.05	.02	.01
	Charlotte Hornets			
☐ 120	Alex English	.10	.05	.01
	Denver Nuggets			
☐ 121	Dennis Johnson	.10	.05	.01
	Boston Celtics			
☐ 122	Wayne Cooper SP	.15	.07	.02
	Denver Nuggets			
☐ 123A	Don Chaney CO	.30	.14	.04
	Houston Rockets			
	(Line next to NBA			

(coaching record)
☐ 123B	Don Chaney CO	.05	.02	.01
	Houston Rockets			
	(No line)			
☐ 124	A.C. Green	.20	.09	.03
	Los Angeles Lakers			
☐ 125	Adrian Dantley	.10	.05	.01
	Dallas Mavericks			
☐ 126	Del Harris CO	.05	.02	.01
	Milwaukee Bucks			
☐ 127	Dick Harter CO	.05	.02	.01
	Charlotte Hornets			
☐ 128	Reggie Williams	.25	.11	.03
	Los Angeles Clippers			
☐ 129	Bill Hanzlik	.05	.02	.01
	Denver Nuggets			
☐ 130	Dominique Wilkins	.40	.18	.05
	Atlanta Hawks			
☐ 131	Herb Williams	.05	.02	.01
	Dallas Mavericks			
☐ 132	Steve Johnson SP	.15	.07	.02
	Portland Trail Blazers			
☐ 133	Alex English AS	.08	.04	.01
	Denver Nuggets			
☐ 134	Darrell Walker	.05	.02	.01
	Washington Bullets			
☐ 135	Bill Laimbeer	.10	.05	.01
	Detroit Pistons			
☐ 136	Fred Roberts	.05	.02	.01
	Milwaukee Bucks			
☐ 137	Hersey Hawkins	.50	.23	.06
	Philadelphia 76ers			
☐ 138	David Robinson SP	25.00	11.50	3.10
	San Antonio Spurs			
☐ 139	Brad Sellers SP	.15	.07	.02
	Chicago Bulls			
☐ 140	John Stockton	.50	.23	.06
	Utah Jazz			
☐ 141	Grant Long	.25	.11	.03
	Miami Heat			
☐ 142	Marc Iavaroni SP	.15	.07	.02
	Utah Jazz			
☐ 143	Steve Alford SP	.25	.11	.03
	Golden State Warriors			
☐ 144	Jeff Lamp SP	.15	.07	.02
	Los Angeles Lakers			
☐ 145	Buck Williams SP UER	.25	.11	.03
	New Jersey Nets			
	(Won ROY in '81,			
	should say '82)			
☐ 146	Mark Jackson AS	.08	.04	.01
	New York Knicks			
☐ 147	Jim Petersen	.05	.02	.01
	Sacramento Kings			
☐ 148	Steve Stipanovich SP	.15	.07	.02
	Indiana Pacers			
☐ 149	Sam Vincent SP	.15	.07	.02
	Chicago Bulls			
☐ 150	Larry Bird	1.00	.45	.13
	Boston Celtics			
☐ 151	Jon Koncak	.15	.07	.02
	Atlanta Hawks			
☐ 152	Olden Polynice	.25	.11	.03
	Seattle Supersonics			
☐ 153	Randy Breuer	.05	.02	.01
	Milwaukee Bucks			
☐ 154	John Battle	.15	.07	.02
	Atlanta Hawks			
☐ 155	Mark Eaton	.08	.04	.01
	Utah Jazz			
☐ 156	Kevin McHale AS UER	.10	.05	.01
	Boston Celtics			
	(No TM on Celtics			
	logo on back)			

☐ 157	Jerry Sichting SP .... Portland Trail Blazers	.15	.07	.02
☐ 158	Pat Cummings SP .... Miami Heat	.15	.07	.02
☐ 159	Patrick Ewing AS .... New York Knicks	.25	.11	.03
☐ 160	Mark Price .... Cleveland Cavaliers	.25	.11	.03
☐ 161	Jerry Reynolds CO .... Sacramento Kings	.05	.02	.01
☐ 162	Ken Norman .... Los Angeles Clippers	.25	.11	.03
☐ 163	John Bagley SP UER .... New Jersey Nets (Picked in '83, should say '82)	.15	.07	.02
☐ 164	Christian Welp SP .... Philadelphia 76ers	.15	.07	.02
☐ 165	Reggie Theus SP .... Atlanta Hawks	.20	.09	.03
☐ 166	Magic Johnson AS .... Los Angeles Lakers	.40	.18	.05
☐ 167	John Long UER .... Detroit Pistons (Picked in '79, should say '78)	.05	.02	.01
☐ 168	Larry Smith SP .... Golden State Warriors	.20	.09	.03
☐ 169	Charles Shackleford .... New Jersey Nets	.05	.02	.01
☐ 170	Tom Chambers .... Phoenix Suns	.10	.05	.01
☐ 171A	John MacLeod CO SP .... Dallas Mavericks ERR (NBA logo in wrong place)	.30	.14	.04
☐ 171B	John MacLeod CO .... Dallas Mavericks COR (Second series)	.05	.02	.01
☐ 172	Ron Rothstein CO .... Miami Heat	.05	.02	.01
☐ 173	Joe Wolf .... Los Angeles Clippers	.05	.02	.01
☐ 174	Mark Eaton AS .... Utah Jazz	.05	.02	.01
☐ 175	Jon Sundvold .... Miami Heat	.05	.02	.01
☐ 176	Scott Hastings SP .... Miami Heat	.15	.07	.02
☐ 177	Isiah Thomas AS .... Detroit Pistons	.15	.07	.02
☐ 178	Hakeem Olajuwon AS .... Houston Rockets	.50	.23	.06
☐ 179	Mike Fratello CO .... Atlanta Hawks	.05	.02	.01
☐ 180	Hakeem Olajuwon .... Houston Rockets	1.00	.45	.13
☐ 181	Randolph Keys .... Cleveland Cavaliers	.05	.02	.01
☐ 182	Richard Anderson UER .... Portland Trail Blazers (Trail Blazers on front should be all caps)	.05	.02	.01
☐ 183	Dan Majerle .... Phoenix Suns	1.25	.55	.16
☐ 184	Derek Harper .... Dallas Mavericks	.08	.04	.01
☐ 185	Robert Parish .... Boston Celtics	.15	.07	.02
☐ 186	Ricky Berry SP .... Sacramento Kings	.15	.07	.02
☐ 187	Michael Cooper .... Los Angeles Lakers	.10	.05	.01

☐ 188	Vinnie Johnson	.08	.04	.01
	Detroit Pistons			
☐ 189	James Donaldson	.05	.02	.01
	Dallas Mavericks			
☐ 190	Clyde Drexler UER	.25	.11	.03
	Portland Trail Blazers			
	(4th pick, should			
	be 14th)			
☐ 191	Jay Vincent SP	.15	.07	.02
	San Antonio Spurs			
☐ 192	Nate McMillan	.08	.04	.01
	Seattle Supersonics			
☐ 193	Kevin Duckworth AS	.05	.02	.01
	Portland Trail Blazers			
☐ 194	Ledell Eackles	.05	.02	.01
	Washington Bullets			
☐ 195	Eddie Johnson	.08	.04	.01
	Phoenix Suns			
☐ 196	Terry Teagle	.05	.02	.01
	Golden State Warriors			
☐ 197	Tom Chambers AS	.10	.05	.01
	Phoenix Suns			
☐ 198	Joe Barry Carroll	.05	.02	.01
	New Jersey Nets			
☐ 199	Dennis Hopson	.05	.02	.01
	New Jersey Nets			
☐ 200	Michael Jordan	3.00	1.35	.40
	Chicago Bulls			
☐ 201	Jerome Lane	.05	.02	.01
	Denver Nuggets			
☐ 202	Greg Kite	.05	.02	.01
	Charlotte Hornets			
☐ 203	David Rivers SP	.20	.09	.03
	Los Angeles Lakers			
☐ 204	Sylvester Gray	.05	.02	.01
	Miami Heat			
☐ 205	Ron Harper	.10	.05	.01
	Cleveland Cavaliers			
☐ 206	Frank Brickowski	.08	.04	.01
	San Antonio Spurs			
☐ 207	Rory Sparrow	.05	.02	.01
	Miami Heat			
☐ 208	Gerald Henderson	.05	.02	.01
	Philadelphia 76ers			
☐ 209	Rod Higgins UER	.05	.02	.01
	Golden State Warriors			
	('85-86 stats should			
	also include San			
	Antonio and Seattle)			
☐ 210	James Worthy	.15	.07	.02
	Los Angeles Lakers			
☐ 211	Dennis Rodman	.25	.11	.03
	Detroit Pistons			
☐ 212	Ricky Pierce	.10	.05	.01
	Milwaukee Bucks			
☐ 213	Charles Oakley	.10	.05	.01
	New York Knicks			
☐ 214	Steve Colter	.05	.02	.01
	Washington Bullets			
☐ 215	Danny Ainge	.15	.07	.02
	Sacramento Kings			
☐ 216	Lenny Wilkens CO UER	.08	.04	.01
	Cleveland Cavaliers			
	(No NBA logo on back			
	in bottom right)			
☐ 217	Larry Nance AS	.08	.04	.01
	Cleveland Cavaliers			
☐ 218	Muggsy Bogues	.10	.05	.01
	Charlotte Hornets			
☐ 219	James Worthy AS	.08	.04	.01
	Los Angeles Lakers			
☐ 220	Lafayette Lever	.05	.02	.01
	Denver Nuggets			

☐ 221	Quintin Dailey SP	.15	.07	.02
	Los Angeles Clippers			
☐ 222	Lester Conner	.05	.02	.01
	New Jersey Nets			
☐ 223	Jose Ortiz	.05	.02	.01
	Utah Jazz			
☐ 224	Micheal Williams SP	.75	.35	.09
	Detroit Pistons			
	UER (Misspelled			
	Michael on card)			
☐ 225	Wayman Tisdale	.08	.04	.01
	Sacramento Kings			
☐ 226	Mike Sanders SP	.15	.07	.02
	Cleveland Cavaliers			
☐ 227	Jim Farmer SP	.15	.07	.02
	Utah Jazz			
☐ 228	Mark West	.05	.02	.01
	Phoenix Suns			
☐ 229	Jeff Hornacek	.50	.23	.06
	Phoenix Suns			
☐ 230	Chris Mullin AS	.15	.07	.02
	Golden State Warriors			
☐ 231	Vern Fleming	.08	.04	.01
	Indiana Pacers			
☐ 232	Kenny Smith	.08	.04	.01
	Sacramento Kings			
☐ 233	Derrick McKey	.08	.04	.01
	Seattle Supersonics			
☐ 234	Dominique Wilkins AS	.20	.09	.03
	Atlanta Hawks			
☐ 235	Willie Anderson	.25	.11	.03
	San Antonio Spurs			
☐ 236	Keith Lee SP	.15	.07	.02
	New Jersey Nets			
☐ 237	Buck Johnson	.15	.07	.02
	Houston Rockets			
☐ 238	Randy Wittman	.05	.02	.01
	Indiana Pacers			
☐ 239	Terry Catledge SP	.15	.07	.02
	Washington Bullets			
☐ 240	Bernard King	.10	.05	.01
	Washington Bullets			
☐ 241	Darrell Griffith	.08	.04	.01
	Utah Jazz			
☐ 242	Horace Grant	.25	.11	.03
	Chicago Bulls			
☐ 243	Rony Seikaly	.60	.25	.08
	Miami Heat			
☐ 244	Scottie Pippen	1.25	.55	.16
	Chicago Bulls			
☐ 245	Michael Cage UER	.05	.02	.01
	Seattle Supersonics			
	(Picked in '85,			
	should say '84)			
☐ 246	Kurt Rambis	.08	.04	.01
	Charlotte Hornets			
☐ 247	Morlon Wiley SP	.15	.07	.02
	Dallas Mavericks			
☐ 248	Ronnie Grandison	.05	.02	.01
	Boston Celtics			
☐ 249	Scott Skiles SP	.75	.35	.09
	Indiana Pacers			
☐ 250	Isiah Thomas	.20	.09	.03
	Detroit Pistons			
☐ 251	Thurl Bailey	.05	.02	.01
	Utah Jazz			
☐ 252	Doc Rivers	.08	.04	.01
	Atlanta Hawks			
☐ 253	Stuart Gray SP	.15	.07	.02
	Indiana Pacers			
☐ 254	John Williams	.05	.02	.01
	Washington Bullets			
☐ 255	Bill Cartwright	.08	.04	.01

	Chicago Bulls			
☐ 256	Terry Cummings AS	.05	.02	.01
	Milwaukee Bucks			
☐ 257	Rodney McCray	.05	.02	.01
	Sacramento Kings			
☐ 258	Larry Krystkowiak	.15	.07	.02
	Milwaukee Bucks			
☐ 259	Will Perdue	.15	.07	.02
	Chicago Bulls			
☐ 260	Mitch Richmond	1.25	.55	.16
	Golden State Warriors			
☐ 261	Blair Rasmussen	.05	.02	.01
	Denver Nuggets			
☐ 262	Charles Smith	.25	.11	.03
	Los Angeles Clippers			
☐ 263	Tyrone Corbin SP	.50	.23	.06
	Phoenix Suns			
☐ 264	Kelvin Upshaw	.05	.02	.01
	Boston Celtics			
☐ 265	Otis Thorpe	.08	.04	.01
	Houston Rockets			
☐ 266	Phil Jackson CO	.08	.04	.01
	Chicago Bulls			
☐ 267	Jerry Sloan CO	.05	.02	.01
	Utah Jazz			
☐ 268	John Shasky	.05	.02	.01
	Miami Heat			
☐ 269A	B. Bickerstaff CO SP	.30	.14	.04
	Seattle Supersonics			
	ERR (Born 2/11/44)			
☐ 269B	B. Bickerstaff CO	.05	.02	.01
	Seattle Supersonics			
	COR (Second series;			
	Born 11/2/43)			
☐ 270	Magic Johnson	.75	.35	.09
	Los Angeles Lakers			
☐ 271	Vernon Maxwell	.60	.25	.08
	San Antonio Spurs			
☐ 272	Tim McCormick	.05	.02	.01
	Houston Rockets			
☐ 273	Don Nelson CO	.08	.04	.01
	Golden State Warriors			
☐ 274	Gary Grant	.15	.07	.02
	Los Angeles Clippers			
☐ 275	Sidney Moncrief SP	.25	.11	.03
	Milwaukee Bucks			
☐ 276	Roy Hinson	.05	.02	.01
	New Jersey Nets			
☐ 277	Jimmy Rodgers CO	.05	.02	.01
	Boston Celtics			
☐ 278	Antoine Carr	.08	.04	.01
	Atlanta Hawks			
☐ 279A	Orlando Woolridge SP	.30	.14	.04
	Los Angeles Lakers			
	ERR (No Trademark)			
☐ 279B	Orlando Woolridge	.08	.04	.01
	Los Angeles Lakers			
	COR (Second series)			
☐ 280	Kevin McHale	.15	.07	.02
	Boston Celtics			
☐ 281	LaSalle Thompson	.08	.04	.01
	Indiana Pacers			
☐ 282	Detlef Schrempf	.35	.16	.04
	Indiana Pacers			
☐ 283	Doug Moe CO	.05	.02	.01
	Denver Nuggets			
☐ 284A	James Edwards	.30	.14	.04
	Detroit Pistons			
	(Small black line			
	next to card number)			
☐ 284B	James Edwards	.08	.04	.01
	Detroit Pistons			
	(No small black line)			

☐ 285	Jerome Kersey	.08	.04	.01
	Portland Trail Blazers			
☐ 286	Sam Perkins	.08	.04	.01
	Dallas Mavericks			
☐ 287	Sedale Threatt	.08	.04	.01
	Seattle Supersonics			
☐ 288	Tim Kempton SP	.15	.07	.02
	Charlotte Hornets			
☐ 289	Mark McNamara	.05	.02	.01
	Los Angeles Lakers			
☐ 290	Moses Malone	.15	.07	.02
	Atlanta Hawks			
☐ 291	Rick Adelman CO UER	.08	.04	.01
	Portland Trail Blazers			
	(Chemekata misspelled			
	as Chemketa)			
☐ 292	Dick Versace CO	.05	.02	.01
	Indiana Pacers			
☐ 293	Alton Lister SP	.15	.07	.02
	Seattle Supersonics			
☐ 294	Winston Garland	.05	.02	.01
	Golden State Warriors			
☐ 295	Kiki Vandeweghe	.08	.04	.01
	New York Knicks			
☐ 296	Brad Davis	.05	.02	.01
	Dallas Mavericks			
☐ 297	John Stockton AS	.25	.11	.03
	Utah Jazz			
☐ 298	Jay Humphries	.05	.02	.01
	Milwaukee Bucks			
☐ 299	Dell Curry	.08	.04	.01
	Charlotte Hornets			
☐ 300	Mark Jackson	.08	.04	.01
	New York Knicks			
☐ 301	Morlon Wiley	.05	.02	.01
	Orlando Magic			
☐ 302	Reggie Theus	.10	.05	.01
	Orlando Magic			
☐ 303	Otis Smith	.05	.02	.01
	Orlando Magic			
☐ 304	Tod Murphy	.05	.02	.01
	Minnesota Timberwolves			
☐ 305	Sidney Green	.05	.02	.01
	Orlando Magic			
☐ 306	Shelton Jones	.05	.02	.01
	Milwaukee Bucks			
☐ 307	Mark Acres	.05	.02	.01
	Orlando Magic			
☐ 308	Terry Catledge	.05	.02	.01
	Orlando Magic			
☐ 309	Larry Smith	.08	.04	.01
	Houston Rockets			
☐ 310	David Robinson IA	4.00	1.80	.50
	San Antonio Spurs			
☐ 311	Johnny Dawkins	.08	.04	.01
	Philadelphia 76ers			
☐ 312	Terry Cummings	.08	.04	.01
	San Antonio Spurs			
☐ 313	Sidney Lowe	.08	.04	.01
	Minnesota Timberwolves			
☐ 314	Bill Musselman CO	.05	.02	.01
	Minnesota Timberwolves			
☐ 315	Buck Williams UER	.10	.05	.01
	Portland Trail Blazers			
	(Won ROY in '81,			
	should say '82)			
☐ 316	Mel Turpin	.08	.04	.01
	Washington Bullets			
☐ 317	Scott Hastings	.05	.02	.01
	Detroit Pistons			
☐ 318	Scott Skiles	.15	.07	.02
	Orlando Magic			
☐ 319	Tyrone Corbin	.15	.07	.02

	Minnesota Timberwolves			
☐ 320	Maurice Cheeks	.10	.05	.01
	San Antonio Spurs			
☐ 321	Matt Goukas CO	.05	.02	.01
	Orlando Magic			
☐ 322	Jeff Turner	.05	.02	.01
	Orlando Magic			
☐ 323	David Wingate	.05	.02	.01
	San Antonio Spurs			
☐ 324	Steve Johnson	.05	.02	.01
	Minnesota Timberwolves			
☐ 325	Alton Lister	.05	.02	.01
	Golden State Warriors			
☐ 326	Ken Bannister	.05	.02	.01
	Los Angeles Clippers			
☐ 327	Bill Fitch CO UER	.05	.02	.01
	New Jersey Nets			
	(Copyright missing			
	on bottom of back)			
☐ 328	Sam Vincent	.05	.02	.01
	Orlando Magic			
☐ 329	Larry Drew	.05	.02	.01
	Los Angeles Lakers			
☐ 330	Rick Mahorn	.05	.02	.01
	Minnesota Timberwolves			
☐ 331	Christian Welp	.05	.02	.01
	San Antonio Spurs			
☐ 332	Brad Lohaus	.05	.02	.01
	Minnesota Timberwolves			
☐ 333	Frank Johnson	.08	.04	.01
	Orlando Magic			
☐ 334	Jim Farmer	.05	.02	.01
	Minnesota Timberwolves			
☐ 335	Wayne Cooper	.05	.02	.01
	Portland Trail Blazers			
☐ 336	Mike Brown	.05	.02	.01
	Utah Jazz			
☐ 337	Sam Bowie	.08	.04	.01
	New Jersey Nets			
☐ 338	Kevin Gamble	.25	.11	.03
	Boston Celtics			
☐ 339	Jerry Ice Reynolds	.05	.02	.01
	Orlando Magic			
☐ 340	Mike Sanders	.05	.02	.01
	Indiana Pacers			
☐ 341	Bill Jones UER	.05	.02	.01
	New Jersey Nets			
	(Center on front,			
	should be F)			
☐ 342	Greg Anderson	.05	.02	.01
	Milwaukee Bucks			
☐ 343	Dave Corzine	.05	.02	.01
	Orlando Magic			
☐ 344	Micheal Williams UER	.25	.11	.03
	Phoenix Suns			
	(Misspelled Michael			
	on card)			
☐ 345	Jay Vincent	.05	.02	.01
	Philadelphia 76ers			
☐ 346	David Rivers	.05	.02	.01
	Minnesota Timberwolves			
☐ 347	Caldwell Jones UER	.08	.04	.01
	San Antonio Spurs			
	(He was not starting			
	center on '83 Sixers)			
☐ 348	Brad Sellers	.05	.02	.01
	Seattle Supersonics			
☐ 349	Scott Roth	.05	.02	.01
	Minnesota Timberwolves			
☐ 350	Alvin Robertson	.08	.04	.01
	Milwaukee Bucks			
☐ 351	Steve Kerr	.25	.11	.03
	Cleveland Cavaliers			

		MINT	EXC	G-VG
☐ 352	Stuart Gray.................................... Charlotte Hornets	.05	.02	.01
☐ 353A	World Champions SP Detroit Pistons	6.00	2.70	.75
☐ 353B	World Champions UER Detroit Pistons (George Blaha misspelled Blanha)	.50	.23	.06

1990-91 Hoops

The complete 1990-91 Hoops basketball set contains 440 cards measuring the standard size (2 1/2" by 3 1/2"). The set was distributed in two series of 336 and 104 cards, respectively. The cards were issued exclusively in 15-card plastic-wrap packs, which came 36 to a box. On the front the color action player photo appears in the shape of a basketball lane, bordered by gold on the All-Star cards (1-26) and by silver on the regular issues (27-331, 336). The player's name and the stripe below the picture are printed in one of the team's colors. The team logo at the lower right corner rounds out the card face. The back of the regular issue has a color head shot and biographical information as well as college and pro statistics, framed by a basketball lane. The cards are numbered on the back and arranged alphabetically according to teams as follows: Atlanta Hawks (27-37), Boston Celtics (38-48), Charlotte Hornets (49-59), Chicago Bulls (60-69), Cleveland Cavaliers (70-80), Dallas Mavericks (81-90), Denver Nuggets (91-100), Detroit Pistons (101-111), Golden State Warriors (112-122), Houston Rockets (123-131), Indiana Pacers (132-141), Los Angeles Clippers (142-152), Los Angeles Lakers (153-163), Miami Heat (164-172), Milwaukee Bucks (173-183), Minnesota Timberwolves (184-192), New Jersey Nets (193-201), New York Knicks (202-212), Orlando Magic (213-223), Philadelphia 76ers (224-232), Phoenix Suns (233-242), Portland Trail Blazers (243-252), Sacramento Kings (253-262), San Antonio Spurs (263-273), Seattle Supersonics (274-284), Utah Jazz (285-294), Washington Bullets (295-304), Coaches (305-331), NBA Finals (337-342), Coaches (343-354), Team checklists (355-381), Inside Stuff (382-385), Stay in School (386-387), Don't Foul Out (388-389), Lottery Selections (390-400), and Updates (401-438). Some of the All-Star cards (card numbers 2, 6, and 8) can be found with or without a printing mistake, i.e., no T in the the trademark logo on the card back. A few of the cards (card numbers 14, 66, 144, and 279) refer to the player as "all America" rather than "All America". The following cards can be found with or without a black line under the card number, height, and birthplace: 20, 23, 24, 29, and 87. Rookie Cards included in the set are Nick Anderson, B.J. Armstrong, Mookie Blaylock, Derrick Coleman, Vlade Divac, Sherman Douglas, Blue Edwards, Sean Elliott, Pervis Ellison, Danny Ferry, Kendall Gill, Tim Hardaway, Chris Jackson, Shawn Kemp, Sarunas Marciulionis, Gary Payton, Drazen Petrovic, Glen Rice, Pooh Richardson, Cliff Robinson, Dennis Scott, and Lionel Simmons. The short prints (SP below) in the first series are those cards which were dropped to make room for the new second series cards on the printing sheet.

	MINT	EXC	G-VG
COMPLETE SET (440)...	15.00	6.75	1.90
COMPLETE SERIES 1 (336).....................................	10.00	4.50	1.25
COMPLETE SERIES 2 (104).....................................	5.00	2.30	.60
COMMON PLAYER (1-336).......................................	.05	.02	.01
COMMON PLAYER (337-440)...................................	.05	.02	.01

☐ 1 Charles Barkley AS SP Philadelphia 76ers	.50	.23	.06
☐ 2 Larry Bird AS SP Boston Celtics	.75	.35	.09
☐ 3 Joe Dumars AS SP Detroit Pistons	.15	.07	.02
☐ 4 Patrick Ewing AS SP New York Knicks (A-S blocks listed as 1, should be 5) UER	.30	.14	.04
☐ 5 Michael Jordan AS SP Chicago Bulls (Won Slam Dunk in '87 and '88, not '86 and '88) UER	2.50	1.15	.30
☐ 6 Kevin McHale AS SP Boston Celtics	.10	.05	.01
☐ 7 Reggie Miller AS SP Indiana Pacers	.15	.07	.02
☐ 8 Robert Parish AS SP Boston Celtics	.10	.05	.01
☐ 9 Scottie Pippen AS SP Chicago Bulls	.40	.18	.05
☐ 10 Dennis Rodman AS SP Detroit Pistons	.07	.03	.01
☐ 11 Isiah Thomas AS SP Detroit Pistons	.15	.07	.02
☐ 12 Dominique Wilkins AS SP Atlanta Hawks	.25	.11	.03
☐ 13A All-Star Checklist SP ERR (No card number)	.40	.18	.05
☐ 13B All-Star Checklist SP COR (Card number on back)	.10	.05	.01
☐ 14 Rolando Blackman AS SP Dallas Mavericks	.07	.03	.01
☐ 15 Tom Chambers AS SP Phoenix Suns	.10	.05	.01
☐ 16 Clyde Drexler AS SP Portland Trail Blazers	.15	.07	.02
☐ 17 A.C. Green AS SP Los Angeles Lakers	.07	.03	.01
☐ 18 Magic Johnson AS SP Los Angeles Lakers	.50	.23	.06
☐ 19 Kevin Johnson AS SP Phoenix Suns	.20	.09	.03
☐ 20 Lafayette Lever AS SP Denver Nuggets	.07	.03	.01
☐ 21 Karl Malone AS SP Utah Jazz	.20	.09	.03
☐ 22 Chris Mullin AS SP Golden State Warriors	.15	.07	.02
☐ 23 Hakeem Olajuwon AS SP Houston Rockets	.60	.25	.08
☐ 24 David Robinson AS SP San Antonio Spurs	1.00	.45	.13
☐ 25 John Stockton AS SP Utah Jazz	.15	.07	.02
☐ 26 James Worthy AS SP Los Angeles Lakers	.10	.05	.01
☐ 27 John Battle	.05	.02	.01
☐ 28 Jon Koncak	.05	.02	.01
☐ 29 Cliff Levingston SP	.07	.03	.01
☐ 30 John Long SP	.07	.03	.01
☐ 31 Moses Malone	.10	.05	.01
☐ 32 Doc Rivers	.08	.04	.01
☐ 33 Kenny Smith SP	.07	.03	.01
☐ 34 Alexander Volkov	.05	.02	.01
☐ 35 Spud Webb	.10	.05	.01
☐ 36 Dominique Wilkins	.25	.11	.03
☐ 37 Kevin Willis	.08	.04	.01
☐ 38 John Bagley	.05	.02	.01
☐ 39 Larry Bird	.75	.35	.09

☐	40	Kevin Gamble	.05	.02	.01
☐	41	Dennis Johnson SP	.10	.05	.01
☐	42	Joe Kleine	.05	.02	.01
☐	43	Reggie Lewis	.15	.07	.02
☐	44	Kevin McHale	.10	.05	.01
☐	45	Robert Parish	.10	.05	.01
☐	46	Jim Paxson SP	.07	.03	.01
☐	47	Ed Pinckney	.05	.02	.01
☐	48	Brian Shaw	.05	.02	.01
☐	49	Richard Anderson SP	.07	.03	.01
☐	50	Muggsy Bogues	.10	.05	.01
☐	51	Rex Chapman	.08	.04	.01
☐	52	Dell Curry	.05	.02	.01
☐	53	Kenny Gattison	.05	.02	.01
☐	54	Armon Gilliam	.05	.02	.01
☐	55	Dave Hoppen	.05	.02	.01
☐	56	Randolph Keys	.05	.02	.01
☐	57	J.R. Reid	.15	.07	.02
☐	58	Robert Reid SP	.07	.03	.01
☐	59	Kelly Tripucka	.08	.04	.01
☐	60	B.J. Armstrong	.75	.35	.09
☐	61	Bill Cartwright	.08	.04	.01
☐	62	Charles Davis SP	.07	.03	.01
☐	63	Horace Grant	.10	.05	.01
☐	64	Craig Hodges	.05	.02	.01
☐	65	Michael Jordan	2.50	1.15	.30
☐	66	Stacey King	.10	.05	.01
☐	67	John Paxson	.08	.04	.01
☐	68	Will Perdue	.05	.02	.01
☐	69	Scottie Pippen	.40	.18	.05
☐	70	Winston Bennett	.05	.02	.01
☐	71	Chucky Brown	.05	.02	.01
☐	72	Derrick Chievous	.05	.02	.01
☐	73	Brad Daugherty	.10	.05	.01
☐	74	Craig Ehlo	.08	.04	.01
☐	75	Steve Kerr	.05	.02	.01
☐	76	Paul Mokeski SP	.07	.03	.01
☐	77	John Morton	.05	.02	.01
☐	78	Larry Nance	.08	.04	.01
☐	79	Mark Price	.10	.05	.01
☐	80	Hot Rod Williams	.05	.02	.01
☐	81	Steve Alford	.05	.02	.01
☐	82	Rolando Blackman	.08	.04	.01
☐	83	Adrian Dantley SP	.10	.05	.01
☐	84	Brad Davis	.05	.02	.01
☐	85	James Donaldson	.05	.02	.01
☐	86	Derek Harper	.08	.04	.01
☐	87	Sam Perkins SP	.10	.05	.01
☐	88	Roy Tarpley	.05	.02	.01
☐	89	Bill Wennington SP	.07	.03	.01
☐	90	Herb Williams	.05	.02	.01
☐	91	Michael Adams	.08	.04	.01
☐	92	Joe Barry Carroll SP	.07	.03	.01
☐	93	Walter Davis UER	.10	.05	.01
		(Born NC, not PA)			
☐	94	Alex English SP	.10	.05	.01
☐	95	Bill Hanzlik	.05	.02	.01
☐	96	Jerome Lane	.05	.02	.01
☐	97	Lafayette Lever SP	.07	.03	.01
☐	98	Todd Lichti	.05	.02	.01
☐	99	Blair Rasmussen	.05	.02	.01
☐	100	Danny Schayes SP	.07	.03	.01
☐	101	Mark Aguirre	.10	.05	.01
☐	102	William Bedford	.05	.02	.01
☐	103	Joe Dumars	.15	.07	.02
☐	104	James Edwards	.05	.02	.01
☐	105	Scott Hastings	.05	.02	.01
☐	106	Gerald Henderson SP	.07	.03	.01
☐	107	Vinnie Johnson	.08	.04	.01
☐	108	Bill Laimbeer	.10	.05	.01
☐	109	Dennis Rodman	.08	.04	.01
☐	110	John Salley	.08	.04	.01
☐	111	Isiah Thomas UER	.15	.07	.02

(No position listed
on the card)

☐ 112	Manute Bol SP	.07	.03	.01
☐ 113	Tim Hardaway	.75	.35	.09
☐ 114	Rod Higgins	.05	.02	.01
☐ 115	Sarunas Marciulionis	.10	.05	.01
☐ 116	Chris Mullin UER	.15	.07	.02
	(Born Brooklyn, NY, not New York, NY)			
☐ 117	Jim Petersen	.05	.02	.01
☐ 118	Mitch Richmond	.20	.09	.03
☐ 119	Mike Smrek	.05	.02	.01
☐ 120	Terry Teagle SP	.07	.03	.01
☐ 121	Tom Tolbert	.05	.02	.01
☐ 122	Christian Welp SP	.07	.03	.01
☐ 123	Byron Dinkins SP	.07	.03	.01
☐ 124	Eric(Sleepy) Floyd	.08	.04	.01
☐ 125	Buck Johnson	.05	.02	.01
☐ 126	Vernon Maxwell	.08	.04	.01
☐ 127	Hakeem Olajuwon	.75	.35	.09
☐ 128	Larry Smith	.08	.04	.01
☐ 129	Otis Thorpe	.08	.04	.01
☐ 130	Mitchell Wiggins SP	.07	.03	.01
☐ 131	Mike Woodson	.05	.02	.01
☐ 132	Greg Dreiling	.05	.02	.01
☐ 133	Vern Fleming	.05	.02	.01
☐ 134	Rickey Green SP	.07	.03	.01
☐ 135	Reggie Miller	.15	.07	.02
☐ 136	Chuck Person	.08	.04	.01
☐ 137	Mike Sanders	.05	.02	.01
☐ 138	Detlef Schrempf	.10	.05	.01
☐ 139	Rik Smits	.10	.05	.01
☐ 140	LaSalle Thompson	.08	.04	.01
☐ 141	Randy Wittman	.05	.02	.01
☐ 142	Benoit Benjamin	.05	.02	.01
☐ 143	Winston Garland	.05	.02	.01
☐ 144	Tom Garrick	.05	.02	.01
☐ 145	Gary Grant	.05	.02	.01
☐ 146	Ron Harper	.08	.04	.01
☐ 147	Danny Manning	.25	.11	.03
☐ 148	Jeff Martin	.05	.02	.01
☐ 149	Ken Norman	.08	.04	.01
☐ 150	David Rivers SP	.07	.03	.01
☐ 151	Charles Smith	.08	.04	.01
☐ 152	Joe Wolf SP	.07	.03	.01
☐ 153	Michael Cooper SP	.10	.05	.01
☐ 154	Vlade Divac UER	.25	.11	.03
	(Height 6'11" should be 7'1")			
☐ 155	Larry Drew	.05	.02	.01
☐ 156	A.C. Green	.08	.04	.01
☐ 157	Magic Johnson	.50	.23	.06
☐ 158	Mark McNamara SP	.07	.03	.01
☐ 159	Byron Scott	.08	.04	.01
☐ 160	Mychal Thompson	.08	.04	.01
☐ 161	Jay Vincent SP	.07	.03	.01
☐ 162	Orlando Woolridge SP	.10	.05	.01
☐ 163	James Worthy	.10	.05	.01
☐ 164	Sherman Douglas	.20	.09	.03
☐ 165	Kevin Edwards	.08	.04	.01
☐ 166	Tellis Frank SP	.07	.03	.01
☐ 167	Grant Long	.08	.04	.01
☐ 168	Glen Rice	.75	.35	.09
☐ 169A	Rony Seikaly	.10	.05	.01
	(Athens)			
☐ 169B	Rony Seikaly	.10	.05	.01
	(Beirut)			
☐ 170	Rory Sparrow SP	.07	.03	.01
☐ 171A	Jon Sundvold	.07	.03	.01
	(First series)			
☐ 171B	Billy Thompson	.07	.03	.01
	(Second series)			
☐ 172A	Billy Thompson	.07	.03	.01
	(First series)			

☐ 172B Jon Sundvold	.07	.03	.01
(Second series)			
☐ 173 Greg Anderson	.05	.02	.01
☐ 174 Jeff Grayer	.05	.02	.01
☐ 175 Jay Humphries	.05	.02	.01
☐ 176 Frank Kornet	.05	.02	.01
☐ 177 Larry Krystkowiak	.05	.02	.01
☐ 178 Brad Lohaus	.05	.04	.01
☐ 179 Ricky Pierce	.08	.04	.01
☐ 180 Paul Pressey SP	.07	.03	.01
☐ 181 Fred Roberts	.05	.02	.01
☐ 182 Alvin Robertson	.08	.04	.01
☐ 183 Jack Sikma	.10	.05	.01
☐ 184 Randy Breuer	.05	.02	.01
☐ 185 Tony Campbell	.05	.02	.01
☐ 186 Tyrone Corbin	.08	.04	.01
☐ 187 Sidney Lowe SP	.07	.03	.01
☐ 188 Sam Mitchell	.05	.02	.01
☐ 189 Tod Murphy	.05	.02	.01
☐ 190 Pooh Richardson	.15	.07	.02
☐ 191 Scott Roth SP	.07	.03	.01
☐ 192 Brad Sellers SP	.07	.03	.01
☐ 193 Mookie Blaylock	.50	.23	.06
☐ 194 Sam Bowie	.08	.04	.01
☐ 195 Lester Conner	.05	.02	.01
☐ 196 Derrick Gervin	.05	.02	.01
☐ 197 Jack Haley	.05	.02	.01
☐ 198 Roy Hinson	.05	.02	.01
☐ 199 Dennis Hopson SP	.07	.03	.01
☐ 200 Chris Morris	.05	.02	.01
☐ 201 Purvis Short SP	.07	.03	.01
☐ 202 Maurice Cheeks	.10	.05	.01
☐ 203 Patrick Ewing	.30	.14	.04
☐ 204 Stuart Gray	.05	.02	.01
☐ 205 Mark Jackson	.08	.04	.01
☐ 206 Johnny Newman SP	.07	.03	.01
☐ 207 Charles Oakley	.10	.05	.01
☐ 208 Trent Tucker	.05	.02	.01
☐ 209 Kiki Vandeweghe	.08	.04	.01
☐ 210 Kenny Walker	.05	.02	.01
☐ 211 Eddie Lee Wilkins	.05	.02	.01
☐ 212 Gerald Wilkins	.08	.04	.01
☐ 213 Mark Acres	.05	.02	.01
☐ 214 Nick Anderson	.40	.18	.05
☐ 215 Michael Ansley UER	.05	.02	.01
(Ranked first, not third)			
☐ 216 Terry Catledge	.05	.02	.01
☐ 217 Dave Corzine SP	.07	.03	.01
☐ 218 Sidney Green SP	.07	.03	.01
☐ 219 Jerry Reynolds	.05	.02	.01
☐ 220 Scott Skiles	.08	.04	.01
☐ 221 Otis Smith	.05	.02	.01
☐ 222 Reggie Theus SP	.10	.05	.01
☐ 223A Sam Vincent	.50	.23	.06
(First series, shows			
12 Michael Jordan)			
☐ 223B Sam Vincent	.05	.02	.01
(Second series, shows			
Sam dribbling)			
☐ 224 Ron Anderson	.05	.02	.01
☐ 225 Charles Barkley	.50	.23	.06
☐ 226 Scott Brooks SP UER	.07	.03	.01
(Born French Camp,			
not Lathron, Cal.)			
☐ 227 Johnny Dawkins	.05	.02	.01
☐ 228 Mike Gminski	.05	.02	.01
☐ 229 Hersey Hawkins	.10	.05	.01
☐ 230 Rick Mahorn	.05	.02	.01
☐ 231 Derek Smith SP	.07	.03	.01
☐ 232 Bob Thornton	.05	.02	.01
☐ 233 Kenny Battle	.05	.02	.01
☐ 234A Tom Chambers	.15	.07	.02
(First series;			

		Forward on front)			
☐	234B	Tom Chambers	.15	.07	.02
		(Second series;			
		Guard on front)			
☐	235	Greg Grant SP	.07	.03	.01
☐	236	Jeff Hornacek	.10	.05	.01
☐	237	Eddie Johnson	.05	.02	.01
☐	238A	Kevin Johnson	.25	.11	.03
		(First series;			
		Guard on front)			
☐	238B	Kevin Johnson	.25	.11	.03
		(Second series;			
		Forward on front)			
☐	239	Dan Majerle	.20	.09	.03
☐	240	Tim Perry	.05	.02	.01
☐	241	Kurt Rambis	.08	.04	.01
☐	242	Mark West	.05	.02	.01
☐	243	Mark Bryant	.05	.02	.01
☐	244	Wayne Cooper	.05	.02	.01
☐	245	Clyde Drexler	.20	.09	.03
☐	246	Kevin Duckworth	.05	.02	.01
☐	247	Jerome Kersey	.05	.02	.01
☐	248	Drazen Petrovic	.35	.16	.04
☐	249A	Terry Porter ERR	1.00	.45	.13
		(No NBA symbol on back)			
☐	249B	Terry Porter COR	.10	.05	.01
☐	250	Cliff Robinson	.75	.35	.09
☐	251	Buck Williams	.10	.05	.01
☐	252	Danny Young	.05	.02	.01
☐	253	Danny Ainge SP UER	.10	.05	.01
		(Middle name Ray mis-spelled as Rae on back)			
☐	254	Randy Allen SP	.07	.03	.01
☐	255	Antoine Carr	.05	.02	.01
☐	256	Vinny Del Negro SP	.07	.03	.01
☐	257	Pervis Ellison SP	.20	.09	.03
☐	258	Greg Kite SP	.07	.03	.01
☐	259	Rodney McCray SP	.07	.03	.01
☐	260	Harold Pressley SP	.07	.03	.01
☐	261	Ralph Sampson	.08	.04	.01
☐	262	Wayman Tisdale	.08	.04	.01
☐	263	Willie Anderson	.05	.02	.01
☐	264	Uwe Blab SP	.07	.03	.01
☐	265	Frank Brickowski SP	.10	.05	.01
☐	266	Terry Cummings	.08	.04	.01
☐	267	Sean Elliott	.25	.11	.03
☐	268	Caldwell Jones SP	.10	.05	.01
☐	269	Johnny Moore SP	.07	.03	.01
☐	270	David Robinson	1.00	.45	.13
☐	271	Rod Strickland	.08	.04	.01
☐	272	Reggie Williams	.08	.04	.01
☐	273	David Wingate SP	.07	.03	.01
☐	274	Dana Barros UER	.15	.07	.02
		(Born April, not March)			
☐	275	Michael Cage UER	.05	.02	.01
		(Drafted '84, not '85)			
☐	276	Quintin Dailey	.05	.02	.01
☐	277	Dale Ellis	.08	.04	.01
☐	278	Steve Johnson SP	.07	.03	.01
☐	279	Shawn Kemp	2.50	1.15	.30
☐	280	Xavier McDaniel	.10	.05	.01
☐	281	Derrick McKey	.05	.02	.01
☐	282	Nate McMillan	.08	.04	.01
☐	283	Olden Polynice	.05	.02	.01
☐	284	Sedale Threatt	.08	.04	.01
☐	285	Thurl Bailey	.05	.02	.01
☐	286	Mike Brown	.05	.02	.01
☐	287	Mark Eaton UER	.08	.04	.01
		(72nd pick, not 82nd)			
☐	288	Blue Edwards	.15	.07	.02
☐	289	Darrell Griffith	.08	.04	.01
☐	290	Robert Hansen SP	.07	.03	.01
☐	291	Eric Leckner SP	.07	.03	.01

☐ 292	Karl Malone	.25	.11	.03
☐ 293	Delaney Rudd	.05	.02	.01
☐ 294	John Stockton	.20	.09	.03
☐ 295	Mark Alarie	.05	.02	.01
☐ 296	Ledell Eackles SP	.07	.03	.01
☐ 297	Harvey Grant	.05	.02	.01
☐ 298A	Tom Hammonds (No rookie logo on front)	.10	.05	.01
☐ 298B	Tom Hammonds (Rookie logo on front)	.10	.05	.01
☐ 299	Charles Jones	.05	.02	.01
☐ 300	Bernard King	.10	.05	.01
☐ 301	Jeff Malone SP	.07	.03	.01
☐ 302	Mel Turpin SP	.07	.02	.01
☐ 303	Darrell Walker	.05	.02	.01
☐ 304	John Williams	.05	.02	.01
☐ 305	Bob Weiss CO	.05	.02	.01
	Atlanta Hawks			
☐ 306	Chris Ford CO	.08	.04	.01
	Boston Celtics			
☐ 307	Gene Littles CO	.05	.02	.01
	Charlotte Hornets			
☐ 308	Phil Jackson CO	.08	.04	.01
	Chicago Bulls			
☐ 309	Lenny Wilkens CO	.08	.04	.01
	Cleveland Cavaliers			
☐ 310	Richie Adubato CO	.05	.02	.01
	Dallas Mavericks			
☐ 311	Doug Moe CO SP	.07	.03	.01
	Denver Nuggets			
☐ 312	Chuck Daly CO	.08	.04	.01
	Detroit Pistons			
☐ 313	Don Nelson CO	.08	.04	.01
	Golden State Warriors			
☐ 314	Don Chaney CO	.05	.02	.01
	Houston Rockets			
☐ 315	Dick Versace CO	.05	.02	.01
	Indiana Pacers			
☐ 316	Mike Schuler CO	.05	.02	.01
	Los Angeles Clippers			
☐ 317	Pat Riley CO SP	.10	.05	.01
	Los Angeles Lakers			
☐ 318	Ron Rothstein CO	.05	.02	.01
	Miami Heat			
☐ 319	Del Harris CO	.05	.02	.01
	Milwaukee Bucks			
☐ 320	Bill Musselman CO	.05	.02	.01
	Minnesota Timberwolves			
☐ 321	Bill Fitch CO	.05	.02	.01
	New Jersey Nets			
☐ 322	Stu Jackson CO	.05	.02	.01
	New York Knicks			
☐ 323	Matt Guokas CO	.05	.02	.01
	Orlando Magic			
☐ 324	Jim Lynam CO	.05	.02	.01
	Philadelphia 76ers			
☐ 325	Cotton Fitzsimmons CO	.05	.02	.01
	Phoenix Suns			
☐ 326	Rick Adelman CO	.08	.04	.01
	Portland Trail Blazers			
☐ 327	Dick Motta CO	.05	.02	.01
	Sacramento Kings			
☐ 328	Larry Brown CO	.08	.04	.01
	San Antonio Spurs			
☐ 329	K.C. Jones CO	.08	.04	.01
	Seattle Supersonics			
☐ 330	Jerry Sloan CO	.05	.02	.01
	Utah Jazz			
☐ 331	Wes Unseld CO	.08	.04	.01
	Washington Bullets			
☐ 332	Checklist 1 SP	.07	.03	.01
☐ 333	Checklist 2 SP	.07	.03	.01
☐ 334	Checklist 3 SP	.07	.03	.01

☐ 335 Checklist 4 SP	.07	.03	.01
☐ 336 Danny Ferry SP	.15	.07	.02
Cleveland Cavaliers			
☐ 337 NBA Final Game 1	.05	.02	.01
☐ 338 NBA Final Game 2	.05	.02	.01
☐ 339 NBA Final Game 3	.05	.02	.01
☐ 340 NBA Final Game 4	.05	.02	.01
☐ 341A NBA Final Game 5 ERR	.10	.05	.01
(No headline on back)			
☐ 341B NBA Final Game 5 COR	.10	.05	.01
☐ 342 Championship Card UER	.10	.05	.01
(Player named as Sidney			
Green is really			
David Greenwood)			
☐ 343 K.C. Jones CO	.08	.04	.01
Seattle Supersonics			
☐ 344 Wes Unseld CO	.08	.04	.01
Washington Bullets			
☐ 345 Don Nelson CO	.08	.04	.01
Golden State Warriors			
☐ 346 Bob Weiss CO	.08	.04	.01
Atlanta Hawks			
☐ 347 Chris Ford CO	.05	.02	.01
Boston Celtics			
☐ 348 Phil Jackson CO	.08	.04	.01
Chicago Bulls			
☐ 349 Lenny Wilkens CO	.08	.04	.01
Cleveland Cavaliers			
☐ 350 Don Chaney CO	.08	.04	.01
Houston Rockets			
☐ 351 Mike Dunleavy CO	.05	.02	.01
Los Angeles Lakers			
☐ 352 Matt Guokas CO	.05	.02	.01
Orlando Magic			
☐ 353 Rick Adelman CO	.08	.04	.01
Portland Trail Blazers			
☐ 354 Jerry Sloan CO	.05	.02	.01
Utah Jazz			
☐ 355 Dominique Wilkins TC	.15	.07	.02
Atlanta Hawks			
☐ 356 Larry Bird TC	.40	.18	.05
Boston Celtics			
☐ 357 Rex Chapman TC	.05	.02	.01
Charlotte Hornets			
☐ 358 Michael Jordan TC	1.25	.55	.16
Chicago Bulls			
☐ 359 Mark Price TC	.08	.04	.01
Cleveland Cavaliers			
☐ 360 Rolando Blackman TC	.05	.02	.01
Dallas Mavericks			
☐ 361 Michael Adams TC UER	.05	.02	.01
Denver Nuggets			
(Westhead should be			
card 422, not 440)			
☐ 362 Joe Dumars TC UER	.10	.05	.01
Detroit Pistons			
(Gerald Henderson's name			
and number not listed)			
☐ 363 Chris Mullin TC	.10	.05	.01
Golden State Warriors			
☐ 364 Hakeem Olajuwon TC	.30	.14	.04
Houston Rockets			
☐ 365 Reggie Miller TC	.10	.05	.01
Indiana Pacers			
☐ 366 Danny Manning TC	.08	.04	.01
Los Angeles Clippers			
☐ 367 Magic Johnson TC UER	.25	.11	.03
Los Angeles Lakers			
(Dunleavy listed as 439,			
should be 351)			
☐ 368 Rony Seikaly TC	.08	.04	.01
Miami Heat			
☐ 369 Alvin Robertson TC	.05	.02	.01

	Milwaukee Bucks		.02	.01
☐ 370	Pooh Richardson TC	.05	.02	.01
	Minnesota Timberwolves			
☐ 371	Chris Morris TC	.05	.02	.01
	New Jersey Nets			
☐ 372	Patrick Ewing TC	.15	.07	.02
	New York Knicks			
☐ 373	Nick Anderson TC	.15	.07	.02
	Orlando Magic			
☐ 374	Charles Barkley TC	.25	.11	.03
	Philadelphia 76ers			
☐ 375	Kevin Johnson TC	.12	.05	.02
	Phoenix Suns			
☐ 376	Clyde Drexler TC	.10	.05	.01
	Portland Trail Blazers			
☐ 377	Wayman Tisdale TC	.05	.02	.01
	Sacramento Kings			
☐ 378A	David Robinson TC	.50	.23	.06
	San Antonio Spurs (Basketball fully visible)			
☐ 378B	David Robinson TC	.50	.23	.06
	San Antonio Spurs (Basketball partially visible)			
☐ 379	Xavier McDaniel TC	.08	.04	.01
	Seattle Supersonics			
☐ 380	Karl Malone TC	.12	.05	.02
	Utah Jazz			
☐ 381	Bernard King TC	.08	.04	.01
	Washington Bullets			
☐ 382	Michael Jordan	1.25	.55	.16
	Playground			
☐ 383	Lights, Camera,	.10	.05	.01
	NBA Action (Karl Malone on horseback)			
☐ 384	European Imports	.05	.02	.01
	(Vlade Divac and Sarunas Marciulionis)			
☐ 385	Super Streaks	1.00	.45	.13
	Stay In School (Magic Johnson and Michael Jordan)			
☐ 386	Johnny Newman	.05	.02	.01
	Charlotte Hornets (Stay in School)			
☐ 387	Dell Curry	.05	.02	.01
	Charlotte Hornets (Stay in School)			
☐ 388	Patrick Ewing	.15	.07	.02
	New York Knicks (Don't Foul Out)			
☐ 389	Isiah Thomas	.10	.05	.01
	Detroit Pistons (Don't Foul Out)			
☐ 390	Derrick Coleman LS	1.50	.65	.19
	New Jersey Nets			
☐ 391	Gary Payton LS	.75	.35	.09
	Seattle Supersonics			
☐ 392	Chris Jackson LS	.60	.25	.08
	Denver Nuggets			
☐ 393	Dennis Scott LS	.30	.14	.04
	Los Angeles Lakers			
☐ 394	Kendall Gill LS	.60	.25	.08
	Charlotte Hornets			
☐ 395	Felton Spencer LS	.15	.07	.02
	Minnesota Timberwolves			
☐ 396	Lionel Simmons LS	.30	.14	.04
	Sacramento Kings			
☐ 397	Bo Kimble LS	.10	.05	.01
	Los Angeles Clippers			
☐ 398	Willie Burton LS	.10	.05	.01
	Miami Heat			

☐ 399	Rumeal Robinson LS Atlanta Hawks	.10	.05	.01
☐ 400	Tyrone Hill LS Golden State Warriors	.25	.11	.03
☐ 401	Tim McCormick Atlanta Hawks	.05	.02	.01
☐ 402	Sidney Moncrief Atlanta Hawks	.10	.05	.01
☐ 403	Johnny Newman Charlotte Hornets	.05	.02	.01
☐ 404	Dennis Hopson Chicago Bulls	.05	.02	.01
☐ 405	Cliff Levingston Chicago Bulls	.05	.02	.01
☐ 406A	Danny Ferry ERR Cleveland Cavaliers (No position on front of card)	.50	.23	.06
☐ 406B	Danny Ferry COR Cleveland Cavaliers	.10	.05	.01
☐ 407	Alex English Dallas Mavericks	.10	.05	.01
☐ 408	Lafayette Lever Dallas Mavericks	.05	.02	.01
☐ 409	Rodney McCray Dallas Mavericks	.05	.02	.01
☐ 410	Mike Dunleavy CO Los Angeles Lakers	.05	.02	.01
☐ 411	Orlando Woolridge Denver Nuggets	.08	.04	.01
☐ 412	Joe Wolf Denver Nuggets	.05	.02	.01
☐ 413	Tree Rollins Detroit Pistons	.05	.02	.01
☐ 414	Kenny Smith Houston Rockets	.05	.02	.01
☐ 415	Sam Perkins Los Angeles Lakers	.10	.05	.01
☐ 416	Terry Teagle Los Angeles Lakers	.05	.02	.01
☐ 417	Frank Brickowski Milwaukee Bucks	.08	.04	.01
☐ 418	Danny Schayes Milwaukee Bucks	.05	.02	.01
☐ 419	Scott Brooks Minnesota Timberwolves	.05	.02	.01
☐ 420	Reggie Theus New Jersey Nets	.08	.04	.01
☐ 421	Greg Grant New York Knicks	.05	.02	.01
☐ 422	Paul Westhead CO Denver Nuggets	.08	.04	.01
☐ 423	Greg Kite Orlando Magic	.05	.02	.01
☐ 424	Manute Bol Philadelphia 76ers	.05	.02	.01
☐ 425	Rickey Green Philadelphia 76ers	.05	.02	.01
☐ 426	Ed Nealy Phoenix Suns	.05	.02	.01
☐ 427	Danny Ainge Portland Trail Blazers	.10	.05	.01
☐ 428	Bobby Hansen Sacramento Kings	.05	.02	.01
☐ 429	Eric Leckner Charlotte Hornets	.05	.02	.01
☐ 430	Rory Sparrow Sacramento Kings	.05	.02	.01
☐ 431	Bill Wennington Sacramento Kings	.05	.02	.01
☐ 432	Paul Pressey San Antonio Spurs	.05	.02	.01
☐ 433	David Greenwood	.05	.02	.01

San Antonio Spurs
- [ ] 434 Mark McNamara.................... .05 .02 .01
  Orlando Magic
- [ ] 435 Sidney Green...................... .05 .02 .01
  Orlando Magic
- [ ] 436 Dave Corzine..................... .05 .02 .01
  Orlando Magic
- [ ] 437 Jeff Malone .... .08 .04 .01
  Utah Jazz
- [ ] 438 Pervis Ellison................... .10 .05 .01
  Washington Bullets
- [ ] 439 Checklist 5...................... .05 .02 .01
- [ ] 440 Checklist 6...................... .05 .02 .01
- [ ] NNO David Robinson and........... 2.00 .90 .25
  All-Rookie Team
  (No stats on back)
- [ ] NNO David Robinson and........... 10.00 4.50 1.25
  All-Rookie Team
  (Stats on back)

1991-92 Hoops

The complete 1991-92 Hoops basketball set contains 590 cards measuring the standard size (2 1/2" by 3 1/2"). The set was released in two series of 330 and 260 cards, respectively. The fronts feature color action player photos, with different color borders on a white card face. The player's name is printed in black lettering in the upper left corner, and the team logo is superimposed over the lower left corner of the picture. In a horizontal format the backs have color head shots and biographical information on the left side, while the right side presents college and pro statistics. The cards are numbered on the back and checklisted below alphabetically within and according to teams as follows: Atlanta Hawks (1-8), Boston Celtics (9-17), Charlotte Hornets (18-25), Chicago Bulls (26-34), Cleveland Cavaliers (35-42), Dallas Mavericks (43-50), Denver Nuggets (51-58), Detroit Pistons (59-66), Golden State Warriors (67-74), Houston Rockets (75-82), Indiana Pacers (83-90), Los Angeles Clippers (91-98), Los Angeles Lakers (99-106), Miami Heat (107-114), Milwaukee Bucks (115-122), Minnesota Timberwolves (123-130), New Jersey Nets (131-138), New York Knicks (139-146), Orlando Magic (147-154), Philadelphia 76ers (155-162), Phoenix Suns (163-170), Portland Trail Blazers (171-179), Sacramento Kings (180-187), San Antonio Spurs (188-196), Seattle Supersonics (197-204), Utah Jazz (205-212), Washington Bullets (213-220), Coaches (221-247), All-Stars East (248-260), All-Stars West (261-273), Teams (274-300), Centennial Card honoring James Naismith (301), Inside Stuff (302-305), League Leaders (306-313), Milestones (314-318), NBA yearbook (319-324), Stay in School (325-326), Don't Drive and Drink (327), Checklists (328-330), Atlanta Hawks (331-337), Boston Celtics (338-341), Charlotte Hornets (342-344), Chicago Bulls (345-346), Cleveland Cavaliers (347-351), Dallas Mavericks (352-353), Denver Nuggets (354-359), Detroit Pistons (360-367), Houston Rockets (368-371), Indiana Pacers (372-375), Los Angeles

Clippers (376-381), Los Angeles Lakers (382-385), Miami Heat (386-389), Milwaukee Bucks (390-394), Minnesota Timberwolves (395-397), New Jersey Nets (398-401), New York Knicks (402-406), Orlando Magic (407-410), Philadelphia 76ers (411-416), Phoenix Suns (417-422), Portland Trail Blazers (423-425), Sacramento Kings (426-431), San Antonio Spurs (432-437), Seattle Supersonics (438-441), Utah Jazz (442-448), Supreme Court (449-502), Art Cards (503-529), Active Leaders (530-537), NBA Hoops Tribune (538-543), Stay in School (544-545), Draft Picks (546-556), USA Basketball 1976 (557), USA Basketball 1984 (558-564), USA Basketball 1988 (565-574), and USA Basketball 1992 (575-588). A special short-printed Naismith card, numbered CC1, was inserted into wax packs. It features a colorized photo of Dr. Naismith standing between two peach baskets like those used in the first basketball game. The back narrates the invention of the game of basketball. An unnumbered Centennial Card featuring the Centennial Logo was also available via a mail-in offer. Series II packs also featured a randomly packed Gold Foil USA Basketball logo card. Part of the second series, the USA Basketball subset cards have white borders with fronts that feature color player photos inside different color frames. The player's name appears above the picture, while the team logo appears at the lower left corner. In a horizontal format, the backs have a color head shot, biography, and complete statistics (college and pro). Rookie Cards include Kenny Anderson, Stacey Augmon, Larry Johnson, Mike Krzyzewski (USA coach), Dikembe Mutombo, Billy Owens, Steve Smith, and John Starks. A special individually numbered (out of 10,000) "Head of the Class" (showing the top six draft picks from 1991) card was made available to the first 10,000 fans requesting one along with three wrappers from each series of 1991-92 Hoops cards.

	MINT	EXC	G-VG
COMPLETE SET (590)	20.00	9.00	2.50
COMPLETE SERIES 1 (330)	8.00	3.60	1.00
COMPLETE SERIES 2 (260)	12.00	5.50	1.50
COMMON PLAYER (1-330)	.05	.02	.01
COMMON PLAYER (331-590)	.05	.02	.01
☐ 1 John Battle	.05	.02	.01
☐ 2 Moses Malone UER	.10	.05	.01
(119 rebounds 1982-83, should be 1194)			
☐ 3 Sidney Moncrief	.10	.05	.01
☐ 4 Doc Rivers	.08	.04	.01
☐ 5 Rumeal Robinson UER	.05	.02	.01
(Back says 11th pick in 1990, should be 10th)			
☐ 6 Spud Webb	.10	.05	.01
☐ 7 Dominique Wilkins	.20	.09	.03
☐ 8 Kevin Willis	.08	.04	.01
☐ 9 Larry Bird	.60	.25	.08
☐ 10 Dee Brown	.08	.04	.01
☐ 11 Kevin Gamble	.05	.02	.01
☐ 12 Joe Kleine	.05	.02	.01
☐ 13 Reggie Lewis	.10	.05	.01
☐ 14 Kevin McHale	.10	.05	.01
☐ 15 Robert Parish	.10	.05	.01
☐ 16 Ed Pinckney	.05	.02	.01
☐ 17 Brian Shaw	.05	.02	.01
☐ 18 Muggsy Bogues	.10	.05	.01
☐ 19 Rex Chapman	.05	.02	.01
☐ 20 Dell Curry	.08	.04	.01
☐ 21 Kendall Gill	.08	.04	.01
☐ 22 Mike Gminski	.05	.02	.01
☐ 23 Johnny Newman	.05	.02	.01
☐ 24 J.R. Reid	.05	.02	.01
☐ 25 Kelly Tripucka	.08	.04	.01
☐ 26 B.J. Armstrong	.15	.07	.02
(B.J. on front, Benjamin Roy on back)			
☐ 27 Bill Cartwright	.08	.04	.01
☐ 28 Horace Grant	.10	.05	.01
☐ 29 Craig Hodges	.05	.02	.01
☐ 30 Michael Jordan	2.00	.90	.25
☐ 31 Stacey King	.05	.02	.01
☐ 32 Cliff Levingston	.05	.02	.01
☐ 33 John Paxson	.08	.04	.01
☐ 34 Scottie Pippen	.25	.11	.03
☐ 35 Chucky Brown	.05	.02	.01
☐ 36 Brad Daugherty	.10	.05	.01
☐ 37 Craig Ehlo	.05	.02	.01

☐ 38	Danny Ferry	.05	.02	.01
☐ 39	Larry Nance	.08	.04	.01
☐ 40	Mark Price	.10	.05	.01
☐ 41	Darnell Valentine	.05	.02	.01
☐ 42	Hot Rod Williams	.05	.02	.01
☐ 43	Rolando Blackman	.08	.04	.01
☐ 44	Brad Davis	.05	.02	.01
☐ 45	James Donaldson	.05	.02	.01
☐ 46	Derek Harper	.08	.04	.01
☐ 47	Fat Lever	.05	.02	.01
☐ 48	Rodney McCray	.05	.02	.01
☐ 49	Roy Tarpley	.05	.02	.01
☐ 50	Herb Williams	.05	.02	.01
☐ 51	Michael Adams	.08	.04	.01
☐ 52	Chris Jackson UER	.05	.02	.01
	(Born in Mississippi, not Michigan)			
☐ 53	Jerome Lane	.05	.02	.01
☐ 54	Todd Lichti	.05	.02	.01
☐ 55	Blair Rasmussen	.05	.02	.01
☐ 56	Reggie Williams	.08	.04	.01
☐ 57	Joe Wolf	.05	.02	.01
☐ 58	Orlando Woolridge	.08	.04	.01
☐ 59	Mark Aguirre	.10	.05	.01
☐ 60	Joe Dumars	.15	.07	.02
☐ 61	James Edwards	.05	.02	.01
☐ 62	Vinnie Johnson	.08	.04	.01
☐ 63	Bill Laimbeer	.10	.05	.01
☐ 64	Dennis Rodman	.08	.04	.01
☐ 65	John Salley	.05	.02	.01
☐ 66	Isiah Thomas	.15	.07	.02
☐ 67	Tim Hardaway	.15	.07	.02
☐ 68	Rod Higgins	.05	.02	.01
☐ 69	Tyrone Hill	.05	.02	.01
☐ 70	Alton Lister	.05	.02	.01
☐ 71	Sarunas Marciulionis	.08	.04	.01
☐ 72	Chris Mullin	.15	.07	.02
☐ 73	Mitch Richmond	.10	.05	.01
☐ 74	Tom Tolbert	.05	.02	.01
☐ 75	Eric(Sleepy) Floyd	.05	.02	.01
☐ 76	Buck Johnson	.05	.02	.01
☐ 77	Vernon Maxwell	.08	.04	.01
☐ 78	Hakeem Olajuwon	.60	.25	.08
☐ 79	Kenny Smith	.05	.02	.01
☐ 80	Larry Smith	.08	.04	.01
☐ 81	Otis Thorpe	.08	.04	.01
☐ 82	David Wood	.05	.02	.01
☐ 83	Vern Fleming	.05	.02	.01
☐ 84	Reggie Miller	.15	.07	.02
☐ 85	Chuck Person	.08	.04	.01
☐ 86	Mike Sanders	.05	.02	.01
☐ 87	Detlef Schrempf	.10	.05	.01
☐ 88	Rik Smits	.08	.04	.01
☐ 89	LaSalle Thompson	.08	.04	.01
☐ 90	Micheal Williams	.08	.04	.01
☐ 91	Winston Garland	.05	.02	.01
☐ 92	Gary Grant	.05	.02	.01
☐ 93	Ron Harper	.08	.04	.01
☐ 94	Danny Manning	.15	.07	.02
☐ 95	Jeff Martin	.05	.02	.01
☐ 96	Ken Norman	.08	.04	.01
☐ 97	Olden Polynice	.05	.02	.01
☐ 98	Charles Smith	.08	.04	.01
☐ 99	Vlade Divac	.08	.04	.01
☐ 100	A.C. Green	.08	.04	.01
☐ 101	Magic Johnson	.40	.18	.05
☐ 102	Sam Perkins	.08	.04	.01
☐ 103	Byron Scott	.08	.04	.01
☐ 104	Terry Teagle	.05	.02	.01
☐ 105	Mychal Thompson	.08	.04	.01
☐ 106	James Worthy	.10	.05	.01
☐ 107	Willie Burton	.05	.02	.01
☐ 108	Bimbo Coles	.05	.02	.01

☐	109	Terry Davis	.05	.02	.01
☐	110	Sherman Douglas	.05	.02	.01
☐	111	Kevin Edwards	.05	.02	.01
☐	112	Alec Kessler	.05	.02	.01
☐	113	Glen Rice	.15	.07	.02
☐	114	Rony Seikaly	.10	.05	.01
☐	115	Frank Brickowski	.08	.04	.01
☐	116	Dale Ellis	.08	.04	.01
☐	117	Jay Humphries	.05	.02	.01
☐	118	Brad Lohaus	.05	.02	.01
☐	119	Fred Roberts	.05	.02	.01
☐	120	Alvin Robertson	.08	.04	.01
☐	121	Danny Schayes	.05	.02	.01
☐	122	Jack Sikma	.10	.05	.01
☐	123	Randy Breuer	.05	.02	.01
☐	124	Tony Campbell	.05	.02	.01
☐	125	Tyrone Corbin	.05	.02	.01
☐	126	Gerald Glass	.05	.02	.01
☐	127	Sam Mitchell	.05	.02	.01
☐	128	Tod Murphy	.05	.02	.01
☐	129	Pooh Richardson	.05	.02	.01
☐	130	Felton Spencer	.05	.02	.01
☐	131	Mookie Blaylock	.08	.04	.01
☐	132	Sam Bowie	.08	.04	.01
☐	133	Jud Buechler	.05	.02	.01
☐	134	Derrick Coleman	.30	.14	.04
☐	135	Chris Dudley	.05	.02	.01
☐	136	Chris Morris	.05	.02	.01
☐	137	Drazen Petrovic	.08	.04	.01
☐	138	Reggie Theus	.08	.04	.01
☐	139	Maurice Cheeks	.10	.05	.01
☐	140	Patrick Ewing	.25	.11	.03
☐	141	Mark Jackson	.08	.04	.01
☐	142	Charles Oakley	.10	.05	.01
☐	143	Trent Tucker	.05	.02	.01
☐	144	Kiki Vandeweghe	.08	.04	.01
☐	145	Kenny Walker	.05	.02	.01
☐	146	Gerald Wilkins	.08	.04	.01
☐	147	Nick Anderson	.10	.05	.01
☐	148	Michael Ansley	.05	.02	.01
☐	149	Terry Catledge	.05	.02	.01
☐	150	Jerry Reynolds	.05	.02	.01
☐	151	Dennis Scott	.08	.04	.01
☐	152	Scott Skiles	.08	.04	.01
☐	153	Otis Smith	.05	.02	.01
☐	154	Sam Vincent	.05	.02	.01
☐	155	Ron Anderson	.05	.02	.01
☐	156	Charles Barkley	.40	.18	.05
☐	157	Manute Bol	.05	.02	.01
☐	158	Johnny Dawkins	.05	.02	.01
☐	159	Armon Gilliam	.05	.02	.01
☐	160	Rickey Green	.05	.02	.01
☐	161	Hersey Hawkins	.08	.04	.01
☐	162	Rick Mahorn	.08	.04	.01
☐	163	Tom Chambers	.10	.05	.01
☐	164	Jeff Hornacek	.10	.05	.01
☐	165	Kevin Johnson	.15	.07	.02
☐	166	Andrew Lang	.05	.02	.01
☐	167	Dan Majerle	.10	.05	.01
☐	168	Xavier McDaniel	.10	.05	.01
☐	169	Kurt Rambis	.08	.04	.01
☐	170	Mark West	.05	.02	.01
☐	171	Danny Ainge	.10	.05	.01
☐	172	Mark Bryant	.05	.02	.01
☐	173	Walter Davis	.10	.05	.01
☐	174	Clyde Drexler	.15	.07	.02
☐	175	Kevin Duckworth	.05	.02	.01
☐	176	Jerome Kersey	.05	.02	.01
☐	177	Terry Porter	.08	.04	.01
☐	178	Cliff Robinson	.15	.07	.02
☐	179	Buck Williams	.10	.05	.01
☐	180	Anthony Bonner	.05	.02	.01
☐	181	Antoine Carr	.05	.02	.01

☐ 182	Duane Causwell	.05	.02	.01
☐ 183	Bobby Hansen	.05	.02	.01
☐ 184	Travis Mays	.05	.02	.01
☐ 185	Lionel Simmons	.08	.04	.01
☐ 186	Rory Sparrow	.05	.02	.01
☐ 187	Wayman Tisdale	.08	.04	.01
☐ 188	Willie Anderson	.05	.02	.01
☐ 189	Terry Cummings	.08	.04	.01
☐ 190	Sean Elliott	.08	.04	.01
☐ 191	Sidney Green	.05	.02	.01
☐ 192	David Greenwood	.05	.02	.01
☐ 193	Paul Pressey	.05	.02	.01
☐ 194	David Robinson	.50	.23	.06
☐ 195	Dwayne Schintzius	.05	.02	.01
☐ 196	Rod Strickland	.08	.04	.01
☐ 197	Benoit Benjamin	.05	.02	.01
☐ 198	Michael Cage	.05	.02	.01
☐ 199	Eddie Johnson	.08	.04	.01
☐ 200	Shawn Kemp	.75	.35	.09
☐ 201	Derrick McKey	.05	.02	.01
☐ 202	Gary Payton	.15	.07	.02
☐ 203	Ricky Pierce	.08	.04	.01
☐ 204	Sedale Threatt	.05	.02	.01
☐ 205	Thurl Bailey	.05	.02	.01
☐ 206	Mike Brown	.05	.02	.01
☐ 207	Mark Eaton	.05	.02	.01
☐ 208	Blue Edwards UER (Forward/guard on front, guard on back)	.08	.04	.01
☐ 209	Darrell Griffith	.08	.04	.01
☐ 210	Jeff Malone	.08	.04	.01
☐ 211	Karl Malone	.20	.09	.03
☐ 212	John Stockton	.15	.07	.02
☐ 213	Ledell Eackles	.05	.02	.01
☐ 214	Pervis Ellison	.08	.04	.01
☐ 215	A.J. English	.05	.02	.01
☐ 216	Harvey Grant (Shown boxing out twin brother Horace)	.05	.02	.01
☐ 217	Charles Jones	.05	.02	.01
☐ 218	Bernard King	.10	.05	.01
☐ 219	Darrell Walker	.05	.02	.01
☐ 220	John Williams	.05	.02	.01
☐ 221	Bob Weiss CO	.05	.02	.01
☐ 222	Chris Ford CO	.08	.04	.01
☐ 223	Gene Littles CO	.05	.02	.01
☐ 224	Phil Jackson CO	.08	.04	.01
☐ 225	Lenny Wilkens CO	.08	.04	.01
☐ 226	Richie Adubato CO	.05	.02	.01
☐ 227	Paul Westhead CO	.08	.04	.01
☐ 228	Chuck Daly CO	.08	.04	.01
☐ 229	Don Nelson CO	.08	.04	.01
☐ 230	Don Chaney CO	.05	.02	.01
☐ 231	Bob Hill CO UER (Coached under Ted Owens, not Ted Owen)	.05	.02	.01
☐ 232	Mike Schuler CO	.05	.02	.01
☐ 233	Mike Dunleavy CO	.08	.04	.01
☐ 234	Kevin Loughery CO	.08	.04	.01
☐ 235	Del Harris CO	.05	.02	.01
☐ 236	Jimmy Rodgers CO	.05	.02	.01
☐ 237	Bill Fitch CO	.05	.02	.01
☐ 238	Pat Riley CO	.08	.04	.01
☐ 239	Matt Guokas CO	.05	.02	.01
☐ 240	Jim Lynam CO	.05	.02	.01
☐ 241	Cotton Fitzsimmons CO	.05	.02	.01
☐ 242	Rick Adelman CO	.08	.04	.01
☐ 243	Dick Motta CO	.05	.02	.01
☐ 244	Larry Brown CO	.08	.04	.01
☐ 245	K.C. Jones CO	.08	.04	.01
☐ 246	Jerry Sloan CO	.05	.02	.01
☐ 247	Wes Unseld CO	.08	.04	.01
☐ 248	Charles Barkley AS	.20	.09	.03

☐ 249	Brad Daugherty AS	.08	.04	.01
☐ 250	Joe Dumars AS	.08	.04	.01
☐ 251	Patrick Ewing AS	.15	.07	.02
☐ 252	Hersey Hawkins AS	.05	.02	.01
☐ 253	Michael Jordan AS	1.00	.45	.13
☐ 254	Bernard King AS	.08	.04	.01
☐ 255	Kevin McHale AS	.08	.04	.01
☐ 256	Robert Parish AS	.08	.04	.01
☐ 257	Ricky Pierce AS	.05	.02	.01
☐ 258	Alvin Robertson AS	.05	.02	.01
☐ 259	Dominique Wilkins AS	.10	.05	.01
☐ 260	Chris Ford CO AS	.05	.02	.01
☐ 261	Tom Chambers AS	.08	.04	.01
☐ 262	Clyde Drexler AS	.10	.05	.01
☐ 263	Kevin Duckworth AS	.05	.02	.01
☐ 264	Tim Hardaway AS	.10	.05	.01
☐ 265	Kevin Johnson AS	.10	.05	.01
☐ 266	Magic Johnson AS	.20	.09	.03
☐ 267	Karl Malone AS	.10	.05	.01
☐ 268	Chris Mullen AS	.10	.05	.01
☐ 269	Terry Porter AS	.05	.02	.01
☐ 270	David Robinson AS	.25	.11	.03
☐ 271	John Stockton AS	.10	.05	.01
☐ 272	James Worthy AS	.08	.04	.01
☐ 273	Rick Adelman CO AS	.05	.02	.01
☐ 274	Atlanta Hawks Team Card UER (Actually began as Tri-Cities Blackhawks)	.05	.02	.01
☐ 275	Boston Celtics Team Card UER (No NBA Hoops logo on card front)	.05	.02	.01
☐ 276	Charlotte Hornets Team Card	.05	.02	.01
☐ 277	Chicago Bulls Team Card	.05	.02	.01
☐ 278	Cleveland Cavaliers Team Card	.05	.02	.01
☐ 279	Dallas Mavericks Team Card	.05	.02	.01
☐ 280	Denver Nuggets Team Card	.05	.02	.01
☐ 281	Detroit Pistons Team Card UER (Pistons not NBA Finalists until 1988; Ft. Ft. Wayne Pistons in Finals in 1955 and 1956)	.05	.02	.01
☐ 282	Golden State Warriors Team Card	.05	.02	.01
☐ 283	Houston Rockets Team Card	.05	.02	.01
☐ 284	Indiana Pacers Team Card	.05	.02	.01
☐ 285	Los Angeles Clippers Team Card	.05	.02	.01
☐ 286	Los Angeles Lakers Team Card	.05	.02	.01
☐ 287	Miami Heat Team Card	.05	.02	.01
☐ 288	Milwaukee Bucks Team Card	.05	.02	.01
☐ 289	Minnesota Timberwolves Team Card	.05	.02	.01
☐ 290	New Jersey Nets Team Card	.05	.02	.01
☐ 291	New York Knicks Team Card UER (Golden State not mentioned as an active charter member of NBA)	.05	.02	.01
☐ 292	Orlando Magic	.05	.02	.01

Team Card			
☐ 293 Philadelphia 76ers	.05	.02	.01
Team Card			
☐ 294 Phoenix Suns	.05	.02	.01
Team Card			
☐ 295 Portland Trail Blazers	.05	.02	.01
Team Card			
☐ 296 Sacramento Kings	.05	.02	.01
Team Card			
☐ 297 San Antonio Spurs	.05	.02	.01
Team Card			
☐ 298 Seattle Supersonics	.05	.02	.01
Team Card			
☐ 299 Utah Jazz	.05	.02	.01
Team Card			
☐ 300 Washington Bullets	.05	.02	.01
Team Card			
☐ 301 Centennial Card	.05	.02	.01
James Naismith			
☐ 302 Kevin Johnson IS	.08	.04	.01
☐ 303 Reggie Miller IS	.10	.05	.01
☐ 304 Hakeem Olajuwon IS	.30	.14	.04
☐ 305 Robert Parish IS	.08	.04	.01
☐ 306 Scoring Leaders	.50	.23	.06
Michael Jordan			
Karl Malone			
☐ 307 3-Point FG Percent	.05	.02	.01
League Leaders			
Jim Les			
Trent Tucker			
☐ 308 Free Throw Percent	.10	.05	.01
League Leaders			
Reggie Miller			
Jeff Malone			
☐ 309 Blocks League Leaders	.35	.16	.04
Hakeem Olajuwon			
David Robinson			
☐ 310 Steals League Leaders	.08	.04	.01
Alvin Robertson			
John Stockton			
☐ 311 Rebounds LL UER	.15	.07	.02
David Robinson			
Dennis Rodman			
(Robinson credited as			
playing for Houston)			
☐ 312 Assists League Leaders	.25	.11	.03
John Stockton			
Magic Johnson			
☐ 313 Field Goal Percent	.08	.04	.01
League Leaders			
Buck Williams			
Robert Parish			
☐ 314 Larry Bird UER	.30	.14	.04
Milestone			
(Should be card 315 to			
fit Milestone sequence)			
☐ 315 A.English/M.Malone	.08	.04	.01
Milestone UER			
(Should be card 314 and			
be a League Leader card)			
☐ 316 Magic Johnson	.20	.09	.03
Milestone			
☐ 317 Michael Jordan	1.00	.45	.13
Milestone			
☐ 318 Moses Malone	.08	.04	.01
Milestone			
☐ 319 Larry Bird	.30	.14	.04
NBA Yearbook			
Look Back			
☐ 320 Maurice Cheeks	.08	.04	.01
NBA Yearbook			
Look Back			
☐ 321 Magic Johnson	.20	.09	.03
NBA Yearbook			

	Look Back			
☐ 322	Bernard King	.08	.04	.01
	NBA Yearbook			
	Look Back			
☐ 323	Moses Malone	.08	.04	.01
	NBA Yearbook			
	Look Back			
☐ 324	Robert Parish	.08	.04	.01
	NBA Yearbook			
	Look Back			
☐ 325	All-Star Jam	.05	.02	.01
	Jammin' With Will Smith			
	(Stay in School)			
☐ 326	All-Star Jam	.05	.02	.01
	Jammin' With The Boys			
	and Will Smith			
	(Stay in School)			
☐ 327	David Robinson	.25	.11	.03
	Leave Alcohol Out			
☐ 328	Checklist 1	.05	.02	.01
☐ 329	Checklist 2 UER	.05	.02	.01
	(Card front is from 330)			
☐ 330	Checklist 3 UER	.05	.02	.01
	(Card front is from 329;			
	card 327 listed oper-			
	ation, should be			
	celebration)			
☐ 331	Maurice Cheeks	.10	.05	.01
☐ 332	Duane Ferrell	.05	.02	.01
☐ 333	Jon Koncak	.05	.02	.01
☐ 334	Gary Leonard	.05	.02	.01
☐ 335	Travis Mays	.05	.02	.01
☐ 336	Blair Rasmussen	.05	.02	.01
☐ 337	Alexander Volkov	.05	.02	.01
☐ 338	John Bagley	.05	.02	.01
☐ 339	Rickey Green UER	.05	.02	.01
	(Ricky on front)			
☐ 340	Derek Smith	.05	.02	.01
☐ 341	Stojko Vrankovic	.05	.02	.01
☐ 342	Anthony Frederick	.05	.02	.01
☐ 343	Kenny Gattison	.05	.02	.01
☐ 344	Eric Leckner	.05	.02	.01
☐ 345	Will Perdue	.05	.02	.01
☐ 346	Scott Williams	.15	.07	.02
☐ 347	John Battle	.05	.02	.01
☐ 348	Winston Bennett	.05	.02	.01
☐ 349	Henry James	.05	.02	.01
☐ 350	Steve Kerr	.05	.02	.01
☐ 351	John Morton	.05	.02	.01
☐ 352	Terry Davis	.05	.02	.01
☐ 353	Randy White	.05	.02	.01
☐ 354	Greg Anderson	.05	.02	.01
☐ 355	Anthony Cook	.05	.02	.01
☐ 356	Walter Davis	.10	.05	.01
☐ 357	Winston Garland	.05	.02	.01
☐ 358	Scott Hastings	.05	.02	.01
☐ 359	Marcus Liberty	.05	.02	.01
☐ 360	William Bedford	.05	.02	.01
☐ 361	Lance Blanks	.05	.02	.01
☐ 362	Brad Sellers	.05	.02	.01
☐ 363	Darrell Walker	.05	.02	.01
☐ 364	Orlando Woolridge	.08	.04	.01
☐ 365	Vincent Askew	.05	.02	.01
☐ 366	Mario Elie	.20	.09	.03
☐ 367	Jim Petersen	.05	.02	.01
☐ 368	Matt Bullard	.05	.02	.01
☐ 369	Gerald Henderson	.05	.02	.01
☐ 370	Dave Jamerson	.05	.02	.01
☐ 371	Tree Rollins	.05	.02	.01
☐ 372	Greg Dreiling	.05	.02	.01
☐ 373	George McCloud	.05	.02	.01
☐ 374	Kenny Williams	.05	.02	.01
☐ 375	Randy Wittman	.05	.02	.01

☐	376	Tony Brown	.05	.02	.01
☐	377	Lanard Copeland	.05	.02	.01
☐	378	James Edwards	.05	.02	.01
☐	379	Bo Kimble	.08	.04	.01
☐	380	Doc Rivers	.08	.04	.01
☐	381	Loy Vaught	.05	.02	.01
☐	382	Elden Campbell	.05	.02	.01
☐	383	Jack Haley	.05	.02	.01
☐	384	Tony Smith	.05	.02	.01
☐	385	Sedale Threatt	.05	.02	.01
☐	386	Keith Askins	.05	.02	.01
☐	387	Grant Long	.05	.02	.01
☐	388	Alan Ogg	.05	.02	.01
☐	389	Jon Sundvold	.05	.02	.01
☐	390	Lester Conner	.05	.02	.01
☐	391	Jeff Grayer	.05	.02	.01
☐	392	Steve Henson	.05	.02	.01
☐	393	Larry Krystkowiak	.05	.02	.01
☐	394	Moses Malone	.10	.05	.01
☐	395	Scott Brooks	.05	.02	.01
☐	396	Tellis Frank	.05	.02	.01
☐	397	Doug West	.08	.04	.01
☐	398	Rafael Addison	.05	.02	.01
☐	399	Dave Feitl	.05	.02	.01
☐	400	Tate George	.05	.02	.01
☐	401	Terry Mills	.40	.18	.05
☐	402	Tim McCormick	.05	.02	.01
☐	403	Xavier McDaniel	.10	.05	.01
☐	404	Anthony Mason	.30	.14	.04
☐	405	Brian Quinnett	.05	.02	.01
☐	406	John Starks	.50	.23	.06
☐	407	Mark Acres	.05	.02	.01
☐	408	Greg Kite	.05	.02	.01
☐	409	Jeff Turner	.05	.02	.01
☐	410	Morlon Wiley	.05	.02	.01
☐	411	Dave Hoppen	.05	.02	.01
☐	412	Brian Oliver	.05	.02	.01
☐	413	Kenny Payne	.05	.02	.01
☐	414	Charles Shackleford	.05	.02	.01
☐	415	Mitchell Wiggins	.05	.02	.01
☐	416	Jayson Williams	.05	.02	.01
☐	417	Cedric Ceballos	.10	.05	.01
☐	418	Negele Knight	.05	.02	.01
☐	419	Andrew Lang	.05	.02	.01
☐	420	Jerrod Mustaf	.05	.02	.01
☐	421	Ed Nealy	.05	.02	.01
☐	422	Tim Perry	.05	.02	.01
☐	423	Alaa Abdelnaby	.05	.02	.01
☐	424	Wayne Cooper	.05	.02	.01
☐	425	Danny Young	.05	.02	.01
☐	426	Dennis Hopson	.05	.02	.01
☐	427	Les Jepsen	.05	.02	.01
☐	428	Jim Les	.05	.02	.01
☐	429	Mitch Richmond	.10	.05	.01
☐	430	Dwayne Schintzius	.05	.02	.01
☐	431	Spud Webb	.10	.05	.01
☐	432	Jud Buechler	.05	.02	.01
☐	433	Antoine Carr	.05	.02	.01
☐	434	Tom Garrick	.05	.02	.01
☐	435	Sean Higgins	.08	.04	.01
☐	436	Avery Johnson	.08	.04	.01
☐	437	Tony Massenburg	.05	.02	.01
☐	438	Dana Barros	.05	.02	.01
☐	439	Quintin Dailey	.05	.02	.01
☐	440	Bart Kofoed	.05	.02	.01
☐	441	Nate McMillan	.08	.04	.01
☐	442	Delaney Rudd	.05	.02	.01
☐	443	Michael Adams	.08	.04	.01
☐	444	Mark Alarie	.05	.02	.01
☐	445	Greg Foster	.05	.02	.01
☐	446	Tom Hammonds	.05	.02	.01
☐	447	Andre Turner	.05	.02	.01
☐	448	David Wingate	.05	.02	.01

☐	449	Dominique Wilkins SC	.10	.05	.01
☐	450	Kevin Willis SC	.05	.02	.01
☐	451	Larry Bird SC	.30	.14	.04
☐	452	Robert Parish SC	.08	.04	.01
☐	453	Rex Chapman SC	.05	.02	.01
☐	454	Kendall Gill SC	.08	.04	.01
☐	455	Michael Jordan SC	1.00	.45	.13
☐	456	Scottie Pippen SC	.15	.07	.02
☐	457	Brad Daugherty SC	.08	.04	.01
☐	458	Larry Nance SC	.05	.02	.01
☐	459	Rolando Blackman SC	.05	.02	.01
☐	460	Derek Harper SC	.05	.02	.01
☐	461	Chris Jackson SC	.08	.04	.01
☐	462	Todd Lichti SC	.05	.02	.01
☐	463	Joe Dumars SC	.08	.04	.01
☐	464	Isiah Thomas SC	.10	.05	.01
☐	465	Tim Hardaway SC	.10	.05	.01
☐	466	Chris Mullin SC	.10	.05	.01
☐	467	Hakeem Olajuwon SC	.30	.14	.04
☐	468	Otis Thorpe SC	.05	.02	.01
☐	469	Reggie Miller SC	.10	.05	.01
☐	470	Detlef Schrempf SC	.08	.04	.01
☐	471	Ron Harper SC	.05	.02	.01
☐	472	Charles Smith SC	.05	.02	.01
☐	473	Magic Johnson SC	.20	.09	.03
☐	474	James Worthy SC	.08	.04	.01
☐	475	Sherman Douglas SC	.05	.02	.01
☐	476	Rony Seikaly SC	.08	.04	.01
☐	477	Jay Humphries SC	.05	.02	.01
☐	478	Alvin Robertson SC	.05	.02	.01
☐	479	Tyrone Corbin SC	.05	.02	.01
☐	480	Pooh Richardson SC	.05	.02	.01
☐	481	Sam Bowie SC	.05	.02	.01
☐	482	Derrick Coleman SC	.15	.07	.02
☐	483	Patrick Ewing SC	.15	.07	.02
☐	484	Charles Oakley SC	.08	.04	.01
☐	485	Dennis Scott SC	.05	.02	.01
☐	486	Scott Skiles SC	.05	.02	.01
☐	487	Charles Barkley SC	.20	.09	.03
☐	488	Hersey Hawkins SC	.05	.02	.01
☐	489	Tom Chambers SC	.08	.04	.01
☐	490	Kevin Johnson SC	.10	.05	.01
☐	491	Clyde Drexler SC	.10	.05	.01
☐	492	Terry Porter SC	.05	.02	.01
☐	493	Lionel Simmons SC	.05	.02	.01
☐	494	Wayman Tisdale SC	.05	.02	.01
☐	495	Terry Cummings SC	.05	.02	.01
☐	496	David Robinson SC	.25	.11	.03
☐	497	Shawn Kemp SC	.40	.18	.05
☐	498	Ricky Pierce SC	.05	.02	.01
☐	499	Karl Malone SC	.10	.05	.01
☐	500	John Stockton SC	.10	.05	.01
☐	501	Harvey Grant SC	.05	.02	.01
☐	502	Bernard King SC	.08	.04	.01
☐	503	Travis Mays Art	.05	.02	.01
☐	504	Kevin McHale Art	.08	.04	.01
☐	505	Muggsy Bogues Art	.08	.04	.01
☐	506	Scottie Pippen Art	.15	.07	.02
☐	507	Brad Daugherty Art	.08	.04	.01
☐	508	Derek Harper Art	.05	.02	.01
☐	509	Chris Jackson Art	.08	.04	.01
☐	510	Isiah Thomas Art	.10	.05	.01
☐	511	Tim Hardaway Art	.10	.05	.01
☐	512	Otis Thorpe Art	.05	.02	.01
☐	513	Chuck Person Art	.05	.02	.01
☐	514	Ron Harper Art	.05	.02	.01
☐	515	James Worthy Art	.08	.04	.01
☐	516	Sherman Douglas Art	.05	.02	.01
☐	517	Dale Ellis Art	.05	.02	.01
☐	518	Tony Campbell Art	.05	.02	.01
☐	519	Derrick Coleman Art	.15	.07	.02
☐	520	Gerald Wilkins Art	.05	.02	.01
☐	521	Scott Skiles Art	.05	.02	.01

☐ 522	Manute Bol Art	.05	.02	.01
☐ 523	Tom Chambers Art	.08	.04	.01
☐ 524	Terry Porter Art	.05	.02	.01
☐ 525	Lionel Simmons Art	.05	.02	.01
☐ 526	Sean Elliott Art	.05	.02	.01
☐ 527	Shawn Kemp Art	.40	.18	.05
☐ 528	John Stockton Art	.10	.05	.01
☐ 529	Harvey Grant Art	.05	.02	.01
☐ 530	Michael Adams	.06	.03	.01
	All-Time Active Leader			
	Three-Point Field Goals			
☐ 531	Charles Barkley	.20	.09	.03
	All-Time Active Leader			
	Field Goal Percentage			
☐ 532	Larry Bird	.30	.14	.04
	All-Time Active Leader			
	Free Throw Percentage			
☐ 533	Maurice Cheeks	.08	.04	.01
	All-Time Active Leader			
	Steals			
☐ 534	Mark Eaton	.06	.03	.01
	All-Time Active Leader			
	Blocks			
☐ 535	Magic Johnson	.20	.09	.03
	All-Time Active Leader			
	Assists			
☐ 536	Michael Jordan	1.00	.45	.13
	All-Time Active Leader			
	Scoring Average			
☐ 537	Moses Malone	.08	.04	.01
	All-Time Active Leader			
	Rebounds			
☐ 538	NBA Finals Game 1	.06	.03	.01
	Perkins' Three Pointer			
	(Sam Perkins)			
☐ 539	NBA Finals Game 2	.08	.04	.01
	Bulls Rout Lakers			
	(Pippen against Worthy)			
☐ 540	NBA Finals Game 3	.06	.03	.01
	Bulls Win OT Thriller			
	(Vlade Divac lay-in)			
☐ 541	NBA Finals Game 4	.06	.03	.01
	Bulls One Game Away			
	(John Paxson jumper)			
☐ 542	NBA Finals Game 5	.75	.35	.09
	Jordan, Bulls Win			
	First Title			
	(Jordan reverses			
	over Vlade Divac)			
☐ 543	Championship Card	.75	.35	.09
	Chicago Bulls Champs			
	(Michael Jordan			
	kissing trophy)			
☐ 544	Otis Smith	.05	.02	.01
	Stay in School			
☐ 545	Jeff Turner	.05	.02	.01
	Stay in School			
☐ 546	Larry Johnson	2.00	.90	.25
☐ 547	Kenny Anderson	.75	.35	.09
☐ 548	Billy Owens	.40	.18	.05
☐ 549	Dikembe Mutombo	1.00	.45	.13
☐ 550	Steve Smith	.50	.23	.06
☐ 551	Doug Smith	.15	.07	.02
☐ 552	Luc Longley	.15	.07	.02
☐ 553	Mark Macon	.10	.05	.01
☐ 554	Stacey Augmon	.40	.18	.05
☐ 555	Brian Williams	.20	.09	.03
☐ 556	Terrell Brandon	.15	.07	.02
☐ 557	Walter Davis	.12	.05	.02
	Team USA 1976			
☐ 558	Vern Fleming	.10	.05	.01
	Team USA 1984			
☐ 559	Joe Kleine	.10	.05	.01

	Team USA 1984		
☐ 560	Jon Koncak	.10	.05	.01
	Team USA 1984		
☐ 561	Sam Perkins	.10	.05	.01
	Team USA 1984		
☐ 562	Alvin Robertson	.10	.05	.01
	Team USA 1984		
☐ 563	Wayman Tisdale	.10	.05	.01
	Team USA 1984		
☐ 564	Jeff Turner	.10	.05	.01
	Team USA 1984		
☐ 565	Willie Anderson	.10	.05	.01
	Team USA 1988		
☐ 566	Stacey Augmon	.25	.11	.03
	Team USA 1988		
☐ 567	Bimbo Coles	.10	.05	.01
	Team USA 1988		
☐ 568	Jeff Grayer	.10	.05	.01
	Team USA 1988		
☐ 569	Hersey Hawkins	.10	.05	.01
	Team USA 1988		
☐ 570	Dan Majerle	.12	.05	.02
	Team USA 1988		
☐ 571	Danny Manning	.12	.05	.02
	Team USA 1988		
☐ 572	J.R. Reid	.10	.05	.01
	Team USA 1988		
☐ 573	Mitch Richmond	.12	.05	.02
	Team USA 1988		
☐ 574	Charles Smith	.10	.05	.01
	Team USA 1988		
☐ 575	Charles Barkley	.75	.35	.09
	Team USA 1992		
☐ 576	Larry Bird	1.25	.55	.16
	Team USA 1992		
☐ 577	Patrick Ewing	.50	.23	.06
	Team USA 1992		
☐ 578	Magic Johnson	.75	.35	.09
	Team USA 1992		
☐ 579	Michael Jordan	3.50	1.55	.45
	Team USA 1992		
☐ 580	Karl Malone	.40	.18	.05
	Team USA 1992		
☐ 581	Chris Mullin	.25	.11	.03
	Team USA 1992		
☐ 582	Scottie Pippen	.50	.23	.06
	Team USA 1992		
☐ 583	David Robinson	1.00	.45	.13
	Team USA 1992		
☐ 584	John Stockton	.25	.11	.03
	Team USA 1992		
☐ 585	Chuck Daly CO	.12	.05	.02
	Team USA 1992		
☐ 586	Lenny Wilkens CO	.12	.05	.02
	Team USA 1992		
☐ 587	P.J. Carlesimo CO	.15	.07	.02
	Team USA 1992		
☐ 588	Mike Krzyzewski CO	.50	.23	.06
	Team USA 1992		
☐ 589	Checklist Card 1	.05	.02	.01
☐ 590	Checklist Card 2	.05	.02	.01
☐ CC1	Dr.James Naismith	5.00	2.30	.60
	Title Card		
☐ NNO	Team USA SP	.50	.23	.06
☐ NNO	Centennial Card	3.00	1.35	.40
	(Sendaway)		
☐ XX	Head of the Class	25.00	11.50	3.10
	Kenny Anderson		
	Larry Johnson		
	Dikembe Mutombo		
	Billy Owens		
	Doug Smith		
	Steve Smith		

1991-92 Hoops Slam Dunk

This six-card insert set of "Slam Dunk Champions" features the winners of the All-Star weekend slam dunk competition from 1986 to 1991. The cards measure the standard size (2 1/2" by 3 1/2") and were only available as inserts one per first series 47-card rack pack. The front has a color photo of the player dunking the ball, with royal blue borders on a white card face. The player's name appears in orange lettering in a purple stripe above the picture, and the year the player won is given in a "Slam Dunk Champion" emblem overlaying the lower left corner of the picture. The design of the back is similar to the front, only with an extended caption on a yellow-green background. A drawing of a basketball entering a rim appears at the upper left corner. The cards are numbered on the back by Roman numerals.

	MINT	EXC	G-VG
COMPLETE SET (6)	20.00	9.00	2.50
COMMON PLAYER (1-6)	1.00	.45	.13
☐ 1 Larry Nance (Numbered I)	1.25	.55	.16
☐ 2 Dominique Wilkins (Numbered II)	3.00	1.35	.40
☐ 3 Spud Webb (Numbered III)	1.25	.55	.16
☐ 4 Michael Jordan (Numbered IV)	15.00	6.75	1.90
☐ 5 Kenny Walker (Numbered V)	1.00	.45	.13
☐ 6 Dee Brown (Numbered VI)	1.25	.55	.16

1991-92 Hoops All-Star MVP's

This six-card standard-size (2 1/2" by 3 1/2") set commemorates the most valuable player of the NBA All-Star games from 1986 to 1991. One card was inserted in each second series rack pack. On a white card face, the front features non-action color photos framed by either a blue (7, 9, 12) or red (8, 10, 11) border. The top thicker border is jagged and displays the player's name, while the year the award was received appears in a colored box in the lower left corner. The backs have the same design and feature a color action photo from the All-Star game. The cards are numbered on the back by Roman numerals.

	MINT	EXC	G-VG
COMPLETE SET (6)	25.00	11.50	3.10
COMMON PLAYER (7-12)	1.00	.45	.13

☐ 7 Isiah Thomas (Numbered VII)	1.50	.65	.19
☐ 8 Tom Chambers (Numbered VIII)	1.00	.45	.13
☐ 9 Michael Jordan (Numbered IX)	15.00	6.75	1.90
☐ 10 Karl Malone (Numbered X)	2.50	1.15	.30
☐ 11 Magic Johnson (Numbered XI)	4.00	1.80	.50
☐ 12 Charles Barkley (Numbered XII)	4.00	1.80	.50

1992-93 Hoops

The complete 1992-93 Hoops basketball set contains 490 cards measuring the standard size (2 1/2" by 3 1/2"). The set was released in two series of 350 and 140 cards, respectively. Both series packs contained 12 cards each; suggested retail price for both series packs was 79 cents each. A Magic Johnson "Commemorative Card" and a Patrick Ewing "Ultimate Game" card were randomly inserted in the foil packs, of which 1,000 of each were personally autographed according to representatives of National Media Group (SkyBox International's PR firm). The odds of pulling a signed Ewing or Magic are reportedly approximately one per 14,400 packs. Also randomly inserted were a USA Basketball Team card and a NBA Draft Lottery Exchange card. The latter card could have been redeemed for a ten card set of 1992 lottery picks. The Draft Exchange card was reportedly available at a rate of approximately one per 360 packs (or two per case). A Barcelona Plastic card was

also randomly inserted in first series packs at a rate of approximately one per 720 packs. The basic card fronts display color action player photos enclosed by white borders. A color stripe reflecting one of the team's colors cuts across the picture, and the player's name is printed vertically in a transparent stripe bordering the left side of the picture. The horizontally oriented backs carry a color head shot, biography, career highlights, and complete statistics (college and pro). The cards are checklisted below alphabetically according to teams as follows: Atlanta Hawks (1-9), Boston Celtics (10-18), Charlotte Hornets (19-26), Chicago Bulls (27-35), Cleveland Cavaliers (36-44), Dallas Mavericks (45-53), Denver Nuggets (54-61), Detroit Pistons (62-70), Golden State Warriors (71-79), Houston Rockets (80-88), Indiana Pacers (89-97), Los Angeles Clippers (98-106), Los Angeles Lakers (107-115), Miami Heat (116-124), Milwaukee Bucks (125-133), Minnesota Timberwolves (134-142), New Jersey Nets (143-151), New York Knicks (152-159), Orlando Magic (160-168), Philadelphia 76ers (169-177), Phoenix Suns (178-186), Portland Trail Blazers (187-195), Sacramento Kings (196-203), San Antonio Spurs (204-211), Seattle Supersonics (212-220), Utah Jazz (221-229), Washington Bullets (230-238) Coaches (239-265), Team cards (266-292), NBA All-Stars East (293-305), NBA All-Stars West (306-319), League Leaders (320-327), Magic Moments (328-331), NBA Inside Stuff (332-333), NBA Stay in School (334-335), Basketball Tournament of the Americas (336-347), Checklists (348-350), Atlanta Hawks (351-354), Boston Celtics (355-357), Charlotte Hornets (358-361), Chicago Bulls (362-364), Cleveland Cavaliers (365-369), Dallas Mavericks (370-373), Denver Nuggets (374-379), Detroit Pistons (380-385), Golden State Warriors (386-389), Houston Rockets (390-394), Indiana Pacers (395-400), Los Angeles Clippers (401-407), Los Angeles Lakers (408-410), Miami Heat (411-414), Milwaukee Bucks (415-420), Minnesota Timberwolves (421-426), New Jersey Nets (427-432), New York Knicks (433-438), Orlando Magic (439-443), Philadelphia 76ers (444-449), Phoenix Suns (450-453), Portland Trail Blazers (454-458), Sacramento Kings (459-463), San Antonio Spurs (464-469), Seattle Supersonics (470), Utah Jazz (471-475), Washington Bullets (476-480), Trivia (481-485) and Miscellaneous (486-490) cards. Randomly inserted throughout the second series foil packs were a ten-card Supreme Court subset, a ten-card Magic's All-Rookie Team subset, a Patrick Ewing Art card (reported odds were one per 21 packs), a Chicago Bulls Championship card (reported odds were one per 32 packs), and a John Stockton "Ultimate Game" card (reported odds were one per 92 packs). Commemorating each steal in his career, John Stockton autographed 1,633 of these cards (reported odds were one per 5,732 packs). Also a three-card "More Magic" random insert set captured Magic's brief return to the NBA. Rookie cards, scattered throughout the set, have a gold rather than a ghosted white stripe. The team logo appears in the lower left corner and intersects a team color-coded stripe that contains the player's position. The horizontal backs show a white background and include statistics (collegiate and pro), biographies, and career summaries. A close-up photo is at the upper left. The key Rookie Cards in the set are LaPhonso Ellis, Tom Gugliotta, Robert Horry, Christian Laettner, Don McLean, Harold Miner, Alonzo Mourning, Shaquille O'Neal, Latrell Sprewell, Clarence Weatherspoon, and Walt Williams. Reported production quantities were 20,000 20-box wax cases of the first series and approximately 14,000 20-box wax cases of the second series.

	MINT	EXC	G-VG
COMPLETE SET (490)	40.00	18.00	5.00
COMPLETE SERIES 1 (350)	15.00	6.75	1.90
COMPLETE SERIES 2 (140)	25.00	11.50	3.10
COMMON PLAYER (1-350)	.05	.02	.01
COMMON PLAYER (351-490)	.08	.04	.01
☐ 1 Stacey Augmon	.10	.05	.01
☐ 2 Maurice Cheeks	.10	.05	.01
☐ 3 Duane Ferrell	.05	.02	.01
☐ 4 Paul Graham	.05	.02	.01
☐ 5 Jon Koncak	.05	.02	.01
☐ 6 Blair Rasmussen	.05	.02	.01
☐ 7 Rumeal Robinson	.05	.02	.01
☐ 8 Dominique Wilkins	.30	.14	.04
☐ 9 Kevin Willis	.08	.04	.01
☐ 10 Larry Bird	.75	.35	.09
☐ 11 Dee Brown	.05	.02	.01
☐ 12 Sherman Douglas	.05	.02	.01
☐ 13 Rick Fox	.08	.04	.01
☐ 14 Kevin Gamble	.05	.02	.01
☐ 15 Reggie Lewis	.10	.05	.01
☐ 16 Kevin McHale	.10	.05	.01
☐ 17 Robert Parish	.10	.05	.01
☐ 18 Ed Pinckney UER	.05	.02	.01
(Wrong trade info, Kleine to Sacramento and Lohaus to Boston)			
☐ 19 Muggsy Bogues	.10	.05	.01
☐ 20 Dell Curry	.08	.04	.01

☐ 21	Kenny Gattison	.05	.02	.01
☐ 22	Kendall Gill	.08	.04	.01
☐ 23	Mike Gminski	.05	.02	.01
☐ 24	Larry Johnson	.50	.23	.06
☐ 25	Johnny Newman	.05	.02	.01
☐ 26	J.R. Reid	.05	.02	.01
☐ 27	B.J. Armstrong	.10	.05	.01
☐ 28	Bill Cartwright	.08	.04	.01
☐ 29	Horace Grant	.10	.05	.01
☐ 30	Michael Jordan	2.00	.90	.25
☐ 31	Stacey King	.05	.02	.01
☐ 32	John Paxson	.08	.04	.01
☐ 33	Will Perdue	.05	.02	.01
☐ 34	Scottie Pippen	.40	.18	.05
☐ 35	Scott Williams	.05	.02	.01
☐ 36	John Battle	.05	.02	.01
☐ 37	Terrell Brandon	.05	.02	.01
☐ 38	Brad Daugherty	.10	.05	.01
☐ 39	Craig Ehlo	.05	.02	.01
☐ 40	Danny Ferry	.05	.02	.01
☐ 41	Henry James	.05	.02	.01
☐ 42	Larry Nance	.08	.04	.01
☐ 43	Mark Price	.10	.05	.01
☐ 44	Hot Rod Williams	.05	.02	.01
☐ 45	Rolando Blackman	.08	.04	.01
☐ 46	Terry Davis	.05	.02	.01
☐ 47	Derek Harper	.08	.04	.01
☐ 48	Mike Iuzzolino	.05	.02	.01
☐ 49	Fat Lever	.05	.02	.01
☐ 50	Rodney McCray	.05	.02	.01
☐ 51	Doug Smith	.05	.02	.01
☐ 52	Randy White	.05	.02	.01
☐ 53	Herb Williams	.05	.02	.01
☐ 54	Greg Anderson	.05	.02	.01
☐ 55	Winston Garland	.05	.02	.01
☐ 56	Chris Jackson	.08	.04	.01
☐ 57	Marcus Liberty	.05	.02	.01
☐ 58	Todd Lichti	.05	.02	.01
☐ 59	Mark Macon	.05	.02	.01
☐ 60	Dikembe Mutombo	.20	.09	.03
☐ 61	Reggie Williams	.08	.04	.01
☐ 62	Mark Aguirre	.10	.05	.01
☐ 63	William Bedford	.05	.02	.01
☐ 64	Joe Dumars	.15	.07	.02
☐ 65	Bill Laimbeer	.10	.05	.01
☐ 66	Dennis Rodman	.08	.04	.01
☐ 67	John Salley	.05	.02	.01
☐ 68	Isiah Thomas	.15	.07	.02
☐ 69	Darrell Walker	.05	.02	.01
☐ 70	Orlando Woolridge	.08	.04	.01
☐ 71	Victor Alexander	.05	.02	.01
☐ 72	Mario Elie	.05	.02	.01
☐ 73	Chris Gatling	.05	.02	.01
☐ 74	Tim Hardaway	.10	.05	.01
☐ 75	Tyrone Hill	.05	.02	.01
☐ 76	Alton Lister	.05	.02	.01
☐ 77	Sarunas Marciulionis	.08	.04	.01
☐ 78	Chris Mullin	.15	.07	.02
☐ 79	Billy Owens	.10	.05	.01
☐ 80	Matt Bullard	.05	.02	.01
☐ 81	Sleepy Floyd	.05	.02	.01
☐ 82	Avery Johnson	.05	.02	.01
☐ 83	Buck Johnson	.05	.02	.01
☐ 84	Vernon Maxwell	.08	.04	.01
☐ 85	Hakeem Olajuwon	.75	.35	.09
☐ 86	Kenny Smith	.05	.02	.01
☐ 87	Larry Smith	.08	.04	.01
☐ 88	Otis Thorpe	.08	.04	.01
☐ 89	Dale Davis	.08	.04	.01
☐ 90	Vern Fleming	.05	.02	.01
☐ 91	George McCloud	.05	.02	.01
☐ 92	Reggie Miller	.20	.09	.03
☐ 93	Chuck Person	.08	.04	.01

☐ 94	Detlef Schrempf	.10	.05	.01
☐ 95	Rik Smits	.08	.04	.01
☐ 96	LaSalle Thompson	.08	.04	.01
☐ 97	Micheal Williams	.08	.04	.01
☐ 98	James Edwards	.05	.02	.01
☐ 99	Gary Grant	.05	.02	.01
☐ 100	Ron Harper	.08	.04	.01
☐ 101	Danny Manning	.15	.07	.02
☐ 102	Ken Norman	.05	.02	.01
☐ 103	Olden Polynice	.05	.02	.01
☐ 104	Doc Rivers	.08	.04	.01
☐ 105	Charles Smith	.05	.02	.01
☐ 106	Loy Vaught	.08	.04	.01
☐ 107	Elden Campbell	.05	.02	.01
☐ 108	Vlade Divac	.08	.04	.01
☐ 109	A.C. Green	.08	.04	.01
☐ 110	Sam Perkins	.08	.04	.01
☐ 111	Byron Scott	.08	.04	.01
☐ 112	Tony Smith	.05	.02	.01
☐ 113	Terry Teagle	.05	.02	.01
☐ 114	Sedale Threatt	.05	.02	.01
☐ 115	James Worthy	.10	.05	.01
☐ 116	Willie Burton	.05	.02	.01
☐ 117	Bimbo Coles	.05	.02	.01
☐ 118	Kevin Edwards	.05	.02	.01
☐ 119	Alec Kessler	.05	.02	.01
☐ 120	Grant Long	.05	.02	.01
☐ 121	Glen Rice	.10	.05	.01
☐ 122	Rony Seikaly	.10	.05	.01
☐ 123	Brian Shaw	.05	.02	.01
☐ 124	Steve Smith	.15	.07	.02
☐ 125	Frank Brickowski	.08	.04	.01
☐ 126	Dale Ellis	.08	.04	.01
☐ 127	Jeff Grayer	.05	.02	.01
☐ 128	Jay Humphries	.05	.02	.01
☐ 129	Larry Krystkowiak	.05	.02	.01
☐ 130	Moses Malone	.10	.05	.01
☐ 131	Fred Roberts	.05	.02	.01
☐ 132	Alvin Robertson	.08	.04	.01
☐ 133	Dan Schayes	.05	.02	.01
☐ 134	Thurl Bailey	.05	.02	.01
☐ 135	Scott Brooks	.05	.02	.01
☐ 136	Tony Campbell	.05	.02	.01
☐ 137	Gerald Glass	.05	.02	.01
☐ 138	Luc Longley	.05	.02	.01
☐ 139	Sam Mitchell	.05	.02	.01
☐ 140	Pooh Richardson	.05	.02	.01
☐ 141	Felton Spencer	.05	.02	.01
☐ 142	Doug West	.05	.02	.01
☐ 143	Rafael Addison	.08	.04	.01
☐ 144	Kenny Anderson	.20	.09	.03
☐ 145	Mookie Blaylock	.08	.04	.01
☐ 146	Sam Bowie	.05	.02	.01
☐ 147	Derrick Coleman	.20	.09	.03
☐ 148	Chris Dudley	.05	.02	.01
☐ 149	Terry Mills	.10	.05	.01
☐ 150	Chris Morris	.05	.02	.01
☐ 151	Drazen Petrovic	.08	.04	.01
☐ 152	Greg Anthony	.05	.02	.01
☐ 153	Patrick Ewing	.40	.18	.05
☐ 154	Mark Jackson	.08	.04	.01
☐ 155	Anthony Mason	.08	.04	.01
☐ 156	Xavier McDaniel	.08	.04	.01
☐ 157	Charles Oakley	.10	.05	.01
☐ 158	John Starks	.10	.05	.01
☐ 159	Gerald Wilkins	.05	.02	.01
☐ 160	Nick Anderson	.08	.04	.01
☐ 161	Terry Catledge	.05	.02	.01
☐ 162	Jerry Reynolds	.05	.02	.01
☐ 163	Stanley Roberts	.05	.02	.01
☐ 164	Dennis Scott	.08	.04	.01
☐ 165	Scott Skiles	.08	.04	.01
☐ 166	Jeff Turner	.05	.02	.01

#	Player			
☐ 167	Sam Vincent	.05	.02	.01
☐ 168	Brian Williams	.05	.02	.01
☐ 169	Ron Anderson	.05	.02	.01
☐ 170	Charles Barkley	.50	.23	.06
☐ 171	Manute Bol	.05	.02	.01
☐ 172	Johnny Dawkins	.05	.02	.01
☐ 173	Armon Gilliam	.05	.02	.01
☐ 174	Hersey Hawkins	.08	.04	.01
☐ 175	Brian Oliver	.05	.02	.01
☐ 176	Charles Shackleford	.05	.02	.01
☐ 177	Jayson Williams	.05	.02	.01
☐ 178	Cedric Ceballos	.10	.05	.01
☐ 179	Tom Chambers	.08	.04	.01
☐ 180	Jeff Hornacek	.08	.04	.01
☐ 181	Kevin Johnson	.10	.05	.01
☐ 182	Negele Knight	.05	.02	.01
☐ 183	Andrew Lang	.05	.02	.01
☐ 184	Dan Majerle	.10	.05	.01
☐ 185	Tim Perry	.05	.02	.01
☐ 186	Mark West	.05	.02	.01
☐ 187	Alaa Abdelnaby	.05	.02	.01
☐ 188	Danny Ainge	.10	.05	.01
☐ 189	Clyde Drexler	.20	.09	.03
☐ 190	Kevin Duckworth	.05	.02	.01
☐ 191	Jerome Kersey	.05	.02	.01
☐ 192	Robert Pack	.05	.02	.01
☐ 193	Terry Porter	.08	.04	.01
☐ 194	Cliff Robinson	.10	.05	.01
☐ 195	Buck Williams	.10	.05	.01
☐ 196	Anthony Bonner	.05	.02	.01
☐ 197	Duane Causwell	.05	.02	.01
☐ 198	Pete Chilcutt	.05	.02	.01
☐ 199	Dennis Hopson	.05	.02	.01
☐ 200	Mitch Richmond	.10	.05	.01
☐ 201	Lionel Simmons	.08	.04	.01
☐ 202	Wayman Tisdale	.08	.04	.01
☐ 203	Spud Webb	.10	.05	.01
☐ 204	Willie Anderson	.05	.02	.01
☐ 205	Antoine Carr	.05	.02	.01
☐ 206	Terry Cummings	.08	.04	.01
☐ 207	Sean Elliott	.08	.04	.01
☐ 208	Sidney Green	.05	.02	.01
☐ 209	David Robinson	.50	.23	.06
☐ 210	Rod Strickland	.08	.04	.01
☐ 211	Greg Sutton	.05	.02	.01
☐ 212	Dana Barros	.05	.02	.01
☐ 213	Benoit Benjamin	.05	.02	.01
☐ 214	Michael Cage	.05	.02	.01
☐ 215	Eddie Johnson	.05	.02	.01
☐ 216	Shawn Kemp	.75	.35	.09
☐ 217	Derrick McKey	.05	.02	.01
☐ 218	Nate McMillan	.05	.02	.01
☐ 219	Gary Payton	.10	.05	.01
☐ 220	Ricky Pierce	.08	.04	.01
☐ 221	David Benoit	.05	.02	.01
☐ 222	Mike Brown	.05	.02	.01
☐ 223	Tyrone Corbin	.05	.02	.01
☐ 224	Mark Eaton	.05	.02	.01
☐ 225	Blue Edwards	.08	.04	.01
☐ 226	Jeff Malone	.08	.04	.01
☐ 227	Karl Malone	.25	.11	.03
☐ 228	Eric Murdock	.08	.04	.01
☐ 229	John Stockton	.20	.09	.03
☐ 230	Michael Adams	.08	.04	.01
☐ 231	Rex Chapman	.05	.02	.01
☐ 232	Ledell Eackles	.05	.02	.01
☐ 233	Pervis Ellison	.05	.02	.01
☐ 234	A.J. English	.05	.02	.01
☐ 235	Harvey Grant	.05	.02	.01
☐ 236	Charles Jones	.05	.02	.01
☐ 237	LaBradford Smith	.05	.02	.01
☐ 238	Larry Stewart	.05	.02	.01
☐ 239	Bob Weiss CO	.05	.02	.01

☐	240	Chris Ford CO	.08	.04	.01
☐	241	Allan Bristow CO	.05	.02	.01
☐	242	Phil Jackson CO	.08	.04	.01
☐	243	Lenny Wilkens CO	.08	.04	.01
☐	244	Richie Adubato CO	.05	.02	.01
☐	245	Dan Issel CO	.08	.04	.01
☐	246	Ron Rothstein CO	.05	.02	.01
☐	247	Don Nelson CO	.08	.04	.01
☐	248	Rudy Tomjanovich CO	.08	.04	.01
☐	249	Bob Hill CO	.05	.02	.01
☐	250	Larry Brown CO	.08	.04	.01
☐	251	Randy Pfund CO	.05	.02	.01
☐	252	Kevin Loughery CO	.08	.04	.01
☐	253	Mike Dunleavy CO	.08	.04	.01
☐	254	Jimmy Rodgers CO	.05	.02	.01
☐	255	Chuck Daly CO	.08	.04	.01
☐	256	Pat Riley CO	.08	.04	.01
☐	257	Matt Guokas CO	.05	.02	.01
☐	258	Doug Moe CO	.05	.02	.01
☐	259	Paul Westphal CO	.08	.04	.01
☐	260	Rick Adelman CO	.05	.02	.01
☐	261	Garry St. Jean CO	.05	.02	.01
☐	262	Jerry Tarkanian CO	.20	.09	.03
☐	263	George Karl CO	.05	.02	.01
☐	264	Jerry Sloan CO	.05	.02	.01
☐	265	Wes Unseld CO	.08	.04	.01
☐	266	Atlanta Hawks Team Card	.05	.02	.01
☐	267	Boston Celtics Team Card	.05	.02	.01
☐	268	Charlotte Hornets Team Card	.05	.02	.01
☐	269	Chicago Bulls Team Card	.05	.02	.01
☐	270	Cleveland Cavaliers Team Card	.05	.02	.01
☐	271	Dallas Mavericks Team Card	.05	.02	.01
☐	272	Denver Nuggets Team Card	.05	.02	.01
☐	273	Detroit Pistons Team Card	.05	.02	.01
☐	274	Golden State Warriors Team Card	.05	.02	.01
☐	275	Houston Rockets Team Card	.05	.02	.01
☐	276	Indiana Pacers Team Card	.05	.02	.01
☐	277	Los Angeles Clippers Team Card	.05	.02	.01
☐	278	Los Angeles Lakers Team Card	.05	.02	.01
☐	279	Miami Heat Team Card	.05	.02	.01
☐	280	Milwaukee Bucks Team Card	.05	.02	.01
☐	281	Minnesota Timberwolves Team Card	.05	.02	.01
☐	282	New Jersey Nets Team Card	.05	.02	.01
☐	283	New York Knicks Team Card	.05	.02	.01
☐	284	Orlando Magic Team Card	.05	.02	.01
☐	285	Philadelphia 76ers Team Card	.05	.02	.01
☐	286	Phoenix Suns Team Card	.05	.02	.01
☐	287	Portland Trail Blazers Team Card	.05	.02	.01
☐	288	Sacramento Kings Team Card	.05	.02	.01
☐	289	San Antonio Spurs	.05	.02	.01

☐ 335	Kevin Johnson	.08	.04	.01
	Stay in School			
☐ 336	Charles Barkley	.25	.11	.03
	Tournament of The Americas			
☐ 337	Larry Bird	.40	.18	.05
	Tournament of The Americas			
☐ 338	Clyde Drexler	.10	.05	.01
	Tournament of The Americas			
☐ 339	Patrick Ewing	.20	.09	.03
	Tournament of The Americas			
☐ 340	Magic Johnson	.25	.11	.03
	Tournament of The Americas			
☐ 341	Michael Jordan	1.25	.55	.16
	Tournament of The Americas			
☐ 342	Christian Laettner	1.00	.45	.13
	Tournament of The Americas			
☐ 343	Karl Malone	.12	.05	.02
	Tournament of The Americas			
☐ 344	Chris Mullin	.10	.05	.01
	Tournament of The Americas			
☐ 345	Scottie Pippen	.20	.09	.03
	Tournament of The Americas			
☐ 346	David Robinson	.25	.11	.03
	Tournament of The Americas			
☐ 347	John Stockton	.10	.05	.01
	Tournament of The Americas			
☐ 348	Checklist 1	.05	.02	.01
☐ 349	Checklist 2	.05	.02	.01
☐ 350	Checklist 3	.05	.02	.01
☐ 351	Mookie Blaylock	.12	.05	.02
☐ 352	Adam Keefe	.15	.07	.02
☐ 353	Travis Mays	.08	.04	.01
☐ 354	Morlon Wiley	.08	.04	.01
☐ 355	Joe Kleine	.08	.04	.01
☐ 356	Bart Kofoed	.08	.04	.01
☐ 357	Xavier McDaniel	.15	.07	.02
☐ 358	Tony Bennett	.15	.07	.02
☐ 359	Tom Hammonds	.08	.04	.01
☐ 360	Kevin Lynch	.08	.04	.01
☐ 361	Alonzo Mourning	6.00	2.70	.75
☐ 362	Rodney McCray	.08	.04	.01
☐ 363	Trent Tucker	.08	.04	.01
☐ 364	Corey Williams	.08	.04	.01
☐ 365	Steve Kerr	.08	.04	.01
	Traded to Orlando			
☐ 366	Jerome Lane	.08	.04	.01
☐ 367	Bobby Phills	.25	.11	.03
☐ 368	Mike Sanders	.08	.04	.01
☐ 369	Gerald Wilkins	.08	.04	.01
☐ 370	Donald Hodge	.08	.04	.01
☐ 371	Brian Howard	.08	.04	.01
☐ 372	Tracy Moore	.08	.04	.01
☐ 373	Sean Rooks	.25	.11	.03
☐ 374	Kevin Brooks	.08	.04	.01
☐ 375	LaPhonso Ellis	1.25	.55	.16
☐ 376	Scott Hastings	.08	.04	.01
☐ 377	Robert Pack	.08	.04	.01
☐ 378	Bryant Stith	.60	.25	.08
☐ 379	Robert Werdann	.08	.04	.01
☐ 380	Lance Blanks	.08	.04	.01
	Traded to Minnesota			

☐ 381 Terry Mills	.12	.05	.02
☐ 382 Isaiah Morris	.08	.04	.01
☐ 383 Olden Polynice	.08	.04	.01
☐ 384 Brad Sellers	.08	.04	.01
Traded to Minnesota			
☐ 385 Jud Buechler	.08	.04	.01
☐ 386 Jeff Grayer	.08	.04	.01
☐ 387 Byron Houston	.20	.09	.03
☐ 388 Keith Jennings	.20	.09	.03
☐ 389 Latrell Sprewell	4.00	1.80	.50
☐ 390 Scott Brooks	.08	.04	.01
☐ 391 Carl Herrera	.08	.04	.01
☐ 392 Robert Horry	1.25	.55	.16
☐ 393 Tree Rollins	.08	.04	.01
☐ 394 Kennard Winchester	.08	.04	.01
☐ 395 Greg Dreiling	.08	.04	.01
☐ 396 Sean Green	.08	.04	.01
☐ 397 Sam Mitchell	.08	.04	.01
☐ 398 Pooh Richardson	.08	.04	.01
☐ 399 Malik Sealy	.20	.09	.03
☐ 400 Kenny Williams	.08	.04	.01
☐ 401 Jaren Jackson	.08	.04	.01
☐ 402 Mark Jackson	.12	.05	.02
☐ 403 Stanley Roberts	.08	.04	.01
☐ 404 Elmore Spencer	.25	.11	.03
☐ 405 Kiki Vandeweghe	.12	.05	.02
☐ 406 John Williams	.08	.04	.01
☐ 407 Randy Woods	.08	.04	.01
☐ 408 Alex Blackwell	.08	.04	.01
☐ 409 Duane Cooper	.08	.04	.01
☐ 410 Anthony Peeler	.50	.23	.06
☐ 411 Keith Askins	.08	.04	.01
☐ 412 Matt Geiger	.20	.09	.03
☐ 413 Harold Miner	.60	.25	.08
☐ 414 John Salley	.08	.04	.01
☐ 415 Alaa Abdelnaby	.08	.04	.01
Traded to Boston			
☐ 416 Todd Day	.60	.25	.08
☐ 417 Blue Edwards	.12	.05	.02
☐ 418 Brad Lohaus	.08	.04	.01
☐ 419 Lee Mayberry	.20	.09	.03
☐ 420 Eric Murdock	.12	.05	.02
☐ 421 Christian Laettner	1.25	.55	.16
☐ 422 Bob McCann	.08	.04	.01
☐ 423 Chuck Person	.12	.05	.02
☐ 424 Chris Smith	.20	.09	.03
☐ 425 Gundars Vetra	.08	.04	.01
☐ 426 Micheal Williams	.11	.05	.01
☐ 427 Chucky Brown	.08	.04	.01
☐ 428 Tate George	.08	.04	.01
☐ 429 Rick Mahorn	.12	.05	.02
☐ 430 Rumeal Robinson	.08	.04	.01
☐ 431 Jayson Williams	.08	.04	.01
☐ 432 Eric Anderson	.08	.04	.01
☐ 433 Rolando Blackman	.12	.05	.02
☐ 434 Tony Campbell	.08	.04	.01
☐ 435 Hubert Davis	.60	.25	.08
☐ 436 Bo Kimble	.08	.04	.01
☐ 437 Doc Rivers	.12	.05	.02
☐ 438 Charles Smith	.08	.04	.01
☐ 439 Anthony Bowie	.08	.04	.01
☐ 440 Litterial Green	.15	.07	.02
☐ 441 Greg Kite	.08	.04	.01
☐ 442 Shaquille O'Neal	10.00	4.50	1.25
☐ 443 Donald Royal	.08	.04	.01
☐ 444 Greg Grant	.08	.04	.01
☐ 445 Jeff Hornacek	.12	.05	.02
☐ 446 Andrew Lang	.08	.04	.01
☐ 447 Kenny Payne	.08	.04	.01
☐ 448 Tim Perry	.08	.04	.01
☐ 449 Clarence Weatherspoon	1.25	.55	.16
☐ 450 Danny Ainge	.15	.07	.02
☐ 451 Charles Barkley	.75	.35	.09

☐ 452	Tim Kempton	.08	.04	.01
☐ 453	Oliver Miller	.60	.25	.08
☐ 454	Mark Bryant	.08	.04	.01
☐ 455	Mario Elie	.08	.04	.01
☐ 456	Dave Jamerson	.08	.04	.01
☐ 457	Tracy Murray	.20	.09	.03
☐ 458	Rod Strickland	.12	.05	.02
☐ 459	Vincent Askew	.08	.04	.01
	Traded to Seattle			
☐ 460	Randy Brown	.08	.04	.01
☐ 461	Marty Conlon	.08	.04	.01
☐ 462	Jim Les	.08	.04	.01
☐ 463	Walt Williams	.60	.25	.08
☐ 464	William Bedford	.08	.04	.01
☐ 465	Lloyd Daniels	.20	.09	.03
☐ 466	Vinny Del Negro	.08	.04	.01
☐ 467	Dale Ellis	.12	.05	.02
☐ 468	Larry Smith	.12	.05	.02
☐ 469	David Wood	.08	.04	.01
☐ 470	Rich King	.08	.04	.01
☐ 471	Isaac Austin	.08	.04	.01
☐ 472	John Crotty	.08	.04	.01
☐ 473	Stephen Howard	.08	.04	.01
☐ 474	Jay Humphries	.08	.04	.01
☐ 475	Larry Krystowiak	.08	.04	.01
☐ 476	Tom Gugliotta	1.25	.55	.16
☐ 477	Buck Johnson	.08	.04	.01
☐ 478	Don MacLean	.75	.35	.09
☐ 479	Doug Overton	.08	.04	.01
☐ 480	Brent Price	.20	.09	.03
☐ 481	David Robinson TRIV	.40	.18	.05
	San Antonio Spurs			
	Blocks			
☐ 482	Magic Johnson TRIV	.40	.18	.05
	Los Angeles Lakers			
	Assists			
☐ 483	John Stockton TRIV	.12	.05	.02
	Utah Jazz			
	Steals			
☐ 484	Patrick Ewing TRIV	.25	.11	.03
	New York Knicks			
	Points			
☐ 485	Answer Card TRIV	.25	.11	.03
	Magic Johnson			
	David Robinson			
	Patrick Ewing			
	John Stockton			
☐ 486	John Stockton	.12	.05	.02
	Utah Jazz			
	Stay in School			
☐ 487	Ahmad Rashad	.12	.05	.02
	Willow Bay			
	Inside Stuff			
☐ 488	Rookie Checklist	.08	.04	.01
☐ 489	Checklist 1	.08	.04	.01
☐ 490	Checklist 2	.08	.04	.01
☐ AC1	Patrick Ewing Art	1.00	.45	.13
☐ NNO	Barcelona Plastic	30.00	13.50	3.80
☐ NNO	Magic Johnson Comm	2.00	.90	.25
☐ NNO	Patrick Ewing Game	1.00	.45	.13
☐ NNO	Patrick Ewing AU	125.00	57.50	15.50
	(Certified autograph)			
☐ NNO	Team USA	2.00	.90	.25
☐ SU1	John Stockton Game	3.00	1.35	.40
	Utah Jazz			
	His Ultimate Game			
☐ SU1AU	John Stockton AU	100.00	45.00	12.50
	(Certified autograph)			
☐ TR1	NBA Championship	1.50	.65	.19
	Michael Jordan			
	Clyde Drexler			

1992-93 Hoops Draft Redemption

A "Lottery Exchange Card" randomly inserted (reportedly at a rate of one per 360 packs) in 1992-93 Hoops first series foil packs entitled the collector to receive this NBA Draft Redemption Lottery Exchange Insert set, consisting of ten standard size (2 1/2" by 3 1/2") cards of the top NBA Draft Picks. The first eleven players drafted are represented, with the exception of Jim Jackson, the late-signing fourth pick. Insert sets began to be mailed out during the week of January 4, 1993, and the redemption period expired on March 31, 1993. According to SkyBox International media releases a total of 25,876 sets were released to the public; 24,461 Lottery Exchange cards were redeemed. An additional 415 sets were claimed through a second chance drawing (selected from 149,166 mail-in entries). Finally, 1,000 more sets were released for public relations and promotional use. A reserve of 1,000 sets were held for replacement of damaged sets and 500 sets were kept for SkyBox International archives. In the color photos on the fronts, the players appear in dress attire in front of a gray studio background, except for cards C and J. The player's name is printed in white in a hardwood floor border design at the bottom of the card. A NBA Draft icon overlaps the border and the photo. A one inch tall hardwood design number at the upper left corner indicates the order the players were drafted. The horizontal backs display white backgrounds with a similar hardwood stripe containing the player's name across the top. A shadowed close-up photo is displayed next to college statistics and a player profile. The cards are lettered on the back. Sets still in the factory-sealed bags are valued at a premium of up to 20 percent above the complete set price below.

	MINT	EXC	G-VG
COMPLETE BAG SET (10)	150.00	70.00	19.00
COMMON PLAYER (A-J)	1.50	.65	.19
*OPENED SET: .75X to 1.0X VALUE			
☐ A Shaquille O'Neal	70.00	32.00	8.75
Orlando Magic			
☐ B Alonzo Mourning	40.00	18.00	5.00
Charlotte Hornets			
☐ C Christian Laettner	10.00	4.50	1.25
Minnesota Timberwolves			
☐ D LaPhonso Ellis	12.00	5.50	1.50
Denver Nuggets			
☐ E Tom Gugliotta	10.00	4.50	1.25
Washington Bullets			
☐ F Walt Williams	5.00	2.30	.60
Sacramento Kings			
☐ G Todd Day	5.00	2.30	.60
Milwaukee Bucks			
☐ H Clarence Weatherspoon	10.00	4.50	1.25
Philadelphia 76ers			
☐ I Adam Keefe	1.50	.65	.19
Atlanta Hawks			
☐ J Robert Horry	10.00	4.50	1.25
Houston Rockets			
☐ NNO Draft Redemption Card	5.00	2.30	.60
(Stamped)			

☐ NNO Draft Redemption Card.................................... 20.00   9.00   2.50
    (Unstamped)

1992-93 Hoops Magic's All-Rookies

This ten-card, standard size (2 1/2" by 3 1/2"), set was randomly inserted (at a reported rate of one card per 30 packs) into Hoops second series 12-card foil packs. The set features ten top rookies. The cards show color action player photos and have a gold foil stripe containing the player's name down the left edge and a thinner stripe across the bottom printed with the city's name. The Magic's All-Rookie Team logo appears in the lower left corner. The backs display a small close-up picture of Magic Johnson in a yellow Los Angeles Lakers' warmup jacket. A yellow stripe down the left edge contains the set name (Magic's All-Rookie Team) and the card number. The white background is printed in black with Magic's evaluation of the player.

	MINT	EXC	G-VG
COMPLETE SET (10)...............................	275.00	125.00	34.00
COMMON PLAYER (1-10)........................	10.00	4.50	1.25
☐ 1 Shaquille O'Neal............................ Orlando Magic	125.00	57.50	15.50
☐ 2 Alonzo Mourning........................... Charlotte Hornets	75.00	34.00	9.50
☐ 3 Christian Laettner........................... Minnesota Timberwolves	20.00	9.00	2.50
☐ 4 LaPhonso Ellis.............................. Denver Nuggets	25.00	11.50	3.10
☐ 5 Tom Gugliotta............................... Washington Bullets	20.00	9.00	2.50
☐ 6 Walt Williams................................ Sacramento Kings	10.00	4.50	1.25
☐ 7 Todd Day..................................... Milwaukee Bucks	10.00	4.50	1.25
☐ 8 Clarence Weatherspoon................... Philadelphia 76ers	20.00	9.00	2.50
☐ 9 Robert Horry................................. Houston Rockets	20.00	9.00	2.50
☐ 10 Harold Miner............................... Miami Heat	10.00	4.50	1.25

1992-93 Hoops More Magic Moments

Randomly inserted (at a reported rate of one card per 195 packs) into 1992-93 Hoops second series 12-card packs, this three-card standard-size (2 1/2" by 3 1/2") set commemorates Magic Johnson's return to training camp and pre-season game action. Each card fea-

tures a color player photo bordered in white. Team color-coded bars and lettering accent the picture on the left edge and below, and a team color-coded star overwritten with the words "More Magic" appears at the lower left corner. Over ghosted photos similar or identical to the front photos, the backs summarize Magic's return, his performance in his first game, his performance in his last game, and his decision to retire again. The cards are numbered on the back with an "M" prefix.

	MINT	EXC	G-VG
COMPLETE SET (3)	35.00	16.00	4.40
COMMON CARD (M1-M3)	12.00	5.50	1.50
☐ M1 Magic in Training Camp Fall 1992	12.00	5.50	1.50
☐ M2 L.A. Lakers vs. Philadelphia October 20, 1992	12.00	5.50	1.50
☐ M3 L.A. Lakers vs. Cleveland October 30, 1992	12.00	5.50	1.50

1992-93 Hoops Supreme Court

This ten-card, standard size (2 1/2" by 3 1/2"), set was randomly inserted (at a reported rate of one card per 11 packs) in Hoops second series 12-card foil packs and features color action player photos on the front. A gold foil stripe frames the pictures which are surrounded by a hardwood floor design. The player's name is printed in gold foil down the left side. A gray and burnt-orange logo printed with the words "Supreme Court 1992-93" appears in the lower left corner. A purple stripe containing the phrase "The Fan's Choice" runs across the bottom of the picture. Hoops promoted The Supreme Court Sweepstakes, which offered fans the opportunity to select the ten players who appeared in this subset. The backs are *white with black print. A small color player photo with rounded corners is displayed next to a personal profile. The cards are numbered on the back with an "SC" prefix.*

	MINT	EXC	G-VG
COMPLETE SET (10)	20.00	9.00	2.50
COMMON PLAYER (SC1-SC10)	1.00	.45	.13
☐ SC1 Michael Jordan Chicago Bulls	12.00	5.50	1.50
☐ SC2 Scottie Pippen Chicago Bulls	3.00	1.35	.40
☐ SC3 David Robinson San Antonio Spurs	4.00	1.80	.50
☐ SC4 Patrick Ewing New York Knicks	3.00	1.35	.40
☐ SC5 Clyde Drexler Portland Trail Blazers	1.25	.55	.16
☐ SC6 Karl Malone Utah Jazz	2.00	.90	.25
☐ SC7 Charles Barkley Phoenix Suns	4.00	1.80	.50
☐ SC8 John Stockton Utah Jazz	1.25	.55	.16
☐ SC9 Chris Mullin Golden State Warriors	1.00	.45	.13
☐ SC10 Magic Johnson Los Angeles Lakers	4.00	1.80	.50

1993-94 Hoops

This 421-card standard-size (2 1/2" by 3 1/2") set features full-bleed glossy color player photos on the fronts. Each player's name and team logo appear in team colors along a ghosted band at the bottom. The back presents a color head shot of the player in a small rectangle bordered with a team color in the top right corner. Alongside is his jersey number and position within a team-colored bar. The player's name and a short biography are printed on a hardwood floor design at the top. Below, the player's college and NBA stats, displayed in separate tables on a white background, round out the card. The cards were distributed in 13 card foil packs (12 basic cards plus one fifth anniversary gold foil card). The cards are numbered on the back and listed alphabetically according to and within teams as follows: Atlanta Hawks (1-8), Boston Celtics (9-16), Charlotte Hornets (17-24), Chicago Bulls (25-34), Cleveland Cavaliers (35-43), Dallas Mavericks (44-51), Denver Nuggets (52-59), Detroit Pistons (60-67), Golden State Warriors (68-75), Houston Rockets (76-83), Indiana Pacers (84-92), Los Angeles Clippers (93-102), Los Angeles Lakers (103-110), Miami Heat (111-118), Milwaukee Bucks (119-127), Minnesota Timberwolves (128-135), New Jersey Nets (136-142), New York Knicks (143-151), Orlando Magic (152-160), Philadelphia 76ers (161-167), Phoenix Suns (168-175), Portland Trail Blazers (176-185), Sacramento Kings (186-194), San Antonio Spurs (195-203), Seattle Supersonics (204-212), Utah Jazz (213-219), and Washington Bullets (220-229), Coaches (230-256), All-

Stars (257-282), League Leaders (283-290), Boys and Girls Club (291), Hoops Tribune (292-297), and Checklists (298-300). Second series cards (301-421) include rookies not in the first series and traded players with their new teams as well as three more checklists (419-421). Rookie Cards include Vin Baker, Shawn Bradley, Sam Cassell, Calbert Cheaney, Anfernee Hardaway, Bobby Hurley, Jamal Mashburn and Chris Webber.

		MINT	EXC	G-VG
	COMPLETE SET (421)	20.00	9.00	2.50
	COMPLETE SERIES 1 (300)	12.00	5.50	1.50
	COMPLETE SERIES 2 (121)	8.00	3.60	1.00
	COMMON PLAYER (1-300)	.05	.02	.01
	COMMON PLAYER (301-421)	.05	.02	.01
☐ 1	Stacey Augmon	.10	.05	.01
☐ 2	Mookie Blaylock	.08	.04	.01
☐ 3	Duane Ferrell	.05	.02	.01
☐ 4	Paul Graham	.05	.02	.01
☐ 5	Adam Keefe	.05	.02	.01
☐ 6	Blair Rasmussen	.05	.02	.01
☐ 7	Dominique Wilkins	.25	.11	.03
☐ 8	Kevin Willis	.08	.04	.01
☐ 9	Alaa Abdelnaby	.05	.02	.01
☐ 10	Dee Brown	.05	.02	.01
☐ 11	Sherman Douglas	.05	.02	.01
☐ 12	Rick Fox	.05	.02	.01
☐ 13	Kevin Gamble	.05	.02	.01
☐ 14	Joe Kleine	.05	.02	.01
☐ 15	Xavier McDaniel	.08	.04	.01
☐ 16	Robert Parish	.10	.05	.01
☐ 17	Tony Bennett	.05	.02	.01
☐ 18	Muggsy Bogues	.10	.05	.01
☐ 19	Dell Curry	.08	.04	.01
☐ 20	Kenny Gattison	.05	.02	.01
☐ 21	Kendall Gill	.08	.04	.01
☐ 22	Larry Johnson	.25	.11	.03
☐ 23	Alonzo Mourning	.50	.23	.06
☐ 24	Johnny Newman	.05	.02	.01
☐ 25	B.J. Armstrong	.10	.05	.01
☐ 26	Bill Cartwright	.08	.04	.01
☐ 27	Horace Grant	.10	.05	.01
☐ 28	Michael Jordan	2.00	.90	.25
☐ 29	Stacey King	.05	.02	.01
☐ 30	John Paxson	.08	.04	.01
☐ 31	Will Perdue	.05	.02	.01
☐ 32	Scottie Pippen	.30	.14	.04
☐ 33	Scott Williams	.05	.02	.01
☐ 34	Moses Malone	.05	.02	.01
☐ 35	John Battle	.10	.02	.01
☐ 36	Terrell Brandon	.05	.02	.01
☐ 37	Brad Daugherty	.10	.05	.01
☐ 38	Craig Ehlo	.05	.02	.01
☐ 39	Danny Ferry	.05	.02	.01
☐ 40	Larry Nance	.08	.04	.01
☐ 41	Mark Price	.10	.05	.01
☐ 42	Gerald Wilkins	.05	.02	.01
☐ 43	John Williams	.05	.02	.01
☐ 44	Terry Davis	.05	.02	.01
☐ 45	Derek Harper	.08	.04	.01
☐ 46	Donald Hodge	.05	.02	.01
☐ 47	Mike Iuzzolino	.05	.02	.01
☐ 48	Jim Jackson	.25	.11	.03
☐ 49	Sean Rooks	.05	.02	.01
☐ 50	Doug Smith	.05	.02	.01
☐ 51	Randy White	.05	.02	.01
☐ 52	Mahmoud Abdul-Rauf	.05	.02	.01
☐ 53	LaPhonso Ellis	.10	.05	.01
☐ 54	Marcus Liberty	.05	.02	.01
☐ 55	Mark Macon	.05	.02	.01
☐ 56	Dikembe Mutombo	.10	.05	.01
☐ 57	Robert Pack	.05	.02	.01
☐ 58	Bryant Stith	.08	.04	.01
☐ 59	Reggie Williams	.05	.02	.01
☐ 60	Mark Aguirre	.10	.05	.01

☐	61	Joe Dumars	.15	.07	.02
☐	62	Bill Laimbeer	.10	.05	.01
☐	63	Terry Mills	.08	.04	.01
☐	64	Olden Polynice	.05	.02	.01
☐	65	Alvin Robertson	.08	.04	.01
☐	66	Dennis Rodman	.08	.04	.01
☐	67	Isiah Thomas	.15	.07	.02
☐	68	Victor Alexander	.05	.02	.01
☐	69	Tim Hardaway	.10	.05	.01
☐	70	Tyrone Hill	.05	.02	.01
☐	71	Byron Houston	.05	.02	.01
☐	72	Sarunas Marciulionis	.08	.04	.01
☐	73	Chris Mullin	.15	.07	.02
☐	74	Billy Owens	.08	.04	.01
☐	75	Latrell Sprewell	.40	.18	.05
☐	76	Scott Brooks	.05	.02	.01
☐	77	Matt Bullard	.05	.02	.01
☐	78	Carl Herrera	.05	.02	.01
☐	79	Robert Horry	.10	.05	.01
☐	80	Vernon Maxwell	.08	.04	.01
☐	81	Hakeem Olajuwon	.75	.35	.09
☐	82	Kenny Smith	.05	.02	.01
☐	83	Otis Thorpe	.08	.04	.01
☐	84	Dale Davis	.08	.04	.01
☐	85	Vern Fleming	.05	.02	.01
☐	86	George McCloud	.05	.02	.01
☐	87	Reggie Miller	.15	.07	.02
☐	88	Sam Mitchell	.05	.02	.01
☐	89	Pooh Richardson	.05	.02	.01
☐	90	Detlef Schrempf	.10	.05	.01
☐	91	Malik Sealy	.08	.04	.01
☐	92	Rik Smits	.08	.04	.01
☐	93	Gary Grant	.05	.02	.01
☐	94	Ron Harper	.08	.04	.01
☐	95	Mark Jackson	.08	.04	.01
☐	96	Danny Manning	.10	.05	.01
☐	97	Ken Norman	.05	.02	.01
☐	98	Stanley Roberts	.05	.02	.01
☐	99	Elmore Spencer	.05	.02	.01
☐	100	Loy Vaught	.08	.04	.01
☐	101	John Williams	.05	.02	.01
☐	102	Randy Woods	.05	.02	.01
☐	103	Benoit Benjamin	.05	.02	.01
☐	104	Elden Campbell	.05	.02	.01
☐	105	Doug Christie UER	.08	.04	.01
		(Has uniform on front and 35 on back)			
☐	106	Vlade Divac	.05	.02	.01
☐	107	Anthony Peeler	.08	.04	.01
☐	108	Tony Smith	.05	.02	.01
☐	109	Sedale Threatt	.05	.02	.01
☐	110	James Worthy	.10	.05	.01
☐	111	Bimbo Coles	.05	.02	.01
☐	112	Grant Long	.08	.04	.01
☐	113	Harold Miner	.08	.04	.01
☐	114	Glen Rice	.10	.05	.01
☐	115	John Salley	.05	.02	.01
☐	116	Rony Seikaly	.10	.05	.01
☐	117	Brian Shaw	.05	.02	.01
☐	118	Steve Smith	.08	.04	.01
☐	119	Anthony Avent	.05	.02	.01
☐	120	Jon Barry	.08	.04	.01
☐	121	Frank Brickowski	.08	.04	.01
☐	122	Todd Day	.08	.04	.01
☐	123	Blue Edwards	.05	.02	.01
☐	124	Brad Lohaus	.05	.02	.01
☐	125	Lee Mayberry	.05	.02	.01
☐	126	Eric Murdock	.08	.04	.01
☐	127	Derek Strong	.10	.05	.01
☐	128	Thurl Bailey	.05	.02	.01
☐	129	Christian Laettner	.08	.04	.01
☐	130	Luc Longley	.05	.02	.01

□				
□ 131	Marlon Maxey	.05	.02	.01
□ 132	Chuck Person	.08	.04	.01
□ 133	Chris Smith	.05	.02	.01
□ 134	Doug West	.05	.02	.01
□ 135	Micheal Williams	.05	.02	.01
□ 136	Rafael Addison	.05	.02	.01
□ 137	Kenny Anderson	.15	.07	.02
□ 138	Sam Bowie	.05	.02	.01
□ 139	Chucky Brown	.05	.02	.01
□ 140	Derrick Coleman	.20	.09	.03
□ 141	Chris Morris	.05	.02	.01
□ 142	Rumeal Robinson	.05	.02	.01
□ 143	Greg Anthony	.05	.02	.01
□ 144	Rolando Blackman	.08	.04	.01
□ 145	Hubert Davis	.05	.02	.01
□ 146	Patrick Ewing	.30	.14	.04
□ 147	Anthony Mason	.05	.02	.01
□ 148	Charles Oakley	.10	.05	.01
□ 149	Doc Rivers	.08	.04	.01
□ 150	Charles Smith	.05	.02	.01
□ 151	John Starks	.10	.05	.01
□ 152	Nick Anderson	.08	.04	.01
□ 153	Anthony Bowie	.05	.02	.01
□ 154	Litterial Green	.05	.02	.01
□ 155	Shaquille O'Neal	1.50	.65	.19
□ 156	Donald Royal	.05	.02	.01
□ 157	Dennis Scott	.08	.04	.01
□ 158	Scott Skiles	.05	.02	.01
□ 159	Tom Tolbert	.05	.02	.01
□ 160	Jeff Turner	.05	.02	.01
□ 161	Ron Anderson	.05	.02	.01
□ 162	Johnny Dawkins	.05	.02	.01
□ 163	Hersey Hawkins	.08	.04	.01
□ 164	Jeff Hornacek	.08	.04	.01
□ 165	Andrew Lang	.05	.02	.01
□ 166	Tim Perry	.05	.02	.01
□ 167	Clarence Weatherspoon	.10	.05	.01
□ 168	Danny Ainge	.10	.05	.01
□ 169	Charles Barkley	.40	.18	.05
□ 170	Cedric Ceballos	.10	.05	.01
□ 171	Richard Dumas	.08	.04	.01
□ 172	Kevin Johnson	.10	.05	.01
□ 173	Dan Majerle	.10	.05	.01
□ 174	Oliver Miller	.10	.05	.01
□ 175	Mark West	.05	.02	.01
□ 176	Clyde Drexler	.15	.07	.02
□ 177	Kevin Duckworth	.05	.02	.01
□ 178	Mario Elie	.05	.02	.01
□ 179	Dave Johnson	.05	.02	.01
□ 180	Jerome Kersey	.05	.02	.01
□ 181	Tracy Murray	.05	.02	.01
□ 182	Terry Porter	.08	.04	.01
□ 183	Cliff Robinson	.10	.05	.01
□ 184	Rod Strickland	.08	.04	.01
□ 185	Buck Williams	.10	.05	.01
□ 186	Anthony Bonner	.05	.02	.01
□ 187	Randy Brown	.05	.02	.01
□ 188	Duane Causwell	.05	.02	.01
□ 189	Pete Chilcutt	.05	.02	.01
□ 190	Mitch Richmond	.10	.05	.01
□ 191	Lionel Simmons	.08	.04	.01
□ 192	Wayman Tisdale	.08	.04	.01
□ 193	Spud Webb	.10	.05	.01
□ 194	Walt Williams	.08	.04	.01
□ 195	Willie Anderson	.05	.02	.01
□ 196	Antoine Carr	.05	.02	.01
□ 197	Terry Cummings	.08	.04	.01
□ 198	Lloyd Daniels	.05	.02	.01
□ 199	Sean Elliott	.08	.04	.01
□ 200	Dale Ellis	.08	.04	.01
□ 201	Avery Johnson	.05	.02	.01
□ 202	J.R. Reid	.05	.02	.01
□ 203	David Robinson	.40	.18	.05

☐	204	Dana Barros	.05	.02	.01
☐	205	Michael Cage	.05	.02	.01
☐	206	Eddie Johnson	.05	.02	.01
☐	207	Shawn Kemp	.30	.14	.04
☐	208	Derrick McKey	.05	.02	.01
☐	209	Nate McMillan	.05	.02	.01
☐	210	Gary Payton	.10	.05	.01
☐	211	Sam Perkins	.08	.04	.01
☐	212	Ricky Pierce	.08	.04	.01
☐	213	David Benoit	.05	.02	.01
☐	214	Tyrone Corbin	.05	.02	.01
☐	215	Mark Eaton	.05	.02	.01
☐	216	Jay Humphries	.05	.02	.01
☐	217	Jeff Malone	.08	.04	.01
☐	218	Karl Malone	.25	.11	.03
☐	219	John Stockton	.15	.07	.02
☐	220	Michael Adams	.08	.04	.01
☐	221	Rex Chapman	.05	.02	.01
☐	222	Pervis Ellison	.05	.02	.01
☐	223	Harvey Grant	.05	.02	.01
☐	224	Tom Gugliotta	.08	.04	.01
☐	225	Don MacLean	.08	.04	.01
☐	226	Doug Overton	.05	.02	.01
☐	227	Brent Price	.05	.02	.01
☐	228	LaBradford Smith	.05	.02	.01
☐	229	Larry Stewart	.05	.02	.01
☐	230	Lenny Wilkens CO	.08	.04	.01
☐	231	Chris Ford CO	.05	.02	.01
☐	232	Allan Bristow CO	.05	.02	.01
☐	233	Phil Jackson CO	.08	.04	.01
☐	234	Mike Fratello CO	.05	.02	.01
☐	235	Quinn Buckner CO	.05	.02	.01
☐	236	Dan Issel CO	.08	.04	.01
☐	237	Dan Chaney CO	.05	.02	.01
☐	238	Don Nelson CO	.08	.04	.01
☐	239	Rudy Tomjanovich CO	.08	.04	.01
☐	240	Larry Brown CO	.08	.04	.01
☐	241	Bob Weiss CO	.05	.02	.01
☐	242	Randy Pfund CO	.05	.02	.01
☐	243	Kevin Loughery CO	.05	.02	.01
☐	244	Mike Dunleavy CO	.05	.02	.01
☐	245	Sidney Lowe CO	.05	.02	.01
☐	246	Chuck Daly CO	.08	.04	.01
☐	247	Pat Riley CO	.08	.04	.01
☐	248	Brian Hill CO	.05	.02	.01
☐	249	Fred Carter CO	.05	.02	.01
☐	250	Paul Westphal CO	.05	.02	.01
☐	251	Rick Adelman CO	.08	.04	.01
☐	252	Garry St. Jean CO	.05	.02	.01
☐	253	John Lucas CO	.05	.02	.01
☐	254	George Karl CO	.05	.02	.01
☐	255	Jerry Sloan CO	.05	.02	.01
☐	256	Wes Unseld CO	.08	.04	.01
☐	257	Michael Jordan AS	1.00	.45	.13
☐	258	Isiah Thomas AS	.10	.05	.01
☐	259	Scottie Pippen AS	.15	.07	.02
☐	260	Larry Johnson AS	.12	.05	.02
☐	261	Dominique Wilkins AS	.12	.05	.02
☐	262	Joe Dumars AS	.10	.05	.01
☐	263	Mark Price AS	.08	.04	.01
☐	264	Shaquille O'Neal AS	.75	.35	.09
☐	265	Patrick Ewing AS	.15	.07	.02
☐	266	Larry Nance AS	.05	.02	.01
☐	267	Detlef Schrempf AS	.08	.04	.01
☐	268	Brad Daugherty AS	.08	.04	.01
☐	269	Charles Barkley AS	.20	.09	.03
☐	270	Clyde Drexler AS	.10	.05	.01
☐	271	Sean Elliott AS	.05	.02	.01
☐	272	Tim Hardaway AS	.08	.04	.01
☐	273	Shawn Kemp AS	.15	.07	.02
☐	274	Dan Majerle AS	.08	.04	.01
☐	275	Karl Malone AS	.12	.05	.02
☐	276	Danny Manning AS	.08	.04	.01

☐ 277	Hakeem Olajuwon AS	.40	.18	.05
☐ 278	Terry Porter AS	.05	.02	.01
☐ 279	David Robinson AS	.20	.09	.03
☐ 280	John Stockton AS	.10	.05	.01
☐ 281	East Team Photo	.08	.04	.01
☐ 282	West Team Photo	.08	.04	.01
☐ 283	Scoring	.30	.14	.04
	Michael Jordan			
	Dominique Wilkins			
	Karl Malone			
☐ 284	Rebounding	.25	.11	.03
	Dennis Rodman			
	Shaquille O'Neal			
	Dikembe Mutombo			
☐ 285	Field Goal Percentage	.05	.02	.01
	Cedric Ceballos			
	Brad Daugherty			
	Dale Davis			
☐ 286	Assists	.05	.02	.01
	John Stockton			
	Tim Hardaway			
	Scott Skiles			
☐ 287	Free Throw Percentage	.10	.05	.01
	Mark Price			
	Mahmoud Abdul-Rauf			
	Eddie Johnson			
☐ 288	3-point FG Percentage	.08	.04	.01
	B.J. Armstrong			
	Chris Mullin			
	Kenny Smith			
☐ 289	Steals	.25	.11	.03
	Michael Jordan			
	Mookie Blaylock			
	John Stockton			
☐ 290	Blocks	.30	.14	.04
	Hakeem Olajuwon			
	Shaquille O'Neal			
	Dikembe Mutombo			
☐ 291	Boys and Girls Club	.20	.09	.03
	David Robinson			
☐ 292	Tribune 1	.05	.02	.01
	B.J. Armstrong			
☐ 293	Tribune 2	.15	.07	.02
	Scottie Pippen			
☐ 294	Tribune 3	.08	.04	.01
	Kevin Johnson			
☐ 295	Tribune 4	.20	.09	.03
	Charles Barkley			
☐ 296	Tribune 5	.05	.02	.01
	Richard Dumas			
☐ 297	Tribune 6	.05	.02	.01
	Horace Grant			
☐ 298	Checklist 1	.08	.04	.01
	David Robinson			
☐ 299	Checklist 2	.08	.04	.01
	David Robinson			
☐ 300	Checklist 3	.08	.04	.01
	David Robinson			
☐ 301	Craig Ehlo	.05	.02	.01
☐ 302	Jon Koncak	.05	.02	.01
☐ 303	Andrew Lang	.05	.02	.01
☐ 304	Chris Corchiani	.05	.02	.01
☐ 305	Acie Earl	.10	.05	.01
☐ 306	Dino Radja	.40	.18	.05
☐ 307	Scott Burrell	.15	.07	.02
☐ 308	Hersey Hawkins	.08	.04	.01
☐ 309	Eddie Johnson	.05	.02	.01
☐ 310	David Wingate	.05	.02	.01
☐ 311	Corie Blount	.10	.05	.01
☐ 312	Steve Kerr	.05	.02	.01
☐ 313	Toni Kukoc	.40	.18	.05
☐ 314	Pete Myers	.05	.02	.01
☐ 315	Jay Guidinger	.05	.02	.01

☐ 316	Tyrone Hill	.05	.02	.01
☐ 317	Gerald Madkins	.10	.05	.01
☐ 318	Chris Mills	.25	.11	.03
☐ 319	Bobby Phils	.05	.02	.01
☐ 320	Lucious Harris	.10	.05	.01
☐ 321	Popeye Jones	.15	.07	.02
☐ 322	Fat Lever	.05	.02	.01
☐ 323	Jamal Mashburn	1.00	.45	.13
☐ 324	Darren Morningstar	.10	.05	.01
	(See also 334)			
☐ 325	Kevin Brooks	.05	.02	.01
☐ 326	Tom Hammonds	.05	.02	.01
☐ 327	Darnell Mee	.10	.05	.01
☐ 328	Rodney Rodgers	.25	.11	.03
☐ 329	Brian Williams	.05	.02	.01
☐ 330	Greg Anderson	.05	.02	.01
☐ 331	Sean Elliott	.08	.04	.01
☐ 332	Allan Houston	.15	.07	.02
☐ 333	Lindsey Hunter	.40	.18	.05
☐ 334	David Wood UER	.05	.02	.01
	(Card misnumbered 324)			
☐ 335	Jud Buechler	.05	.02	.01
☐ 336	Chris Gatling	.05	.02	.01
☐ 337	Josh Grant	.10	.05	.01
☐ 338	Jeff Grayer	.05	.02	.01
☐ 339	Keith Jennings	.05	.02	.01
☐ 340	Avery Johnson	.05	.02	.01
☐ 341	Chris Webber	2.50	1.15	.30
☐ 342	Sam Cassell	.50	.23	.06
☐ 343	Mario Elie	.05	.02	.01
☐ 344	Eric Riley	.10	.05	.01
☐ 345	Antonio Davis	.25	.11	.03
☐ 346	Scott Haskin	.10	.05	.01
☐ 347	Gerald Paddio	.05	.02	.01
☐ 348	LaSalle Thompson	.08	.04	.01
☐ 349	Ken Williams	.05	.02	.01
☐ 350	Mark Aguirre	.10	.05	.01
☐ 351	Terry Dehere	.10	.05	.01
☐ 352	Henry James	.05	.02	.01
☐ 353	Sam Bowie	.05	.02	.01
☐ 354	George Lynch	.25	.11	.03
☐ 355	Kurt Rambis	.05	.02	.01
☐ 356	Nick Van Exel	.40	.18	.05
☐ 357	Trevor Wilson	.05	.02	.01
☐ 358	Keith Askins	.05	.02	.01
☐ 359	Manute Bol	.05	.02	.01
☐ 360	Willie Burton	.05	.02	.01
☐ 361	Matt Geiger	.05	.02	.01
☐ 362	Alec Kessler	.05	.02	.01
☐ 363	Vin Baker	.60	.25	.08
☐ 364	Ken Norman	.05	.02	.01
☐ 365	Dan Schayes	.05	.02	.01
☐ 366	Mike Brown	.05	.02	.01
☐ 367	Isaiah Rider	1.00	.45	.13
☐ 368	Benoit Benjamin	.05	.02	.01
☐ 369	P.J. Brown	.15	.07	.02
☐ 370	Kevin Edwards	.05	.02	.01
☐ 371	Armon Gilliam	.05	.02	.01
☐ 372	Rick Mahorn	.05	.02	.01
☐ 373	Dwayne Schintzius	.05	.02	.01
☐ 374	Rex Walters	.10	.05	.01
☐ 375	Jayson Williams	.05	.02	.01
☐ 376	Eric Anderson	.05	.02	.01
☐ 377	Anthony Bonner	.05	.02	.01
☐ 378	Tony Campbell	.05	.02	.01
☐ 379	Herb Williams	.05	.02	.01
☐ 380	Anfernee Hardaway	2.00	.90	.25
☐ 381	Greg Kite	.05	.02	.01
☐ 382	Larry Krystkowiak	.05	.02	.01
☐ 383	Todd Lichti	.05	.02	.01
☐ 384	Dana Barros	.05	.02	.01
☐ 385	Shawn Bradley	.40	.18	.05
☐ 386	Greg Graham	.10	.05	.01

☐	387	Warren Kidd	.10	.05	.01
☐	388	Eric Leckner	.05	.02	.01
☐	389	Moses Malone	.10	.05	.01
☐	390	A.C. Green	.08	.04	.01
☐	391	Frank Johnson	.05	.02	.01
☐	392	Joe Kleine	.05	.02	.01
☐	393	Malcolm Mackey	.10	.05	.01
☐	394	Jerrod Mustaf	.05	.02	.01
☐	395	Mark Bryant	.05	.02	.01
☐	396	Chris Dudley	.05	.02	.01
☐	397	Harvey Grant	.05	.02	.01
☐	398	James Robinson	.15	.07	.02
☐	399	Reggie Smith	.05	.02	.01
☐	400	Randy Brown	.05	.02	.01
☐	401	Bobby Hurley	.40	.18	.05
☐	402	Jim Les	.05	.02	.01
☐	403	Vinny Del Negro	.05	.02	.01
☐	404	Sleepy Floyd	.05	.02	.01
☐	405	Dennis Rodman	.08	.04	.01
☐	406	Chris Whitney	.10	.05	.01
☐	407	Vincent Askew	.05	.02	.01
☐	408	Kendall Gill	.08	.04	.01
☐	409	Ervin Johnson	.10	.05	.01
☐	410	Rich King	.05	.02	.01
☐	411	Detlef Schrempf	.10	.05	.01
☐	412	Tom Chambers	.08	.04	.01
☐	413	John Crotty	.05	.02	.01
☐	414	Felton Spencer	.05	.02	.01
☐	415	Luther Wright	.10	.05	.01
☐	416	Calbert Cheaney	.40	.18	.05
☐	417	Kevin Duckworth	.05	.02	.01
☐	418	Gheorghe Muresan	.15	.07	.02
☐	419	Checklist 1	.05	.02	.01
☐	420	Checklist 2	.05	.02	.01
☐	421	Rookie Checklist	.05	.02	.01
☐	DR1	David Robinson Commemorative 1989 Rookie Card	.50	.23	.06
☐	MB1	Magic Johnson Larry Bird Commemorative	.50	.23	.06
☐	NNO	Lottery Exchange Card	150.00	70.00	19.00
☐	NNO	David Robinson Voucher	150.00	70.00	19.00
☐	NNO	Magic Johnson Larry Bird Expired Voucher	100.00	45.00	12.50
☐	NNO	Magic Johnson Larry Bird Autograph Card	400.00	180.00	50.00

1993-94 Hoops Fifth Anniversary Gold

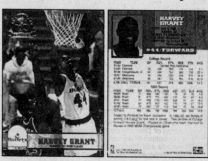

Inserted one per pack and two per jumbo pack, this 421-card set parallels the regular issue 1993-1994 Hoops. The only difference is the Fifth Anniversary embossed gold-foil seal and gold-foil stripes highlighting the player's name on the front. The cards are numbered on the back.

	MINT	EXC	G-VG
COMPLETE SET (421)	80.00	36.00	10.00
COMPLETE SERIES 1 (300)	45.00	20.00	5.75
COMPLETE SERIES 2 (121)	35.00	16.00	4.40
COMMON GOLD (1-300)	.10	.05	.01
COMMON GOLD (301-421)	.10	.05	.01

*GOLD STARS: 2.5X to 5X VALUE
*GOLD ROOKIES: 1.5X to 3X VALUE

1993-94 Hoops Admiral's Choice

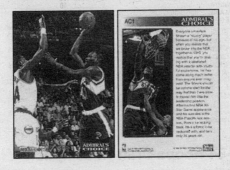

Randomly inserted in packs, this five-card standard-size (2 1/2" by 3 1/2") set features borderless fronts with color player photos. The player's name appears in gold-foil lettering at the top. The white back features a color player photo on the left with the player profile on the right. The cards are numbered on the back with an "AC" prefix.

	MINT	EXC	G-VG
COMPLETE SET (5)	6.00	2.70	.75
COMMON PLAYER (AC1-AC5)	.25	.11	.03
☐ AC1 Shawn Kemp	.75	.35	.09
Seattle Supersonics			
☐ AC2 Derrick Coleman	.25	.11	.03
New Jersey Nets			
☐ AC3 Kenny Anderson	.25	.11	.03
New Jersey Nets			
☐ AC4 Shaquille O'Neal	3.00	1.35	.40
Orlando Magic			
☐ AC5 Chris Webber	3.00	1.35	.40
Golden State Warriors			

1993-94 Hoops David's Best

Inserted into one in every ten first series 1993-94 Hoops foil packs, these UV-coated cards feature color action photos of David Robinson against featured opponents. The "David's Best" logo runs across the bottom of the card in "golden crystal-foil" lettering. The flipside of the cards present Robinson's stat line from the selected game and a brief synopsis of the highlights. The cards are numbered on the back with a "DB" prefix.

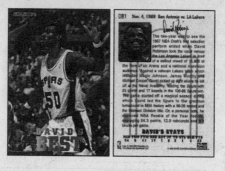

	MINT	EXC	G-VG
COMPLETE SET (5)	3.00	1.35	.40
COMMON ROBINSON (DB1-DB5)	.75	.35	.09
☐ DB1 David Robinson (Vs. Lakers)	.75	.35	.09
☐ DB2 David Robinson (Vs. Magic)	.75	.35	.09
☐ DB3 David Robinson (Vs. Trail Blazers)	.75	.35	.09
☐ DB4 David Robinson (Vs. Warriors)	.75	.35	.09
☐ DB5 David Robinson (Vs. Hornets)	.75	.35	.09

1993-94 Hoops Draft Redemption

A redemption card was randomly inserted into series one packs, which could be sent in for this 11-card standard-size (2 1/2" by 3 1/2") set, which features a full-color posed player photo on the front. The player's name appears centered at the top in gold foil. The player's draft number also appears in gold foil at the upper right. The horizontal back features a color player head shot on the left, with player statistics and biography alongside on the right. The cards are numbered on the back with an "LP" prefix.

	MINT	EXC	G-VG
COMPLETE SET (11)	50.00	23.00	6.25
COMMON PLAYER (LP1-LP11)	1.00	.45	.13

☐ LP1 Chris Webber	20.00	9.00	2.50
Golden State Warriors			
☐ LP2 Shawn Bradley	3.00	1.35	.40
Philadelphia 76ers			
☐ LP3 Anfernee Hardaway	15.00	6.75	1.90
Orlando Magic			
☐ LP4 Jamal Mashburn	8.00	3.60	1.00
Dallas Mavericks			
☐ LP5 Isaiah Rider	8.00	3.60	1.00
Minnesota Timberwolves			
☐ LP6 Calbert Cheaney	3.00	1.35	.40
Washington Bullets			
☐ LP7 Bobby Hurley	3.00	1.35	.40
Sacramento Kings			
☐ LP8 Vin Baker	6.00	2.70	.75
Milwaukee Bucks			
☐ LP9 Rodney Rogers	1.75	.80	.22
Denver Nuggets			
☐ LP10 Lindsey Hunter	3.00	1.35	.40
Detroit Pistons			
☐ LP11 Allan Houston	1.00	.45	.13
Detroit Pistons			
☐ NNO Redeemed Lottery Card	.50	.23	.06
☐ NNO Unredeemed Lottery Card	3.00	1.35	.40

1993-94 Hoops Face to Face

*Randomly inserted in first series 12-card foil packs, these 12 standard-size (2 1/2" by 3 1/2")
cards feature a promising rookie standout on one side and a veteran all-star on the other.
The full-bleed glossy color player action photos on both sides are reproduced over metallic-
type backgrounds. On both sides, the Face to Face logo and the player's name appears at
the bottom. The cards are numbered on the second side with an "FTF" prefix.*

	MINT	EXC	G-VG
COMPLETE SET (12)	40.00	18.00	5.00
COMMON PAIR (1-12)	2.00	.90	.25
☐ 1 Shaquille O'Neal	12.00	5.50	1.50
David Robinson			
☐ 2 Alonzo Mourning	7.00	3.10	.85
Patrick Ewing			
☐ 3 Christian Laettner	4.00	1.80	.50
Shawn Kemp			
☐ 4 Jim Jackson	4.00	1.80	.50
Clyde Drexler			
☐ 5 LaPhonso Ellis	3.00	1.35	.40
Larry Johnson			
☐ 6 Clarence Weatherspoon	4.00	1.80	.50

	Charles Barkley		
☐ 7	Tom Gugliotta	3.00	1.35	.40
	Karl Malone		
☐ 8	Walt Williams	3.00	1.35	.40
	Magic Johnson		
☐ 9	Robert Horry	3.00	1.35	.40
	Scottie Pippen		
☐ 10	Harold Miner	12.00	5.50	1.50
	Michael Jordan		
☐ 11	Todd Day	2.00	.90	.25
	Chris Mullin		
☐ 12	Richard Dumas	2.00	.90	.25
	Dominique Wilkins		

1993-94 Hoops Magic's All-Rookies

Randomly inserted in second-series packs, this 10-card standard size (2 1/2" by 3 1/2") set features Magic Johnson's projected All-Rookie team. The borderless front features a full-color action shot with the player's name in a gold-foil strip at the bottom. The borderless back features an italicized player profile written by Magic Johnson and set against a ghosted background photo. The cards are numbered on the back.

		MINT	EXC	G-VG
COMPLETE SET (10)	....	100.00	45.00	12.50
COMMON PLAYER (1-10)	....	5.00	2.30	.60
☐ 1	Chris Webber	30.00	13.50	3.80
	Golden State Warriors			
☐ 2	Shawn Bradley	5.00	2.30	.60
	Philadelphia 76ers			
☐ 3	Anfernee Hardaway	25.00	11.50	3.10
	Orlando Magic			
☐ 4	Jamal Mashburn	12.00	5.50	1.50
	Dallas Mavericks			
☐ 5	Isaiah Rider	12.00	5.50	1.50
	Minnesota Timberwolves			
☐ 6	Calbert Cheaney	5.00	2.30	.60
	Washington Bullets			
☐ 7	Bobby Hurley	5.00	2.30	.60
	Sacramento Kings			
☐ 8	Vin Baker	9.00	4.00	1.15
	Milwaukee Bucks			
☐ 9	Lindsey Hunter	5.00	2.30	.60
	Detroit Pistons			
☐ 10	Toni Kukoc	5.00	2.30	.60
	Chicago Bulls			

1993-94 Hoops Scoops

Randomly inserted in Series II foil packs, this 28-card set measures the standard size (2 1/2" by 3 1/2"). The horizontal and vertical fronts feature color action player photos taken from around the rim. The player's name, his team's name, and logo appear in a black bar under the photo, while the NBA Hoops Scoops logo appears in the upper right or left corner. On a white background, the backs carry trivia questions about the teams. The cards are numbered on the back with an "HS" prefix.

	MINT	EXC	G-VG
COMPLETE SET (28)	1.00	.45	.13
COMMON PLAYER (HS1-HS28)	.05	.02	.01
☐ HS1 Dominique Wilkins	.12	.05	.02
Atlanta Hawks			
☐ HS2 Robert Parish	.10	.05	.01
Boston Celtics			
☐ HS3 Alonzo Mourning	.25	.11	.03
Charlotte Hornets			
☐ HS4 Scottie Pippen	.15	.07	.02
Chicago Bulls			
☐ HS5 Larry Nance	.05	.02	.01
Cleveland Cavaliers			
☐ HS6 Derek Harper	.10	.05	.01
Dallas Mavericks			
☐ HS7 Reggie Williams	.05	.02	.01
Denver Nuggets			
☐ HS8 Bill Laimbeer	.05	.02	.01
Detroit Pistons			
☐ HS9 Tim Hardaway	.05	.02	.01
Golden State Warriors			
☐ HS10 Hakeem Olajuwon UER	.40	.18	.05
Houston Rockets			
(Robert Horry is featured player)			
☐ HS11 LaSalle Thompson	.05	.02	.01
Indiana Pacers			
☐ HS12 Danny Manning	.05	.02	.01
Los Angeles Clippers			
☐ HS13 James Worthy	.05	.02	.01
Los Angeles Lakers			
☐ HS14 Grant Long	.05	.02	.01
Miami Heat			
☐ HS15 Blue Edwards	.05	.02	.01
Milwaukee Bucks			
☐ HS16 Christian Laettner	.10	.05	.01
Minnesota Timberwolves			
☐ HS17 Derrick Coleman	.10	.05	.01
New Jersey Nets			
☐ HS18 Patrick Ewing	.15	.07	.02
New York Knicks			

☐ HS19 Nick Anderson	.05	.02	.01
Orlando Magic			
☐ HS20 Clarence Weatherspoon	.10	.05	.01
Philadelphia 76ers			
☐ HS21 Charles Barkley	.20	.09	.03
Phoenix Suns			
☐ HS22 Cliff Robinson	.10	.05	.01
Portland Trail Blazers			
☐ HS23 Lionel Simmons	.05	.02	.01
Sacramento Kings			
☐ HS24 David Robinson	.20	.09	.03
San Antonio Spurs			
☐ HS25 Shawn Kemp	.15	.07	.02
Seattle Supersonics			
☐ HS26 Karl Malone	.12	.05	.02
Utah Jazz			
☐ HS27 Rex Chapman	.05	.02	.01
Washington Bullets			
☐ HS28 Answer Card	.05	.02	.01

1993-94 Hoops Scoops Fifth Anniversary Gold

Randomly inserted in Series II foil packs, this 28-card parallel set to the regular Hoops Scoops set measures the standard size (2 1/2" by 3 1/2"). Aside from the gold-foil logo and special glossy coating, the cards are identical to the regular issue Hoops Scoops cards. The cards are numbered on the back with an "HS" prefix.

	MINT	EXC	G-VG
COMPLETE SET (28)	5.00	2.30	.60
COMMON PLAYER (HS1-HS28)	.10	.05	.01
*STARS: 2.5X to 5X VALUE			

1993-94 Hoops Supreme Court

Randomly inserted into second-series packs, this 11-card standard size (2 1/2" by 3 1/2") set features full-color action player photos with the player's name centered at the top in silver-foil lettering. The backs carry color player action shots along the left side and player statistics along the right side. The cards are numbered on the back with an "SC" prefix.

	MINT	EXC	G-VG
COMPLETE SET (11)	10.00	4.50	1.25
COMMON PLAYER (SC1-SC11)	.50	.23	.06

☐ SC1 Charles Barkley	1.50	.65	.19
Phoenix Suns			
☐ SC2 David Robinson	1.50	.65	.19
San Antonio Spurs			
☐ SC3 Patrick Ewing	1.25	.55	.16
New York Knicks			
☐ SC4 Shaquille O'Neal	4.00	1.80	.50
Orlando Magic			
☐ SC5 Larry Johnson	1.00	.45	.13
Charlotte Hornets			
☐ SC6 Karl Malone	1.00	.45	.13
Utah Jazz			
☐ SC7 Alonzo Mourning	1.50	.65	.19
Charlotte Hornets			
☐ SC8 John Stockton	.50	.23	.06
Utah Jazz			
☐ SC9 Hakeem Olajuwon UER	2.00	.90	.25
Houston Rockets			
(Name spelled Olajwon on front)			
☐ SC10 Scottie Pippen	1.25	.55	.16
Chicago Bulls			
☐ SC11 Michael Jordan	6.00	2.70	.75
Chicago Bulls			

1993-94 Jam Session

This 240-card set was issued in 1993 by Fleer and features oversized cards measuring approximately 2 1/2" by 4 3/4". The full-bleed fronts feature glossy color action player photos. Across the bottom edge of the picture appears a team color-coded bar with the player's name, position and team. The NBA Jam Session logo is superposed on the lower right corner. The backs are divided in half vertically with the left side carrying a second action shot and on the right side a panel with a background that fades from green to white. On the panel appears biography, career highlights, statistics and team logo. The cards are numbered on the back and checklisted below alphabetically within and according to teams as follows: Atlanta Hawks (1-9), Boston Celtics (10-16), Charlotte Hornets (17-26), Chicago Bulls (27-35), Cleveland Cavaliers (36-44), Dallas Mavericks (45-51), Denver Nuggets (52-59), Detroit Pistons (60-66), Golden State Warriors (67-75), Houston Rockets (76-85), Indiana Pacers (86-94), Los Angeles Clippers (95-101), Los Angeles Lakers (102-110), Miami Heat (111-118), Milwaukee Bucks (119-128), Minnesota Timberwolves (129-136), New Jersey Nets (137-144), New York Knicks (145-155), Orlando Magic (156-164), Philadelphia 76ers (165-172), Phoenix Suns (173-183), Portland Trail Blazers (184-192), Sacramento Kings (193-200), San Antonio Spurs (201-210), Seattle Supersonics (211-219), Utah Jazz (220-229), and Washington Bullets (230-238).

	MINT	EXC	G-VG
COMPLETE SET (240)	30.00	13.50	3.80
COMMON PLAYER (1-240)	.10	.05	.01

☐ 1	Stacey Augmon	.15	.07	.02
☐ 2	Mookie Blaylock	.12	.05	.02
☐ 3	Doug Edwards	.15	.07	.02
☐ 4	Duane Ferrell	.10	.05	.01
☐ 5	Paul Graham	.10	.05	.01
☐ 6	Adam Keefe	.10	.05	.01
☐ 7	Jon Koncak	.10	.05	.01
☐ 8	Dominique Wilkins	.40	.18	.05
☐ 9	Kevin Willis	.12	.05	.02
☐ 10	Alaa Abdelnaby	.10	.05	.01
☐ 11	Dee Brown	.10	.05	.01
☐ 12	Sherman Douglas	.10	.05	.01
☐ 13	Rick Fox	.10	.05	.01
☐ 14	Kevin Gamble	.10	.05	.01
☐ 15	Xavier McDaniel	.10	.05	.01
☐ 16	Robert Parish	.15	.07	.02
☐ 17	Muggsy Bogues	.15	.07	.02
☐ 18	Scott Burrell	.25	.11	.03
☐ 19	Dell Curry	.12	.05	.02
☐ 20	Kenny Gattison	.10	.05	.01
☐ 21	Hersey Hawkins	.12	.05	.02
☐ 22	Eddie Johnson	.10	.05	.01
☐ 23	Larry Johnson	.40	.18	.05
☐ 24	Alonzo Mourning	1.00	.45	.13
☐ 25	Johnny Newman	.10	.05	.01
☐ 26	David Wingate	.10	.05	.01
☐ 27	B.J. Armstrong	.15	.07	.02
☐ 28	Corie Blount	.15	.07	.02
☐ 29	Bill Cartwright	.10	.05	.01
☐ 30	Horace Grant	.15	.07	.02
☐ 31	Stacey King	.10	.05	.01
☐ 32	John Paxson	.10	.05	.01
☐ 33	Michael Jordan	3.00	1.35	.40
☐ 34	Scottie Pippen	.50	.23	.06
☐ 35	Scott Williams	.10	.05	.01
☐ 36	Terrell Brandon	.10	.05	.01
☐ 37	Brad Daugherty	.15	.07	.02
☐ 38	Danny Ferry	.10	.05	.01
☐ 39	Tyrone Hill	.10	.05	.01
☐ 40	Chris Mills	.40	.18	.05
☐ 41	Larry Nance	.12	.05	.02
☐ 42	Mark Price	.15	.07	.02
☐ 43	Gerald Wilkins	.10	.05	.01
☐ 44	John Williams	.10	.05	.01

☐	45	Terry Davis	.10	.05	.01
☐	46	Derek Harper	.12	.05	.02
☐	47	Donald Hodge	.10	.05	.01
☐	48	Jim Jackson	.40	.18	.05
☐	49	Jamal Mashburn	1.50	.65	.19
☐	50	Sean Rooks	.10	.05	.01
☐	51	Doug Smith	.10	.05	.01
☐	52	Mahmoud Abdul-Rauf	.10	.05	.01
☐	53	Kevin Brooks	.15	.07	.02
☐	54	LaPhonso Ellis	.10	.05	.01
☐	55	Mark Macon	.15	.07	.02
☐	56	Dikembe Mutombo	.40	.18	.05
☐	57	Rodney Rogers	.12	.05	.02
☐	58	Bryant Stith	.10	.05	.01
☐	59	Reggie Williams	.25	.11	.03
☐	60	Joe Dumars	.12	.05	.02
☐	61	Sean Elliott	.15	.07	.02
☐	62	Bill Laimbeer	.12	.05	.02
☐	63	Terry Mills	.10	.05	.01
☐	64	Olden Polynice	.10	.05	.01
☐	65	Alvin Robertson	.25	.11	.03
☐	66	Isiah Thomas	.10	.05	.01
☐	67	Victor Alexander	.10	.05	.01
☐	68	Chris Gatling	.15	.07	.02
☐	69	Tim Hardaway	.10	.05	.01
☐	70	Byron Houston	.10	.05	.01
☐	71	Sarunas Marciulionis	.25	.11	.03
☐	72	Chris Mullin	.12	.05	.02
☐	73	Billy Owens	.60	.25	.08
☐	74	Latrell Sprewell	4.00	1.80	.50
☐	75	Chris Webber	.10	.05	.01
☐	76	Scott Brooks	.10	.05	.01
☐	77	Matt Bullard	.75	.35	.09
☐	78	Sam Cassell	.10	.05	.01
☐	79	Mario Elie	.10	.05	.01
☐	80	Carl Herrera	.15	.07	.02
☐	81	Robert Horry	.10	.05	.02
☐	82	Vernon Maxwell	1.25	.55	.16
☐	83	Hakeem Olajuwon	.10	.05	.01
☐	84	Kenny Smith	.12	.05	.02
☐	85	Otis Thorpe	.10	.05	.01
☐	86	Dale Davis	.15	.07	.02
☐	87	Vern Fleming	.30	.14	.04
☐	88	Scott Haskin	.10	.05	.01
☐	89	Reggie Miller	.10	.05	.01
☐	90	Sam Mitchell	.15	.07	.02
☐	91	Pooh Richardson	.10	.05	.01
☐	92	Detlef Schrempf	.12	.05	.02
☐	93	Malik Sealy	.20	.09	.03
☐	94	Rik Smits	.12	.05	.02
☐	95	Terry Dehere	.12	.05	.02
☐	96	Ron Harper	.15	.07	.02
☐	97	Mark Jackson	.12	.05	.02
☐	98	Danny Manning	.10	.05	.01
☐	99	Stanley Roberts	.10	.05	.01
☐	100	Loy Vaught	.10	.05	.01
☐	101	John Williams	.10	.05	.01
☐	102	Sam Bowie	.12	.05	.02
☐	103	Elden Campbell	.10	.05	.01
☐	104	Doug Christie	.10	.05	.01
☐	105	Vlade Divac	.35	.16	.04
☐	106	James Edwards	.12	.05	.02
☐	107	George Lynch	.10	.05	.01
☐	108	Anthony Peeler	.15	.07	.02
☐	109	Sedale Threatt	.10	.05	.01
☐	110	James Worthy	.10	.05	.01
☐	111	Bimbo Coles	.12	.05	.02
☐	112	Grant Long	.10	.05	.01
☐	113	Harold Miner	.15	.07	.02
☐	114	Glen Rice	.10	.05	.01
☐	115	John Salley	.15	.07	.02
☐	116	Rony Seikaly	.10	.05	.01
☐	117	Brian Shaw			

☐	118 Steve Smith	.12	.05	.02
☐	119 Anthony Avent	.10	.05	.01
☐	120 Vin Baker	1.00	.45	.13
☐	121 Jon Barry	.10	.05	.01
☐	122 Frank Brickowski	.12	.05	.02
☐	123 Todd Day	.12	.05	.02
☐	124 Blue Edwards	.10	.05	.01
☐	125 Brad Lohaus	.10	.05	.01
☐	126 Lee Mayberry	.10	.05	.01
☐	127 Eric Murdock	.12	.05	.02
☐	128 Ken Norman	.10	.05	.01
☐	129 Thurl Bailey	.10	.05	.01
☐	130 Mike Brown	.10	.05	.01
☐	131 Christian Laettner	.12	.05	.02
☐	132 Luc Longley	.10	.05	.01
☐	133 Chuck Person	.12	.05	.02
☐	134 Chris Smith	.10	.05	.01
☐	135 Doug West	.10	.05	.01
☐	136 Micheal Williams	.12	.05	.02
☐	137 Kenny Anderson	.25	.11	.03
☐	138 Benoit Benjamin	.10	.05	.01
☐	139 Derrick Coleman	.30	.14	.04
☐	140 Armon Gilliam	.10	.05	.01
☐	141 Rick Mahorn	.10	.05	.01
☐	142 Chris Morris	.10	.05	.01
☐	143 Rumeal Robinson	.10	.05	.01
☐	144 Rex Walters	.15	.07	.02
☐	145 Greg Anthony	.10	.05	.01
☐	146 Rolando Blackman	.10	.05	.01
☐	147 Tony Campbell	.10	.05	.01
☐	148 Hubert Davis	.10	.05	.01
☐	149 Patrick Ewing	.50	.23	.06
☐	150 Anthony Mason	.10	.05	.01
☐	151 Charles Oakley	.15	.07	.02
☐	152 Doc Rivers	.12	.05	.02
☐	153 Charles Smith	.10	.05	.01
☐	154 John Starks	.15	.07	.02
☐	155 Herb Williams	.10	.05	.01
☐	156 Nick Anderson	.12	.05	.02
☐	157 Anthony Bowie	.10	.05	.01
☐	158 Litterial Green	.10	.05	.01
☐	159 Anfernee Hardaway	3.00	1.35	.40
☐	160 Shaquille O'Neal	2.50	1.15	.30
☐	161 Donald Royal	.10	.05	.01
☐	162 Dennis Scott	.12	.05	.02
☐	163 Scott Skiles	.10	.05	.01
☐	164 Jeff Turner	.10	.05	.01
☐	165 Dana Barros	.10	.05	.01
☐	166 Shawn Bradley	.60	.25	.08
☐	167 Johnny Dawkins	.10	.05	.01
☐	168 Greg Graham	.15	.07	.02
☐	169 Jeff Hornacek	.12	.05	.02
☐	170 Moses Malone	.15	.07	.02
☐	171 Tim Perry	.10	.05	.01
☐	172 Clarence Weatherspoon	.15	.07	.02
☐	173 Danny Ainge	.15	.07	.02
☐	174 Charles Barkley	.75	.35	.09
☐	175 Cedric Ceballos	.15	.07	.02
☐	176 A.C. Green	.12	.05	.02
☐	177 Frank Johnson	.10	.05	.01
☐	178 Kevin Johnson	.15	.07	.02
☐	179 Negele Knight	.10	.05	.01
☐	180 Malcolm Mackey	.15	.07	.02
☐	181 Dan Majerle	.15	.07	.02
☐	182 Oliver Miller	.15	.07	.02
☐	183 Mark West	.10	.05	.01
☐	184 Clyde Drexler	.30	.14	.04
☐	185 Chris Dudley	.10	.05	.01
☐	186 Harvey Grant	.10	.05	.01
☐	187 Jerome Kersey	.10	.05	.01
☐	188 Terry Porter	.12	.05	.02
☐	189 Clifford Robinson	.15	.07	.02
☐	190 James Robinson	.25	.11	.03

☐ 191	Rod Strickland	.12	.05	.02
☐ 192	Buck Williams	.15	.07	.02
☐ 193	Randy Brown	.10	.05	.01
☐ 194	Duane Causwell	.10	.05	.01
☐ 195	Bobby Hurley	.60	.25	.08
☐ 196	Mitch Richmond	.15	.07	.02
☐ 197	Lionel Simmons	.12	.05	.02
☐ 198	Wayman Tisdale	.12	.05	.02
☐ 199	Spud Webb	.15	.07	.02
☐ 200	Walt Williams	.12	.05	.02
☐ 201	Willie Anderson	.10	.05	.01
☐ 202	Antoine Carr	.10	.05	.01
☐ 203	Terry Cummings	.12	.05	.02
☐ 204	Lloyd Daniels	.10	.05	.01
☐ 205	Vinny Del Negro	.10	.05	.01
☐ 206	Sleepy Floyd	.10	.05	.01
☐ 207	Avery Johnson	.10	.05	.01
☐ 208	J.R. Reid	.10	.05	.01
☐ 209	David Robinson	.75	.35	.09
☐ 210	Dennis Rodman	.12	.05	.02
☐ 211	Michael Cage	.10	.05	.01
☐ 212	Kendall Gill	.12	.05	.02
☐ 213	Ervin Johnson	.15	.07	.02
☐ 214	Shawn Kemp	.50	.23	.06
☐ 215	Derrick McKey	.10	.05	.01
☐ 216	Nate McMillan	.10	.05	.01
☐ 217	Gary Payton	.15	.07	.02
☐ 218	Sam Perkins	.12	.05	.02
☐ 219	Ricky Pierce	.12	.05	.02
☐ 220	Isaac Austin	.10	.05	.01
☐ 221	David Benoit	.10	.05	.01
☐ 222	Tom Chambers	.12	.05	.02
☐ 223	Tyrone Corbin	.10	.05	.01
☐ 224	Mark Eaton	.10	.05	.01
☐ 225	Jay Humphries	.10	.05	.01
☐ 226	Jeff Malone	.12	.05	.02
☐ 227	Karl Malone	.40	.18	.05
☐ 228	John Stockton	.30	.14	.04
☐ 229	Luther Wright	.15	.07	.02
☐ 230	Michael Adams	.12	.05	.02
☐ 231	Calbert Cheaney	.60	.25	.08
☐ 232	Kevin Duckworth	.10	.05	.01
☐ 233	Pervis Ellison	.10	.05	.01
☐ 234	Tom Gugliotta	.12	.05	.02
☐ 235	Buck Johnson	.10	.05	.01
☐ 236	Doug Overton	.10	.05	.01
☐ 237	LaBradford Smith	.10	.05	.01
☐ 238	Larry Stewart	.10	.05	.01
☐ 239	Checklist	.10	.05	.01
☐ 240	Checklist	.10	.05	.01

1993-94 Jam Session Gamebreakers

Randomly inserted into packs, this 8-card 2 1/2" by 4 3/4" set features some of the NBA's top players. The borderless fronts feature color action cutouts on multicolored backgrounds highlighted by grid lines. The player's name appears in gold foil at the lower left. The back features a color player head shot with a screened background similar to the front. The player's name appears above the photo, career highlights appear below. The cards are numbered on the back as "X of 8."

	MINT	EXC	G-VG
COMPLETE SET (8)	4.00	1.80	.50
COMMON PLAYER (1-8)	.25	.11	.03
☐ 1 Charles Barkley	1.50	.65	.19
Phoenix Suns			

□				
□	2 Tim Hardaway	.25	.11	.03
	Golden State Warriors			
□	3 Kevin Johnson	.25	.11	.03
	Phoenix Suns			
□	4 Dan Majerle	.25	.11	.03
	Phoenix Suns			
□	5 Scottie Pippen	1.25	.55	.16
	Chicago Bulls			
□	6 Mark Price	.25	.11	.03
	Cleveland Cavaliers			
□	7 John Starks	.25	.11	.03
	New York Knicks			
□	8 Dominique Wilkins	1.00	.45	.13
	Atlanta Hawks			

1993-94 Jam Session Rookie Standouts

Randomly inserted into packs, this oversized (2 1/2" by 4 3/4") 8-card set features border-less fronts with full-color player action photos. The player's name appears in gold-foil letter-ing in the lower left corner. The back features a color player action headshot with the play-er's statistics below. The cards are numbered on the back as "X of 8."

	MINT	EXC	G-VG
COMPLETE SET (8)	20.00	9.00	2.50
COMMON PLAYER (1-8)	1.00	.45	.13
☐ 1 Vin Baker	2.50	1.15	.30
Milwaukee Bucks			
☐ 2 Shawn Bradley	1.50	.65	.19
Philadelphia 76ers			
☐ 3 Calbert Cheaney	1.50	.65	.19
Washington Bullets			
☐ 4 Anfernee Hardaway UER	7.00	3.10	.85
Orlando Magic			
(Text states he drafted after			
senior year instead of junior)			
☐ 5 Bobby Hurley	1.50	.65	.19
Sacramento Kings			
☐ 6 Jamal Mashburn	3.50	1.55	.45
Dallas Mavericks			
☐ 7 Rodney Rogers	1.00	.45	.13
Denver Nuggets			
☐ 8 Chris Webber	8.00	3.60	1.00
Golden State Warriors			

1993-94 Jam Session Second Year Stars

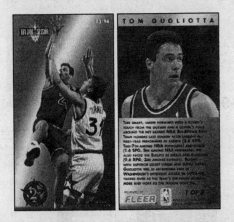

Randomly inserted into Jam Session packs, this 8-card 2 1/2" by 4 3/4" set features some of the NBA's top second-year players. The borderless fronts feature a color action cutout on a rainbow-colored background. The player's name appears in gold foil in the lower right. The back features a color player head shot with screened rainbow background. The players name appears above the photo with a player profile displayed below. The cards are num-bered on the back as "X of 8."

	MINT	EXC	G-VG
COMPLETE SET (8)	7.00	3.10	.85
COMMON PLAYER (1-8)	.25	.11	.03
☐ 1 Tom Gugliotta	.50	.23	.06
Washington Bullets			

☐ 2 Jim Jackson	1.25	.55	.16
Dallas Mavericks			
☐ 3 Christian Laettner	.50	.23	.06
Minnesota Timberwolves			
☐ 4 Oliver Miller	.25	.11	.03
Phoenix Suns			
☐ 5 Harold Miner	.50	.23	.06
Miami Heat			
☐ 6 Alonzo Mourning	2.00	.90	.25
Charlotte Hornets			
☐ 7 Shaquille O'Neal	4.00	1.80	.50
Orlando Magic			
☐ 8 Walt Williams	.25	.11	.03
Sacramento Kings			

1993-94 Jam Session Slam Dunk Heroes

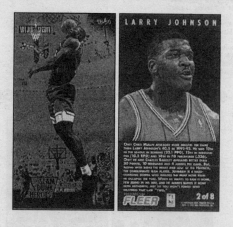

Randomly inserted into packs, this 8-card 2 1/2" by 4 3/4" set features some of the NBA's top slam dunkers. The borderless fronts feature color action cutouts on multicolored poster-ized background. The player's name appears vertically in gold foil near the bottom. The back features a color player head shot. The player's name appears above the photo, a play-er profile is displayed below. The cards are numbered on the back as "X of 8."

	MINT	EXC	G-VG
COMPLETE SET (8)	12.00	5.50	1.50
COMMON PLAYER (1-8)	1.00	.45	.13
☐ 1 Patrick Ewing	1.25	.55	.16
New York Knicks			
☐ 2 Larry Johnson	1.25	.55	.16
Charlotte Hornets			
☐ 3 Shawn Kemp	1.25	.55	.16
Seattle Supersonics			
☐ 4 Karl Malone	1.00	.45	.13
Utah Jazz			
☐ 5 Alonzo Mourning	2.00	.90	.25
Charlotte Hornets			
☐ 6 Hakeem Olajuwon	2.00	.90	.25
Houston Rockets			
☐ 7 Shaquille O'Neal	4.00	1.80	.50
Orlando Magic			
☐ 8 David Robinson	1.50	.65	.19
San Antonio Spurs			

1990-91 SkyBox

The complete 1990-91 SkyBox set contains 423 cards featuring NBA players. The set was released in two series of 300 and 123 cards, respectively. Both series foil packs contained 15 cards, however the second series packs contained a mix of players from both series. The new second series cards replaced 123 cards from the first series, which then became short-prints compared to other cards in the first series. The cards measure the standard size (2 1/2" by 3 1/2"). The front features an action shot of the player on a computer-generated background consisting of various color stripes and geometric shapes. The player's name appears in a black stripe below the photo, with the team logo superimposed at the left lower corner. The photo is bordered in gold. The back presents head shots of the player, with gold borders on white background. Player statistics are given in a box below the photo. The cards are numbered on the back and checklisted below alphabetically according to team names as follows: Atlanta Hawks (1-12), Boston Celtics (13-24), Charlotte Hornets (25-36), Chicago Bulls (37-47), Cleveland Cavaliers (48-58), Dallas Mavericks (59-70), Denver Nuggets (71-81), Detroit Pistons (82-93), Golden State Warriors (94-104), Houston Rockets (105-113), Indiana Pacers (114-123), Los Angeles Clippers (124-133), Los Angeles Lakers (134-143), Miami Heat (144-154), Milwaukee Bucks (155-166), Minnesota Timberwolves (167-175), New Jersey Nets (176-185), New York Knicks (186-197), Orlando Magic (198-209), Philadelphia 76ers (210-219), Phoenix Suns (220-230), Portland Trail Blazers (231-241), Sacramento Kings (242-251), San Antonio Spurs (252-262), Seattle Supersonics (263-273), Utah Jazz (274-284), Washington Bullets (285-294), Coaches (301-327), Team Checklists (328-354), Lottery Picks (355-365), Updates (366-420), and Checklists (421-423). The backs of the coaches' cards each feature a quote. Rookie Cards included in the set are Nick Anderson, B.J. Armstrong, Mookie Blaylock, Derrick Coleman, Vlade Divac, Sherman Douglas, Blue Edwards, Sean Elliott, Pervis Ellison, Danny Ferry, Kendall Gill, Tim Hardaway, Chris Jackson, Shawn Kemp, Sarunas Marciulionis, Gary Payton, Drazen Petrovic, Glen Rice, Pooh Richardson, and Cliff Robinson, Dennis Scott, Lionel Simmons, and Doug West. Cards that were deleted by SkyBox for the second series are marked in the checklist below by SP.

	MINT	EXC	G-VG
COMPLETE SET (423)	20.00	9.00	2.50
COMPLETE SERIES 1 (300)	12.00	5.50	1.50
COMPLETE SERIES 2 (123)	8.00	3.60	1.00
COMMON PLAYER (1-300)	.05	.02	.01
COMMON PLAYER (301-423)	.05	.02	.01
☐ 1 John Battle	.05	.02	.01
☐ 2 Duane Ferrell SP	.25	.11	.03
☐ 3 Jon Koncak	.05	.02	.01
☐ 4 Cliff Levingston SP	.08	.04	.01
☐ 5 John Long SP	.08	.04	.01
☐ 6 Moses Malone	.10	.05	.01
☐ 7 Glenn Rivers	.08	.04	.01
☐ 8 Kenny Smith SP	.08	.04	.01
☐ 9 Alexander Volkov	.05	.02	.01
☐ 10 Spud Webb	.10	.05	.01
☐ 11 Dominique Wilkins	.40	.18	.05
☐ 12 Kevin Willis	.08	.04	.01
☐ 13 John Bagley	.05	.02	.01

☐ 14 Larry Bird	1.00	.45	.13
☐ 15 Kevin Gamble	.05	.02	.01
☐ 16 Dennis Johnson SP	.12	.05	.02
☐ 17 Joe Kleine	.05	.02	.01
☐ 18 Reggie Lewis	.25	.11	.03
☐ 19 Kevin McHale	.10	.05	.01
☐ 20 Robert Parish	.10	.05	.01
☐ 21 Jim Paxson SP	.08	.04	.01
☐ 22 Ed Pinckney	.05	.02	.01
☐ 23 Brian Shaw	.05	.02	.01
☐ 24 Michael Smith	.05	.02	.01
☐ 25 Richard Anderson SP	.08	.04	.01
☐ 26 Tyrone Bogues	.10	.05	.01
☐ 27 Rex Chapman	.08	.04	.01
☐ 28 Dell Curry	.08	.04	.01
☐ 29 Armon Gilliam	.05	.02	.01
☐ 30 Michael Holton SP	.08	.04	.01
☐ 31 Dave Hoppen	.05	.02	.01
☐ 32 J.R. Reid	.20	.09	.03
☐ 33 Robert Reid SP	.08	.04	.01
☐ 34 Brian Rowsom SP	.08	.04	.01
☐ 35 Kelly Tripucka	.08	.04	.01
☐ 36 Micheal Williams SP	.12	.05	.02
UER (Misspelled Michael on card)			
☐ 37 B.J. Armstrong	1.00	.45	.13
☐ 38 Bill Cartwright	.08	.04	.01
☐ 39 Horace Grant	.10	.05	.01
☐ 40 Craig Hodges	.05	.02	.01
☐ 41 Michael Jordan	3.00	1.35	.40
☐ 42 Stacey King	.15	.07	.02
☐ 43 Ed Nealy SP	.08	.04	.01
☐ 44 John Paxson	.08	.04	.01
☐ 45 Will Perdue	.05	.02	.01
☐ 46 Scottie Pippen	.60	.25	.08
☐ 47 Jeff Sanders SP	.08	.04	.01
☐ 48 Winston Bennett	.05	.02	.01
☐ 49 Chucky Brown	.05	.02	.01
☐ 50 Brad Daugherty	.10	.05	.01
☐ 51 Craig Ehlo	.08	.04	.01
☐ 52 Steve Kerr	.05	.02	.01
☐ 53 Paul Mokeski SP	.08	.04	.01
☐ 54 John Morton	.08	.04	.01
☐ 55 Larry Nance	.08	.04	.01
☐ 56 Mark Price	.10	.05	.01
☐ 57 Tree Rollins SP	.08	.04	.01
☐ 58 Hot Rod Williams	.05	.02	.01
☐ 59 Steve Alford	.05	.02	.01
☐ 60 Rolando Blackman	.08	.04	.01
☐ 61 Adrian Dantley SP	.15	.07	.02
☐ 62 Brad Davis	.05	.02	.01
☐ 63 James Donaldson	.05	.02	.01
☐ 64 Derek Harper	.08	.04	.01
☐ 65 Anthony Jones SP	.08	.04	.01
☐ 66 Sam Perkins SP	.12	.05	.02
☐ 67 Roy Tarpley	.05	.02	.01
☐ 68 Bill Wennington SP	.08	.04	.01
☐ 69 Randy White	.15	.07	.02
☐ 70 Herb Williams	.05	.02	.01
☐ 71 Michael Adams	.08	.04	.01
☐ 72 Joe Barry Carroll SP	.08	.04	.01
☐ 73 Walter Davis	.10	.05	.01
☐ 74 Alex English SP	.15	.07	.02
☐ 75 Bill Hanzlik	.05	.02	.01
☐ 76 Tim Kempton SP	.08	.04	.01
☐ 77 Jerome Lane	.05	.02	.01
☐ 78 Lafayette Lever SP	.08	.04	.01
☐ 79 Todd Lichti	.05	.02	.01
☐ 80 Blair Rasmussen	.05	.02	.01
☐ 81 Dan Schayes SP	.08	.04	.01
☐ 82 Mark Aguirre	.10	.05	.01
☐ 83 William Bedford	.05	.02	.01
☐ 84 Joe Dumars	.20	.09	.03

☐ 85 James Edwards	.05	.02	.01
☐ 86 David Greenwood SP	.08	.04	.01
☐ 87 Scott Hastings	.05	.02	.01
☐ 88 Gerald Henderson SP	.08	.04	.01
☐ 89 Vinnie Johnson	.08	.04	.01
☐ 90 Bill Laimbeer	.10	.05	.01
☐ 91A Dennis Rodman	.25	.11	.03
(SkyBox logo in upper right corner)			
☐ 91B Dennis Rodman	.25	.11	.03
(SkyBox logo in upper left corner)			
☐ 92 John Salley	.08	.04	.01
☐ 93 Isiah Thomas	.20	.09	.03
☐ 94 Manute Bol SP	.08	.04	.01
☐ 95 Tim Hardaway	1.00	.45	.13
☐ 96 Rod Higgins	.05	.02	.01
☐ 97 Sarunas Marciulionis	.15	.07	.02
☐ 98 Chris Mullin	.20	.09	.03
☐ 99 Jim Petersen	.05	.02	.01
☐ 100 Mitch Richmond	.30	.14	.04
☐ 101 Mike Smrek	.05	.02	.01
☐ 102 Terry Teagle SP	.08	.04	.01
☐ 103 Tom Tolbert	.05	.02	.01
☐ 104 Kelvin Upshaw SP	.08	.04	.01
☐ 105 Anthony Bowie SP	.25	.11	.03
☐ 106 Adrian Caldwell	.05	.02	.01
☐ 107 Eric(Sleepy) Floyd	.05	.02	.01
☐ 108 Buck Johnson	.05	.02	.01
☐ 109 Vernon Maxwell	.08	.04	.01
☐ 110 Hakeem Olajuwon	1.00	.45	.13
☐ 111 Larry Smith	.08	.04	.01
☐ 112A Otis Thorpe ERR	.75	.35	.09
(Front photo actually Mitchell Wiggins)			
☐ 112B Otis Thorpe COR	.08	.04	.01
☐ 113A M. Wiggins SP ERR	.75	.35	.09
(Front photo actually Otis Thorpe)			
☐ 113B M. Wiggins SP COR	.05	.02	.01
☐ 114 Vern Fleming	.05	.02	.01
☐ 115 Rickey Green SP	.08	.04	.01
☐ 116 George McCloud	.05	.02	.01
☐ 117 Reggie Miller	.25	.11	.03
☐ 118A Dyron Nix SP ERR	2.00	.90	.25
(Back photo actually Wayman Tisdale)			
☐ 118B Dyron Nix SP COR	.08	.04	.01
☐ 119 Chuck Person	.08	.04	.01
☐ 120 Mike Sanders	.05	.02	.01
☐ 121 Detlef Schrempf	.10	.05	.01
☐ 122 Rik Smits	.10	.05	.01
☐ 123 LaSalle Thompson	.08	.04	.01
☐ 124 Benoit Benjamin	.05	.02	.01
☐ 125 Winston Garland	.05	.02	.01
☐ 126 Tom Garrick	.05	.02	.01
☐ 127 Gary Grant	.05	.02	.01
☐ 128 Ron Harper	.08	.04	.01
☐ 129 Danny Manning	.35	.16	.04
☐ 130 Jeff Martin	.05	.02	.01
☐ 131 Ken Norman	.08	.04	.01
☐ 132 Charles Smith	.08	.04	.01
☐ 133 Joe Wolf SP	.08	.04	.01
☐ 134 Michael Cooper SP	.15	.07	.02
☐ 135 Vlade Divac	.35	.16	.04
☐ 136 Larry Drew	.08	.04	.01
☐ 137 A.C. Green	.08	.04	.01
☐ 138 Magic Johnson	.75	.35	.09
☐ 139 Mark McNamara SP	.08	.04	.01
☐ 140 Byron Scott	.08	.04	.01
☐ 141 Mychal Thompson	.08	.04	.01
☐ 142 Orlando Woolridge SP	.12	.05	.02
☐ 143 James Worthy	.10	.05	.01

☐ 144	Terry Davis	.10	.05	.01
☐ 145	Sherman Douglas	.30	.14	.04
☐ 146	Kevin Edwards	.08	.04	.01
☐ 147	Tellis Frank SP	.08	.04	.01
☐ 148	Scott Haffner SP	.08	.04	.01
☐ 149	Grant Long	.08	.04	.01
☐ 150	Glen Rice	1.00	.45	.13
☐ 151	Rony Seikaly	.10	.05	.01
☐ 152	Rory Sparrow SP	.08	.04	.01
☐ 153	Jon Sundvold	.05	.02	.01
☐ 154	Billy Thompson	.05	.02	.01
☐ 155	Greg Anderson	.05	.02	.01
☐ 156	Ben Coleman SP	.08	.04	.01
☐ 157	Jeff Grayer	.05	.02	.01
☐ 158	Jay Humphries	.05	.02	.01
☐ 159	Frank Kornet	.05	.02	.01
☐ 160	Larry Krystkowiak	.05	.02	.01
☐ 161	Brad Lohaus	.05	.02	.01
☐ 162	Ricky Pierce	.08	.04	.01
☐ 163	Paul Pressey SP	.08	.04	.01
☐ 164	Fred Roberts	.05	.02	.01
☐ 165	Alvin Robertson	.08	.04	.01
☐ 166	Jack Sikma	.10	.05	.01
☐ 167	Randy Breuer	.05	.02	.01
☐ 168	Tony Campbell	.05	.02	.01
☐ 169	Tyrone Corbin	.08	.04	.01
☐ 170	Sidney Lowe SP	.08	.04	.01
☐ 171	Sam Mitchell	.05	.02	.01
☐ 172	Tod Murphy	.05	.02	.01
☐ 173	Pooh Richardson	.25	.11	.03
☐ 174	Donald Royal SP	.25	.11	.03
☐ 175	Brad Sellers SP	.08	.04	.01
☐ 176	Mookie Blaylock	.75	.35	.09
☐ 177	Sam Bowie	.08	.04	.01
☐ 178	Lester Conner	.05	.02	.01
☐ 179	Derrick Gervin	.05	.02	.01
☐ 180	Jack Haley	.05	.02	.01
☐ 181	Roy Hinson	.05	.02	.01
☐ 182	Dennis Hopson SP	.08	.04	.01
☐ 183	Chris Morris	.05	.02	.01
☐ 184	Pete Myers SP	.25	.11	.03
☐ 185	Purvis Short SP	.08	.04	.01
☐ 186	Maurice Cheeks	.10	.05	.01
☐ 187	Patrick Ewing	.50	.23	.06
☐ 188	Stuart Gray	.05	.02	.01
☐ 189	Mark Jackson	.08	.04	.01
☐ 190	Johnny Newman SP	.08	.04	.01
☐ 191	Charles Oakley	.10	.05	.01
☐ 192	Brian Quinnett	.05	.02	.01
☐ 193	Trent Tucker	.05	.02	.01
☐ 194	Kiki Vandeweghe	.08	.04	.01
☐ 195	Kenny Walker	.05	.02	.01
☐ 196	Eddie Lee Wilkins	.05	.02	.01
☐ 197	Gerald Wilkins	.08	.04	.01
☐ 198	Mark Acres	.05	.02	.01
☐ 199	Nick Anderson	.60	.25	.08
☐ 200	Michael Ansley	.05	.02	.01
☐ 201	Terry Catledge	.05	.02	.01
☐ 202	Dave Corzine SP	.08	.04	.01
☐ 203	Sidney Green SP	.08	.04	.01
☐ 204	Jerry Reynolds	.05	.02	.01
☐ 205	Scott Skiles	.08	.04	.01
☐ 206	Otis Smith	.05	.02	.01
☐ 207	Reggie Theus SP	.12	.05	.02
☐ 208	Jeff Turner	.05	.02	.01
☐ 209	Sam Vincent	.05	.02	.01
☐ 210	Ron Anderson	.05	.02	.01
☐ 211	Charles Barkley	.75	.35	.09
☐ 212	Scott Brooks SP	.08	.04	.01
☐ 213	Lanard Copeland SP	.08	.04	.01
☐ 214	Johnny Dawkins	.05	.02	.01
☐ 215	Mike Gminski	.05	.02	.01
☐ 216	Hersey Hawkins	.10	.05	.01

☐	217	Rick Mahorn	.08	.04	.01
☐	218	Derek Smith SP	.08	.04	.01
☐	219	Bob Thornton	.05	.02	.01
☐	220	Tom Chambers	.10	.05	.01
☐	221	Greg Grant SP	.08	.04	.01
☐	222	Jeff Hornacek	.10	.05	.01
☐	223	Eddie Johnson	.08	.04	.01
☐	224A	Kevin Johnson	.35	.16	.04
		(SkyBox logo in lower right corner)			
☐	224B	Kevin Johnson	.35	.16	.04
		(SkyBox logo in upper right corner)			
☐	225	Andrew Lang	.25	.11	.03
☐	226	Dan Majerle	.30	.14	.04
☐	227	Mike McGee SP	.08	.04	.01
☐	228	Tim Perry	.05	.02	.01
☐	229	Kurt Rambis	.05	.04	.01
☐	230	Mark West	.05	.02	.01
☐	231	Mark Bryant	.05	.02	.01
☐	232	Wayne Cooper	.05	.02	.01
☐	233	Clyde Drexler	.25	.11	.03
☐	234	Kevin Duckworth	.05	.02	.01
☐	235	Byron Irvin SP	.08	.04	.01
☐	236	Jerome Kersey	.05	.02	.01
☐	237	Drazen Petrovic	.60	.25	.08
☐	238	Terry Porter	.10	.05	.01
☐	239	Cliff Robinson	1.00	.45	.13
☐	240	Buck Williams	.10	.05	.01
☐	241	Danny Young	.05	.02	.01
☐	242	Danny Ainge SP	.12	.05	.02
☐	243	Randy Allen SP	.08	.04	.01
☐	244A	Antoine Carr SP	.08	.04	.01
		(Wearing Atlanta jersey on back)			
☐	244B	Antoine Carr	.05	.02	.01
		(Wearing Sacramento jersey on back)			
☐	245	Vinny Del Negro SP	.08	.04	.01
☐	246	Pervis Ellison	.40	.18	.05
☐	247	Greg Kite SP	.08	.04	.01
☐	248	Rodney McCray SP	.08	.04	.01
☐	249	Harold Pressley SP	.08	.04	.01
☐	250	Ralph Sampson	.08	.04	.01
☐	251	Wayman Tisdale	.08	.04	.01
☐	252	Willie Anderson	.05	.02	.01
☐	253	Uwe Blab SP	.08	.04	.01
☐	254	Frank Brickowski	.12	.05	.02
☐	255	Terry Cummings	.08	.04	.01
☐	256	Sean Elliott	.35	.16	.04
☐	257	Caldwell Jones SP	.12	.05	.02
☐	258	Johnny Moore SP	.08	.04	.01
☐	259	Zarko Paspalj SP	.08	.04	.01
☐	260	David Robinson	1.50	.65	.19
☐	261	Rod Strickland	.08	.04	.01
☐	262	David Wingate SP	.08	.04	.01
☐	263	Dana Barros	.25	.11	.03
☐	264	Michael Cage	.05	.02	.01
☐	265	Quintin Dailey	.05	.02	.01
☐	266	Dale Ellis	.08	.04	.01
☐	267	Steve Johnson SP	.08	.04	.01
☐	268	Shawn Kemp	3.50	1.55	.45
☐	269	Xavier McDaniel	.10	.05	.01
☐	270	Derrick McKey	.05	.02	.01
☐	271A	Nate McMillan SP ERR	.12	.05	.02
		(Back photo actually Olden Polynice; first series)			
☐	271B	Nate McMillan COR	.08	.04	.01
		(second series)			
☐	272	Olden Polynice	.05	.02	.01
☐	273	Sedale Threatt	.08	.04	.01
☐	274	Thurl Bailey	.05	.02	.01

☐	275	Mike Brown	.05	.02	.01
☐	276	Mark Eaton	.08	.04	.01
☐	277	Blue Edwards	.25	.11	.03
☐	278	Darrell Griffith	.08	.04	.01
☐	279	Bobby Hansen SP	.08	.04	.01
☐	280	Eric Johnson	.05	.02	.01
☐	281	Eric Leckner SP	.08	.04	.01
☐	282	Karl Malone	.35	.16	.04
☐	283	Delaney Rudd	.05	.02	.01
☐	284	John Stockton	.30	.14	.04
☐	285	Mark Alarie	.05	.02	.01
☐	286	Steve Colter SP	.08	.04	.01
☐	287	Ledell Eackles SP	.08	.04	.01
☐	288	Harvey Grant	.05	.02	.01
☐	289	Tom Hammonds	.15	.07	.02
☐	290	Charles Jones	.05	.02	.01
☐	291	Bernard King	.10	.05	.01
☐	292	Jeff Malone SP	.12	.05	.02
☐	293	Darrell Walker	.05	.02	.01
☐	294	John Williams	.05	.02	.01
☐	295	Checklist 1 SP	.08	.04	.01
☐	296	Checklist 2 SP	.08	.04	.01
☐	297	Checklist 3 SP	.08	.04	.01
☐	298	Checklist 4 SP	.08	.04	.01
☐	299	Checklist 5 SP	.08	.04	.01
☐	300	Danny Ferry SP	.25	.11	.03
		Cleveland Cavaliers			
☐	301	Bob Weiss CO	.05	.02	.01
		Atlanta Hawks			
☐	302	Chris Ford CO	.08	.04	.01
		Boston Celtics			
☐	303	Gene Littles CO	.05	.02	.01
		Charlotte Hornets			
☐	304	Phil Jackson CO	.08	.04	.01
		Chicago Bulls			
☐	305	Lenny Wilkens CO	.08	.04	.01
		Cleveland Cavaliers			
☐	306	Richie Adubato CO	.05	.02	.01
		Dallas Mavericks			
☐	307	Paul Westhead CO	.08	.04	.01
		Denver Nuggets			
☐	308	Chuck Daly CO	.08	.04	.01
		Detroit Pistons			
☐	309	Don Nelson CO	.08	.04	.01
		Golden State Warriors			
☐	310	Don Chaney CO	.05	.02	.01
		Houston Rockets			
☐	311	Dick Versace CO	.05	.02	.01
		Indiana Pacers			
☐	312	Mike Schuler CO	.05	.02	.01
		Los Angeles Clippers			
☐	313	Mike Dunleavy CO	.08	.04	.01
		Los Angeles Lakers			
☐	314	Ron Rothstein CO	.05	.02	.01
		Miami Heat			
☐	315	Del Harris CO	.05	.02	.01
		Milwaukee Bucks			
☐	316	Bill Musselman CO	.05	.02	.01
		Minnesota Timberwolves			
☐	317	Bill Fitch CO	.05	.02	.01
		Houston Rockets			
☐	318	Stu Jackson CO	.05	.02	.01
		New York Knicks			
☐	319	Matt Guokas CO	.05	.02	.01
		Orlando Magic			
☐	320	Jim Lynam CO	.05	.02	.01
		Philadelphia 76ers			
☐	321	Cotton Fitzsimmons CO	.05	.02	.01
		Phoenix Suns			
☐	322	Rick Adelman CO	.08	.04	.01
		Portland Trail Blazers			
☐	323	Dick Motta CO	.05	.02	.01
		Sacramento Kings			

☐ 324 Larry Brown CO	.08	.04	.01
San Antonio Spurs			
☐ 325 K.C. Jones CO	.08	.04	.01
Seattle Supersonics			
☐ 326 Jerry Sloan CO	.05	.02	.01
Utah Jazz			
☐ 327 Wes Unseld CO	.08	.04	.01
Washington Bullets			
☐ 328 Atlanta Hawks TC	.05	.02	.01
☐ 329 Boston Celtics TC	.05	.02	.01
☐ 330 Charlotte Hornets TC	.05	.02	.01
☐ 331 Chicago Bulls TC	.05	.02	.01
☐ 332 Cleveland Cavaliers TC	.05	.02	.01
☐ 333 Dallas Mavericks TC	.05	.02	.01
☐ 334 Denver Nuggets TC	.05	.02	.01
☐ 335 Detroit Pistons TC	.05	.02	.01
☐ 336 Golden State Warriors TC	.05	.02	.01
☐ 337 Houston Rockets TC	.05	.02	.01
☐ 338 Indiana Pacers TC	.05	.02	.01
☐ 339 Los Angeles Clippers TC	.05	.02	.01
☐ 340 Los Angeles Lakers TC	.05	.02	.01
☐ 341 Miami Heat TC	.05	.02	.01
☐ 342 Milwaukee Bucks TC	.05	.02	.01
☐ 343 Minnesota Timberwolves TC	.05	.02	.01
☐ 344 New Jersey Nets TC	.05	.02	.01
☐ 345 New York Knicks TC	.05	.02	.01
☐ 346 Orlando Magic TC	.05	.02	.01
☐ 347 Philadelphia 76ers TC	.05	.02	.01
☐ 348 Phoenix Suns TC	.05	.02	.01
☐ 349 Portland Trail Blazers TC	.05	.02	.01
☐ 350 Sacramento Kings TC	.05	.02	.01
☐ 351 San Antonio Spurs TC	.05	.02	.01
☐ 352 Seattle SuperSonics TC	.05	.02	.01
☐ 353 Utah Jazz TC	.05	.02	.01
☐ 354 Washington Bullets TC	.05	.02	.01
☐ 355 Rumeal Robinson LP	.15	.07	.02
Atlanta Hawks			
☐ 356 Kendall Gill LP	1.00	.45	.13
Charlotte Hornets			
☐ 357 Chris Jackson LP	1.00	.45	.13
Denver Nuggets			
☐ 358 Tyrone Hill LP	.30	.14	.04
Golden State Warriors			
☐ 359 Bo Kimble LP	.05	.02	.01
Los Angeles Clippers			
☐ 360 Willie Burton LP	.10	.05	.01
Miami Heat			
☐ 361 Felton Spencer LP	.20	.09	.03
Minnesota Timberwolves			
☐ 362 Derrick Coleman LP	2.50	1.15	.30
New Jersey Nets			
☐ 363 Dennis Scott LP	.50	.23	.06
Orlando Magic			
☐ 364 Lionel Simmons LP	.75	.35	.09
Sacramento Kings			
☐ 365 Gary Payton LP	1.25	.55	.16
Seattle Supersonics			
☐ 366 Tim McCormick	.05	.02	.01
Atlanta Hawks			
☐ 367 Sidney Moncrief	.10	.05	.01
Atlanta Hawks			
☐ 368 Kenny Gattison	.05	.02	.01
Charlotte Hornets			
☐ 369 Randolph Keys	.05	.02	.01
Charlotte Hornets			
☐ 370 Johnny Newman	.05	.02	.01
Charlotte Hornets			
☐ 371 Dennis Hopson	.05	.02	.01
Chicago Bulls			
☐ 372 Cliff Levingston	.05	.02	.01
Chicago Bulls			
☐ 373 Derrick Chievous	.05	.02	.01
Cleveland Cavaliers			

☐ 374	Danny Ferry Cleveland Cavaliers	.05	.02	.01
☐ 375	Alex English Dallas Mavericks	.10	.05	.01
☐ 376	Lafayette Lever Dallas Mavericks	.05	.02	.01
☐ 377	Rodney McCray Dallas Mavericks	.05	.02	.01
☐ 378	T.R. Dunn Denver Nuggets	.05	.02	.01
☐ 379	Corey Gaines Denver Nuggets	.05	.02	.01
☐ 380	Avery Johnson San Antonio Spurs	.20	.09	.03
☐ 381	Joe Wolf Denver Nuggets	.05	.02	.01
☐ 382	Orlando Woolridge Denver Nuggets	.08	.04	.01
☐ 383	Tree Rollins Detroit Pistons	.08	.04	.01
☐ 384	Steve Johnson Seattle Supersonics	.05	.02	.01
☐ 385	Kenny Smith Houston Rockets	.05	.02	.01
☐ 386	Mike Woodson Cleveland Cavaliers	.05	.02	.01
☐ 387	Greg Dreiling Indiana Pacers	.05	.02	.01
☐ 388	Micheal Williams Indiana Pacers	.08	.04	.01
☐ 389	Randy Wittman Indiana Pacers	.05	.02	.01
☐ 390	Ken Bannister Los Angeles Clippers	.05	.02	.01
☐ 391	Sam Perkins Los Angeles Lakers	.10	.05	.01
☐ 392	Terry Teagle Los Angeles Lakers	.05	.02	.01
☐ 393	Milt Wagner Miami Heat	.05	.02	.01
☐ 394	Frank Brickowski Milwaukee Bucks	.08	.04	.01
☐ 395	Dan Schayes Milwaukee Bucks	.05	.02	.01
☐ 396	Scott Brooks Minnesota Timberwolves	.05	.02	.01
☐ 397	Doug West Minnesota Timberwolves	.60	.25	.08
☐ 398	Chris Dudley New Jersey Nets	.15	.07	.02
☐ 399	Reggie Theus New Jersey Nets	.08	.04	.01
☐ 400	Greg Grant New York Knicks	.05	.02	.01
☐ 401	Greg Kite Orlando Magic	.05	.02	.01
☐ 402	Mark McNamara Orlando Magic	.05	.02	.01
☐ 403	Manute Bol Philadelphia 76ers	.05	.02	.01
☐ 404	Rickey Green Philadelphia 76ers	.05	.02	.01
☐ 405	Kenny Battle Denver Nuggets	.05	.02	.01
☐ 406	Ed Nealy Phoenix Suns	.05	.02	.01
☐ 407	Danny Ainge Portland Trail Blazers	.10	.05	.01
☐ 408	Steve Colter Sacramento Kings	.05	.02	.01
☐ 409	Bobby Hansen Sacramento Kings	.05	.02	.01
☐ 410	Eric Leckner	.05	.02	.01

Charlotte Hornets				
☐ 411 Rory Sparrow..............................	.05	.02	.01
Sacramento Kings				
☐ 412 Bill Wennington...........................	.05	.02	.01
Sacramento Kings				
☐ 413 Sidney Green..............................	.05	.02	.01
San Antonio Spurs				
☐ 414 David Greenwood.........................	.05	.02	.01
San Antonio Spurs				
☐ 415 Paul Pressey..............................	.05	.02	.01
San Antonio Spurs				
☐ 416 Reggie Williams...........................	.08	.04	.01
San Antonio Spurs				
☐ 417 Dave Corzine..............................	.05	.02	.01
Orlando Magic				
☐ 418 Jeff Malone................................	.08	.04	.01
Utah Jazz				
☐ 419 Pervis Ellison.............................	.10	.05	.01
Washington Bullets				
☐ 420 Byron Irvin................................	.05	.02	.01
Washington Bullets				
☐ 421 Checklist 1.................................	.05	.02	.01
☐ 422 Checklist 2.................................	.05	.02	.01
☐ 423 Checklist 3.................................	.05	.02	.01
☐ NNO SkyBox Salutes..........................	5.00	2.30	.60
the NBA				

1991-92 SkyBox

The complete 1991-92 SkyBox basketball set contains 659 cards measuring the standard size (2 1/2" by 3 1/2"). The set was released in two series of 350 and 309 cards, respectively. This year SkyBox did not co-mingle first and second series cards in the second series packs. The cards were available in 15-card fin-sealed foil packs that feature four different mail-in offers on the back, or 62-card blister packs that contain two (of four) SkyBox logo cards not available in the 15-card foil packs. The fronts feature color action player photos overlaying multi-colored computer-generated geometric shapes and stripes. The pictures are borderless and the card face is white. The player's name appears in different color lettering at the bottom of each card, with the team logo in the lower right corner. In a trapezoid shape, the backs have non-action color player photos. At the bottom biographical and statistical information appear inside a color-striped diagonal. The cards are numbered and checklisted below alphabetically within and according to teams as follows: Atlanta Hawks (1-11), Boston Celtics (12-22), Charlotte Hornets (23-33), Chicago Bulls (34-44), Cleveland Cavaliers (45-55), Dallas Mavericks (56-66), Denver Nuggets (67-77), Detroit Pistons (78-88), Golden State Warriors (89-99), Houston Rockets (100-110), Indiana Pacers (111-121), Los Angeles Clippers (122-132), Los Angeles Lakers (133-143), Miami Heat (144-154), Milwaukee Bucks (155-165), Minnesota Timberwolves (166-176), New Jersey Nets (177-187), New York Knicks (188-198), Orlando Magic (199-209), Philadelphia 76ers (210-220), Phoenix Suns (221-231), Portland Trail Blazers (232-242), Sacramento Kings (243-253), San Antonio Spurs (254-264), Seattle Supersonics (265-275), Utah Jazz (276-286),

Washington Bullets (287-297), Stats (298-307), Best Single Game Performance (308-312), NBA All-Star Weekend Highlights (313-317), NBA All-Rookie Team (318-322), GQ's "NBA All-Star Style Team" (323-327), Centennial Highlights (328-332), Great Moments from the NBA Finals (333-337), Stay in School (338-344), Checklists (345-350), Team Logos (351-377), Coaches (378-404), Game Frames (405-431), Sixth Man (432-458), Teamwork (459-485), Rising Stars (486-512), Lottery Picks (513-523), Centennial (524-529), 1992 USA Basketball Team (530-546), 1988 USA Basketball Team (547-556), 1984 USA Basketball Team (557-563), The Magic of SkyBox (564-571), SkyBox Salutes (572-576), Skymasters (577-588), Shooting Stars (589-602), Small School Sensations (603-609), NBA Stay in School (610-614), Player Updates (615-653), and Checklists (654-659). As part of a promotion with Cheerios, four SkyBox cards were inserted into specially marked 10-ounce and 15-ounce cereal boxes. These cereal boxes appeared on store shelves in December 1991 and January 1992, and they depicted images of SkyBox cards on the front, back, and side panels. An unnumbered gold foil-stamped 1992 USA Basketball Team card was randomly inserted into second series foil packs, while the blister packs featured two-card sets of NBA MVPs from the same team for consecutive years. As a mail-in offer a limited Clyde Drexler Olympic card was sent to the first 10,000 respondents in return for ten SkyBox wrappers and 1.00 for postage and handling. Rookie Cards include Kenny Anderson, Stacey Augmon, Larry Johnson, Mike Krzyzewski (USA coach), Terry Mills, Dikembe Mutumbo, Steve Smith and John Starks.

		MINT	EXC	G-VG
	COMPLETE SET (659)	25.00	11.50	3.10
	COMPLETE SERIES 1 (350)	8.00	3.60	1.00
	COMPLETE SERIES 2 (309)	17.00	7.75	2.10
	COMMON PLAYER (1-350)	.05	.02	.01
	COMMON PLAYER (351-659)	.05	.02	.01
☐ 1	John Battle	.05	.02	.01
☐ 2	Duane Ferrell	1.25	.55	.16
☐ 3	Jon Koncak	.05	.02	.01
☐ 4	Moses Malone	1.05	.45	.13
☐ 5	Tim McCormick	.05	.02	.01
☐ 6	Sidney Moncrief	.10	.05	.01
☐ 7	Doc Rivers	.08	.04	.01
☐ 8	Rumeal Robinson UER	.05	.02	.01
	(Drafted 11th, should say 10th)			
☐ 9	Spud Webb	.10	.05	.01
☐ 10	Dominique Wilkins	.25	.11	.03
☐ 11	Kevin Willis	.08	.04	.01
☐ 12	Larry Bird	.75	.35	.09
☐ 13	Dee Brown	.08	.04	.01
☐ 14	Kevin Gamble	.05	.02	.01
☐ 15	Joe Kleine	.05	.02	.01
☐ 16	Reggie Lewis	.10	.05	.01
☐ 17	Kevin McHale	.10	.05	.01
☐ 18	Robert Parish	.10	.05	.01
☐ 19	Ed Pinckney	.05	.02	.01
☐ 20	Brian Shaw	.05	.02	.01
☐ 21	Michael Smith	.05	.02	.01
☐ 22	Stojko Vrankovic	.05	.02	.01
☐ 23	Muggsy Bogues	.10	.05	.01
☐ 24	Rex Chapman	.05	.02	.01
☐ 25	Dell Curry	.08	.04	.01
☐ 26	Kenny Gattison	.05	.02	.01
☐ 27	Kendall Gill	.08	.04	.01
☐ 28	Mike Gminski	.05	.02	.01
☐ 29	Randolph Keys	.05	.02	.01
☐ 30	Eric Leckner	.05	.02	.01
☐ 31	Johnny Newman	.05	.02	.01
☐ 32	J.R. Reid	.05	.02	.01
☐ 33	Kelly Tripucka	.08	.04	.01
☐ 34	B.J. Armstrong	.20	.09	.03
☐ 35	Bill Cartwright	.08	.04	.01
☐ 36	Horace Grant	.10	.05	.01
☐ 37	Craig Hodges	.05	.02	.01
☐ 38	Dennis Hopson	.05	.02	.01
☐ 39	Michael Jordan	2.50	1.15	.30
☐ 40	Stacey King	.05	.02	.01
☐ 41	Cliff Levingston	.05	.02	.01
☐ 42	John Paxson	.08	.04	.01
☐ 43	Will Perdue	.05	.02	.01

☐ 44	Scottie Pippen	.30	.14	.04
☐ 45	Winston Bennett	.05	.02	.01
☐ 46	Chucky Brown	.05	.02	.01
☐ 47	Brad Daugherty	.10	.05	.01
☐ 48	Craig Ehlo	.05	.02	.01
☐ 49	Danny Ferry	.05	.02	.01
☐ 50	Steve Kerr	.05	.02	.01
☐ 51	John Morton	.05	.02	.01
☐ 52	Larry Nance	.08	.04	.01
☐ 53	Mark Price	.10	.05	.01
☐ 54	Darnell Valentine	.05	.02	.01
☐ 55	John Williams	.08	.04	.01
☐ 56	Steve Alford	.05	.02	.01
☐ 57	Rolando Blackman	.08	.04	.01
☐ 58	Brad Davis	.05	.02	.01
☐ 59	James Donaldson	.05	.02	.01
☐ 60	Derek Harper	.08	.04	.01
☐ 61	Fat Lever	.05	.02	.01
☐ 62	Rodney McCray	.05	.02	.01
☐ 63	Roy Tarpley	.05	.02	.01
☐ 64	Kelvin Upshaw	.05	.02	.01
☐ 65	Randy White	.05	.02	.01
☐ 66	Herb Williams	.05	.02	.01
☐ 67	Michael Adams	.08	.04	.01
☐ 68	Greg Anderson	.05	.02	.01
☐ 69	Anthony Cook	.05	.02	.01
☐ 70	Chris Jackson	.05	.02	.01
☐ 71	Jerome Lane	.05	.02	.01
☐ 72	Marcus Liberty	.05	.02	.01
☐ 73	Todd Lichti	.05	.02	.01
☐ 74	Blair Rasmussen	.05	.02	.01
☐ 75	Reggie Williams	.08	.04	.01
☐ 76	Joe Wolf	.05	.02	.01
☐ 77	Orlando Woolridge	.08	.04	.01
☐ 78	Mark Aguirre	.10	.05	.01
☐ 79	William Bedford	.05	.02	.01
☐ 80	Lance Blanks	.05	.02	.01
☐ 81	Joe Dumars	.20	.09	.03
☐ 82	James Edwards	.05	.02	.01
☐ 83	Scott Hastings	.05	.02	.01
☐ 84	Vinnie Johnson	.08	.04	.01
☐ 85	Bill Laimbeer	.10	.05	.01
☐ 86	Dennis Rodman	.08	.04	.01
☐ 87	John Salley	.05	.02	.01
☐ 88	Isiah Thomas	.20	.09	.03
☐ 89	Mario Elie	.30	.14	.04
☐ 90	Tim Hardaway	.20	.09	.03
☐ 91	Rod Higgins	.05	.02	.01
☐ 92	Tyrone Hill	.05	.02	.01
☐ 93	Les Jepsen	.05	.02	.01
☐ 94	Alton Lister	.05	.02	.01
☐ 95	Sarunas Marciulionis	.08	.04	.01
☐ 96	Chris Mullin	.20	.09	.03
☐ 97	Jim Petersen	.05	.02	.01
☐ 98	Mitch Richmond	.10	.05	.01
☐ 99	Tom Tolbert	.05	.02	.01
☐ 100	Adrian Caldwell	.05	.02	.01
☐ 101	Eric(Sleepy) Floyd	.05	.02	.01
☐ 102	Dave Jamerson	.05	.02	.01
☐ 103	Buck Johnson	.05	.02	.01
☐ 104	Vernon Maxwell	.08	.04	.01
☐ 105	Hakeem Olajuwon	.75	.35	.09
☐ 106	Kenny Smith	.05	.02	.01
☐ 107	Larry Smith	.08	.04	.01
☐ 108	Otis Thorpe	.08	.04	.01
☐ 109	Kennard Winchester	.05	.02	.01
☐ 110	David Wood	.05	.02	.01
☐ 111	Greg Dreiling	.05	.02	.01
☐ 112	Vern Fleming	.05	.02	.01
☐ 113	George McCloud	.05	.02	.01
☐ 114	Reggie Miller	.20	.09	.03
☐ 115	Chuck Person	.08	.04	.01
☐ 116	Mike Sanders	.05	.02	.01

☐	117	Detlef Schrempf	.10	.05	.01
☐	118	Rik Smits	.08	.04	.01
☐	119	LaSalle Thompson	.08	.04	.01
☐	120	Kenny Williams	.05	.02	.01
☐	121	Micheal Williams	.08	.04	.01
☐	122	Ken Bannister	.05	.02	.01
☐	123	Winston Garland	.05	.02	.01
☐	124	Gary Grant	.05	.02	.01
☐	125	Ron Harper	.08	.04	.01
☐	126	Bo Kimble	.05	.02	.01
☐	127	Danny Manning	.20	.09	.03
☐	128	Jeff Martin	.05	.02	.01
☐	129	Ken Norman	.08	.04	.01
☐	130	Olden Polynice	.05	.02	.01
☐	131	Charles Smith	.08	.04	.01
☐	132	Loy Vaught	.08	.04	.01
☐	133	Elden Campbell	.05	.02	.01
☐	134	Vlade Divac	.08	.04	.01
☐	135	Larry Drew	.08	.04	.01
☐	136	A.C. Green	.08	.04	.01
☐	137	Magic Johnson	.50	.23	.06
☐	138	Sam Perkins	.08	.04	.01
☐	139	Byron Scott	.08	.04	.01
☐	140	Tony Smith	.05	.02	.01
☐	141	Terry Teagle	.05	.02	.01
☐	142	Mychal Thompson	.08	.04	.01
☐	143	James Worthy	.10	.05	.01
☐	144	Willie Burton	.05	.02	.01
☐	145	Bimbo Coles	.05	.02	.01
☐	146	Terry Davis	.05	.02	.01
☐	147	Sherman Douglas	.05	.02	.01
☐	148	Kevin Edwards	.05	.02	.01
☐	149	Alec Kessler	.05	.02	.01
☐	150	Grant Long	.05	.02	.01
☐	151	Glen Rice	.20	.09	.03
☐	152	Rony Seikaly	.10	.05	.01
☐	153	Jon Sundvold	.05	.02	.01
☐	154	Billy Thompson	.05	.02	.01
☐	155	Frank Brickowski	.08	.04	.01
☐	156	Lester Conner	.05	.02	.01
☐	157	Jeff Grayer	.05	.02	.01
☐	158	Jay Humphries	.05	.02	.01
☐	159	Larry Krystkowiak	.05	.02	.01
☐	160	Brad Lohaus	.05	.02	.01
☐	161	Dale Ellis	.08	.04	.01
☐	162	Fred Roberts	.05	.02	.01
☐	163	Alvin Robertson	.08	.04	.01
☐	164	Danny Schayes	.05	.02	.01
☐	165	Jack Sikma	.10	.05	.01
☐	166	Randy Breuer	.05	.02	.01
☐	167	Scott Brooks	.05	.02	.01
☐	168	Tony Campbell	.05	.02	.01
☐	169	Tyrone Corbin	.05	.02	.01
☐	170	Gerald Glass	.05	.02	.01
☐	171	Sam Mitchell	.05	.02	.01
☐	172	Tod Murphy	.05	.02	.01
☐	173	Pooh Richardson	.05	.02	.01
☐	174	Felton Spencer	.05	.02	.01
☐	175	Bob Thornton	.05	.02	.01
☐	176	Doug West	.08	.04	.01
☐	177	Mookie Blaylock	.08	.04	.01
☐	178	Sam Bowie	.08	.04	.01
☐	179	Jud Buechler	.05	.02	.01
☐	180	Derrick Coleman	.40	.18	.05
☐	181	Chris Dudley	.05	.02	.01
☐	182	Tate George	.05	.02	.01
☐	183	Jack Haley	.05	.02	.01
☐	184	Terry Mills	.75	.35	.09
☐	185	Chris Morris	.05	.02	.01
☐	186	Drazen Petrovic	.08	.04	.01
☐	187	Reggie Theus	.08	.04	.01
☐	188	Maurice Cheeks	.10	.05	.01
☐	189	Patrick Ewing	.30	.14	.04

☐	190	Mark Jackson	.08	.04	.01
☐	191	Jerrod Mustaf	.05	.02	.01
☐	192	Charles Oakley	.10	.05	.01
☐	193	Brian Quinnett	.05	.02	.01
☐	194	John Starks	1.00	.45	.13
☐	195	Trent Tucker	.05	.02	.01
☐	196	Kiki Vandeweghe	.08	.04	.01
☐	197	Kenny Walker	.05	.02	.01
☐	198	Gerald Wilkins	.08	.04	.01
☐	199	Mark Acres	.05	.02	.01
☐	200	Nick Anderson	.10	.05	.01
☐	201	Michael Ansley	.05	.02	.01
☐	202	Terry Catledge	.05	.02	.01
☐	203	Greg Kite	.05	.02	.01
☐	204	Jerry Reynolds	.05	.02	.01
☐	205	Dennis Scott	.08	.04	.01
☐	206	Scott Skiles	.08	.04	.01
☐	207	Otis Smith	.05	.02	.01
☐	208	Jeff Turner	.05	.02	.01
☐	209	Sam Vincent	.05	.02	.01
☐	210	Ron Anderson	.05	.02	.01
☐	211	Charles Barkley	.50	.23	.06
☐	212	Manute Bol	.05	.02	.01
☐	213	Johnny Dawkins	.05	.02	.01
☐	214	Armon Gilliam	.05	.02	.01
☐	215	Rickey Green	.05	.02	.01
☐	216	Hersey Hawkins	.08	.04	.01
☐	217	Rick Mahorn	.08	.04	.01
☐	218	Brian Oliver	.05	.02	.01
☐	219	Andre Turner	.05	.02	.01
☐	220	Jayson Williams	.05	.02	.01
☐	221	Joe Barry Carroll	.05	.02	.01
☐	222	Cedric Ceballos	.10	.05	.01
☐	223	Tom Chambers	.10	.05	.01
☐	224	Jeff Hornacek	.10	.05	.01
☐	225	Kevin Johnson	.20	.09	.03
☐	226	Negele Knight	.05	.02	.01
☐	227	Andrew Lang	.05	.02	.01
☐	228	Dan Majerle	.10	.05	.01
☐	229	Xavier McDaniel	.10	.05	.01
☐	230	Kurt Rambis	.08	.04	.01
☐	231	Mark West	.05	.02	.01
☐	232	Alaa Abdelnaby	.05	.02	.01
☐	233	Danny Ainge	.10	.05	.01
☐	234	Mark Bryant	.05	.02	.01
☐	235	Wayne Cooper	.05	.02	.01
☐	236	Walter Davis	.10	.05	.01
☐	237	Clyde Drexler	.20	.09	.03
☐	238	Kevin Duckworth	.05	.02	.01
☐	239	Jerome Kersey	.05	.02	.01
☐	240	Terry Porter	.08	.04	.01
☐	241	Cliff Robinson	.20	.09	.03
☐	242	Buck Williams	.10	.05	.01
☐	243	Anthony Bonner	.05	.02	.01
☐	244	Antoine Carr	.05	.02	.01
☐	245	Duane Causwell	.05	.02	.01
☐	246	Bobby Hansen	.05	.02	.01
☐	247	Jim Les	.05	.02	.01
☐	248	Travis Mays	.05	.02	.01
☐	249	Ralph Sampson	.08	.04	.01
☐	250	Lionel Simmons	.08	.04	.01
☐	251	Rory Sparrow	.05	.02	.01
☐	252	Wayman Tisdale	.08	.04	.01
☐	253	Bill Wennington	.05	.02	.01
☐	254	Willie Anderson	.05	.02	.01
☐	255	Terry Cummings	.08	.04	.01
☐	256	Sean Elliott	.08	.04	.01
☐	257	Sidney Green	.05	.02	.01
☐	258	David Greenwood	.05	.02	.01
☐	259	Avery Johnson	.08	.04	.01
☐	260	Paul Pressey	.05	.02	.01
☐	261	David Robinson	.60	.25	.08
☐	262	Dwayne Schintzius	.05	.02	.01

☐	263	Rod Strickland	.08	.04	.01
☐	264	David Wingate	.05	.02	.01
☐	265	Dana Barros	.05	.02	.01
☐	266	Benoit Benjamin	.05	.02	.01
☐	267	Michael Cage	.05	.02	.01
☐	268	Quintin Dailey	.05	.02	.01
☐	269	Ricky Pierce	.08	.04	.01
☐	270	Eddie Johnson	.08	.04	.01
☐	271	Shawn Kemp	1.00	.45	.13
☐	272	Derrick McKey	.05	.02	.01
☐	273	Nate McMillan	.08	.04	.01
☐	274	Gary Payton	.20	.09	.03
☐	275	Sedale Threatt	.05	.02	.01
☐	276	Thurl Bailey	.05	.02	.01
☐	277	Mike Brown	.05	.02	.01
☐	278	Tony Brown	.05	.02	.01
☐	279	Mark Eaton	.05	.02	.01
☐	280	Blue Edwards	.08	.04	.01
☐	281	Darrell Griffith	.08	.04	.01
☐	282	Jeff Malone	.08	.04	.01
☐	283	Karl Malone	.25	.11	.03
☐	284	Delaney Rudd	.05	.02	.01
☐	285	John Stockton	.20	.09	.03
☐	286	Andy Toolson	.05	.02	.01
☐	287	Mark Alarie	.05	.02	.01
☐	288	Ledell Eackles	.05	.02	.01
☐	289	Pervis Ellison	.08	.04	.01
☐	290	A.J. English	.05	.02	.01
☐	291	Harvey Grant	.05	.02	.01
☐	292	Tom Hammonds	.05	.02	.01
☐	293	Charles Jones	.05	.02	.01
☐	294	Bernard King	.10	.05	.01
☐	295	Darrell Walker	.05	.02	.01
☐	296	John Williams	.05	.02	.01
☐	297	Haywoode Workman	.20	.09	.03
☐	298	Muggsy Bogues Charlotte Hornets Assist-to-Turnover Ratio Leader	.08	.04	.01
☐	299	Lester Conner Milwaukee Bucks Steal-to-Turnover Ratio Leader	.05	.02	.01
☐	300	Michael Adams Denver Nuggets Largest One-Year Scoring Improvement	.05	.02	.01
☐	301	Chris Mullin Golden State Warriors Most Minutes Per Game	.10	.05	.01
☐	302	Otis Thorpe Houston Rockets Most Consecutive Games Played	.08	.04	.01
☐	303	Mitch Richmond Chris Mullin Tim Hardaway Highest Scoring Trio	.10	.05	.01
☐	304	Darrell Walker Washington Bullets Top Rebounding Guard	.05	.02	.01
☐	305	Jerome Lane Denver Nuggets Rebounds Per 48 Minutes	.05	.02	.01
☐	306	John Stockton Utah Jazz Assists Per 48 Minutes	.10	.05	.01
☐	307	Michael Jordan Chicago Bulls Points Per 48 Minutes	1.25	.55	.16
☐	308	Michael Adams Denver Nuggets Best Single Game	.05	.02	.01

Performance: Points			
☐ 309 Larry Smith	.05	.02	.01
Houston Rockets			
Jerome Lane			
Denver Nuggets			
Best Single Game			
Performance: Rebounds			
☐ 310 Scott Skiles	.05	.02	.01
Orlando Magic			
Best Single Game			
Performance: Assists			
☐ 311 Hakeem Olajuwon	.50	.23	.06
David Robinson			
Best Single Game			
Performance: Blocks			
☐ 312 Alvin Robertson	.05	.02	.01
Milwaukee Bucks			
Best Single Game			
Performance: Steals			
☐ 313 Stay In School Jam	.05	.02	.01
☐ 314 Craig Hodges	.05	.02	.01
Chicago Bulls			
Three-Point Shootout			
☐ 315 Dee Brown	.08	.04	.01
Boston Celtics			
Slam-Dunk Championship			
☐ 316 Charles Barkley	.20	.09	.03
Philadelphia 76ers			
All-Star Game MVP			
☐ 317 Behind the Scenes	.05	.02	.01
Charles Barkley			
Joe Dumars			
Kevin McHale			
☐ 318 Derrick Coleman ART	.20	.09	.03
New Jersey Nets			
☐ 319 Lionel Simmons ART	.05	.02	.01
Sacramento Kings			
☐ 320 Dennis Scott ART	.05	.02	.01
Orlando Magic			
☐ 321 Kendall Gill ART	.05	.02	.01
Charlotte Hornets			
☐ 322 Dee Brown ART	.08	.04	.01
Boston Celtics			
☐ 323 Magic Johnson	.25	.11	.03
GQ All-Star Style Team			
☐ 324 Hakeem Olajuwon	.40	.18	.05
GQ All-Star Style Team			
☐ 325 Kevin Willis	.10	.05	.01
Dominique Wilkins			
GQ All-Star Style Team			
☐ 326 Kevin Willis	.10	.05	.01
Dominique Wilkins			
GQ All-Star Style Team			
☐ 327 Gerald Wilkins	.05	.02	.01
GQ All-Star Style Team			
☐ 328 1891-1991 Basketball	.05	.02	.01
Centennial Logo			
☐ 329 Old-Fashioned Ball	.05	.02	.01
☐ 330 Women Take the Court	.05	.02	.01
☐ 331 The Peach Basket	.05	.02	.01
☐ 332 James A. Naismith	.10	.05	.01
Founder of Basketball			
☐ 333 Magic Johnson	1.00	.45	.13
and Michael Jordan			
Great Moments from			
the NBA Finals			
☐ 334 Michael Jordan	1.25	.55	.16
Chicago Bulls			
Great Moments from			
the NBA Finals			
☐ 335 Vlade Divac	.08	.04	.01
Los Angeles Lakers			
Great Moments from			
the NBA Finals			

☐ 336 John Paxson	.05	.02	.01
Chicago Bulls			
Great Moments from			
the NBA Finals			
☐ 337 Bulls Starting Five	.15	.07	.02
Great Moments from			
the NBA Finals			
☐ 338 Language Arts	.05	.02	.01
Stay in School			
☐ 339 Mathematics	.05	.02	.01
Stay in School			
☐ 340 Vocational Education	.05	.02	.01
Stay in School			
☐ 341 Social Studies	.05	.02	.01
Stay in School			
☐ 342 Physical Education	.05	.02	.01
Stay in School			
☐ 343 Art	.05	.02	.01
Stay in School			
☐ 344 Science	.05	.02	.01
Stay in School			
☐ 345 Checklist 1 (1-60)	.05	.02	.01
☐ 346 Checklist 2 (61-120)	.05	.02	.01
☐ 347 Checklist 3 (121-180)	.05	.02	.01
☐ 348 Checklist 4 (181-244)	.05	.02	.01
☐ 349 Checklist 5 (245-305)	.05	.02	.01
☐ 350 Checklist 6 (306-350)	.05	.02	.01
☐ 351 Atlanta Hawks	.05	.02	.01
Team Logo			
☐ 352 Boston Celtics	.05	.02	.01
Team Logo			
☐ 353 Charlotte Hornets	.05	.02	.01
Team Logo			
☐ 354 Chicago Bulls	.05	.02	.01
Team Logo			
☐ 355 Cleveland Cavaliers	.05	.02	.01
Team Logo			
☐ 356 Dallas Mavericks	.05	.02	.01
Team Logo			
☐ 357 Denver Nuggets	.05	.02	.01
Team Logo			
☐ 358 Detroit Pistons	.05	.02	.01
Team Logo			
☐ 359 Golden State Warriors	.05	.02	.01
Team Logo			
☐ 360 Houston Rockets	.05	.02	.01
Team Logo			
☐ 361 Indiana Pacers	.05	.02	.01
Team Logo			
☐ 362 Los Angeles Clippers	.05	.02	.01
Team Logo			
☐ 363 Los Angeles Lakers	.05	.02	.01
Team Logo			
☐ 364 Miami Heat	.05	.02	.01
Team Logo			
☐ 365 Milwaukee Bucks	.05	.02	.01
Team Logo			
☐ 366 Minnesota Timberwolves	.05	.02	.01
Team Logo			
☐ 367 New Jersey Nets	.05	.02	.01
Team Logo			
☐ 368 New York Knicks	.05	.02	.01
Team Logo			
☐ 369 Orlando Magic	.05	.02	.01
Team Logo			
☐ 370 Philadelphia 76ers	.05	.02	.01
Team Logo			
☐ 371 Phoenix Suns	.05	.02	.01
Team Logo			
☐ 372 Portland Trail Blazers	.05	.02	.01
Team Logo			
☐ 373 Sacramento Kings	.05	.02	.01
Team Logo			

☐ 374 San Antonio Spurs	.05	.02	.01
Team Logo			
☐ 375 Seattle Supersonics	.05	.02	.01
Team Logo			
☐ 376 Utah Jazz	.05	.02	.01
Team Logo			
☐ 377 Washington Bullets	.05	.02	.01
Team Logo			
☐ 378 Bob Weiss CO	.05	.02	.01
Atlanta Hawks			
☐ 379 Chris Ford CO	.05	.02	.01
Boston Celtics			
☐ 380 Allan Bristow CO	.05	.02	.01
Charlotte Hornets			
☐ 381 Phil Jackson CO	.08	.04	.01
Chicago Bulls			
☐ 382 Lenny Wilkens CO	.08	.04	.01
Cleveland Cavaliers			
☐ 383 Richie Adubato CO	.05	.02	.01
Dallas Mavericks			
☐ 384 Paul Westhead CO	.05	.02	.01
Denver Nuggets			
☐ 385 Chuck Daly CO	.08	.04	.01
Detroit Pistons			
☐ 386 Don Nelson CO	.08	.04	.01
Golden State Warriors			
☐ 387 Don Chaney CO	.08	.04	.01
Houston Rockets			
☐ 388 Bob Hill CO	.05	.02	.01
Indiana Pacers			
☐ 389 Mike Schuler CO	.05	.02	.01
Los Angeles Clippers			
☐ 390 Mike Dunleavy CO	.05	.02	.01
Los Angeles Lakers			
☐ 391 Kevin Loughery CO	.05	.02	.01
Miami Heat			
☐ 392 Del Harris CO	.05	.02	.01
Milwaukee Bucks			
☐ 393 Jimmy Rodgers CO	.05	.02	.01
Minnesota Timberwolves			
☐ 394 Bill Fitch CO	.05	.02	.01
New Jersey Nets			
☐ 395 Pat Riley CO	.08	.04	.01
New York Knicks			
☐ 396 Matt Guokas CO	.05	.02	.01
Orlando Magic			
☐ 397 Jim Lynam CO	.05	.02	.01
Philadelphia 76ers			
☐ 398 Cotton Fitzsimmons CO	.05	.02	.01
Phoenix Suns			
☐ 399 Rick Adelman CO	.08	.04	.01
Portland Trail Blazers			
☐ 400 Dick Motta CO	.05	.02	.01
Sacramento Kings			
☐ 401 Larry Brown CO	.08	.04	.01
San Antonio Spurs			
☐ 402 K.C. Jones CO	.08	.04	.01
Seattle Supersonics			
☐ 403 Jerry Sloan CO	.05	.02	.01
Utah Jazz			
☐ 404 Wes Unseld CO	.08	.04	.01
Washington Bullets			
☐ 405 Atlanta Hawks	.05	.02	.01
Game Frame (Mo Cheeks drives around pick)			
☐ 406 Boston Celtics	.05	.02	.01
Game Frame (Dee Brown drives and shoots)			
☐ 407 Charlotte Hornets	.05	.02	.01
Game Frame (Rex Chapman dunking)			

☐ 408	Chicago Bulls 1.25 Game Frame (Michael Jordan swipes Reggie Lewis)	.55	.16
☐ 409	Cleveland Cavaliers .05 Game Frame (John Williams ties up Eddie Lee Wilkins)	.02	.01
☐ 410	Dallas Mavericks .05 Game Frame (James Donaldson block)	.02	.01
☐ 411	Denver Nuggets .40 Game Frame (Dikembe Mutombo blocking Kenny Smith)	.18	.05
☐ 412	Detroit Pistons .10 Game Frame (Isiah Thomas)	.05	.01
☐ 413	Golden State Warriors .10 Game Frame (Tim Hardaway and Magic Johnson)	.05	.01
☐ 414	Houston Rockets .40 Game Frame (Hakeem Olajuwon sets pick)	.18	.05
☐ 415	Indiana Pacers .05 Game Frame (Detlef Schrempf block)	.02	.01
☐ 416	Los Angeles Clippers .05 Game Frame (Danny Manning sets pick)	.02	.01
☐ 417	Los Angeles Lakers .25 Game Frame (Magic Johnson no-look pass)	.11	.03
☐ 418	Miami Heat .05 Game Frame (Bimbo Coles rebounds)	.02	.01
☐ 419	Milwaukee Bucks .05 Game Frame (Alvin Robertson rebounds)	.02	.01
☐ 420	Minnesota Timberwolves .05 Game Frame (Sam Mitchell drives)	.02	.01
☐ 421	New Jersey Nets .05 Game Frame (Sam Bowie blocking Mark Eaton's shot)	.02	.01
☐ 422	New York Knicks .05 Game Frame (Mark Jackson dribbles between legs)	.02	.01
☐ 423	Orlando Magic .05 Game Frame	.02	.01
☐ 424	Philadelphia 76ers .20 Game Frame (Charles Barkley in rebounding position)	.09	.03
☐ 425	Phoenix Suns .05 Game Frame (Dan Majerle drives)	.02	.01
☐ 426	Portland Trail Blazers .05 Game Frame (Robert Pack drives)	.02	.01
☐ 427	Sacramento Kings .05 Game Frame (Wayman Tisdale drives)	.02	.01
☐ 428	San Antonio Spurs .30 Game Frame (David Robinson scoop)	.14	.04

☐ 429	Seattle Supersonics Game Frame (Nate McMillan protecting ball)	.05	.02	.01
☐ 430	Utah Jazz Game Frame (Karl Malone blocks out)	.15	.07	.02
☐ 431	Washington Bullets Game Frame (Michael Adams drives)	.05	.02	.01
☐ 432	Duane Ferrell 6M Atlanta Hawks	.05	.02	.01
☐ 433	Kevin McHale 6M Boston Celtics	.08	.04	.01
☐ 434	Dell Curry 6M Charlotte Hornets	.05	.02	.01
☐ 435	B.J. Armstrong 6M Chicago Bulls	.10	.05	.01
☐ 436	John Williams 6M Cleveland Cavaliers	.05	.02	.01
☐ 437	Brad Davis 6M Dallas Mavericks	.05	.02	.01
☐ 438	Marcus Liberty 6M Denver Nuggets	.05	.02	.01
☐ 439	Mark Aguirre 6M Detroit Pistons	.08	.04	.01
☐ 440	Rod Higgins 6M Golden State Warriors	.05	.02	.01
☐ 441	Eric(Sleepy) Floyd 6M Houston Rockets	.05	.02	.01
☐ 442	Detlef Schrempf 6M Indiana Pacers	.08	.04	.01
☐ 443	Loy Vaught 6M Los Angeles Clippers	.05	.02	.01
☐ 444	Terry Teagle 6M Los Angeles Lakers	.05	.02	.01
☐ 445	Kevin Edwards 6M Miami Heat	.05	.02	.01
☐ 446	Dale Ellis 6M Milwaukee Bucks	.05	.02	.01
☐ 447	Tod Murphy 6M Minnesota Timberwolves	.05	.02	.01
☐ 448	Chris Dudley 6M New Jersey Nets	.05	.02	.01
☐ 449	Mark Jackson 6M New York Knicks	.05	.02	.01
☐ 450	Jerry Reynolds 6M Orlando Magic	.05	.02	.01
☐ 451	Ron Anderson 6M Philadelphia 76ers	.05	.02	.01
☐ 452	Dan Majerle 6M Phoenix Suns	.08	.04	.01
☐ 453	Danny Ainge 6M Portland Trail Blazers	.10	.05	.01
☐ 454	Jim Les 6M Sacramento Kings	.05	.02	.01
☐ 455	Paul Pressey 6M San Antonio Spurs	.05	.02	.01
☐ 456	Ricky Pierce 6M Seattle Supersonics	.05	.02	.01
☐ 457	Mike Brown 6M Utah Jazz	.05	.02	.01
☐ 458	Ledell Eackles 6M Washington Bullets	.05	.02	.01
☐ 459	Atlanta Hawks Teamwork (Dominique Wilkins and Kevin Willis)	.10	.05	.01
☐ 460	Boston Celtics Teamwork (Larry Bird and Robert Parish)	.25	.11	.03

- [ ] 461 Charlotte Hornets .... .05 .02 .01
  Teamwork
  (Rex Chapman and
  Kendall Gill)
- [ ] 462 Chicago Bulls .... .75 .35 .09
  Teamwork
  (Michael Jordan and
  Scottie Pippen)
- [ ] 463 Cleveland Cavaliers .... .05 .02 .01
  Teamwork
  (Craig Ehlo and
  Mark Price)
- [ ] 464 Dallas Mavericks .... .05 .02 .01
  Teamwork
  (Derek Harper and
  Rolando Blackman)
- [ ] 465 Denver Nuggets .... .05 .02 .01
  Teamwork
  (Reggie Williams and
  Chris Jackson)
- [ ] 466 Detroit Pistons .... .10 .05 .01
  Teamwork
  (Isiah Thomas and
  Bill Laimbeer)
- [ ] 467 Golden State Warriors .... .15 .07 .02
  Teamwork
  (Tim Hardaway and
  Chris Mullin)
- [ ] 468 Houston Rockets .... .05 .02 .01
  Teamwork
  (Vernon Maxwell and
  Kenny Smith)
- [ ] 469 Indiana Pacers .... .10 .05 .01
  Teamwork
  (Detlef Schrempf and
  Reggie Miller)
- [ ] 470 Los Angeles Clippers .... .05 .02 .01
  Teamwork
  (Charles Smith and
  Danny Manning)
- [ ] 471 Los Angeles Lakers .... .20 .09 .03
  Teamwork
  (Magic Johnson and
  James Worthy)
- [ ] 472 Miami Heat .... .05 .02 .01
  Teamwork
  (Glen Rice and
  Rony Seikaly)
- [ ] 473 Milwaukee Bucks .... .05 .02 .01
  Teamwork
  (Jay Humphries and
  Alvin Robertson)
- [ ] 474 Minnesota Timberwolves .... .05 .02 .01
  Teamwork
  (Tony Campbell and
  Pooh Richardson)
- [ ] 475 New Jersey Nets .... .15 .07 .02
  Teamwork
  (Derrick Coleman and
  Sam Bowie)
- [ ] 476 New York Knicks .... .12 .05 .02
  Teamwork
  (Patrick Ewing and
  Charles Oakley)
- [ ] 477 Orlando Magic .... .05 .02 .01
  Teamwork
  (Dennis Scott and
  Scott Skiles)
- [ ] 478 Philadelphia 76ers .... .15 .07 .02
  Teamwork
  (Charles Barkley and
  Hersey Hawkins)
- [ ] 479 Phoenix Suns .... .10 .05 .01

	Teamwork (Kevin Johnson and Tom Chambers)		
☐ 480	Portland Trail Blazers .10	.05	.01
	Teamwork (Clyde Drexler and Terry Porter)		
☐ 481	Sacramento Kings .05	.02	.01
	Teamwork (Lionel Simmons and Wayman Tisdale)		
☐ 482	San Antonio Spurs .05	.02	.01
	Teamwork (Terry Cummings and Sean Elliott)		
☐ 483	Seattle Supersonics .05	.02	.01
	Teamwork (Eddie Johnson and Ricky Pierce)		
☐ 484	Utah Jazz .15	.07	.02
	Teamwork (Karl Malone and John Stockton)		
☐ 485	Washington Bullets .05	.02	.01
	Teamwork (Harvey Grant and Bernard King)		
☐ 486	Rumeal Robinson RS .06	.03	.01
	Atlanta Hawks		
☐ 487	Dee Brown RS .08	.04	.01
	Boston Celtics		
☐ 488	Kendall Gill RS .06	.03	.01
	Charlotte Hornets		
☐ 489	B.J. Armstrong RS .10	.05	.01
	Chicago Bulls		
☐ 490	Danny Ferry RS .06	.03	.01
	Cleveland Cavaliers		
☐ 491	Randy White RS .06	.03	.01
	Dallas Mavericks		
☐ 492	Chris Jackson RS .08	.04	.01
	Denver Nuggets		
☐ 493	Lance Blanks RS .06	.03	.01
	Detroit Pistons		
☐ 494	Tim Hardaway RS .10	.05	.01
	Golden State Warriors		
☐ 495	Vernon Maxwell RS .08	.04	.01
	Houston Rockets		
☐ 496	Micheal Williams RS .06	.03	.01
	Indiana Pacers		
☐ 497	Charles Smith RS .06	.03	.01
	Los Angeles Clippers		
☐ 498	Vlade Divac RS .06	.03	.01
	Los Angeles Lakers		
☐ 499	Willie Burton RS .06	.03	.01
	Miami Heat		
☐ 500	Jeff Grayer RS .06	.03	.01
	Milwaukee Bucks		
☐ 501	Pooh Richardson RS .06	.03	.01
	Minnesota Timberwolves		
☐ 502	Derrick Coleman RS .20	.09	.03
	New Jersey Nets		
☐ 503	John Starks RS .25	.11	.03
	New York Knicks		
☐ 504	Dennis Scott RS .06	.03	.01
	Orlando Magic		
☐ 505	Hersey Hawkins RS .08	.04	.01
	Philadelphia 76ers		
☐ 506	Negele Knight RS .06	.03	.01
	Phoenix Suns		
☐ 507	Cliff Robinson RS .10	.05	.01
	Portland Trail Blazers		
☐ 508	Lionel Simmons RS .06	.03	.01
	Sacramento Kings		

☐ 509	David Robinson RS	.30	.14	.04
	San Antonio Spurs			
☐ 510	Gary Payton RS	.10	.05	.01
	Seattle Supersonics			
☐ 511	Blue Edwards RS	.06	.03	.01
	Utah Jazz			
☐ 512	Harvey Grant RS	.06	.03	.01
	Washington Bullets			
☐ 513	Larry Johnson	4.00	1.80	.50
	Charlotte Hornets			
☐ 514	Kenny Anderson	1.50	.65	.19
	New Jersey Nets			
☐ 515	Billy Owens	.75	.35	.09
	Golden State Warriors			
☐ 516	Dikembe Mutombo	1.50	.65	.19
	Denver Nuggets			
☐ 517	Steve Smith	1.00	.45	.13
	Miami Heat			
☐ 518	Doug Smith	.30	.14	.04
	Dallas Mavericks			
☐ 519	Luc Longley	.20	.09	.03
	Minnesota Timberwolves			
☐ 520	Mark Macon	.12	.05	.02
	Denver Nuggets			
☐ 521	Stacey Augmon	.75	.35	.09
	Atlanta Hawks			
☐ 522	Brian Williams	.30	.14	.04
	Orlando Magic			
☐ 523	Terrell Brandon	.30	.14	.04
	Cleveland Cavaliers			
☐ 524	The Ball	.05	.02	.01
☐ 525	The Basket	.05	.02	.01
☐ 526	The 24-second Shot	.05	.02	.01
	Clock			
☐ 527	The Game Program	.05	.02	.01
☐ 528	The Championship Gift	.05	.02	.01
☐ 529	Championship Trophy	.05	.02	.01
☐ 530	Charles Barkley USA	1.00	.45	.13
☐ 531	Larry Bird USA	1.50	.65	.19
☐ 532	Patrick Ewing USA	.75	.35	.09
☐ 533	Magic Johnson USA	1.00	.45	.13
☐ 534	Michael Jordan USA	4.00	1.80	.50
☐ 535	Karl Malone USA	.50	.23	.06
☐ 536	Chris Mullin USA	.40	.18	.05
☐ 537	Scottie Pippen USA	.75	.35	.09
☐ 538	David Robinson USA	1.25	.55	.16
☐ 539	John Stockton USA	.40	.18	.05
☐ 540	Chuck Daly CO USA	.10	.05	.01
☐ 541	P.J. Carlesimo CO USA	.25	.11	.03
☐ 542	Mike Krzyzewski CO USA	1.00	.45	.13
☐ 543	Lenny Wilkens CO USA	.12	.05	.02
☐ 544	Team USA Card 1	1.50	.65	.19
☐ 545	Team USA Card 2	1.50	.65	.19
☐ 546	Team USA Card 3	1.50	.65	.19
☐ 547	Willie Anderson USA	.10	.05	.01
☐ 548	Stacey Augmon USA	.30	.14	.04
☐ 549	Bimbo Coles USA	.10	.05	.01
☐ 550	Jeff Grayer USA	.10	.05	.01
☐ 551	Hersey Hawkins USA	.12	.05	.02
☐ 552	Dan Majerle USA	.12	.05	.02
☐ 553	Danny Manning USA	.12	.05	.02
☐ 554	J.R. Reid USA	.10	.05	.01
☐ 555	Mitch Richmond USA	.12	.05	.02
☐ 556	Charles Smith USA	.12	.05	.02
☐ 557	Vern Fleming USA	.10	.05	.01
☐ 558	Joe Kleine USA	.10	.05	.01
☐ 559	Jon Koncak USA	.10	.05	.01
☐ 560	Sam Perkins USA	.12	.05	.02
☐ 561	Alvin Robertson USA	.12	.05	.02
☐ 562	Wayman Tisdale USA	.12	.05	.02
☐ 563	Jeff Turner USA	.10	.05	.01
☐ 564	Tony Campbell	.05	.02	.01
	Minnesota Timberwolves			

		Magic of SkyBox			
☐	565	Joe Dumars	.08	.04	.01
		Detroit Pistons			
		Magic of SkyBox			
☐	566	Horace Grant	.10	.05	.01
		Chicago Bulls			
		Magic of SkyBox			
☐	567	Reggie Lewis	.08	.04	.01
		Boston Celtics			
		Magic of SkyBox			
☐	568	Hakeem Olajuwon	.40	.18	.05
		Houston Rockets			
		Magic of SkyBox			
☐	569	Sam Perkins	.08	.04	.01
		Los Angeles Lakers			
		Magic of SkyBox			
☐	570	Chuck Person	.08	.04	.01
		Indiana Pacers			
		Magic of SkyBox			
☐	571	Buck Williams	.10	.05	.01
		Portland Trail Blazers			
		Magic of SkyBox			
☐	572	Michael Jordan	1.25	.55	.16
		Chicago Bulls			
		SkyBox Salutes			
☐	573	Bernard King	.08	.04	.01
		NBA All-Star			
		SkyBox Salutes			
☐	574	Moses Malone	.08	.04	.01
		Milwaukee Bucks			
		SkyBox Salutes			
☐	575	Robert Parish	.08	.04	.01
		Boston Celtics			
		SkyBox Salutes			
☐	576	Pat Riley CO	.08	.04	.01
		Los Angeles Lakers			
		SkyBox Salutes			
☐	577	Dee Brown	.08	.04	.01
		Boston Celtics			
		SkyMaster			
☐	578	Rex Chapman	.05	.02	.01
		Charlotte Hornets			
		SkyMaster			
☐	579	Clyde Drexler	.10	.05	.01
		Portland Trail Blazers			
		SkyMaster			
☐	580	Blue Edwards	.05	.02	.01
		Utah Jazz			
		SkyMaster			
☐	581	Ron Harper	.08	.04	.01
		Los Angeles Clippers			
		SkyMaster			
☐	582	Kevin Johnson	.10	.05	.01
		Phoenix Suns			
		SkyMaster			
☐	583	Michael Jordan	1.25	.55	.16
		Chicago Bulls			
		SkyMaster			
☐	584	Shawn Kemp	.50	.23	.06
		Seattle Supersonics			
		SkyMaster			
☐	585	Xavier McDaniel	.08	.04	.01
		New York Knicks			
		SkyMaster			
☐	586	Scottie Pippen	.15	.07	.02
		Chicago Bulls			
		SkyMaster			
☐	587	Kenny Smith	.05	.02	.01
		Houston Rockets			
		SkyMaster			
☐	588	Dominique Wilkins	.12	.05	.02
		Atlanta Hawks			
		SkyMaster			

☐ 589	Michael Adams Denver Nuggets Shooting Star	.05	.02	.01
☐ 590	Danny Ainge Denver Nuggets Shooting Star	.10	.05	.01
☐ 591	Larry Bird Boston Celtics Shooting Star	.40	.18	.05
☐ 592	Dale Ellis Milwaukee Bucks Shooting Star	.05	.02	.01
☐ 593	Hersey Hawkins Philadelphia 76ers Shooting Star	.08	.04	.01
☐ 594	Jeff Hornacek Phoenix Suns Shooting Star	.10	.05	.01
☐ 595	Jeff Malone Utah Jazz Shooting Star	.08	.04	.01
☐ 596	Reggie Miller Indiana Pacers Shooting Star	.10	.05	.01
☐ 597	Chris Mullin Golden State Warriors Shooting Star	.10	.05	.01
☐ 598	John Paxson Chicago Bulls Shooting Star	.05	.02	.01
☐ 599	Drazen Petrovic New Jersey Nets Shooting Star	.08	.04	.01
☐ 600	Ricky Pierce Milwaukee Bucks Shooting Star	.08	.04	.01
☐ 601	Mark Price Cleveland Cavaliers Shooting Star	.08	.04	.01
☐ 602	Dennis Scott Orlando Magic Shooting Star	.05	.02	.01
☐ 603	Manute Bol Philadelphia 76ers Small School Sensation	.05	.02	.01
☐ 604	Jerome Kersey Portland Trail Blazers Small School Sensation	.05	.02	.01
☐ 605	Charles Oakley New York Knicks Small School Sensation	.10	.05	.01
☐ 606	Scottie Pippen Chicago Bulls Small School Sensation	.15	.07	.02
☐ 607	Terry Porter Portland Trail Blazers Small School Sensation	.08	.04	.01
☐ 608	Dennis Rodman Detroit Pistons Small School Sensation	.05	.02	.01
☐ 609	Sedale Threatt Los Angeles Lakers Small School Sensation	.05	.02	.01
☐ 610	Business Stay in School	.05	.02	.01
☐ 611	Engineering Stay in School	.05	.02	.01
☐ 612	Law Stay in School	.05	.02	.01
☐ 613	Liberal Arts Stay in School	.05	.02	.01
☐ 614	Medicine Stay in School	.05	.02	.01

☐ 615 Maurice Cheeks	.10	.05	.01
Atlanta Hawks			
☐ 616 Travis Mays	.05	.02	.01
Atlanta Hawks			
☐ 617 Blair Rasmussen	.05	.02	.01
Atlanta Hawks			
☐ 618 Alexander Volkov	.05	.02	.01
Atlanta Hawks			
☐ 619 Rickey Green	.05	.02	.01
Boston Celtics			
☐ 620 Bobby Hansen	.05	.02	.01
Chicago Bulls			
☐ 621 John Battle	.05	.02	.01
Cleveland Cavaliers			
☐ 622 Terry Davis	.05	.02	.01
Dallas Mavericks			
☐ 623 Walter Davis	.10	.05	.01
Denver Nuggets			
☐ 624 Winston Garland	.05	.02	.01
Denver Nuggets			
☐ 625 Scott Hastings	.05	.02	.01
Denver Nuggets			
☐ 626 Brad Sellers	.05	.02	.01
Denver Nuggets			
☐ 627 Darrell Walker	.05	.02	.01
Detroit Pistons			
☐ 628 Orlando Woolridge	.08	.04	.01
Detroit Pistons			
☐ 629 Tony Brown	.05	.02	.01
Los Angeles Clippers			
☐ 630 James Edwards	.05	.02	.01
Los Angeles Clippers			
☐ 631 Doc Rivers	.08	.04	.01
Los Angeles Clippers			
☐ 632 Jack Haley	.05	.02	.01
Los Angeles Lakers			
☐ 633 Sedale Threatt	.05	.02	.01
Los Angeles Lakers			
☐ 634 Moses Malone	.10	.05	.01
Milwaukee Bucks			
☐ 635 Thurl Bailey	.05	.02	.01
Minnesota Timberwolves			
☐ 636 Rafael Addison	.05	.02	.01
New Jersey Nets			
☐ 637 Tim McCormick	.05	.02	.01
New York Knicks			
☐ 638 Xavier McDaniel	.10	.05	.01
New York Knicks			
☐ 639 Charles Shackleford	.05	.02	.01
Philadelphia 76ers			
☐ 640 Mitchell Wiggins	.05	.02	.01
Philadelphia 76ers			
☐ 641 Jerrod Mustaf	.05	.02	.01
Phoenix Suns			
☐ 642 Dennis Hopson	.05	.02	.01
Sacramento Kings			
☐ 643 Les Jepsen	.05	.02	.01
Sacramento Kings			
☐ 644 Mitch Richmond	.10	.05	.01
Sacramento Kings			
☐ 645 Dwayne Schintzius	.05	.02	.01
Sacramento Kings			
☐ 646 Spud Webb	.10	.05	.01
Sacramento Kings			
☐ 647 Jud Buechler	.05	.02	.01
San Antonio Spurs			
☐ 648 Antoine Carr	.05	.02	.01
San Antonio Spurs			
☐ 649 Tyrone Corbin	.05	.02	.01
Utah Jazz			
☐ 650 Michael Adams	.08	.04	.01
Washington Bullets			
☐ 651 Ralph Sampson	.08	.04	.01

	Washington Bullets				
☐ 652	Andre Turner	.05	.02	.01	
	Washington Bullets				
☐ 653	David Wingate	.05	.02	.01	
	Washington Bullets				
☐ 654	Checklist "S" (351-404)	.05	.02	.01	
☐ 655	Checklist "K" (405-458)	.05	.02	.01	
☐ 656	Checklist "Y" (459-512)	.05	.02	.01	
☐ 657	Checklist "B" (513-563)	.05	.02	.01	
☐ 658	Checklist "O" (564-614)	.05	.02	.01	
☐ 659	Checklist "X" (615-659)	.05	.02	.01	
☐ NNO	Clyde Drexler USA (Send-away)	50.00	23.00	6.25	
☐ NNO	Team USA Card	15.00	6.75	1.90	

1992-93 SkyBox

The complete 1992-93 SkyBox basketball set contains 413 cards, measuring the standard size (2 1/2" by 3 1/2"). The set was released in two series of 327 and 86 cards, respectively. Both series foil packs contained 12 cards each with 36 packs to a box; suggested retail price was 1.15 per pack. The new front design features computer-generated screens of color blended with full-bleed color action photos. The backs carry full-bleed nonaction close-up photos, overlayed by a column displaying complete statistics and a color stripe with a personal "bio-bit." The cards are checklisted below alphabetically according to and within teams as follows: Atlanta Hawks (1-9), Boston Celtics (10-18), Charlotte Hornets (19-27), Chicago Bulls (28-36), Cleveland Cavaliers (37-46), Dallas Mavericks (47-56), Denver Nuggets (57-65), Detroit Pistons (66-75), Golden State Warriors (76-84), Houston Rockets (85-93), Indiana Pacers (94-102), Los Angeles Clippers (103-112), Los Angeles Lakers (113-121), Miami Heat (122-131), Milwaukee Bucks (132-140), Minnesota Timberwolves (141-149), New Jersey Nets (150-159), New York Knicks (160-168), Orlando Magic (169-177), Philadelphia 76ers (178-187), Phoenix Suns (188-197), Portland Trail Blazers (198-207), Sacramento Kings (208-217), San Antonio Spurs (218-226), Seattle Supersonics (227-235), Utah Jazz (236-244), and Washington Bullets (245-254). Other cards featured include Coaches (255-281), Team Tix (282-308), 1992 NBA All-Star Weekend Highlights (309-313), 1992 NBA Finals (314-318), 1992 NBA All-Rookie Team (319), and Public Service (230-321). The set concludes with checklist cards (322-327). The cards are numbered on the back. Special gold-foil stamped cards of Magic Johnson and David Robinson, some personally autographed, were randomly inserted in first series foil packs. Versions of these Johnson and Robinson cards with silver light defraction foil were also produced and one of each accompanied the first 7,500 cases ordered exclusively by hobby accounts. According to SkyBox approximately one of every 36 packs contained either a Magic Johnson or David Robinson SP card. Four special insert sets, NBA First Round Draft Picks, School Ties, The David Robinson Flagship Series, and Thunder and Lightning, were randomly packed in second series 12-card foil packs. The "Head of the Class" mail-away card features the first six 1992 NBA draft picks. The card was made available to the first 20,000 fans through a mail-in offer for three wrappers from each series of 1992-93 SkyBox cards plus 3.25 for postage and handling. The horizontal front features three color, cut-out player photos against a black background. Three wide vertical stripes in shades of red and violet run behind the players. A gold bar near the bottom carries the phrase "Head of the Class 1992 Top NBA Draft Picks." The back features three player photos similar to the ones on the front. The background design is the same except the wide stripes are green, orange, and blue. A white bar at the lower right corner carries the serial number and production run (20,000). Cards of second series rookies have a gold seal in the other lower corner. In addition, the second series Draft Pick rookie cards were printed in shorter supply than the other cards in the second series set. Rookie Cards include Tom Gugliotta, Robert Horry, Christian Laettner, Don McLean, Harold Miner, Alonzo Mourning, Shaquille O'Neal, Clarence Weatherspoon and Walt Williams. Reported production quantities were approximately 15,000 20-box cases for the first series and 15,000 20-box cases for the second series.

	MINT	EXC	G-VG
COMPLETE SET (413)	55.00	25.00	7.00
COMPLETE SERIES 1 (327)	25.00	11.50	3.10
COMPLETE SERIES 2 (86)	30.00	13.50	3.80
COMMON PLAYER (1-327)	.05	.02	.01
COMMON PLAYER (328-413)	.05	.02	.01
☐ 1 Stacey Augmon	.10	.05	.01
☐ 2 Maurice Cheeks	.10	.05	.01
☐ 3 Duane Ferrell	.05	.02	.01
☐ 4 Paul Graham	.05	.02	.01
☐ 5 Jon Koncak	.05	.02	.01
☐ 6 Blair Rasmussen	.05	.02	.01
☐ 7 Rumeal Robinson	.05	.02	.01
☐ 8 Dominique Wilkins	.50	.23	.06
☐ 9 Kevin Willis	.08	.04	.01
☐ 10 Larry Bird	1.25	.55	.16
☐ 11 Dee Brown	.05	.02	.01
☐ 12 Sherman Douglas	.05	.02	.01
☐ 13 Rick Fox	.08	.04	.01
☐ 14 Kevin Gamble	.05	.02	.01
☐ 15 Reggie Lewis	.10	.05	.01
☐ 16 Kevin McHale	.10	.05	.01
☐ 17 Robert Parish	.05	.02	.01
☐ 18 Ed Pinckney	.05	.02	.01
☐ 19 Muggsy Bogues	.10	.05	.01
☐ 20 Dell Curry	.08	.04	.01
☐ 21 Kenny Gattison	.05	.02	.01
☐ 22 Kendall Gill	.08	.04	.01
☐ 23 Mike Gminski	.05	.02	.01
☐ 24 Tom Hammonds	.75	.35	.09
☐ 25 Larry Johnson	.05	.02	.01
☐ 26 Johnny Newman	.05	.02	.01
☐ 27 J.R. Reid	.05	.02	.01
☐ 28 B.J. Armstrong	.10	.05	.01
☐ 29 Bill Cartwright	.08	.04	.01
☐ 30 Horace Grant	.10	.05	.01
☐ 31 Michael Jordan	3.00	1.35	.40
☐ 32 Stacey King	.05	.02	.01
☐ 33 John Paxson	.08	.04	.01
☐ 34 Will Perdue	.05	.02	.01
☐ 35 Scottie Pippen	.60	.25	.08
☐ 36 Scott Williams	.05	.02	.01
☐ 37 John Battle	.05	.02	.01
☐ 38 Terrell Brandon	.05	.02	.01
☐ 39 Brad Daugherty	.10	.05	.01
☐ 40 Craig Ehlo	.05	.02	.01
☐ 41 Danny Ferry	.05	.02	.01
☐ 42 Henry James	.05	.02	.01
☐ 43 Larry Nance	.08	.04	.01
☐ 44 Mark Price	.10	.05	.01
☐ 45 Mike Sanders	.05	.02	.01
☐ 46 Hot Rod Williams	.05	.02	.01
☐ 47 Rolando Blackman	.08	.04	.01
☐ 48 Terry Davis	.05	.02	.01
☐ 49 Derek Harper	.08	.04	.01

☐ 50	Donald Hodge	.05	.02	.01
☐ 51	Mike Iuzzolino	.05	.02	.01
☐ 52	Fat Lever	.05	.02	.01
☐ 53	Rodney McCray	.05	.02	.01
☐ 54	Doug Smith	.05	.02	.01
☐ 55	Randy White	.05	.02	.01
☐ 56	Herb Williams	.05	.02	.01
☐ 57	Greg Anderson	.05	.02	.01
☐ 58	Walter Davis	.10	.05	.01
☐ 59	Winston Garland	.05	.02	.01
☐ 60	Chris Jackson	.08	.04	.01
☐ 61	Marcus Liberty	.05	.02	.01
☐ 62	Todd Lichti	.05	.02	.01
☐ 63	Mark Macon	.05	.02	.01
☐ 64	Dikembe Mutombo	.30	.14	.04
☐ 65	Reggie Williams	.08	.04	.01
☐ 66	Mark Aguirre	.10	.05	.01
☐ 67	William Bedford	.05	.02	.01
☐ 68	Lance Blanks	.05	.02	.01
☐ 69	Joe Dumars	.20	.09	.03
☐ 70	Bill Laimbeer	.10	.05	.01
☐ 71	Dennis Rodman	.08	.04	.01
☐ 72	John Salley	.05	.02	.01
☐ 73	Isiah Thomas	.20	.09	.03
☐ 74	Darrell Walker	.05	.02	.01
☐ 75	Orlando Woolridge	.08	.04	.01
☐ 76	Victor Alexander	.05	.02	.01
☐ 77	Mario Elie	.05	.02	.01
☐ 78	Chris Gatling	.05	.02	.01
☐ 79	Tim Hardaway	.10	.05	.01
☐ 80	Tyrone Hill	.05	.02	.01
☐ 81	Alton Lister	.05	.02	.01
☐ 82	Sarunas Marciulionis	.08	.04	.01
☐ 83	Chris Mullin	.20	.09	.03
☐ 84	Billy Owens	.10	.05	.01
☐ 85	Matt Bullard	.05	.02	.01
☐ 86	Sleepy Floyd	.05	.02	.01
☐ 87	Avery Johnson	.05	.02	.01
☐ 88	Buck Johnson	.05	.02	.01
☐ 89	Vernon Maxwell	.08	.04	.01
☐ 90	Hakeem Olajuwon	1.25	.55	.16
☐ 91	Kenny Smith	.05	.02	.01
☐ 92	Larry Smith	.08	.04	.01
☐ 93	Otis Thorpe	.08	.04	.01
☐ 94	Dale Davis	.08	.04	.01
☐ 95	Vern Fleming	.05	.02	.01
☐ 96	George McCloud	.05	.02	.01
☐ 97	Reggie Miller	.25	.11	.03
☐ 98	Chuck Person	.08	.04	.01
☐ 99	Detlef Schrempf	.10	.05	.01
☐ 100	Rik Smits	.08	.04	.01
☐ 101	LaSalle Thompson	.08	.04	.01
☐ 102	Micheal Williams	.08	.04	.01
☐ 103	James Edwards	.05	.02	.01
☐ 104	Gary Grant	.05	.02	.01
☐ 105	Ron Harper	.08	.04	.01
☐ 106	Bo Kimble	.05	.02	.01
☐ 107	Danny Manning	.20	.09	.03
☐ 108	Ken Norman	.05	.02	.01
☐ 109	Olden Polynice	.05	.02	.01
☐ 110	Doc Rivers	.08	.04	.01
☐ 111	Charles Smith	.05	.02	.01
☐ 112	Loy Vaught	.08	.04	.01
☐ 113	Elden Campbell	.05	.02	.01
☐ 114	Vlade Divac	.08	.04	.01
☐ 115	A.C. Green	.08	.04	.01
☐ 116	Jack Haley	.05	.02	.01
☐ 117	Sam Perkins	.08	.04	.01
☐ 118	Byron Scott	.08	.04	.01
☐ 119	Tony Smith	.05	.02	.01
☐ 120	Sedale Threatt	.05	.02	.01
☐ 121	James Worthy	.10	.05	.01
☐ 122	Keith Askins	.05	.02	.01

☐ 123	Willie Burton	.05	.02	.01
☐ 124	Bimbo Coles	.05	.02	.01
☐ 125	Kevin Edwards	.05	.02	.01
☐ 126	Alec Kessler	.05	.02	.01
☐ 127	Grant Long	.05	.02	.01
☐ 128	Glen Rice	.10	.05	.01
☐ 129	Rony Seikaly	.10	.05	.01
☐ 130	Brian Shaw	.05	.02	.01
☐ 131	Steve Smith	.25	.11	.03
☐ 132	Frank Brickowski	.08	.04	.01
☐ 133	Dale Ellis	.08	.04	.01
☐ 134	Jeff Grayer	.05	.02	.01
☐ 135	Jay Humphries	.05	.02	.01
☐ 136	Larry Krystkowiak	.05	.02	.01
☐ 137	Moses Malone	.10	.05	.01
☐ 138	Fred Roberts	.05	.02	.01
☐ 139	Alvin Robertson	.08	.04	.01
☐ 140	Dan Schayes	.05	.02	.01
☐ 141	Thurl Bailey	.05	.02	.01
☐ 142	Scott Brooks	.05	.02	.01
☐ 143	Tony Campbell	.05	.02	.01
☐ 144	Gerald Glass	.05	.02	.01
☐ 145	Luc Longley	.05	.02	.01
☐ 146	Sam Mitchell	.05	.02	.01
☐ 147	Pooh Richardson	.05	.02	.01
☐ 148	Felton Spencer	.05	.02	.01
☐ 149	Doug West	.05	.02	.01
☐ 150	Rafael Addison	.05	.02	.01
☐ 151	Kenny Anderson	.30	.14	.04
☐ 152	Mookie Blaylock	.08	.04	.01
☐ 153	Sam Bowie	.05	.02	.01
☐ 154	Derrick Coleman	.25	.11	.03
☐ 155	Chris Dudley	.05	.02	.01
☐ 156	Tate George	.05	.02	.01
☐ 157	Terry Mills	.10	.05	.01
☐ 158	Chris Morris	.05	.02	.01
☐ 159	Drazen Petrovic	.08	.04	.01
☐ 160	Greg Anthony	.05	.02	.01
☐ 161	Patrick Ewing	.60	.25	.08
☐ 162	Mark Jackson	.08	.04	.01
☐ 163	Anthony Mason	.08	.04	.01
☐ 164	Tim McCormick	.05	.02	.01
☐ 165	Xavier McDaniel	.08	.04	.01
☐ 166	Charles Oakley	.10	.05	.01
☐ 167	John Starks	.10	.05	.01
☐ 168	Gerald Wilkins	.05	.02	.01
☐ 169	Nick Anderson	.08	.04	.01
☐ 170	Terry Catledge	.05	.02	.01
☐ 171	Jerry Reynolds	.05	.02	.01
☐ 172	Stanley Roberts	.05	.02	.01
☐ 173	Dennis Scott	.08	.04	.01
☐ 174	Scott Skiles	.08	.04	.01
☐ 175	Jeff Turner	.05	.02	.01
☐ 176	Sam Vincent	.05	.02	.01
☐ 177	Brian Williams	.05	.02	.01
☐ 178	Ron Anderson	.05	.02	.01
☐ 179	Charles Barkley	.75	.35	.09
☐ 180	Manute Bol	.05	.02	.01
☐ 181	Johnny Dawkins	.05	.02	.01
☐ 182	Armon Gilliam	.05	.02	.01
☐ 183	Greg Grant	.05	.02	.01
☐ 184	Hersey Hawkins	.08	.04	.01
☐ 185	Brian Oliver	.05	.02	.01
☐ 186	Charles Shackleford	.05	.02	.01
☐ 187	Jayson Williams	.05	.02	.01
☐ 188	Cedric Ceballos	.10	.05	.01
☐ 189	Tom Chambers	.08	.04	.01
☐ 190	Jeff Hornacek	.08	.04	.01
☐ 191	Kevin Johnson	.10	.05	.01
☐ 192	Negele Knight	.05	.02	.01
☐ 193	Andrew Lang	.05	.02	.01
☐ 194	Dan Majerle	.10	.05	.01
☐ 195	Jerrod Mustaf	.05	.02	.01

☐ 196	Tim Perry	.05	.02	.01
☐ 197	Mark West	.05	.02	.01
☐ 198	Alaa Abdelnaby	.05	.02	.01
☐ 199	Danny Ainge	.10	.05	.01
☐ 200	Mark Bryant	.05	.02	.01
☐ 201	Clyde Drexler	.25	.11	.03
☐ 202	Kevin Duckworth	.05	.02	.01
☐ 203	Jerome Kersey	.05	.02	.01
☐ 204	Robert Pack	.05	.02	.01
☐ 205	Terry Porter	.08	.04	.01
☐ 206	Cliff Robinson	.10	.05	.01
☐ 207	Buck Williams	.10	.05	.01
☐ 208	Anthony Bonner	.05	.02	.01
☐ 209	Randy Brown	.05	.02	.01
☐ 210	Duane Causwell	.05	.02	.01
☐ 211	Pete Chilcutt	.05	.02	.01
☐ 212	Dennis Hopson	.05	.02	.01
☐ 213	Jim Les	.05	.02	.01
☐ 214	Mitch Richmond	.10	.05	.01
☐ 215	Lionel Simmons	.08	.04	.01
☐ 216	Wayman Tisdale	.08	.04	.01
☐ 217	Spud Webb	.10	.05	.01
☐ 218	Willie Anderson	.05	.02	.01
☐ 219	Antoine Carr	.05	.02	.01
☐ 220	Terry Cummings	.08	.04	.01
☐ 221	Sean Elliott	.08	.04	.01
☐ 222	Sidney Green	.05	.02	.01
☐ 223	Vinnie Johnson	.08	.04	.01
☐ 224	David Robinson	.75	.35	.09
☐ 225	Rod Strickland	.08	.04	.01
☐ 226	Greg Sutton	.05	.02	.01
☐ 227	Dana Barros	.05	.02	.01
☐ 228	Benoit Benjamin	.05	.02	.01
☐ 229	Michael Cage	.05	.02	.01
☐ 230	Eddie Johnson	.05	.02	.01
☐ 231	Shawn Kemp	1.25	.55	.16
☐ 232	Derrick McKey	.05	.02	.01
☐ 233	Nate McMillan	.05	.02	.01
☐ 234	Gary Payton	.10	.05	.01
☐ 235	Ricky Pierce	.08	.04	.01
☐ 236	David Benoit	.05	.02	.01
☐ 237	Mike Brown	.05	.02	.01
☐ 238	Tyrone Corbin	.05	.02	.01
☐ 239	Mark Eaton	.05	.02	.01
☐ 240	Blue Edwards	.08	.04	.01
☐ 241	Jeff Malone	.08	.04	.01
☐ 242	Karl Malone	.40	.18	.05
☐ 243	Eric Murdock	.08	.04	.01
☐ 244	John Stockton	.25	.11	.03
☐ 245	Michael Adams	.08	.04	.01
☐ 246	Rex Chapman	.05	.02	.01
☐ 247	Ledell Eackles	.05	.02	.01
☐ 248	Pervis Ellison	.05	.02	.01
☐ 249	A.J. English	.05	.02	.01
☐ 250	Harvey Grant	.05	.02	.01
☐ 251	Charles Jones	.05	.02	.01
☐ 252	Bernard King	.10	.05	.01
☐ 253	LaBradford Smith	.05	.02	.01
☐ 254	Larry Stewart	.05	.02	.01
☐ 255	Bob Weiss CO Atlanta Hawks	.05	.02	.01
☐ 256	Chris Ford CO Boston Celtics	.08	.04	.01
☐ 257	Allan Bristow CO Charlotte Hornets	.05	.02	.01
☐ 258	Phil Jackson CO Chicago Bulls	.08	.04	.01
☐ 259	Lenny Wilkens CO Cleveland Cavaliers	.08	.04	.01
☐ 260	Richie Adubato CO Dallas Mavericks	.05	.02	.01
☐ 261	Dan Issel CO Denver Nuggets	.08	.04	.01

☐ 262	Ron Rothstein CO	.05	.02	.01
	Detroit Pistons			
☐ 263	Don Nelson CO	.08	.04	.01
	Golden State Warriors			
☐ 264	Rudy Tomjanovich CO	.08	.04	.01
	Houston Rockets			
☐ 265	Bob Hill CO	.05	.02	.01
	Indiana Pacers			
☐ 266	Larry Brown CO	.08	.04	.01
	Los Angeles Clippers			
☐ 267	Randy Pfund CO	.05	.02	.01
	Los Angeles Lakers			
☐ 268	Kevin Loughery CO	.08	.04	.01
	Miami Heat			
☐ 269	Mike Dunleavy CO	.08	.04	.01
	Milwaukee Bucks			
☐ 270	Jimmy Rodgers CO	.05	.02	.01
	Minnesota Timberwolves			
☐ 271	Chuck Daly CO	.08	.04	.01
	New Jersey Nets			
☐ 272	Pat Riley CO	.08	.04	.01
	New York Knicks			
☐ 273	Matt Guokas CO	.05	.02	.01
	Orlando Magic			
☐ 274	Doug Moe CO	.05	.02	.01
	Philadelphia 76ers			
☐ 275	Paul Westphal CO	.08	.04	.01
	Phoenix Suns			
☐ 276	Rick Adelman CO	.05	.02	.01
	Portland Trail Blazers			
☐ 277	Garry St. Jean CO	.05	.02	.01
	Sacramento Kings			
☐ 278	Jerry Tarkanian CO	.25	.11	.03
	San Antonio Spurs			
☐ 279	George Karl CO	.05	.02	.01
	Seattle Supersonics			
☐ 280	Jerry Sloan CO	.05	.02	.01
	Utah Jazz			
☐ 281	Wes Unseld CO	.08	.04	.01
	Washington Bullets			
☐ 282	Dominique Wilkins TT	.25	.11	.03
	Atlanta Hawks			
☐ 283	Reggie Lewis TT	.10	.05	.01
	Boston Celtics			
☐ 284	Kendall Gill TT	.06	.03	.01
	Charlotte Hornets			
☐ 285	Horace Grant TT	.06	.03	.01
	Chicago Bulls			
☐ 286	Brad Daugherty TT	.10	.05	.01
	Cleveland Cavaliers			
☐ 287	Derek Harper TT	.06	.03	.01
	Dallas Mavericks			
☐ 288	Chris Jackson TT	.10	.05	.01
	Denver Nuggets			
☐ 289	Isiah Thomas TT	.10	.05	.01
	Detroit Pistons			
☐ 290	Chris Mullin TT	.10	.05	.01
	Golden State Warriors			
☐ 291	Kenny Smith TT	.06	.03	.01
	Houston Rockets			
☐ 292	Reggie Miller TT	.12	.05	.02
	Indiana Pacers			
☐ 293	Ron Harper TT	.06	.03	.01
	Los Angeles Clippers			
☐ 294	Vlade Divac TT	.06	.03	.01
	Los Angeles Lakers			
☐ 295	Glen Rice TT	.10	.05	.01
	Miami Heat			
☐ 296	Moses Malone TT	.10	.05	.01
	Milwaukee Bucks			
☐ 297	Doug West TT	.06	.03	.01
	Minnesota Timberwolves			
☐ 298	Derrick Coleman TT	.12	.05	.02

New Jersey Nets
- ☐ 299 Patrick Ewing TT ... .30 / .14 / .04
  (See also card 305)
  New York Knicks
- ☐ 300 Scott Skiles TT ... .06 / .03 / .01
  Orlando Magic
- ☐ 301 Hersey Hawkins TT ... .06 / .03 / .01
  Philadelphia 76ers
- ☐ 302 Kevin Johnson TT ... .10 / .05 / .01
  Phoenix Suns
- ☐ 303 Cliff Robinson TT ... .10 / .05 / .01
  Portland Trail Blazers
- ☐ 304 Anthony Webb TT ... .06 / .03 / .01
  Sacramento Kings
- ☐ 305A David Robinson TT ERR ... .40 / .18 / .05
  (Card misnumbered as 299)
  San Antonio Spurs
- ☐ 305B David Robinson TT COR ... .40 / .18 / .05
  San Antonio Spurs
- ☐ 306 Shawn Kemp TT ... .60 / .25 / .08
  Seattle Supersonics
- ☐ 307 John Stockton TT ... .12 / .05 / .02
  Utah Jazz
- ☐ 308 Pervis Ellison TT ... .06 / .03 / .01
  Washington Bullets
- ☐ 309 Craig Hodges ... .06 / .03 / .01
- ☐ 310 Magic Johnson A-S MVP ... .40 / .18 / .05
- ☐ 311 Cedric Ceballos ... .10 / .05 / .01
  Slam Dunk Champ
- ☐ 312 West in Action ... .06 / .03 / .01
- ☐ 313 East in Action ... .06 / .03 / .01
- ☐ 314 Michael Jordan MVP ... 1.50 / .65 / .19
- ☐ 315 Clyde Drexler ... .12 / .05 / .02
  NBA Finals
- ☐ 316 Western Conference ... .06 / .03 / .01
  Danny Ainge
- ☐ 317 Eastern Conference ... .30 / .14 / .04
  Scottie Pippen
- ☐ 318 NBA Champs ... .10 / .05 / .01
  Chicago Bulls
- ☐ 319 NBA Rookie of the Year ... .40 / .18 / .05
  All-Rookie Team
  Larry Johnson
  Dikembe Mutombo
- ☐ 320 NBA Stay in School ... .06 / .03 / .01
- ☐ 321 Boys and Girls ... .06 / .03 / .01
  Clubs of America
- ☐ 322 Checklist 1 ... .06 / .03 / .01
- ☐ 323 Checklist 2 ... .06 / .03 / .01
- ☐ 324 Checklist 3 ... .06 / .03 / .01
- ☐ 325 Checklist 4 ... .06 / .03 / .01
- ☐ 326 Checklist 5 ... .06 / .03 / .01
- ☐ 327 Checklist 6 ... .06 / .03 / .01
- ☐ 328 Adam Keefe ... .15 / .07 / .02
  Atlanta Hawks
- ☐ 329 Sean Rooks ... .25 / .11 / .03
  Dallas Mavericks
- ☐ 330 Xavier McDaniel ... .08 / .04 / .01
  Boston Celtics
- ☐ 331 Kiki Vandeweghe ... .08 / .04 / .01
  Los Angeles Clippers
- ☐ 332 Alonzo Mourning ... 6.00 / 2.70 / .75
  Charlotte Hornets
- ☐ 333 Rodney McCray ... .05 / .02 / .01
  Chicago Bulls
- ☐ 334 Gerald Wilkins ... .05 / .02 / .01
  Cleveland Cavaliers
- ☐ 335 Tony Bennett ... .20 / .09 / .03
  Charlotte Hornets
- ☐ 336 LaPhonso Ellis ... 1.25 / .55 / .16
  Denver Nuggets
- ☐ 337 Bryant Stith ... .60 / .25 / .08
  Denver Nuggets

☐ 338	Isaiah Morris ..... Detroit Pistons	.05	.02	.01
☐ 339	Olden Polynice ..... Detroit Pistons	.05	.02	.01
☐ 340	Jeff Grayer ..... Golden State Warriors	.05	.02	.01
☐ 341	Byron Houston ..... Golden State Warriors	.20	.09	.03
☐ 342	Latrell Sprewell ..... Golden State Warriors	4.00	1.80	.50
☐ 343	Scott Brooks ..... Houston Rockets	.05	.02	.01
☐ 344	Frank Johnson ..... Phoenix Suns	.08	.04	.01
☐ 345	Robert Horry ..... Houston Rockets	1.25	.55	.16
☐ 346	David Wood ..... San Antonio Spurs	.05	.02	.01
☐ 347	Sam Mitchell ..... Indiana Pacers	.05	.02	.01
☐ 348	Pooh Richardson ..... Indiana Pacers	.05	.02	.01
☐ 349	Malik Sealy ..... Indiana Pacers	.20	.09	.03
☐ 350	Morlon Wiley ..... Los Angeles Clippers	.05	.02	.01
☐ 351	Mark Jackson ..... Los Angeles Clippers	.08	.04	.01
☐ 352	Stanley Roberts ..... Los Angeles Clippers	.05	.02	.01
☐ 353	Elmore Spencer ..... Los Angeles Clippers	.25	.11	.03
☐ 354	John Williams ..... Los Angeles Clippers	.05	.02	.01
☐ 355	Randy Woods ..... Los Angeles Clippers	.05	.02	.01
☐ 356	James Edwards ..... Los Angeles Lakers	.05	.02	.01
☐ 357	Jeff Sanders ..... Atlanta Hawks	.05	.02	.01
☐ 358	Magic Johnson ..... Los Angeles Lakers	.40	.18	.05
☐ 359	Anthony Peeler ..... Los Angeles Lakers	.50	.23	.06
☐ 360	Harold Miner ..... Miami Heat	.60	.25	.08
☐ 361	John Salley ..... Miami Heat	.05	.02	.01
☐ 362	Alaa Abdelnaby ..... Milwaukee Bucks	.05	.02	.01
☐ 363	Todd Day ..... Milwaukee Bucks	.60	.25	.08
☐ 364	Blue Edwards ..... Milwaukee Bucks	.08	.04	.01
☐ 365	Lee Mayberry ..... Milwaukee Bucks	.20	.09	.03
☐ 366	Eric Murdock ..... Milwaukee Bucks	.08	.04	.01
☐ 367	Mookie Blaylock ..... Atlanta Hawks	.08	.04	.01
☐ 368	Anthony Avent ..... Milwaukee Bucks	.20	.09	.03
☐ 369	Christian Laettner ..... Minnesota Timberwolves	1.25	.55	.16
☐ 370	Chuck Person ..... Minnesota Timberwolves	.08	.04	.01
☐ 371	Chris Smith ..... Minnesota Timberwolves	.20	.09	.03
☐ 372	Micheal Williams ..... Minnesota Timberwolves	.08	.04	.01
☐ 373	Rolando Blackman ..... New York Knicks	.08	.04	.01
☐ 374	Tony Campbell UER	.05	.02	.01

(Back photo actually
Alvin Robertson)
New York Knicks

☐ 375	Hubert Davis	.60	.25	.08
	New York Knicks			
☐ 376	Travis Mays	.05	.02	.01
	Atlanta Hawks			
☐ 377	Doc Rivers	.08	.04	.01
	New York Knicks			
☐ 378	Charles Smith	.05	.02	.01
	New York Knicks			
☐ 379	Rumeal Robinson	.05	.02	.01
	New Jersey Nets			
☐ 380	Vinny Del Negro	.05	.02	.01
	San Antonio Spurs			
☐ 381	Steve Kerr	.05	.02	.01
	Orlando Magic			
☐ 382	Shaquille O'Neal	10.00	4.50	1.25
	Orlando Magic			
☐ 383	Donald Royal	.05	.02	.01
	Orlando Magic			
☐ 384	Jeff Hornacek	.08	.04	.01
	Philadelphia 76ers			
☐ 385	Andrew Lang	.05	.02	.01
	Philadelphia 76ers			
☐ 386	Tim Perry UER	.05	.02	.01
	Philadelphia 76ers			
	(Alvin Robertson pictured on back)			
☐ 387	Clarence Weatherspoon	1.25	.55	.16
	Philadelphia 76ers			
☐ 388	Danny Ainge	.10	.05	.01
	Phoenix Suns			
☐ 389	Charles Barkley	.40	.18	.05
	Phoenix Suns			
☐ 390	Tim Kempton	.05	.02	.01
	Phoenix Suns			
☐ 391	Oliver Miller	.60	.25	.08
	Phoenix Suns			
☐ 392	Dave Johnson	.05	.02	.01
	Portland Trail Blazers			
☐ 393	Tracy Murray	.20	.09	.03
	Portland Trail Blazers			
☐ 394	Rod Strickland	.08	.04	.01
	Portland Trail Blazers			
☐ 395	Marty Conlon	.05	.02	.01
	Sacramento Kings			
☐ 396	Walt Williams	.60	.25	.08
	Sacramento Kings			
☐ 397	Lloyd Daniels	.20	.09	.03
	San Antonio Spurs			
☐ 398	Dale Ellis	.08	.04	.01
	San Antonio Spurs			
☐ 399	Dave Hoppen	.05	.02	.01
	San Antonio Spurs			
☐ 400	Larry Smith	.08	.04	.01
	San Antonio Spurs			
☐ 401	Doug Overton	.05	.02	.01
	Washington Bullets			
☐ 402	Isaac Austin	.05	.02	.01
	Utah Jazz			
☐ 403	Jay Humphries	.05	.02	.01
	Utah Jazz			
☐ 404	Larry Krystowiak	.05	.02	.01
	Utah Jazz			
☐ 405	Tom Gugliotta	1.25	.55	.16
	Washington Bullets			
☐ 406	Buck Johnson	.05	.02	.01
	Washington Bullets			
☐ 407	Don MacLean	.75	.35	.09
	Washington Bullets			
☐ 408	Marlon Maxey	.05	.02	.01
	Minnesota Timberwolves			
☐ 409	Corey Williams	.05	.02	.01
	Chicago Bulls			

☐ 410	Special Olympics	.09	.04	.01
	Dan Majerle			
	Phoenix Suns			
☐ 411	Checklist 1	.06	.03	.01
☐ 412	Checklist 2	.06	.03	.01
☐ 413	Checklist 3	.06	.03	.01
☐ NNO	David Robinson	10.00	4.50	1.25
	The Admiral Comes Prepared			
☐ NNO	Head of the Class	50.00	23.00	6.25
	Alonzo Mourning			
	Charlotte Hornets			
	Shaquille O'Neal			
	Orlando Magic			
	Christian Laettner			
	Minnesota Timberwolves			
	LaPhonso Ellis			
	Denver Nuggets			
	Jim Jackson			
	Dallas Mavericks			
	Tom Gugliotta			
	Washington Bullets			
☐ NNO	Magic Johnson	10.00	4.50	1.25
	The Magic Never Ends			

1992-93 SkyBox Draft Picks

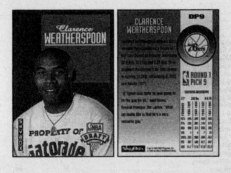

This subset showcases the first round picks from the 1992 NBA Draft. The card numbering (1-27) reflects the actual order in which each player was selected. Six players (2, 10-11, 15-16, 18) available by the cut-off date were issued in first series foil packs, while the rest of the first round picks who signed NBA contracts were issued in second series packs. DP4 and DP17, intended for Jim Jackson and Doug Christie respectively, were not issued with this set because neither player signed a professional contract. The cards were randomly insert-ed into 12-card (both series) foil packs. According to SkyBox approximately one out of every eight packs will contain a Draft Pick insert card. The fronts display an opaque metallic gold rectangle set off from the player. On a gradated gold background, the backs present player profiles. A white rectangle that runs vertically the length of the card contains statistics. The team logo is superimposed on this rectangle. The cards are num-bered on the back with a "DP" prefix.

	MINT	EXC	G-VG
COMPLETE SET (25)	90.00	40.00	11.50
COMPLETE SERIES 1 (6)	25.00	11.50	3.10
COMPLETE SERIES 2 (19)	65.00	29.00	8.25
COMMON (2/10/11/15/16/18)	1.00	.45	.13
COMMON (1/3/5-9/12-14/19-27)	1.00	.45	.13
☐ 1 Shaquille O'Neal	35.00	16.00	4.40
Orlando Magic			

		MINT	EXC	G-VG
☐ 2	Alonzo Mourning	18.00	8.00	2.30
	Charlotte Hornets			
☐ 3	Christian Laettner	5.00	2.30	.60
	Minnesota Timberwolves			
☐ 4	Not issued	.00	.00	.00
	(Player unsigned)			
☐ 5	LaPhonso Ellis	5.00	2.30	.60
	Denver Nuggets			
☐ 6	Tom Gugliotta	5.00	2.30	.60
	Washington Bullets			
☐ 7	Walt Williams	2.50	1.15	.30
	Sacramento Kings			
☐ 8	Todd Day	2.50	1.15	.30
	Milwaukee Bucks			
☐ 9	Clarence Weatherspoon	5.00	2.30	.60
	Philadelphia 76ers			
☐ 10	Adam Keefe	1.00	.45	.13
	Atlanta Hawks			
☐ 11	Robert Horry	5.00	2.30	.60
	Houston Rockets			
☐ 12	Harold Miner	2.50	1.15	.30
	Miami Heat			
☐ 13	Bryant Stith	2.50	1.15	.30
	Denver Nuggets			
☐ 14	Malik Sealy	1.25	.55	.16
	Indiana Pacers			
☐ 15	Anthony Peeler	2.00	.90	.25
	Los Angeles Lakers			
☐ 16	Randy Woods	1.00	.45	.13
	San Diego Clippers			
☐ 17	Not issued	.00	.00	.00
	(Player unsigned)			
☐ 18	Tracy Murray	1.00	.45	.13
	San Antonio Spurs			
☐ 19	Don MacLean	4.00	1.80	.50
	Washington Bullets			
☐ 20	Hubert Davis	3.00	1.35	.40
	New York Knicks			
☐ 21	Jon Barry	1.00	.45	.13
	Milwaukee Bucks			
☐ 22	Oliver Miller	2.50	1.15	.30
	Phoenix Suns			
☐ 23	Lee Mayberry	1.00	.45	.13
	Milwaukee Bucks			
☐ 24	Latrell Sprewell	12.00	5.50	1.50
	Golden State Warriors			
☐ 25	Elmore Spencer	1.00	.45	.13
	Los Angeles Clippers			
☐ 26	Dave Johnson	1.00	.45	.13
	Portland Trail Blazers			
☐ 27	Byron Houston	1.25	.55	.16
	Golden State Warriors			

1992-93 SkyBox Olympic Team

Each card in this 12-card set features an action photo of a team member and his complete statistics from the Olympic Games. According to SkyBox, the cards were randomly inserted into 12-card first series foil packs at an approximate rate of one per six packs. The backs tell the story of U.S. Men's Olympic Team, from scrimmage in Monte Carlo to the medal cere- mony in Barcelona. These standard size (2 1/2" by 3 1/2") cards are numbered on the back with a "USA" prefix.

	MINT	EXC	G-VG
COMPLETE SET (12)	30.00	13.50	3.80
COMMON PLAYER (1-12)	1.25	.55	.16
☐ 1 Clyde Drexler	1.50	.65	.19
☐ 2 Chris Mullin	1.25	.55	.16
☐ 3 John Stockton	1.50	.65	.19
☐ 4 Karl Malone	2.00	.90	.25

☐ 5 Scottie Pippen	3.50	1.55	.45
☐ 6 Larry Bird	6.00	2.70	.75
☐ 7 Charles Barkley	5.00	2.30	.60
☐ 8 Patrick Ewing	3.50	1.55	.45
☐ 9 Christian Laettner	4.00	1.80	.50
☐ 10 David Robinson	5.00	2.30	.60
☐ 11 Michael Jordan	15.00	6.75	1.90
☐ 12 Magic Johnson	4.00	1.80	.50

1992-93 SkyBox David Robinson

This ten-card subset captures moments in Robinson's life, beginning with his childhood and ending with his present day super stardom. The first five cards were randomly inserted in first series 12-card foil packs, while the second five were found in second series packs. According to SkyBox, approximately one of every eight packs contains a David Robinson insert card. The standard-size (2 1/2" by 3 1/2") cards feature a different design than the regular issue cards. The fronts display color photos tilted slightly to the left with a special seal overlaying the upper left corner. The surrounding card face show two colors

	MINT	EXC	G-VG
COMPLETE SET (10)	4.00	1.80	.50
COMPLETE SERIES 1 (5)	2.00	.90	.25
COMPLETE SERIES 2 (5)	2.00	.90	.25
COMMON D.ROBINSON (R1-R5)	.50	.23	.06
COMMON D.ROBINSON (R6-R10)	.50	.23	.06
☐ R1 David Robinson	.50	.23	.06
Childhood			

		MINT	EXC	G-VG
☐ R2	David Robinson .... At Ease	.50	.23	.06
☐ R3	David Robinson .... College	.50	.23	.06
☐ R4	David Robinson .... College	.50	.23	.06
☐ R5	David Robinson .... At Ease	.50	.23	.06
☐ R6	David Robinson .... College	.50	.23	.06
☐ R7	David Robinson .... College	.50	.23	.06
☐ R8	David Robinson .... Awards	.50	.23	.06
☐ R9	David Robinson .... Awards	.50	.23	.06
☐ R10	David Robinson .... At Ease	.50	.23	.06

1992-93 SkyBox School Ties

Randomly inserted in 1992-93 SkyBox second series 12-card foil packs at a reported rate of one per four packs, this 18-card set consists of six different three-card "School Ties" puzzles. When the three cards in each puzzle are placed together, they create a montage of active NBA players from one particular college. The cards measure the standard size (2 1/2" by 3 1/2"). The fronts feature several color player photos that are tilted slightly and have team color-coded picture frames. The team logo appears in a team color-coded banner that is superimposed across the bottom of the picture. The backs have brightly colored backgrounds and display information about the college, the players, and a checklist of the players on the three-card puzzle. The cards are numbered on the back with an "ST" prefix.

		MINT	EXC	G-VG
COMPLETE SET (18)	....	8.00	3.60	1.00
COMMON PLAYER (ST1-ST18)	....	.25	.11	.03
☐ ST1	Patrick Ewing .... Alonzo Mourning Georgetown	3.00	1.35	.40
☐ ST2	Dikembe Mutombo .... Eric Floyd Georgetown	.35	.16	.04
☐ ST3	Reggie Williams .... David Wingate Georgetown	.25	.11	.03
☐ ST4	Kenny Anderson .... Duane Ferrell Georgia Tech	.50	.23	.06
☐ ST5	Tom Hammonds	.30	.14	.04

		MINT	EXC	G-VG
	Jon Barry			
	Mark Price			
	Georgia Tech			
☐ ST6	John Salley	.30	.14	.04
	Dennis Scott			
	Georgia Tech			
☐ ST7	Rafael Addison	.25	.11	.03
	Dave Johsnon			
	Syracuse			
☐ ST8	Billy Owens	.50	.23	.06
	Derrick Coleman			
	Rony Seikaly			
	Syracuse			
☐ ST9	Sherman Douglas	.30	.14	.04
	Danny Schayes			
	Syracuse			
☐ ST10	Nick Anderson	.30	.14	.04
	Kendall Gill			
	Illinois			
☐ ST11	Derek Harper	.30	.14	.04
	Eddie Johnson			
	Illinois			
☐ ST12	Marcus Liberty	.25	.11	.03
	Ken Norman			
	Illinois			
☐ ST13	Greg Anthony	.25	.11	.03
	Stacey Augmon			
	Nevada-Las Vegas			
☐ ST14	Armon Gilliam	.75	.35	.09
	Larry Johnson			
	Sidney Green			
	Nevada-Las Vegas			
☐ ST15	Elmore Spencer	.25	.11	.03
	Gerald Paddio			
	Nevada-Las Vegas			
☐ ST16	James Worthy	1.50	.65	.19
	Michael Jordan			
	Sam Perkins			
	North Carolina			
☐ ST17	J.R. Reid	.35	.16	.04
	Pete Chilcutt			
	Brad Daugherty			
	Rick Fox			
	North Carolina			
☐ ST18	Hubert Davis	.25	.11	.03
	Kenny Smith			
	Scott Williams			
	North Carolina			

1992-93 SkyBox Thunder and Lightning

Randomly inserted into second series 12-card foil packs at a reported rate of one card per 40 packs, each card in this nine-card set features a pair of teammates, one on each side. The catchword on the front is "Thunder", referring to a dominant power player, while "Lightning" on the back captures the speed of a guard. The cards are highlighted by a litho-foil printing which gives a foil-look to the graphics around the basketball. The cards measure the standard size (2 1/2" by 3 1/2") and have color action player photos against a dark background, with computer enhancement around the ball and player. On the front, the power player's name appears at the bottom and is underlined by a thin yellow stripe. The word "Thunder" appears below the stripe. On the horizontal backs, the speed player's name is displayed in the upper right with the same yellow underline, but the word "Lightning" appears below it. The cards are numbered on the back with a "TL" prefix.

	MINT	EXC	G-VG
COMPLETE SET (9)	75.00	34.00	9.50
COMMON PAIR (TL1-TL9)	2.00	.90	.25
☐ TL1 Dikembe Mutombo	8.00	3.60	1.00
Mark Macon			
Denver Nuggets			

☐ TL2	Buck Williams Clyde Drexler Portland Trail Blazers	5.00	2.30	.60
☐ TL3	Charles Barkley Kevin Johnson Phoenix Suns	20.00	9.00	2.50
☐ TL4	Pervis Ellison Michael Adams Washington Bullets	2.00	.90	.25
☐ TL5	Larry Johnson Tyrone Bogues Charlotte Hornets	20.00	9.00	2.50
☐ TL6	Brad Daugherty Mark Price Cleveland Cavaliers	3.00	1.35	.40
☐ TL7	Shawn Kemp Gary Payton Seattle Supersonics	20.00	9.00	2.50
☐ TL8	Karl Malone John Stockton Utah Jazz	10.00	4.50	1.25
☐ TL9	Billy Owens Tim Hardaway Golden State Warriors	3.00	1.35	.40

1993-94 SkyBox

The 1993-94 SkyBox basketball set contains 341 cards that measure standard size (2 1/2" by 3 1/2"). The fronts feature full-bleed color action photos with a wide white stripe down one side of the front containing the player's name, position, and team. The SkyBox Premium foil stamp logo appears superimposed on the front. The backs display a second player close-up shot on the top half, and the player's statistics and scouting report on the bottom half. The cards are numbered on the back, grouped alphabetically within teams, and checklisted below alphabetically according to teams as follows: Atlanta Hawks (24-29; 192-195), Boston Celtics (30-35; 196-199), Charlotte Hornets (36-41; 200-204), Chicago Bulls (42-48; 205-208), Cleveland Cavaliers (49-54; 209-212), Dallas Mavericks (55-59; 213-215), Denver Nuggets (60-65; 216-218), Detroit Pistons (66-71; 219-222), Golden State Warriors (72-78; 223-227), Houston Rockets (79-83; 228-231), Indiana Pacers (84-89; 232-234), Los Angeles Clippers (92-95; 235-238), Los Angeles Lakers (96-101; 239-241), Miami Heat (102-107; 242-243), Milwaukee Bucks (108-114; 244-248), Minnesota Timberwolves (115-119; 249-251), New Jersey Nets (120-124; 252-253), New York Knicks (125-131; 254-257), Orlando Magic (132-137; 258-261), Philadelphia 76ers (138-143; 262-265), Phoenix Suns (144-149; 266-268), Portland Trail Blazers (150-156; 269-272), Sacramento Kings (157-161; 273-275), San Antonio Spurs (162-168; 276-280), Seattle Supersonics (169-174; 281-284), Utah Jazz (175-179; 285-287), and Washington Bullets (180-185; 288-291). The following subsets are also included in this set: 1993 Playoff Performances (4-21), Changing Faces (292-318), and Costacos Brothers Poster Cards (319-338). The odds of finding a Tip-off Exchange Card are one in every 240 packs.

	MINT	EXC	G-VG
COMPLETE SET (341)	30.00	13.50	3.80
COMPLETE SERIES 1 (191)	15.00	6.75	1.90
COMPLETE SERIES 2 (150)	15.00	6.75	1.90
COMMON PLAYER (1-191)	.05	.02	.01
COMMON PLAYER (192-341)	.05	.02	.01
☐ 1 Checklist	.05	.02	.01
☐ 2 Checklist	.05	.02	.01
☐ 3 Checklist	.05	.02	.01
☐ 4 Larry Johnson	.20	.09	.03
Charlotte Hornets			
☐ 5 Alonzo Mourning	.40	.18	.05
Charlotte Hornets			
☐ 6 Hakeem Olajuwon	.50	.23	.06
Houston Rockets			
☐ 7 Brad Daugherty	.05	.02	.01
Cleveland Cavaliers			
☐ 8 Oliver Miller	.08	.04	.01
Phoenix Suns			
☐ 9 David Robinson	.25	.11	.03
San Antonio Spurs			
☐ 10 Patrick Ewing	.20	.09	.03
New York Knicks			
☐ 11 Ricky Pierce	.05	.02	.01
Seattle Supersonics			
☐ 12 Sam Perkins	.08	.04	.01
Seattle Supersonics			
☐ 13 John Starks	.10	.05	.01
Seattle Supersonics			
☐ 14 Michael Jordan	1.25	.55	.16
Chicago Bulls			
☐ 15 Dan Majerle	.08	.04	.01
Phoenix Suns			
☐ 16 Scottie Pippen	.20	.09	.03
Chicago Bulls			
☐ 17 Shawn Kemp	.20	.09	.03
Seattle Supersonics			
☐ 18 Charles Barkley	.25	.11	.03
Phoenix Suns			
☐ 19 Horace Grant	.08	.04	.01
Chicago Bulls			
☐ 20 Kevin Johnson	.08	.04	.01
Phoenix Suns			
☐ 21 John Paxson	.05	.02	.01
Chicago Bulls			
☐ 22 Inside Stuff	.05	.02	.01
☐ 23 NBA On NBC	.05	.02	.01
☐ 24 Stacey Augmon	.10	.05	.01
☐ 25 Mookie Blaylock	.08	.04	.01
☐ 26 Craig Ehlo	.05	.02	.01

☐ 27	Adam Keefe	.05	.02	.01
☐ 28	Dominique Wilkins	.30	.14	.04
☐ 29	Kevin Willis	.08	.04	.01
☐ 30	Dee Brown	.05	.02	.01
☐ 31	Sherman Douglas	.05	.02	.01
☐ 32	Rick Cox	.05	.02	.01
☐ 33	Kevin Gamble	.05	.02	.01
☐ 34	Xavier McDaniel	.08	.04	.01
☐ 35	Robert Parish	.10	.05	.01
☐ 36	Muggsy Bogues	.10	.05	.01
☐ 37	Dell Curry	.08	.04	.01
☐ 38	Kendall Gill	.08	.04	.01
☐ 39	Larry Johnson	.35	.16	.04
☐ 40	Alonzo Mourning	.75	.35	.09
☐ 41	Johnny Newman	.05	.02	.01
☐ 42	B.J. Armstrong	.10	.05	.01
☐ 43	Bill Cartwright	.05	.02	.01
☐ 44	Horace Grant	.10	.05	.01
☐ 45	Michael Jordan	2.50	1.15	.30
☐ 46	John Paxson	.05	.02	.01
☐ 47	Scottie Pippen	.40	.18	.05
☐ 48	Scott Williams	.05	.02	.01
☐ 49	Terrell Brandon	.05	.02	.01
☐ 50	Brad Daugherty	.10	.05	.01
☐ 51	Larry Nance	.08	.04	.01
☐ 52	Mark Price	.10	.05	.01
☐ 53	Gerald Wilkins	.05	.02	.01
☐ 54	John Williams	.05	.02	.01
☐ 55	Terry Davis	.05	.02	.01
☐ 56	Derek Harper	.08	.04	.01
☐ 57	Jim Jackson	.35	.16	.04
☐ 58	Sean Rooks	.05	.02	.01
☐ 59	Doug Smith	.05	.02	.01
☐ 60	Mahmoud Abdul-Rauf	.05	.02	.01
☐ 61	LaPhonso Ellis	.10	.05	.01
☐ 62	Mark Macon	.05	.02	.01
☐ 63	Dikembe Mutombo	.10	.05	.01
☐ 64	Bryant Stith	.08	.04	.01
☐ 65	Reggie Williams	.05	.02	.01
☐ 66	Joe Dumars	.20	.09	.03
☐ 67	Bill Laimbeer	.10	.05	.01
☐ 68	Terry Mills	.08	.04	.01
☐ 69	Alvin Robertson	.05	.02	.01
☐ 70	Dennis Rodman	.08	.04	.01
☐ 71	Isiah Thomas	.20	.09	.03
☐ 72	Victor Alexander	.05	.02	.01
☐ 73	Tim Hardaway	.10	.05	.01
☐ 74	Tyrone Hill	.05	.02	.01
☐ 75	Sarunas Marciulionis	.05	.02	.01
☐ 76	Chris Mullin	.20	.09	.03
☐ 77	Billy Owens	.08	.04	.01
☐ 78	Latrell Sprewell	.50	.23	.06
☐ 79	Robert Horry	.10	.05	.01
☐ 80	Vernon Maxwell	.08	.04	.01
☐ 81	Hakeem Olajuwon	1.00	.45	.13
☐ 82	Kenny Smith	.05	.02	.01
☐ 83	Otis Thorpe	.08	.04	.01
☐ 84	Dale Davis	.08	.04	.01
☐ 85	Reggie Miller	.25	.11	.03
☐ 86	Pooh Richardson	.05	.02	.01
☐ 87	Detlef Schrempf	.10	.05	.01
☐ 88	Malik Sealy	.05	.02	.01
☐ 89	Rik Smits	.08	.04	.01
☐ 90	Ron Harper	.08	.04	.01
☐ 91	Mark Jackson	.08	.04	.01
☐ 92	Danny Manning	.10	.05	.01
☐ 93	Stanley Roberts	.05	.02	.01
☐ 94	Loy Vaught	.08	.04	.01
☐ 95	Randy Woods	.05	.02	.01
☐ 96	Sam Bowie	.05	.02	.01
☐ 97	Doug Christie	.08	.04	.01
☐ 98	Vlade Divac	.05	.02	.01
☐ 99	Anthony Peeler	.08	.04	.01

☐ 100	Sedale Threatt	.05	.02	.01
☐ 101	James Worthy	.10	.05	.01
☐ 102	Grant Long	.05	.02	.01
☐ 103	Harold Miner	.08	.04	.01
☐ 104	Glen Rice	.10	.05	.01
☐ 105	John Salley	.05	.02	.01
☐ 106	Rony Seikaly	.10	.05	.01
☐ 107	Steve Smith	.08	.04	.01
☐ 108	Anthony Avent	.05	.02	.01
☐ 109	Jon Barry	.05	.02	.01
☐ 110	Frank Brickowski	.08	.04	.01
☐ 111	Blue Edwards	.05	.02	.01
☐ 112	Todd Day	.08	.04	.01
☐ 113	Lee Mayberry	.05	.02	.01
☐ 114	Eric Murdock	.08	.04	.01
☐ 115	Thurl Bailey	.05	.02	.01
☐ 116	Christian Laettner	.08	.04	.01
☐ 117	Chuck Person	.08	.04	.01
☐ 118	Doug West	.05	.02	.01
☐ 119	Micheal Williams	.08	.04	.01
☐ 120	Kenny Anderson	.20	.09	.03
☐ 121	Benoit Benjamin	.05	.02	.01
☐ 122	Derrick Coleman	.25	.11	.03
☐ 123	Chris Morris	.05	.02	.01
☐ 124	Rumeal Robinson	.05	.02	.01
☐ 125	Rolando Blackman	.05	.02	.01
☐ 126	Patrick Ewing	.40	.18	.05
☐ 127	Anthony Mason	.05	.02	.01
☐ 128	Charles Oakley	.10	.05	.01
☐ 129	Doc Rivers	.08	.04	.01
☐ 130	Charles Smith	.05	.05	.01
☐ 131	John Starks	.10	.05	.01
☐ 132	Nick Anderson	.08	.04	.01
☐ 133	Shaquille O'Neal	2.00	.90	.25
☐ 134	Donald Royal	.05	.02	.01
☐ 135	Dennis Scott	.08	.04	.01
☐ 136	Scott Skiles	.05	.02	.01
☐ 137	Brian Williams	.05	.02	.01
☐ 138	Johnny Dawkins	.05	.02	.01
☐ 139	Hersey Hawkins	.08	.04	.01
☐ 140	Jeff Hornacek	.08	.04	.01
☐ 141	Andrew Lang	.05	.02	.01
☐ 142	Tim Perry	.05	.02	.01
☐ 143	Clarence Weatherspoon	.10	.05	.01
☐ 144	Danny Ainge	.10	.05	.01
☐ 145	Charles Barkley	.60	.25	.08
☐ 146	Cedric Ceballos	.10	.05	.01
☐ 147	Kevin Johnson	.10	.05	.01
☐ 148	Oliver Miller	.10	.05	.01
☐ 149	Dan Majerle	.10	.05	.01
☐ 150	Clyde Drexler	.20	.09	.03
☐ 151	Harvey Grant	.05	.02	.01
☐ 152	Jerome Kersey	.05	.02	.01
☐ 153	Terry Porter	.08	.04	.01
☐ 154	Cliff Robinson	.10	.05	.01
☐ 155	Rod Strickland	.08	.04	.01
☐ 156	Buck Williams	.10	.05	.01
☐ 157	Mitch Richmond	.10	.05	.01
☐ 158	Lionel Simmons	.08	.04	.01
☐ 159	Wayman Tisdale	.08	.04	.01
☐ 160	Spud Webb	.10	.05	.01
☐ 161	Walt Williams	.10	.05	.01
☐ 162	Antoine Carr	.05	.02	.01
☐ 163	Lloyd Daniels	.05	.02	.01
☐ 164	Sean Elliott	.08	.04	.01
☐ 165	Dale Ellis	.08	.04	.01
☐ 166	Avery Johnson	.05	.02	.01
☐ 167	J.R. Reid	.05	.02	.01
☐ 168	David Robinson	.60	.25	.08
☐ 169	Shawn Kemp	.40	.18	.05
☐ 170	Derrick McKey	.05	.02	.01
☐ 171	Nate McMillan	.05	.02	.01
☐ 172	Gary Payton	.10	.05	.01

☐ 173	Sam Perkins	.08	.04	.01
☐ 174	Ricky Pierce	.08	.04	.01
☐ 175	Tyrone Corbin	.05	.02	.01
☐ 176	Jay Humphries	.05	.02	.01
☐ 177	Jeff Malone	.08	.04	.01
☐ 178	Karl Malone	.30	.14	.04
☐ 179	John Stockton	.20	.09	.03
☐ 180	Michael Adams	.08	.04	.01
☐ 181	Kevin Duckworth	.05	.02	.01
☐ 182	Pervis Ellison	.05	.02	.01
☐ 183	Tom Gugliotta	.08	.04	.01
☐ 184	Don MacLean	.05	.02	.01
☐ 185	Brent Price	.05	.02	.01
☐ 186	George Lynch Los Angeles Lakers	.30	.14	.04
☐ 187	Rex Walters New Jersey Nets	.15	.07	.02
☐ 188	Shawn Bradley Philadelphia 76ers	.50	.23	.06
☐ 189	Ervin Johnson Seattle Supersonics	.15	.07	.02
☐ 190	Luther Wright Utah Jazz	.15	.07	.02
☐ 191	Calbert Cheaney Washington Bullets	.50	.23	.06
☐ 192	Craig Ehlo	.05	.02	.01
☐ 193	Duane Ferrell	.05	.02	.01
☐ 194	Paul Graham	.05	.02	.01
☐ 195	Andrew Lang	.05	.02	.01
☐ 196	Chris Corchiani	.05	.02	.01
☐ 197	Acie Earl	.15	.07	.02
☐ 198	Dino Radja	.50	.23	.06
☐ 199	Ed Pinckney	.05	.02	.01
☐ 200	Tony Bennett	.05	.02	.01
☐ 201	Scott Burrell	.20	.09	.03
☐ 202	Kenny Gattison	.05	.02	.01
☐ 203	Hersey Hawkins	.08	.04	.01
☐ 204	Eddie Johnson	.05	.02	.01
☐ 205	Corie Blount	.15	.07	.02
☐ 206	Steve Kerr	.05	.02	.01
☐ 207	Toni Kukoc	.50	.23	.06
☐ 208	Pete Myers	.05	.02	.01
☐ 209	Danny Ferry	.05	.02	.01
☐ 210	Tyrone Hill	.05	.02	.01
☐ 211	Gerald Madkins	.15	.07	.02
☐ 212	Chris Mills	.30	.14	.04
☐ 213	Lucious Harris	.15	.07	.02
☐ 214	Ron Jones	.20	.09	.03
☐ 215	Jamal Mashburn	1.25	.55	.16
☐ 216	Darnell Mee	.15	.07	.02
☐ 217	Rodney Rodgers	.30	.14	.04
☐ 218	Brian Williams	.05	.02	.01
☐ 219	Greg Anderson	.05	.02	.01
☐ 220	Sean Elliott	.08	.04	.01
☐ 221	Allan Houston	.20	.09	.03
☐ 222	Lindsey Hunter	.50	.23	.06
☐ 223	Chris Gatling	.05	.02	.01
☐ 224	Josh Grant	.15	.07	.02
☐ 225	Keith Jennings	.05	.02	.01
☐ 226	Avery Johnson	.05	.02	.01
☐ 227	Chris Webber	3.00	1.35	.40
☐ 228	Sam Cassell	.60	.25	.08
☐ 229	Mario Elie	.05	.02	.01
☐ 230	Richard Petruska	.15	.07	.02
☐ 231	Eric Riley	.15	.07	.02
☐ 232	Antonio Davis	.30	.14	.04
☐ 233	Scott Haskin	.15	.07	.02
☐ 234	Derrick McKey	.08	.04	.01
☐ 235	Mark Aguirre	.10	.05	.01
☐ 236	Terry Dehere	.15	.07	.02
☐ 237	Gary Grant	.05	.02	.01
☐ 238	Randy Woods	.05	.02	.01
☐ 239	Sam Bowie	.05	.02	.01

☐ 240 Elden Campbell	.05	.02	.01
☐ 241 Nick Van Exel	.50	.23	.06
☐ 242 Manute Bol	.05	.02	.01
☐ 243 Brian Shaw	.05	.02	.01
☐ 244 Vin Baker	.75	.35	.09
☐ 245 Brad Lohaus	.05	.02	.01
☐ 246 Ken Norman	.05	.02	.01
☐ 247 Derek Strong	.15	.07	.02
☐ 248 Dan Schayes	.05	.02	.01
☐ 249 Mike Brown	.05	.02	.01
☐ 250 Luc Longley	.05	.02	.01
☐ 251 Isaiah Rider	1.25	.55	.16
☐ 252 Kevin Edwards	.05	.02	.01
☐ 253 Armon Gilliam	.05	.02	.01
☐ 254 Greg Anthony	.05	.02	.01
☐ 255 Anthony Bonner	.05	.02	.01
☐ 256 Tony Campbell	.05	.02	.01
☐ 257 Hubert Davis	.05	.02	.01
☐ 258 Litterial Green	.05	.02	.01
☐ 259 Anfernee Hardaway	2.50	1.15	.30
☐ 260 Larry Krystkowiak	.05	.02	.01
☐ 261 Todd Lichti	.05	.02	.01
☐ 262 Dana Barros	.05	.02	.01
☐ 263 Greg Graham	.15	.07	.02
☐ 264 Warren Kidd	.15	.07	.02
☐ 265 Moses Malone	.10	.05	.01
☐ 266 A.C. Green	.08	.04	.01
☐ 267 Joe Kleine	.05	.02	.01
☐ 268 Malcolm Mackey	.15	.07	.02
☐ 269 Mark Bryant	.05	.02	.01
☐ 270 Chris Dudley	.05	.02	.01
☐ 271 Harvey Grant	.05	.02	.01
☐ 272 James Robinson	.20	.09	.03
☐ 273 Duane Causwell	.05	.02	.01
☐ 274 Bobby Hurley	.50	.23	.06
☐ 275 Jim Les	.05	.02	.01
☐ 276 Willie Anderson	.05	.02	.01
☐ 277 Terry Cummings	.08	.04	.01
☐ 278 Vinny Del Negro	.05	.02	.01
☐ 279 Sleepy Floyd	.05	.02	.01
☐ 280 Dennis Rodman	.08	.04	.01
☐ 281 Vincent Askew	.05	.02	.01
☐ 282 Kendall Gill	.08	.04	.01
☐ 283 Steve Scheffler	.05	.02	.01
☐ 284 Detlef Schrempf	.10	.05	.01
☐ 285 David Benoit	.05	.02	.01
☐ 286 Tom Chambers	.08	.04	.01
☐ 287 Felton Spencer	.05	.02	.01
☐ 288 Rex Chapman	.05	.02	.01
☐ 289 Kevin Duckworth	.05	.02	.01
☐ 290 Gheorghe Muresan	.20	.09	.03
☐ 291 Kenny Walker	.05	.02	.01
☐ 292 Andrew Lang CF	.05	.02	.01
Craig Ehlo			
Atlanta Hawks			
☐ 293 Dino Radja CF	.15	.07	.02
Acie Earl			
Boston Celtics			
☐ 294 Eddie Johnson CF	.05	.02	.01
Hersey Hawkins			
Charlotte Hornets			
☐ 295 Toni Kukoc CF	.15	.07	.02
Corie Blount			
Chicago Bulls			
☐ 296 Tyrone Hill CF	.05	.02	.01
Chris Mills			
Cleveland Cavaliers			
☐ 297 Jamal Mashburn CF	.40	.18	.05
Ron Jones			
Dallas Mavericks			
☐ 298 Darnell Mee CF	.05	.02	.01
Rodney Rodgers			
Denver Nuggets			

☐ 299 Lindsey Hunter CF Allan Houston Detroit Pistons	.20	.09	.03
☐ 300 Chris Webber CF Avery Johnson Golden State Warriors	1.00	.45	.13
☐ 301 Sam Cassell CF Mario Elie Houston Rockets	.05	.02	.01
☐ 302 Derrick McKey CF Antonio Davis Indiana Pacers	.05	.02	.01
☐ 303 Terry Dehere CF Mark Aguirre Los Angeles Clippers	.05	.02	.01
☐ 304 Nick Van Exel CF George Lynch Los Angeles Lakers	.20	.09	.03
☐ 305 Harold Miner CF Steve Smith Miami Heat	.05	.02	.01
☐ 306 Ken Norman CF Vin Baker Milwaukee Bucks	.25	.11	.03
☐ 307 Mike Brown CF Isaiah Rider Minnesota Timberwolves	.40	.18	.05
☐ 308 Kevin Edwards CF Rex Walters New Jersey Nets	.05	.02	.01
☐ 309 Hubert Davis CF Anthony Bonner New York Knicks	.05	.02	.01
☐ 310 Anfernee Hardaway CF Larry Krystkowiak Orlando Magic	.75	.35	.09
☐ 311 Moses Malone CF Shawn Bradley Philadelphia 76ers	.15	.07	.02
☐ 312 Joe Kleine CF A.C. Green Phoenix Suns	.05	.02	.01
☐ 313 Harvey Grant CF Chris Dudley Portland Trail Blazers	.05	.02	.01
☐ 314 Bobby Hurley CF Mitch Richmond Sacramento Kings	.15	.07	.02
☐ 315 Sleepy Floyd CF Dennis Rodman San Antonio Spurs	.05	.02	.01
☐ 316 Kendall Gill CF Detlef Schrempf Seattle Supersonics	.05	.02	.01
☐ 317 Felton Spencer CF Luther Wright Utah Jazz	.05	.02	.01
☐ 318 Calbert Cheaney CF Kevin Duckworth Washington Bullets	.15	.07	.02
☐ 319 Karl Malone PC Utah Jazz	.15	.07	.02
☐ 320 Alonzo Mourning PC Charlotte Hornets	.40	.18	.05
☐ 321 Scottie Pippen PC Chicago Bulls	.20	.09	.03
☐ 322 Mark Price PC Cleveland Cavaliers	.08	.04	.01
☐ 323 LaPhonso Ellis PC Denver Nuggets	.10	.05	.01
☐ 324 Joe Dumars PC Detroit Pistons	.10	.05	.01
☐ 325 Chris Mullin PC	.10	.05	.01

	Golden State Warriors			
☐ 326	Ron Harper PC	.05	.02	.01
	Los Angeles Clippers			
☐ 327	Glen Rice PC	.05	.02	.01
	Miami Heat			
☐ 328	Christian Laettner PC	.08	.04	.01
	Minnesota Timberwolves			
☐ 329	Kenny Anderson PC	.12	.05	.02
	New Jersey Nets			
☐ 330	John Starks PC	.08	.04	.01
	New York Knicks			
☐ 331	Shaquille O'Neal PC	1.00	.45	.13
	Orlando Magic			
☐ 332	Charles Barkley PC	.30	.14	.04
	Phoenix Suns			
☐ 333	Clifford Robinson PC	.10	.05	.01
	Portland Trail Blazers			
☐ 334	Clyde Drexler PC	.12	.05	.02
	Portland Trail Blazers			
☐ 335	Mitch Richmond PC	.08	.04	.01
	Sacramento Kings			
☐ 336	David Robinson PC	.30	.14	.04
	San Antonio Spurs			
☐ 337	Shawn Kemp PC	.20	.09	.03
	Seattle Supersonics			
☐ 338	John Stockton PC	.12	.05	.02
	Utah Jazz			
☐ 339	Checklist 4	.05	.02	.01
☐ 340	Checklist 5	.05	.02	.01
☐ 341	Checklist 6	.05	.02	.01
☐ DP4	Jim Jackson	5.00	2.30	.60
	Dallas Mavericks			
☐ DP17	Doug Christie	1.00	.45	.13
	Los Angeles Lakers			
☐ NNO	Expired Head of the	4.00	1.80	.50
	Class Exchange Card			
☐ NNO	Head of the Class Card	50.00	23.00	6.25

1993-94 SkyBox All-Rookies

Randomly inserted in Series I packs, this standard-size (2 1/2" by 3 1/2") 5-card set features borderless fronts with color action player cutouts set against metallic game-crowd backgrounds. The player's name appears in gold-foil lettering at the upper left. The white back carries a color player head shot along with career highlights. The cards are numbered on the back with an "AR" prefix.

	MINT	EXC	G-VG
COMPLETE SET (5)	30.00	13.50	3.80
COMMON PLAYER (AR1-AR5)	2.00	.90	.25

☐ AR1 Shaquille O'Neal	20.00	9.00	2.50
Orlando Magic			
☐ AR2 Alonzo Mourning	8.00	3.60	1.00
Charlotte Hornets			
☐ AR3 Christian Laettner	2.00	.90	.25
Minnesota Timberwolves			
☐ AR4 Tom Gugliotta	2.00	.90	.25
Washington Bullets			
☐ AR5 LaPhonso Ellis	2.00	.90	.25
Denver Nuggets			

1993-94 SkyBox Center Stage

Randomly inserted in Series I packs, this 9-card standard-size (2 1/2" by 3 1/2") set features borderless fronts with color action player cutouts placed against black backgrounds. The player's name is centered at the top in prismatic silver-foil lettering. The white back features a color action player cutout and player biography. The cards are numbered on the back with a "CS" prefix.

	MiNT	EXC	G-VG
COMPLETE SET (9)	30.00	13.50	3.80
COMMON PLAYER (CS1-CS9)	.75	.35	.09
☐ CS1 Michael Jordan	12.00	5.50	1.50
Chicago Bulls			
☐ CS2 Shaquille O'Neal	8.00	3.60	1.00
Orlando Magic			
☐ CS3 Charles Barkley	3.00	1.35	.40
Phoenix Suns			
☐ CS4 John Starks	.75	.35	.09
New York Knicks			
☐ CS5 Larry Johnson	2.00	.90	.25
Charlotte Hornets			
☐ CS6 Hakeem Olajuwon	4.00	1.80	.50
Houston Rockets			
☐ CS7 Kenny Anderson	1.00	.45	.13
New Jersey Nets			
☐ CS8 Mahmoud Abdul-Rauf	.75	.35	.09
Denver Nuggets			
☐ CS9 Cliff Robinson	.75	.35	.09
Portland Trail Blazers			

1993-94 SkyBox Draft Picks

These 26 standard-size (2 1/2" by 3 1/2") cards were random inserts in both series I and series II packs. The odds of finding one of these cards are one in every 12 packs. The fronts feature a color player action cutout set off to one side and superposed upon a ghosted

posed color player photo. The player's name, the team that drafted him, and his draft pick number appear at the top. The white back carries the player's name, career highlights, and pre-NBA statistics. The cards are numbered on the back with a "DP" prefix.

	MINT	EXC	G-VG
COMPLETE SET (26)	90.00	40.00	11.50
COMPLETE SERIES 1 (9)	20.00	9.00	2.50
COMPLETE SERIES 2 (17)	70.00	32.00	8.75
COMMON 1 (2/6-8/12/15)	1.00	.45	.13
COMMON 1 (16/18/23)	1.00	.45	.13
COMMON 2 (1/3-5/9/10/13/14)	1.00	.45	.13
COMMON 2 (17/19-22/24-27)	1.00	.45	.13
☐ 1 Chris Webber Golden State Warriors	25.00	11.50	3.10
☐ 2 Shawn Bradley Philadelphia 76ers	4.00	1.80	.50
☐ 3 Anfernee Hardaway Orlando Magic	20.00	9.00	2.50
☐ 4 Jamal Mashburn Dallas Mavericks	10.00	4.50	1.25
☐ 5 Isaiah Rider Minnesota Timberwolves	10.00	4.50	1.25
☐ 6 Calbert Cheaney Washington Bullets	4.00	1.80	.50
☐ 7 Bobby Hurley Seattle Supersonics	4.00	1.80	.50
☐ 8 Vin Baker Minnesota Timberwolves	7.00	3.10	.85
☐ 9 Rodney Rodgers Denver Nuggets	2.50	1.15	.30
☐ 10 Lindsey Hunter Detroit Pistons	4.00	1.80	.50
☐ 11 Allan Houston Detroit Pistons	1.50	.65	.19
☐ 12 George Lynch Los Angeles Lakers	2.00	.90	.25
☐ 13 Terry Dehere Los Angeles Clippers	1.50	.65	.19
☐ 14 Scott Haskins Indiana Pacers	1.00	.45	.13
☐ 15 Doug Edwards Atlanta Hawks	1.00	.45	.13
☐ 16 Rex Walters New Jersey Nets	1.00	.45	.13
☐ 17 Greg Graham Philadelphia 76ers	1.00	.45	.13
☐ 18 Luther Wright Utah Jazz	1.00	.45	.13
☐ 19 Acie Earl Boston Celtics	1.00	.45	.13
☐ 20 Scott Burrell Charlotte Hornets	1.50	.65	.19

☐ 21	James Robinson	1.50	.65	.19
	Portland Trail Blazers			
☐ 22	Chris Mills	2.00	.90	.25
	Cleveland Cavaliers			
☐ 23	Ervin Johnson	1.00	.45	.13
	Seattle Supersonics			
☐ 24	Sam Cassell	5.00	2.30	.60
	Houston Rockets			
☐ 25	Corie Blount	1.00	.45	.13
	Chicago Bulls			
☐ 26	Not Issued	.00	.00	.00
☐ 27	Malcolm Mackey	1.00	.45	.13
	Phoenix Suns			

1993-94 SkyBox Dynamic Dunks

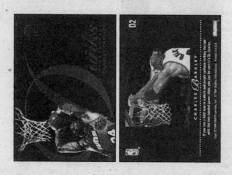

These nine standard-size (2 1/2" by 3 1/2") cards were random inserts in Series II packs. The odds of finding one of these cards are one in every 36 packs. The horizontal fronts feature color dunking-action player cutouts superposed upon borderless black and gold metallic backgrounds. The player's name appears in gold lettering at the bottom right. The horizontal black back carries another color dunking-action player photo. The player's name and a comment on his dunking style appear in white lettering beneath the photo. The cards are numbered on the back with a "D" prefix.

	MINT	EXC	G-VG
COMPLETE SET (9)	60.00	27.00	7.50
COMMON PLAYER (D1-D9)	2.00	.90	.25
☐ D1 Nick Anderson	2.00	.90	.25
Orlando Magic			
☐ D2 Charles Barkley	10.00	4.50	1.25
Phoenix Suns			
☐ D3 Robert Horry	3.00	1.35	.40
Houston Rockets			
☐ D4 Michael Jordan	35.00	16.00	4.40
Chicago Bulls			
☐ D5 Shawn Kemp	8.00	3.60	1.00
Seattle Supersonics			
☐ D6 Anthony Mason	2.00	.90	.25
New York Knicks			
☐ D7 Alonzo Mourning	10.00	4.50	1.25
Charlotte Hornets			
☐ D8 Hakeem Olajuwon	12.00	5.50	1.50
Houston Rockets			
☐ D9 Dominique Wilkins	6.00	2.70	.75
Atlanta Hawks			

1993-94 SkyBox Shaq Talk

The 1993-94 SkyBox Shaq Talk set consists of ten cards that were randomly inserted in Series 1 (1-5) and Series 2 (6-10) packs. The odds of finding one of these cards are reportedly one in every 36 packs. The standard size (2 1/2" by 3 1/2") cards spotlight Shaquille O'Neal. The fronts feature cut-out action shots of Shaq over a ghosted background. The set title is superimposed across the top of the card in red lettering. The white backs have a ghosted SkyBox Premium logo. At the top is a quote from Shaquille regarding game strategy and below is player critique by a basketball analyst. The cards are numbered on the back with a "Shaq Talk" prefix.

	MINT	EXC	G-VG
COMPLETE SET (10)	40.00	18.00	5.00
COMPLETE SERIES 1 (5)	20.00	9.00	2.50
COMPLETE SERIES 2 (5)	20.00	9.00	2.50
COMMON O'NEAL (1-5)	5.00	2.30	.60
COMMON O'NEAL (6-10)	5.00	2.30	.60
☐ 1 Shaq Talk 1 The Rebound	5.00	2.30	.60
☐ 2 Shaq Talk 2 The Block (Blocking David Robinson's shot)	5.00	2.30	.60
☐ 3 Shaq Talk 3 The Postup	5.00	2.30	.60
☐ 4 Shaq Talk 4 The Bunk	5.00	2.30	.60
☐ 5 Shaq Talk 5 Defense	5.00	2.30	.60
☐ 6 Shaq Talk Scoring	5.00	2.30	.60
☐ 7 Shaq Talk Passing	5.00	2.30	.60
☐ 8 Shaq Talk Rejections	5.00	2.30	.60
☐ 9 Shaq Talk Confidence	5.00	2.30	.60
☐ 10 Shaq Talk Legends	5.00	2.30	.60

1993-94 SkyBox Showdown Series

These 12 standard-size (2 1/2" by 3 1/2") cards were random inserts in first-series (1-6) and second-series (7-12) packs. The odds of finding one of these cards are one in every six packs. Each front features a borderless color action photo of the two players involved in the "Showdown." Both players' names appear, one vs. the other, in gold lettering within a metal-

lic black stripe near the bottom. The horizontal white back carries a color player close-up for each player on each side. The players' names appear beneath each photo. Comparative statistics fill in the area between the two player photos. The cards are numbered on the back with an "SS" prefix.

	MINT	EXC	G-VG
COMPLETE SET (12)	10.00	4.50	1.25
COMPLETE SERIES 1 (6)	6.00	2.70	.75
COMPLETE SERIES 2 (6)	4.00	1.80	.50
COMMON PAIR (SS1-SS6)	.75	.35	.09
COMMON PAIR (SS7-SS12)	.40	.18	.05
☐ SS1 Alonzo Mourning Patrick Ewing	1.50	.65	.19
☐ SS2 Shaquille O'Neal Patrick Ewing	2.50	1.15	.30
☐ SS3 Alonzo Mourning Shaquille O'Neal	3.00	1.35	.40
☐ SS4 Hakeem Olajuwon Dikembe Mutombo	1.00	.45	.13
☐ SS5 David Robinson Hakeem Olajuwon	1.50	.65	.19
☐ SS6 David Robinson Dikembe Mutombo	.75	.35	.09
☐ SS7 Shawn Kemp Karl Malone	1.00	.45	.13
☐ SS8 Larry Johnson Charles Barkley	1.00	.45	.13
☐ SS9 Dominique Wilkins Scottie Pippen	.75	.35	.09
☐ SS10 Joe Dumars Reggie Miller	.40	.18	.05
☐ SS11 Clyde Drexler Michael Jordan	2.00	.90	.25
☐ SS12 Magic Johnson Larry Bird	2.00	.90	.25

1993-94 SkyBox Thunder and Lightning

Randomly inserted in series two packs, this standard-size (2 1/2" by 3 1/2") 9-card set features players pictured on both borderless sides with color action player cutouts set against metallic backgrounds. The cards are numbered on the back with a "TL" prefix.

	MINT	EXC	G-VG
COMPLETE SET (9)	35.00	16.00	4.40
COMMON PAIR (1-9)	1.00	.45	.13
☐ TL1 Jamal Mashburn Jim Jackson Dallas Mavericks	6.00	2.70	.75

	MINT	EXC	G-VG
☐ TL2 Harold Miner	1.00	.45	.13
Steve Smith			
Miami Heat			
☐ TL3 Isaiah Rider	4.00	1.80	.50
Micheal Williams			
Minnesota Timberwolves			
☐ TL4 Derrick Coleman	2.00	.90	.25
Kenny Anderson			
New Jersey Nets			
☐ TL5 Patrick Ewing	2.50	1.15	.30
John Starks			
New York Knicks			
☐ TL6 Shaquille O'Neal	20.00	9.00	2.50
Anfernee Hardaway			
Orlando Magic			
☐ TL7 Shawn Bradley	1.50	.65	.19
Jeff Hornacek			
Philadelphia 76ers			
☐ TL8 Walt Williams	1.50	.65	.19
Bobby Hurley			
Sacramento Kings			
☐ TL9 Dennis Rodman	3.00	1.35	.40
David Robinson			
San Antonio Spurs			

1993-94 SkyBox USA Tip-Off

The 13-card 1993-94 SkyBox USA Tip-Off set could be acquired by sending in one USA Exchange card. The USA Exchange cards were randomly inserted in SkyBox series two packs. The Tip-Off redemption expiration was 6/15/94. Two players are featured on the front of each card with quotes from either player on the back. Players were chosen to share a card based on similar styles of play. It should be noted that Michael Jordan is not part of the set.

	MINT	EXC	G-VG
COMPLETE SET (14)	30.00	13.50	3.80
COMMON CARD (1-13)	1.00	.45	.13
☐ 1 Steve Smith	3.00	1.35	.40
Magic Johnson			
☐ 2 Larry Johnson	4.00	1.80	.50
Charles Barkley			
☐ 3 Patrick Ewing	5.00	2.30	.60
Alonzo Mourning			
☐ 4 Shawn Kemp	3.00	1.35	.40
Karl Malone			
☐ 5 Chris Mullin	1.00	.45	.13
Dan Majerle			

				8 ☐
☐ 6	John Stockton	1.50	.65	.19 ☐
	Mark Price			
☐ 7	Christian Laettner	1.50	.65	.19
	Derrick Coleman			
☐ 8	Dominique Wilkins	2.00	.90	.25
	Clyde Drexler			
☐ 9	Joe Dumars	2.00	.90	.25
	Scottie Pippen			
☐ 10	David Robinson	10.00	4.50	1.25
	Shaquille O'Neal			
☐ 11	Reggie Miller	4.00	1.80	.50
	Larry Bird			
☐ 12	Tim Hardaway	1.00	.45	.13
☐ 13	Isiah Thomas	1.50	.65	.19
☐ NNO	Checklist	3.00	1.35	.40
☐ NNO	Expired USA Exchange	.25	.11	.03

1994 SkyBox USA

These 89 standard-size (2 1/2" by 3 1/2") cards honor the '94 Team USA players. The border-less fronts feature color posed and action player shots. The player's name appears in sil-ver-foil lettering within a red stripe near the bottom. Each player has a subset of six cards, the backs of which carry information about each player's international experience, NBA rookie year, best game, NBA update, trademark move, and comments on the player by Magic Johnson. The cards are numbered on the back.

	MINT	EXC	G-VG
COMPLETE SET (89)	15.00	6.75	1.90
COMMON PLAYER (1-89)	.10	.05	.01
☐ 1 Alonzo Mourning International	.60	.25	.08
☐ 2 Alonzo Mourning NBA Rookie	.60	.25	.08
☐ 3 Alonzo Mourning Best Game	.60	.25	.08
☐ 4 Alonzo Mourning NBA Update	.60	.25	.08
☐ 5 Alonzo Mourning Trademark Move	.60	.25	.08
☐ 6 Alonzo Mourning Magic On	.30	.14	.04
☐ 7 Larry Johnson International	.40	.18	.05
☐ 8 Larry Johnson NBA Rookie	.40	.18	.05
☐ 9 Larry Johnson Best Game	.40	.18	.05
☐ 10 Larry Johnson NBA Update	.40	.18	.05
☐ 11 Larry Johnson Trademark Move	.40	.18	.05
☐ 12 Larry Johnson Magic On	.40	.18	.05
☐ 13 Shawn Kemp International	.40	.18	.05
☐ 14 Shawn Kemp NBA Rookie	.40	.18	.05
☐ 15 Shawn Kemp Best Game	.40	.18	.05
☐ 16 Shawn Kemp NBA Update	.40	.18	.05
☐ 17 Shawn Kemp Trademark Move	.40	.18	.05
☐ 18 Shawn Kemp Magic On	.40	.18	.05
☐ 19 Mark Price International	.10	.05	.01
☐ 20 Mark Price NBA Rookie	.10	.05	.01
☐ 21 Mark Price Best Game	.10	.05	.01
☐ 22 Mark Price NBA Update	.10	.05	.01
☐ 23 Mark Price Trademark Move	.10	.05	.01
☐ 24 Mark Price Magic On	.10	.05	.01
☐ 25 Steve Smith International	.10	.05	.01
☐ 26 Steve Smith NBA Rookie	.10	.05	.01
☐ 27 Steve Smith Best Game	.10	.05	.01
☐ 28 Steve Smith NBA Update	.10	.05	.01
☐ 29 Steve Smith Trademark Move	.10	.05	.01
☐ 30 Steve Smith Magic On	.10	.05	.01
☐ 31 Dominique Wilkins International	.30	.14	.04
☐ 32 Dominique Wilkins NBA Rookie	.30	.14	.04
☐ 33 Dominique Wilkins Best Game	.30	.14	.04
☐ 34 Dominique Wilkins NBA Update	.30	.14	.04
☐ 35 Dominique Wilkins Trademark Move	.30	.14	.04

☐ 36	Dominique Wilkins Magic On	.30	.14	.04
☐ 37	Derrick Coleman International	.20	.09	.03
☐ 38	Derrick Coleman NBA Rookie	.20	.09	.03
☐ 39	Derrick Coleman Best Game	.20	.09	.03
☐ 40	Derrick Coleman NBA Update	.20	.09	.03
☐ 41	Derrick Coleman Trademark Move	.20	.09	.03
☐ 42	Derrick Coleman Magic On	.20	.09	.03
☐ 43	Isiah Thomas International	.15	.07	.02
☐ 44	Isiah Thomas NBA Rookie	.15	.07	.02
☐ 45	Isiah Thomas Best Game	.15	.07	.02
☐ 46	Isiah Thomas NBA Update	.15	.07	.02
☐ 47	Isiah Thomas Trademark Move	.15	.07	.02
☐ 48	Isiah Thomas Magic On	.15	.07	.02
☐ 49	Joe Dumars International	.15	.07	.02
☐ 50	Joe Dumars NBA Rookie	.15	.07	.02
☐ 51	Joe Dumars Best Game	.15	.07	.02
☐ 52	Joe Dumars NBA Update	.15	.07	.02
☐ 53	Joe Dumars Trademark Move	.15	.07	.02
☐ 54	Joe Dumars Magic On	.15	.07	.02
☐ 55	Dan Majerle International	.10	.05	.01
☐ 56	Dan Majerle NBA Rookie	.10	.05	.01
☐ 57	Dan Majerle Best Game	.10	.05	.01
☐ 58	Dan Majerle NBA Update	.10	.05	.01
☐ 59	Dan Majerle Trademark Move	.10	.05	.01
☐ 60	Dan Majerle Magic On	.10	.05	.01
☐ 61	Tim Hardaway International	.10	.05	.01
☐ 62	Tim Hardaway NBA Rookie	.10	.05	.01
☐ 63	Tim Hardaway Best Game	.10	.05	.01
☐ 64	Tim Hardaway NBA Update	.10	.05	.01
☐ 65	Tim Hardaway Trademark Move	.10	.05	.01
☐ 66	Tim Hardaway Magic On	.10	.05	.01
☐ 67	Shaquille O'Neal International	1.50	.65	.19
☐ 68	Shaquille O'Neal NBA Rookie	1.50	.65	.19
☐ 69	Shaquille O'Neal Best Game	1.50	.65	.19
☐ 70	Shaquille O'Neal NBA Update	1.50	.65	.19
☐ 71	Shaquille O'Neal Trademark Move	1.50	.65	.19
☐ 72	Shaquille O'Neal	1.50	.65	.19

			MINT	EXC	G-VG
☐ 73	Reggie Miller		.20	.09	.03
	Magic On International				
☐ 74	Reggie Miller		.20	.09	.03
	NBA Rookie				
☐ 75	Reggie Miller		.20	.09	.03
	Best Game				
☐ 76	Reggie Miller		.20	.09	.03
	NBA Update				
☐ 77	Reggie Miller		.20	.09	.03
	Trademark Move				
☐ 78	Reggie Miller		.20	.09	.03
	Magic On				
☐ 79	Don Chaney CO		.10	.05	.01
☐ 80	Pete Gillen CO		.10	.05	.01
☐ 81	Rick Majerus CO		.10	.05	.01
☐ 82	Don Nelson CO		.10	.05	.01
☐ 83	'94 USA Team		.25	.11	.03
☐ 84	International Rules		.10	.05	.01
	Time				
☐ 85	International Rules		.10	.05	.01
	Court Dimensions				
☐ 86	International Rules		.10	.05	.01
	Rules				
☐ 87	Earvin(Magic) Johnson		.50	.23	.06
	Passing the Torch				
☐ 88	David Robinson		.50	.23	.06
	Passing the Torch				
☐ 89	Checklist		.10	.05	.01
☐ NNO	T-shirt Exchange Card		15.00	6.75	1.90
☐ NNO	On The Court Exchange		40.00	18.00	5.00

1994 SkyBox USA Champion Gold

Randomly inserted in packs, this parallel set features standard-size (2 1/2" by 3 1/2") cards that differ from their '94 SkyBox USA counterparts only by the embossed gold-foil highlights. The cards are numbered on the back.

	MINT	EXC	G-VG
COMPLETE SET (89)	100.00	45.00	12.50
COMMON GOLD (1-89)	.50	.23	.06
*GOLD CARDS: 2.5X to 5X VALUE			

1994 SkyBox USA Dream Play

Randomly inserted in packs, these 13 standard-size (2 1/2" by 3 1/2") cards feature on their borderless fronts posed action color cutouts of the players in their Team USA uniforms set on a dark play diagram background. The player's name appears in prismatic silver-foil lettering at the top. The white back carries play diagrams and descriptions. The cards are numbered on the back with a "DP" prefix.

	MINT	EXC	G-VG
COMPLETE SET (13)	100.00	45.00	12.50
COMMON PLAYER (DP1-DP13)	4.00	1.80	.50
☐ DP1 Alonzo Mourning	15.00	6.75	1.90
☐ DP2 Larry Johnson	10.00	4.50	1.25
☐ DP3 Shawn Kemp	12.00	5.50	1.50
☐ DP4 Mark Price	4.00	1.80	.50
☐ DP5 Steve Smith	4.00	1.80	.50
☐ DP6 Dominique Wilkins	10.00	4.50	1.25
☐ DP7 Derrick Coleman	6.00	2.70	.75
☐ DP8 Isiah Thomas	5.00	2.30	.60
☐ DP9 Joe Dumars	5.00	2.30	.60
☐ DP10 Dan Majerle	4.00	1.80	.50
☐ DP11 Tim Hardaway	4.00	1.80	.50
☐ DP12 Shaquille O'Neal	35.00	16.00	4.40
☐ DP13 Reggie Miller	6.00	2.70	.75

1994 SkyBox USA Portraits

Randomly inserted in packs, these 13 standard-size (2 1/2" by 3 1/2") cards feature on their embossed gold foil-bordered fronts posed color retouched photo portraits of the players in their Team USA uniforms. The player's name appears in embossed lettering within the gold-foil lower margin. The red, white, and blue back carries a quote from the player. The cards are numbered on the back with a "PT" prefix.

	MINT	EXC	G-VG
COMPLETE SET (13)	300.00	135.00	38.00
COMMON PLAYER (PT1-PT13)	10.00	4.50	1.25
☐ PT1 Alonzo Mourning	40.00	18.00	5.00
☐ PT2 Larry Johnson	25.00	11.50	3.10
☐ PT3 Shawn Kemp	30.00	13.50	3.80
☐ PT4 Mark Price	10.00	4.50	1.25
☐ PT5 Steve Smith	10.00	4.50	1.25
☐ PT6 Dominique Wilkins	25.00	11.50	3.10
☐ PT7 Derrick Coleman	15.00	6.75	1.90
☐ PT8 Isiah Thomas	12.00	5.50	1.50

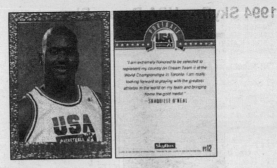

☐ PT9	Joe Dumars	12.00	5.50	1.50
☐ PT10	Dan Majerle	10.00	4.50	1.25
☐ PT11	Tim Hardaway	10.00	4.50	1.25
☐ PT12	Shaquille O'Neal	100.00	47.50	13.00
☐ PT13	Reggie Miller	15.00	6.75	1.90

1992-93 Stadium Club

The complete 1992-93 Topps Stadium Club basketball set consists of 400 cards, having been issued in two 200-card series. Both first and second series packs contained 15 cards with a suggested retail price of 1.79 per pack. Topps also issued, late in the season, second series 23-card jumbo packs. The cards measure the standard size (2 1/2" by 3 1/2" inches). A Stadium Club membership form was inserted in every 15-card pack. In the second series, "Beam Team" cards were randomly inserted approximately one in every 36 15-card packs. The basic card fronts feature full-bleed color action player photos. The team name and player's name appear in gold foil stripes that cut across the bottom of the card and intersect the Stadium Club logo. On a colorful background of a basketball in a net, the horizontal backs present biography, The Sporting News Skills Rating System, player evaluation, 1991-92 season and career statistics, and a miniature representation of the player's first Topps card, which is confusingly referenced as "Topps Rookie Card" by Topps. The first series closes and the second series begins with a Members Choice (191-211) sub-set. The cards are numbered on the back. Rookie Cards include LaPhonso Ellis, Tom Gugliotta, Robert Horry, Christian Laettner, Don McLean, Harold Miner, Alonzo Mourning, Shaquille O'Neal, Latrell Sprewell, Clarence Weatherspoon, and Walt Williams.

	MINT	EXC	G-VG
COMPLETE SET (400)	60.00	27.00	7.50
COMPLETE SERIES 1 (200)	25.00	11.50	3.10
COMPLETE SERIES 2 (200)	35.00	16.00	4.40
COMMON PLAYER (1-200)	.10	.05	.01
COMMON PLAYER (201-400)	.10	.05	.01
☐ 1 Michael Jordan	4.00	1.80	.50
Chicago Bulls			
☐ 2 Greg Anthony	.10	.05	.01
New York Knicks			
☐ 3 Otis Thorpe	.15	.07	.02
Houston Rockets			
☐ 4 Jim Les	.10	.05	.01
Sacramento Kings			
☐ 5 Kevin Willis	.15	.07	.02
Atlanta Hawks			
☐ 6 Derek Harper	.15	.07	.02
Dallas Mavericks			
☐ 7 Elden Campbell	.10	.05	.01
Los Angeles Lakers			
☐ 8 A.J. English	.10	.05	.01
Washington Bullets			
☐ 9 Kenny Gattison	.10	.05	.01
Charlotte Hornets			
☐ 10 Drazen Petrovic	.15	.07	.02
New Jersey Nets			
☐ 11 Chris Mullin	.30	.14	.04
Golden State Warriors			
☐ 12 Mark Price	.20	.09	.03
Cleveland Cavaliers			
☐ 13 Karl Malone	.50	.23	.06
Utah Jazz			
☐ 14 Gerald Glass	.10	.05	.01
Minnesota Timberwolves			
☐ 15 Negele Knight	.10	.05	.01
Phoenix Suns			
☐ 16 Mark Macon	.10	.05	.01
Denver Nuggets			
☐ 17 Michael Cage	.10	.05	.01
Seattle Supersonics			
☐ 18 Kevin Edwards	.10	.05	.01
Miami Heat			
☐ 19 Sherman Douglas	.10	.05	.01
Boston Celtics			
☐ 20 Ron Harper	.15	.07	.02
Los Angeles Clippers			
☐ 21 Cliff Robinson	.20	.09	.03
Portland Trail Blazers			
☐ 22 Byron Scott	.15	.07	.02
Los Angeles Lakers			
☐ 23 Antoine Carr	.10	.05	.01
San Antonio Spurs			
☐ 24 Greg Dreiling	.10	.05	.01
Indiana Pacers			
☐ 25 Bill Laimbeer	.20	.09	.03
Detroit Pistons			
☐ 26 Hersey Hawkins	.15	.07	.02
Philadelphia 76ers			
☐ 27 Will Perdue	.10	.05	.01
Chicago Bulls			
☐ 28 Todd Lichti	.10	.05	.01
Denver Nuggets			
☐ 29 Gary Grant	.10	.05	.01
Los Angeles Clippers			
☐ 30 Sam Perkins	.15	.07	.02
Los Angeles Lakers			
☐ 31 Jayson Williams	.10	.05	.01
Philadelphia 76ers			
☐ 32 Magic Johnson	1.00	.45	.13
Los Angeles Lakers			
☐ 33 Larry Bird	1.50	.65	.19
Boston Celtics			

☐ 34 Chris Morris	.10	.05	.01
New Jersey Nets			
☐ 35 Nick Anderson	.15	.07	.02
Orlando Magic			
☐ 36 Scott Hastings	.10	.05	.01
Denver Nuggets			
☐ 37 Ledell Eackles	.10	.05	.01
Washington Bullets			
☐ 38 Robert Pack	.10	.05	.01
Portland Trail Blazers			
☐ 39 Dana Barros	.10	.05	.01
Seattle Supersonics			
☐ 40 Anthony Bonner	.10	.05	.01
Sacramento Kings			
☐ 41 J.R. Reid	.10	.05	.01
Charlotte Hornets			
☐ 42 Tyrone Hill	.10	.05	.01
Golden State Warriors			
☐ 43 Rik Smits	.15	.07	.02
Indiana Pacers			
☐ 44 Kevin Duckworth	.10	.05	.01
Portland Trail Blazers			
☐ 45 LaSalle Thompson	.15	.07	.02
Indiana Pacers			
☐ 46 Brian Williams	.10	.05	.01
Orlando Magic			
☐ 47 Willie Anderson	.10	.05	.01
San Antonio Spurs			
☐ 48 Ken Norman	.10	.05	.01
Los Angeles Clippers			
☐ 49 Mike Iuzzolino	.10	.05	.01
Dallas Mavericks			
☐ 50 Isiah Thomas	.30	.14	.04
Detroit Pistons			
☐ 51 Alec Kessler	.10	.05	.01
Miami Heat			
☐ 52 Johnny Dawkins	.10	.05	.01
Philadelphia 76ers			
☐ 53 Avery Johnson	.10	.05	.01
Houston Rockets			
☐ 54 Stacey Augmon	.20	.09	.03
Atlanta Hawks			
☐ 55 Charles Oakley	.20	.09	.03
New York Knicks			
☐ 56 Rex Chapman	.10	.05	.01
Washington Bullets			
☐ 57 Charles Shackleford	.10	.05	.01
Philadelphia 76ers			
☐ 58 Jeff Ruland	.15	.07	.02
Philadelphia 76ers			
☐ 59 Craig Ehlo	.10	.05	.01
Cleveland Cavaliers			
☐ 60 Jon Koncak	.10	.05	.01
Atlanta Hawks			
☐ 61 Danny Schayes	.10	.05	.01
Milwaukee Bucks			
☐ 62 David Benoit	.10	.05	.01
Utah Jazz			
☐ 63 Robert Parish	.20	.09	.03
Boston Celtics			
☐ 64 Mookie Blaylock	.15	.07	.02
New Jersey Nets			
☐ 65 Sean Elliott	.10	.05	.01
San Antonio Spurs			
☐ 66 Mark Aguirre	.20	.09	.03
Detroit Pistons			
☐ 67 Scott Williams	.10	.05	.01
Chicago Bulls			
☐ 68 Doug West	.10	.05	.01
Minnesota Timberwolves			
☐ 69 Kenny Anderson	.40	.18	.05
New Jersey Nets			
☐ 70 Randy Brown	.10	.05	.01

	Sacramento Kings			
☐ 71	Muggsy Bogues	.20	.09	.03
	Charlotte Hornets			
☐ 72	Spud Webb	.20	.09	.03
	Sacramento Kings			
☐ 73	Sedale Threatt	.10	.05	.01
	Los Angeles Lakers			
☐ 74	Chris Gatling	.10	.05	.01
	Golden State Warriors			
☐ 75	Derrick McKey	.10	.05	.01
	Seattle Supersonics			
☐ 76	Sleepy Floyd	.10	.05	.01
	Houston Rockets			
☐ 77	Chris Jackson	.15	.07	.02
	Denver Nuggets			
☐ 78	Thurl Bailey	.10	.05	.01
	Minnesota Timberwolves			
☐ 79	Steve Smith	.25	.11	.03
	Miami Heat			
☐ 80	Jerrod Mustaf	.10	.05	.01
	Phoenix Suns			
☐ 81	Anthony Bowie	.10	.05	.01
	Orlando Magic			
☐ 82	John Williams	.10	.05	.01
	Washington Bullets			
☐ 83	Paul Graham	.10	.05	.01
	Atlanta Hawks			
☐ 84	Willie Burton	.10	.05	.01
	Miami Heat			
☐ 85	Vernon Maxwell	.15	.07	.02
	Houston Rockets			
☐ 86	Stacey King	.10	.05	.01
	Chicago Bulls			
☐ 87	B.J. Armstrong	.20	.09	.03
	Chicago Bulls			
☐ 88	Kevin Gamble	.10	.05	.01
	Boston Celtics			
☐ 89	Terry Catledge	.10	.05	.01
	Orlando Magic			
☐ 90	Jeff Malone	.15	.07	.02
	Utah Jazz			
☐ 91	Sam Bowie	.10	.05	.01
	New Jersey Nets			
☐ 92	Orlando Woolridge	.15	.07	.02
	Detroit Pistons			
☐ 93	Steve Kerr	.10	.05	.01
	Cleveland Cavaliers			
☐ 94	Eric Leckner	.10	.05	.01
	Charlotte Hornets			
☐ 95	Loy Vaught	.15	.07	.02
	Los Angeles Clippers			
☐ 96	Jud Buechler	.10	.05	.01
	Golden State Warriors			
☐ 97	Doug Smith	.10	.05	.01
	Dallas Mavericks			
☐ 98	Sidney Green	.10	.05	.01
	San Antonio Spurs			
☐ 99	Jerome Kersey	.10	.05	.01
	Portland Trail Blazers			
☐ 100	Patrick Ewing	.75	.35	.09
	New York Knicks			
☐ 101	Ed Nealy	.10	.05	.01
	Phoenix Suns			
☐ 102	Shawn Kemp	1.50	.65	.19
	Seattle Supersonics			
☐ 103	Luc Longley	.10	.05	.01
	Minnesota Timberwolves			
☐ 104	George McCloud	.10	.05	.01
	Indiana Pacers			
☐ 105	Ron Anderson	.10	.05	.01
	Philadelphia 76ers			
☐ 106	Moses Malone UER	.20	.09	.03
	(Rookie Card is 1975-76, not 1976-77)			

Milwaukee Bucks
☐ 107 Tony Smith... .10 .05 .01
Los Angeles Lakers
☐ 108 Terry Porter...................................... .15 .07 .02
Portland Trail Blazers
☐ 109 Blair Rasmussen............................... .10 .05 .01
Atlanta Hawks
☐ 110 Bimbo Coles..................................... .10 .05 .01
Miami Heat
☐ 111 Grant Long....................................... .10 .05 .01
Miami Heat
☐ 112 John Battle....................................... .10 .05 .01
Cleveland Cavaliers
☐ 113 Brian Oliver...................................... .10 .05 .01
Philadelphia 76ers
☐ 114 Tyrone Corbin................................... .10 .05 .01
Utah Jazz
☐ 115 Benoit Benjamin................................ .10 .05 .01
Seattle Supersonics
☐ 116 Rick Fox... .10 .05 .01
Boston Celtics
☐ 117 Rafael Addison.................................. .10 .05 .01
New Jersey Nets
☐ 118 Danny Young..................................... .10 .05 .01
Los Angeles Clippers
☐ 119 Fat Lever.. .10 .05 .01
Dallas Mavericks
☐ 120 Terry Cummings................................ .15 .07 .02
San Antonio Spurs
☐ 121 Felton Spencer................................. .10 .05 .01
Minnesota Timberwolves
☐ 122 Joe Kleine.. .10 .05 .01
Boston Celtics
☐ 123 Johnny Newman................................ .10 .05 .01
Charlotte Hornets
☐ 124 Gary Payton...................................... .20 .09 .03
Seattle Supersonics
☐ 125 Kurt Rambis...................................... .15 .07 .02
Phoenix Suns
☐ 126 Vlade Divac....................................... .15 .07 .02
Los Angeles Lakers
☐ 127 John Paxson...................................... .15 .07 .02
Chicago Bulls
☐ 128 Lionel Simmons................................. .15 .07 .02
Sacramento Kings
☐ 129 Randy Wittman.................................. .10 .05 .01
Indiana Pacers
☐ 130 Winston Garland............................... .10 .05 .01
Denver Nuggets
☐ 131 Jerry Reynolds.................................. .10 .05 .01
Orlando Magic
☐ 132 Dell Curry... .15 .07 .02
Charlotte Hornets
☐ 133 Fred Roberts..................................... .10 .05 .01
Milwaukee Bucks
☐ 134 Michael Adams.................................. .15 .07 .02
Washington Bullets
☐ 135 Charles Jones................................... .10 .05 .01
Washington Bullets
☐ 136 Frank Brickowski............................... .15 .07 .02
Milwaukee Bucks
☐ 137 Alton Lister....................................... .10 .05 .01
Golden State Warriors
☐ 138 Horace Grant.................................... .20 .09 .03
Chicago Bulls
☐ 139 Greg Sutton...................................... .10 .05 .01
San Antonio Spurs
☐ 140 John Starks....................................... .20 .09 .03
New York Knicks
☐ 141 Detlef Schrempf................................ .20 .09 .03
Indiana Pacers
☐ 142 Rodney Monroe................................. .10 .05 .01
Atlanta Hawks

☐ 143	Pete Chilcutt Sacramento Kings	.10	.05	.01
☐ 144	Mike Brown Utah Jazz	.10	.05	.01
☐ 145	Rony Seikaly Miami Heat	.20	.09	.03
☐ 146	Donald Hodge Dallas Mavericks	.10	.05	.01
☐ 147	Kevin McHale Boston Celtics	.20	.09	.03
☐ 148	Ricky Pierce Seattle Supersonics	.15	.07	.02
☐ 149	Brian Shaw Miami Heat	.10	.05	.01
☐ 150	Reggie Williams Denver Nuggets	.15	.07	.02
☐ 151	Kendall Gill Charlotte Hornets	.15	.07	.02
☐ 152	Tom Chambers Phoenix Suns	.15	.07	.02
☐ 153	Jack Haley Los Angeles Lakers	.10	.05	.01
☐ 154	Terrell Brandon Cleveland Cavaliers	.10	.05	.01
☐ 155	Dennis Scott Orlando Magic	.15	.07	.02
☐ 156	Mark Randall Minnesota Timberwolves	.10	.05	.01
☐ 157	Kenny Payne Philadelphia 76ers	.10	.05	.01
☐ 158	Bernard King Washington Bullets	.20	.09	.03
☐ 159	Tate George New Jersey Nets	.10	.05	.01
☐ 160	Scott Skiles Orlando Magic	.10	.05	.01
☐ 161	Pervis Ellison Washington Bullets	.10	.05	.01
☐ 162	Marcus Liberty Denver Nuggets	.10	.05	.01
☐ 163	Rumeal Robinson Atlanta Hawks	.10	.05	.01
☐ 164	Anthony Mason New York Knicks	.15	.07	.02
☐ 165	Les Jepsen Sacramento Kings	.10	.05	.01
☐ 166	Kenny Smith Houston Rockets	.10	.05	.01
☐ 167	Randy White Dallas Mavericks	.10	.05	.01
☐ 168	Dee Brown Boston Celtics	.10	.05	.01
☐ 169	Chris Dudley New Jersey Nets	.10	.05	.01
☐ 170	Armon Gilliam Philadelphia 76ers	.10	.05	.01
☐ 171	Eddie Johnson Seattle Supersonics	.10	.05	.01
☐ 172	A.C. Green Los Angeles Lakers	.15	.07	.02
☐ 173	Darrell Walker Detroit Pistons	.10	.05	.01
☐ 174	Bill Cartwright Chicago Bulls	.15	.07	.02
☐ 175	Mike Gminski Charlotte Hornets	.10	.05	.01
☐ 176	Tom Tolbert Golden State Warriors	.10	.05	.01
☐ 177	Buck Williams Portland Trail Blazers	.20	.09	.03
☐ 178	Mark Eaton Utah Jazz	.10	.05	.01
☐ 179	Danny Manning	.30	.14	.04

		Los Angeles Clippers		
☐	180	Glen Rice .20	.09	.03
		Miami Heat		
☐	181	Sarunas Marciulionis .15	.07	.02
		Golden State Warriors		
☐	182	Danny Ferry .10	.05	.01
		Cleveland Cavaliers		
☐	183	Chris Corchiani .10	.05	.01
		Orlando Magic		
☐	184	Dan Majerle .20	.09	.03
		Phoenix Suns		
☐	185	Alvin Robertson .15	.07	.02
		Milwaukee Bucks		
☐	186	Vern Fleming .10	.05	.01
		Indiana Pacers		
☐	187	Kevin Lynch .10	.05	.01
		Charlotte Hornets		
☐	188	John Williams .15	.07	.02
☐	189	Checklist 1-100 .10	.05	.01
☐	190	Checklist 101-200 .10	.05	.01
☐	191	David Robinson MC .50	.23	.06
		San Antonio Spurs		
☐	192	Larry Johnson MC .60	.25	.08
		Charlotte Hornets		
☐	193	Derrick Coleman MC .20	.09	.03
		New Jersey Nets		
☐	194	Larry Bird MC 1.00	.45	.13
		Boston Celtics		
☐	195	Billy Owens MC .20	.09	.03
		Golden State Warriors		
☐	196	Dikembe Mutombo MC .20	.09	.03
		Denver Nuggets		
☐	197	Charles Barkley MC .50	.23	.06
		Philadelphia 76ers		
☐	198	Scottie Pippen MC .40	.18	.05
		Chicago Bulls		
☐	199	Clyde Drexler MC .20	.09	.03
		Portland Trail Blazers		
☐	200	John Stockton MC .20	.09	.03
		Utah Jazz		
☐	201	Shaquille O'Neal MC 4.00	1.80	.50
		Orlando Magic		
☐	202	Chris Mullin MC .20	.09	.03
		Golden State Warriors		
☐	203	Glen Rice MC .10	.05	.01
		Miami Heat		
☐	204	Isiah Thomas MC .15	.07	.02
		Detroit Pistons		
☐	205	Karl Malone MC .25	.11	.03
		Utah Jazz		
☐	206	Christian Laettner MC .60	.25	.08
		Minnesota Timberwolves		
☐	207	Patrick Ewing MC .40	.18	.05
		New York Knicks		
☐	208	Dominique Wilkins MC .30	.14	.04
		Atlanta Hawks		
☐	209	Alonzo Mourning MC 2.50	1.15	.30
		Charlotte Hornets		
☐	210	Michael Jordan MC 2.00	.90	.25
		Chicago Bulls		
☐	211	Tim Hardaway MC .20	.09	.03
		Golden State Warriors		
☐	212	Rodney McCray .10	.05	.01
		Chicago Bulls		
☐	213	Larry Johnson 1.00	.45	.13
		Charlotte Hornets		
☐	214	Charles Smith .10	.05	.01
		New York Knicks		
☐	215	Kevin Brooks .10	.05	.01
		Indiana Pacers		
☐	216	Kevin Johnson .20	.09	.03
		Phoenix Suns		
☐	217	Duane Cooper .10	.05	.01
		Los Angeles Lakers		

☐ 218 Christian Laettner UER (Missing '92 Draft Pick logo) Minnesota Timberwolves	1.50	.65	.19
☐ 219 Tim Perry Philadelphia 76ers	.10	.05	.01
☐ 220 Hakeem Olajuwon Houston Rockets	1.50	.65	.19
☐ 221 Lee Mayberry Milwaukee Bucks	.20	.09	.03
☐ 222 Mark Bryant Portland Trail Blazers	.10	.05	.01
☐ 223 Robert Horry Houston Rockets	1.50	.65	.19
☐ 224 Tracy Murray UER (Missing '92 Draft Pick logo) Portland Trail Blazers	.20	.09	.03
☐ 225 Greg Grant Philadelphia 76ers	.10	.05	.01
☐ 226 Rolando Blackman New York Knicks	.15	.07	.02
☐ 227 James Edwards UER (Rookie Card is 1978-79, not 1980-81) Los Angeles Lakers	.10	.05	.01
☐ 228 Sean Green Indiana Pacers	.10	.05	.01
☐ 229 Buck Johnson Washington Bullets	.10	.05	.01
☐ 230 Andrew Lang Philadelphia 76ers	.10	.05	.01
☐ 231 Tracy Moore Dallas Mavericks	.10	.05	.01
☐ 232 Adam Keefe UER (Missing '92 Draft Pick logo) Atlanta Hawks	.20	.09	.03
☐ 233 Tony Campbell New York Knicks	.10	.05	.01
☐ 234 Rod Strickland Portland Trail Blazers	.15	.07	.02
☐ 235 Terry Mills Detroit Pistons	.20	.09	.03
☐ 236 Billy Owens Golden State Warriors	.20	.09	.03
☐ 237 Bryant Stith UER (Missing '92 Draft Pick logo) Denver Nuggets	.75	.35	.09
☐ 238 Tony Bennett UER (Missing '92 Draft Pick logo) Charlotte Hornets	.20	.09	.03
☐ 239 David Wood San Antonio Spurs	.10	.05	.01
☐ 240 Jay Humphries Utah Jazz	.10	.05	.01
☐ 241 Doc Rivers New York Knicks	.15	.07	.02
☐ 242 Wayman Tisdale Sacramento Kings	.15	.07	.02
☐ 243 Litterial Green Orlando Magic	.20	.09	.03
☐ 244 Jon Barry Milwaukee Bucks	.20	.09	.03
☐ 245 Brad Daugherty Cleveland Cavaliers	.20	.09	.03
☐ 246 Nate McMillan Seattle Supersonics	.10	.05	.01
☐ 247 Shaquille O'Neal Orlando Magic	12.00	5.50	1.50
☐ 248 Chris Smith	.25	.11	.03

	Minnesota Timberwolves		
☐ 249	Duane Ferrell .10	.05	.01
	Atlanta Hawks		
☐ 250	Anthony Peeler .60	.25	.08
	Los Angeles Lakers		
☐ 251	Gundars Vetra .10	.05	.01
	Minnesota Timberwolves		
☐ 252	Danny Ainge .20	.09	.03
	Phoenix Suns		
☐ 253	Mitch Richmond .20	.09	.03
	Sacramento Kings		
☐ 254	Malik Sealy .20	.09	.03
	Indiana Pacers		
☐ 255	Brent Price .20	.09	.03
	Washington Bullets		
☐ 256	Xavier McDaniel .15	.07	.02
	Boston Celtics		
☐ 257	Bobby Phills .25	.11	.03
	Cleveland Cavaliers		
☐ 258	Donald Royal .10	.05	.01
	Orlando Magic		
☐ 259	Olden Polynice .10	.05	.01
	Detroit Pistons		
☐ 260	Dominique Wilkins UER .60	.25	.08
	(Scoring 10,000th point, should be 20,000th)		
	Atlanta Hawks		
☐ 261	Larry Krystkowiak .10	.05	.01
	Utah Jazz		
☐ 262	Duane Causwell .10	.05	.01
	Sacramento Kings		
☐ 263	Todd Day .75	.35	.09
	Milwaukee Bucks		
☐ 264	Sam Mack .10	.05	.01
	San Antonio Spurs		
☐ 265	John Stockton .35	.16	.04
	Utah Jazz		
☐ 266	Eddie Lee Wilkins .10	.05	.01
	Philadelphia 76ers		
☐ 267	Gerald Glass .10	.05	.01
	Detroit Pistons		
☐ 268	Robert Pack .10	.05	.01
	Denver Nuggets		
☐ 269	Gerald Wilkins .10	.05	.01
	Cleveland Cavaliers		
☐ 270	Reggie Lewis .20	.09	.03
	Boston Celtics		
☐ 271	Scott Brooks .10	.05	.01
	Houston Rockets		
☐ 272	Randy Woods UER .10	.05	.01
	(Missing '92 Draft Pick logo)		
	Los Angeles Clippers		
☐ 273	Dikembe Mutombo .40	.18	.05
	Denver Nuggets		
☐ 274	Kiki Vandeweghe .15	.07	.02
	Los Angeles Clippers		
☐ 275	Rich King .10	.05	.01
	Seattle Supersonics		
☐ 276	Jeff Turner .10	.05	.01
	Orlando Magic		
☐ 277	Vinny Del Negro .10	.05	.01
	San Antonio Spurs		
☐ 278	Marlon Maxey .10	.05	.01
	Minnesota Timberwolves		
☐ 279	Elmore Spencer UER .30	.14	.04
	(Missing '92 Draft Pick logo)		
	Los Angeles Clippers		
☐ 280	Cedric Ceballos .20	.09	.03
	Phoenix Suns		
☐ 281	Alex Blackwell .10	.05	.01
	Los Angeles Lakers		

☐ 282 Terry Davis	.10	.05	.01
Dallas Mavericks			
☐ 283 Morlon Wiley	.10	.05	.01
Atlanta Hawks			
☐ 284 Trent Tucker	.10	.05	.01
Washington Bullets			
☐ 285 Carl Herrera	.10	.05	.01
Houston Rockets			
☐ 286 Eric Anderson	.10	.05	.01
New York Knicks			
☐ 287 Clyde Drexler	.35	.16	.04
Portland Trail Blazers			
☐ 288 Tom Gugliotta	1.50	.65	.19
Washington Bullets			
☐ 289 Dale Ellis	.15	.07	.02
San Antonio Spurs			
☐ 290 Lance Blanks	.10	.05	.01
Minnesota Timberwolves			
☐ 291 Tom Hammonds	.10	.05	.01
Charlotte Hornets			
☐ 292 Eric Murdock	.15	.07	.02
Milwaukee Bucks			
☐ 293 Walt Williams	.75	.35	.09
Sacramento Kings			
☐ 294 Gerald Paddio	.10	.05	.01
Seattle Supersonics			
☐ 295 Brian Howard	.10	.05	.01
Dallas Mavericks			
☐ 296 Ken Williams	.10	.05	.01
Indiana Pacers			
☐ 297 Alonzo Mourning	7.00	3.10	.85
Charlotte Hornets			
☐ 298 Larry Nance	.15	.07	.02
Cleveland Cavaliers			
☐ 299 Jeff Grayer	.10	.05	.01
Golden State Warriors			
☐ 300 Dave Johnson	.10	.05	.01
Portland Trail Blazers			
☐ 301 Bob McCann	.10	.05	.01
Minnesota Timberwolves			
☐ 302 Bart Kofoed	.10	.05	.01
Boston Celtics			
☐ 303 Anthony Cook	.10	.05	.01
Denver Nuggets			
☐ 304 Radisav Curcic	.10	.05	.01
Dallas Mavericks			
☐ 305 John Crotty	.10	.05	.01
Utah Jazz			
☐ 306 Brad Sellers	.10	.05	.01
Detroit Pistons			
☐ 307 Marcus Webb	.10	.05	.01
Boston Celtics			
☐ 308 Winston Garland	.10	.05	.01
Houston Rockets			
☐ 309 Walter Palmer	.10	.05	.01
Dallas Mavericks			
☐ 310 Rod Higgins	.10	.05	.01
Sacramento Kings			
☐ 311 Travis Mays	.10	.05	.01
Atlanta Hawks			
☐ 312 Alex Stivrins	.10	.05	.01
Atlanta Hawks			
☐ 313 Greg Kite	.10	.05	.01
Orlando Magic			
☐ 314 Dennis Rodman	.15	.07	.02
Detroit Pistons			
☐ 315 Mike Sanders	.10	.05	.01
Cleveland Cavaliers			
☐ 316 Ed Pinckney	.10	.05	.01
Boston Celtics			
☐ 317 Harold Miner	.75	.35	.09
Miami Heat			
☐ 318 Pooh Richardson	.10	.05	.01

	Indiana Pacers			
☐ 319	Oliver Miller	.75	.35	.09
	Phoenix Suns			
☐ 320	Latrell Sprewell	5.00	2.30	.60
	Golden State Warriors			
☐ 321	Anthony Pullard	.10	.05	.01
	Milwaukee Bucks			
☐ 322	Mark Randall	.10	.05	.01
	Detroit Pistons			
☐ 323	Jeff Hornacek	.15	.07	.02
	Philadelphia 76ers			
☐ 324	Rick Mahorn UER	.15	.07	.02
	(Rookie Card is 1981-82, not 1992-93)			
	New Jersey Nets			
☐ 325	Sean Rooks	.30	.14	.04
	Dallas Mavericks			
☐ 326	Paul Pressey	.10	.05	.01
	Golden State Warriors			
☐ 327	James Worthy	.20	.09	.03
	Los Angeles Lakers			
☐ 328	Matt Bullard	.10	.05	.01
	Houston Rockets			
☐ 329	Reggie Smith	.10	.05	.01
	Portland Trail Blazers			
☐ 330	Don MacLean UER	1.00	.45	.13
	(Missing '92 Draft Pick logo)			
	Washington Bullets			
☐ 331	John Williams UER	.10	.05	.01
	(Rookie Card erroneously shows Hot Rod)			
	Los Angeles Clippers			
☐ 332	Frank Johnson	.15	.07	.02
	Phoenix Suns			
☐ 333	Hubert Davis UER	.75	.35	.09
	(Missing '92 Draft Pick logo)			
	New York Knicks			
☐ 334	Lloyd Daniels	.25	.11	.03
	San Antonio Spurs			
☐ 335	Steve Bardo	.10	.05	.01
	Dallas Mavericks			
☐ 336	Jeff Sanders	.10	.05	.01
	Atlanta Hawks			
☐ 337	Tree Rollins	.10	.05	.01
	Houston Rockets			
☐ 338	Micheal Williams	.15	.07	.02
	Minnesota Timberwolves			
☐ 339	Lorenzo Williams	.15	.07	.02
	Boston Celtics			
☐ 340	Harvey Grant	.10	.05	.01
	Washington Bullets			
☐ 341	Avery Johnson	.10	.05	.01
	San Antonio Spurs			
☐ 342	Bo Kimble	.10	.05	.01
	New York Knicks			
☐ 343	LaPhonso Ellis UER	1.50	.65	.19
	(Missing '92 Draft Pick logo)			
	Denver Nuggets			
☐ 344	Mookie Blaylock	.15	.07	.02
	Atlanta Hawks			
☐ 345	Isaiah Morris UER	.10	.05	.01
	(Missing '92 Draft Pick logo)			
	Detroit Pistons			
☐ 346	Clarence Weatherspoon	1.50	.65	.19
	Philadelphia 76ers			
☐ 347	Manute Bol	.10	.05	.01
	Philadelphia 76ers			
☐ 348	Victor Alexander	.10	.05	.01
	Golden State Warriors			

☐ 349 Corey Williams	.10	.05	.01
Washington Bullets			
☐ 350 Byron Houston	.20	.09	.03
Golden State Warriors			
☐ 351 Stanley Roberts	.10	.05	.01
Los Angeles Clippers			
☐ 352 Anthony Avent	.20	.09	.03
Milwaukee Bucks			
☐ 353 Vincent Askew	.10	.05	.01
Golden State Warriors			
☐ 354 Herb Williams	.10	.05	.01
New York Knicks			
☐ 355 J.R. Reid	.10	.05	.01
San Antonio Spurs			
☐ 356 Brad Lohaus	.10	.05	.01
Milwaukee Bucks			
☐ 357 Reggie Miller	.35	.16	.04
Indiana Pacers			
☐ 358 Blue Edwards	.15	.07	.02
Milwaukee Bucks			
☐ 359 Tom Tolbert	.10	.05	.01
Orlando Magic			
☐ 360 Charles Barkley	1.00	.45	.13
Phoenix Suns			
☐ 361 David Robinson	1.00	.45	.13
San Antonio Spurs			
☐ 362 Dale Davis	.15	.07	.02
Indiana Pacers			
☐ 363 Robert Werdann UER	.10	.05	.01
(Missing '92 Draft			
Pick logo)			
Denver Nuggets			
☐ 364 Chuck Person	.15	.07	.02
Minnesota Timberwolves			
☐ 365 Alaa Abdelnaby	.10	.05	.01
Boston Celtics			
☐ 366 Dave Jamerson	.10	.05	.01
Houston Rockets			
☐ 367 Scottie Pippen	.75	.35	.09
Washington Bullets			
☐ 368 Mark Jackson	.15	.07	.02
Los Angeles Clippers			
☐ 369 Keith Askins	.10	.05	.01
Miami Heat			
☐ 370 Marty Conlon	.10	.05	.01
Sacramento Kings			
☐ 371 Chucky Brown	.10	.05	.01
New Jersey Nets			
☐ 372 LaBradford Smith	.10	.05	.01
Washington Bullets			
☐ 373 Tim Kempton	.10	.05	.01
Phoenix Suns			
☐ 374 Sam Mitchell	.10	.05	.01
Indiana Pacers			
☐ 375 John Salley	.10	.05	.01
Miami Heat			
☐ 376 Mario Elie	.10	.05	.01
Portland Trail Blazers			
☐ 377 Mark West	.10	.05	.01
Phoenix Suns			
☐ 378 David Wingate	.10	.05	.01
Charlotte Hornets			
☐ 379 Jaren Jackson	.10	.05	.01
Los Angeles Clippers			
☐ 380 Rumeal Robinson	.10	.05	.01
New Jersey Nets			
☐ 381 Kennard Winchester	.10	.05	.01
Houston Rockets			
☐ 382 Walter Bond	.10	.05	.01
Dallas Mavericks			
☐ 383 Isaac Austin	.10	.05	.01
Utah Jazz			
☐ 384 Derrick Coleman	.35	.16	.04

	New Jersey Nets			
☐ 385	Larry Smith	.15	.07	.02
	San Antonio Spurs			
☐ 386	Joe Dumars	.30	.14	.04
	Detroit Pistons			
☐ 387	Matt Geiger UER	.25	.11	.03
	(Missing '92 Draft			
	Pick logo)			
	Miami Heat			
☐ 388	Stephen Howard	.10	.05	.01
	Utah Jazz			
☐ 389	William Bedford	.10	.05	.01
	Los Angeles Clippers			
☐ 390	Jayson Williams	.10	.05	.01
	New Jersey Nets			
☐ 391	Kurt Rambis	.15	.07	.02
	Sacramento Kings			
☐ 392	Keith Jennings	.15	.07	.02
	Golden State Warriors			
☐ 393	Steve Kerr UER	.10	.05	.01
	(The words key stat			
	are repeated on back)			
	Orlando Magic			
☐ 394	Larry Stewart	.10	.05	.01
	Washington Bullets			
☐ 395	Danny Young	.10	.05	.01
	Los Angeles Clippers			
☐ 396	Doug Overton	.10	.05	.01
	Washington Bullets			
☐ 397	Mark Acres	.10	.05	.01
	Orlando Magic			
☐ 398	John Bagley	.10	.05	.01
	Boston Celtics			
☐ 399	Checklist 201-300	.10	.05	.01
☐ 400	Checklist 301-400	.10	.05	.01

1992-93 Stadium Club Beam Team

Comprised of some of the NBA's biggest stars, the second series of Stadium Club included these special "Beam Team" insert cards to commemorate Topps' 1993 sponsorship of a six-minute NBA laser animation show called Beams Above the Rim, premiering at the NBA All-Star Game on Feb. 21. Afterwards, the laser show embarked on a ten-city tour and was featured in either the pre-game or half-time events in ten NBA arenas. These cards were randomly inserted approximately one in every 36 15-card packs of second series Stadium Club. The cards measure the standard size (2 1/2" by 3 1/2"). The color action player photos on the fronts are bordered on two sides by an angled silver light beam border design with a

light refracting pattern. The player's name appears on a white-outlined burnt orange bar superimposed over a basketball icon at the bottom. The backs present a color headshot and, on a basketball icon, career highlights. The cards are numbered on the back. For an annual fee, collectors could join the Stadium Club Members Only club and were invited to purchase (for 199.95 plus handling) the special "Members Only" set, which included all regular-issue 1992-93 Stadium Club cards and Beam Team cards. All these cards carry the Members Only logo on the card front. This offer was limited to the first 12,000 responses and sold out quickly. Beam Team "Members Only" cards are valued at 50 to 75 percent of the regular-issue Stadium Club Beam Team cards.

	MINT	EXC	G-VG
COMPLETE SET (21)	225.00	100.00	28.00
COMMON PLAYER (1-21)	2.00	.90	.25
☐ 1 Michael Jordan Chicago Bulls	60.00	27.00	7.50
☐ 2 Dominique Wilkins Atlanta Hawks	10.00	4.50	1.25
☐ 3 Shawn Kemp Seattle Supersonics	25.00	11.50	3.10
☐ 4 Clyde Drexler Portland Trail Blazers	5.00	2.30	.60
☐ 5 Scottie Pippen Chicago Bulls	12.00	5.50	1.50
☐ 6 Chris Mullin Golden State Warriors	4.00	1.80	.50
☐ 7 Reggie Miller Indiana Pacers	5.00	2.30	.60
☐ 8 Glen Rice Miami Heat	3.00	1.35	.40
☐ 9 Jeff Hornacek Philadelphia 76ers	2.00	.90	.25
☐ 10 Jeff Malone Utah Jazz	2.00	.90	.25
☐ 11 John Stockton Utah Jazz	5.00	2.30	.60
☐ 12 Kevin Johnson Phoenix Suns	4.00	1.80	.50
☐ 13 Mark Price Cleveland Cavaliers	3.00	1.35	.40
☐ 14 Tim Hardaway Golden State Warriors	3.00	1.35	.40
☐ 15 Charles Barkley Phoenix Suns	15.00	6.75	1.90
☐ 16 Hakeem Olajuwon Houston Rockets	20.00	9.00	2.50
☐ 17 Karl Malone Utah Jazz	8.00	3.60	1.00
☐ 18 Patrick Ewing New York Knicks	12.00	5.50	1.50
☐ 19 Dennis Rodman Detroit Pistons	2.00	.90	.25
☐ 20 David Robinson San Antonio Spurs	15.00	6.75	1.90
☐ 21 Shaquille O'Neal Orlando Magic	100.00	45.00	12.50

1993-94 Stadium Club

The 1993-94 Stadium Club set consists of 360 standard-size (2 1/2" by 3 1/2") cards. The full-bleed fronts feature glossy color action photos. The player's name is superimposed on the lower portion of the picture in white and gold foil lettering. The borderless backs are divided in half vertically with a torn effect. The left side sports a vertical player photo, and on the right side, over a purple background, is biography, and player's name and team. A brief section named "The Buzz" provides career highlights. A multi-colored box lists the 1992-93 statistics, career statistics and a Topps Skills Rating System that provides a score including player intimidation, mobility, shooting range and defense. Topical subsets featured are Triple Double (1-11, 101-111) and High Court (61-69, 170-178), with NBA Draft Picks (30, 36, 53, 82, 97,127, 139, 150, 159) scattered throughout the set. The cards are numbered on the back.

	MINT	EXC	G-VG
COMPLETE SET (360)	50.00	23.00	6.25
COMPLETE SERIES 1 (180)	25.00	11.50	3.10
COMPLETE SERIES 2 (180)	25.00	11.50	3.10
COMMON PLAYER (1-180)	.10	.05	.01
COMMON PLAYER (181-360)	.10	.05	.01

		MINT	EXC	G-VG
☐ 1	Michael Jordan TD Chicago Bulls	1.50	.65	.19
☐ 2	Kenny Anderson TD New Jersey Nets	.15	.07	.02
☐ 3	Steve Smith TD Miami Heat	.12	.05	.02
☐ 4	Kevin Gamble TD Boston Celtics	.10	.05	.01
☐ 5	Detlef Schrempf TD Indiana Pacers	.12	.05	.02
☐ 6	Larry Johnson TD Charlotte Hornets	.20	.09	.03
☐ 7	Brad Daugherty TD Cleveland Cavaliers	.12	.05	.02
☐ 8	Rumeal Robinson TD Atlanta Hawks	.10	.05	.01
☐ 9	Micheal Williams TD Minnesota Timberwolves	.10	.05	.01
☐ 10	David Robinson TD San Antonio Spurs	.40	.18	.05
☐ 11	Sam Perkins TD San Antonio Spurs	.10	.05	.01
☐ 12	Thurl Bailey Minnesota Timberwolves	.10	.05	.01
☐ 13	Sherman Douglas Boston Celtics	.10	.05	.01
☐ 14	Larry Stewart Washington Bullets	.10	.05	.01
☐ 15	Kevin Johnson Phoenix Suns	.15	.07	.02
☐ 16	Bill Cartwright Chicago Bulls	.10	.05	.01
☐ 17	Larry Nance Cleveland Cavaliers	.12	.05	.02
☐ 18	P.J. Brown New Jersey Nets	.25	.11	.03
☐ 19	Tony Bennett Charlotte Hornets	.10	.05	.01
☐ 20	Robert Parish Boston Celtics	.15	.07	.02
☐ 21	David Benoit Utah Jazz	.10	.05	.01
☐ 22	Detlef Schrempf Indiana Pacers	.15	.07	.02
☐ 23	Hubert Davis	.10	.05	.01

	New York Knicks		
☐ 24 Donald Hodge	.10	.05	.01
	Dallas Mavericks		
☐ 25 Hersey Hawkins	.12	.05	.02
	Philadelphia 76ers		
☐ 26 Mark Jackson	.12	.05	.02
	Los Angeles Clippers		
☐ 27 Reggie Williams	.10	.05	.01
	Denver Nuggets		
☐ 28 Lionel Simmons	.12	.05	.02
	Sacramento Kings		
☐ 29 Ron Harper	.12	.05	.02
	Los Angeles Clippers		
☐ 30 Chris Mills DP	.40	.18	.05
	Cleveland Cavaliers		
☐ 31 Danny Schayes	.10	.05	.01
	Milwaukee Bucks		
☐ 32 J.R. Reid	.10	.05	.01
	San Antonio Spurs		
☐ 33 Willie Burton	.10	.05	.01
	Miami Heat		
☐ 34 Greg Anthony	.10	.05	.01
	New York Knicks		
☐ 35 Elden Campbell	.10	.05	.01
	Los Angeles Lakers		
☐ 36 Ervin Johnson DP	.15	.07	.02
	Seattle Supersonics		
☐ 37 Scott Brooks	.10	.05	.01
	Houston Rockets		
☐ 38 Johnny Newman	.10	.05	.01
	Charlotte Hornets		
☐ 39 Rex Chapman	.10	.05	.01
	Washington Bullets		
☐ 40 Chuck Person	.12	.05	.02
	Minnesota Timberwolves		
☐ 41 John Williams	.12	.05	.02
	Cleveland Cavaliers		
☐ 42 Anthony Bowie	.10	.05	.01
	Orlando Magic		
☐ 43 Negele Knight	.10	.05	.01
	Phoenix Suns		
☐ 44 Tyrone Corbin	.10	.05	.01
	Utah Jazz		
☐ 45 Jud Buechler	.10	.05	.01
	Golden State Warriors		
☐ 46 Adam Keefe	.10	.05	.01
	Atlanta Hawks		
☐ 47 Glen Rice	.15	.07	.02
	Miami Heat		
☐ 48 Tracy Murray	.10	.05	.01
	Portland Trail Blazers		
☐ 49 Rick Mahorn	.10	.05	.01
	New Jersey Nets		
☐ 50 Vlade Divac	.10	.05	.01
	Los Angeles Lakers		
☐ 51 Eric Murdock	.12	.05	.02
	Milwaukee Bucks		
☐ 52 Isaiah Morris	.10	.05	.01
	Detroit Pistons		
☐ 53 Bobby Hurley DP	.60	.25	.08
	Sacramento Kings		
☐ 54 Mitch Richmond	.15	.07	.02
	Golden State Warriors		
☐ 55 Danny Ainge	.15	.07	.02
	Phoenix Suns		
☐ 56 Dikembe Mutombo	.15	.07	.02
	Denver Nuggets		
☐ 57 Jeff Hornacek	.12	.05	.02
	Philadelphia 76ers		
☐ 58 Tony Campbell	.10	.05	.01
	New York Knicks		
☐ 59 Vinny Del Negro	.10	.05	.01
	San Antonio Spurs		

☐ 60	Xavier McDaniel HC	.12	.05	.02
	Boston Celtics			
☐ 61	Scottie Pippen HC	.25	.11	.03
	Chicago Bulls			
☐ 62	Larry Nance HC	.10	.05	.01
	Cleveland Cavaliers			
☐ 63	Dikembe Mutombo HC	.12	.05	.02
	Denver Nuggets			
☐ 64	Hakeem Olajuwon HC	.60	.25	.08
	Houston Rockets			
☐ 65	Dominique Wilkins HC	.20	.09	.03
	Atlanta Hawks			
☐ 66	Clarence Weatherspoon HC	.12	.05	.02
	Philadelphia 76ers			
☐ 67	Chris Morris HC	.10	.05	.01
	New Jersey Nets			
☐ 68	Patrick Ewing HC	.25	.11	.03
	New York Knicks			
☐ 69	Kevin Willis HC	.10	.05	.01
	Atlanta Hawks			
☐ 70	Jon Barry	.10	.05	.01
	Milwaukee Bucks			
☐ 71	Jerry Reynolds	.10	.05	.01
	Orlando Magic			
☐ 72	Sarunas Marciulionis	.10	.05	.01
	Golden State Warriors			
☐ 73	Mark West	.10	.05	.01
	Phoenix Suns			
☐ 74	B.J. Armstrong	.15	.07	.02
	Chicago Bulls			
☐ 75	Greg Kite	.10	.05	.01
	Orlando Magic			
☐ 76	LaSalle Thompson	.12	.05	.02
	Indiana Pacers			
☐ 77	Randy White	.10	.05	.01
	Dallas Mavericks			
☐ 78	Alaa Abdelnaby	.10	.05	.01
	Boston Celtics			
☐ 79	Kevin Brooks	.10	.05	.01
	Denver Nuggets			
☐ 80	Vern Fleming	.10	.05	.01
	Indiana Pacers			
☐ 81	Doc Rivers	.12	.05	.02
	New York Knicks			
☐ 82	Shawn Bradley DP	.60	.25	.08
	Philadelphia 76ers			
☐ 83	Wayman Tisdale	.12	.05	.02
	Sacramento Kings			
☐ 84	Olden Polynice	.10	.05	.01
	Detroit Pistons			
☐ 85	Michael Cage	.10	.05	.01
	Seattle Supersonics			
☐ 86	Harold Miner	.12	.05	.02
	Orlando Magic			
☐ 87	Doug Smith	.10	.05	.01
	Dallas Mavericks			
☐ 88	Tom Gugliotta	.12	.05	.02
	Washington Bullets			
☐ 89	Hakeem Olajuwon	1.25	.55	.16
	Houston Rockets			
☐ 90	Loy Vaught	.12	.05	.02
	Los Angeles Clippers			
☐ 91	James Worthy	.15	.07	.02
	Los Angeles Lakers			
☐ 92	John Paxson	.10	.05	.01
	Chicago Bulls			
☐ 93	Jon Koncak	.10	.05	.01
	Atlanta Hawks			
☐ 94	Lee Mayberry	.10	.05	.01
	Milwaukee Bucks			
☐ 95	Clarence Weatherspoon	.15	.07	.02
	Philadelphia 76ers			

☐ 96	Mark Eaton	.10	.05	.01
	Utah Jazz			
☐ 97	Rex Walters DP	.15	.07	.02
	New Jersey Nets			
☐ 98	Alvin Robertson	.10	.05	.01
	Detroit Pistons			
☐ 99	Dan Majerle	.15	.07	.02
	Phoenix Suns			
☐ 100	Shaquille O'Neal	2.50	1.15	.30
	Orlando Magic			
☐ 101	Derrick Coleman TD	.15	.07	.02
	New Jersey Nets			
☐ 102	Hersey Hawkins TD	.12	.05	.02
	Philadelphia 76ers			
☐ 103	Scottie Pippen TD	.25	.11	.03
	Chicago Bulls			
☐ 104	Scott Skiles TD	.10	.05	.01
	Orlando Magic			
☐ 105	Rod Strickland TD	.10	.05	.01
	Portland Trail Blazers			
☐ 106	Pooh Richardson TD	.10	.05	.01
	Indiana Pacers			
☐ 107	Tom Gugliotta TD	.12	.05	.02
	Washington Bullets			
☐ 108	Mark Jackson TD	.10	.05	.01
	Los Angeles Clippers			
☐ 109	Dikembe Mutombo TD	.12	.05	.02
	Denver Nuggets			
☐ 110	Charles Barkley TD	.40	.18	.05
	Phoenix Suns			
☐ 111	Otis Thorpe TD	.10	.05	.01
	Houston Rockets			
☐ 112	Malik Sealy	.10	.05	.01
	Indiana Pacers			
☐ 113	Mark Macon	.10	.05	.01
	Denver Nuggets			
☐ 114	Dee Brown	.10	.05	.01
	Boston Celtics			
☐ 115	Nate McMillan	.10	.05	.01
	Seattle Supersonics			
☐ 116	John Starks	.15	.07	.02
	New York Knicks			
☐ 117	Clyde Drexler	.25	.11	.03
	Portland Trail Blazers			
☐ 118	Antoine Carr	.10	.05	.01
	San Antonio Spurs			
☐ 119	Doug West	.10	.05	.01
	Minnesota Timberwolves			
☐ 120	Victor Alexander	.10	.05	.01
	Golden State Warriors			
☐ 121	Kenny Gattison	.10	.05	.01
	Charlotte Hornets			
☐ 122	Spud Webb	.15	.07	.02
	Atlanta Hawks			
☐ 123	Rumeal Robinson	.10	.05	.01
	New Jersey Nets			
☐ 124	Tim Kempton	.10	.05	.01
	Phoenix Suns			
☐ 125	Karl Malone	.40	.18	.05
	Utah Jazz			
☐ 126	Randy Woods	.10	.05	.01
	Los Angeles Clippers			
☐ 127	Calbert Cheaney DP	.60	.25	.08
	Washington Bullets			
☐ 128	Johnny Dawkins	.10	.05	.01
	Philadelphia 76ers			
☐ 129	Dominique Wilkins	.40	.18	.05
	Atlanta Hawks			
☐ 130	Horace Grant	.15	.07	.02
	Chicago Bulls			
☐ 131	Bill Laimbeer	.15	.07	.02
	Detroit Pistons			
☐ 132	Kenny Smith	.10	.05	.01

		Houston Rockets			
☐	133	Sedale Threatt	.10	.05	.01
		Los Angeles Lakers			
☐	134	Brian Shaw	.10	.05	.01
		Miami Heat			
☐	135	Dennis Scott	.12	.05	.02
		Orlando Magic			
☐	136	Mark Bryant	.10	.05	.01
		Portland Trail Blazers			
☐	137	Xavier McDaniel	.12	.05	.02
		Boston Celtics			
☐	138	David Wood	.10	.05	.01
		Houston Rockets			
☐	139	Luther Wright DP	.15	.07	.02
		Utah Jazz			
☐	140	Lloyd Daniels	.10	.05	.01
		San Antonio Spurs			
☐	141	Marlon Maxey UER	.10	.05	.01
		Minnesota Timberwolves			
		(Name spelled Maxley on the front)			
☐	142	Pooh Richardson	.10	.05	.01
		Indiana Pacers			
☐	143	Jeff Grayer	.10	.05	.01
		Golden State Warriors			
☐	144	LaPhonso Ellis	.15	.07	.02
		Denver Nuggets			
☐	145	Gerald Wilkins	.10	.05	.01
		Cleveland Cavaliers			
☐	146	Dell Curry	.12	.05	.02
		Charlotte Hornets			
☐	147	Duane Causwell	.10	.05	.01
		Sacramento Kings			
☐	148	Tim Hardaway	.15	.07	.02
		Golden State Warriors			
☐	149	Isiah Thomas	.25	.11	.03
		Detroit Pistons			
☐	150	Doug Edwards DP	.15	.07	.02
		Atlanta Hawks			
☐	151	Anthony Peeler	.12	.05	.02
		Los Angeles Lakers			
☐	152	Tate George	.10	.05	.01
		New Jersey Nets			
☐	153	Terry Davis	.10	.05	.01
		Dallas Mavericks			
☐	154	Sam Perkins	.12	.05	.02
		Seattle Supersonics			
☐	155	John Salley	.10	.05	.01
		Miami Heat			
☐	156	Vernon Maxwell	.12	.05	.02
		Houston Rockets			
☐	157	Anthony Avent	.10	.05	.01
		Milwaukee Bucks			
☐	158	Cliff Robinson	.15	.07	.02
		Portland Trail Blazers			
☐	159	Corie Blount DP	.15	.07	.02
		Chicago Bulls			
☐	160	Gerald Paddio	.10	.05	.01
		Seattle Supersonics			
☐	161	Blair Rasmussen	.10	.05	.01
		Atlanta Hawks			
☐	162	Carl Herrera	.10	.05	.01
		Houston Rockets			
☐	163	Chris Smith	.10	.05	.01
		Minnesota Timberwolves			
☐	164	Pervis Ellison	.10	.05	.01
		Washington Bullets			
☐	165	Rod Strickland	.12	.05	.02
		Portland Trail Blazers			
☐	166	Jeff Malone	.12	.05	.02
		Utah Jazz			
☐	167	Danny Ferry	.10	.05	.01
		Cleveland Cavaliers			
☐	168	Kevin Lynch	.10	.05	.01
		Charlotte Hornets			

☐ 169	Michael Jordan	3.00	1.35	.40
	Chicago Bulls			
☐ 170	Derrick Coleman HC	.15	.07	.02
	New Jersey Nets			
☐ 171	Jerome Kersey HC	.10	.05	.01
	Portland Trail Blazers			
☐ 172	David Robinson HC	.40	.18	.05
	San Antonio Spurs			
☐ 173	Shawn Kemp HC	.25	.11	.03
	Seattle Supersonics			
☐ 174	Karl Malone HC	.20	.09	.03
	Utah Jazz			
☐ 175	Shaquille O'Neal HC	1.25	.55	.16
	Orlando Magic			
☐ 176	Alonzo Mourning HC	.50	.23	.06
	Charlotte Hornets			
☐ 177	Charles Barkley HC	.40	.18	.05
	Phoenix Suns			
☐ 178	Larry Johnson HC	.20	.09	.03
	Charlotte Hornets			
☐ 179	Checklist 1-90	.10	.05	.01
☐ 180	Checklist 91-180	.10	.05	.01
☐ 181	Michael Jordan	1.50	.65	.19
	Chicago Bulls			
☐ 182	Dominique Wilkins	.20	.09	.03
	Atlanta Hawks			
☐ 183	Dennis Rodman	.12	.05	.02
	San Antonio Spurs			
☐ 184	Scottie Pippen	.25	.11	.03
	Chicago Bulls			
☐ 185	Larry Johnson	.20	.09	.03
	Charlotte Hornets			
☐ 186	Karl Malone	.20	.09	.03
	Utah Jazz			
☐ 187	Clarence Weatherspoon	.12	.05	.02
	Philadelphia 76ers			
☐ 188	Charles Barkley	.40	.18	.05
	Phoenix Suns			
☐ 189	Patrick Ewing	.25	.11	.03
	New York Knicks			
☐ 190	Derrick Coleman	.15	.07	.02
	New Jersey Nets			
☐ 191	LaBradford Smith	.10	.05	.01
	San Antonio Spurs			
☐ 192	Derek Harper	.12	.05	.02
	New York Knicks			
☐ 193	Ken Norman	.10	.05	.01
	Milwaukee Bucks			
☐ 194	Rodney Rogers	.40	.18	.05
	Denver Nuggets			
☐ 195	Chris Dudley	.10	.05	.01
	Portland Trail Blazers			
☐ 196	Gary Payton	.15	.07	.02
	Seattle Supersonics			
☐ 197	Andrew Lang	.10	.05	.01
	Atlanta Hawks			
☐ 198	Billy Owens	.12	.05	.02
	Golden State Warriors			
☐ 199	Bryon Russell	.25	.11	.03
	Utah Jazz			
☐ 200	Patrick Ewing	.50	.23	.06
	New York Knicks			
☐ 201	Stacey King	.10	.05	.01
	Chicago Bulls			
☐ 202	Grant Long	.10	.05	.01
	Miami Heat			
☐ 203	Sean Elliott	.12	.05	.02
	Detroit Pistons			
☐ 204	Muggsy Bogues	.15	.07	.02
	Charlotte Hornets			
☐ 205	Kevin Edwards	.10	.05	.01
	New Jersey Nets			
☐ 206	Dale Davis	.12	.05	.02

	Indiana Pacers			
☐ 207	Dale Ellis	.12	.05	.02
	San Antonio Spurs			
☐ 208	Terrell Brandon	.10	.05	.01
	Cleveland Cavaliers			
☐ 209	Kevin Gamble	.10	.05	.01
	Boston Celtics			
☐ 210	Robert Horry	.15	.07	.02
	Houston Rockets			
☐ 211	Moses Malone UER	.15	.07	.02
	Philadelphia 76ers			
	(Birthdate on back is 1993)			
☐ 212	Gary Grant	.10	.05	.01
	Los Angeles Clippers			
☐ 213	Bobby Hurley	.30	.14	.04
	Sacramento Kings			
☐ 214	Larry Krystkowiak	.10	.05	.01
	Orlando Magic			
☐ 215	A.C. Green	.12	.05	.02
	Phoenix Suns			
☐ 216	Christian Laettner	.12	.05	.02
	Minnesota Timberwolves			
☐ 217	Orlando Woolridge	.12	.05	.02
	Philadelphia 76ers			
☐ 218	Craig Ehlo	.10	.05	.01
	Atlanta Hawks			
☐ 219	Terry Porter	.12	.05	.02
	Portland Trail Blazers			
☐ 220	Jamal Mashburn	1.50	.65	.19
	Dallas Mavericks			
☐ 221	Kevin Duckworth	.10	.05	.01
	Washington Bullets			
☐ 222	Shawn Kemp	.50	.23	.06
	Seattle Supersonics			
☐ 223	Frank Brickowski	.12	.05	.02
	Milwaukee Bucks			
☐ 224	Chris Webber	4.00	1.80	.50
	Golden State Warriors			
☐ 225	Charles Oakley	.15	.07	.02
	New York Knicks			
☐ 226	Jay Humphries	.10	.05	.01
	Utah Jazz			
☐ 227	Steve Kerr	.10	.05	.01
	Chicago Bulls			
☐ 228	Tim Perry	.10	.05	.01
	Philadelphia 76ers			
☐ 229	Sleepy Floyd	.10	.05	.01
	San Antonio Spurs			
☐ 230	Bimbo Coles	.10	.05	.01
	Miami Heat			
☐ 231	Eddie Johnson	.10	.05	.01
	Charlotte Hornets			
☐ 232	Terry Mills	.12	.05	.02
	Detroit Pistons			
☐ 233	Danny Manning	.20	.09	.03
	Los Angeles Clippers			
☐ 234	Isaiah Rider	1.50	.65	.19
	Minnesota Timberwolves			
☐ 235	Darnell Mee	.15	.07	.02
	Denver Nuggets			
☐ 236	Haywoode Workman	.10	.05	.01
	Indiana Pacers			
☐ 237	Scott Skiles	.10	.05	.01
	Orlando Magic			
☐ 238	Otis Thorpe	.12	.05	.02
	Houston Rockets			
☐ 239	Mike Peplowski	.15	.07	.02
	Sacramento Kings			
☐ 240	Eric Leckner	.10	.05	.01
	Philadelphia 76ers			
☐ 241	Johnny Newman	.10	.05	.01
	New Jersey Nets			
☐ 242	Benoit Benjamin	.10	.05	.01
	New Jersey Nets			

☐ 243	Doug Christie	.12	.05	.02
	Los Angeles Lakers			
☐ 244	Acie Earl	.15	.07	.02
	Boston Celtics			
☐ 245	Luc Longley	.10	.05	.01
	Minnesota Timberwolves			
☐ 246	Tyrone Hill	.10	.05	.01
	Cleveland Cavaliers			
☐ 247	Allan Houston	.25	.11	.03
	Detroit Pistons			
☐ 248	Joe Kleine	.10	.05	.01
	Phoenix Suns			
☐ 249	Mookie Blaylock	.12	.05	.02
	Atlanta Hawks			
☐ 250	Anthony Bonner	.10	.05	.01
	New York Knicks			
☐ 251	Luther Wright	.10	.05	.01
	Utah Jazz			
☐ 252	Todd Day	.12	.05	.02
	Milwaukee Bucks			
☐ 253	Kendall Gill	.12	.05	.02
	Seattle Supersonics			
☐ 254	Mario Elie	.10	.05	.01
	Houston Rockets			
☐ 255	Pete Myers	.10	.05	.01
	Chicago Bulls			
☐ 256	Jim Les	.10	.05	.01
	Sacramento Kings			
☐ 257	Stanley Roberts	.10	.05	.01
	Los Angeles Clippers			
☐ 258	Michael Adams	.12	.05	.02
	Washington Bullets			
☐ 259	Hersey Hawkins	.12	.05	.02
	Charlotte Hornets			
☐ 260	Shawn Bradley	.30	.14	.04
	Philadelphia 76ers			
☐ 261	Scott Haskin	.15	.07	.02
	Indiana Pacers			
☐ 262	Corie Blount	.10	.05	.01
	Chicago Bulls			
☐ 263	Charles Smith	.10	.05	.01
	New York Knicks			
☐ 264	Armon Gilliam	.10	.05	.01
	New Jersey Nets			
☐ 265	Jamal Mashburn	.60	.25	.08
	Dallas Mavericks			
☐ 266	Anfernee Hardaway	1.25	.55	.16
	Orlando Magic			
☐ 267	Shawn Bradley	.25	.11	.03
	Philadelphia 76ers			
☐ 268	Chris Webber	1.50	.65	.19
	Golden State Warriors			
☐ 269	Bobby Hurley	.25	.11	.03
	Sacramento Kings			
☐ 270	Isaiah Rider	.60	.25	.08
	Minnesota Timberwolves			
☐ 271	Dino Radja	.25	.11	.03
	Boston Celtics			
☐ 272	Chris Mills	.15	.07	.02
	Cleveland Cavaliers			
☐ 273	Nick Van Exel	.25	.11	.03
	Los Angeles Lakers			
☐ 274	Lindsey Hunter	.25	.11	.03
	Detroit Pistons			
☐ 275	Toni Kukoc	.25	.11	.03
	Chicago Bulls			
☐ 276	Popeye Jones	.10	.05	.01
	Dallas Mavericks			
☐ 277	Chris Mills	.20	.09	.03
	Cleveland Cavaliers			
☐ 278	Ricky Pierce	.12	.05	.02
	Seattle Supersonics			
☐ 279	Negele Knight	.10	.05	.01

☐ 280	San Antonio Spurs Kenny Walker	.10	.05	.01
☐ 281	New Jersey Nets Nick Van Exel	.60	.25	.08
☐ 282	Los Angeles Lakers Derrick Coleman UER	.30	.14	.04
☐ 283	New Jersey Nets (Career stats listed under `92-93) Popeye Jones	.25	.11	.03
☐ 284	Dallas Mavericks Derrick McKey	.10	.05	.01
☐ 285	Indiana Pacers Rick Fox	.10	.05	.01
☐ 286	Boston Celtics Jerome Kersey	.10	.05	.01
☐ 287	Portland Trail Blazers Steve Smith	.12	.05	.02
☐ 288	Miami Heat Brian Williams	.10	.05	.01
☐ 289	Denver Nuggets Chris Mullin	.25	.11	.03
☐ 290	Golden State Warriors Terry Cummings	.12	.05	.02
☐ 291	San Antonio Spurs Donald Royal	.10	.05	.01
☐ 292	Orlando Magic Alonzo Mourning	1.00	.45	.13
☐ 293	Charlotte Hornets Mike Brown	.10	.05	.01
☐ 294	Minnesota Timberwolves Latrell Sprewell	.60	.25	.08
☐ 295	Golden State Warriors Oliver Miller	.15	.07	.02
☐ 296	Phoenix Suns Terry Dehere	.15	.07	.02
☐ 297	Los Angeles Clippers Detlef Schrempf	.15	.07	.02
☐ 298	Seattle Supersonics Sam Bowie UER	.10	.05	.01
☐ 299	Los Angeles Lakers (Last name Bowe on front) Chris Morris	.10	.05	.01
☐ 300	New Jersey Nets Scottie Pippen	.50	.23	.06
☐ 301	Chicago Bulls Warren Kidd	.15	.07	.02
☐ 302	Philadelphia 76ers Don MacLean	.12	.05	.02
☐ 303	Washington Bullets Sean Rooks	.10	.05	.01
☐ 304	Dallas Mavericks Matt Geiger	.10	.05	.01
☐ 305	Miami Heat Dennis Rodman	.12	.05	.02
☐ 306	San Antonio Spurs Reggie Miller	.30	.14	.04
☐ 307	Indiana Pacers Vin Baker	1.00	.45	.13
☐ 308	Miami Heat Anfernee Hardaway	3.00	1.35	.40
☐ 309	Orlando Magic Lindsey Hunter	.60	.25	.08
☐ 310	Detroit Pistons Stacey Augmon	.15	.07	.02
☐ 311	Atlanta Hawks Randy Brown	.10	.05	.01
☐ 312	Sacramento Kings Anthony Mason	.10	.05	.01
☐ 313	New York Knicks John Stockton	.25	.11	.03
☐ 314	Utah Jazz Sam Cassell	.75	.35	.09
	Houston Rockets			

☐ 315	Buck Williams	.15	.07	.02
	Portland Trail Blazers			
☐ 316	Bryant Stith	.12	.05	.02
	Denver Nuggets			
☐ 317	Brad Daugherty	.15	.07	.02
	Cleveland Cavaliers			
☐ 318	Dino Radja	.60	.25	.08
	Boston Celtics			
☐ 319	Rony Seikaly	.15	.07	.02
	Miami Heat			
☐ 320	Charles Barkley	.75	.35	.09
	Phoenix Suns			
☐ 321	Avery Johnson	.10	.05	.01
	Golden State Warriors			
☐ 322	Mahmoud Abdul Rauf	.12	.05	.02
	Denver Nuggets			
☐ 323	Larry Johnson	.50	.23	.06
	Charlotte Hornets			
☐ 324	Micheal Williams	.12	.05	.02
	Minnesota Timberwolves			
☐ 325	Mark Aguirre	.15	.07	.02
	Los Angeles Clippers			
☐ 326	Jim Jackson	.50	.23	.06
	Dallas Mavericks			
☐ 327	Antonio Harvey	.15	.07	.02
	Los Angeles Lakers			
☐ 328	David Robinson	.75	.35	.09
	San Antonio Spurs			
☐ 329	Calbert Cheaney	.30	.14	.04
	Washington Bullets			
☐ 330	Kenny Anderson	.25	.11	.03
	New Jersey Nets			
☐ 331	Walt Williams	.12	.05	.02
	Sacramento Kings			
☐ 332	Kevin Willis	.12	.05	.02
	Atlanta Hawks			
☐ 333	Nick Anderson	.12	.05	.02
	Orlando Magic			
☐ 334	Rik Smits	.12	.05	.02
	Indiana Pacers			
☐ 335	Joe Dumars	.25	.11	.03
	Detroit Pistons			
☐ 336	Toni Kukoc	.75	.35	.09
	Chicago Bulls			
☐ 337	Harvey Grant	.10	.05	.01
	Portland Trail Blazers			
☐ 338	Tom Chambers	.12	.05	.02
	Utah Jazz			
☐ 339	Blue Edwards	.10	.05	.01
	Milwaukee Bucks			
☐ 340	Mark Price	.15	.07	.02
	Cleveland Cavaliers			
☐ 341	Ervin Johnson	.10	.05	.01
	Seattle Supersonics			
☐ 342	Rolando Blackman	.10	.05	.01
	New York Knicks			
☐ 343	Scott Burrell	.25	.11	.03
	Charlotte Hornets			
☐ 344	Gheorghe Muresan	.25	.11	.03
	Washington Bullets			
☐ 345	Chris Corchiani	.10	.05	.01
	Boston Celtics			
☐ 346	Richard Petruska	.15	.07	.02
	Houston Rockets			
☐ 347	Dana Barros	.10	.05	.01
	Philadelphia 76ers			
☐ 348	Hakeem Olajuwon	.60	.25	.08
	Houston Rockets			
☐ 349	Dee Brown	.10	.05	.01
	Boston Celtics			
☐ 350	John Starks	.15	.07	.02
	New York Knicks			
☐ 351	Ron Harper	.10	.05	.01

	Los Angeles Clippers			
☐ 352	Chris Webber	1.50	.65	.19
	Golden State Warriors			
☐ 353	Dan Majerle	.12	.05	.02
	Phoenix Suns			
☐ 354	Clyde Drexler	.15	.07	.02
	Portland Trail Blazers			
☐ 355	Shawn Kemp	.25	.11	.03
	Seattle Supersonics			
☐ 356	David Robinson	.40	.18	.05
	San Antonio Spurs			
☐ 357	Chris Morris	.10	.05	.01
	New Jersey Nets			
☐ 358	Shaquille O'Neal	1.25	.55	.16
	Orlando Magic			
☐ 359	Checklist	.10	.05	.01
☐ 360	Checklist	.10	.05	.01

1993-94 Stadium Club First Day Issue

Randomly inserted in regular packs, the parallel First Day Issue set consists of 360 standard-size (2 1/2'' by 3 1/2'') cards. The full-bleed fronts feature glossy color action photos, with the prismatic silver-foil First Day logo in one corner. The player's name is superimposed on the lower portion of the picture in white and gold foil lettering. The borderless backs are divided in half vertically with a torn effect. The left side sports a vertical player photo, and on the right side, over a purple background, is a biography, and player's name and team. Abrief section named "The Buzz" provides career highlights. A multi colored box lists the 1992-93 statistics, career statistics and a Topps Skills Rating System that provides a score including player intimidation, mobility, shooting range and defense. Topical subsets featured are Triple Double (1-11, 101-111) and High Court (61-69, 170-178), with NBA Draft Picks (30, 36, 53, 82, 97, 127, 139, 150, 159) scattered throughout the set. Cards 265-276 belong to the New Wave subset. The cards are numbered on the back.

	MINT	EXC	G-VG
COMPLETE SET (360)	2500.00	1150.00	325.00
COMPLETE SERIES 1 (180)	1250.00	575.00	160.00
COMPLETE SERIES 2 (180)	1250.00	575.00	160.00
COMMON PLAYER (1-180)	2.00	.90	.25
COMMON PLAYER (181-360)	2.00	.90	.25
*FDI STARS:30X to 60X VALUE			
*FDI ROOKIES: 15X to 30X VALUE			
☐ 1 Michael Jordan TD	100.00	45.00	12.50
Chicago Bulls			

☐ 10	David Robinson TD San Antonio Spurs	25.00	11.50	3.10
☐ 64	Hakeem Olajuwon HC Houston Rockets	35.00	16.00	4.40
☐ 89	Hakeem Olajuwon Houston Rockets	70.00	32.00	8.75
☐ 100	Shaquille O'Neal Orlando Magic	150.00	70.00	19.00
☐ 110	Charles Barkley TD Phoenix Suns	25.00	11.50	3.10
☐ 125	Karl Malone Utah Jazz	25.00	11.50	3.10
☐ 129	Dominique Wilkins Atlanta Hawks	30.00	13.50	3.80
☐ 169	Michael Jordan Chicago Bulls	200.00	90.00	25.00
☐ 172	David Robinson HC San Antonio Spurs	25.00	11.50	3.10
☐ 175	Shaquille O'Neal HC Orlando Magic	75.00	34.00	9.50
☐ 176	Alonzo Mourning HC Charlotte Hornets	30.00	13.50	3.80
☐ 177	Charles Barkley HC Phoenix Suns	25.00	11.50	3.10
☐ 181	Michael Jordan Chicago Bulls	100.00	45.00	12.50
☐ 188	Charles Barkley Phoenix Suns	25.00	11.50	3.10
☐ 200	Patrick Ewing New York Knicks	35.00	16.00	4.40
☐ 220	Jamal Mashburn Dallas Mavericks	40.00	18.00	5.00
☐ 222	Shawn Kemp Seattle Supersonics	35.00	16.00	4.40
☐ 224	Chris Webber Golden State Warriors	150.00	70.00	19.00
☐ 234	Isaiah Rider Minnesota Timberwolves	40.00	18.00	5.00
☐ 266	Anfernee Hardaway Orlando Magic	40.00	18.00	5.00
☐ 268	Chris Webber Golden State Warriors	60.00	27.00	7.50
☐ 292	Alonzo Mourning Charlotte Hornets	60.00	27.00	7.50
☐ 294	Latrell Sprewell Golden State Warriors	40.00	18.00	5.00
☐ 300	Scottie Pippen Chicago Bulls	35.00	16.00	4.40
☐ 307	Vin Baker Miami Heat	30.00	13.50	3.80
☐ 308	Anfernee Hardaway Orlando Magic	100.00	45.00	12.50
☐ 320	Charles Barkley Phoenix Suns	50.00	23.00	6.25
☐ 323	Larry Johnson Charlotte Hornets	30.00	13.50	3.80
☐ 326	Jim Jackson Dallas Mavericks	30.00	13.50	3.80
☐ 328	David Robinson San Antonio Spurs	50.00	23.00	6.25
☐ 348	Hakeem Olajuwon Houston Rockets	35.00	16.00	4.40
☐ 352	Chris Webber Golden State Warriors	60.00	27.00	7.50
☐ 356	David Robinson San Antonio Spurs	25.00	11.50	3.10
☐ 358	Shaquille O'Neal Orlando Magic	75.00	34.00	9.50

1993-94 Stadium Club Beam Team

KARL MALONE

Randomly inserted in packs, this standard-size (2 1/2" by 3 1/2") 27-card set features borderless fronts with color player action photos set against game-crowd backgrounds. Silver metallic beams appear near the bottom above the player's name. The horizontal back carries a color action photo on one side, with player profile on the other. The cards are numbered on the back as "X of 27."

	MINT	EXC	G-VG
COMPLETE SET (27)	200.00	90.00	25.00
COMPLETE SERIES 1 (13)	100.00	45.00	12.50
COMPLETE SERIES 2 (14)	100.00	45.00	12.50
COMMON PLAYER (1-13)	2.00	.90	.25
COMMON PLAYER (14-27)	2.00	.90	.25
☐ 1 Shaquille O'Neal	22.00	10.00	2.80
Orlando Magic			
☐ 2 Mark Price	2.50	1.15	.30
Cleveland Cavaliers			
☐ 3 Patrick Ewing	8.00	3.60	1.00
New York Knicks			
☐ 4 Michael Jordan	35.00	16.00	4.40
Chicago Bulls			
☐ 5 Charles Barkley	10.00	4.50	1.25
Phoenix Suns			
☐ 6 Reggie Miller	4.00	1.80	.50
Indiana Pacers			
☐ 7 Derrick Coleman	4.00	1.80	.50
New Jersey Nets			
☐ 8 Dominique Wilkins	6.00	2.70	.75
Atlanta Hawks			
☐ 9 Karl Malone	5.00	2.30	.60
Utah Jazz			
☐ 10 Alonzo Mourning	10.00	4.50	1.25
Charlotte Hornets			
☐ 11 Tim Hardaway	2.50	1.15	.30
Golden State Warriors			
☐ 12 Hakeem Olajuwon	12.00	5.50	1.50
Houston Rockets			
☐ 13 David Robinson	10.00	4.50	1.25
San Antonio Spurs			
☐ 14 Dan Majerle	2.50	1.15	.30
Phoenix Suns			
☐ 15 Larry Johnson	6.00	2.70	.75
Charlotte Hornets			
☐ 16 LaPhonso Ellis	3.00	1.35	.40
Denver Nuggets			
☐ 17 Nick Van Exel	4.00	1.80	.50
Los Angeles Lakers			
☐ 18 Scottie Pippen	8.00	3.60	1.00
Chicago Bulls			

☐ 19 John Stockton Utah Jazz	4.00	1.80	.50
☐ 20 Bobby Hurley Sacramento Kings	4.00	1.80	.50
☐ 21 Chris Webber Golden State Warriors	25.00	11.50	3.10
☐ 22 Jamal Mashburn Dallas Mavericks	10.00	4.50	1.25
☐ 23 Anfernee Hardaway Orlando Magic	20.00	9.00	2.50
☐ 24 Isaiah Rider Minnesota Timberwolves	10.00	4.50	1.25
☐ 25 Ken Norman Milwaukee Bucks	2.00	.90	.25
☐ 26 Danny Manning Los Angeles Clippers	3.00	1.35	.40
☐ 27 Calbert Cheaney Washington Bullets	4.00	1.80	.50

1993-94 Stadium Club
Frequent Flyer Upgrades

Upon collecting 50 points or more for one particular player from the Frequent Flyer Point Cards set, the collector could send the cards to Topps and receive a limited edition Frequent Flyer Upgrade card for the same player. Aside from the chromium-type metallic finish and the "Upgrades" logo on the fronts, the Upgrade cards are identical to the cards from the Frequent Flyers subset in the '93 Stadium Club set. The cards are numbered on the back.

	MINT	EXC	G-VG
COMPLETE SET (20)	200.00	90.00	25.00
COMMON PLAYER (182-190)	4.00	1.80	.50
COMMON PLAYER (348-358)	4.00	1.80	.50
☐ 182 Dominique Wilkins Atlanta Hawks	10.00	4.50	1.25
☐ 183 Dennis Rodman San Antonio Spurs	4.00	1.80	.50
☐ 184 Scottie Pippen Chicago Bulls	12.00	5.50	1.50
☐ 185 Larry Johnson Charlotte Hornets	10.00	4.50	1.25
☐ 186 Karl Malone Utah Jazz	8.00	3.60	1.00
☐ 187 Clarence Weatherspoon Philadelphia 76ers	4.00	1.80	.50
☐ 188 Charles Barkley Phoenix Suns	15.00	6.75	1.90
☐ 189 Patrick Ewing	12.00	5.50	1.50

	New York Knicks				
☐ 190	Derrick Coleman	5.00	2.30	.60
	New Jersey Nets				
☐ 348	Hakeem Olajuwon	20.00	9.00	2.50
	Houston Rockets				
☐ 349	Dee Brown	4.00	1.80	.50
	Boston Celtics				
☐ 350	John Starks	4.00	1.80	.50
	New York Knicks				
☐ 351	Ron Harper	4.00	1.80	.50
	Los Angeles Clippers				
☐ 352	Chris Webber	40.00	18.00	5.00
	Golden State Warriors				
☐ 353	Dan Majerle	4.00	1.80	.50
	Phoenix Suns				
☐ 354	Clyde Drexler	5.00	2.30	.60
	Portland Trail Blazers				
☐ 355	Shawn Kemp	12.00	5.50	1.50
	Seattle Supersonics				
☐ 356	David Robinson	15.00	6.75	1.90
	San Antonio Spurs				
☐ 357	Chris Morris	4.00	1.80	.50
	New Jersey Nets				
☐ 358	Shaquille O'Neal	40.00	18.00	5.00
	Orlando Magic				

1993-94 Stadium Club Rim Rockers

Randomly inserted in Series 2 packs, these six standard-size (2 1/2" by 3 1/2") cards feature color player action shots on their borderless fronts. The player's name appears near the bottom. His first name is printed in white lowercase lettering; his last is gold-foil stamped in uppercase lettering. The back carries another borderless color player action shot, but its right side is ghosted, blue-screened, and overprinted with career highlights in white lettering. The cards are numbered on the back as "X of 6."

		MINT	EXC	G-VG
	COMPLETE SET (6)	20.00	9.00	2.50
	COMMON PLAYER (1-6)	1.00	.45	.13
☐ 1	Shaquille O'Neal	12.00	5.50	1.50
	Orlando Magic			
☐ 2	Harold Miner	1.00	.45	.13
	Miami Heat			
☐ 3	Charles Barkley	5.00	2.30	.60
	Phoenix Suns			
☐ 4	Dominique Wilkins	3.00	1.35	.40
	Atlanta Hawks			
☐ 5	Shawn Kemp	3.50	1.55	.45
	Seattle Supersonics			
☐ 6	Robert Horry	1.50	.65	.19
	Houston Rockets			

1993-94 Stadium Club Super Teams

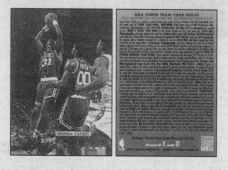

Randomly inserted in regular packs, this standard-size (2 1/2" by 3 1/2") 27-card set features borderless fronts with color team action photos. The team name appears in gold-foil lettering at the bottom. The back features the NBA Super Team Card rules. If the team shown on the card wins its division, conference title, or the NBA Finals, the collector could redeem it for special prizes until Nov. 1, 1994. The cards are numbered on the back as "X of 27."

	MINT	EXC	G-VG
COMPLETE SET (27)	175.00	80.00	22.00
COMMON PLAYER (1-27)	2.00	.90	.25
☐ 1 Atlanta Hawks	15.00	6.75	1.90
☐ 2 Boston Celtics	3.00	1.35	.40
☐ 3 Charlotte Hornets	3.00	1.35	.40
☐ 4 Chicago Bulls	2.00	.90	.25
☐ 5 Cleveland Cavaliers	2.00	.90	.25
☐ 6 Dallas Mavericks	2.00	.90	.25
☐ 7 Denver Nuggets	2.00	.90	.25
☐ 8 Detroit Pistons	2.00	.90	.25
☐ 9 Golden State Warriors	2.00	.90	.25
☐ 10 Houston Rockets	100.00	45.00	12.50
☐ 11 Indiana Pacers	2.00	.90	.25
☐ 12 Los Angeles Clippers	2.00	.90	.25
☐ 13 Los Angeles Lakers	2.00	.90	.25
☐ 14 Miami Heat	2.00	.90	.25
☐ 15 Milwaukee Bucks	2.00	.90	.25
☐ 16 Minnesota Timberwolves	2.00	.90	.25
☐ 17 New Jersey Nets	2.00	.90	.25
☐ 18 New York Knicks	40.00	18.00	5.00
☐ 19 Orlando Magic	5.00	2.30	.60
☐ 20 Philadelphia 76ers	2.00	.90	.25
☐ 21 Phoenix Suns	5.00	2.30	.60
☐ 22 Portland Trail Blazers	2.00	.90	.25
☐ 23 Sacramento Kings	2.00	.90	.25
☐ 24 San Antonio Spurs	5.00	2.30	.60
☐ 25 Seattle Supersonics	15.00	6.75	1.90
☐ 26 Utah Jazz	2.00	.90	.25
☐ 27 Washington Bullets	2.00	.90	.25

1983-84 Star NBA

This set of 276 cards was issued in four series during the first six months of 1984. Several teams in the first series (1-100) are difficult to obtain due to extensive miscuts (all of which, according to the company, were destroyed) in the initial production process. The team sets were issued in clear sealed bags. Many of the team bags were distributed to hobby dealers

through a small group of Star Co. master distributors. The original wholesale price per bag was 2.00 to 3.00 for most of the teams. Cards measure 2 1/2" by 3 1/2". Color borders around the fronts and color printing on the backs correspond to team colors. Cards are numbered according to team order, e.g., Philadelphia 76ers (1-12), Los Angeles Lakers (13-25), Boston Celtics (26-37), Milwaukee Bucks (38-48), Dallas Mavericks (49-60), New York Knicks (61-72), Houston Rockets (73-84), Detroit Pistons (85-96), Portland Trail Blazers (97-108), Phoenix Suns (109-120), San Diego Clippers (121-132), Utah Jazz (133-144), New Jersey Nets (145-156), Indiana Pacers (157-168), Chicago Bulls (169-180), Denver Nuggets (181-192), Seattle Supersonics (193-203), Washington Bullets (204-215), Kansas City Kings (216-227), Cleveland Cavaliers (228-240), San Antonio Spurs (241-251), Golden State Warriors (252-263), and Atlanta Hawks (264-276). Extended Rookie Cards include Mark Aguirre, Danny Ainge, Rolando Blackman, Tom Chambers, Clyde Drexler, Dale Ellis, Derek Harper, Larry Nance, Rickey Pierce, Isiah Thomas, Dominique Wilkins, and Buck Williams and James Worthy. A promotional card of Sidney Moncrief was produced in limited quantities, but it was numbered 39 rather than 38 as it was in the regular set. According to Star Company's original sales materials and order forms, reportedly 5,000 team bags were printed for each team although quality control problems with the early sets apparently shrunk that number considerably. There is typically a slight discount on sales of opened team bags.

	MINT	EXC	G-VG
COMPLETE BAG SET (276)	3000.00	1350.00	375.00
COMP.BAG 76ERS (12)	150.00	70.00	19.00
COMP.BAG LAKERS (13)	200.00	90.00	25.00
COMP.BAG CELTICS (12)	650.00	300.00	80.00
COMP.BAG BUCKS (11)	70.00	32.00	8.75
COMP.BAG MAVS (12)	700.00	325.00	90.00
COMP.BAG KNICKS (12)	45.00	20.00	5.75
COMP.BAG ROCKETS (12)	25.00	11.50	3.10
COMP.BAG PISTONS (12)	200.00	90.00	25.00
COMP.BAG BLAZERS (12)	250.00	115.00	31.00
COMP.BAG SUNS (12)	75.00	34.00	9.50
COMP.BAG CLIPPERS (12)	75.00	34.00	9.50
COMP.BAG JAZZ (12)	35.00	16.00	4.40
COMP.BAG NETS (12)	50.00	23.00	6.25
COMP.BAG PACERS (12)	25.00	11.50	3.10
COMP.BAG BULLS (12)	45.00	20.00	5.75
COMP.BAG NUGGETS (12)	45.00	20.00	5.75
COMP.BAG SONICS (11)	70.00	32.00	8.75
COMP.BAG BULLETS (12)	40.00	18.00	5.00
COMP.BAG KINGS (12)	40.00	18.00	5.00
COMP.BAG CAVS (13)	35.00	16.00	4.40
COMP.BAG SPURS (11)	50.00	23.00	6.25
COMP.BAG WARRIORS (11)	25.00	11.50	3.10
COMP.BAG HAWKS (14)	400.00	180.00	50.00
COMMON 76ERS SP (1-12) !	5.00	2.30	.60
COMMON LAKERS SP (13-25)	5.00	2.30	.60
COMMON CELTICS SP (26-37)	9.00	4.00	1.15
COMMON BUCKS SP (38-48)	5.00	2.30	.60
COMMON MAVS SP (49-60) !	30.00	13.50	3.80
COMMON KNICKS (61-72)	2.50	1.15	.30
COMMON ROCKETS (73-84)	2.50	1.15	.30
COMMON PISTONS (85-96)	2.50	1.15	.30
COMMON BLAZERS (97-108)	2.50	1.15	.30

COMMON SUNS (109-120)	2.50	1.15	.30
COMMON CLIPPERS (121-132)	2.50	1.15	.30
COMMON JAZZ (133-144)	2.50	1.15	.30
COMMON NETS (145-156)	2.50	1.15	.30
COMMON PACERS (157-168)	2.50	1.15	.30
COMMON BULLS (169-180)	2.50	1.15	.30
COMMON NUGGETS (181-192)	2.50	1.15	.30
COMMON SONICS (193-203)	2.50	1.15	.30
COMMON BULLETS (204-215)	2.50	1.15	.30
COMMON KINGS (216-227)	2.50	1.15	.30
COMMON CAVS (228-240)	2.50	1.15	.30
COMMON SPURS (241-251)	2.50	1.15	.30
COMMON WARRIORS (252-262)	2.50	1.15	.30
COMMON HAWKS (263-276)	2.50	1.15	.30
*OPENED TEAM SETS: .75X to 1.0 VALUE			

☐	1 Julius Erving	90.00	40.00	11.50
☐	2 Maurice Cheeks	15.00	6.75	1.90
☐	3 Franklin Edwards	5.00	2.30	.60
☐	4 Marc Iavaroni	5.00	2.30	.60
☐	5 Clemon Johnson	5.00	2.30	.60
☐	6 Bobby Jones	10.00	4.50	1.25
☐	7 Moses Malone	30.00	13.50	3.80
☐	8 Leo Rautins	5.00	2.30	.60
☐	9 Clint Richardson	5.00	2.30	.60
☐	10 Sedale Threatt	25.00	11.50	3.10
☐	11 Andrew Toney	10.00	4.50	1.25
☐	12 Sam Williams	5.00	2.30	.60
☐	13 Magic Johnson	150.00	70.00	19.00
☐	14 Kareem Abdul-Jabbar	45.00	20.00	5.75
☐	15 Michael Cooper	12.00	5.50	1.50
☐	16 Calvin Garrett	5.00	2.30	.60
☐	17 Mitch Kupchak	5.50	2.50	.70
☐	18 Bob McAdoo	15.00	6.75	1.90
☐	19 Mike McGee	5.00	2.30	.60
☐	20 Swen Nater	5.00	2.30	.60
☐	21 Kurt Rambis	12.00	5.50	1.50
☐	22 Byron Scott	30.00	13.50	3.80
☐	23 Larry Spriggs	5.00	2.30	.60
☐	24 Jamaal Wilkes	8.00	3.60	1.00
☐	25 James Worthy	65.00	29.00	8.25
☐	26 Larry Bird	400.00	180.00	50.00
☐	27 Danny Ainge	100.00	45.00	12.50
☐	28 Quinn Buckner	10.00	4.50	1.25
☐	29 M.L. Carr	10.00	4.50	1.25
☐	30 Carlos Clark	9.00	4.00	1.15
☐	31 Gerald Henderson	9.00	4.00	1.15
☐	32 Dennis Johnson	25.00	11.50	3.10
☐	33 Cedric Maxwell	15.00	6.75	1.90
☐	34 Kevin McHale	65.00	29.00	8.25
☐	35 Robert Parish	65.00	29.00	8.25
☐	36 Scott Wedman	9.00	4.00	1.15
☐	37 Greg Kite	12.00	5.50	1.50
☐	38 Sidney Moncrief	15.00	6.75	1.90
☐	39A Sidney Moncrief (Promotional card)	45.00	20.00	5.75
☐	39B Nate Archibald	20.00	9.00	2.50
☐	40 Randy Breuer	6.00	2.70	.75
☐	41 Junior Bridgeman	5.50	2.50	.70
☐	42 Harvey Catchings	5.00	2.30	.60
☐	43 Kevin Grevey	5.00	2.30	.60
☐	44 Marques Johnson	10.00	4.50	1.25
☐	45 Bob Lanier	20.00	9.00	2.50
☐	46 Alton Lister	6.00	2.70	.75
☐	47 Paul Mokeski	5.00	2.30	.60
☐	48 Paul Pressey	7.00	3.10	.85
☐	49 Mark Aguirre	85.00	38.00	10.50
☐	50 Rolando Blackman	85.00	38.00	10.50
☐	51 Pat Cummings	30.00	13.50	3.80
☐	52 Brad Davis	40.00	18.00	5.00
☐	53 Dale Ellis	100.00	45.00	12.50
☐	54 Bill Garnett	30.00	13.50	3.80
☐	55 Derek Harper	125.00	57.50	15.50

	#	Player			
☐	56	Kurt Nimphius	30.00	13.50	3.80
☐	57	Jim Spanarkel	30.00	13.50	3.80
☐	58	Elston Turner	30.00	13.50	3.80
☐	59	Jay Vincent	30.00	13.50	3.80
☐	60	Mark West	40.00	18.00	5.00
☐	61	Bernard King	10.00	4.50	1.25
☐	62	Bill Cartwright	7.00	3.10	.85
☐	63	Len Elmore	3.00	1.35	.40
☐	64	Eric Fernsten	2.50	1.15	.30
☐	65	Ernie Grunfeld	3.00	1.35	.40
☐	66	Louis Orr	2.50	1.15	.30
☐	67	Leonard Robinson	3.50	1.55	.45
☐	68	Rory Sparrow	2.50	1.15	.30
☐	69	Trent Tucker	6.00	2.70	.75
☐	70	Darrell Walker	6.00	2.70	.75
☐	71	Marvin Webster	3.50	1.55	.45
☐	72	Ray Williams	2.50	1.15	.30
☐	73	Ralph Sampson	6.00	2.70	.75
☐	74	James Bailey	2.50	1.15	.30
☐	75	Phil Ford	4.00	1.80	.50
☐	76	Elvin Hayes	12.00	5.50	1.50
☐	77	Caldwell Jones	3.50	1.55	.45
☐	78	Major Jones	2.50	1.15	.30
☐	79	Allen Leavell	2.50	1.15	.30
☐	80	Lewis Lloyd	2.50	1.15	.30
☐	81	Rodney McCray	4.00	1.80	.50
☐	82	Robert Reid	2.50	1.15	.30
☐	83	Terry Teagle	4.00	1.80	.50
☐	84	Wally Walker	2.50	1.15	.30
☐	85	Kelly Tripucka	4.00	1.80	.50
☐	86	Kent Benson	3.00	1.35	.40
☐	87	Earl Cureton	2.50	1.15	.30
☐	88	Lionel Hollins	2.50	1.15	.30
☐	89	Vinnie Johnson	4.00	1.80	.50
☐	90	Bill Laimbeer	8.00	3.60	1.00
☐	91	Cliff Levingston	4.00	1.80	.50
☐	92	John Long	2.50	1.15	.30
☐	93	David Thirdkill	2.50	1.15	.30
☐	94	Isiah Thomas	175.00	80.00	22.00
☐	95	Ray Tolbert	2.50	1.15	.30
☐	96	Terry Tyler	2.50	1.15	.30
☐	97	Jim Paxson	2.50	1.15	.30
☐	98	Kenny Carr	3.00	1.35	.40
☐	99	Wayne Cooper	2.50	1.15	.30
☐	100	Clyde Drexler	200.00	90.00	25.00
☐	101	Jeff Lamp	4.00	1.80	.50
☐	102	Lafayette Lever	5.00	2.30	.60
☐	103	Calvin Natt	2.50	1.15	.30
☐	104	Audie Norris	2.50	1.15	.30
☐	105	Tom Piotrowski	2.50	1.15	.30
☐	106	Mychal Thompson	4.00	1.80	.50
☐	107	Darnell Valentine	2.50	1.15	.30
☐	108	Pete Verhoeven	2.50	1.15	.30
☐	109	Walter Davis	8.00	3.60	1.00
☐	110	Alvan Adams	3.00	1.35	.40
☐	111	James Edwards	3.00	1.35	.40
☐	112	Rod Foster	2.50	1.15	.30
☐	113	Maurice Lucas	5.00	2.30	.60
☐	114	Kyle Macy	3.00	1.35	.40
☐	115	Larry Nance	45.00	20.00	5.75
☐	116	Charles Pittman	2.50	1.15	.30
☐	117	Rick Robey	3.00	1.35	.40
☐	118	Mike Sanders	4.00	1.80	.50
☐	119	Alvin Scott	2.50	1.15	.30
☐	120	Paul Westphal	10.00	4.50	1.25
☐	121	Bill Walton	20.00	9.00	2.50
☐	122	Michael Brooks	2.50	1.15	.30
☐	123	Terry Cummings	15.00	6.75	1.90
☐	124	James Donaldson	3.00	1.35	.40
☐	125	Craig Hodges	6.00	2.70	.75
☐	126	Greg Kelser	2.50	1.15	.30
☐	127	Hank McDowell	2.50	1.15	.30
☐	128	Billy McKinney	2.50	1.15	.30

☐	129	Norm Nixon	5.00	2.30	.60
☐	130	Ricky Pierce UER	35.00	16.00	4.40
		(Misspelled Rickey			
		on both sides)			
☐	131	Derek Smith	2.50	1.15	.30
☐	132	Jerome Whitehead	2.50	1.15	.30
☐	133	Adrian Dantley	8.00	3.60	1.00
☐	134	Mitch Anderson	2.50	1.15	.30
☐	135	Thurl Bailey	6.00	2.70	.75
☐	136	Tom Boswell	2.50	1.15	.30
☐	137	John Drew	2.50	1.15	.30
☐	138	Mark Eaton	10.00	4.50	1.25
☐	139	Jerry Eaves	2.50	1.15	.30
☐	140	Rickey Green	4.00	1.80	.50
☐	141	Darrell Griffith	4.00	1.80	.50
☐	142	Bobby Hansen	4.00	1.80	.50
☐	143	Rich Kelley	2.50	1.15	.30
☐	144	Jeff Wilkins	2.50	1.15	.30
☐	145	Buck Williams	35.00	16.00	4.40
☐	146	Otis Birdsong	3.00	1.35	.40
☐	147	Darwin Cook	2.50	1.15	.30
☐	148	Darryl Dawkins	6.00	2.70	.75
☐	149	Mike Gminski	4.00	1.80	.50
☐	150	Reggie Johnson	2.50	1.15	.30
☐	151	Albert King	4.00	1.80	.50
☐	152	Mike O'Koren	3.00	1.35	.40
☐	153	Kelvin Ransey	2.50	1.15	.30
☐	154	Michael Ray Richardson	2.50	1.15	.30
☐	155	Clarence Walker	2.50	1.15	.30
☐	156	Bill Willoughby	2.50	1.15	.30
☐	157	Steve Stipanovich	4.00	1.80	.50
☐	158	Butch Carter	2.50	1.15	.30
☐	159	Edwin Leroy Combs	2.50	1.15	.30
☐	160	George L. Johnson	2.50	1.15	.30
☐	161	Clark Kellogg	5.00	2.30	.60
☐	162	Sidney Lowe	5.00	2.30	.60
☐	163	Kevin McKenna	2.50	1.15	.30
☐	164	Jerry Sichting	3.00	1.35	.40
☐	165	Brook Steppe	2.50	1.15	.30
☐	166	Jimmy Thomas	2.50	1.15	.30
☐	167	Granville Waiters	2.50	1.15	.30
☐	168	Herb Williams	5.00	2.30	.60
☐	169	Dave Corzine	3.00	1.35	.40
☐	170	Wallace Bryant	2.50	1.15	.30
☐	171	Quintin Dailey	2.50	1.15	.30
☐	172	Sidney Green	4.00	1.80	.50
☐	173	David Greenwood	3.00	1.35	.40
☐	174	Rod Higgins	5.00	2.30	.60
☐	175	Clarence Johnson	2.50	1.15	.30
☐	176	Ronnie Lester	2.50	1.15	.30
☐	177	Jawann Oldham	2.50	1.15	.30
☐	178	Ennis Whatley	4.00	1.80	.50
☐	179	Mitchell Wiggins	2.50	1.15	.30
☐	180	Orlando Woolridge	10.00	4.50	1.25
☐	181	Kiki Vandeweghe	12.00	5.50	1.50
☐	182	Richard Anderson	2.50	1.15	.30
☐	183	Howard Carter	2.50	1.15	.30
☐	184	T.R. Dunn	2.50	1.15	.30
☐	185	Keith Edmonson	2.50	1.15	.30
☐	186	Alex English	10.00	4.50	1.25
☐	187	Mike Evans	2.50	1.15	.30
☐	188	Bill Hanzlik	4.00	1.80	.50
☐	189	Dan Issel	15.00	6.75	1.90
☐	190	Anthony Roberts	2.50	1.15	.30
☐	191	Danny Schayes	6.00	2.70	.75
☐	192	Rob Williams	2.50	1.15	.30
☐	193	Jack Sikma	8.00	3.60	1.00
☐	194	Fred Brown	4.00	1.80	.50
☐	195	Tom Chambers	35.00	16.00	4.40
☐	196	Steve Hawes	2.50	1.15	.30
☐	197	Steve Hayes	2.50	1.15	.30
☐	198	Reggie King	2.50	1.15	.30
☐	199	Scooter McCray	3.00	1.35	.40

☐ 200	Jon Sundvold	4.00	1.80	.50
☐ 201	Danny Vranes	2.50	1.15	.30
☐ 202	Gus Williams	3.00	1.35	.40
☐ 203	Al Wood	2.50	1.15	.30
☐ 204	Jeff Ruland	4.00	1.80	.50
☐ 205	Greg Ballard	2.50	1.15	.30
☐ 206	Charles Davis	2.50	1.15	.30
☐ 207	Darren Daye	2.50	1.15	.30
☐ 208	Michael Gibson	2.50	1.15	.30
☐ 209	Frank Johnson	6.00	2.70	.75
☐ 210	Joe Kopicki	2.50	1.15	.30
☐ 211	Rick Mahorn	4.00	1.80	.50
☐ 212	Jeff Malone	25.00	11.50	3.10
☐ 213	Tom McMillen	4.00	1.80	.50
☐ 214	Ricky Sobers	2.50	1.15	.30
☐ 215	Bryan Warrick	2.50	1.15	.30
☐ 216	Billy Knight	3.00	1.35	.40
☐ 217	Don Buse	3.00	1.35	.40
☐ 218	Larry Drew	3.00	1.35	.40
☐ 219	Eddie Johnson	20.00	9.00	2.50
☐ 220	Joe Meriweather	2.50	1.15	.30
☐ 221	Larry Micheaux	2.50	1.15	.30
☐ 222	Ed Nealy	2.50	1.15	.30
☐ 223	Mark Olberding	2.50	1.15	.30
☐ 224	Dave Robisch	3.00	1.35	.40
☐ 225	Reggie Theus	5.00	2.30	.60
☐ 226	LaSalle Thompson	4.00	1.80	.50
☐ 227	Mike Woodson	2.50	1.15	.30
☐ 228	World B. Free	5.00	2.30	.60
☐ 229	John Bagley	5.00	2.30	.60
☐ 230	Jeff Cook	2.50	1.15	.30
☐ 231	Geoff Crompton	2.50	1.15	.30
☐ 232	John Garris	2.50	1.15	.30
☐ 233	Stewart Granger	2.50	1.15	.30
☐ 234	Roy Hinson	4.00	1.80	.50
☐ 235	Phil Hubbard	2.50	1.15	.30
☐ 236	Geoff Huston	2.50	1.15	.30
☐ 237	Ben Poquette	2.50	1.15	.30
☐ 238	Cliff Robinson	2.50	1.15	.30
☐ 239	Lonnie Shelton	3.00	1.35	.40
☐ 240	Paul Thompson	2.50	1.15	.30
☐ 241	George Gervin	15.00	6.75	1.90
☐ 242	Gene Banks	3.00	1.35	.40
☐ 243	Ron Brewer	2.50	1.15	.30
☐ 244	Artis Gilmore	7.00	3.10	.85
☐ 245	Edgar Jones	2.50	1.15	.30
☐ 246	John Lucas	8.00	3.60	1.00
☐ 247A	Mike Mitchell ERR (Photo actually Mark McNamara)	4.00	1.80	.50
☐ 247B	Mike Mitchell COR	6.00	2.70	.75
☐ 248A	Mark McNamara ERR (Photo actually Mike Mitchell)	4.00	1.80	.50
☐ 248B	Mark McNamara COR	6.00	2.70	.75
☐ 249	Johnny Moore	2.50	1.15	.30
☐ 250	John Paxson	20.00	9.00	2.50
☐ 251	Fred Roberts	4.00	1.80	.50
☐ 252	Joe Barry Carroll	3.00	1.35	.40
☐ 253	Mike Bratz	2.50	1.15	.30
☐ 254	Don Collins	2.50	1.15	.30
☐ 255	Lester Conner	2.50	1.15	.30
☐ 256	Chris Engler	2.50	1.15	.30
☐ 257	Sleepy Floyd	10.00	4.50	1.25
☐ 258	Wallace Johnson	2.50	1.15	.30
☐ 259	Pace Mannion	2.50	1.15	.30
☐ 260	Purvis Short	2.50	1.15	.30
☐ 261	Larry Smith	3.00	1.35	.40
☐ 262	Darren Tillis	2.50	1.15	.30
☐ 263	Dominique Wilkins	350.00	160.00	45.00
☐ 264	Rickey Brown	2.50	1.15	.30
☐ 265	Johnny Davis	2.50	1.15	.30
☐ 266	Mike Glenn	4.00	1.80	.50

☐ 267	Scott Hastings	4.00	1.80	.50
☐ 268	Eddie Johnson	2.50	1.15	.30
☐ 269	Mark Landsberger	2.50	1.15	.30
☐ 270	Billy Paultz	3.50	1.55	.45
☐ 271	Doc Rivers	25.00	11.50	3.10
☐ 272	Tree Rollins	3.50	1.55	.45
☐ 273	Dan Roundfield	3.50	1.55	.45
☐ 274	Sly Williams	2.50	1.15	.30
☐ 275	Randy Wittman	2.50	1.15	.30

1983-84 Star All-Rookies

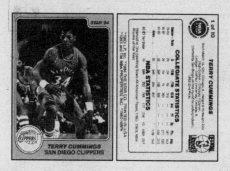

This set features the ten members of the 1982-83 NBA All-Rookie Team. Cards measure 2 1/2" by 3 1/2" and have a yellow border around the fronts of the cards. The set was issued in late Summer of 1983 and features the Star '84 logo on the front of each card. The cards are numbered on the backs with the order of the numbering alphabetical according to the player's last name.

	MINT	EXC	G-VG
COMPLETE BAG SET (10)	75.00	34.00	9.50
COMMON PLAYER (1-10)	2.50	1.15	.30
*OPENED SET: .75X to 1.0X VALUE			

☐ 1	Terry Cummings	5.00	2.30	.60
☐ 2	Quintin Dailey	2.50	1.15	.30
☐ 3	Roderick Higgins	2.50	1.15	.30
☐ 4	Clark Kellogg	3.00	1.35	.40
☐ 5	Lafayette Lever	3.00	1.35	.40
☐ 6	Paul Pressey	2.50	1.15	.30
☐ 7	Trent Tucker	2.50	1.15	.30
☐ 8	Dominique Wilkins	50.00	23.00	6.25
☐ 9	Rob Williams	2.50	1.15	.30
☐ 10	James Worthy	12.00	5.50	1.50

1983-84 Star Sixers Champs

This set of 25 cards is devoted to Philadelphia's NBA Championship victory over the Los Angeles Lakers in 1983. Reportedly 10,000 sets were printed with majority of distribution done through the Spectrum, the 76ers home court. Cards measure 2 1/2" by 3 1/2" and have a red border around the fronts of the cards and red printing on the backs. The set was issued in late Summer of 1983 and features the Star '84 logo on the front of each card.

	MINT	EXC	G-VG
COMPLETE BAG SET (25)	40.00	18.00	5.00
COMMON PLAYER (1-25)	2.50	1.15	.30
*OPENED SET: .75X to 1.0X VALUE			
☐ 1 Sixers 1982-83 NBA	3.50	1.55	.45
World Champs			
(Checklist back)			
☐ 2 Billy Cunningham	3.00	1.35	.40
Head Coach			
☐ 3 Clash of the Titans	4.00	1.80	.50
Malone vs. Abdul-Jabbar			
☐ 4 The Quest Begins	6.00	2.70	.75
Julius Erving			
☐ 5 Philly Super-Sub	2.50	1.15	.30
Clint Richardson			
☐ 6 Laker Killer	2.75	1.25	.35
Andrew Toney			
☐ 7 Phila. 113, LA 107	2.50	1.15	.30
Game 1 Boxscore			
☐ 8 Secretary of Defense	3.00	1.35	.40
Bobby Jones			
☐ 9 Mo Can Go	3.00	1.35	.40
Maurice Cheeks			
☐ 10 Doc for 2	6.00	2.70	.75
Julius Erving			
☐ 11 Toney on the Drive	2.75	1.25	.35
Andrew Toney			
☐ 12 Phila. 103, LA 93	2.50	1.15	.30
Game 2 Boxscore			
☐ 13 Serious Sixers	2.50	1.15	.30
(Pre-Game Lineup)			
☐ 14 Moses Leads Sixers	3.50	1.55	.45
Moses Malone			
☐ 15 Bench Strength	2.50	1.15	.30
Clemon Johnson			
☐ 16 One Mo Time	3.00	1.35	.40
Maurice Cheeks			
☐ 17 Phila. 111, LA 94	2.50	1.15	.30
Game 3 Boxscore			
☐ 18 Julius Scoops	6.00	2.70	.75
Julius Erving			
☐ 19 Sixth Man of Year	3.00	1.35	.40
Bobby Jones			
☐ 20 Coast to Coast	3.50	1.55	.45
Moses Malone			
☐ 21 World Champs	2.50	1.15	.30
Phila. 115, LA 108			
Game 4 Boxscore			
☐ 22 Doc Gets the Ring	6.00	2.70	.75
(Julius Erving)			
Series Stats			

☐ 23	Philly in a Sweep	3.50	1.55	.45
	Prior World Champs			
☐ 24	Basking in Glory	6.00	2.70	.75
	Profile: Dr.J			
☐ 25	The NBA's MVP	4.00	1.80	.50
	Profile: Moses Malone			

1983 Star All-Star Game

This was the first NBA set issued by the Star Company. The 30-card set was issued in a clear, sealed plastic bag and distributed through hobby dealers. According to information provided on the order forms, Star Company printed 15,000 sets. The sets originally retailed for 2.50 to 5.00 each. Each card measures 2 1/2" by 3 1/2". The cards have a blue border on the front of each card and blue print is used on the back of each card. The set commemorates the 1983 NBA All-Star Game held in Los Angeles. Many of the cards feature players in their all-star uniforms. There are two unnumbered cards in the set listed at the end of the checklist below. The cards are numbered on the backs with the order of the numbering essentially alphabetical according to the player's name. The set features the first professional card of Isiah Thomas.

	MINT	EXC	G-VG
COMPLETE BAG SET (32)	80.00	36.00	10.00
COMMON PLAYER (1-30)	2.50	1.15	.30
*OPENED SET: .75X to 1.0X VALUE			

			MINT	EXC	G-VG
☐ 1	Checklist (Julius Erving on front)		8.00	3.60	1.00
☐ 2	Larry Bird		35.00	16.00	4.40
☐ 3	Maurice Cheeks		3.00	1.35	.40
☐ 4	Julius Erving		12.00	5.50	1.50
☐ 5	Marques Johnson		2.75	1.25	.35
☐ 6	Bill Laimbeer		3.00	1.35	.40
☐ 7	Moses Malone		5.00	2.30	.60
☐ 8	Sidney Moncrief		3.00	1.35	.40
☐ 9	Robert Parish		5.00	2.30	.60
☐ 10	Reggie Theus		2.75	1.25	.35
☐ 11	Isiah Thomas		20.00	9.00	2.50
☐ 12	Andrew Toney		2.50	1.15	.30
☐ 13	Buck Williams		6.00	2.70	.75
☐ 14	Kareem Abdul-Jabbar		9.00	4.00	1.15
☐ 15	Alex English		3.00	1.35	.40
☐ 16	George Gervin		4.00	1.80	.50
☐ 17	Artis Gilmore		3.00	1.35	.40
☐ 18	Magic Johnson		25.00	11.50	3.10
☐ 19	Maurice Lucas		2.75	1.25	.35
☐ 20	Jim Paxson		2.50	1.15	.30
☐ 21	Jack Sikma		2.75	1.25	.35
☐ 22	David Thompson		4.00	1.80	.50

☐ 23 Kiki Vandeweghe	3.00	1.35	.40
☐ 24 Jamaal Wilkes	3.00	1.35	.40
☐ 25 Gus Williams	2.50	1.15	.30
☐ 26 All-Star MVPs (Dr. J, '77, '83)	8.00	3.60	1.00
☐ 27 One Player, Single Game Records (Theus and Malone)	3.00	1.35	.40
☐ 28 All-Star All-Time Leaders (East Coast Line)	3.00	1.35	.40
☐ 29 East Box Score (Boston Bombers: Bird and Parish)	15.00	6.75	1.90
☐ 30 West Box Score (Moncrief Soars)	2.50	1.15	.30
☐ xx Gilmore and English (Ad on back)	3.00	1.35	.40
☐ xx Kareem Abdul-Jabbar (Uncut sheet offer on back)	9.00	4.00	1.15

1984 Star All-Star Game

This set of 25 cards features participants in the 34th Annual 1984 NBA All-Star Game held in Denver. Cards measure 2 1/2" by 3 1/2" and have a white border around the fronts of the cards and blue printing on the backs. Cards feature the Star '84 logo on the front. The cards are ordered with the East All-Stars on cards 2-13 and the West All-Stars on cards 14-25. The cards are numbered on the backs and are in order by division. Within each division, the cards are alphabetical by player's last name.

	MINT	EXC	G-VG
COMPLETE BAG SET (1-25)	100.00	45.00	12.50
COMMON PLAYER (1-25)	2.50	1.15	.30
*OPENED SET: .75X to 1.0X VALUE			
☐ 1 1984 NBA All-Star Game Checklist (Isiah Thomas)	5.00	2.30	.60
☐ 2 Larry Bird	45.00	20.00	5.75
☐ 3 Otis Birdsong	2.50	1.15	.30
☐ 4 Julius Erving	18.00	8.00	2.30
☐ 5 Bernard King	3.50	1.55	.45
☐ 6 Bill Laimbeer	3.00	1.35	.40
☐ 7 Kevin McHale	8.00	3.60	1.00
☐ 8 Sidney Moncrief	3.00	1.35	.40
☐ 9 Robert Parish	8.00	3.60	1.00
☐ 10 Jeff Ruland	2.50	1.15	.30
☐ 11 Isiah Thomas (Magic Johnson also	12.00	5.50	1.50

shown on card)

		MINT	EXC	G-VG
☐ 12	Andrew Toney	2.75	1.25	.35
☐ 13	Kelly Tripucka	2.75	1.25	.35
☐ 14	Kareem Abdul-Jabbar	9.00	4.00	1.15
☐ 15	Mark Aguirre	3.00	1.35	.40
☐ 16	Adrian Dantley	3.00	1.35	.40
☐ 17	Walter Davis	3.00	1.35	.40
☐ 18	Alex English	3.00	1.35	.40
☐ 19	George Gervin	4.00	1.80	.50
☐ 20	Rickey Green	2.75	1.25	.35
☐ 21	Magic Johnson	32.00	14.50	4.00
☐ 22	Jim Paxson	2.50	1.15	.30
☐ 23	Ralph Sampson	2.75	1.25	.35
☐ 24	Jack Sikma	3.00	1.35	.40
☐ 25	Kiki Vandeweghe	2.75	1.25	.35

1984 Star All-Star Game Denver Police

This 34-card set was distributed as individual cards by the Denver Police in the months following the NBA All-Star Game (ASG) held in Denver. Reportedly 10,000 sets were produced. The set was composed of participants in the All-Star Game (1-25) and the Slam Dunk contest (26-34). Cards measure 2 1/2" by 3 1/2" and have a white border around the fronts and blue printing on the backs. Cards feature the Star '84 logo on the fronts and safety tips on the backs.

		MINT	EXC	G-VG
COMPLETE SET (34)		200.00	90.00	25.00
COMMON PLAYER (1-25)		2.50	1.15	.30
COMMON PLAYER (26-34)		2.50	1.15	.30
☐ 1	Checklist Card	8.00	3.60	1.00
☐ 2	Larry Bird	55.00	25.00	7.00
☐ 3	Otis Birdsong	2.50	1.15	.30
☐ 4	Julius Erving	25.00	11.50	3.10
☐ 5	Bernard King	4.00	1.80	.50
☐ 6	Bill Laimbeer	4.00	1.80	.50
☐ 7	Kevin McHale	12.00	5.50	1.50
☐ 8	Sidney Moncrief	4.00	1.80	.50
☐ 9	Robert Parish	12.00	5.50	1.50
☐ 10	Jeff Ruland	2.50	1.15	.30
☐ 11	Isiah Thomas	15.00	6.75	1.90
	(Magic Johnson also shown on card)			
☐ 12	Andrew Toney	3.00	1.35	.40
☐ 13	Kelly Tripucka	3.00	1.35	.40
☐ 14	Kareem Abdul-Jabbar	12.00	5.50	1.50
☐ 15	Mark Aguirre	4.00	1.80	.50

☐ 16 Adrian Dantley	4.00	1.80	.50
☐ 17 Walter Davis	4.00	1.80	.50
☐ 18 Alex English	4.00	1.80	.50
☐ 19 George Gervin	6.00	2.70	.75
☐ 20 Rickey Green	3.00	1.35	.40
☐ 21 Magic Johnson	40.00	18.00	5.00
☐ 22 Jim Paxson	2.50	1.15	.30
☐ 23 Ralph Sampson	3.00	1.35	.40
☐ 24 Jack Sikma	4.00	1.80	.50
☐ 25 Kiki Vandeweghe	3.00	1.35	.40
☐ 26 Michael Cooper	4.00	1.80	.50
☐ 27 Clyde Drexler	25.00	11.50	3.10
☐ 28 Julius Erving	25.00	11.50	3.10
☐ 29 Darrell Griffith	3.00	1.35	.40
☐ 30 Edgar Jones	2.50	1.15	.30
☐ 31 Larry Nance	6.00	2.70	.75
☐ 32 Ralph Sampson	3.00	1.35	.40
☐ 33 Dominique Wilkins	40.00	18.00	5.00
☐ 34 Orlando Woolridge	2.50	1.15	.30

1984 Star Slam Dunk

An 11-card set highlighting the revival of the Slam Dunk contest (during the 1984 All-Star Weekend in Denver) was produced by the Star Company in 1984. Cards measure 2 1/2" by 3 1/2" and have a white border around the fronts and blue printing on the backs. The Star '84 logo are featured on the front. The cards are numbered on the back.

	MINT	EXC	G-VG
COMPLETE BAG SET (11)	90.00	40.00	11.50
COMMON PLAYER (1-11)	2.50	1.15	.30
*OPENED SET: .75X to 1.0X VALUE			
☐ 1 Group Photo	14.00	6.25	1.75
(checklist back)			
☐ 2 Michael Cooper	4.00	1.80	.50
☐ 3 Clyde Drexler	25.00	11.50	3.10
☐ 4 Julius Erving	25.00	11.50	3.10
☐ 5 Darrell Griffith	2.75	1.25	.35
☐ 6 Edgar Jones	2.50	1.15	.30
☐ 7 Larry Nance	6.00	2.70	.75
☐ 8 Ralph Sampson	2.75	1.25	.35
☐ 9 Dominique Wilkins	40.00	18.00	5.00
☐ 10 Orlando Woolridge	3.00	1.35	.40
☐ 11 Larry Nance,	8.00	3.60	1.00
1984 Slam Dunk Champ			

1984 Star Celtics Champs

This set of 25 cards is devoted to Boston's NBA Championship victory over the Los Angeles Lakers in 1984. Cards measure 2 1/2" by 3 1/2" and have a green border around the fronts of the cards and green printing on the backs. The set was issued in Summer of 1984 and features the Star '84 logo on the front of each card. The set includes two of the three Red Auerbach cards ever printed.

	MINT	EXC	G-VG
COMPLETE BAG SET (25)	225.00	100.00	28.00
COMMON PLAYER (1-25)	3.00	1.35	.40
*OPENED SET: .75X to 1.0X VALUE			
☐ 1 Celtics Champs (Red Auerbach/Maxwell) (Checklist back)	8.00	3.60	1.00
☐ 2 Game 1 (Abdul-Jabbar over Parish)	8.00	3.60	1.00
☐ 3 Game 1 (McHale drives)	6.00	2.70	.75
☐ 4 LA 115, Boston 109 (Larry Bird)	35.00	16.00	4.40
☐ 5 Game 2 (Magic Johnson)	25.00	11.50	3.10
☐ 6 Game 2 (K.C. Jones and Danny Ainge)	7.00	3.10	.85
☐ 7 Boston 124, LA 121 (OT) (Larry Bird)	35.00	16.00	4.40
☐ 8 Game 3 (Abdul-Jabbar and McHale)	7.00	3.10	.85
☐ 9 Game 3 (J.Worthy)	6.00	2.70	.75
☐ 10 LA 137, Boston 104 (Magic Johnson)	25.00	11.50	3.10
☐ 11 Game 4 (Magic blocks Bird)	60.00	27.00	7.50
☐ 12 Game 4 (Ainge scuffle)	6.00	2.70	.75
☐ 13 Boston 129, LA 125 Overtime (Carr and Maxwell)	3.00	1.35	.40
☐ 14 Game 5 (Larry Bird)	35.00	16.00	4.40
☐ 15 Game 5 (Pat Riley)	7.00	3.10	.85
☐ 16 Boston 121, LA 103 (Kareem Abdul-Jabbar)	8.00	3.60	1.00
☐ 17 Game 6 (Parish sandwich)	6.00	2.70	.75
☐ 18 Game 6 (Kareem Abdul-Jabbar)	7.00	3.10	.85
☐ 19 LA 119, Boston 108 (Dennis Johnson)	4.00	1.80	.50
☐ 20 Game 7 (Kareem sky hook)	7.00	3.10	.85

			MINT	EXC	G-VG
☐	21	Game 7 (K.C. Jones)	4.00	1.80	.50
☐	22	World Champs; Boston 111, LA 102 (M.L. Carr)	3.00	1.35	.40
☐	23	Prior Celtic Championships (Red Auerbach)	10.00	4.50	1.25
☐	24	Bird: Championship Series MVP	40.00	18.00	5.00
☐	25	The Road to the Title (Boston Garden)	5.00	2.30	.60

1984 Star Award Banquet

This 24-card set was produced for the NBA to be given away at the Awards Banquet which took place following the conclusion of the 1983-84 season. According to a 1984 Star Company press release, only 3,000 sets were produced. The cards highlighted award winners from the 1983-84 season. Cards measure 2 1/2" by 3 1/2" and have a blue border around the fronts of the cards and pink and blue printing on the backs. The set was issued in June of 1984 and features the Star '84 logo on the front of each card.

		MINT	EXC	G-VG
COMPLETE BAG SET (24)		75.00	34.00	9.50
COMMON PLAYER (1-24)		2.50	1.15	.30
*OPENED SET: .75X to 1.0X VALUE				
☐ 1	1984 Award Winners Checklist	2.50	1.15	.30
☐ 2	Frank Layden CO	3.00	1.35	.40
☐ 3	Ralph Sampson ROY	2.75	1.25	.35
☐ 4	Comeback Player of the Year; Adrian Dantley	3.00	1.35	.40
☐ 5	Sixth Man; Kevin McHale	6.00	2.70	.75
☐ 6	Pivotal Player of the Year; Magic Johnson	15.00	6.75	1.90
☐ 7	Defensive Player; Sidney Moncrief	3.00	1.35	.40
☐ 8	MVP: Larry Bird	25.00	11.50	3.10
☐ 9	Slam Dunk Champ; Larry Nance	3.50	1.55	.45
☐ 10	Statistical Leaders	8.00	3.60	1.00
☐ 11	Statistical Leaders II	6.00	2.70	.75
☐ 12	All-Star Game MVP; Isiah Thomas	6.00	2.70	.75
☐ 13	Leading Scorer;	3.00	1.35	.40

☐ 14	Adrian Dantley Field Goal Percent Leader; Artis Gilmore	3.00	1.35	.40
☐ 15	Free Throw Percent Leader; Larry Bird	25.00	11.50	3.10
☐ 16	Three Point Field Goal Percent Leader; Darrell Griffith	2.50	1.15	.30
☐ 17	Assists Leader; Magic Johnson	15.00	6.75	1.90
☐ 18	Steals Leader; Rickey Green	2.50	1.15	.30
☐ 19	Most Blocked Shots; Mark Eaton	2.50	1.15	.30
☐ 20	Leading Rebounder; Moses Malone	3.50	1.55	.45
☐ 21	Most Career Points; Kareem Abdul-Jabbar	8.00	3.60	1.00
☐ 22	NBA All-Defensive Team	3.00	1.35	.40
☐ 23	NBA All-Rookie Team	4.00	1.80	.50
☐ 24	NBA All-NBA Team	20.00	9.00	2.50

1984 Star Larry Bird

This set contains 18 cards highlighting the career of basketball great Larry Bird. Cards measure 2 1/2" by 3 1/2" and have a green border around the fronts of the cards and green printing on the backs. Cards feature Star '84 logo on the front as they were released in May of 1984.

	MINT	**EXC**	**G-VG**
COMPLETE BAG SET (18)	100.00	45.00	12.50
COMMON L.BIRD (1-18)	8.00	3.60	1.00
*OPENED SET: .75X to 1.0X VALUE			

☐ 1	Checklist	8.00	3.60	1.00
☐ 2	Collegiate Stats	8.00	3.60	1.00
☐ 3	1980 Rookie of the Year	8.00	3.60	1.00
☐ 4	Regular Season Stats	8.00	3.60	1.00
☐ 5	Playoff Stats	8.00	3.60	1.00
☐ 6	All-Star Stats	8.00	3.60	1.00
☐ 7	The 1979-80 Season	8.00	3.60	1.00
☐ 8	The 1980-81 Season	8.00	3.60	1.00
☐ 9	The 1981-82 Season	8.00	3.60	1.00
☐ 10	The 1982-83 Season	8.00	3.60	1.00
☐ 11	The 1983-84 Season	8.00	3.60	1.00
☐ 12	The 1984 NBA MVP	8.00	3.60	1.00
☐ 13	Member - 1984 All NBA Team	8.00	3.60	1.00

☐	14	World Champions	8.00	3.60	1.00
		1981, 1984			
☐	15	1984 Free Throw	8.00	3.60	1.00
		Percentage Leader			
☐	16	Career Data	8.00	3.60	1.00
☐	17	Personal Data	8.00	3.60	1.00
☐	18	The Future	8.00	3.60	1.00

1984-85 Star NBA

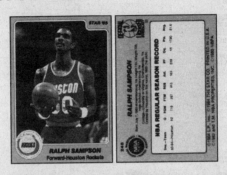

This set of 288 cards was issued in three series during the first five months of 1985 by the Star Company. The set features players by team throughout the NBA. The team sets were issued in clear sealed bags. Many of these team bags were distributed to hobby dealers through a small group of Star Co. master distributors. The original wholesale price per bag was 2.00 to 3.00 for most of the teams. Cards measure 2 1/2" by 3 1/2" and have a colored border around the fronts of the cards according to the team with corresponding color printing on the backs. Cards are organized numerically by team, i.e., Boston Celtics (1-12), Los Angeles Clippers (13-24), New York Knicks (25-37), Phoenix Suns (38-51), Indiana Pacers (52-63), San Antonio Spurs (64-75), Atlanta Hawks (76-87), New Jersey Nets (88-100), Chicago Bulls (101-112), Seattle Supersonics (113-124), Milwaukee Bucks (125-136), Denver Nuggets (137-148), Golden State Warriors (149-160), Portland Trail Blazers (161-171), Los Angeles Lakers (172-184), Washington Bullets (185-194), Philadelphia 76ers (201-212), Cleveland Cavaliers (213-224), Utah Jazz (225-236), Houston Rockets (237-249), Dallas Mavericks (250-260), Detroit Pistons (261-269), and Sacramento Kings (270-280). The set also features a special subset (195-200) honoring Gold Medal-winning players from the 1984 Olympic basketball competition as well as a subset of NBA specials (281-288). Extended Rookie Cards include Charles Barkley, Craig Ehlo, Michael Jordan, Hakeem Olajuwon, Alvin Robertson, Sam Perkins, John Stockton and Otis Thorpe. According to Star original sales materials and order forms, reportedly 3,000 team bags were printed for each team. There is typically a slight discount on sales of opened team bags.

	MINT	EXC	G-VG
COMPLETE BAG SET (288)	6000.00	2700.00	750.00
COMP.BAG CELTICS (12)	300.00	135.00	38.00
COMP.BAG CLIPPERS (12)	25.00	11.50	3.10
COMP.BAG KNICKS (13)	30.00	13.50	3.80
COMP.BAG SUNS (14)	40.00	18.00	5.00
COMP.BAG PACERS SP (12)	75.00	34.00	9.50
COMP.BAG SPURS (12)	40.00	18.00	5.00
COMP.BAG HAWKS (12)	175.00	80.00	22.00
COMP.BAG NETS (13)	25.00	11.50	3.10
COMP.BAG BULLS (12)	3200.00	1450.00	400.00
COMP.BAG SONICS (12)	30.00	13.50	3.80
COMP.BAG BUCKS (12)	25.00	11.50	3.10
COMP.BAG NUGGETS (12)	30.00	13.50	3.80
COMP.BAG WARRIORS (12)	25.00	11.50	3.10
COMP.BAG BLAZERS (11)	110.00	50.00	14.00
COMP.BAG LAKERS (13)	175.00	80.00	22.00

COMP.BAG BULLETS (10)	25.00	11.50	3.10
COMP.BAG OLY/SPEC (14)	900.00	400.00	115.00
COMP.BAG 76ERS (12)	500.00	230.00	65.00
COMP.BAG CAVS (12)	25.00	11.50	3.10
COMP.BAG JAZZ (12)	200.00	90.00	25.00
COMP.BAG ROCKETS (13)	600.00	275.00	75.00
COMP.BAG MAVS (11) !	65.00	29.00	8.25
COMP.BAG PISTONS (9)	55.00	25.00	7.00
COMP.BAG KINGS (11)	45.00	20.00	5.75
COMMON CELTICS (1-12)	2.50	1.15	.30
COMMON CLIPPERS (13-24) !	2.50	1.15	.30
COMMON KNICKS (25-37)	2.50	1.15	.30
COMMON SUNS (38-51)	2.50	1.15	.30
COMMON PACERS SP (52-63)	6.00	2.70	.75
COMMON SPURS (64-75)	2.50	1.15	.30
COMMON HAWKS (76-87)	2.50	1.15	.30
COMMON NETS (88-100)	2.50	1.15	.30
COMMON BULLS (101-112) !	2.50	1.15	.30
COMMON SONICS (113-124)	2.50	1.15	.30
COMMON BUCKS (125-136)	2.50	1.15	.30
COMMON NUGGETS (137-148)	2.50	1.15	.30
COMMON WARRIORS (149-160)	2.50	1.15	.30
COMMON BLAZERS (161-171)	2.50	1.15	.30
COMMON LAKERS (172-184)	2.50	1.15	.30
COMMON BULLETS (185-194)	2.50	1.15	.30
COMMON OLYMPIANS (195-200)	2.50	1.15	.30
COMMON 76ERS (201-212)	2.50	1.15	.30
COMMON CAVS (213-224)	2.50	1.15	.30
COMMON JAZZ (225-236)	2.50	1.15	.30
COMMON ROCKETS (237-249)	2.50	1.15	.30
COMMON MAVS (250-260) !	2.50	1.15	.30
COMMON PISTONS (261-269)	2.50	1.15	.30
COMMON KINGS (270-280)	2.50	1.15	.30
COMMON SPECIALS (281-288)	2.50	1.15	.30

*OPENED TEAM SETS: .75X to 1.0 VALUE

☐	1	Larry Bird	180.00	80.00	23.00
☐	2	Danny Ainge	25.00	11.50	3.10
☐	3	Quinn Buckner	3.00	1.35	.40
☐	4	Rick Carlisle	2.50	1.15	.30
☐	5	M.L. Carr	3.50	1.55	.45
☐	6	Dennis Johnson	7.00	3.10	.85
☐	7	Greg Kite	2.50	1.15	.30
☐	8	Cedric Maxwell	4.00	1.80	.50
☐	9	Kevin McHale	20.00	9.00	2.50
☐	10	Robert Parish	20.00	9.00	2.50
☐	11	Scott Wedman	2.50	1.15	.30
☐	12	Larry Bird	90.00	40.00	11.50
		1983-84 NBA MVP			
☐	13	Marques Johnson	4.00	1.80	.50
☐	14	Junior Bridgeman	3.00	1.35	.40
☐	15	Michael Cage	8.00	3.60	1.00
☐	16	Harvey Catchings	2.50	1.15	.30
☐	17	James Donaldson	3.00	1.35	.40
☐	18	Lancaster Gordon	2.50	1.15	.30
☐	19	Jay Murphy	2.50	1.15	.30
☐	20	Norm Nixon	5.00	2.30	.60
☐	21	Derek Smith	2.50	1.15	.30
☐	22	Bill Walton	20.00	9.00	2.50
☐	23	Bryan Warrick	2.50	1.15	.30
☐	24	Rory White	2.50	1.15	.30
☐	25	Bernard King	7.00	3.10	.85
☐	26	James Bailey	2.50	1.15	.30
☐	27	Ken Bannister	2.50	1.15	.30
☐	28	Butch Carter	2.50	1.15	.30
☐	29	Bill Cartwright	5.00	2.30	.60
☐	30	Pat Cummings	2.50	1.15	.30
☐	31	Ernie Grunfeld	3.00	1.35	.40
☐	32	Louis Orr	2.50	1.15	.30
☐	33	Leonard Robinson	3.50	1.55	.45
☐	34	Rory Sparrow	2.50	1.15	.30
☐	35	Trent Tucker	3.00	1.35	.40
☐	36	Darrell Walker	2.50	1.15	.30

☐ 37 Eddie Lee Wilkins	2.50	1.15	.30
☐ 38 Alvan Adams	3.00	1.35	.40
☐ 39 Walter Davis	6.00	2.70	.75
☐ 40 James Edwards	3.00	1.35	.40
☐ 41 Rod Foster	2.50	1.15	.30
☐ 42 Michael Holton	2.50	1.15	.30
☐ 43 Jay Humphries	8.00	3.60	1.00
☐ 44 Charles Jones	2.50	1.15	.30
☐ 45 Maurice Lucas	4.00	1.80	.50
☐ 46 Kyle Macy	3.00	1.35	.40
☐ 47 Larry Nance	15.00	6.75	1.90
☐ 48 Charles Pittman	2.50	1.15	.30
☐ 49 Rick Robey	3.00	1.35	.40
☐ 50 Mike Sanders	2.50	1.15	.30
☐ 51 Alvin Scott	2.50	1.15	.30
☐ 52 Clark Kellogg	7.00	3.10	.85
☐ 53 Tony Brown	6.00	2.70	.75
☐ 54 Devin Durrant	6.00	2.70	.75
☐ 55 Vern Fleming	15.00	6.75	1.90
☐ 56 Bill Garnett	6.00	2.70	.75
☐ 57 Stuart Gray UER	6.00	2.70	.75
(Photo actually			
Tony Brown)			
☐ 58 Jerry Sichting	7.00	3.10	.85
☐ 59 Terence Stansbury	6.00	2.70	.75
☐ 60 Steve Stipanovich	7.00	3.10	.85
☐ 61 Jimmy Thomas	6.00	2.70	.75
☐ 62 Granville Waiters	6.00	2.70	.75
☐ 63 Herb Williams	7.00	3.10	.85
☐ 64 Artis Gilmore	5.00	2.30	.60
☐ 65 Gene Banks	3.00	1.35	.40
☐ 66 Ron Brewer	2.50	1.15	.30
☐ 67 George Gervin	15.00	6.75	1.90
☐ 68 Edgar Jones	2.50	1.15	.30
☐ 69 Ozell Jones	2.50	1.15	.30
☐ 70 Mark McNamara	2.50	1.15	.30
☐ 71 Mike Mitchell	2.50	1.15	.30
☐ 72 Johnny Moore	2.50	1.15	.30
☐ 73 John Paxson	7.00	3.10	.85
☐ 74 Fred Roberts	2.50	1.15	.30
☐ 75 Alvin Robertson	20.00	9.00	2.50
☐ 76 Dominique Wilkins	150.00	70.00	19.00
☐ 77 Rickey Brown	2.50	1.15	.30
☐ 78 Antoine Carr	8.00	3.60	1.00
☐ 79 Mike Glenn	2.50	1.15	.30
☐ 80 Scott Hastings	2.50	1.15	.30
☐ 81 Eddie Johnson	2.50	1.15	.30
☐ 82 Cliff Levingston	2.50	1.15	.30
☐ 83 Leo Rautins	2.50	1.15	.30
☐ 84 Doc Rivers	8.00	3.60	1.00
☐ 85 Tree Rollins	3.50	1.55	.45
☐ 86 Randy Wittman	2.50	1.15	.30
☐ 87 Sly Williams	2.50	1.15	.30
☐ 88 Darryl Dawkins	6.00	2.70	.75
☐ 89 Otis Birdsong	3.00	1.35	.40
☐ 90 Darwin Cook	2.50	1.15	.30
☐ 91 Mike Gminski	4.00	1.80	.50
☐ 92 George L. Johnson	2.50	1.15	.30
☐ 93 Albert King	2.50	1.15	.30
☐ 94 Mike O'Koren	3.00	1.35	.40
☐ 95 Kelvin Ransey	2.50	1.15	.30
☐ 96 M.R. Richardson	2.50	1.15	.30
☐ 97 Wayne Sappleton	2.50	1.15	.30
☐ 98 Jeff Turner	4.00	1.80	.50
☐ 99 Buck Williams	12.00	5.50	1.50
☐ 100 Michael Wilson	2.50	1.15	.30
☐ 101 Michael Jordan	2800.00	1250.00	350.00
☐ 102 Dave Corzine	3.00	1.35	.40
☐ 103 Quintin Dailey	2.50	1.15	.30
☐ 104 Sidney Green	2.50	1.15	.30
☐ 105 David Greenwood	3.00	1.35	.40
☐ 106 Rod Higgins	2.50	1.15	.30
☐ 107 Steve Johnson	2.50	1.15	.30

☐ 108	Caldwell Jones	3.50	1.55	.45
☐ 109	Wes Matthews	2.50	1.15	.30
☐ 110	Jawann Oldham	2.50	1.15	.30
☐ 111	Ennis Whatley	2.50	1.15	.30
☐ 112	Orlando Woolridge	4.00	1.80	.50
☐ 113	Tom Chambers	9.00	4.00	1.15
☐ 114	Cory Blackwell	2.50	1.15	.30
☐ 115	Frank Brickowski	9.00	4.00	1.15
☐ 116	Gerald Henderson	2.50	1.15	.30
☐ 117	Reggie King	2.50	1.15	.30
☐ 118	Tim McCormick	2.50	1.15	.30
☐ 119	John Schweitz	2.50	1.15	.30
☐ 120	Jack Sikma	6.00	2.70	.75
☐ 121	Ricky Sobers	2.50	1.15	.30
☐ 122	Jon Sundvold	2.50	1.15	.30
☐ 123	Danny Vranes	2.50	1.15	.30
☐ 124	Al Wood	2.50	1.15	.30
☐ 125	Terry Cummings UER (Robert Cummings on card back)	7.00	3.10	.85
☐ 126	Randy Breuer	2.50	1.15	.30
☐ 127	Charles Davis	2.50	1.15	.30
☐ 128	Mike Dunleavy	4.00	1.80	.50
☐ 129	Kenny Fields	2.50	1.15	.30
☐ 130	Kevin Grevey	2.50	1.15	.30
☐ 131	Craig Hodges	4.00	1.80	.50
☐ 132	Alton Lister	3.00	1.35	.40
☐ 133	Larry Micheaux	2.50	1.15	.30
☐ 134	Paul Mokeski	2.50	1.15	.30
☐ 135	Sidney Moncrief	7.00	3.10	.85
☐ 136	Paul Pressey	2.50	1.15	.30
☐ 137	Alex English	8.00	3.60	1.00
☐ 138	Wayne Cooper	2.50	1.15	.30
☐ 139	T.R. Dunn	2.50	1.15	.30
☐ 140	Mike Evans	2.50	1.15	.30
☐ 141	Bill Hanzlik	2.50	1.15	.30
☐ 142	Dan Issel	15.00	6.75	1.90
☐ 143	Joe Kopicki	2.50	1.15	.30
☐ 144	Lafayette Lever	3.00	1.35	.40
☐ 145	Calvin Natt	2.50	1.15	.30
☐ 146	Danny Schayes	2.50	1.15	.30
☐ 147	Elston Turner	2.50	1.15	.30
☐ 148	Willie White	2.50	1.15	.30
☐ 149	Purvis Short	2.50	1.15	.30
☐ 150	Chuck Aleksinas	2.50	1.15	.30
☐ 151	Mike Bratz	2.50	1.15	.30
☐ 152	Steve Burtt	2.50	1.15	.30
☐ 153	Lester Conner	2.50	1.15	.30
☐ 154	Sleepy Floyd	4.00	1.80	.50
☐ 155	Mickey Johnson	3.00	1.35	.40
☐ 156	Gary Plummer	2.50	1.15	.30
☐ 157	Larry Smith	3.00	1.35	.40
☐ 158	Peter Thibeaux	2.50	1.15	.30
☐ 159	Jerome Whitehead	2.50	1.15	.30
☐ 160	Othell Wilson	2.50	1.15	.30
☐ 161	Kiki Vandeweghe	5.00	2.30	.60
☐ 162	Sam Bowie	9.00	4.00	1.15
☐ 163	Kenny Carr	3.00	1.35	.40
☐ 164	Steve Colter	2.50	1.15	.30
☐ 165	Clyde Drexler	100.00	45.00	12.50
☐ 166	Audie Norris	2.50	1.15	.30
☐ 167	Jim Paxson	2.50	1.15	.30
☐ 168	Tom Scheffler	2.50	1.15	.30
☐ 169	Bernard Thompson	2.50	1.15	.30
☐ 170	Mychal Thompson	4.00	1.80	.50
☐ 171	Darnell Valentine	2.50	1.15	.30
☐ 172	Magic Johnson	125.00	57.50	15.50
☐ 173	Kareem Abdul-Jabbar	25.00	11.50	3.10
☐ 174	Michael Cooper	5.00	2.30	.60
☐ 175	Earl Jones	2.50	1.15	.30
☐ 176	Mitch Kupchak	3.00	1.35	.40
☐ 177	Ronnie Lester	2.50	1.15	.30
☐ 178	Bob McAdoo	6.00	2.70	.75

☐	179	Mike McGee	2.50	1.15	.30
☐	180	Kurt Rambis	4.00	1.80	.50
☐	181	Byron Scott	8.00	3.60	1.00
☐	182	Larry Spriggs	2.50	1.15	.30
☐	183	Jamaal Wilkes	5.00	2.30	.60
☐	184	James Worthy	25.00	11.50	3.10
☐	185	Gus Williams	3.00	1.35	.40
☐	186	Greg Ballard	2.50	1.15	.30
☐	187	Dudley Bradley	2.50	1.15	.30
☐	188	Darren Daye	2.50	1.15	.30
☐	189	Frank Johnson	3.00	1.35	.40
☐	190	Charles Jones	2.50	1.15	.30
☐	191	Rick Mahorn	4.00	1.80	.50
☐	192	Jeff Malone	9.00	4.00	1.15
☐	193	Tom McMillen	4.00	1.80	.50
☐	194	Jeff Ruland	3.00	1.35	.40
☐	195	Michael Jordan	400.00	180.00	50.00
☐	196	Vern Fleming	4.00	1.80	.50
☐	197	Sam Perkins	14.00	6.25	1.75
☐	198	Alvin Robertson	8.00	3.60	1.00
☐	199	Jeff Turner	2.50	1.15	.30
☐	200	Leon Wood	2.50	1.15	.30
☐	201	Moses Malone	14.00	6.25	1.75
☐	202	Charles Barkley	400.00	180.00	50.00
☐	203	Maurice Cheeks	7.00	3.10	.85
☐	204	Julius Erving	40.00	18.00	5.00
☐	205	Clemon Johnson	2.50	1.15	.30
☐	206	George Johnson	2.50	1.15	.30
☐	207	Bobby Jones	5.00	2.30	.60
☐	208	Clint Richardson	2.50	1.15	.30
☐	209	Sedale Threatt	7.00	3.10	.85
☐	210	Andrew Toney	4.00	1.80	.50
☐	211	Sam Williams	2.50	1.15	.30
☐	212	Leon Wood	2.50	1.15	.30
☐	213	Mel Turpin	4.00	1.80	.50
☐	214	Ron Anderson	4.00	1.80	.50
☐	215	John Bagley	2.50	1.15	.30
☐	216	Johnny Davis	2.50	1.15	.30
☐	217	World B. Free	4.00	1.80	.50
☐	218	Roy Hinson	2.50	1.15	.30
☐	219	Phil Hubbard	2.50	1.15	.30
☐	220	Edgar Jones	2.50	1.15	.30
☐	221	Ben Poquette	2.50	1.15	.30
☐	222	Lonnie Shelton	3.00	1.35	.40
☐	223	Mark West	2.50	1.15	.30
☐	224	Kevin Williams	2.50	1.15	.30
☐	225	Mark Eaton	4.00	1.80	.50
☐	226	Mitchell Anderson	2.50	1.15	.30
☐	227	Thurl Bailey	4.00	1.80	.50
☐	228	Adrian Dantley	7.00	3.10	.85
☐	229	Rickey Green	3.00	1.35	.40
☐	230	Darrell Griffith	4.00	1.80	.50
☐	231	Rich Kelley	2.50	1.15	.30
☐	232	Pace Mannion	2.50	1.15	.30
☐	233	Billy Paultz	3.50	1.55	.45
☐	234	Fred Roberts	2.50	1.15	.30
☐	235	John Stockton	175.00	80.00	22.00
☐	236	Jeff Wilkins	2.50	1.15	.30
☐	237	Hakeem Olajuwon	500.00	230.00	65.00
☐	238	Craig Ehlo	25.00	11.50	3.10
☐	239	Lionel Hollins	2.50	1.15	.30
☐	240	Allen Leavell	2.50	1.15	.30
☐	241	Lewis Lloyd	2.50	1.15	.30
☐	242	John Lucas	7.00	3.10	.85
☐	243	Rodney McCray	3.00	1.35	.40
☐	244	Hank McDowell	2.50	1.15	.30
☐	245	Larry Micheaux	2.50	1.15	.30
☐	246	Jim Peterson	2.50	1.15	.30
☐	247	Robert Reid	2.50	1.15	.30
☐	248	Ralph Sampson	4.00	1.80	.50
☐	249	Mitchell Wiggins	2.50	1.15	.30
☐	250	Mark Aguirre	7.00	3.10	.85
☐	251	Rolando Blackman	7.00	3.10	.85

☐	252	Wallace Bryant	2.50	1.15	.30
☐	253	Brad Davis	3.00	1.35	.40
☐	254	Dale Ellis	8.00	3.60	1.00
☐	255	Derek Harper	14.00	6.25	1.75
☐	256	Kurt Nimphius	2.50	1.15	.30
☐	257	Sam Perkins	35.00	16.00	4.40
☐	258	Charlie Sitton	2.50	1.15	.30
☐	259	Tom Sluby	2.50	1.15	.30
☐	260	Jay Vincent	2.50	1.15	.30
☐	261	Isiah Thomas	50.00	23.00	6.25
☐	262	Kent Benson	3.00	1.35	.40
☐	263	Earl Cureton	2.50	1.15	.30
☐	264	Vinnie Johnson	4.00	1.80	.50
☐	265	Bill Laimbeer	5.00	2.30	.60
☐	266	John Long	2.50	1.15	.30
☐	267	Dan Roundfield	3.50	1.55	.45
☐	268	Kelly Tripucka	3.00	1.35	.40
☐	269	Terry Tyler	2.50	1.15	.30
☐	270	Reggie Theus	4.00	1.80	.50
☐	271	Don Buse	3.00	1.35	.40
☐	272	Larry Drew	3.00	1.35	.40
☐	273	Eddie Johnson	7.00	3.10	.85
☐	274	Billy Knight	3.00	1.35	.40
☐	275	Joe Meriweather	2.50	1.15	.30
☐	276	Mark Olberding	2.50	1.15	.30
☐	277	LaSalle Thompson	3.00	1.35	.40
☐	278	Otis Thorpe	40.00	18.00	5.00
☐	279	Pete Verhoeven	2.50	1.15	.30
☐	280	Mike Woodson	2.50	1.15	.30
☐	281	Julius Erving	20.00	9.00	2.50
☐	282	Kareem Abdul-Jabbar	12.00	5.50	1.50
☐	283	Dan Issel	8.00	3.60	1.00
☐	284	Bernard King	4.00	1.80	.50
☐	285	Moses Malone	8.00	3.60	1.00
☐	286	Mark Eaton	4.00	1.80	.50
☐	287	Isiah Thomas	20.00	9.00	2.50
☐	288	Michael Jordan	400.00	180.00	50.00

1984-85 Star Arena

These sets were produced to be sold in the arena of each of the five teams. Each set is different from the team's regular issue set in that the photography and card backs are different. Shortly after distribution began, Bob Lanier announced his retirement plans and his cards were withdrawn from the Milwaukee set. Cards measure 2 1/2" by 3 1/2" and have a colored border around the fronts according to team. Corresponding color printing is on the backs. Celtics feature Star '85 logo on the front while the other four teams feature the Star '84 logo on the front. The cards are ordered below by teams, for example, Boston Celtics A, Dallas Mavericks B, Milwaukee Bucks C, Los Angeles Lakers D, and Philadelphia 76ers E.

	MINT	EXC	G-VG
COMPLETE BAG SET (48)	300.00	135.00	38.00
COMPLETE SET (49) w/Lanier	700.00	325.00	90.00
COMP.BAG CELTICS (9)	100.00	45.00	12.50
COMP.BAG MAVERICKS (11)	25.00	11.50	3.10
COMP.BAG BUCKS (8)	25.00	11.50	3.10
COMP.BAG LAKERS (10)	100.00	45.00	12.50
COMP.BAG 76ERS (10)	50.00	23.00	6.25
COMMON CELTICS (A1-A9)	2.50	1.15	.30
COMMON MAVS (B1-B11)	2.50	1.15	.30
COMMON BUCKS (C1-C9)	2.50	1.15	.30
COMMON LAKERS (D1-D10)	2.50	1.15	.30
COMMON 76ERS (E1-E10)	2.50	1.15	.30

*OPENED TEAM SETS: .75X to 1.0 VALUE

		MINT	EXC	G-VG
☐	A1 Larry Bird	50.00	23.00	6.25
☐	A2 Danny Ainge	10.00	4.50	1.25
☐	A3 Rick Carlisle	2.50	1.15	.30
☐	A4 Dennis Johnson	5.00	2.30	.60
☐	A5 Cedric Maxwell	3.00	1.35	.40
☐	A6 Kevin McHale	8.00	3.60	1.00
☐	A7 Robert Parish	8.00	3.60	1.00
☐	A8 Scott Wedman	2.50	1.15	.30
☐	A9 World Champs	25.00	11.50	3.10
	1981, 1984			
	Robert Parish			
	Larry Bird			
	Kevin McHale			
	Jimmy Rodgers CO			
	K.C. Jones CO			
	Chris Ford CO			
☐	B1 Mark Aguirre	4.00	1.80	.50
☐	B2 Rolando Blackman	4.00	1.80	.50
☐	B3 Brad Davis	2.50	1.15	.30
☐	B4 Dale Ellis	5.00	2.30	.60
☐	B5 Bill Garnett	2.50	1.15	.30
☐	B6 Derek Harper UER	7.00	3.10	.85
	(Mike Harper on both			
	sides with Mike's			
	birthdate, etc.)			
☐	B7 Kurt Nimphius	2.50	1.15	.30
☐	B8 Jim Spanarkel	2.50	1.15	.30
☐	B9 Elston Turner	2.50	1.15	.30
☐	B10 Jay Vincent	2.50	1.15	.30
☐	B11 Mark West	2.75	1.25	.35
☐	C1 Nate Archibald	8.00	3.60	1.00
☐	C2 Junior Bridgeman	2.50	1.15	.30
☐	C3 Mike Dunleavy	3.50	1.55	.45
☐	C4 Kevin Grevey	2.50	1.15	.30
☐	C5 Marques Johnson	3.00	1.35	.40
☐	C6 Bob Lanier SP	450.00	200.00	57.50
☐	C7 Alton Lister	2.50	1.15	.30
☐	C8 Sidney Moncrief	5.00	2.30	.60
☐	C9 Paul Pressey	2.50	1.15	.30
☐	D1 Kareem Abdul-Jabbar	20.00	9.00	2.50
☐	D2 Michael Cooper	5.00	2.30	.60
☐	D3 Magic Johnson	50.00	23.00	6.25
☐	D4 Mike McGee	2.75	1.25	.35
☐	D5 Swen Nater	2.50	1.15	.30
☐	D6 Kurt Rambis	3.00	1.35	.40
☐	D7 Byron Scott	5.00	2.30	.60
☐	D8 James Worthy	10.00	4.50	1.25
☐	D9 Laker All-Stars	35.00	16.00	4.40
	(Magic Johnson and			
	Kareem Abdul-Jabbar)			
☐	D10 Kareem Abdul-Jabbar	10.00	4.50	1.25
	NBA Scoring Leader			
☐	E1 Julius Erving	25.00	11.50	3.10
☐	E2 Maurice Cheeks	5.00	2.30	.60
☐	E3 Franklin Edwards	2.50	1.15	.30
☐	E4 Marc Iavaroni	2.50	1.15	.30
☐	E5 Clemon Johnson	2.50	1.15	.30
☐	E6 Bobby Jones	4.00	1.80	.50

☐ E7 Moses Malone	10.00	4.50	1.25
☐ E8 Clint Richardson	2.50	1.15	.30
☐ E9 Andrew Toney	2.75	1.25	.35
☐ E10 Sam Williams	2.50	1.15	.30

1984-85 Star Julius Erving

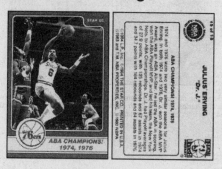

This set contains 18 cards highlighting the career of basketball great Julius Erving. Cards measure 2 1/2" by 3 1/2" and have a red border around the fronts of the cards and red printing on the backs. Cards feature Star '85 logo on the front although they were released in the Summer of 1984.

	MINT	EXC	G-VG
COMPLETE BAG SET (18)	100.00	45.00	12.50
COMMON J.ERVING (1-18)	8.00	3.60	1.00
*OPENED SET: .75X to 1.0X VALUE			
☐ 1 Checklist	8.00	3.60	1.00
☐ 2 NBA Regular	8.00	3.60	1.00
Season Stats			
☐ 3 ABA Regular	8.00	3.60	1.00
Season Stats			
☐ 4 NBA All-Star	8.00	3.60	1.00
Eight Times			
☐ 5 ABA All-Star	8.00	3.60	1.00
Five Times			
☐ 6 NBA Playoff Stats	8.00	3.60	1.00
☐ 7 ABA Playoff Stats	8.00	3.60	1.00
☐ 8 NBA MVP, 1981	8.00	3.60	1.00
☐ 9 ABA MVP, 1974,	8.00	3.60	1.00
1975, and 1976			
☐ 10 Collegiate Stats	8.00	3.60	1.00
☐ 11 NBA All-Star MVP,	8.00	3.60	1.00
1977 and 1983			
☐ 12 NBA Career Highlights	8.00	3.60	1.00
☐ 13 ABA Career Highlights	8.00	3.60	1.00
☐ 14 1983 World Champs	8.00	3.60	1.00
☐ 15 ABA Champions	8.00	3.60	1.00
1974 and 1976			
☐ 16 All-Time Scoring	8.00	3.60	1.00
☐ 17 Personal Data	8.00	3.60	1.00
☐ 18 The Future	8.00	3.60	1.00

1985 Star Gatorade Slam Dunk

This nine-card set was given to the people who attended the 1985 All-Star Weekend Banquet at Indianapolis. Cards measure 2 1/2" by 3 1/2" and have a green border around the fronts of the cards and green printing on the backs. Cards feature the Star '85 and

Gatorade logos on the fronts. Since Terence Stansbury was a late substitute in the Slam Dunk contest for Charles Barkley, both cards were produced, but the Barkley card was never released. The Barkley card is unnumbered and shows him dunking.

	MINT	EXC	G-VG
COMPLETE BAG SET (9)	325.00	145.00	40.00
COMMON PLAYER (1-9)	3.00	1.35	.40
*OPENED SET: .75X to 1.0X VALUE			
☐ 1 Gatorade 2nd Annual	5.00	2.30	.60
Slam Dunk			
Championship			
(Checklist back)			
☐ 2 Larry Nance	6.00	2.70	.75
☐ 3 Terence Stansbury	3.00	1.35	.40
☐ 4 Clyde Drexler	30.00	13.50	3.80
☐ 5 Julius Erving	30.00	13.50	3.80
☐ 6 Darrell Griffith	3.50	1.55	.45
☐ 7 Michael Jordan	250.00	115.00	31.00
☐ 8 Dominique Wilkins	50.00	23.00	6.25
☐ 9 Orlando Woolridge	3.50	1.55	.45
☐ NNO Charles Barkley SP	400.00	180.00	50.00
(Withdrawn)			

1985 Star Crunch'n'Munch All-Stars

The 1985 Star Crunch'n'Munch NBA All-Stars set is an 11-card set featuring the ten starting players in the 1985 NBA All-Star Game, plus a checklist card. The set was produced for the Crunch 'n' Munch Food Company and was originally available to the hobby exclusively through Don Guilbert of Woonsocket, Rhode Island. The set's basic design is identical to

those of the Star Company's regular NBA sets. The cards measure approximately 2 1/2" by 3 1/2". The cards show a Star '85 logo in the upper right corner. The front borders are yellowish orange, and the backs show each player's All-Star Game record.

	MINT	EXC	G-VG
COMPLETE BAG SET (11)	500.00	230.00	65.00
COMMON PLAYER (1-11)	5.00	2.30	.60
*OPENED SET: .75X to 1.0X VALUE			

		MINT	EXC	G-VG
☐ 1	Checklist Card	10.00	4.50	1.25
☐ 2	Larry Bird	100.00	45.00	12.50
☐ 3	Julius Erving	35.00	16.00	4.40
☐ 4	Michael Jordan	300.00	135.00	38.00
☐ 5	Moses Malone	10.00	4.50	1.25
☐ 6	Isiah Thomas	18.00	8.00	2.30
☐ 7	Kareem Abdul-Jabbar	20.00	9.00	2.50
☐ 8	Adrian Dantley	6.00	2.70	.75
☐ 9	George Gervin	10.00	4.50	1.25
☐ 10	Magic Johnson	75.00	34.00	9.50
☐ 11	Ralph Sampson	5.00	2.30	.60

1985 Star Kareem Abdul-Jabbar

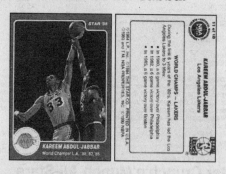

The 1985 Star Kareem Abdul-Jabbar set is an 18-card tribute highlighting the career of Abdul-Jabbar. Most of the photos on the fronts are from the early 1980s. Card backs provide various statistics and tidbits of information about Abdul-Jabbar. The set's basic design is identical to those of the Star Company's regular NBA sets. The cards show a Star '85 logo in the upper right corner. The cards measure approximately 2 1/2" by 3 1/2". The front borders are Lakers' purple.

	MINT	EXC	G-VG
COMPLETE BAG SET (18)	60.00	27.00	7.50
COMMON PLAYER (1-18)	4.00	1.80	.50
OPENED SET: .75X to 1.0X VALUE			

		MINT	EXC	G-VG
☐ 1	Checklist Card	4.00	1.80	.50
☐ 2	Collegiate Stats	4.00	1.80	.50
☐ 3	Regular Season Stats	4.00	1.80	.50
☐ 4	Playoff Stats	4.00	1.80	.50
☐ 5	All Star Stats	4.00	1.80	.50
☐ 6	All-Time Scoring King	4.00	1.80	.50
☐ 7	NBA MVP 71/72/74	4.00	1.80	.50
☐ 8	NBA MVP 76/77/80	4.00	1.80	.50
☐ 9	Defensive Star	4.00	1.80	.50
☐ 10	World Champs 71	4.00	1.80	.50
☐ 11	World Champs 80/82/85	4.00	1.80	.50
☐ 12	All-Time Records	4.00	1.80	.50
☐ 13	Rookie-of-the-Year 70	4.00	1.80	.50

☐ 14 Playoff MVP 71/85	4.00	1.80	.50
☐ 15 The League Leader	4.00	1.80	.50
☐ 16 Career Highlights	4.00	1.80	.50
☐ 17 Personal Data	4.00	1.80	.50
☐ 18 The Future	4.00	1.80	.50

1985 Star Last 11 ROY's

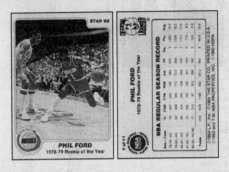

The 1985 Star Rookies of the Year set is an 11-card set depicting each of the NBA's ROY award winners from the 1974-75 through 1984-85 seasons. Michael Jordan's card only shows his collegiate statistics; all others provide NBA statistics (but only up through the 1983-84 NBA season). Cards of Darrell Griffith and Jamaal Wilkes show the Star '86 logo in the upper right corner; all others in the set show Star '85. The set's basic design is identical to those of the Star Company's regular NBA sets, and the front borders are off-white. The cards measure approximately 2 1/2" by 3 1/2". The cards are numbered on the back in reverse chronological order according to when each player won the ROY.

	MINT	EXC	G-VG
COMPLETE BAG SET (11)	350.00	160.00	45.00
COMMON PLAYER (1-11)	3.00	1.35	.40
*OPENED SET: .75X to 1.0X VALUE			

☐ 1 Michael Jordan	250.00	115.00	31.00
☐ 2 Ralph Sampson	3.00	1.35	.40
☐ 3 Terry Cummings	4.00	1.80	.50
☐ 4 Buck Williams	5.00	2.30	.60
☐ 5 Darrell Griffith	3.00	1.35	.40
☐ 6 Larry Bird	100.00	45.00	12.50
☐ 7 Phil Ford	3.00	1.35	.40
☐ 8 Walter Davis	5.00	2.30	.60
☐ 9 Adrian Dantley	5.00	2.30	.60
☐ 10 Alvan Adams	3.00	1.35	.40
☐ 11 Keith/Jamaal Wilkes	5.00	2.30	.60

1985 Star Lite All-Stars

This 13-card set was given to the people who attended the 1985 All-Star Weekend Banquet at Indianapolis. The set was issued in a clear, sealed plastic bag. Cards measure 2 1/2" by 3 1/2" and have a blue border around the fronts of the cards and blue printing on the backs. Cards feature the Star '85 and Lite Beer logos on the fronts. Players featured are the 1985 NBA All-Star starting line-ups and coaches.

	MINT	EXC	G-VG
COMPLETE BAG SET (13)	350.00	160.00	45.00
COMMON PLAYER (1-13)	4.00	1.80	.50
*OPENED SET: .75X to 1.0X VALUE			

☐ 1 1985 NBA All-Stars Starting Line-Ups	4.00	1.80	.50
☐ 2 Larry Bird	90.00	40.00	11.50
☐ 3 Julius Erving	30.00	13.50	3.80
☐ 4 Michael Jordan	250.00	115.00	31.00
☐ 5 Moses Malone	8.00	3.60	1.00
☐ 6 Isiah Thomas	15.00	6.75	1.90
☐ 7 K.C. Jones CO	4.00	1.80	.50
☐ 8 Kareem Abdul-Jabbar	15.00	6.75	1.90
☐ 9 Adrian Dantley	5.00	2.30	.60
☐ 10 George Gervin	8.00	3.60	1.00
☐ 11 Magic Johnson	60.00	27.00	7.50
☐ 12 Ralph Sampson	4.50	2.00	.55
☐ 13 Pat Riley CO	12.00	5.50	1.50

1985-86 Star NBA

This 172-card set was produced by the Star Company and features players in the NBA.
Cards are numbered in team order and measure the standard 2 1/2" by 3 1/2". The team
ordering is as follows, Philadelphia 76ers (1-9), Detroit Pistons (10-17), Houston Rockets
(18-25), Los Angeles Lakers (26-33), Phoenix Suns (34-41), Atlanta Hawks (42-49), Denver
Nuggets (50-57), New Jersey Nets (58-65), Seattle Supersonics (66-73), Sacramento Kings
(74-80), Indiana Pacers (81-87), Los Angeles Clippers (88-94), Boston Celtics (95-102),
Portland Trail Blazers (103-109), Washington Bullets (110-116), Chicago Bulls (117-123),
Milwaukee Bucks (124-130), Golden State Warriors (131-136), Utah Jazz (137-144), San
Antonio Spurs (145-151), Cleveland Cavaliers (152-158), Dallas Mavericks (159-165), and
New York Knicks (166-172). Borders are colored according to team. Cards were released in

two groups, 1-94 and 95-172. The team sets were issued in clear sealed bags. Many of these team bags were distributed to hobby dealers through a small group of Star Co. master distributors. The original wholesale price per bag was 2.00 to 3.00 for most of the teams. Card backs are very similar to the other Star basketball sets except that the player statistics go up through the 1984-85 season. Extended Rookie Cards in this set include Patrick Ewing, Jerome Kersey, and Kevin Willis. According to Star original sales materials and order forms, reportedly 2,000 team bags were printed for each team and an additional 2,200 team sets were printed for the more popular teams of that time. There is typically a slight discount on sales of opened team bags. Cards of Celtics players (95-102) have either green or white borders. There is no difference in value as neither more difficult to obtain than the other.

	MINT	EXC	G-VG
COMPLETE BAG SET (172)	2500.00	1150.00	325.00
COMP.BAG 76ERS (9)	200.00	90.00	25.00
COMP.BAG PISTONS (8)	50.00	23.00	6.25
COMP.BAG ROCKETS (8)	250.00	115.00	31.00
COMP.BAG LAKERS SP (8)	300.00	135.00	38.00
COMP.BAG SUNS (8)	35.00	16.00	4.40
COMP.BAG HAWKS (8)	150.00	70.00	19.00
COMP.BAG NUGGETS (8)	25.00	11.50	3.10
COMP.BAG NETS (8)	25.00	11.50	3.10
COMP.BAG SONICS (8)	25.00	11.50	3.10
COMP.BAG KINGS (7)	25.00	11.50	3.10
COMP.BAG PACERS (7)	25.00	11.50	3.10
COMP.BAG CLIPPERS (7)	25.00	11.50	3.10
COMP.BAG CELTICS (8)	150.00	70.00	19.00
COMP.BAG BLAZERS (7)	100.00	45.00	12.50
COMP.BAG BULLETS (7)	25.00	11.50	3.10
COMP.BAG BULLS (7)	900.00	400.00	115.00
COMP.BAG BUCKS (7)	25.00	11.50	3.10
COMP.BAG WARRIORS (7)	25.00	11.50	3.10
COMP.BAG JAZZ (7)	100.00	45.00	12.50
COMP.BAG SPURS (7)	25.00	11.50	3.10
COMP.BAG CAVS (7)	25.00	11.50	3.10
COMP.BAG MAVS (7)	35.00	16.00	4.40
COMP.BAG KNICKS (7)	400.00	180.00	50.00
COMMON 76ERS (1-9)	2.50	1.15	.30
COMMON PISTONS (10-17)	2.50	1.15	.30
COMMON ROCKETS (18-25)	2.50	1.15	.30
COMMON LAKERS SP (26-33)	5.00	2.30	.60
COMMON SUNS (34-41)	2.50	1.15	.30
COMMON HAWKS (42-49)	2.50	1.15	.30
COMMON NUGGETS (50-57)	2.50	1.15	.30
COMMON NETS (58-65)	2.50	1.15	.30
COMMON SONICS (66-73)	2.50	1.15	.30
COMMON KINGS (74-80)	2.50	1.15	.30
COMMON PACERS (81-87)	2.50	1.15	.30
COMMON CLIPPERS (88-94)	2.50	1.15	.30
COMMON CELTICS (95-102)	2.50	1.15	.30
COMMON BLAZERS (103-109)	2.50	1.15	.30
COMMON BULLETS (110-116)	2.50	1.15	.30
COMMON BULLS (117-123)	2.50	1.15	.30
COMMON BUCKS (124-130)	2.50	1.15	.30
COMMON WARRIORS (131-137)	2.50	1.15	.30
COMMON JAZZ (138-144)	2.50	1.15	.30
COMMON SPURS (145-151)	2.50	1.15	.30
COMMON CAVS (152-158)	2.50	1.15	.30
COMMON MAVS (159-165)	2.50	1.15	.30
COMMON KNICKS (166-172) !	2.50	1.15	.30

*OPENED TEAM SETS: .75X to 1.0 VALUE
*GREEN OR WHITE CELTICS: EQUAL VALUE

☐ 1	Maurice Cheeks	6.00	2.70	.75
☐ 2	Charles Barkley	175.00	80.00	22.00
☐ 3	Julius Erving	35.00	16.00	4.40
☐ 4	Clemon Johnson	2.50	1.15	.30
☐ 5	Bobby Jones	5.00	2.30	.60
☐ 6	Moses Malone	10.00	4.50	1.25
☐ 7	Sedale Threatt	6.00	2.70	.75
☐ 8	Andrew Toney	3.00	1.35	.40
☐ 9	Leon Wood	2.50	1.15	.30
☐ 10	Isiah Thomas UER	35.00	16.00	4.40

(No Pistons logo
on card front)

☐ 11	Kent Benson	3.00	1.35	.40
☐ 12	Earl Cureton	2.50	1.15	.30
☐ 13	Vinnie Johnson	4.00	1.80	.50
☐ 14	Bill Laimbeer	5.00	2.30	.60
☐ 15	John Long	2.50	1.15	.30
☐ 16	Rick Mahorn	4.00	1.80	.50
☐ 17	Kelly Tripucka	3.00	1.35	.40
☐ 18	Hakeem Olajuwon	200.00	90.00	25.00
☐ 19	Allen Leavell	2.50	1.15	.30
☐ 20	Lewis Lloyd	2.50	1.15	.30
☐ 21	John Lucas	6.00	2.70	.75
☐ 22	Rodney McCray	2.50	1.15	.30
☐ 23	Robert Reid	2.50	1.15	.30
☐ 24	Ralph Sampson	4.00	1.80	.50
☐ 25	Mitchell Wiggins	2.50	1.15	.30
☐ 26	Kareem Abdul-Jabbar	45.00	20.00	5.75
☐ 27	Michael Cooper	10.00	4.50	1.25
☐ 28	Magic Johnson	200.00	90.00	25.00
☐ 29	Mitch Kupchak	5.50	2.50	.70
☐ 30	Maurice Lucas	6.00	2.70	.75
☐ 31	Kurt Rambis	6.00	2.70	.75
☐ 32	Byron Scott	8.00	3.60	1.00
☐ 33	James Worthy	25.00	11.50	3.10
☐ 34	Larry Nance	15.00	6.75	1.90
☐ 35	Alvan Adams	3.00	1.35	.40
☐ 36	Walter Davis	5.00	2.30	.60
☐ 37	James Edwards	3.00	1.35	.40
☐ 38	Jay Humphries	4.00	1.80	.50
☐ 39	Charles Pittman	2.50	1.15	.30
☐ 40	Rick Robey	3.00	1.35	.40
☐ 41	Mike Sanders	2.50	1.15	.30
☐ 42	Dominique Wilkins	110.00	50.00	14.00
☐ 43	Scott Hastings	2.50	1.15	.30
☐ 44	Eddie Johnson	2.50	1.15	.30
☐ 45	Cliff Levingston	2.50	1.15	.30
☐ 46	Tree Rollins	3.50	1.55	.45
☐ 47	Doc Rivers UER	7.00	3.10	.85

(Ray Williams is
pictured on the front)

☐ 48	Kevin Willis	40.00	18.00	5.00
☐ 49	Randy Wittman	2.50	1.15	.30
☐ 50	Alex English	6.00	2.70	.75
☐ 51	Wayne Cooper	2.50	1.15	.30
☐ 52	T.R. Dunn	2.50	1.15	.30
☐ 53	Mike Evans	2.50	1.15	.30
☐ 54	Lafayette Lever	4.00	1.80	.50
☐ 55	Calvin Natt	2.50	1.15	.30
☐ 56	Danny Schayes	4.00	1.80	.50
☐ 57	Elston Turner	2.50	1.15	.30
☐ 58	Buck Williams	10.00	4.50	1.25
☐ 59	Otis Birdsong	3.00	1.35	.40
☐ 60	Darwin Cook	2.50	1.15	.30
☐ 61	Darryl Dawkins	4.00	1.80	.50
☐ 62	Mike Gminski	4.00	1.80	.50
☐ 63	Mickey Johnson	3.00	1.35	.40
☐ 64	Mike O'Koren	3.00	1.35	.40
☐ 65	Micheal R. Richardson	2.50	1.15	.30
☐ 66	Tom Chambers	9.00	4.00	1.15
☐ 67	Gerald Henderson	2.50	1.15	.30
☐ 68	Tim McCormick	2.50	1.15	.30
☐ 69	Jack Sikma	5.00	2.30	.60
☐ 70	Ricky Sobers	2.50	1.15	.30
☐ 71	Danny Vranes	2.50	1.15	.30
☐ 72	Al Wood	2.50	1.15	.30
☐ 73	Danny Young	2.50	1.15	.30
☐ 74	Reggie Theus	4.00	1.80	.50
☐ 75	Larry Drew	3.00	1.35	.40
☐ 76	Eddie Johnson	6.00	2.70	.75
☐ 77	Mark Olberding	2.50	1.15	.30
☐ 78	LaSalle Thompson	3.00	1.35	.40
☐ 79	Otis Thorpe	16.00	7.25	2.00

☐ 80	Mike Woodson	2.50	1.15	.30
☐ 81	Clark Kellogg	3.00	1.35	.40
☐ 82	Quinn Buckner	3.00	1.35	.40
☐ 83	Vern Fleming	4.00	1.80	.50
☐ 84	Bill Garnett	2.50	1.15	.30
☐ 85	Terence Stansbury	2.50	1.15	.30
☐ 86	Steve Stipanovich	2.50	1.15	.30
☐ 87	Herb Williams	3.00	1.35	.40
☐ 88	Marques Johnson	4.00	1.80	.50
☐ 89	Michael Cage	4.00	1.80	.50
☐ 90	Franklin Edwards	2.50	1.15	.30
☐ 91	Cedric Maxwell	4.00	1.80	.50
☐ 92	Derek Smith	2.50	1.15	.30
☐ 93	Rory White	2.50	1.15	.30
☐ 94	Jamaal Wilkes	5.00	2.30	.60
☐ 95	Larry Bird	125.00	57.50	15.50
	(Green or whote border)			
☐ 96	Danny Ainge	20.00	9.00	2.50
	(Green or white border)			
☐ 97	Dennis Johnson	6.00	2.70	.75
	(Green or white border)			
☐ 98	Kevin McHale	15.00	6.75	1.90
	(Green or white border)			
☐ 99	Robert Parish ERR	15.00	6.75	1.90
	(Green or white border;			
	no number on back)			
☐ 100	Jerry Sichting	2.50	1.15	.30
	(Green or white border)			
☐ 101	Bill Walton	15.00	6.75	1.90
	(Green or white border)			
☐ 102	Scott Wedman	2.50	1.15	.30
	(Green or white border)			
☐ 103	Kiki Vandeweghe	4.00	1.80	.50
☐ 104	Sam Bowie	5.00	2.30	.60
☐ 105	Kenny Carr	3.00	1.35	.40
☐ 106	Clyde Drexler	75.00	34.00	9.50
☐ 107	Jerome Kersey	10.00	4.50	1.25
☐ 108	Jim Paxson	2.50	1.15	.30
☐ 109	Mychal Thompson	4.00	1.80	.50
☐ 110	Gus Williams	3.00	1.35	.40
☐ 111	Darren Daye	2.50	1.15	.30
☐ 112	Jeff Malone	6.00	2.70	.75
☐ 113	Tom McMillen	4.00	1.80	.50
☐ 114	Cliff Robinson	2.50	1.15	.30
☐ 115	Dan Roundfield	3.50	1.55	.45
☐ 116	Jeff Ruland	3.00	1.35	.40
☐ 117	Michael Jordan	800.00	350.00	100.00
☐ 118	Gene Banks	3.00	1.35	.40
☐ 119	Dave Corzine	2.50	1.15	.30
☐ 120	Quintin Dailey	2.50	1.15	.30
☐ 121	George Gervin	10.00	4.50	1.25
☐ 122	Jawann Oldham	2.50	1.15	.30
☐ 123	Orlando Woolridge	4.00	1.80	.50
☐ 124	Terry Cummings	6.00	2.70	.75
☐ 125	Craig Hodges	4.00	1.80	.50
☐ 126	Alton Lister	3.00	1.35	.40
☐ 127	Paul Mokeski	2.50	1.15	.30
☐ 128	Sidney Moncrief	6.00	2.70	.75
☐ 129	Ricky Pierce	10.00	4.50	1.25
☐ 130	Paul Pressey	2.50	1.15	.30
☐ 131	Purvis Short	2.50	1.15	.30
☐ 132	Joe Barry Carroll	3.00	1.35	.40
☐ 133	Lester Conner	2.50	1.15	.30
☐ 134	Sleepy Floyd	4.00	1.80	.50
☐ 135	Geoff Huston	2.50	1.15	.30
☐ 136	Larry Smith	3.00	1.35	.40
☐ 137	Jerome Whitehead	2.50	1.15	.30
☐ 138	Adrian Dantley	6.00	2.70	.75
☐ 139	Mitchell Anderson	2.50	1.15	.30
☐ 140	Thurl Bailey	4.00	1.80	.50
☐ 141	Mark Eaton	4.00	1.80	.50
☐ 142	Rickey Green	3.00	1.35	.40
☐ 143	Darrell Griffith	4.00	1.80	.50

		MINT	EXC	G-VG
☐ 144	John Stockton	90.00	40.00	11.50
☐ 145	Artis Gilmore	6.00	2.70	.75
☐ 146	Marc Iavaroni	2.50	1.15	.30
☐ 147	Steve Johnson	2.50	1.15	.30
☐ 148	Mike Mitchell	2.50	1.15	.30
☐ 149	Johnny Moore	2.50	1.15	.30
☐ 150	Alvin Robertson	6.00	2.70	.75
☐ 151	Jon Sundvold	2.50	1.15	.30
☐ 152	World B. Free	4.00	1.80	.50
☐ 153	John Bagley	2.50	1.15	.30
☐ 154	Johnny Davis	2.50	1.15	.30
☐ 155	Roy Hinson	2.50	1.15	.30
☐ 156	Phil Hubbard	2.50	1.15	.30
☐ 157	Ben Poquette	2.50	1.15	.30
☐ 158	Mel Turpin	3.00	1.35	.40
☐ 159	Rolando Blackman	6.00	2.70	.75
☐ 160	Mark Aguirre	6.00	2.70	.75
☐ 161	Brad Davis	3.00	1.35	.40
☐ 162	Dale Ellis	7.00	3.10	.85
☐ 163	Derek Harper	12.00	5.50	1.50
☐ 164	Sam Perkins	14.00	6.25	1.75
☐ 165	Jay Vincent	2.50	1.15	.30
☐ 166	Patrick Ewing	350.00	160.00	45.00
☐ 167	Bill Cartwright	5.00	2.30	.60
☐ 168	Pat Cummings	2.50	1.15	.30
☐ 169	Ernie Grunfeld	3.00	1.35	.40
☐ 170	Rory Sparrow	2.50	1.15	.30
☐ 171	Trent Tucker	3.00	1.35	.40
☐ 172	Darrell Walker	2.50	1.15	.30

1985-86 Star All-Rookie Team

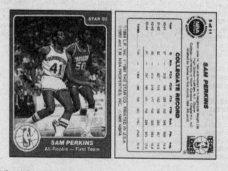

The 1985-86 Star NBA All-Rookie Team is an 11-card set that features 11 top rookies from the previous (1984-85) season. The set's basic design is identical to those of the Star Company's regular NBA sets. The cards measure approximately 2 1/2" by 3 1/2". The front borders are red, and the backs include each player's collegiate statistics. Alvin Robertson's card shows the Star '86 logo in the upper right corner; all others in the set show Star '85.

	MINT	EXC	G-VG
COMPLETE BAG SET (11)	500.00	230.00	65.00
COMMON PLAYER (1-11)	5.00	2.30	.60
*OPENED SET: .75X to 1.0X VALUE			

		MINT	EXC	G-VG
☐ 1	Hakeem Olajuwon	125.00	57.50	15.50
☐ 2	Michael Jordan	300.00	135.00	38.00
☐ 3	Charles Barkley	100.00	45.00	12.50
☐ 4	Sam Bowie	6.00	2.70	.75
☐ 5	Sam Perkins	14.00	6.25	1.75
☐ 6	Vern Fleming	6.00	2.70	.75

☐ 7	Otis Thorpe	15.00	6.75	1.90
☐ 8	John Stockton	40.00	18.00	5.00
☐ 9	Kevin Willis	20.00	9.00	2.50
☐ 10	Tim McCormick	5.00	2.30	.60
☐ 11	Alvin Robertson	7.00	3.10	.85

1985-86 Star Lakers Champs

The 1985-86 Star Lakers NBA Champs set is an 18-card set commemorating the Los Angeles Lakers' 1985 NBA Championship. Each card depicts action from the Championship series. The front borders are off-white. The backs feature game and series summaries plus other related information. The set's basic design is identical to those of the Star Company's regular NBA sets. The cards show a Star '86 logo in the upper right corner. The cards measure approximately 2 1/2" by 3 1/2". The cards are numbered in the upper left corner of the reverse.

	MINT	EXC	G-VG
COMPLETE BAG SET (18)	100.00	45.00	12.50
COMMON PLAYER (1-18)	2.50	1.15	.30
*OPENED SET: .75X to 1.0X VALUE			
☐ 1 Lakers 1985 NBA Champs	8.00	3.60	1.00
(Kareem and Buss with trophy)			
☐ 2 Boston 148, L.A. 114	30.00	13.50	3.80
(Bird under basket)			
☐ 3 L.A. 109, Boston 102	5.00	2.30	.60
(Dennis Johnson)			
☐ 4 L.A. 136, Boston 111	8.00	3.60	1.00
(Danny Ainge)			
☐ 5 Boston 107, L.A. 105	4.00	1.80	.50
(Byron Scott driving)			
☐ 6 L.A. 120, Boston 111	6.00	2.70	.75
(McHale under basket)			
☐ 7 L.A. 111, Boston 100	20.00	9.00	2.50
(Magic driving)			
☐ 8 Kareem	6.00	2.70	.75
1985 Series MVP			
☐ 9 Playoff Highs	30.00	13.50	3.80
(Larry Bird)			
☐ 10 Top Playoff Scorers	7.00	3.10	.85
(Kareem holding ball)			
☐ 11 Title Fight	5.00	2.30	.60
(Ainge/Michael Cooper)			
☐ 12 Laker Series Stats	8.00	3.60	1.00
(Riley in huddle)			
☐ 13 Boston Series Stats	2.50	1.15	.30
(K.C. Jones in huddle)			

☐	14	L.A. Playoff Stats..........	20.00	9.00	2.50
		(Magic driving)			
☐	15	Boston Playoff Stats..........	4.00	1.80	.50
		(action under basket)			
☐	16	Road To The Title..........	2.50	1.15	.30
☐	17	Prior World Champs I..........	2.50	1.15	.30
		(riding on float)			
☐	18	Prior World Champs II..........	20.00	9.00	2.50
		(with Ronald Reagan)			

1986 Star Best of the Best

The Star Co. reportedly produced only 1,400 sets and planned to release them in 1986. However, they were not issued until perhaps as late as 1990. This set and the Magic Johnson set were printed on the same uncut sheet. No factory-sealed bags exist for this set due to the fact that the sets were cut from the sheets years after the original printing. The cards measure the standard size (2 1/2" by 3 1/2"). The fronts feature color action photos with white inner borders and a blue card face. The player's name, position, and team name appear at the bottom. The set title "Best of the Best" appears in a white circle at the lower left corner. The backs are white with blue borders and contain biography and statistics. The cards are numbered and arranged in alphabetical order.

	MINT	EXC	G-VG
COMPLETE SET (15)............	700.00	325.00	90.00
COMMON PLAYER (1-15)............	8.00	3.60	1.00

☐	1	Kareem Abdul-Jabbar............	25.00	11.50	3.10
☐	2	Charles Barkley............	125.00	57.50	15.50
☐	3	Larry Bird............	125.00	57.50	15.50
☐	4	Tom Chambers............	8.00	3.60	1.00
☐	5	Terry Cummings............	8.00	3.60	1.00
☐	6	Julius Erving............	40.00	18.00	5.00
☐	7	Patrick Ewing............	100.00	45.00	12.50
☐	8	Magic Johnson............	85.00	38.00	10.50
☐	9	Michael Jordan............	350.00	160.00	45.00
☐	10	Moses Malone............	10.00	4.50	1.25
☐	11	Hakeem Olajuwon............	150.00	70.00	19.00
☐	12	John Stockton............	45.00	20.00	5.75
☐	13	Isiah Thomas............	25.00	11.50	3.10
☐	14	Dominique Wilkins............	75.00	34.00	9.50
☐	15	James Worthy............	12.00	5.50	1.50

1986 Star Court Kings

The 1986 Star Court Kings set contains 33 cards which feature many of the NBA's top players. The set's basic design is identical to those of the Star Company's regular NBA sets. The front borders are yellow, and the backs have career narrative summaries of each player

but no statistics. The cards show a Star '86 logo in the upper right corner. The cards measure approximately 2 1/2" by 3 1/2". The cards are numbered in the upper left corner of the reverse. The numbering is alphabetical and by last name.

		MINT	EXC	G-VG
	COMPLETE BAG SET (33)	350.00	160.00	45.00
	COMMON PLAYER (1-33)	2.50	1.15	.30
	*OPENED SET: .75X to 1.0X VALUE			
☐ 1	Mark Aguirre	3.00	1.35	.40
☐ 2	Kareem Abdul-Jabbar	10.00	4.50	1.25
☐ 3	Charles Barkley	50.00	23.00	6.25
☐ 4	Larry Bird	60.00	27.00	7.50
☐ 5	Rolando Blackman	3.00	1.35	.40
☐ 6	Tom Chambers	3.50	1.55	.45
☐ 7	Maurice Cheeks	3.00	1.35	.40
☐ 8	Terry Cummings	3.00	1.35	.40
☐ 9	Adrian Dantley	3.00	1.35	.40
☐ 10	Darryl Dawkins	3.00	1.35	.40
☐ 11	Mark Eaton	2.50	1.15	.30
☐ 12	Alex English	3.00	1.35	.40
☐ 13	Julius Erving	18.00	8.00	2.30
☐ 14	Patrick Ewing	50.00	23.00	6.25
☐ 15	George Gervin	5.00	2.30	.60
☐ 16	Darrell Griffith	2.50	1.15	.30
☐ 17	Magic Johnson	40.00	18.00	5.00
☐ 18	Michael Jordan	175.00	80.00	22.00
☐ 19	Clark Kellogg	2.50	1.15	.30
☐ 20	Bernard King	3.00	1.35	.40
☐ 21	Moses Malone	5.00	2.30	.60
☐ 22	Kevin McHale	8.00	3.60	1.00
☐ 23	Sidney Moncrief	3.00	1.35	.40
☐ 24	Larry Nance	5.00	2.30	.60
☐ 25	Hakeem Olajuwon	70.00	32.00	8.75
☐ 26	Robert Parish	8.00	3.60	1.00
☐ 27	Ralph Sampson	2.75	1.25	.35
☐ 28	Isiah Thomas	12.00	5.50	1.50
☐ 29	Andrew Toney	2.50	1.15	.30
☐ 30	Kelly Tripucka	2.75	1.25	.35
☐ 31	Kiki Vandeweghe	2.75	1.25	.35
☐ 32	Dominique Wilkins	40.00	18.00	5.00
☐ 33	James Worthy	7.00	3.10	.85

1986 Star Magic Johnson

The Star Co. reportedly produced only 1,400 sets of these cards and planned to release them in 1986; however, they were not issued until perhaps as late as 1990. This set and the Best of the Best set were printed on the same uncut sheet. The cards measure the standard size (2 1/2" by 3 1/2"). The cards are unnumbered and checklisted below in alphabetical order.

	MINT	EXC	G-VG
COMPLETE SET (10)	150.00	70.00	19.00
COMMON M.JOHNSON (1-10)	20.00	9.00	2.50
☐ 1 Checklist	20.00	9.00	2.50
☐ 2 Collegiate Stats	20.00	9.00	2.50
☐ 3 Regular Season Stats	20.00	9.00	2.50
☐ 4 Playoff Stats	20.00	9.00	2.50
☐ 5 All-Star Stats	20.00	9.00	2.50
☐ 6 Career Info 1	20.00	9.00	2.50
☐ 7 Career Info 2	20.00	9.00	2.50
☐ 8 Top Performance	20.00	9.00	2.50
☐ 9 1980 Playoff MVP	20.00	9.00	2.50
☐ 10 1982 Playoff MVP	20.00	9.00	2.50

1986 Star Michael Jordan

The 1986 Star Michael Jordan set contains ten cards highlighting the career of Michael Jordan. There were reportedly only 2,800 sets produced, which were originally available to the hobby exclusively through Dan Stickney of Michigan. The card backs contain various information about Jordan. The set's basic design is identical to those of the Star Company's regular NBA sets. The front borders are red. The cards show a Star '86 logo in the upper right corner. The cards measure approximately 2 1/2" by 3 1/2". The cards are numbered in the upper left corner of the reverse.

	MINT	EXC	G-VG
COMPLETE BAG SET (10)	650.00	300.00	80.00
COMMON M.JORDAN (1-10)	75.00	34.00	9.50
*OPENED SET: .75X to 1.0X VALUE			
☐ 1 Michael Jordan	75.00	34.00	9.50

			MINT	EXC	G-VG
]	2	Collegiate Stats	75.00	34.00	9.50
]	3	1984 Olympian	75.00	34.00	9.50
]	4	Pro Stats	75.00	34.00	9.50
]	5	1985 All-Star	75.00	34.00	9.50
]	6	1985 Rookie of Year	75.00	34.00	9.50
]	7	Career Highlights	75.00	34.00	9.50
]	8	The 1986 Playoffs	75.00	34.00	9.50
]	9	Personal Data	75.00	34.00	9.50
]	10	The Future	75.00	34.00	9.50

1986 Star Best of the New/Old

It was reported that Star Company produced only 440 of these sets. They were distributed to dealers who purchased 1985-86 complete sets. Dealers received one set for every five regular sets purchased. The cards measure the standard size (2 1/2" by 3 1/2"). The cards are unnumbered and checklisted below in alphabetical order. The Best of the New are numbered 1-4 and the Best of the Old are numbered 5-8. The numbering is alphabetical within each group.

		MINT	EXC	G-VG
COMPLETE SET (8)		1800.00	800.00	230.00
COMPLETE NEW SET (4)		1400.00	650.00	180.00
COMPLETE OLD SET (4)		400.00	180.00	50.00
COMMON NEW PLAYER (1-4)		40.00	18.00	5.00
COMMON OLD PLAYER (5-8)		75.00	34.00	9.50
*BAGGED SETS: 1.0X to 1.5X VALUE				

			MINT	EXC	G-VG
□	1	Patrick Ewing	300.00	135.00	38.00
□	2	Michael Jordan	900.00	400.00	115.00
□	3	Hakeem Olajuwon	300.00	135.00	38.00
□	4	Ralph Sampson	40.00	18.00	5.00
□	5	Kareem Abdul-Jabbar	150.00	70.00	19.00
□	6	Julius Erving	175.00	80.00	22.00
□	7	George Gervin	75.00	34.00	9.50
□	8	Bill Walton	90.00	40.00	11.50

1990 Star Pics

This premier edition showcases sixty of college basketball's top pro prospects. The cards were issued exclusively in complete factory set boxes distributed by hobby dealers. The cards measure the standard size (2 1/2" by 3 1/2"). The front features a color action player photo, with the player shown in his college uniform. A white border separates the picture from the surrounding "basketball" background. The player's name appears in an aqua box at the bottom. The back has a head shot of the player in the upper left corner and the card number in a red star in the upper right corner. On a tan-colored basketball court design, the back presents biography, accomplishments, and a mini-scouting report that assesses a player's strengths and weaknesses. The more limited "Medallion" edition (sup-

posedly only 25,000 Medallion sets were produced, each with its own serial number) is valued at approximately one and a half times the prices listed below. The Medallion cards are distinguished by their more glossy feel and gold metallic print. The Medallion sets did not contain any random autographed cards inserted. The autographed cards are valued at 25 to 50 times the prices listed below.

	MINT	**EXC**	**G-VG**
COMPLETE SET (70)	12.00	5.00	1.20
COMMON PLAYER (1-70)	.05	.02	.00
☐ 1 Checklist Card	.05	.02	.00
☐ 2 David Robinson	3.50	1.40	.35
(Mr. Robinson)			
☐ 3 Antonio Davis	.75	.30	.07
UTEP			
☐ 4 Steve Bardo	.05	.02	.00
Illinois			
☐ 5 Jayson Williams	.10	.04	.01
St. John's			
☐ 6 Alaa Abdelnaby	.12	.05	.01
Duke			
☐ 7 Trevor Wilson	.12	.05	.01
UCLA			
☐ 8 Dee Brown	.90	.36	.09
Jacksonville			
☐ 9 Dennis Scott	.50	.20	.05
Georgia Tech			
☐ 10 Danny Ferry	.12	.05	.01
(Flashback)			
☐ 11 Stevie Thompson	.05	.02	.00
Syracuse			
☐ 12 Anthony Bonner	.25	.10	.02
St. Louis			
☐ 13 Keith Robinson	.05	.02	.00
Notre Dame			
☐ 14 Sean Higgins	.08	.03	.01
Michigan			
☐ 15 Bo Kimble	.08	.03	.01
Loyola Marymount			
☐ 16 David Jamerson	.08	.03	.01
Ohio University			
☐ 17 Anthony Pullard	.05	.02	.00
McNeese State			
☐ 18 Phil Henderson	.05	.02	.00
Duke			
☐ 19 Mike Mitchell	.05	.02	.00
Colorado State			
☐ 20 Vanderbilt Team	.05	.02	.00
☐ 21 Gary Payton	1.50	.60	.15
Oregon State			
☐ 22 Tony Massenburg	.05	.02	.00
Maryland			
☐ 23 Cedric Ceballos	1.50	.60	.15
Cal State-Fullerton			
☐ 24 Dwayne Schintzius	.10	.04	.01
Florida			
☐ 25 Bimbo Coles	.30	.12	.03
Virginia Tech			
☐ 26 Scott Williams	.40	.16	.04
North Carolina			
☐ 27 Willie Burton	.12	.05	.01
Minnesota			
☐ 28 Tate George	.08	.03	.01
U Conn			
☐ 29 Mark Stevenson	.05	.02	.00
Duquesne			
☐ 30 UNLV Team	1.00	.40	.10
☐ 31 Earl Wise	.05	.02	.00
Tennessee Tech			
☐ 32 Alec Kessler	.10	.04	.01
Georgia			
☐ 33 Les Jepsen	.05	.02	.00
Iowa			

☐ 34	Boo Harvey	.05	.02	.00
	St. John's			
☐ 35	Elden Campbell	.50	.20	.05
	Clemson			
☐ 36	Jud Buechler	.10	.04	.01
	Arizona			
☐ 37	Loy Vaught	.50	.20	.05
	Michigan			
☐ 38	Tyrone Hill	.30	.12	.03
	Xavier			
☐ 39	Toni Kukoc	2.50	1.00	.25
	Jugoplastika			
☐ 40	Jim Calhoun CO	.10	.04	.01
	U Conn			
☐ 41	Felton Spencer	.50	.20	.05
	Louisville			
☐ 42	Dan Godfread	.05	.02	.00
	Evansville			
☐ 43	Derrick Coleman	4.00	1.60	.40
	Syracuse			
☐ 44	Terry Mills	.90	.36	.09
	Michigan			
☐ 45	Kendall Gill	1.50	.60	.15
	Illinois			
☐ 46	A.J. English	.08	.03	.01
	Virginia Union			
☐ 47	Duane Causwell	.12	.05	.01
	Temple			
☐ 48	Jerrod Mustaf	.10	.04	.01
	Maryland			
☐ 49	Alan Ogg	.05	.02	.00
	Alabama Birmingham			
☐ 50	Pervis Ellison	.40	.16	.04
	(Flashback)			
☐ 51	Matt Bullard	.12	.05	.01
	Iowa			
☐ 52	Melvin Newbern	.05	.02	.00
	Minnesota			
☐ 53	Marcus Liberty	.10	.04	.01
	Ilinois			
☐ 54	Walter Palmer	.05	.02	.00
	Dartmouth			
☐ 55	Negele Knight	.25	.10	.02
	Dayton			
☐ 56	Steve Henson	.05	.02	.00
	Kansas State			
☐ 57	Greg Foster	.05	.02	.00
	UTEP			
☐ 58	Brian Oliver	.05	.02	.00
	Georgia Tech			
☐ 59	Travis Mays	.08	.03	.01
	Texas			
☐ 60	All-Rookie Team	.60	.24	.06
☐ 61	Steve Scheffler	.10	.04	.01
	Purdue			
☐ 62	Chris Jackson	1.50	.60	.15
	LSU			
☐ 63	Derek Strong	.12	.05	.01
	Xavier			
☐ 64	David Butler	.05	.02	.00
	UNLV			
☐ 65	Kevin Pritchard	.05	.02	.00
	Kansas			
☐ 66	Lionel Simmons	.90	.36	.09
	LaSalle			
☐ 67	Gerald Glass	.08	.03	.01
	Mississippi			
☐ 68	Tony Harris	.05	.02	.00
	New Orleans			
☐ 69	Lance Blanks	.08	.03	.01
	Texas			
☐ 70	Draft Overview	.05	.02	.00
☐ 71	Medallion special card	1.00	.40	.10

1991 Star Pics

This 73-card set was produced by Star Pics, subtitled "Pro Prospects," and features 45 of the 54 players picked in the 1991 NBA draft. The cards were issued exclusively in complete factory set boxes distributed by hobby dealers. The cards measure the standard size (2 1/2" by 3 1/2"). The front features a color action photo of player in his college uniform. This picture overlays a black background with a basketball partially in view. The back has a color head shot of the player in the upper left corner and an orange border. On a two color jersey background, the back presents biographical information, accomplishments, and a mini scouting report assessing the player's strengths and weaknesses. The cards are numbered on the back. The Medallion version of this set is tougher to find than that of the previous year and is valued at triple the prices listed below. The Medallion sets again did not contain any random autographed cards inserted. The autographed cards are valued at 20 to 40 times the prices listed below for draft picks; 150 to 250 times for flashback players.

	MINT	EXC	G-VG
COMPLETE SET (73).................................	5.00	2.00	.50
COMMON PLAYER (1-72)...........................	.04	.02	.00
☐ 1 Draft Overview...................................	.04	.02	.00
☐ 2 Derrick Coleman................................	.30	.12	.03
Flashback			
☐ 3 Treg Lee..	.07	.03	.01
Ohio State			
☐ 4 Rich King...	.10	.04	.01
Nebraska			
☐ 5 Kenny Anderson.................................	.75	.30	.07
Georgia Tech			
☐ 6 John Crotty......................................	.10	.04	.01
Virginia			
☐ 7 Mark Randall....................................	.07	.03	.01
Kansas			
☐ 8 Kevin Brooks.....................................	.04	.02	.00
Southwestern Lousiana			
☐ 9 Lamont Strothers...............................	.04	.02	.00
Christopher Newport			
☐ 10 Tim Hardaway..................................	.15	.06	.01
Flashback			
☐ 11 Eric Murdock...................................	.35	.14	.03
Providence			
☐ 12 Melvin Cheatum................................	.04	.02	.00
Alabama			
☐ 13 Pete Chilcutt...................................	.15	.06	.01

☐ 14	Zan Tabak North Carolina Jugoplastika	.04	.02	.00
☐ 15	Greg Anthony UNLV	.15	.06	.01
☐ 16	George Ackles UNLV	.07	.03	.01
☐ 17	Stacey Augmon UNLV	.50	.20	.05
☐ 18	Larry Johnson UNLV	1.50	.60	.15
☐ 19	Alvaro Teheran Houston	.04	.02	.00
☐ 20	Reggie Miller Flashback	.20	.08	.02
☐ 21	Steve Smith Michigan State	.50	.20	.05
☐ 22	Sean Green Iona	.04	.02	.00
☐ 23	Johnny Pittman Oklahoma State	.04	.02	.00
☐ 24	Anthony Avent Seton Hall	.15	.06	.01
☐ 25	Chris Gatling Old Dominion	.15	.06	.01
☐ 26	Mark Macon Temple	.10	.04	.01
☐ 27	Joey Wright Texas	.04	.02	.00
☐ 28	Von McDade Wisconsin (Milwaukee)	.04	.02	.00
☐ 29	Bobby Phills Southern U	.15	.06	.01
☐ 30	Larry Fleisher HOF and Lawyer (In Memoriam)	.04	.02	.00
☐ 31	Luc Longley New Mexico	.20	.08	.02
☐ 32	Jean Derouillere Kansas State	.04	.02	.00
☐ 33	Doug Smith Missouri	.15	.06	.01
☐ 34	Chad Gallagher Creighton	.04	.02	.00
☐ 35	Marty Dow San Diego State	.04	.02	.00
☐ 36	Tony Farmer Nebraska	.04	.02	.00
☐ 37	John Taft Marshall	.04	.02	.00
☐ 38	Reggie Hanson Kentucky	.07	.03	.01
☐ 39	Terrell Brandon Oregon	.20	.08	.02
☐ 40	Dee Brown Flashback	.10	.04	.01
☐ 41	Doug Overton La Salle	.10	.04	.01
☐ 42	Joe Wylie Miami	.04	.02	.00
☐ 43	Myron Brown Slippery Rock	.04	.02	.00
☐ 44	Steve Hood James Madison	.04	.02	.00
☐ 45	Randy Brown New Mexico State	.10	.04	.01
☐ 46	Chris Corchiani NC State	.10	.04	.01
☐ 47	Kevin Lynch Minnesota	.07	.03	.01
☐ 48	Donald Hodge Temple	.07	.03	.01
☐ 49	LaBradford Smith Louisville	.07	.03	.01

☐ 50	Shawn Kemp	.30	.12	.03
	Flashback			
☐ 51	Brian Shorter	.04	.02	.00
	Pittsburgh			
☐ 52	Gary Waites	.04	.02	.00
	Alabama			
☐ 53	Mike Iuzzolino	.07	.03	.01
	St. Francis			
☐ 54	LeRon Ellis	.10	.04	.01
	Syracuse			
☐ 55	Perry Carter	.07	.03	.01
	Ohio State			
☐ 56	Keith Hughes	.04	.02	.00
	Rutgers			
☐ 57	John Turner	.04	.02	.00
	Phillips University			
☐ 58	Marcus Kennedy	.04	.02	.00
	Eastern Michigan			
☐ 59	Randy Ayers CO	.10	.04	.01
	Ohio State			
☐ 60	All-Rookie Team	.30	.12	.03
☐ 61	Jackie Jones	.04	.02	.00
	Oklahoma			
☐ 62	Shaun Vandiver	.04	.02	.00
	Colorado			
☐ 63	Dale Davis	.40	.16	.04
	Clemson			
☐ 64	Jimmy Oliver	.04	.02	.00
	Purdue			
☐ 65	Elliot Perry	.07	.03	.01
	Memphis State			
☐ 66	Jerome Harmon	.07	.03	.01
	Louisville			
☐ 67	Darrin Chancellor	.04	.02	.00
	Southern Mississippi			
☐ 68	Roy Fisher	.04	.02	.00
	California (Berkeley)			
☐ 69	Rick Fox	.30	.12	.03
	North Carolina			
☐ 70	Kenny Anderson	.30	.12	.03
	Special Second Card.			
☐ 71	Richard Dumas	.10	.04	.01
	Oklahoma State			
☐ 72	Checklist Card	.04	.02	.00
☐ NNO	Salute/American Flag	.07	.03	.01

1992 Star Pics

The 1992 Star Pics Pro Prospects Basketball HotPics set contains 90 cards measuring the standard size (2 1/2" by 3 1/2"). The set includes 47 of the 54 players selected in the 1992 NBA Draft as well as some free agents who had a chance to make NBA rosters. Special cards featured in the set include eight StarStats (10, 31, 36, 43, 74, 78, 81, 89), five Flashbacks (30, 40, 50, 60, 70), three Kid cards (33, 68, 83), and two coaches cards (5, 15). Each nine-card foil StarPak included one "Jump At The Chance" game card, with which collectors could win various prizes. The fronts display color action player photos with white borders. The player's position and name are printed vertically in the right border, with the latter in a colored stripe. The Star Pics logo in the lower right corner rounds out the card face. The backs present accomplishments, strengths, weaknesses, and biographical information. A close-up photo appears at the lower right corner inside the Star Pics logo. The cards are numbered on the back. The unnumbered Bonus card of Steve Smith features a full-bleed color illustration by artist Rip Evans. The autographed cards are valued at 25 to 50 times the prices listed below for draft picks; 125 to 200 times for flashback players.

	MINT	EXC	G-VG
COMPLETE SET (90)	8.00	3.25	.80
COMMON PLAYER (1-90)	.04	.02	.00
☐ 1 Draft Overview	.07	.03	.01
☐ 2 Bryant Stith	.50	.20	.05
Virginia			
☐ 3 Reggie Smith	.10	.04	.01
Texas Christian			
☐ 4 Todd Day	.30	.12	.03
Arkansas			
☐ 5 Bobby Knight CO	.20	.08	.02
Indiana			
☐ 6 Darren Morningstar	.04	.02	.00
Pittsburgh			
☐ 7 Clarence Weatherspoon	.90	.36	.09
Southern Mississippi			
☐ 8 Matt Geiger	.25	.10	.02
Georgia Tech			
☐ 9 Marlon Maxey	.12	.05	.01
Texas El Paso			
☐ 10 Christian Laettner SS	.20	.08	.02
Duke			
☐ 11 Tony Bennett	.15	.06	.01
Wisconsin (Green Bay)			
☐ 12 Sean Rooks	.20	.08	.02
Arizona			
☐ 13 Tom Gugliotta	.75	.30	.07
North Carolina State			
☐ 14 Chris King	.10	.04	.01
Wake Forest			
☐ 15 Mike Krzyzewski CO	.25	.10	.02
Duke			
☐ 16 Sam Mack	.04	.02	.00
Houston			
☐ 17 Matt Fish	.04	.02	.00
NC (Wilmington)			
☐ 18 Brian Davis	.10	.04	.01
Duke			
☐ 19 Oliver Miller	.35	.14	.03
Arkansas			
☐ 20 Daimon Sweet	.07	.03	.01
Notre Dame			
☐ 21 Eric Anderson	.10	.04	.01
Indiana			
☐ 22 Henry Williams	.04	.02	.00
NC (Charlotte)			
☐ 23 David Johnson	.07	.03	.01
Syracuse			
☐ 24 Duane Cooper	.07	.03	.01
USC			
☐ 25 Lucius Davis	.07	.03	.01
UC Santa Barbara			
☐ 26 Matt Steigenga	.07	.03	.01
Michigan State			
☐ 27 Robert Horry	.90	.36	.09
Alabama			
☐ 28 Brent Price	.12	.05	.01

		Oklahoma			
☐	29	Chris Smith	.25	.10	.02
		Connecticut			
☐	30	Vlade Divac FLB	.07	.03	.01
☐	31	Adam Keefe SS	.07	.03	.01
		Stanford			
☐	32	Christian Laettner	.60	.24	.06
		Duke			
☐	33	LaPhonso Ellis	.30	.12	.03
		Notre Dame			
		Kid Card			
☐	34	Alex Blackwell	.04	.02	.00
		Monmouth			
☐	35	Popeye Jones	.07	.03	.01
		Murray State			
☐	36	Walt Williams SS	.10	.04	.01
		Maryland			
☐	37	Radenko Dobras	.04	.02	.00
		South Florida			
☐	38	Latrell Sprewell	1.75	.70	.17
		Alabama			
☐	39	Isaiah Morris	.07	.03	.01
		Arkansas			
☐	40	Horace Grant FLB	.12	.05	.01
☐	41	Craig Upchurch	.04	.02	.00
		Houston			
☐	42	Alonzo Jamison	.07	.03	.01
		Kansas			
☐	43	Bryant Stith SS	.20	.08	.02
		Virginia			
☐	44	Jon Barry	.20	.08	.02
		Georgia Tech			
☐	45	Litterial Green	.10	.04	.01
		Georgia			
☐	46	Malik Sealy	.15	.06	.01
		St. John's			
☐	47	Anthony Peeler	.35	.14	.03
		Missouri			
☐	48	Dexter Cambridge	.04	.02	.00
		Texas			
☐	49	Eric Manuel	.04	.02	.00
		Oklahoma City			
☐	50	Kendall Gill FLB	.15	.06	.01
☐	51	Hubert Davis	.30	.12	.03
		North Carolina			
☐	52	Steve Rogers	.04	.02	.00
		Alabama State			
☐	53	Byron Houston	.15	.06	.01
		Oklahoma State			
☐	54	Randy Woods	.10	.04	.01
		LaSalle			
☐	55	Elmer Bennett	.07	.03	.01
		Notre Dame			
☐	56	Smokey McCovery	.04	.02	.00
		Oklahoma City			
☐	57	George Gilmore	.04	.02	.00
		Chaminade			
☐	58	Predrag Danilovic	.04	.02	.00
		Belgrade			
☐	59	John Pelphrey	.07	.03	.01
		Kentucky			
☐	60	Dan Majerle FLB	.15	.06	.01
		Central Michigan			
☐	61	Elmore Spencer	.25	.10	.02
		UNLV			
☐	62	Calvin Talford	.04	.02	.00
		East Tennessee State			
☐	63	David Booth	.07	.03	.01
		DePaul			
☐	64	Herb Jones	.07	.03	.01
		Cincinnati			
☐	65	Benford Williams	.04	.02	.00
		Texas			

☐ 66	Greg Dennis	.04	.02	.00
	East Tennessee State			
☐ 67	James McCoy	.04	.02	.00
	Massachusetts			
☐ 68	Clarence Weatherspoon	.30	.12	.03
	Southern Mississippi Kid Card			
☐ 69	LaPhonso Ellis	.90	.36	.09
	Notre Dame			
☐ 70	Sarun.Marciulionis FLB	.07	.03	.01
☐ 71	Walt Williams	.30	.12	.03
	Maryland			
☐ 72	Lee Mayberry	.20	.08	.02
	Arkansas			
☐ 73	Doug Christie	.40	.16	.04
	Pepperdine			
☐ 74	Jon Barry SS	.07	.03	.01
	Georgia Tech			
☐ 75	Adam Keefe	.12	.05	.01
	Stanford			
☐ 76	Robert Werdann	.07	.03	.01
	St. John's			
☐ 77	P.J. Brown	.04	.02	.00
	Louisiana Tech			
☐ 78	Tom Gugliotta SS	.25	.10	.02
	North Carolina State			
☐ 79	Terrell Lowery	.25	.10	.02
	Loyola Marymount			
☐ 80	Tracy Murray	.20	.08	.02
	UCLA			
☐ 81	Clar.Weatherspoon SS	.30	.12	.03
	Southern Mississippi			
☐ 82	Melvin Robinson	.04	.02	.00
	St. Louis			
☐ 83	Todd Day	.10	.04	.01
	Arkansas Kid Card			
☐ 84	Harold Miner	.40	.16	.04
	USC			
☐ 85	Tim Burroughs	.04	.02	.00
	Jacksonville			
☐ 86	Damon Patterson	.04	.02	.00
	Oklahoma			
☐ 87	Corey Williams	.04	.02	.00
	Oklahoma State			
☐ 88	Harold Ellis	.25	.10	.02
	Morehouse College			
☐ 89	LaPhonso Ellis SS	.30	.12	.03
	Notre Dame			
☐ 90	Checklist	.07	.03	.01
☐ BONU	Steve Smith Art	2.50	1.00	.25
	Miami Heat			

1957-58 Topps

*The 1957-58 Topps basketball set of 80 cards was Topps' first basketball issue. Topps did not release another basketball set until 1969. Cards in the set measure approximately 2 1/2"
by 3 1/2". A number of cards in the set were double printed (indicated by DP in checklist below) and are more plentiful. In fact there are 49 double prints, 30 single prints, and one quadruple print in the set. Card backs give statistical information from the 1956-57 NBA season. Rookie Cards include Paul Arizin, Nat Clifton, Bob Cousy, Cliff Hagan, Tom Heinsohn, Rod Hundley, Red Kerr, Clyde Lovellette, Bob Pettit, Bill Russell, Dolph Schayes, Bill*

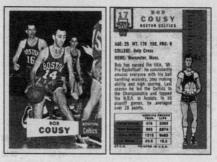

Sharman and Jack Twyman. The set contains the only card of Maurice Stokes. Topps also produced a three-card advertising panel featuring the fronts of Walt Davis, Joe Graboski, and Bob Cousy with an advertisement for the upcoming Topps basketball set on the combined reverse.

	NRMT	VG-E	GOOD
COMPLETE SET (80)	5500.00	2500.00	700.00
COMMON PLAYER (1-80)	35.00	16.00	4.40
☐ 1 Nat Clifton DP Detroit Pistons	250.00	115.00	31.00
☐ 2 George Yardley DP Detroit Pistons	50.00	23.00	6.25
☐ 3 Neil Johnston DP Philadelphia Warriors	60.00	27.00	7.50
☐ 4 Carl Braun DP New York Knicks	35.00	16.00	4.40
☐ 5 Bill Sharman DP Boston Celtics	150.00	70.00	19.00
☐ 6 George King DP Cincinnati Royals	32.00	14.50	4.00
☐ 7 Kenny Sears DP New York Knicks	35.00	16.00	4.40
☐ 8 Dick Ricketts DP Cincinnati Royals	35.00	16.00	4.40
☐ 9 Jack Nichols DP Boston Celtics	25.00	11.50	3.10
☐ 10 Paul Arizin DP Philadelphia Warriors	100.00	45.00	12.50
☐ 11 Chuck Noble DP Detroit Pistons	25.00	11.50	3.10
☐ 12 Slater Martin DP St. Louis Hawks	60.00	27.00	7.50
☐ 13 Dolph Schayes DP Syracuse Nationals	125.00	57.50	15.50
☐ 14 Dick Atha DP Detroit Pistons	25.00	11.50	3.10
☐ 15 Frank Ramsey DP Boston Celtics	80.00	36.00	10.00
☐ 16 Dick McGuire DP Detroit Pistons	50.00	23.00	6.25
☐ 17 Bob Cousy DP Boston Celtics	550.00	250.00	70.00
☐ 18 Larry Foust DP Minneapolis Lakers	32.00	14.50	4.00
☐ 19 Tom Heinsohn Boston Celtics	300.00	135.00	38.00
☐ 20 Bill Thieben DP Detroit Pistons	25.00	11.50	3.10
☐ 21 Don Meineke DP Cincinnati Royals	35.00	16.00	4.40
☐ 22 Tom Marshall Cincinnati Royals	35.00	16.00	4.40

☐ 23	Dick Garmaker	35.00	16.00	4.40
	Minneapolis Lakers			
☐ 24	Bob Pettit QP	200.00	90.00	25.00
	St. Louis Hawks			
☐ 25	Jim Krebs DP	32.00	14.50	4.00
	Minneapolis Lakers			
☐ 26	Gene Shue DP	60.00	27.00	7.50
	Detroit Pistons			
☐ 27	Ed Macauley DP	60.00	27.00	7.50
	St. Louis Hawks			
☐ 28	Vern Mikkelsen	60.00	27.00	7.50
	Minneapolis Lakers			
☐ 29	Willie Naulls	60.00	27.00	7.50
	New York Knicks			
☐ 30	Walter Dukes DP	35.00	16.00	4.40
	Detroit Pistons			
☐ 31	Dave Piontek DP	25.00	11.50	3.10
	Cincinnati Royals			
☐ 32	John Kerr	125.00	57.50	15.50
	Syracuse Nationals			
☐ 33	Larry Costello DP	50.00	23.00	6.25
	Syracuse Nationals			
☐ 34	Woody Sauldsberry DP	35.00	16.00	4.40
	Philadelphia Warriors			
☐ 35	Ray Felix	40.00	18.00	5.00
	New York Knicks			
☐ 36	Ernie Beck	35.00	16.00	4.40
	Philadelphia Warriors			
☐ 37	Cliff Hagan	120.00	55.00	15.00
	St. Louis Hawks			
☐ 38	Guy Sparrow DP	25.00	11.50	3.10
	New York Knicks			
☐ 39	Jim Loscutoff	50.00	23.00	6.25
	Boston Celtics			
☐ 40	Arnie Risen DP	35.00	16.00	4.40
	Boston Celtics			
☐ 41	Joe Graboski	35.00	16.00	4.40
	Philadelphia Warriors			
☐ 42	Maurice Stokes DP UER	120.00	55.00	15.00
	Cincinnati Royals			
	(Text refers to			
	N.F.L. Record)			
☐ 43	Rod Hundley DP	120.00	55.00	15.00
	Minneapolis Lakers			
☐ 44	Tom Gola DP	80.00	36.00	10.00
	Philadelphia Warriors			
☐ 45	Med Park	40.00	18.00	5.00
	St. Louis Hawks			
☐ 46	Mel Hutchins DP	25.00	11.50	3.10
	New York Knicks			
☐ 47	Larry Friend DP	25.00	11.50	3.10
	New York Knicks			
☐ 48	Lennie Rosenbluth DP	60.00	27.00	7.50
	Philadelphia Warriors			
☐ 49	Walt Davis	35.00	16.00	4.40
	Philadelphia Warriors			
☐ 50	Richie Regan	40.00	18.00	5.00
	Cincinnati Royals			
☐ 51	Frank Selvy DP	40.00	18.00	5.00
	St. Louis Hawks			
☐ 52	Art Spoelstra DP	25.00	11.50	3.10
	Minneapolis Lakers			
☐ 53	Bob Hopkins	40.00	18.00	5.00
	Syracuse Nationals			
☐ 54	Earl Lloyd	40.00	18.00	5.00
	Syracuse Nationals			
☐ 55	Phil Jordan DP	25.00	11.50	3.10
	New York Knicks			
☐ 56	Bob Houbregs DP	35.00	16.00	4.40
	Detroit Pistons			
☐ 57	Lou Tsioropoulas DP	25.00	11.50	3.10
	Boston Celtics			
☐ 58	Ed Conlin	40.00	18.00	5.00

		NRMT	VG-E	GOOD
	Syracuse Nationals			
☐ 59	Al Bianchi	80.00	36.00	10.00
	Syracuse Nationals			
☐ 60	George Dempsey	40.00	18.00	5.00
	Philadelphia Warriors			
☐ 61	Chuck Share	35.00	16.00	4.40
	St. Louis Hawks			
☐ 62	Harry Gallatin DP	50.00	23.00	6.25
	Detroit Pistons			
☐ 63	Bob Harrison	35.00	16.00	4.40
	Syracuse Nationals			
☐ 64	Bob Burrow DP	25.00	11.50	3.10
	Minneapolis Lakers			
☐ 65	Win Wilfong DP	25.00	11.50	3.10
	St. Louis Hawks			
☐ 66	Jack McMahon DP	35.00	16.00	4.40
	St. Louis Hawks			
☐ 67	Jack George	35.00	16.00	4.40
	Philadelphia Warriors			
☐ 68	Charlie Tyra DP	25.00	11.50	3.10
	New York Knicks			
☐ 69	Ron Sobie	35.00	16.00	4.40
	New York Knicks			
☐ 70	Jack Coleman	35.00	16.00	4.40
	St. Louis Hawks			
☐ 71	Jack Twyman DP	120.00	55.00	15.00
	Cincinnati Royals			
☐ 72	Paul Seymour	40.00	18.00	5.00
	Syracuse Nationals			
☐ 73	Jim Paxson DP	55.00	25.00	7.00
	Cincinnati Royals			
☐ 74	Bob Leonard	40.00	18.00	5.00
	Minneapolis Lakers			
☐ 75	Andy Phillip	40.00	18.00	5.00
	Boston Celtics			
☐ 76	Joe Holup	35.00	16.00	4.40
	Syracuse Nationals			
☐ 77	Bill Russell	2000.00	900.00	250.00
	Boston Celtics			
☐ 78	Clyde Lovellette DP	100.00	45.00	12.50
	Cincinnati Royals			
☐ 79	Ed Fleming DP	25.00	11.50	3.10
	Minneapolis Lakers			
☐ 80	Dick Schnittker	90.00	40.00	11.50
	Minneapolis Lakers			

1969-70 Topps

The 1969-70 Topps set of 99 cards was Topps' first regular basketball issue since 1958. These tall cards measure 2 1/2" by 4 11/16". The cards are much larger than the standard card size. The set features the first card of Lew Alcindor (later Kareem Abdul-Jabbar). Other notable Rookie Cards in the set are Dave Bing, Bill Bradley, Billy Cunningham, Dave DeBusschere, Walt Frazier, John Havlicek, Connie Hawkins, Elvin Hayes, Jerry Lucas, Earl Monroe, Don Nelson, Willis Reed, Nate Thurmond, and Wes Unseld. The set was printed on a sheet of 99 cards (nine rows of eleven across) with the checklist card occupying the lower right corner of the sheet. As a result, the checklist is very difficult to obtain in Near Mint or better condition.

		NRMT	VG-E	GOOD
	COMPLETE SET (99)	1800.00	800.00	230.00
	COMMON PLAYER (1-99)	4.00	1.80	.50
☐ 1	Wilt Chamberlain	200.00	65.00	20.00
	Los Angeles Lakers			
☐ 2	Gail Goodrich	35.00	16.00	4.40
	Phoenix Suns			
☐ 3	Cazzie Russell	15.00	6.75	1.90
	New York Knicks			
☐ 4	Darrall Imhoff	5.00	2.30	.60
	Philadelphia 76ers			

☐ 5	Bailey Howell	5.00	2.30	.60
	Boston Celtics			
☐ 6	Lucius Allen	9.00	4.00	1.15
	Seattle Supersonics			
☐ 7	Tom Boerwinkle	8.00	3.60	1.00
	Chicago Bulls			
☐ 8	Jimmy Walker	7.00	3.10	.85
	Detroit Pistons			
☐ 9	John Block	5.00	2.30	.60
	San Diego Rockets			
☐ 10	Nate Thurmond	30.00	13.50	3.80
	San Francisco Warriors			
☐ 11	Gary Gregor	4.00	1.80	.50
	Atlanta Hawks			
☐ 12	Gus Johnson	15.00	6.75	1.90
	Baltimore Bullets			
☐ 13	Luther Rackley	4.00	1.80	.50
	Cincinnati Royals			
☐ 14	Jon McGlocklin	7.00	3.10	.85
	Milwaukee Bucks			
☐ 15	Connie Hawkins	40.00	18.00	5.00
	Phoenix Suns			
☐ 16	Johnny Egan	4.00	1.80	.50
	Los Angeles Lakers			
☐ 17	Jim Washington	4.00	1.80	.50
	Philadelphia 76ers			
☐ 18	Dick Barnett	9.00	4.00	1.15
	New York Knicks			
☐ 19	Tom Meschery	4.00	1.80	.50
	Seattle Supersonics			
☐ 20	John Havlicek	175.00	80.00	22.00
	Boston Celtics			
☐ 21	Eddie Miles	4.00	1.80	.50
	Detroit Pistons			
☐ 22	Walt Wesley	4.00	1.80	.50
	Chicago Bulls			
☐ 23	Rick Adelman	12.00	5.50	1.50
	San Diego Rockets			
☐ 24	Al Attles	5.00	2.30	.60
	San Francisco Warriors			
☐ 25	Lew Alcindor	550.00	250.00	70.00
	Milwaukee Bucks			
☐ 26	Jack Marin	8.00	3.60	1.00
	Baltimore Bullets			
☐ 27	Walt Hazzard	12.00	5.50	1.50

	Atlanta Hawks			
☐ 28	Connie Dierking	4.00	1.80	.50
	Cincinnati Royals			
☐ 29	Keith Erickson	10.00	4.50	1.25
	Los Angeles Lakers			
☐ 30	Bob Rule	6.00	2.70	.75
	Seattle Supersonics			
☐ 31	Dick Van Arsdale	10.00	4.50	1.25
	Phoenix Suns			
☐ 32	Archie Clark	9.00	4.00	1.15
	Philadelphia 76ers			
☐ 33	Terry Dischinger	8.00	3.60	1.00
	Detroit Pistons			
☐ 34	Henry Finkel	5.00	2.30	.60
	Boston Celtics			
☐ 35	Elgin Baylor	55.00	25.00	7.00
	Los Angeles Lakers			
☐ 36	Ron Williams	4.00	1.80	.50
	San Francisco Warriors			
☐ 37	Loy Petersen	4.00	1.80	.50
	Chicago Bulls			
☐ 38	Guy Rodgers	5.00	2.30	.60
	Milwaukee Bucks			
☐ 39	Toby Kimball	4.00	1.80	.50
	San Diego Rockets			
☐ 40	Billy Cunningham	50.00	23.00	6.25
	Philadelphia 76ers			
☐ 41	Joe Caldwell	7.00	3.10	.85
	Atlanta Hawks			
☐ 42	Leroy Ellis	6.00	2.70	.75
	Baltimore Bullets			
☐ 43	Bill Bradley	150.00	70.00	19.00
	New York Knicks			
☐ 44	Len Wilkens UER	30.00	13.50	3.80
	Seattle Supersonics			
	(Misspelled Wilkins			
	on card back)			
☐ 45	Jerry Lucas	35.00	16.00	4.40
	San Francisco Warriors			
☐ 46	Neal Walk	5.50	2.50	.70
	Phoenix Suns			
☐ 47	Emmette Bryant	5.00	2.30	.60
	Boston Celtics			
☐ 48	Bob Kauffman	5.00	2.30	.60
	Chicago Bulls			
☐ 49	Mel Counts	5.00	2.30	.60
	Los Angeles Lakers			
☐ 50	Oscar Robertson	70.00	32.00	8.75
	Cincinnati Royals			
☐ 51	Jim Barnett	5.00	2.30	.60
	San Diego Rockets			
☐ 52	Don Smith	4.00	1.80	.50
	Milwaukee Bucks			
☐ 53	Jim Davis	4.00	1.80	.50
	Atlanta Hawks			
☐ 54	Wally Jones	6.00	2.70	.75
	Philadelphia 76ers			
☐ 55	Dave Bing	40.00	18.00	5.00
	Detroit Pistons			
☐ 56	Wes Unseld	45.00	20.00	5.75
	Baltimore Bullets			
☐ 57	Joe Ellis	4.00	1.80	.50
	San Francisco Warriors			
☐ 58	John Tresvant	4.00	1.80	.50
	Seattle Supersonics			
☐ 59	Larry Siegfried	8.00	3.60	1.00
	Boston Celtics			
☐ 60	Willis Reed	50.00	23.00	6.25
	New York Knicks			
☐ 61	Paul Silas	15.00	6.75	1.90
	Phoenix Suns			
☐ 62	Bob Weiss	8.00	3.60	1.00
	Chicago Bulls			

☐ 63 Willie McCarter	4.00	1.80	.50
Los Angeles Lakers			
☐ 64 Don Kojis	5.00	2.30	.60
San Diego Rockets			
☐ 65 Lou Hudson	20.00	9.00	2.50
Atlanta Hawks			
☐ 66 Jim King	4.00	1.80	.50
Cincinnati Royals			
☐ 67 Luke Jackson	5.00	2.30	.60
Philadelphia 76ers			
☐ 68 Len Chappell	5.50	2.50	.70
Milwaukee Bucks			
☐ 69 Ray Scott	4.00	1.80	.50
Baltimore Bullets			
☐ 70 Jeff Mullins	9.00	4.00	1.15
San Francisco Warriors			
☐ 71 Howie Komives	4.00	1.80	.50
Detroit Pistons			
☐ 72 Tom Sanders	8.00	3.60	1.00
Boston Celtics			
☐ 73 Dick Snyder	4.00	1.80	.50
Seattle Supersonics			
☐ 74 Dave Stallworth	5.00	2.30	.60
New York Knicks			
☐ 75 Elvin Hayes	75.00	34.00	9.50
San Diego Rockets			
☐ 76 Art Harris	4.00	1.80	.50
Phoenix Suns			
☐ 77 Don Ohl	4.00	1.80	.50
Atlanta Hawks			
☐ 78 Bob Love	30.00	13.50	3.80
Chicago Bulls			
☐ 79 Tom Van Arsdale	10.00	4.50	1.25
Cincinnati Royals			
☐ 80 Earl Monroe	40.00	18.00	5.00
Baltimore Bullets			
☐ 81 Greg Smith	4.00	1.80	.50
Milwaukee Bucks			
☐ 82 Don Nelson	35.00	16.00	4.40
Boston Celtics			
☐ 83 Happy Hairston	9.00	4.00	1.15
Detroit Pistons			
☐ 84 Hal Greer	10.00	4.50	1.25
Philadelphia 76ers			
☐ 85 Dave DeBusschere	45.00	20.00	5.75
New York Knicks			
☐ 86 Bill Bridges	7.00	3.10	.85
Atlanta Hawks			
☐ 87 Herm Gilliam	5.00	2.30	.60
Cincinnati Royals			
☐ 88 Jim Fox	4.00	1.80	.50
Phoenix Suns			
☐ 89 Bob Boozer	5.00	2.30	.60
Seattle Supersonics			
☐ 90 Jerry West	100.00	45.00	12.50
Los Angeles Lakers			
☐ 91 Chet Walker	15.00	6.75	1.90
Chicago Bulls			
☐ 92 Flynn Robinson	5.00	2.30	.60
Milwaukee Bucks			
☐ 93 Clyde Lee	4.00	1.80	.50
San Francisco Warriors			
☐ 94 Kevin Loughery	15.00	6.75	1.90
Baltimore Bullets			
☐ 95 Walt Bellamy	9.00	4.00	1.15
Detroit Pistons			
☐ 96 Art Williams	4.00	1.80	.50
San Diego Rockets			
☐ 97 Adrian Smith	5.00	2.30	.60
Cincinnati Royals			
☐ 98 Walt Frazier	70.00	32.00	8.75
New York Knicks			
☐ 99 Checklist 1-99	250.00	30.00	7.50

1970-71 Topps

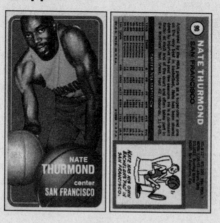

The 1970-71 Topps basketball card set of 175 full-color cards continued the larger-size card format established the previous year. These tall cards measure approximately 2 1/2" by 4 11/16". Cards numbered 106 to 115 contained the previous season's NBA first and second team All-Star selections. The first six cards in the set (1-6) feature the statistical league leaders from the previous season. The last eight cards in the set (168-175) summarize the results of the previous season's NBA championship playoff series won by the Knicks over the Lakers. The key Rookie Cards in this set are Pete Maravich, Calvin Murphy, and Pat Riley. There are 22 short-printed cards in the first series which are marked SP in the checklist below.

	NRMT	VG-E	GOOD
COMPLETE SET (175)	1200.00	550.00	150.00
COMMON PLAYER (1-110)	2.50	1.15	.30
COMMON PLAYER (111-175)	3.25	1.45	.40
☐ 1 NBA Scoring Leaders	32.00	8.00	1.60
Lew Alcindor			
Jerry West			
Elvin Hayes			
☐ 2 NBA Scoring SP	20.00	9.00	2.50
Average Leaders			
Jerry West			
Lew Alcindor			
Elvin Hayes			
☐ 3 NBA FG Pct Leaders	5.00	2.30	.60
Johnny Green			
Darrall Imhoff			
Lou Hudson			
☐ 4 NBA FT Pct Leaders SP	10.00	4.50	1.25
Flynn Robinson			
Chet Walker			
Jeff Mullins			
☐ 5 NBA Rebound Leaders	15.00	6.75	1.90
Elvin Hayes			
Wes Unseld			
Lew Alcindor			
☐ 6 NBA Assist Leaders SP	10.00	4.50	1.25
Len Wilkens			
Walt Frazier			
Clem Haskins			
☐ 7 Bill Bradley	55.00	25.00	7.00
New York Knicks			

☐ 8 Ron Williams	2.50	1.15	.30
San Francisco Warriors			
☐ 9 Otto Moore	2.50	1.15	.30
Detroit Pistons			
☐ 10 John Havlicek SP	70.00	32.00	8.75
Boston Celtics			
☐ 11 George Wilson	3.50	1.55	.45
Buffalo Braves			
☐ 12 John Trapp	2.50	1.15	.30
San Diego Rockets			
☐ 13 Pat Riley	60.00	27.00	7.50
Portland Trail Blazers			
☐ 14 Jim Washington	2.50	1.15	.30
Philadelphia 76ers			
☐ 15 Bob Rule	3.00	1.35	.40
Seattle Supersonics			
☐ 16 Bob Weiss	3.50	1.55	.45
Chicago Bulls			
☐ 17 Neil Johnson	2.50	1.15	.30
Phoenix Suns			
☐ 18 Walt Bellamy	5.50	2.50	.70
Atlanta Hawks			
☐ 19 McCoy McLemore	2.50	1.15	.30
Cleveland Cavaliers			
☐ 20 Earl Monroe	14.00	6.25	1.75
Baltimore Bullets			
☐ 21 Wally Anderzunas	2.50	1.15	.30
Cincinnati Royals			
☐ 22 Guy Rodgers	3.50	1.55	.45
Milwaukee Bucks			
☐ 23 Rick Roberson	2.50	1.15	.30
Los Angeles Lakers			
☐ 24 Checklist 1-110	45.00	6.75	2.30
☐ 25 Jimmy Walker	2.50	1.15	.30
Detroit Pistons			
☐ 26 Mike Riordan	5.00	2.30	.60
New York Knicks			
☐ 27 Henry Finkel	2.50	1.15	.30
Boston Celtics			
☐ 28 Joe Ellis	2.50	1.15	.30
San Francisco Warriors			
☐ 29 Mike Davis	2.50	1.15	.30
Buffalo Braves			
☐ 30 Lou Hudson	5.00	2.30	.60
Atlanta Hawks			
☐ 31 Lucius Allen SP	7.00	3.10	.85
Seattle Supersonics			
☐ 32 Toby Kimball SP	5.00	2.30	.60
San Diego Rockets			
☐ 33 Luke Jackson SP	5.00	2.30	.60
Philadelphia 76ers			
☐ 34 Johnny Egan	2.50	1.15	.30
Cleveland Cavaliers			
☐ 35 Leroy Ellis SP	5.00	2.30	.60
Portland Trail Blazers			
☐ 36 Jack Marin SP	7.00	3.10	.85
Baltimore Bullets			
☐ 37 Joe Caldwell SP	7.00	3.10	.85
Atlanta Hawks			
☐ 38 Keith Erickson	5.00	2.30	.60
Los Angeles Lakers			
☐ 39 Don Smith	2.50	1.15	.30
Milwaukee Bucks			
☐ 40 Flynn Robinson	2.50	1.15	.30
Cincinnati Royals			
☐ 41 Bob Boozer	2.50	1.15	.30
Seattle Supersonics			
☐ 42 Howie Komives	2.50	1.15	.30
Detroit Pistons			
☐ 43 Dick Barnett	5.00	2.30	.60
New York Knicks			
☐ 44 Stu Lantz	5.00	2.30	.60
San Diego Rockets			

☐ 45	Dick Van Arsdale	5.00	2.30	.60
	Phoenix Suns			
☐ 46	Jerry Lucas	12.00	5.50	1.50
	San Francisco Warriors			
☐ 47	Don Chaney	10.00	4.50	1.25
	Boston Celtics			
☐ 48	Ray Scott	2.50	1.15	.30
	Buffalo Braves			
☐ 49	Dick Cunningham SP	5.00	2.30	.60
	Milwaukee Bucks			
☐ 50	Wilt Chamberlain	90.00	40.00	11.50
	Los Angeles Lakers			
☐ 51	Kevin Loughery	5.50	2.50	.70
	Baltimore Bullets			
☐ 52	Stan McKenzie	2.50	1.15	.30
	Portland Trail Blazers			
☐ 53	Fred Foster	2.50	1.15	.30
	Cincinnati Royals			
☐ 54	Jim Davis	2.50	1.15	.30
	Atlanta Hawks			
☐ 55	Walt Wesley	2.50	1.15	.30
	Cleveland Cavaliers			
☐ 56	Bill Hewitt	2.50	1.15	.30
	Detroit Pistons			
☐ 57	Darrall Imhoff	2.50	1.15	.30
	Philadelphia 76ers			
☐ 58	John Block	2.50	1.15	.30
	San Diego Rockets			
☐ 59	Al Attles SP	7.00	3.10	.85
	San Francisco Warriors			
☐ 60	Chet Walker	6.00	2.70	.75
	Chicago Bulls			
☐ 61	Luther Rackley	2.50	1.15	.30
	Cleveland Cavaliers			
☐ 62	Jerry Chambers SP	7.00	3.10	.85
	Atlanta Hawks			
☐ 63	Bob Dandridge	8.00	3.60	1.00
	Milwaukee Bucks			
☐ 64	Dick Snyder	2.50	1.15	.30
	Seattle Supersonics			
☐ 65	Elgin Baylor	35.00	16.00	4.40
	Los Angeles Lakers			
☐ 66	Connie Dierking	2.50	1.15	.30
	Cincinnati Royals			
☐ 67	Steve Kuberski	3.50	1.55	.45
	Boston Celtics			
☐ 68	Tom Boerwinkle	3.50	1.55	.45
	Chicago Bulls			
☐ 69	Paul Silas	6.00	2.70	.75
	Phoenix Suns			
☐ 70	Elvin Hayes	30.00	13.50	3.80
	San Diego Rockets			
☐ 71	Bill Bridges	3.50	1.55	.45
	Atlanta Hawks			
☐ 72	Wes Unseld	10.00	4.50	1.25
	Baltimore Bullets			
☐ 73	Herm Gilliam	2.50	1.15	.30
	Buffalo Braves			
☐ 74	Bobby Smith SP	8.00	3.60	1.00
	Cleveland Cavaliers			
☐ 75	Lew Alcindor	90.00	40.00	11.50
	Milwaukee Bucks			
☐ 76	Jeff Mullins	3.50	1.55	.45
	San Francisco Warriors			
☐ 77	Happy Hairston	3.50	1.55	.45
	Los Angeles Lakers			
☐ 78	Dave Stallworth SP	5.00	2.30	.60
	New York Knicks			
☐ 79	Fred Hetzel	2.50	1.15	.30
	Portland Trail Blazers			
☐ 80	Len Wilkens SP	20.00	9.00	2.50
	Seattle Supersonics			
☐ 81	Johnny Green	4.50	2.00	.55

	Cincinnati Royals				
☐ 82	Erwin Mueller	2.50	1.15	.30
	Detroit Pistons			
☐ 83	Wally Jones	2.50	1.15	.30
	Philadelphia 76ers			
☐ 84	Bob Love	8.00	3.60	1.00
	Chicago Bulls			
☐ 85	Dick Garrett	3.50	1.55	.45
	Buffalo Braves			
☐ 86	Don Nelson SP	18.00	8.00	2.30
	Boston Celtics			
☐ 87	Neal Walk SP	5.00	2.30	.60
	Phoenix Suns			
☐ 88	Larry Siegfried	4.50	2.00	.55
	San Diego Rockets			
☐ 89	Gary Gregor	2.50	1.15	.30
	Portland Trail Blazers			
☐ 90	Nate Thurmond	9.00	4.00	1.15
	San Francisco Warriors			
☐ 91	John Warren	2.50	1.15	.30
	Cleveland Cavaliers			
☐ 92	Gus Johnson	5.00	2.30	.60
	Baltimore Bullets			
☐ 93	Gail Goodrich	8.00	3.60	1.00
	Los Angeles Lakers			
☐ 94	Dorrie Murrey	2.50	1.15	.30
	Portland Trail Blazers			
☐ 95	Cazzie Russell SP	10.00	4.50	1.25
	New York Knicks			
☐ 96	Terry Dischinger	4.50	2.00	.55
	Detroit Pistons			
☐ 97	Norm Van Lier SP	14.00	6.25	1.75
	Cincinnati Royals			
☐ 98	Jim Fox	2.50	1.15	.30
	Chicago Bulls			
☐ 99	Tom Meschery	2.50	1.15	.30
	Seattle Supersonics			
☐ 100	Oscar Robertson	35.00	16.00	4.40
	Milwaukee Bucks			
☐ 101A	Checklist 111-175	30.00	4.50	1.50
	(1970-71 in black)			
☐ 101B	Checklist 111-175	30.00	4.50	1.50
	(1970-71 in white)			
☐ 102	Rich Johnson	2.50	1.15	.30
	Boston Celtics			
☐ 103	Mel Counts	3.00	1.35	.40
	Phoenix Suns			
☐ 104	Bill Hosket SP	7.00	3.10	.85
	Buffalo Braves			
☐ 105	Archie Clark	3.50	1.55	.45
	Philadelphia 76ers			
☐ 106	Walt Frazier AS	12.00	5.50	1.50
	New York Knicks			
☐ 107	Jerry West AS	28.00	12.50	3.50
	Los Angeles Lakers			
☐ 108	Bill Cunningham AS	10.00	4.50	1.25
	Philadelphia 76ers			
☐ 109	Connie Hawkins AS	6.00	2.70	.75
	Phoenix Suns			
☐ 110	Willis Reed AS	10.00	4.50	1.25
	New York Knicks			
☐ 111	Nate Thurmond AS	4.25	1.90	.55
	San Francisco Warriors			
☐ 112	John Havlicek AS	30.00	13.50	3.80
	Boston Celtics			
☐ 113	Elgin Baylor AS	18.00	8.00	2.30
	Los Angeles Lakers			
☐ 114	Oscar Robertson AS	20.00	9.00	2.50
	Milwaukee Bucks			
☐ 115	Lou Hudson AS	4.25	1.90	.55
	Atlanta Hawks			
☐ 116	Emmette Bryant	3.25	1.45	.40
	Buffalo Braves			

☐ 117	Greg Howard	Phoenix Suns	3.25	1.45	.40
☐ 118	Rick Adelman	Portland Trail Blazers	5.00	2.30	.60
☐ 119	Barry Clemens	Seattle Supersonics	3.25	1.45	.40
☐ 120	Walt Frazier	New York Knicks	28.00	12.50	3.50
☐ 121	Jim Barnes	Boston Celtics	5.00	2.30	.60
☐ 122	Bernie Williams	San Diego Rockets	3.25	1.45	.40
☐ 123	Pete Maravich	Atlanta Hawks	180.00	80.00	23.00
☐ 124	Matt Guokas	Philadelphia 76ers	11.00	4.90	1.40
☐ 125	Dave Bing	Detroit Pistons	12.00	5.50	1.50
☐ 126	John Tresvant	Los Angeles Lakers	3.25	1.45	.40
☐ 127	Shaler Halimon	Chicago Bulls	3.25	1.45	.40
☐ 128	Don Ohl	Cleveland Cavaliers	3.25	1.45	.40
☐ 129	Fred Carter	Baltimore Bullets	5.00	2.30	.60
☐ 130	Connie Hawkins	Phoenix Suns	13.00	5.75	1.65
☐ 131	Jim King	Cincinnati Royals	3.25	1.45	.40
☐ 132	Ed Manning	Portland Trail Blazers	6.00	2.70	.75
☐ 133	Adrian Smith	San Francisco Warriors	3.25	1.45	.40
☐ 134	Walt Hazzard	Atlanta Hawks	6.00	2.70	.75
☐ 135	Dave DeBusschere	New York Knicks	16.00	7.25	2.00
☐ 136	Don Kojis	Seattle Supersonics	3.25	1.45	.40
☐ 137	Calvin Murphy	San Diego Rockets	40.00	18.00	5.00
☐ 138	Nate Bowman	Buffalo Braves	3.25	1.45	.40
☐ 139	Jon McGlocklin	Milwaukee Bucks	5.00	2.30	.60
☐ 140	Billy Cunningham	Philadelphia 76ers	16.00	7.25	2.00
☐ 141	Willie McCarter	Los Angeles Lakers	3.25	1.45	.40
☐ 142	Jim Barnett	Portland Trail Blazers	4.00	1.80	.50
☐ 143	JoJo White	Boston Celtics	20.00	9.00	2.50
☐ 144	Clyde Lee	San Francisco Warriors	3.25	1.45	.40
☐ 145	Tom Van Arsdale	Cincinnati Royals	5.00	2.30	.60
☐ 146	Len Chappell	Cleveland Cavaliers	3.25	1.45	.40
☐ 147	Lee Winfield	Seattle Supersonics	3.25	1.45	.40
☐ 148	Jerry Sloan	Chicago Bulls	13.00	5.75	1.65
☐ 149	Art Harris	Phoenix Suns	3.25	1.45	.40
☐ 150	Willis Reed	New York Knicks	18.00	8.00	2.30
☐ 151	Art Williams	San Diego Rockets	3.25	1.45	.40
☐ 152	Don May	Buffalo Braves	3.25	1.45	.40
☐ 153	Loy Petersen		3.25	1.45	.40

		NRMT	VG-E	GOOD
	Cleveland Cavaliers			
□ 154	Dave Gambee	3.25	1.45	.40
	San Francisco Warriors			
□ 155	Hal Greer	6.00	2.70	.75
	Philadelphia 76ers			
□ 156	Dave Newmark	3.25	1.45	.40
	Atlanta Hawks			
□ 157	Jimmy Collins	3.25	1.45	.40
	Chicago Bulls			
□ 158	Bill Turner	3.25	1.45	.40
	Cincinnati Royals			
□ 159	Eddie Miles	3.25	1.45	.40
	Baltimore Bullets			
□ 160	Jerry West	55.00	25.00	7.00
	Los Angeles Lakers			
□ 161	Bob Quick	3.25	1.45	.40
	Detroit Pistons			
□ 162	Fred Crawford	3.25	1.45	.40
	Buffalo Braves			
□ 163	Tom Sanders	5.00	2.30	.60
	Boston Celtics			
□ 164	Dale Schlueter	3.25	1.45	.40
	Portland Trail Blazers			
□ 165	Clem Haskins	8.00	3.60	1.00
	Phoenix Suns			
□ 166	Greg Smith	3.25	1.45	.40
	Milwaukee Bucks			
□ 167	Rod Thorn	9.00	4.00	1.15
	Seattle Supersonics			
□ 168	Playoff Game 1	7.00	3.10	.85
	(Willis Reed)			
□ 169	Playoff Game 2	5.00	2.30	.60
	(Dick Garrett)			
□ 170	Playoff Game 3	7.00	3.10	.85
	(Dave DeBusschere)			
□ 171	Playoff Game 4	15.00	6.75	1.90
	(Jerry West)			
□ 172	Playoff Game 5	14.00	6.25	1.75
	(Bill Bradley)			
□ 173	Playoff Game 6	15.00	6.75	1.90
	(Wilt Chamberlain)			
□ 174	Playoff Game 7	9.00	4.00	1.15
	(Walt Frazier)			
□ 175	Knicks Celebrate	20.00	5.00	1.00
	(New York Knicks, World Champs)			

1971-72 Topps

The 1971-72 Topps basketball set of 233 witnessed a return to the standard-sized card, i.e., 2 1/2" by 3 1/2". National Basketball Association (NBA) players are depicted on cards 1 to 144 and American Basketball Association (ABA) players are depicted on cards 145 to 233. The set was produced on two sheets. The second production sheet contained the ABA players (145-233) as well as 31 double-printed cards (essentially NBA players) from the first sheet. These DP's are indicated in the checklist below. Special subseries within this set include NBA Playoffs (133-137), NBA Statistical Leaders (138-143), and ABA Statistical Leaders (146-151). The key Rookie Cards in this set are Nate Archibald, Rick Barry, Larry Brown, Dave Cowens, Spencer Haywood, Dan Issel, Bob Lanier, Rudy Tomjanovich and Doug Moe.

	NRMT	VG-E	GOOD
COMPLETE SET (233)	800.00	350.00	100.00
COMMON NBA PLAYER (1-144)	1.50	.65	.19
COMMON ABA PLAYER (145-233)	2.00	.90	.25
□ 1 Oscar Robertson	45.00	14.50	2.70
Milwaukee Bucks			
□ 2 Bill Bradley	30.00	13.50	3.80
New York Knicks			

☐ 3 Jim Fox 1.50		.65	.19
Chicago Bulls			
☐ 4 John Johnson 3.00		1.35	.40
Cleveland Cavaliers			
☐ 5 Luke Jackson 1.50		.65	.19
Philadelphia 76ers			
☐ 6 Don May DP 1.00		.45	.13
Atlanta Hawks			
☐ 7 Kevin Loughery 3.50		1.55	.45
Baltimore Bullets			
☐ 8 Terry Dischinger 1.75		.80	.22
Detroit Pistons			
☐ 9 Neal Walk 1.75		.80	.22
Phoenix Suns			
☐ 10 Elgin Baylor 25.00		11.50	3.10
Los Angeles Lakers			
☐ 11 Rick Adelman 2.00		.90	.25
Portland Trail Blazers			
☐ 12 Clyde Lee 1.50		.65	.19
Golden State Warriors			
☐ 13 Jerry Chambers 1.50		.65	.19
Buffalo Braves			
☐ 14 Fred Carter 1.75		.80	.22
Baltimore Bullets			
☐ 15 Tom Boerwinkle DP 1.00		.45	.13
Chicago Bulls			
☐ 16 John Block 1.50		.65	.19
Houston Rockets			
☐ 17 Dick Barnett 2.00		.90	.25
New York Knicks			
☐ 18 Henry Finkel 1.50		.65	.19
Boston Celtics			
☐ 19 Norm Van Lier 4.00		1.80	.50
Cincinnati Royals			
☐ 20 Spencer Haywood 15.00		6.75	1.90
Seattle Supersonics			
☐ 21 George Johnson 1.50		.65	.19
Baltimore Bullets			
☐ 22 Bobby Lewis 1.50		.65	.19
Cleveland Cavaliers			
☐ 23 Bill Hewitt 1.50		.65	.19
Detroit Pistons			
☐ 24 Walt Hazzard DP 3.00		1.35	.40
Buffalo Braves			
☐ 25 Happy Hairston 2.00		.90	.25
Los Angeles Lakers			
☐ 26 George Wilson 1.50		.65	.19
Buffalo Braves			
☐ 27 Lucius Allen 2.00		.90	.25
Milwaukee Bucks			
☐ 28 Jim Washington 1.50		.65	.19
Philadelphia 76ers			

☐ 29	Nate Archibald	35.00	16.00	4.40
	Cincinnati Royals			
☐ 30	Willis Reed	10.00	4.50	1.25
	New York Knicks			
☐ 31	Erwin Mueller	1.50	.65	.19
	Detroit Pistons			
☐ 32	Art Harris	1.50	.65	.19
	Phoenix Suns			
☐ 33	Pete Cross	1.50	.65	.19
	Seattle Supersonics			
☐ 34	Geoff Petrie	6.00	2.70	.75
	Portland Trail Blazers			
☐ 35	John Havlicek	30.00	13.50	3.80
	Boston Celtics			
☐ 36	Larry Siegfried	1.50	.65	.19
	Houston Rockets			
☐ 37	John Tresvant DP	1.00	.45	.13
	Baltimore Bullets			
☐ 38	Ron Williams	1.50	.65	.19
	Golden State Warriors			
☐ 39	Lamar Green DP	1.00	.45	.13
	Phoenix Suns			
☐ 40	Bob Rule DP	1.00	.45	.13
	Seattle Supersonics			
☐ 41	Jim McMillian	3.00	1.35	.40
	Los Angeles Lakers			
☐ 42	Wally Jones	1.50	.65	.19
	Philadelphia 76ers			
☐ 43	Bob Boozer	1.50	.65	.19
	Milwaukee Bucks			
☐ 44	Eddie Miles	1.50	.65	.19
	Baltimore Bullets			
☐ 45	Bob Love DP	3.50	1.55	.45
	Chicago Bulls			
☐ 46	Claude English	1.50	.65	.19
	Portland Trail Blazers			
☐ 47	Dave Cowens	50.00	23.00	6.25
	Boston Celtics			
☐ 48	Emmette Bryant	1.50	.65	.19
	Buffalo Braves			
☐ 49	Dave Stallworth	1.50	.65	.19
	New York Knicks			
☐ 50	Jerry West	40.00	18.00	5.00
	Los Angeles Lakers			
☐ 51	Joe Ellis	1.50	.65	.19
	Golden State Warriors			
☐ 52	Walt Wesley DP	1.00	.45	.13
	Cleveland Cavaliers			
☐ 53	Howie Komives	1.50	.65	.19
	Detroit Pistons			
☐ 54	Paul Silas	4.00	1.80	.50
	Phoenix Suns			
☐ 55	Pete Maravich DP	40.00	18.00	5.00
	Atlanta Hawks			
☐ 56	Gary Gregor	1.50	.65	.19
	Portland Trail Blazers			
☐ 57	Sam Lacey	3.00	1.35	.40
	Cincinnati Royals			
☐ 58	Calvin Murphy DP	6.00	2.70	.75
	Houston Rockets			
☐ 59	Bob Dandridge	2.50	1.15	.30
	Milwaukee Bucks			
☐ 60	Hal Greer	4.00	1.80	.50
	Philadelphia 76ers			
☐ 61	Keith Erickson	2.00	.90	.25
	Los Angeles Lakers			
☐ 62	Joe Cooke	1.50	.65	.19
	Cleveland Cavaliers			
☐ 63	Bob Lanier	40.00	18.00	5.00
	Detroit Pistons			
☐ 64	Don Kojis	1.50	.65	.19
	Seattle Supersonics			
☐ 65	Walt Frazier	15.00	6.75	1.90

	New York Knicks			
☐ 66	Chet Walker DP	3.00	1.35	.40
	Chicago Bulls			
☐ 67	Dick Garrett	1.50	.65	.19
	Buffalo Braves			
☐ 68	John Trapp	1.75	.80	.22
	Houston Rockets			
☐ 69	JoJo White	6.00	2.70	.75
	Boston Celtics			
☐ 70	Wilt Chamberlain	50.00	23.00	6.25
	Los Angeles Lakers			
☐ 71	Dave Sorenson	1.50	.65	.19
	Cleveland Cavaliers			
☐ 72	Jim King	1.50	.65	.19
	Chicago Bulls			
☐ 73	Cazzie Russell	4.00	1.80	.50
	Golden State Warriors			
☐ 74	Jon McGlocklin	1.75	.80	.22
	Milwaukee Bucks			
☐ 75	Tom Van Arsdale	1.75	.80	.22
	Cincinnati Royals			
☐ 76	Dale Schlueter	1.50	.65	.19
	Portland Trail Blazers			
☐ 77	Gus Johnson DP	2.00	.90	.25
	Baltimore Bullets			
☐ 78	Dave Bing	7.00	3.10	.85
	Detroit Pistons			
☐ 79	Billy Cunningham	9.00	4.00	1.15
	Philadelphia 76ers			
☐ 80	Len Wilkens	10.00	4.50	1.25
	Seattle Supersonics			
☐ 81	Jerry Lucas DP	6.50	2.90	.80
	New York Knicks			
☐ 82	Don Chaney	3.50	1.55	.45
	Boston Celtics			
☐ 83	McCoy McLemore	1.50	.65	.19
	Milwaukee Bucks			
☐ 84	Bob Kauffman DP	1.00	.45	.13
	Buffalo Braves			
☐ 85	Dick Van Arsdale	1.75	.80	.22
	Phoenix Suns			
☐ 86	Johnny Green	1.50	.65	.19
	Cincinnati Royals			
☐ 87	Jerry Sloan	5.00	2.30	.60
	Chicago Bulls			
☐ 88	Luther Rackley DP	1.00	.45	.13
	Cleveland Cavaliers			
☐ 89	Shaler Halimon	1.50	.65	.19
	Portland Trail Blazers			
☐ 90	Jimmy Walker	1.50	.65	.19
	Detroit Pistons			
☐ 91	Rudy Tomjanovich	25.00	11.50	3.10
	Houston Rockets			
☐ 92	Levi Fontaine	1.50	.65	.19
	Golden State Warriors			
☐ 93	Bobby Smith	1.75	.80	.22
	Cleveland Cavaliers			
☐ 94	Bob Arnzen	1.50	.65	.19
	Cincinnati Royals			
☐ 95	Wes Unseld DP	6.00	2.70	.75
	Baltimore Bullets			
☐ 96	Clem Haskins DP	1.75	.80	.22
	Phoenix Suns			
☐ 97	Jim Davis	1.50	.65	.19
	Atlanta Hawks			
☐ 98	Steve Kuberski	1.75	.80	.22
	Boston Celtics			
☐ 99	Mike Davis DP	1.00	.45	.13
	Buffalo Braves			
☐ 100	Lew Alcindor	50.00	23.00	6.25
	Milwaukee Bucks			
☐ 101	Willie McCarter	1.50	.65	.19
	Los Angeles Lakers			

☐ 102	Charlie Paulk Chicago Bulls	1.50	.65	.19
☐ 103	Lee Winfield Seattle Supersonics	1.50	.65	.19
☐ 104	Jim Barnett Golden State Warriors	1.50	.65	.19
☐ 105	Connie Hawkins DP Phoenix Suns	6.00	2.70	.75
☐ 106	Archie Clark DP Philadelphia 76ers	1.75	.80	.22
☐ 107	Dave DeBusschere New York Knicks	9.00	4.00	1.15
☐ 108	Stu Lantz DP Houston Rockets	1.25	.55	.16
☐ 109	Don Smith Seattle Supersonics	1.50	.65	.19
☐ 110	Lou Hudson Atlanta Hawks	2.50	1.15	.30
☐ 111	Leroy Ellis Portland Trail Blazers	1.75	.80	.22
☐ 112	Jack Marin Baltimore Bullets	2.00	.90	.25
☐ 113	Matt Guokas Cincinnati Royals	3.50	1.55	.45
☐ 114	Don Nelson Boston Celtics	7.00	3.10	.85
☐ 115	Jeff Mullins DP Golden State Warriors	1.75	.80	.22
☐ 116	Walt Bellamy Atlanta Hawks	4.00	1.80	.50
☐ 117	Bob Quick Detroit Pistons	1.50	.65	.19
☐ 118	John Warren Cleveland Cavaliers	1.50	.65	.19
☐ 119	Barry Clemens Seattle Supersonics	1.50	.65	.19
☐ 120	Elvin Hayes DP Houston Rockets	12.00	5.50	1.50
☐ 121	Gail Goodrich Los Angeles Lakers	6.00	2.70	.75
☐ 122	Ed Manning Portland Trail Blazers	1.75	.80	.22
☐ 123	Herm Gilliam DP Atlanta Hawks	1.00	.45	.13
☐ 124	Dennis Awtrey Philadelphia 76ers	2.00	.90	.25
☐ 125	John Hummer DP Buffalo Braves	1.00	.45	.13
☐ 126	Mike Riordan New York Knicks	1.75	.80	.22
☐ 127	Mel Counts Phoenix Suns	1.50	.65	.19
☐ 128	Bob Weiss DP Chicago Bulls	1.75	.80	.22
☐ 129	Greg Smith DP Milwaukee Bucks	1.00	.45	.13
☐ 130	Earl Monroe Baltimore Bullets	10.00	4.50	1.25
☐ 131	Nate Thurmond DP Golden State Warriors	5.00	2.30	.60
☐ 132	Bill Bridges DP Atlanta Hawks	1.75	.80	.22
☐ 133	NBA Playoffs G1 Alcindor scores 31	11.00	4.90	1.40
☐ 134	NBA Playoffs G2 Bucks make it Two Straight	3.00	1.35	.40
☐ 135	NBA Playoffs G3 Dandridge makes It Three in a Row	3.00	1.35	.40
☐ 136	NBA Playoffs G4 A Clean Sweep (Oscar Robertson)	7.00	3.10	.85

☐ 137	NBA Champs Celebrate	3.50	1.55	.45
	Bucks sweep Bullets			
☐ 138	NBA Scoring Leaders	14.00	6.25	1.75
	Lew Alcindor			
	Elvin Hayes			
	John Havlicek			
☐ 139	NBA Scoring Average	14.00	6.25	1.75
	Leaders			
	Lew Alcindor			
	John Havlicek			
	Elvin Hayes			
☐ 140	NBA FG Pct Leaders	12.00	5.50	1.50
	Johnny Green			
	Lew Alcindor			
	Wilt Chamberlain			
☐ 141	NBA FT Pct Leaders	3.00	1.35	.40
	Chet Walker			
	Oscar Robertson			
	Ron Williams			
☐ 142	NBA Rebound Leaders	22.00	10.00	2.80
	Wilt Chamberlain			
	Elvin Hayes			
	Lew Alcindor			
☐ 143	NBA Assist Leaders	8.00	3.60	1.00
	Norm Van Lier			
	Oscar Robertson			
	Jerry West			
☐ 144A	NBA Checklist 1-144	18.00	2.30	.45
	(Copyright notation			
	extends up to			
	card 110)			
☐ 144B	NBA Checklist 1-144	18.00	2.30	.45
	(Copyright notation			
	extends up to			
	card 108)			
☐ 145	ABA Checklist 145-233	18.00	2.30	.45
☐ 146	ABA Scoring Leaders	6.00	2.70	.75
	Dan Issel			
	John Brisker			
	Charlie Scott			
☐ 147	ABA Scoring Average	12.00	5.50	1.50
	Leaders			
	Dan Issel			
	Rick Barry			
	John Brisker			
☐ 148	ABA 2pt FG Pct Leaders	4.00	1.80	.50
	Zelmo Beaty			
	Bill Paultz			
	Roger Brown			
☐ 149	ABA FT Pct Leaders	9.00	4.00	1.15
	Rick Barry			
	Darrell Carrier			
	Billy Keller			
☐ 150	ABA Rebound Leaders	4.00	1.80	.50
	Mel Daniels			
	Julius Keye			
	Mike Lewis			
☐ 151	ABA Assist Leaders	4.00	1.80	.50
	Bill Melchionni			
	Mack Calvin			
	Charlie Scott			
☐ 152	Larry Brown	25.00	11.50	3.10
	Denver Rockets			
☐ 153	Bob Bedell	2.00	.90	.25
	Dallas Chaparrals			
☐ 154	Merv Jackson	2.00	.90	.25
	Utah Stars			
☐ 155	Joe Caldwell	3.00	1.35	.40
	Carolina Cougars			
☐ 156	Billy Paultz	4.00	1.80	.50
	New York Nets			
☐ 157	Les Hunter	2.00	.90	.25
	Kentucky Colonels			

☐ 158 Charlie Williams	2.00	.90	.25
Memphis Pros			
☐ 159 Stew Johnson	2.00	.90	.25
Pittsburgh Condors			
☐ 160 Mack Calvin	5.00	2.30	.60
Florida Floridians			
☐ 161 Don Sidle	2.00	.90	.25
Indiana Pacers			
☐ 162 Mike Barrett	2.00	.90	.25
Virginia Squires			
☐ 163 Tom Workman	2.00	.90	.25
Denver Rockets			
☐ 164 Joe Hamilton	2.00	.90	.25
Dallas Chaparrals			
☐ 165 Zelmo Beaty	7.00	3.10	.85
Utah Stars			
☐ 166 Dan Hester	2.00	.90	.25
Kentucky Colonels			
☐ 167 Bob Verga	2.00	.90	.25
Carolina Cougars			
☐ 168 Wilbert Jones	2.00	.90	.25
Memphis Pros			
☐ 169 Skeeter Swift	2.00	.90	.25
Pittsburgh Condors			
☐ 170 Rick Barry	60.00	27.00	7.50
New York Nets			
☐ 171 Billy Keller	4.00	1.80	.50
Indiana Pacers			
☐ 172 Ron Franz	2.00	.90	.25
Florida Floridians			
☐ 173 Roland Taylor	2.50	1.15	.30
Virginia Squires			
☐ 174 Julian Hammond	2.00	.90	.25
Denver Rockets			
☐ 175 Steve Jones	5.00	2.30	.60
Dallas Chaparrals			
☐ 176 Gerald Govan	2.00	.90	.25
Memphis Pros			
☐ 177 Darrell Carrier	3.00	1.35	.40
Kentucky Colonels			
☐ 178 Ron Boone	4.00	1.80	.50
Utah Stars			
☐ 179 George Peeples	2.00	.90	.25
Carolina Cougars			
☐ 180 John Brisker	2.00	.90	.25
Pittsburgh Condors			
☐ 181 Doug Moe	12.00	5.50	1.50
Virginia Squires			
☐ 182 Ollie Taylor	2.00	.90	.25
New York Nets			
☐ 183 Bob Netolicky	2.50	1.15	.30
Indiana Pacers			
☐ 184 Sam Robinson	2.00	.90	.25
Florida Floridians			
☐ 185 James Jones	2.00	.90	.25
Memphis Pros			
☐ 186 Julius Keye	2.00	.90	.25
Denver Rockets			
☐ 187 Wayne Hightower	2.00	.90	.25
Dallas Chaparrals			
☐ 188 Warren Armstrong	2.50	1.15	.30
Indiana Pacers			
☐ 189 Mike Lewis	2.00	.90	.25
Pittsburgh Condors			
☐ 190 Charlie Scott	8.00	3.60	1.00
Virginia Squires			
☐ 191 Jim Ard	2.00	.90	.25
New York Nets			
☐ 192 George Lehmann	2.00	.90	.25
Carolina Cougars			
☐ 193 Ira Harge	2.00	.90	.25
Florida Floridians			
☐ 194 Willie Wise	5.00	2.30	.60

	#	Player			
		Utah Stars			
☐	195	Mel Daniels	9.00	4.00	1.15
		Indiana Pacers			
☐	196	Larry Cannon	2.00	.90	.25
		Denver Rockets			
☐	197	Jim Eakins	2.00	.90	.25
		Virginia Squires			
☐	198	Rich Jones	2.00	.90	.25
		Dallas Chaparrals			
☐	199	Bill Melchionni	4.00	1.80	.50
		New York Nets			
☐	200	Dan Issel	50.00	23.00	6.25
		Kentucky Colonels			
☐	201	George Stone	2.00	.90	.25
		Utah Stars			
☐	202	George Thompson	2.00	.90	.25
		Pittsburgh Condors			
☐	203	Craig Raymond	2.00	.90	.25
		Memphis Pros			
☐	204	Freddie Lewis	3.00	1.35	.40
		Indiana Pacers			
☐	205	George Carter	2.00	.90	.25
		Virginia Squires			
☐	206	Lonnie Wright	2.00	.90	.25
		Florida Floridians			
☐	207	Cincy Powell	2.00	.90	.25
		Kentucky Colonels			
☐	208	Larry Miller	2.00	.90	.25
		Carolina Cougars			
☐	209	Sonny Dove	2.00	.90	.25
		New York Nets			
☐	210	Byron Beck	2.50	1.15	.30
		Denver Rockets			
☐	211	John Beasley	2.00	.90	.25
		Dallas Chaparrals			
☐	212	Lee Davis	2.00	.90	.25
		Memphis Pros			
☐	213	Rick Mount	8.00	3.60	1.00
		Indiana Pacers			
☐	214	Walt Simon	2.00	.90	.25
		Kentucky Colonels			
☐	215	Glen Combs	2.00	.90	.25
		Utah Stars			
☐	216	Neil Johnson	2.00	.90	.25
		Virginia Squires			
☐	217	Manny Leaks	2.00	.90	.25
		New York Nets			
☐	218	Chuck Williams	2.00	.90	.25
		Pittsburgh Condors			
☐	219	Warren Davis	2.00	.90	.25
		Florida Floridians			
☐	220	Donnie Freeman	4.00	1.80	.50
		Dallas Chaparrals			
☐	221	Randy Mahaffey	2.00	.90	.25
		Carolina Cougars			
☐	222	John Barnhill	2.00	.90	.25
		Denver Rockets			
☐	223	Al Cueto	2.00	.90	.25
		Memphis Pros			
☐	224	Louie Dampier	8.00	3.60	1.00
		Kentucky Colonels			
☐	225	Roger Brown	4.00	1.80	.50
		Indiana Pacers			
☐	226	Joe DePre	2.00	.90	.25
		New York Nets			
☐	227	Ray Scott	2.00	.90	.25
		Virginia Squires			
☐	228	Arvesta Kelly	2.00	.90	.25
		Pittsburgh Condors			
☐	229	Vann Williford	2.00	.90	.25
		Carolina Cougars			
☐	230	Larry Jones	2.25	1.00	.30
		Florida Floridians			

			NRMT	VG-E	GOOD
☐	231	Gene Moore	2.00	.90	.25
		Dallas Chaparrals			
☐	232	Ralph Simpson	4.00	1.80	.50
		Denver Rockets			
☐	233	Red Robbins	3.00	.90	.25
		Utah Stars			

1972-73 Topps

The 1972-73 Topps set of 264 cards contains NBA players (1-176) and ABA players (177-264). The cards in the set measure standard size, 2 1/2" by 3 1/2". All-Star selections are depicted for the NBA on cards numbered 161 to 170 and for the ABA on cards numbered 249 to 258. Special subseries within this set include NBA Playoffs (154-159), NBA Statistical Leaders (171-176), ABA Playoffs (241-247), and ABA Statistical Leaders (259-264). The key Rookie Cards in this set are Julius Erving, Artis Gilmore, and Phil Jackson.

			NRMT	VG-E	GOOD
	COMPLETE SET (264)		800.00	350.00	100.00
	COMMON NBA PLAYER (1-176)		1.25	.55	.16
	COMMON ABA PLAYER (177-264)		1.50	.65	.19
☐	1	Wilt Chamberlain	40.00	12.50	2.50
		Los Angeles Lakers			
☐	2	Stan Love	1.25	.55	.16
		Baltimore Bullets			
☐	3	Geoff Petrie	2.00	.90	.25
		Portland Trail Blazers			
☐	4	Curtis Perry	2.00	.90	.25
		Milwaukee Bucks			
☐	5	Pete Maravich	35.00	16.00	4.40
		Atlanta Hawks			
☐	6	Gus Johnson	2.00	.90	.25
		Phoenix Suns			
☐	7	Dave Cowens	15.00	6.75	1.90
		Boston Celtics			
☐	8	Randy Smith	3.50	1.55	.45
		Buffalo Braves			
☐	9	Matt Guokas	2.50	1.15	.30
		Kansas City-Omaha Kings			
☐	10	Spencer Haywood	3.50	1.55	.45
		Seattle Supersonics			
☐	11	Jerry Sloan	3.50	1.55	.45
		Chicago Bulls			
☐	12	Dave Sorenson	1.25	.55	.16
		Cleveland Cavaliers			
☐	13	Howie Komives	1.25	.55	.16
		Detroit Pistons			
☐	14	Joe Ellis	1.25	.55	.16

	Golden State Warriors			
☐ 15	Jerry Lucas	6.00	2.70	.75
	New York Knicks			
☐ 16	Stu Lantz	1.50	.65	.19
	Detroit Pistons			
☐ 17	Bill Bridges	1.50	.65	.19
	Philadelphia 76ers			
☐ 18	Leroy Ellis	1.50	.65	.19
	Los Angeles Lakers			
☐ 19	Art Williams	1.25	.55	.16
	Boston Celtics			
☐ 20	Sidney Wicks	10.00	4.50	1.25
	Portland Trail Blazers			
☐ 21	Wes Unseld	6.00	2.70	.75
	Baltimore Bullets			
☐ 22	Jim Washington	1.25	.55	.16
	Atlanta Hawks			
☐ 23	Fred Hilton	1.25	.55	.16
	Buffalo Braves			
☐ 24	Curtis Rowe	3.00	1.35	.40
	Detroit Pistons			
☐ 25	Oscar Robertson	20.00	9.00	2.50
	Milwaukee Bucks			
☐ 26	Larry Steele	2.00	.90	.25
	Portland Trail Blazers			
☐ 27	Charlie Davis	1.25	.55	.16
	Cleveland Cavaliers			
☐ 28	Nate Thurmond	4.50	2.00	.55
	Golden State Warriors			
☐ 29	Fred Carter	1.50	.65	.19
	Philadelphia 76ers			
☐ 30	Connie Hawkins	5.00	2.30	.60
	Phoenix Suns			
☐ 31	Calvin Murphy	4.50	2.00	.55
	Houston Rockets			
☐ 32	Phil Jackson	25.00	11.50	3.10
	New York Knicks			
☐ 33	Lee Winfield	1.25	.55	.16
	Seattle Supersonics			
☐ 34	Jim Fox	1.25	.55	.16
	Seattle Supersonics			
☐ 35	Dave Bing	6.00	2.70	.75
	Detroit Pistons			
☐ 36	Gary Gregor	1.25	.55	.16
	Portland Trail Blazers			
☐ 37	Mike Riordan	1.50	.65	.19
	Baltimore Bullets			
☐ 38	George Trapp	1.25	.55	.16
	Atlanta Hawks			
☐ 39	Mike Davis	1.25	.55	.16
	Buffalo Braves			
☐ 40	Bob Rule	1.25	.55	.16
	Philadelphia 76ers			
☐ 41	John Block	1.25	.55	.16
	Philadelphia 76ers			
☐ 42	Bob Dandridge	2.00	.90	.25
	Milwaukee Bucks			
☐ 43	John Johnson	1.50	.65	.19
	Cleveland Cavaliers			
☐ 44	Rick Barry	18.00	8.00	2.30
	Golden State Warriors			
☐ 45	JoJo White	3.50	1.55	.45
	Boston Celtics			
☐ 46	Cliff Meely	1.25	.55	.16
	Houston Rockets			
☐ 47	Charlie Scott	2.00	.90	.25
	Phoenix Suns			
☐ 48	Johnny Green	1.25	.55	.16
	Kansas City-Omaha Kings			
☐ 49	Pete Cross	1.25	.55	.16
	Kansas City-Omaha Kings			
☐ 50	Gail Goodrich	4.00	1.80	.50
	Los Angeles Lakers			

☐ 51 Jim Davis	1.25	.55	.16
Detroit Pistons			
☐ 52 Dick Barnett	1.50	.65	.19
New York Knicks			
☐ 53 Bob Christian	1.25	.55	.16
Atlanta Hawks			
☐ 54 Jon McGlocklin	1.50	.65	.19
Milwaukee Bucks			
☐ 55 Paul Silas	2.00	.90	.25
Boston Celtics			
☐ 56 Hal Greer	3.50	1.55	.45
Philadelphia 76ers			
☐ 57 Barry Clemens	1.25	.55	.16
Seattle Supersonics			
☐ 58 Nick Jones	1.25	.55	.16
Golden State Warriors			
☐ 59 Cornell Warner	1.25	.55	.16
Buffalo Braves			
☐ 60 Walt Frazier	10.00	4.50	1.25
New York Knicks			
☐ 61 Dorrie Murray	1.25	.55	.16
Baltimore Bullets			
☐ 62 Dick Cunningham	1.25	.55	.16
Houston Rockets			
☐ 63 Sam Lacey	1.50	.65	.19
Kansas City-Omaha Kings			
☐ 64 John Warren	1.25	.55	.16
Cleveland Cavaliers			
☐ 65 Tom Boerwinkle	1.50	.65	.19
Chicago Bulls			
☐ 66 Fred Foster	1.25	.55	.16
Detroit Pistons			
☐ 67 Mel Counts	1.25	.55	.16
Phoenix Suns			
☐ 68 Toby Kimball	1.25	.55	.16
Milwaukee Bucks			
☐ 69 Dale Schlueter	1.25	.55	.16
Portland Trail Blazers			
☐ 70 Jack Marin	1.50	.65	.19
Houston Rockets			
☐ 71 Jim Barnett	1.25	.55	.16
Golden State Warriors			
☐ 72 Clem Haskins	2.00	.90	.25
Phoenix Suns			
☐ 73 Earl Monroe	6.00	2.70	.75
New York Knicks			
☐ 74 Tom Sanders	1.25	.55	.16
Boston Celtics			
☐ 75 Jerry West	25.00	11.50	3.10
Los Angeles Lakers			
☐ 76 Elmore Smith	2.00	.90	.25
Buffalo Braves			
☐ 77 Don Adams	1.25	.55	.16
Atlanta Hawks			
☐ 78 Wally Jones	1.25	.55	.16
Milwaukee Bucks			
☐ 79 Tom Van Arsdale	1.50	.65	.19
Kansas City-Omaha Kings			
☐ 80 Bob Lanier	12.00	5.50	1.50
Detroit Pistons			
☐ 81 Len Wilkens	6.00	2.70	.75
Seattle Supersonics			
☐ 82 Neal Walk	1.50	.65	.19
Phoenix Suns			
☐ 83 Kevin Loughery	2.50	1.15	.30
Philadelphia 76ers			
☐ 84 Stan McKenzie	1.25	.55	.16
Portland Trail Blazers			
☐ 85 Jeff Mullins	1.50	.65	.19
Golden State Warriors			
☐ 86 Otto Moore	1.25	.55	.16
Houston Rockets			
☐ 87 John Tresvant	1.25	.55	.16

	Baltimore Bullets		
☐ 88	Dean Meminger	.90	.25
	New York Knicks		2.00
☐ 89	Jim McMillian	.65	.19
	Los Angeles Lakers		1.50
☐ 90	Austin Carr	3.10	.85
	Cleveland Cavaliers		7.00
☐ 91	Clifford Ray	1.15	.30
	Chicago Bulls		2.50
☐ 92	Don Nelson	2.70	.75
	Boston Celtics		6.00
☐ 93	Mahdi Abdul-Rahman	.90	.25
	Buffalo Braves		2.00
	(formerly Walt Hazzard)		
☐ 94	Willie Norwood	.55	.16
	Detroit Pistons		1.25
☐ 95	Dick Van Arsdale	.65	.19
	Phoenix Suns		1.50
☐ 96	Don May	.55	.16
	Atlanta Hawks		1.25
☐ 97	Walt Bellamy	1.55	.45
	Atlanta Hawks		3.50
☐ 98	Garfield Heard	1.80	.50
	Seattle Supersonics		4.00
☐ 99	Dave Wohl	.55	.16
	Philadelphia 76ers		1.25
☐ 100	Kareem Abdul-Jabbar	16.00	4.40
	Milwaukee Bucks		35.00
☐ 101	Ron Knight	.55	.16
	Portland Trail Blazers		1.25
☐ 102	Phil Chenier	2.00	.55
	Baltimore Bullets		4.50
☐ 103	Rudy Tomjanovich	4.50	1.25
	Houston Rockets		10.00
☐ 104	Flynn Robinson	.55	.16
	Los Angeles Lakers		1.25
☐ 105	Dave DeBusschere	3.10	.85
	New York Knicks		7.00
☐ 106	Dennis Layton	.55	.16
	Phoenix Suns		1.25
☐ 107	Bill Hewitt	.55	.16
	Detroit Pistons		1.25
☐ 108	Dick Garrett	.55	.16
	Buffalo Braves		1.25
☐ 109	Walt Wesley	.55	.16
	Cleveland Cavaliers		1.25
☐ 110	John Havlicek	11.50	3.10
	Boston Celtics		25.00
☐ 111	Norm Van Lier	.90	.25
	Chicago Bulls		2.00
☐ 112	Cazzie Russell	1.15	.30
	Golden State Warriors		2.50
☐ 113	Herm Gilliam	.55	.16
	Atlanta Hawks		1.25
☐ 114	Greg Smith	.55	.16
	Houston Rockets		1.25
☐ 115	Nate Archibald	3.60	1.00
	Kansas City-Omaha Kings		8.00
☐ 116	Don Kojis	.55	.16
	Kansas City-Omaha Kings		1.25
☐ 117	Rick Adelman	.90	.25
	Portland Trail Blazers		2.00
☐ 118	Luke Jackson	.55	.16
	Philadelphia 76ers		1.25
☐ 119	Lamar Green	.55	.16
	Phoenix Suns		1.25
☐ 120	Archie Clark	.65	.19
	Baltimore Bullets		1.50
☐ 121	Happy Hairston	.65	.19
	Los Angeles Lakers		1.50
☐ 122	Bill Bradley	9.00	2.50
	New York Knicks		20.00
☐ 123	Ron Williams	.55	.16
	Golden State Warriors		1.25

☐ 124	Jimmy Walker	1.25	.55	.16
	Houston Rockets			
☐ 125	Bob Kauffman	1.25	.55	.16
	Buffalo Braves			
☐ 126	Rick Roberson	1.25	.55	.16
	Cleveland Cavaliers			
☐ 127	Howard Porter	2.50	1.15	.30
	Chicago Bulls			
☐ 128	Mike Newlin	2.00	.90	.25
	Houston Rockets			
☐ 129	Willis Reed	8.00	3.60	1.00
	New York Knicks			
☐ 130	Lou Hudson	2.00	.90	.25
	Atlanta Hawks			
☐ 131	Don Chaney	2.00	.90	.25
	Boston Celtics			
☐ 132	Dave Stallworth	1.25	.55	.16
	Baltimore Bullets			
☐ 133	Charlie Yelverton	1.25	.55	.16
	Portland Trail Blazers			
☐ 134	Ken Durrett	1.25	.55	.16
	Kansas City-Omaha Kings			
☐ 135	John Brisker	1.25	.55	.16
	Seattle Supersonics			
☐ 136	Dick Snyder	1.25	.55	.16
	Seattle Supersonics			
☐ 137	Jim McDaniels	1.25	.55	.16
	Seattle Supersonics			
☐ 138	Clyde Lee	1.25	.55	.16
	Golden State Warriors			
☐ 139	Dennis Awtrey UER	1.50	.65	.19
	Philadelphia 76ers			
	(Misspelled Awtry			
	on card front)			
☐ 140	Keith Erickson	2.00	.90	.25
	Los Angeles Lakers			
☐ 141	Bob Weiss	2.00	.90	.25
	Chicago Bulls			
☐ 142	Butch Beard	3.00	1.35	.40
	Cleveland Cavaliers			
☐ 143	Terry Dischinger	1.50	.65	.19
	Portland Trail Blazers			
☐ 144	Pat Riley	15.00	6.75	1.90
	Los Angeles Lakers			
☐ 145	Lucius Allen	2.00	.90	.25
	Milwaukee Bucks			
☐ 146	John Mengelt	2.00	.90	.25
	Kansas City-Omaha Kings			
☐ 147	John Hummer	1.25	.55	.16
	Buffalo Braves			
☐ 148	Bob Love	4.00	1.80	.50
	Chicago Bulls			
☐ 149	Bobby Smith	1.50	.65	.19
	Cleveland Cavaliers			
☐ 150	Elvin Hayes	12.00	5.50	1.50
	Baltimore Bullets			
☐ 151	Nate Williams	1.25	.55	.16
	Kansas City-Omaha Kings			
☐ 152	Chet Walker	3.50	1.55	.45
	Chicago Bulls			
☐ 153	Steve Kuberski	1.50	.65	.19
	Boston Celtics			
☐ 154	NBA Playoffs G1	3.00	1.35	.40
	Knicks win Opener			
	(Earl Monroe)			
☐ 155	NBA Playoffs G2	2.50	1.15	.30
	Lakers Come Back			
	(under the basket)			
☐ 156	NBA Playoffs G3	2.50	1.15	.30
	Two in a Row			
	(under the basket)			
☐ 157	NBA Playoffs G4	2.50	1.15	.30
	Ellis provides			

bench strength
- [ ] 158 NBA Playoffs G5.................................... 7.00 — 3.10 — .85
  Jerry drives in
  (Jerry West)
- [ ] 159 NBA Champs-Lakers................................ 8.00 — 3.60 — 1.00
  (Wilt rebounding)
- [ ] 160 NBA Checklist 1-176............................... 16.00 — 1.90 — .50
  UER (135 Jim King)
- [ ] 161 John Havlicek AS................................... 12.00 — 5.50 — 1.50
  Boston Celtics
- [ ] 162 Spencer Haywood AS............................. 2.00 — .90 — .25
  Seattle Supersonics
- [ ] 163 Kareem Abdul-Jabbar AS...................... 20.00 — 9.00 — 2.50
  Milwaukee Bucks
- [ ] 164 Jerry West AS...................................... 15.00 — 6.75 — 1.90
  Los Angeles Lakers
- [ ] 165 Walt Frazier AS................................... 4.50 — 2.00 — .55
  New York Knicks
- [ ] 166 Bob Love AS... 2.00 — .90 — .25
  Chicago Bulls
- [ ] 167 Billy Cunningham AS............................ 3.50 — 1.55 — .45
  Philadelphia 76ers
- [ ] 168 Wilt Chamberlain AS............................ 20.00 — 9.00 — 2.50
  Los Angeles Lakers
- [ ] 169 Nate Archibald AS............................... 4.50 — 2.00 — .55
  Kansas City-Omaha Kings
- [ ] 170 Archie Clark AS................................... 1.75 — .80 — .22
  Baltimore Bullets
- [ ] 171 NBA Scoring Leaders........................... 10.00 — 4.50 — 1.25
  Kareem Abdul-Jabbar
  John Havlicek
  Nate Archibald
- [ ] 172 NBA Scoring Average.......................... 10.00 — 4.50 — 1.25
  Leaders
  Kareem Abdul-Jabbar
  Nate Archibald
  John Havlicek
- [ ] 173 NBA FG Pct Leaders............................ 12.00 — 5.50 — 1.50
  Wilt Chamberlain
  Kareem Abdul-Jabbar
  Walt Bellamy
- [ ] 174 NBA FT Pct Leaders............................ 2.50 — 1.15 — .30
  Jack Marin
  Calvin Murphy
  Gail Goodrich
- [ ] 175 NBA Rebound Leaders......................... 14.00 — 6.25 — 1.75
  Wilt Chamberlain
  Kareem Abdul-Jabbar
  Wes Unseld
- [ ] 176 NBA Assist Leaders............................ 8.00 — 3.60 — 1.00
  Len Wilkens
  Jerry West
  Nate Archibald
- [ ] 177 Roland Taylor...................................... 1.50 — .65 — .19
  Virginia Squires
- [ ] 178 Art Becker.. 1.50 — .65 — .19
  San Diego Conquistadors
- [ ] 179 Mack Calvin... 2.50 — 1.15 — .30
  Carolina Cougars
- [ ] 180 Artis Gilmore....................................... 35.00 — 16.00 — 4.40
  Kentucky Colonels
- [ ] 181 Collis Jones.. 1.50 — .65 — .19
  Dallas Chaparrals
- [ ] 182 John Roche... 2.50 — 1.15 — .30
  New York Nets
- [ ] 183 George McGinnis.................................. 14.00 — 6.25 — 1.75
  Indiana Pacers
- [ ] 184 Johnny Neumann................................. 1.75 — .80 — .22
  Memphis Tams
- [ ] 185 Willie Wise.. 2.00 — .90 — .25
  Utah Stars
- [ ] 186 Bernie Williams.................................... 1.50 — .65 — .19
  Virginia Squires

☐ 187	Byron Beck	1.75	.80	.22
	Denver Rockets			
☐ 188	Larry Miller	1.50	.65	.19
	San Diego Conquistadors			
☐ 189	Cincy Powell	1.50	.65	.19
	Kentucky Colonels			
☐ 190	Donnie Freeman	1.75	.80	.22
	Dallas Chaparrals			
☐ 191	John Baum	1.50	.65	.19
	New York Nets			
☐ 192	Billy Keller	2.00	.90	.25
	Indiana Pacers			
☐ 193	Wilbert Jones	1.50	.65	.19
	Memphis Tams			
☐ 194	Glen Combs	1.50	.65	.19
	Utah Stars			
☐ 195	Julius Erving	300.00	135.00	38.00
	Virginia Squires (Forward on front, but Center on back)			
☐ 196	Al Smith	1.50	.65	.19
	Denver Rockets			
☐ 197	George Carter	1.50	.65	.19
	New York Nets			
☐ 198	Louie Dampier	2.50	1.15	.30
	Kentucky Colonels			
☐ 199	Rich Jones	1.50	.65	.19
	Dallas Chaparrals			
☐ 200	Mel Daniels	4.00	1.80	.50
	Indiana Pacers			
☐ 201	Gene Moore	1.50	.65	.19
	San Diego Conquistadors			
☐ 202	Randy Denton	1.50	.65	.19
	Memphis Tams			
☐ 203	Larry Jones	1.75	.80	.22
	Utah Stars			
☐ 204	Jim Ligon	1.50	.65	.19
	Virginia Squires			
☐ 205	Warren Jabali	1.50	.65	.19
	Denver Rockets			
☐ 206	Joe Caldwell	1.50	.65	.19
	Carolina Cougars			
☐ 207	Darrell Carrier	1.75	.80	.22
	Kentucky Colonels			
☐ 208	Gene Kennedy	1.50	.65	.19
	Dallas Chaparrals			
☐ 209	Ollie Taylor	1.50	.65	.19
	San Diego Conquistadors			
☐ 210	Roger Brown	2.00	.90	.25
	Indiana Pacers			
☐ 211	George Lehmann	1.50	.65	.19
	Memphis Tams			
☐ 212	Red Robbins	1.50	.65	.19
	San Diego Conquistadors			
☐ 213	Jim Eakins	1.50	.65	.19
	Virginia Squires			
☐ 214	Willie Long	1.50	.65	.19
	Denver Rockets			
☐ 215	Billy Cunningham	7.00	3.10	.85
	Carolina Cougars			
☐ 216	Steve Jones	2.50	1.15	.30
	Dallas Chaparrals			
☐ 217	Les Hunter	1.50	.65	.19
	San Diego Conquistadors			
☐ 218	Billy Paultz	2.00	.90	.25
	New York Nets			
☐ 219	Freddie Lewis	2.00	.90	.25
	Indiana Pacers			
☐ 220	Zelmo Beaty	2.50	1.15	.30
	Utah Stars			
☐ 221	George Thompson	1.50	.65	.19
	Memphis Tams			
☐ 222	Neil Johnson	1.50	.65	.19

	Virginia Squires			
☐ 223	Dave Robisch	3.00	1.35	.40
	Denver Rockets			
☐ 224	Walt Simon	1.50	.65	.19
	Kentucky Colonels			
☐ 225	Bill Melchionni	1.75	.80	.22
	New York Nets			
☐ 226	Wendell Ladner	2.50	1.15	.30
	Memphis Tams			
☐ 227	Joe Hamilton	1.50	.65	.19
	Dallas Chaparrals			
☐ 228	Bob Netolicky	1.50	.65	.19
	Dallas Chaparrals			
☐ 229	James Jones	1.75	.80	.22
	Utah Stars			
☐ 230	Dan Issel	15.00	6.75	1.90
	Kentucky Colonels			
☐ 231	Charlie Williams	1.50	.65	.19
	San Diego Conquistadors			
☐ 232	Willie Sojourner	1.50	.65	.19
	Virginia Squires			
☐ 233	Merv Jackson	1.50	.65	.19
	Utah Stars			
☐ 234	Mike Lewis	1.50	.65	.19
	Carolina Cougars			
☐ 235	Ralph Simpson	2.00	.90	.25
	Denver Rockets			
☐ 236	Darnell Hillman	1.75	.80	.22
	Indiana Pacers			
☐ 237	Rick Mount	4.00	1.80	.50
	Kentucky Colonels			
☐ 238	Gerald Govan	1.50	.65	.19
	Memphis Tams			
☐ 239	Ron Boone	2.00	.90	.25
	Utah Stars			
☐ 240	Tom Washington	1.50	.65	.19
	New York Nets			
☐ 241	ABA Playoffs G1	2.50	1.15	.30
	Pacers take lead			
	(under the basket)			
☐ 242	ABA Playoffs G2	4.50	2.00	.55
	Barry evens things			
☐ 243	ABA Playoffs G3	4.00	1.80	.50
	McGinnis blocks			
	a jumper			
☐ 244	ABA Playoffs G4	4.50	2.00	.55
	Rick (Barry) scores			
	on fast break			
☐ 245	ABA Playoffs G5	2.50	1.15	.30
	Keller becomes			
	Net killer			
☐ 246	ABA Playoffs G6	2.50	1.15	.30
	Tight Defense			
☐ 247	ABA Champs: Pacers	3.00	1.35	.40
☐ 248	ABA Checklist 177-264	16.00	1.90	.50
	UER (236 John Brisker)			
☐ 249	Dan Issel AS	7.00	3.10	.85
	Kentucky Colonels			
☐ 250	Rick Barry AS	10.00	4.50	1.25
	New York Nets			
☐ 251	Artis Gilmore AS	7.00	3.10	.85
	Kentucky Colonels			
☐ 252	Donnie Freeman AS	2.00	.90	.25
	Dallas Chaparrals			
☐ 253	Bill Melchionni AS	2.00	.90	.25
	New York Nets			
☐ 254	Willie Wise AS	2.00	.90	.25
	Utah Stars			
☐ 255	Julius Erving AS	60.00	27.00	7.50
	Virginia Squires			
☐ 256	Zelmo Beaty AS	2.00	.90	.25
	Utah Stars			
☐ 257	Ralph Simpson AS	2.00	.90	.25
	Denver Rockets			

☐ 258	Charlie Scott AS	2.25	1.00	.30
	Virginia Squires			
☐ 259	ABA Scoring Average	5.00	2.30	.60
	Leaders			
	Charlie Scott			
	Rick Barry			
	Dan Issel			
☐ 260	ABA 2pt FG Pct.	4.00	1.80	.50
	Leaders			
	Artis Gilmore			
	Tom Washington			
	Larry Jones			
☐ 261	ABA 3pt FG Pct.	2.50	1.15	.30
	Leaders			
	Glen Combs			
	Louie Dampier			
	Warren Jabali			
☐ 262	ABA FT Pct Leaders	4.00	1.80	.50
	Rick Barry			
	Mack Calvin			
	Steve Jones			
☐ 263	ABA Rebound Leaders	20.00	9.00	2.50
	Artis Gilmore			
	Julius Erving			
	Mel Daniels			
☐ 264	ABA Assist Leaders	4.50	1.80	.35
	Bill Melchionni			
	Larry Brown			
	Louie Dampier			

1973-74 Topps

The 1973-74 Topps set of 264 contains NBA players on cards numbered 1 to 176 and ABA players on cards numbered 177 to 264. The cards in the set measure the standard 2 1/2" by 3 1/2". All-Star selections (first and second team) for both leagues are noted on the respective player's regular cards. Card backs are printed in red and green on gray card stock. The backs feature year-by-year ABA and NBA statistics. Subseries within the set include NBA Playoffs (62-68), NBA League Leaders (153-158), ABA Playoffs (202-208), and ABA League Leaders (234-239). The only notable Rookie Cards in this set are Chris Ford, Bob McAdoo, and Paul Westphal.

		NRMT	VG-E	GOOD
	COMPLETE SET (264)	375.00	170.00	47.50
	COMMON NBA PLAYER (1-176)	.60	.25	.08
	COMMON ABA PLAYER (177-264)	1.00	.45	.13
☐ 1	Nate Archibald AS1	8.00	2.20	.50
	Kansas City-Omaha Kings			
☐ 2	Steve Kuberski	.75	.35	.09
	Boston Celtics			
☐ 3	John Mengelt	.60	.25	.08
	Detroit Pistons			
☐ 4	Jim McMillian	.75	.35	.09
	Los Angeles Lakers			
☐ 5	Nate Thurmond	3.50	1.55	.45
	Golden State Warriors			
☐ 6	Dave Wohl	.60	.25	.08
	Buffalo Braves			
☐ 7	John Brisker	.60	.25	.08
	Seattle Supersonics			
☐ 8	Charlie Davis	.60	.25	.08
	Portland Trail Blazers			
☐ 9	Lamar Green	.60	.25	.08
	Phoenix Suns			
☐ 10	Walt Frazier AS2	7.00	3.10	.85
	New York Knicks			
☐ 11	Bob Christian	.60	.25	.08
	Atlanta Hawks			
☐ 12	Cornell Warner	.60	.25	.08
	Cleveland Cavaliers			

☐ 13	Calvin Murphy	4.00	1.80	.50
	Houston Rockets			
☐ 14	Dave Sorenson	.60	.25	.08
	Philadelphia 76ers			
☐ 15	Archie Clark	1.00	.45	.13
	Capital Bullets			
☐ 16	Clifford Ray	1.00	.45	.13
	Chicago Bulls			
☐ 17	Terry Driscoll	.60	.25	.08
	Milwaukee Bucks			
☐ 18	Matt Guokas	1.50	.65	.19
	Kansas City-Omaha Kings			
☐ 19	Elmore Smith	1.00	.45	.13
	Buffalo Braves			
☐ 20	John Havlicek AS1	14.00	6.25	1.75
	Boston Celtics			
☐ 21	Pat Riley	12.00	5.50	1.50
	Los Angeles Lakers			
☐ 22	George Trapp	.60	.25	.08
	Detroit Pistons			
☐ 23	Ron Williams	.60	.25	.08
	Golden State Warriors			
☐ 24	Jim Fox	.60	.25	.08
	Seattle Supersonics			
☐ 25	Dick Van Arsdale	.75	.35	.09
	Phoenix Suns			
☐ 26	John Tresvant	.60	.25	.08
	Capital Bullets			
☐ 27	Rick Adelman	1.00	.45	.13
	Portland Trail Blazers			
☐ 28	Eddie Mast	.60	.25	.08
	Atlanta Hawks			
☐ 29	Jim Cleamons	.60	.25	.08
	Cleveland Cavaliers			
☐ 30	Dave DeBusschere AS2	6.00	2.70	.75
	New York Knicks			
☐ 31	Norm Van Lier	1.50	.65	.19
	Chicago Bulls			
☐ 32	Stan McKenzie	.60	.25	.08
	Houston Rockets			
☐ 33	Bob Dandridge	1.00	.45	.13
	Milwaukee Bucks			
☐ 34	Leroy Ellis	.75	.35	.09
	Philadelphia 76ers			
☐ 35	Mike Riordan	.75	.35	.09
	Capital Bullets			
☐ 36	Fred Hilton	.60	.25	.08
	Buffalo Braves			
☐ 37	Toby Kimball	.60	.25	.08
	Kansas City-Omaha Kings			
☐ 38	Jim Price	.60	.25	.08

	Los Angeles Lakers		
☐ 39	Willie Norwood .... .60	.25	.08
	Detroit Pistons		
☐ 40	Dave Cowens AS2 .... 7.00	3.10	.85
	Boston Celtics		
☐ 41	Cazzie Russell 2.00	.90	.25
	Golden State Warriors		
☐ 42	Lee Winfield .... .60	.25	.08
	Seattle Supersonics		
☐ 43	Connie Hawkins 4.50	2.00	.55
	Phoenix Suns		
☐ 44	Mike Newlin .... .75	.35	.09
	Houston Rockets		
☐ 45	Chet Walker 2.00	.90	.25
	Chicago Bulls		
☐ 46	Walt Bellamy 2.00	.90	.25
	Atlanta Hawks		
☐ 47	John Johnson 1.00	.45	.13
	Portland Trail Blazers		
☐ 48	Henry Bibby 4.00	1.80	.50
	New York Knicks		
☐ 49	Bobby Smith .... .60	.25	.08
	Cleveland Cavaliers		
☐ 50	Kareem Abdul-Jabbar AS1 .... 25.00	11.50	3.10
	Milwaukee Bucks		
☐ 51	Mike Price .... .60	.25	.08
	Philadelphia 76ers		
☐ 52	John Hummer .... .60	.25	.08
	Buffalo Braves		
☐ 53	Kevin Porter 5.00	2.30	.60
	Capital Bullets		
☐ 54	Nate Williams .... .60	.25	.08
	Kansas City-Omaha Kings		
☐ 55	Gail Goodrich 3.50	1.55	.45
	Los Angeles Lakers		
☐ 56	Fred Foster .... .60	.25	.08
	Detroit Pistons		
☐ 57	Don Chaney 2.00	.90	.25
	Boston Celtics		
☐ 58	Bud Stallworth .... .60	.25	.08
	Seattle Supersonics		
☐ 59	Clem Haskins 1.00	.45	.13
	Phoenix Suns		
☐ 60	Bob Love AS2 .... 2.50	1.15	.30
	Chicago Bulls		
☐ 61	Jimmy Walker .... .60	.25	.08
	Houston Rockets		
☐ 62	NBA Eastern Semis 1.00	.45	.13
	Knicks shoot down		
	Bullets in 5		
☐ 63	NBA Eastern Semis 1.00	.45	.13
	Celts oust Hawks		
	2nd Straight Year		
☐ 64	NBA Western Semis 7.00	3.10	.85
	Lakers outlast		
	Bulls at Wire		
	(W.Chamberlain)		
☐ 65	NBA Western Semis 1.00	.45	.13
	Warriors over-		
	whelm Milwaukee		
☐ 66	NBA Eastern Finals 3.00	1.35	.40
	Knicks stun		
	Celtics at Boston		
	(W.Reed/Finkel)		
☐ 67	NBA Western Finals 1.00	.45	.13
	Lakers Breeze Past		
	Golden State		
☐ 68	NBA Championship 4.00	1.80	.50
	Knicks Do It,		
	Repeat '70 Miracle		
	(W.Frazier/Erickson)		
☐ 69	Larry Steele .... .60	.25	.08
	Portland Trail Blazers		

☐ 70	Oscar Robertson	20.00	9.00	2.50
	Milwaukee Bucks			
☐ 71	Phil Jackson	6.00	2.70	.75
	New York Knicks			
☐ 72	John Wetzel	.60	.25	.08
	Atlanta Hawks			
☐ 73	Steve Patterson	2.00	.90	.25
	Cleveland Cavaliers			
☐ 74	Manny Leaks	.60	.25	.08
	Philadelphia 76ers			
☐ 75	Jeff Mullins	1.00	.45	.13
	Golden State Warriors			
☐ 76	Stan Love	.60	.25	.08
	Capital Bullets			
☐ 77	Dick Garrett	.60	.25	.08
	Buffalo Braves			
☐ 78	Don Nelson	4.00	1.80	.50
	Boston Celtics			
☐ 79	Chris Ford	6.00	2.70	.75
	Detroit Pistons			
☐ 80	Wilt Chamberlain	25.00	11.50	3.10
	Los Angeles Lakers			
☐ 81	Dennis Layton	.60	.25	.08
	Phoenix Suns			
☐ 82	Bill Bradley	14.00	6.25	1.75
	New York Knicks			
☐ 83	Jerry Sloan	2.00	.90	.25
	Chicago Bulls			
☐ 84	Cliff Meely	.60	.25	.08
	Houston Rockets			
☐ 85	Sam Lacey	.60	.25	.08
	Kansas City-Omaha Kings			
☐ 86	Dick Snyder	.60	.25	.08
	Seattle Supersonics			
☐ 87	Jim Washington	.60	.25	.08
	Atlanta Hawks			
☐ 88	Lucius Allen	1.25	.55	.16
	Milwaukee Bucks			
☐ 89	LaRue Martin	.60	.25	.08
	Portland Trail Blazers			
☐ 90	Rick Barry	14.00	6.25	1.75
	Golden State Warriors			
☐ 91	Fred Boyd	.60	.25	.08
	Philadelphia 76ers			
☐ 92	Barry Clemens	.60	.25	.08
	Cleveland Cavaliers			
☐ 93	Dean Meminger	.60	.25	.08
	New York Knicks			
☐ 94	Henry Finkel	.60	.25	.08
	Boston Celtics			
☐ 95	Elvin Hayes	8.00	3.60	1.00
	Capital Bullets			
☐ 96	Stu Lantz	.75	.35	.09
	Detroit Pistons			
☐ 97	Bill Hewitt	.60	.25	.08
	Buffalo Braves			
☐ 98	Neal Walk	.75	.35	.09
	Phoenix Suns			
☐ 99	Garfield Heard	1.00	.45	.13
	Chicago Bulls			
☐ 100	Jerry West AS1	24.00	11.00	3.00
	Los Angeles Lakers			
☐ 101	Otto Moore	.60	.25	.08
	Houston Rockets			
☐ 102	Don Kojis	.60	.25	.08
	Kansas City-Omaha Kings			
☐ 103	Fred Brown	5.00	2.30	.60
	Seattle Supersonics			
☐ 104	Dwight Davis	.60	.25	.08
	Cleveland Cavaliers			
☐ 105	Willis Reed	6.50	2.90	.80
	New York Knicks			
☐ 106	Herm Gilliam	.60	.25	.08

	Atlanta Hawks			
☐ 107	Mickey Davis	.60	.25	.08
	Milwaukee Bucks			
☐ 108	Jim Barnett	.60	.25	.08
	Golden State Warriors			
☐ 109	Ollie Johnson	.60	.25	.08
	Portland Trail Blazers			
☐ 110	Bob Lanier	6.50	2.90	.80
	Detroit Pistons			
☐ 111	Fred Carter	.75	.35	.09
	Philadelphia 76ers			
☐ 112	Paul Silas	2.00	.90	.25
	Boston Celtics			
☐ 113	Phil Chenier	1.50	.65	.19
	Capital Bullets			
☐ 114	Dennis Awtrey	.60	.25	.08
	Chicago Bulls			
☐ 115	Austin Carr	2.00	.90	.25
	Cleveland Cavaliers			
☐ 116	Bob Kauffman	.60	.25	.08
	Buffalo Braves			
☐ 117	Keith Erickson	.75	.35	.09
	Los Angeles Lakers			
☐ 118	Walt Wesley	.60	.25	.08
	Phoenix Suns			
☐ 119	Steve Bracey	.60	.25	.08
	Atlanta Hawks			
☐ 120	Spencer Haywood AS1	2.50	1.15	.30
	Seattle Supersonics			
☐ 121	NBA Checklist 1-176	12.00	1.00	.20
☐ 122	Jack Marin	.75	.35	.09
	Houston Rockets			
☐ 123	Jon McGlocklin	.60	.25	.08
	Milwaukee Bucks			
☐ 124	Johnny Green	.60	.25	.08
	Kansas City-Omaha Kings			
☐ 125	Jerry Lucas	5.00	2.30	.60
	New York Knicks			
☐ 126	Paul Westphal	25.00	11.50	3.10
	Boston Celtics			
☐ 127	Curtis Rowe	1.25	.55	.16
	Detroit Pistons			
☐ 128	Mahdi Abdul-Rahman	1.50	.65	.19
	Seattle Supersonics			
	(formerly Walt Hazzard)			
☐ 129	Lloyd Neal	2.00	.90	.25
	Portland Trail Blazers			
☐ 130	Pete Maravich AS1	20.00	9.00	2.50
	Atlanta Hawks			
☐ 131	Don May	.60	.25	.08
	Philadelphia 76ers			
☐ 132	Bob Weiss	1.25	.55	.16
	Chicago Bulls			
☐ 133	Dave Stallworth	.60	.25	.08
	Capital Bullets			
☐ 134	Dick Cunningham	.60	.25	.08
	Milwaukee Bucks			
☐ 135	Bob McAdoo	22.00	10.00	2.80
	Buffalo Braves			
☐ 136	Butch Beard	1.25	.55	.16
	Golden State Warriors			
☐ 137	Happy Hairston	1.00	.45	.13
	Los Angeles Lakers			
☐ 138	Bob Rule	.60	.25	.08
	Cleveland Cavaliers			
☐ 139	Don Adams	.60	.25	.08
	Detroit Pistons			
☐ 140	Charlie Scott	1.25	.55	.16
	Phoenix Suns			
☐ 141	Ron Riley	.60	.25	.08
	Kansas City-Omaha Kings			
☐ 142	Earl Monroe	6.00	2.70	.75
	New York Knicks			

☐ 143 Clyde Lee	.60	.25	.08
Golden State Warriors			
☐ 144 Rick Roberson	.60	.25	.08
Portland Trail Blazers			
☐ 145 Rudy Tomjanovich	7.00	3.10	.85
Houston Rockets			
(Printed without			
Houston on basket)			
☐ 146 Tom Van Arsdale	.75	.35	.09
Philadelphia 76ers			
☐ 147 Art Williams	.60	.25	.08
Boston Celtics			
☐ 148 Curtis Perry	.60	.25	.08
Milwaukee Bucks			
☐ 149 Rich Rinaldi	.60	.25	.08
Capital Bullets			
☐ 150 Lou Hudson	1.25	.55	.16
Atlanta Hawks			
☐ 151 Mel Counts	.60	.25	.08
Los Angeles Lakers			
☐ 152 Jim McDaniels	.60	.25	.08
Seattle Supersonics			
☐ 153 NBA Scoring Leaders	6.00	2.70	.75
Nate Archibald			
Kareem Abdul-Jabbar			
Spencer Haywood			
☐ 154 NBA Scoring Average	6.00	2.70	.75
Leaders			
Nate Archibald			
Kareem Abdul-Jabbar			
Spencer Haywood			
☐ 155 NBA FG Pct Leaders	8.00	3.60	1.00
Wilt Chamberlain			
Matt Guokas			
Kareem Abdul-Jabbar			
☐ 156 NBA FT Pct Leaders	2.50	1.15	.30
Rick Barry			
Calvin Murphy			
Mike Newlin			
☐ 157 NBA Rebound Leaders	6.50	2.90	.80
Wilt Chamberlain			
Nate Thurmond			
Dave Cowens			
☐ 158 NBA Assist Leaders	2.50	1.15	.30
Nate Archibald			
Len Wilkens			
Dave Bing			
☐ 159 Don Smith	.60	.25	.08
Houston Rockets			
☐ 160 Sidney Wicks	2.50	1.15	.30
Portland Trail Blazers			
☐ 161 Howie Komives	.60	.25	.08
Buffalo Braves			
☐ 162 John Gianelli	.60	.25	.08
New York Knicks			
☐ 163 Jeff Halliburton	.60	.25	.08
Philadelphia 76ers			
☐ 164 Kennedy McIntosh	.60	.25	.08
Seattle Supersonics			
☐ 165 Len Wilkens	5.00	2.30	.60
Cleveland Cavaliers			
☐ 166 Corky Calhoun	.75	.35	.09
Phoenix Suns			
☐ 167 Howard Porter	1.00	.45	.13
Chicago Bulls			
☐ 168 JoJo White	2.50	1.15	.30
Boston Celtics			
☐ 169 John Block	.60	.25	.08
Kansas City-Omaha Kings			
☐ 170 Dave Bing	4.00	1.80	.50
Detroit Pistons			
☐ 171 Joe Ellis	.60	.25	.08
Golden State Warriors			

☐ 172	Chuck Terry	.60	.25	.08
	Milwaukee Bucks			
☐ 173	Randy Smith	1.00	.45	.13
	Buffalo Braves			
☐ 174	Bill Bridges	.75	.35	.09
	Los Angeles Lakers			
☐ 175	Geoff Petrie	1.50	.65	.19
	Portland Trail Blazers			
☐ 176	Wes Unseld	5.00	2.30	.60
	Capital Bullets			
☐ 177	Skeeter Swift	1.00	.45	.13
	San Antonio Spurs			
☐ 178	Jim Eakins	1.00	.45	.13
	Virginia Squires			
☐ 179	Steve Jones	1.25	.55	.16
	Carolina Cougars			
☐ 180	George McGinnis AS1	3.50	1.55	.45
	Indiana Pacers			
☐ 181	Al Smith	1.00	.45	.13
	Denver Rockets			
☐ 182	Tom Washington	1.00	.45	.13
	New York Nets			
☐ 183	Louie Dampier	2.00	.90	.25
	Kentucky Colonels			
☐ 184	Simmie Hill	1.00	.45	.13
	San Diego Conquistadors			
☐ 185	George Thompson	1.00	.45	.13
	Memphis Tams			
☐ 186	Cincy Powell	1.00	.45	.13
	Utah Stars			
☐ 187	Larry Jones	1.25	.55	.16
	San Antonio Spurs			
☐ 188	Neil Johnson	1.00	.45	.13
	Virginia Squires			
☐ 189	Tom Owens	1.00	.45	.13
	Carolina Cougars			
☐ 190	Ralph Simpson AS2	1.25	.55	.16
	Denver Rockets			
☐ 191	George Carter	1.00	.45	.13
	Virginia Squires			
☐ 192	Rick Mount	2.00	.90	.25
	Kentucky Colonels			
☐ 193	Red Robbins	1.00	.45	.13
	San Diego Conquistadors			
☐ 194	George Lehmann	1.00	.45	.13
	Memphis Tams			
☐ 195	Mel Daniels AS2	2.00	.90	.25
	Indiana Pacers			
☐ 196	Bob Warren	1.00	.45	.13
	Utah Stars			
☐ 197	Gene Kennedy	1.00	.45	.13
	San Antonio Spurs			
☐ 198	Mike Barr	1.00	.45	.13
	Virginia Squires			
☐ 199	Dave Robisch	1.50	.65	.19
	Denver Rockets			
☐ 200	Billy Cunningham AS1	6.00	2.70	.75
	Carolina Cougars			
☐ 201	John Roche	1.00	.45	.13
	New York Nets			
☐ 202	ABA Western Semis	1.75	.80	.22
	Pacers Oust Injured Rockets			
☐ 203	ABA Western Semis	1.75	.80	.22
	Stars sweep Q's in Four Straight			
☐ 204	ABA Eastern Semis	1.75	.80	.22
	Kentucky overcomes Squires and Dr. J. (Issel jump shot)			
☐ 205	ABA Eastern Semis	1.75	.80	.22
	Cougars in strong finish over Nets			

☐ 206	ABA Western Finals Pacers nip bitter rival, Stars	1.75	.80	.22
☐ 207	ABA Eastern Finals Colonels prevail in grueling Series (Gilmore shooting)	3.00	1.35	.40
☐ 208	ABA Championship McGinnis leads Pacers to Title (center jump)	1.75	.80	.22
☐ 209	Glen Combs Utah Stars	1.00	.45	.13
☐ 210	Dan Issel AS2 Kentucky Colonels	7.00	3.10	.85
☐ 211	Randy Denton Memphis Tams	1.00	.45	.13
☐ 212	Freddie Lewis Indiana Pacers	1.25	.55	.16
☐ 213	Stew Johnson San Diego Conquistadors	1.00	.45	.13
☐ 214	Roland Taylor Virginia Squires	1.00	.45	.13
☐ 215	Rich Jones San Antonio Spurs	1.00	.45	.13
☐ 216	Billy Paultz New York Nets	1.50	.65	.19
☐ 217	Ron Boone Utah Stars	1.25	.55	.16
☐ 218	Walt Simon Kentucky Colonels	1.00	.45	.13
☐ 219	Mike Lewis Carolina Cougars	1.00	.45	.13
☐ 220	Warren Jabali AS1 Denver Rockets	1.25	.55	.16
☐ 221	Wilbert Jones Memphis Tams	1.00	.45	.13
☐ 222	Don Buse Indiana Pacers	2.00	.90	.25
☐ 223	Gene Moore San Diego Conquistadors	1.00	.45	.13
☐ 224	Joe Hamilton San Antonio Spurs	1.00	.45	.13
☐ 225	Zelmo Beaty Utah Stars	1.25	.55	.16
☐ 226	Brian Taylor New York Nets	2.00	.90	.25
☐ 227	Julius Keye Denver Rockets	1.00	.45	.13
☐ 228	Mike Gale Kentucky Colonels	1.50	.65	.19
☐ 229	Warren Davis Memphis Tams	1.00	.45	.13
☐ 230	Mack Calvin AS2 Carolina Cougars	1.50	.65	.19
☐ 231	Roger Brown Indiana Pacers	1.25	.55	.16
☐ 232	Chuck Williams San Diego Conquistadors	1.00	.45	.13
☐ 233	Gerald Govan Utah Stars	1.00	.45	.13
☐ 234	ABA Scoring Average Leaders Julius Erving George McGinnis Dan Issel	8.00	3.60	1.00
☐ 235	ABA 2 Pt. Pct. Leaders Artis Gilmore Gene Kennedy Tom Owens	2.00	.90	.25
☐ 236	ABA 3 Pt. Pct. Leaders	1.75	.80	.22

	Glen Combs			
	Roger Brown			
	Louie Dampier			
☐ 237	ABA F.T. Pct. Leaders	1.75	.80	.22
	Billy Keller			
	Ron Boone			
	Bob Warren			
☐ 238	ABA Rebound Leaders	2.00	.90	.25
	Artis Gilmore			
	Mel Daniels			
	Bill Paultz			
☐ 239	ABA Assist Leaders	1.75	.80	.22
	Bill Melchionni			
	Chuck Williams			
	Warren Jabali			
☐ 240	Julius Erving AS2	70.00	32.00	8.75
	Virginia Squires			
☐ 241	Jimmy O'Brien	1.00	.45	.13
	Kentucky Colonels			
☐ 242	ABA Checklist 177-264	12.00	1.20	.24
☐ 243	Johnny Neumann	1.25	.55	.16
	Memphis Tams			
☐ 244	Darnell Hillman	1.25	.55	.16
	Indiana Pacers			
☐ 245	Willie Wise	1.25	.55	.16
	Utah Stars			
☐ 246	Collis Jones	1.00	.45	.13
	San Antonio Spurs			
☐ 247	Ted McClain	1.00	.45	.13
	Carolina Cougars			
☐ 248	George Irvine	1.50	.65	.19
	Virginia Squires			
☐ 249	Bill Melchionni	1.25	.55	.16
	New York Nets			
☐ 250	Artis Gilmore AS1	7.00	3.10	.85
	Kentucky Colonels			
☐ 251	Willie Long	1.00	.45	.13
	Denver Rockets			
☐ 252	Larry Miller	1.00	.45	.13
	San Diego Conquistadors			
☐ 253	Lee Davis	1.00	.45	.13
	Memphis Tams			
☐ 254	Donnie Freeman	1.00	.45	.13
	Indiana Pacers			
☐ 255	Joe Caldwell	1.25	.55	.16
	Carolina Cougars			
☐ 256	Bob Netolicky	1.00	.45	.13
	San Antonio Spurs			
☐ 257	Bernie Williams	1.00	.45	.13
	Virginia Squires			
☐ 258	Byron Beck	1.25	.55	.16
	Denver Rockets			
☐ 259	Jim Chones	3.00	1.35	.40
	New York Nets			
☐ 260	James Jones AS1	1.25	.55	.16
	Utah Stars			
☐ 261	Wendell Ladner	1.25	.55	.16
	Kentucky Colonels			
☐ 262	Ollie Taylor	1.00	.45	.13
	San Diego Conquistadors			
☐ 263	Les Hunter	1.00	.45	.13
	Memphis Tams			
☐ 264	Billy Keller	2.00	.90	.25
	Indiana Pacers			

1974-75 Topps

The 1974-75 Topps set of 264 cards contains NBA players on cards numbered 1 to 176 and ABA players on cards numbered 177 to 264. For the first time Team Leader (TL) cards are provided for each team. The cards in the set measure the standard 2 1/2" by 3 1/2". All-Star selections (first and second team) for both leagues are noted on the respective player's reg-

ular cards. The card backs are printed in blue and red on gray card stock. Subseries within the set include NBA Team Leaders (81-98), NBA Statistical Leaders (144-149), NBA Playoffs (161-164), ABA Statistical Leaders (207-212), ABA Team Leaders (221-230), and ABA Playoffs (246-249). The key Rookie Cards in this set are Doug Collins, George Gervin, and Bill Walton.

	NRMT	VG-E	GOOD
COMPLETE SET (264)	375.00	170.00	47.50
COMMON NBA PLAYER (1-176)	.50	.23	.06
COMMON ABA PLAYER (177-264)	1.00	.45	.13
☐ 1 Kareem Abdul-Jabbar AS1	30.00	9.00	1.80
Milwaukee Bucks			
☐ 2 Don May	.50	.23	.06
Philadelphia 76ers			
☐ 3 Bernie Fryer	1.00	.45	.13
Portland Trail Blazers			
☐ 4 Don Adams	.50	.23	.06
Detroit Pistons			
☐ 5 Herm Gilliam	.50	.23	.06
Atlanta Hawks			
☐ 6 Jim Chones	.60	.25	.08
Cleveland Cavaliers			
☐ 7 Rick Adelman	1.00	.45	.13
Chicago Bulls			
☐ 8 Randy Smith	.60	.25	.08
Buffalo Braves			
☐ 9 Paul Silas	1.50	.65	.19
Boston Celtics			
☐ 10 Pete Maravich	20.00	9.00	2.50
New Orleans Jazz			
☐ 11 Ron Behagen	.50	.23	.06
Kansas City-Omaha Kings			
☐ 12 Kevin Porter	1.00	.45	.13
Washington Bullets			
☐ 13 Bill Bridges	.60	.25	.08
Los Angeles Lakers			
(On back team shown as			
Los And., should			
be Los Ang.)			
☐ 14 Charles Johnson	1.50	.65	.19
Golden State Warriors			
☐ 15 Bob Love	1.50	.65	.19
Chicago Bulls			
☐ 16 Henry Bibby	1.00	.45	.13
New York Knicks			
☐ 17 Neal Walk	.60	.25	.08
Phoenix Suns			
☐ 18 John Brisker	.50	.23	.06
Seattle Supersonics			
☐ 19 Lucius Allen	1.00	.45	.13
Milwaukee Bucks			
☐ 20 Tom Van Arsdale	.60	.25	.08

	Philadelphia 76ers			
☐ 21	Larry Steele	.50	.23	.06
	Portland Trail Blazers			
☐ 22	Curtis Rowe	1.00	.45	.13
	Detroit Pistons			
☐ 23	Dean Meminger	.50	.23	.06
	Atlanta Hawks			
☐ 24	Steve Patterson	.50	.23	.06
	Cleveland Cavaliers			
☐ 25	Earl Monroe	6.00	2.70	.75
	New York Knicks			
☐ 26	Jack Marin	.60	.25	.08
	Buffalo Braves			
☐ 27	JoJo White	2.00	.90	.25
	Boston Celtics			
☐ 28	Rudy Tomjanovich	6.00	2.70	.75
	Houston Rockets			
☐ 29	Otto Moore	.50	.23	.06
	Kansas City-Omaha Kings			
☐ 30	Elvin Hayes AS2	7.50	3.40	.95
	Washington Bullets			
☐ 31	Pat Riley	8.00	3.60	1.00
	Los Angeles Lakers			
☐ 32	Clyde Lee	.50	.23	.06
	Golden State Warriors			
☐ 33	Bob Weiss	1.00	.45	.13
	Chicago Bulls			
☐ 34	Jim Fox	.50	.23	.06
	Seattle Supersonics			
☐ 35	Charlie Scott	1.00	.45	.13
	Phoenix Suns			
☐ 36	Cliff Meely	.50	.23	.06
	Houston Rockets			
☐ 37	Jon McGlocklin	.50	.23	.06
	Milwaukee Bucks			
☐ 38	Jim McMillian	.60	.25	.08
	Buffalo Braves			
☐ 39	Bill Walton	65.00	29.00	8.25
	Portland Trail Blazers			
☐ 40	Dave Bing AS2	4.00	1.80	.50
	Detroit Pistons			
☐ 41	Jim Washington	.50	.23	.06
	Atlanta Hawks			
☐ 42	Jim Cleamons	.50	.23	.06
	Cleveland Cavaliers			
☐ 43	Mel Davis	.50	.23	.06
	New York Knicks			
☐ 44	Garfield Heard	.60	.25	.08
	Buffalo Braves			
☐ 45	Jimmy Walker	.50	.23	.06
	Kansas City-Omaha Kings			
☐ 46	Don Nelson	3.50	1.55	.45
	Boston Celtics			
☐ 47	Jim Barnett	.50	.23	.06
	New Orleans Jazz			
☐ 48	Manny Leaks	.50	.23	.06
	Washington Bullets			
☐ 49	Elmore Smith	.75	.35	.09
	Los Angeles Lakers			
☐ 50	Rick Barry AS1	10.00	4.50	1.25
	Golden State Warriors			
☐ 51	Jerry Sloan	1.50	.65	.19
	Chicago Bulls			
☐ 52	John Hummer	.50	.23	.06
	Seattle Supersonics			
☐ 53	Keith Erickson	.60	.25	.08
	Phoenix Suns			
☐ 54	George E. Johnson	.50	.23	.06
	Houston Rockets			
☐ 55	Oscar Robertson	10.00	4.50	1.25
	Milwaukee Bucks			
☐ 56	Steve Mix	1.50	.65	.19
	Philadelphia 76ers			

☐ 57	Rick Roberson Portland Trail Blazers	.50	.23	.06
☐ 58	John Mengelt Detroit Pistons	.50	.23	.06
☐ 59	Dwight Jones Atlanta Hawks	1.00	.45	.13
☐ 60	Austin Carr Cleveland Cavaliers	2.00	.90	.25
☐ 61	Nick Weatherspoon Washington Bullets	1.25	.55	.16
☐ 62	Clem Haskins Phoenix Suns	1.00	.45	.13
☐ 63	Don Kojis Kansas City-Omaha Kings	.50	.23	.06
☐ 64	Paul Westphal Boston Celtics	10.00	4.50	1.25
☐ 65	Walt Bellamy New Orleans Jazz	2.00	.90	.25
☐ 66	John Johnson Portland Trail Blazers	.50	.23	.06
☐ 67	Butch Beard Golden State Warriors	1.00	.45	.13
☐ 68	Happy Hairston Los Angeles Lakers	1.00	.45	.13
☐ 69	Tom Boerwinkle Chicago Bulls	.50	.23	.06
☐ 70	Spencer Haywood AS2 Seattle Supersonics	2.00	.90	.25
☐ 71	Gary Melchionni Phoenix Suns	.50	.23	.06
☐ 72	Ed Ratleff Houston Rockets	1.00	.45	.13
☐ 73	Mickey Davis Milwaukee Bucks	.50	.23	.06
☐ 74	Dennis Awtrey New Orleans Jazz	.50	.23	.06
☐ 75	Fred Carter Philadelphia 76ers	.60	.25	.08
☐ 76	George Trapp Detroit Pistons	.50	.23	.06
☐ 77	John Wetzel Atlanta Hawks	.50	.23	.06
☐ 78	Bobby Smith Cleveland Cavaliers	.50	.23	.06
☐ 79	John Gianelli New York Knicks	.50	.23	.06
☐ 80	Bob McAdoo AS2 Buffalo Braves	7.50	3.40	.95
☐ 81	Atlanta Hawks TL Pete Maravich Lou Hudson Walt Bellamy Pete Maravich	4.50	2.00	.55
☐ 82	Boston Celtics TL John Havlicek JoJo White Dave Cowens JoJo White	4.50	2.00	.55
☐ 83	Buffalo Braves TL Bob McAdoo Ernie DiGregorio Bob McAdoo Ernie DiGregorio	1.25	.55	.16
☐ 84	Chicago Bulls TL Bob Love Chet Walker Clifford Ray Norm Van Lier	2.50	1.15	.30
☐ 85	Cleveland Cavs TL Austin Carr Austin Carr Dwight Davis Len Wilkens	1.25	.55	.16

☐ 86	Detroit Pistons TL	1.25	.55	.16
	Bob Lanier			
	Stu Lantz			
	Bob Lanier			
	Dave Bing			
☐ 87	Golden State	2.50	1.15	.30
	Warriors TL			
	Rick Barry			
	Rick Barry			
	Nate Thurmond			
	Rick Barry			
☐ 88	Houston Rockets TL	1.25	.55	.16
	Rudy Tomjanovich			
	Calvin Murphy			
	Don Smith			
	Calvin Murphy			
☐ 89	Kansas City Omaha TL	1.00	.45	.13
	Jimmy Walker			
	Jimmy Walker			
	Sam Lacey			
	Jimmy Walker			
☐ 90	Los Angeles Lakers TL	1.50	.65	.19
	Gail Goodrich			
	Gail Goodrich			
	Happy Hairston			
	Gail Goodrich			
☐ 91	Milwaukee Bucks TL	7.50	3.40	.95
	Kareem Abdul-Jabbar			
	Oscar Robertson			
	Kareem Abdul-Jabbar			
	Oscar Robertson			
☐ 92	New Orleans Jazz	1.00	.45	.13
	Emblem; Expansion			
	Draft Picks on Back			
☐ 93	New York Knicks TL	5.00	2.30	.60
	Walt Frazier			
	Bill Bradley			
	Dave DeBusschere			
	Walt Frazier			
☐ 94	Philadelphia 76ers TL	1.25	.55	.16
	Fred Carter			
	Tom Van Arsdale			
	Leroy Ellis			
	Fred Carter			
☐ 95	Phoenix Suns TL	1.25	.55	.16
	Charlie Scott			
	Dick Van Arsdale			
	Neal Walk			
	Neal Walk			
☐ 96	Portland Trail	1.50	.65	.19
	Blazers TL			
	Geoff Petrie			
	Geoff Petrie			
	Rick Roberson			
	Sidney Wicks			
☐ 97	Seattle Supersonics TL	1.25	.55	.16
	Spencer Haywood			
	Dick Snyder			
	Spencer Haywood			
	Fred Brown			
☐ 98	Capitol Bullets TL	1.25	.55	.16
	Phil Chenier			
	Phil Chenier			
	Elvin Hayes			
	Kevin Porter			
☐ 99	Sam Lacey	.50	.23	.06
	Kansas City-Omaha Kings			
☐ 100	John Havlicek AS1	10.00	4.50	1.25
	Boston Celtics			
☐ 101	Stu Lantz	.60	.25	.08
	New Orleans Jazz			
☐ 102	Mike Riordan	.60	.25	.08
	Washington Bullets			

□ 103	Larry Jones	.60	.25	.08
	Philadelphia 76ers			
□ 104	Connie Hawkins	4.00	1.80	.50
	Los Angeles Lakers			
□ 105	Nate Thurmond	3.00	1.35	.40
	Golden State Warriors			
□ 106	Dick Gibbs	.50	.23	.06
	Seattle Supersonics			
□ 107	Corky Calhoun	.60	.25	.08
	Phoenix Suns			
□ 108	Dave Wohl	.50	.23	.06
	Houston Rockets			
□ 109	Cornell Warner	.50	.23	.06
	Milwaukee Bucks			
□ 110	Geoff Petrie UER	1.00	.45	.13
	Portland Trail Blazers			
	(Misspelled Patrie			
	on card front)			
□ 111	Leroy Ellis	.60	.25	.08
	Philadelphia 76ers			
□ 112	Chris Ford	2.00	.90	.25
	Detroit Pistons			
□ 113	Bill Bradley	10.00	4.50	1.25
	New York Knicks			
□ 114	Clifford Ray	.60	.25	.08
	Chicago Bulls			
□ 115	Dick Snyder	.50	.23	.06
	Cleveland Cavaliers			
□ 116	Nate Williams	.50	.23	.06
	Kansas City-Omaha Kings			
□ 117	Matt Guokas	1.25	.55	.16
	Buffalo Braves			
□ 118	Henry Finkel	.50	.23	.06
	Boston Celtics			
□ 119	Curtis Perry	.50	.23	.06
	New Orleans Jazz			
□ 120	Gail Goodrich AS1	2.50	1.15	.30
	Los Angeles Lakers			
□ 121	Wes Unseld	4.00	1.80	.50
	Washington Bullets			
□ 122	Howard Porter	.60	.25	.08
	New York Knicks			
□ 123	Jeff Mullins	1.00	.45	.13
	Golden State Warriors			
□ 124	Mike Bantom	.75	.35	.09
	Phoenix Suns			
□ 125	Fred Brown	2.00	.90	.25
	Seattle Supersonics			
□ 126	Bob Dandridge	.60	.25	.08
	Milwaukee Bucks			
□ 127	Mike Newlin	.60	.25	.08
	Houston Rockets			
□ 128	Greg Smith	.50	.23	.06
	Portland Trail Blazers			
□ 129	Doug Collins	15.00	6.75	1.90
	Philadelphia 76ers			
□ 130	Lou Hudson	1.25	.55	.16
	Atlanta Hawks			
□ 131	Bob Lanier	5.00	2.30	.60
	Detroit Pistons			
□ 132	Phil Jackson	5.00	2.30	.60
	New York Knicks			
□ 133	Don Chaney	1.25	.55	.16
	Boston Celtics			
□ 134	Jim Brewer	.75	.35	.09
	Cleveland Cavaliers			
□ 135	Ernie DiGregorio	4.50	2.00	.55
	Buffalo Braves			
□ 136	Steve Kuberski	.60	.25	.08
	New Orleans Jazz			
□ 137	Jim Price	.50	.23	.06
	Los Angeles Lakers			
□ 138	Mike D'Antoni	.50	.23	.06

	Kansas City-Omaha Kings			
☐ 139	John Brown	.50	.23	.06
	Atlanta Hawks			
☐ 140	Norm Van Lier AS2	1.25	.55	.16
	Chicago Bulls			
☐ 141	NBA Checklist 1-176	10.00	1.00	.20
☐ 142	Don(Slick) Watts	2.00	.90	.25
	Seattle Supersonics			
☐ 143	Walt Wesley	.50	.23	.06
	Washington Bullets			
☐ 144	NBA Scoring Leaders	8.00	3.60	1.00
	Bob McAdoo			
	Kareem Abdul-Jabbar			
	Pete Maravich			
☐ 145	NBA Scoring	8.00	3.60	1.00
	Average Leaders			
	Bob McAdoo			
	Pete Maravich			
	Kareem Abdul-Jabbar			
☐ 146	NBA F.G. Pct. Leaders	5.00	2.30	.60
	Bob McAdoo			
	Kareem Abdul-Jabbar			
	Rudy Tomjanovich			
☐ 147	NBA F.T. Pct. Leaders	1.00	.45	.13
	Ernie DiGregorio			
	Rick Barry			
	Jeff Mullins			
☐ 148	NBA Rebound Leaders	3.00	1.35	.40
	Elvin Hayes			
	Dave Cowens			
	Bob McAdoo			
☐ 149	NBA Assist Leaders	1.00	.45	.13
	Ernie DiGregorio			
	Calvin Murphy			
	Len Wilkens			
☐ 150	Walt Frazier AS1	6.00	2.70	.75
	New York Knicks			
☐ 151	Cazzie Russell	2.00	.90	.25
	Golden State Warriors			
☐ 152	Calvin Murphy	3.00	1.35	.40
	Houston Rockets			
☐ 153	Bob Kauffman	.50	.23	.06
	Atlanta Hawks			
☐ 154	Fred Boyd	.50	.23	.06
	Philadelphia 76ers			
☐ 155	Dave Cowens	6.00	2.70	.75
	Boston Celtics			
☐ 156	Willie Norwood	.50	.23	.06
	Detroit Pistons			
☐ 157	Lee Winfield	.50	.23	.06
	Buffalo Braves			
☐ 158	Dwight Davis	.50	.23	.06
	Cleveland Cavaliers			
☐ 159	George T. Johnson	.50	.23	.06
	Golden State Warriors			
☐ 160	Dick Van Arsdale	.60	.25	.08
	Phoenix Suns			
☐ 161	NBA Eastern Semis	1.00	.45	.13
	Celts over Braves			
	Knicks edge Bullets			
☐ 162	NBA Western Semis	1.00	.45	.13
	Bucks over Lakers			
	Bulls edge Pistons			
☐ 163	NBA Div. Finals	1.00	.45	.13
	Celts over Knicks			
	Bucks sweep Bulls			
☐ 164	NBA Championship	1.25	.55	.16
	Celtics over Bucks			
☐ 165	Phil Chenier	1.25	.55	.16
	Washington Bullets			
☐ 166	Kermit Washington	2.00	.90	.25
	Los Angeles Lakers			
☐ 167	Dale Schlueter	.50	.23	.06
	Atlanta Hawks			

☐ 168	John Block	50	.23	.06
	New Orleans Jazz			
☐ 169	Don Smith	50	.23	.06
	Houston Rockets			
☐ 170	Nate Archibald	4.00	1.80	.50
	Kansas City-Omaha Kings			
☐ 171	Chet Walker	1.75	.80	.22
	Chicago Bulls			
☐ 172	Archie Clark	1.25	.55	.16
	Washington Bullets			
☐ 173	Kennedy McIntosh	50	.23	.06
	Seattle Supersonics			
☐ 174	George Thompson	50	.23	.06
	Milwaukee Bucks			
☐ 175	Sidney Wicks	2.00	.90	.25
	Portland Trail Blazers			
☐ 176	Jerry West	20.00	9.00	2.50
	Los Angeles Lakers			
☐ 177	Dwight Lamar	1.25	.55	.16
	San Diego Conquistadors			
☐ 178	George Carter	1.00	.45	.13
	Virginia Squires			
☐ 179	Wil Robinson	1.00	.45	.13
	Memphis Sounds			
☐ 180	Artis Gilmore AS1	5.00	2.30	.60
	Kentucky Colonels			
☐ 181	Brian Taylor	1.25	.55	.16
	New York Nets			
☐ 182	Darnell Hillman	1.25	.55	.16
	Indiana Pacers			
☐ 183	Dave Robisch	1.25	.55	.16
	Denver Nuggets			
☐ 184	Gene Littles	1.25	.55	.16
	St. Louis Spirits			
☐ 185	Willie Wise AS2	1.25	.55	.16
	Utah Stars			
☐ 186	James Silas	3.00	1.35	.40
	San Antonio Spurs			
☐ 187	Caldwell Jones	5.00	2.30	.60
	San Diego Conquistadors			
☐ 188	Roland Taylor	1.00	.45	.13
	Virginia Squires			
☐ 189	Randy Denton	1.00	.45	.13
	Memphis Sounds			
☐ 190	Dan Issel AS2	6.00	2.70	.75
	Kentucky Colonels			
☐ 191	Mike Gale	1.00	.45	.13
	New York Nets			
☐ 192	Mel Daniels	2.00	.90	.25
	Memphis Sounds			
☐ 193	Steve Jones	1.25	.55	.16
	Denver Nuggets			
☐ 194	Marv Roberts	1.00	.45	.13
	St. Louis Spirits			
☐ 195	Ron Boone AS2	1.25	.55	.16
	Utah Stars			
☐ 196	George Gervin	40.00	18.00	5.00
	San Antonio Spurs			
☐ 197	Flynn Robinson	1.00	.45	.13
	San Diego Conquistadors			
☐ 198	Cincy Powell	1.00	.45	.13
	Virginia Squires			
☐ 199	Glen Combs	1.00	.45	.13
	Memphis Sounds			
☐ 200	Julius Erving AS1 UER	50.00	23.00	6.25
	New York Nets			
	(Misspelled Irving			
	on card back)			
☐ 201	Billy Keller	1.25	.55	.16
	Indiana Pacers			
☐ 202	Willie Long	1.00	.45	.13
	Denver Nuggets			
☐ 203	ABA Checklist 177-264	10.00	1.00	.20

☐ 204	Joe Caldwell	1.25	.55	.16
	St. Louis Spirits			
☐ 205	Swen Nater AS2	3.50	1.55	.45
	San Antonio Spurs			
☐ 206	Rick Mount	2.00	.90	.25
	Utah Stars			
☐ 207	ABA Scoring	8.00	3.60	1.00
	Avg. Leaders			
	Julius Erving			
	George McGinnis			
	Dan Issel			
☐ 208	ABA Two-Point Field	1.75	.80	.22
	Goal Percent Leaders			
	Swen Nater			
	James Jones			
	Tom Owens			
☐ 209	ABA Three-Point Field	1.75	.80	.22
	Goal Percent Leaders			
	Louie Dampier			
	Billy Keller			
	Roger Brown			
☐ 210	ABA Free Throw	1.75	.80	.22
	Percent Leaders			
	James Jones			
	Mack Calvin			
	Ron Boone			
☐ 211	ABA Rebound Leaders	2.00	.90	.25
	Artis Gilmore			
	George McGinnis			
	Caldwell Jones			
☐ 212	ABA Assist Leaders	1.75	.80	.22
	Al Smith			
	Chuck Williams			
	Louie Dampier			
☐ 213	Larry Miller	1.00	.45	.13
	Virginia Squires			
☐ 214	Stew Johnson	1.00	.45	.13
	San Diego Conquistadors			
☐ 215	Larry Finch	3.00	1.35	.40
	Memphis Sounds			
☐ 216	Larry Kenon	3.00	1.35	.40
	New York Nets			
☐ 217	Joe Hamilton	1.00	.45	.13
	Kentucky Colonels			
☐ 218	Gerald Govan	1.00	.45	.13
	Utah Stars			
☐ 219	Ralph Simpson	1.25	.55	.16
	Denver Nuggets			
☐ 220	George McGinnis AS1	3.00	1.35	.40
	Indiana Pacers			
☐ 221	Carolina Cougars TL	2.00	.90	.25
	Billy Cunningham			
	Mack Calvin			
	Tom Owens			
	Joe Caldwell			
☐ 222	Denver Nuggets TL	2.00	.90	.25
	Ralph Simpson			
	Byron Beck			
	Dave Robisch			
	Al Smith			
☐ 223	Indiana Pacers TL	2.00	.90	.25
	George McGinnis			
	Billy Keller			
	George McGinnis			
	Freddie Lewis			
☐ 224	Kentucky Colonels TL	3.00	1.35	.40
	Dan Issel			
	Louie Dampier			
	Artis Gilmore			
	Louie Dampier			
☐ 225	Memphis Sounds TL	1.75	.80	.22
	George Thompson			
	Larry Finch			

	Randy Denton			
	George Thompson			
☐ 226	New York Nets TL	9.00	4.00	1.15
	Julius Erving			
	John Roche			
	Larry Kenon			
	Julius Erving			
☐ 227	San Antonio Spurs TL	5.00	2.30	.60
	George Gervin			
	George Gervin			
	Swen Nater			
	James Silas			
☐ 228	San Diego Conq. TL	1.75	.80	.22
	Dwight Lamar			
	Stew Johnson			
	Caldwell Jones			
	Chuck Williams			
☐ 229	Utah Stars TL	2.00	.90	.25
	Willie Wise			
	James Jones			
	Gerald Govan			
	James Jones			
☐ 230	Virginia Squires TL	1.75	.80	.22
	George Carter			
	George Irvine			
	Jim Eakins			
	Roland Taylor			
☐ 231	Bird Averitt	1.00	.45	.13
	Kentucky Colonels			
☐ 232	John Roche	1.00	.45	.13
	Kentucky Colonels			
☐ 233	George Irvine	1.00	.45	.13
	Virginia Squires			
☐ 234	John Williamson	1.50	.65	.19
	New York Nets			
☐ 235	Billy Cunningham	4.50	2.00	.55
	St. Louis Spirits			
☐ 236	Jimmy O'Brien	1.00	.45	.13
	San Diego Conquistadors			
☐ 237	Wilbert Jones	1.00	.45	.13
	Kentucky Colonels			
☐ 238	Johnny Neumann	1.25	.55	.16
	Utah Stars			
☐ 239	Al Smith	1.00	.45	.13
	Denver Nuggets			
☐ 240	Roger Brown	1.25	.55	.16
	Memphis Sounds			
☐ 241	Chuck Williams	1.00	.45	.13
	Kentucky Colonels			
☐ 242	Rich Jones	1.00	.45	.13
	San Antonio Spurs			
☐ 243	Dave Twardzik	2.00	.90	.25
	Virginia Squires			
☐ 244	Wendell Ladner	1.25	.55	.16
	New York Nets			
☐ 245	Mack Calvin AS1	1.50	.65	.19
	St. Louis Spirits			
☐ 246	ABA Eastern Semis	1.75	.80	.22
	Nets over Squires			
	Colonels sweep Cougars			
☐ 247	ABA Western Semis	1.75	.80	.22
	Stars over Conquistadors			
	Pacers over Spurs			
☐ 248	ABA Div. Finals	1.75	.80	.22
	Nets sweep Colonels			
	Stars edge Pacers			
☐ 249	ABA Championship	9.00	4.00	1.15
	Nets over Stars			
	(Julius Erving)			
☐ 250	Wilt Chamberlain CO	25.00	11.50	3.10
	San Diego Conquistadors			
☐ 251	Ron Robinson	1.00	.45	.13
	Memphis Sounds			

		NRMT	VG-E	GOOD
☐ 252	Zelmo Beaty	1.25	.55	.16
	Utah Stars			
☐ 253	Donnie Freeman	1.25	.55	.16
	Indiana Pacers			
☐ 254	Mike Green	1.00	.45	.13
	Denver Nuggets			
☐ 255	Louie Dampier AS2	1.25	.55	.16
	Kentucky Colonels			
☐ 256	Tom Owens	1.00	.45	.13
	St. Louis Spirits			
☐ 257	George Karl	9.00	4.00	1.15
	San Antonio Spurs			
☐ 258	Jim Eakins	1.00	.45	.13
	Virginia Squires			
☐ 259	Travis Grant	1.00	.45	.13
	San Diego Conquistadors			
☐ 260	James Jones AS1	1.25	.55	.16
	Utah Stars			
☐ 261	Mike Jackson	1.00	.45	.13
	Memphis Sounds			
☐ 262	Billy Paultz	1.25	.55	.16
	New York Nets			
☐ 263	Freddie Lewis	1.25	.55	.16
	Memphis Sounds			
☐ 264	Byron Beck	1.50	.65	.19
	Denver Nuggets			
	(Back refers to ANA,			
	should be ABA)			

1975-76 Topps

The 1975-76 Topps basketball card set of 330 was the largest basketball set ever produced to that time. NBA players are depicted on cards 1-220 and ABA players on cards 221-330. The cards in the set measure the standard 2 1/2" by 3 1/2". Team Leader (TL) cards are provided for each team on cards 116-133 and 278-287. Other subseries in this set include NBA Statistical Leaders (1-6), NBA Playoffs (188-189), NBA Team Checklists (203-220), ABA Statistical Leaders (221-226), ABA Playoffs (309-310), and ABA Team Checklists (321-330). All-Star selections (first and second team) for both leagues are noted on the respective player's regular cards. Card backs are printed in blue and green on gray card stock. The set is particularly hard to sort numerically, as the small card number on the back is printed in blue on a dark green background. The set was printed on three large sheets each containing 110 different cards. Investigation of the second (series) sheet reveals that 22 of the cards were double printed; they are marked DP in the checklist below. The key Rookie Card in this set is Moses Malone.

	NRMT	VG-E	GOOD
COMPLETE SET (330)	500.00	230.00	65.00
COMMON NBA PLAYER (1-110)	.60	.25	.08
COMMON NBA PLAYER (111-220)	.60	.25	.08
COMMON ABA PLAYER (221-330)	1.00	.45	.13

☐ 1	NBA Scoring Average	10.00	2.80	.60
	Leaders			
	Bob McAdoo			
	Rick Barry			
	Kareem Abdul-Jabbar			
☐ 2	NBA Field Goal	2.00	.90	.25
	Percentage Leaders			
	Don Nelson			
	Butch Beard			
	Rudy Tomjanovich			
☐ 3	NBA Free Throw	4.00	1.80	.50
	Percentage Leaders			
	Rick Barry			
	Calvin Murphy			
	Bill Bradley			
☐ 4	NBA Rebounds Leaders	1.50	.65	.19
	Wes Unseld			
	Dave Cowens			
	Sam Lacey			
☐ 5	NBA Assists Leaders	2.00	.90	.25
	Kevin Porter			
	Dave Bing			
	Nate Archibald			
☐ 6	NBA Steals Leaders	3.00	1.35	.40
	Rick Barry			
	Walt Frazier			
	Larry Steele			
☐ 7	Tom Van Arsdale	.75	.35	.09
	Atlanta Hawks			
☐ 8	Paul Silas	1.25	.55	.16
	Boston Celtics			
☐ 9	Jerry Sloan	1.25	.55	.16
	Chicago Bulls			
☐ 10	Bob McAdoo AS1	6.00	2.70	.75
	Buffalo Braves			
☐ 11	Dwight Davis	.60	.25	.08
	Golden State Warriors			
☐ 12	John Mengelt	.60	.25	.08
	Detroit Pistons			
☐ 13	George Johnson	.60	.25	.08
	Golden State Warriors			
☐ 14	Ed Ratleff	.60	.25	.08
	Houston Rockets			
☐ 15	Nate Archibald AS1	4.00	1.80	.50
	Kansas City Kings			
☐ 16	Elmore Smith	.75	.35	.09
	Milwaukee Bucks			
☐ 17	Bob Dandridge	.75	.35	.09
	Milwaukee Bucks			
☐ 18	Louie Nelson	.75	.35	.09
	New Orleans Jazz			
☐ 19	Neal Walk	.75	.35	.09
	New York Knicks			
☐ 20	Billy Cunningham	4.50	2.00	.55
	Philadelphia 76ers			
☐ 21	Gary Melchionni	.60	.25	.08
	Phoenix Suns			
☐ 22	Barry Clemens	.60	.25	.08
	Portland Trail Blazers			
☐ 23	Jimmy Jones	.60	.25	.08
	Washington Bullets			
☐ 24	Tom Burleson	2.50	1.15	.30
	Seattle Supersonics			
☐ 25	Lou Hudson	1.00	.45	.13
	Atlanta Hawks			
☐ 26	Henry Finkel	.60	.25	.08
	Boston Celtics			
☐ 27	Jim McMillian	.75	.35	.09
	Buffalo Braves			
☐ 28	Matt Guokas	1.25	.55	.16
	Chicago Bulls			
☐ 29	Fred Foster DP	.60	.25	.08
	Cleveland Cavaliers			

☐ 30	Bob Lanier	4.50	2.00	.55
	Detroit Pistons			
☐ 31	Jimmy Walker	.60	.25	.08
	Kansas City Kings			
☐ 32	Cliff Meely	.60	.25	.08
	Houston Rockets			
☐ 33	Butch Beard	.75	.35	.09
	Cleveland Cavaliers			
☐ 34	Cazzie Russell	1.25	.55	.16
	Los Angeles Lakers			
☐ 35	Jon McGlocklin	.60	.25	.08
	Milwaukee Bucks			
☐ 36	Bernie Fryer	.75	.35	.09
	New Orleans Jazz			
☐ 37	Bill Bradley	10.00	4.50	1.25
	New York Knicks			
☐ 38	Fred Carter	.75	.35	.09
	Philadelphia 76ers			
☐ 39	Dennis Awtrey DP	.60	.25	.08
	Phoenix Suns			
☐ 40	Sidney Wicks	2.00	.90	.25
	Portland Trail Blazers			
☐ 41	Fred Brown	1.00	.45	.13
	Seattle Supersonics			
☐ 42	Rowland Garrett	.60	.25	.08
	Chicago Bulls			
☐ 43	Herm Gilliam	.60	.25	.08
	Atlanta Hawks			
☐ 44	Don Nelson	3.00	1.35	.40
	Boston Celtics			
☐ 45	Ernie DiGregorio	.75	.35	.09
	Buffalo Braves			
☐ 46	Jim Brewer	.60	.25	.08
	Cleveland Cavaliers			
☐ 47	Chris Ford	1.25	.55	.16
	Detroit Pistons			
☐ 48	Nick Weatherspoon	.75	.35	.09
	Washington Bullets			
☐ 49	Zaid Abdul-Aziz	.60	.25	.08
	(formerly Don Smith)			
	Houston Rockets			
☐ 50	Keith Wilkes	15.00	6.75	1.90
	Golden State Warriors			
☐ 51	Ollie Johnson DP	.60	.25	.08
	Kansas City Kings			
☐ 52	Lucius Allen	1.00	.45	.13
	Los Angeles Lakers			
☐ 53	Mickey Davis	.60	.25	.08
	Milwaukee Bucks			
☐ 54	Otto Moore	.60	.25	.08
	New Orleans Jazz			
☐ 55	Walt Frazier AS1	7.00	3.10	.85
	New York Knicks			
☐ 56	Steve Mix	.75	.35	.09
	Philadelphia 76ers			
☐ 57	Nate Hawthorne	.60	.25	.08
	Phoenix Suns			
☐ 58	Lloyd Neal	.60	.25	.08
	Portland Trail Blazers			
☐ 59	Don Watts	.75	.35	.09
	Seattle Supersonics			
☐ 60	Elvin Hayes	7.00	3.10	.85
	Washington Bullets			
☐ 61	Checklist 1-110	8.00	.80	.15
☐ 62	Mike Sojourner	.60	.25	.08
	Atlanta Hawks			
☐ 63	Randy Smith	.75	.35	.09
	Buffalo Braves			
☐ 64	John Block DP	.60	.25	.08
	Chicago Bulls			
☐ 65	Charlie Scott	1.00	.45	.13
	Boston Celtics			
☐ 66	Jim Chones	.75	.35	.09

		Cleveland Cavaliers			
☐ 67	Rick Adelman		1.00	.45	.13
		Kansas City Kings			
☐ 68	Curtis Rowe		1.00	.45	.13
		Detroit Pistons			
☐ 69	Derrek Dickey		.75	.35	.09
		Golden State Warriors			
☐ 70	Rudy Tomjanovich		6.00	2.70	.75
		Houston Rockets			
☐ 71	Pat Riley		8.00	3.60	1.00
		Los Angeles Lakers			
☐ 72	Cornell Warner		.60	.25	.08
		Milwaukee Bucks			
☐ 73	Earl Monroe		6.00	2.70	.75
		New York Knicks			
☐ 74	Allan Bristow		4.00	1.80	.50
		Philadelphia 76ers			
☐ 75	Pete Maravich DP		12.00	5.50	1.50
		New Orleans Jazz			
☐ 76	Curtis Perry		.60	.25	.08
		Phoenix Suns			
☐ 77	Bill Walton		25.00	11.50	3.10
		Portland Trail Blazers			
☐ 78	Leonard Gray		.60	.25	.08
		Seattle Supersonics			
☐ 79	Kevin Porter		1.00	.45	.13
		Washington Bullets			
☐ 80	John Havlicek AS2		10.00	4.50	1.25
		Boston Celtics			
☐ 81	Dwight Jones		.60	.25	.08
		Atlanta Hawks			
☐ 82	Jack Marin		.75	.35	.09
		Buffalo Braves			
☐ 83	Dick Snyder		.60	.25	.08
		Cleveland Cavaliers			
☐ 84	George Trapp		.60	.25	.08
		Detroit Pistons			
☐ 85	Nate Thurmond		2.50	1.15	.30
		Chicago Bulls			
☐ 86	Charles Johnson		.60	.25	.08
		Golden State Warriors			
☐ 87	Ron Riley		.60	.25	.08
		Houston Rockets			
☐ 88	Stu Lantz		.75	.35	.09
		Los Angeles Lakers			
☐ 89	Scott Wedman		2.50	1.15	.30
		Kansas City Kings			
☐ 90	Kareem Abdul-Jabbar		20.00	9.00	2.50
		Los Angeles Lakers			
☐ 91	Aaron James		.60	.25	.08
		New Orleans Jazz			
☐ 92	Jim Barnett		.60	.25	.08
		New York Knicks			
☐ 93	Clyde Lee		.60	.25	.08
		Philadelphia 76ers			
☐ 94	Larry Steele		.60	.25	.08
		Portland Trail Blazers			
☐ 95	Mike Riordan		.75	.35	.09
		Washington Bullets			
☐ 96	Archie Clark		.75	.35	.09
		Seattle Supersonics			
☐ 97	Mike Bantom		.75	.35	.09
		Phoenix Suns			
☐ 98	Bob Kauffman		.60	.25	.08
		Atlanta Hawks			
☐ 99	Kevin Stacom		1.00	.45	.13
		Boston Celtics			
☐ 100	Rick Barry AS1		8.00	3.60	1.00
		Golden State Warriors			
☐ 101	Ken Charles		.60	.25	.08
		Buffalo Braves			
☐ 102	Tom Boerwinkle		.60	.25	.08
		Chicago Bulls			

☐ 103	Mike Newlin	.75	.35	.09
	Houston Rockets			
☐ 104	Leroy Ellis	.75	.35	.09
	Philadelphia 76ers			
☐ 105	Austin Carr	1.50	.65	.19
	Cleveland Cavaliers			
☐ 106	Ron Behagen	.60	.25	.08
	New Orleans Jazz			
☐ 107	Jim Price	.60	.25	.08
	Milwaukee Bucks			
☐ 108	Bud Stallworth	.60	.25	.08
	New Orleans Jazz			
☐ 109	Earl Williams	.60	.25	.08
	Detroit Pistons			
☐ 110	Gail Goodrich	2.50	1.15	.30
	Los Angeles Lakers			
☐ 111	Phil Jackson	4.50	2.00	.55
	New York Knicks			
☐ 112	Rod Derline	.60	.25	.08
	Seattle Supersonics			
☐ 113	Keith Erickson	.75	.35	.09
	Phoenix Suns			
☐ 114	Phil Lumpkin	.60	.25	.08
	Phoenix Suns			
☐ 115	Wes Unseld	4.00	1.80	.50
	Washington Bullets			
☐ 116	Atlanta Hawks TL	1.50	.65	.19
	Lou Hudson			
	Lou Hudson			
	John Drew			
	Dean Meminger			
☐ 117	Boston Celtics TL	2.00	.90	.25
	Dave Cowens			
	Kevin Stacom			
	Paul Silas			
	JoJo White			
☐ 118	Buffalo Braves TL	1.75	.80	.22
	Bob McAdoo			
	Jack Marin			
	Bob McAdoo			
	Randy Smith			
☐ 119	Chicago Bulls TL	2.00	.90	.25
	Bob Love			
	Chet Walker			
	Nate Thurmond			
	Norm Van Lier			
☐ 120	Cleveland Cavs TL	1.50	.65	.19
	Bobby Smith			
	Dick Snyder			
	Jim Chones			
	Jim Cleamons			
☐ 121	Detroit Pistons TL	2.00	.90	.25
	Bob Lanier			
	John Mengelt			
	Bob Lanier			
	Dave Bing			
☐ 122	Golden State TL	2.00	.90	.25
	Rick Barry			
	Rick Barry			
	Clifford Ray			
	Rick Barry			
☐ 123	Houston Rockets TL	1.75	.80	.22
	Rudy Tomjanovich			
	Calvin Murphy			
	Kevin Kunnert			
	Mike Newlin			
☐ 124	Kansas City Kings TL	1.75	.80	.22
	Nate Archibald			
	Ollie Johnson			
	Sam Lacey UER			
	(Lacy on front)			
	Nate Archibald			
☐ 125	Los Angeles Lakers TL	1.50	.65	.19

	Gail Goodrich			
	Cazzie Russell			
	Happy Hairston			
	Gail Goodrich			
☐ 126	Milwaukee Bucks TL	4.50	2.00	.55
	Kareem Abdul-Jabbar			
	Mickey Davis			
	Kareem Abdul-Jabbar			
	Kareem Abdul-Jabbar			
☐ 127	New Orleans Jazz TL	3.00	1.35	.40
	Pete Maravich			
	Stu Lantz			
	E.C. Coleman			
	Pete Maravich			
☐ 128	New York Knicks TL DP	3.00	1.35	.40
	Walt Frazier			
	Bill Bradley			
	John Gianelli			
	Walt Frazier			
☐ 129	Phila. 76ers TL DP	1.75	.80	.22
	Fred Carter			
	Doug Collins			
	Billy Cunningham			
	Billy Cunningham			
☐ 130	Phoenix Suns TL DP	1.50	.65	.19
	Charlie Scott			
	Keith Erickson			
	Curtis Perry			
	Dennis Awtrey			
☐ 131	Portland Blazers TL DP	1.50	.65	.19
	Sidney Wicks			
	Geoff Petrie			
	Sidney Wicks			
	Geoff Petrie			
☐ 132	Seattle Sonics TL	1.75	.80	.22
	Spencer Haywood			
	Archie Clark			
	Spencer Haywood			
	Don Watts			
☐ 133	Washington Bullets TL	2.00	.90	.25
	Elvin Hayes			
	Clem Haskins			
	Wes Unseld			
	Kevin Porter			
☐ 134	John Drew	2.50	1.15	.30
	Atlanta Hawks			
☐ 135	JoJo White AS2	2.00	.90	.25
	Boston Celtics			
☐ 136	Garfield Heard	.75	.35	.09
	Buffalo Braves			
☐ 137	Jim Cleamons	.60	.25	.08
	Cleveland Cavaliers			
☐ 138	Howard Porter	.75	.35	.09
	Detroit Pistons			
☐ 139	Phil Smith	1.00	.45	.13
	Golden State Warriors			
☐ 140	Bob Love	1.50	.65	.19
	Chicago Bulls			
☐ 141	John Gianelli DP	.60	.25	.08
	New York Knicks			
☐ 142	Larry McNeill	.75	.35	.09
	Kansas City Kings			
☐ 143	Brian Winters	2.00	.90	.25
	Milwaukee Bucks			
☐ 144	George Thompson	.60	.25	.08
	Milwaukee Bucks			
☐ 145	Kevin Kunnert	.60	.25	.08
	Houston Rockets			
☐ 146	Henry Bibby	.75	.35	.09
	New Orleans Jazz			
☐ 147	John Johnson	.60	.25	.08
	Portland Trail Blazers			
☐ 148	Doug Collins	4.50	2.00	.55
	Philadelphia 76ers			

☐ 149	John Brisker	.60	.25	.08
	Seattle Supersonics			
☐ 150	Dick Van Arsdale	.75	.35	.09
	Phoenix Suns			
☐ 151	Leonard Robinson	2.50	1.15	.30
	Washington Bullets			
☐ 152	Dean Meminger	.60	.25	.08
	Atlanta Hawks			
☐ 153	Phil Hankinson	.60	.25	.08
	Boston Celtics			
☐ 154	Dale Schlueter	.60	.25	.08
	Buffalo Braves			
☐ 155	Norm Van Lier	1.25	.55	.16
	Chicago Bulls			
☐ 156	Campy Russell	3.00	1.35	.40
	Cleveland Cavaliers			
☐ 157	Jeff Mullins	1.00	.45	.13
	Golden State Warriors			
☐ 158	Sam Lacey	.60	.25	.08
	Kansas City Kings			
☐ 159	Happy Hairston	1.00	.45	.13
	Los Angeles Lakers			
☐ 160	Dave Bing DP	3.00	1.35	.40
	Detroit Pistons			
☐ 161	Kevin Restani	.75	.35	.09
	Milwaukee Bucks			
☐ 162	Dave Wohl	.60	.25	.08
	Houston Rockets			
☐ 163	E.C. Coleman	.60	.25	.08
	New Orleans Jazz			
☐ 164	Jim Fox	.60	.25	.08
	Seattle Supersonics			
☐ 165	Geoff Petrie	1.25	.55	.16
	Portland Trail Blazers			
☐ 166	Hawthorne Wingo DP UER	.60	.25	.08
	New York Knicks			
	(Misspelled Harthorne			
	on card front)			
☐ 167	Fred Boyd	.60	.25	.08
	Philadelphia 76ers			
☐ 168	Willie Norwood	.60	.25	.08
	Phoenix Suns			
☐ 169	Bob Wilson	.60	.25	.08
	Chicago Bulls			
☐ 170	Dave Cowens	7.00	3.10	.85
	Boston Celtics			
☐ 171	Tom Henderson	.75	.35	.09
	Atlanta Hawks			
☐ 172	Jim Washington	.60	.25	.08
	Buffalo Braves			
☐ 173	Clem Haskins	.75	.35	.09
	Washington Bullets			
☐ 174	Jim Davis	.60	.25	.08
	Detroit Pistons			
☐ 175	Bobby Smith DP	.60	.25	.08
	Cleveland Cavaliers			
☐ 176	Mike D'Antoni	.60	.25	.08
	Kansas City Kings			
☐ 177	Zelmo Beaty	.75	.35	.09
	Los Angeles Lakers			
☐ 178	Gary Brokaw	1.25	.55	.16
	Milwaukee Bucks			
☐ 179	Mel Davis	.60	.25	.08
	New York Knicks			
☐ 180	Calvin Murphy	2.50	1.15	.30
	Houston Rockets			
☐ 181	Checklist 111-220 DP	8.00	.80	.15
☐ 182	Nate Williams	.60	.25	.08
	New Orleans Jazz			
☐ 183	LaRue Martin	.60	.25	.08
	Portland Trail Blazers			
☐ 184	George McGinnis	2.50	1.15	.30
	Philadelphia 76ers			

☐ 185	Clifford Ray	.75	.35	.09
	Golden State Warriors			
☐ 186	Paul Westphal	6.00	2.70	.75
	Phoenix Suns			
☐ 187	Talvin Skinner	.60	.25	.08
	Seattle Supersonics			
☐ 188	NBA Playoff Semis DP	1.50	.65	.19
	Warriors edge Bulls			
	Bullets over Celts			
☐ 189	NBA Playoff Finals	1.50	.65	.19
	Warriors sweep Bullets			
	(C.Ray blocks shot)			
☐ 190	Phil Chenier AS2 DP	.75	.35	.09
	Washington Bullets			
☐ 191	John Brown	.60	.25	.08
	Atlanta Hawks			
☐ 192	Lee Winfield	.60	.25	.08
	Buffalo Braves			
☐ 193	Steve Patterson	.60	.25	.08
	Cleveland Cavaliers			
☐ 194	Charles Dudley	.60	.25	.08
	Golden State Warriors			
☐ 195	Connie Hawkins DP	2.00	.90	.25
	Los Angeles Lakers			
☐ 196	Leon Benbow	.60	.25	.08
	Chicago Bulls			
☐ 197	Don Kojis	.60	.25	.08
	Kansas City Kings			
☐ 198	Ron Williams	.60	.25	.08
	Milwaukee Bucks			
☐ 199	Mel Counts	.60	.25	.08
	New Orleans Jazz			
☐ 200	Spencer Haywood AS2	2.00	.90	.25
	Seattle Supersonics			
☐ 201	Greg Jackson	.60	.25	.08
	Phoenix Suns			
☐ 202	Tom Kozelko DP	.60	.25	.08
	Washington Bullets			
☐ 203	Atlanta Hawks	1.50	.65	.19
	Checklist			
☐ 204	Boston Celtics	2.00	.90	.25
	Checklist			
☐ 205	Buffalo Braves	1.50	.65	.19
	Checklist			
☐ 206	Chicago Bulls	2.50	1.15	.30
	Checklist			
☐ 207	Cleveland Cavs	1.50	.65	.19
	Checklist			
☐ 208	Detroit Pistons	1.50	.65	.19
	Checklist			
☐ 209	Golden State	1.50	.65	.19
	Checklist			
☐ 210	Houston Rockets	1.50	.65	.19
	Checklist			
☐ 211	Kansas City Kings DP	1.50	.65	.19
	Checklist			
☐ 212	Los Angeles Lakers DP	1.50	.65	.19
	Checklist			
☐ 213	Milwaukee Bucks	1.50	.65	.19
	Checklist			
☐ 214	New Orleans Jazz	1.50	.65	.19
	Checklist			
☐ 215	New York Knicks	1.50	.65	.19
	Checklist			
☐ 216	Philadelphia 76ers	1.50	.65	.19
	Checklist			
☐ 217	Phoenix Suns DP	1.50	.65	.19
	Checklist			
☐ 218	Portland Blazers	1.50	.65	.19
	Checklist			
☐ 219	Seattle Sonics DP	7.00	3.10	.85
	Checklist			
☐ 220	Washington Bullets	1.50	.65	.19

	Checklist			
☐ 221	ABA Scoring	6.00	2.70	.75
	Average Leaders			
	George McGinnis			
	Julius Erving			
	Ron Boone			
☐ 222	ABA 2 Pt. Field Goal	6.00	2.70	.75
	Percentage Leaders			
	Bobby Jones			
	Artis Gilmore			
	Moses Malone			
☐ 223	ABA 3 Pt. Field Goal	2.00	.90	.25
	Percentage Leaders			
	Billy Shepherd			
	Louie Dampier			
	Al Smith			
☐ 224	ABA Free Throw	2.00	.90	.25
	Percentage Leaders			
	Mack Calvin			
	James Silas			
	Dave Robisch			
☐ 225	ABA Rebounds Leaders	2.00	.90	.25
	Swen Nater			
	Artis Gilmore			
	Marvin Barnes			
☐ 226	ABA Assists Leaders	2.00	.90	.25
	Mack Calvin			
	Chuck Williams			
	George McGinnis			
☐ 227	Mack Calvin AS1	2.00	.90	.25
	Virginia Squires			
☐ 228	Billy Knight AS1	4.00	1.80	.50
	Indiana Pacers			
☐ 229	Bird Averitt	1.00	.45	.13
	Kentucky Colonels			
☐ 230	George Carter	1.00	.45	.13
	Memphis Sounds			
☐ 231	Swen Nater AS2	2.00	.90	.25
	New York Nets			
☐ 232	Steve Jones	1.25	.55	.16
	St. Louis Spirits			
☐ 233	George Gervin	12.00	5.50	1.50
	San Antonio Spurs			
☐ 234	Lee Davis	1.00	.45	.13
	San Diego Sails			
☐ 235	Ron Boone AS1	1.25	.55	.16
	Utah Stars			
☐ 236	Mike Jackson	1.00	.45	.13
	Virginia Squires			
☐ 237	Kevin Joyce	2.00	.90	.25
	Indiana Pacers			
☐ 238	Marv Roberts	1.00	.45	.13
	Kentucky Colonels			
☐ 239	Tom Owens	1.00	.45	.13
	Memphis Sounds			
☐ 240	Ralph Simpson	1.25	.55	.16
	Denver Nuggets			
☐ 241	Gus Gerard	1.00	.45	.13
	St. Louis Spirits			
☐ 242	Brian Taylor AS2	1.00	.45	.13
	New York Nets			
☐ 243	Rich Jones	1.00	.45	.13
	San Antonio Spurs			
☐ 244	John Roche	1.00	.45	.13
	Utah Stars			
☐ 245	Travis Grant	1.25	.55	.16
	San Diego Sails			
☐ 246	Dave Twardzik	1.25	.55	.16
	Virginia Squires			
☐ 247	Mike Green	1.00	.45	.13
	Virginia Squires			
☐ 248	Billy Keller	1.00	.45	.13
	Indiana Pacers			

☐ 249	Stew Johnson	1.00	.45	.13
	Memphis Sounds			
☐ 250	Artis Gilmore AS1	5.00	2.30	.60
	Kentucky Colonels			
☐ 251	John Williamson	1.25	.55	.16
	New York Nets			
☐ 252	Marvin Barnes AS2	6.50	2.90	.80
	St. Louis Spirits			
☐ 253	James Silas AS2	2.00	.90	.25
	San Antonio Spurs			
☐ 254	Moses Malone	65.00	29.00	8.25
	Utah Stars			
☐ 255	Willie Wise	1.25	.55	.16
	Virginia Squires			
☐ 256	Dwight Lamar	1.00	.45	.13
	San Diego Sails			
☐ 257	Checklist 221-330	8.00	.80	.15
☐ 258	Byron Beck	1.25	.55	.16
	Denver Nuggets			
☐ 259	Len Elmore	5.00	2.30	.60
	Indiana Pacers			
☐ 260	Dan Issel	6.00	2.70	.75
	Kentucky Colonels			
☐ 261	Rick Mount	1.25	.55	.16
	Memphis Sounds			
☐ 262	Billy Paultz	1.25	.55	.16
	New York Nets			
☐ 263	Donnie Freeman	1.25	.55	.16
	San Antonio Spurs			
☐ 264	George Adams	1.00	.45	.13
	San Diego Sails			
☐ 265	Don Chaney	2.00	.90	.25
	St. Louis Spirits			
☐ 266	Randy Denton	1.00	.45	.13
	Utah Stars			
☐ 267	Don Washington	1.00	.45	.13
	Denver Nuggets			
☐ 268	Roland Taylor	1.00	.45	.13
	Denver Nuggets			
☐ 269	Charlie Edge	1.00	.45	.13
	Indiana Pacers			
☐ 270	Louie Dampier	1.25	.55	.16
	Kentucky Colonels			
☐ 271	Collis Jones	1.00	.45	.13
	Memphis Sounds			
☐ 272	Al Skinner	1.50	.65	.19
	New York Nets			
☐ 273	Coby Dietrick	1.00	.45	.13
	San Antonio Spurs			
☐ 274	Tim Bassett	1.00	.45	.13
	San Diego Sails			
☐ 275	Freddie Lewis	1.25	.55	.16
	St. Louis Spirits			
☐ 276	Gerald Govan	1.00	.45	.13
	Utah Stars			
☐ 277	Ron Thomas	1.00	.45	.13
	Kentucky Colonels			
☐ 278	Denver Nuggets TL	2.00	.90	.25
	Ralph Simpson			
	Mack Calvin			
	Mike Green			
	Mack Calvin			
☐ 279	Indiana Pacers TL	2.50	1.15	.30
	George McGinnis			
	Billy Keller			
	George McGinnis			
	George McGinnis			
☐ 280	Kentucky Colonels TL	2.50	1.15	.30
	Artis Gilmore			
	Louie Dampier			
	Artis Gilmore			
	Louie Dampier			
☐ 281	Memphis Sounds TL	2.00	.90	.25

	George Carter			
	Larry Finch			
	Tom Owens			
	Chuck Williams			
☐ 282 New York Nets TL	8.00	3.60	1.00
	Julius Erving			
	John Williamson			
	Julius Erving			
	Julius Erving			
☐ 283 St. Louis Spirits TL	2.50	1.15	.30
	Marvin Barnes			
	Freddie Lewis			
	Marvin Barnes			
	Freddie Lewis			
☐ 284 San Antonio Spurs TL	4.00	1.80	.50
	George Gervin			
	James Silas			
	Swen Nater			
	James Silas			
☐ 285 San Diego Sails TL	2.00	.90	.25
	Travis Grant			
	Jimmy O'Brien			
	Caldwell Jones			
	Jimmy O'Brien			
☐ 286 Utah Stars TL	9.00	4.00	1.15
	Ron Boone			
	Ron Boone			
	Moses Malone			
	Al Smith			
☐ 287 Virginia Squires TL	2.00	.90	.25
	Willie Wise			
	Red Robbins			
	Dave Vaughn			
	Dave Twardzik			
☐ 288 Claude Terry	1.00	.45	.13
	Denver Nuggets			
☐ 289 Wilbert Jones	1.00	.45	.13
	Kentucky Colonels			
☐ 290 Darnell Hillman	1.25	.55	.16
	Indiana Pacers			
☐ 291 Bill Melchionni	1.25	.55	.16
	New York Nets			
☐ 292 Mel Daniels	3.00	1.35	.40
	Memphis Sounds			
☐ 293 Fly Williams	3.00	1.35	.40
	St. Louis Spirits			
☐ 294 Larry Kenon	1.25	.55	.16
	San Antonio Spurs			
☐ 295 Red Robbins	1.00	.45	.13
	Virginia Squires			
☐ 296 Warren Jabali	1.00	.45	.13
	San Diego Sails			
☐ 297 Jim Eakins	1.00	.45	.13
	Utah Stars			
☐ 298 Bobby Jones	12.00	5.50	1.50
	Denver Nuggets			
☐ 299 Don Buse	1.25	.55	.16
	Indiana Pacers			
☐ 300 Julius Erving AS1	50.00	23.00	6.25
	New York Nets			
☐ 301 Billy Shepherd	1.00	.45	.13
	Memphis Sounds			
☐ 302 Maurice Lucas	12.00	5.50	1.50
	St. Louis Spirits			
☐ 303 George Karl	3.00	1.35	.40
	San Antonio Spurs			
☐ 304 Jim Bradley	1.00	.45	.13
	Kentucky Colonels			
☐ 305 Caldwell Jones	3.00	1.35	.40
	San Diego Sails			
☐ 306 Al Smith	1.00	.45	.13
	Utah Stars			
☐ 307 Jan Van Breda Kolff	2.00	.90	.25
	Virginia Squires			

		NRMT	VG-E	GOOD
☐ 308	Darrell Elston Virginia Squires	1.00	.45	.13
☐ 309	ABA Playoff Semifinals Colonels over Spirits; Pacers edge Nuggets	2.00	.90	.25
☐ 310	ABA Playoff Finals Colonels over Pacers (Gilmore hooking)	2.00	.90	.25
☐ 311	Ted McClain Kentucky Colonels	1.00	.45	.13
☐ 312	Willie Sojourner New York Nets	1.00	.45	.13
☐ 313	Bob Warren San Antonio Spurs	1.00	.45	.13
☐ 314	Bob Netolicky Indiana Pacers	1.00	.45	.13
☐ 315	Chuck Williams Memphis Sounds	1.00	.45	.13
☐ 316	Gene Kennedy St. Louis Spirits	1.00	.45	.13
☐ 317	Jimmy O'Brien San Diego Sails	1.00	.45	.13
☐ 318	Dave Robisch Denver Nuggets	1.25	.55	.16
☐ 319	Wali Jones Utah Stars	1.00	.45	.13
☐ 320	George Irvine Denver Nuggets	1.00	.45	.13
☐ 321	Denver Nuggets Checklist	1.75	.80	.22
☐ 322	Indiana Pacers Checklist	1.75	.80	.22
☐ 323	Kentucky Colonels Checklist	1.75	.80	.22
☐ 324	Memphis Sounds Checklist	1.75	.80	.22
☐ 325	New York Nets Checklist	1.75	.80	.22
☐ 326	St. Louis Spirits Checklist (Spirits of St. Louis on card back)	1.75	.80	.22
☐ 327	San Antonio Spurs Checklist	1.75	.80	.22
☐ 328	San Diego Sails Checklist	1.75	.80	.22
☐ 329	Utah Stars Checklist	1.75	.80	.22
☐ 330	Virginia Squires Checklist	4.00	1.05	.30

1976-77 Topps

The 144-card 1976-77 Topps set witnesses a return to the larger-sized cards, with each card measuring approximately 3 1/8" by 5 1/4". Cards numbered 126-135 are the previous season's NBA All-Star selections. The cards were printed on two large sheets, each with eight rows and nine columns. The checklist card was located in the lower right corner of the second sheet. The key Rookie Card in this set is David Thompson.

		NRMT	VG-E	GOOD
	COMPLETE SET (144)	350.00	160.00	45.00
	COMMON PLAYER (1-144)	1.50	.65	.19
☐ 1	Julius Erving New York Nets	60.00	22.00	4.90
☐ 2	Dick Snyder Cleveland Cavaliers	1.50	.65	.19
☐ 3	Paul Silas Boston Celtics	2.00	.90	.25

☐ 4	Keith Erickson	1.75	.80	.22
	Phoenix Suns			
☐ 5	Wes Unseld	4.00	1.80	.50
	Washington Bullets			
☐ 6	Butch Beard	2.00	.90	.25
	New York Knicks			
☐ 7	Lloyd Neal	1.50	.65	.19
	Portland Trail Blazers			
☐ 8	Tom Henderson	1.50	.65	.19
	Atlanta Hawks			
☐ 9	Jim McMillian	1.75	.80	.22
	Buffalo Braves			
☐ 10	Bob Lanier	4.50	2.00	.55
	Detroit Pistons			
☐ 11	Junior Bridgeman	2.50	1.15	.30
	Milwaukee Bucks			
☐ 12	Corky Calhoun	1.75	.80	.22
	Los Angeles Lakers			
☐ 13	Billy Keller	1.50	.65	.19
	Indiana Pacers			
☐ 14	Mickey Johnson	2.00	.90	.25
	Chicago Bulls			
☐ 15	Fred Brown	2.00	.90	.25
	Seattle Supersonics			
☐ 16	Jamaal Wilkes	3.00	1.35	.40
	Golden State Warriors			
☐ 17	Louie Nelson	1.50	.65	.19
	New Orleans Jazz			
☐ 18	Ed Ratleff	1.50	.65	.19
	Houston Rockets			
☐ 19	Billy Paultz	2.00	.90	.25
	San Antonio Spurs			
☐ 20	Nate Archibald	4.00	1.80	.50
	Kansas City Kings			
☐ 21	Steve Mix	1.75	.80	.22
	Philadelphia 76ers			
☐ 22	Ralph Simpson	1.75	.80	.22
	Denver Nuggets			
☐ 23	Campy Russell	2.00	.90	.25
	Cleveland Cavaliers			
☐ 24	Charlie Scott	2.00	.90	.25
	Boston Celtics			
☐ 25	Artis Gilmore	5.00	2.30	.60
	Chicago Bulls			
☐ 26	Dick Van Arsdale	1.75	.80	.22
	Phoenix Suns			
☐ 27	Phil Chenier	1.75	.80	.22
	Washington Bullets			
☐ 28	Spencer Haywood	2.50	1.15	.30

	New York Knicks			
☐ 29	Chris Ford	2.00	.90	.25
	Detroit Pistons			
☐ 30	Dave Cowens	8.00	3.60	1.00
	Boston Celtics			
☐ 31	Sidney Wicks	2.00	.90	.25
	Portland Trail Blazers			
☐ 32	Jim Price	1.50	.65	.19
	Milwaukee Bucks			
☐ 33	Dwight Jones	1.50	.65	.19
	Houston Rockets			
☐ 34	Lucius Allen	2.00	.90	.25
	Los Angeles Lakers			
☐ 35	Marvin Barnes	2.00	.90	.25
	Detroit Pistons			
☐ 36	Henry Bibby	1.75	.80	.22
	New Orleans Jazz			
☐ 37	Joe Meriweather	2.00	.90	.25
	Atlanta Hawks			
☐ 38	Doug Collins	6.00	2.70	.75
	Philadelphia 76ers			
☐ 39	Garfield Heard	1.50	.65	.19
	Phoenix Suns			
☐ 40	Randy Smith	1.75	.80	.22
	Buffalo Braves			
☐ 41	Tom Burleson	1.75	.80	.22
	Seattle Supersonics			
☐ 42	Dave Twardzik	1.75	.80	.22
	Portland Trail Blazers			
☐ 43	Bill Bradley	14.00	6.25	1.75
	New York Knicks			
☐ 44	Calvin Murphy	2.50	1.15	.30
	Houston Rockets			
☐ 45	Bob Love	2.50	1.15	.30
	Chicago Bulls			
☐ 46	Brian Winters	1.75	.80	.22
	Milwaukee Bucks			
☐ 47	Glenn McDonald	1.50	.65	.19
	Boston Celtics			
☐ 48	Checklist 1-144	18.00	2.00	.50
☐ 49	Bird Averitt	1.50	.65	.19
	Buffalo Braves			
☐ 50	Rick Barry	10.00	4.50	1.25
	Golden State Warriors			
☐ 51	Ticky Burden	1.50	.65	.19
	New York Knicks			
☐ 52	Rich Jones	1.50	.65	.19
	New York Nets			
☐ 53	Austin Carr	2.00	.90	.25
	Cleveland Cavaliers			
☐ 54	Steve Kuberski	1.75	.80	.22
	Boston Celtics			
☐ 55	Paul Westphal	8.00	3.60	1.00
	Phoenix Suns			
☐ 56	Mike Riordan	1.75	.80	.22
	Washington Bullets			
☐ 57	Bill Walton	25.00	11.50	3.10
	Portland Trail Blazers			
☐ 58	Eric Money	2.00	.90	.25
	Detroit Pistons			
☐ 59	John Drew	2.00	.90	.25
	Atlanta Hawks			
☐ 60	Pete Maravich	25.00	11.50	3.10
	New Orleans Jazz			
☐ 61	John Shumate	2.50	1.15	.30
	Buffalo Braves			
☐ 62	Mack Calvin	2.00	.90	.25
	Los Angeles Lakers			
☐ 63	Bruce Seals	1.50	.65	.19
	Seattle Supersonics			
☐ 64	Walt Frazier	6.50	2.90	.80
	New York Knicks			
☐ 65	Elmore Smith	1.75	.80	.22
	Milwaukee Bucks			

☐	66	Rudy Tomjanovich	7.00	3.10	.85
		Houston Rockets			
☐	67	Sam Lacey	1.50	.65	.19
		Kansas City Kings			
☐	68	George Gervin	10.00	4.50	1.25
		San Antonio Spurs			
☐	69	Gus Williams	6.00	2.70	.75
		Golden State Warriors			
☐	70	George McGinnis	3.00	1.35	.40
		Philadelphia 76ers			
☐	71	Len Elmore	2.00	.90	.25
		Indiana Pacers			
☐	72	Jack Marin	1.75	.80	.22
		Chicago Bulls			
☐	73	Brian Taylor	1.50	.65	.19
		New York Nets			
☐	74	Jim Brewer	1.50	.65	.19
		Cleveland Cavaliers			
☐	75	Alvan Adams	5.00	2.30	.60
		Phoenix Suns			
☐	76	Dave Bing	3.00	1.35	.40
		Washington Bullets			
☐	77	Phil Jackson	6.00	2.70	.75
		New York Knicks			
☐	78	Geoff Petrie	2.00	.90	.25
		Portland Trail Blazers			
☐	79	Mike Sojourner	1.50	.65	.19
		Atlanta Hawks			
☐	80	James Silas	2.00	.90	.25
		San Antonio Spurs			
☐	81	Bob Dandridge	1.75	.80	.22
		Milwaukee Bucks			
☐	82	Ernie DiGregorio	1.75	.80	.22
		Buffalo Braves			
☐	83	Cazzie Russell	2.00	.90	.25
		Los Angeles Lakers			
☐	84	Kevin Porter	2.00	.90	.25
		Detroit Pistons			
☐	85	Tom Boerwinkle	1.50	.65	.19
		Chicago Bulls			
☐	86	Darnell Hillman	1.75	.80	.22
		Indiana Pacers			
☐	87	Herm Gilliam	1.50	.65	.19
		Seattle Supersonics			
☐	88	Nate Williams	1.50	.65	.19
		New Orleans Jazz			
☐	89	Phil Smith	1.50	.65	.19
		Golden State Warriors			
☐	90	John Havlicek	14.00	6.25	1.75
		Boston Celtics			
☐	91	Kevin Kunnert	1.50	.65	.19
		Houston Rockets			
☐	92	Jimmy Walker	1.50	.65	.19
		Kansas City Kings			
☐	93	Billy Cunningham	4.00	1.80	.50
		Philadelphia 76ers			
☐	94	Dan Issel	6.00	2.70	.75
		Denver Nuggets			
☐	95	Ron Boone	1.75	.80	.22
		Kansas City Kings			
☐	96	Lou Hudson	2.00	.90	.25
		Atlanta Hawks			
☐	97	Jim Chones	1.75	.80	.22
		Cleveland Cavaliers			
☐	98	Earl Monroe	5.00	2.30	.60
		New York Knicks			
☐	99	Tom Van Arsdale	1.75	.80	.22
		Buffalo Braves			
☐	100	Kareem Abdul-Jabbar	30.00	13.50	3.80
		Los Angeles Lakers			
☐	101	Moses Malone	30.00	13.50	3.80
		Portland Trail Blazers			
☐	102	Ricky Sobers	2.00	.90	.25

	Phoenix Suns			
☐ 103	Swen Nater	1.75	.80	.22
	Milwaukee Bucks			
☐ 104	Leonard Robinson	2.00	.90	.25
	Washington Bullets			
☐ 105	Don Watts	1.75	.80	.22
	Seattle Supersonics			
☐ 106	Otto Moore	1.50	.65	.19
	New Orleans Jazz			
☐ 107	Maurice Lucas	3.00	1.35	.40
	Portland Trail Blazers			
☐ 108	Norm Van Lier	2.00	.90	.25
	Chicago Bulls			
☐ 109	Clifford Ray	1.75	.80	.22
	Golden State Warriors			
☐ 110	David Thompson	30.00	13.50	3.80
	Denver Nuggets			
☐ 111	Fred Carter	1.75	.80	.22
	Philadelphia 76ers			
☐ 112	Caldwell Jones	2.00	.90	.25
	Philadelphia 76ers			
☐ 113	John Williamson	1.75	.80	.22
	New York Nets			
☐ 114	Bobby Smith	1.50	.65	.19
	Cleveland Cavaliers			
☐ 115	JoJo White	2.00	.90	.25
	Boston Celtics			
☐ 116	Curtis Perry	1.50	.65	.19
	Phoenix Suns			
☐ 117	John Gianelli	1.50	.65	.19
	New York Knicks			
☐ 118	Curtis Rowe	2.00	.90	.25
	Detroit Pistons			
☐ 119	Lionel Hollins	4.00	1.80	.50
	Portland Trail Blazers			
☐ 120	Elvin Hayes	6.00	2.70	.75
	Washington Bullets			
☐ 121	Ken Charles	1.50	.65	.19
	Atlanta Hawks			
☐ 122	Dave Meyers	3.00	1.35	.40
	Milwaukee Bucks			
☐ 123	Jerry Sloan	3.00	1.35	.40
	Chicago Bulls			
☐ 124	Billy Knight	1.75	.80	.22
	Indiana Pacers			
☐ 125	Gail Goodrich	3.00	1.35	.40
	Los Angeles Lakers			
☐ 126	Kareem Abdul-Jabbar AS	20.00	9.00	2.50
	Los Angeles Lakers			
☐ 127	Julius Erving AS	25.00	11.50	3.10
	New York Nets			
☐ 128	George McGinnis AS	2.50	1.15	.30
	Philadelphia 76ers			
☐ 129	Nate Archibald AS	2.50	1.15	.30
	Kansas City Kings			
☐ 130	Pete Maravich AS	14.00	6.25	1.75
	New Orleans Jazz			
☐ 131	Dave Cowens AS	4.50	2.00	.55
	Boston Celtics			
☐ 132	Rick Barry AS	4.50	2.00	.55
	Golden State Warriors			
☐ 133	Elvin Hayes AS	4.00	1.80	.50
	Washington Bullets			
☐ 134	James Silas AS	2.00	.90	.25
	San Antonio Spurs			
☐ 135	Randy Smith AS	2.00	.90	.25
	Buffalo Braves			
☐ 136	Leonard Gray	1.50	.65	.19
	Seattle Supersonics			
☐ 137	Charles Johnson	1.50	.65	.19
	Golden State Warriors			
☐ 138	Ron Behagen	1.50	.65	.19
	New Orleans Jazz			

		NRMT	VG-E	GOOD
☐ 139	Mike Newlin Houston Rockets	1.75	.80	.22
☐ 140	Bob McAdoo Buffalo Braves	7.00	3.10	.85
☐ 141	Mike Gale San Antonio Spurs	1.50	.65	.19
☐ 142	Scott Wedman Kansas City Kings	2.00	.90	.25
☐ 143	Lloyd Free Philadelphia 76ers	6.00	2.70	.75
☐ 144	Bobby Jones Denver Nuggets	5.00	1.75	.40

1977-78 Topps

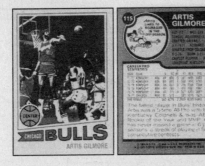

The 1977-78 Topps basketball card set consists of 132 standard-sized (2 1/2" by 3 1/2") cards. Card backs are printed in green and black on either white or gray card stock. The white card stock is considered more desirable by most collectors and may even be a little tougher to find. The key Rookie Cards in this set are Adrian Dantley, John Lucas, and Robert Parish.

		NRMT	VG-E	GOOD
COMPLETE SET (132)		120.00	55.00	15.00
COMMON PLAYER (1-132)		.30	.14	.04
*GRAY AND WHITE BACKS: EQUAL VALUE				
☐ 1	Kareem Abdul-Jabbar Los Angeles Lakers	18.00	6.50	1.75
☐ 2	Henry Bibby Philadelphia 76ers	.35	.16	.04
☐ 3	Curtis Rowe Boston Celtics	.40	.18	.05
☐ 4	Norm Van Lier Chicago Bulls	.35	.16	.04
☐ 5	Darnell Hillman New Jersey Nets	.35	.16	.04
☐ 6	Earl Monroe New York Knicks	3.00	1.35	.40
☐ 7	Leonard Gray Washington Bullets	.30	.14	.04
☐ 8	Bird Averitt Buffalo Braves	.30	.14	.04
☐ 9	Jim Brewer Cleveland Cavaliers	.30	.14	.04
☐ 10	Paul Westphal Phoenix Suns	3.00	1.35	.40
☐ 11	Bob Gross Portland Trail Blazers	.75	.35	.09

☐ 12	Phil Smith	.30	.14	.04
	Golden State Warriors			
☐ 13	Dan Roundfield	1.00	.45	.13
	Indiana Pacers			
☐ 14	Brian Taylor	.30	.14	.04
	Denver Nuggets			
☐ 15	Rudy Tomjanovich	1.50	.65	.19
	Houston Rockets			
☐ 16	Kevin Porter	.40	.18	.05
	Detroit Pistons			
☐ 17	Scott Wedman	.50	.23	.06
	Kansas City Kings			
☐ 18	Lloyd Free	.75	.35	.09
	Philadelphia 76ers			
☐ 19	Tom Boswell	.40	.18	.05
	Boston Celtics			
☐ 20	Pete Maravich	8.00	3.60	1.00
	New Orleans Jazz			
☐ 21	Cliff Poindexter	.30	.14	.04
	Chicago Bulls			
☐ 22	Bubbles Hawkins	.30	.14	.04
	New Jersey Nets			
☐ 23	Kevin Grevey	1.50	.65	.19
	Washington Bullets			
☐ 24	Ken Charles	.30	.14	.04
	Atlanta Hawks			
☐ 25	Bob Dandridge	.35	.16	.04
	Washington Bullets			
☐ 26	Lonnie Shelton	.60	.25	.08
	New York Knicks			
☐ 27	Don Chaney	.35	.16	.04
	Los Angeles Lakers			
☐ 28	Larry Kenon	.35	.16	.04
	San Antonio Spurs			
☐ 29	Checklist 1-132	3.00	.30	.06
☐ 30	Fred Brown	.50	.23	.06
	Seattle Supersonics			
☐ 31	John Gianelli UER	.30	.14	.04
	Cleveland Cavaliers			
	(Listed as Cavaliers,			
	should be Buffalo Braves)			
☐ 32	Austin Carr	.75	.35	.09
	Cleveland Cavaliers			
☐ 33	Jamaal Wilkes	1.00	.45	.13
	Los Angeles Lakers			
☐ 34	Caldwell Jones	.40	.18	.05
	Philadelphia 76ers			
☐ 35	JoJo White	1.00	.45	.13
	Boston Celtics			
☐ 36	Scott May	1.50	.65	.19
	Chicago Bulls			
☐ 37	Mike Newlin	.35	.16	.04
	Houston Rockets			
☐ 38	Mel Davis	.30	.14	.04
	New Jersey Nets			
☐ 39	Lionel Hollins	.75	.35	.09
	Portland Trail Blazers			
☐ 40	Elvin Hayes	4.00	1.80	.50
	Washington Bullets			
☐ 41	Dan Issel	2.50	1.15	.30
	Denver Nuggets			
☐ 42	Ricky Sobers	.30	.14	.04
	Phoenix Suns			
☐ 43	Don Ford	.30	.14	.04
	Los Angeles Lakers			
☐ 44	John Williamson	.35	.16	.04
	Indiana Pacers			
☐ 45	Bob McAdoo	1.75	.80	.22
	New York Knicks			
☐ 46	Geoff Petrie	.35	.16	.04
	Atlanta Hawks			
☐ 47	M.L. Carr	2.50	1.15	.30
	Detroit Pistons			

☐ 48	Brian Winters	.35	.16	.04
	Milwaukee Bucks			
☐ 49	Sam Lacey	.30	.14	.04
	Kansas City Kings			
☐ 50	George McGinnis	1.00	.45	.13
	Philadelphia 76ers			
☐ 51	Don Watts	.35	.16	.04
	Seattle Supersonics			
☐ 52	Sidney Wicks	.75	.35	.09
	Boston Celtics			
☐ 53	Wilbur Holland	.30	.14	.04
	Chicago Bulls			
☐ 54	Tim Bassett	.30	.14	.04
	New Jersey Nets			
☐ 55	Phil Chenier	.35	.16	.04
	Washington Bullets			
☐ 56	Adrian Dantley	12.00	5.50	1.50
	Buffalo Braves			
☐ 57	Jim Chones	.35	.16	.04
	Cleveland Cavaliers			
☐ 58	John Lucas	12.00	5.50	1.50
	Houston Rockets			
☐ 59	Cazzie Russell	.75	.35	.09
	Los Angeles Lakers			
☐ 60	David Thompson	3.00	1.35	.40
	Denver Nuggets			
☐ 61	Bob Lanier	2.00	.90	.25
	Detroit Pistons			
☐ 62	Dave Twardzik	.30	.14	.04
	Portland Trail Blazers			
☐ 63	Wilbert Jones	.35	.16	.04
	Indiana Pacers			
☐ 64	Clifford Ray	.35	.16	.04
	Golden State Warriors			
☐ 65	Doug Collins	1.50	.65	.19
	Philadelphia 76ers			
☐ 66	Tom McMillen	4.00	1.80	.50
	New York Knicks			
☐ 67	Rich Kelley	.40	.18	.05
	New Orleans Jazz			
☐ 68	Mike Bantom	.30	.14	.04
	New Jersey Nets			
☐ 69	Tom Boerwinkle	.30	.14	.04
	Chicago Bulls			
☐ 70	John Havlicek	6.00	2.70	.75
	Boston Celtics			
☐ 71	Marvin Webster	.75	.35	.09
	Seattle Supersonics			
☐ 72	Curtis Perry	.30	.14	.04
	Phoenix Suns			
☐ 73	George Gervin	6.00	2.70	.75
	San Antonio Spurs			
☐ 74	Leonard Robinson	.40	.18	.05
	New Orleans Jazz			
☐ 75	Wes Unseld	1.75	.80	.22
	Washington Bullets			
☐ 76	Dave Meyers	.60	.25	.08
	Milwaukee Bucks			
☐ 77	Gail Goodrich	1.25	.55	.16
	New Orleans Jazz			
☐ 78	Richard Washington	1.00	.45	.13
	Kansas City Kings			
☐ 79	Mike Gale	.30	.14	.04
	San Antonio Spurs			
☐ 80	Maurice Lucas	1.00	.45	.13
	Portland Trail Blazers			
☐ 81	Harvey Catchings	.40	.18	.05
	Philadelphia 76ers			
☐ 82	Randy Smith	.35	.16	.04
	Buffalo Braves			
☐ 83	Campy Russell	.35	.16	.04
	Cleveland Cavaliers			
☐ 84	Kevin Kunnert	.30	.14	.04

	Houston Rockets				
☐ 85	Lou Hudson	.75	.35	.09
	Atlanta Hawks				
☐ 86	Mickey Johnson	.35	.16	.04
	Chicago Bulls				
☐ 87	Lucius Allen	.35	.16	.04
	Kansas City Kings				
☐ 88	Spencer Haywood	1.00	.45	.13
	New York Knicks				
☐ 89	Gus Williams	1.00	.45	.13
	Golden State Warriors				
☐ 90	Dave Cowens	3.00	1.35	.40
	Boston Celtics				
☐ 91	Al Skinner	.30	.14	.04
	New Jersey Nets				
☐ 92	Swen Nater	.30	.14	.04
	Buffalo Braves				
☐ 93	Tom Henderson	.30	.14	.04
	Washington Bullets				
☐ 94	Don Buse	.35	.16	.04
	Indiana Pacers				
☐ 95	Alvan Adams	1.25	.55	.16
	Phoenix Suns				
☐ 96	Mack Calvin	.50	.23	.06
	Denver Nuggets				
☐ 97	Tom Burleson	.35	.16	.04
	Kansas City Kings				
☐ 98	John Drew	.35	.16	.04
	Atlanta Hawks				
☐ 99	Mike Green	.30	.14	.04
	Seattle Supersonics				
☐ 100	Julius Erving	20.00	9.00	2.50
	Philadelphia 76ers				
☐ 101	John Mengelt	.30	.14	.04
	Chicago Bulls				
☐ 102	Howard Porter	.35	.16	.04
	Detroit Pistons				
☐ 103	Billy Paultz	.40	.18	.05
	San Antonio Spurs				
☐ 104	John Shumate	.60	.25	.08
	Buffalo Braves				
☐ 105	Calvin Murphy	1.25	.55	.16
	Houston Rockets				
☐ 106	Elmore Smith	.35	.16	.04
	Cleveland Cavaliers				
☐ 107	Jim McMillian	.35	.16	.04
	New York Knicks				
☐ 108	Kevin Stacom	.30	.14	.04
	Boston Celtics				
☐ 109	Jan Van Breda Kolff	.30	.14	.04
	New Jersey Nets				
☐ 110	Billy Knight	.35	.16	.04
	Indiana Pacers				
☐ 111	Robert Parish	45.00	20.00	5.75
	Golden State Warriors				
☐ 112	Larry Wright	.30	.14	.04
	Washington Bullets				
☐ 113	Bruce Seals	.30	.14	.04
	Seattle Supersonics				
☐ 114	Junior Bridgeman	.40	.18	.05
	Milwaukee Bucks				
☐ 115	Artis Gilmore	2.00	.90	.25
	Chicago Bulls				
☐ 116	Steve Mix	.35	.16	.04
	Philadelphia 76ers				
☐ 117	Ron Lee	.30	.14	.04
	Phoenix Suns				
☐ 118	Bobby Jones	1.00	.45	.13
	Denver Nuggets				
☐ 119	Ron Boone	.35	.16	.04
	Kansas City Kings				
☐ 120	Bill Walton	10.00	4.50	1.25
	Portland Trail Blazers				

		NRMT	VG-E	GOOD
☐ 121	Chris Ford	.75	.35	.09
	Detroit Pistons			
☐ 122	Earl Tatum	.30	.14	.04
	Los Angeles Lakers			
☐ 123	E.C. Coleman	.30	.14	.04
	New Orleans Jazz			
☐ 124	Moses Malone	10.00	4.50	1.25
	Houston Rockets			
☐ 125	Charlie Scott	.35	.16	.04
	Boston Celtics			
☐ 126	Bobby Smith	.30	.14	.04
	Cleveland Cavaliers			
☐ 127	Nate Archibald	2.00	.90	.25
	New Jersey Nets			
☐ 128	Mitch Kupchak	3.00	1.35	.40
	Washington Bullets			
☐ 129	Walt Frazier	3.50	1.55	.45
	New York Knicks			
☐ 130	Rick Barry	5.00	2.30	.60
	Golden State Warriors			
☐ 131	Ernie DiGregorio	.35	.16	.04
	Buffalo Braves			
☐ 132	Darryl Dawkins	8.00	2.00	.40
	Philadelphia 76ers			

1978-79 Topps

The 1978-79 Topps basketball card set contains 132 cards. The cards in the set measure the standard 2 1/2" by 3 1/2". Card backs are printed in orange and brown on gray card stock. The key Rookie Cards in this set are Quinn Buckner, Walter Davis, Dennis Johnson, Marques Johnson, Bernard King, Norm Nixon and Jack Sikma.

		NRMT	VG-E	GOOD
COMPLETE SET (132)		80.00	36.00	10.00
COMMON PLAYER (1-132)		.30	.14	.04
☐ 1	Bill Walton	12.00	3.60	.70
	Portland Trail Blazers			
☐ 2	Doug Collins	1.25	.55	.16
	Philadelphia 76ers			
☐ 3	Jamaal Wilkes	1.00	.45	.13
	Los Angeles Lakers			
☐ 4	Wilbur Holland	.30	.14	.04
	Chicago Bulls			
☐ 5	Bob McAdoo	1.50	.65	.19
	New York Knicks			
☐ 6	Lucius Allen	.35	.16	.04
	Kansas City Kings			

☐ 7 Wes Unseld Washington Bullets	1.50	.65	.19
☐ 8 Dave Meyers Milwaukee Bucks	.35	.16	.04
☐ 9 Austin Carr Cleveland Cavaliers	.35	.16	.04
☐ 10 Walter Davis Phoenix Suns	8.00	3.60	1.00
☐ 11 John Williamson New Jersey Nets	.35	.16	.04
☐ 12 E.C. Coleman Golden State Warriors	.30	.14	.04
☐ 13 Calvin Murphy Houston Rockets	1.25	.55	.16
☐ 14 Bobby Jones Denver Nuggets	1.00	.45	.13
☐ 15 Chris Ford Detroit Pistons	.60	.25	.08
☐ 16 Kermit Washington Boston Celtics	.35	.16	.04
☐ 17 Butch Beard New York Knicks	.35	.16	.04
☐ 18 Steve Mix Philadelphia 76ers	.35	.16	.04
☐ 19 Marvin Webster Seattle Supersonics	.40	.18	.05
☐ 20 George Gervin San Antonio Spurs	3.00	1.35	.40
☐ 21 Steve Hawes Atlanta Hawks	.30	.14	.04
☐ 22 Johnny Davis Portland Trail Blazers	.35	.16	.04
☐ 23 Swen Nater San Diego Clippers	.30	.14	.04
☐ 24 Lou Hudson Los Angeles Lakers	.50	.23	.06
☐ 25 Elvin Hayes Washington Bullets	3.50	1.55	.45
☐ 26 Nate Archibald San Diego Clippers	1.50	.65	.19
☐ 27 James Edwards Indiana Pacers	2.50	1.15	.30
☐ 28 Howard Porter New Jersey Nets	.35	.16	.04
☐ 29 Quinn Buckner Milwaukee Bucks	3.00	1.35	.40
☐ 30 Leonard Robinson New Orleans Jazz	.40	.18	.05
☐ 31 Jim Cleamons New York Knicks	.30	.14	.04
☐ 32 Campy Russell Cleveland Cavaliers	.35	.16	.04
☐ 33 Phil Smith Golden State Warriors	.30	.14	.04
☐ 34 Darryl Dawkins Philadelphia 76ers	1.50	.65	.19
☐ 35 Don Buse Phoenix Suns	.35	.16	.04
☐ 36 Mickey Johnson Chicago Bulls	.35	.16	.04
☐ 37 Mike Gale San Antonio Spurs	.30	.14	.04
☐ 38 Moses Malone Houston Rockets	6.00	2.70	.75
☐ 39 Gus Williams Seattle Supersonics	.60	.25	.08
☐ 40 Dave Cowens Boston Celtics	2.50	1.15	.30
☐ 41 Bobby Wilkerson Denver Nuggets	.50	.23	.06
☐ 42 Wilbert Jones San Diego Clippers	.30	.14	.04
☐ 43 Charlie Scott	.35	.16	.04

	Los Angeles Lakers			
☐ 44	John Drew	.35	.16	.04
	Atlanta Hawks			
☐ 45	Earl Monroe	2.50	1.15	.30
	New York Knicks			
☐ 46	John Shumate	.35	.16	.04
	Detroit Pistons			
☐ 47	Earl Tatum	.30	.14	.04
	Indiana Pacers			
☐ 48	Mitch Kupchak	.50	.23	.06
	Washington Bullets			
☐ 49	Ron Boone	.35	.16	.04
	Kansas City Kings			
☐ 50	Maurice Lucas	1.00	.45	.13
	Portland Trail Blazers			
☐ 51	Louie Dampier	.35	.16	.04
	San Antonio Spurs			
☐ 52	Aaron James	.30	.14	.04
	New Orleans Jazz			
☐ 53	John Mengelt	.30	.14	.04
	Chicago Bulls			
☐ 54	Garfield Heard	.30	.14	.04
	Phoenix Suns			
☐ 55	George Johnson	.30	.14	.04
	New Jersey Nets			
☐ 56	Junior Bridgeman	.35	.16	.04
	Milwaukee Bucks			
☐ 57	Elmore Smith	.35	.16	.04
	Cleveland Cavaliers			
☐ 58	Rudy Tomjanovich	1.25	.55	.16
	Houston Rockets			
☐ 59	Fred Brown	.60	.25	.08
	Seattle Supersonics			
☐ 60	Rick Barry UER	3.00	1.35	.40
	Golden State Warriors			
	(reversed negative)			
☐ 61	Dave Bing	1.50	.65	.19
	Boston Celtics			
☐ 62	Anthony Roberts	.30	.14	.04
	Denver Nuggets			
☐ 63	Norm Nixon	4.00	1.80	.50
	Los Angeles Lakers			
☐ 64	Leon Douglas	.35	.16	.04
	Detroit Pistons			
☐ 65	Henry Bibby	.35	.16	.04
	Philadelphia 76ers			
☐ 66	Lonnie Shelton	.35	.16	.04
	New York Knicks			
☐ 67	Checklist 1-132	2.00	.25	.05
☐ 68	Tom Henderson	.30	.14	.04
	Washington Bullets			
☐ 69	Dan Roundfield	.40	.18	.05
	Indiana Pacers			
☐ 70	Armond Hill	.35	.16	.04
	Atlanta Hawks			
☐ 71	Larry Kenon	.35	.16	.04
	San Antonio Spurs			
☐ 72	Billy Knight	.35	.16	.04
	San Diego Clippers			
☐ 73	Artis Gilmore	1.50	.65	.19
	Chicago Bulls			
☐ 74	Lionel Hollins	.35	.16	.04
	Portland Trail Blazers			
☐ 75	Bernard King	10.00	4.50	1.25
	New Jersey Nets			
☐ 76	Brian Winters	.35	.16	.04
	Milwaukee Bucks			
☐ 77	Alvan Adams	.75	.35	.09
	Phoenix Suns			
☐ 78	Dennis Johnson	15.00	6.75	1.90
	Seattle Supersonics			
☐ 79	Scott Wedman	.30	.14	.04
	Kansas City Kings			

☐ 80 Pete Maravich	6.00	2.70	.75
New Orleans Jazz			
☐ 81 Dan Issel	1.75	.80	.22
Denver Nuggets			
☐ 82 M.L. Carr	.40	.18	.05
Detroit Pistons			
☐ 83 Walt Frazier	2.50	1.15	.30
Cleveland Cavaliers			
☐ 84 Dwight Jones	.30	.14	.04
Houston Rockets			
☐ 85 JoJo White	.75	.35	.09
Boston Celtics			
☐ 86 Robert Parish	8.00	3.60	1.00
Golden State Warriors			
☐ 87 Charlie Criss	.40	.18	.05
Atlanta Hawks			
☐ 88 Jim McMillian	.35	.16	.04
New York Knicks			
☐ 89 Chuck Williams	.30	.14	.04
San Diego Clippers			
☐ 90 George McGinnis	.75	.35	.09
Philadelphia 76ers			
☐ 91 Billy Paultz	.40	.18	.05
San Antonio Spurs			
☐ 92 Bob Dandridge	.35	.16	.04
Washington Bullets			
☐ 93 Ricky Sobers	.30	.14	.04
Indiana Pacers			
☐ 94 Paul Silas	.35	.16	.04
Seattle Supersonics			
☐ 95 Gail Goodrich	1.00	.45	.13
New Orleans Jazz			
☐ 96 Tim Bassett	.30	.14	.04
New Jersey Nets			
☐ 97 Ron Lee	.30	.14	.04
Phoenix Suns			
☐ 98 Bob Gross	.30	.14	.04
Portland Trail Blazers			
☐ 99 Sam Lacey	.30	.14	.04
Kansas City Kings			
☐ 100 David Thompson	2.50	1.15	.30
Denver Nuggets			
(College North Carolina,			
should be NC State)			
☐ 101 John Gianelli	.30	.14	.04
Milwaukee Bucks			
☐ 102 Norm Van Lier	.35	.16	.04
Chicago Bulls			
☐ 103 Caldwell Jones	.40	.18	.05
Philadelphia 76ers			
☐ 104 Eric Money	.30	.14	.04
Detroit Pistons			
☐ 105 Jim Chones	.35	.16	.04
Cleveland Cavaliers			
☐ 106 John Lucas	2.50	1.15	.30
Houston Rockets			
☐ 107 Spencer Haywood	.75	.35	.09
New York Knicks			
☐ 108 Eddie Johnson	.60	.25	.08
Atlanta Hawks			
☐ 109 Sidney Wicks	.50	.23	.06
Boston Celtics			
☐ 110 Kareem Abdul-Jabbar	8.00	3.60	1.00
Los Angeles Lakers			
☐ 111 Sonny Parker	.40	.18	.05
Golden State Warriors			
☐ 112 Randy Smith	.35	.16	.04
San Diego Clippers			
☐ 113 Kevin Grevey	.30	.14	.04
Washington Bullets			
☐ 114 Rich Kelley	.30	.14	.04
New Orleans Jazz			
☐ 115 Scott May	.50	.23	.06

	Chicago Bulls		
☐ 116	Lloyd Free .... .40	.18	.05
	Philadelphia 76ers		
☐ 117	Jack Sikma 7.00	3.10	.85
	Seattle Supersonics		
☐ 118	Kevin Porter .... .40	.18	.05
	New Jersey Nets		
☐ 119	Darnell Hillman .... .35	.16	.04
	Denver Nuggets		
☐ 120	Paul Westphal 2.50	1.15	.30
	Phoenix Suns		
☐ 121	Richard Washington .... .30	.14	.04
	Kansas City Kings		
☐ 122	Dave Twardzik .... .35	.16	.04
	Portland Trail Blazers		
☐ 123	Mike Bantom .... .30	.14	.04
	Indiana Pacers		
☐ 124	Mike Newlin .... .35	.16	.04
	Houston Rockets		
☐ 125	Bob Lanier 1.50	.65	.19
	Detroit Pistons		
☐ 126	Marques Johnson 3.50	1.55	.45
	Milwaukee Bucks		
☐ 127	Foots Walker .... .40	.18	.05
	Cleveland Cavaliers		
☐ 128	Cedric Maxwell 2.50	1.15	.30
	Boston Celtics		
☐ 129	Ray Williams .... .75	.35	.09
	New York Knicks		
☐ 130	Julius Erving 15.00	6.75	1.90
	Philadelphia 76ers		
☐ 131	Clifford Ray .... .35	.16	.04
	Golden State Warriors		
☐ 132	Adrian Dantley 3.00	1.00	.25
	Los Angeles Lakers		

1979-80 Topps

The 1979-80 Topps basketball card set contains 132 cards of NBA players. The cards in the set measure the standard 2 1/2" by 3 1/2". Card backs are printed in red and black on gray card stock. All-Star selections are designated as AS1 for first team selections and AS2 for second team selections and are denoted on the front of the player's regular card. Notable Rookie Cards in this set include Alex English, Reggie Theus, and Mychal Thompson.

		MINT	EXC	G-VG
	COMPLETE SET (132)	80.00	36.00	10.00
	COMMON PLAYER (1-132)	.30	.14	.04
☐ 1	George Gervin	3.00	1.00	.25
	San Antonio Spurs			
☐ 2	Mitch Kupchak	.35	.16	.04
	Washington Bullets			
☐ 3	Henry Bibby	.35	.16	.04
	Philadelphia 76ers			
☐ 4	Bob Gross	.30	.14	.04
	Portland Trail Blazers			
☐ 5	Dave Cowens	2.00	.90	.25
	Boston Celtics			
☐ 6	Dennis Johnson	2.00	.90	.25
	Seattle Supersonics			
☐ 7	Scott Wedman	.30	.14	.04
	Kansas City Kings			
☐ 8	Earl Monroe	2.00	.90	.25
	New York Knicks			
☐ 9	Mike Bantom	.30	.14	.04
	Indiana Pacers			
☐ 10	Kareem Abdul-Jabbar AS	8.00	3.60	1.00
	Los Angeles Lakers			
☐ 11	JoJo White	.60	.25	.08
	Golden State Warriors			

☐ 12	Spencer Haywood	.50	.23	.06
	Utah Jazz			
☐ 13	Kevin Porter	.35	.16	.04
	Detroit Pistons			
☐ 14	Bernard King	2.00	.90	.25
	New Jersey Nets			
☐ 15	Mike Newlin	.35	.16	.04
	Houston Rockets			
☐ 16	Sidney Wicks	.50	.23	.06
	San Diego Clippers			
☐ 17	Dan Issel	1.25	.55	.16
	Denver Nuggets			
☐ 18	Tom Henderson	.30	.14	.04
	Washington Bullets			
☐ 19	Jim Chones	.35	.16	.04
	Cleveland Cavaliers			
☐ 20	Julius Erving	14.00	6.25	1.75
	Philadelphia 76ers			
☐ 21	Brian Winters	.30	.14	.04
	Milwaukee Bucks			
☐ 22	Billy Paultz	.40	.18	.05
	San Antonio Spurs			
☐ 23	Cedric Maxwell	.60	.25	.08
	Boston Celtics			
☐ 24	Eddie Johnson	.30	.14	.04
	Atlanta Hawks			
☐ 25	Artis Gilmore	1.00	.45	.13
	Chicago Bulls			
☐ 26	Maurice Lucas	.60	.25	.08
	Portland Trail Blazers			
☐ 27	Gus Williams	.50	.23	.06
	Seattle Supersonics			
☐ 28	Sam Lacey	.30	.14	.04
	Kansas City Kings			
☐ 29	Toby Knight	.30	.14	.04
	New York Knicks			
☐ 30	Paul Westphal AS1	1.50	.65	.19
	Phoenix Suns			
☐ 31	Alex English	14.00	6.25	1.75
	Indiana Pacers			
☐ 32	Gail Goodrich	.60	.25	.08
	Utah Jazz			
☐ 33	Caldwell Jones	.40	.18	.05
	Philadelphia 76ers			
☐ 34	Kevin Grevey	.30	.14	.04
	Washington Bullets			
☐ 35	Jamaal Wilkes	.60	.25	.08
	Los Angeles Lakers			
☐ 36	Sonny Parker	.30	.14	.04
	Golden State Warriors			

☐ 37	John Gianelli	.30	.14	.04
	New Jersey Nets			
☐ 38	John Long	.75	.35	.09
	Detroit Pistons			
☐ 39	George Johnson	.30	.14	.04
	New Jersey Nets			
☐ 40	Lloyd Free AS2	.40	.18	.05
	San Diego Clippers			
☐ 41	Rudy Tomjanovich	1.00	.45	.13
	Houston Rockets			
☐ 42	Foots Walker	.35	.16	.04
	Cleveland Cavaliers			
☐ 43	Dan Roundfield	.40	.18	.05
	Atlanta Hawks			
☐ 44	Reggie Theus	3.50	1.55	.45
	Chicago Bulls			
☐ 45	Bill Walton	6.00	2.70	.75
	San Diego Clippers			
☐ 46	Fred Brown	.40	.18	.05
	Seattle Supersonics			
☐ 47	Darnell Hillman	.35	.16	.04
	Kansas City Kings			
☐ 48	Ray Williams	.35	.16	.04
	New York Knicks			
☐ 49	Larry Kenon	.35	.16	.04
	San Antonio Spurs			
☐ 50	David Thompson	2.00	.90	.25
	Denver Nuggets			
☐ 51	Billy Knight	.35	.16	.04
	Indiana Pacers			
☐ 52	Alvan Adams	.40	.18	.05
	Phoenix Suns			
☐ 53	Phil Smith	.30	.14	.04
	Golden State Warriors			
☐ 54	Adrian Dantley	1.25	.55	.16
	Los Angeles Lakers			
☐ 55	John Williamson	.35	.16	.04
	New Jersey Nets			
☐ 56	Campy Russell	.35	.16	.04
	Cleveland Cavaliers			
☐ 57	Armond Hill	.30	.14	.04
	Atlanta Hawks			
☐ 58	Bob Lanier	1.25	.55	.16
	Detroit Pistons			
☐ 59	Mickey Johnson	.35	.16	.04
	Chicago Bulls			
☐ 60	Pete Maravich	6.00	2.70	.75
	Utah Jazz			
☐ 61	Nick Weatherspoon	.30	.14	.04
	San Diego Clippers			
☐ 62	Robert Reid	.75	.35	.09
	Houston Rockets			
☐ 63	Mychal Thompson	3.00	1.35	.40
	Portland Trail Blazers			
☐ 64	Doug Collins	1.00	.45	.13
	Philadelphia 76ers			
☐ 65	Wes Unseld	1.00	.45	.13
	Washington Bullets			
☐ 66	Jack Sikma	1.50	.65	.19
	Seattle Supersonics			
☐ 67	Bobby Wilkerson	.30	.14	.04
	Denver Nuggets			
☐ 68	Bill Robinzine	.30	.14	.04
	Kansas City Kings			
☐ 69	Joe Meriweather	.30	.14	.04
	New York Knicks			
☐ 70	Marques Johnson AS1	.75	.35	.09
	Milwaukee Bucks			
☐ 71	Ricky Sobers	.30	.14	.04
	Indiana Pacers			
☐ 72	Clifford Ray	.35	.16	.04
	Golden State Warriors			
☐ 73	Tim Bassett	.30	.14	.04

	New Jersey Nets			
☐ 74	James Silas	.35	.16	.04
	San Antonio Spurs			
☐ 75	Bob McAdoo	1.00	.45	.13
	Boston Celtics			
☐ 76	Austin Carr	.35	.16	.04
	Cleveland Cavaliers			
☐ 77	Don Ford	.30	.14	.04
	Los Angeles Lakers			
☐ 78	Steve Hawes	.30	.14	.04
	Atlanta Hawks			
☐ 79	Ron Brewer	.35	.16	.04
	Portland Trail Blazers			
☐ 80	Walter Davis	1.25	.55	.16
	Phoenix Suns			
☐ 81	Calvin Murphy	1.00	.45	.13
	Houston Rockets			
☐ 82	Tom Boswell	.30	.14	.04
	Denver Nuggets			
☐ 83	Lonnie Shelton	.35	.16	.04
	Seattle Supersonics			
☐ 84	Terry Tyler	.35	.16	.04
	Detroit Pistons			
☐ 85	Randy Smith	.35	.16	.04
	San Diego Clippers			
☐ 86	Rich Kelley	.30	.14	.04
	Utah Jazz			
☐ 87	Otis Birdsong	.60	.25	.08
	Kansas City Kings			
☐ 88	Marvin Webster	.40	.18	.05
	New York Knicks			
☐ 89	Eric Money	.30	.14	.04
	Philadelphia 76ers			
☐ 90	Elvin Hayes AS1	3.00	1.35	.40
	Washington Bullets			
☐ 91	Junior Bridgeman	.35	.16	.04
	Milwaukee Bucks			
☐ 92	Johnny Davis	.30	.14	.04
	Indiana Pacers			
☐ 93	Robert Parish	5.00	2.30	.60
	Golden State Warriors			
☐ 94	Eddie Jordan	.30	.14	.04
	New Jersey Nets			
☐ 95	Leonard Robinson	.40	.18	.05
	Phoenix Suns			
☐ 96	Rick Robey	.40	.18	.05
	Boston Celtics			
☐ 97	Norm Nixon	.60	.25	.08
	Los Angeles Lakers			
☐ 98	Mark Olberding	.30	.14	.04
	San Antonio Spurs			
☐ 99	Wilbur Holland	.30	.14	.04
	Utah Jazz			
☐ 100	Moses Malone AS1	5.00	2.30	.60
	Houston Rockets			
☐ 101	Checklist 1-132	2.00	.16	.04
☐ 102	Tom Owens	.30	.14	.04
	Portland Trail Blazers			
☐ 103	Phil Chenier	.35	.16	.04
	Washington Bullets			
☐ 104	John Johnson	.30	.14	.04
	Seattle Supersonics			
☐ 105	Darryl Dawkins	1.00	.45	.13
	Philadelphia 76ers			
☐ 106	Charlie Scott	.35	.16	.04
	Denver Nuggets			
☐ 107	M.L. Carr	.40	.18	.05
	Detroit Pistons			
☐ 108	Phil Ford	3.00	1.35	.40
	Kansas City Kings			
☐ 109	Swen Nater	.30	.14	.04
	San Diego Clippers			
☐ 110	Nate Archibald	1.25	.55	.16
	Boston Celtics			

☐ 111 Aaron James	.30	.14	.04
Utah Jazz			
☐ 112 Jim Cleamons	.30	.14	.04
New York Knicks			
☐ 113 James Edwards	.60	.25	.08
Indiana Pacers			
☐ 114 Don Buse	.35	.16	.04
Phoenix Suns			
☐ 115 Steve Mix	.35	.16	.04
Philadelphia 76ers			
☐ 116 Charles Johnson	.30	.14	.04
Washington Bullets			
☐ 117 Elmore Smith	.35	.16	.04
Cleveland Cavaliers			
☐ 118 John Drew	.35	.16	.04
Atlanta Hawks			
☐ 119 Lou Hudson	.50	.23	.06
Los Angeles Lakers			
☐ 120 Rick Barry	2.00	.90	.25
Houston Rockets			
☐ 121 Kent Benson	.50	.23	.06
Milwaukee Bucks			
☐ 122 Mike Gale	.30	.14	.04
San Antonio Spurs			
☐ 123 Jan Van Breda Kolff	.30	.14	.04
New Jersey Nets			
☐ 124 Chris Ford	.50	.23	.06
Boston Celtics			
☐ 125 George McGinnis	.75	.35	.09
Denver Nuggets			
☐ 126 Leon Douglas	.30	.14	.04
Detroit Pistons			
☐ 127 John Lucas	1.50	.65	.19
Golden State Warriors			
☐ 128 Kermit Washington	.35	.16	.04
San Diego Clippers			
☐ 129 Lionel Hollins	.35	.16	.04
Portland Trail Blazers			
☐ 130 Bob Dandridge AS2	.35	.16	.04
Washington Bullets			
☐ 131 James McElroy	.30	.14	.04
Utah Jazz			
☐ 132 Bobby Jones	1.00	.35	.08
Philadelphia 76ers			

1980-81 Topps

The 1980-81 Topps basketball card set contains 264 different individual players (1 1/6" by 2 1/2") on 176 different panels of three (2 1/2" by 3 1/2"). The cards come with three individual

players per standard card. A perforation line segments each card into three players. In all, there are 176 different complete cards; however, the same player will be on more than one card. The variations stem from the fact that the cards in this set were printed on two separate sheets. In the checklist below, the first 88 cards comprise a complete set of all 264 players. The second 88 cards (89-176) provide a slight rearrangement of players within the card, but still contain the same 264 players. The cards are numbered within each series of 88 by any ordering of the left-hand player's name when the card is viewed from the back. In the checklist below, SD refers to a "Slam Dunk" star card. The letters AS in the checklist refer to an All-Star selection pictured on the front of the checklist card. There are a number of Team Leader (TL) cards which depict the team's leader in assists scoring or rebounds. Prices given below are for complete panels, as that is the typical way these cards are collected; cards which have been separated into the three parts are relatively valueless. The key card in this set is the combination of Larry Bird, Julius Erving, and Magic Johnson which features both rookie type cards of Bird and Johnson together on the same card. Since this confusing set was issued in three-player panels, there are no single-player Rookie Cards as the other basketball sets have. In addition to Larry Bird and Magic Johnson, other noteworthy players making their first card appearance in this set include Bill Cartwright, Maurice Cheeks, Michael Cooper, Sidney Moncrief and Tree Rollins. Other lesser-known players making their first card appearance include James Bailey, Greg Ballard, Dudley Bradley, Mike Bratz, Joe Bryant, Kenny Carr, Wayne Cooper, David Greenwood, Phil Hubbard, Geoff Huston, Abdul Jeelani, Greg Kelser, Reggie King, Tom LaGarde, Mark Landsberger, Allen Leavell, Calvin Natt, Roger Phegley, Ben Poquette, Micheal Ray Richardson, Cliff Robinson, Purvis Short, Jerome Whitehead, and Freeman Williams.

	MINT	EXC	G-VG
COMPLETE SET (176)	600.00	275.00	75.00
COMMON PANEL (1-176)	.30	.14	.04
☐ 1 3 Dan Roundfield 181 Julius Erving 258 Ron Brewer SD	7.00	3.10	.85
☐ 2 7 Moses Malone AS 185 Steve Mix 92 Robert Parish TL	2.00	.90	.25
☐ 3 12 Gus Williams AS 67 Geoff Huston 5 John Drew AS	.35	.16	.04
☐ 4 24 Steve Hawes 32 Nate Archibald TL 248 Elvin Hayes	1.00	.45	.13
☐ 5 29 Dan Roundfield 73 Dan Issel TL 152 Brian Winters	.40	.18	.05
☐ 6 34 Larry Bird 174 Julius Erving TL 139 Magic Johnson	400.00	180.00	50.00
☐ 7 36 Dave Cowens 186 Paul Westphal TL 142 Jamaal Wilkes	1.00	.45	.13
☐ 8 38 Pete Maravich 264 Lloyd Free SD 194 Dennis Johnson	3.00	1.35	.40
☐ 9 40 Rick Robey 234 Ad.Dantley TL 26 Eddie Johnson	.40	.18	.05
☐ 10 47 Scott May 196 K.Washington TL 177 Henry Bibby	.30	.14	.04
☐ 11 55 Don Ford 145 Quinn Buckner TL 138 Brad Holland	.30	.14	.04
☐ 12 58 Campy Russell 247 Kevin Grevey 52 Dave Robisch TL	.30	.14	.04
☐ 13 60 Foots Walker 113 Mick.Johnson TL 130 Bill Robinzine	.30	.14	.04
☐ 14 61 Austin Carr 8 Kareem Abdul-Jabbar AS 200 Calvin Natt	2.50	1.15	.30
☐ 15 63 Jim Cleamons 256 Robert Reid SD 22 Charlie Criss	.30	.14	.04

☐ 16	69 Tom LaGarde	.30		.14	.04
	215 Swen Nater TL				
	213 James Silas				
☐ 17	71 Jerome Whitehead	.40		.18	.05
	259 Artis Gilmore SD				
	184 Caldwell Jones				
☐ 18	74 John Roche TL	.30		.14	.04
	99 Clifford Ray				
	235 Ben Poquette TL				
☐ 19	75 Alex English	2.00		.90	.25
	2 Marques Johnson AS				
	68 Jeff Judkins				
☐ 20	82 Terry Tyler TL	.30		.14	.04
	21 Armond Hill TL				
	171 M.R. Richardson				
☐ 21	84 Kent Benson	.40		.18	.05
	212 John Shumate				
	229 Paul Westphal				
☐ 22	86 Phil Hubbard	1.50		.65	.19
	93 Robert Parish TL				
	126 Tom Burleson				
☐ 23	88 John Long	3.00		1.35	.40
	1 Julius Erving AS				
	49 Ricky Sobers				
☐ 24	90 Eric Money	.30		.14	.04
	57 Dave Robisch				
	254 Rick Robey SD				
☐ 25	95 Wayne Cooper	.30		.14	.04
	226 John Johnson TL				
	45 David Greenwood				
☐ 26	97 Robert Parish	4.00		1.80	.50
	187 Leon.Robinson TL				
	46 Dwight Jones				
☐ 27	98 Sonny Parker	.30		.14	.04
	197 Dave Twardzik TL				
	39 Cedric Maxwell				
☐ 28	105 Rick Barry	1.00		.45	.13
	122 Otis Birdsong TL				
	48 John Mengelt				
☐ 29	106 Allen Leavell	.30		.14	.04
	53 Foots Walker TL				
	223 Freeman Williams				
☐ 30	108 Calvin Murphy	1.00		.45	.13
	176 Maur.Cheeks TL				
	87 Greg Kelser				
☐ 31	110 Robert Reid	.40		.18	.05
	243 Wes Unseld TL				
	50 Reggie Theus				
☐ 32	111 Rudy Tomjanovich	.40		.18	.05
	13 Eddie Johnson AS				
	179 Doug Collins				
☐ 33	112 Mickey Johnson TL	1.00		.45	.13
	28 Wayne Rollins				
	15 M.R.Richardson AS				
☐ 34	115 Mike Bantom	.35		.16	.04
	6 Adrian Dantley AS				
	227 James Bailey				
☐ 35	116 Dudley Bradley	.30		.14	.04
	155 Eddie Jordan TL				
	239 Allan Bristow				
☐ 36	118 James Edwards	.30		.14	.04
	153 Mike Newlin TL				
	182 Lionel Hollins				
☐ 37	119 Mickey Johnson	.30		.14	.04
	154 Geo.Johnson TL				
	193 Leonard Robinson				
☐ 38	120 Billy Knight	.40		.18	.05
	16 Paul Westphal AS				
	59 Randy Smith				
☐ 39	121 George McGinnis	.35		.16	.04
	83 Eric Money TL				
	65 Mike Bratz				
☐ 40	124 Phil Ford TL	.30		.14	.04

	101 Phil Smith				
	224 Gus Williams TL				
☐ 41	127 Phil Ford	.30	.14	.04
	19 John Drew TL				
	209 Larry Kenon				
☐ 42	131 Scott Wedman	.35	.16	.04
	164 B.Cartwright TL				
	23 John Drew				
☐ 43	132 K.Abdul-Jabbar TL	2.50	1.15	.30
	56 Mike Mitchell				
	81 Terry Tyler TL				
☐ 44	135 K.Abdul-Jabbar	5.50	2.50	.70
	79 David Thompson				
	216 Brian Taylor TL				
☐ 45	137 Michael Cooper	3.00	1.35	.40
	148 George Johnson				
	103 Moses Malone TL				
☐ 46	140 Mark Landsberger	1.50	.65	.19
	10 Bob Lanier AS				
	222 Bill Walton				
☐ 47	141 Norm Nixon	.30	.14	.04
	123 Sam Lacey TL				
	54 Kenny Carr				
☐ 48	143 Marq.Johnson TL	25.00	11.50	3.10
	30 Larry Bird TL				
	232 Jack Sikma				
☐ 49	146 Junior Bridgeman	25.00	11.50	3.10
	31 Larry Bird TL				
	198 Ron Brewer				
☐ 50	147 Quinn Buckner	2.50	1.15	.30
	133 K.Abdul-Jabbar TL				
	207 Mike Gale				
☐ 51	149 Marques Johnson	3.00	1.35	.40
	262 Julius Erving SD				
	62 Abdul Jeelani				
☐ 52	151 Sidney Moncrief	4.50	2.00	.55
	260 Lonnie Shelton SD				
	220 Paul Silas				
☐ 53	156 George Johnson	.35	.16	.04
	9 Bill Cartwright AS				
	199 Bob Gross				
☐ 54	158 Maurice Lucas	.35	.16	.04
	261 James Edwards SD				
	157 Eddie Jordan				
☐ 55	159 Mike Newlin	.30	.14	.04
	134 Norm Nixon TL				
	180 Darryl Dawkins				
☐ 56	160 Roger Phegley	.30	.14	.04
	206 James Silas TL				
	91 Terry Tyler UER				
	(First name spelled Jams)				
☐ 57	161 Cliff Robinson	.30	.14	.04
	51 Mike Mitchell TL				
	80 Bobby Wilkerson				
☐ 58	162 Jan V.Breda Kolff	.35	.16	.04
	204 George Gervin TL				
	117 Johnny Davis				
☐ 59	165 M.R.Richardson TL	.50	.23	.06
	214 Lloyd Free TL				
	44 Artis Gilmore				
☐ 60	166 Bill Cartwright	3.00	1.35	.40
	244 Kevin Porter TL				
	25 Armond Hill				
☐ 61	168 Toby Knight	.50	.23	.06
	14 Lloyd Free AS				
	240 Adrian Dantley				
☐ 62	169 Joe Meriweather	.35	.16	.04
	218 Lloyd Free				
	42 D.Greenwood TL				
☐ 63	170 Earl Monroe	1.00	.45	.13
	27 James McElroy				
	85 Leon Douglas				
☐ 64	172 Marvin Webster	.35	.16	.04
	175 Caldwell Jones TL				

	129 Sam Lacey				
☐ 65	173 Ray Williams	.30	.14	.04
	94 John Lucas TL				
	202 Dave Twardzik				
☐ 66	178 Maurice Cheeks	30.00	13.50	3.80
	18 Magic Johnson AS				
	237 Ron Boone				
☐ 67	183 Bobby Jones	.40	.18	.05
	37 Chris Ford				
	66 Joe Hassett				
☐ 68	189 Alvan Adams	1.00	.45	.13
	163 B.Cartwright TL				
	76 Dan Issel				
☐ 69	190 Don Buse	.35	.16	.04
	242 Elvin Hayes TL				
	35 M.L. Carr				
☐ 70	191 Walter Davis	.50	.23	.06
	11 George Gervin AS				
	136 Jim Chones				
☐ 71	192 Rich Kelley	1.00	.45	.13
	102 Moses Malone TL				
	64 Winford Boynes				
☐ 72	201 Tom Owens	.30	.14	.04
	225 Jack Sikma TL				
	100 Purvis Short				
☐ 73	208 George Gervin	1.00	.45	.13
	72 Dan Issel TL				
	249 Mitch Kupchak				
☐ 74	217 Joe Bryant	2.50	1.15	.30
	263 Bobby Jones SD				
	107 Moses Malone				
☐ 75	219 Swen Nater	.35	.16	.04
	17 Calvin Murphy AS				
	70 Rich.Washington				
☐ 76	221 Brian Taylor	.30	.14	.04
	253 John Shumate SD				
	167 Larry Demic				
☐ 77	228 Fred Brown	.30	.14	.04
	205 Larry Kenon TL				
	203 Kerm.Washington				
☐ 78	230 John Johnson	.75	.35	.09
	4 Walter Davis AS				
	33 Nate Archibald				
☐ 79	231 Lonnie Shelton	.35	.16	.04
	104 Allen Leavell TL				
	96 John Lucas				
☐ 80	233 Gus Williams	.30	.14	.04
	20 Dan Roundfield TL				
	211 Kevin Restani				
☐ 81	236 Allan Bristow TL	.30	.14	.04
	210 Mark Olberding				
	255 James Bailey SD				
☐ 82	238 Tom Boswell	.75	.35	.09
	109 Billy Paultz				
	150 Bob Lanier				
☐ 83	241 Ben Poquette	.40	.18	.05
	188 Paul Westphal TL				
	77 Charlie Scott				
☐ 84	245 Greg Ballard	.30	.14	.04
	43 Reggie Theus TL				
	252 John Williamson				
☐ 85	246 Bob Dandridge	.35	.16	.04
	41 Reggie Theus TL				
	128 Reggie King				
☐ 86	250 Kevin Porter	.30	.14	.04
	114 Johnny Davis TL				
	125 Otis Birdsong				
☐ 87	251 Wes Unseld	.60	.25	.08
	195 Tom Owens TL				
	78 John Roche				
☐ 88	257 Elvin Hayes SD	.60	.25	.08
	144 Marq.Johnson TL				
	89 Bob McAdoo				

☐ 89	3 Dan Roundfield	.35	.16	.04
	218 Lloyd Free			
	42 D.Greenwood TL			
☐ 90	7 Moses Malone	1.00	.45	.13
	247 Kevin Grevey			
	52 Dave Robisch TL			
☐ 91	12 Gus Williams	.30	.14	.04
	210 Mark Olberding			
	255 James Bailey SD			
☐ 92	24 Steve Hawes	.30	.14	.04
	226 John Johnson TL			
	45 David Greenwood			
☐ 93	29 Dan Roundfield	.30	.14	.04
	113 Mick.Johnson TL			
	130 Bill Robinzine			
☐ 94	34 Larry Bird	80.00	36.00	10.00
	164 B.Cartwright TL			
	23 John Drew			
☐ 95	36 Dave Cowens	1.00	.45	.13
	16 Paul Westphal AS			
	59 Randy Smith			
☐ 96	38 Pete Maravich	2.00	.90	.25
	187 Leon.Robinson TL			
	46 Dwight Jones			
☐ 97	40 Rick Robey	.35	.16	.04
	37 Chris Ford			
	66 Joe Hassett			
☐ 98	47 Scott May	25.00	11.50	3.10
	30 Larry Bird TL			
	232 Jack Sikma			
☐ 99	55 Don Ford	.40	.18	.05
	144 Marq.Johnson TL			
	89 Bob McAdoo			
☐ 100	58 Campy Russell	.35	.16	.04
	21 Armond Hill TL			
	171 M.R.Richardson			
☐ 101	60 Foots Walker	.30	.14	.04
	122 Otis Birdsong TL			
	48 John Mengelt			
☐ 102	61 Austin Carr	.30	.14	.04
	56 Mike Mitchell			
	81 Terry Tyler TL			
☐ 103	63 Jim Cleamons	.30	.14	.04
	261 James Edwards SD			
	157 Eddie Jordan			
☐ 104	69 Tom LaGarde	.75	.35	.09
	109 Billy Paultz			
	150 Bob Lanier			
☐ 105	71 Jerome Whitehead	.35	.16	.04
	17 Calvin Murphy AS			
	70 Rich.Washington			
☐ 106	74 John Roche TL	1.00	.45	.13
	28 Wayne Rollins			
	15 M.R.Richardson AS			
☐ 107	75 Alex English	2.50	1.15	.30
	102 Moses Malone TL			
	64 Winford Boynes			
☐ 108	82 Terry Tyler TL	.30	.14	.04
	79 David Thompson			
	216 Brian Taylor TL			
☐ 109	84 Kent Benson	.35	.16	.04
	259 Artis Gilmore SD			
	184 Caldwell Jones			
☐ 110	86 Phil Hubbard	.30	.14	.04
	195 Tom Owens TL			
	78 John Roche			
☐ 111	88 John Long	25.00	11.50	3.10
	18 Magic Johnson AS			
	237 Ron Boone			
☐ 112	90 Eric Money	.30	.14	.04
	215 Swen Nater TL			
	213 James Silas			
☐ 113	95 Wayne Cooper	.30	.14	.04

		154 Geo.Johnson TL			
		193 Leon.Robinson			
☐	114	97 Robert Parish	5.00	2.30	.60
		103 Moses Malone TL			
		148 George Johnson			
☐	115	98 Sonny Parker	.35	.16	.04
		94 John Lucas TL			
		202 Dave Twardzik			
☐	116	105 Rick Barry	1.00	.45	.13
		123 Sam Lacey TL			
		54 Kenny Carr			
☐	117	106 Allen Leavell	.30	.14	.04
		197 Dave Twardzik TL			
		39 Cedric Maxwell			
☐	118	108 Calvin Murphy	.35	.16	.04
		51 Mike Mitchell TL			
		80 Bobby Wilkerson			
☐	119	110 Robert Reid	.35	.16	.04
		153 Mike Newlin TL			
		182 Lionel Hollins			
☐	120	111 Rudy Tomjanovich	.40	.18	.05
		73 Dan Issel TL			
		152 Brian Winters			
☐	121	112 Mick.Johnson TL	.60	.25	.08
		264 Lloyd Free SD			
		194 Dennis Johnson			
☐	122	115 Mike Bantom	.35	.16	.04
		204 George Gervin TL			
		117 Johnny Davis			
☐	123	116 Dudley Bradley	.40	.18	.05
		186 Paul Westphal TL			
		142 Jamaal Wilkes			
☐	124	118 James Edwards	1.25	.55	.16
		32 Nate Archibald TL			
		248 Elvin Hayes			
☐	125	119 Mickey Johnson	.40	.18	.05
		72 Dan Issel TL			
		249 Mitch Kupchak			
☐	126	120 Billy Knight	.30	.14	.04
		104 Allen Leavell TL			
		96 John Lucas			
☐	127	121 George McGinnis	1.50	.65	.19
		10 Bob Lanier AS			
		222 Bill Walton			
☐	128	124 Phil Ford TL	.35	.16	.04
		234 Adr.Dantley TL			
		26 Eddie Johnson			
☐	129	127 Phil Ford	.35	.16	.04
		43 Reggie Theus TL			
		252 John Williamson			
☐	130	131 Scott Wedman	.30	.14	.04
		244 Kevin Porter TL			
		25 Armond Hill			
☐	131	132 K.Abdul-Jabbar TL	4.00	1.80	.50
		93 Robert Parish TL			
		126 Tom Burleson			
☐	132	135 K.Abdul-Jabbar	5.50	2.50	.70
		253 John Shumate SD			
		167 Larry Demic			
☐	133	137 Michael Cooper	2.00	.90	.25
		212 John Shumate			
		229 Paul Westphal			
☐	134	140 Mark Landsberger	.50	.23	.06
		214 Lloyd Free TL			
		44 Artis Gilmore			
☐	135	141 Norm Nixon	.35	.16	.04
		242 Elvin Hayes TL			
		35 M.L. Carr			
☐	136	143 Marq.Johnson TL	.30	.14	.04
		57 Dave Robisch			
		254 Rick Robey SD			
☐	137	146 Junior Bridgeman	3.00	1.35	.40
		1 Julius Erving AS			
		49 Ricky Sobers			

☐ 138	147 Quinn Buckner .... .35	.16	.04
	2 Marques Johnson AS		
	68 Jeff Judkins		
☐ 139	149 Marques Johnson .... .30	.14	.04
	83 Eric Money TL		
	65 Mike Bratz		
☐ 140	151 Sidney Moncrief 5.50	2.50	.70
	133 K.Abdul-Jabbar TL		
	207 Mike Gale		
☐ 141	156 George Johnson .... .30	.14	.04
	175 Caldw.Jones TL		
	129 Sam Lacey		
☐ 142	158 Maurice Lucas 3.00	1.35	.40
	262 Julius Erving SD		
	62 Abdul Jeelani		
☐ 143	159 Mike Newlin .... .35	.16	.04
	243 Wes Unseld TL		
	50 Reggie Theus		
☐ 144	160 Roger Phegley .... .30	.14	.04
	145 Quinn Buckner TL		
	138 Brad Holland		
☐ 145	161 Cliff Robinson .... .30	.14	.04
	114 Johnny Davis TL		
	125 Otis Birdsong		
☐ 146	162 Jan V.Breda Kolff 80.00	36.00	10.00
	139 Magic Johnson		
	174 Julius Erving TL		
☐ 147	165 M.R.Richardson TL 1.50	.65	.19
	185 Steve Mix		
	92 Robert Parish TL		
☐ 148	166 Bill Cartwright 3.00	1.35	.40
	13 Eddie Johnson AS		
	179 Doug Collins		
☐ 149	168 Toby Knight .... .40	.18	.05
	188 Paul Westphal TL		
	77 Charlie Scott		
☐ 150	169 Joe Meriweather .... .30	.14	.04
	196 K.Washington TL		
	177 Henry Bibby		
☐ 151	170 Earl Monroe 1.00	.45	.13
	206 James Silas TL		
	91 Terry Tyler		
☐ 152	172 Marvin Webster .... .35	.16	.04
	155 Eddie Jordan TL		
	239 Allan Bristow		
☐ 153	173 Ray Williams .... .30	.14	.04
	225 Jack Sikma TL		
	100 Purvis Short		
☐ 154	178 Maurice Cheeks 6.00	2.70	.75
	11 George Gervin AS		
	136 Jim Chones		
☐ 155	183 Bobby Jones .... .35	.16	.04
	99 Clifford Ray		
	235 Ben Poquette TL		
☐ 156	189 Alvan Adams .... .50	.23	.06
	14 Lloyd Free AS		
	240 Adrian Dantley		
☐ 157	190 Don Buse .... .35	.16	.04
	6 Adrian Dantley AS		
	227 James Bailey		
☐ 158	191 Walter Davis .... .35	.16	.04
	9 Bill Cartwright AS		
	199 Bob Gross		
☐ 159	192 Rich Kelley 2.50	1.15	.30
	263 Bobby Jones SD		
	107 Moses Malone		
☐ 160	201 Tom Owens .... .35	.16	.04
	134 Norm Nixon TL		
	180 Darryl Dawkins		
☐ 161	208 George Gervin 1.00	.45	.13
	53 Foots Walker TL		
	223 Freeman Williams		
☐ 162	217 Joe Bryant 2.50	1.15	.30

	8 K.Abdul-Jabbar AS			
	200 Calvin Natt			
☐ 163	219 Swen Nater	.30	.14	.04
	101 Phil Smith			
	224 Gus Williams TL			
☐ 164	221 Brian Taylor	.30	.14	.04
	256 Robert Reid SD			
	22 Charlie Criss			
☐ 165	228 Fred Brown	25.00	11.50	3.10
	31 Larry Bird TL			
	198 Ron Brewer			
☐ 166	230 John Johnson	1.00	.45	.13
	163 B.Cartwright TL			
	76 Dan Issel			
☐ 167	231 Lonnie Shelton	.30	.14	.04
	205 Larry Kenon TL			
	203 Kermit Washington			
☐ 168	233 Gus Williams	.35	.16	.04
	41 Reggie Theus TL			
	128 Reggie King			
☐ 169	236 Allan Bristow TL	.30	.14	.04
	260 Lonnie Shelton SD			
	220 Paul Silas			
☐ 170	238 Tom Boswell	.30	.14	.04
	27 James McElroy			
	85 Leon Douglas			
☐ 171	241 Ben Poquette	1.00	.45	.13
	176 Maurice Cheeks TL			
	87 Greg Kelser			
☐ 172	245 Greg Ballard	.75	.35	.09
	4 Walter Davis AS			
	33 Nate Archibald			
☐ 173	246 Bob Dandridge	.30	.14	.04
	19 John Drew TL			
	209 Larry Kenon			
☐ 174	250 Kevin Porter	.30	.14	.04
	20 Dan Roundfield TL			
	211 Kevin Restani			
☐ 175	251 Wes Unseld	.60	.25	.08
	67 Geoff Huston			
	5 John Drew AS			
☐ 176	257 Elvin Hayes SD	7.00	3.10	.85
	181 Julius Erving			
	258 Ron Brewer SD			

1981-82 Topps

The 1981-82 Topps basketball card set contains a total of 198 cards. The cards in the set measure the standard 2 1/2" by 3 1/2". These cards are numbered depending upon the regional distribution used in the issue. A 66-card national set was issued to all parts of the

country; however, subsets of 44 cards each were issued in the East, Midwest, and West. Card numbers over 66 are prefaced on the card by the region in which they were distributed, e.g., East 96. The cards themselves feature the Topps logo in the frame line and a quarter-round sunburst in the lower left-hand corner which lists the name, position, and team of the player depicted. Cards 44-66 are Team Leader (TL) cards picturing each team's statistical leaders. The back, printed in orange and brown on gray stock, features standard Topps biographical data and career statistics. There are a number of Super Action (SA) cards in the set. Rookie Cards included in this set are Joe Barry Carroll, Mike Dunleavy, Mike Gminski, Darrell Griffith, Ernie Grunfeld, Vinnie Johnson, Bill Laimbeer, Rick Mahorn, Kevin McHale, Jim Paxson and Larry Smith. The card numbering sequence is alphabetical within team within series. This was Topps' last basketball card issue until 1992.

	MINT	EXC	G-VG
COMPLETE SET (198)	90.00	40.00	11.50
COMMON PLAYER (1-66)	.12	.05	.02
COMMON PLAYER (E67-E110)	.15	.07	.02
COMMON PLAYER (MW67-MW110)	.15	.07	.02
COMMON PLAYER (W67-W110)	.15	.07	.02
☐ 1 John Drew Atlanta Hawks	.12	.05	.02
☐ 2 Dan Roundfield Atlanta Hawks	.15	.07	.02
☐ 3 Nate Archibald Boston Celtics	.75	.35	.09
☐ 4 Larry Bird Boston Celtics	25.00	11.50	3.10
☐ 5 Cedric Maxwell Boston Celtics	.25	.11	.03
☐ 6 Robert Parish Boston Celtics	3.00	1.35	.40
☐ 7 Artis Gilmore Chicago Bulls	.60	.25	.08
☐ 8 Ricky Sobers Chicago Bulls	.12	.05	.02
☐ 9 Mike Mitchell Cleveland Cavaliers	.12	.05	.02
☐ 10 Tom LaGarde Dallas Mavericks	.12	.05	.02
☐ 11 Dan Issel Denver Nuggets	.90	.40	.11
☐ 12 David Thompson Denver Nuggets	.50	.23	.06
☐ 13 Lloyd Free Golden State Warriors	.20	.09	.03
☐ 14 Moses Malone Houston Rockets	2.00	.90	.25
☐ 15 Calvin Murphy Houston Rockets	.30	.14	.04
☐ 16 Johnny Davis Indiana Pacers	.12	.05	.02
☐ 17 Otis Birdsong Milwaukee Bucks	.15	.07	.02
☐ 18 Phil Ford Kansas City Kings	.25	.11	.03
☐ 19 Scott Wedman Cleveland Cavaliers	.12	.05	.02
☐ 20 Kareem Abdul-Jabbar Los Angeles Lakers	4.00	1.80	.50
☐ 21 Magic Johnson Los Angeles Lakers	25.00	11.50	3.10
☐ 22 Norm Nixon Los Angeles Lakers	.25	.11	.03
☐ 23 Jamaal Wilkes Los Angeles Lakers	.25	.11	.03
☐ 24 Marques Johnson Milwaukee Bucks	.25	.11	.03
☐ 25 Bob Lanier Milwaukee Bucks	.75	.35	.09
☐ 26 Bill Cartwright New York Knicks	.75	.35	.09
☐ 27 Michael Ray Richardson New York Knicks	.12	.05	.02

☐ 28 Ray Williams New York Knicks	.12	.05	.02
☐ 29 Darryl Dawkins Philadelphia 76ers	.35	.16	.04
☐ 30 Julius Erving Philadelphia 76ers	6.00	2.70	.75
☐ 31 Lionel Hollins Philadelphia 76ers	.12	.05	.02
☐ 32 Bobby Jones Philadelphia 76ers	.20	.09	.03
☐ 33 Walter Davis Phoenix Suns	.30	.14	.04
☐ 34 Dennis Johnson Phoenix Suns	.50	.23	.06
☐ 35 Leonard Robinson Phoenix Suns	.15	.07	.02
☐ 36 Mychal Thompson Portland Trail Blazers	.30	.14	.04
☐ 37 George Gervin San Antonio Spurs	.90	.40	.11
☐ 38 Swen Nater San Diego Clippers	.12	.05	.02
☐ 39 Jack Sikma Seattle Supersonics	.50	.23	.06
☐ 40 Adrian Dantley Utah Jazz	.60	.25	.08
☐ 41 Darrell Griffith Utah Jazz	1.50	.65	.19
☐ 42 Elvin Hayes Houston Rockets	1.00	.45	.13
☐ 43 Fred Brown Seattle Supersonics	.25	.11	.03
☐ 44 Atlanta Hawks TL John Drew Dan Roundfield Eddie Johnson	.15	.07	.02
☐ 45 Boston Celtics TL Larry Bird Larry Bird Nate Archibald	2.00	.90	.25
☐ 46 Chicago Bulls TL Reggie Theus Artis Gilmore Reggie Theus	.25	.11	.03
☐ 47 Cleveland Cavs TL Mike Mitchell Kenny Carr Mike Bratz	.15	.07	.02
☐ 48 Dallas Mavericks TL Jim Spanarkel Tom LaGarde Brad Davis	.15	.07	.02
☐ 49 Denver Nuggets TL David Thompson Dan Issel Kenny Higgs	.25	.11	.03
☐ 50 Detroit Pistons TL John Long Phil Hubbard Ron Lee	.15	.07	.02
☐ 51 Golden State TL Lloyd Free Larry Smith John Lucas	.25	.11	.03
☐ 52 Houston Rockets TL Moses Malone Moses Malone Allen Leavell	.40	.18	.05
☐ 53 Indiana Pacers TL Billy Knight James Edwards Johnny Davis	.20	.09	.03
☐ 54 Kansas City Kings TL	.15	.07	.02

	Otis Birdsong		
	Reggie King		
	Phil Ford		
☐ 55 Los Angeles Lakers TL	1.00	.45	.13
	Kareem Abdul-Jabbar		
	Kareem Abdul-Jabbar		
	Norm Nixon		
☐ 56 Milwaukee Bucks TL	.25	.11	.03
	Marques Johnson		
	Mickey Johnson		
	Quinn Buckner		
☐ 57 New Jersey Nets TL	.15	.07	.02
	Mike Newlin		
	Maurice Lucas		
	Mike Newlin		
☐ 58 New York Knicks TL	.20	.09	.03
	Bill Cartwright		
	Bill Cartwright		
	M.R. Richardson		
☐ 59 Philadelphia 76ers TL	1.25	.55	.16
	Julius Erving		
	Caldwell Jones		
	Maurice Cheeks		
☐ 60 Phoenix Suns TL	.20	.09	.03
	Truck Robinson		
	Truck Robinson		
	Alvan Adams		
☐ 61 Portland Blazers TL	.35	.16	.04
	Jim Paxson		
	Mychal Thompson		
	Kermit Washington		
	Kelvin Ransey		
☐ 62 San Antonio Spurs TL	.20	.09	.03
	George Gervin		
	Dave Corzine		
	Johnny Moore		
☐ 63 San Diego Clippers TL	.15	.07	.02
	Freeman Williams		
	Swen Nater		
	Brian Taylor		
☐ 64 Seattle Sonics TL	.25	.11	.03
	Jack Sikma		
	Jack Sikma		
	Vinnie Johnson		
☐ 65 Utah Jazz TL	.25	.11	.03
	Adrian Dantley		
	Ben Poquette		
	Allan Bristow		
☐ 66 Washington Bullets TL	.25	.11	.03
	Elvin Hayes		
	Elvin Hayes		
	Kevin Porter		
☐ E67 Charlie Criss	.20	.09	.03
	Atlanta Hawks		
☐ E68 Eddie Johnson	.15	.07	.02
	Atlanta Hawks		
☐ E69 Wes Matthews	.15	.07	.02
	Atlanta Hawks		
☐ E70 Tom McMillen	.40	.18	.05
	Atlanta Hawks		
☐ E71 Tree Rollins	.30	.14	.04
	Atlanta Hawks		
☐ E72 M.L. Carr	.25	.11	.03
	Boston Celtics		
☐ E73 Chris Ford	.50	.23	.06
	Boston Celtics		
☐ E74 Gerald Henderson	.50	.23	.06
	Boston Celtics		
☐ E75 Kevin McHale	20.00	9.00	2.50
	Boston Celtics		
☐ E76 Rick Robey	.20	.09	.03
	Boston Celtics		
☐ E77 Darwin Cook	.30	.14	.04
	Milwaukee Bucks		

☐ E78 Mike Gminski	1.25	.55	.16
Milwaukee Bucks			
☐ E79 Maurice Lucas	.30	.14	.04
Milwaukee Bucks			
☐ E80 Mike Newlin	.20	.09	.03
New York Knicks			
☐ E81 Mike O'Koren	.40	.18	.05
Milwaukee Bucks			
☐ E82 Steve Hawes	.15	.07	.02
Atlanta Hawks			
☐ E83 Foots Walker	.20	.09	.03
Milwaukee Bucks			
☐ E84 Campy Russell	.20	.09	.03
New York Knicks			
☐ E85 DeWayne Scales	.15	.07	.02
New York Knicks			
☐ E86 Randy Smith	.20	.09	.03
New York Knicks			
☐ E87 Marvin Webster	.25	.11	.03
New York Knicks			
☐ E88 Sly Williams	.15	.07	.02
New York Knicks			
☐ E89 Mike Woodson	.40	.18	.05
Milwaukee Bucks			
☐ E90 Maurice Cheeks	1.75	.80	.22
Philadelphia 76ers			
☐ E91 Caldwell Jones	.25	.11	.03
Philadelphia 76ers			
☐ E92 Steve Mix	.20	.09	.03
Philadelphia 76ers			
☐ E93A Checklist 1-110 ERR	2.00	.90	.25
(WEST above card number)			
☐ E93B Checklist 1-110 COR	1.00	.45	.13
☐ E94 Greg Ballard	.15	.07	.02
Washington Bullets			
☐ E95 Don Collins	.15	.07	.02
Washington Bullets			
☐ E96 Kevin Grevey	.15	.07	.02
Washington Bullets			
☐ E97 Mitch Kupchak	.20	.09	.03
Washington Bullets			
☐ E98 Rick Mahorn	1.00	.45	.13
Washington Bullets			
☐ E99 Kevin Porter	.20	.09	.03
Washington Bullets			
☐ E100 Nate Archibald SA	.40	.18	.05
Boston Celtics			
☐ E101 Larry Bird SA	12.00	5.50	1.50
Boston Celtics			
☐ E102 Bill Cartwright SA	.40	.18	.05
New York Knicks			
☐ E103 Darryl Dawkins SA	.25	.11	.03
Philadelphia 76ers			
☐ E104 Julius Erving SA	3.00	1.35	.40
Philadelphia 76ers			
☐ E105 Kevin Porter SA	.20	.09	.03
Washington Bullets			
☐ E106 Bobby Jones SA	.25	.11	.03
Philadelphia 76ers			
☐ E107 Cedric Maxwell SA	.20	.09	.03
Boston Celtics			
☐ E108 Robert Parish SA	2.50	1.15	.30
Boston Celtics			
☐ E109 M.R.Richardson SA	.15	.07	.02
New York Knicks			
☐ E110 Dan Roundfield SA	.20	.09	.03
Atlanta Hawks			
☐ MW67 David Greenwood	.20	.09	.03
Chicago Bulls			
☐ MW68 Dwight Jones	.15	.07	.02
Chicago Bulls			
☐ MW69 Reggie Theus	.25	.11	.03
Chicago Bulls			

☐ MW70 Bobby Wilkerson	.15	.07	.02
Cleveland Cavaliers			
☐ MW71 Mike Bratz	.15	.07	.02
Cleveland Cavaliers			
☐ MW72 Kenny Carr	.15	.07	.02
Cleveland Cavaliers			
☐ MW73 Geoff Huston	.15	.07	.02
Cleveland Cavaliers			
☐ MW74 Bill Laimbeer	4.00	1.80	.50
Cleveland Cavaliers			
☐ MW75 Roger Phegley	.15	.07	.02
Cleveland Cavaliers			
☐ MW76 Checklist 1-110	1.00	.45	.13
Dallas Mavericks			
☐ MW77 Abdul Jeelani	.15	.07	.02
Dallas Mavericks			
☐ MW78 Bill Robinzine	.15	.07	.02
Dallas Mavericks			
☐ MW79 Jim Spanarkel	.15	.07	.02
Dallas Mavericks			
☐ MW80 Kent Benson	.20	.09	.03
Detroit Pistons			
☐ MW81 Keith Herron	.15	.07	.02
Detroit Pistons			
☐ MW82 Phil Hubbard	.15	.07	.02
Detroit Pistons			
☐ MW83 John Long	.15	.07	.02
Detroit Pistons			
☐ MW84 Terry Tyler	.15	.07	.02
Detroit Pistons			
☐ MW85 Mike Dunleavy	1.75	.80	.22
Houston Rockets			
☐ MW86 Tom Henderson	.15	.07	.02
Houston Rockets			
☐ MW87 Billy Paultz	.25	.11	.03
Houston Rockets			
☐ MW88 Robert Reid	.15	.07	.02
Houston Rockets			
☐ MW89 Mike Bantom	.15	.07	.02
Indiana Pacers			
☐ MW90 James Edwards	.35	.16	.04
Cleveland Cavaliers			
☐ MW91 Billy Knight	.20	.09	.03
Indiana Pacers			
☐ MW92 George McGinnis	.35	.16	.04
Indiana Pacers			
☐ MW93 Louis Orr	.15	.07	.02
Indiana Pacers			
☐ MW94 Ernie Grunfeld	.60	.25	.08
Kansas City Kings			
☐ MW95 Reggie King	.15	.07	.02
Kansas City Kings			
☐ MW96 Sam Lacey	.15	.07	.02
Kansas City Kings			
☐ MW97 Junior Bridgeman	.20	.09	.03
Milwaukee Bucks			
☐ MW98 Mickey Johnson	.20	.09	.03
Milwaukee Bucks			
☐ MW99 Sidney Moncrief	1.50	.65	.19
Milwaukee Bucks			
☐ MW100 Brian Winters	.15	.07	.02
Milwaukee Bucks			
☐ MW101 Dave Corzine	.30	.14	.04
San Antonio Spurs			
☐ MW102 Paul Griffin	.15	.07	.02
San Antonio Spurs			
☐ MW103 Johnny Moore	.30	.14	.04
San Antonio Spurs			
☐ MW104 Mark Olberding	.15	.07	.02
San Antonio Spurs			
☐ MW105 James Silas	.20	.09	.03
Cleveland Cavaliers			
☐ MW106 George Gervin SA	.50	.23	.06
San Antonio Spurs			

☐ MW107 Artis Gilmore SA	.25	.11	.03
Chicago Bulls			
☐ MW108 Marques Johnson SA	.20	.09	.03
Milwaukee Bucks			
☐ MW109 Bob Lanier SA	.40	.18	.05
Milwaukee Bucks			
☐ MW110 Moses Malone SA	1.50	.65	.19
Houston Rockets			
☐ W67 T.R. Dunn	.35	.16	.04
Denver Nuggets			
☐ W68 Alex English	1.50	.65	.19
Denver Nuggets			
☐ W69 Billy McKinney	.30	.14	.04
Denver Nuggets			
☐ W70 Dave Robisch	.20	.09	.03
Denver Nuggets			
☐ W71 Joe Barry Carroll	.60	.25	.08
Golden State Warriors			
☐ W72 Bernard King	1.50	.65	.19
Golden State Warriors			
☐ W73 Sonny Parker	.15	.07	.02
Golden State Warriors			
☐ W74 Purvis Short	.20	.09	.03
Golden State Warriors			
☐ W75 Larry Smith	.75	.35	.09
Golden State Warriors			
☐ W76 Jim Chones	.20	.09	.03
Los Angeles Lakers			
☐ W77 Michael Cooper	1.75	.80	.22
Los Angeles Lakers			
☐ W78 Mark Landsberger	.15	.07	.02
Los Angeles Lakers			
☐ W79 Alvan Adams	.25	.11	.03
Phoenix Suns			
☐ W80 Jeff Cook	.15	.07	.02
Phoenix Suns			
☐ W81 Rich Kelley	.15	.07	.02
Phoenix Suns			
☐ W82 Kyle Macy	.50	.23	.06
Phoenix Suns			
☐ W83 Billy Ray Bates	.50	.23	.06
Portland Trail Blazers			
☐ W84 Bob Gross	.15	.07	.02
Portland Trail Blazers			
☐ W85 Calvin Natt	.25	.11	.03
Portland Trail Blazers			
☐ W86 Lonnie Shelton	.20	.09	.03
Seattle Supersonics			
☐ W87 Jim Paxson	1.50	.65	.19
Portland Trail Blazers			
☐ W88 Kelvin Ransey	.15	.07	.02
Portland Trail Blazers			
☐ W89 Kermit Washington	.20	.09	.03
Portland Trail Blazers			
☐ W90 Henry Bibby	.20	.09	.03
San Diego Clippers			
☐ W91 Michael Brooks	.25	.11	.03
San Diego Clippers			
☐ W92 Joe Bryant	.15	.07	.02
San Diego Clippers			
☐ W93 Phil Smith	.15	.07	.02
San Diego Clippers			
☐ W94 Brian Taylor	.15	.07	.02
San Diego Clippers			
☐ W95 Freeman Williams	.30	.14	.04
San Diego Clippers			
☐ W96 James Bailey	.15	.07	.02
Seattle Supersonics			
☐ W97 Checklist 1-110	1.00	.45	.13
☐ W98 John Johnson	.15	.07	.02
Seattle Supersonics			
☐ W99 Vinnie Johnson	1.50	.65	.19
Seattle Supersonics			

☐ W100 Wally Walker..30		.14	.04
Seattle Supersonics			
☐ W101 Paul Westphal......................................25		.11	.03
Seattle Supersonics			
☐ W102 Allan Bristow..20		.09	.03
Utah Jazz			
☐ W103 Wayne Cooper......................................15		.07	.02
Utah Jazz			
☐ W104 Carl Nicks..15		.07	.02
Utah Jazz			
☐ W105 Ben Poquette..15		.07	.02
Utah Jazz			
☐ W106 Kareem Abdul-Jabbar SA..................2.50		1.15	.30
Los Angeles Lakers			
☐ W107 Dan Issel SA..50		.23	.06
Denver Nuggets			
☐ W108 Dennis Johnson SA..............................40		.18	.05
Phoenix Suns			
☐ W109 Magic Johnson SA.............................12.00		5.50	1.50
Los Angeles Lakers			
☐ W110 Jack Sikma SA......................................30		.14	.04
Seattle Supersonics			

1992-93 Topps

The complete 1992-93 Topps basketball set consists of 396 cards, issued in two 198-card series. Each card measures the standard size (2 1/2" by 3 1/2"). Gold foil versions of the cards were inserted one per 15-card plastic-wrap pack (suggested retail price 79 cents with 36 packs per box) , except if the pack contained a Beam Team card. Gold foil cards were also inserted two per 18-card mini-jumbo pack, three per 45-card retail rack pack, five per 41-card magazine jumbo pack, and 12 per factory set. On a white card face, the fronts display color action player photos framed by two-color border stripes. The player's name and team name appear in two different colored bars across the bottom of the picture. In addition to a color close-up photo, the horizontal backs have biography on a light blue panel as well as statistics and brief player profile on a yellow panel. Most Rookie Cards have the a gold-foil "'92 Draft Pix" emblem on their card fronts. Topical subsets included are Highlight (2-4), All-Star (100-126), 50 Point Club (199-215), and 20 Assist Club (216-224). The cards are numbered on the back in a basketball icon at the upper left corner. Rookie Cards include LaPhonso Ellis, Tom Gugliotta, Robert Horry, Christian Laettner, Harold Miner, Alonzo Mourning, Shaquille O'Neal, Latrell Sprewell, Clarence Weatherspoon and Walt Williams.

	MINT	EXC	G-VG
COMPLETE SET (396)......................................	15.00	6.75	1.90
COMPLETE FACT.SET (408).............................	20.00	9.00	2.50
COMPLETE SERIES 1 (198).............................	5.00	2.30	.60

		4.50	1.25
COMPLETE SERIES 2 (198)	10.00	4.50	1.25
COMMON PLAYER (1-198)	.05	.02	.01
COMMON PLAYER (199-396)	.05	.02	.01

☐ 1 Larry Bird .... .40 .18 .05
  Boston Celtics
☐ 2 Magic Johnson HL .... .12 .05 .02
  Earvin's Magical
  Moment 2/9/92
  Los Angeles Lakers
☐ 3 Michael Jordan HL .... .50 .23 .06
  Michael Lights It
  Up 6/3/92
  Chicago Bulls
☐ 4 David Robinson HL .... .12 .05 .02
  Admiral Ranks High
  In Five 4/19/92
  San Antonio Spurs
☐ 5 Johnny Newman .... .05 .02 .01
  Charlotte Hornets
☐ 6 Mike Iuzzolino .... .05 .02 .01
  Dallas Mavericks
☐ 7 Ken Norman .... .05 .02 .01
  Los Angeles Clippers
☐ 8 Chris Jackson .... .08 .04 .01
  Denver Nuggets
☐ 9 Duane Ferrell .... .05 .02 .01
  Atlanta Hawks
☐ 10 Sean Elliott .... .08 .04 .01
  San Antonio Spurs
☐ 11 Bernard King .... .10 .05 .01
  Washington Bullets
☐ 12 Armon Gilliam .... .05 .02 .01
  Philadelphia 76ers
☐ 13 Reggie Williams .... .08 .04 .01
  Denver Nuggets
☐ 14 Steve Kerr .... .05 .02 .01
  Cleveland Cavaliers
☐ 15 Anthony Bowie .... .05 .02 .01
  Orlando Magic
☐ 16 Alton Lister .... .05 .02 .01
  Golden State Warriors
☐ 17 Dee Brown .... .05 .02 .01
  Boston Celtics
☐ 18 Tom Chambers .... .08 .04 .01
  Phoenix Suns
☐ 19 Otis Thorpe .... .08 .04 .01
  Houston Rockets
☐ 20 Karl Malone .... .15 .07 .02
  Utah Jazz
☐ 21 Kenny Gattison .... .05 .02 .01
  Charlotte Hornets
☐ 22 Lionel Simmons UER .... .08 .04 .01
  (Misspelled Lionell
  on card front)
  Sacramento Kings
☐ 23 Vern Fleming .... .05 .02 .01
  Indiana Pacers
☐ 24 John Paxson .... .08 .04 .01
  Chicago Bulls
☐ 25 Mitch Richmond .... .10 .05 .01
  Sacramento Kings
☐ 26 Danny Schayes .... .05 .02 .01
  Milwaukee Bucks
☐ 27 Derrick McKey .... .05 .02 .01
  Seattle Supersonics
☐ 28 Mark Randall .... .05 .02 .01
  Minnesota Timberwolves
☐ 29 Bill Laimbeer .... .10 .05 .01
  Detroit Pistons
☐ 30 Chris Morris .... .05 .02 .01
  New Jersey Nets
☐ 31 Alex Kessler .... .05 .02 .01
  Miami Heat

☐ 32	Vlade Divac Los Angeles Lakers	.08	.04	.01
☐ 33	Rick Fox Boston Celtics	.08	.04	.01
☐ 34	Charles Shackleford Philadelphia 76ers	.05	.02	.01
☐ 35	Dominique Wilkins Atlanta Hawks	.15	.07	.02
☐ 36	Sleepy Floyd Houston Rockets	.05	.02	.01
☐ 37	Doug West Minnesota Timberwolves	.05	.02	.01
☐ 38	Pete Chilcutt Sacramento Kings	.05	.02	.01
☐ 39	Orlando Woolridge Detroit Pistons	.08	.04	.01
☐ 40	Eric Leckner Charlotte Hornets	.05	.02	.01
☐ 41	Joe Kleine Boston Celtics	.05	.02	.01
☐ 42	Scott Skiles Orlando Magic	.08	.04	.01
☐ 43	Jerrod Mustaf Phoenix Suns	.05	.02	.01
☐ 44	John Starks New York Knicks	.10	.05	.01
☐ 45	Sedale Threatt Los Angeles Lakers	.05	.02	.01
☐ 46	Doug Smith Dallas Mavericks	.05	.02	.01
☐ 47	Byron Scott Los Angeles Lakers	.08	.04	.01
☐ 48	Willie Anderson San Antonio Spurs	.05	.02	.01
☐ 49	David Benoit Utah Jazz	.05	.02	.01
☐ 50	Scott Hastings Denver Nuggets	.05	.02	.01
☐ 51	Terry Porter Portland Trail Blazers	.08	.04	.01
☐ 52	Sidney Green San Antonio Spurs	.05	.02	.01
☐ 53	Danny Young Los Angeles Clippers	.05	.02	.01
☐ 54	Magic Johnson Los Angeles Lakers	.25	.11	.03
☐ 55	Brian Williams Orlando Magic	.05	.02	.01
☐ 56	Randy Wittman Indiana Pacers	.05	.02	.01
☐ 57	Kevin McHale Boston Celtics	.10	.05	.01
☐ 58	Dana Barros Seattle Supersonics	.05	.02	.01
☐ 59	Thurl Bailey Minnesota Timberwolves	.05	.02	.01
☐ 60	Kevin Duckworth Portland Trail Blazers	.05	.02	.01
☐ 61	John Williams Cleveland Cavaliers	.08	.04	.01
☐ 62	Willie Burton Miami Heat	.05	.02	.01
☐ 63	Spud Webb Sacramento Kings	.10	.05	.01
☐ 64	Detlef Schrempf Indiana Pacers	.10	.05	.01
☐ 65	Sherman Douglas Boston Celtics	.05	.02	.01
☐ 66	Patrick Ewing New York Knicks	.20	.09	.03
☐ 67	Michael Adams Washington Bullets	.08	.04	.01
☐ 68	Vernon Maxwell	.08	.04	.01

	Houston Rockets			
☐ 69	Terrell Brandon	.05	.02	.01
	Cleveland Cavaliers			
☐ 70	Terry Catledge	.05	.02	.01
	Orlando Magic			
☐ 71	Mark Eaton	.05	.02	.01
	Utah Jazz			
☐ 72	Tony Smith	.05	.02	.01
	Los Angeles Lakers			
☐ 73	B.J. Armstrong	.10	.05	.01
	Chicago Bulls			
☐ 74	Moses Malone	.10	.05	.01
	Milwaukee Bucks			
☐ 75	Anthony Bonner	.05	.02	.01
	Sacramento Kings			
☐ 76	George McCloud	.05	.02	.01
	Indiana Pacers			
☐ 77	Glen Rice	.10	.05	.01
	Miami Heat			
☐ 78	Jon Koncak	.05	.02	.01
	Atlanta Hawks			
☐ 79	Michael Cage	.05	.02	.01
	Seattle Supersonics			
☐ 80	Ron Harper	.08	.04	.01
	Los Angeles Clippers			
☐ 81	Tom Tolbert	.05	.02	.01
	Golden State Warriors			
☐ 82	Brad Sellers	.05	.02	.01
	Detroit Pistons			
☐ 83	Winston Garland	.05	.02	.01
	Denver Nuggets			
☐ 84	Negele Knight	.05	.02	.01
	Phoenix Suns			
☐ 85	Ricky Pierce	.08	.04	.01
	Seattle Supersonics			
☐ 86	Mark Aguirre	.10	.05	.01
	Detroit Pistons			
☐ 87	Ron Anderson	.05	.02	.01
	Philadelphia 76ers			
☐ 88	Loy Vaught	.08	.04	.01
	Los Angeles Clippers			
☐ 89	Luc Longley	.05	.02	.01
	Minnesota Timberwolves			
☐ 90	Jerry Reynolds	.05	.02	.01
	Orlando Magic			
☐ 91	Terry Cummings	.08	.04	.01
	San Antonio Spurs			
☐ 92	Rony Seikaly	.10	.05	.01
	Miami Heat			
☐ 93	Derek Harper	.08	.04	.01
	Dallas Mavericks			
☐ 94	Cliff Robinson	.10	.05	.01
	Portland Trail Blazers			
☐ 95	Kenny Anderson	.10	.05	.01
	New Jersey Nets			
☐ 96	Chris Gatling	.05	.02	.01
	Golden State Warriors			
☐ 97	Stacey Augmon	.10	.05	.01
	Atlanta Hawks			
☐ 98	Chris Corchiani	.05	.02	.01
	Orlando Magic			
☐ 99	Pervis Ellison	.05	.02	.01
	Washington Bullets			
☐ 100	Larry Bird AS	.20	.09	.03
	Boston Celtics			
☐ 101	John Stockton AS UER	.10	.05	.01
	(Listed as Center on card back)			
	Phoenix Suns			
☐ 102	Clyde Drexler AS	.10	.05	.01
	Portland Trail Blazers			
☐ 103	Scottie Pippen AS	.10	.05	.01
	Chicago Bulls			

☐ 104	Reggie Lewis AS	.08	.04	.01
	Boston Celtics			
☐ 105	Hakeem Olajuwon AS	.20	.09	.03
	Houston Rockets			
☐ 106	David Robinson AS	.12	.05	.02
	San Antonio Spurs			
☐ 107	Charles Barkley AS	.12	.05	.02
	Philadelphia 76ers			
☐ 108	James Worthy AS	.08	.04	.01
	Los Angeles Lakers			
☐ 109	Kevin Willis AS	.05	.02	.01
	Atlanta Hawks			
☐ 110	Dikembe Mutombo AS	.10	.05	.01
	Denver Nuggets			
☐ 111	Joe Dumars AS	.08	.04	.01
	Detroit Pistons			
☐ 112	Jeff Hornacek AS UER	.08	.04	.01
	(5 or 7 shots should			
	be 5 of 7 shots)			
	Phoenix Suns			
☐ 113	Mark Price AS	.08	.04	.01
	Cleveland Cavaliers			
☐ 114	Michael Adams AS	.05	.02	.01
	Washington Bullets			
☐ 115	Michael Jordan AS	.50	.23	.06
	Chicago Bulls			
☐ 116	Brad Daugherty AS	.08	.04	.01
	Cleveland Cavaliers			
☐ 117	Dennis Rodman AS	.05	.02	.01
	Detroit Pistons			
☐ 118	Isiah Thomas AS	.10	.05	.01
	Detroit Pistons			
☐ 119	Tim Hardaway AS	.08	.04	.01
	Golden State Warriors			
☐ 120	Chris Mullin AS	.10	.05	.01
	Golden State Warriors			
☐ 121	Patrick Ewing AS	.10	.05	.01
	New York Knicks			
☐ 122	Dan Majerle AS	.08	.04	.01
	Phoenix Suns			
☐ 123	Karl Malone AS	.10	.05	.01
	Utah Jazz			
☐ 124	Otis Thorpe AS	.08	.04	.01
	Houston Rockets			
☐ 125	Dominique Wilkins AS	.10	.05	.01
	Atlanta Hawks			
☐ 126	Magic Johnson AS	.15	.07	.02
	Los Angeles Lakers			
☐ 127	Charles Oakley	.10	.05	.01
	New York Knicks			
☐ 128	Robert Pack	.05	.02	.01
	Portland Trail Blazers			
☐ 129	Billy Owens	.10	.05	.01
	Golden State Warriors			
☐ 130	Jeff Malone	.08	.04	.01
	Utah Jazz			
☐ 131	Danny Ferry	.05	.02	.01
	Cleveland Cavaliers			
☐ 132	Sam Bowie	.05	.02	.01
	New Jersey Nets			
☐ 133	Avery Johnson	.05	.02	.01
	Houston Rockets			
☐ 134	Jayson Williams	.05	.02	.01
	Philadelphia 76ers			
☐ 135	Fred Roberts	.05	.02	.01
	Milwaukee Bucks			
☐ 136	Greg Sutton	.05	.02	.01
	San Antonio Spurs			
☐ 137	Dennis Rodman	.08	.04	.01
	Detroit Pistons			
☐ 138	John Williams	.05	.02	.01
	Washington Bullets			
☐ 139	Greg Dreiling	.05	.02	.01

☐ 140	Indiana Pacers Rik Smits	.08	.04	.01
☐ 141	Indiana Pacers Michael Jordan	1.00	.45	.13
☐ 142	Chicago Bulls Nick Anderson	.08	.04	.01
☐ 143	Orlando Magic Jerome Kersey	.05	.02	.01
☐ 144	Portland Trail Blazers Fat Lever	.05	.02	.01
☐ 145	Dallas Mavericks Tyrone Corbin	.05	.02	.01
☐ 146	Utah Jazz Robert Parish	.10	.05	.01
☐ 147	Boston Celtics Steve Smith	.10	.05	.01
☐ 148	Miami Heat Chris Dudley	.05	.02	.01
☐ 149	New Jersey Nets Antoine Carr	.05	.02	.01
☐ 150	San Antonio Spurs Elden Campbell	.05	.02	.01
☐ 151	Los Angeles Lakers Randy White	.05	.02	.01
☐ 152	Dallas Mavericks Felton Spencer	.05	.02	.01
☐ 153	Minnesota Timberwolves Cedric Ceballos	.10	.05	.01
☐ 154	Phoenix Suns Mark Macon	.05	.02	.01
☐ 155	Denver Nuggets Jack Haley	.05	.02	.01
☐ 156	Los Angeles Lakers Bimbo Coles	.05	.02	.01
☐ 157	Miami Heat A.J. English	.05	.02	.01
☐ 158	Washington Bullets Kendall Gill	.08	.04	.01
☐ 159	Charlotte Hornets A.C. Green	.08	.04	.01
☐ 160	Los Angeles Lakers Mark West	.05	.02	.01
☐ 161	Phoenix Suns Benoit Benjamin	.05	.02	.01
☐ 162	Seattle Supersonics Tyrone Hill	.05	.02	.01
☐ 163	Golden State Warriors Larry Nance	.08	.04	.01
☐ 164	Cleveland Cavaliers Gary Grant	.05	.02	.01
☐ 165	Los Angeles Clippers Bill Cartwright	.08	.04	.01
☐ 166	Chicago Bulls Greg Anthony	.05	.02	.01
☐ 167	New York Knicks Jim Les	.05	.02	.01
☐ 168	Sacramento Kings Johnny Dawkins	.05	.02	.01
☐ 169	Philadelphia 76ers Alvin Robertson	.08	.04	.01
☐ 170	Milwaukee Bucks Kenny Smith	.05	.02	.01
☐ 171	Houston Rockets Gerald Glass	.05	.02	.01
☐ 172	Minnesota Timberwolves Harvey Grant	.05	.02	.01
☐ 173	Washington Bullets Paul Graham	.05	.02	.01
☐ 174	Atlanta Hawks Sam Perkins	.08	.04	.01
☐ 175	Los Angeles Lakers Manute Bol	.05	.02	.01
	Philadelphia 76ers			

☐ 176	Muggsy Bogues	.10	.05	.01
	Charlotte Hornets			
☐ 177	Mike Brown	.05	.02	.01
	Utah Jazz			
☐ 178	Donald Hodge	.05	.02	.01
	Dallas Mavericks			
☐ 179	Dave Jamerson	.05	.02	.01
	Houston Rockets			
☐ 180	Mookie Blaylock	.08	.04	.01
	New Jersey Nets			
☐ 181	Randy Brown	.05	.02	.01
	Sacramento Kings			
☐ 182	Todd Lichti	.05	.02	.01
	Denver Nuggets			
☐ 183	Kevin Gamble	.05	.02	.01
	Boston Celtics			
☐ 184	Gary Payton	.10	.05	.01
	Seattle Supersonics			
☐ 185	Brian Shaw	.05	.02	.01
	Miami Heat			
☐ 186	Grant Long	.05	.02	.01
	Miami Heat			
☐ 187	Frank Brickowski	.08	.04	.01
	Milwaukee Bucks			
☐ 188	Tim Hardaway	.10	.05	.01
	Golden State Warriors			
☐ 189	Danny Manning	.10	.05	.01
	Los Angeles Clippers			
☐ 190	Kevin Johnson	.10	.05	.01
	Phoenix Suns			
☐ 191	Craig Ehlo	.05	.02	.01
	Cleveland Cavaliers			
☐ 192	Dennis Scott	.08	.04	.01
	Orlando Magic			
☐ 193	Reggie Miller	.10	.05	.01
	Indiana Pacers			
☐ 194	Darrell Walker	.05	.02	.01
	Detroit Pistons			
☐ 195	Anthony Mason	.08	.04	.01
	New York Knicks			
☐ 196	Buck Williams	.10	.05	.01
	Portland Trail Blazers			
☐ 197	Checklist 1-99	.05	.02	.01
☐ 198	Checklist 100-198	.05	.02	.01
☐ 199	Karl Malone	.10	.05	.01
	Utah Jazz			
☐ 200	Dominique Wilkins	.10	.05	.01
	Atlanta Hawks			
☐ 201	Tom Chambers	.08	.04	.01
	Phoenix Suns			
☐ 202	Bernard King	.08	.04	.01
	Washington Bullets			
☐ 203	Kiki Vandeweghe	.05	.02	.01
	Los Angeles Clippers			
☐ 204	Dale Ellis	.05	.02	.01
	San Antonio Spurs			
☐ 205	Michael Jordan	.50	.23	.06
	Chicago Bulls			
☐ 206	Michael Adams	.05	.02	.01
	Washington Bullets			
☐ 207	Charles Smith	.05	.02	.01
	New York Knicks			
☐ 208	Moses Malone	.08	.04	.01
	Milwaukee Bucks			
☐ 209	Terry Cummings	.05	.02	.01
	San Antonio Spurs			
☐ 210	Vernon Maxwell	.05	.02	.01
	Houston Rockets			
☐ 211	Patrick Ewing	.10	.05	.01
	New York Knicks			
☐ 212	Clyde Drexler	.10	.05	.01
	Portland Trail Blazers			
☐ 213	Kevin McHale	.08	.04	.01

Boston Celtics					
☐ 214	Hakeem Olajuwon	.20	.09	.03
Houston Rockets					
☐ 215	Reggie Miller	.10	.05	.01
Indiana Pacers					
☐ 216	Gary Grant	.05	.02	.01
Los Angeles Clippers					
☐ 217	Doc Rivers	.05	.02	.01
New York Knicks					
☐ 218	Mark Price	.08	.04	.01
Cleveland Cavaliers					
☐ 219	Isiah Thomas	.10	.05	.01
Detroit Pistons					
☐ 220	Nate McMillan	.05	.02	.01
Seattle Supersonics					
☐ 221	Fat Lever	.05	.02	.01
Dallas Mavericks					
☐ 222	Kevin Johnson	.08	.04	.01
Phoenix Suns					
☐ 223	John Stockton	.10	.05	.01
Utah Jazz					
☐ 224	Scott Skiles	.05	.02	.01
Orlando Magic					
☐ 225	Kevin Brooks	.05	.02	.01
Indiana Pacers					
☐ 226	Bobby Phills	.12	.05	.02
Cleveland Cavaliers					
☐ 227	Oliver Miller	.20	.09	.03
Phoenix Suns					
☐ 228	John Williams	.05	.02	.01
Los Angeles Clippers					
☐ 229	Brad Lohaus	.05	.02	.01
Milwaukee Bucks					
☐ 230	Derrick Coleman	.12	.05	.02
New Jersey Nets					
☐ 231	Ed Pinckney	.05	.02	.01
Boston Celtics					
☐ 232	Trent Tucker	.05	.02	.01
Chicago Bulls					
☐ 233	Lance Blanks	.05	.02	.01
Minnesota Timberwolves					
☐ 234	Drazen Petrovic	.08	.04	.01
New Jersey Nets					
☐ 235	Mark Bryant	.05	.02	.01
Portland Trail Blazers					
☐ 236	Lloyd Daniels	.10	.05	.01
San Antonio Spurs					
☐ 237	Dale Davis	.08	.04	.01
Indiana Pacers					
☐ 238	Jayson Williams	.05	.02	.01
New Jersey Nets					
☐ 239	Mike Sanders	.05	.02	.01
Cleveland Cavaliers					
☐ 240	Mike Gminski	.05	.02	.01
Charlotte Hornets					
☐ 241	William Bedford	.05	.02	.01
Los Angeles Clippers					
☐ 242	Dell Curry	.08	.04	.01
Charlotte Hornets					
☐ 243	Gerald Paddio	.05	.02	.01
Seattle Supersonics					
☐ 244	Chris Smith	.10	.05	.01
Minnesota Timberwolves					
☐ 245	Jud Buechler	.05	.02	.01
Golden State Warriors					
☐ 246	Walter Palmer	.05	.02	.01
Dallas Mavericks					
☐ 247	Larry Krystkowiak	.05	.02	.01
Utah Jazz					
☐ 248	Marcus Liberty	.05	.02	.01
Denver Nuggets					
☐ 249	Sam Mitchell	.05	.02	.01
Indiana Pacers					

☐ 250 Kiki Vandeweghe	.08	.04	.01
Los Angeles Clippers			
☐ 251 Vincent Askew	.05	.02	.01
Seattle Supersonics			
☐ 252 Travis Mays	.05	.02	.01
Atlanta Hawks			
☐ 253 Charles Smith	.05	.02	.01
New York Knicks			
☐ 254 John Bagley	.05	.02	.01
Boston Celtics			
☐ 255 James Worthy	.10	.05	.01
Los Angeles Lakers			
☐ 256 Paul Pressey P/CO	.05	.02	.01
Golden State Warriors			
☐ 257 Rumeal Robinson	.05	.02	.01
New Jersey Nets			
☐ 258 Tom Gugliotta	.40	.18	.05
Washington Bullets			
☐ 259 Eric Anderson	.05	.02	.01
New York Knicks			
☐ 260 Hersey Hawkins	.08	.04	.01
Philadelphia 76ers			
☐ 261 Terry Davis	.05	.02	.01
Dallas Mavericks			
☐ 262 Rex Chapman	.05	.02	.01
Washington Bullets			
☐ 263 Chucky Brown	.05	.02	.01
New Jersey Nets			
☐ 264 Danny Young	.05	.02	.01
Detroit Pistons			
☐ 265 Olden Polynice	.05	.02	.01
Detroit Pistons			
☐ 266 Kevin Willis	.08	.04	.01
Atlanta Hawks			
☐ 267 Shawn Kemp	.40	.18	.05
Seattle Supersonics			
☐ 268 Mookie Blaylock	.08	.04	.01
Atlanta Hawks			
☐ 269 Malik Sealy	.10	.05	.01
Indiana Pacers			
☐ 270 Charles Barkley	.25	.11	.03
Phoenix Suns			
☐ 271 Corey Williams	.05	.02	.01
Chicago Bulls			
☐ 272 Stephen Howard	.05	.02	.01
(See also card 286)			
Utah Jazz			
☐ 273 Keith Askins	.05	.02	.01
Miami Heat			
☐ 274 Matt Bullard	.05	.02	.01
Houston Rockets			
☐ 275 John Battle	.05	.02	.01
Cleveland Cavaliers			
☐ 276 Andrew Lang	.05	.02	.01
Philadelphia 76ers			
☐ 277 David Robinson	.25	.11	.03
San Antonio Spurs			
☐ 278 Harold Miner	.20	.09	.03
Miami Heat			
☐ 279 Tracy Murray	.10	.05	.01
Portland Trail Blazers			
☐ 280 Pooh Richardson	.05	.02	.01
Indiana Pacers			
☐ 281 Dikembe Mutombo	.15	.07	.02
Denver Nuggets			
☐ 282 Wayman Tisdale	.08	.04	.01
Sacramento Kings			
☐ 283 Larry Johnson	.30	.14	.04
Charlotte Hornets			
☐ 284 Todd Day	.15	.07	.02
Milwaukee Bucks			
☐ 285 Stanley Roberts	.05	.02	.01
Los Angeles Clippers			

□	286	Randy Woods UER	.10	.05	.01
		Los Angeles Clippers			
		(Card misnumbered 272; run he show should be run the show)			
□	287	Avery Johnson	.05	.02	.01
		San Antonio Spurs			
□	288	Anthony Peeler	.15	.07	.02
		Los Angeles Lakers			
□	289	Mario Elie	.05	.02	.01
		Portland Trail Blazers			
□	290	Doc Rivers	.08	.04	.01
		New York Knicks			
□	291	Blue Edwards	.08	.04	.01
		Milwaukee Bucks			
□	292	Sean Rooks	.12	.05	.02
		Dallas Mavericks			
□	293	Xavier McDaniel	.08	.04	.01
		Boston Celtics			
□	294	Clarence Weatherspoon	.40	.18	.05
		Philadelphia 76ers			
□	295	Morlon Wiley	.05	.02	.01
		Atlanta Hawks			
□	296	LaBradford Smith	.05	.02	.01
		Washington Bullets			
□	297	Reggie Lewis	.10	.05	.01
		Boston Celtics			
□	298	Chris Mullin	.10	.05	.01
		Golden State Warriors			
□	299	Litterial Green	.10	.05	.01
		Orlando Magic			
□	300	Elmore Spencer	.15	.07	.02
		Los Angeles Clippers			
□	301	John Stockton	.12	.05	.02
		Utah Jazz			
□	302	Walt Williams	.20	.09	.03
		Sacramento Kings			
□	303	Anthony Pullard	.05	.02	.01
		Milwaukee Bucks			
□	304	Gundars Vetra	.05	.02	.01
		Minnesota Timberwolves			
□	305	LaSalle Thompson	.08	.04	.01
		Indiana Pacers			
□	306	Nate McMillan	.05	.02	.01
		Seattle Supersonics			
□	307	Steve Bardo	.05	.02	.01
		Dallas Mavericks			
□	308	Robert Horry	.40	.18	.05
		Houston Rockets			
□	309	Scott Williams	.05	.02	.01
		Chicago Bulls			
□	310	Bo Kimble	.05	.02	.01
		New York Knicks			
□	311	Tree Rollins	.05	.02	.01
		Houston Rockets			
□	312	Tim Perry	.05	.02	.01
		Philadelphia 76ers			
□	313	Isaac Austin	.05	.02	.01
		Utah Jazz			
□	314	Tate George	.05	.02	.01
		New Jersey Nets			
□	315	Kevin Lynch	.05	.02	.01
		Charlotte Hornets			
□	316	Victor Alexander	.05	.02	.01
		Golden State Warriors			
□	317	Doug Overton	.05	.02	.01
		Washington Bullets			
□	318	Tom Hammonds	.05	.02	.01
		Charlotte Hornets			
□	319	LaPhonso Ellis	.40	.18	.05
		Denver Nuggets			
□	320	Scott Brooks	.05	.02	.01
		Houston Rockets			

☐ 321 Anthony Avent UER (Front photo actually Blue Edwards) Milwaukee Bucks	.10	.05	.01
☐ 322 Matt Geiger Miami Heat	.10	.05	.01
☐ 323 Duane Causwell Sacramento Kings	.05	.02	.01
☐ 324 Horace Grant Chicago Bulls	.10	.05	.01
☐ 325 Mark Jackson Los Angeles Clippers	.08	.04	.01
☐ 326 Dan Majerle Phoenix Suns	.10	.05	.01
☐ 327 Chuck Person Minnesota Timberwolves	.08	.04	.01
☐ 328 Buck Johnson Washington Bullets	.05	.02	.01
☐ 329 Duane Cooper Los Angeles Lakers	.05	.02	.01
☐ 330 Rod Strickland Portland Trail Blazers	.08	.04	.01
☐ 331 Isiah Thomas Detroit Pistons	.10	.05	.01
☐ 332 Greg Kite (See also card 387) Orlando Magic	.05	.02	.01
☐ 333 Don MacLean Washington Bullets	.30	.14	.04
☐ 334 Christian Laettner Minnesota Timberwolves	.40	.18	.05
☐ 335 John Crotty Utah Jazz	.05	.02	.01
☐ 336 Tracy Moore Dallas Mavericks	.05	.02	.01
☐ 337 Hakeem Olajuwon Houston Rockets	.40	.18	.05
☐ 338 Byron Houston Golden State Warriors	.10	.05	.01
☐ 339 Walter Bond Dallas Mavericks	.05	.02	.01
☐ 340 Brent Price Washington Bullets	.10	.05	.01
☐ 341 Bryant Stith Denver Nuggets	.15	.07	.02
☐ 342 Will Perdue Chicago Bulls	.05	.02	.01
☐ 343 Jeff Hornacek Philadelphia 76ers	.08	.04	.01
☐ 344 Adam Keefe Atlanta Hawks	.10	.05	.01
☐ 345 Rafael Addison New Jersey Nets	.05	.02	.01
☐ 346 Marlon Maxey Minnesota Timberwolves	.05	.02	.01
☐ 347 Joe Dumars Detroit Pistons	.10	.05	.01
☐ 348 Jon Barry Milwaukee Bucks	.10	.05	.01
☐ 349 Marty Conlon Sacramento Kings	.05	.02	.01
☐ 350 Alaa Abdelnaby Boston Celtics	.05	.02	.01
☐ 351 Micheal Williams Minnesota Timberwolves	.08	.04	.01
☐ 352 Brad Daugherty Cleveland Cavaliers	.10	.05	.01
☐ 353 Tony Bennett Charlotte Hornets	.10	.05	.01
☐ 354 Clyde Drexler Portland Trail Blazers	.12	.05	.02
☐ 355 Rolando Blackman New York Knicks	.08	.04	.01

☐ 356 Tom Tolbert	.05	.02	.01
Orlando Magic			
☐ 357 Sarunas Marciulionis	.08	.04	.01
Golden State Warriors			
☐ 358 Jaren Jackson	.05	.02	.01
Los Angeles Clippers			
☐ 359 Stacey King	.05	.02	.01
Chicago Bulls			
☐ 360 Danny Ainge	.10	.05	.01
Phoenix Suns			
☐ 361 Dale Ellis	.08	.04	.01
San Antonio Spurs			
☐ 362 Shaquille O'Neal	3.00	1.35	.40
Orlando Magic			
☐ 363 Bob McCann	.05	.02	.01
Minnesota Timberwolves			
☐ 364 Reggie Smith	.05	.02	.01
Portland Trail Blazers			
☐ 365 Vinny Del Negro	.05	.02	.01
San Antonio Spurs			
☐ 366 Robert Pack	.05	.02	.01
Denver Nuggets			
☐ 367 David Wood	.05	.02	.01
San Antonio Spurs			
☐ 368 Rodney McCray	.05	.02	.01
Chicago Bulls			
☐ 369 Terry Mills	.10	.05	.01
Detroit Pistons			
☐ 370 Eric Murdock UER	.08	.04	.01
Milwaukee Bucks			
(Jazz on back spelled Jass)			
☐ 371 Alex Blackwell	.05	.02	.01
Los Angeles Lakers			
☐ 372 Jay Humphries	.05	.02	.01
Utah Jazz			
☐ 373 Eddie Lee Wilkins	.05	.02	.01
Philadelphia 76ers			
☐ 374 James Edwards	.05	.02	.01
Los Angeles Lakers			
☐ 375 Tim Kempton	.05	.02	.01
Phoenix Suns			
☐ 376 J.R. Reid	.05	.02	.01
San Antonio Spurs			
☐ 377 Sam Mack	.05	.02	.01
San Antonio Spurs			
☐ 378 Donald Royal	.05	.02	.01
Orlando Magic			
☐ 379 Mark Price	.10	.05	.01
Cleveland Cavaliers			
☐ 380 Mark Acres	.05	.02	.01
Orlando Magic			
☐ 381 Hubert Davis	.20	.09	.03
New York Knicks			
☐ 382 Dave Johnson	.05	.02	.01
Portland Trail Blazers			
☐ 383 John Salley	.05	.02	.01
Miami Heat			
☐ 384 Eddie Johnson	.05	.02	.01
Seattle Supersonics			
☐ 385 Brian Howard	.05	.02	.01
Dallas Mavericks			
☐ 386 Isaiah Morris	.05	.02	.01
Detroit Pistons			
☐ 387 Frank Johnson	.05	.02	.01
Phoenix Suns			
(Card misnumbered 332)			
☐ 388 Rick Mahorn	.08	.04	.01
New Jersey Nets			
☐ 389 Scottie Pippen	.20	.09	.03
Chicago Bulls			
☐ 390 Lee Mayberry	.10	.05	.01
Milwaukee Bucks			
☐ 391 Tony Campbell	.05	.02	.01

	New York Knicks			
☐ 392	Latrell Sprewell	1.00	.45	.13
	Golden State Warriors			
☐ 393	Alonzo Mourning	1.50	.65	.19
	Charlotte Hornets			
☐ 394	Robert Werdann	.05	.02	.01
	Denver Nuggets			
☐ 395	Checklist 199-297 UER	.05	.02	.01
	(286 Kennard Winchester; should be Randy Woods)			
☐ 396	Checklist 298-396	.05	.02	.01

1992-93 Topps Beam Team

Comprised of some of the NBA's biggest stars, the second series packs of Topps regular basketball cards included these special "Topps Beam Team" bonus cards to commemorate Topps' 1993 sponsorship of a six-minute NBA laser animation show called Beams Above the Rim, premiering at the NBA All-Star Game on Feb. 21. Afterwards, the laser show embarked on a ten-city tour and was featured in either the pre-game or half-time events in ten NBA arenas. These cards were randomly inserted approximately one in every 18 15-card packs of Topps Basketball second series. Three players are featured on each Topps Beam Team card. Measuring the standard-size (2 1/2" by 3 1/2"), the horizontal fronts display three color action player photos on a dark blue background with a grid of brightly colored light beams. The set title "Beam Team" appears in pastel green block lettering across the top. The backs carry three light blue panels, with a close-up color photo, biography, and player profile on each panel. The cards are numbered on the back.

		MINT	EXC	G-VG
COMPLETE SET (7)		6.00	2.70	.75
COMMON PLAYER (1-7)		.75	.35	.09
COMP.GOLD BEAM TEAM (7)		12.00	5.50	1.50
*GOLD CARDS: 1X to 2X VALUE				
☐ 1	Reggie Miller	1.25	.55	.16
	Indiana Pacers			
	Charles Barkley			
	Phoenix Suns			
	Clyde Drexler			
	Portland Trail Blazers			
☐ 2	Patrick Ewing	.75	.35	.09
	New York Knicks			
	Tim Hardaway			
	Golden State Warriors			
	Jeff Hornacek			
	Philadelphia 76ers			
☐ 3	Kevin Johnson	2.00	.90	.25
	Phoenix Suns			
	Michael Jordan			
	Chicago Bulls			

Dennis Rodman
Detroit Pistons
☐ 4 Dominique Wilkins...............................1.00   .45   .13
   Atlanta Hawks
   John Stockton
   Utah Jazz
   Karl Malone
   Utah Jazz
☐ 5 Hakeem Olajuwon.............................1.50   .65   .19
   Houston Rockets
   Mark Price
   Cleveland Cavaliers
   Shawn Kemp
   Seattle Supersonics
☐ 6 Scottie Pippen.................................1.25   .55   .16
   Chicago Bulls
   David Robinson
   San Antonio Spurs
   Jeff Malone
   Utah Jazz
☐ 7 Chris Mullin....................................3.00   1.35   .40
   Golden State Warriors
   Shaquille O'Neal
   Orlando Magic
   Glen Rice
   Miami Heat

1992-93 Topps Gold

Topps produced a gold factory set version that includes all 396 cards of the 1992-93 Topps series plus all seven Beam Team cards in gold. All the cards are embossed with gold foil. The cards are standard size, 2 1/2" by 3 1/2". Reportedly only 5,000 cases of factory sets were produced making for a total of 10,000 factory sets. Four different player cards replaced the checklist cards found in the regular 396-card set. Gold foil versions of the regular cards were inserted one per 15-card plastic-wrap pack, except if the pack contained a Beam Team card. Gold foil cards were also inserted two per 18-card mini-jumbo pack, three per 45-card retail rack pack, five per 41-card magazine jumbo pack, and 12 per factory set. The cards are identical in design to the regular issue, except that on the fronts the team color-coded stripes carrying player information are replaced by gold foil stripes. The cards are numbered on the back without a "G" suffix.

	MINT	EXC	G-VG
COMPLETE GOLD SET (396)......................	90.00	40.00	11.50
COMPLETE FACT.SET (403)......................	100.00	45.00	12.50
COMPLETE SERIES 1 (198)......................	30.00	13.50	3.80
COMPLETE SERIES 2 (198)......................	60.00	27.00	7.50
COMMON GOLD (1-198)...........................	.10	.05	.01
COMMON GOLD (199-396)........................	.10	.05	.01

*GOLD STARS: 3X to 8X VALUE
*GOLD ROOKIES: 2X to 5X VALUE

☐ 197G Jeff Sanders	.50	.23	.06
Atlanta Hawks			
☐ 198G Elliott Perry UER	.50	.23	.06
Charlotte Hornets			
(Misspelled Elliot			
on front)			
☐ 395G David Wingate	.50	.23	.06
Washington Bullets			
☐ 396G Carl Herrera	.50	.23	.06
Houston Rockets			

1992-93 Topps Archives

Featuring the missing years of Topps basketball from 1981 through 1991, this 150-card set consists of 139 current NBA players and an 11-card subset of the Number One draft picks from 1981 to 1991. Production was limited to 10,000 24-box cases (24 packs per box). Each pack contained 14 cards and one Stadium Club membership card, and in one pack out of 24, the Stadium Club membership card was replaced by a mini Master Photo offer card good for three full-size Master Photos. The cards measure the standard size (2 1/2" by 3 1/2"). Since Topps did not produce basketball cards when the photos were taken, the front designs are patterned after the Topps baseball cards issued during the same year. The horizontal backs display a small, square, current action player photo that overlaps a red, yellow, and white box containing biographical information, and statistics from college and the NBA. The set name, player's name, and team are printed in the upper left portion. The background is in varying shades of blue with a light beam design. After opening with a No. 1 Draft Pick (1-11) subset, the player cards are arranged by year in ascending chronological order and alphabetically within each season as follows: 1981-82 (12-22), 1982-83 (23-31), 1983-84 (32-42), 1984-85 (43-59), 1985-86 (60-76), 1986-87 (77-88), 1987-88 (89-100), 1988-89 (101-114), 1989-90 (115-130), 1990-91 (131-139), and 1991-92 (140-148). The set closes with checklist (149-150) cards. Topps also produced a Topps Gold Archive set, which is the same as regular set but with gold-stamped player names and a Topps Archives Gold Logo. These cards were available only in full set form and quantities were limited to no more than 5,000 cases.

	MINT	EXC	G-VG
COMPLETE SET (150)	10.00	4.50	1.25
COMMON PLAYER (1-150)	.05	.02	.01
☐ 1 Mark Aguirre	.10	.05	.01
Dallas Mavericks			
1981 No. 1 Draft Pick			
☐ 2 James Worthy	.08	.04	.01
Los Angeles Lakers			
1982 No. 1 Draft Pick			
☐ 3 Ralph Sampson	.05	.02	.01
Houston Rockets			
1983 No. 1 Draft Pick			
☐ 4 Hakeem Olajuwon	.40	.18	.05

	Houston Rockets		
	1984 No. 1 Draft Pick		
☐ 5	Patrick Ewing 20	.09	.03
	New York Knicks		
	1985 No. 1 Draft Pick		
☐ 6	Brad Daugherty 10	.05	.01
	Cleveland Cavaliers		
	1986 No. 1 Draft Pick		
☐ 7	David Robinson 25	.11	.03
	San Antonio Spurs		
	1987 No. 1 Draft Pick		
☐ 8	Danny Manning 10	.05	.01
	Los Angeles Clippers		
	1988 No. 1 Draft Pick		
☐ 9	Pervis Ellison UER 05	.02	.01
	Sacramento Kings		
	1989 No. 1 Draft Pick		
	(Text on back: Clippers		
	not Lakers had 2nd pick)		
☐ 10	Derrick Coleman 10	.05	.01
	New Jersey Nets		
	1990 No. 1 Draft Pick		
☐ 11	Larry Johnson 25	.11	.03
	Charlotte Hornets		
	1991 No. 1 Draft Pick		
☐ 12	Mark Aguirre 10	.05	.01
	Dallas Mavericks		
☐ 13	Danny Ainge 10	.05	.01
	Boston Celtics		
☐ 14	Rolando Blackman 08	.04	.01
	Dallas Mavericks		
☐ 15	Tom Chambers 08	.04	.01
	San Diego Clippers		
☐ 16	Eddie Johnson 05	.02	.01
	Kansas City Kings		
☐ 17	Alton Lister 05	.02	.01
	Milwaukee Bucks		
☐ 18	Larry Nance 08	.04	.01
	Phoenix Suns		
☐ 19	Kurt Rambis 08	.04	.01
	Los Angeles Lakers		
☐ 20	Isiah Thomas 15	.07	.02
	Detroit Pistons		
☐ 21	Buck Williams 10	.05	.01
	New Jersey Nets		
☐ 22	Orlando Woolridge 08	.04	.01
	Chicago Bulls		
☐ 23	John Bagley 05	.02	.01
	Cleveland Cavaliers		
☐ 24	Terry Cummings 08	.04	.01
	San Diego Clippers		
☐ 25	Mark Eaton 05	.02	.01
	Utah Jazz		
☐ 26	Sleepy Floyd 05	.02	.01
	New Jersey Nets		
☐ 27	Fat Lever 05	.02	.01
	Portland Trail Blazers		
☐ 28	Ricky Pierce 08	.04	.01
	Detroit Pistons		
☐ 29	Trent Tucker 05	.02	.01
	New York Knicks		
☐ 30	Dominique Wilkins 30	.14	.04
	Atlanta Hawks		
☐ 31	James Worthy 10	.05	.01
	Los Angeles Lakers		
☐ 32	Thurl Bailey 05	.02	.01
	Utah Jazz		
☐ 33	Clyde Drexler 20	.09	.03
	Portland Trail Blazers		
☐ 34	Dale Ellis 08	.04	.01
	Dallas Mavericks		
☐ 35	Sidney Green 05	.02	.01
	Chicago Bulls		

☐ 36	Derek Harper .08 Dallas Mavericks	.04	.01
☐ 37	Jeff Malone .08 Washington Bullets	.04	.01
☐ 38	Rodney McCray .05 Houston Rockets	.02	.01
☐ 39	John Paxson .08 San Antonio Spurs	.04	.01
☐ 40	Doc Rivers .08 Atlanta Hawks	.04	.01
☐ 41	Byron Scott .08 Los Angeles Lakers	.04	.01
☐ 42	Sedale Threatt .05 Philadelphia 76ers	.02	.01
☐ 43	Ron Anderson .05 Cleveland Cavaliers	.02	.01
☐ 44	Charles Barkley .50 Philadelphia 76ers	.23	.06
☐ 45	Sam Bowie .05 Portland Trail Blazers	.02	.01
☐ 46	Michael Cage .05 Los Angeles Clippers	.02	.01
☐ 47	Tony Campbell .05 Detroit Pistons	.02	.01
☐ 48	Antoine Carr .05 Atlanta Hawks	.02	.01
☐ 49	Craig Ehlo .05 Houston Rockets	.02	.01
☐ 50	Vern Fleming .05 Indiana Pacers	.02	.01
☐ 51	Jay Humphries .05 Phoenix Suns	.02	.01
☐ 52	Michael Jordan 2.00 Chicago Bulls	.90	.25
☐ 53	Jerome Kersey .05 Portland Trail Blazers	.02	.01
☐ 54	Hakeem Olajuwon .75 Houston Rockets	.35	.09
☐ 55	Sam Perkins .08 Dallas Mavericks	.04	.01
☐ 56	Alvin Robertson .08 San Antonio Spurs	.04	.01
☐ 57	John Stockton .15 Utah Jazz	.07	.02
☐ 58	Otis Thorpe .08 Kansas City Kings	.04	.01
☐ 59	Kevin Willis .08 Atlanta Hawks	.04	.01
☐ 60	Michael Adams .08 Sacramento Kings	.04	.01
☐ 61	Benoit Benjamin .05 Los Angeles Clippers	.02	.01
☐ 62	Terry Catledge .05 Philadelphia 76ers	.02	.01
☐ 63	Joe Dumars .15 Detroit Pistons	.07	.02
☐ 64	Patrick Ewing .40 New York Knicks	.18	.05
☐ 65	A.C. Green .08 Los Angeles Lakers	.04	.01
☐ 66	Karl Malone .25 Utah Jazz	.11	.03
☐ 67	Reggie Miller .15 Indiana Pacers	.07	.02
☐ 68	Chris Mullin .15 Golden State Warriors	.07	.02
☐ 69	Xavier McDaniel .08 Seattle Supersonics	.04	.01
☐ 70	Charles Oakley .10 Chicago Bulls	.05	.01
☐ 71	Terry Porter .08 Portland Trail Blazers	.04	.01
☐ 72	Jerry Reynolds .05	.02	.01

	Milwaukee Bucks			
☐ 73	Detlef Schrempf	.10	.05	.01
	Dallas Mavericks			
☐ 74	Wayman Tisdale	.08	.04	.01
	Indiana Pacers			
☐ 75	Spud Webb	.10	.05	.01
	Atlanta Hawks			
☐ 76	Gerald Wilkins	.05	.02	.01
	New York Knicks			
☐ 77	Dell Curry	.08	.04	.01
	Utah Jazz			
☐ 78	Brad Daugherty	.10	.05	.01
	Cleveland Cavaliers			
☐ 79	Johnny Dawkins	.05	.02	.01
	San Antonio Spurs			
☐ 80	Kevin Duckworth	.05	.02	.01
	Portland Trail Blazers			
☐ 81	Ron Harper	.08	.04	.01
	Cleveland Cavaliers			
☐ 82	Jeff Hornacek	.10	.05	.01
	Phoenix Suns			
☐ 83	Johnny Newman	.05	.02	.01
	Cleveland Cavaliers			
☐ 84	Chuck Person	.08	.04	.01
	Indiana Pacers			
☐ 85	Mark Price	.08	.04	.01
	Cleveland Cavaliers			
☐ 86	Dennis Rodman	.08	.04	.01
	Detroit Pistons			
☐ 87	John Salley	.05	.02	.01
	Detroit Pistons			
☐ 88	Scott Skiles	.08	.04	.01
	Milwaukee Bucks			
☐ 89	Muggsy Bogues	.10	.05	.01
	Washington Bullets			
☐ 90	Armon Gilliam	.05	.02	.01
	Phoenix Suns			
☐ 91	Horace Grant	.10	.05	.01
	Chicago Bulls			
☐ 92	Mark Jackson	.08	.04	.01
	New York Knicks			
☐ 93	Kevin Johnson	.10	.05	.01
	Cleveland Cavaliers			
☐ 94	Reggie Lewis	.10	.05	.01
	Boston Celtics			
☐ 95	Derrick McKey	.05	.02	.01
	Seattle Supersonics			
☐ 96	Ken Norman	.05	.02	.01
	Los Angeles Clippers			
☐ 97	Scottie Pippen	.35	.16	.04
	Chicago Bulls			
☐ 98	Olden Polynice	.05	.02	.01
	Seattle Supersonics			
☐ 99	Kenny Smith	.05	.02	.01
	Sacramento Kings			
☐ 100	John Williams	.08	.04	.01
	Cleveland Cavaliers			
☐ 101	Willie Anderson	.05	.02	.01
	San Antonio Spurs			
☐ 102	Rex Chapman	.05	.02	.01
	Charlotte Hornets			
☐ 103	Harvey Grant	.05	.02	.01
	Washington Bullets			
☐ 104	Hersey Hawkins	.08	.04	.01
	Philadelphia 76ers			
☐ 105	Dan Majerle	.10	.05	.01
	Phoenix Suns			
☐ 106	Danny Manning	.15	.07	.02
	Los Angeles Clippers			
☐ 107	Vernon Maxwell	.08	.04	.01
	San Antonio Spurs			
☐ 108	Chris Morris	.05	.02	.01
	New Jersey Nets			

☐ 109	Mitch Richmond UER	.10	.05	.01
	Golden State Warriors			
	(Tim Hardaway pictured on front)			
☐ 110	Rony Seikaly	.10	.05	.01
	Miami Heat			
☐ 111	Brian Shaw	.05	.02	.01
	Boston Celtics			
☐ 112	Charles Smith	.05	.02	.01
	Los Angeles Clippers			
☐ 113	Rod Strickland	.08	.04	.01
	New York Knicks			
☐ 114	Micheal Williams	.08	.04	.01
	Detroit Pistons			
☐ 115	Nick Anderson	.05	.02	.01
	Orlando Magic			
☐ 116	B.J. Armstrong	.10	.05	.01
	Chicago Bulls			
☐ 117	Mookie Blaylock	.08	.04	.01
	New Jersey Nets			
☐ 118	Vlade Divac	.08	.04	.01
	Los Angeles Lakers			
☐ 119	Sherman Douglas	.05	.02	.01
	Miami Heat			
☐ 120	Blue Edwards	.08	.04	.01
	Utah Jazz			
☐ 121	Sean Elliott	.08	.04	.01
	San Antonio Spurs			
☐ 122	Pervis Ellison	.05	.02	.01
	Sacramento Kings			
☐ 123	Tim Hardaway	.10	.05	.01
	Golden State Warriors			
☐ 124	Sarunas Marciulionis	.08	.04	.01
	Golden State Warriors			
☐ 125	Drazen Petrovic	.08	.04	.01
	Portland Trail Blazers			
☐ 126	J.R. Reid	.05	.02	.01
	Charlotte Hornets			
☐ 127	Glen Rice	.10	.05	.01
	Miami Heat			
☐ 128	Pooh Richardson	.05	.02	.01
	Minnesota Timberwolves			
☐ 129	Cliff Robinson	.10	.05	.01
	Portland Trail Blazers			
☐ 130	David Robinson	.50	.23	.06
	San Antonio Spurs			
☐ 131	Dee Brown	.05	.02	.01
	Boston Celtics			
☐ 132	Cedric Ceballos	.10	.05	.01
	Phoenix Suns			
☐ 133	Derrick Coleman	.20	.09	.03
	New Jersey Nets			
☐ 134	Kendall Gill	.08	.04	.01
	Charlotte Hornets			
☐ 135	Chris Jackson	.08	.04	.01
	Denver Nuggets			
☐ 136	Shawn Kemp	.60	.25	.08
	Seattle Supersonics			
☐ 137	Gary Payton	.10	.05	.01
	Seattle Supersonics			
☐ 138	Dennis Scott	.08	.04	.01
	Orlando Magic			
☐ 139	Lionel Simmons	.08	.04	.01
	Sacramento Kings			
☐ 140	Kenny Anderson	.20	.09	.03
	New Jersey Nets			
☐ 141	Greg Anthony	.05	.02	.01
	New York Knicks			
☐ 142	Stacey Augmon	.10	.05	.01
	Atlanta Hawks			
☐ 143	Rick Fox	.08	.04	.01
	Boston Celtics			
☐ 144	Larry Johnson	.50	.23	.06
	Charlotte Hornets			

☐ 145	Luc Longley...	.05	.02	.01
	Minnesota Timberwolves			
☐ 146	Dikembe Mutombo.................................	.20	.09	.03
	Denver Nuggets			
☐ 147	Billy Owens..	.10	.05	.01
	Golden State Warriors			
☐ 148	Steve Smith...	.15	.07	.02
	Miami Heat			
☐ 149	Checklist 1-75..	.05	.02	.01
☐ 150	Checklist 76-150....................................	.05	.02	.01

1992-93 Topps Archives Gold

Only 10,000 factory sets were made of the 1992-93 Topps Archives Gold. The factory sets were sold to dealers in eight-set cases. The 150 cards comprising this set have identical player selection and numbering as the regular-issue Topps Archives set, except that the checklist cards from the regular Archives set (149 and 150) have been replaced by cards of Rumeal Robinson and Shaquille O'Neal, respectively. Like the regular-issue Archive cards, the fronts are designed to mimic the layouts of several Topps' baseball issues of the 1980s; the only differences being that the Topps Archives logo, which doesn't appear on the regular-issue set, and the player's name are stamped in gold foil. The horizontal backs, however, all have the same design, with player action photos displayed in the upper right, the NBA and Topps Archives logos to the left of the picture, and the player's name and team beneath the logos. A brief biography is printed within a red rectangle, a complete college record appears beneath within a yellow rectangle, and the player's record of his NBA rookie year on the bottom rounds out the back. The cards are standard size, 2 1/2" by 3 1/2".

	MINT	EXC	G-VG
COMPLETE FACT.SET (150)..	35.00	16.00	4.40
COMMON PLAYER (1-150)...	.10	.05	.01
*GOLD STARS: 1.5X to 3X VALUE			
☐ 149 Rumeal Robinson...	.50	.23	.06
☐ 150 Shaquille O'Neal...	20.00	9.00	2.50

1992-93 Topps Archives Master Photos

In one out of 24 '92-93 Archives packs, the Stadium Club membership card was replaced by a mini-Master Photo offer card good for three of these full-size Master Photos. Showcasing the 11 No. 1 NBA draft picks from the missing years of Topps basketball from 1981 through 1991, these 12 oversized cards measure 5" by 7" and feature on their fronts white-bordered color player action shots framed by prismatic silver-foil lines. The player's name, team name, and year of his being the No. 1 pick appear in diagonal red, yellow, and blue stripes near the bottom. The words "1 Draft Pick" followed by a curving cometlike prismatic silver-

foil tail appear in one of the photo's upper corners. Aside from the Topps and NBA trade-marks, the white backs are blank. The cards are numbered on the front by year.

	MINT	EXC	G-VG
COMPLETE SET (12)	10.00	4.50	1.25
COMMON PLAYER (1981-1991)	.25	.11	.03
☐ 1981 Mark Aguirre	.25	.11	.03
Dallas Mavericks			
1981 No. 1 Draft Pick			
☐ 1982 James Worthy	.35	.16	.04
Los Angeles Lakers			
1982 No. 1 Draft Pick			
☐ 1983 Ralph Sampson	.25	.11	.03
Houston Rockets			
1983 No. 1 Draft Pick			
☐ 1984 Hakeem Olajuwon	2.50	1.15	.30
Houston Rockets			
1984 No. 1 Draft Pick			
☐ 1985 Patrick Ewing	1.50	.65	.19
New York Knicks			
1985 No. 1 Draft Pick			
☐ 1986 Brad Daugherty	.25	.11	.03
Cleveland Cavaliers			
1986 No. 1 Draft Pick			
☐ 1987 David Robinson	2.00	.90	.25
San Antonio Spurs			
1987 No. 1 Draft Pick			
☐ 1988 Danny Manning	.50	.23	.06
Los Angeles Clippers			
1988 No. 1 Draft Pick			
☐ 1989 Pervis Ellison	.25	.11	.03
Sacramento Kings			
1989 No. 1 Draft Pick			
☐ 1990 Derrick Coleman	.75	.35	.09
New Jersey Nets			
1990 No. 1 Draft Pick			
☐ 1991 Larry Johnson	2.00	.90	.25
Charlotte Hornets			
1991 No. 1 Draft Pick			
☐ NNO First Picks 1981-91	.50	.23	.06

1993-94 Topps

The complete 1993-94 Topps basketball set consists of 396 cards issued in two 198-card series. Factory sets contain 410 cards including a pack a 14 Gold cards. The cards are standard size (2 1/2" by 3 1/2"). The white bordered fronts display color action player photos

with a team color coded inner border three quarters the way down the left side and curving along the bottom of the picture. The player's name is printed in white script at the lower left corner with the team name appearing on a team color coded bar at the very bottom. The horizontal backs carry a close-up player photo on the right with complete NBA statistics, biography, and career highlights on the left on a beige panel. Topical subsets featured are Highlights (1-5), 50 Point Club (50, 57, 64), Topps All-Star 1st Team (100-104), Topps All-Star 2nd Team (115-119), Topps All-Star 3rd Team (130-134), Topps All-Rookie 1st Team (150-154), and Topps All-Rookie 2nd Team (175-179). The cards are numbered on the back.

	MINT	EXC	G-VG
COMPLETE SET (396)	20.00	9.00	2.50
COMPLETE FACT.SET (410)	25.00	11.50	3.10
COMPLETE SERIES 1 (198)	10.00	4.50	1.25
COMPLETE SERIES 2 (198)	10.00	4.50	1.25
COMMON PLAYER (1-198)	.05	.02	.01
COMMON PLAYER (199-396)	.05	.02	.01
☐ 1 Charles Barkley HL	.20	.09	.03
Phoenix Suns			
☐ 2 Hakeem Olajuwon HL	.40	.18	.05
Houston Rockets			
☐ 3 Shaquille O'Neal HL	.75	.35	.09
Orlando Magic			
☐ 4 Chris Jackson HL	.05	.02	.01
Denver Nuggets			
☐ 5 Cliff Robinson HL	.10	.05	.01
Portland Trail Blazers			
☐ 6 Donald Hodge	.05	.02	.01
Dallas Mavericks			
☐ 7 Victor Alexander	.05	.02	.01
Golden State Warriors			
☐ 8 Chris Morris	.05	.02	.01
New Jersey Nets			
☐ 9 Muggsy Bogues	.10	.05	.01
Charlotte Hornets			
☐ 10 Steve Smith UER	.08	.04	.01
Miami Heat			
(Listed with Kings in '90-91;			
was not in NBA that year)			
☐ 11 Dave Johnson	.05	.02	.01
Portland Trail Blazers			
☐ 12 Tom Gugliotta	.08	.04	.01
Washington Bullets			
☐ 13 Doug Edwards	.10	.05	.01
Atlanta Hawks			
☐ 14 Vlade Divac	.05	.02	.01
Los Angeles Lakers			
☐ 15 Corie Blount	.10	.05	.01
Chicago Bulls			
☐ 16 Derek Harper	.08	.04	.01
Dallas Mavericks			
☐ 17 Matt Bullard	.05	.02	.01

Houston Rockets
☐ 18	Terry Catledge	.05	.02	.01
	Orlando Magic			
☐ 19	Mark Eaton	.05	.02	.01
	Utah Jazz			
☐ 20	Mark Jackson	.08	.04	.01
	Los Angeles Clippers			
☐ 21	Terry Mills	.08	.04	.01
	Detroit Pistons			
☐ 22	Johnny Dawkins	.05	.02	.01
	Philadelphia 76ers			
☐ 23	Michael Jordan UER	2.00	.90	.25
	Chicago Bulls (Listed as a forward with birthdate of 1968; he is a guard with bithdate of 1963)			
☐ 24	Rick Fox UER	.05	.02	.01
	Boston Celtics (Listed with Kings in `91-92)			
☐ 25	Charles Oakley	.10	.05	.01
	New York Knicks			
☐ 26	Derrick McKey	.05	.02	.01
	Seattle Supersonics			
☐ 27	Christian Laettner	.08	.04	.01
	Minnesota Timberwolves			
☐ 28	Todd Day	.08	.04	.01
	Milwaukee Bucks			
☐ 29	Danny Ferry	.05	.02	.01
	Cleveland Cavaliers			
☐ 30	Kevin Johnson	.10	.05	.01
	Phoenix Suns			
☐ 31	Vinny Del Negro	.05	.02	.01
	San Antonio Spurs			
☐ 32	Kevin Brooks	.05	.02	.01
	Denver Nuggets			
☐ 33	Pete Chilcutt	.05	.02	.01
	Sacramento Kings			
☐ 34	Larry Stewart	.05	.02	.01
	Washington Bullets			
☐ 35	Dave Jamerson	.05	.02	.01
	Houston Rockets			
☐ 36	Sidney Green	.05	.02	.01
	Philadelphia 76ers			
☐ 37	J.R. Reid	.05	.02	.01
	San Antonio Spurs			
☐ 38	Jimmy Jackson	.30	.14	.04
	Dallas Mavericks			
☐ 39	Micheal Williams UER	.08	.04	.01
	Minnesota Timberwolves (350.2 minutes per game)			
☐ 40	Rex Walters	.10	.05	.01
	New Jersey Nets			
☐ 41	Shawn Bradley	.40	.18	.05
	Philadelphia 76ers			
☐ 42	Jon Koncak	.05	.02	.01
	Atlanta Hawks			
☐ 43	Byron Houston	.05	.02	.01
	Golden State Warriors			
☐ 44	Brian Shaw	.05	.02	.01
	Miami Heat			
☐ 45	Bill Cartwright	.05	.02	.01
	Chicago Bulls			
☐ 46	Jerome Kersey	.05	.02	.01
	Portland Trail Blazers			
☐ 47	Danny Schayes	.05	.02	.01
	Milwaukee Bucks			
☐ 48	Olden Polynice	.05	.02	.01
	Detroit Pistons			
☐ 49	Anthony Peeler	.08	.04	.01
	Los Angeles Lakers			
☐ 50	Nick Anderson 50	.08	.04	.01
	Orlando Magic			
☐ 51	David Benoit	.05	.02	.01
	Utah Jazz			

☐ 52 David Robinson	.20	.09	.03
San Antonio Spurs			
☐ 53 Greg Kite	.05	.02	.01
Orlando Magic			
☐ 54 Gerald Paddio	.05	.02	.01
Seattle Supersonics			
☐ 55 Don MacLean	.08	.04	.01
Washington Bullets			
☐ 56 Randy Woods	.05	.02	.01
Los Angeles Clippers			
☐ 57 Reggie Miller 50	.10	.05	.01
Indiana Pacers			
☐ 58 Kevin Gamble	.05	.02	.01
Boston Celtics			
☐ 59 Sean Green	.05	.02	.01
Indiana Pacers			
☐ 60 Jeff Hornacek	.08	.04	.01
Philadelphia 76ers			
☐ 61 John Starks	.10	.05	.01
New York Knicks			
☐ 62 Gerald Wilkins	.05	.02	.01
Cleveland Cavaliers			
☐ 63 Jim Les	.05	.02	.01
Sacramento Kings			
☐ 64 Michael Jordan 50	1.00	.45	.13
Chicago Bulls			
☐ 65 Alvin Robertson	.05	.02	.01
Detroit Pistons			
☐ 66 Tim Kempton	.05	.02	.01
Phoenix Suns			
☐ 67 Bryant Stith	.08	.04	.01
Denver Nuggets			
☐ 68 Jeff Turner	.05	.02	.01
Orlando Magic			
☐ 69 Malik Sealy	.05	.02	.01
Indiana Pacers			
☐ 70 Dell Curry	.08	.04	.01
Charlotte Hornets			
☐ 71 Brent Price	.05	.02	.01
Washington Bullets			
☐ 72 Kevin Lynch	.05	.02	.01
Charlotte Hornets			
☐ 73 Bimbo Coles	.05	.02	.01
Miami Heat			
☐ 74 Larry Nance	.08	.04	.01
Cleveland Cavaliers			
☐ 75 Luther Wright	.10	.05	.01
Utah Jazz			
☐ 76 Willie Anderson	.05	.02	.01
San Antonio Spurs			
☐ 77 Dennis Rodman	.08	.04	.01
Detroit Pistons			
☐ 78 Anthony Mason	.05	.02	.01
New York Knicks			
☐ 79 Chris Gatling	.05	.02	.01
Golden State Warriors			
☐ 80 Antoine Carr	.05	.02	.01
San Antonio Spurs			
☐ 81 Kevin Willis	.08	.04	.01
Atlanta Hawks			
☐ 82 Thurl Bailey	.05	.02	.01
Minnesota Timberwolves			
☐ 83 Reggie Williams	.05	.02	.01
Denver Nuggets			
☐ 84 Rod Strickland	.08	.04	.01
Portland Trail Blazers			
☐ 85 Rolando Blackman	.05	.02	.01
New York Knicks			
☐ 86 Bobby Hurley	.40	.18	.05
Sacramento Kings			
☐ 87 Jeff Malone	.08	.04	.01
Utah Jazz			
☐ 88 James Worthy	.10	.05	.01

	Los Angeles Lakers			
☐ 89 Alaa Abdelnaby	.05	.02	.01
	Boston Celtics			
☐ 90 Duane Ferrell	.05	.02	.01
	Atlanta Hawks			
☐ 91 Anthony Avent	.05	.02	.01
	Milwaukee Bucks			
☐ 92 Scottie Pippen	.30	.14	.04
	Chicago Bulls			
☐ 93 Ricky Pierce	.08	.04	.01
	Seattle Supersonics			
☐ 94 P.J. Brown	.15	.07	.02
	New Jersey Nets			
☐ 95 Jeff Grayer	.05	.02	.01
	Golden State Warriors			
☐ 96 Jerrod Mustaf	.05	.02	.01
	Phoenix Suns			
☐ 97 Elmore Spencer	.05	.02	.01
	Los Angeles Clippers			
☐ 98 Walt Williams	.08	.04	.01
	Sacramento Kings			
☐ 99 Otis Thorpe	.08	.04	.01
	Houston Rockets			
☐ 100 Patrick Ewing AS	.15	.07	.02
	New York Knicks			
☐ 101 Michael Jordan AS	1.00	.45	.13
	Chicago Bulls			
☐ 102 John Stockton AS	.10	.05	.01
	Utah Jazz			
☐ 103 Dominique Wilkins AS	.12	.05	.02
	Atlanta Hawks			
☐ 104 Charles Barkley AS	.20	.09	.03
	Phoenix Suns			
☐ 105 Lee Mayberry	.05	.02	.01
	Milwaukee Bucks			
☐ 106 James Edwards	.05	.02	.01
	Los Angeles Lakers			
☐ 107 Scott Brooks	.05	.02	.01
	Houston Rockets			
☐ 108 John Battle	.05	.02	.01
	Cleveland Cavaliers			
☐ 109 Kenny Gattison	.05	.02	.01
	Charlotte Hornets			
☐ 110 Pooh Richardson	.05	.02	.01
	Indiana Pacers			
☐ 111 Rony Seikaly	.10	.05	.01
	Miami Heat			
☐ 112 Mahmoud Abdul-Rauf	.05	.02	.01
	Denver Nuggets			
☐ 113 Nick Anderson	.08	.04	.01
	Orlando Magic			
☐ 114 Gundars Vetra	.05	.02	.01
	Minnesota Timberwolves			
☐ 115 Joe Dumars AS	.10	.05	.01
	Detroit Pistons			
☐ 116 Hakeem Olajuwon AS	.40	.18	.05
	Houston Rockets			
☐ 117 Scottie Pippen AS	.15	.07	.02
	Chicago Bulls			
☐ 118 Mark Price AS	.08	.04	.01
	Cleveland Cavaliers			
☐ 119 Karl Malone AS	.12	.05	.02
	Utah Jazz			
☐ 120 Michael Cage	.05	.02	.01
	Seattle Supersonics			
☐ 121 Ed Pinckney	.05	.02	.01
	Boston Celtics			
☐ 122 Jay Humphries	.05	.02	.01
	Utah Jazz			
☐ 123 Dale Davis	.08	.04	.01
	Indiana Pacers			
☐ 124 Sean Rooks	.05	.02	.01
	Dallas Mavericks			

☐ 125 Mookie Blaylock	.08	.04	.01
Atlanta Hawks			
☐ 126 Buck Williams	.10	.05	.01
Portland Trail Blazers			
☐ 127 John Williams	.05	.02	.01
Los Angeles Clippers			
☐ 128 Stacey King	.05	.02	.01
Chicago Bulls			
☐ 129 Tim Perry	.05	.02	.01
Philadelphia 76ers			
☐ 130 Tim Hardaway AS	.08	.04	.01
Golden State Warriors			
☐ 131 Larry Johnson AS	.15	.07	.02
Charlotte Hornets			
☐ 132 Detlef Schrempf AS	.08	.04	.01
Indiana Pacers			
☐ 133 Reggie Miller AS	.10	.05	.01
Indiana Pacers			
☐ 134 Shaquille O'Neal	.75	.35	.09
Orlando Magic			
☐ 135 Dale Ellis	.08	.04	.01
San Antonio Spurs			
☐ 136 Duane Causwell	.05	.02	.01
Sacramento Kings			
☐ 137 Rumeal Robinson	.05	.02	.01
New Jersey Nets			
☐ 138 Billy Owens	.08	.04	.01
Golden State Warriors			
☐ 139 Malcolm Mackey	.10	.05	.01
Phoenix Suns			
☐ 140 Vernon Maxwell	.08	.04	.01
Houston Rockets			
☐ 141 LaPhonso Ellis	.10	.05	.01
Denver Nuggets			
☐ 142 Robert Parish	.10	.05	.01
Boston Celtics			
☐ 143 LaBradford Smith	.05	.02	.01
Washington Bullets			
☐ 144 Charles Smith	.05	.02	.01
New York Knicks			
☐ 145 Terry Porter	.08	.04	.01
Portland Trail Blazers			
☐ 146 Elden Campbell	.05	.02	.01
Los Angeles Lakers			
☐ 147 Bill Laimbeer	.10	.05	.01
Detroit Pistons			
☐ 148 Chris Mills	.25	.11	.03
Cleveland Cavaliers			
☐ 149 Brad Lohaus	.05	.02	.01
Milwaukee Bucks			
☐ 150 Jimmy Jackson ART	.15	.07	.02
Dallas Mavericks			
☐ 151 Tom Gugliotta ART	.12	.05	.02
Washington Bullets			
☐ 152 Shaquille O'Neal ART	.75	.35	.09
Orlando Magic			
☐ 153 Latrell Sprewell ART	.20	.09	.03
Golden State Warriors			
☐ 154 Walt Williams ART	.12	.05	.02
Sacramento Kings			
☐ 155 Gary Payton	.10	.05	.01
Seattle Supersonics			
☐ 156 Orlando Woolridge	.08	.04	.01
Milwaukee Bucks			
☐ 157 Adam Keefe	.05	.02	.01
Atlanta Hawks			
☐ 158 Calbert Cheaney	.40	.18	.05
Washington Bullets			
☐ 159 Rick Mahorn	.05	.02	.01
New Jersey Nets			
☐ 160 Robert Horry	.10	.05	.01
Houston Rockets			
☐ 161 John Salley	.05	.02	.01

	Miami Heat			
☐ 162	Sam Mitchell	.05	.02	.01
	Indiana Pacers			
☐ 163	Stanley Roberts	.05	.02	.01
	Los Angeles Clippers			
☐ 164	Clarence Weatherspoon	.10	.05	.01
	Philadelphia 76ers			
☐ 165	Anthony Bowie	.05	.02	.01
	Orlando Magic			
☐ 166	Derrick Coleman	.20	.09	.03
	New Jersey Nets			
☐ 167	Negele Knight	.05	.02	.01
	Phoenix Suns			
☐ 168	Marlon Maxey	.05	.02	.01
	Minnesota Timberwolves			
☐ 169	Spud Webb UER	.10	.05	.01
	Sacramento Kings			
	(Listed as center instead of guard)			
☐ 170	Alonzo Mourning	.50	.23	.06
	Charlotte Hornets			
☐ 171	Ervin Johnson	.10	.05	.01
	Seattle Supersonics			
☐ 172	Sedale Threatt	.05	.02	.01
	Los Angeles Lakers			
☐ 173	Mark Macon	.05	.02	.01
	Denver Nuggets			
☐ 174	B.J. Armstrong	.10	.05	.01
	Chicago Bulls			
☐ 175	Harold Miner ART	.05	.02	.01
	Miami Heat			
☐ 176	Anthony Peeler ART	.05	.02	.01
	Los Angeles Lakers			
☐ 177	Alonzo Mourning ART	.25	.11	.03
	Charlotte Hornets			
☐ 178	Christian Laettner ART	.08	.04	.01
	Minnesota Timberwolves			
☐ 179	Clarence Weatherspoon ART	.08	.04	.01
	Philadelphia 76ers			
☐ 180	Dee Brown	.05	.02	.01
	Boston Celtics			
☐ 181	Shaquille O'Neal	1.50	.65	.19
	Orlando Magic			
☐ 182	Loy Vaught	.08	.04	.01
	Los Angeles Clippers			
☐ 183	Terrell Brandon	.05	.02	.01
	Cleveland Cavaliers			
☐ 184	Lionel Simmons	.08	.04	.01
	Sacramento Kings			
☐ 185	Mark Aguirre	.10	.05	.01
	Detroit Pistons			
☐ 186	Danny Ainge	.10	.05	.01
	Phoenix Suns			
☐ 187	Reggie Miller	.20	.09	.03
	Indiana Pacers			
☐ 188	Terry Davis	.05	.02	.01
	Dallas Mavericks			
☐ 189	Mark Bryant	.05	.02	.01
	Portland Trail Blazers			
☐ 190	Tyrone Corbin	.05	.02	.01
	Utah Jazz			
☐ 191	Chris Mullin	.15	.07	.02
	Golden State Warriors			
☐ 192	Johnny Newman	.05	.02	.01
	Charlotte Hornets			
☐ 193	Doug West	.05	.02	.01
	Minnesota Timberwolves			
☐ 194	Keith Askins	.05	.02	.01
	Miami Heat			
☐ 195	Bo Kimble	.05	.02	.01
	New York Knicks			
☐ 196	Sean Elliott	.08	.04	.01
	San Antonio Spurs			

☐ 197	Checklist 1-99 UER	.05	.02	.01
	(No. 18 listed as Terry Mills instead of Terry Cummings and No. 23 listed as Sam Mitchell instead of Michael Jordan)			
☐ 198	Checklist 100-198	.05	.02	.01
☐ 199	Michael Jordan	1.00	.45	.13
	Chicago Bulls			
☐ 200	Patrick Ewing	.15	.07	.02
	New York Knicks			
☐ 201	John Stockton	.10	.05	.01
	Utah Jazz			
☐ 202	Shawn Kemp	.15	.07	.02
	Seattle Supersonics			
☐ 203	Mark Price	.08	.04	.01
	Cleveland Cavaliers			
☐ 204	Charles Barkley	.20	.09	.03
	Phoenix Suns			
☐ 205	Hakeem Olajuwon	.40	.18	.05
	Houston Rockets			
☐ 206	Clyde Drexler	.10	.05	.01
	Portland Trail Blazers			
☐ 207	Kevin Johnson	.10	.05	.01
	Phoenix Suns			
☐ 208	John Starks	.08	.04	.01
	New York Knicks			
☐ 209	Chris Mullin	.10	.05	.01
	Golden State Warriors			
☐ 210	Doc Rivers	.08	.04	.01
	New York Knicks			
☐ 211	Kenny Walker	.05	.02	.01
	New Jersey Nets			
☐ 212	Doug Christie	.08	.04	.01
	Los Angeles Lakers			
☐ 213	James Robinson	.15	.07	.02
	Portland Trail Blazers			
☐ 214	Larry Krystkowiak	.05	.02	.01
	Orlando Magic			
☐ 215	Manute Bol	.05	.02	.01
	Miami Heat			
☐ 216	Carl Herrera	.05	.02	.01
	Houston Rockets			
☐ 217	Paul Graham	.05	.02	.01
	Atlanta Hawks			
☐ 218	Jud Buechler	.05	.02	.01
	Golden State Warriors			
☐ 219	Mike Brown	.05	.02	.01
	Minnesota Timberwolves			
☐ 220	Tom Chambers	.08	.04	.01
	Utah Jazz			
☐ 221	Kendall Gill	.08	.04	.01
	Seattle Supersonics			
☐ 222	Kenny Anderson	.15	.07	.02
	New Jersey Nets			
☐ 223	Larry Johnson	.30	.14	.04
	Charlotte Hornets			
☐ 224	Chris Webber	2.50	1.15	.30
	Golden State Warriors			
☐ 225	Randy White	.05	.02	.01
	Dallas Mavericks			
☐ 226	Rik Smits	.08	.04	.01
	Indiana Pacers			
☐ 227	A.C. Green	.08	.04	.01
	Phoenix Suns			
☐ 228	David Robinson	.40	.18	.05
	San Antonio Spurs			
☐ 229	Sean Elliott	.08	.04	.01
	Detroit Pistons			
☐ 230	Gary Grant	.05	.02	.01
	Los Angeles Clippers			
☐ 231	Dana Barros	.05	.02	.01
	Philadelphia 76ers			
☐ 232	Bobby Hurley	.20	.09	.03

	Sacramento Kings			
☐ 233	Blue Edwards	.05	.02	.01
	Milwaukee Bucks			
☐ 234	Tom Hammonds	.05	.02	.01
	Denver Nuggets			
☐ 235	Pete Myers	.05	.02	.01
	Chicago Bulls			
☐ 236	Acie Earl	.10	.05	.01
	Boston Celtics			
☐ 237	Tony Smith	.05	.02	.01
	Los Angeles Lakers			
☐ 238	Bill Wennington	.05	.02	.01
	Chicago Bulls			
☐ 239	Andrew Lang	.05	.02	.01
	Atlanta Hawks			
☐ 240	Ervin Johnson	.05	.02	.01
	Seattle Supersonics			
☐ 241	Byron Scott	.08	.04	.01
	Indiana Pacers			
☐ 242	Eddie Johnson	.05	.02	.01
	Charlotte Hornets			
☐ 243	Anthony Bonner	.05	.02	.01
	New York Knicks			
☐ 244	Luther Wright	.05	.02	.01
	Utah Jazz			
☐ 245	LaSalle Thompson	.08	.04	.01
	Indiana Pacers			
☐ 246	Harold Miner	.08	.04	.01
	Miami Heat			
☐ 247	Chris Smith	.05	.02	.01
	Minnesota Timberwolves			
☐ 248	John Williams	.08	.04	.01
	Cleveland Cavaliers			
☐ 249	Clyde Drexler	.20	.09	.03
	Portland Trail Blazers			
☐ 250	Calbert Cheaney	.20	.09	.03
	Washington Bullets			
☐ 251	Avery Johnson	.05	.02	.01
	Golden State Warriors			
☐ 252	Steve Kerr	.05	.02	.01
	Chicago Bulls			
☐ 253	Warren Kidd	.10	.05	.01
	Philadelphia 76ers			
☐ 254	Wayman Tisdale	.08	.04	.01
	Sacramento Kings			
☐ 255	Bob Martin	.10	.05	.01
	Los Angeles Clippers			
☐ 256	Popeye Jones	.15	.07	.02
	Dallas Mavericks			
☐ 257	Jimmy Oliver	.05	.02	.01
	Boston Celtics			
☐ 258	Kevin Edwards	.05	.02	.01
	New Jersey Nets			
☐ 259	Dan Majerle	.10	.05	.01
	Phoenix Suns			
☐ 260	Jon Barry	.05	.02	.01
	Milwaukee Bucks			
☐ 261	Allan Houston	.15	.07	.02
	Detroit Pistons			
☐ 262	Dikembe Mutombo	.10	.05	.01
	Denver Nuggets			
☐ 263	Sleepy Floyd	.05	.02	.01
	San Antonio Spurs			
☐ 264	George Lynch	.25	.11	.03
	Los Angeles Lakers			
☐ 265	Stacey Augmon UER	.10	.05	.01
	Atlanta Hawks			
	(Listed with Heat in stats)			
☐ 266	Hakeem Olajuwon	.75	.35	.09
	Houston Rockets			
☐ 267	Scott Skiles	.05	.02	.01
	Orlando Magic			
☐ 268	Detlef Schrempf	.10	.05	.01
	Seattle Supersonics			

☐ 269	Brian Davis	.10	.05	.01
	Minnesota Timberwolves			
☐ 270	Tracy Murray	.05	.02	.01
	Portland Trail Blazers			
☐ 271	Gheorghe Muresan	.15	.07	.02
	Washington Bullets			
☐ 272	Terry Dehere	.10	.05	.01
	Los Angeles Clippers			
☐ 273	Terry Cummings	.08	.04	.01
	San Antonio Spurs			
☐ 274	Keith Jennings	.05	.02	.01
	Golden State Warriors			
☐ 275	Tyrone Hill	.05	.02	.01
	Cleveland Cavaliers			
☐ 276	Hersey Hawkins	.08	.04	.01
	Charlotte Hornets			
☐ 277	Grant Long	.05	.02	.01
	Miami Heat			
☐ 278	Herb Williams	.05	.02	.01
	New York Knicks			
☐ 279	Karl Malone	.25	.11	.03
	Utah Jazz			
☐ 280	Mitch Richmond	.10	.05	.01
	Sacramento Kings			
☐ 281	Derek Strong	.10	.05	.01
	Milwaukee Bucks			
☐ 282	Dino Radja	.40	.18	.05
	Boston Celtics			
☐ 283	Jack Haley	.05	.02	.01
	San Antonio Spurs			
☐ 284	Derek Harper	.08	.04	.01
	New York Knicks			
☐ 285	Dwayne Schintzius	.05	.02	.01
	New Jersey Nets			
☐ 286	Michael Curry	.10	.05	.01
	Philadelphia 76ers			
☐ 287	Rodney Rogers	.25	.11	.03
	Denver Nuggets			
☐ 288	Horace Grant	.10	.05	.01
	Chicago Bulls			
☐ 289	Oliver Miller	.10	.05	.01
	Phoenix Suns			
☐ 290	Luc Longley	.05	.02	.01
	Minnesota Timberwolves			
☐ 291	Walter Bond	.05	.02	.01
	Utah Jazz			
☐ 292	Dominique Wilkins	.25	.11	.03
	Atlanta Hawks			
☐ 293	Vern Fleming	.05	.02	.01
	Indiana Pacers			
☐ 294	Mark Price	.10	.05	.01
	Cleveland Cavaliers			
☐ 295	Mark Aguirre	.10	.05	.01
	Los Angeles Clippers			
☐ 296	Shawn Kemp	.30	.14	.04
	Seattle Supersonics			
☐ 297	Pervis Ellison	.05	.02	.01
	Washington Bullets			
☐ 298	Josh Grant	.10	.05	.01
	Golden State Warriors			
☐ 299	Scott Burrell	.15	.07	.02
	Charlotte Hornets			
☐ 300	Patrick Ewing	.30	.14	.04
	New York Knicks			
☐ 301	Sam Cassell	.50	.23	.06
	Houston Rockets			
☐ 302	Nick Van Exel	.40	.18	.05
	Los Angeles Lakers			
☐ 303	Clifford Robinson	.10	.05	.01
	Portland Trail Blazers			
☐ 304	Frank Johnson	.05	.02	.01
	Phoenix Suns			
☐ 305	Matt Geiger	.05	.02	.01

	Miami Heat				
☐ 306	Vin Baker	.60		.25	.08
	Milwaukee Bucks				
☐ 307	Benoit Benjamin	.05		.02	.01
	New Jersey Nets				
☐ 308	Shawn Bradley	.20		.09	.03
	Philadelphia 76ers				
☐ 309	Chris Whitney	.10		.05	.01
	San Antonio Spurs				
☐ 310	Eric Riley	.10		.05	.01
	Houston Rockets				
☐ 311	Isiah Thomas	.15		.07	.02
	Detroit Pistons				
☐ 312	Jamal Mashburn	1.00		.45	.13
	Dallas Mavericks				
☐ 313	Xavier McDaniel	.08		.04	.01
	Boston Celtics				
☐ 314	Mike Peplowski	.10		.05	.01
	Sacramento Kings				
☐ 315	Darnell Mee	.10		.05	.01
	Denver Nuggets				
☐ 316	Toni Kukoc	.40		.18	.05
	Chicago Bulls				
☐ 317	Felton Spencer	.05		.02	.01
	Utah Jazz				
☐ 318	Sam Bowie	.05		.02	.01
	Los Angeles Lakers				
☐ 319	Mario Elie	.05		.02	.01
	Houston Rockets				
☐ 320	Tim Hardaway	.10		.05	.01
	Golden State Warriors				
☐ 321	Ken Norman	.05		.02	.01
	Milwaukee Bucks				
☐ 322	Isaiah Rider	1.00		.45	.13
	Minnesota Timberwolves				
☐ 323	Rex Chapman	.05		.02	.01
	Washington Bullets				
☐ 324	Dennis Rodman	.08		.04	.01
	San Antonio Spurs				
☐ 325	Derrick McKey	.05		.02	.01
	Indiana Pacers				
☐ 326	Corie Blount	.05		.02	.01
	Chicago Bulls				
☐ 327	Fat Lever	.05		.02	.01
	Dallas Mavericks				
☐ 328	Ron Harper	.08		.04	.01
	Los Angeles Clippers				
☐ 329	Eric Anderson	.05		.02	.01
	New York Knicks				
☐ 330	Armon Gilliam	.05		.02	.01
	New Jersey Nets				
☐ 331	Lindsey Hunter	.40		.18	.05
	Detroit Pistons				
☐ 332	Eric Leckner	.05		.02	.01
	Philadelphia 76ers				
☐ 333	Chris Corchiani	.05		.02	.01
	Boston Celtics				
☐ 334	Anfernee Hardaway	2.00		.90	.25
	Orlando Magic				
☐ 335	Randy Brown	.05		.02	.01
	Sacramento Kings				
☐ 336	Sam Perkins	.08		.04	.01
	Seattle Supersonics				
☐ 337	Glen Rice	.10		.05	.01
	Miami Heat				
☐ 338	Orlando Woolridge	.08		.04	.01
	Philadelphia 76ers				
☐ 339	Mike Gminski	.05		.02	.01
	Charlotte Hornets				
☐ 340	Latrell Sprewell	.40		.18	.05
	Golden State Warriors				
☐ 341	Harvey Grant	.05		.02	.01
	Portland Trail Blazers				

☐ 342	Doug Smith	.05	.02	.01
	Dallas Mavericks			
☐ 343	Kevin Duckworth	.05	.02	.01
	Washington Bullets			
☐ 344	Cedric Ceballos	.10	.05	.01
	Phoenix Suns			
☐ 345	Chuck Person	.08	.04	.01
	Minnesota Timberwolves			
☐ 346	Scott Haskin	.10	.05	.01
	Indiana Pacers			
☐ 347	Frank Brickowski	.08	.04	.01
	Milwaukee Bucks			
☐ 348	Scott Williams	.05	.02	.01
	Chicago Bulls			
☐ 349	Brad Daugherty	.10	.05	.01
	Cleveland Cavaliers			
☐ 350	Willie Burton	.05	.02	.01
	Miami Heat			
☐ 351	Joe Dumars	.15	.07	.02
	Detroit Pistons			
☐ 352	Craig Ehlo	.05	.02	.01
	Atlanta Hawks			
☐ 353	Lucious Harris	.10	.05	.01
	Dallas Mavericks			
☐ 354	Danny Manning	.10	.05	.01
	Los Angeles Clippers			
☐ 355	Litterial Green	.05	.02	.01
	Orlando Magic			
☐ 356	John Stockton	.15	.07	.02
	Utah Jazz			
☐ 357	Nate McMillan	.05	.02	.01
	Seattle Supersonics			
☐ 358	Greg Graham	.10	.05	.01
	Philadelphia 76ers			
☐ 359	Rex Walters	.05	.02	.01
	New Jersey Nets			
☐ 360	Lloyd Daniels	.05	.02	.01
	San Antonio Spurs			
☐ 361	Antonio Harvey	.10	.05	.01
	Los Angeles Lakers			
☐ 362	Brian Williams	.05	.02	.01
	Denver Nuggets			
☐ 363	LeRon Ellis	.05	.02	.01
	Charlotte Hornets			
☐ 364	Chris Dudley	.05	.02	.01
	Portland Trail Blazers			
☐ 365	Hubert Davis	.05	.02	.01
	New York Knicks			
☐ 366	Evers Burns	.10	.05	.01
	Sacramento Kings			
☐ 367	Sherman Douglas	.05	.02	.01
	Boston Celtics			
☐ 368	Sarunas Marciulionis	.05	.02	.01
	Golden State Warriors			
☐ 369	Tom Tolbert	.05	.02	.01
	Orlando Magic			
☐ 370	Robert Pack	.05	.02	.01
	Denver Nuggets			
☐ 371	Michael Adams	.08	.04	.01
	Washington Bullets			
☐ 372	Negele Knight	.05	.02	.01
	San Antonio Spurs			
☐ 373	Charles Barkley	.40	.18	.05
	Phoenix Suns			
☐ 374	Bryon Russell	.15	.07	.02
	Utah Jazz			
☐ 375	Greg Anthony	.05	.02	.01
	New York Knicks			
☐ 376	Ken Williams	.05	.02	.01
	Indiana Pacers			
☐ 377	John Paxson	.05	.02	.01
	Chicago Bulls			
☐ 378	Corey Gaines	.05	.02	.01

☐ 379 Eric Murdock	.08	.04	.01
New York Knicks			
☐ 380 Kevin Thompson	.10	.05	.01
Milwaukee Bucks			
☐ 381 Moses Malone	.10	.05	.01
Portland Trail Blazers			
☐ 382 Kenny Smith	.05	.02	.01
Philadelphia 76ers			
☐ 383 Dennis Scott	.08	.04	.01
Houston Rockets			
☐ 384 Michael Jordan	1.00	.45	.13
Orlando Magic			
☐ 385 Hakeem Olajuwon	.40	.18	.05
Chicago Bulls			
☐ 386 Shaquille O'Neal	.75	.35	.09
Houston Rockets			
☐ 387 David Robinson	.20	.09	.03
Orlando Magic			
☐ 388 Derrick Coleman	.10	.05	.01
San Antonio Spurs			
☐ 389 Karl Malone	.12	.05	.02
New Jersey Nets			
☐ 390 Patrick Ewing	.15	.07	.02
Utah Jazz			
☐ 391 Scottie Pippen	.15	.07	.02
New York Knicks			
☐ 392 Dominique Wilkins	.12	.05	.02
Chicago Bulls			
☐ 393 Charles Barkley	.20	.09	.03
Atlanta Hawks			
☐ 394 Larry Johnson	.15	.07	.02
Phoenix Suns			
☐ 395 Checklist	.05	.02	.01
Charlotte Hornets			
☐ 396 Checklist	.05	.02	.01
☐ NNO Expired Finest	1.50	.65	.19
Redemption Card			

1993-94 Topps Gold

Each pack of '93-94 Topps contained at least one Gold card. Aside from the gold-foil highlights the Gold cards are identical to their regular issue counterparts, except the four regular issue checklists were replaced by Gold cards featuring the players listed below.

	MINT	EXC	G-VG
COMPLETE SET (396)	75.00	34.00	9.50
COMPLETE SERIES 1 (198)	30.00	13.50	3.80
COMPLETE SERIES 2 (198)	45.00	20.00	5.75
COMMON GOLD (1-198)	.10	.05	.01
COMMON GOLD (199-396)	.10	.05	.01
*GOLD STARS: 2.5X to 5X VALUE			
*GOLD ROOKIES: 1.5X to 3X VALUE			

☐ 197	Frank Johnson.............	.50	.23	.06
	Phoenix Suns			
☐ 198	David Wingate.............	.50	.23	.06
	Charlotte Hornets			
☐ 395	Will Perdue.................	.50	.23	.06
	Chicago Bulls			
☐ 396	Mark West..................	.50	.23	.06
	Phoenix Suns			

1993-94 Topps Black Gold

Randomly inserted into packs or three per factory set, this 25-card standard-size (2 1/2" by 3 1/2") set features the NBA's top young stars. Each white-bordered front displays a color action player shot with the background tinted in black. Gold prismatic wavy stripes appear above and below the photo with the player's name reversed out of the black bar near the bottom. The white-bordered horizontal backs carry a close-up color cutout on a black background with white concentric stripes. The players name appears on a wood textured bar in gold foil in the upper right with the team name directly to the right in black. Player statistics appear below on the left on an orange background. The cards are numbered on the back.

	MINT	EXC	G-VG
COMPLETE SET (25)......................	25.00	11.50	3.10
COMPLETE SERIES 1 (13)...............	5.00	2.30	.60
COMPLETE SERIES 2 (12)...............	20.00	9.00	2.50
COMMON PLAYER (1-13).................	.50	.23	.06
COMMON PLAYER (14-25)...............	.50	.23	.06
☐ 1 Sean Elliott..........................	.50	.23	.06
San Antonio Spurs			
☐ 2 Dennis Scott.........................	.50	.23	.06
Orlando Magic			
☐ 3 Kenny Anderson....................	1.00	.45	.13
New Jersey Nets			
☐ 4 Alonzo Mourning...................	3.50	1.55	.45
Charlotte Hornets			
☐ 5 Glen Rice.............................	.50	.23	.06
Miami Heat			
☐ 6 Billy Owens...........................	.50	.23	.06
Golden State Warriors			
☐ 7 Jim Jackson..........................	2.00	.90	.25
Dallas Mavericks			
☐ 8 Derrick Coleman....................	1.00	.45	.13
New Jersey Nets			
☐ 9 Larry Johnson.......................	2.00	.90	.25
Charlotte Hornets			
☐ 10 Gary Payton.........................	.50	.23	.06
Seattle Supersonics			
☐ 11 Christian Laettner..................	.75	.35	.09

		Minnesota Timberwolves			
☐	12	Dikembe Mutombo	.75	.35	.09
		Denver Nuggets			
☐	13	Mahmoud Abdul-Rauf	.50	.23	.06
		Denver Nuggets			
☐	14	Isaiah Rider	3.00	1.35	.40
		Minnesota Timberwolves			
☐	15	Steve Smith	.75	.35	.09
		Miami Heat			
☐	16	LaPhonso Ellis	.75	.35	.09
		Denver Nuggets			
☐	17	Danny Ferry	.50	.23	.06
		Cleveland Cavaliers			
☐	18	Shaquille O'Neal	8.00	3.60	1.00
		Orlando Magic			
☐	19	Anfernee Hardaway	6.00	2.70	.75
		Orlando Magic			
☐	20	J.R. Reid	.50	.23	.06
		San Antonio Spurs			
☐	21	Shawn Bradley	1.25	.55	.16
		Philadelphia 76ers			
☐	22	Pervis Ellison	.50	.23	.06
		Washington Bullets			
☐	23	Chris Webber	8.00	3.60	1.00
		Golden State Warriors			
☐	24	Jamal Mashburn	3.00	1.35	.40
		Dallas Mavericks			
☐	25	Kendall Gill	.50	.23	.06
		Seattle Supersonics			
☐	A	Expired Winner A	1.00	.45	.13
☐	AB	Expired Winner A/B	3.00	1.35	.40
☐	B	Expired Winner B	2.00	.90	.25

1992-93 Ultra

DENVER NUGGETS • CENTER

*The complete 1992-93 Ultra basketball set consists of 375 standard-size (2 1/2" by 3 1/2")
cards. The set was released in two series of 200 and 175 cards, respectively. Both series
packs contained 14 cards each with 36 packs to a box. Suggested retail pack price was
1.79 to 1.99. The glossy color action player photos on the fronts are full-bleed except at the
bottom where a diagonal gold-foil stripe edges a pale green variegated border. The player's
name and team appear on two team color-coded bars that overlay the bottom border. The
horizontal backs display action and close-up cut-out player photos against a basketball
court background. The team logo and biographical information appear in a pale green bar
like that on the front that edges the right side, while the player's name and statistics are
given in bars running across the card bottom. The cards are numbered on the back,
grouped alphabetically within teams, and checklisted below alphabetically according to
teams as follows: Atlanta Hawks (1-7), Boston Celtics (8-16), Charlotte Hornets (17-23),
Chicago Bulls (24-32), Cleveland Cavaliers (33-40), Dallas Mavericks (41-47), Denver
Nuggets (48-54), Detroit Pistons (55-61), Golden State Warriors (62-68), Houston Rockets*

(69-74), Indiana Pacers (75-81), Los Angeles Clippers (82-88), Los Angeles Lakers (89-96), Miami Heat (97-104), Milwaukee Bucks (105-108), Minnesota Timberwolves (109-113), New Jersey Nets (114-120), New York Knicks (121-127), Orlando Magic (128-134), Philadelphia 76ers (135-141), Phoenix Suns (142-147), Portland Trail Blazers (148-155), Sacramento Kings (156-161), San Antonio Spurs (162-167), Seattle Supersonics (168-176), Utah Jazz (177-183), and Washington Bullets (184-192). The first series closes with NBA Draft Picks (193-198) and checklists (199-200). The second series contains more than 40 rookies, 30 trades, free agent signings, and other veterans omitted from the first series. The second series opens with an NBA Jam Session (201-220) subset. Three players from this Jam Session subset, Duane Causwell, Pervis Ellison, and Stacey Augmon, autographed a total of more than 2,500 cards that were randomly inserted in second series foil packs. On the back, a mail-in offer provided the opportunity to acquire two more exclusive Jam Session cards, showing all 20 players in the set, for ten wrappers and 1.00 for postage and handling. According to Fleer, they anticipated about 100,000 requests. Key Rookie Cards include LaPhonso Ellis, Tom Gugliotta, Robert Horry, Christian Laettner, Alonzo Mourning, Shaquille O'Neal, Latrell Sprewell and Clarence Weatherspoon.

		MINT	EXC	G-VG
	COMPLETE SET (375)	50.00	23.00	6.25
	COMPLETE SERIES 1 (200)	25.00	11.50	3.10
	COMPLETE SERIES 2 (175)	25.00	11.50	3.10
	COMMON PLAYER (1-200)	.10	.05	.01
	COMMON PLAYER (201-375)	.05	.02	.01
☐ 1	Stacey Augmon	.20	.09	.03
☐ 2	Duane Ferrell	.10	.05	.01
☐ 3	Paul Graham	.10	.05	.01
☐ 4	Blair Rasmussen	.10	.05	.01
☐ 5	Rumeal Robinson	.10	.05	.01
☐ 6	Dominique Wilkins	.60	.25	.08
☐ 7	Kevin Willis	.15	.07	.02
☐ 8	John Bagley	.10	.05	.01
☐ 9	Dee Brown	.15	.07	.02
☐ 10	Rick Fox	.10	.05	.01
☐ 11	Kevin Gamble	.10	.05	.01
☐ 12	Joe Kleine	.10	.05	.01
☐ 13	Reggie Lewis	.20	.09	.03
☐ 14	Kevin McHale	.20	.09	.03
☐ 15	Robert Parish	.20	.09	.03
☐ 16	Ed Pinckney	.10	.05	.01
☐ 17	Muggsy Bogues	.20	.09	.03
☐ 18	Dell Curry	.15	.07	.02
☐ 19	Kenny Gattison	.10	.05	.01
☐ 20	Kendall Gill	.15	.07	.02
☐ 21	Larry Johnson	1.00	.45	.13
☐ 22	Johnny Newman	.10	.05	.01
☐ 23	J.R. Reid	.10	.05	.01
☐ 24	B.J. Armstrong	.20	.09	.03
☐ 25	Bill Cartwright	.15	.07	.02
☐ 26	Horace Grant	.20	.09	.03
☐ 27	Michael Jordan	4.00	1.80	.50
☐ 28	Stacey King	.10	.05	.01
☐ 29	John Paxson	.15	.07	.02
☐ 30	Will Perdue	.10	.05	.01
☐ 31	Scottie Pippen	.75	.35	.09
☐ 32	Scott Williams	.10	.05	.01
☐ 33	John Battle	.10	.05	.01
☐ 34	Terrell Brandon	.10	.05	.01
☐ 35	Brad Daugherty	.20	.09	.03
☐ 36	Craig Ehlo	.10	.05	.01
☐ 37	Larry Nance	.15	.07	.02
☐ 38	Mark Price	.20	.09	.03
☐ 39	Mike Sanders	.10	.05	.01
☐ 40	John Williams	.15	.07	.02
☐ 41	Terry Davis	.10	.05	.01
☐ 42	Derek Harper	.15	.07	.02
☐ 43	Donald Hodge	.10	.05	.01
☐ 44	Mike Iuzzolino	.10	.05	.01
☐ 45	Fat Lever	.10	.05	.01
☐ 46	Doug Smith	.10	.05	.01
☐ 47	Randy White	.10	.05	.01
☐ 48	Winston Garland	.10	.05	.01
☐ 49	Chris Jackson	.15	.07	.02

☐ 50 Marcus Liberty	.10	.05	.01
☐ 51 Todd Lichti	.10	.05	.01
☐ 52 Mark Macon	.10	.05	.01
☐ 53 Dikembe Mutombo	.40	.18	.05
☐ 54 Reggie Williams	.15	.07	.02
☐ 55 Mark Aguirre	.20	.09	.03
☐ 56 Joe Dumars	.30	.14	.04
☐ 57 Bill Laimbeer	.20	.09	.03
☐ 58 Dennis Rodman	.15	.07	.02
☐ 59 Isiah Thomas	.30	.14	.04
☐ 60 Darrell Walker	.10	.05	.01
☐ 61 Orlando Woolridge	.15	.07	.02
☐ 62 Victor Alexander	.10	.05	.01
☐ 63 Chris Gatling	.10	.05	.01
☐ 64 Tim Hardaway	.20	.09	.03
☐ 65 Tyrone Hill	.10	.05	.01
☐ 66 Sarunas Marciulionis	.15	.07	.02
☐ 67 Chris Mullin	.30	.14	.04
☐ 68 Billy Owens	.20	.09	.03
☐ 69 Sleepy Floyd	.10	.05	.01
☐ 70 Avery Johnson	.10	.05	.01
☐ 71 Vernon Maxwell	.15	.07	.02
☐ 72 Hakeem Olajuwon	1.50	.65	.19
☐ 73 Kenny Smith	.10	.05	.01
☐ 74 Otis Thorpe	.15	.07	.02
☐ 75 Dale Davis	.15	.07	.02
☐ 76 Vern Fleming	.10	.05	.01
☐ 77 George McCloud	.10	.05	.01
☐ 78 Reggie Miller	.35	.16	.04
☐ 79 Detlef Schrempf	.20	.09	.03
☐ 80 Rik Smits	.15	.07	.02
☐ 81 LaSalle Thompson	.15	.07	.02
☐ 82 Gary Grant	.10	.05	.01
☐ 83 Ron Harper	.15	.07	.02
☐ 84 Mark Jackson	.15	.07	.02
☐ 85 Danny Manning	.30	.14	.04
☐ 86 Ken Norman	.10	.05	.01
☐ 87 Stanley Roberts	.10	.05	.01
☐ 88 Loy Vaught	.15	.07	.02
☐ 89 Elden Campbell	.10	.05	.01
☐ 90 Vlade Divac	.15	.07	.02
☐ 91 A.C. Green	.15	.07	.02
☐ 92 Sam Perkins	.15	.07	.02
☐ 93 Byron Scott	.15	.07	.02
☐ 94 Tony Smith	.10	.05	.01
☐ 95 Sedale Threatt	.10	.05	.01
☐ 96 James Worthy	.20	.09	.03
☐ 97 Willie Burton	.10	.05	.01
☐ 98 Vernell Coles	.10	.05	.01
☐ 99 Kevin Edwards	.10	.05	.01
☐ 100 Grant Long	.10	.05	.01
☐ 101 Glen Rice	.20	.09	.03
☐ 102 Rony Seikaly	.20	.09	.03
☐ 103 Brian Shaw	.10	.05	.01
☐ 104 Steve Smith	.25	.11	.03
☐ 105 Frank Brickowski	.15	.07	.02
☐ 106 Moses Malone	.20	.09	.03
☐ 107 Fred Roberts	.10	.05	.01
☐ 108 Alvin Robertson	.15	.07	.02
☐ 109 Thurl Bailey	.10	.05	.01
☐ 110 Gerald Glass	.10	.05	.01
☐ 111 Luc Longley	.10	.05	.01
☐ 112 Felton Spencer	.10	.05	.01
☐ 113 Doug West	.10	.05	.01
☐ 114 Kenny Anderson	.40	.18	.05
☐ 115 Mookie Blaylock	.15	.07	.02
☐ 116 Sam Bowie	.10	.05	.01
☐ 117 Derrick Coleman	.35	.16	.04
☐ 118 Chris Dudley	.10	.05	.01
☐ 119 Chris Morris	.10	.05	.01
☐ 120 Drazen Petrovic	.15	.07	.02
☐ 121 Greg Anthony	.10	.05	.01
☐ 122 Patrick Ewing	.75	.35	.09

☐	123	Anthony Mason	.15	.07	.02
☐	124	Charles Oakley	.20	.09	.03
☐	125	Glenn Rivers	.15	.07	.02
☐	126	Charles Smith	.10	.05	.01
☐	127	John Starks	.20	.09	.03
☐	128	Nick Anderson	.15	.07	.02
☐	129	Anthony Bowie	.15	.07	.02
☐	130	Terry Catledge	.10	.05	.01
☐	131	Jerry Reynolds	.10	.05	.01
☐	132	Dennis Scott	.15	.07	.02
☐	133	Scott Skiles	.15	.07	.02
☐	134	Brian Williams	.10	.05	.01
☐	135	Ron Anderson	.10	.05	.01
☐	136	Manute Bol	.10	.05	.01
☐	137	Johnny Dawkins	.10	.05	.01
☐	138	Armon Gilliam	.10	.05	.01
☐	139	Hersey Hawkins	.15	.07	.02
☐	140	Jeff Ruland	.15	.07	.02
☐	141	Charles Shackleford	.10	.05	.01
☐	142	Cedric Ceballos	.20	.09	.03
☐	143	Tom Chambers	.15	.07	.02
☐	144	Kevin Johnson	.20	.09	.03
☐	145	Negele Knight	.10	.05	.01
☐	146	Dan Majerle	.20	.09	.03
☐	147	Mark West	.10	.05	.01
☐	148	Mark Bryant	.10	.05	.01
☐	149	Clyde Drexler	.35	.16	.04
☐	150	Kevin Duckworth	.10	.05	.01
☐	151	Jerome Kersey	.10	.05	.01
☐	152	Robert Pack	.10	.05	.01
☐	153	Terry Porter	.15	.07	.02
☐	154	Cliff Robinson	.20	.09	.03
☐	155	Buck Williams	.20	.09	.03
☐	156	Anthony Bonner	.10	.05	.01
☐	157	Duane Causwell	.10	.05	.01
☐	158	Mitch Richmond	.20	.09	.03
☐	159	Lionel Simmons	.15	.07	.02
☐	160	Wayman Tisdale	.15	.07	.02
☐	161	Spud Webb	.20	.09	.03
☐	162	Willie Anderson	.10	.05	.01
☐	163	Antoine Carr	.10	.05	.01
☐	164	Terry Cummings	.15	.07	.02
☐	165	Sean Elliott	.15	.07	.02
☐	166	Sidney Green	.10	.05	.01
☐	167	David Robinson	1.00	.45	.13
☐	168	Dana Barros	.10	.05	.01
☐	169	Benoit Benjamin	.10	.05	.01
☐	170	Michael Cage	.10	.05	.01
☐	171	Eddie Johnson	.10	.05	.01
☐	172	Shawn Kemp	1.50	.65	.19
☐	173	Derrick McKey	.10	.05	.01
☐	174	Nate McMillan	.10	.05	.01
☐	175	Gary Payton	.20	.09	.03
☐	176	Ricky Pierce	.15	.07	.02
☐	177	David Benoit	.10	.05	.01
☐	178	Mike Brown	.10	.05	.01
☐	179	Tyrone Corbin	.10	.05	.01
☐	180	Mark Eaton	.10	.05	.01
☐	181	Jeff Malone	.15	.07	.02
☐	182	Karl Malone	.50	.23	.06
☐	183	John Stockton	.35	.16	.04
☐	184	Michael Adams	.15	.07	.02
☐	185	Ledell Eackles	.10	.05	.01
☐	186	Pervis Ellison	.10	.05	.01
☐	187	A.J. English	.10	.05	.01
☐	188	Harvey Grant	.10	.05	.01
☐	189	Buck Johnson	.10	.05	.01
☐	190	LaBradford Smith	.10	.05	.01
☐	191	Larry Stewart	.10	.05	.01
☐	192	David Wingate	.10	.05	.01
☐	193	Alonzo Mourning	7.00	3.10	.85
☐	194	Adam Keefe	.20	.09	.03
☐	195	Robert Horry	1.50	.65	.19

☐ 196 Anthony Peeler	.60	.25	.08
☐ 197 Tracy Murray	.20	.09	.03
☐ 198 Dave Johnson	.10	.05	.01
☐ 199 Checklist 1-104	.10	.05	.01
☐ 200 Checklist 105-200	.10	.05	.01
☐ 201 David Robinson JS	.30	.14	.04
San Antonio Spurs			
☐ 202 Dikembe Mutombo JS	.15	.07	.02
Denver Nuggets			
☐ 203 Otis Thorpe JS	.15	.07	.02
Houston Rockets			
☐ 204 Hakeem Olajuwon JS	.50	.23	.06
Houston Rockets			
☐ 205 Shawn Kemp JS	.50	.23	.06
Seattle Supersonics			
☐ 206 Charles Barkley JS	.30	.14	.04
Phoenix Suns			
☐ 207 Pervis Ellison JS	.10	.05	.01
Washington Bullets			
☐ 208 Chris Morris JS	.10	.05	.01
New Jersey Nets			
☐ 209 Brad Daugherty JS	.15	.07	.02
Cleveland Cavaliers			
☐ 210 Derrick Coleman JS	.15	.07	.02
New Jersey Nets			
☐ 211 Tim Perry JS	.10	.05	.01
Philadelphia 76ers			
☐ 212 Duane Causwell JS	.10	.05	.01
Sacramento Kings			
☐ 213 Scottie Pippen JS	.25	.11	.03
Chicago Bulls			
☐ 214 Robert Parish JS	.15	.07	.02
Boston Celtics			
☐ 215 Stacey Augmon JS	.10	.05	.01
Atlanta Hawks			
☐ 216 Michael Jordan JS	1.25	.55	.16
Chicago Bulls			
☐ 217 Karl Malone JS	.20	.09	.03
Utah Jazz			
☐ 218 John Williams JS	.10	.05	.01
Cleveland Cavaliers			
☐ 219 Horace Grant JS	.10	.05	.01
Chicago Bulls			
☐ 220 Orlando Woolridge JS	.10	.05	.01
Detroit Pistons			
☐ 221 Mookie Blaylock	.08	.04	.01
☐ 222 Greg Foster	.05	.02	.01
☐ 223 Steve Henson	.05	.02	.01
☐ 224 Adam Keefe	.05	.02	.01
☐ 225 Jon Koncak	.05	.02	.01
☐ 226 Travis Mays	.05	.02	.01
☐ 227 Alaa Abdelnaby	.05	.02	.01
☐ 228 Sherman Douglas	.05	.02	.01
☐ 229 Xavier McDaniel	.10	.05	.01
☐ 230 Marcus Webb	.05	.02	.01
☐ 231 Tony Bennett	.10	.05	.01
☐ 232 Mike Gminski	.05	.02	.01
☐ 233 Kevin Lynch	.05	.02	.01
☐ 234 Alonzo Mourning	1.50	.65	.19
☐ 235 David Wingate	.05	.02	.01
☐ 236 Rodney McCray	.05	.02	.01
☐ 237 Trent Tucker	.05	.02	.01
☐ 238 Corey Williams	.05	.02	.01
☐ 239 Danny Ferry	.05	.02	.01
☐ 240 Jay Guidinger	.05	.02	.01
☐ 241 Jerome Lane	.05	.02	.01
☐ 242 Bobby Phills	.20	.09	.03
☐ 243 Gerald Wilkins	.05	.02	.01
☐ 244 Walter Bond	.05	.02	.01
☐ 245 Dexter Cambridge	.05	.02	.01
☐ 246 Radisav Curcic UER	.05	.02	.01
(Misspelled Radislav			
on card front)			

☐ 247 Brian Howard	.05	.02	.01
☐ 248 Tracy Moore	.05	.02	.01
☐ 249 Sean Rooks	.20	.09	.03
☐ 250 Kevin Brooks	.05	.02	.01
☐ 251 LaPhonso Ellis	1.25	.55	.16
☐ 252 Scott Hastings	.05	.02	.01
☐ 253 Robert Pack	.05	.02	.01
☐ 254 Gary Plummer	.05	.02	.01
☐ 255 Bryant Stith	.50	.23	.06
☐ 256 Robert Werdann	.05	.02	.01
☐ 257 Gerald Glass	.05	.02	.01
☐ 258 Terry Mills	.10	.05	.01
☐ 259 Olden Polynice	.05	.02	.01
☐ 260 Danny Young	.05	.02	.01
☐ 261 Jud Buechler	.05	.02	.01
☐ 262 Jeff Grayer	.05	.02	.01
☐ 263 Bryon Houston	.15	.07	.02
☐ 264 Keith Jennings	.10	.05	.01
☐ 265 Ed Nealy	.05	.02	.01
☐ 266 Latrell Sprewell	3.00	1.35	.40
☐ 267 Scott Brooks	.05	.02	.01
☐ 268 Matt Bullard	.05	.02	.01
☐ 269 Winston Garland	.05	.02	.01
☐ 270 Carl Herrera	.05	.02	.01
☐ 271 Robert Horry	.40	.18	.05
☐ 272 Tree Rollins	.05	.02	.01
☐ 273 Greg Dreiling	.05	.02	.01
☐ 274 Sean Green	.05	.02	.01
☐ 275 Sam Mitchell	.05	.02	.01
☐ 276 Pooh Richardson	.05	.02	.01
☐ 277 Malik Sealy	.15	.07	.02
☐ 278 Kenny Williams	.05	.02	.01
☐ 279 Mark Jackson	.08	.04	.01
☐ 280 Stanley Roberts	.05	.02	.01
☐ 281 Elmore Spencer	.15	.07	.02
☐ 282 Kiki Vandeweghe	.08	.04	.01
☐ 283 John S. Williams	.05	.02	.01
☐ 284 Randy Woods	.05	.02	.01
☐ 285 Alex Blackwell	.05	.02	.01
☐ 286 Duane Cooper	.05	.02	.01
☐ 287 James Edwards	.05	.02	.01
☐ 288 Jack Haley	.05	.02	.01
☐ 289 Anthony Peeler	.15	.07	.02
☐ 290 Keith Askins	.05	.02	.01
☐ 291 Matt Geiger	.15	.07	.02
☐ 292 Alec Kessler	.05	.02	.01
☐ 293 Harold Miner	.50	.23	.06
☐ 294 John Salley	.05	.02	.01
☐ 295 Anthony Avent	.15	.07	.02
☐ 296 Jon Barry	.15	.07	.02
☐ 297 Todd Day	.50	.23	.06
☐ 298 Blue Edwards	.08	.04	.01
☐ 299 Brad Lohaus	.05	.02	.01
☐ 300 Lee Mayberry	.15	.07	.02
☐ 301 Eric Murdock	.08	.04	.01
☐ 302 Dan Schayes	.05	.02	.01
☐ 303 Lance Blanks	.05	.02	.01
☐ 304 Christian Laettner	1.25	.55	.16
☐ 305 Marlon Maxey	.05	.02	.01
☐ 306 Bob McCann	.05	.02	.01
☐ 307 Chuck Person	.08	.04	.01
☐ 308 Brad Sellers	.05	.02	.01
☐ 309 Chris Smith	.15	.07	.02
☐ 310 Gundars Vetra	.05	.02	.01
☐ 311 Micheal Williams	.10	.05	.01
☐ 312 Rafael Addison	.05	.02	.01
☐ 313 Chucky Brown	.05	.02	.01
☐ 314 Maurice Cheeks	.10	.05	.01
☐ 315 Tate George	.05	.02	.01
☐ 316 Rick Mahorn	.08	.04	.01
☐ 317 Rumeal Robinson	.05	.02	.01
☐ 318 Eric Anderson	.05	.02	.01
☐ 319 Rolando Blackman	.08	.04	.01

☐	320	Tony Campbell	.05	.02	.01
☐	321	Hubert Davis	.50	.23	.06
☐	322	Doc Rivers	.08	.04	.01
☐	323	Charles Smith	.05	.02	.01
☐	324	Herb Williams	.05	.02	.01
☐	325	Litterial Green	.10	.05	.01
☐	326	Steve Kerr	.05	.02	.01
☐	327	Greg Kite	.05	.02	.01
☐	328	Shaquille O'Neal	8.00	3.60	1.00
☐	329	Tom Tolbert	.05	.02	.01
☐	330	Jeff Turner	.05	.02	.01
☐	331	Greg Grant	.05	.02	.01
☐	332	Jeff Hornacek	.10	.05	.01
☐	333	Andrew Lang	.05	.02	.01
☐	334	Tim Perry	.05	.02	.01
☐	335	Clarence Weatherspoon	1.25	.55	.16
		(Shaquille O'Neal			
		also pictured)			
☐	336	Danny Ainge	.10	.05	.01
☐	337	Charles Barkley	.60	.25	.08
☐	338	Richard Dumas	.40	.18	.05
☐	339	Frank Johnson	.05	.02	.01
☐	340	Tim Kempton	.05	.02	.01
☐	341	Oliver Miller	.50	.23	.06
☐	342	Jerrod Mustaf	.05	.02	.01
☐	343	Mario Elie	.05	.02	.01
☐	344	Dave Johnson	.05	.02	.01
☐	345	Tracy Murray	.05	.02	.01
☐	346	Rod Strickland	.08	.04	.01
☐	347	Randy Brown	.05	.02	.01
☐	348	Pete Chilcutt	.05	.02	.01
☐	349	Marty Conlon	.05	.02	.01
☐	350	Jim Les	.05	.02	.01
☐	351	Kurt Rambis	.08	.04	.01
☐	352	Walt Williams	.50	.23	.06
☐	353	Lloyd Daniels	.15	.07	.02
☐	354	Vinny Del Negro	.05	.02	.01
☐	355	Dale Ellis	.08	.04	.01
☐	356	Avery Johnson	.05	.02	.01
☐	357	Sam Mack	.05	.02	.01
☐	358	J.R. Reid	.05	.02	.01
☐	359	David Wood	.05	.02	.01
☐	360	Vincent Askew	.05	.02	.01
☐	361	Isaac Austin	.05	.02	.01
☐	362	John Crotty	.05	.02	.01
☐	363	Stephen Howard	.05	.02	.01
☐	364	Jay Humphries	.05	.02	.01
☐	365	Larry Krystkowiak	.05	.02	.01
☐	366	Rex Chapman	.05	.02	.01
☐	367	Tom Gugliotta	1.25	.55	.16
☐	368	Buck Johnson	.05	.02	.01
☐	369	Charles Jones	.05	.02	.01
☐	370	Don MacLean	.75	.35	.09
☐	371	Doug Overton	.05	.02	.01
☐	372	Brent Price	.15	.07	.02
☐	373	Checklist 201-266	.10	.05	.01
☐	374	Checklist 267-330	.10	.05	.01
☐	375	Checklist 331-375	.10	.05	.01
☐	JS207	Pervis Ellison AU	20.00	9.00	2.50
		(Certified Autograph)			
		Washington Bullets			
☐	JS212	Duane Causwell AU	10.00	4.50	1.25
		(Certified Autograph)			
		Sacramento Kings			
☐	JS215	Stacey Augmon AU	50.00	23.00	6.25
		(Certified Autograph)			
		Atlanta Hawks			
☐	NNO	Jam Session Rank 1-10	2.50	1.15	.30
		David Robinson			
		Dikembe Mutombo			
		Otis Thorpe			
		Hakeem Olajuwon			
		Shawn Kemp			

Charles Barkley
Pervis Ellison
Chris Morris
Brad Daugherty
Derrick Coleman

☐ NNO Jam Session Rank 11-20	2.50	1.15	.30

Tim Perry
Duane Causwell
Scottie Pippen
Robert Parish
Stacey Augmon
Michael Jordan
Karl Malone
John Williams
Horace Grant
Orlando Woolridge

1992-93 Ultra All-NBA

This set features 15 cards, one for each All-NBA first, second, and third-team player. The standard-size (2 1/2" by 3 1/2") cards were randomly inserted into approximately one out of every 14 first series foil packs according to information printed on the wrapper. The fronts feature color action player photos which are full-bleed except at the bottom, where a gold foil stripe separates a marbleized diagonal bottom border. A crest showing which All-NBA team the player was on overlaps the border and picture. The player's name is gold-foil stamped at the bottom. The horizontal backs carry a cut-out player close-up and career highlights on a marbleized background. The cards are numbered on the back.

	MINT	EXC	G-VG
COMPLETE SET (15)	30.00	13.50	3.80
COMMON PLAYER (1-15)	.75	.35	.09
☐ 1 Karl Malone	2.00	.90	.25
Utah Jazz			
☐ 2 Chris Mullin	1.25	.55	.16
Golden State Warriors			
☐ 3 David Robinson	5.00	2.30	.60
San Antonio Spurs			
☐ 4 Michael Jordan	15.00	6.75	1.90
Chicago Bulls			
☐ 5 Clyde Drexler	1.50	.65	.19
Portland Trail Blazers			
☐ 6 Scottie Pippen	3.50	1.55	.45
Chicago Bulls			
☐ 7 Charles Barkley	5.00	2.30	.60
Phoenix Suns			
☐ 8 Patrick Ewing	3.50	1.55	.45
New York Knicks			
☐ 9 Tim Hardaway	1.00	.45	.13

Golden State Warriors			
☐ 10 John Stockton	1.50	.65	.19
Utah Jazz			
☐ 11 Dennis Rodman	.75	.35	.09
Detroit Pistons			
☐ 12 Kevin Willis	.75	.35	.09
Atlanta Hawks			
☐ 13 Brad Daugherty	.75	.35	.09
Cleveland Cavaliers			
☐ 14 Mark Price	1.00	.45	.13
Cleveland Cavaliers			
☐ 15 Kevin Johnson	1.00	.45	.13
Phoenix Suns			

1992-93 Ultra All-Rookies

Randomly inserted in second series foil packs at a reported rate of approximately one card per nine packs, this ten-card standard-size (2 1/2" by 3 1/2") set focuses on last year's class of outstanding rookies. A color action shot on the front has been cut out and superimposed on grid of identical close-up shots of the player, which resemble the effect produced by a wall of TV sets displaying the same image. The "All-Rookie" logo and the player's name are gold-foil stamped across the bottom of the picture. On the backs, a wheat-colored panel carrying a player profile overlays a second full-bleed color action photo. The cards are numbered in the lower left corner of the panel.

	MINT	EXC	G-VG
COMPLETE SET (10)	40.00	18.00	5.00
COMMON PLAYER (1-10)	2.00	.90	.25
☐ 1 LaPhonso Ellis	3.00	1.35	.40
Denver Nuggets			
☐ 2 Tom Gugliotta	3.00	1.35	.40
Washington Bullets			
☐ 3 Robert Horry	3.00	1.35	.40
Houston Rockets			
☐ 4 Christian Laettner	3.00	1.35	.40
Minnesota Timberwolves			
☐ 5 Harold Miner	2.00	.90	.25
Miami Heat			
☐ 6 Alonzo Mourning	12.00	5.50	1.50
Charlotte Hornets			
☐ 7 Shaquille O'Neal	20.00	9.00	2.50
Orlando Magic			
☐ 8 Latrell Sprewell	8.00	3.60	1.00
Golden State Warriors			
☐ 9 Clarence Weatherspoon	3.00	1.35	.40
Philadelphia 76ers			
☐ 10 Walt Williams	2.00	.90	.25
Sacramento Kings			

1992-93 Ultra Award Winners

This five-card Ultra Award Winners subset spotlights last season's MVP, Rookie of the Year, Defensive Player of the Year, top "6th Man" and Most Improved Player. These cards were randomly inserted into first series packs at a rate of one card per every 42 packs according to information printed on the wrappers. The cards are standard size (2 1/2" by 3 1/2").

	MINT	EXC	G-VG
COMPLETE SET (5)	30.00	13.50	3.80
COMMON PLAYER (1-5)	1.50	.65	.19
☐ 1 Michael Jordan	20.00	9.00	2.50
Chicago Bulls			
☐ 2 David Robinson	6.00	2.70	.75
San Antonio Spurs			
☐ 3 Larry Johnson	6.00	2.70	.75
Charlotte Hornets			
☐ 4 Detlef Schrempf	2.00	.90	.25
Indiana Pacers			
☐ 5 Pervis Ellison	1.50	.65	.19
Washington Bullets			

1992-93 Ultra Scottie Pippen

This 12-card "Career Highlights" subset chronicles Scottie Pippen's rise to NBA stardom. The cards were inserted at a rate of one card per every 21 packs according to information

printed on the wrappers. Moreover Scottie autographed more than 2,000 of these cards for random insertion in first series packs. Through a special mail-in offer only, two additional Pippen cards were made available to collectors who sent in ten wrappers and 1.00 for postage and handling. On the front, the standard-size (2 1/2" by 3 1/2") cards feature color action player photos with brownish-green marbleized borders. The player's name and the words "Career Highlights" are stamped in gold foil below the picture. On the same marbleized background, the backs carry a color headshot as well as biography and career summary. The cards are numbered on the back.

	MINT	EXC	G-VG
COMPLETE SET (10)	8.00	3.60	1.00
COMMON S.PIPPEN (1-10)	1.00	.45	.13
COMMON SEND-OFF (11-12)	1.00	.45	.13
☐ 1 Scottie Pippen	1.00	.45	.13
(Dribbling, right index finger pointing down)			
☐ 2 Scottie Pippen	1.00	.45	.13
(Dribbling, Magnavox ad in background)			
☐ 3 Scottie Pippen	1.00	.45	.13
(Preparing to dunk)			
☐ 4 Scottie Pippen	1.00	.45	.13
(Dribbling, defender's hand reaching in)			
☐ 5 Scottie Pippen	1.00	.45	.13
(In air, ball in both hands, vs. Bucks)			
☐ 6 Scottie Pippen	1.00	.45	.13
(Driving toward basket, vs. Nuggets)			
☐ 7 Scottie Pippen	1.00	.45	.13
(Shooting over McDaniel of the Knicks)			
☐ 8 Scottie Pippen	1.00	.45	.13
(Dribbling, Laker cheerleader in background)			
☐ 9 Scottie Pippen	1.00	.45	.13
(Defending against McDaniel of the Knicks)			
☐ 10 Scottie Pippen	1.00	.45	.13
(Driving toward basket, vs. Nets)			
☐ 11 Scottie Pippen	1.00	.45	.13
(Defended by Rodman; ball in left hand)			
☐ 12 Scottie Pippen	1.00	.45	.13
(Dunking over Nugget player)			
☐ AU Scottie Pippen	125.00	57.50	15.50
(Certified autograph)			

1992-93 Ultra Playmakers

Randomly inserted in second series foil packs at a reported rate of one card per 13 packs, this ten-card standard-size (2 1/2" by 3 1/2") set features the NBA's top point guards. The glossy color action photos on the fronts are full-bleed except at the bottom where a lavender stripe edges the picture. The "Playmaker" logo and the player's name are gold-foil stamped across the bottom of the picture. On the backs, a wheat-colored panel carrying a player profile overlays a second full-bleed color action photo. The cards are numbered in the lower left corner of the panel.

	MINT	EXC	G-VG
COMPLETE SET (10)	5.00	2.30	.60
COMMON PLAYER (1-10)	.50	.23	.06
☐ 1 Kenny Anderson	1.25	.55	.16
New Jersey Nets			
☐ 2 Muggsy Bogues	.60	.25	.08
Charlotte Hornets			

1992-93 Ultra Rejectors

Randomly inserted in second series foil packs at a reported rate of one card per 26 packs, this five-card set showcases defensive big men who are aptly dubbed "Rejectors." The cards measure the standard size (2 1/2" by 3 1/2"). The glossy color action photos on the fronts are full-bleed except at the bottom where a gold stripe edges the picture. The player's name and the "Rejector" logo are gold-foil stamped across the bottom of the picture. On a black panel inside gold borders, the horizontal backs carry text describing the player's defensive accomplishments and a color close-up photo. The cards are numbered on the back.

	MINT	EXC	G-VG
COMPLETE SET (5)	30.00	13.50	3.80
COMMON PLAYER (1-5)	1.25	.55	.16
☐ 1 Alonzo Mourning	10.00	4.50	1.25
Charlotte Hornets			
☐ 2 Dikembe Mutombo	1.25	.55	.16
Denver Nuggets			
☐ 3 Hakeem Olajuwon	3.50	1.55	.45
Houston Rockets			
☐ 4 Shaquille O'Neal	18.00	8.00	2.30
Orlando Magic			
☐ 5 David Robinson	3.00	1.35	.40
San Antonio Spurs			

1993-94 Ultra

The complete 1993-94 Ultra basketball set consists of 375 standard-size (2 1/2" by 3 1/2") cards. The glossy color action player photos on the fronts are full-bleed except at the bottom. The bottom of the front consists of player name, team name and a peach colored border. The horizontal backs feature a player photos against a basketball court background. The team logo and biographical information appear a pale peach bar, while the player's name and statistics are printed in team color-coded bars running across the card bottom. The cards are alphabetically arranged by team and are numbered alphabetically within teams: Atlanta Hawks (1-8), Boston Celtics (9-15), Charlotte Hornets (16-25), Chicago Bulls (26-34), Cleveland Cavaliers (35-42), Dallas Mavericks (43-48), Denver Nuggets (49-54), Detroit Pistons (55-62), Golden State Warriors (63-70), Houston Rockets (71-78), Indiana Pacers (79-85), Los Angeles Clippers (86-91), Los Angeles Lakers (92-97), Miami Heat (98-104), Milwaukee Bucks (105-112), Minnesota Timberwolves (113-117), New Jersey Nets (118-123), New York Knicks (124-132), Orlando Magic (133-138), Philadelphia 76ers (139-143), Phoenix Suns (144-152), Portland Trail Blazers (153-159), Sacramento Kings (160-166), San Antonio Spurs (167-174), Seattle Supersonics (175-183), Utah Jazz (184-191), and Washington Bullets (192-198). The second series cards are also grouped alphabetically within teams as follows: Atlanta Hawks (201-205), Boston Celtics (206-211), Charlotte Hornets (212-217), Chicago Bulls (218-224), Cleveland Cavaliers (225-229), Dallas Mavericks (230-235), Denver Nuggets (236-240), Detroit Pistons (241-246), Golden State Warriors (247-252), Houston Rockets (253-257), Indiana Pacers (258-264), Los Angeles Clippers (265-271), Los Angeles Lakers (272-278), Miami Heat (279-281), Milwaukee Bucks (282-286), Minnesota Timberwolves (287-293), New Jersey Nets (294-300), New York Knicks (301-303), Orlando Magic (304-308), Philadelphia 76ers (309-316), Phoenix Suns (317-321), Portland Trail Blazers (322-328), Sacramento Kings (329-335), San Antonio Spurs (336-341), Seattle Supersonics (342-346), Utah Jazz (347-351), and Washington Bullets (352-360). The set closes with a USA Basketball (361-372) subset and checklists (373-374).

	MINT	EXC	G-VG
COMPLETE SET (375)	35.00	16.00	4.40
COMPLETE SERIES 1 (200)	18.00	8.00	2.30
COMPLETE SERIES 2 (175)	18.00	8.00	2.30

COMMON PLAYER (1-200)	.10	.05	.01
COMMON PLAYER (201-375)	.10	.05	.01

☐ 1 Stacey Augmon	.15	.07	.02
☐ 2 Mookie Blaylock	.12	.05	.02
☐ 3 Doug Edwards	.15	.07	.02
☐ 4 Duane Ferrell	.10	.05	.01
☐ 5 Paul Graham	.10	.05	.01
☐ 6 Adam Keefe	.10	.05	.01
☐ 7 Dominique Wilkins	.40	.18	.05
☐ 8 Kevin Willis	.12	.05	.02
☐ 9 Alaa Abdelnaby	.10	.05	.01
☐ 10 Dee Brown	.10	.05	.01
☐ 11 Sherman Douglas	.10	.05	.01
☐ 12 Rick Fox	.10	.05	.01
☐ 13 Kevin Gamble	.10	.05	.01
☐ 14 Xavier McDaniel	.12	.05	.02
☐ 15 Robert Parish	.15	.07	.02
☐ 16 Muggsy Bogues	.15	.07	.02
☐ 17 Scott Burrell	.25	.11	.03
☐ 18 Dell Curry	.12	.05	.02
☐ 19 Kenny Gattison	.10	.05	.01
☐ 20 Hersey Hawkins	.12	.05	.02
☐ 21 Eddie Johnson	.10	.05	.01
☐ 22 Larry Johnson	.50	.23	.06
☐ 23 Alonzo Mourning	1.00	.45	.13
☐ 24 Johnny Newman	.10	.05	.01
☐ 25 David Wingate	.10	.05	.01
☐ 26 B.J. Armstrong	.15	.07	.02
☐ 27 Corie Blount	.15	.07	.02
☐ 28 Bill Cartwright	.10	.05	.01
☐ 29 Horace Grant	.15	.07	.02
☐ 30 Michael Jordan	3.00	1.35	.40
☐ 31 Stacey King	.10	.05	.01
☐ 32 John Paxson	.10	.05	.01
☐ 33 Will Perdue	.10	.05	.01
☐ 34 Scottie Pippen	.50	.23	.06
☐ 35 Terrell Brandon	.10	.05	.01
☐ 36 Brad Daugherty	.15	.07	.02
☐ 37 Danny Ferry	.10	.05	.01
☐ 38 Chris Mills	.40	.18	.05
☐ 39 Larry Nance	.12	.05	.02
☐ 40 Mark Price	.15	.07	.02
☐ 41 Gerald Wilkins	.10	.05	.01
☐ 42 John Williams	.10	.05	.01
☐ 43 Terry Davis	.10	.05	.01
☐ 44 Derek Harper	.12	.05	.02
☐ 45 Donald Hodge	.10	.05	.01
☐ 46 Jim Jackson	.50	.23	.06
☐ 47 Sean Rooks	.10	.05	.01
☐ 48 Doug Smith	.10	.05	.01
☐ 49 Mahmoud Abdul-Rauf	.10	.05	.01
☐ 50 LaPhonso Ellis	.15	.07	.02
☐ 51 Mark Macon	.10	.05	.01
☐ 52 Dikembe Mutombo	.15	.07	.02
☐ 53 Bryant Stith	.12	.05	.02
☐ 54 Reggie Williams	.10	.05	.01
☐ 55 Mark Aguirre	.15	.07	.02
☐ 56 Joe Dumars	.25	.11	.03
☐ 57 Bill Laimbeer	.15	.07	.02
☐ 58 Terry Mills	.12	.05	.02
☐ 59 Olden Polynice	.10	.05	.01
☐ 60 Alvin Robertson	.10	.05	.01
☐ 61 Dennis Rodman	.12	.05	.02
☐ 62 Isiah Thomas	.25	.11	.03
☐ 63 Victor Alexander	.10	.05	.01
☐ 64 Chris Gatling	.10	.05	.01
☐ 65 Tim Hardaway	.15	.07	.02
☐ 66 Byron Houston	.10	.05	.01
☐ 67 Sarunas Marciulionis	.10	.05	.01
☐ 68 Chris Mullin	.25	.11	.03
☐ 69 Billy Owens	.12	.05	.02
☐ 70 Latrell Sprewell	.60	.25	.08

☐	71	Matt Bullard	.10	.05	.01
☐	72	Sam Cassell	.75	.35	.09
☐	73	Carl Herrera	.10	.05	.01
☐	74	Robert Horry	.15	.07	.02
☐	75	Vernon Maxwell	.12	.05	.02
☐	76	Hakeem Olajuwon	1.25	.55	.16
☐	77	Kenny Smith	.10	.05	.01
☐	78	Otis Thorpe	.12	.05	.02
☐	79	Dale Davis	.12	.05	.02
☐	80	Vern Fleming	.10	.05	.01
☐	81	Reggie Miller	.30	.14	.04
☐	82	Sam Mitchell	.10	.05	.01
☐	83	Pooh Richardson	.10	.05	.01
☐	84	Detlef Schrempf	.15	.07	.02
☐	85	Rik Smits	.12	.05	.02
☐	86	Ron Harper	.12	.05	.02
☐	87	Mark Jackson	.12	.05	.02
☐	88	Danny Manning	.15	.07	.02
☐	89	Stanley Roberts	.10	.05	.01
☐	90	Loy Vaught	.12	.05	.02
☐	91	John Williams	.10	.05	.01
☐	92	Sam Bowie	.10	.05	.01
☐	93	Doug Christie	.12	.05	.02
☐	94	Vlade Divac	.10	.05	.01
☐	95	George Lynch	.40	.18	.05
☐	96	Anthony Peeler	.12	.05	.02
☐	97	James Worthy	.15	.07	.02
☐	98	Bimbo Coles	.10	.05	.01
☐	99	Grant Long	.10	.05	.01
☐	100	Harold Miner	.12	.05	.02
☐	101	Glen Rice	.15	.07	.02
☐	102	Rony Seikaly	.15	.07	.02
☐	103	Brian Shaw	.10	.05	.01
☐	104	Steve Smith	.12	.05	.02
☐	105	Anthony Avent	.10	.05	.01
☐	106	Vin Baker	1.00	.45	.13
☐	107	Frank Brickowski	.12	.05	.02
☐	108	Todd Day	.12	.05	.02
☐	109	Blue Edwards	.10	.05	.01
☐	110	Lee Mayberry	.10	.05	.01
☐	111	Eric Murdock	.12	.05	.02
☐	112	Orlando Woolridge	.12	.05	.02
☐	113	Thurl Bailey	.10	.05	.01
☐	114	Christian Laettner	.12	.05	.02
☐	115	Chuck Person	.12	.05	.02
☐	116	Doug West	.10	.05	.01
☐	117	Micheal Williams	.12	.05	.02
☐	118	Kenny Anderson	.25	.11	.03
☐	119	Derrick Coleman	.30	.14	.04
☐	120	Rick Mahorn	.10	.05	.01
☐	121	Chris Morris	.10	.05	.01
☐	122	Rumeal Robinson	.10	.05	.01
☐	123	Rex Walters	.15	.07	.02
☐	124	Greg Anthony	.10	.05	.01
☐	125	Rolando Blackman	.10	.05	.01
☐	126	Hubert Davis	.10	.05	.01
☐	127	Patrick Ewing	.50	.23	.06
☐	128	Anthony Mason	.10	.05	.01
☐	129	Charles Oakley	.15	.07	.02
☐	130	Doc Rivers	.12	.05	.02
☐	131	Charles Smith	.10	.05	.01
☐	132	John Starks	.15	.07	.02
☐	133	Nick Anderson	.12	.05	.02
☐	134	Anthony Bowie	.10	.05	.01
☐	135	Shaquille O'Neal	2.50	1.15	.30
☐	136	Dennis Scott	.12	.05	.02
☐	137	Scott Skiles	.10	.05	.01
☐	138	Jeff Turner	.10	.05	.01
☐	139	Shawn Bradley	.60	.25	.08
☐	140	Johnny Dawkins	.10	.05	.01
☐	141	Jeff Hornacek	.12	.05	.02
☐	142	Tim Perry	.10	.05	.01
☐	143	Clarence Weatherspoon	.15	.07	.02

☐	144	Danny Ainge	.15	.07	.02
☐	145	Charles Barkley	.75	.35	.09
☐	146	Cedric Ceballos	.15	.07	.02
☐	147	Kevin Johnson	.15	.07	.02
☐	148	Negele Knight	.10	.05	.01
☐	149	Malcolm Mackey	.15	.07	.02
☐	150	Dan Majerle	.15	.07	.02
☐	151	Oliver Miller	.15	.07	.02
☐	152	Mark West	.10	.05	.01
☐	153	Mark Bryant	.10	.05	.01
☐	154	Clyde Drexler	.25	.11	.03
☐	155	Jerome Kersey	.10	.05	.01
☐	156	Terry Porter	.12	.05	.02
☐	157	Cliff Robinson	.15	.07	.02
☐	158	Rod Strickland	.12	.05	.02
☐	159	Buck Williams	.15	.07	.02
☐	160	Duane Causwell	.10	.05	.01
☐	161	Bobby Hurley	.60	.25	.08
☐	162	Mitch Richmond	.15	.07	.02
☐	163	Lionel Simmons	.12	.05	.02
☐	164	Wayman Tisdale	.12	.05	.02
☐	165	Spud Webb	.15	.07	.02
☐	166	Walt Williams	.12	.05	.02
☐	167	Willie Anderson	.10	.05	.01
☐	168	Antoine Carr	.10	.05	.01
☐	169	Lloyd Daniels	.10	.05	.01
☐	170	Sean Elliott	.12	.05	.02
☐	171	Dale Ellis	.12	.05	.02
☐	172	Avery Johnson	.10	.05	.01
☐	173	J.R. Reid	.10	.05	.01
☐	174	David Robinson	.75	.35	.09
☐	175	Michael Cage	.10	.05	.01
☐	176	Kendall Gill	.12	.05	.02
☐	177	Ervin Johnson	.15	.07	.02
☐	178	Shawn Kemp	.50	.23	.06
☐	179	Derrick McKey	.10	.05	.01
☐	180	Nate McMillan	.10	.05	.01
☐	181	Gary Payton	.15	.07	.02
☐	182	Sam Perkins	.12	.05	.02
☐	183	Ricky Pierce	.12	.05	.02
☐	184	David Benoit	.10	.05	.01
☐	185	Tyrone Corbin	.10	.05	.01
☐	186	Mark Eaton	.10	.05	.01
☐	187	Jay Humphries	.10	.05	.01
☐	188	Jeff Malone	.12	.05	.02
☐	189	Karl Malone	.40	.18	.05
☐	190	John Stockton	.25	.11	.03
☐	191	Luther Wright	.15	.07	.02
☐	192	Michael Adams	.12	.05	.02
☐	193	Calbert Cheaney	.60	.25	.08
☐	194	Pervis Ellison	.10	.05	.01
☐	195	Tom Gugliotta	.12	.05	.02
☐	196	Buck Johnson	.10	.05	.01
☐	197	LaBradford Smith	.10	.05	.01
☐	198	Larry Stewart	.10	.05	.01
☐	199	Checklist	.10	.05	.01
☐	200	Checklist	.10	.05	.01
☐	201	Doug Edwards	.10	.05	.01
☐	202	Craig Ehlo	.10	.05	.01
☐	203	Jon Koncak	.10	.05	.01
☐	204	Andrew Lang	.10	.05	.01
☐	205	Ennis Whatley	.10	.05	.01
☐	206	Chris Corchiani	.10	.05	.01
☐	207	Acie Earl	.15	.07	.02
☐	208	Jimmy Oliver	.10	.05	.01
☐	209	Ed Pinckney	.10	.05	.01
☐	210	Dino Radja	.60	.25	.08
☐	211	Matt Wenstrom	.15	.07	.02
☐	212	Tony Bennett	.10	.05	.01
☐	213	Scott Burrell	.10	.05	.01
☐	214	LeRon Ellis	.10	.05	.01
☐	215	Hersey Hawkins	.12	.05	.02
☐	216	Eddie Johnson	.10	.05	.01

☐ 217	Rumeal Robinson	.10	.05	.01
☐ 218	Corie Blount	.10	.05	.01
☐ 219	Dave Johnson	.10	.05	.01
☐ 220	Steve Kerr	.10	.05	.01
☐ 221	Toni Kukoc	.75	.35	.09
☐ 222	Pete Myers	.10	.05	.01
☐ 223	Bill Wennington	.10	.05	.01
☐ 224	Scott Williams	.10	.05	.01
☐ 225	John Battle	.10	.05	.01
☐ 226	Tyrone Hill	.10	.05	.01
☐ 227	Gerald Madkins	.15	.07	.02
☐ 228	Chris Mills	.20	.09	.03
☐ 229	Bobby Phills	.10	.05	.01
☐ 230	Greg Dreiling	.10	.05	.01
☐ 231	Lucious Harris	.15	.07	.02
☐ 232	Popeye Jones	.25	.11	.03
☐ 233	Tim Legler	.15	.07	.02
☐ 234	Fat Lever	.10	.05	.01
☐ 235	Jamal Mashburn	1.50	.65	.19
☐ 236	Tom Hammonds	.10	.05	.01
☐ 237	Darnell Mee	.15	.07	.02
☐ 238	Robert Pack	.10	.05	.01
☐ 239	Rodney Rogers	.40	.18	.05
☐ 240	Brian Williams	.10	.05	.01
☐ 241	Greg Anderson	.10	.05	.01
☐ 242	Sean Elliott	.12	.05	.02
☐ 243	Allan Houston	.25	.11	.03
☐ 244	Lindsey Hunter	.60	.25	.08
☐ 245	Mark Macon	.10	.05	.01
☐ 246	David Wood	.10	.05	.01
☐ 247	Jud Buechler	.10	.05	.01
☐ 248	Josh Grant	.15	.07	.02
☐ 249	Jeff Grayer	.10	.05	.01
☐ 250	Keith Jennings	.10	.05	.01
☐ 251	Avery Johnson	.10	.05	.01
☐ 252	Chris Webber	4.00	1.80	.50
☐ 253	Scott Brooks	.10	.05	.01
☐ 254	Sam Cassell	.40	.18	.05
☐ 255	Mario Elie	.10	.05	.01
☐ 256	Richard Petruska	.15	.07	.02
☐ 257	Eric Riley	.15	.07	.02
☐ 258	Antonio Davis	.40	.18	.05
☐ 259	Scott Haskin	.15	.07	.02
☐ 260	Derrick McKey	.10	.05	.01
☐ 261	Byron Scott	.12	.05	.02
☐ 262	Malik Sealy	.10	.05	.01
☐ 263	Kenny Williams	.10	.05	.01
☐ 264	Haywoode Workman	.10	.05	.01
☐ 265	Mark Aguirre	.15	.07	.02
☐ 266	Terry Dehere	.15	.07	.02
☐ 267	Harold Ellis	.15	.07	.02
☐ 268	Gary Grant	.10	.05	.01
☐ 269	Bob Martin	.15	.07	.02
☐ 270	Elmore Spencer	.10	.05	.01
☐ 271	Tom Tolbert	.10	.05	.01
☐ 272	Sam Bowie	.10	.05	.01
☐ 273	Elden Campbell	.10	.05	.01
☐ 274	Antonio Harvey	.15	.07	.02
☐ 275	George Lynch	.15	.07	.02
☐ 276	Tony Smith	.10	.05	.01
☐ 277	Sedale Threatt	.10	.05	.01
☐ 278	Nick Van Exel	.60	.25	.08
☐ 279	Willie Burton	.10	.05	.01
☐ 280	Matt Geiger	.10	.05	.01
☐ 281	John Salley	.10	.05	.01
☐ 282	Vin Baker	.50	.23	.06
☐ 283	Jon Barry	.10	.05	.01
☐ 284	Brad Lohaus	.10	.05	.01
☐ 285	Ken Norman	.10	.05	.01
☐ 286	Derek Strong	.15	.07	.02
☐ 287	Mike Brown	.10	.05	.01
☐ 288	Brian Davis	.15	.07	.02
☐ 289	Tellis Frank	.10	.05	.01

☐ 290	Luc Longley	.10	.05	.01
☐ 291	Marlon Maxey	.10	.05	.01
☐ 292	Isaiah Rider	1.50	.65	.19
☐ 293	Chris Smith	.10	.05	.01
☐ 294	P.J. Brown	.25	.11	.03
☐ 295	Kevin Edwards	.10	.05	.01
☐ 296	Armon Gilliam	.10	.05	.01
☐ 297	Johnny Newman	.10	.05	.01
☐ 298	Rex Walters	.10	.05	.01
☐ 299	David Wesley	.15	.07	.02
☐ 300	Jayson Williams	.10	.05	.01
☐ 301	Anthony Bonner	.10	.05	.01
☐ 302	Derek Harper	.12	.05	.02
☐ 303	Herb Williams	.10	.05	.01
☐ 304	Litterial Green	.10	.05	.01
☐ 305	Anfernee Hardaway	3.00	1.35	.40
☐ 306	Greg Kite	.10	.05	.01
☐ 307	Larry Krystkowiak	.10	.05	.01
☐ 308	Keith Tower	.15	.07	.02
☐ 309	Dana Barros	.10	.05	.01
☐ 310	Shawn Bradley	.30	.14	.04
☐ 311	Greg Graham	.15	.07	.02
☐ 312	Sean Green	.10	.05	.01
☐ 313	Warren Kidd	.15	.07	.02
☐ 314	Eric Leckner	.10	.05	.01
☐ 315	Moses Malone	.15	.07	.02
☐ 316	Orlando Woolridge	.12	.05	.02
☐ 317	Duane Cooper	.10	.05	.01
☐ 318	Joe Courtney	.15	.07	.02
☐ 319	A.C. Green	.12	.05	.02
☐ 320	Frank Johnson	.10	.05	.01
☐ 321	Joe Kleine	.10	.05	.01
☐ 322	Chris Dudley	.10	.05	.01
☐ 323	Harvey Grant	.10	.05	.01
☐ 324	Jaren Jackson	.10	.05	.01
☐ 325	Tracy Murray	.10	.05	.01
☐ 326	James Robinson	.25	.11	.03
☐ 327	Reggie Smith	.10	.05	.01
☐ 328	Kevin Thompson	.15	.07	.02
☐ 329	Randy Brown	.10	.05	.01
☐ 330	Evers Burns	.15	.07	.02
☐ 331	Pete Chilcutt	.10	.05	.01
☐ 332	Bobby Hurley	.30	.14	.04
☐ 333	Mike Peplowski	.15	.07	.02
☐ 334	LaBradford Smith	.10	.05	.01
☐ 335	Trevor Wilson	.10	.05	.01
☐ 336	Terry Cummings	.12	.05	.02
☐ 337	Vinny Del Negro	.10	.05	.01
☐ 338	Sleepy Floyd	.10	.05	.01
☐ 339	Negele Knight	.10	.05	.01
☐ 340	Dennis Rodman	.12	.05	.02
☐ 341	Chris Whitney	.15	.07	.02
☐ 342	Vincent Askew	.10	.05	.01
☐ 343	Kendall Gill	.12	.05	.02
☐ 344	Ervin Johnson	.10	.05	.01
☐ 345	Chris King	.15	.07	.02
☐ 346	Detlef Schrempf	.15	.07	.02
☐ 347	Walter Bond	.10	.05	.01
☐ 348	Tom Chambers	.12	.05	.02
☐ 349	John Crotty	.10	.05	.01
☐ 350	Bryon Russell	.25	.11	.03
☐ 351	Felton Spencer	.10	.05	.01
☐ 352	Mitchell Butler	.15	.07	.02
☐ 353	Rex Chapman	.10	.05	.01
☐ 354	Calbert Cheaney	.30	.14	.04
☐ 355	Kevin Duckworth	.10	.05	.01
☐ 356	Don MacLean	.12	.05	.02
☐ 357	Gheorghe Muresan	.25	.11	.03
☐ 358	Doug Overton	.10	.05	.01
☐ 359	Brent Price	.10	.05	.01
☐ 360	Kenny Walker	.10	.05	.01
☐ 361	Derrick Coleman	.30	.14	.04
☐ 362	Joe Dumars	.25	.11	.03

☐ 363	Tim Hardaway	.20	.09	.03
☐ 364	Larry Johnson	.50	.23	.06
☐ 365	Shawn Kemp	.50	.23	.06
☐ 366	Dan Majerle	.20	.09	.03
☐ 367	Alonzo Mourning	1.00	.45	.13
☐ 368	Mark Price	.20	.09	.03
☐ 369	Steve Smith	.20	.09	.03
☐ 370	Isiah Thomas	.25	.11	.03
☐ 371	Dominique Wilkins	.40	.18	.05
☐ 372	Don Nelson	.15	.07	.02
	Don Chaney			
☐ 373	Checklist	.10	.05	.01
☐ 374	Checklist	.10	.05	.01
☐ 375	Checklist	.10	.05	.01
☐ M1	Reggie Miller USA	.50	.23	.06
☐ M2	Shaquille O'Neal USA	4.00	1.80	.50
☐ M3	Team Checklist USA	1.00	.45	.13

1993-94 Ultra All-Defensive

Randomly inserted in Series I jumbo packs, this standard-size (2 1/2" by 3 1/2") 10-card set features on each borderless front a color player action cutout set against a background of an enlarged and ghosted version of the same photo. The player's name appears in gold-foil lettering at the bottom. The back features a color player photo at the lower left, along with his career highlights set against the same ghosted photo background. The cards are numbered on the back as "X of 10." The set is arranged according to First Team (1-5) and Second Team (6-10).

		MINT	EXC	G-VG
	COMPLETE SET (10)	225.00	100.00	28.00
	COMMON PLAYER (1-10)	12.00	5.50	1.50
☐ 1	Joe Dumars	12.00	5.50	1.50
	Detroit Pistons			
☐ 2	Michael Jordan	100.00	45.00	12.50
	Chicago Bulls			
☐ 3	Hakeem Olajuwon	40.00	18.00	5.00
	Houston Rockets			
☐ 4	Scottie Pippen	22.00	10.00	2.80
	Chicago Bulls			
☐ 5	Dennis Rodman	12.00	5.50	1.50
	Detroit Pistons			
☐ 6	Horace Grant	12.00	5.50	1.50
	Chicago Bulls			
☐ 7	Dan Majerle	12.00	5.50	1.50
	Phoenix Suns			
☐ 8	Larry Nance	12.00	5.50	1.50
	Cleveland Cavaliers			

☐ 9	David Robinson	30.00	13.50	3.80
	San Antonio Spurs			
☐ 10	John Starks	12.00	5.50	1.50
	New York Knicks			

1993-94 Ultra All-NBA

Randomly inserted in Series I packs, this 14-card standard-size (2 1/2" by 3 1/2") set features one card for each All-NBA first-, second-, and third-team player, with the exception of Drazen Petrovic. The fronts display full-bleed glossy color action photos with a series of three smaller photos along the left side. The player's name appears in gold-foil lettering at the lower right. The back carries a hardwood floor-design background with three small photos along the left side that progressively zoom in on the player. Career highlights appear alongside. The cards are numbered on the back as "X of 14." The set is arranged according to First Team (1-5), Second Team (6-10), and Third Team (11-14).

	MINT	EXC	G-VG
COMPLETE SET (14)	40.00	18.00	5.00
COMMON PLAYER (1-14)	1.00	.45	.13
☐ 1 Charles Barkley	5.00	2.30	.60
Phoenix Suns			
☐ 2 Michael Jordan	15.00	6.75	1.90
Chicago Bulls			
☐ 3 Karl Malone	3.00	1.35	.40
Utah Jazz			
☐ 4 Hakeem Olajuwon	6.00	2.70	.75
Houston Rockets			
☐ 5 Mark Price	1.00	.45	.13
Cleveland Cavaliers			
☐ 6 Joe Dumars	1.00	.45	.13
Detroit Pistons			
☐ 7 Patrick Ewing	4.00	1.80	.50
New York Knicks			
☐ 8 Larry Johnson	3.50	1.55	.45
Charlotte Hornets			
☐ 9 John Stockton	1.75	.80	.22
Utah Jazz			
☐ 10 Dominique Wilkins	3.50	1.55	.45
Atlanta Hawks			
☐ 11 Derrick Coleman	1.75	.80	.22
New Jersey Nets			
☐ 12 Tim Hardaway	1.00	.45	.13
Golden State Warriors			
☐ 13 Scottie Pippen	4.00	1.80	.50
Chicago Bulls			
☐ 14 David Robinson	5.00	2.30	.60
San Antonio Spurs			

1993-94 Ultra All-Rookie Series

*Randomly inserted in Series II packs, this 15-card standard-size (2 1/2" by 3 1/2") set fea-
tures some of the NBA's top draft picks. Each borderless front features a color action photo.
The player's name appears in silver foil near the bottom. The horizontal borderless back
carries a color player action shot on one side and career highlights on the other. The cards
are numbered on the back "X of 15."*

	MINT	EXC	G-VG
COMPLETE SET (15)	40.00	18.00	5.00
COMMON PLAYER (1-15)	.75	.35	.09
☐ 1 Vin Baker	3.50	1.55	.45
Milwaukee Bucks			
☐ 2 Shawn Bradley	2.00	.90	.25
Philadelphia 76ers			
☐ 3 Calbert Cheaney	2.00	.90	.25
Washington Bullets			
☐ 4 Anfernee Hardaway	10.00	4.50	1.25
Orlando Magic			
☐ 5 Lindsey Hunter	2.00	.90	.25
Detroit Pistons			
☐ 6 Bobby Hurley	2.00	.90	.25
Sacramento Kings			
☐ 7 Popeye Jones	.75	.35	.09
Dallas Mavericks			
☐ 8 Toni Kukoc	2.00	.90	.25
Chicago Bulls			
☐ 9 Jamal Mashburn	5.00	2.30	.60
Dallas Mavericks			
☐ 10 Chris Mills	1.25	.55	.16
Cleveland Cavaliers			
☐ 11 Dino Radja	2.00	.90	.25
Boston Celtics			
☐ 12 Isaiah Rider	5.00	2.30	.60
Minnesota Timberwolves			
☐ 13 Rodney Rogers	1.25	.55	.16
Denver Nuggets			
☐ 14 Nick Van Exel	2.00	.90	.25
Los Angeles Lakers			
☐ 15 Chris Webber	12.00	5.50	1.50
Golden State Warriors			

1993-94 Ultra All-Rookie Team

*Randomly inserted in Series I packs, this 5-card standard-size (2 1/2" by 3 1/2") set features
on its borderless fronts color player action cutouts breaking out of hardwood floor backgrounds. The player's name appears in gold foil at the bottom. The horizontal borderless
back carries a color player cutout and career highlights on a hardwood floor background.
The cards are numbered on the back "X of 5."*

	MINT	EXC	G-VG
COMPLETE SET (5)	20.00	9.00	2.50
COMMON PLAYER (1-5)	1.25	.55	.16
☐ 1 LaPhonso Ellis	1.25	.55	.16
Denver Nuggets			
☐ 2 Tom Gugliotta	2.50	1.15	.30
Washington Bullets			
(with Michael Jordan)			
☐ 3 Christian Laettner	1.25	.55	.16
Minnesota Timberwolves			
☐ 4 Alonzo Mourning	5.00	2.30	.60
Charlotte Hornets			
☐ 5 Shaquille O'Neal	12.00	5.50	1.50
Orlando Magic			

1993-94 Ultra Award Winners

Randomly inserted in Series I jumbo packs, this 5-card standard-size (2 1/2" by 3 1/2") set features on its fronts color player action cutouts on borderless metallic backgrounds highlighted by radial streaks. On a radially streaked background, the back carries a color player close-up and career highlights. The cards are numbered on the back "X of 5."

	MINT	EXC	G-VG
COMPLETE SET (5)	110.00	50.00	14.00
COMMON PLAYER (1-5)	10.00	4.50	1.25
☐ 1 Mahmoud Abdul-Rauf	10.00	4.50	1.25
Denver Nuggets			
☐ 2 Charles Barkley	25.00	11.50	3.10
Phoenix Suns			

☐ 3 Hakeem Olajuwon	35.00	16.00	4.40
Houston Rockets			
☐ 4 Shaquille O'Neal	65.00	29.00	8.25
Orlando Magic			
☐ 5 Cliff Robinson	10.00	4.50	1.25
Portland Trail Blazers			

1993-94 Ultra Famous Nicknames

Randomly inserted in Series II packs, this 15-card standard-size (2 1/2" by 3 1/2") set features on its borderless fronts color action cutouts on hardwood-floor and basket-net backgrounds. The player's nickname appears in silver foil on the right. The borderless back carries a color player photo on one side. On the other, the shot's game background blends into a hardwood-floor background for the player's name in vertical silver-foil lettering and his career highlights. The cards are numbered on the back "X of 15."

	MINT	EXC	G-VG
COMPLETE SET (15)	25.00	11.50	3.10
COMMON PLAYER (1-15)	.50	.23	.06
☐ 1 Charles Barkley	3.00	1.35	.40
Sir Charles			
Phoenix Suns			
☐ 2 Tyrone Bogues	.50	.23	.06
Muggsy			
Charlotte Hornets			
☐ 3 Derrick Coleman	1.00	.45	.13
D.C.			
New Jersey Nets			
☐ 4 Clyde Drexler	1.00	.45	.13
The Glide			
Portland Trail Blazers			
☐ 5 Anfernee Hardaway	7.00	3.10	.85
Penny			
Orlando Magic			
☐ 6 Larry Johnson	2.00	.90	.25
L.J.			
Charlotte Hornets			
☐ 7 Michael Jordan	12.00	5.50	1.50
Air			
Chicago Bulls			
☐ 8 Toni Kukoc	1.25	.55	.16
The Pink Panther			
Chicago Bulls			
☐ 9 Karl Malone	1.75	.80	.22
The Mailman			
Utah Jazz			

			MINT	EXC	G-VG
☐ 10	Harold Miner	.50	.23	.06
	Baby Jordan			
	Miami Heat			
☐ 11	Alonzo Mourning	3.00	1.35	.40
	Zo			
	Charlotte Hornets			
☐ 12	Hakeem Olajuwon	4.00	1.80	.50
	The Dream			
	Houston Rockets			
☐ 13	Shaquille O'Neal	8.00	3.60	1.00
	Shaq			
	Orlando Magic			
☐ 14	David Robinson	3.00	1.35	.40
	The Admiral			
	San Antonio Spurs			
☐ 15	Dominique Wilkins	2.00	.90	.25
	Human Highlight Film			
	Atlanta Hawks			

1993-94 Ultra Inside/Outside

Randomly inserted in Series II packs, this 10-card standard-size (2 1/2" by 3 1/2") set features on each borderless front a color player action cutout over a shot of a cometlike basketball going through the basket, all on a black background. The player's name appears in gold foil near the bottom. This design, but with a different action cutout, is mirrored somewhat on the borderless back, which also carries to the left of the player photo his career highlights within a ghosted box framed by a purple line. The cards are numbered on the back "X of 10."

		MINT	EXC	G-VG
	COMPLETE SET (10)	10.00	4.50	1.25
	COMMON PLAYER (1-10)	.50	.23	.06
☐ 1	Patrick Ewing	1.25	.55	.16
	New York Knicks			
☐ 2	Jim Jackson	1.00	.45	.13
	Dallas Mavericks			
☐ 3	Larry Johnson	1.00	.45	.13
	Charlotte Hornets			
☐ 4	Michael Jordan	6.00	2.70	.75
	Chicago Bulls			
☐ 5	Dan Majerle	.50	.23	.06
	Phoenix Suns			
☐ 6	Hakeem Olajuwon	2.00	.90	.25
	Houston Rockets			
☐ 7	Scottie Pippen	1.25	.55	.16
	Chicago Bulls			
☐ 8	Latrell Sprewell	1.50	.65	.19
	Golden State Warriors			

☐ 9 John Starks..................... New York Knicks	.50	.23	.06
☐ 10 Walt Williams................ Sacramento Kings	.50	.23	.06

1993-94 Ultra Jam City

Randomly inserted in Series II jumbo packs, this 9-card standard-size (2 1/2" by 3 1/2") set features on its borderless fronts color player action cutouts on black and purple metallic cityscape backgrounds. The player's name appears in gold foil in a lower corner. The borderless back carries a color player action cutout on a nonmetallic background otherwise similar to the front. The player's name and career highlights appear in a ghosted box to the left of the photo. The cards are numbered on the back as "X of 10."

	MINT	EXC	G-VG
COMPLETE SET (9)............................	90.00	40.00	11.50
COMMON PLAYER (1-9).....................	2.00	.90	.25
☐ 1 Charles Barkley.......................... Phoenix Suns	15.00	6.75	1.90
☐ 2 Derrick Coleman......................... New Jersey Nets	5.00	2.30	.60
☐ 3 Clyde Drexler.............................. Portland Trail Blazers	5.00	2.30	.60
☐ 4 Patrick Ewing.............................. New York Knicks	12.00	5.50	1.50
☐ 5 Shawn Kemp............................... Seattle Supersonics	12.00	5.50	1.50
☐ 6 Harold Miner.............................. Miami Heat	2.00	.90	.25
☐ 7 Shaquille O'Neal......................... Orlando Magic	40.00	18.00	5.00
☐ 8 David Robinson.......................... San Antonio Spurs	15.00	6.75	1.90
☐ 9 Dominique Wilkins....................... Atlanta Hawks	10.00	4.50	1.25

1993-94 Ultra Karl Malone

This ten-card set of Career Highlights issued by Fleer Ultra in 1993, spotlights Utah Jazz forward, Karl Malone. The cards in this set were randomly inserted in Ultra packs. The cards measure standard size (2 1/2" by 3 1/2"). The full-bleed color fronts have purple tinted ghosted backgrounds with Malone portrayed in normal color action and posed photos. Across the bottom edge is a marbleized border with the subset title "Career Highlights",

above the lower border is a silver and black box containing Malone's name. The backs carry information about Malone within a purple tinted ghosted box that is superimposed over a color photo. The cards are numbered on the back. Cards 11 and 12 were mail-aways.

	MINT	EXC	G-VG
COMPLETE SET (10)	8.00	3.60	1.00
COMMON MALONE (1-10)	1.00	.45	.13
COMMON SEND-OFF (11-12)	2.00	.90	.25
☐ 1 Karl Malone	1.00	.45	.13
Power Rig			
☐ 2 Karl Malone	1.00	.45	.13
Summerfield			
☐ 3 Karl Malone	1.00	.45	.13
Mailman-Born			
☐ 4 Karl Malone	1.00	.45	.13
Luck of the Draw			
☐ 5 Karl Malone	1.00	.45	.13
Double-Double			
☐ 6 Karl Malone	1.00	.45	.13
Dynamic Duo			
☐ 7 Karl Malone	1.00	.45	.13
Mt. Malone			
☐ 8 Karl Malone	1.00	.45	.13
Salt Lake Slammer			
☐ 9 Karl Malone	1.00	.45	.13
Overhead Delivery			
☐ 10 Karl Malone	1.00	.45	.13
Truckin'			
☐ 11 Karl Malone	2.00	.90	.25
Role Player			
☐ 12 Karl Malone	2.00	.90	.25
Rigged			

1993-94 Ultra Power In The Key

Randomly inserted in second-series hobby packs, this 9-card standard-size (2 1/2" by 3 1/2") set features on its borderless fronts color player action cutouts on multicolored and multitextured metallic backgrounds that depict the key area of a basketball court. The player's name appears in gold foil at the lower right. The borderless horizontal back carries on its right side a color player close-up on a nonmetallic background otherwise similar to the front. The player's name and career highlights appear in a ghosted box to the left of the photo. The cards are numbered on the back as "X of 9."

	MINT	EXC	G-VG
COMPLETE SET (9)	90.00	40.00	11.50
COMMON PLAYER (1-9)	2.00	.90	.25
☐ 1 Larry Johnson	6.00	2.70	.75
Charlotte Hornets			

☐	2 Michael Jordan	35.00	16.00	4.40
	Chicago Bulls			
☐	3 Karl Malone	5.00	2.30	.60
	Utah Jazz			
☐	4 Oliver Miller	2.00	.90	.25
	Phoenix Suns			
☐	5 Alonzo Mourning	10.00	4.50	1.25
	Charlotte Hornets			
☐	6 Hakeem Olajuwon	12.00	5.50	1.50
	Houston Rockets			
☐	7 Shaquille O'Neal	22.00	10.00	2.80
	Orlando Magic			
☐	8 Otis Thorpe	2.50	1.15	.30
	Houston Rockets			
☐	9 Chris Webber	22.00	10.00	2.80
	Golden State Warriors			

1993-94 Ultra Rebound Kings

*Randomly inserted in Series II packs, this 10-card standard-size (2 1/2" by 3 1/2") set fea-
tures on its borderless fronts color player action shots on backgrounds that blend from the
actual background at the bottom to a ghosted and color-screened player close-up at the top.
The player's name appears vertically in gold foil on one side. The borderless horizontal back
carries a color player cutout on one side, and the player's name in gold foil and career highlights on the other, all on a ghosted and color-screened background. The cards are numbered on the back as "X of 10."*

	MINT	EXC	G-VG
COMPLETE SET (10)	10.00	4.50	1.25
COMMON PLAYER (1-10)	.25	.11	.03
☐ 1 Charles Barkley	1.50	.65	.19
Phoenix Suns			
☐ 2 Derrick Coleman	.50	.23	.06
New Jersey Nets			
☐ 3 Shawn Kemp	1.25	.55	.16
Seattle Supersonics			
☐ 4 Karl Malone	1.00	.45	.13
Utah Jazz			
☐ 5 Alonzo Mourning	1.50	.65	.19
Charlotte Hornets			
☐ 6 Dikembe Mutombo	.40	.18	.05
Denver Nuggets			
☐ 7 Charles Oakley	.25	.11	.03
New York Knicks			
☐ 8 Hakeem Olajuwon	2.00	.90	.25
Houston Rockets			
☐ 9 Shaquille O'Neal	4.00	1.80	.50
Orlando Magic			
☐ 10 Dennis Rodman	.25	.11	.03
San Antonio Spurs			

1993-94 Ultra Scoring Kings

Randomly inserted in Series I hobby packs, this 10-card, standard size (2 1/2" by 3 1/2") set features on its fronts color player action cutouts on borderless metallic backgrounds highlighted by lightning filaments. The player's name appears in silver-foil lettering in a lower corner. The horizontal back carries a color player close-up on the right, with the player's name appearing in silver-foil lettering at the upper left, followed below by career highlights, all on a dark borderless background again highlighted by lightning filaments. The cards are numbered on the back as "X of 10."

	MINT	EXC	G-VG
COMPLETE SET (10)	200.00	90.00	25.00
COMMON PLAYER (1-10)	5.00	2.30	.60
☐ 1 Charles Barkley	18.00	8.00	2.30
Phoenix Suns			
☐ 2 Joe Dumars	5.00	2.30	.60
Detroit Pistons			
☐ 3 Patrick Ewing	15.00	6.75	1.90
New York Knicks			
☐ 4 Larry Johnson	12.00	5.50	1.50
Charlotte Hornets			
☐ 5 Michael Jordan	75.00	34.00	9.50
Chicago Bulls			
☐ 6 Karl Malone	9.00	4.00	1.15

Utah Jazz
☐ 7 Alonzo Mourning	22.00	10.00	2.80
Charlotte Hornets			
☐ 8 Shaquille O'Neal	50.00	23.00	6.25
Orlando Magic			
☐ 9 David Robinson	18.00	8.00	2.30
San Antonio Spurs			
☐ 10 Dominique Wilkins	12.00	5.50	1.50
Atlanta Hawks			

1991-92 Upper Deck

The 1991-92 Upper Deck basketball set contains 500 cards, measuring the standard size (2 1/2" by 3 1/2"). The set was released in two series of 400 and 100 cards, respectively. High series cards are in relatively shorter supply (than low series cards) because high series packs contained a mix of both high and low series cards. The fronts feature glossy color player photos, bordered below and on the right by a hardwood basketball floor design. The player's name appears beneath the picture, while the team name is printed vertically alongside the picture. The backs display a second color player photo as well as biographical and statistical information. Special subsets featured include Draft Choices (1-21), Classic Confrontations (30-34), All-Rookie Team (35-39), All-Stars (49-72), and Team Checklists (73-99). Inserted in the high series were cards of Hall of Famer Jerry West, who is highlighted in a nine-card Basketball Heroes subset. West signed 2,500 of the set's checklist cards. High series lockers contained seven 12-card packs of cards 1-500 and a special "Rookie Standouts" card. Both low and high series were offered in a 500-card factory set. The fronts feature glossy color player photos, bordered below and on the right by a hardwood basketball floor design. The player's name appears beneath the picture, while the team name is printed vertically alongside the picture. The backs display a second color player photo as well as biographical and statistical information. In addition to rookie and traded players, the high series includes the following topical subsets: Top Prospects (438-448), All-Star Skills (476-484), capturing players who participated in the slam dunk competition as well as the three-point shootout winner, Eastern All-Star Team (449, 451-462), and Western All-Star Team (450, 463-475). The cards are numbered on the back and checklisted below accordingly. Rookie Cards include Kenny Anderson, Stacey Augmon, Dale Davis, Larry Johnson, Terry Mills, Dikembe Mutombo, Billy Owens, Steve Smith, and John Starks.

	MINT	EXC	G-VG
COMPLETE SET (500)	25.00	11.50	3.10
COMPLETE FACT.SET (500)	25.00	11.50	3.10
COMPLETE SERIES 1 (400)	15.00	6.75	1.90
COMPLETE SERIES 2 (100)	10.00	4.50	1.25
COMMON PLAYER (1-400)	.05	.02	.01
COMMON PLAYER (401-500)	.06	.03	.01
☐ 1 Draft Checklist	.15	.07	.02
(Stacey Augmon and			
Rodney Monroe)			
☐ 2 Larry Johnson UER	4.00	1.80	.50
Charlotte Hornets			

	(Career FG Percentage is .643, not .648)		
☐ 3	Dikembe Mutombo 1.50	.65	.19
	Denver Nuggets		
☐ 4	Steve Smith 1.00	.45	.13
	Miami Heat		
☐ 5	Stacey Augmon .... .75	.35	.09
	Atlanta Hawks		
☐ 6	Terrell Brandon .... .30	.14	.04
	Cleveland Cavaliers		
☐ 7	Greg Anthony .... .20	.09	.03
	New York Knicks		
☐ 8	Rich King .... .08	.04	.01
	Seattle Supersonics		
☐ 9	Chris Gatling .... .20	.09	.03
	Golden State Warriors		
☐ 10	Victor Alexander .... .20	.09	.03
	Golden State Warriors		
☐ 11	John Turner .... .08	.04	.01
	Houston Rockets		
☐ 12	Eric Murdock .... .75	.35	.09
	Utah Jazz		
☐ 13	Mark Randall .... .08	.04	.01
	Chicago Bulls		
☐ 14	Rodney Monroe .... .08	.04	.01
	Atlanta Hawks		
☐ 15	Myron Brown .... .08	.04	.01
	Minnesota Timberwolves		
☐ 16	Mike Iuzzolino .... .08	.04	.01
	Dallas Mavericks		
☐ 17	Chris Corchiani .... .15	.07	.02
	Orlando Magic		
☐ 18	Elliot Perry .... .08	.04	.01
	Los Angeles Clippers		
☐ 19	Jimmy Oliver .... .08	.04	.01
	Cleveland Cavaliers		
☐ 20	Doug Overton .... .08	.04	.01
	Detroit Pistons		
☐ 21	Steve Hood UER .... .08	.04	.01
	Sacramento Kings (Card has NBA record, but he's a rookie)		
☐ 22	Michael Jordan .... .75	.35	.09
	Stay In School		
☐ 23	Kevin Johnson .... .10	.05	.01
	Stay In School		
☐ 24	Kurk Lee .... .05	.02	.01
	New Jersey Nets		
☐ 25	Sean Higgins .... .05	.02	.01
	San Antonio Spurs		
☐ 26	Morlon Wiley .... .05	.02	.01
	Orlando Magic		
☐ 27	Derek Smith .... .05	.02	.01
	Boston Celtics		
☐ 28	Kenny Payne .... .05	.02	.01
	Philadelphia 76ers		
☐ 29	Magic Johnson .... .25	.11	.03
	Assist Record		
☐ 30	Larry Bird CC .... .25	.11	.03
	and Chuck Person		
☐ 31	Karl Malone CC .... .25	.11	.03
	and Charles Barkley		
☐ 32	Kevin Johnson CC .... .15	.07	.02
	and John Stockton		
☐ 33	Hakeem Olajuwon CC .... .35	.16	.04
	and Patrick Ewing		
☐ 34	Magic Johnson CC 1.00	.45	.13
	and Michael Jordan		
☐ 35	Derrick Coleman ART .... .20	.09	.03
	New Jersey Nets		
☐ 36	Lionel Simmons ART .... .05	.02	.01
	Sacramento Kings		
☐ 37	Dee Brown ART .... .05	.02	.01
	Boston Celtics		

☐ 38	Dennis Scott ART .... Orlando Magic	.05	.02	.01
☐ 39	Kendall Gill ART .... Charlotte Hornets	.08	.04	.01
☐ 40	Winston Garland .... Los Angeles Clippers	.05	.02	.01
☐ 41	Danny Young .... Portland Trail Blazers	.05	.02	.01
☐ 42	Rick Mahorn .... Philadelphia 76ers	.08	.04	.01
☐ 43	Michael Adams .... Denver Nuggets	.08	.04	.01
☐ 44	Michael Jordan .... Chicago Bulls	2.50	1.15	.30
☐ 45	Magic Johnson .... Los Angeles Lakers	.50	.23	.06
☐ 46	Doc Rivers .... Atlanta Hawks	.08	.04	.01
☐ 47	Moses Malone .... Atlanta Hawks	.10	.05	.01
☐ 48	Michael Jordan .... All-Star Checklist	1.25	.55	.16
☐ 49	James Worthy AS .... Los Angeles Lakers	.08	.04	.01
☐ 50	Tim Hardaway AS .... Golden State Warriors	.10	.05	.01
☐ 51	Karl Malone AS .... Utah Jazz	.12	.05	.02
☐ 52	John Stockton AS .... Utah Jazz	.10	.05	.01
☐ 53	Clyde Drexler AS .... Portland Trail Blazers	.10	.05	.01
☐ 54	Terry Porter AS .... Portland Trail Blazers	.05	.02	.01
☐ 55	Kevin Duckworth AS .... Portland Trail Blazers	.05	.02	.01
☐ 56	Tom Chambers AS .... Phoenix Suns	.08	.04	.01
☐ 57	Magic Johnson AS .... Los Angeles Lakers	.25	.11	.03
☐ 58	David Robinson AS .... San Antonio Spurs	.30	.14	.04
☐ 59	Kevin Johnson AS .... Phoenix Suns	.10	.05	.01
☐ 60	Chris Mullin AS .... Golden State Warriors	.10	.05	.01
☐ 61	Joe Dumars AS .... Detroit Pistons	.08	.04	.01
☐ 62	Kevin McHale AS .... Boston Celtics	.08	.04	.01
☐ 63	Brad Daugherty AS .... Cleveland Cavaliers	.08	.04	.01
☐ 64	Alvin Robertson AS .... Milwaukee Bucks	.05	.02	.01
☐ 65	Bernard King AS .... Washington Bullets	.08	.04	.01
☐ 66	Dominique Wilkins AS .... Atlanta Hawks	.12	.05	.02
☐ 67	Ricky Pierce AS .... Milwaukee Bucks	.05	.02	.01
☐ 68	Patrick Ewing AS .... New York Knicks	.15	.07	.02
☐ 69	Michael Jordan AS .... Chicago Bulls	1.25	.55	.16
☐ 70	Charles Barkley AS .... Philadelphia 76ers	.25	.11	.03
☐ 71	Hersey Hawkins AS .... Philadelphia 76ers	.05	.02	.01
☐ 72	Robert Parish AS .... Boston Celtics	.08	.04	.01
☐ 73	Alvin Robertson TC .... Milwaukee Bucks	.05	.02	.01
☐ 74	Bernard King TC	.08	.04	.01

	Washington Bullets				
☐ 75	Michael Jordan TC	1.25	.55	.16
	Chicago Bulls				
☐ 76	Brad Daugherty TC	.08	.04	.01
	Cleveland Cavaliers				
☐ 77	Larry Bird TC	.40	.18	.05
	Boston Celtics				
☐ 78	Ron Harper TC	.05	.02	.01
	Los Angeles Clippers				
☐ 79	Dominique Wilkins TC	.12	.05	.02
	Atlanta Hawks				
☐ 80	Rony Seikaly TC	.08	.04	.01
	Miami Heat				
☐ 81	Rex Chapman TC	.05	.02	.01
	Charlotte Hornets				
☐ 82	Mark Eaton TC	.05	.02	.01
	Utah Jazz				
☐ 83	Lionel Simmons TC	.05	.02	.01
	Sacramento Kings				
☐ 84	Gerald Wilkins TC	.05	.02	.01
	New York Knicks				
☐ 85	James Worthy TC	.08	.04	.01
	Los Angeles Lakers				
☐ 86	Scott Skiles TC	.05	.02	.01
	Orlando Magic				
☐ 87	Rolando Blackman TC	.05	.02	.01
	Dallas Mavericks				
☐ 88	Derrick Coleman TC	.20	.09	.03
	New Jersey Nets				
☐ 89	Chris Jackson TC	.08	.04	.01
	Denver Nuggets				
☐ 90	Reggie Miller TC	.10	.05	.01
	Indiana Pacers				
☐ 91	Isiah Thomas TC	.10	.05	.01
	Detroit Pistons				
☐ 92	Hakeem Olajuwon TC	.40	.18	.05
	Houston Rockets				
☐ 93	Hersey Hawkins TC	.05	.02	.01
	Philadelphia 76ers				
☐ 94	David Robinson TC	.30	.14	.04
	San Antonio Spurs				
☐ 95	Tom Chambers TC	.08	.04	.01
	Phoenix Suns				
☐ 96	Shawn Kemp TC	.50	.23	.06
	Seattle Supersonics				
☐ 97	Pooh Richardson TC	.05	.02	.01
	Minnesota Timberwolves				
☐ 98	Clyde Drexler TC	.10	.05	.01
	Portland Trail Blazers				
☐ 99	Chris Mullin TC	.10	.05	.01
	Golden State Warriors				
☐ 100	Checklist 1-100	.05	.02	.01
☐ 101	John Shasky	.05	.02	.01
	Dallas Mavericks				
☐ 102	Dana Barros	.05	.02	.01
	Seattle Supersonics				
☐ 103	Stojko Vrankovic	.05	.02	.01
	Boston Celtics				
☐ 104	Larry Drew	.05	.02	.01
	Los Angeles Lakers				
☐ 105	Randy White	.05	.02	.01
	Dallas Mavericks				
☐ 106	Dave Corzine	.05	.02	.01
	Seattle Supersonics				
☐ 107	Joe Kleine	.05	.02	.01
	Boston Celtics				
☐ 108	Lance Blanks	.05	.02	.01
	Detroit Pistons				
☐ 109	Rodney McCray	.05	.02	.01
	Dallas Mavericks				
☐ 110	Sedale Threatt	.05	.02	.01
	Seattle Supersonics				
☐ 111	Ken Norman	.08	.04	.01
	Los Angeles Clippers				

☐ 112	Rickey Green Philadelphia 76ers	.05	.02	.01
☐ 113	Andy Toolson Utah Jazz	.05	.02	.01
☐ 114	Bo Kimble Los Angeles Clippers	.05	.02	.01
☐ 115	Mark West Phoenix Suns	.05	.02	.01
☐ 116	Mark Eaton Utah Jazz	.05	.02	.01
☐ 117	John Paxson Chicago Bulls	.08	.04	.01
☐ 118	Mike Brown Utah Jazz	.05	.02	.01
☐ 119	Brian Oliver Philadelphia 76ers	.05	.02	.01
☐ 120	Will Perdue Chicago Bulls	.05	.02	.01
☐ 121	Michael Smith Boston Celtics	.05	.02	.01
☐ 122	Sherman Douglas Miami Heat	.05	.02	.01
☐ 123	Reggie Lewis Boston Celtics	.10	.05	.01
☐ 124	James Donaldson Dallas Mavericks	.05	.02	.01
☐ 125	Scottie Pippen Chicago Bulls	.30	.14	.04
☐ 126	Elden Campbell Los Angeles Lakers	.05	.02	.01
☐ 127	Michael Cage Seattle Supersonics	.05	.02	.01
☐ 128	Tony Smith Los Angeles Lakers	.05	.02	.01
☐ 129	Ed Pinckney Boston Celtics	.05	.02	.01
☐ 130	Keith Askins Miami Heat	.05	.02	.01
☐ 131	Darrell Griffith Utah Jazz	.08	.04	.01
☐ 132	Vinnie Johnson Detroit Pistons	.08	.04	.01
☐ 133	Ron Harper Los Angeles Clippers	.08	.04	.01
☐ 134	Andre Turner Philadelphia 76ers	.05	.02	.01
☐ 135	Jeff Hornacek Phoenix Suns	.10	.05	.01
☐ 136	John Stockton Utah Jazz	.20	.09	.03
☐ 137	Derek Harper Dallas Mavericks	.08	.04	.01
☐ 138	Loy Vaught Los Angeles Clippers	.08	.04	.01
☐ 139	Thurl Bailey Utah Jazz	.05	.02	.01
☐ 140	Olden Polynice Los Angeles Clippers	.05	.02	.01
☐ 141	Kevin Edwards Miami Heat	.05	.02	.01
☐ 142	Byron Scott Los Angeles Lakers	.08	.04	.01
☐ 143	Dee Brown Boston Celtics	.08	.04	.01
☐ 144	Sam Perkins Los Angeles Lakers	.08	.04	.01
☐ 145	Rony Seikaly Miami Heat	.10	.05	.01
☐ 146	James Worthy Los Angeles Lakers	.10	.05	.01
☐ 147	Glen Rice Miami Heat	.20	.09	.03
☐ 148	Craig Hodges	.05	.02	.01

	Chicago Bulls			
☐ 149	Bimbo Coles	.05	.02	.01
	Miami Heat			
☐ 150	Mychal Thompson	.08	.04	.01
	Los Angeles Lakers			
☐ 151	Xavier McDaniel	.10	.05	.01
	Phoenix Suns			
☐ 152	Roy Tarpley	.05	.02	.01
	Dallas Mavericks			
☐ 153	Gary Payton	.20	.09	.03
	Seattle Supersonics			
☐ 154	Rolando Blackman	.08	.04	.01
	Dallas Mavericks			
☐ 155	Hersey Hawkins	.08	.04	.01
	Philadelphia 76ers			
☐ 156	Ricky Pierce	.08	.04	.01
	Seattle Supersonics			
☐ 157	Fat Lever	.05	.02	.01
	Dallas Mavericks			
☐ 158	Andrew Lang	.05	.02	.01
	Phoenix Suns			
☐ 159	Benoit Benjamin	.05	.02	.01
	Seattle Supersonics			
☐ 160	Cedric Ceballos	.10	.05	.01
	Phoenix Suns			
☐ 161	Charles Smith	.08	.04	.01
	Los Angeles Clippers			
☐ 162	Jeff Martin	.05	.02	.01
	Los Angeles Clippers			
☐ 163	Robert Parish	.10	.05	.01
	Boston Celtics			
☐ 164	Danny Manning	.20	.09	.03
	Los Angeles Clippers			
☐ 165	Mark Aguirre	.10	.05	.01
	Detroit Pistons			
☐ 166	Jeff Malone	.08	.04	.01
	Utah Jazz			
☐ 167	Bill Laimbeer	.10	.05	.01
	Detroit Pistons			
☐ 168	Willie Burton	.05	.02	.01
	Miami Heat			
☐ 169	Dennis Hopson	.05	.02	.01
	Chicago Bulls			
☐ 170	Kevin Gamble	.05	.02	.01
	Boston Celtics			
☐ 171	Terry Teagle	.05	.02	.01
	Los Angeles Lakers			
☐ 172	Dan Majerle	.10	.05	.01
	Phoenix Suns			
☐ 173	Shawn Kemp	1.00	.45	.13
	Seattle Supersonics			
☐ 174	Tom Chambers	.10	.05	.01
	Phoenix Suns			
☐ 175	Vlade Divac	.08	.04	.01
	Los Angeles Lakers			
☐ 176	Johnny Dawkins	.05	.02	.01
	Philadelphia 76ers			
☐ 177	A.C. Green	.08	.04	.01
	Los Angeles Lakers			
☐ 178	Manute Bol	.05	.02	.01
	Philadelphia 76ers			
☐ 179	Terry Davis	.05	.02	.01
	Miami Heat			
☐ 180	Ron Anderson	.05	.02	.01
	Philadelphia 76ers			
☐ 181	Horace Grant	.10	.05	.01
	Chicago Bulls			
☐ 182	Stacey King	.05	.02	.01
	Chicago Bulls			
☐ 183	William Bedford	.05	.02	.01
	Detroit Pistons			
☐ 184	B.J. Armstrong	.20	.09	.03
	Chicago Bulls			

☐ 185 Dennis Rodman	.08	.04	.01
Detroit Pistons			
☐ 186 Nate McMillan	.08	.04	.01
Seattle Supersonics			
☐ 187 Cliff Levingston	.05	.02	.01
Chicago Bulls			
☐ 188 Quintin Dailey	.05	.02	.01
Seattle Supersonics			
☐ 189 Bill Cartwright	.08	.04	.01
Chicago Bulls			
☐ 190 John Salley	.05	.02	.01
Detroit Pistons			
☐ 191 Jayson Williams	.05	.02	.01
Philadelphia 76ers			
☐ 192 Grant Long	.05	.02	.01
Miami Heat			
☐ 193 Negele Knight	.05	.02	.01
Phoenix Suns			
☐ 194 Alec Kessler	.05	.02	.01
Miami Heat			
☐ 195 Gary Grant	.05	.02	.01
Los Angeles Clippers			
☐ 196 Billy Thompson	.05	.02	.01
Miami Heat			
☐ 197 Delaney Rudd	.05	.02	.01
Utah Jazz			
☐ 198 Alan Ogg	.05	.02	.01
Miami Heat			
☐ 199 Blue Edwards	.08	.04	.01
Utah Jazz			
☐ 200 Checklist 101-200	.05	.02	.01
☐ 201 Mark Acres	.05	.02	.01
Orlando Magic			
☐ 202 Craig Ehlo	.05	.02	.01
Cleveland Cavaliers			
☐ 203 Anthony Cook	.05	.02	.01
Denver Nuggets			
☐ 204 Eric Leckner	.05	.02	.01
Charlotte Hornets			
☐ 205 Terry Catledge	.05	.02	.01
Orlando Magic			
☐ 206 Reggie Williams	.08	.04	.01
Denver Nuggets			
☐ 207 Greg Kite	.05	.02	.01
Orlando Magic			
☐ 208 Steve Kerr	.05	.02	.01
Cleveland Cavaliers			
☐ 209 Kenny Battle	.05	.02	.01
Denver Nuggets			
☐ 210 John Morton	.05	.02	.01
Cleveland Cavaliers			
☐ 211 Kenny Williams	.05	.02	.01
Indiana Pacers			
☐ 212 Mark Jackson	.08	.04	.01
New York Knicks			
☐ 213 Alaa Abdelnaby	.05	.02	.01
Portland Trail Blazers			
☐ 214 Rod Strickland	.08	.04	.01
San Antonio Spurs			
☐ 215 Micheal Williams	.08	.04	.01
Indiana Pacers			
☐ 216 Kevin Duckworth	.05	.02	.01
Portland Trail Blazers			
☐ 217 David Wingate	.05	.02	.01
San Antonio Spurs			
☐ 218 LaSalle Thompson	.08	.04	.01
Indiana Pacers			
☐ 219 John Starks	1.00	.45	.13
New York Knicks			
☐ 220 Cliff Robinson	.20	.09	.03
Portland Trail Blazers			
☐ 221 Jeff Grayer	.05	.02	.01
Milwaukee Bucks			

☐ 222	Marcus Liberty	.05	.02	.01
	Denver Nuggets			
☐ 223	Larry Nance	.08	.04	.01
	Cleveland Cavaliers			
☐ 224	Michael Ansley	.05	.02	.01
	Orlando Magic			
☐ 225	Kevin McHale	.10	.05	.01
	Boston Celtics			
☐ 226	Scott Skiles	.08	.04	.01
	Orlando Magic			
☐ 227	Darnell Valentine	.05	.02	.01
	Cleveland Cavaliers			
☐ 228	Nick Anderson	.10	.05	.01
	Orlando Magic			
☐ 229	Brad Davis	.05	.02	.01
	Dallas Mavericks			
☐ 230	Gerald Paddio	.05	.02	.01
	Cleveland Cavaliers			
☐ 231	Sam Bowie	.08	.04	.01
	New Jersey Nets			
☐ 232	Sam Vincent	.05	.02	.01
	Orlando Magic			
☐ 233	George McCloud	.05	.02	.01
	Indiana Pacers			
☐ 234	Gerald Wilkins	.08	.04	.01
	New York Knicks			
☐ 235	Mookie Blaylock	.08	.04	.01
	New Jersey Nets			
☐ 236	Jon Koncak	.05	.02	.01
	Atlanta Hawks			
☐ 237	Danny Ferry	.05	.02	.01
	Cleveland Cavaliers			
☐ 238	Vern Fleming	.05	.02	.01
	Indiana Pacers			
☐ 239	Mark Price	.10	.05	.01
	Cleveland Cavaliers			
☐ 240	Sidney Moncrief	.10	.05	.01
	Atlanta Hawks			
☐ 241	Jay Humphries	.05	.02	.01
	Milwaukee Bucks			
☐ 242	Muggsy Bogues	.10	.05	.01
	Charlotte Hornets			
☐ 243	Tim Hardaway	.20	.09	.03
	Golden State Warriors			
☐ 244	Alvin Robertson	.08	.04	.01
	Milwaukee Bucks			
☐ 245	Chris Mullin	.20	.09	.03
	Golden State Warriors			
☐ 246	Pooh Richardson	.05	.02	.01
	Minnesota Timberwolves			
☐ 247	Winston Bennett	.05	.02	.01
	Cleveland Cavaliers			
☐ 248	Kelvin Upshaw	.05	.02	.01
	Dallas Mavericks			
☐ 249	John Williams	.08	.04	.01
	Cleveland Cavaliers			
☐ 250	Steve Alford	.05	.02	.01
	Dallas Mavericks			
☐ 251	Spud Webb	.10	.05	.01
	Atlanta Hawks			
☐ 252	Sleepy Floyd	.08	.04	.01
	Houston Rockets			
☐ 253	Chuck Person	.08	.04	.01
	Indiana Pacers			
☐ 254	Hakeem Olajuwon	.75	.35	.09
	Houston Rockets			
☐ 255	Dominique Wilkins	.25	.11	.03
	Atlanta Hawks			
☐ 256	Reggie Miller	.20	.09	.03
	Indiana Pacers			
☐ 257	Dennis Scott	.08	.04	.01
	Orlando Magic			
☐ 258	Charles Oakley	.10	.05	.01

New York Knicks
- ☐ 259 Sidney Green .... .05 .02 .01
  San Antonio Spurs
- ☐ 260 Detlef Schrempf .... .10 .05 .01
  Indiana Pacers
- ☐ 261 Rod Higgins .... .05 .02 .01
  Golden State Warriors
- ☐ 262 J.R. Reid .... .05 .02 .01
  Charlotte Hornets
- ☐ 263 Tyrone Hill .... .05 .02 .01
  Golden State Warriors
- ☐ 264 Reggie Theus .... .08 .04 .01
  New Jersey Nets
- ☐ 265 Mitch Richmond .... .10 .05 .01
  Golden State Warriors
- ☐ 266 Dale Ellis .... .08 .04 .01
  Milwaukee Bucks
- ☐ 267 Terry Cummings .... .08 .04 .01
  San Antonio Spurs
- ☐ 268 Johnny Newman .... .05 .02 .01
  Charlotte Hornets
- ☐ 269 Doug West .... .08 .04 .01
  Minnesota Timberwolves
- ☐ 270 Jim Petersen .... .05 .02 .01
  Golden State Warriors
- ☐ 271 Otis Thorpe .... .08 .04 .01
  Houston Rockets
- ☐ 272 John Williams .... .05 .02 .01
  Washington Bullets
- ☐ 273 Kennard Winchester .... .05 .02 .01
  Houston Rockets
- ☐ 274 Duane Ferrell .... .05 .02 .01
  Atlanta Hawks
- ☐ 275 Vernon Maxwell .... .08 .04 .01
  Houston Rockets
- ☐ 276 Kenny Smith .... .05 .02 .01
  Houston Rockets
- ☐ 277 Jerome Kersey .... .05 .02 .01
  Portland Trail Blazers
- ☐ 278 Kevin Willis .... .08 .04 .01
  Atlanta Hawks
- ☐ 279 Danny Ainge .... .10 .05 .01
  Portland Trail Blazers
- ☐ 280 Larry Smith .... .08 .04 .01
  Houston Rockets
- ☐ 281 Maurice Cheeks .... .10 .05 .01
  New York Knicks
- ☐ 282 Willie Anderson .... .05 .02 .01
  San Antonio Spurs
- ☐ 283 Tom Tolbert .... .05 .02 .01
  Golden State Warriors
- ☐ 284 Jerrod Mustaf .... .05 .02 .01
  New York Knicks
- ☐ 285 Randolph Keys .... .05 .02 .01
  Charlotte Hornets
- ☐ 286 Jerry Reynolds .... .05 .02 .01
  Orlando Magic
- ☐ 287 Sean Elliott .... .08 .04 .01
  San Antonio Spurs
- ☐ 288 Otis Smith .... .05 .02 .01
  Orlando Magic
- ☐ 289 Terry Mills .... .75 .35 .09
  New Jersey Nets
- ☐ 290 Kelly Tripucka .... .08 .04 .01
  Charlotte Hornets
- ☐ 291 Jon Sundvold .... .05 .02 .01
  Miami Heat
- ☐ 292 Rumeal Robinson .... .05 .02 .01
  Atlanta Hawks
- ☐ 293 Fred Roberts .... .05 .02 .01
  Milwaukee Bucks
- ☐ 294 Rik Smits .... .08 .04 .01
  Indiana Pacers

☐	295	Jerome Lane	.05	.02	.01
		Denver Nuggets			
☐	296	Dave Jamerson	.05	.02	.01
		Houston Rockets			
☐	297	Joe Wolf	.05	.02	.01
		Denver Nuggets			
☐	298	David Wood	.05	.02	.01
		Houston Rockets			
☐	299	Todd Lichti	.05	.02	.01
		Denver Nuggets			
☐	300	Checklist 201-300	.05	.02	.01
☐	301	Randy Breuer	.05	.02	.01
		Minnesota Timberwolves			
☐	302	Buck Johnson	.05	.02	.01
		Houston Rockets			
☐	303	Scott Brooks	.05	.02	.01
		Minnesota Timberwolves			
☐	304	Jeff Turner	.05	.02	.01
		Orlando Magic			
☐	305	Felton Spencer	.05	.02	.01
		Minnesota Timberwolves			
☐	306	Greg Dreiling	.05	.02	.01
		Indiana Pacers			
☐	307	Gerald Glass	.05	.02	.01
		Minnesota Timberwolves			
☐	308	Tony Brown	.05	.02	.01
		Utah Jazz			
☐	309	Sam Mitchell	.05	.02	.01
		Minnesota Timberwolves			
☐	310	Adrian Caldwell	.05	.02	.01
		Houston Rockets			
☐	311	Chris Dudley	.05	.02	.01
		New Jersey Nets			
☐	312	Blair Rasmussen	.05	.02	.01
		Denver Nuggets			
☐	313	Antoine Carr	.05	.02	.01
		Sacramento Kings			
☐	314	Greg Anderson	.05	.02	.01
		Denver Nuggets			
☐	315	Drazen Petrovic	.08	.04	.01
		New Jersey Nets			
☐	316	Alton Lister	.05	.02	.01
		Golden State Warriors			
☐	317	Jack Haley	.05	.02	.01
		New Jersey Nets			
☐	318	Bobby Hansen	.05	.02	.01
		Sacramento Kings			
☐	319	Chris Jackson	.08	.04	.01
		Denver Nuggets			
☐	320	Herb Williams	.05	.02	.01
		Dallas Mavericks			
☐	321	Kendall Gill	.08	.04	.01
		Charlotte Hornets			
☐	322	Tyrone Corbin	.05	.02	.01
		Minnesota Timberwolves			
☐	323	Kiki Vandeweghe	.08	.04	.01
		New York Knicks			
☐	324	David Robinson	.60	.25	.08
		San Antonio Spurs			
☐	325	Rex Chapman	.05	.02	.01
		Charlotte Hornets			
☐	326	Tony Campbell	.05	.02	.01
		Minnesota Timberwolves			
☐	327	Dell Curry	.08	.04	.01
		Charlotte Hornets			
☐	328	Charles Jones	.05	.02	.01
		Washington Bullets			
☐	329	Kenny Gattison	.05	.02	.01
		Charlotte Hornets			
☐	330	Haywoode Workman	.25	.11	.03
		Washington Bullets			
☐	331	Travis Mays	.05	.02	.01
		Sacramento Kings			

☐ 332	Derrick Coleman New Jersey Nets	.40	.18	.05
☐ 333	Isiah Thomas Detroit Pistons	.20	.09	.03
☐ 334	Jud Buechler New Jersey Nets	.05	.02	.01
☐ 335	Joe Dumars Detroit Pistons	.20	.09	.03
☐ 336	Tate George New Jersey Nets	.05	.02	.01
☐ 337	Mike Sanders Indiana Pacers	.05	.02	.01
☐ 338	James Edwards Detroit Pistons	.05	.02	.01
☐ 339	Chris Morris New Jersey Nets	.05	.02	.01
☐ 340	Scott Hastings Detroit Pistons	.05	.02	.01
☐ 341	Trent Tucker New York Knicks	.05	.02	.01
☐ 342	Harvey Grant Washington Bullets	.05	.02	.01
☐ 343	Patrick Ewing New York Knicks	.30	.14	.04
☐ 344	Larry Bird Boston Celtics	.75	.35	.09
☐ 345	Charles Barkley Philadelphia 76ers	.50	.23	.06
☐ 346	Brian Shaw Boston Celtics	.05	.02	.01
☐ 347	Kenny Walker New York Knicks	.05	.02	.01
☐ 348	Danny Schayes Milwaukee Bucks	.05	.02	.01
☐ 349	Tom Hammonds Washington Bullets	.05	.02	.01
☐ 350	Frank Brickowski Milwaukee Bucks	.08	.04	.01
☐ 351	Terry Porter Portland Trail Blazers	.08	.04	.01
☐ 352	Orlando Woolridge Denver Nuggets	.08	.04	.01
☐ 353	Buck Williams Portland Trail Blazers	.10	.05	.01
☐ 354	Sarunas Marciulionis Golden State Warriors	.08	.04	.01
☐ 355	Karl Malone Utah Jazz	.25	.11	.03
☐ 356	Kevin Johnson Phoenix Suns	.20	.09	.03
☐ 357	Clyde Drexler Portland Trail Blazers	.20	.09	.03
☐ 358	Duane Causwell Sacramento Kings	.05	.02	.01
☐ 359	Paul Pressey San Antonio Spurs	.05	.02	.01
☐ 360	Jim Les Sacramento Kings	.05	.02	.01
☐ 361	Derrick McKey Seattle Supersonics	.05	.02	.01
☐ 362	Scott Williams Chicago Bulls	.20	.09	.03
☐ 363	Mark Alarie Washington Bullets	.05	.02	.01
☐ 364	Brad Daugherty Cleveland Cavaliers	.10	.05	.01
☐ 365	Bernard King Washington Bullets	.10	.05	.01
☐ 366	Steve Henson Milwaukee Bucks	.05	.02	.01
☐ 367	Darrell Walker Washington Bullets	.05	.02	.01
☐ 368	Larry Krystkowiak	.05	.02	.01

	Milwaukee Bucks			
☐ 369	Henry James UER	.05	.02	.01
	Cleveland Cavaliers			
	(Scored 20 points vs.			
	Pistons, not Jazz)			
☐ 370	Jack Sikma	.10	.05	.01
	Milwaukee Bucks			
☐ 371	Eddie Johnson	.05	.02	.01
	Seattle Supersonics			
☐ 372	Wayman Tisdale	.08	.04	.01
	Sacramento Kings			
☐ 373	Joe Barry Carroll	.05	.02	.01
	Phoenix Suns			
☐ 374	David Greenwood	.05	.02	.01
	San Antonio Spurs			
☐ 375	Lionel Simmons	.05	.02	.01
	Sacramento Kings			
☐ 376	Dwayne Schintzius	.05	.02	.01
	San Antonio Spurs			
☐ 377	Tod Murphy	.05	.02	.01
	Minnesota Timberwolves			
☐ 378	Wayne Cooper	.05	.02	.01
	Portland Trail Blazers			
☐ 379	Anthony Bonner	.05	.02	.01
	Sacramento Kings			
☐ 380	Walter Davis	.10	.05	.01
	Portland Trail Blazers			
☐ 381	Lester Conner	.05	.02	.01
	Milwaukee Bucks			
☐ 382	Ledell Eackles	.05	.02	.01
	Washington Bullets			
☐ 383	Brad Lohaus	.05	.02	.01
	Milwaukee Bucks			
☐ 384	Derrick Gervin	.05	.02	.01
	New Jersey Nets			
☐ 385	Pervis Ellison	.08	.04	.01
	Washington Bullets			
☐ 386	Tim McCormick	.05	.02	.01
	Atlanta Hawks			
☐ 387	A.J. English	.05	.02	.01
	Washington Bullets			
☐ 388	John Battle	.05	.02	.01
	Atlanta Hawks			
☐ 389	Roy Hinson	.05	.02	.01
	New Jersey Nets			
☐ 390	Armon Gilliam	.05	.02	.01
	Philadelphia 76ers			
☐ 391	Kurt Rambis	.08	.04	.01
	Phoenix Suns			
☐ 392	Mark Bryant	.05	.02	.01
	Portland Trail Blazers			
☐ 393	Chucky Brown	.05	.02	.01
	Cleveland Cavaliers			
☐ 394	Avery Johnson	.08	.04	.01
	San Antonio Spurs			
☐ 395	Rory Sparrow	.05	.02	.01
	Sacramento Kings			
☐ 396	Mario Elie	.30	.14	.04
	Golden State Warriors			
☐ 397	Ralph Sampson	.08	.04	.01
	Sacramento Kings			
☐ 398	Mike Gminski	.05	.02	.01
	Charlotte Hornets			
☐ 399	Bill Wennington	.05	.02	.01
	Sacramento Kings			
☐ 400	Checklist 301-400	.05	.02	.01
☐ 401	David Wingate	.06	.03	.01
	Washington Bullets			
☐ 402	Moses Malone	.10	.05	.01
	Milwaukee Bucks			
☐ 403	Darrell Walker	.06	.03	.01
	Detroit Pistons			
☐ 404	Antoine Carr	.06	.03	.01
	San Antonio Spurs			

☐ 405	Charles Shackleford	.06	.03	.01
	Philadelphia 76ers			
☐ 406	Orlando Woolridge	.08	.04	.01
	Detroit Pistons			
☐ 407	Robert Pack	.40	.18	.05
	Portland Trail Blazers			
☐ 408	Bobby Hansen	.06	.03	.01
	Chicago Bulls			
☐ 409	Dale Davis	.75	.35	.09
	Indiana Pacers			
☐ 410	Vincent Askew	.06	.03	.01
	Golden State Warriors			
☐ 411	Alexander Volkov	.06	.03	.01
	Atlanta Hawks			
☐ 412	Dwayne Schintzius	.06	.03	.01
	Sacramento Kings			
☐ 413	Tim Perry	.06	.03	.01
	Phoenix Suns			
☐ 414	Tyrone Corbin	.06	.03	.01
	Utah Jazz			
☐ 415	Pete Chilcutt	.06	.03	.01
	Sacramento Kings			
☐ 416	James Edwards	.06	.03	.01
	Los Angeles Clippers			
☐ 417	Jerrod Mustaf	.06	.03	.01
	Phoenix Suns			
☐ 418	Thurl Bailey	.06	.03	.01
	Minnesota Timberwolves			
☐ 419	Spud Webb	.10	.05	.01
	Sacramento Kings			
☐ 420	Doc Rivers	.08	.04	.01
	Los Angeles Clippers			
☐ 421	Sean Green	.06	.03	.01
	Indiana Pacers			
☐ 422	Walter Davis	.10	.05	.01
	Denver Nuggets			
☐ 423	Terry Davis	.06	.03	.01
	Dallas Mavericks			
☐ 424	John Battle	.06	.03	.01
	Cleveland Cavaliers			
☐ 425	Vinnie Johnson	.08	.04	.01
	San Antonio Spurs			
☐ 426	Sherman Douglas	.06	.03	.01
	Boston Celtics			
☐ 427	Kevin Brooks	.06	.03	.01
	Denver Nuggets			
☐ 428	Greg Sutton	.06	.03	.01
	San Antonio Spurs			
☐ 429	Rafael Addison	.06	.03	.01
	New Jersey Nets			
☐ 430	Anthony Mason	.75	.35	.09
	New York Knicks			
☐ 431	Paul Graham	.15	.07	.02
	Atlanta Hawks			
☐ 432	Anthony Frederick	.06	.03	.01
	Charlotte Hornets			
☐ 433	Dennis Hopson	.06	.03	.01
	Sacramento Kings			
☐ 434	Rory Sparrow	.06	.03	.01
	Los Angeles Lakers			
☐ 435	Michael Adams	.08	.04	.01
	Washington Bullets			
☐ 436	Kevin Lynch	.06	.03	.01
	Charlotte Hornets			
☐ 437	Randy Brown	.15	.07	.02
	Sacramento Kings			
☐ 438	NBA Top Prospects	.50	.23	.06
	Checklist			
	(Larry Johnson			
	and Billy Owens)			
☐ 439	Stacey Augmon TP	.40	.18	.05
	Atlanta Hawks			
☐ 440	Larry Stewart TP	.15	.07	.02

	Washington Bullets		
☐ 441	Terrell Brandon TP	.10	.05	.01
	Cleveland Cavaliers		
☐ 442	Billy Owens TP	1.00	.45	.13
	Golden State Warriors		
☐ 443	Rick Fox TP	.50	.23	.06
	Boston Celtics		
☐ 444	Kenny Anderson TP	2.00	.90	.25
	New Jersey Nets		
☐ 445	Larry Johnson TP	2.00	.90	.25
	Charlotte Hornets		
☐ 446	Dikembe Mutombo TP	.75	.35	.09
	Denver Nuggets		
☐ 447	Steve Smith TP	.50	.23	.06
	Miami Heat		
☐ 448	Greg Anthony TP	.10	.05	.01
	New York Knicks		
☐ 449	East All-Star	.10	.05	.01
	Checklist		
☐ 450	West All-Star	.10	.05	.01
	Checklist		
☐ 451	Isiah Thomas AS	.25	.11	.03
	(Magic Johnson		
	also shown)		
☐ 452	Michael Jordan AS	2.00	.90	.25
☐ 453	Scottie Pippen AS	.25	.11	.03
☐ 454	Charles Barkley AS	.40	.18	.05
☐ 455	Patrick Ewing AS	.25	.11	.03
☐ 456	Michael Adams AS	.06	.03	.01
☐ 457	Dennis Rodman AS	.06	.03	.01
☐ 458	Reggie Lewis AS	.10	.05	.01
☐ 459	Joe Dumars AS	.10	.05	.01
☐ 460	Mark Price AS	.10	.05	.01
☐ 461	Brad Daugherty AS	.10	.05	.01
☐ 462	Kevin Willis AS	.06	.03	.01
☐ 463	Clyde Drexler AS	.15	.07	.02
☐ 464	Magic Johnson AS	.40	.18	.05
☐ 465	Chris Mullin AS	.15	.07	.02
☐ 466	Karl Malone AS	.20	.09	.03
☐ 467	David Robinson AS	.50	.23	.06
☐ 468	Tim Hardaway AS	.15	.07	.02
☐ 469	Jeff Hornacek AS	.08	.04	.01
☐ 470	John Stockton AS	.15	.07	.02
☐ 471	Dikembe Mutombo AS UER	.40	.18	.05
	(Drafted in 1992,		
	should be 1991)		
☐ 472	Hakeem Olajuwon AS	.60	.25	.08
☐ 473	James Worthy AS	.10	.05	.01
☐ 474	Otis Thorpe AS	.10	.05	.01
☐ 475	Dan Majerle AS	.10	.05	.01
☐ 476	Cedric Ceballos CL	.10	.05	.01
	Phoenix Suns		
	All-Star Skills		
☐ 477	Nick Anderson SD	.10	.05	.01
	Orlando Magic		
☐ 478	Stacey Augmon SD	.20	.09	.03
	Atlanta Hawks		
☐ 479	Cedric Ceballos SD	.10	.05	.01
	Phoenix Suns		
☐ 480	Larry Johnson SD	1.00	.45	.13
	Charlotte Hornets		
☐ 481	Shawn Kemp SD	.75	.35	.09
	Seattle Supersonics		
☐ 482	John Starks SD	.50	.23	.06
	New York Knicks		
☐ 483	Doug West SD	.06	.03	.01
	Minnesota Timberwolves		
☐ 484	Craig Hodges	.06	.03	.01
	Long Distance Shoot Out		
☐ 485	LaBradford Smith	.15	.07	.02
	Washington Bullets		
☐ 486	Winston Garland	.06	.03	.01
	Denver Nuggets		

			MINT	EXC	G-VG
☐	487	David Benoit	.25	.11	.03
		Utah Jazz			
☐	488	John Bagley	.06	.03	.01
		Boston Celtics			
☐	489	Mark Macon	.06	.03	.01
		Denver Nuggets			
☐	490	Mitch Richmond	.10	.05	.01
		Sacramento Kings			
☐	491	Luc Longley	.40	.18	.05
		Minnesota Timberwolves			
☐	492	Sedale Threatt	.06	.03	.01
		Los Angeles Lakers			
☐	493	Doug Smith	.40	.18	.05
		Dallas Mavericks			
☐	494	Travis Mays	.06	.03	.01
		Atlanta Hawks			
☐	495	Xavier McDaniel	.10	.05	.01
		New York Knicks			
☐	496	Brian Shaw	.06	.03	.01
		Miami Heat			
☐	497	Stanley Roberts	.25	.11	.03
		Orlando Magic			
☐	498	Blair Rasmussen	.06	.03	.01
		Atlanta Hawks			
☐	499	Brian Williams	.40	.18	.05
		Orlando Magic			
☐	500	Checklist Card	.06	.03	.01

1991-92 Upper Deck Award Winner Holograms

These holograms feature NBA statistical leaders in nine different categories. The first six holograms were random inserts in 1991-92 Upper Deck low series foil and jumbo packs, while the last three were inserted in high series foil and jumbo packs. The standard-size (2 1/2" by 3 1/2") holograms have the player's name and award received in the lower right corner on the front. The back has a color player photo and a summary of the player's performance. The cards are numbered on the back with an "AW" prefix before the number.

		MINT	EXC	G-VG
COMPLETE SET (9)		12.00	5.50	1.50
COMMON PLAYER (AW1-AW9)		.50	.23	.06
☐ AW1	Michael Jordan	5.00	2.30	.60
	Scoring Leader			
☐ AW2	Alvin Robertson	.50	.23	.06
	Steals Leader			

		MINT	EXC	G-VG
☐ AW3	John Stockton	.75	.35	.09
	Assists Leader			
☐ AW4	Michael Jordan	5.00	2.30	.60
	MVP			
☐ AW5	Detlef Schrempf	.60	.25	.08
	Sixth Man			
☐ AW6	David Robinson	1.50	.65	.19
	Rebounds Leader			
☐ AW7	Derrick Coleman	1.00	.45	.13
	Rookie of the Year			
☐ AW8	Hakeem Olajuwon	1.75	.80	.22
	Blocked Shots Leader			
☐ AW9	Dennis Rodman	.50	.23	.06
	Defensive POY			

1991-92 Upper Deck Rookie Standouts

The first 20 cards of this subset were randomly inserted (one per pack) in 1991-92 Upper Deck low series jumbo packs and locker series boxes, while the second 20 cards were offered in the same packaging (also one per pack) in the high series. The fronts of the standard-size (2 1/2" by 3 1/2") cards feature color action player photos, bordered on the right and below by a hardwood basketball court and with the "'91-92 Rookie Standouts" emblem in the lower right corner. The back features a second color player photo and player profile. The cards are numbered on the back with an R prefix on the card number.

		MINT	EXC	G-VG
COMPLETE SET (40)		20.00	9.00	2.50
COMPLETE SERIES 1 (20)		5.00	2.30	.60
COMPLETE SERIES 2 (20)		15.00	6.75	1.90
COMMON PLAYER (R1-R20)		.25	.11	.03
COMMON PLAYER (R21-R40)		.25	.11	.03
☐ R1	Gary Payton	1.00	.45	.13
	Seattle Supersonics			
☐ R2	Dennis Scott	.35	.16	.04
	Orlando Magic			
☐ R3	Kendall Gill	.75	.35	.09
	Charlotte Hornets			
☐ R4	Felton Spencer	.25	.11	.03
	Minnesota Timberwolves			
☐ R5	Bo Kimble	.25	.11	.03
	Los Angeles Clippers			
☐ R6	Willie Burton	.25	.11	.03
	Miami Heat			
☐ R7	Tyrone Hill	.25	.11	.03
	Golden State Warriors			
☐ R8	Loy Vaught	.35	.16	.04
	Los Angeles Clippers			
☐ R9	Travis Mays	.25	.11	.03

	Sacramento Kings			
☐ R10	Derrick Coleman	2.00	.90	.25
	New Jersey Nets			
☐ R11	Duane Causwell	.25	.11	.03
	Sacramento Kings			
☐ R12	Dee Brown	.60	.25	.08
	Boston Celtics			
☐ R13	Gerald Glass	.25	.11	.03
	Minnesota Timberwolves			
☐ R14	Jayson Williams	.25	.11	.03
	Philadelphia 76ers			
☐ R15	Elden Campbell	.25	.11	.03
	Los Angeles Lakers			
☐ R16	Negele Knight	.25	.11	.03
	Phoenix Suns			
☐ R17	Chris Jackson	1.00	.45	.13
	Denver Nuggets			
☐ R18	Danny Ferry	.25	.11	.03
	Cleveland Cavaliers			
☐ R19	Tony Smith	.25	.11	.03
	Los Angeles Lakers			
☐ R20	Cedric Ceballos	1.00	.45	.13
	Phoenix Suns			
☐ R21	Victor Alexander	.25	.11	.03
	Golden State Warriors			
☐ R22	Terrell Brandon	.50	.23	.06
	Cleveland Cavaliers			
☐ R23	Rick Fox	.50	.23	.06
	Boston Celtics			
☐ R24	Stacey Augmon	1.00	.45	.13
	Atlanta Hawks			
☐ R25	Mark Macon	.25	.11	.03
	Denver Nuggets			
☐ R26	Larry Johnson	6.00	2.70	.75
	Charlotte Hornets			
☐ R27	Paul Graham	.25	.11	.03
	Atlanta Hawks			
☐ R28	Stanley Roberts UER	.25	.11	.03
	Orlando Magic			
	(Not the Magic's 1st			
	pick in 1991)			
☐ R29	Dikembe Mutombo	2.50	1.15	.30
	Denver Nuggets			
☐ R30	Robert Pack	.50	.23	.06
	Portland Trail Blazers			
☐ R31	Doug Smith	.25	.11	.03
	Dallas Mavericks			
☐ R32	Steve Smith	1.50	.65	.19
	Miami Heat			
☐ R33	Billy Owens	1.00	.45	.13
	Golden State Warriors			
☐ R34	David Benoit	.25	.11	.03
	Utah Jazz			
☐ R35	Brian Williams	.50	.23	.06
	Orlando Magic			
☐ R36	Kenny Anderson	2.50	1.15	.30
	New Jersey Nets			
☐ R37	Greg Anthony	.25	.11	.03
	New York Knicks			
☐ R38	Dale Davis	.75	.35	.09
	Indiana Pacers			
☐ R39	Larry Stewart	.25	.11	.03
	Washington Bullets			
☐ R40	Mike Iuzzolino	.25	.11	.03
	Dallas Mavericks			

1991-92 Upper Deck Jerry West Heroes

This ten-card insert set was randomly inserted in Upper Deck's high series basketball foil packs. Also included in the packs were 2,500 checklist cards autographed by West. The fronts of the standard-size (2 1/2" by 3 1/2") cards capture memorable moments from his

college and professional career. The player photos are cut out and superimposed over a jump ball circle on a hardwood basketball floor design. The card backs present commentary. The cards are numbered on the back.

	MINT	EXC	G-VG
COMPLETE SET (10)	10.00	4.50	1.25
COMMON WEST HEROES (1-9)	1.00	.45	.13
☐ 1 Jerry West	1.00	.45	.13
1959 NCAA Tournament MVP			
☐ 2 Jerry West	1.00	.45	.13
1960 U.S. Team			
☐ 3 Jerry West	1.00	.45	.13
1968-69 NBA Playoff MVP			
☐ 4 Jerry West	1.00	.45	.13
1969-70 NBA Scoring Leader			
☐ 5 Jerry West	1.00	.45	.13
1972 NBA World Championship			
☐ 6 Jerry West	1.00	.45	.13
1973-74 25,000 Points			
☐ 7 Jerry West	1.00	.45	.13
1979 Basketball Hall of Fame			
☐ 8 Jerry West	1.00	.45	.13
1982 to the present Front Office Success			
☐ 9 Jerry West	1.00	.45	.13
Portrait Card			
☐ AU Jerry West AU	200.00	90.00	25.00
(Certified autograph)			
☐ NNO Jerry West	2.00	.90	.25
Cover/Title Card			

1992-93 Upper Deck

The complete 1992-93 Upper Deck basketball set consists of 510 standard-size (2 1/2" by 3 1/2") cards issued in two series of 310 and 200 cards, respectively. High series cards are slightly tougher to find (compared to the low numbers) because high series packs contained a mix of high and low series cards. No factory sets were produced by Upper Deck for this issue. Card number 1A is a "Trade Upper Deck" card that the collector could trade to Upper Deck for a Shaquille O'Neal mail-away trade card beginning on Jan. 1, 1993. The offer expired June 30, 1993. Randomly inserted throughout all low series packs (both foil and jumbo) were a Magic/Bird "SP" card and a ten-card Wilt Chamberlain Basketball Heroes subset. One card from a 27-card Team MVPs subset was inserted into each low series

jumbo pack; a ten-card NBA All-Rookie Team was randomly featured in low series foil packs only; and a ten-card All-NBA team was featured in each pack of the low series "Locker Box" packs. The fronts feature color action player photos with white borders. The team name is gold-foil stamped across the top of the picture. The border design at the bottom consists of a team colored stripe that shades from one team color to the other with diagonal stripes within the larger stripe that add texture. The entire design is edged in gold foil. The right end is off-set slightly by the Upper Deck logo. The backs show an action player photo that runs down the left side of the card. The right side displays statistics printed on a ghosted NBA logo. Topical subsets featured include NBA Draft (2-21), Team Checklists (35-61), and Scoring Threats (62-66). The set also includes two art cards (67-68) and one Stay in School card (69). The cards are numbered on the back. Randomly inserted into series II packs were a 20,000-point "SP2" card, three Award Winner holograms, a 20-card 15,000-Point Club subset (hobby only), a 20-card Rookie Standouts subset (only in retail foil packs), a ten-card Foreign Exchange set (one card per pack in series II locker boxes), a 20-card All-Division subset (retail jumbo only), and a Larry Bird Basketball Heroes subset. Topical subsets featured are Team Fact Cards (350-376), NBA East All-Star Game (421-433), NBA West All-Star Game (434-445), In Your Face (446-454), Top Prospects (455-482), NBA Game Faces (483-497), Scoring Threats (498-505), and Fanimation (506-510). The cards are numbered on the back. Rookie Cards include Doug Christie, Richard Dumas, LaPhonso Ellis, Tom Gugliotta, Jim Jackson, Christian Laettner, Harold Miner, Alonzo Mourning, Shaquille O'Neal, Latrell Sprewell, Clarence Weatherspoon and Walt Williams.

	MINT	EXC	G-VG
COMPLETE SET (514)	60.00	27.00	7.50
COMPLETE LO SERIES (311)	25.00	11.50	3.10
COMPLETE HI SERIES (203)	35.00	16.00	4.40
COMMON PLAYER (1-310)	.05	.02	.01
COMMON PLAYER (311-510)	.06	.03	.01
☐ 1 Shaquille O'Neal SP	12.00	5.50	1.50
Orlando Magic			
NBA First Draft Pick			
☐ 1A 1992 NBA Draft Trade	1.00	.45	.13
Card SP			
☐ 1AX 1992 NBA Draft Trade	.25	.11	.03
Card (Stamped)			
☐ 1B Shaquille O'Neal Trade	8.00	3.60	1.00
☐ 2 Alonzo Mourning	3.00	1.35	.40
Charlotte Hornets			
☐ 3 Christian Laettner	.75	.35	.09
Minnesota Timberwolves			
☐ 4 LaPhonso Ellis	.75	.35	.09
Denver Nuggets			
☐ 5 Clarence Weatherspoon	.75	.35	.09
Philadelphia 76ers			
☐ 6 Adam Keefe	.10	.05	.01
Atlanta Hawks			
☐ 7 Robert Horry	.75	.35	.09
Houston Rockets			
☐ 8 Harold Miner	.35	.16	.04
Miami Heat			
☐ 9 Bryant Stith	.30	.14	.04
Denver Nuggets			

☐ 10 Malik Sealy	.10	.05	.01
Indiana Pacers			
☐ 11 Anthony Peeler	.25	.11	.03
Los Angeles Lakers			
☐ 12 Randy Woods	.05	.02	.01
Los Angeles Clippers			
☐ 13 Tracy Murray	.10	.05	.01
Portland Trail Blazers			
☐ 14 Tom Gugliotta	.75	.35	.09
Washington Bullets			
☐ 15 Hubert Davis	.30	.14	.04
New York Knicks			
☐ 16 Don MacLean	.50	.23	.06
Washington Bullets			
☐ 17 Lee Mayberry	.10	.05	.01
Milwaukee Bucks			
☐ 18 Corey Williams	.05	.02	.01
Chicago Bulls			
☐ 19 Sean Rooks	.15	.07	.02
Dallas Mavericks			
☐ 20 Todd Day	.30	.14	.04
Milwaukee Bucks			
☐ 21 NBA Draft Card CL	.15	.07	.02
Bryant Stith			
LaPhonso Ellis			
☐ 22 Jeff Hornacek	.08	.04	.01
Phoenix Suns			
☐ 23 Michael Jordan	2.00	.90	.25
Chicago Bulls			
☐ 24 John Salley	.05	.02	.01
Detroit Pistons			
☐ 25 Andre Turner	.05	.02	.01
Washington Bullets			
☐ 26 Charles Barkley	.50	.23	.06
Philadelphia 76ers			
☐ 27 Anthony Frederick	.05	.02	.01
Charlotte Hornets			
☐ 28 Mario Elie	.05	.02	.01
Golden State Warriors			
☐ 29 Olden Polynice	.05	.02	.01
Los Angeles Clippers			
☐ 30 Rodney Monroe	.05	.02	.01
Atlanta Hawks			
☐ 31 Tim Perry	.05	.02	.01
Phoenix Suns			
☐ 32 Doug Christie SP	1.00	.45	.13
Los Angeles Lakers			
☐ 32A Magic Johnson SP	1.00	.45	.13
Los Angeles Lakers			
☐ 33 Jim Jackson SP	6.00	2.70	.75
Dallas Mavericks			
☐ 33A Larry Bird SP	1.50	.65	.19
Boston Celtics			
☐ 34 Randy White	.05	.02	.01
Dallas Mavericks			
☐ 35 Frank Brickowski TC	.05	.02	.01
Milwaukee Bucks			
☐ 36 Michael Adams TC	.05	.02	.01
Washington Bullets			
☐ 37 Scottie Pippen TC	.20	.09	.03
Chicago Bulls			
☐ 38 Mark Price TC	.08	.04	.01
Cleveland Cavaliers			
☐ 39 Robert Parish TC	.08	.04	.01
Boston Celtics			
☐ 40 Danny Manning TC	.08	.04	.01
Los Angeles Clippers			
☐ 41 Kevin Willis TC	.05	.02	.01
Atlanta Hawks			
☐ 42 Glen Rice TC	.05	.02	.01
Miami Heat			
☐ 43 Kendall Gill TC	.05	.02	.01
Charlotte Hornets			

☐ 44 Karl Malone TC	.12	.05	.02
Utah Jazz			
☐ 45 Mitch Richmond TC	.08	.04	.01
Sacramento Kings			
☐ 46 Patrick Ewing TC	.20	.09	.03
New York Knicks			
☐ 47 Sam Perkins TC	.05	.02	.01
Los Angeles Lakers			
☐ 48 Dennis Scott TC	.05	.02	.01
Orlando Magic			
☐ 49 Derek Harper TC	.05	.02	.01
Dallas Mavericks			
☐ 50 Drazen Petrovic TC	.05	.02	.01
New Jersey Nets			
☐ 51 Reggie Williams TC	.05	.02	.01
Denver Nuggets			
☐ 52 Rik Smits TC	.05	.02	.01
Indiana Pacers			
☐ 53 Joe Dumars TC	.08	.04	.01
Detroit Pistons			
☐ 54 Otis Thorpe TC	.08	.04	.01
Houston Rockets			
☐ 55 Johnny Dawkins TC	.05	.02	.01
Philadelphia 76ers			
☐ 56 Sean Elliott TC	.05	.02	.01
San Antonio Spurs			
☐ 57 Kevin Johnson TC	.08	.04	.01
Phoenix Suns			
☐ 58 Ricky Pierce TC	.05	.02	.01
Seattle Supersonics			
☐ 59 Doug West TC	.05	.02	.01
Minnesota Timberwolves			
☐ 60 Terry Porter TC	.05	.02	.01
Portland Trail Blazers			
☐ 61 Tim Hardaway TC	.08	.04	.01
Golden State Warriors			
☐ 62 Michael Jordan ST	.50	.23	.06
Scottie Pippen ST			
Chicago Bulls			
☐ 63 Kendall Gill ST	.15	.07	.02
Larry Johnson ST			
Charlotte Hornets			
☐ 64 Tom Chambers ST	.12	.05	.02
Kevin Johnson ST			
Phoenix Suns			
☐ 65 Tim Hardaway ST	.12	.05	.02
Chris Mullin ST			
Golden State Warriors			
☐ 66 Karl Malone ST	.15	.07	.02
John Stockton ST			
Utah Jazz			
☐ 67 Michael Jordan MVP	1.00	.45	.13
Chicago Bulls			
☐ 68 Stacey Augmon	.10	.05	.01
Atlanta Hawks			
Six Million Point Man			
☐ 69 Bob Lanier	.05	.02	.01
Stay in School			
☐ 70 Alaa Abdelnaby	.05	.02	.01
Portland Trail Blazers			
☐ 71 Andrew Lang	.05	.02	.01
Phoenix Suns			
☐ 72 Larry Krystkowiak	.05	.02	.01
Milwaukee Bucks			
☐ 73 Gerald Wilkins	.05	.02	.01
New York Knicks			
☐ 74 Rod Strickland	.08	.04	.01
San Antonio Spurs			
☐ 75 Danny Ainge	.10	.05	.01
Portland Trail Blazers			
☐ 76 Chris Corchiani	.05	.02	.01
Orlando Magic			
☐ 77 Jeff Grayer	.05	.02	.01

	Milwaukee Bucks			
☐ 78	Eric Murdock	.08	.04	.01
	Utah Jazz			
☐ 79	Rex Chapman	.05	.02	.01
	Washington Bullets			
☐ 80	LaBradford Smith	.05	.02	.01
	Washington Bullets			
☐ 81	Jay Humphries	.05	.02	.01
	Milwaukee Bucks			
☐ 82	David Robinson	.50	.23	.06
	San Antonio Spurs			
☐ 83	William Bedford	.05	.02	.01
	Detroit Pistons			
☐ 84	James Edwards	.05	.02	.01
	Los Angeles Clippers			
☐ 85	Dan Schayes	.05	.02	.01
	Milwaukee Bucks			
☐ 86	Lloyd Daniels	.10	.05	.01
	San Antonio Spurs			
☐ 87	Blue Edwards	.08	.04	.01
	Utah Jazz			
☐ 88	Dale Ellis	.08	.04	.01
	Milwaukee Bucks			
☐ 89	Rolando Blackman	.08	.04	.01
	Dallas Mavericks			
☐ 90	Form Checklist 1	.25	.11	.03
	Michael Jordan			
	Chicago Bulls			
☐ 91	Rik Smits	.08	.04	.01
	Indiana Pacers			
☐ 92	Terry Davis	.05	.02	.01
	Dallas Mavericks			
☐ 93	Bill Cartwright	.08	.04	.01
	Chicago Bulls			
☐ 94	Avery Johnson	.05	.02	.01
	Houston Rockets			
☐ 95	Micheal Williams	.08	.04	.01
	Indiana Pacers			
☐ 96	Spud Webb	.10	.05	.01
	Sacramento Kings			
☐ 97	Benoit Benjamin	.05	.02	.01
	Seattle Supersonics			
☐ 98	Derek Harper	.08	.04	.01
	Dallas Mavericks			
☐ 99	Matt Bullard	.05	.02	.01
	Houston Rockets			
☐ 100A	Tyrone Corbin ERR	5.00	2.30	.60
	(Heat on front)			
	Utah Jazz			
☐ 100B	Tyrone Corbin COR	.10	.05	.01
	Utah Jazz			
☐ 101	Doc Rivers	.08	.04	.01
	Los Angeles Clippers			
☐ 102	Tony Smith	.05	.02	.01
	Los Angeles Lakers			
☐ 103	Doug West	.05	.02	.01
	Minnesota Timberwolves			
☐ 104	Kevin Duckworth	.05	.02	.01
	Portland Trail Blazers			
☐ 105	Luc Longley	.05	.02	.01
	Minnesota Timberwolves			
☐ 106	Antoine Carr	.05	.02	.01
	San Antonio Spurs			
☐ 107	Cliff Robinson	.10	.05	.01
	Portland Trail Blazers			
☐ 108	Grant Long	.05	.02	.01
	Miami Heat			
☐ 109	Terry Porter	.08	.04	.01
	Portland Trail Blazers			
☐ 110A	Steve Smith ERR	10.00	4.50	1.25
	(Jazz on front)			
	Miami Heat			
☐ 110B	Steve Smith COR	.15	.07	.02
	Miami Heat			

☐ 111	Brian Williams	.05	.02	.01
	Orlando Magic			
☐ 112	Karl Malone	.25	.11	.03
	Utah Jazz			
☐ 113	Reggie Williams	.08	.04	.01
	Denver Nuggets			
☐ 114	Tom Chambers	.08	.04	.01
	Phoenix Suns			
☐ 115	Winston Garland	.05	.02	.01
	Denver Nuggets			
☐ 116	John Stockton	.20	.09	.03
	Utah Jazz			
☐ 117	Chris Jackson	.08	.04	.01
	Denver Nuggets			
☐ 118	Mike Brown	.05	.02	.01
	Utah Jazz			
☐ 119	Kevin Johnson	.10	.05	.01
	Phoenix Suns			
☐ 120	Reggie Lewis	.10	.05	.01
	Boston Celtics			
☐ 121	Bimbo Coles	.05	.02	.01
	Miami Heat			
☐ 122	Drazen Petrovic	.08	.04	.01
	New Jersey Nets			
☐ 123	Reggie Miller	.20	.09	.03
	Indiana Pacers			
☐ 124	Derrick Coleman	.20	.09	.03
	New Jersey Nets			
☐ 125	Chuck Person	.08	.04	.01
	Indiana Pacers			
☐ 126	Glen Rice	.10	.05	.01
	Miami Heat			
☐ 127	Kenny Anderson	.20	.09	.03
	New Jersey Nets			
☐ 128	Willie Burton	.05	.02	.01
	Miami Heat			
☐ 129	Chris Morris	.05	.02	.01
	New Jersey Nets			
☐ 130	Patrick Ewing	.40	.18	.05
	New York Knicks			
☐ 131	Sean Elliott	.08	.04	.01
	San Antonio Spurs			
☐ 132	Clyde Drexler	.20	.09	.03
	Portland Trail Blazers			
☐ 133	Scottie Pippen	.40	.18	.05
	Chicago Bulls			
☐ 134	Pooh Richardson	.05	.02	.01
	Minnesota Timberwolves			
☐ 135	Horace Grant	.10	.05	.01
	Chicago Bulls			
☐ 136	Hakeem Olajuwon	.75	.35	.09
	Houston Rockets			
☐ 137	John Paxson	.08	.04	.01
	Chicago Bulls			
☐ 138	Kendall Gill	.08	.04	.01
	Charlotte Hornets			
☐ 139	Michael Adams	.08	.04	.01
	Washington Bullets			
☐ 140	Otis Thorpe	.08	.04	.01
	Houston Rockets			
☐ 141	Dennis Scott	.08	.04	.01
	Orlando Magic			
☐ 142	Stacey Augmon	.10	.05	.01
	Atlanta Hawks			
☐ 143	Robert Pack	.05	.02	.01
	Portland Trail Blazers			
☐ 144	Kevin Willis	.08	.04	.01
	Atlanta Hawks			
☐ 145	Jerome Kersey	.05	.02	.01
	Portland Trail Blazers			
☐ 146	Paul Graham	.05	.02	.01
	Atlanta Hawks			
☐ 147	Stanley Roberts	.05	.02	.01

	Orlando Magic			
☐ 148	Dominique Wilkins	.30	.14	.04
	Atlanta Hawks			
☐ 149	Scott Skiles	.08	.04	.01
	Orlando Magic			
☐ 150	Rumeal Robinson	.05	.02	.01
	Atlanta Hawks			
☐ 151	Mookie Blaylock	.08	.04	.01
	New Jersey Nets			
☐ 152	Elden Campbell	.05	.02	.01
	Los Angeles Lakers			
☐ 153	Chris Dudley	.05	.02	.01
	New Jersey Nets			
☐ 154	Sedale Threatt	.05	.02	.01
	Los Angeles Lakers			
☐ 155	Tate George	.05	.02	.01
	New Jersey Nets			
☐ 156	James Worthy	.10	.05	.01
	Los Angeles Lakers			
☐ 157	B.J. Armstrong	.10	.05	.01
	Chicago Bulls			
☐ 158	Gary Payton	.10	.05	.01
	Seattle Supersonics			
☐ 159	Ledell Eackles	.05	.02	.01
	Washington Bullets			
☐ 160	Sam Perkins	.08	.04	.01
	Los Angeles Lakers			
☐ 161	Nick Anderson	.08	.04	.01
	Orlando Magic			
☐ 162	Mitch Richmond	.10	.05	.01
	Sacramento Kings			
☐ 163	Buck Williams	.10	.05	.01
	Portland Trail Blazers			
☐ 164	Blair Rasmussen	.05	.02	.01
	Atlanta Hawks			
☐ 165	Vern Fleming	.05	.02	.01
	Indiana Pacers			
☐ 166	Duane Ferrell	.05	.02	.01
	Atlanta Hawks			
☐ 167	George McCloud	.05	.02	.01
	Indiana Pacers			
☐ 168	Terry Cummings	.08	.04	.01
	San Antonio Spurs			
☐ 169	Detlef Schrempf	.10	.05	.01
	Indiana Pacers			
☐ 170	Willie Anderson	.05	.02	.01
	San Antonio Spurs			
☐ 171	Scott Williams	.05	.02	.01
	Chicago Bulls			
☐ 172	Vernon Maxwell	.08	.04	.01
	Houston Rockets			
☐ 173	Todd Lichti	.05	.02	.01
	Denver Nuggets			
☐ 174	David Benoit	.05	.02	.01
	Utah Jazz			
☐ 175	Marcus Liberty	.05	.02	.01
	Denver Nuggets			
☐ 176	Kenny Smith	.05	.02	.01
	Houston Rockets			
☐ 177	Dan Majerle	.10	.05	.01
	Phoenix Suns			
☐ 178	Jeff Malone	.08	.04	.01
	Utah Jazz			
☐ 179	Robert Parish	.10	.05	.01
	Boston Celtics			
☐ 180	Mark Eaton	.05	.02	.01
	Utah Jazz			
☐ 181	Rony Seikaly	.10	.05	.01
	Miami Heat			
☐ 182	Tony Campbell	.05	.02	.01
	Minnesota Timberwolves			
☐ 183	Kevin McHale	.10	.05	.01
	Boston Celtics			

☐ 184	Thurl Bailey Minnesota Timberwolves	.05	.02	.01
☐ 185	Kevin Edwards Miami Heat	.05	.02	.01
☐ 186	Gerald Glass Minnesota Timberwolves	.05	.02	.01
☐ 187	Hersey Hawkins Philadelphia 76ers	.08	.04	.01
☐ 188	Sam Mitchell Minnesota Timberwolves	.05	.02	.01
☐ 189	Brian Shaw Miami Heat	.05	.02	.01
☐ 190	Felton Spencer Minnesota Timberwolves	.05	.02	.01
☐ 191	Mark Macon Denver Nuggets	.05	.02	.01
☐ 192	Jerry Reynolds Orlando Magic	.05	.02	.01
☐ 193	Dale Davis Indiana Pacers	.08	.04	.01
☐ 194	Sleepy Floyd Houston Rockets	.05	.02	.01
☐ 195	A.C. Green Los Angeles Lakers	.08	.04	.01
☐ 196	Terry Catledge Orlando Magic	.05	.02	.01
☐ 197	Byron Scott Los Angeles Lakers	.08	.04	.01
☐ 198	Sam Bowie New Jersey Nets	.05	.02	.01
☐ 199	Vlade Divac Los Angeles Lakers	.08	.04	.01
☐ 200	Form Checklist 2 Michael Jordan Chicago Bulls	.25	.11	.03
☐ 201	Brad Lohaus Milwaukee Bucks	.05	.02	.01
☐ 202	Johnny Newman Charlotte Hornets	.05	.02	.01
☐ 203	Gary Grant Los Angeles Clippers	.05	.02	.01
☐ 204	Sidney Green San Antonio Spurs	.05	.02	.01
☐ 205	Frank Brickowski Milwaukee Bucks	.08	.04	.01
☐ 206	Anthony Bowie Orlando Magic	.05	.02	.01
☐ 207	Duane Causwell Sacramento Kings	.05	.02	.01
☐ 208	A.J. English Washington Bullets	.05	.02	.01
☐ 209	Mark Aguirre Detroit Pistons	.10	.05	.01
☐ 210	Jon Koncak Atlanta Hawks	.05	.02	.01
☐ 211	Kevin Gamble Boston Celtics	.05	.02	.01
☐ 212	Craig Ehlo Cleveland Cavaliers	.05	.02	.01
☐ 213	Herb Williams Dallas Mavericks	.05	.02	.01
☐ 214	Cedric Ceballos Phoenix Suns	.10	.05	.01
☐ 215	Mark Jackson New York Knicks	.08	.04	.01
☐ 216	John Bagley Boston Celtics	.05	.02	.01
☐ 217	Ron Anderson Philadelphia 76ers	.05	.02	.01
☐ 218	John Battle Cleveland Cavaliers	.05	.02	.01
☐ 219	Kevin Lynch Charlotte Hornets	.05	.02	.01

☐ 220 Donald Hodge	.05	.02	.01
Dallas Mavericks			
☐ 221 Chris Gatling	.05	.02	.01
Golden State Warriors			
☐ 222 Muggsy Bogues	.10	.05	.01
Charlotte Hornets			
☐ 223 Bill Laimbeer	.10	.05	.01
Detroit Pistons			
☐ 224 Anthony Bonner	.05	.02	.01
Sacramento Kings			
☐ 225 Fred Roberts	.05	.02	.01
Milwaukee Bucks			
☐ 226 Larry Stewart	.05	.02	.01
Washington Bullets			
☐ 227 Darrell Walker	.05	.02	.01
Detroit Pistons			
☐ 228 Larry Smith	.08	.04	.01
Houston Rockets			
☐ 229 Billy Owens	.10	.05	.01
Golden State Warriors			
☐ 230 Vinnie Johnson	.08	.04	.01
San Antonio Spurs			
☐ 231 Johnny Dawkins	.05	.02	.01
Philadelphia 76ers			
☐ 232 Rick Fox	.08	.04	.01
Boston Celtics			
☐ 233 Travis Mays	.05	.02	.01
Atlanta Hawks			
☐ 234 Mark Price	.10	.05	.01
Cleveland Cavaliers			
☐ 235 Derrick McKey	.05	.02	.01
Seattle Supersonics			
☐ 236 Greg Anthony	.05	.02	.01
New York Knicks			
☐ 237 Doug Smith	.05	.02	.01
Dallas Mavericks			
☐ 238 Alec Kessler	.05	.02	.01
Miami Heat			
☐ 239 Anthony Mason	.08	.04	.01
New York Knicks			
☐ 240 Shawn Kemp	.75	.35	.09
Seattle Supersonics			
☐ 241 Jim Les	.05	.02	.01
Sacramento Kings			
☐ 242 Dennis Rodman	.08	.04	.01
Detroit Pistons			
☐ 243 Lionel Simmons	.08	.04	.01
Sacramento Kings			
☐ 244 Pervis Ellison	.05	.02	.01
Washington Bullets			
☐ 245 Terrell Brandon	.05	.02	.01
Cleveland Cavaliers			
☐ 246 Mark Bryant	.05	.02	.01
Portland Trail Blazers			
☐ 247 Brad Daugherty	.10	.05	.01
Cleveland Cavaliers			
☐ 248 Scott Brooks	.05	.02	.01
Minnesota Timberwolves			
☐ 249 Sarunas Marciulionis	.08	.04	.01
Golden State Warriors			
☐ 250 Danny Ferry	.05	.02	.01
Cleveland Cavaliers			
☐ 251 Loy Vaught	.08	.04	.01
Los Angeles Clippers			
☐ 252 Dee Brown	.05	.02	.01
Boston Celtics			
☐ 253 Alvin Robertson	.08	.04	.01
Milwaukee Bucks			
☐ 254 Charles Smith	.05	.02	.01
Los Angeles Clippers			
☐ 255 Dikembe Mutombo	.20	.09	.03
Denver Nuggets			
☐ 256 Greg Kite	.05	.02	.01

Orlando Magic			
☐ 257 Ed Pinckney	.05	.02	.01
Boston Celtics			
☐ 258 Ron Harper	.08	.04	.01
Los Angeles Clippers			
☐ 259 Elliot Perry	.05	.02	.01
Charlotte Hornets			
☐ 260 Rafael Addison	.05	.02	.01
New Jersey Nets			
☐ 261 Tim Hardaway	.10	.05	.01
Golden State Warriors			
☐ 262 Randy Brown	.05	.02	.01
Sacramento Kings			
☐ 263 Isiah Thomas	.15	.07	.02
Detroit Pistons			
☐ 264 Victor Alexander	.05	.02	.01
Golden State Warriors			
☐ 265 Wayman Tisdale	.08	.04	.01
Sacramento Kings			
☐ 266 Harvey Grant	.05	.02	.01
Washington Bullets			
☐ 267 Mike Iuzzolino	.05	.02	.01
Dallas Mavericks			
☐ 268 Joe Dumars	.15	.07	.02
Detroit Pistons			
☐ 269 Xavier McDaniel	.08	.04	.01
New York Knicks			
☐ 270 Jeff Sanders	.05	.02	.01
Atlanta Hawks			
☐ 271 Danny Manning	.10	.05	.01
Los Angeles Clippers			
☐ 272 Jayson Williams	.05	.02	.01
Philadelphia 76ers			
☐ 273 Ricky Pierce	.08	.04	.01
Seattle Supersonics			
☐ 274 Will Perdue	.05	.02	.01
Chicago Bulls			
☐ 275 Dana Barros	.05	.02	.01
Seattle Supersonics			
☐ 276 Randy Breuer	.05	.02	.01
Minnesota Timberwolves			
☐ 277 Manute Bol	.05	.02	.01
Philadelphia 76ers			
☐ 278 Negele Knight	.05	.02	.01
Phoenix Suns			
☐ 279 Rodney McCray	.05	.02	.01
Dallas Mavericks			
☐ 280 Greg Sutton	.05	.02	.01
San Antonio Spurs			
☐ 281 Larry Nance	.08	.04	.01
Cleveland Cavaliers			
☐ 282 John Starks	.10	.05	.01
New York Knicks			
☐ 283 Pete Chilcutt	.05	.02	.01
Sacramento Kings			
☐ 284 Kenny Gattison	.05	.02	.01
Charlotte Hornets			
☐ 285 Stacey King	.05	.02	.01
Chicago Bulls			
☐ 286 Bernard King	.10	.05	.01
Washington Bullets			
☐ 287 Larry Johnson	.50	.23	.06
Charlotte Hornets			
☐ 288 John Williams	.08	.04	.01
Cleveland Cavaliers			
☐ 289 Dell Curry	.08	.04	.01
Charlotte Hornets			
☐ 290 Orlando Woolridge	.08	.04	.01
Detroit Pistons			
☐ 291 Nate McMillan	.05	.02	.01
Seattle Supersonics			
☐ 292 Terry Mills	.10	.05	.01
New Jersey Nets			

☐ 293	Sherman Douglas	.05	.02	.01
	Boston Celtics			
☐ 294	Charles Shackleford	.05	.02	.01
	Philadelphia 76ers			
☐ 295	Ken Norman	.05	.02	.01
	Los Angeles Clippers			
☐ 296	LaSalle Thompson	.08	.04	.01
	Indiana Pacers			
☐ 297	Chris Mullin	.15	.07	.02
	Golden State Warriors			
☐ 298	Eddie Johnson	.05	.02	.01
	Seattle Supersonics			
☐ 299	Armon Gilliam	.05	.02	.01
	Philadelphia 76ers			
☐ 300	Michael Cage	.05	.02	.01
	Seattle Supersonics			
☐ 301	Moses Malone	.10	.05	.01
	Milwaukee Bucks			
☐ 302	Charles Oakley	.10	.05	.01
	New York Knicks			
☐ 303	David Wingate	.05	.02	.01
	Washington Bullets			
☐ 304	Steve Kerr	.05	.02	.01
	Cleveland Cavaliers			
☐ 305	Tyrone Hill	.05	.02	.01
	Golden State Warriors			
☐ 306	Mark West	.05	.02	.01
	Phoenix Suns			
☐ 307	Fat Lever	.05	.02	.01
	Dallas Mavericks			
☐ 308	J.R. Reid	.05	.02	.01
	Charlotte Hornets			
☐ 309	Ed Nealy	.05	.02	.01
	Phoenix Suns			
☐ 310	Form Checklist 3	.25	.11	.03
	Michael Jordan			
	Chicago Bulls			
☐ 311	Alaa Abdelnaby	.06	.03	.01
	Boston Celtics			
☐ 312	Stacey Augmon	.10	.05	.01
	Atlanta Hawks			
☐ 313	Anthony Avent	.15	.07	.02
	Milwaukee Bucks			
☐ 314	Walter Bond	.06	.03	.01
	Dallas Mavericks			
☐ 315	Byron Houston	.15	.07	.02
	Golden State Warriors			
☐ 316	Rick Mahorn	.08	.04	.01
	New Jersey Nets			
☐ 317	Sam Mitchell	.06	.03	.01
	Indiana Pacers			
☐ 318	Mookie Blaylock	.08	.04	.01
	Atlanta Hawks			
☐ 319	Lance Blanks	.06	.03	.01
	Minnesota Timberwolves			
☐ 320	John Williams	.06	.03	.01
	Los Angeles Clippers			
☐ 321	Rolando Blackman	.08	.04	.01
	New York Knicks			
☐ 322	Danny Ainge	.10	.05	.01
	Phoenix Suns			
☐ 323	Gerald Glass	.06	.03	.01
	Detroit Pistons			
☐ 324	Robert Pack	.06	.03	.01
	Denver Nuggets			
☐ 325	Oliver Miller	.35	.16	.04
	Phoenix Suns			
☐ 326	Charles Smith	.06	.03	.01
	New York Knicks			
☐ 327	Duane Ferrell	.06	.03	.01
	Atlanta Hawks			
☐ 328	Pooh Richardson	.06	.03	.01
	Indiana Pacers			

☐ 329	Scott Brooks Houston Rockets	.06	.03	.01
☐ 330	Walt Williams Sacramento Kings	.35	.16	.04
☐ 331	Andrew Lang Philadelphia 76ers	.06	.03	.01
☐ 332	Eric Murdock Milwaukee Bucks	.08	.04	.01
☐ 333	Vinny Del Negro San Antonio Spurs	.06	.03	.01
☐ 334	Charles Barkley Phoenix Suns	.50	.23	.06
☐ 335	James Edwards Los Angeles Lakers	.06	.03	.01
☐ 336	Xavier McDaniel Boston Celtics	.10	.05	.01
☐ 337	Paul Graham Atlanta Hawks	.06	.03	.01
☐ 338	David Wingate Charlotte Hornets	.06	.03	.01
☐ 339	Richard Dumas Phoenix Suns	.30	.14	.04
☐ 340	Jay Humphries Utah Jazz	.06	.03	.01
☐ 341	Mark Jackson Los Angeles Clippers	.08	.04	.01
☐ 342	John Salley Miami Heat	.06	.03	.01
☐ 343	Jon Koncak Atlanta Hawks	.06	.03	.01
☐ 344	Rodney McCray Chicago Bulls	.06	.03	.01
☐ 345	Chuck Person Minnesota Timberwolves	.08	.04	.01
☐ 346	Mario Elie Portland Trail Blazers	.06	.03	.01
☐ 347	Frank Johnson Phoenix Suns	.06	.03	.01
☐ 348	Rumeal Robinson New Jersey Nets	.06	.03	.01
☐ 349	Terry Mills Detroit Pistons	.10	.05	.01
☐ 350	Kevin Willis TFC Atlanta Hawks	.06	.03	.01
☐ 351	Dee Brown TFC Boston Celtics	.06	.03	.01
☐ 352	Muggsy Bogues TFC Charlotte Hornets	.08	.04	.01
☐ 353	B.J. Armstrong TFC Chicago Bulls	.08	.04	.01
☐ 354	Larry Nance TFC Cleveland Cavaliers	.08	.04	.01
☐ 355	Doug Smith TFC Dallas Mavericks	.06	.03	.01
☐ 356	Robert Pack TFC Denver Nuggets	.06	.03	.01
☐ 357	Joe Dumars TFC Detroit Pistons	.08	.04	.01
☐ 358	Sarunas Marciulionis TFC Golden State Warriors	.06	.03	.01
☐ 359	Kenny Smith TFC Houston Rockets	.06	.03	.01
☐ 360	Pooh Richardson TFC Indiana Pacers	.06	.03	.01
☐ 361	Mark Jackson TFC Los Angeles Clippers	.06	.03	.01
☐ 362	Sedale Threatt TFC Los Angeles Lakers	.06	.03	.01
☐ 363	Grant Long TFC Miami Heat	.06	.03	.01
☐ 364	Eric Murdock TFC Milwaukee Bucks	.06	.03	.01
☐ 365	Doug West TFC	.06	.03	.01

Minnesota Timberwolves				
☐ 366 Kenny Anderson TFC	.10	.05	.01
New Jersey Nets				
☐ 367 Anthony Mason TFC	.06	.03	.01
New York Knicks				
☐ 368 Nick Anderson TFC	.08	.04	.01
Orlando Magic				
☐ 369 Jeff Hornacek TFC	.08	.04	.01
Philadelphia 76ers				
☐ 370 Dan Majerle TFC	.08	.04	.01
Phoenix Suns				
☐ 371 Cliff Robinson TFC	.08	.04	.01
Portland Trail Blazers				
☐ 372 Lionel Simmons TFC	.06	.03	.01
Sacramento Kings				
☐ 373 Dale Ellis TFC	.06	.03	.01
San Antonio Spurs				
☐ 374 Gary Payton TFC	.08	.04	.01
Seattle Supersonics				
☐ 375 David Benoit TFC	.06	.03	.01
Utah Jazz				
☐ 376 Harvey Grant TFC	.06	.03	.01
Washington Bullets				
☐ 377 Buck Johnson	.06	.03	.01
Washington Bullets				
☐ 378 Brian Howard	.06	.03	.01
Dallas Mavericks				
☐ 379 Travis Mays	.06	.03	.01
Atlanta Hawks				
☐ 380 Jud Buechler	.06	.03	.01
Golden State Warriors				
☐ 381 Matt Geiger	.15	.07	.02
Miami Heat				
☐ 382 Bob McCann	.06	.03	.01
Minnesota Timberwolves				
☐ 383 Cedric Ceballos	.08	.04	.01
Phoenix Suns				
☐ 384 Rod Strickland	.08	.04	.01
Portland Trail Blazers				
☐ 385 Kiki Vandeweghe	.08	.04	.01
Los Angeles Clippers				
☐ 386 Latrell Sprewell	2.00	.90	.25
Golden State Warriors				
☐ 387 Larry Krystkowiak	.06	.03	.01
Utah Jazz				
☐ 388 Dale Ellis	.08	.04	.01
San Antonio Spurs				
☐ 389 Trent Tucker	.06	.03	.01
Chicago Bulls				
☐ 390 Negele Knight	.06	.03	.01
Phoenix Suns				
☐ 391 Stanley Roberts	.06	.03	.01
Los Angeles Clippers				
☐ 392 Tony Campbell	.06	.03	.01
New York Knicks				
☐ 393 Tim Perry	.06	.03	.01
Philadelphia 76ers				
☐ 394 Doug Overton	.06	.03	.01
Washington Bullets				
☐ 395 Dan Majerle	.10	.05	.01
Phoenix Suns				
☐ 396 Duane Cooper	.06	.03	.01
Los Angeles Lakers				
☐ 397 Kevin Willis	.08	.04	.01
Atlanta Hawks				
☐ 398 Micheal Williams	.08	.04	.01
Minnesota Timberwolves				
☐ 399 Avery Johnson	.06	.03	.01
San Antonio Spurs				
☐ 400 Dominique Wilkins	.30	.14	.04
Atlanta Hawks				
☐ 401 Chris Smith	.15	.07	.02
Minnesota Timberwolves				

☐ 402	Blair Rasmussen	.06	.03	.01
	Atlanta Hawks			
☐ 403	Jeff Hornacek	.08	.04	.01
	Philadelphia 76ers			
☐ 404	Blue Edwards	.08	.04	.01
	Milwaukee Bucks			
☐ 405	Olden Polynice	.06	.03	.01
	Detroit Pistons			
☐ 406	Jeff Grayer	.06	.03	.01
	Golden State Warriors			
☐ 407	Tony Bennett	.10	.05	.01
	Charlotte Hornets			
☐ 408	Don MacLean	.30	.14	.04
	Washington Bullets			
☐ 409	Tom Chambers	.10	.05	.01
	Phoenix Suns			
☐ 410	Keith Jennings	.10	.05	.01
	Golden State Warriors			
☐ 411	Gerald Wilkins	.06	.03	.01
	Cleveland Cavaliers			
☐ 412	Kennard Winchester	.06	.03	.01
	Houston Rockets			
☐ 413	Doc Rivers	.08	.04	.01
	New York Knicks			
☐ 414	Brent Price	.15	.07	.02
	Washington Bullets			
☐ 415	Mark West	.06	.03	.01
	Phoenix Suns			
☐ 416	J.R. Reid	.06	.03	.01
	San Antonio Spurs			
☐ 417	Jon Barry	.15	.07	.02
	Milwaukee Bucks			
☐ 418	Kevin Johnson	.10	.05	.01
	Phoenix Suns			
☐ 419	Checklist	.15	.07	.02
☐ 420	Checklist	.15	.07	.02
☐ 421	John Stockton	.07	.03	.01
	Karl Malone			
	NBA All-Star Game			
	Checklist			
☐ 422	Scottie Pippen AS	.20	.09	.03
☐ 423	Larry Johnson AS	.25	.11	.03
☐ 424	Shaquille O'Neal AS	3.00	1.35	.40
☐ 425	Michael Jordan AS	1.00	.45	.13
☐ 426	Isiah Thomas AS	.10	.05	.01
☐ 427	Brad Daugherty AS	.10	.05	.01
☐ 428	Joe Dumars AS	.10	.05	.01
☐ 429	Patrick Ewing AS	.20	.09	.03
☐ 430	Larry Nance AS	.10	.05	.01
☐ 431	Mark Price AS	.10	.05	.01
☐ 432	Detlef Schrempf AS	.10	.05	.01
☐ 433	Dominique Wilkins AS	.15	.07	.02
☐ 434	Karl Malone AS	.12	.05	.02
☐ 435	Charles Barkley AS	.25	.11	.03
☐ 436	David Robinson AS	.25	.11	.03
☐ 437	John Stockton AS	.10	.05	.01
☐ 438	Clyde Drexler AS	.10	.05	.01
☐ 439	Sean Elliott AS	.07	.03	.01
☐ 440	Tim Hardaway AS	.10	.05	.01
☐ 441	Shawn Kemp AS	.40	.18	.05
☐ 442	Dan Majerle AS	.10	.05	.01
☐ 443	Danny Manning AS	.12	.05	.02
☐ 444	Hakeem Olajuwon AS	.40	.18	.05
☐ 445	Terry Porter AS	.07	.03	.01
☐ 446	Harold Miner FACE	.15	.07	.02
	Miami Heat			
☐ 447	David Benoit FACE	.07	.03	.01
	Utah Jazz			
☐ 448	Cedric Ceballos FACE	.10	.05	.01
	Phoenix Suns			
☐ 449	Chris Jackson FACE	.10	.05	.01
	Denver Nuggets			
☐ 450	Tim Perry FACE	.07	.03	.01

	Philadelphia 76ers			
☐ 451	Kenny Smith FACE	.07	.03	.01
	Houston Rockets			
☐ 452	Clarence Weatherspoon	.40	.18	.05
	FACE			
	Philadelphia 76ers			
☐ 453A	Michael Jordan FACE	2.00	.90	.25
	ERR (Slam Dunk Champ			
	in 1985 and 1990)			
	Chicago Bulls			
☐ 453B	Michael Jordan FACE	1.00	.45	.13
	COR (Slam Dunk Champ			
	in 1987 and 1988)			
	Chicago Bulls			
☐ 454A	Dominique Wilkins	.50	.23	.06
	FACE ERR (Slam Dunk Champ			
	in 1987 and 1988)			
	Atlanta Hawks			
☐ 454B	Dominique Wilkins	.15	.07	.02
	FACE COR (Slam Dunk Champ			
	in 1985 and 1990)			
	Atlanta Hawks			
☐ 455	Anthony Peeler	.15	.07	.02
	Duane Cooper CL			
	Los Angeles Lakers			
☐ 456	Adam Keefe TP	.10	.05	.01
	Atlanta Hawks			
☐ 457	Alonzo Mourning TP	1.50	.65	.19
	Charlotte Hornets			
☐ 458	Jim Jackson TP	1.00	.45	.13
	Dallas Mavericks			
☐ 459	Sean Rooks TP	.10	.05	.01
	Dallas Mavericks			
☐ 460	LaPhonso Ellis TP	.40	.18	.05
	Denver Nuggets			
☐ 461	Bryant Stith TP	.15	.07	.02
	Denver Nuggets			
☐ 462	Byron Houston TP	.10	.05	.01
	Golden State Warriors			
☐ 463	Latrell Sprewell TP	1.00	.45	.13
	Golden State Warriors			
☐ 464	Robert Horry TP	.40	.18	.05
	Houston Rockets			
☐ 465	Malik Sealy TP	.10	.05	.01
	Indiana Pacers			
☐ 466	Doug Christie TP	.15	.07	.02
	Los Angeles Lakers			
☐ 467	Duane Cooper TP	.10	.05	.01
	Los Angeles Lakers			
☐ 468	Anthony Peeler TP	.12	.05	.02
	Los Angeles Lakers			
☐ 469	Harold Miner TP	.15	.07	.02
	Miami Heat			
☐ 470	Todd Day TP	.15	.07	.02
	Milwaukee Bucks			
☐ 471	Lee Mayberry TP	.10	.05	.01
	Milwaukee Bucks			
☐ 472	Christian Laettner TP	.40	.18	.05
	Minnesota Timberwolves			
☐ 473	Hubert Davis TP	.15	.07	.02
	New York Knicks			
☐ 474	Shaquille O'Neal TP	3.00	1.35	.40
	Orlando Magic			
☐ 475	Clarence Weatherspoon TP	.40	.18	.05
	Philadelphia 76ers			
☐ 476	Richard Dumas TP	.12	.05	.02
	Phoenix Suns			
☐ 477	Oliver Miller TP	.15	.07	.02
	Phoenix Suns			
☐ 478	Tracy Murray TP	.10	.05	.01
	Portland Trail Blazers			
☐ 479	Walt Williams TP	.15	.07	.02
	Sacramento Kings			

☐ 480	Lloyd Daniels TP	.10	.05	.01
	San Antonio Spurs			
☐ 481	Tom Gugliotta TP	.40	.18	.05
	Washington Bullets			
☐ 482	Brent Price TP	.10	.05	.01
	Washington Bullets			
☐ 483	Mark Aguirre GF	.10	.05	.01
	Detroit Pistons			
☐ 484	Frank Brickowski GF	.07	.03	.01
	Milwaukee Bucks			
☐ 485	Derrick Coleman GF	.10	.05	.01
	New Jersey Nets			
☐ 486	Clyde Drexler GF	.10	.05	.01
	Portland Trail Blazers			
☐ 487	Harvey Grant GF	.07	.03	.01
	Washington Bullets			
☐ 488	Michael Jordan GF	1.00	.45	.13
	Chicago Bulls			
☐ 489	Karl Malone GF	.12	.05	.02
	Utah Jazz			
☐ 490	Xavier McDaniel GF	.10	.05	.01
	Boston Celtics			
☐ 491	Drazen Petrovic GF	.10	.05	.01
	New Jersey Nets			
☐ 492	John Starks GF	.10	.05	.01
	New York Knicks			
☐ 493	Robert Parish GF	.10	.05	.01
	Boston Celtics			
☐ 494	Christian Laettner GF	.40	.18	.05
	Minnesota Timberwolves			
☐ 495	Ron Harper GF	.07	.03	.01
	Los Angeles Clippers			
☐ 496	David Robinson GF	.25	.11	.03
	San Antonio Spurs			
☐ 497	John Salley GF	.07	.03	.01
	Miami Heat			
☐ 498	Brad Daugherty ST	.10	.05	.01
	Mark Price			
	Cleveland Cavaliers			
☐ 499	Dikembe Mutombo ST	.10	.05	.01
	Chris Jackson			
	Denver Nuggets			
☐ 500	Isiah Thomas ST	.10	.05	.01
	Joe Dumars			
	Detroit Pistons			
☐ 501	Hakeem Olajuwon	.30	.14	.04
	Otis Thorpe ST			
	Houston Rockets			
☐ 502	Derrick Coleman ST	.10	.05	.01
	Drazen Petrovic			
	New Jersey Nets			
☐ 503	Terry Porter ST	.07	.03	.01
	Clyde Drexler			
	Portland Trail Blazers			
☐ 504	Lionel Simmons ST	.07	.03	.01
	Mitch Richmond			
	Sacramento Kings			
☐ 505	David Robinson ST	.15	.07	.02
	Sean Elliott			
	San Antonio Spurs			
☐ 506	Michael Jordan FAN	1.00	.45	.13
	Chicago Bulls			
☐ 507	Larry Bird FAN	.40	.18	.05
	Boston Celtics			
☐ 508	Karl Malone FAN	.12	.05	.02
	Utah Jazz			
☐ 509	Dikembe Mutombo FAN	.10	.05	.01
	Denver Nuggets			
☐ 510	Fanimation	.50	.23	.06
	Explanation Card			
☐ SP1	Bird/Magic Retirement	5.00	2.30	.60
	Larry Bird			
	Magic Johnson			

☐ SP2 20,000 Points .... 5.00   2.30   .60
     Dominique Wilkins
     Atlanta Hawks
     (Nov. 6, 1992)
     Michael Jordan
     Chicago Bulls
     (Jan. 8, 1993)

1992-93 Upper Deck All-Division

Inserted one card per second series jumbo pack, this 20-card set consists of Upper Deck's selection of the top five players in each of the NBA's four divisions. There is a special logo representing each division. The cards are arranged according to division as follows: Atlantic (1-5), Central (6-10), Midwest (11-15), and Pacific (16-20). These standard size (2 1/2" by 3 1/2") cards are numbered with an "AD" prefix. The fronts feature full-bleed, color, action player photos. A black and team color-coded bar outlined with gold foil carries the player's name and position. These cards can be distinguished by an All-Division Team icon in the lower left corner above the player's name. The backs display career highlights against a light blue panel. A U.S. map shows the player's division. The cards are numbered on the back.

	MINT	EXC	G-VG
COMPLETE SET (20)	20.00	9.00	2.50
COMMON PLAYER (AD1-AD20)	.25	.11	.03
☐ AD1 Shaquille O'Neal	10.00	4.50	1.25
Orlando Magic			
☐ AD2 Derrick Coleman	.50	.23	.06
New Jersey Nets			
☐ AD3 Glen Rice	.35	.16	.04
Miami Heat			
☐ AD4 Reggie Lewis	.35	.16	.04
Boston Celtics			
☐ AD5 Kenny Anderson	.50	.23	.06
New Jersey Nets			
☐ AD6 Brad Daugherty	.35	.16	.04
Cleveland Cavaliers			
☐ AD7 Dominique Wilkins	1.00	.45	.13
Atlanta Hawks			
☐ AD8 Larry Johnson	1.50	.65	.19
Charlotte Hornets			
☐ AD9 Michael Jordan	6.00	2.70	.75
Chicago Bulls			
☐ AD10 Mark Price	.35	.16	.04
Cleveland Cavaliers			
☐ AD11 David Robinson	1.50	.65	.19
San Antonio Spurs			
☐ AD12 Karl Malone	.75	.35	.09

Utah Jazz			
☐ AD13 Sean Elliott	.25	.11	.03
San Antonio Spurs			
☐ AD14 John Stockton	.50	.23	.06
Utah Jazz			
☐ AD15 Derek Harper	.25	.11	.03
Dallas Mavericks			
☐ AD16 Kevin Duckworth	.25	.11	.03
Portland Trail Blazers			
☐ AD17 Chris Mullin	.40	.18	.05
Golden State Warriors			
☐ AD18 Charles Barkley	1.50	.65	.19
Phoenix Suns			
☐ AD19 Tim Hardaway	.35	.16	.04
Golden State Warriors			
☐ AD20 Clyde Drexler	.50	.23	.06
Portland Trail Blazers			

1992-93 Upper Deck All-NBA

This ten-card insert set featuring the 1991-92 All-NBA team was available in the "Locker Box" low series. Each plastic locker contained four specially wrapped 27-card foil packs, including one "All-NBA team" insert card per pack. The cards measure the standard size (2 1/2" by 3 1/2"). The fronts feature full-bleed color action player photos with black bottom borders. The player's name is foil-stamped in the border, and the words "All-NBA Team" are foil-stamped at the top. Gold and silver foil stamping are used to designate the First (1-5) and Second Teams (6-10) respectively. The backs carry a close-up player photo and career summary. The cards are numbered on the back with an "AN" prefix.

	MINT	EXC	G-VG
COMPLETE SET (10)	25.00	11.50	3.10
COMMON PLAYER (AN1-AN10)	1.00	.45	.13
☐ AN1 Michael Jordan	15.00	6.75	1.90
Chicago Bulls			
☐ AN2 Clyde Drexler	1.50	.65	.19
Portland Trail Blazers			
☐ AN3 David Robinson	5.00	2.30	.60
San Antonio Spurs			
☐ AN4 Karl Malone	2.00	.90	.25
Utah Jazz			
☐ AN5 Chris Mullin	1.25	.55	.16
Golden State Warriors			
☐ AN6 John Stockton	1.25	.55	.16
Utah Jazz			

☐ AN7 Tim Hardaway	1.00	.45	.13
Golden State Warriors			
☐ AN8 Patrick Ewing	3.50	1.55	.45
New York Knicks			
☐ AN9 Scottie Pippen	3.50	1.55	.45
Chicago Bulls			
☐ AN10 Charles Barkley	5.00	2.30	.60
Philadelphia 76ers			

1992-93 Upper Deck All-Rookies

Randomly inserted in retail foil packs at a reported rate of one card for every nine packs, this ten-card subset features the top ten first-year players for the 1991-92 season. Card numbers 1-5 present the first team and card numbers 6-10 the second team. The cards measure the standard size (2 1/2" by 3 1/2"). The cards are numbered with an "AR" prefix. The fronts feature full-bleed, color, action player photos. A gold and red bottom border design carries the player's name, position, the number team (first or second), and an NBA All-Rookie Team icon. The backs carry player profiles. The cards are numbered on the back.

	MINT	EXC	G-VG
COMPLETE SET (10)	10.00	4.50	1.25
COMMON PLAYER (AR1-AR10)	.50	.23	.06
☐ AR1 Larry Johnson	5.00	2.30	.60
Charlotte Hornets			
☐ AR2 Dikembe Mutombo	2.00	.90	.25
Denver Nuggets			
☐ AR3 Billy Owens	1.00	.45	.13
Golden State Warriors			
☐ AR4 Steve Smith	1.25	.55	.16
Miami Heat			
☐ AR5 Stacey Augmon	1.00	.45	.13
Atlanta Hawks			
☐ AR6 Rick Fox	.50	.23	.06
Boston Celtics			
☐ AR7 Terrell Brandon	.50	.23	.06
Cleveland Cavaliers			
☐ AR8 Larry Stewart	.50	.23	.06
Washington Bullets			
☐ AR9 Stanley Roberts	.50	.23	.06
Orlando Magic			
☐ AR10 Mark Macon	.50	.23	.06
Denver Nuggets			

1992-93 Upper Deck Award Winner Holograms

The 1992-93 Upper Deck set features nine holograms depicting league leaders in various statistical categories and honoring award winners such as top Sixth Man, Rookie of the Year, Defensive Player of the Year, and Most Valuable Player. Card numbers 1-6 were randomly inserted in all forms of low series packs while card numbers 7-9 were included in all forms of high series packs. The card numbers have an "AW" prefix. The fronts feature holographic cut-out images of the player against a game-action photo of the player. The player's name and award are displayed at the bottom. The backs carry vertical, color player photos. A light blue plaque-style panel contains information about the player and the award won. The cards are numbered on the back.

	MINT	EXC	G-VG
COMPLETE SET (9)	18.00	8.00	2.30
COMPLETE LO SERIES (6)	10.00	4.50	1.25
COMPLETE HI SERIES (3)	8.00	3.60	1.00
COMMON PLAYER (AW1-AW6)	.75	.35	.09
COMMON PLAYER (AW7-AW9)	.75	.35	.09
☐ AW1 Michael Jordan Chicago Bulls Scoring	6.00	2.70	.75
☐ AW2 John Stockton Utah Jazz Steals	1.00	.45	.13
☐ AW3 Dennis Rodman Detroit Pistons Rebounds	.75	.35	.09
☐ AW4 Detlef Schrempf Indiana Pacers Sixth Man	.75	.35	.09
☐ AW5 Larry Johnson Charlotte Hornets Rookie of the Year	1.50	.65	.19
☐ AW6 David Robinson San Antonio Spurs Blocked Shots	1.75	.80	.22
☐ AW7 David Robinson San Antonio Spurs Def. Player of Year	1.75	.80	.22
☐ AW8 John Stockton Utah Jazz Assists	.75	.35	.09
☐ AW9 Michael Jordan Chicago Bulls Most Valuable Player	6.00	2.70	.75

1992-93 Upper Deck Larry Bird Heroes

Randomly inserted into all forms of high series packs, this ten-card set chronicles the career of Larry Bird from his college days at Indiana State University to pro stardom with the Boston Celtics. The cards measure the standard size (2 1/2" by 3 1/2"). The color action player photos on the fronts are bordered on the left and bottom by black borders that carry the card subtitle and "Basketball Heroes, Larry Bird" respectively. On a background shading from white to green, brief summaries of Bird's career are presented on a center panel. The cards are numbered on the back in continuation of the Upper Deck Basketball Heroes.

	MINT	EXC	G-VG
COMPLETE SET (10)	10.00	4.50	1.25
COMMON BIRD (19-27)	1.00	.45	.13
☐ 19 Larry Bird 1979 College Player of the Year	1.00	.45	.13
☐ 20 Larry Bird 1979-80 Rookie of the Year	1.00	.45	.13
☐ 21 Larry Bird 1980-92 12-Time NBA All-Star	1.00	.45	.13
☐ 22 Larry Bird 1981-86 Three NBA Championships	1.00	.45	.13
☐ 23 Larry Bird 1984-86 3-Time NBA MVP	1.00	.45	.13
☐ 24 Larry Bird 1986-88 3-Point King	1.00	.45	.13
☐ 25 Larry Bird 1990 20,000 Points	1.00	.45	.13
☐ 26 Larry Bird Larry Legend	1.00	.45	.13
☐ 27 Larry Bird (Portrait by Alan Studt)	1.00	.45	.13
☐ NNO Larry Bird Title/Header Card	3.00	1.35	.40

1992-93 Upper Deck Wilt Chamberlain Heroes

This ten-card set honors Wilt Chamberlain by highlighting various points in his career. The cards were randomly inserted in all forms of low series packs. The cards are standard size (2 1/2" by 3 1/2").

	MINT	EXC	G-VG
COMPLETE SET (10)	5.00	2.30	.60
COMMON CHAMBERLAIN (10-18)	.50	.23	.06
☐ 10 1956-58 College Star	.50	.23	.06
☐ 11 1958-59 Harlem Globetrotter	.50	.23	.06
☐ 12 1960 NBA ROY	.50	.23	.06
☐ 13 1962 100-Point Game	.50	.23	.06
☐ 14 1960-68 Four-time NBA MVP	.50	.23	.06
☐ 15 1960-66 Seven consecutive scoring titles	.50	.23	.06
☐ 16 1971-72 30,000-Point Plateau	.50	.23	.06
☐ 17 1978 Basketball HOF	.50	.23	.06
☐ 18 Basketball Heroes CL	.50	.23	.06
☐ NNO Basketball Heroes (Header card)	1.50	.65	.19

1992-93 Upper Deck 15000 Point Club

Randomly inserted in high series hobby packs at a reported rate of one card per nine packs, this 20-card set spotlights active NBA players who have scored more than 15,000 points in their career. The fronts feature full-bleed color action player photos accented at the top and bottom by team color-coded stripes carrying the phrase "15,000 Point Club" and the player's name respectively. A gold 15,000-Point club logo at the lower left corner carries the season the player joined this elite club. The backs display a small player photo and year-by-year scoring totals. The cards are numbered on the back. These standard size (2 1/2" by 3 1/2") cards are numbered with an "PC" prefix.

	MINT	EXC	G-VG
COMPLETE SET (20)	35.00	16.00	4.40
COMMON PLAYER (PC1-PC20)	.75	.35	.09
☐ PC1 Dominique Wilkins Atlanta Hawks	3.00	1.35	.40
☐ PC2 Kevin McHale Boston Celtics	1.00	.45	.13
☐ PC3 Robert Parish Boston Celtics	1.00	.45	.13
☐ PC4 Michael Jordan Chicago Bulls	20.00	9.00	2.50
☐ PC5 Isiah Thomas Detroit Pistons	1.50	.65	.19
☐ PC6 Mark Aguirre Detroit Pistons	1.00	.45	.13

Michael Jordan • G

☐ PC7 Kiki Vandeweghe....................	.75	.35	.09
Los Angeles Clippers			
☐ PC8 James Worthy......................	1.00	.45	.13
Los Angeles Lakers			
☐ PC9 Rolando Blackman.................	.75	.35	.09
New York Knicks			
☐ PC10 Moses Malone.....................	1.00	.45	.13
Milwaukee Bucks			
☐ PC11 Charles Barkley...................	6.00	2.70	.75
Phoenix Suns			
☐ PC12 Tom Chambers...................	.75	.35	.09
Phoenix Suns			
☐ PC13 Clyde Drexler.....................	1.50	.65	.19
Portland Trail Blazers			
☐ PC14 Terry Cummings..................	.75	.35	.09
San Antonio Spurs			
☐ PC15 Eddie Johnson....................	.75	.35	.09
Seattle Supersonics			
☐ PC16 Karl Malone.......................	2.50	1.15	.30
Utah Jazz			
☐ PC17 Bernard King......................	1.00	.45	.13
Washington Bullets			
☐ PC18 Larry Nance.......................	1.00	.45	.13
Cleveland Cavaliers			
☐ PC19 Jeff Malone.......................	.75	.35	.09
Utah Jazz			
☐ PC20 Hakeem Olajuwon................	7.00	3.10	.85
Houston Rockets			

1992-93 Upper Deck Foreign Exchange

Inserted one card per pack in second series locker boxes, this ten-card set showcases foreign players who are stars in the NBA. Each card uses the colors of the flag from the player's homeland as well as a "Foreign Exchange" logo. These standard size (2 1/2" by 3 1/2") cards are numbered with an "FE" prefix. The fronts carry full-bleed, color, action player photos. The player's name, position, and place of birth appear in border stripes at the bottom. The backs display either an action or close-up player photo on a pale beige panel along with a player profile. A small representation of the player's home flag appears at the lower right corner of the picture. The cards are numbered on the back.

	MINT	EXC	G-VG
COMPLETE SET (10)......................	15.00	6.75	1.90
COMMON PLAYER (FE1-FE10)...........	.75	.35	.09
☐ FE1 Manute Bol......................	.75	.35	.09
Philadelphia 76ers			
☐ FE2 Vlade Divac......................	.75	.35	.09
Los Angeles Lakers			

☐	FE3	Patrick Ewing	4.00	1.80	.50
		New York Knicks			
☐	FE4	Sarunas Marciulionis	.75	.35	.09
		Golden State Warriors			
☐	FE5	Dikembe Mutombo	2.00	.90	.25
		Denver Nuggets			
☐	FE6	Hakeem Olajuwon	7.00	3.10	.85
		Houston Rockets			
☐	FE7	Drazen Petrovic	1.00	.45	.13
		New Jersey Nets			
☐	FE8	Detlef Schrempf	1.00	.45	.13
		Indiana Pacers			
☐	FE9	Rik Smits	1.00	.45	.13
		Indiana Pacers			
☐	FE10	Dominique Wilkins	3.00	1.35	.40
		Atlanta Hawks			

1992-93 Upper Deck Rookie Standouts

Randomly inserted in high series retail and jumbo packs at a reported rate of one card per nine packs, this 20-card set honors top rookies who have made the most impact during the 1992-93 NBA season. These standard size (2 1/2" by 3 1/2") cards are numbered on the back with an "RS" prefix. The fronts feature full-bleed, color, action player photos. The player's name and position appear in a teal stripe across the bottom. A "Rookie Standouts" icon overlaps the stripe and the picture at the lower right corner. The backs have a vertical action photo and career highlights within a gold box. A red banner over a gold basketball icon accent the top of the box. The cards are numbered on the back.

	MINT	EXC	G-VG
COMPLETE SET (20)	40.00	18.00	5.00
COMMON PLAYER (RS1-RS20)	.50	.23	.06
□ RS1 Adam Keefe	.50	.23	.06
Atlanta Hawks			
□ RS2 Alonzo Mourning	10.00	4.50	1.25
Charlotte Hornets			
□ RS3 Sean Rooks	.50	.23	.06
Dallas Mavericks			
□ RS4 LaPhonso Ellis	2.50	1.15	.30
Denver Nuggets			
□ RS5 Latrell Sprewell	8.00	3.60	1.00
Golden State Warriors			
□ RS6 Robert Horry	2.50	1.15	.30
Houston Rockets			
□ RS7 Malik Sealy	.75	.35	.09
Indiana Pacers			
□ RS8 Anthony Peeler	1.00	.45	.13
Los Angeles Lakers			
□ RS9 Harold Miner	1.25	.55	.16
Miami Heat			
□ RS10 Anthony Avent	.50	.23	.06
Milwaukee Bucks			
□ RS11 Todd Day	1.25	.55	.16
Milwaukee Bucks			
□ RS12 Lee Mayberry	.50	.23	.06
Milwaukee Bucks			
□ RS13 Christian Laettner	2.50	1.15	.30
Minnesota Timberwolves			
□ RS14 Hubert Davis	1.50	.65	.19
New York Knicks			
□ RS15 Shaquille O'Neal	18.00	8.00	2.30
Orlando Magic			
□ RS16 Clarence Weatherspoon	2.50	1.15	.30
Philadelphia 76ers			
□ RS17 Richard Dumas	.75	.35	.09
Phoenix Suns			
□ RS18 Walt Williams	1.25	.55	.16
Sacramento Kings			
□ RS19 Lloyd Daniels	.50	.23	.06
San Antonio Spurs			
□ RS20 Tom Gugliotta	2.50	1.15	.30
Washington Bullets			

1992-93 Upper Deck Team MVPs

This 28-card set honors a top player from each NBA team. One "Team MVP" card was inserted into each 1992-93 Upper Deck low series jumbo pack. These standard size (2 1/2" by 3 1/2") cards are numbered on the back with a "TM" prefix.

	MINT	EXC	G-VG
COMPLETE SET (28)	35.00	16.00	4.40
COMMON PLAYER (TM1-TM28)	.75	.35	.09
□ TM1 Checklist Card	8.00	3.60	1.00
Michael Jordan			
Chicago Bulls			
□ TM2 Dominique Wilkins	2.50	1.15	.30
Atlanta Hawks			
□ TM3 Reggie Lewis	1.00	.45	.13
Boston Celtics			
□ TM4 Kendall Gill	1.00	.45	.13
Charlotte Hornets			
□ TM5 Michael Jordan	15.00	6.75	1.90
Chicago Bulls			
□ TM6 Brad Daugherty	1.00	.45	.13
Cleveland Cavaliers			
□ TM7 Derek Harper	.75	.35	.09
Dallas Mavericks			

☐ TM8 Dikembe Mutombo	1.75	.80	.22
Denver Nuggets			
☐ TM9 Isiah Thomas	1.25	.55	.16
Detroit Pistons			
☐ TM10 Chris Mullin	1.25	.55	.16
Golden State Warriors			
☐ TM11 Hakeem Olajuwon	6.00	2.70	.75
Houston Rockets			
☐ TM12 Reggie Miller	1.25	.55	.16
Indiana Pacers			
☐ TM13 Ron Harper	.75	.35	.09
Los Angeles Clippers			
☐ TM14 James Worthy	1.00	.45	.13
Los Angeles Lakers			
☐ TM15 Rony Seikaly	1.00	.45	.13
Miami Heat			
☐ TM16 Alvin Robertson	.75	.35	.09
Milwaukee Bucks			
☐ TM17 Pooh Richardson	.75	.35	.09
Minnesota Timberwolves			
☐ TM18 Derrick Coleman	1.50	.65	.19
New Jersey Nets			
☐ TM19 Patrick Ewing	3.50	1.55	.45
New York Knicks			
☐ TM20 Scott Skiles	.75	.35	.09
Orlando Magic			
☐ TM21 Hersey Hawkins	.75	.35	.09
Philadelphia 76ers			
☐ TM22 Kevin Johnson	1.00	.45	.13
Phoenix Suns			
☐ TM23 Clyde Drexler	1.50	.65	.19
Portland Trail Blazers			
☐ TM24 Mitch Richmond	1.00	.45	.13
Sacramento Kings			
☐ TM25 David Robinson	5.00	2.30	.60
San Antonio Spurs			
☐ TM26 Ricky Pierce	.75	.35	.09
Seattle Supersonics			
☐ TM27 John Stockton	1.50	.65	.19
Utah Jazz			
☐ TM28 Pervis Ellison	.75	.35	.09
Washington Bullets			

1992-93 Upper Deck Jerry West Selects

Randomly inserted in low series hobby packs at a reported rate of one card per nine packs, this 20-card set pays tribute to Jerry West's selection of NBA players who are the most dominant in ten different basketball skills. The cards measure the standard size (2 1/2" by 3 1/2")

and feature color action player photos bordered on the right edge by a white stripe containing the player's name. Two stripes border the bottom of the cards, a black stripe containing a gold foil facsimile autograph of Jerry West and the word "Select," and a gradated team-colored stripe. This second stripe contains the player's specific achievement. The backs show a smaller color action shot of the player above a pale gray panel containing comments by West. The right edge of the card has a 1/2" white border containing the player's name. A small cut-out action image of Jerry West appears at the lower right corner. Card numbers 1-10 feature his present selections for best in ten different categories while card numbers 11-20 are his future selections. The cards are numbered on the back with a "JW" prefix.

	MINT	EXC	G-VG
COMPLETE SET (20)	50.00	23.00	6.25
COMMON PLAYER (JW1-JW20)	.75	.35	.09
☐ JW1 Michael Jordan	10.00	4.50	1.25
Chicago Bulls			
Best Shooter			
☐ JW2 Dennis Rodman	.75	.35	.09
Detroit Pistons			
Best Rebounder			
☐ JW3 David Robinson	5.00	2.30	.60
San Antonio Spurs			
Best Shot Blocker			
☐ JW4 Michael Jordan	10.00	4.50	1.25
Chicago Bulls			
Best Defender			
☐ JW5 Magic Johnson	4.00	1.80	.50
Los Angeles Lakers			
Best Point Guard			
☐ JW6 Detlef Schrempf	.75	.35	.09
Indiana Pacers			
Best Sixth Man			
☐ JW7 Magic Johnson	4.00	1.80	.50
Los Angeles Lakers			
Most Inspirational			
Player			
☐ JW8 Michael Jordan	10.00	4.50	1.25
Chicago Bulls			
Best All-Around Player			
☐ JW9 Michael Jordan	10.00	4.50	1.25
Chicago Bulls			
Best Clutch Player			
☐ JW10 Magic Johnson	4.00	1.80	.50
Los Angeles Lakers			
Best Court Leader			
☐ JW11 Glen Rice	1.00	.45	.13
Miami Heat			
Best Shooter			
☐ JW12 Dikembe Mutombo	2.00	.90	.25
Denver Nuggets			
Best Rebounder			
☐ JW13 Dikembe Mutombo	2.00	.90	.25
Denver Nuggets			

		MINT	EXC	G-VG
	Best Shot Blocker			
☐ JW14	Stacey Augmon	1.00	.45	.13
	Atlanta Hawks			
	Best Defender			
☐ JW15	Tim Hardaway	1.00	.45	.13
	Golden State Warriors			
	Best Point Guard			
☐ JW16	Shawn Kemp	8.00	3.60	1.00
	Seattle Supersonics			
	Best Sixth Man			
☐ JW17	Danny Manning	1.00	.45	.13
	Los Angeles Clippers			
	Most Inspirational Player			
☐ JW18	Larry Johnson	5.00	2.30	.60
	Charlotte Hornets			
	Best All-Around Player			
☐ JW19	Reggie Lewis	1.00	.45	.13
	Boston Celtics			
	Best Clutch Player			
☐ JW20	Tim Hardaway	1.00	.45	.13
	Golden State Warriors			
	Best Court Leader			

1993-94 Upper Deck

This 510-card standard-size (2 1/2" by 3 1/2") UV-coated set features glossy color player action photos on the fronts. The left and bottom borders (team colors) contain the team and player's name respectively. The backs feature another color action player photo at the top. At bottom, player stats are shaded in team colors. Topical subsets featured are the following: Season Leaders (166-177), NBA Playoffs Highlights (178-197), NBA Finals Highlights (198-209), Schedules (210-236), Signature Moves (237-251), Executive Board (421-435), Breakaway Threats (436-455), Game Images (456-465), Skylights (467-480), Top Prospects (482-497) and McDonald's Open (498-507). The cards are numbered on the back. The SP3 card was inserted randomly in all forms of first series packaging with the SP4 in the second series. The silver version of the "Trade Upper Deck" card was reportedly available at a ratio of one per.72 packs, could be exchanged for the silver-foil ten-card "NBA Rookie Exchange" set. The gold version, which is four times as scarce as the silver version, could be traded for a gold-foil version of the "NBA Rookie Exchange" set. The "Trade Upper Deck" cards could be mailed in until Dec. 31, 1993, and their redemption for the "NBA Rookie Exchange" set began Jan. 3, 1994. Rookie Cards include Vin Baker, Shawn Bradley, Sam Cassell, Calbert Cheaney, Anfernee Hardaway, Lindsey Hunter, Bobby Hurley, Toni Kukoc, Jamal Mashburn, Dino Radja, Isaiah Rider, Nick Van Exel and Chris Webber.

	MINT	EXC	G-VG
COMPLETE SET (510)	35.00	16.00	4.40
COMPLETE SERIES 1 (255)	15.00	6.75	1.90
COMPLETE SERIES 2 (255)	20.00	9.00	2.50

COMMON PLAYER (1-255)		.05	.02	.01
COMMON PLAYER (256-510)		.05	.02	.01
☐ 1	Muggsy Bogues Charlotte Hornets	.10	.05	.01
☐ 2	Kenny Anderson New Jersey Nets	.20	.09	.03
☐ 3	Dell Curry Charlotte Hornets	.08	.04	.01
☐ 4	Charles Smith New York Knicks	.05	.02	.01
☐ 5	Chuck Person Minnesota Timberwolves	.08	.04	.01
☐ 6	Chucky Brown New Jersey Nets	.05	.02	.01
☐ 7	Kevin Johnson Phoenix Suns	.10	.05	.01
☐ 8	Winston Garland Houston Rockets	.05	.02	.01
☐ 9	John Salley Miami Heat	.05	.02	.01
☐ 10	Dale Ellis San Antonio Spurs	.08	.04	.01
☐ 11	Otis Thorpe Houston Rockets	.08	.04	.01
☐ 12	John Stockton Utah Jazz	.20	.09	.03
☐ 13	Kendall Gill Charlotte Hornets	.08	.04	.01
☐ 14	Randy White Dallas Mavericks	.05	.02	.01
☐ 15	Mark Jackson Los Angeles Clippers	.08	.04	.01
☐ 16	Vlade Divac Los Angeles Lakers	.05	.02	.01
☐ 17	Scott Skiles Miami Heat	.05	.02	.01
☐ 18	Xavier McDaniel Boston Celtics	.10	.05	.01
☐ 19	Jeff Hornacek Philadelphia 76ers	.08	.04	.01
☐ 20	Stanley Roberts Los Angeles Clippers	.05	.02	.01
☐ 21	Harold Miner Miami Heat	.08	.04	.01
☐ 22	Terrell Brandon Cleveland Cavaliers	.05	.02	.01
☐ 23	Michael Jordan Chicago Bulls	2.50	1.15	.30
☐ 24	Jim Jackson Dallas Mavericks	.35	.16	.04
☐ 25	Keith Askins Miami Heat	.05	.02	.01
☐ 26	Corey Williams Chicago Bulls	.05	.02	.01
☐ 27	David Benoit Utah Jazz	.05	.02	.01
☐ 28	Charles Oakley New York Knicks	.10	.05	.01
☐ 29	Michael Adams Washington Bullets	.08	.04	.01
☐ 30	Clarence Weatherspoon Philadelphia 76ers	.10	.05	.01
☐ 31	Jon Koncak Atlanta Hawks	.05	.02	.01
☐ 32	Gerald Wilkins Cleveland Cavaliers	.05	.02	.01
☐ 33	Anthony Bowie Orlando Magic	.05	.02	.01
☐ 34	Willie Burton Miami Heat	.05	.02	.01
☐ 35	Stacey Augmon Atlanta Hawks	.10	.05	.01

☐ 36	Doc Rivers	.08	.04	.01
	New York Knicks			
☐ 37	Luc Longley	.05	.02	.01
	Minnesota Timberwolves			
☐ 38	Dee Brown	.05	.02	.01
	Boston Celtics			
☐ 39	Litterial Green	.05	.02	.01
	Orlando Magic			
☐ 40	Dan Majerle	.10	.05	.01
	Phoenix Suns			
☐ 41	Doug West	.05	.02	.01
	Minnesota Timberwolves			
☐ 42	Joe Dumars	.20	.09	.03
	Detroit Pistons			
☐ 43	Dennis Scott	.08	.04	.01
	Orlando Magic			
☐ 44	Mahmoud Abdul-Rauf	.05	.02	.01
	Denver Nuggets			
	(formerly Chris Jackson)			
☐ 45	Mark Eaton	.05	.02	.01
	Utah Jazz			
☐ 46	Danny Ferry	.05	.02	.01
	Cleveland Cavaliers			
☐ 47	Kenny Smith	.05	.02	.01
	Houston Rockets			
☐ 48	Ron Harper	.08	.04	.01
	Los Angeles Clippers			
☐ 49	Adam Keefe	.05	.02	.01
	Atlanta Hawks			
☐ 50	David Robinson	.60	.25	.08
	San Antonio Spurs			
☐ 51	John Starks	.10	.05	.01
	New York Knicks			
☐ 52	Jeff Malone	.08	.04	.01
	Utah Jazz			
☐ 53	Vern Fleming	.05	.02	.01
	Indiana Pacers			
☐ 54	Olden Polynice	.05	.02	.01
	Los Angeles Clippers			
☐ 55	Dikembe Mutombo	.10	.05	.01
	Denver Nuggets			
☐ 56	Chris Morris	.05	.02	.01
	New Jersey Nets			
☐ 57	Paul Graham	.05	.02	.01
	Atlanta Hawks			
☐ 58	Richard Dumas	.08	.04	.01
	Phoenix Suns			
☐ 59	J.R. Reid	.05	.02	.01
	San Antonio Spurs			
☐ 60	Brad Daugherty	.10	.05	.01
	Cleveland Cavaliers			
☐ 61	Blue Edwards	.05	.02	.01
	Milwaukee Bucks			
☐ 62	Mark Macon	.05	.02	.01
	Denver Nuggets			
☐ 63	Latrell Sprewell	.50	.23	.06
	Golden State Warriors			
☐ 64	Mitch Richmond	.10	.05	.01
	Sacramento Kings			
☐ 65	David Wingate	.05	.02	.01
	Charlotte Hornets			
☐ 66	LaSalle Thompson	.08	.04	.01
	Indiana Pacers			
☐ 67	Sedale Threatt	.05	.02	.01
	Los Angeles Lakers			
☐ 68	Larry Krystkowiak	.05	.02	.01
	Utah Jazz			
☐ 69	John Paxson	.08	.04	.01
	Chicago Bulls			
☐ 70	Frank Brickowski	.08	.04	.01
	Milwaukee Bucks			
☐ 71	Duane Causwell	.05	.02	.01
	Sacramento Kings			

☐ 72 Fred Roberts	.05	.02	.01
Milwaukee Bucks			
☐ 73 Rod Strickland	.08	.04	.01
Portland Trail Blazers			
☐ 74 Willie Anderson	.05	.02	.01
San Antonio Spurs			
☐ 75 Thurl Bailey	.05	.02	.01
Utah Jazz			
☐ 76 Ricky Pierce	.08	.04	.01
Seattle Supersonics			
☐ 77 Todd Day	.08	.04	.01
Milwaukee Bucks			
☐ 78 Hot Rod Williams	.05	.02	.01
Cleveland Cavaliers			
☐ 79 Danny Ainge	.10	.05	.01
Phoenix Suns			
☐ 80 Mark West	.05	.02	.01
Phoenix Suns			
☐ 81 Marcus Liberty	.05	.02	.01
Denver Nuggets			
☐ 82 Keith Jennings	.05	.02	.01
Golden State Warriors			
☐ 83 Derrick Coleman	.25	.11	.03
New Jersey Nets			
☐ 84 Larry Stewart	.05	.02	.01
Washington Bullets			
☐ 85 Tracy Murray	.05	.02	.01
Portland Trail Blazers			
☐ 86 Robert Horry	.10	.05	.01
Houston Rockets			
☐ 87 Derek Harper	.08	.04	.01
Dallas Mavericks			
☐ 88 Scott Hastings	.05	.02	.01
Denver Nuggets			
☐ 89 Sam Perkins	.08	.04	.01
Seattle Supersonics			
☐ 90 Clyde Drexler	.20	.09	.03
Seattle Supersonics			
☐ 91 Brent Price	.05	.02	.01
Washington Bullets			
☐ 92 Chris Mullin	.20	.09	.03
Golden State Warriors			
☐ 93 Rafael Addison	.05	.02	.01
New Jersey Nets			
☐ 94 Tyrone Corbin	.05	.02	.01
Minnesota Timberwolves			
☐ 95 Sarunas Marciulionis	.08	.04	.01
Golden State Warriors			
☐ 96 Antoine Carr	.05	.02	.01
San Antonio Spurs			
☐ 97 Tony Bennett	.05	.02	.01
Charlotte Hornets			
☐ 98 Sam Mitchell	.05	.02	.01
Indiana Pacers			
☐ 99 Lionel Simmons	.08	.04	.01
Sacramento Kings			
☐ 100 Tim Perry	.05	.02	.01
Phoenix Suns			
☐ 101 Horace Grant	.10	.05	.01
Chicago Bulls			
☐ 102 Tom Hammonds	.05	.02	.01
Denver Nuggets			
☐ 103 Walter Bond	.05	.02	.01
Dallas Mavericks			
☐ 104 Detlef Schrempf	.10	.05	.01
Indiana Pacers			
☐ 105 Terry Porter	.08	.04	.01
Portland Trail Blazers			
☐ 106 Dan Schayes	.05	.02	.01
Milwaukee Bucks			
☐ 107 Rumeal Robinson	.05	.02	.01
New Jersey Nets			
☐ 108 Gerald Glass	.05	.02	.01

☐	109	Mike Gminski Detroit Pistons	.05	.02	.01
☐	110	Terry Mills Charlotte Hornets	.08	.04	.01
☐	111	Loy Vaught Detroit Pistons	.08	.04	.01
☐	112	Jim Les Los Angeles Clippers	.05	.02	.01
☐	113	Byron Houston Sacramento Kings	.05	.02	.01
☐	114	Randy Brown Golden State Warriors	.05	.02	.01
☐	115	Anthony Avent Sacramento Kings	.05	.02	.01
☐	116	Donald Hodge Milwaukee Bucks	.05	.02	.01
☐	117	Kevin Willis Dallas Mavericks	.08	.04	.01
☐	118	Robert Pack Atlanta Hawks	.05	.02	.01
☐	119	Dale Davis Denver Nuggets	.08	.04	.01
☐	120	Grant Long Indiana Pacers	.05	.02	.01
☐	121	Anthony Bonner Miami Heat	.05	.02	.01
☐	122	Chris Smith Sacramento Kings	.05	.02	.01
☐	123	Elden Campbell Minnesota Timberwolves	.05	.02	.01
☐	124	Cliff Robinson Los Angeles Lakers	.10	.05	.01
☐	125	Sherman Douglas Portland Trail Blazers	.05	.02	.01
☐	126	Alvin Robertson Boston Celtics	.08	.04	.01
☐	127	Rolando Blackman Milwaukee Bucks	.08	.04	.01
☐	128	Malik Sealy New York Knicks	.05	.02	.01
☐	129	Ed Pinckney Indiana Pacers	.05	.02	.01
☐	130	Anthony Peeler Boston Celtics	.08	.04	.01
☐	131	Scott Brooks Los Angeles Lakers	.05	.02	.01
☐	132	Rik Smits Houston Rockets	.08	.04	.01
☐	133	Derrick McKey Indiana Pacers	.05	.02	.01
☐	134	Alaa Abdelnaby Seattle Supersonics	.05	.02	.01
☐	135	Rex Chapman Boston Celtics	.05	.02	.01
☐	136	Tony Campbell Washington Bullets	.05	.02	.01
☐	137	John Williams New York Knicks	.05	.02	.01
☐	138	Vincent Askew Los Angeles Clippers	.05	.02	.01
☐	139	LaBradford Smith Seattle Supersonics	.05	.02	.01
☐	140	Vinny Del Negro Washington Bullets	.05	.02	.01
☐	141	Darrell Walker San Antonio Spurs	.05	.02	.01
☐	142	James Worthy Chicago Bulls	.10	.05	.01
☐	143	Jeff Turner Los Angeles Lakers	.05	.02	.01
☐	144	Duane Ferrell Orlando Magic	.05	.02	.01
		Atlanta Hawks			

☐ 145	Larry Smith	.08	.04	.01
	Houston Rockets			
☐ 146	Eddie Johnson	.05	.02	.01
	Seattle Supersonics			
☐ 147	Chris Gatling	.05	.02	.01
	Golden State Warriors			
☐ 148	Buck Williams	.10	.05	.01
	Portland Trail Blazers			
☐ 149	Donald Royal	.05	.02	.01
	Orlando Magic			
☐ 150	Dino Radja	.50	.23	.06
	Boston Celtics			
☐ 151	Johnny Dawkins	.05	.02	.01
	Philadelphia 76ers			
☐ 152	Tim Legler	.15	.07	.02
	Dallas Mavericks			
☐ 153	Bill Laimbeer	.10	.05	.01
	Detroit Pistons			
☐ 154	Glen Rice	.10	.05	.01
	Miami Heat			
☐ 155	Bill Cartwright	.08	.04	.01
	Chicago Bulls			
☐ 156	Luther Wright	.15	.07	.02
	Utah Jazz			
☐ 157	Rex Walters	.15	.07	.02
	New Jersey Nets			
☐ 158	Doug Edwards	.15	.07	.02
	Atlanta Hawks			
☐ 159	George Lynch	.25	.11	.03
	Los Angeles Lakers			
☐ 160	Chris Mills	.30	.14	.04
	Cleveland Cavaliers			
☐ 161	Sam Cassell	.60	.25	.08
	Houston Rockets			
☐ 162	Nick Van Exel	.50	.23	.06
	Los Angeles Lakers			
☐ 163	Shawn Bradley	.50	.23	.06
	Philadelphia 76ers			
☐ 164	Calbert Cheaney	.50	.23	.06
	Washington Bullets			
☐ 165	Corie Blount	.15	.07	.02
	Chicago Bulls			
☐ 166	Michael Jordan SL	1.25	.55	.16
	Chicago Bulls			
	Scoring			
☐ 167	Dennis Rodman SL	.05	.02	.01
	Detroit Pistons			
	Rebounds			
☐ 168	John Stockton SL	.12	.05	.02
	Utah Jazz			
	Assists			
☐ 169	B.J. Armstrong SL	.10	.05	.01
	Chicago Bulls			
	3-pt. field goals			
☐ 170	Hakeem Olajuwon SL	.40	.18	.05
	Houston Rockets			
	Blocked shots			
☐ 171	Michael Jordan SL	1.25	.55	.16
	Chicago Bulls			
	Steals			
☐ 172	Cedric Ceballos SL	.08	.04	.01
	Phoenix Suns			
	Field goal percentage			
☐ 173	Mark Price SL	.08	.04	.01
	Cleveland Cavaliers			
	Free-throw percentage			
☐ 174	Charles Barkley SL	.30	.14	.04
	Phoenix Suns			
	MVP			
☐ 175	Cliff Robinson SL	.08	.04	.01
	Portland Trail Blazers			
	Sixth man			
☐ 176	Hakeem Olajuwon SL	.40	.18	.05

Houston Rockets
Defensive player
- [ ] 177 Shaquille O'Neal SL............ 1.00   .45   .13
Orlando Magic
ROY
- [ ] 178 1st Round: Knicks 3,............ .08   .04   .01
Pacers 1 PH
Charles Oakley
Reggie Miller
Doc Rivers
- [ ] 179 1st Round: Hornets 3,............ .05   .02   .01
Celtics 1 PH
Rick Fox
Kenny Gattison
- [ ] 180 1st Round: Bulls 3,............ .50   .23   .06
Hawks 0 PH
Michael Jordan
Stacey Augmon
- [ ] 181 1st Round: Cavs 3,............ .05   .02   .01
Nets 2 PH
Brad Daugherty
- [ ] 182 1st Round: Suns 3,............ .05   .02   .01
Lakers 2 PH
Byron Scott
Oliver Miller
- [ ] 183 1st Round: Spurs 3,............ .15   .07   .02
Trail Blazers 1 PH
Sean Elliott
David Robinson
- [ ] 184 1st Round: Rockets 3,............ .05   .02   .01
Clippers 2 PH
Kenny Smith
Mark Jackson
- [ ] 185 1st Round: Sonics............ .05   .02   .01
3, Jazz 2 PH
Eddie Johnson
- [ ] 186 East Semis: Knicks............ .08   .04   .01
4, Hornets 1 PH
Anthony Mason
Patrick Ewing
Alonzo Mourning
- [ ] 187 East Semis: Bulls 4,............ .50   .23   .06
Cavaliers 0 PH
Michael Jordan
Gerald Wilkins
- [ ] 188 West Semis: Suns 4,............ .05   .02   .01
Spurs 2 PH
Oliver Miller
- [ ] 189 West Semis: Sonics 4,............ .08   .04   .01
Rockets 3 PH
Sam Perkins
Hakeem Olajuwon
- [ ] 190 East Finals: Bulls 4,............ .08   .04   .01
Knicks 2 PH
Bill Cartwright
- [ ] 191 West Finals: Suns 4,............ .08   .04   .01
Supersonics 3 PH
Kevin Johnson
- [ ] 192 Majerle hits record............ .05   .02   .01
eight treys PH
Dan Majerle
- [ ] 193 Jordan scores 54............ 1.25   .55   .16
points PH
Michael Jordan
Charles Oakley
John Starks
- [ ] 194 Hornets win first............ .15   .07   .02
series PH
Larry Johnson
Muggsy Bogues
- [ ] 195 Miller ties Playoffs............ .08   .04   .01
free-throw mark PH
Reggie Miller

☐ 196	Bulls and Knicks renew rivalry PH John Starks Scottie Pippen	.08	.04	.01
☐ 197	Lakers give Suns wake-up call PH Sedale Threatt Vlade Divac Charles Barkley	.08	.04	.01
☐ 198	Michael Jordan G1 Game One Finals	1.25	.55	.16
☐ 199	Scottie Pippen G2 Game Two Finals	.20	.09	.03
☐ 200	Kevin Johnson G3 Game Three Finals	.08	.04	.01
☐ 201	Michael Jordan G4 Game Four Finals	1.25	.55	.16
☐ 202	Richard Dumas G5 Game Five Finals	.05	.02	.01
☐ 203	Horace Grant G6 Game Six Finals	.08	.04	.01
☐ 204	Michael Jordan 1993 Finals MVP	1.25	.55	.16
☐ 205	Triple Overtime 1993 Finals Charles Barkley Scottie Pippen Tom Chambers Scott Williams	.08	.04	.01
☐ 206	John Paxson Hits 3 for title	.08	.04	.01
☐ 207	B.J. Armstrong Finals records	.10	.05	.01
☐ 208	1992-93 Bulls Road to 1993 Finals	.08	.04	.01
☐ 209	1992-93 Suns Road to 1993 Finals	.08	.04	.01
☐ 210	Atlanta Hawks Sked	.05	.02	.01
☐ 211	Boston Celtics Sked	.08	.04	.01
☐ 212	Charlotte Hornets Sked	.05	.02	.01
☐ 213	Chicago Bulls Sked (Michael Jordan)	.10	.05	.01
☐ 214	Cleveland Cavaliers Sked (Mark Price)	.05	.02	.01
☐ 215	Dallas Mavericks Sked (Jim Jackson and Sean Rooks)	.15	.07	.02
☐ 216	Denver Nuggets Sked	.05	.02	.01
☐ 217	Detroit Pistons Sked (Isiah Thomas)	.08	.04	.01
☐ 218	Golden State Warriors Sked	.05	.02	.01
☐ 219	Houston Rockets Sked (Hakeem Olajuwon)	.08	.04	.01
☐ 220	Indiana Pacers Sked (Rik Smits)	.08	.04	.01
☐ 221	L.A. Clippers Sked	.05	.02	.01
☐ 222	L.A. Lakers Sked	.05	.02	.01
☐ 223	Miami Heat Sked	.05	.02	.01
☐ 224	Milwaukee Bucks Sked	.05	.02	.01
☐ 225	Minnesota Timberwolves Sked	.05	.02	.01
☐ 226	New Jersey Nets Sked	.05	.02	.01
☐ 227	New York Knicks Sked	.05	.02	.01
☐ 228	Orlando Magic Sked (Shaquille O'Neal)	.50	.23	.06
☐ 229	Philadelphia 76ers Sked (Hersey Hawkins)	.08	.04	.01
☐ 230	Phoenix Suns Sked (Charles Barkley)	.05	.02	.01
☐ 231	Portland Trail Blazers Sked (Jerome Kersey) and Terry Porter)	.05	.02	.01

☐ 232	Sacramento Kings Sked	.05	.02	.01
☐ 233	San Antonio Spurs Sked	.08	.04	.01
	(David Robinson)			
☐ 234	Seattle SuperSonics	.05	.02	.01
	Sked			
☐ 235	Utah Jazz Sked	.05	.02	.01
☐ 236	Washington Bullets	.05	.02	.01
	Sked (Michael Adams)			
☐ 237	Michael Jordan SM	1.25	.55	.16
	Chicago Bulls			
☐ 238	Clyde Drexler SM	.12	.05	.02
	Portland Trail Blazers			
☐ 239	Tim Hardaway SM	.08	.04	.01
	Golden State Warriors			
☐ 240	Dominique Wilkins SM	.15	.07	.02
	Atlanta Hawks			
☐ 241	Brad Daugherty SM	.08	.04	.01
	Cleveland Cavaliers			
☐ 242	Chris Mullin SM	.10	.05	.01
	Golden State Warriors			
☐ 243	Kenny Anderson SM	.08	.04	.01
	New Jersey Nets			
☐ 244	Patrick Ewing SM	.20	.09	.03
	New York Knicks			
☐ 245	Isiah Thomas SM	.10	.05	.01
	Detroit Pistons			
☐ 246	Dikembe Mutombo SM	.08	.04	.01
	Denver Nuggets			
☐ 247	Danny Manning SM	.08	.04	.01
	Los Angeles Clippers			
☐ 248	David Robinson SM	.30	.14	.04
	San Antonio Spurs			
☐ 249	Karl Malone SM	.15	.07	.02
	Utah Jazz			
☐ 250	James Worthy SM	.08	.04	.01
	Los Angeles Lakers			
☐ 251	Shawn Kemp SM	.20	.09	.03
	Seattle Supersonics			
☐ 252	Checklist 1-64	.05	.02	.01
☐ 253	Checklist 65-128	.05	.02	.01
☐ 254	Checklist 129-192	.05	.02	.01
☐ 255	Checklist 193-255	.05	.02	.01
☐ 256	Patrick Ewing	.40	.18	.05
	New York Knicks			
☐ 257	B.J. Armstrong	.10	.05	.01
	Chicago Bulls			
☐ 258	Oliver Miller	.10	.05	.01
	Phoenix Suns			
☐ 259	Jud Buechler	.05	.02	.01
	Golden State Warriors			
☐ 260	Pooh Richardson	.05	.02	.01
	Indiana Pacers			
☐ 261	Victor Alexander	.05	.02	.01
	Golden State Warriors			
☐ 262	Kevin Gamble	.05	.02	.01
	Boston Celtics			
☐ 263	Doug Smith	.05	.02	.01
	Dallas Mavericks			
☐ 264	Isiah Thomas	.20	.09	.03
	Detroit Pistons			
☐ 265	Doug Christie	.08	.04	.01
	Los Angeles Lakers			
☐ 266	Mark Bryant	.05	.02	.01
	Portland Trail Blazers			
☐ 267	Lloyd Daniels	.05	.02	.01
	San Antonio Spurs			
☐ 268	Micheal Williams	.08	.04	.01
	Minnesota Timberwolves			
☐ 269	Nick Anderson	.08	.04	.01
	Orlando Magic			
☐ 270	Tom Gugliotta	.08	.04	.01
	Washington Bullets			
☐ 271	Kenny Gattison	.05	.02	.01

	Charlotte Hornets			
☐ 272	Vernon Maxwell	.08	.04	.01
	Houston Rockets			
☐ 273	Terry Cummings	.08	.04	.01
	San Antonio Spurs			
☐ 274	Karl Malone	.30	.14	.04
	Utah Jazz			
☐ 275	Rick Fox	.05	.02	.01
	Boston Celtics			
☐ 276	Matt Bullard	.05	.02	.01
	Houston Rockets			
☐ 277	Johnny Newman	.05	.02	.01
	Charlotte Hornets			
☐ 278	Mark Price	.10	.05	.01
	Cleveland Cavaliers			
☐ 279	Mookie Blaylock	.08	.04	.01
	Atlanta Hawks			
☐ 280	Charles Barkley	.60	.25	.08
	Phoenix Suns			
☐ 281	Larry Nance	.08	.04	.01
	Cleveland Cavaliers			
☐ 282	Walt Williams	.08	.04	.01
	Sacramento Kings			
☐ 283	Brian Shaw	.05	.02	.01
	Miami Heat			
☐ 284	Robert Parish	.10	.05	.01
	Boston Celtics			
☐ 285	Pervis Ellison	.05	.02	.01
	Washington Bullets			
☐ 286	Spud Webb	.10	.05	.01
	Sacramento Kings			
☐ 287	Hakeem Olajuwon	1.00	.45	.13
	Houston Rockets			
☐ 288	Jerome Kersey	.05	.02	.01
	Portland Trail Blazers			
☐ 289	Carl Herrera	.05	.02	.01
	Houston Rockets			
☐ 290	Dominique Wilkins	.30	.14	.04
	Atlanta Hawks			
☐ 291	Billy Owens	.08	.04	.01
	Golden State Warriors			
☐ 292	Greg Anthony	.05	.02	.01
	New York Knicks			
☐ 293	Nate McMillan	.05	.02	.01
	Seattle Supersonics			
☐ 294	Christian Laettner	.08	.04	.01
	Minnesota Timberwolves			
☐ 295	Gary Payton	.10	.05	.01
	Seattle Supersonics			
☐ 296	Steve Smith	.08	.04	.01
	Miami Heat			
☐ 297	Anthony Mason	.05	.02	.01
	New York Knicks			
☐ 298	Sean Rooks	.05	.02	.01
	Dallas Mavericks			
☐ 299	Toni Kukoc	.50	.23	.06
	Chicago Bulls			
☐ 300	Shaquille O'Neal	2.00	.90	.25
	Orlando Magic			
☐ 301	Jay Humphries	.05	.02	.01
	Utah Jazz			
☐ 302	Sleepy Floyd	.05	.02	.01
	San Antonio Spurs			
☐ 303	Bimbo Coles	.05	.02	.01
	Miami Heat			
☐ 304	John Battle	.05	.02	.01
	Atlanta Hawks			
☐ 305	Shawn Kemp	.40	.18	.05
	Seattle Supersonics			
☐ 306	Scott Williams	.05	.02	.01
	Chicago Bulls			
☐ 307	Wayman Tisdale	.08	.04	.01
	Sacramento Kings			

☐ 308	Rony Seikaly Miami Heat	.10	.05	.01
☐ 309	Reggie Miller Indiana Pacers	.25	.11	.03
☐ 310	Scottie Pippen Chicago Bulls	.40	.18	.05
☐ 311	Chris Webber Golden State Warriors	3.00	1.35	.40
☐ 312	Trevor Wilson Los Angeles Lakers	.05	.02	.01
☐ 313	Derek Strong Milwaukee Bucks	.15	.07	.02
☐ 314	Bobby Hurley Sacramento Kings	.50	.23	.06
☐ 315	Herb Williams New York Knicks	.05	.02	.01
☐ 316	Rex Walters New Jersey Nets	.05	.02	.01
☐ 317	Doug Edwards Atlanta Hawks	.05	.02	.01
☐ 318	Ken Williams Indiana Pacers	.05	.02	.01
☐ 319	Jon Barry Milwaukee Bucks	.05	.02	.01
☐ 320	Joe Courtney Phoenix Suns	.15	.07	.02
☐ 321	Ervin Johnson Seattle Supersonics	.15	.07	.02
☐ 322	Sam Cassell Houston Rockets	.30	.14	.04
☐ 323	Tim Hardaway Golden State Warriors	.10	.05	.01
☐ 324	Ed Stokes Miami Heat	.05	.02	.01
☐ 325	Steve Kerr Chicago Bulls	.05	.02	.01
☐ 326	Doug Overton Washington Bullets	.05	.02	.01
☐ 327	Reggie Williams Portland Trail Blazers	.05	.02	.01
☐ 328	Avery Johnson Golden State Warriors	.05	.02	.01
☐ 329	Stacey King Chicago Bulls	.05	.02	.01
☐ 330	Vin Baker Milwaukee Bucks	.75	.35	.09
☐ 331	Greg Kite Orlando Magic	.05	.02	.01
☐ 332	Michael Cage Seattle Supersonics	.05	.02	.01
☐ 333	Alonzo Mourning Charlotte Hornets	.75	.35	.09
☐ 334	Acie Earl Boston Celtics	.15	.07	.02
☐ 335	Terry Dehere Los Angeles Clippers	.15	.07	.02
☐ 336	Negele Knight San Antonio Spurs	.05	.02	.01
☐ 337	Gerald Madkins Cleveland Cavaliers	.15	.07	.02
☐ 338	Lindsey Hunter Detroit Pistons	.50	.23	.06
☐ 339	Luther Wright Utah Jazz	.05	.02	.01
☐ 340	Mike Peplowski Sacramento Kings	.15	.07	.02
☐ 341	Gerald Paddio Indiana Pacers	.25	.11	.03
☐ 342	Danny Manning Los Angeles Clippers	.10	.05	.01
☐ 343	Chris Mills Cleveland Cavaliers	.15	.07	.02
☐ 344	Kevin Lynch	.05	.02	.01

	Charlotte Hornets			
☐ 345	Shawn Bradley	.25	.11	.03
	Philadelphia 76ers			
☐ 346	Evers Burns	.15	.07	.02
	Sacramento Kings			
☐ 347	Rodney Rogers	.30	.14	.04
	Denver Nuggets			
☐ 348	Cedric Ceballos	.10	.05	.01
	Phoenix Suns			
☐ 349	Warren Kidd	.15	.07	.02
	Philadelphia 76ers			
☐ 350	Darnell Mee	.15	.07	.02
	Denver Nuggets			
☐ 351	Matt Geiger	.05	.02	.01
	Miami Heat			
☐ 352	Jamal Mashburn	1.25	.55	.16
	Dallas Mavericks			
☐ 353	Antonio Davis	.30	.14	.04
	Indiana Pacers			
☐ 354	Calbert Cheaney	.25	.11	.03
	Washington Bullets			
☐ 355	George Lynch	.15	.07	.02
	Los Angeles Lakers			
☐ 356	Derrick McKey	.05	.02	.01
	Indiana Pacers			
☐ 357	Jerry Reynolds	.05	.02	.01
	Orlando Magic			
☐ 358	Don MacLean	.08	.04	.01
	Washington Bullets			
☐ 359	Scott Haskin	.15	.07	.02
	Indiana Pacers			
☐ 360	Malcolm Mackey	.15	.07	.02
	Phoenix Suns			
☐ 361	Isaiah Rider	1.25	.55	.16
	Minnesota Timberwolves			
☐ 362	Detlef Schrempf	.10	.05	.01
	Seattle Supersonics			
☐ 363	Josh Grant	.15	.07	.02
	Golden State Warriors			
☐ 364	Richard Petruska	.05	.02	.01
	Houston Rockets			
☐ 365	Larry Johnson	.35	.16	.04
	Charlotte Hornets			
☐ 366	Felton Spencer	.15	.07	.02
	Utah Jazz			
☐ 367	Ken Norman	.05	.02	.01
	Milwaukee Bucks			
☐ 368	Anthony Cook	.05	.02	.01
	Orlando Magic			
☐ 369	James Robinson	.20	.09	.03
	Portland Trail Blazers			
☐ 370	Kevin Duckworth	.05	.02	.01
	Washington Bullets			
☐ 371	Chris Whitney	.15	.07	.02
	San Antonio Spurs			
☐ 372	Moses Malone	.10	.05	.01
	Philadelphia 76ers			
☐ 373	Nick Van Exel	.25	.11	.03
	Los Angeles Lakers			
☐ 374	Scott Burrell	.20	.09	.03
	Charlotte Hornets			
☐ 375	Harvey Grant	.05	.02	.01
	Portland Trail Blazers			
☐ 376	Benoit Benjamin	.05	.02	.01
	New Jersey Nets			
☐ 377	Henry James	.05	.02	.01
	Los Angeles Clippers			
☐ 378	Craig Ehlo	.05	.02	.01
	Atlanta Hawks			
☐ 379	Ennis Whatley	.05	.02	.01
	Atlanta Hawks			
☐ 380	Sean Green	.05	.02	.01
	Philadelphia 76ers			

☐ 381	Eric Murdock	.08	.04	.01
	Milwaukee Bucks			
☐ 382	Anfernee Hardaway	2.50	1.15	.30
	Orlando Magic			
☐ 383	Gheorghe Muresan	.20	.09	.03
	Washington Bullets			
☐ 384	Kendall Gill	.08	.04	.01
	Seattle Supersonics			
☐ 385	David Wood	.05	.02	.01
	Detroit Pistons			
☐ 386	Mario Elie	.05	.02	.01
	Houston Rockets			
☐ 387	Chris Corchiani	.05	.02	.01
	Boston Celtics			
☐ 388	Greg Graham	.15	.07	.02
	Philadelphia 76ers			
☐ 389	Hersey Hawkins	.08	.04	.01
	Charlotte Hornets			
☐ 390	Mark Aguirre	.10	.05	.01
	Los Angeles Clippers			
☐ 391	LaPhonso Ellis	.10	.05	.01
	Denver Nuggets			
☐ 392	Anthony Bonner	.05	.02	.01
	New York Knicks			
☐ 393	Lucious Harris	.15	.07	.02
	Dallas Mavericks			
☐ 394	Andrew Lang	.05	.02	.01
	Atlanta Hawks			
☐ 395	Chris Dudley	.05	.02	.01
	Portland Trail Blazers			
☐ 396	Dennis Rodman	.08	.04	.01
	San Antonio Spurs			
☐ 397	Larry Krystkowiak	.05	.02	.01
	Orlando Magic			
☐ 398	A.C. Green	.08	.04	.01
	Phoenix Suns			
☐ 399	Eddie Johnson	.05	.02	.01
	Charlotte Hornets			
☐ 400	Kevin Edwards	.05	.02	.01
	New Jersey Nets			
☐ 401	Tyrone Hill	.05	.02	.01
	Cleveland Cavaliers			
☐ 402	Greg Anderson	.05	.02	.01
	Detroit Pistons			
☐ 403	P.J. Brown	.20	.09	.03
	New Jersey Nets			
☐ 404	Dana Barros	.05	.02	.01
	Philadelphia 76ers			
☐ 405	Allan Houston	.20	.09	.03
	Detroit Pistons			
☐ 406	Mike Brown	.05	.02	.01
	Minnesota Timberwolves			
☐ 407	Lee Mayberry	.05	.02	.01
	Milwaukee Bucks			
☐ 408	Fat Lever	.05	.02	.01
	Dallas Mavericks			
☐ 409	Tony Smith	.05	.02	.01
	Los Angeles Lakers			
☐ 410	Tom Chambers	.08	.04	.01
	Utah Jazz			
☐ 411	Manute Bol	.05	.02	.01
	Miami Heat			
☐ 412	Joe Kleine	.05	.02	.01
	Phoenix Suns			
☐ 413	Bryant Smith	.05	.02	.01
	Denver Nuggets			
☐ 414	Eric Riley	.05	.02	.01
	Houston Rockets			
☐ 415	Pete Myers	.15	.07	.02
	Chicago Bulls			
☐ 416	Sean Elliott	.08	.04	.01
	Detroit Pistons			
☐ 417	Sam Bowie	.05	.02	.01

	Los Angeles Lakers			
☐ 418	Armon Gilliam	.05	.02	.01
	New Jersey Nets			
☐ 419	Brian Williams	.05	.02	.01
	Denver Nuggets			
☐ 420	Popeye Jones	.20	.09	.03
	Dallas Mavericks			
☐ 421	Dennis Rodman EB	.05	.02	.01
	San Antonio Spurs			
☐ 422	Karl Malone EB	.15	.07	.02
	Utah Jazz			
☐ 423	Tom Gugliotta EB	.08	.04	.01
	Washington Bullets			
☐ 424	Kevin Willis EB	.05	.02	.01
	Atlanta Hawks			
☐ 425	Hakeem Olajuwon EB	.50	.23	.06
	Houston Rockets			
☐ 426	Charles Oakley EB	.10	.05	.01
	New York Knicks			
☐ 427	Clarence Weatherspoon EB	.08	.04	.01
	Philadelphia 76ers			
☐ 428	Derrick Coleman EB	.12	.05	.02
	New Jersey Nets			
☐ 429	Buck Williams EB	.08	.04	.01
	Portland Trail Blazers			
☐ 430	Christian Laettner EB	.08	.04	.01
	Minnesota Timberwolves			
☐ 431	Dikembe Mutombo EB	.08	.04	.01
	Denver Nuggets			
☐ 432	Rony Seikaly EB	.08	.04	.01
	Miami Heat			
☐ 433	Brad Daugherty EB	.08	.04	.01
	Cleveland Cavaliers			
☐ 434	Horace Grant EB	.08	.04	.01
	Chicago Bulls			
☐ 435	Larry Johnson EB	.20	.09	.03
	Charlotte Hornets			
☐ 436	Dee Brown BT	.05	.02	.01
	Boston Celtics			
☐ 437	Muggsy Bogues BT	.08	.04	.01
	Charlotte Hornets			
☐ 438	Michael Jordan BT	1.25	.55	.16
	Chicago Bulls			
☐ 439	Tim Hardaway BT	.08	.04	.01
	Golden State Warriors			
☐ 440	Micheal Williams BT	.05	.02	.01
	Minnesota Timberwolves			
☐ 441	Gary Payton BT	.05	.02	.01
	Seattle Supersonics			
☐ 442	Mookie Blaylock BT	.08	.04	.01
	Atlanta Hawks			
☐ 443	Doc Rivers BT	.05	.02	.01
	New York Knicks			
☐ 444	Kenny Smith BT	.05	.02	.01
	Houston Rockets			
☐ 445	John Stockton BT	.12	.05	.02
	Utah Jazz			
☐ 446	Alvin Robertson BT	.05	.02	.01
	Detroit Pistons			
☐ 447	Mark Jackson BT	.05	.02	.01
	Los Angeles Clippers			
☐ 448	Kenny Anderson BT	.12	.05	.02
	New Jersey Nets			
☐ 449	Scottie Pippen BT	.20	.09	.03
	Chicago Bulls			
☐ 450	Isiah Thomas BT	.10	.05	.01
	Detroit Pistons			
☐ 451	Mark Price BT	.08	.04	.01
	Cleveland Cavaliers			
☐ 452	Latrell Sprewell BT	.25	.11	.03
	Golden State Warriors			
☐ 453	Sedale Threatt BT	.05	.02	.01
	Los Angeles Lakers			

☐ 490	Vin Baker TP	.30	.14	.04
	Sacramento Kings Milwaukee Bucks			
☐ 491	Rodney Rogers TP	.10	.05	.01
	Denver Nuggets			
☐ 492	Lindsey Hunter TP	.15	.07	.02
	Detroit Pistons			
☐ 493	Allan Houston TP	.10	.05	.01
	Detroit Pistons			
☐ 494	Terry Dehere TP	.10	.05	.01
	Los Angeles Clippers			
☐ 495	George Lynch TP	.10	.05	.01
	Los Angeles Lakers			
☐ 496	Scott Burrell TP	.15	.07	.02
	Charlotte Hornets			
☐ 497	Rex Walters TP	.15	.07	.02
	New Jersey Nets			
☐ 498	Charles Barkley MO	.30	.14	.04
	Phoenix Suns			
☐ 499	A.C. Green MO	.05	.02	.01
	Phoenix Suns			
☐ 500	Dan Majerle MO	.08	.04	.01
	Phoenix Suns			
☐ 501	Jerrod Mustaf MO	.05	.02	.01
	Phoenix Suns			
☐ 502	Kevin Johnson MO	.08	.04	.01
	Phoenix Suns			
☐ 503	Negele Knight MO	.05	.02	.01
	Phoenix Suns			
☐ 504	Danny Ainge MO	.08	.04	.01
	Phoenix Suns			
☐ 505	Oliver Miller MO	.08	.04	.01
	Phoenix Suns			
☐ 506	Joe Courtney MO	.05	.02	.01
	Phoenix Suns			
☐ 507	Checklist	.05	.02	.01
☐ 508	Checklist	.05	.02	.01
☐ 509	Checklist	.05	.02	.01
☐ 510	Checklist	.05	.02	.01
☐ SP3	Michael Jordan	5.00	2.30	.60
	Chicago Bulls Wilt Chamberlain			
☐ SP4	Chicago Bull's Third	5.00	2.30	.60
	NBA Championship			

1993-94 Upper Deck All-NBA

Randomly inserted in jumbo packs only, this 15-card set spotlights All-NBA first, second and third teams. Measuring the standard size (3 1/2" by 2 1/2"), the cards feature a borderless front with a color action photo set against a game-crowd background. The player's name appears in a red vertical stripe along the right side. The All NBA Team appears in a blue vertical stripe along the right side. The back features a color action photo along the left side with player's statistics along the right side. The cards are numbered on the back with an "AN" prefix.

		MINT	EXC	G-VG
COMPLETE SET (15)		15.00	6.75	1.90
COMMON PLAYER (AN1-AN15)		.25	.11	.03
☐ AN1	Charles Barkley	1.50	.65	.19
	Phoenix Suns			
☐ AN2	Karl Malone	1.00	.45	.13
	Utah Jazz			
☐ AN3	Hakeem Olajuwon	2.00	.90	.25
	Houston Rockets			
☐ AN4	Michael Jordan	6.00	2.70	.75
	Chicago Bulls			
☐ AN5	Mark Price	.25	.11	.03
	Cleveland Cavaliers			

☐ AN6 Dominique Wilkins	1.00	.45	.13
Atlanta Hawks			
☐ AN7 Larry Johnson	1.00	.45	.13
Charlotte Hornets			
☐ AN8 Patrick Ewing	1.25	.55	.16
New York Knicks			
☐ AN9 John Stockton	.50	.23	.06
Utah Jazz			
☐ AN10 Joe Dumars	.25	.11	.03
Detroit Pistons			
☐ AN11 Scottie Pippen	1.25	.55	.16
Chicago Bulls			
☐ AN12 Derrick Coleman	.50	.23	.06
New Jersey Nets			
☐ AN13 David Robinson	1.50	.65	.19
San Antonio Spurs			
☐ AN14 Tim Hardaway	.25	.11	.03
Golden State Warriors			
☐ AN15 Michael Jordan CL	3.00	1.35	.40
Chicago Bulls			

1993-94 Upper Deck All-Rookies

Randomly inserted in Series I retail packs, this 10-card standard-size (2 1/2" by 3 1/2") set features the NBA All-Rookie first (1-5) and second (6-10) teams. The cards feature color game-action player photos on their fronts. They are borderless, except at the top, where a red stripe edges the cards of the first team and a blue one edges those of the second. The

player's name appears in white lettering within a red or blue stripe near the bottom. The back carries a color player action photo on the left and career highlights on the right. The cards are numbered on the back with an "AR" prefix.

	MINT	EXC	G-VG
COMPLETE SET (10)	50.00	23.00	6.25
COMMON PLAYER (AR1-AR10)	1.00	.45	.13
☐ AR1 Shaquille O'Neal	25.00	11.50	3.10
Orlando Magic			
☐ AR2 Alonzo Mourning	12.00	5.50	1.50
Charlotte Hornets			
☐ AR3 Christian Laettner	3.00	1.35	.40
Minnesota Timberwolves			
☐ AR4 Tom Gugliotta	3.00	1.35	.40
Washington Bullets			
☐ AR5 LaPhonso Ellis	3.00	1.35	.40
Denver Nuggets			
☐ AR6 Walt Williams	1.50	.65	.19
Sacramento Kings			
☐ AR7 Robert Horry	3.00	1.35	.40
Houston Rockets			
☐ AR8 Latrell Sprewell	8.00	3.60	1.00
Golden State Warriors			
☐ AR9 Clarence Weatherspoon	3.00	1.35	.40
Philadelphia 76ers			
☐ AR10 Richard Dumas	1.00	.45	.13
Phoenix Suns			

1993-94 Upper Deck Flight Team

Michael Jordan reportedly selected the league's best dunkers for this 20-card insert set, randomly inserted only in Series I hobby packs. The standard-size (2 1/2" by 3 1/2") cards feature on their fronts full-bleed color action player photos. The words "Michael Jordan's Flight Team" appear in ghosted block lettering over the background. The player's name is gold-foil stamped at the bottom, with the Flight Team insignia displayed immediately above carrying his team's city name and the his uniform number. On a background consisting of blue sky and clouds, the back carries a color player action cutout and an evaluative quote by Jordan. The cards are numbered on the back with an "FT" prefix.

	MINT	EXC	G-VG
COMPLETE SET (20)	125.00	57.50	15.50
COMMON PLAYER (FT1-FT20)	2.00	.90	.25
☐ FT1 Stacey Augmon	2.00	.90	.25
Atlanta Hawks			
☐ FT2 Charles Barkley	12.00	5.50	1.50
Phoenix Suns			

☐ FT3 David Benoit .... Utah Jazz	2.00	.90	.25
☐ FT4 Dee Brown .... Boston Celtics	2.00	.90	.25
☐ FT5 Cedric Ceballos .... Phoenix Suns	2.50	1.15	.30
☐ FT6 Derrick Coleman .... New Jersey Nets	4.00	1.80	.50
☐ FT7 Clyde Drexler .... Portland Trail Blazers	4.00	1.80	.50
☐ FT8 Sean Elliott .... San Antonio Spurs	2.00	.90	.25
☐ FT9 LaPhonso Ellis .... Denver Nuggets	3.50	1.55	.45
☐ FT10 Kendall Gill .... Charlotte Hornets	2.50	1.15	.30
☐ FT11 Larry Johnson .... Charlotte Hornets	8.00	3.60	1.00
☐ FT12 Shawn Kemp .... Seattle Supersonics	10.00	4.50	1.25
☐ FT13 Karl Malone .... Utah Jazz	6.00	2.70	.75
☐ FT14 Harold Miner .... Miami Heat	2.50	1.15	.30
☐ FT15 Alonzo Mourning .... Charlotte Hornets	12.00	5.50	1.50
☐ FT16 Shaquille O'Neal .... Orlando Magic	30.00	13.50	3.80
☐ FT17 Scottie Pippen .... Chicago Bulls	10.00	4.50	1.25
☐ FT18 Clarence Weatherspoon .... Philadelphia 76ers	3.50	1.55	.45
☐ FT19 Spud Webb .... Sacramento Kings	2.50	1.15	.30
☐ FT20 Dominique Wilkins .... Atlanta Hawks	8.00	3.60	1.00

1993-94 Upper Deck Future Heroes

Inserted one per Series I locker pack, this 10-card standard-size (2 1/2" by 3 1/2") set features color player action shots on its fronts. The photos are bordered on the left and bottom by gray and team color-coded stripes. The player's name and position appear in white lettering in the color-coded stripe at the bottom. An embossed silver-foil basketball appears at the lower left. The white back carries the player's career highlights. The cards are numbered on the back as "X of 36."

	MINT	EXC	G-VG
COMPLETE SET (10)	30.00	13.50	3.80
COMMON PLAYER (28-36)	.75	.35	.09
☐ 28 Derrick Coleman	1.50	.65	.19
New Jersey Nets			
☐ 29 LaPhonso Ellis	1.25	.55	.16
Denver Nuggets			
☐ 30 Jim Jackson	3.00	1.35	.40
Dallas Mavericks			
☐ 31 Larry Johnson	3.00	1.35	.40
Charlotte Hornets			
☐ 32 Shawn Kemp	3.50	1.55	.45
Seattle Supersonics			
☐ 33 Christian Laettner	1.25	.55	.16
Minnesota Timberwolves			
☐ 34 Alonzo Mourning	5.00	2.30	.60
Charlotte Hornets			
☐ 35 Shaquille O'Neal	12.00	5.50	1.50
Orlando Magic			
☐ 36 Walt Williams	.75	.35	.09
Sacramento Kings			
☐ NNO Checklist Card	1.00	.45	.13
LaPhonso Ellis			
Christian Laettner			

1993-94 Upper Deck Locker Talk

Inserted one per Series II locker pack, this 15-card standard-size (2 1/2" by 3 1/2") set features color player action photos on their fronts. The player's name appears in white lettering within the gold stripe that edges the left side. A personal player quote appears in white lettering within the photo's "torn" lower right corner. The back carries the same quote at the upper right, within a shot of a locker that has a print of the front's action shot taped to the door. Another player photo and more personal player quotes round out the back. The cards are numbered on the back with an "LT" prefix.

	MINT	EXC	G-VG
COMPLETE SET (15)	30.00	13.50	3.80
COMMON PLAYER (LT1-LT15)	.50	.23	.06
☐ LT1 Michael Jordan	15.00	6.75	1.90
Chicago Bulls			
☐ LT2 Stacey Augmon	.50	.23	.06
Atlanta Hawks			
☐ LT3 Shaquille O'Neal	10.00	4.50	1.25
Orlando Magic			
☐ LT4 Alonzo Mourning	4.00	1.80	.50
Charlotte Hornets			
☐ LT5 Harold Miner	.75	.35	.09

		MINT	EXC	G-VG
	Miami Heat			
☐ LT6	Clarence Weatherspoon	1.00	.45	.13
	Philadelphia 76ers			
☐ LT7	Derrick Coleman	1.25	.55	.16
	New Jersey Nets			
☐ LT8	Charles Barkley	4.00	1.80	.50
	Phoenix Suns			
☐ LT9	David Robinson	4.00	1.80	.50
	San Antonio Spurs			
☐ LT10	Chuck Person	.50	.23	.06
	Minnesota Timberwolves			
☐ LT11	Karl Malone	2.00	.90	.25
	Utah Jazz			
☐ LT12	Muggsy Bogues	.50	.23	.06
	Charlotte Hornets			
☐ LT13	Latrell Sprewell	4.00	1.80	.50
	Golden State Warriors			
☐ LT14	John Starks	.75	.35	.09
	New York Knicks			
☐ LT15	Jim Jackson	2.50	1.15	.30
	Dallas Mavericks			

1993-94 Upper Deck Mr. June

Randomly inserted in Series II hobby packs, this 10-card standard-size (2 1/2" by 3 1/2") set focuses on Michael Jordan's performance while leading his team to three consecutive NBA Championships. The front features a color action shot of Michael Jordan with his name, accomplishment, and year thereof printed in the team-colored (Chicago Bulls) stripe at the bottom. The back features a color action photo at the upper right with a description of his accomplishments printed alongside and below. The cards are numbered on the back with an "MJ" prefix.

		MINT	EXC	G-VG
COMPLETE SET (10)		175.00	80.00	22.00
COMMON JORDAN (MJ1-MJ10)		20.00	9.00	2.50
☐ MJ1	Michael Jordan	20.00	9.00	2.50
	Jordan's a Steal			
☐ MJ2	Michael Jordan	20.00	9.00	2.50
	M.J.'s High Five			
☐ MJ3	Michael Jordan	20.00	9.00	2.50
	1991 NBA Finals MVP			
☐ MJ4	Michael Jordan	20.00	9.00	2.50
	35 Points in One Half			
☐ MJ5	Michael Jordan	20.00	9.00	2.50
	Three-Points King			
☐ MJ6	Michael Jordan	20.00	9.00	2.50
	Back-To-Back Finals MVP			

	MINT	EXC	G-VG
☐ MJ7 Michael Jordan	20.00	9.00	2.50
55-Point Game			
☐ MJ8 Michael Jordan	20.00	9.00	2.50
Record Scoring Average			
☐ MJ9 Michael Jordan	20.00	9.00	2.50
Jordan's Three-Peat			
☐ MJ10 Checklist	20.00	9.00	2.50

1993-94 Upper Deck Rookie Exchange Silver

This 10-card standard-size (2 1/2" by 3 1/2") set could be obtained by mail for the exchange card. The Silver Exchange expiration date was 12/31/93. The borderless front features a color player action photo with the his name printed in white lettering within a red stripe near the bottom. The word "Exchange" runs vertically along the left side in silver-foil lettering. The white and gray back carries a color player photo at the upper left and career highlights and statistics alongside and below. The cards are numbered on the back with an "RE" prefix.

	MINT	EXC	G-VG
COMPLETE SET (10)	12.00	5.50	1.50
COMMON PLAYER (RE1-RE10)	.50	.23	.06
☐ RE1 Chris Webber	5.00	2.30	.60
Golden State Warriors			
☐ RE2 Shawn Bradley	.75	.35	.09
Philadelphia 76ers			
☐ RE3 Anfernee Hardaway	4.00	1.80	.50
Orlando Magic			
☐ RE4 Jamal Mashburn	2.00	.90	.25
Dallas Mavericks			
☐ RE5 Isaiah Rider	2.00	.90	.25
Minnesota Timberwolves			
☐ RE6 Calbert Cheaney	.75	.35	.09
Washington Bullets			
☐ RE7 Bobby Hurley	.75	.35	.09
Sacramento Kings			
☐ RE8 Vin Baker	1.50	.65	.19
Milwaukee Bucks			
☐ RE9 Rodney Rogers	.50	.23	.06
Denver Nuggets			
☐ RE10 Lindsey Hunter	.75	.35	.09
Detroit Pistons			
☐ TC2 Redeemed Silver Trade	.25	.11	.03
☐ TC2 Unredeemed Silver Trade	1.00	.45	.13

1993-94 Upper Deck Rookie Exchange Gold

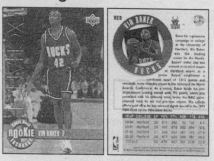

This 10-card standard-size (2-1/2" by 3 1/2") set could be obtained by mail for the exchange card. The Gold Exchange expiration date was 12/31/93. The borderless front features a color player action photo with the his name printed in white lettering within a red stripe near the bottom. The word "Exchange" runs vertically along the left side in gold-foil lettering. The white and gray back carries a color player photo at the upper left and career highlights and statistics alongside and below. The cards are numbered on the back with an "RE" prefix.

	MINT	EXC	G-VG
COMPLETE SET (10)	25.00	11.50	3.10
COMMON PLAYER (RE1-RE10)	1.00	.45	.13
*GOLD CARDS: 2X SILVER VALUE			
☐ TC1 Redeemed Gold Trade	.50	.23	.06
☐ TC1 Unredeemed Gold Trade	2.00	.90	.25

1993-94 Upper Deck Rookie Standouts

Randomly inserted in second-series retail packs and inserted one per second-series purple jumbo, this 20-card standard-size (2 1/2" by 3 1/2") set showcases the top rookies of the 1993-94 NBA season. The borderless front features a color player action photo with his name printed in a gold-foil banner beneath the silver-foil set logo in a lower corner. The gray back carries a color player photo on one side and career highlights on the other. The cards are numbered on the back with an "RS" prefix.

	MINT	EXC	G-VG
COMPLETE SET (20)	75.00	34.00	9.50
COMMON PLAYER (RS1-RS20)	.75	.35	.09
☐ RS1 Chris Webber Golden State Warriors	20.00	9.00	2.50
☐ RS2 Bobby Hurley Sacramento Kings	3.00	1.35	.40
☐ RS3 Isaiah Rider Minnesota Timberwolves	8.00	3.60	1.00
☐ RS4 Terry Dehere Los Angeles Clippers	.75	.35	.09
☐ RS5 Toni Kukoc Chicago Bulls	3.00	1.35	.40
☐ RS6 Shawn Bradley Philadelphia 76ers	3.00	1.35	.40
☐ RS7 Allan Houston Detroit Pistons	1.00	.45	.13
☐ RS8 Chris Mills Cleveland Cavaliers	1.75	.80	.22
☐ RS9 Jamal Mashburn Dallas Mavericks	8.00	3.60	1.00
☐ RS10 Acie Earl Boston Celtics	.75	.35	.09
☐ RS11 George Lynch Los Angeles Lakers	1.50	.65	.19
☐ RS12 Scott Burrell Charlotte Hornets	1.00	.45	.13
☐ RS13 Calbert Cheaney Washington Bullets	3.00	1.35	.40
☐ RS14 Lindsey Hunter Detroit Pistons	3.00	1.35	.40
☐ RS15 Nick Van Exel Los Angeles Lakers	3.00	1.35	.40
☐ RS16 Rex Walters New Jersey Nets	.75	.35	.09
☐ RS17 Anfernee Hardaway Orlando Magic	15.00	6.75	1.90
☐ RS18 Sam Cassell Houston Rockets	3.50	1.55	.45
☐ RS19 Vin Baker Milwaukee Bucks	6.00	2.70	.75
☐ RS20 Rodney Rogers Denver Nuggets	1.50	.65	.19

1993-94 Upper Deck Team MVPs

This 27-card standard size (3 1/2" by 2 1/2") set was inserted one per Series II and purple jumbo packs. The white- and prismatic team-colored foil-bordered front features a color player action shot, with the player's name printed vertically in the foil border at the upper right. The horizontal back is bordered in white and a team color and carries a color action shot on the left with career highlights appearing in a gray panel alongside on the right. The cards are numbered on the back with a "TM" prefix.

	MINT	EXC	G-VG
COMPLETE SET (27)	20.00	9.00	2.50
COMMON PLAYER (TM1-TM27)	.25	.11	.03
☐ TM1 Dominique Wilkins Atlanta Hawks	1.00	.45	.13
☐ TM2 Robert Parish Boston Celtics	.35	.16	.04
☐ TM3 Larry Johnson Charlotte Hornets	1.00	.45	.13
☐ TM4 Scottie Pippen Chicago Bulls	1.25	.55	.16
☐ TM5 Mark Price Cleveland Cavaliers	.35	.16	.04
☐ TM6 Jim Jackson Dallas Mavericks	1.00	.45	.13

☐ TM7 Mahmoud Abdul-Rauf .... Denver Nuggets	.25	.11	.03
☐ TM8 Joe Dumars .... Detroit Pistons	.35	.16	.04
☐ TM9 Chris Mullin .... Golden State Warriors	.40	.18	.05
☐ TM10 Hakeem Olajuwon .... Houston Rockets	2.00	.90	.25
☐ TM11 Reggie Miller .... Indiana Pacers	.50	.23	.06
☐ TM12 Danny Manning .... Los Angeles Clippers	.40	.18	.05
☐ TM13 James Worthy .... Los Angeles Lakers	.35	.16	.04
☐ TM14 Glen Rice .... Miami Heat	.35	.16	.04
☐ TM15 Blue Edwards .... Milwaukee Bucks	.25	.11	.03
☐ TM16 Christian Laettner .... Minnesota Timberwolves	.40	.18	.05
☐ TM17 Derrick Coleman .... New Jersey Nets	.50	.23	.06
☐ TM18 Patrick Ewing .... New York Knicks	1.25	.55	.16
☐ TM19 Shaquille O'Neal .... Orlando Magic	4.00	1.80	.50
☐ TM20 Clarence Weatherspoon .... Philadelphia 76ers	.40	.18	.05
☐ TM21 Charles Barkley .... Phoenix Suns	1.50	.65	.19
☐ TM22 Clyde Drexler .... Portland Trail Blazers	.50	.23	.06
☐ TM23 Mitch Richmond .... Sacramento Kings	.25	.11	.03
☐ TM24 David Robinson .... San Antonio Spurs	1.50	.65	.19
☐ TM25 Shawn Kemp .... Seattle Supersonics	1.25	.55	.16
☐ TM26 John Stockton .... Utah Jazz	.50	.23	.06
☐ TM27 Tom Gugliotta .... Washington Bullets	.40	.18	.05

1993-94 Upper Deck Triple Double

Randomly inserted in first-series packs and inserted one per first-series green jumbo, this 10-card set features the NBA leaders in triple-doubles from the 1992-93 season. The standard-size (2 1/2" by 3 1/2") horizontal hologram cards feature one color player action cutout

and two hologram action shots on their fronts. Each of the three images show the player performing three different skills (scoring, rebounding, passing or blocking) necessary to achieve a triple-double. The words "Triple Double" appear vertically on the left. The player's name appears at the upper right of the hologram. The horizontal back displays another color player action shot on the left, with a story of the player's triple-double feat on the right. The player's name appears in a team-colored bar at the bottom. The cards are numbered on the back with a "TD" prefix.

	MINT	EXC	G-VG
COMPLETE SET (10)	25.00	11.50	3.10
COMMON PLAYER (TD1-TD10)	.50	.23	.06
☐ TD1 Charles Barkley	4.00	1.80	.50
Phoenix Suns			
☐ TD2 Michael Jordan	15.00	6.75	1.90
Chicago Bulls			
☐ TD3 Scottie Pippen	3.00	1.35	.40
Chicago Bulls			
☐ TD4 Detlef Schrempf	.75	.35	.09
Indiana Pacers			
☐ TD5 Mark Jackson	.50	.23	.06
Los Angeles Clippers			
☐ TD6 Kenny Anderson	1.25	.55	.16
New Jersey Nets			
☐ TD7 Larry Johnson	2.50	1.15	.30
Charlotte Hornets			
☐ TD8 Dikembe Mutombo	.75	.35	.09
Denver Nuggets			
☐ TD9 Rumeal Robinson	.50	.23	.06
New Jersey Nets			
☐ TD10 Micheal Williams	.50	.23	.06
Minnesota Timberwolves			

1993-94 Upper Deck Pro View

This 110-card standard-size (2 1/2" by 3 1/2"') set features on its fronts white-bordered 3-D color player action shots, with the player's name appearing within a vertical ghosted strip on the left. Each pack came with a pair of 3-D glasses. The back carries a color player action shot on the left, with career highlights horizontally printed alongside on the right. The set closes with the following subsets: 3-D Playground Legends (71-79), 3-D Rookies (80-88) and 3-D Jams (89-108). The cards are numbered on the back.

	MINT	EXC	G-VG
COMPLETE SET (110)	20.00	9.00	2.50
COMMON PLAYER (1-110)	.05	.02	.01
☐ 1 Karl Malone	.25	.11	.03
Utah Jazz			
☐ 2 Chuck Person	.08	.04	.01
Minnesota Timberwolves			
☐ 3 Latrell Sprewell	.40	.18	.05
Golden State Warriors			

☐ 4	Dominique Wilkins	.25	.11	.03
	Atlanta Hawks			
☐ 5	Reggie Miller	.20	.09	.03
	Indiana Pacers			
☐ 6	Vlade Divac	.05	.02	.01
	Los Angeles Lakers			
☐ 7	Otis Thorpe	.08	.04	.01
	Houston Rockets			
☐ 8	Patrick Ewing	.30	.14	.04
	New York Knicks			
☐ 9	Ron Harper	.05	.02	.01
	Los Angeles Clippers			
☐ 10	Brad Daugherty	.05	.02	.01
	Cleveland Cavaliers			
☐ 11	Robert Parish	.05	.02	.01
	Boston Celtics			
☐ 12	Glen Rice	.05	.02	.01
	Miami Heat			
☐ 13	Kevin Johnson	.10	.05	.01
	Phoenix Suns			
☐ 14	Christian Laettner	.08	.04	.01
	Minnesota Timberwolves			
☐ 15	Ricky Pierce	.08	.04	.01
	Seattle Supersonics			
☐ 16	Joe Dumars	.15	.07	.02
	Detroit Pistons			
☐ 17	James Worthy	.10	.05	.01
	Los Angeles Lakers			
☐ 18	John Stockton	.15	.07	.02
	Utah Jazz			
☐ 19	Robert Horry	.10	.05	.01
	Houston Rockets			
☐ 20	John Starks	.10	.05	.01
	New York Knicks			
☐ 21	Danny Manning	.05	.02	.01
	Los Angeles Clippers			
☐ 22	Alonzo Mourning	.50	.23	.06
	Charlotte Hornets			
☐ 23	Michael Jordan	2.00	.90	.25
	Chicago Bulls			
☐ 24	Hakeem Olajuwon	.75	.35	.09
	Houston Rockets			
☐ 25	Scott Skiles	.05	.02	.01
	Orlando Magic			
☐ 26	Stacey Augmon	.10	.05	.01
	Atlanta Hawks			
☐ 27	Mitch Richmond	.10	.05	.01
	Sacramento Kings			
☐ 28	Derrick Coleman	.20	.09	.03
	New Jersey Nets			
☐ 29	Jeff Malone	.08	.04	.01

			Utah Jazz		
☐	30	Larry Johnson	.30	.14	.04
			Charlotte Hornets		
☐	31	Sam Perkins	.08	.04	.01
			Seattle Supersonics		
☐	32	Shaquille O'Neal	1.50	.65	.19
			Orlando Magic		
☐	33	Walt Williams	.08	.04	.01
			Sacramento Kings		
☐	34	Doug West	.05	.02	.01
			Minnesota Timberwolves		
☐	35	Mark Price	.10	.05	.01
			Cleveland Cavaliers		
☐	36	Rony Seikaly	.10	.05	.01
			Miami Heat		
☐	37	Michael Adams	.08	.04	.01
			Washington Bullets		
☐	38	Anthony Peeler	.08	.04	.01
			Los Angeles Lakers		
☐	39	Larry Nance	.05	.02	.01
			Cleveland Cavaliers		
☐	40	Shawn Kemp	.30	.14	.04
			Seattle Supersonics		
☐	41	Terry Porter	.08	.04	.01
			Portland Trail Blazers		
☐	42	Dan Majerle	.05	.02	.01
			Phoenix Suns		
☐	43	Dennis Rodman	.08	.04	.01
			San Antonio Spurs		
☐	44	Isiah Thomas	.15	.07	.02
			Detroit Pistons		
☐	45	Spud Webb	.10	.05	.01
			Sacramento Kings		
☐	46	Pooh Richardson	.05	.02	.01
			Indiana Pacers		
☐	47	Tim Hardaway	.10	.05	.01
			Golden State Warriors		
☐	48	Derek Harper	.08	.04	.01
			Dallas Mavericks		
☐	49	Pervis Ellison	.05	.02	.01
			Washington Bullets		
☐	50	Xavier McDaniel	.05	.02	.01
			Boston Celtics		
☐	51	Jeff Hornacek	.08	.04	.01
			Philadelphia 76ers		
☐	52	Ken Norman	.05	.02	.01
			Milwaukee Bucks		
☐	53	LaPhonso Ellis	.10	.05	.01
			Denver Nuggets		
☐	54	Charles Barkley	.40	.18	.05
			Phoenix Suns		
☐	55	Tom Gugliotta	.08	.04	.01
			Washington Bullets		
☐	56	Clifford Robinson	.10	.05	.01
			Portland Trail Blazers		
☐	57	Mark Jackson	.05	.02	.01
			Los Angeles Clippers		
☐	58	Mahmoud Abdul-Rauf	.05	.02	.01
			Denver Nuggets		
☐	59	Todd Day	.05	.02	.01
			Milwaukee Bucks		
☐	60	Kenny Anderson	.15	.07	.02
			New Jersey Nets		
☐	61	Jim Jackson	.30	.14	.04
			Dallas Mavericks		
☐	62	Chris Mullin	.15	.07	.02
			Golden State Warriors		
☐	63	Scottie Pippen	.30	.14	.04
			Chicago Bulls		
☐	64	Dikembe Mutombo	.10	.05	.01
			Denver Nuggets		
☐	65	Sean Elliott	.05	.02	.01
			Detroit Pistons		

☐ 66 Clarence Weatherspoon Philadelphia 76ers	.10	.05	.01
☐ 67 Chris Morris New Jersey Nets	.05	.02	.01
☐ 68 Clyde Drexler Portland Trail Blazers	.15	.07	.02
☐ 69 Dennis Scott Orlando Magic	.08	.04	.01
☐ 70 David Robinson San Antonio Spurs	.40	.18	.05
☐ 71 Larry Johnson Charlotte Hornets	.12	.05	.02
☐ 72 Chris Webber Golden State Warriors	.75	.35	.09
☐ 73 Alonzo Mourning Charlotte Hornets	.30	.14	.04
☐ 74 Lloyd Daniels San Antonio Spurs	.05	.02	.01
☐ 75 Derrick Coleman New Jersey Nets	.10	.05	.01
☐ 76 Tim Hardaway Golden State Warriors	.10	.05	.01
☐ 77 Isiah Thomas Detroit Pistons	.10	.05	.01
☐ 78 Chris Mullin Golden State Warriors	.10	.05	.01
☐ 79 Shaquille O'Neal Orlando Magic	.75	.35	.09
☐ 80 Shawn Bradley Philadelphia 76ers	.40	.18	.05
☐ 81 Chris Webber Golden State Warriors	2.50	1.15	.30
☐ 82 Jamal Mashburn Dallas Mavericks	1.00	.45	.13
☐ 83 Anfernee Hardaway Orlando Magic	2.00	.90	.25
☐ 84 Calbert Cheaney Washington Bullets	.40	.18	.05
☐ 85 Vin Baker Milwaukee Bucks	.60	.25	.08
☐ 86 Isaiah Rider Minnesota Timberwolves	1.00	.45	.13
☐ 87 Lindsey Hunter Detroit Pistons	.40	.18	.05
☐ 88 Bobby Hurley Sacramento Kings	.40	.18	.05
☐ 89 Dominique Wilkins Atlanta Hawks	.12	.05	.02
☐ 90 Charles Barkley Phoenix Suns	.20	.09	.03
☐ 91 Michael Jordan Chicago Bulls	1.00	.45	.13
☐ 92 Derrick Coleman New Jersey Nets	.10	.05	.01
☐ 93 Scottie Pippen Chicago Bulls	.15	.07	.02
☐ 94 Karl Malone Utah Jazz	.12	.05	.02
☐ 95 Larry Johnson Charlotte Hornets	.12	.05	.02
☐ 96 Cedric Ceballos Phoenix Suns	.10	.05	.01
☐ 97 David Robinson San Antonio Spurs	.20	.09	.03
☐ 98 Patrick Ewing New York Knicks	.15	.07	.02
☐ 99 Clarence Weatherspoon Philadelphia 76ers	.08	.04	.01
☐ 100 Alonzo Mourning Charlotte Hornets	.25	.11	.03
☐ 101 Stacey Augmon Atlanta Hawks	.10	.05	.01
☐ 102 Shaquille O'Neal	.75	.35	.09

	Orlando Magic			
☐ 103	Clyde Drexler	.10	.05	.01
	Portland Trail Blazers			
☐ 104	Shawn Kemp	.15	.07	.02
	Seattle Supersonics			
☐ 105	Harold Miner	.08	.04	.01
	Miami Heat			
☐ 106	Chris Webber	.75	.35	.09
	Golden State Warriors			
☐ 107	Dikembe Mutombo	.08	.04	.01
	Denver Nuggets			
☐ 108	Doug West	.05	.02	.01
	Minnesota Timberwolves			
☐ 109	Checklist 1	.05	.02	.01
☐ 110	Checklist 2	.05	.02	.01

1993-94 Upper Deck SE

This 225-card standard-size (2 1/2" by 3 1/2") set features on its fronts color player action shots that are borderless, except on the left, where a strip carries the player's name in gold foil along with his position and a vertically distorted black-and-white version of the action shot. The player's team name appears in vertical gold-foil lettering near the right edge. The back carries a color player action photo, with his name, position, and brief biography appearing in stripes across the top. Statistics and career highlights are displayed horizontally in a ghosted panel on the left. Collectors could redeem the "USA Basketball Trade Card" for a set of 25 cards, depicting the 12 players selected by USA Basketball for "Dream Team II" plus Tim Hardaway, who was originally selected to the team but will be unable to participate due to injury, and 12 players from the original Dream Team. Three Michael Jordan insert cards are included in the set: a Kilroy card, a retirement tribute card numbered MJR1, and a "Behind The Glass" insert card. These Jordan insert cards were randomly inserted at a rate of one card per 72 foil packs; the "Behind The Glass" insert card was found in foil packs available at retail locations only. The set closes with the following topical subsets: NBA All-Star Weekend Highlights (181-198) and Team Headlines (199-225). They are noted as such in the checklist below.

	MINT	EXC	G-VG
COMPLETE SET (225)	25.00	11.50	3.10
COMMON PLAYER (1-225)	.10	.05	.01
☐ 1 Scottie Pippen	.50	.23	.06
Chicago Bulls			
☐ 2 Todd Day	.15	.07	.02
Milwaukee Bucks			
☐ 3 Detlef Schrempf	.20	.09	.03
Seattle Supersonics			
☐ 4 Chris Webber	4.00	1.80	.50
Golden State Warriors			
☐ 5 Michael Adams	.15	.07	.02
Washington Bullets			

☐ 6 Loy Vaught	.15	.07	.02
Los Angeles Clippers			
☐ 7 Doug West	.10	.05	.01
Minnesota Timberwolves			
☐ 8 A.C. Green	.15	.07	.02
Phoenix Suns			
☐ 9 Anthony Mason	.10	.05	.01
New York Knicks			
☐ 10 Clyde Drexler	.30	.14	.04
Portland Trail Blazers			
☐ 11 Popeye Joenes	.25	.11	.03
Dallas Mavericks			
☐ 12 Vlade Divac	.10	.05	.01
Los Angeles Lakers			
☐ 13 Armon Gilliam	.10	.05	.01
New Jersey Nets			
☐ 14 Hersey Hawkins	.15	.07	.02
Charlotte Hornets			
☐ 15 Dennis Scott	.15	.07	.02
Orlando Magic			
☐ 16 Bimbo Coles	.10	.05	.01
Miami Heat			
☐ 17 Blue Edwards	.10	.05	.01
Milwaukee Bucks			
☐ 18 Negele Knight	.10	.05	.01
San Antonio Spurs			
☐ 19 Dale Davis	.10	.05	.01
Indiana Pacers			
☐ 20 Isiah Thomas	.25	.11	.03
Detroit Pistons			
☐ 21 Latrell Sprewell	.60	.25	.08
Golden State Warriors			
☐ 22 Kenny Smith	.10	.05	.01
Houston Rockets			
☐ 23 Bryant Stith	.15	.07	.02
Denver Nuggets			
☐ 24 Terry Porter	.15	.07	.02
Portland Trail Blazers			
☐ 25 Spud Webb	.20	.09	.03
Sacramento Kings			
☐ 26 John Battle	.10	.05	.01
Cleveland Cavaliers			
☐ 27 Jeff Malone	.15	.07	.02
Philadelphia 76ers			
☐ 28 Olden Polynice	.10	.05	.01
Sacramento Kings			
☐ 29 Kevin Willis	.15	.07	.02
Atlanta Hawks			
☐ 30 Robert Parish	.20	.09	.03
Boston Celtics			
☐ 31 Kevin Johnson	.20	.09	.03
Phoenix Suns			
☐ 32 Shaquille O'Neal	2.50	1.15	.30
Orlando Magic			
☐ 33 Willie Anderson	.10	.05	.01
San Antonio Spurs			
☐ 34 Micheal Williams	.15	.07	.02
Minnesota Timberwolves			
☐ 35 Steve Smith	.15	.07	.02
Miami Heat			
☐ 36 Rik Smits	.15	.07	.02
Indiana Pacers			
☐ 37 Pete Myers	.10	.05	.01
Chicago Bulls			
☐ 38 Oliver Miller	.20	.09	.03
Phoenix Suns			
☐ 39 Eddie Johnson	.10	.05	.01
Charlotte Hornets			
☐ 40 Calbert Cheaney	.60	.25	.08
Washington Bullets			
☐ 41 Vernon Maxwell	.10	.05	.01
Houston Rockets			
☐ 42 James Worthy	.20	.09	.03

☐ 43	Dino Radja	.60	.25	.08
	Los Angeles Lakers			
	Boston Celtics			
☐ 44	Derrick Coleman	.30	.14	.04
	New Jersey Nets			
☐ 45	Reggie Williams	.10	.05	.01
	Denver Nuggets			
☐ 46	Dale Ellis	.15	.07	.02
	San Antonio Spurs			
☐ 47	Clifford Robinson	.20	.09	.03
	Portland Trail Blazers			
☐ 48	Doug Christie	.15	.07	.02
	Los Angeles Lakers			
☐ 49	Ricky Pierce	.15	.07	.02
	Seattle Supersonics			
☐ 50	Sean Elliott	.15	.07	.02
	Detroit Pistons			
☐ 51	Anfernee Hardaway	3.00	1.35	.40
	Orlando Magic			
☐ 52	Dana Barros	.10	.05	.01
	Philadelphia 76ers			
☐ 53	Reggie Miller	.30	.14	.04
	Indiana Pacers			
☐ 54	Brian Williams	.10	.05	.01
	Denver Nuggets			
☐ 55	Otis Thorpe	.15	.07	.02
	Houston Rockets			
☐ 56	Jerome Kersey	.10	.05	.01
	Portland Trail Blazers			
☐ 57	Larry Johnson	.40	.18	.05
	Charlotte Hornets			
☐ 58	Rex Chapman	.10	.05	.01
	Washington Bullets			
☐ 59	Kevin Edwards	.10	.05	.01
	New Jersey Nets			
☐ 60	Nate McMillan	.10	.05	.01
	Seattle Supersonics			
☐ 61	Chris Mullin	.25	.11	.03
	Golden State Warriors			
☐ 62	Bill Cartwright	.10	.05	.01
	Chicago Bulls			
☐ 63	Dennis Rodman	.15	.07	.02
	San Antonio Spurs			
☐ 64	Pooh Richardson	.10	.05	.01
	Indiana Pacers			
☐ 65	Tyrone Hill	.10	.05	.01
	Cleveland Cavaliers			
☐ 66	Scott Brooks	.10	.05	.01
	Houston Rockets			
☐ 67	Brad Daugherty	.20	.09	.03
	Cleveland Cavaliers			
☐ 68	Joe Dumars	.25	.11	.03
	Detroit Pistons			
☐ 69	Vin Baker	1.00	.45	.13
	Milwaukee Bucks			
☐ 70	Rod Strickland	.15	.07	.02
	Portland Trail Blazers			
☐ 71	Tom Chambers	.15	.07	.02
	Utah Jazz			
☐ 72	Charles Oakley	.20	.09	.03
	New York Knicks			
☐ 73	Craig Ehlo	.10	.05	.01
	Atlanta Hawks			
☐ 74	LaPhonso Ellis	.20	.09	.03
	Denver Nuggets			
☐ 75	Kevin Gamble	.10	.05	.01
	Boston Celtics			
☐ 76	Shawn Bradley	.60	.25	.08
	Philadelphia 76ers			
☐ 77	Kendall Gill	.15	.07	.02
	Seattle Supersonics			
☐ 78	Hakeem Olajuwon	1.25	.55	.16
	Houston Rockets			

☐ 79 Nick Anderson	.15	.07	.02
Orlando Magic			
☐ 80 Anthony Peeler	.15	.07	.02
Los Angeles Lakers			
☐ 81 Wayman Tisdale	.15	.07	.02
Sacramento Kings			
☐ 82 Danny Manning	.20	.09	.03
Los Angeles Clippers			
☐ 83 John Starks	.20	.09	.03
New York Knicks			
☐ 84 Jeff Hornacek	.15	.07	.02
Utah Jazz			
☐ 85 Victor Alexander	.10	.05	.01
Golden State Warriors			
☐ 86 Mitch Richmond	.20	.09	.03
Sacramento Kings			
☐ 87 Mookie Blaylock	.15	.07	.02
Atlanta Hawks			
☐ 88 Harvey Grant	.10	.05	.01
Portland Trail Blazers			
☐ 89 Doug Smith	.10	.05	.01
Dallas Mavericks			
☐ 90 John Stockton	.25	.11	.03
Utah Jazz			
☐ 91 Charles Barkley	.75	.35	.09
Phoenix Suns			
☐ 92 Gerald Wilkins	.10	.05	.01
Cleveland Cavaliers			
☐ 93 Mario Elie	.10	.05	.01
Houston Rockets			
☐ 94 Ken Norman	.10	.05	.01
Milwaukee Bucks			
☐ 95 B.J. Armstrong	.20	.09	.03
Chicago Bulls			
☐ 96 John Williams	.15	.07	.02
Cleveland Cavaliers			
☐ 97 Rony Seikaly	.20	.09	.03
Miami Heat			
☐ 98 Sean Rooks	.10	.05	.01
Dallas Mavericks			
☐ 99 Shawn Kemp	.50	.23	.06
Seattle Supersonics			
☐ 100 Danny Ainge	.20	.09	.03
Phoenix Suns			
☐ 101 Terry Mills	.15	.07	.02
Detroit Pistons			
☐ 102 Doc Rivers	.15	.07	.02
New York Knicks			
☐ 103 Chuck Person	.15	.07	.02
Minnesota Timberwolves			
☐ 104 Sam Cassell	.75	.35	.09
Houston Rockets			
☐ 105 Kevin Duckworth	.10	.05	.01
Washington Bullets			
☐ 106 Dan Majerle	.20	.09	.03
Phoenix Suns			
☐ 107 Mark Jackson	.10	.05	.01
Los Angeles Clippers			
☐ 108 Steve Kerr	.10	.05	.01
Chicago Bulls			
☐ 109 Sam Perkins	.15	.07	.02
Seattle Supersonics			
☐ 110 Clarence Weatherspoon	.20	.09	.03
Philadelphia 76ers			
☐ 111 Felton Spencer	.10	.05	.01
Utah Jazz			
☐ 112 Greg Anthony	.10	.05	.01
New York Knicks			
☐ 113 Pete Chilcutt	.10	.05	.01
Sacramento Kings			
☐ 114 Malik Sealy	.10	.05	.01
Indiana Pacers			
☐ 115 Horace Grant	.20	.09	.03

	Chicago Bulls				
☐	116	Chris Morris	.10	.05	.01
	New Jersey Nets				
☐	117	Xavier McDaniel	.15	.07	.02
	Boston Celtics				
☐	118	Lionel Simmons	.15	.07	.02
	Sacramento Kings				
☐	119	Dell Curry	.15	.07	.02
	Charlotte Hornets				
☐	120	Moses Malone	.20	.09	.03
	Philadelphia 76ers				
☐	121	Lindsey Hunter	.60	.25	.08
	Detroit Pistons				
☐	122	Buck Williams	.20	.09	.03
	Portland Trail Blazers				
☐	123	Mahmoud Abdul-Rauf	.10	.05	.01
	Denver Nuggets				
☐	124	Rumeal Robinson	.10	.05	.01
	Charlotte Hornets				
☐	125	Chris Mills	.40	.18	.05
	Cleveland Cavaliers				
☐	126	Scott Skiles	.10	.05	.01
	Orlando Magic				
☐	127	Derrick McKey	.10	.05	.01
	Indiana Pacers				
☐	128	Avery Johnson	.10	.05	.01
	Golden State Warriors				
☐	129	Harold Miner	.15	.07	.02
	Miami Heat				
☐	130	Frank Brickowski	.15	.07	.02
	Charlotte Hornets				
☐	131	Gary Payton	.20	.09	.03
	Seattle Supersonics				
☐	132	Don MacLean	.15	.07	.02
	Washington Bullets				
☐	133	Thurl Bailey	.10	.05	.01
	Minnesota Timberwolves				
☐	134	Nick Van Exel	.60	.25	.08
	Los Angeles Lakers				
☐	135	Matt Geiger	.10	.05	.01
	Miami Heat				
☐	136	Stacey Augmon	.20	.09	.03
	Atlanta Hawks				
☐	137	Sedale Threatt	.10	.05	.01
	Los Angeles Lakers				
☐	138	Patrick Ewing	.50	.23	.06
	New York Knicks				
☐	139	Tyrone Corbin	.10	.05	.01
	Utah Jazz				
☐	140	Jim Jackson	.40	.18	.05
	Dallas Mavericks				
☐	141	Christian Laettner	.15	.07	.02
	Minnesota Timberwolves				
☐	142	Robert Horry	.20	.09	.03
	Houston Rockets				
☐	143	J.R. Reid	.10	.05	.01
	San Antonio Spurs				
☐	144	Eric Murdock	.15	.07	.02
	Milwaukee Bucks				
☐	145	Alonzo Mourning	1.00	.45	.13
	Charlotte Hornets				
☐	146	Sherman Douglas	.10	.05	.01
	Boston Celtics				
☐	147	Tom Gugliotta	.15	.07	.02
	Washington Bullets				
☐	148	Glen Rice	.20	.09	.03
	Miami Heat				
☐	149	Mark Price	.20	.09	.03
	Cleveland Cavaliers				
☐	150	Dikembe Mutombo	.20	.09	.03
	Denver Nuggets				
☐	151	Derek Harper	.15	.07	.02
	New York Knicks				

☐ 152 Karl Malone	.40	.18	.05
Utah Jazz			
☐ 153 Byron Scott	.15	.07	.02
Indiana Pacers			
☐ 154 Reggie Jordan	.15	.07	.02
Los Angeles Lakers			
☐ 155 Dominique Wilkins	.40	.18	.05
Atlanta Hawks			
☐ 156 Bobby Hurley	.60	.25	.08
Sacramento Kings			
☐ 157 Ron Harper	.15	.07	.02
Los Angeles Clippers			
☐ 158 Bryon Russell	.25	.11	.03
Utah Jazz			
☐ 159 Frank Johnson	.10	.05	.01
Phoenix Suns			
☐ 160 Toni Kukoc	.60	.25	.08
Chicago Bulls			
☐ 161 Lloyd Daniels	.10	.05	.01
San Antonio Spurs			
☐ 162 Jeff Turner	.10	.05	.01
Orlando Magic			
☐ 163 Muggsy Bogues	.10	.05	.01
Charlotte Hornets			
☐ 164 Chris Gatling	.10	.05	.01
Golden State Warriors			
☐ 165 Kenny Anderson	.25	.11	.03
New Jersey Nets			
☐ 166 Elmore Spencer	.10	.05	.01
Los Angeles Clippers			
☐ 167 Jamal Mashburn	1.50	.65	.19
Dallas Mavericks			
☐ 168 Tim Perry	.10	.05	.01
Philadelphia 76ers			
☐ 169 Antonio Davis	.40	.18	.05
Indiana Pacers			
☐ 170 Isaiah Rider	1.50	.65	.19
Minnesota Timberwolves			
☐ 171 Dee Brown	.10	.05	.01
Boston Celtics			
☐ 172 Walt Williams	.15	.07	.02
Sacramento Kings			
☐ 173 Elden Cambell	.10	.05	.01
Los Angeles Lakers			
☐ 174 Benoit Benjamin	.10	.05	.01
New Jersey Nets			
☐ 175 Billy Owens	.15	.07	.02
Golden State Warriors			
☐ 176 Andrew Lang	.10	.05	.01
Atlanta Hawks			
☐ 177 David Robinson	.75	.35	.09
San Antonio Spurs			
☐ 178 Checklist 1	.10	.05	.01
☐ 179 Checklist 2	.10	.05	.01
☐ 180 Checklist 3	.10	.05	.01
☐ 181 Shawn Bradley AS	.25	.11	.03
Philadelphia 76ers			
☐ 182 Calbert Cheaney AS	.25	.11	.03
Washington Bullets			
☐ 183 Toni Kukoc AS	.25	.11	.03
Chicago Bulls			
☐ 184 Popeye Jones AS	.15	.07	.02
Dallas Mavericks			
☐ 185 Lindsey Hunter AS	.25	.11	.03
Detroit Pistons			
☐ 186 Chris Webber AS	1.50	.65	.19
Golden State Warriors			
☐ 187 Bryon Russell AS	.15	.07	.02
Utah Jazz			
☐ 188 Anfernee Hardaway AS	1.25	.55	.16
Orlando Magic			
☐ 189 Nick Van Exel AS	.25	.11	.03
Los Angeles Lakers			

☐ 190 P.J. Brown AS	.15	.07	.02
New Jersey Nets			
☐ 191 Isaiah Rider AS	.60	.25	.08
Minnesota Timberwolves			
☐ 192 Chris Mills AS	.15	.07	.02
Cleveland Cavaliers			
☐ 193 Antonio Davis AS	.20	.09	.03
Indiana Pacers			
☐ 194 Jamal Mashburn AS	.60	.25	.08
Dallas Mavericks			
☐ 195 Dino Radja AS	.25	.11	.03
Boston Celtics			
☐ 196 Sam Cassell AS	.30	.14	.04
Houston Rockets			
☐ 197 Isaiah Rider SD	.60	.25	.08
Minnesota Timberwolves			
☐ 198 Mark Price LDS	.20	.09	.03
Cleveland Cavaliers			
☐ 199 Stacey Augmon HDL	.15	.07	.02
Atlanta Hawks			
☐ 200 Celtics Team HDL	.10	.05	.01
Boston Celtics			
☐ 201 Eddie Johnson HDL	.10	.05	.01
Charlotte Hornets			
☐ 202 Scottie Pippen HDL	.25	.11	.03
Chicago Bulls			
☐ 203 Brad Daugherty HDL	.15	.07	.02
Cleveland Cavaliers			
☐ 204 Jamal Mashburn HDL	.40	.18	.05
Dallas Mavericks			
☐ 205 Dikembe Mutombo HDL	.15	.07	.02
Oliver Miller HDL			
Denver Nuggets			
☐ 206 Lindsey Hunter HDL	.10	.05	.01
Detroit Pistons			
☐ 207 Chris Webber HDL	1.00	.45	.13
Golden State Warriors			
☐ 208 Rockets Team HDL	.10	.05	.01
Houston Rockets			
☐ 209 Derrick McKey HDL	.10	.05	.01
Indiana Pacers			
☐ 210 Danny Manning HDL	.15	.07	.02
Los Angeles Clippers			
☐ 211 Doug Christie HDL	.10	.05	.01
Los Angeles Lakers			
☐ 212 Glen Rice HDL	.15	.07	.02
Miami Heat			
☐ 213 Todd Day HDL	.20	.09	.03
Ken Norman HDL			
Vin Baker HDL			
Jon Barry HDL			
Milwaukee Bucks			
☐ 214 Isaiah Rider HDL	.40	.18	.05
Minnesota Timberwolves			
☐ 215 Kenny Anderson HDL	.15	.07	.02
New Jersey Nets			
☐ 216 Patrick Ewing	.25	.11	.03
New York Knicks			
☐ 217 Anfernee Hardaway HDL	.75	.35	.09
Orlando Magic			
☐ 218 Moses Malone HDL	.15	.07	.02
Philadelphia 76ers			
☐ 219 Kevin Johnson HDL	.15	.07	.02
Phoenix Suns			
☐ 220 Clifford Robinson HD	.15	.07	.02
Portland Trail Blazers			
☐ 221 Wayman Tisdale HDL	.10	.05	.01
Sacramento Kings			
☐ 222 David Robinson HDL	.40	.18	.05
San Antonio Spurs			
☐ 223 Sonics Team HDL	.10	.05	.01
Seattle Supersonics			
☐ 224 John Stockton HDL	.15	.07	.02

		MINT	EXC	G-VG
	Utah Jazz			
☐ 225	Don MacLean HDL	.10	.05	.01
	Washington Bullets			
☐ JK1	Johnny Kilroy	10.00	4.50	1.25
☐ MJR1	Michael Jordan	15.00	6.75	1.90
	Retirement Card			

1993-94 Upper Deck SE Electric Court

Inserted one per SE pack, this is a parallel set to '93-94 Upper Deck SE. The 225-card stan-dard-size (2 1/2" by 3 1/2") set features on its fronts color player action shots that are bor-derless, except on the left, where a strip carries the player's name in gold foil along with his position and a vertically distorted black-and-white version of the action shot. The player's team name appears in vertical gold-foil lettering near the right edge. The Electric Court set name appears in prismatic silver foil lettering near the bottom. The back carries a color play-er action photo, with his name, position, and brief biography appearing in stripes across the top. Statistics and career highlights are displayed horizontally in a ghosted panel on the left. The cards are numbered on the back.

	MINT	EXC	G-VG
COMPLETE SET (225)	100.00	45.00	12.50
COMMON PLAYER (1-225)	.15	.07	.02
*EC STARS: 2.5X to 5X VALUE			
*EC ROOKIES: 1.5X to 3X VALUE			

1993-94 Upper Deck SE Electric Gold

Randomly inserted in SE packs, this is a parallel set to '93-94 Upper Deck SE. The 225-card standard-size (2 1/2" by 3 1/2") set features on its fronts color player action shots that are borderless, except on the left, where a strip carries the player's name in gold foil along with his position and a vertically distorted black-and-white version of the action shot. The player's team name appears in vertical gold-foil lettering near the right edge. The Electric Gold set name appears in gold foil lettering near the bottom. The back carries a color player action photo, with his name, position, and brief biography appearing in stripes across the top. Statistics and career highlights are displayed horizontally in a ghosted panel on the left. The cards are numbered on the back.

	MINT	EXC	G-VG
COMPLETE SET (225)	1800.00	800.00	230.00
COMMON PLAYER (1-225)	2.00	.90	.25
*EG STARS: 30X to 60X VALUE			
*EG ROOKIES: 15X to 30X VALUE			

☐	1	Scottie Pippen	35.00	16.00	4.40
		Chicago Bulls			
☐	4	Chris Webber	150.00	70.00	19.00
		Golden State Warriors			
☐	21	Latrell Sprewell	40.00	18.00	5.00
		Golden State Warriors			
☐	32	Shaquille O'Neal	150.00	70.00	19.00
		Orlando Magic			
☐	51	Anfernee Hardaway	100.00	45.00	12.50
		Orlando Magic			
☐	57	Larry Johnson	30.00	13.50	3.80
		Charlotte Hornets			
☐	69	Vin Baker	30.00	13.50	3.80
		Milwaukee Bucks			
☐	78	Hakeem Olajuwon	70.00	32.00	8.75
		Houston Rockets			
☐	91	Charles Barkley	50.00	23.00	6.25
		Phoenix Suns			
☐	99	Shawn Kemp	35.00	16.00	4.40
		Seattle Supersonics			
☐	138	Patrick Ewing	35.00	16.00	4.40
		New York Knicks			
☐	140	Jim Jackson	30.00	13.50	3.80
		Dallas Mavericks			
☐	145	Alonzo Mourning	60.00	27.00	7.50
		Charlotte Hornets			
☐	152	Karl Malone	25.00	11.50	3.10
		Utah Jazz			
☐	155	Dominique Wilkins	30.00	13.50	3.80
		Atlanta Hawks			
☐	167	Jamal Mashburn	40.00	18.00	5.00
		Dallas Mavericks			
☐	170	Isaiah Rider	40.00	18.00	5.00
		Minnesota Timberwolves			
☐	177	David Robinson	50.00	23.00	6.25
		San Antonio Spurs			
☐	186	Chris Webber AS	60.00	27.00	7.50
		Golden State Warriors			
☐	188	Anfernee Hardaway AS	40.00	18.00	5.00
		Orlando Magic			
☐	207	Chris Webber HDL	30.00	13.50	3.80
		Golden State Warriors			
☐	217	Anfernee Hardaway HDL	20.00	9.00	2.50
		Orlando Magic			

1993-94 Upper Deck SE Behind the Glass

Randomly inserted in retail packs, this 15-card standard-size (2 1/2" by 3 1/2") set captures some of the NBA's best dunkers from the unique camera angle behind the backboard glass.

A gold-foil "Behind the Glass Trade Card" was randomly inserted in retail and hobby packs, and the collector could redeem it for the complete 15-card "Behind the Glass" set. The borderless front features a color player action shot on a gold metallic finish. The player's name and position appear vertically along the right side. The back features a color player action shot on the right side with career highlights appearing alongside on the left. The cards are numbered on the back with a "G" prefix.

	MINT	EXC	G-VG
COMPLETE SET (15)	100.00	45.00	12.50
COMMON PLAYER (G1-G15)	2.00	.90	.25
☐ G1 Shawn Kemp	6.00	2.70	.75
Seattle Supersonics			
☐ G2 Patrick Ewing	6.00	2.70	.75
New York Knicks			
☐ G3 Dikembe Mutombo	2.00	.90	.25
Denver Nuggets			
☐ G4 Charles Barkley	8.00	3.60	1.00
Phoenix Suns			
☐ G5 Hakeem Olajuwon	10.00	4.50	1.25
Houston Rockets			
☐ G6 Larry Johnson	5.00	2.30	.60
Charlotte Hornets			
☐ G7 Chris Webber	20.00	9.00	2.50
Golden State Warriors			
☐ G8 John Starks	2.00	.90	.25
New York Knicks			
☐ G9 Kevin Willis	2.00	.90	.25
Atlanta Hawks			
☐ G10 Scottie Pippen	6.00	2.70	.75
Chicago Bulls			
☐ G11 Michael Jordan	30.00	13.50	3.80
Chicago Bulls			
☐ G12 Alonzo Mourning	8.00	3.60	1.00
Charlotte Hornets			
☐ G13 Shaquille O'Neal	20.00	9.00	2.50
Orlando Magic			
☐ G14 Shawn Bradley	3.00	1.35	.40
Philadelphia 76ers			
☐ G15 Ron Harper	2.00	.90	.25
Los Angeles Clippers			
☐ NNO Behind the Glass	3.00	1.35	.40
Trade Card			

1993-94 Upper Deck SE Die-Cut All-Stars

In these two 15-card insert sets, Upper Deck saluted the 1994 NBA All-Star Game by featuring the five starters, five previously active players who were All-Stars, and five who are projected Future All-Stars for each conference. Hobby dealers in the East received cases containing players from the Eastern conference, while hobby dealers in the West received

cases containing players from the Western conference. Measuring the standard-size (2 1/2" by 3 1/2"), these die-cut cards have been inserted in hobby packs only. This unique card design features a partial gold-foil border at the top only. Centered is a color player action photo. The player's name and team appear in red vertical lettering along the left side. The back features brief statistics. The cards are numbered on the back with an "E" or "W" prefix.

		MINT	EXC	G-VG
	COMPLETE EAST SET (15)	210.00	95.00	26.00
	COMPLETE WEST SET (15)	250.00	115.00	31.00
	COMMON EAST (E1-E15)	5.00	2.30	.60
	COMMON WEST (W1-W15)	5.00	2.30	.60
☐ E1	Dominique Wilkins Atlanta Hawks	15.00	6.75	1.90
☐ E2	Alonzo Mourning Charlotte Hornets	30.00	13.50	3.80
☐ E3	B.J. Armstrong Chicago Bulls	5.00	2.30	.60
☐ E4	Scottie Pippen Chicago Bulls	18.00	8.00	2.30
☐ E5	Mark Price Cleveland Cavaliers	5.00	2.30	.60
☐ E6	Isiah Thomas Detroit Pistons	6.00	2.70	.75
☐ E7	Harold Miner Miami Heat	5.00	2.30	.60
☐ E8	Vin Baker Milwaukee Bucks	15.00	6.75	1.90
☐ E9	Kenny Anderson New Jersey Nets	7.00	3.10	.85
☐ E10	Derrick Coleman New Jersey Nets	8.00	3.60	1.00
☐ E11	Patrick Ewing New York Knicks	18.00	8.00	2.30
☐ E12	Anfernee Hardaway Orlando Magic	50.00	23.00	6.25
☐ E13	Shaquille O'Neal Orlando Magic	65.00	29.00	8.25
☐ E14	Shawn Bradley Philadelphia 76ers	9.00	4.00	1.15
☐ E15	Calbert Cheaney Washington Bullets	9.00	4.00	1.15
☐ W1	Jim Jackson Dallas Mavericks	15.00	6.75	1.90
☐ W2	Jamal Mashburn Dallas Mavericks	20.00	9.00	2.50
☐ W3	Dikembe Mutombo Denver Nuggets	7.00	3.10	.85
☐ W4	Latrell Sprewell Golden State Warriors	18.00	8.00	2.30
☐ W5	Chris Webber Golden State Warriors	65.00	29.00	8.25
☐ W6	Hakeem Olajuwon	35.00	16.00	4.40

			Houston Rockets			
☐	W7	Danny Manning		6.00	2.70	.75
			Los Angeles Clippers			
☐	W8	Nick Van Exel		9.00	4.00	1.15
			Los Angeles Lakers			
☐	W9	Isaiah Rider		20.00	9.00	2.50
			Minnesota Timberwolves			
☐	W10	Charles Barkley		25.00	11.50	3.10
			Phoenix Suns			
☐	W11	Clyde Drexler		8.00	3.60	1.00
			Portland Trail Blazers			
☐	W12	Mitch Richmond		5.00	2.30	.60
			Sacramento Kings			
☐	W13	David Robinson		25.00	11.50	3.10
			San Antonio Spurs			
☐	W14	Shawn Kemp		18.00	8.00	2.30
			Seattle Supersonics			
☐	W15	Karl Malone		12.00	5.50	1.50
			Utah Jazz			

1993-94 Upper Deck SE USA Trade

This set previewed the USA Basketball set that was released in the summer of 1994. Collectors could redeem the "USA Basketball Trade Card" for the 24-card set, and approximately two of these redeemable cards were found in each case. The cards depict the 12 players selected by USA Basketball for "Dream Team II" plus Tim Hardaway, who was originally selected to the team was unable to participate due to injury, and 11 from the original Dream Team. Measuring the standard size (2 1/2" by 3 1/2"), each card features a borderless color player action shot on its front. The player's name and position appear in white lettering within red and blue stripes near the bottom. The words "Exchange Set" in vertical gold-foil lettering and the gold-foil Upper Deck logo appear at the upper left. On a background of the American flag, the back carries a posed color shot of the player in his USA uniform and career highlights. The cards are numbered on the back with a "USA" prefix.

		MINT	EXC	G-VG
COMPLETE SET (24)		35.00	16.00	4.40
COMMON PLAYER (1-24)		.25	.11	.03
☐ 1	Charles Barkley	2.50	1.15	.30
☐ 2	Larry Bird	3.50	1.55	.45
☐ 3	Clyde Drexler	.75	.35	.09
☐ 4	Patrick Ewing	2.00	.90	.25
☐ 5	Michael Jordan	10.00	4.50	1.25
☐ 6	Christian Laettner	.50	.23	.06
☐ 7	Karl Malone	1.50	.65	.19
☐ 8	Chris Mullin	.50	.23	.06
☐ 9	Scottie Pippen	2.00	.90	.25
☐ 10	David Robinson	2.50	1.15	.30
☐ 11	John Stockton	.75	.35	.09

☐ 12 Dominique Wilkins	1.75	.80	.22
☐ 13 Isiah Thomas	.50	.23	.06
☐ 14 Dan Majerle	.25	.11	.03
☐ 15 Steve Smith	.25	.11	.03
☐ 16 Alonzo Mourning	2.50	1.15	.30
☐ 17 Shawn Kemp	2.00	.90	.25
☐ 18 Larry Johnson	1.75	.80	.22
☐ 19 Tim Hardaway	.25	.11	.03
☐ 20 Joe Dumars	.50	.23	.06
☐ 21 Mark Price	.25	.11	.03
☐ 22 Derrick Coleman	.75	.35	.09
☐ 23 Reggie Miller	.75	.35	.09
☐ 24 Shaquille O'Neal	7.00	3.10	.85
☐ NNO Expired USA Trade Card	3.00	1.35	.40

1994 Upper Deck USA

These 90 standard-size (2 1/2" by 3 1/2") cards honor the '94 Team USA players. The borderless fronts feature color posed and action player shots. The player's name and position appear in red, white, and blue bars near the bottom. The card's subtitle appears vertically in gold-foil lettering near the left edge, information for which appears on the back. The cards are numbered on the back.

	MINT	EXC	G-VG
COMPLETE SET (90)	18.00	8.00	2.30
COMMON PLAYER (1-90)	.15	.07	.02
☐ 1 Derrick Coleman	.25	.11	.03
Player Quotebook			
☐ 2 Derrick Coleman	.25	.11	.03
DC			
1 Draft Choice			
☐ 3 Derrick Coleman	.25	.11	.03
1991 Rookie of the Year			
☐ 4 Derrick Coleman	.25	.11	.03
1994 All-Star Game			
☐ 5 Derrick Coleman	.25	.11	.03
The Jordan Report			
☐ 6 Derrick Coleman	.25	.11	.03
Career Statistics			
☐ 7 Joe Dumars	.20	.09	.03
Player Quotebook			
☐ 8 Joe Dumars	.20	.09	.03
1986 All-Rookie Team			
☐ 9 Joe Dumars	.20	.09	.03
1989 NBA Finals MVP			
☐ 10 Joe Dumars	.20	.09	.03
4-Time All-Star			

☐ 11	Joe Dumars	.20	.09	.03
	The Jordan Report			
☐ 12	Joe Dumars	.20	.09	.03
	Career Statistics			
☐ 13	Tim Hardaway	.15	.07	.02
	Player Quotebook			
☐ 14	Tim Hardaway	.15	.07	.02
	1990 NBA All-Rookie Team			
☐ 15	Tim Hardaway	.15	.07	.02
	Run TMC			
☐ 16	Tim Hardaway	.15	.07	.02
	3-Time All-Star			
☐ 17	Tim Hardaway	.15	.07	.02
	The Jordan Report			
☐ 18	Tim Hardaway	.15	.07	.02
	Career Statistics			
☐ 19	Larry Johnson	.40	.18	.05
	Player Quotebook			
☐ 20	Larry Johnson	.40	.18	.05
	Franchise Player			
☐ 21	Larry Johnson	.40	.18	.05
	1992 Rookie Of The Year			
☐ 22	Larry Johnson	.40	.18	.05
	2-Time All-Star			
☐ 23	Larry Johnson	.40	.18	.05
	The Jordan Report			
☐ 24	Larry Johnson	.40	.18	.05
	Career Statistics			
☐ 25	Shawn Kemp	.50	.23	.06
	Player Quotebook			
☐ 26	Shawn Kemp	.50	.23	.06
	19-Year-Old Rookie			
☐ 27	Shawn Kemp	.50	.23	.06
	2-Time NBA All-Star			
☐ 28	Shawn Kemp	.50	.23	.06
	Reign Man			
☐ 29	Shawn Kemp	.50	.23	.06
	The Jordan Report			
☐ 30	Shawn Kemp	.50	.23	.06
	Career Statistics			
☐ 31	Dan Majerle	.15	.07	.02
	Player Quotebook			
☐ 32	Dan Majerle	.15	.07	.02
	1988 USAB			
☐ 33	Dan Majerle	.15	.07	.02
	3-Time NBA All-Star			
☐ 34	Dan Majerle	.15	.07	.02
	3-Point King			
☐ 35	Dan Majerle	.15	.07	.02
	The Jordan Report			
☐ 36	Dan Majerle	.15	.07	.02
	Career Statistics			
☐ 37	Reggie Miller	.25	.11	.03
	Player Quotebook			
☐ 38	Reggie Miller	.20	.09	.03
	Miller Bloodlines			
☐ 39	Reggie Miller	.20	.09	.03
	1990 NBA All-Star			
☐ 40	Reggie Miller	.20	.09	.03
	57-Point Game			
☐ 41	Reggie Miller	.20	.09	.03
	The Jordan Report			
☐ 42	Reggie Miller	.20	.09	.03
	Career Statistics			
☐ 43	Alonzo Mourning	.75	.35	.09
	Player Quotebook			
☐ 44	Alonzo Mourning	.75	.35	.09
	1990 World Championships			
☐ 45	Alonzo Mourning	.75	.35	.09
	1994 NBA All-Star			
☐ 46	Alonzo Mourning	.75	.35	.09
	Zo-man's Land			
☐ 47	Alonzo Mourning	.75	.35	.09

☐ 84 Sheryl Swoopes	.15	.07	.02
USAB Women			
☐ 85 Michael Jordan	2.50	1.15	.30
USAB Greats			
Chicago Bulls			
☐ 86 Larry Bird	1.00	.45	.13
USAB Greats			
Boston Celtics			
☐ 87 Jerry West	.50	.23	.06
USAB Greats			
Los Angeles Lakers			
☐ 88 Adrian Dantley	.15	.07	.02
USAB Greats			
☐ 89 Cheryl Miller	.15	.07	.02
USAB Greats			
☐ 90 Henry Iba CO	.15	.07	.02
USAB Greats			
☐ CK1 Checklist 1	2.00	.90	.25
☐ CK2 Checklist 2	2.00	.90	.25

1994 Upper Deck USA Gold Medal

Inserted one per '94 Upper Deck USA pack, these gold cards are identical to the regular issues except for the Upper Deck Gold Medal logos appearing on the fronts. The cards are numbered on the back.

	MINT	EXC	G-VG
COMPLETE SET (90)	45.00	20.00	5.75
COMMON GOLD (1-90)	.25	.11	.03
*GOLD CARDS: 2.5X VALUE			

1994 Upper Deck USA Chalk Talk

Randomly inserted in Upper Deck USA packs, the Chalk Talk set consists of 14 cards. Card fronts include a small hologram of Don Nelson who is also quoted on the back in reference to the player on the card. The card fronts are full-bleed on one side with a gray border on the other that contains the player's name. In addition to Nelson's quote, a small photo of him and a larger photo of the player appear on the back. The cards are numbered with a "CT" prefix.

	MINT	EXC	G-VG
COMPLETE SET (14)	125.00	57.50	15.50
COMMON PLAYER (CT1-CT14)	5.00	2.30	.60

☐ CT1	Derrick Coleman	8.00	3.60	1.00
	New Jersey Nets			
☐ CT2	Joe Dumars	6.00	2.70	.75
	Detroit Pistons			
☐ CT3	Tim Hardaway	5.00	2.30	.60
	Golden State Warriors			
☐ CT4	Larry Johnson	12.00	5.50	1.50
	Charlotte Hornets			
☐ CT5	Shawn Kemp	14.00	6.25	1.75
	Seattle Supersonics			
☐ CT6	Dan Majerle	5.00	2.30	.60
	Phoenix Suns			
☐ CT7	Reggie Miller	8.00	3.60	1.00
	Indiana Pacers			
☐ CT8	Alonzo Mourning	18.00	8.00	2.30
	Charlotte Hornets			
☐ CT9	Shaquille O'Neal	40.00	18.00	5.00
	Orlando Magic			
☐ CT10	Mark Price	5.00	2.30	.60
	Cleveland Cavaliers			
☐ CT11	Steve Smith	5.00	2.30	.60
	Miami Heat			
☐ CT12	Isiah Thomas	6.00	2.70	.75
	Detroit Pistons			
☐ CT13	Dominique Wilkins	12.00	5.50	1.50
	Atlanta Hawks			
☐ CT14	Kevin Johnson	5.00	2.30	.60
	Phoenix Suns			

1994 Upper Deck USA Follow Your Dreams

Randomly inserted in packs, these 14 standard-size (2 1/2" by 3 1/2") game-prize cards feature borderless color player action shots on their fronts. The player's name appears in vertical gold-foil lettering near one edge. The back carries the rules for playing the game. Briefly, each game card depicts one of the 14 players from the '94 USA Dream Team. Each card also designates the player as either a "Top Scorer," "Top Rebounder," or "Top Assists." If the player and category announced at the end of the championship matches one of these, that card would be a winner. The game started June 27, 1994, and ended Nov. 30, 1994. The cards are unnumbered and checklisted below in alphabetical order.

	MINT	EXC	G-VG
COMPLETE ASSISTS (14)	40.00	18.00	5.00
COMPLETE REBOUNDS (14)	40.00	18.00	5.00
COMPLETE SCORING (14)	40.00	18.00	5.00
COMMON CARD (1-14)	1.00	.45	.13

☐ 1	Derrick Coleman	1.75	.80	.22
	New Jersey Nets			
☐ 2	Joe Dumars	1.50	.65	.19
	Detroit Pistons			
☐ 3	Tim Hardaway	1.00	.45	.13
	Golden State Warriors			
☐ 4A	Kevin Johnson	20.00	9.00	2.50
	Assists			
	Phoenix Suns			
☐ 4R	Kevin Johnson	1.00	.45	.13
	Rebounds			
	Phoenix Suns			
☐ 4S	Kevin Johnson	1.00	.45	.13
	Scoring			
	Phoenix Suns			
☐ 5	Larry Johnson	1.75	.80	.22
	Charlotte Hornets			
☐ 6	Shawn Kemp	1.75	.80	.22
	Seattle Supersonics			
☐ 7	Dan Majerle	1.75	.80	.22
	Phoenix Suns			
☐ 8	Reggie Miller	1.75	.80	.22
	Indiana Pacers			
☐ 9	Alonzo Mourning	1.75	.80	.22
	Charlotte Hornets			
☐ 10A	Shaquille O'Neal	12.00	5.50	1.50
	Assists			
	Orlando Magic			
☐ 10R	Shaquille O'Neal	25.00	11.50	3.10
	Rebounds			
	Orlando Magic			
☐ 10S	Shaquille O'Neal	25.00	11.50	3.10
	Scoring			
	Orlando Magic			
☐ 11	Mark Price	1.00	.45	.13
	Cleveland Cavaliers			
☐ 12	Steve Smith	1.00	.45	.13
	Miami Heat			
☐ 13	Isiah Thomas	1.50	.65	.19
	Detroit Pistons			
☐ 14	Dominique Wilkins	3.00	1.35	.40
	Atlanta Hawks			

1994 Upper Deck USA Jordan's Highlights

Randomly inserted in packs, the five-card standard size (2 1/2" by 3 1/2") set features action photos of Michael Jordan representing the United States during international play. A facsimile autograph in gold foil lettering appears near the bottom. On back, the Amercian flag is used as a backdrop to highlights and statistics that pertains to action on the front. The cards are numbered with a "JH" prefix.

	MINT	EXC	G-VG
COMPLETE SET (5)	85.00	38.00	10.50
COMMON JORDAN (JH1-JH5)	18.00	8.00	2.30
☐ JH1 Michael Jordan .... Chicago Bulls 1992 Summer Games	18.00	8.00	2.30
☐ JH2 Michael Jordan .... Chicago Bulls 1992 Tournament of the Americas	18.00	8.00	2.30
☐ JH3 Michael Jordan .... Chicago Bulls 1984 Summer Games	18.00	8.00	2.30
☐ JH4 Michael Jordan .... Chicago Bulls 1983 World University Games	18.00	8.00	2.30
☐ JH5 Michael Jordan .... Chicago Bulls International Games	18.00	8.00	2.30

1991-92 Wild Card Promos

These two standard-size (2 1/2" by 3 1/2") cards were issued to preview the design of 1991-92 Wild Card basketball issue. Two versions of each card were produced; one was marked with and given out at the 1991 San Francisco Sports Card Expo, while the other version

(without the San Francisco Sports Expo emblem) was given to dealers and also available as a random insert in Wild Card College Football foil packs. The color action player photos on the fronts are black-bordered, and colored numbers are displayed in the black border above and to the right of the picture. The backs carry a color headshot, biography, and statistics. The cards are numbered on the back with a "P" prefix. The San Francisco give-away cards are arguably less than valuable than the harder-to-obtain football foil pack insert versions.

	MINT	EXC	G-VG
COMPLETE SET (2)	12.00	5.00	1.20
COMMON PLAYER (P1-P2)	5.00	2.00	.50
☐ P1 Larry Johnson UNLV	8.00	3.25	.80
☐ P2 Kenny Anderson Georgia Tech	5.00	2.00	.50

1991-92 Wild Card Collegiate

The Wild Card Collegiate Basketball set contains 120 cards measuring the standard size (2 1/2" by 3 1/2"). One out of every 100 cards is "Wild", with a numbered stripe to indicate how many cards it can be redeemed for. There are 5, 10, 20, 50, 100, and 1,000 denominations, with the highest numbers the scarcest. Whatever the number, the card can be redeemed for that number of regular cards of the same player, after paying a redemption fee of 4.95 per order. The front design features glossy color action player photos on a black card face, with an orange frame around the picture and different color numbers in the top and right borders. The backs have different shades of purple and a color head shot, biography, and statistics. The cards are numbered on the back. At the San Francisco Card Expo (Aug. 30 to Sept. 2, 1991), promo cards of Kenny Anderson and Larry Johnson were given away. These cards are identical to those inserted in 1991 Wild Card Collegiate football packs, except that they have the San Francisco Expo logo at the lower left corner on the back.

	MINT	EXC	G-VG
COMPLETE w/REDEMPT. (125)	8.00	3.25	.80
COMPLETE w/SURPRISE (120)	7.00	2.80	.70
COMMON PLAYER (1-120)	.04	.02	.00
☐ 1 Larry Johnson First NBA Draft Pick	.40	.16	.04
☐ 2 LeRon Ellis Syracuse	.10	.04	.01
☐ 3 Alvaro Teheran Houston	.04	.02	.00
☐ 4 Eric Murdock Providence	.35	.14	.03
☐ 5A Surprise Card 1	.60	.24	.06
☐ 5B Dikembe Mutombo Georgetown	.75	.30	.07

☐ 6 Anthony Avent .15	.06	.01
Seton Hall		
☐ 7 Isiah Thomas .15	.06	.01
Indiana		
☐ 8 Abdul Shamsid-Deen .04	.02	.00
Providence		
☐ 9 Linton Townes .04	.02	.00
James Madison		
☐ 10 Joe Wylie .04	.02	.00
Miami		
☐ 11 Cozell McQueen .04	.02	.00
North Carolina State		
☐ 12 David Benoit .20	.08	.02
Alabama		
☐ 13 Chris Mullin .15	.06	.01
St. John's		
☐ 14 Dale Davis .40	.16	.04
Clemson		
☐ 15 Patrick Ewing .25	.10	.02
Georgetown		
☐ 16 Greg Anthony .15	.06	.01
UNLV		
☐ 17 Robert Pack .25	.10	.02
USC		
☐ 18 Phil Zevenbergen .04	.02	.00
Washington		
☐ 19 Rick Fox .30	.12	.03
North Carolina		
☐ 20 Chris Corchiani .10	.04	.01
North Carolina State		
☐ 21 Elliot Perry .07	.03	.01
Memphis State		
☐ 22 Kevin Brooks .07	.03	.01
SW Louisiana		
☐ 23 Mark Macon .10	.04	.01
Temple		
☐ 24 Larry Johnson 1.50	.60	.15
UNLV		
☐ 25 George Ackles .07	.03	.01
UNLV		
☐ 26A Surprise Card 5 1.50	.60	.15
☐ 26B Christian Laettner .50	.20	.05
(Promo)		
Duke		
☐ 27 Andy Fields .04	.02	.00
Cheyney State		
☐ 28 Kevin Lynch .07	.03	.01
Minnesota		
☐ 29 Graylin Warner .04	.02	.00
SW Louisiana		
☐ 30 James Bullock .04	.02	.00
Purdue		
☐ 31 Steve Bucknall .04	.02	.00
North Carolina		
☐ 32 Carl Thomas .04	.02	.00
Eastern Michigan		
☐ 33 Doug Overton .10	.04	.01
La Salle		
☐ 34 Brian Shorter .04	.02	.00
Pittsburgh		
☐ 35 Chad Gallagher .04	.02	.00
Creighton		
☐ 36 Antonio Davis .15	.06	.01
Texas-El Paso		
☐ 37 Sean Green .07	.03	.01
Iona		
☐ 38 Randy Brown .10	.04	.01
New Mexico State		
☐ 39 Richard Dumas .10	.04	.01
Oklahoma State		
☐ 40 Terrell Brandon .20	.08	.02
Oregon		
☐ 41 Marty Embry .04	.02	.00

☐ 42	Ronald Coleman (DePaul)	.04	.02	.00
☐ 43	King Rice (USC)	.04	.02	.00
☐ 44	Perry Carter (North Carolina)	.07	.03	.01
☐ 45	Andrew Gaze (Ohio State)	.10	.04	.01
☐ 46A	Surprise Card 2	.60	.24	.06
☐ 46B	Billy Owens (Seton Hall)	.50	.20	.05
☐ 47A	Surprise Card 3	.40	.16	.04
☐ 47B	Stacey Augmon (Syracuse)	.50	.20	.05
☐ 48	Jimmy Oliver (UNLV)	.07	.03	.01
☐ 49	Treg Lee (Purdue)	.07	.03	.01
☐ 50	Ricky Winslow (Ohio State)	.04	.02	.00
☐ 51	Danny Vranes (Houston)	.07	.03	.01
☐ 52	Jay Murphy (Utah)	.04	.02	.00
☐ 53	Adrian Dantley (Boston College)	.07	.03	.01
☐ 54	Joe Arlauckas (Notre Dame)	.04	.02	.00
☐ 55	Moses Scurry (Niagara University)	.07	.03	.01
☐ 56	Andy Toolson (UNLV)	.07	.03	.01
☐ 57	Ramon Rivas (Brigham Young)	.04	.02	.00
☐ 58	Charles Davis (Temple)	.04	.02	.00
☐ 59	Butch Wade (Vanderbilt)	.04	.02	.00
☐ 60	John Pinone (Michigan)	.04	.02	.00
☐ 61	Bill Wennington (Villanova)	.07	.03	.01
☐ 62	Walter Berry (St. John's)	.07	.03	.01
☐ 63	Terry Dozier (St. John's)	.04	.02	.00
☐ 64	Mitchell Anderson (South Carolina)	.04	.02	.00
☐ 65	Pace Mannion (Bradley)	.07	.03	.01
☐ 66	Pete Myers (Utah)	.04	.02	.00
☐ 67	Eddie Lee Wilkins (Little Rock)	.07	.03	.01
☐ 68	Mark Hughes (Gardner Webb)	.04	.02	.00
☐ 69	Darryl Dawkins (Michigan)	.10	.04	.01
☐ 70	Jay Vincent (No College)	.07	.03	.01
☐ 71	Doug Lee (Michigan State)	.04	.02	.00
☐ 72	Russ Schoene (Purdue)	.04	.02	.00
☐ 73	Tim Kempton (Tennessee-Chattanooga)	.04	.02	.00
☐ 74	Earl Cureton (Notre Dame)	.07	.03	.01
☐ 75	Terence Stansbury (Detroit)	.04	.02	.00
☐ 76	Frank Kornet (Temple)	.04	.02	.00
	Vanderbilt			